60,000+
Baby
Names

Bruce Lansky

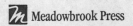 Meadowbrook Press

Distributed by Simon & Schuster
New York

Library of Congress Cataloging-in-Publication Data

Lansky, Bruce.
  60,000+ baby names / by Bruce Lansky.
    p. cm.
  ISBN 0-88166-519-3 (Meadowbrook Press) ISBN 0-684-04702-0 (Simon & Schuster)
  1. Names, Personal--Dictionaries. I. Title. II. Title: Sixty-thousand plus baby names.
  CS2377.L35434 2006
  929.4'4--dc22   2006026226

Editorial Director: Christine Zuchora-Walske
Editors: Megan McGinnis, Angela Wiechmann
Editorial Assistants: Alicia Ester, Andrea Patch, Maureen Burns
Production Manager: Paul Woods
Graphic Design Manager: Tamara Peterson
Researcher and Translator: David Rochelero
Researcher: Kelsey Anderson
Cover Art: © Corbis, © Getty Images, Inc.

© 2006, 2008, 2009 by Bruce Lansky

ISBN 13: 978-0-88166-519-2
ISBN 10: 0-88166-519-3

Published by:
Meadowbrook Press • 5451 Smetana Drive • Minnetonka, MN • 55343

www.meadowbrookpress.com

BOOK TRADE DISTRIBUTION by Simon and Schuster, a division of Simon and Schuster, Inc., 1230 Avenue of the Americas, New York, New York 10020

15 14 13 12 11 10   15 14 13 12 11 10 9 8 7 6

Printed in the United States of America

Contents

Introduction

Searching for just the right name for your baby can be a pleasure if you have just the right book. Let me tell you why I think *60,000+ Baby Names* is the right book.

It contains the most names—complete with origins, meanings, variations, fascinating facts, and famous namesakes—of any book in its price range. Here you'll find the most names from major ethnic origins, such as:

- Nearly 7,000 American names, many of which African-American families choose for their children

- Over 5,000 names Hispanic families commonly use

- Over 4,000 French names; 9,000 English names; 6,000 Latin names; 4,000 Irish names; and 6,000 Greek names

- Nearly 6,000 Hebrew names; 2,500 Arabic names; and 4,000 German names

- Thousands of Scottish, Welsh, Italian, Russian, Scandinavian, Chinese, Japanese, Polish, Native American, Hawaiian, African, and Hindi names.

But there's more in *60,000+ Baby Names* than just pages and pages of names. There are also over 200 fun, helpful lists that will get you brainstorming names without having to read the book cover to cover. You'll find the most recently available lists of the top 100 girls' and boys' names, and I've also included data to help you compare rankings from the previous year's list so you can see which names are climbing, which are falling, and which are holding steady. To quickly see what's hot and what's not, check out the Changes in the Top 100 lists. And to quickly find the most popular names in the Girls' Names and Boys' Names sections, look for the special ☆ icon. If you're expecting a double dose of joy, take a look at the lists of the most popular names for twins. Lastly, if you're interested in tracking names over the years or just looking for a timeless name, you'll love the lists of popular names over the last one hundred years.

Want to know what parents in Canada, Australia, Sweden, and Japan are naming their babies? Want to find that perfect name to reflect your heritage? *60,000+ Baby Names* features lists of popular names around the world as well as lists of common and interesting names from many different origins. Want to name your baby after your favorite movie star, religious figure, or locale? Check out the lists featuring names inspired by people, places, and things. These lists will get you thinking about names that have special meaning to you. Don't miss "How to Pick a Name You and Your Baby Will Love." In three simple steps, complete with easy-to-use worksheets, you can select a name that has personal meaning but is also practical. It's the perfect approach for parents who find the idea of reading over 60,000 baby names a bit overwhelming.

60,000+ Baby Names also has an exclusive new feature to help parents make informed choices about names. Recently, naming trends have been heading in less traditional directions. One such trend is to use traditional boys' names for girls and vice versa. Throughout the Girls' Names and Boys' Names sections, you'll find special icons highlighting names that are shared by both genders. The icons will indicate whether a shared name is used mostly for boys **B**, used mostly for girls **G**, or used about evenly by both genders **BG**. Some parents want androgynous or gender-jumping names and other parents want names with clear gender identification. Either way, the icons will help you make an informed choice.

As you browse the names with these special icons, you may be surprised to learn that certain names are shared. It's important to keep several factors in mind:

1. The data may include errors. Amanda is listed in the boys' section because records show that 1 out of every 100,000 boys are named Amanda. It's reasonable to think that some boy "Amandas" are simply recording errors, but perhaps some aren't.

2. Names have different roles in different cultures. In the U.S., Andrea is primarily a girls' name, whereas in Italy, it's often used as a boys' name (for example, opera star Andrea Bocelli).

3. This book defines a name by its spelling, not by its pronunciation or meaning. This explains why a name like Julian is listed as a shared name. Julian (pronounced "JOO-lee-en") is a form of Julius, and therefore in the Boys' Names section. Julian (pronounced "Joo-lee-ANN") is a form of Julianne, and therefore in the Girls' Names section. You could argue that these are two different names, but because this book defines a name by its spelling, it treats them as one name.

4. The gender "assignment" of names change—often in surprising ways. For years, Ashley was used often for boys. (Remember Ashley Wilkes in *Gone with the Wind?*) Twenty-five years ago, it was in the top 300 of boys' names. Today it doesn't crack the top 1000, whereas it's the eighth-most-popular name for girls. In 2000, over twice as many boys than girls were named Reese. By 2004, actress Reese Witherspoon had helped those numbers switch places—now nearly twice as many girls than boys are named Reese.

I hope you find this book fun, helpful, and easy to use as you search for just the right name that will help your baby put his or her best foot forward in life.

Bruce Lansky

What's Hot, What's Not: The Latest Popularity Trends

Every year around Mother's Day, the Social Security Administration releases the latest baby name popularity information. Here's what I think are the most interesting and salient trends over the past year.

1. The Top 10 Names

Girls: In 2009, the top five girls' names shared one feature: They all ended with an "ah" sound. Isabella passed Emma as the new #1 name, and Olivia, Sophia, and Ava pushed Emily and Madison out of the top 5.

Boys: The top three boy's names (and six of the top 10) come from the Bible. Jacob has had a strong hold on the #1 position since the turn of the 21st century, while Michael (the #1 boys' name in the 1990s) dropped to #3, making room at #2 for Ethan. Alexander, William, Jayden, and particularly Noah moved up the list, while Joshua, Daniel, and Anthony moved down.

2. The Top 100 Names

Girls: The biggest popularity gains were registered by Khloe (+101), Bella (+64), Zoey (+23), Charlotte (+19) Peyton (+17), Serenity (+17), Evelyn (+15), Eva (+15), Arianna (+14), Aaliyah (+13), and Leah (+13). At the same time, the biggest popularity losses were registered by Jessica (-19), Angelina (-17), Gabrielle (17), Lauren (-16) Rachel (-16), Katherine (-14), Vanessa (-14), and Kaitlyn (-14).

Boys: The biggest popularity gains were registered by Levi (+28), Liam (+26), Oliver (+20), Carter (+15), Dominic (+12), and Eli (+10). The biggest popularity losses were registered by Hayden (-15), Sean (-14), Aidan (-13), and Bryan (-10).

3. Name Clusters

When selecting names, parents often consider name clusters. For example, they may weigh root names against their variations (William versus Liam), consider names that sound similar (Audrey sounds like Aubrey), or choose among names with the same theme (nature theme, such as River or Forest; place name, such as Austin or Boston; or religious theme, such as Jacob, Matthew, or Joshua).

Popular culture also affects the popularity of names. Last year, the most prominent cluster of pop-culture names were associated with the *Twilight* series of books and films. The popularity of the names Bella, Alice, Cullen, Jasper, and Emmett has been steadily rising since 2005, when the first book was released. However, of those names only Bella, the female protagonist, cracked the top 100 list to #58 in 2009.

Girls The most dynamic cluster for girls in 2009 were variant spellings of sound-alike names, notably Khloe (+101) & Chloe (+1) and Zoey (+23) & Zoe (+11). "Glamour" names—those ending with an "ah" sound and associated with movie stars—made up another key cluster: Mia (+4) and Sophia (+3) ascended the top 10 list, while Ava held steady at #5. Notice, too, the gains made by names with a religious or spiritual theme: Serenity (+17), Genesis (+12), Faith (+10), and Grace (+4).

Boys: In 2009, sound-alike names were the main cluster parents looked to for monikers to consider or avoid. For example, Jayden (+3), Brayden (+4), and Aiden (+4) all gained, at the expense of Hayden (-15) and Aidan (-13). Notice, too, that parents preferred Landon (+8) to sound-alike Brandon (-5). Another popular cluster was occupation-themed names, such as Carter (+15) and Cooper (+8), although a "traditional occupation" name, Hunter (-2), declined.

4. Paired Names for Twins

Twin Girls: The top 5 paired names for twin girls were: Isabella & Sophia (Mediterranean names that end with an "ah" sound), Faith & Hope (religious/spiritual names), Olivia & Sophia (more names with "ah" endings), Ella & Emma (two nicknames beginning with E and ending with an "ah" sound), and Hailey & Hannah (two names beginning with H). Notably, the #7 paired names are Heaven and Nevaeh, religious/spiritual names that are the same name, with one is the backward spelling of the other.

Twin Boys: The top 5 paired names for twin boys were: Jacob & Joshua (Old Testament names that start with J), Matthew & Michael (New Testament names that start with M), Daniel & David (more Old Testament names that start with D), Jayden & Jordan (names that start with J), and Jayden & Jaylen (sound-alike names that also start with J).

Twin Girl and Boy: The top 5 paired names for twin girl and boy were: Madison & Mason (two names that start with M), Taylor & Tyler (two sound-alike names that start with T), Addison & Aiden (two names that start with A and contain a "dee" sound), Emily & Ethan (two names that start with E), Emma & Evan (two more names that start with E). More than half of the top 50 paired names for twin boy and girl started with the same letter, as do the paired names for twin boys. By contrast, only about a third of the top 50 paired names for twin girls started with the same letter.

5. A Few Predictions

Girls: Isabella is likely to retain its #1 ranking. Olivia and Sophia could challenge Emma for the #2 position. The top 10 girls' names most likely to decline in popularity are Emily and Madison. Names most likely to rise onto the top 10 list are Addison, Alexis, and Ella. Looking at the top 1,000 list, watch for the rise of short names that end with an "ah" sound, such as Leia, Diya, Gia, Malia, Alia, Isla, and Nylah.

Boys: Jacob is sure to keep its #1 ranking. Alexander and William could challenge Michael for the #3 position. The top 10 boys' names most likely to decline in popularity are Joshua, Daniel, and Anthony. The name most likely to rise onto the top 10 list is Aiden. Looking at the top 1,000 list, watch for the rise of names with double consonant endings (such as Tripp, Jett, Maxx, and Emmett) and short, one-syllable names (such as Ace, Chase, Case, Colt, King, and Jax).

Step 2: Narrow the List Based on What Will Work Best for Your Baby

Now that you've each created a list based on personal considerations, it's time to narrow them down based on practical considerations. This way, you'll choose a name that works well for you and for your baby. You may love a particular name, but if it doesn't hold up to these basic criteria, your baby probably won't love it. It can be unpleasant going through life with a name that for whatever reason doesn't work for you.

Make enough copies of the table on the following page for each name on your list. Have your partner do the same. Rate each name on twelve factors. Example: Consider the popularity of the name Jacob—if you think there might be too many Jacobs in his school, check "too popular." Consider nicknames—if you love Jake, check "appealing." Another example: Consider the way Rafael sounds to you—if it's music to your ears, check "pleasing." Consider its fit with your last name—if you don't think it goes so well with Abramovitz, check "doesn't fit."

When you've completed the table, add up the score by giving three points for every check in the Positive column, two points for every check in the Neutral column, and one point for every check in the Negative column. Scoring each name might help make the subjective process of selecting a name more objective to you.

(Note: If you're pinched for time, mentally complete the table for each name, keeping track of a rough score. The important part is to narrow the list to your top five boys' and girls' names.)

Use this Form to Rate Your Favorite Names

Name:_____

Factors	Positive	Neutral	Negative
1. Spelling	❏ easy	❏ medium	❏ hard
2. Pronunciation	❏ easy	❏ medium	❏ hard
3. Sound	❏ pleasing	❏ okay	❏ unpleasing
4. Last name	❏ fits well	❏ fits okay	❏ doesn't fit
5. Gender ID	❏ clear	❏ neutral	❏ confusing
6. Nicknames	❏ appealing	❏ okay	❏ unappealing
7. Popularity	❏ not too popular	❏ popular	❏ too popular
8. Uniqueness	❏ not too unique	❏ unique	❏ too unique
9. Impression	❏ positive	❏ okay	❏ negative
10. Namesakes	❏ positive	❏ okay	❏ negative
11. Initials	❏ pleasing	❏ okay	❏ unpleasing
12. Meaning	❏ positive	❏ okay	❏ negative

Final Score:_____

Step 3: Make the Final Choice

List your top five boys' and girls' names in the chart below, and have your partner do the same. It's now time to share the names. If you have names in common, compare your scores; perhaps average them. If you have different names on your lists, swap names and rate them using the same table as before. In the end, you'll have a handful of names that work well for you, your partner, and your baby. Now all you have to do is make the final decision. Good luck!

Mom's Top Five Names

1._____ Mom's Score: ____ Dad's Score: ____

2._____ Mom's Score: ____ Dad's Score: ____

3._____ Mom's Score: ____ Dad's Score: ____

4._____ Mom's Score: ____ Dad's Score: ____

5._____ Mom's Score: ____ Dad's Score: ____

Dad's Top Five Names

1._____ Dad's Score: ____ Mom's Score: ____

2._____ Dad's Score: ____ Mom's Score: ____

3._____ Dad's Score: ____ Mom's Score: ____

4._____ Dad's Score: ____ Mom's Score: ____

5._____ Dad's Score: ____ Mom's Score: ____

What's Hot, What's Not: The Latest Popularity Trends

Every year around Mother's Day, the Social Security Administration releases the latest baby name popularity information. Here are the most interesting trends in 2008 that I spotted.

1. The Top 10 Names

Girls: After being stuck behind Emily for years, Emma became the most popular name for girls. Emily dropped two places to #3 while Isabella remained at #2. Chloe jumped six spots to #10—easily the biggest move in the top 10. Madison rose from #5 to #4, while Addison fell from #11 to #12. In 2007, Madison slipped from #3 to #5 at the expense of Addison, which leaped from #28 to #11.

Boys: The biggest news was no surprise. The first five boys' names—Jacob, Michael, Ethan, Joshua, and Daniel—retained their positions on the list. The biggest move in the top 10 was made by Alexander, which jumped five spots to #6 at the expense of Christopher, which fell from #6 to #9, and Matthew, which dropped from #9 to #10.

2. The Top 100 Names

Girls: The biggest popularity gains were registered by Payton (+63), Peyton (+61), Camila (+46), Genesis (+43), Madelyn (+41), Layla (+30), Aubrey (+27), Leah (+27), and Valeria (+25). Of these names, only Aubrey gained popularity last year, too. The biggest popularity losses were registered by Megan (-22), Jennifer (-20), Faith (-17), Jocelyn (-17), Jessica (-17), Rachel (-16), Isabelle (-14), Gabrielle (-12), Alexandra (-12), and Sydney (-12).

Boys: The biggest popularity gains were registered by Brody (+35), Eli (+30), Colton (+19), Carter (+15), Liam (+14), Brayden (+13), Henry (+13), Chase (+12), Aiden (+11), Ayden (+11), and Josiah (+10). The biggest popularity losses were registered by Jaden (-13,) Alex (-12), Diego (11), and Kyle (-10).

3. Name Clusters

When selecting names, parents often consider name clusters. For example, they may weigh root names against their variations (William versus Liam), consider names that sound similar (Audrey sounds like

Aubrey), or choose among names with the same theme (city theme, such as Brooklyn or Sydney, or religious theme, such as Jacob, Matthew, or Joshua).

Girls: The most dynamic name cluster was Payton (+63) and Peyton (+61), two names that rocketed onto the top-100 list for the first time. Sound-alike names Layla (+30) and Leah (+27) jumped to mid-list. Rhyming pair Chloe (+6) and Zoey (+14) moved up, as did Riley (+13) and Kylie (+12). Madeline (+5) and its alternative Madelyn (+41) also moved up. Names that end with "-el" or "-elle" endings, including Rachel (-16), Isabelle (-14), and Gabrielle (-12), all declined. Name clusters in which one name gained seemingly at the expense of others were Mariah (+14) and Maria (-11), Mary (-4), and Maya (-10); Brooklyn (+10) and Sydney (-12); and Genesis (+43) and Faith (-17), Destiny (-7), and Neveah (-3), which is *heaven* spelled backward.

Boys: The most dynamic name cluster was Eli (+30) and its root name Elijah (+8), which both moved up. Alex (-12), however, fell as its root name Alexander (+5) rose. Brody (+35) definitely jumped, but it didn't significantly affect the popularity of sound-alike Brady (-1). Brayden (+13), Jayden (+7), Aiden (+11), and Ayden (+11) all moved up, apparently at the expense of Jaden (-13), Aidan (-5), Hayden (-4), Caden (-3), and Kaden (-1).

4. Paired Names for Twins
Twin Girls: The five most popular paired names for twin girls were Gabriella and Isabella (two Italian names with "-a" endings), Madison and Morgan (two names that start with M), Ella and Emma (two nicknames beginning with E), Faith and Hope (two religious/spiritual names), and Isabella and Sophia (two Italian names that end with "-a"). In the top 20, six of the paired girls' names started with the same letters.

Twin Boys: The five most popular paired names for twin boys were Jacob and Joshua (two Old Testament names that start with J), Daniel and David (two Old Testament names that start with D), Jayden and Jordan (two names that start with a J), Ethan and Evan (two names that start with an E), and Isaac and Isaiah (two Old Testament names that start with I). In the top 20, sixteen paired boys' names started with the same letters.

Twin Girl & Boy: The five most popular paired names for girl/boy twins were Taylor and Tyler, Madison and Mason, Emma and Ethan, Emily and Ethan, Jayda and Jayden. In the top 13, twelve paired names started with the same letters—making this an almost universal practice.

5. A Few Surprises

For all the news about what a religious country we are, I was surprised to discover that seven of the nine religious/spiritual names on the girls' top 100 list declined in popularity. With that said, however, four of the five top boys' names are from the Old Testament, and names from the New Testament hold the fifth, ninth, and tenth spots.

For all the news about the growing Latino population in America, I could identify only one traditionally Latino name on the girls' top 100 list (Maria), which lost popularity in 2008. Of the six traditionally Latino names on the boys' list, all moved down: Diego (-11) Jose (-6), Carlos (-3), Juan (-3), Jesus (-2), Angel (-2). More Latino families seem to be choosing names of other origins for their sons.

There continues to be no names of clear African American origin on either top-100 list.

6. A Few Predictions

Girls' Top 10 Names: Chloe could plateau after its big move to #10 and might be challenged by up-and-comers Samantha, Addison, Natalie, Mia, and Alexis.

Boys' Top 10 Names: Fast-rising Jayden and Aiden could challenge Christopher and Matthew for positions in the top 10.

Girls' Top 100 Names: Genesis seems to have become the fastest-rising religious/spiritual name. Nevaeh held this title in 2007, but its popularity may start dropping like a rock. Payton and Peyton should continue to rocket up the list.

Boys' Top 100 Names: Jayden/Brayden and Aiden/Ayden should continue to rise at the expense of Jaden and Aidan.

The Most Popular Names from 1900 to 2009

The popularity of names, like the length of hemlines and the width of ties, is subject to change every year. The changes become even more noticeable when you think about the changes in name "fashions" over long periods.

Think about the names of your grandparents' generation: Margaret, Shirley, George, Harold. Very few of those names are in the current list of top 100 names. Most names from your parents' generation—Susan, Cheryl, Gary, Ronald—don't make the current list of top 100 names either.

It seems that every decade a new group of names rises in popularity and an old group of names declines. So, when choosing a name for your baby, it's wise to consider whether a name's popularity is rising, declining, or holding steady.

To help you assess name popularity trends, we are presenting the latest top 100 names given to baby boys and girls in the United States. The rankings are derived from a survey of new births nationwide conducted by the Social Security Administration. (Alternate spellings of each name are treated as separate names. For example, Sarah and Sara are ranked separately.) You can see from the data how the names have risen or fallen since the previous year's survey. If you're expecting two bundles of joy, don't miss the lists of most popular names for twins in the U.S. In addition, you can track popularity trends over the years with the lists of top 25 names given to girls and boys in each decade since 1900.

Enjoy the following data, but remember that the popularity issue cuts two ways: 1) Psychologists say a child with a common or popular name seems to have better odds of success in life than a child with an uncommon name. 2) A child whose name is at the top of the popularity poll may not feel as unique and special as a child whose name is less common.

Top 100 Girls' Names in 2009

2009 Rank	Name	2008 Rank	Rank Change	2009 Rank	Name	2008 Rank	Rank Change
1	Isabella	2	+1	26	Kaylee	31	+5
2	Emma	1	-1	27	Lillian	29	+2
3	Olivia	6	+3	28	Leah	41	+13
4	Sophia	7	+3	29	Anna	26	-3
5	Ava	5	—	30	Allison	32	+2
6	Emily	3	-3	31	Victoria	27	-4
7	Madison	4	-3	32	Avery	38	+6
8	Abigail	8	—	33	Gabriella	35	+2
9	Chloe	10	+1	34	Nevaeh	34	—
10	Mia	14	+4	35	Kayla	28	-7
11	Elizabeth	9	-2	36	Sofia	36	—
12	Addison	12	—	37	Brooklyn	47	+10
13	Alexis	15	+2	38	Riley	39	+1
14	Ella	19	+5	39	Evelyn	54	+15
15	Samantha	11	-4	40	Savannah	33	-7
16	Natalie	13	-3	41	Aubrey	42	+1
17	Grace	21	+4	42	Alexa	50	+8
18	Lily	24	+6	43	Peyton	60	+17
19	Alyssa	16	-3	44	Makayla	37	-7
20	Ashley	18	-2	45	Layla	55	+10
21	Sarah	20	-1	46	Lauren	30	-16
22	Taylor	22	—	47	Zoe	58	+11
23	Hannah	17	-6	48	Sydney	49	+1
24	Brianna	23	-1	49	Audrey	44	-5
25	Hailey	25	—	50	Julia	40	-10

2009 Rank	Name	2008 Rank	Rank Change	2009 Rank	Name	2008 Rank	Rank Change
51	Jasmine	43	-8	76	Gianna	86	+10
52	Arianna	66	+14	77	Mackenzie	65	-12
53	Claire	62	+9	78	Jessica	59	-19
54	Brooke	52	-2	79	Camila	83	+4
55	Amelia	68	+13	80	Faith	91	+11
56	Morgan	46	-10	81	Autumn	89	+8
57	Destiny	48	-9	82	Ariana	81	-1
58	Bella	122	+64	83	Genesis	95	+12
59	Madelyn	63	+4	84	Payton	90	+6
60	Katherine	45	-15	85	Bailey	82	-3
61	Kylie	51	-10	86	Angelina	69	-17
62	Maya	72	+10	87	Caroline	94	+7
63	Aaliyah	77	+14	88	Mariah	78	-10
64	Madeline	56	-8	89	Katelyn	80	-9
65	Sophie	74	+9	90	Rachel	75	-15
66	Kimberly	57	-9	91	Vanessa	76	-15
67	Kaitlyn	53	-14	92	Molly	104	+12
68	Charlotte	87	+19	93	Melanie	85	-8
69	Alexandra	61	-8	94	Serenity	111	+17
70	Jocelyn	67	-3	95	Khloe	196	+101
71	Maria	64	-7	96	Gabrielle	79	-17
72	Valeria	73	+1	97	Paige	88	-9
73	Andrea	71	-2	98	Mya	101	+3
74	Trinity	70	-4	99	Eva	114	+15
75	Zoey	98	+23	100	Isabelle	93	-7

Top 100 Boys' Names in 2009

2009 Rank	Name	2008 Rank	Rank Change	2009 Rank	Name	2008 Rank	Rank Change
1	Jacob	1	—	26	John	20	-6
2	Ethan	3	+1	27	Samuel	28	+1
3	Michael	2	-1	28	Tyler	27	-1
4	Alexander	6	+2	29	Dylan	31	+2
5	William	8	+3	30	Jonathan	26	-4
6	Joshua	4	-2	31	Caleb	34	+3
7	Daniel	5	-2	32	Nicholas	29	-3
8	Jayden	11	+3	33	Gavin	30	-3
9	Noah	15	+6	34	Mason	35	+1
10	Anthony	7	-3	35	Evan	38	+3
11	Christopher	9	-2	36	Landon	44	+8
12	Aiden	16	+4	37	Angel	36	-1
13	Matthew	10	-3	38	Brandon	33	-5
14	David	14	—	39	Lucas	46	+7
15	Andrew	12	-3	40	Isaac	37	-3
16	Joseph	13	-3	41	Isaiah	42	+1
17	Logan	19	+2	42	Jack	39	-3
18	James	17	-1	43	Jose	41	-2
19	Ryan	18	-1	44	Kevin	40	-4
20	Benjamin	25	+5	45	Jordan	48	+3
21	Elijah	22	+1	46	Justin	45	-1
22	Gabriel	24	+2	47	Brayden	51	+4
23	Christian	23	—	48	Luke	43	-5
24	Nathan	21	-3	49	Liam	75	+26
25	Jackson	32	+7	50	Carter	65	+15

2009 Rank	Name	2008 Rank	Rank Change	2009 Rank	Name	2008 Rank	Rank Change
51	Owen	58	+7	76	Nathaniel	77	+1
52	Connor	57	+5	77	Brody	70	-7
53	Zachary	47	-6	78	Jesus	79	+1
54	Aaron	50	-4	79	Carlos	73	-6
55	Robert	49	-6	80	Tristan	81	+1
56	Hunter	54	-2	81	Dominic	93	+12
57	Thomas	52	-5	82	Cole	84	+2
58	Adrian	56	-2	83	Alex	85	+2
59	Cameron	53	-6	84	Cooper	92	+8
60	Wyatt	62	+2	85	Ayden	91	+6
61	Chase	67	+6	86	Carson	89	+3
62	Julian	61	-1	87	Josiah	96	+9
63	Austin	55	-8	88	Levi	116	+28
64	Charles	63	-1	89	Blake	90	+1
65	Jeremiah	69	+4	90	Eli	100	+10
66	Jason	60	-6	91	Hayden	76	-15
67	Juan	66	-1	92	Bryan	82	-10
68	Xavier	71	+3	93	Colton	98	+5
69	Luis	64	-5	94	Brian	87	-7
70	Sebastian	74	+4	95	Eric	86	-9
71	Henry	78	+7	96	Parker	103	+7
72	Aidan	59	-13	97	Sean	83	-14
73	Ian	80	+7	98	Oliver	118	+20
74	Adam	72	-2	99	Miguel	101	+2
75	Diego	68	-7	100	Kyle	97	-3

Changes in Top 100
from 2008 to 2009

Big Gains

Girls		Boys	
Khloe	+101	Levi	+28
Bella	+64	Liam	+26
Zoey	+23	Oliver	+20
Charlotte	+19	Carter	+15
Peyton	+17	Dominic	+12
Serenity	+17	Eli	+10
Evelyn	+15	Josiah	+9
Eva	+15	Landon	+8
Arianna	+14	Cooper	+8
Aaliyah	+14	Jackson	+7
Leah	+13	Lucas	+7
Amelia	+13	Owen	+7
Genesis	+12	Henry	+7
Molly	+12	Ian	+7
Zoe	+11	Parker	+7
Faith	+11		

Big Losses

Girls		Boys	
Jessica	-19	Hayden	-15
Angelina	-17	Sean	-14
Gabrielle	-17	Aidan	-13
Lauren	-16	Bryan	-10
Katherine	-15	Eric	-9
Rachel	-15	Austin	-8
Vanessa	-15	Diego	-7
Kaitlyn	-14	Brody	-7
Mackenzie	-12	Brian	-7
Julia	-10	John	-6
Morgan	-10	Zachary	-6
Kylie	-10	Robert	-6
Mariah	-10	Cameron	-6
		Jason	-6
		Carlos	-6

New to Top 100

Girls		Boys	
Bella	+64	Levi	+28
Eva	+15	Miguel	+2
Khloe	+101	Oliver	+20
Molly	+12	Parker	+7
Mya	+3		
Serenity	+17		

Out of Top 100

Girls		Boys	
Gracie	-16	Brady	-15
Isabel	-14	Caden	-8
Jennifer	-25	Jaden	-13
Mary	-5	Kaden	-3
Megan	-5		
Sara	-14		

The Most Popular Names for Twins in 2009

Twin Girls	Twin Boys	Twin Girl & Boy
Isabella, Sophia	Jacob, Joshua	Madison, Mason
Faith, Hope	Matthew, Michael	Taylor, Tyler
Olivia, Sophia	Daniel, David	Addison, Aiden
Ella, Emma	Jayden, Jordan	Emily, Ethan
Hailey, Hannah	Jayden, Jaylen	Emma, Evan
Ava, Emma	Elijah, Isaiah	Ella, Ethan
Heaven, Nevaeh	Isaac, Isaiah	Emma, Ethan
Madison, Morgan	Ethan, Evan	Jayda, Jayden
Mackenzie, Madison	Logan, Lucas	Jada, Jaden
Ava, Olivia	Logan, Luke	Aidan, Nadia
Isabella, Olivia	Caleb, Joshua	Aiden, Ava
Makayla, Makenzie	Landon, Logan	Emma, William
Ava, Ella	Andrew, Matthew	Madison, Matthew
Faith, Grace	Nathan, Nicholas	Anna, William
Gabriella, Isabella	Brandon, Bryan	Emily, Evan
Abigail, Olivia	Alexander, Benjamin	Emma, Jacob
Emma, Sophia	Hayden, Hunter	Emma, Noah
London, Paris	Alexander, Nicholas	Isabella, Isaiah
Elizabeth, Emily	Gabriel, Michael	Madison, Michael
Valeria, Vanessa	Christian, Christopher	Addison, Andrew
Emily, Emma	Jordan, Justin	Chloe, Connor
Emma, Grace	Benjamin, Samuel	Emma, Jack
Gabriella, Isabella	James, John	Nicholas, Sophia
Abigail, Allison	Jeremiah, Joshua	Noah, Sophia
Abigail, Emma	John, Joseph	Olivia, Owen
Addison, Ava	Joseph, Joshua	Zachary, Zoe
Anna, Emma	Jeremiah, Josiah	Zachary, Zoey
Ava, Mia	Aiden, Ethan	Brian, Brianna
Ava, Sophia	Jacob, Noah	Caleb, Chloe
Abigail, Emily	Alexander, Anthony	Ethan, Isabella

The Most Popular Names through the Decades

Most Popular 2000–2009		Most Popular 1990–1999		Most Popular 1980–1989	
Girls	**Boys**	**Girls**	**Boys**	**Girls**	**Boys**
Emily	Jacob	Ashley	Michael	Jessica	Michael
Madison	Michael	Jessica	Christopher	Jennifer	Christopher
Emma	Joshua	Emily	Matthew	Amanda	Matthew
Olivia	Matthew	Sarah	Joshua	Ashley	Joshua
Hannah	Daniel	Samantha	Jacob	Sarah	David
Abigail	Christopher	Brittany	Andrew	Stephanie	Daniel
Isabella	Andrew	Amanda	Daniel	Melissa	James
Samantha	Ethan	Elizabeth	Nicholas	Nicole	Robert
Elizabeth	Joseph	Taylor	Tyler	Elizabeth	John
Ashley	William	Megan	Joseph	Heather	Joseph
Alexis	Anthony	Stephanie	David	Tiffany	Jason
Sarah	David	Kayla	Brandon	Michelle	Justin
Sophia	Alexander	Lauren	James	Amber	Andrew
Alyssa	Nicholas	Jennifer	John	Megan	Ryan
Grace	Ryan	Rachel	Ryan	Rachel	William
Ava	Tyler	Hannah	Zachary	Amy	Brian
Taylor	James	Nicole	Justin	Lauren	Jonathan
Brianna	John	Amber	Anthony	Kimberly	Brandon
Lauren	Jonathan	Alexis	William	Christina	Nicholas
Chloe	Noah	Courtney	Robert	Brittany	Anthony
Natalie	Brandon	Victoria	Jonathan	Crystal	Eric
Kayla	Christian	Danielle	Kyle	Rebecca	Adam
Jessica	Dylan	Alyssa	Austin	Laura	Kevin
Anna	Samuel	Rebecca	Alexander	Emily	Steven
Victoria	Benjamin	Jasmine	Kevin	Danielle	Thomas

Most Popular 1970–1979		**Most Popular 1960–1969**		**Most Popular 1950–1959**	
Girls	**Boys**	**Girls**	**Boys**	**Girls**	**Boys**
Jennifer	Michael	Lisa	Michael	Mary	Michael
Amy	Christopher	Mary	David	Linda	James
Melissa	Jason	Karen	John	Patricia	Robert
Michelle	David	Susan	James	Susan	John
Kimberly	James	Kimberly	Robert	Deborah	David
Lisa	John	Patricia	Mark	Barbara	William
Angela	Robert	Linda	William	Debra	Richard
Heather	Brian	Donna	Richard	Karen	Thomas
Stephanie	William	Michelle	Thomas	Nancy	Mark
Jessica	Matthew	Cynthia	Jeffrey	Donna	Charles
Elizabeth	Daniel	Sandra	Steven	Cynthia	Steven
Nicole	Joseph	Deborah	Joseph	Sandra	Gary
Rebecca	Kevin	Pamela	Timothy	Pamela	Joseph
Kelly	Eric	Tammy	Kevin	Sharon	Donald
Mary	Jeffrey	Laura	Scott	Kathleen	Ronald
Christina	Richard	Lori	Brian	Carol	Kenneth
Amanda	Scott	Elizabeth	Charles	Diane	Paul
Sarah	Mark	Julie	Daniel	Brenda	Larry
Laura	Steven	Jennifer	Paul	Cheryl	Daniel
Julie	Timothy	Brenda	Christopher	Elizabeth	Stephen
Shannon	Thomas	Angela	Kenneth	Janet	Dennis
Christine	Anthony	Barbara	Anthony	Kathy	Timothy
Tammy	Charles	Debra	Gregory	Margaret	Edward
Karen	Jeremy	Sharon	Ronald	Janice	Jeffrey
Tracy	Joshua	Teresa	Donald	Carolyn	George

Most Popular 1940–1949		**Most Popular 1930–1939**		**Most Popular 1920–1929**	
Girls	**Boys**	**Girls**	**Boys**	**Girls**	**Boys**
Mary	James	Mary	Robert	Mary	Robert
Linda	Robert	Betty	James	Dorothy	John
Barbara	John	Barbara	John	Helen	James
Patricia	William	Shirley	William	Betty	William
Carol	Richard	Patricia	Richard	Margaret	Charles
Sandra	David	Dorothy	Charles	Ruth	George
Nancy	Charles	Joan	Donald	Virginia	Joseph
Judith	Thomas	Margaret	George	Doris	Richard
Sharon	Michael	Nancy	Thomas	Mildred	Edward
Susan	Ronald	Helen	Joseph	Elizabeth	Donald
Betty	Larry	Carol	David	Frances	Thomas
Carolyn	Donald	Joyce	Edward	Anna	Frank
Shirley	Joseph	Doris	Ronald	Evelyn	Paul
Margaret	Gary	Ruth	Paul	Alice	Harold
Karen	George	Virginia	Kenneth	Marie	Walter
Donna	Kenneth	Marilyn	Frank	Jean	Raymond
Judy	Paul	Elizabeth	Raymond	Shirley	Jack
Kathleen	Edward	Jean	Jack	Barbara	Henry
Joyce	Jerry	Frances	Harold	Irene	Arthur
Dorothy	Dennis	Dolores	Billy	Marjorie	Kenneth
Janet	Frank	Beverly	Gerald	Lois	Albert
Diane	Daniel	Donna	Walter	Florence	David
Elizabeth	Raymond	Alice	Jerry	Rose	Harry
Janice	Stephen	Lois	Eugene	Martha	Ralph
Joan	Roger	Janet	Henry	Louise	Eugene

Most Popular 1910–1919		Most Popular 1900–1909	
Girls	**Boys**	**Girls**	**Boys**
Mary	John	Mary	John
Helen	William	Helen	William
Dorothy	James	Margaret	James
Margaret	Robert	Anna	George
Ruth	Joseph	Ruth	Joseph
Mildred	George	Elizabeth	Charles
Anna	Charles	Dorothy	Robert
Elizabeth	Edward	Marie	Frank
Frances	Frank	Mildred	Edward
Marie	Walter	Alice	Henry
Evelyn	Thomas	Florence	Walter
Virginia	Henry	Ethel	Thomas
Alice	Harold	Lillian	Harry
Florence	Paul	Rose	Arthur
Rose	Raymond	Gladys	Harold
Lillian	Arthur	Frances	Albert
Irene	Richard	Edna	Paul
Louise	Albert	Grace	Clarence
Edna	Harry	Catherine	Fred
Gladys	Donald	Hazel	Carl
Catherine	Ralph	Irene	Louis
Ethel	Louis	Gertrude	Raymond
Josephine	Clarence	Clara	Ralph
Ruby	Carl	Louise	Roy
Martha	Fred	Edith	Richard

Names around the World

Want to track popularity trends across the globe? Want to give your baby a name that reflects your heritage, language, or favorite travel destination? The following lists feature names with international flair. You'll learn the latest popular names given to baby girls and boys in several countries. Just as the U.S. popularity lists come from data compiled by the Social Security Administration, these international lists come from records kept by similar organizations across the globe. You'll also discover a sampling of interesting names from particular cultural origins. Use those lists to get you thinking, but don't forget that there are thousands more names in the Girls' Names and Boys' Names sections with the origins you're looking for.

The Most Popular Names around the World

Most Popular Names in Austria in 2006

Girls	Boys
Lena	Lukas
Leonie	Tobias
Sarah	David
Anna	Florian
Julia	Simon
Katharina	Maximilian
Hannah	Fabian
Sophie	Alexander
Laura	Sebastian
Lisa	Julian

Most Popular Names in Belgium in 2006

Girls	Boys
Emma	Noah
Marie	Thomas
Laura	Nathan
Julie	Lucas
Louise	Louis
Clara	Arthur
Manon	Milan
Léa	Hugo
Sarah	Maxime
Luna	Mohamed
Elise	Nicolas
Charlotte	Simon
Lotte	Théo
Camille	Tom
Lore	Victor
Lisa	Robbe
Chloé	Wout
Lucie	Alexandre
Amber	Senne
Lola	Mathis
Jade	Lars
Lara	Matteo
Hanne	Luca
Emilie	Romain
Zoë	Seppe

Most Popular Names in British Columbia, Canada, in 2007

Girls	Boys
Ava	Ethan
Emily	Jacob
Sophia	Noah
Olivia	Liam
Emma	Matthew
Hannah	Joshua
Ella	Logan
Isabella	Owen
Sarah	Ryan
Chloe	Lucas
Madison	Alexander
Sophie	Benjamin
Lily	Nathan
Grace	Daniel
Abigail	Jack
Brooklyn	William
Taylor	James
Julia	Nicholas
Samantha	Jayden
Claire	Tyler

Most Popular Names in Chile in 2006

Girls	Boys
Martina	Benjamin
Constanza	Vicente
Catalina	Matias
Valentina	Martin
Sofia	Sebastian
Javiera	Joaquin
Antonia	Diego
Maria	Nicolas
Isidora	Jose
Francisca	Cristobal
Fernanda	Bastian
Camila	Juan
Antonella	Ignacio
Florencia	Maximiliano
Josefa	Felipe
Emilia	Tomas
Daniela	Javier
Belen	Francisco
Ignacia	Gabriel
Pia	Luis
Rocio	Lucas
Anais	Daniel
Millaray	Agustin
Maite	Franco
Krishna	Carlos

Most Popular Names in England/Wales in 2007

Girls	Boys
Grace	Jack
Ruby	Thomas
Olivia	Oliver
Emily	Joshua
Jessica	Harry
Sophie	Charlie
Chloe	Daniel
Lily	William
Ella	James
Amelia	Alfie
Lucy	Samuel
Charlotte	George
Ellie	Joseph
Mia	Benjamin
Evie	Ethan
Hannah	Lewis
Megan	Mohammed
Katie	Jake
Isabella	Dylan
Isabelle	Jacob
Millie	Luke
Abigail	Callum
Amy	Alexander
Daisy	Matthew
Freya	Ryan

Most Popular Names in France in 2006

Girls	Boys
Emma	Enzo
Lea	Mathis
Manon	Lucas
Clara	Hugo
Chloe	Matheo
Ines	Nathan
Camille	Theo
Sarah	Noah
Oceane	Matteo
Jade	Thomas
Marie	Louis
Lola	Maxime
Anais	Romain
Eva	Tom
Lucie	Leo
Lilou	Yanis
Julie	Alexis
Lena	Baptiste
Romane	Antoine
Lisa	Raphael
Lou	Alexandre
Laura	Clement
Celia	Quentin
Juliette	Paul
Pauline	Axel

Most Popular Names in Germany in 2007

Girls	Boys
Marie	Leon
Sophie/Sofie	Maximilian
Maria	Alexander
Anna/ Anne	Paul
Leonie	Luca
Lena	Lukas/Lucas
Johanna	Felix
Charlotte	Elias
Hannah/Hanna	David
Sophia/Sofia	Jonas

Most Popular Names in Hungary in 2005

Girls	Boys
Anna	Bence
Viktória	Máté
Réka	Balázs
Vivien	Dávid
Zsófia	Dániel
Petra	Levente
Dorina	Tamás
Fanni	Ádám
Boglárka	Péter
Eszter	Gergö

Most Popular Names in Ireland in 2005

Girls	Boys
Emma	Jack
Sarah	Sean
Katie	Adam
Amy	Conor
Aoife	James
Ciara	Daniel
Sophie	Cian
Chloe	Luke
Leah	Aaron
Ella	Michael
Emily	Dylan
Rachel	Ryan
Niamh	Jamie
Grace	Ben
Rebecca	David
Hannah	Thomas
Caoimhe	John
Ava	Patrick
Lauren	Matthew
Jessica	Darragh
Anna	Eoin
Kate	Oisin
Roisin	Shane
Lucy	Alex
Molly	Evan

Most Popular Names in Japan in 2006

Girls	Boys
Hina	Riku
Haruna	Hiroto
Yuna	Haruto
Miu	Daito
Mihane	Hiroki
Myu	Taiki
Misaki	Daiki
Sakura	Ren
Ai	Tsubasa
Mana	Tasuku

Most Popular Names in the Netherlands in 2007

Girls	Boys
Sanne	Sem
Lotte	Tim
Julia	Daan
Sophie	Ruben
Licke	Thomas
Emma	Jesse
Anna	Milan
Eva	Thijs
Lisa	Lucas
Fleur	Stijn
Iris	Lars
Noa	Sven
Isa	Jayden
Anne	Bram
Maud	Luuk
Femke	Finn
Anouk	Max
Sara	Niels
Jasmijn	Julian
Roos	Jasper

Most Popular Names in New South Wales, Australia, in 2007

Girls	Boys
Isabella	Jack
Ella	William
Emily	Joshua
Chloe	Lachlan
Mia	Thomas
Olivia	Riley
Charlotte	Cooper
Sophie	James
Sienna	Noah
Jessica	Ethan
Ava	Daniel
Lily	Oliver
Hannah	Ryan
Grace	Samuel
Amelia	Benjamin
Sarah	Matthew
Ruby	Liam
Zoe	Lucas
Georgia	Alexander
Emma	Jayden
Jasmine	Jacob
Lucy	Luke
Madison	Nicholas
Sophia	Harrison
Chelsea	Isaac

Most Popular Names in Norway in 2007

Girls	Boys
Thea	Jonas
Emma	Mathias
Julie	Magnus
Ida	Elias
Emilie	Emil
Nora	Henrik
Ingrid	Sander
Anna	Martin
Sara	Tobias
Sofie	Daniel
Maria	Andreas
Vilde	Adrian

Girls	Boys
Mia	Sebastian
Linnea	Oliver
Tuva	Marius
Amalie	Noah
Frida	Benjamin
Malin	Kristian
Leah	William
Mina	Alexander
Oda	Markus
Hedda	Sondre
Andrea	Fredrik
Marie	Ole
Mathilde	Lukas

Most Popular Names in Quebec, Canada, in 2006

Girls	Boys
Lea	William
Jade	Samuel
Rosalie	Alexis
Florence	Nathan
Laurie	Thomas
Gabrielle	Antoine
Sarah	Gabriel
Camille	Justin
Oceane	Olivier
Laurence	Felix
Noemie	Zachary
Emma	Xavier
Emilie	Jeremy
Juliette	Alexandre
Maika	Mathis
Coralie	Anthony
Justine	Jacob
Megane	Raphael
Ariane	Emile
Emy	Vincent
Chloe	Nicolas
Audrey	Benjamin
Annabelle	Maxime
Marianne	Tristan
Charlotte	Noah

Most Popular Names in Scotland in 2007

Girls	Boys
Sophie	Lewis
Emma	Jack
Lucy	Ryan
Katie	James
Erin	Callum
Ellie	Cameron
Amy	Daniel
Emily	Liam
Chloe	Jamie
Olivia	Kyle
Hannah	Matthew
Jessica	Logan
Grace	Finlay
Ava	Adam
Rebecca	Alexander
Isla	Dylan
Brooke	Aiden
Megan	Andrew
Niamh	Ben
Eilidh	Aaron
Eva	Connor
Abbie	Thomas
Skye	Joshua
Aimee	David
Mia	Ross

Most Popular Names in Spain in 2006

Girls	Boys
Lucia	Alejandro
Maria	Daniel
Paula	Pablo
Laura	David
Claudia	Adrian
Irene	Alvaro
Marta	Javier
Alba	Sergio
Sara	Hugo
Carla	Diego
Andrea	Carlos
Nerea	Marcos

Girls	Boys
Julia	Mario
Natalia	Ivan
Elena	Manuel
Ana	Miguel
Sofia	Jorge
Carmen	Ruben
Daniela	Iker
Marina	Raul
Cristina	Victor
Ainhoa	Antonio
Aitana	Juan
Rocio	Hector
Angela	Marc

Most Popular Names in Sweden in 2007

Girls	Boys
Wilma	William
Maja	Lucas
Ella	Elias
Emma	Oscar
Julia	Hugo
Alice	Viktor
Alva	Filip
Linnea	Erik
Ida	Emil
Ebba	Isak
Elin	Anton
Elsa	Alexander
Klara	Liam
Nellie	Gustav
Felicia	Oliver
Agnes	Axel
Amanda	Albin
Emilia	Leo
Moa	Ludvig
Hanna	Simon
Ellen	Melvin
Isabelle	Edvin
Saga	Jonathan
Olivia	Max
Matilda	Linus

Names from around the World

African

Girls	Boys
Afi	Afram
Adia	Axi
Adanna	Bello
Ama	Ekon
Ashanti	Enzi
Batini	Idi
Eshe	Jabari
Fayola	Kayin
Femi	Kitwana
Goma	Kosey
Halla	Kwasi
Imena	Liu
Kameke	Mansa
Kamilah	Moswen
Kia	Mzuzi
Mosi	Nwa
Pita	Nwake
Poni	Ogun
Reta	Ohin
Sharik	Okapi
Siko	Ottah
Tawia	Senwe
Thema	Ulan
Winna	Uzoma
Zina	Zareb

American

Girls	Boys
Abelina	Adarius
Akayla	Buster
Amberlyn	Caden
Betsy	Daevon
Blinda	Dantrell
Coralee	Demarius
Darilynn	Dionte
Doneshia	Jadrien
Emmylou	Jailen
Jaycee	Jamar
Jessalyn	Jareth
Johnessa	Jayce
Karolane	Lashawn
Krystalynn	Lavon
Lakiesha	Montel
Lashana	Mychal
Liza	Reno
Roshawna	Reshawn
Shaniqua	Ryker
Shantel	Tevin
Takayla	Tiger
Tenesha	Treshawn
Teralyn	Tyrees
Trixia	Woody
Tyesha	Ziggy

Arabic

Girls	Boys
Abia	Abdul
Aleah	Ahmad
Cantara	Asad
Emani	Bilal
Fatima	Fadi
Ghada	Fahaad
Habiba	Ferran
Halimah	Ghazi
Imani	Gilad
Jalila	Habib
Kalila	Hadi
Laela	Hakim
Lilith	Hassan
Maja	Imad
Marya	Ismael
Nalia	Jabir

Girls	Boys
Omaira	Jamaal
Qadira	Mohamed
Rabi	Nadim
Rasha	Omar
Rayya	Rafiq
Samira	Rahul
Shahar	Rashad
Tabina	Samír
Vega	Sayyid

Chinese

Girls	Boys
An	Chen
Bo	Cheung
Chultua	Chi
Hua	Chung
Jun	De
Lee	Dewei
Lian	Fai
Lien	Gan
Lin	Guotin
Ling	Ho
Mani	Hu
Marrim	Jin
Meiying	Keung
Nuwa	Kong
Ping	Lei
Shu	Li
Syá	Liang
Sying	On
Tao	Park
Tu	Po Sin
Ushi	Quon
Xiang	Shing
Xiu Mei	Tung
Yáng	Wing
Yen	Yu

English

Girls	Boys
Addison	Alfie
Ashley	Ashton
Beverly	Baxter
Britany	Blake
Cady	Chip
Chelsea	Cody
Ellen	Dawson
Evelyn	Edward
Hailey	Franklin
Holly	Gordon
Hope	Harry
Janet	Jamison
Jill	Jeffrey
Julie	Jeremy
Leigh	Lane
Maddie	Maxwell
Millicent	Ned
Paige	Parker
Piper	Rodney
Robin	Scott
Sally	Slade
Scarlet	Ted
Shelby	Tucker
Sigourney	Wallace
Twyla	William

French

Girls	Boys
Angelique	Adrien
Annette	Alexandre
Aubrey	Andre
Belle	Antoine
Camille	Christophe
Charlotte	Donatien
Christelle	Edouard
Cosette	François
Desiree	Gage
Estelle	Guillaume
Gabrielle	Henri
Genevieve	Jacques
Juliette	Jean
Jolie	Leroy
Lourdes	Luc
Margaux	Marc
Maribel	Marquis
Michelle	Philippe
Monique	Pierre
Nicole	Quincy
Paris	Remy
Raquel	Russel
Salina	Sebastien
Sydney	Stéphane
Yvonne	Sylvian

German

Girls	Boys
Adelaide	Adler
Amelia	Adolf
Christa	Arnold
Edda	Bernard
Elke	Claus
Elsbeth	Conrad
Emma	Derek
Frederica	Dieter
Giselle	Dustin
Gretchen	Frederick
Heidi	Fritz
Hetta	Gerald
Hilda	Harvey
Ida	Johan
Johana	Karl
Katrina	Lance
Klarise	Louis
Lisele	Milo
Lorelei	Philipp
Margret	Roger
Milia	Roland
Monika	Sigmund
Reynalda	Terrell
Velma	Ulrich
Wanda	Walter

Greek

Girls	Boys
Alexandra	Achilles
Amaryllis	Adonis
Anastasia	Alexis
Athena	Christos
Callista	Cristobal
Daphne	Damian
Delia	Darius
Delphine	Demetris
Eleanora	Elias
Eudora	Feoras
Evangelina	Gaylen
Gaea	Georgios
Helena	Julius
Hermione	Krisopher
Ianthe	Leander
Kalliope	Nicholas
Kassandra	Panos
Maia	Paris
Medea	Petros
Oceana	Rhodes
Odelia	Sebastian
Ophelia	Stefanos
Phoebe	Thanos
Rhea	Urian
Selena	Xander

Hebrew

Girls	Boys
Alia	Aaron
Anais	Abel
Becca	Ahab
Beth	Azriel
Cayla	Benjamin
Deborah	Boaz
Dinah	Caleb
Eliane	Coby
Eliza	Daniel
Hannah	Elijah
Ilisha	Emmanuel
Jana	Ira
Judith	Isaak
Kaela	Jacob
Leeza	Jeremiah
Lena	Michael
Mariam	Nathaniel
Mikala	Noah

Girls	Boys
Naomi	Oren
Rachael	Raphael
Rebecca	Reuben
Ruth	Seth
Sarah	Tobin
Tirza	Zachariah
Yael	Zachary

Irish

Girls	Boys
Aileen	Aidan
Alanna	Brenden
Blaine	Clancy
Breanna	Desmond
Brigit	Donovan
Carlin	Eagan
Colleen	Flynn
Dacia	Garret
Dierdre	Grady
Erin	Keegan
Fallon	Keenan
Ilene	Kevin
Kaitlin	Liam
Keara	Logan
Kelly	Mahon
Kyleigh	Makenzie
Maura	Nevin
Maureen	Nolan
Moira	Owen
Quincy	Phinean
Raleigh	Quinn
Reagan	Reilly
Sinead	Ryan
Sloane	Seamus
Taryn	Sedric

Japanese

Girls	Boys
Aiko	Akemi
Aneko	Akira
Dai	Botan
Hachi	Goro
Hoshi	Hiroshi
Ishi	Isas
Jin	Joben
Keiko	Joji
Kioko	Jum
Kumiko	Kaemon
Leiko	Kentaro
Maeko	Masao
Mai	Michio
Mariko	Minoru
Masago	Naoko
Nari	Raiden
Oki	Rei
Raku	Saburo
Ran	Sen
Ruri	Takeo
Seki	Toru
Tazu	Udo
Yasu	Yasuo
Yei	Yóshi
Yoko	Yuki

Latin

Girls	Boys
Allegra	Amadeus
Aurora	Antony
Beatrice	Austin
Bella	Benedict
Cecily	Bennett
Celeste	Camilo
Deana	Cecil
Felicia	Delfino
Imogene	Dominic
Josalyn	Favian
Karmen	Felix
Laurel	Griffin
Luna	Horacio
Mabel	Hugo
Madonna	Ignatius
Maren	Jerome
Maxine	Jude
Nova	Loren
Olivia	Marius
Paxton	Octavio
Persis	Oliver

Pomona	Quentin
Regina	Roman
Rose	Silas
Sabina	Valentin

Native American

Girls	Boys
Aiyana	Ahanu
Cherokee	Anoki
Dakota	Bly
Dena	Delsin
Halona	Demothi
Heta	Elan
Imala	Elsu
Izusa	Etu
Kachina	Hakan
Kanda	Huslu
Kiona	Inteus
Leotie	Istu
Magena	Iye
Netis	Jolon
Nuna	Knoton
Olathe	Lenno
Oneida	Mingan
Sakuna	Motega
Sora	Muraco
Taima	Neka
Tala	Nodin
Utina	Patwin
Wyanet	Sahale
Wyoming	Songan
Yenene	Wingi

Russian

Girls	Boys
Alena	Alexi
Annika	Christoff
Breasha	Dimitri
Duscha	Egor
Galina	Feliks
Irina	Fyodor
Karina	Gena
Katia	Gyorgy
Lelya	Igor

Liolya	Ilya
Marisha	Iosif
Masha	Ivan
Natasha	Kolya
Natalia	Leonid
Nikita	Maxim
Olena	Michail
Orlenda	Panas
Raisa	Pasha
Sasha	Pavel
Shura	Pyotr
Svetlana	Sacha
Tanya	Sergei
Valera	Valerii
Yekaterina	Viktor
Yelena	Vladimir

Scandinavian

Girls	Boys
Anneka	Anders
Birgitte	Burr
Britta	Frans
Carina	Gustaf
Elga	Hadrian
Freja	Halen
Freya	Hilmar
Gala	Kjell
Gerda	Krister
Gunda	Kristofer
Haldana	Lauris
Ingrid	Lennart
Kalle	Lunt
Karena	Mats
Karin	Mikael
Kolina	Nansen
Lena	Niklas
Lusa	Nils
Maija	Per
Malena	Reinhold
Rika	Rikard
Runa	Rolle
Ulla	Steffan
Unn	Torkel
Valma	Valter

Scottish

Girls	Boys
Aili	Adair
Ailsa	Alastair
Ainsley	Angus
Berkley	Boyd
Blair	Bret
Camden	Caelan
Connor	Cameron
Christal	Dougal
Davonna	Duncan
Elspeth	Geordan
Greer	Gregor
Isela	Henderson
Jeana	Ian
Jinny	Kennan
Keita	Kenzie
Kelsea	Lennox
Leslie	Leslie
Maisie	Macaulay
Marjie	Malcolm
Mckenzie	Morgan
Mhairie	Perth
Paisley	Ronald
Rhona	Seumas
Roslyn	Stratton
Tavie	Tavish

Spanish

Girls	Boys
Alejandra	Armando
Benita	Carlos
Clarita	Eduardo
Esmeralda	Enrique
Esperanza	Estéban
Felicia	Felipe
Gracia	Fernando
Isabel	Garcia
Jacinthe	Gerardo
Juana	Heraldo
Lola	Jose
Lucia	Jorge
Madrona	Juan
Marisol	Luis
Marquita	Marcos
Nelia	Mateo
Oleda	Pablo
Pilar	Pedro
Reina	Rafael
Rosalinda	Ramón
Rosita	Renaldo
Salvadora	Salvador
Soledad	Santiago
Toya	Tobal
Ynez	Vincinte

Vietnamese

Girls	Boys
Am	Anh
Bian	Antoan
Cai	Binh
Cam	Cadao
Hoa	Cham
Hoai	Duc
Hong	Dinh
Huong	Gia
Kim	Hai
Kima	Hieu
Lan	Hoang
Le	Huy
Mai	Lap
Nu	Minh
Nue	Nam
Ping	Ngai
Tam	Nguyen
Tao	Nien
Thanh	Phuok
Thao	Pin
Thi	Tai
Thuy	Thanh
Tuyen	Thian
Tuyet	Tuan
Xuan	Tuyen

Welsh

Girls	Boys
Bevanne	Bevan
Bronwyn	Bowen
Carys	Broderick
Deryn	Bryce
Enid	Caddock
Glynnis	Cairn
Guinevere	Davis
Gwyneth	Dylan
Idelle	Eoin
Isolde	Gareth
Linette	Gavin
Mab	Griffith
Meghan	Howell
Meredith	Jestin
Olwen	Kynan
Owena	Lewis
Rhiannon	Llewellyn
Rhonda	Lloyd
Ronelle	Maddock
Rowena	Price
Sulwen	Rhett
Teagan	Rhys
Vanora	Tristan
Wenda	Vaughn
Wynne	Wren

The Impressions Names Make

Consciously or unconsciously, we all have private pictures associated with certain names. Jackie could be sophisticated and beautiful, like Jackie Kennedy, or fat and funny, like Jackie Gleason. These pictures come from personal experience as well as from images we absorb from the mass media, and thus they may conflict in interesting ways. The name Charlton strikes many people as a sissified, passive, whiny brat—until they think of Charlton Heston. Marilyn may personify voluptuous femininity—until you think of Marilyn, your neighbor with the ratty bathrobe, curlers, and a cigarette dangling out of her mouth.

Over the years, researchers have been fascinated by this question of the "real" meanings of names and their effects. When asked to stereotype names by age, trustworthiness, attractiveness, sociability, kindness, aggressiveness, popularity, masculinity/femininity, degree of activity or passivity, etc., people actually do tend to agree on each name's characteristics.

So if people think of Mallory as cute and likeable, does that influence a girl named Mallory to become cute and likeable? Experts agree that names don't guarantee instant success or condemn people to certain failure, but they do affect self-images, influence relationships with others, and help (or hinder) success in work and school.

Robert Rosenthal's classic experiment identified what he named the Pygmalion effect: randomly selected children who'd been labeled "intellectual bloomers" actually did bloom. Here's how the Pygmalion effect works with names: Researcher S. Gray Garwood conducted a study on sixth graders in New Orleans. He found that students given names popular with teachers scored higher in skills tests, were better adjusted and more consistent in their self-perceptions, were more realistic in their evaluations of themselves, and more frequently expected that they would attain their goals—even though their goals were more ambitious than ones set by their peers. A research study in San Diego suggested that average essays by Davids, Michaels, Karens, and Lisas got better grades than average essays written by Elmers, Huberts, Adelles, and Berthas. The reason? Teachers expected kids with popular names to do better, and thus they assigned those kids higher grades in a self-fulfilling prophecy.

The Sinrod Marketing Group's International Opinion panel surveyed over 100,000 parents to discover their opinions about names. Results of this poll are presented in *The Baby Name Survey Book* by Bruce Lansky and Barry Sinrod. Their book contains the names people most often associate with hundreds of personal attributes such as intelligent, athletic, attractive, and nice (as well as dumb, klutzy, ugly, and nasty). It also contains personality profiles of over 1,700 common and unusual boys' and girls' names and includes real or fictional famous namesakes who may have influenced people's perception of each name.

What the authors found was that most names have very clear images; some even have multiple images. The following are lists of boys' and girls' names that were found to have particular image associations.

Athletic

Girls	Boys
Bailey	Alex
Billie	Ali
Bobbie	Alonso
Casey	Bart
Chris	Brian
Colleen	Buck
Dena	Chuck
Gabriella	Connor
Jackie	Cooper
Jessie	Daniel
Jill	Derek
Jody	Emmitt
Josie	Hakeem
Katie	Houston
Kelsey	Jake
Lindsay	Jock
Lola	Kareem
Martina	Kevin
Mia	Kirby
Morgan	Lynn
Natalia	Marcus
Nora	Riley
Steffi	Rod
Sue	Terry
Tammy	Trey

Beautiful/Handsome

Girls	Boys
Adrienne	Adam
Ariel	Ahmad
Aurora	Alejandro
Bella	Alonzo
Bonita	Austin
Carmen	Beau
Cassandra	Blake
Catherine	Bo
Danielle	Bryant
Ebony	Chaz
Farrah	Christopher
Genevieve	Clint
Jasmine	Damian
Jewel	David
Kendra	Demetrius
Kiera	Denzel
Lydia	Douglas
Marisa	Grant
Maya	Humphrey
Sarah	Joe
Scarlett	Jude
Simone	Kiefer
Tanya	Mitchell
Tessa	Tevin
Whitney	Vance

Blonde

Girls	Boys
Bambie	Aubrey
Barbie	Austin
Bianca	Bjorn
Blanche	Brett
Brigitte	Bud
Bunny	Chance
Candy	Chick
Daisy	Colin
Dolly	Corbin
Heidi	Dalton
Inga	Dane
Jillian	Dennis
Krystal	Dwayne
Lara	Eric
Lorna	Josh
Madonna	Keith
Marcia	Kerry
Marnie	Kipp
Olivia	Kyle
Randi	Lars
Sally	Leif
Shannon	Louis
Sheila	Martin
Tracy	Olaf
Vanna	Sven

Cute

Girls	Boys
Annie	Andrew
Becca	Antoine
Bobbie	Antonio
Cheryl	Barry
Christy	Benjamin
Deanna	Chick
Debbie	Cory
Dee Dee	Danny
Emily	Eric
Jennifer	Francisco
Jody	Franky
Kari	Jon
Lacie	Kipp
Mallory	Linus
Mandy	Louis
Megan	Matthew
Peggy	Mike
Porsha	Nicholas
Randi	Rene
Serena	Robbie
Shannon	Rory
Shirley	Sonny
Stacy	Stevie
Tammy	Timothy
Trudy	Wade

Friendly

Girls	Boys
Bernadette	Allen
Bobbie	Aubrey
Bonnie	Barrett
Carol	Bennie
Christy	Bing
Dorothy	Cal
Elaine	Casper
Gwen	Cole
Joy	Dan
Kathy	Denny
Kenya	Donovan
Kim	Ed
Lila	Fred
Marcie	Gary
Millie	Hakeem
Nancy	Jeff
Nikki	Jerry
Opal	Jim
Patricia	Khalil
Rhoda	Rob
Rose	Russ
Ruby	Sandy
Sandy	Tony
Vivian	Vinny
Wendy	Wally

Funny

Girls	Boys
Dionne	Abbott
Ellen	Ace
Erma	Allen
Fanny	Archie
Gilda	Artie
Gillian	Bennie
Jenny	Bobby
Julie	Carson
Lucille	Chase
Lucy	Diego
Maggie	Dudley
Marge	Eddie
Marsha	Edsel
Maud	Eduardo
Melinda	Fletcher
Mickey	Fraser
Patty	Grady
Paula	Jerome
Rosie	Keenan
Roxanne	Rochester
Sally	Rollie
Stevie	Roscoe
Sunny	Sid
Sydney	Tim
Vivian	Vinny

Hippie	Intelligent		Nerdy
Girls and Boys	**Girls**	**Boys**	**Boys**
Angel	Abigail	Adlai	Arnie
Autumn	Agatha	Alexander	Barrett
Baby	Alexis	Barton	Bernie
Breezy	Barbara	Brock	Clarence
Crystal	Dana	Clifford	Clifford
Dawn	Daria	Colin	Creighton
Happy	Diana	Dalton	Dexter
Harmony	Eleanor	David	Egbert
Honey	Grace	Donovan	Khalil
Indigo	Helen	Edward	Marvin
Kharma	Jade	Esteban	Mortimer
Love	Jillian	Fraser	Myron
Lucky	Kate	Jefferson	Newt
Meadow	Kaylyn	Jerome	Norman
Misty	Laura	John	Sanford
Moon	Leah	Kelsey	Seymour
Passion	Lillian	Kenneth	Sheldon
Rainbow	Mackenzie	Merlin	Sinclair
River	Marcella	Ned	Tracy
Serenity	Meredith	Nelson	Truman
Skye	Meryl	Roderick	Ulysses
Sparkle	Michaela	Samuel	Vern
Sprout	Shauna	Sebastian	Vladimir
Star	Shelley	Tim	Waldo
Sunshine	Vanessa	Virgil	Xavier

Old-Fashioned

Girls	Boys
Abigail	Abe
Adelaide	Amos
Adelle	Arthur
Bea	Bertrand
Charlotte	Clarence
Clementine	Cy
Cora	Cyril
Dinah	Dennis
Edith	Erasmus
Elsie	Erskine
Esther	Ezekiel
Eugenia	Giuseppe
Hattie	Grover
Ida	Herbert
Mamie	Herschel
Martha	Jerome
Maureen	Kermit
Meryl	Lloyd
Mildred	Sanford
Nellie	Silas
Prudence	Spencer
Rosalie	Stanley
Thelma	Sven
Verna	Vic
Wilma	Wilfred

Quiet

Girls	Boys
Bernice	Aaron
Beth	Adrian
Cathleen	Angel
Chloe	Benedict
Diana	Bryce
Donna	Carlo
Faith	Curtis
Fawn	Cy
Fay	Douglas
Grace	Gerald
Jocelyn	Gideon
Leona	Jeremiah
Lisa	Jermaine
Lori	Kiefer
Lydia	Kyle
Moira	Riley
Natalia	Robert
Nina	Robin
Rena	Samson
Sheryl	Spencer
Tessa	Toby
Theresa	Tommy
Ursula	Tucker
Violet	Vaughn
Yoko	Virgil

Rich/Wealthy		Sexy
Girls	**Boys**	**Girls**
Alexis	Bartholomew	Alana
Amanda	Bradley	Angie
Ariel	Brock	Bambi
Blair	Bryce	Brooke
Chanel	Burke	Caresse
Chantal	Cameron	Cari
Chastity	Carlos	Carmen
Chelsea	Chet	Dani
Christina	Claybourne	Desiree
Clara	Clinton	Donna
Crystal	Colby	Honey
Darlene	Colin	Jillian
Deandra	Corbin	Kirstie
Jewel	Dane	Kitty
Larissa	Dante	Kyra
Madison	Dillon	Latoya
Marina	Frederick	Leah
Meredith	Geoffrey	Lola
Moira	Hamilton	Marilyn
Porsha	Harper	Marlo
Rachel	Montgomery	Raquel
Taryn	Roosevelt	Sabrina
Tiffany	Sterling	Sandra
Trisha	Winslow	Simone
Zsa Zsa	Winthrop	Zsa Zsa

Southern

Girls	Boys
Ada	Ashley
Alma	Beau
Annabel	Bobby
Belle	Cletus
Carolina	Clint
Charlotte	Dale
Clementine	Earl
Dixie	Jackson
Dolly	Jeb
Dottie	Jed
Ellie	Jefferson
Georgeanne	Jesse
Georgia	Jethro
Jolene	Jimmy
LeeAnn	Johnny
Luella	Lee
Mirabel	Luke
Ophelia	Luther
Patsy	Moses
Polly	Otis
Priscilla	Peyton
Rosalind	Rhett
Scarlet	Robert
Tara	Roscoe
Winona	Wade

Strong/Tough

Boys

Amos
Ben
Brandon
Brock
Bronson
Bruce
Bruno
Cain
Christopher
Clint
Cody
Coleman
Colin
Delbert
Demetrius
Duke
Jed
Judd
Kurt
Nick
Sampson
Stefan
Thor
Vince
Zeb

Sweet	Trendy	
Girls	**Girls**	**Boys**
Abby	Alexia	Adrian
Alyssa	Alia	Alec
Angela	Britney	Angelo
Betsy	Chanel	Bradley
Candy	Char	Carson
Cheryl	Delia	Connor
Cindy	Destiny	Davis
Dana	Gwyneth	Dominic
Desiree	Hannah	Ellery
Elise	India	Garrett
Ellie	Isabella	Harley
Esther	Jen	Harper
Heather	Julianna	Jefferson
Heidi	Keely	Kellan
Kara	Lane	Levi
Kristi	Macy	Liam
Laura	Madeleine	Neil
Linda	Madison	Olaf
Marjorie	Morgan	Omar
Melinda	Nadia	Orlando
Melissa	Natalia	Parker
Olivia	Olivia	Pierce
Rose	Paris	Remington
Shauna	Ricki	Simon
Sue	Taylor	Warren

Weird

Girls	Boys
Abra	Abner
Aida	Barton
Annelise	Boris
Athalie	Cosmo
Belicia	Earl
Calla	Edward
Devonna	Ferris
Dianthe	Gaylord
Elvira	Ira
Garland	Jules
Giselle	Maynard
Happy	Mervin
Hestia	Neville
Keiko	Newt
Kyrene	Nolan
Mahalia	Rod
Modesty	Roscoe
Novia	Seth
Opal	Siegfried
Poppy	Sylvester
Rani	Thaddeus
Sapphire	Tristan
Tierney	Vernon
Twyla	Victor
Velvet	Ward

Wimpy

Boys

Antoine
Archibald
Barton
Bernard
Bradford
Burke
Cecil
Cyril
Dalton
Darren
Duane
Edwin
Gaylord
Homer
Horton
Napoleon
Percival
Prescott
Roosevelt
Rupert
Ulysses
Wesley
Winslow
Winthrop
Yale

Names Inspired by People, Places, and Things

What's in a name? Some parents choose names that carry special meaning. They're sports buffs who name their children after legendary athletes, bookworms who name their children after beloved characters, and nature lovers who name their children after the things they see in their favorite vistas. Then again, some people choose names not because they carry personal significance but simply because they fall in love with them. They may not be sports buffs, bookworms, or nature lovers, but they still choose names like Jordan, Bridget, and Willow.

However you approach it, here are several lists of girls' and boys' names inspired by people, places, and things. (To learn more about choosing names with special meaning, check out the "How to Pick a Name You and Your Baby Will Like" feature on page 5.)

Art and Literature

Artists

Male and Female

Andy (Warhol)
Ansel (Adams)
Claude (Monet)
Edgar (Degas)
Edward (Hopper)
Frida (Kahlo)
Henri (Matisse)
Diego (Rivera)
Georgia (O'Keeffe)
Gustav (Klimt)
Jackson (Pollock)
Jasper (Johns)
Leonardo (da Vinci)

Marc (Chagall)
Mary (Cassatt)
Michelangelo (Buonarroti)
Norman (Rockwell)
Pablo (Picasso)
Paul (Cézanne)
Rembrandt (van Rijn)
Robert (Mapplethorpe)
Roy (Lichtenstein)
Salvador (Dali)
Sandro (Botticelli)
Vincent (van Gogh)

Authors

Female	Male
Anne (Tyler)	Ambrose (Bierce)
Barbara (Kingsolver)	Bram (Stoker)
Carolyn (Keene)	Cormac (McCarthy)
Charlotte (Brontë)	Dan (Brown)
Doris (Lessing)	Ernest (Hemingway)
Elizabeth (Barrett Browning)	George (Orwell)
Emily (Dickinson)	Henry David (Thoreau)
Harper (Lee)	Homer
Harriet (Beecher Stowe)	J. D. (Salinger)
Jane (Austen)	Jules (Verne)
Joanne Kathleen (J. K. Rowling)	Leo (Tolstoy)
Judy (Blume)	Lewis (Carroll)
Katherine (Mansfield)	Mark (Twain)
Louisa (May Alcott)	Mario (Puzo)
Lucy Maud (Montgomery)	Nicholas (Sparks)
Madeleine (L'Engle)	Oscar (Wilde)
Margaret (Atwood)	Ray (Bradbury)
Marge (Piercy)	Scott (Fitzgerald)
Mary (Shelley)	Stephen (King)
Maya (Angelou)	Tennessee (Williams)
Paula (Danziger)	Tom (Clancy)
Rebecca (Wells)	Truman (Capote)
Sylvia (Plath)	Virgil
Virginia (Woolf)	Walt (Whitman)
Willa (Cather)	William (Faulkner)

Fictional Characters

Female	Male
Anna (Karenina)	Atticus (Finch)
Anne (Shirley)	Billy (Coleman)
Antonia (Shimerda)	Boo (Radley)
Bridget (Jones)	Cyrus (Trask)
Cosette (Valjean)	Edmond (Dantés)
Daisy (Buchanan)	Ethan (Frome)
Dorothea (Brooke)	Frodo (Baggins)
Edna (Pontellier)	Guy (Montag)
Elizabeth (Bennet)	Harry (Potter)
Emma (Woodhouse)	Heathcliff
Hermione (Granger)	Henry (Fleming)
Hester (Prynne)	Holden (Caulfield)
Isabel (Archer)	Huck (Finn)
Jane (Eyre)	Jake (Barnes)
Josephine (March)	Jay (Gatsby)
Juliet (Capulet)	Jean (Valjean)
Junie (B. Jones)	John (Proctor)
Mary (Lennox)	Odysseus
Meg (Murry)	Owen (Meany)
Ophelia	Pip (Philip Pirrip)
Phoebe (Caulfield)	Rhett (Butler)
Pippi (Longstocking)	Robinson (Crusoe)
Scarlett (O'Hara)	Romeo (Montague)
Scout (Finch)	Santiago
Serena (Joy)	Victor (Frankenstein)

Shakespearean Characters

Female	Male
Adriana	Angelo
Beatrice	Antony
Cleopatra	Balthasar
Cordelia	Bertram
Emilia	Cicero
Gertrude	Claudio
Helena	Cromwell
Hermia	Duncan
Hero	Edmund
Imogen	Hamlet
Isabella	Iachimo
Juliet	Iago
Katharina	Julius (Caesar)
Lavinia	Lysander
Mariana	Malcolm
Miranda	Oberon
Olivia	Orlando
Ophelia	Othello
Paulina	Paris
Portia	Puck
Regan	Richard
Rosalind	Romeo
Titania	Titus
Ursula	Tybalt
Viola	Vincentio

Nursery Rhyme Characters

Female and Male

Bo (Peep)
Bobby (Shaftoe)
Bonnie
Elsie (Marley)
Fred
Georgie (Porgie)
Jack
Jerry (Hall)
Jill
John (Jacob Jingleheimer Schmidt)
King Cole
Lou
MacDonald
Margery (Daw)
Mary
Michael
Nancy (Etticoat)
Peter (Piper)
Polly (Flinders)
Robin
Taffy
Tommy (Tittlemouse)
Simon
Solomon (Grundy)
Willie (Winkie)

Poets

Female	Male
Adrienne (Rich)	Alfred (Lord Tennyson)
Amy (Lowell)	Allen (Ginsberg)
Anne (Sexton)	Carl (Sandburg)
Christina (Rossetti)	Czeslaw (Milosz)
Denise (Levertov)	Dante (Alighieri)
Dorothy (Parker)	Dylan (Thomas)
Edna (St. Vincent Millay)	Ezra (Pound)
Elizabeth (Barrett Browning)	James (Dickey)
Emily (Dickinson)	John (Keats)
Gertrude (Stein)	Juan (Ramón Jiménez)
Gwendolyn (Brooks)	Langston (Hughes)
Jamaica (Kincaid)	Louis (Simpson)
Joy (Harjo)	Mark (Strand)
Marianne (Moore)	Matsuo (Basho)
Marilyn (Hacker)	Pablo (Neruda)
Mary (Oliver)	Percy (Bysshe Shelley)
Mary Ann ("George Eliot" Evans)	Philip (Larkin)
Maxine (Kumin)	Robert (Frost)
Maya (Angelou)	Seamus (Heaney)
Muriel (Rukeyser)	Theodore (Roethke)
Rita (Dove)	Thomas (Stearns "T. S." Eliot)
Sarah (Teasdale)	Wallace (Stevens)
Sharon (Olds)	Walt (Whitman)
Sylvia (Plath)	William (Butler Yeats)
Wislawa (Szymborska)	Yusef (Komunyakaa)

History

Presidents	Members of First Families	Military Figures
Male	**Female and Male**	**Female and Male**
Abraham (Lincoln)	Abigail (Adams)	Alexander (the Great)
Andrew (Jackson)	Amy (Carter)	Andrew (Johnson)
Bill (Clinton)	Barbara (Bush)	Attila (the Hun)
Calvin (Coolidge)	Benjamin (Pierce)	Charles (de Gaulle)
Chester (Arthur)	Caroline (Kennedy)	Che (Guevara)
Dwight (D. Eisenhower)	Chelsea (Clinton)	Deborah
Franklin (D. Roosevelt)	Dolley (Madison)	Douglas (MacArthur)
George (Washington)	Eleanor (Roosevelt)	Dwight (D. Eisenhower)
Gerald (Ford)	Grace (Coolidge)	Genghis (Khan)
Grover (Cleveland)	Helen (Taft)	George (S. Patton)
Harry (S. Truman)	Hillary (Rodham Clinton)	Ivan (Stepanovich Konev)
Herbert (Hoover)	Jacqueline (Kennedy)	Jennie (Hodgers)
James (Madison)	Jeb (Bush)	Joan (of Arc)
Jimmy (Carter)	Jenna (Bush)	Julius (Caesar)
John (F. Kennedy)	John (Fitzgerald Kennedy, Jr.)	Moshe (Dayan)
Lyndon (B. Johnson)	Julie (Nixon)	Napoleon (Bonaparte)
Martin (Van Buren)	Kermit (Roosevelt)	Norman (Schwarzkopf)
Millard (Fillmore)	Laura (Bush)	Oliver (Cromwell)
Richard (Nixon)	Martha (Washington)	Omar (Bradley)
Ronald (Reagan)	Mary (Todd Lincoln)	Peter (the Great)
Rutherford (B. Hayes)	Maureen (Reagan)	Robert (E. Lee)
Thomas (Jefferson)	Nancy (Reagan)	Tecumseh
Ulysses (S. Grant)	Robert (Lincoln)	Ulysses (S. Grant)
Warren (G. Harding)	Rosalynn (Carter)	William (Wallace)
Woodrow (Wilson)	Steven (Ford)	Winston (Churchill)

Explorers

Female and Male

Amelia (Earhart)
Ann (Bancroft)
Amerigo (Vespucci)
Bartolomeu (Dias)
Christopher (Columbus)
Eric (The Red)
Ferdinand (Magellan)
Francisco (Vásquez de Coronado)
George (Everest)
Gertrude (Bell)
Harriet (Chalmers Adams)
Henry (Hudson)
Hernán (Cortés)
Hernando (de Soto)
Jacques (Cousteau)
Juan (Ponce de León)
James (Cook)
Leif (Ericsson)
Marco (Polo)
Neil (Armstrong)
Samuel (de Champlain)
Thor (Heyerdahl)
Walter (Raleigh)
William (Clark)
Zebulon (Pike)

Activists

Female and Male

Agnes ("Mother Teresa" Gonxha Bojaxhiu)
Albert (Schweitzer)
Anwar (el-Sadat)
Cesar (Chavez)
Che (Guevara)
Desmond (Tutu)
Dorothy (Day)
Elizabeth (Cady Stanton)
Frederick (Douglass)
Gloria (Steinem)
Harriet (Tubman)
Jesse (Jackson)
Jimmy (Carter)
John (Muir)
Kim (Dae-jung)
Lucy (Stone)
Malcolm (X)
Margaret (Sanger)
Martin (Luther King)
Mary (Wollstonecraft)
Nelson (Mandela)
Rachel (Carson)
Rosa (Parks)
Susan (B. Anthony)
William ("W. E. B." Du Bois)

Old West Figures

Female and Male

Annie (Oakley)
Bat (Masterson)
Belle (Starr)
Butch (Cassidy)
Charles ("Black Bart" Boles)
Clay (Allison)
Cole (Younger)
Daniel (Boone)
Davy (Crockett)
Doc (Holliday)
Frank (James)
Harry ("Sundance Kid" Longabaugh)
Henry (Starr)
James ("Wild Bill" Hickok)
Jesse (James)
John (Wesley Hardin)
Kit (Carson)
Martha Jane ("Calamity Jane" Canary)
Pat (Garrett)
Roy (Bean)
Sally (Skull)
Sam (Houston)
Tom (Horn)
William ("Buffalo Bill" Cody)
Wyatt (Earp)

Colleges and Universities

Female and Male

Auburn
Berkeley
Brown
Bryn Mawr
Carleton
Columbia
Cornell
Creighton
Drake
Duke
Emerson
Emory
Kent
Kenyon
Lewis and Clark
Penn
Princeton
Regis
Rhodes
Rice
Sarah Lawrence
Stanford
William and Mary
Xavier
Yale

Entertainment

Movie Stars

Female	Male
Angelina (Jolie)	Benicio (Del Toro)
Anjelica (Huston)	Bing (Crosby)
Audrey (Hepburn)	Bruce (Willis)
Betty (Grable)	Cary (Grant)
Cameron (Diaz)	Chevy (Chase)
Catherine (Zeta-Jones)	Clark (Gable)
Cher	Clint (Eastwood)
Drew (Barrymore)	Dustin (Hoffman)
Elizabeth (Taylor)	Harrison (Ford)
Emma (Thompson)	Jack (Nicholson)
Gwyneth (Paltrow)	John (Wayne)
Halle (Berry)	Leonardo (DiCaprio)
Jodie (Foster)	Martin (Sheen)
Julia (Roberts)	Mel (Gibson)
Katharine (Hepburn)	Mickey (Rooney)
Liv (Tyler)	Orlando (Bloom)
Meg (Ryan)	Patrick (Swayze)
Meryl (Streep)	Robert (De Niro)
Michelle (Pfeiffer)	Robin (Williams)
Nicole (Kidman)	Rock (Hudson)
Penelope (Cruz)	Russell (Crowe)
Reese (Witherspoon)	Sean (Connery)
Salma (Hayek)	Spencer (Tracy)
Sandra (Bullock)	Sylvester (Stallone)
Shirley (Temple)	Tom (Cruise)

Movie Characters

Female	Male
Amélie (Poulain)	Atticus (Finch)
Annie (Hall)	Austin (Powers)
Bonnie (Parker)	Billy (Madison)
Bridget (Jones)	Charles (Foster Kane)
Clarice (Starling)	Forrest (Gump)
Clementine (Kruczynski)	Frodo (Baggins)
Dorothy (Gale)	George (Bailey)
Elaine (Robinson)	Hannibal (Lector)
Eliza (Doolittle)	Harry (Potter)
Ellen (Ripley)	Indiana (Jones)
Erin (Brockovich)	Jack (Sparrow)
Holly (Golightly)	Jacques (Clouseau)
Ilsa (Lund)	James (Bond)
Jean Louise ("Scout" Finch)	Jerry (Maguire)
Lara (Croft)	Judah (Ben-Hur)
Leia (Organa)	Lloyd (Dobler)
Louise (Sawyer)	Luke (Skywalker)
Marge (Gunderson)	Maximus (Decimus Meridius)
Maria (von Trapp)	Napoleon (Dynamite)
Mary (Poppins)	Neo
Norma Rae (Webster)	Norman (Bates)
Sandy (Olsson)	Rhett (Butler)
Scarlett (O'Hara)	Rick (Blaine)
Thelma (Dickerson)	Rocky (Balboa)
Trinity	Vito (Corleone)

Comedians

Female

Carol (Burnett)
Caroline (Rhea)
Cheri (Oteri)
Ellen (DeGeneres)
Fanny (Brice)
Gilda (Radner)
Gracie (Allen)
Jane (Curtain)
Janeane (Garofalo)
Joan (Rivers)
Kathy (Griffin)
Lily (Tomlin)
Lucille (Ball)
Margaret (Cho)
Molly (Shannon)
Paula (Poundstone)
Phyllis (Diller)
Rita (Rudner)
Roseanne (Barr)
Rosie (O'Donnell)
Sandra (Bernhard)
Tina (Fey)
Tracey (Ullman)
Wanda (Sykes)
Whoopi (Goldberg)

Male

Adam (Sandler)
Bernie (Mac)
Bill (Cosby)
Bob (Hope)
Cedric ("The Entertainer" Kyles)
Chevy (Chase)
Chris (Rock)
Dan (Aykroyd)
Dana (Carvey)
Dave (Chappelle)
David (Letterman)
Denis (Leary)
Drew (Carey)
Eddie (Murphy)
George (Burns)
Jay (Leno)
Jerry (Seinfeld)
Johnny (Carson)
Louie (Anderson)
Mike (Myers)
Ray (Romano)
Rodney (Dangerfield)
Steve (Martin)
Tim (Allen)
Will (Ferrell)

Disney Cartoon Characters

Female	Male
Alice	Aladdin
Ariel	Bambi
Aurora	Bob (Parr)
Belle	Buzz (Lightyear)
Boo	Chip
Cinderella	Christopher (Robin)
Daisy (Duck)	Dale
Esmeralda	Dash (Parr)
Fauna	Dewey
Flora	Donald (Duck)
Helen (Parr)	Eric
Jane (Porter)	Gaston
Jasmine	Hercules
Jessie	Huey
Lilo	Ichabod (Crane)
Marian	Jafar
Mary (Poppins)	Louie
Megara	Merlin
Minnie	Mickey
Mulan	Mufasa
Nala	Peter (Pan)
Pocahontas	Robin (Hood)
Ursula	Sebastian
Violet (Parr)	Simba
Wendy	Timon

TV Characters

Female	Male
Abby (Lockhart)	Al (Bundy)
Ally (McBeal)	Alex (P. Keaton)
Buffy (Summers)	Archie (Bunker)
Carmela (Soprano)	Arthur ("Fonzie" Fonzarelli)
Carrie (Bradshaw)	Chandler (Bing)
Claire (Kincaid)	Cliff (Huxtable)
Daphne (Moon Crane)	Cosmo (Kramer)
Darlene (Conner-Healy)	Danny ("Danno" Williams)
Donna (Martin Silver)	Dylan (McKay)
Elaine (Benes)	Fox (Mulder)
Erica (Kane)	Frasier (Crane)
Felicity (Porter)	Gil (Grissom)
Fran (Fine)	Jack (McCoy)
Gabrielle (Solis)	Jean-Luc (Picard)
Grace (Adler)	Jed (Bartlet)
Kelly (Bundy)	Joey (Tribbiani)
Kimberly (Shaw Mancini)	John Ross ("J. R." Ewing, Jr.)
Lucy (Ricardo)	Kevin (Arnold)
Marcia (Brady)	Luka (Kovac)
Margaret ("Hot Lips" Houlihan)	Ricky (Ricardo)
Michelle (Tanner)	Sam (Malone)
Rachel (Green)	Tony (Soprano)
Rebecca (Howe)	Vic (Mackey)
Sydney (Bristow)	Will (Truman)
Vanessa (Huxtable)	Zack (Morris)

TV Personalities

Female	Male
Ann (Curry)	Ahmad (Rashad)
Barbara (Walters)	Al (Roker)
Brooke (Burke)	Alex (Trebek)
Connie (Chung)	Bill (O'Reilly)
Diane (Sawyer)	Bob (Barker)
Ellen (DeGeneres)	Carson (Daly)
Jane (Pauley)	Conan (O'Brien)
Jenny (Jones)	Dan (Rather)
Joan (Rivers)	David (Letterman)
Joy (Behar)	Dick (Clark)
Judy ("Judge Judy" Sheindlin)	Geraldo (Rivera)
Kathie (Lee Gifford)	Harry (Caray)
Katie (Couric)	Howard (Stern)
Kelly (Ripa)	Jay (Leno)
Leeza (Gibbons)	Jerry (Springer)
Lisa (Ling)	Jim (Lehrer)
Martha (Stewart)	Johnny (Carson)
Meredith (Vieira)	Larry (King)
Nancy (O'Dell)	Matt (Lauer)
Oprah (Winfrey)	Montel (Williams)
Paige (Davis)	Peter (Jennings)
Ricki (Lake)	Phil (McGraw)
Sally (Jessy Raphaël)	Regis (Philbin)
Star (Jones Reynolds)	Tom (Brokaw)

Pop Artists

Female	Male
Alanis (Morrisette)	Adam (Duritz)
Annie (Lennox)	Billy (Joel)
Avril (Lavigne)	Chris (Martin)
Britney (Spears)	Darius (Rucker)
Celine (Dion)	Dave (Matthews)
Cher	Edwin (McCain)
Christina (Aguilera)	Elton (John)
Dido	Elvis (Presley)
Fiona (Apple)	Enrique (Iglesias)
Gloria (Estefan)	Eric (Clapton)
Gwen (Stefani)	George (Michael)
Janet (Jackson)	Howie (Day)
Jessica (Simpson)	Jack (Johnson)
Jewel	John (Lennon)
Kelly (Clarkson)	Justin (Timberlake)
Madonna	Marc (Anthony)
Mandy (Moore)	Michael (Jackson)
Natalie (Imbruglia)	Nick (Lachey)
Norah (Jones)	Paul (McCartney)
Paula (Abdul)	Prince
Pink	Ricky (Martin)
Sarah (McLachlan)	Ringo (Starr)
Sheryl (Crow)	Rob (Thomas)
Tori (Amos)	Rod (Stewart)
Vanessa (Carlton)	Sting

Classic Rock Artists

Female and Male
Bob (Dylan)
Brian (Wilson)
Carly (Simon)
Carole (King)
Don (Henley)
George (Harrison)
James (Taylor)
Janis (Joplin)
Jerry (Garcia)
Jim (Morrison)
Jimi (Hendrix)
Jimmy (Page)
Joan (Baez)
John (Lennon)
Joni (Mitchell)
Keith (Richards)
Linda (Ronstadt)
Mick (Jagger)
Neil (Young)
Paul (McCartney)
Pete (Townshend)
Ringo (Starr)
Robert (Plant)
Roger (Daltrey)
Stevie (Nicks)

Country Artists

Female
Alison (Krauss)
Carolyn Dawn (Johnson)
Chely (Wright)
Crystal (Gayle)
Cyndi (Thomson)
Dolly (Parton)
Faith (Hill)
Gretchen (Wilson)
Jamie (O'Neal)
Jo Dee (Messina)
Julie (Roberts)
LeAnn (Rimes)
Loretta (Lynn)
Martie (Maguire)
Martina (McBride)
Mary (Chapin Carpenter)
Mindy (McCready)
Natalie (Maines)
Patsy (Cline)
Patty (Loveless)
Reba (McEntire)
Sara (Evans)
Shania (Twain)
Tammy (Wynette)
Terri (Clark)

Male
Alan (Jackson)
Billy Ray (Cyrus)
Brad (Paisley)
Charley (Pride)
Chet (Atkins)
Clint (Black)
Darryl (Worley)
Don (Everly)
Garth (Brooks)
Gene (Autry)
George (Strait)
Hank (Williams)
Joe (Nichols)
Johnny (Cash)
Keith (Urban)
Kenny (Chesney)
Kix (Brooks)
Randy (Travis)
Ronnie (Dunn)
Tim (McGraw)
Toby (Keith)
Trace (Adkins)
Vince (Gill)
Waylon (Jennings)
Willie (Nelson)

Jazz Artists

Female and Male

Benny (Goodman)
Billie (Holiday)
Cab (Calloway)
Cassandra (Wilson)
Charlie (Parker)
Chet (Baker)
Dave (Koz)
David (Sanborn)
Diana (Krall)
Dizzy (Gillespie)
Duke (Ellington)
Grover (Washington, Jr.)
Harry (Connick, Jr.)
Herbie (Mann)
John (Coltrane)
Louis (Armstrong)
Miles (Davis)
Norah (Jones)
Ornette (Coleman)
Quincy (Jones)
Ray (Charles)
Stan (Getz)
William ("Count" Basie)
Wynton (Marsalis)
Xavier (Cugat)

Classical Composers and Performers

Female and Male

Andrea (Bocelli)
Antonio (Vivaldi)
Camille (Saint-Saëns)
Claude (Debussy)
Felix (Mendelssohn)
Franz (Schubert)
Frédéric (Chopin)
George (Handel)
Giacomo (Puccini)
Giuseppe (Verdi)
Igor (Stravinsky)
Johann (Sebastian Bach)
José (Carreras)
Joseph (Haydn)
Leonard (Bernstein)
Luciano (Pavarotti)
Ludwig (van Beethoven)
Maria (Callas)
Nikolay (Rimsky-Korsakov)
Plácido (Domingo)
Pyotr (Tchaikovsky)
Renata (Scotto)
Richard (Wagner)
Wolfgang (Mozart)
Yo-Yo (Ma)

Notorious Celebrity Baby Names

Female and Male

Ahmet Emuukha Rodan (son of Frank and Gail Zappa)
Apple Blythe Alison (daughter of Gwyneth Paltrow and Chris Martin)
Audio Science (son of Shannyn Sossamon and Dallas Clayton)
Coco Riley (daughter of Courteney Cox Arquette and David Arquette)
Daisy Boo (daughter of Jamie and Jools Oliver)
Dweezil (son of Frank and Gail Zappa)
Elijah Bob Patricus Guggi Q (son of Bono and Alison Stewart)
Fifi Trixiebelle (daughter of Paula Yates and Bob Geldof)
Hazel Patricia (daughter of Julia Roberts and Danny Moder)
Heavenly Hirani Tiger Lily (daughter of Paula Yates and Michael Hutchence)
Lourdes Maria Ciccone (daughter of Madonna and Carlos Leon)
Moon Unit (daughter of Frank and Gail Zappa)
Moxie CrimeFighter (daughter of Penn and Emily Jillette)
Peaches Honeyblossom (daughter of Paula Yates and Bob Geldof)
Phinnaeus Walter (son of Julia Roberts and Danny Moder)
Pilot Inspektor (son of Jason Lee and Beth Riesgraf)
Pirate Howsmon (son of Jonathan and Deven Davis)
Poppy Honey (daughter of Jamie and Jools Oliver)
Prince Michael (son of Michael Jackson and Debbie Rowe)
Prince Michael II (son of Michael Jackson)
Rocco (son of Madonna and Guy Ritchie)
Rumer Glenn (daughter of Demi Moore and Bruce Willis)
Scout LaRue (daughter of Demi Moore and Bruce Willis)
Seven Sirius (son of Andre 3000 and Erykah Badu)
Tallulah Belle (daughter of Demi Moore and Bruce Willis)

Nature and Places

Flowers	Rocks, Gems, Minerals
Female	**Female and Male**
Angelica	Beryl
Calla	Clay
Dahlia	Coal
Daisy	Coral
Fern	Crystal
Flora	Diamond
Flower	Esmerelda
Holly	Flint
Hyacinth	Garnet
Iris	Gemma
Jasmine	Goldie
Laurel	Jade
Lavender	Jasper
Lilac	Jewel
Lily	Mercury
Marigold	Mica
Pansy	Opal
Poppy	Pearl
Posy	Rock
Rose	Ruby
Sage	Sandy
Tulip	Sapphire
Verbena	Steele
Vine	Stone
Violet	Topaz

Natural Elements		Places	
Female	**Male**	**Female**	**Male**
Amber	Ash	Africa	Afton
Autumn	Branch	Asia	Austin
Breezy	Bud	Brooklyn	Boston
Blossom	Burr	Cheyenne	Chad
Briar	Canyon	China	Cleveland
Brook	Cliff	Dakota	Cuba
Delta	Crag	Florence	Dakota
Gale	Dale	Georgia	Dallas
Hailey	Eddy	Holland	Denver
Heather	Field	India	Diego
Ivy	Ford	Italia	Indiana
Marina	Forest	Jamaica	Israel
Rain	Heath	Kenya	Kent
Rainbow	Lake	Lourdes	Laramie
Savannah	Marsh	Madison	London
Sequoia	Moss	Montana	Montreal
Sierra	Oakes	Olympia	Nevada
Skye	Thorne	Paris	Orlando
Star	Ridge	Regina	Phoenix
Summer	River	Savannah	Reno
Sunny	Rye	Siena	Rhodes
Terra	Rock	Sydney	Rio
Tempest	Stone	Tijuana	Sydney
Willow	Storm	Victoria	Tennessee
Windy	Woody	Vienna	Washington

Religion

Water-Themed Names	Celestial Names	Old Testament
Female and Male	**Female and Male**	**Male**
Bay	Andromeda	Abel
Brooke	Antares	Abraham
Chelsea	Aries	Adam
Delmar	Cassiopeia	Cain
Delta	Castor	Caleb
Dewey	Cloud	Daniel
Eddy	Corona	David
Ice	Draco	Eli
Lake	Étoile	Esau
Marin	Leo	Ezekiel
Marina	Luna	Ezra
Marisol	Moona	Isaac
Meri	Nova	Isaiah
Misty	Orion	Jacob
Nile	Pollux	Jeremiah
Oceana	Rigel	Job
Rain	Saturn	Joel
Rio	Scorpio	Joshua
River	Skye	Moses
Seabert	Soleil	Nemiah
Spring	Star	Noah
Storm	Starling	Samson
Tempest	Sunny	Samuel
Tigris	Ursa	Solomon
Wade	Venus	

New Testament	Biblical Women	Saints
Male	**Female**	**Female and Male**
Agrippa	Abigail	Anne
Andrew	Bathsheba	Augustine
Annas	Deborah	Bartholomew
Aquila	Delilah	Benedict
Gabriel	Dinah	Bernadette
Herod	Eden	Catherine
James	Elizabeth	Christopher
Jesus	Esther	Felix
John	Eve	Francis
Joseph	Hagar	Ignatius
Judas	Hannah	Joan
Jude	Jezebel	John
Luke	Judith	Jude
Mark	Julia	Leo
Matthew	Leah	Lucy
Nicolas	Maria	Mary
Paul	Martha	Monica
Peter	Mary	Nicholas
Philip	Miriam	Patrick
Simon	Naomi	Paul
Stephen	Phoebe	Peter
Thomas	Rachel	Stephen
Timothy	Rebekah	Teresa
Titus	Ruth	Thomas
Zechariah	Sarah	Valentine

Jewish Figures	Muslim Figures	Hindu Figures
Female and Male	**Male**	**Female**
Aaron	Adam	Agni
Akiva	Al-Yasa	Arjuna
Abraham	Ayub	Bali
Daniel	Daud	Brahma
David (Ben Gurion)	Harun	Buddha
Deborah	Hud	Chandra
Esther	Ibrahim	Devi
Golda (Meir)	Idris	Dharma
Hillel	Ilyas	Indra
Isaac	Isa	Kali
Jacob	Ishaq	Kama
Joseph	Ismail	Krishna
Judah (Maccabee)	Lut	Maya
Leah	Muhammad	Nala
Maimonides	Musa	Parvati
Miriam	Nuh	Rama
Mordechai	Saleh	Ravi
Moses	Shoaib	Sati
Nachimanides	Sulayman	Shiva
Rachel	Yahya	Sita
Rashi	Yaqub	Surya
Rebecca	Yunus	Uma
Ruth	Yusuf	Ushas
Sarah	Zakariya	Vishnu
Yochanan (ben Zakkai)	Zulkifl	Yama

Mythology

Greek Mythology Figures

Female	Male
Aphrodite	Achilles
Artemis	Adonis
Athena	Apollo
Calliope	Ares
Calypso	Atlas
Chloe	Dionysus
Daphne	Eros
Demeter	Hades
Echo	Hector
Electra	Helios
Europa	Hercules
Gaea	Hermes
Helen	Icarus
Hera	Jason
Hestia	Midas
Io	Morpheus
Leda	Narcissus
Medusa	Odysseus
Nike	Orion
Pandora	Pan
Penelope	Paris
Persephone	Perseus
Phoebe	Poseidon
Psyche	Prometheus
Rhea	Zeus

Roman Mythology Figures

Female	Male
Aurora	Aeneas
Bellona	Aesculapius
Camilla	Amor
Ceres	Bacchus
Clementia	Cupid
Concordia	Faunus
Decima	Honos
Diana	Inuus
Fauna	Janus
Felicitas	Jove
Flora	Jupiter
Fortuna	Liber
Hippona	Mars
Juno	Mercury
Juventus	Neptune
Levana	Orcus
Luna	Pluto
Mania	Remus
Minerva	Romulus
Pax	Saturn
Roma	Silvanus
Venus	Sol
Veritas	Somnus
Vesta	Ulysses
Victoria	Vulcan

Sports

Athletes

Female	Male
Anna (Kournikova)	Andre (Agassi)
Annika (Sorenstam)	Andy (Roddick)
Diana (Taurasi)	Babe (Ruth)
Jackie (Joyner-Kersee)	Bernie (Williams)
Jennie (Finch)	Dale (Earnhardt)
Kerri (Strug)	David (Beckham)
Kristi (Yamaguchi)	Elvis (Stojko)
Florence (Griffith Joyner)	Hulk (Hogan)
Laila (Ali)	Kasey (Kahne)
Lisa (Leslie)	Kobe (Bryant)
Marion (Jones)	Lance (Armstrong)
Martina (Hingis)	Mark (Spitz)
Mary Lou (Retton)	Michael (Jordan)
Mia (Hamm)	Mike (Tyson)
Monica (Seles)	Muhammad (Ali)
Nadia (Comaneci)	Orenthal James ("O. J." Simpson)
Babe (Didrikson Zaharias)	Oscar (De La Hoya)
Oksana (Baiul)	Red (Grange)
Picabo (Street)	Riddick (Bowe)
Rebecca (Lobo)	Rocky (Balboa)
Sarah (Hughes)	Scott (Hamilton)
Serena (Williams)	Tiger (Woods)
Sheryl (Swoopes)	Tony (Hawk)
Steffi (Graf)	Wayne (Gretzky)
Venus (Williams)	Yao (Ming)

Baseball Players

Male

Albert (Pujols)
Alex (Rodriguez)
Babe (Ruth)
Barry (Bonds)
Cy (Young)
Derek (Jeter)
Cal (Ripken, Jr.)
Hank (Aaron)
Ichiro (Suzuki)
Jackie (Robinson)
Ken (Griffey, Jr.)
Kirby (Puckett)
Manny (Ramirez)
Mark (McGwire)
Mickey (Mantle)
Nolan (Ryan)
Pete (Rose)
Randy (Johnson)
Roger (Clemens)
Rollie (Fingers)
Sammy (Sosa)
Ted (Williams)
Torii (Hunter)
Wade (Boggs)
Willie (Mays)

Football Players

Male

Barry (Sanders)
Bart (Starr)
Bo (Jackson)
Brett (Favre)
Dan (Marino)
Deion (Sanders)
Donovan (McNabb)
Eli (Manning)
Emmitt (Smith)
Jeremy (Shockey)
Jerry (Rice)
Jim (Brown)
Joe (Montana)
John (Elway)
Johnny (Unitas)
LaDainian (Tomlinson)
Lawrence (Taylor)
Michael (Vick)
Peyton (Manning)
Priest (Holmes)
Randy (Moss)
Ray (Lewis)
Tiki (Barber)
Tom (Brady)
Troy (Aikman)

Basketball Players

Female	Male
Alana (Beard)	Alonzo (Mourning)
Alicia (Thompson)	Anfernee ("Penny" Hardaway)
Chantelle (Anderson)	Bill (Russell)
Coco (Miller)	Carmelo (Anthony)
Dominique (Canty)	Dennis (Rodman)
Ebony (Hoffman)	Dwyane (Wade)
Felicia (Ragland)	Earvin ("Magic" Johnson)
Giuliana (Mendiola)	Isiah (Thomas)
Gwen (Jackson)	Jerry (West)
Jessie (Hicks)	Julius (Erving)
Kaayla (Chones)	Kareem (Abdul-Jabbar)
Katie (Douglas)	Karl (Malone)
Kiesha (Brown)	Kevin (Garnett)
Lisa (Leslie)	Kobe (Bryant)
Lucienne (Berthieu)	Larry (Bird)
Michele (Van Gorp)	Latrell (Sprewell)
Natalie (Williams)	LeBron (James)
Nykesha (Sales)	Michael (Jordan)
Olympia (Scott-Richardson)	Moses (Malone)
Sheryl (Swoopes)	Patrick (Ewing)
Simone (Edwards)	Scottie (Pippen)
Tai (Dillard)	Shaquille (O'Neal)
Tamicha (Jackson)	Spud (Webb)
Tangela (Smith)	Wilt (Chamberlain)
Tari (Phillips)	Yao (Ming)

Tennis Players

Female	Male
Amanda (Coetzer)	Alex (Corretja)
Amelie (Mauresmo)	Andre (Agassi)
Anna (Kournikova)	Andy (Roddick)
Anastasia (Myskina)	Arthur (Ashe)
Billie Jean (King)	Bill (Tilden)
Chris (Evert)	Bjorn (Borg)
Elena (Dementieva)	Boris (Becker)
Gabriela (Sabatini)	Carlos (Moya)
Jennifer (Capriati)	Greg (Rusedski)
Justine (Henin-Hardenne)	Guillermo (Coria)
Kim (Clijsters)	Gustavo (Kuerten)
Lindsay (Davenport)	Ivan (Lendl)
Maria (Sharapova)	James (Blake)
Martina (Navratilova)	Jimmy (Connors)
Mary (Pierce)	John (McEnroe)
Monica (Seles)	Juan Carlos (Ferrero)
Nadia (Petrova)	Lleyton (Hewitt)
Natasha (Zvereva)	Mark (Philippoussis)
Pam (Shriver)	Michael (Chang)
Serena (Williams)	Pete (Sampras)
Steffi (Graf)	Rod (Laver)
Svetlana (Kuznetsova)	Roger (Federer)
Tatiana (Golovin)	Stefan (Edberg)
Tracy (Austin)	Todd (Woodbridge)
Venus (Williams)	Tommy (Haas)

Golfers

Female	Male
Amy (Alcott)	Arnold (Palmer)
Annika (Sorenstam)	Chi Chi (Rodriguez)
Babe (Didrikson Zaharias)	Claude (Harmon)
Beth (Daniel)	Craig (Stadler)
Betsy (King)	Eldrick ("Tiger" Woods)
Betty (Jameson)	Ernie (Els)
Carol (Mann)	Gene (Littler)
Dinah (Shore)	Greg (Norman)
Donna (Caponi)	Hale (Irwin)
Dottie (Pepper)	Happy (Gilmore)
Hollis (Stacy)	Harvey (Penick)
JoAnne (Carner)	Jack (Nicklaus)
Judy (Rankin)	Jeff (Maggert)
Juli (Inkster)	Jesper (Parnevik)
Karrie (Webb)	Ken (Venturi)
Kathy (Whitworth)	Nick (Price)
Laura (Davies)	Payne (Stewart)
Louise (Suggs)	Phil (Mickelson)
Marlene (Hagge)	Raymond (Floyd)
Michelle (Wie)	Retief (Goosen)
Nancy (Lopez)	Sam (Snead)
Pat (Bradley)	Sergio (Garcia)
Patty (Berg)	Tommy (Bolt)
Sandra (Haynie)	Vijay (Singh)
Se (Ri Pak)	Walter (Hagen)

Hockey Players

Male

Bobby (Orr)
Bret (Hull)
Dominik (Hasek)
Eric (Lindros)
Gordie (Howe)
Grant (Fuhr)
Jacques (Plante)
Jarome (Iginla)
Jaromir (Jagr)
Jeremy (Roenick)
Joe (Sakic)
Mario (Lemieux)
Mark (Messier)
Martin (Brodeur)
Maurice (Richard)
Mike (Modano)
Patrick (Roy)
Paul (Coffey)
Pavel (Bure)
Peter (Forsberg)
Phil (Esposito)
Ray (Bourque)
Sergei (Fedorov)
Steve (Yzerman)
Wayne (Gretzky)

Race Car Drivers

Female and Male

A. J. (Foyt)
Al (Unser, Jr.)
Ashton (Lewis)
Bill (Elliott)
Bobby (Labonte)
Carl (Edwards)
Dale (Earnhardt)
Danica (Patrick)
Darrell (Waltrip)
Jeff (Gordon)
Jimmie (Johnson)
John (Andretti)
Justin (Ashburn)
Kasey (Kahne)
Kenny (Irwin)
Kevin (Harvick)
Kyle (Petty)
Mario (Andretti)
Matt (Kenseth)
Richard (Petty)
Ricky (Rudd)
Rusty (Wallace)
Sterling (Marlin)
Terry (Labonte)
Tony (Stewart)

Olympians

Female	Male
Amanda (Beard)	Alberto (Tomba)
Bonnie (Blair)	Aleksandr (Popov)
Dominique (Dawes)	Alexei (Yagudin)
Dorothy (Hamill)	Bjørn (Dæhlie)
Dot (Richardson)	Brian (Boitano)
Florence (Griffith Joyner)	Carl (Lewis)
Inge (de Bruijn)	Dan (Jansen)
Irina (Slutskaya)	Dmitri (Bilozerchev)
Jackie (Joyner-Kersee)	Elvis (Stojko)
Janet (Evans)	Eric (Heiden)
Janica (Kostelic)	Gary (Hall, Jr.)
Katarina (Witt)	Greg (Louganis)
Kerri (Strug)	Hermann (Maier)
Kristi (Yamaguchi)	Ian (Thorpe)
Larissa (Latynina)	Ingemar (Stenmark)
Mary Lou (Retton)	Ivar (Ballangrud)
Nadia (Comaneci)	Jonny (Moseley)
Nancy (Kerrigan)	Kurt (Browning)
Oksana (Baiul)	Mark (Spitz)
Olga (Korbut)	Matt (Biondi)
Peggy (Fleming)	Michael (Phelps)
Shannon (Miller)	Paul (Hamm)
Summer (Sanders)	Scott (Hamilton)
Svetlana (Boguinskaya)	Stephan (Eberharter)
Tatyana (Gutsu)	Tamas (Darnyi)

Other Ideas for Names

Soccer Players	Trade Names
Female and Male	**Female and Male**
Alexi (Lalas)	Baker
Brandi (Chastain)	Butcher
Carlos (Alberto Torres)	Carver
Cristiano (Ronaldo)	Chandler
David (Beckham)	Cooper
Diego (Maradona)	Cutler
Edson ("Pele"Arantes do Nascimento)	Draper
Filippo (Inzaghi)	Fletcher
Freddy (Adu)	Fowler
Gabriel (Batistuta)	Gardner
Heather (Mitts)	Hunter
Jamie (Carragher)	Marshall
Joy (Fawcett)	Mason
Julie (Foudy)	Miller
Kristine (Lilly)	Painter
Landon (Donovan)	Porter
Mia (Hamm)	Ranger
Michael (Owen)	Sawyer
Pavel (Nedved)	Scribe
Raul (Gonzalez Blanco)	Shepherd
Roberto (Baggio)	Slater
Ronaldo (Luiz Nazario da Silva)	Smith
Ronaldinho (Gaucho)	Stockman
Shannon (Boxx)	Tailor
Zinedine (Zidane)	Tanner

Last Names as First Names | Double Names

Female and Male	Female	Male
Anderson	Anne-Marie	Aaronjames
Bradshaw	Billie-Jean	Billijo
Carter	Billie-Jo	Giancarlo
Chavez	Bobbi-Jo	Gianluca
Chen	Bobbi-Lee	Gianpaolo
Foster	Brandy-Lynn	Jaylee
Gallagher	Brooklyn	Jayquan
Garcia	Carolanne	Jean-Claude
Harper	Clarabelle	Jean-Luc
Jackson	Emmylou	Jean-Paul
Johnson	Hollyann	Jean-Sebastien
Keaton	Jody-Ann	Jimmyjo
Kennedy	Julie-Anne	John-Paul
Mackenzie	Katelyn	Joseluis
Madison	Kellyann	Juancarlos
Meyer	Krystalynn	Kendarius
Parker	Leeann	Keyshawn
Patterson	Mary-Kate	Markanthony
Ramsey	Marylou	Michaelangelo
Rodriguez	Raeann	Miguelangel
Sanchez	Raelynn	Quindarius
Taylor	Roseanne	Rayshawn
Tennyson	Ruthann	Tedrick
Walker	Saralyn	Tyquan
Wang	Terry-Lynn	Tyshawn

Virtue Names	Easily Shortened Names	
Female	**Female**	**Male**
Amity	Abigail	Andrew
Blythe	Angela	Anthony
Charity	Barbara	Benjamin
Chastity	Caroline	Christopher
Constance	Christine	Daniel
Faith	Deborah	Donald
Felicity	Elizabeth	Edward
Fidelity	Gwendolyn	Frederick
Grace	Jacqueline	Gregory
Harmony	Jennifer	Jacob
Honora	Jessica	Jeffery
Hope	Jillian	Jonathan
Innocence	Josephine	Joseph
Joy	Katherine	Kenneth
Justice	Lillian	Leonardo
Love	Margaret	Michael
Mercy	Nicole	Nicholas
Modesty	Pamela	Peter
Passion	Rebecca	Richard
Patience	Samantha	Robert
Prudence	Stephanie	Samuel
Purity	Suzanne	Thomas
Temperance	Valerie	Timothy
Unity	Victoria	Walter
Verity	Vivian	William

Old-Fashioned Names
Now Popular

Female	Male
Abigail	Abraham
Alice	Alexander
Anna	Dominic
Ava	Elijah
Caroline	Ethan
Claire	Gabriel
Claudia	Hector
Elizabeth	Isaac
Emily	Isaiah
Emma	Ivan
Evelyn	Jasper
Grace	Julian
Hannah	Maxwell
Hazel	Nathaniel
Isabella	Noah
Katherine	Omar
Leslie	Oscar
Madeline	Owen
Margaret	Samuel
Maria	Sebastian
Olivia	Vernon
Rebecca	Vincent
Sarah	Wesley
Sofia	Xavier
Victoria	Zachary

Names Used for Both Boys and Girls

More for Girls	More for Boys	Used About Equally
Alexis	Alex	Britt
Ariel	Cameron	Addison
Ashley	Carson	Ashton
Bailey	Chandler	Berwyn
Billie	Chase	Blair
Dominique	Chris	Carey
Guadalupe	Christian	Casey
Holland	Cody	Charley
Jade	Dakota	Derian
Jadyn	Devin	Devyn
Jamie	Drew	Dylan
Kelly	Evan	Gentry
Madison	Hunter	Harley
Morgan	Jaime	Jessie
Payton	Jaylin	Jody
Reagan	Jesse	Kriston
Reese	Jordan	London
Ricki	Logan	Maddox
Robin	Parker	Pat
Shannon	Quinn	Peyton
Shea	Riley	Quincey
Sidney	Ryan	Skylar
Stacy	Skyler	Sunny
Taylor	Terry	Tory
Tegan	Tyler	Tristyn

Girls

A 🅖 (American) an initial used as a first name.

Aaarti (Indian) worship; divine fire in ritual.

Aadab (Indian) hope and need.

Aadarshini (Indian) idealistic.

Aadita (Indian) from the beginning.

Aafreen, Afreen (Indian) encouragement.

Aahana (Indian) first rays of the sun.

Aahna (Indian) exist.

Aakaanksha (Indian) wish, desire.

Aakriti (Indian) shape.

Aaleyah (Hebrew) a form of Aliya.
Aalayah, Aalayaha, Aalea, Aaleah, Aaleaha, Aaleeyah, Aaleyiah, Aaleyyah

Aaliah (Hebrew) a form of Aliya.
Aaliaya, Aaliayah

Aalisha (Greek) a form of Alisha.
Aaleasha, Aaliesha

Aaliyah ☀ 🅖 (Hebrew) a form of Aliya.
Aahliyah, Aailiyah, Aailyah, Aalaiya, Aaleah, Aalia, Aalieyha, Aaliya, Aaliyaha, Aaliyha, Aalliah, Aalliyah, Aalyah, Aalyiah

Aamaal (Indian) hopes, aspirations.

Aanandita (Indian) purveyor of joy.

Aanchal, Anchal (Indian) shelter.

Aani (Chamorro) a form of Ha'ani.

Aaron 🅑 (Hebrew) enlightened. (Arabic) messenger.

Aarushi (Indian) first rays.

Aarzoo (Indian) wish.

Aashi (Indian) smile.

Aashirya (Indian) from the land of God.

Aashiyana (Indian) beautiful home; small dwelling, nest.

Aashna (Indian) beloved; devoted to love.

Aashritha (Indian) somebody who gives shelter.

Aasmaa (Indian) excellent; precious.

Aastha (Indian) faith.

Aathmika (Indian) related to the soul.

Aatmaja, Atmaja (Indian) daughter.

Aayushi (Indian) one with long life.

Abagail (Hebrew) a form of Abigail.
Abagael, Abagaile, Abagale, Abagayle, Abageal, Abagil, Abaigael, Abaigeal

Abani (Indian) earth.

Abbagail (Hebrew) a form of Abigail.
Abbagale, Abbagayle, Abbegail, Abbegale, Abbegayle

Abbey, Abbie, Abby 🅖 (Hebrew) familiar forms of Abigail.
Aabbee, Abbe, Abbea, Abbeigh, Abbi, Abbye, Abeey, Abey, Abi, Abia, Abie, Aby

Abbigail 🅖 (Hebrew) a form of Abigail.

Abbygail (Hebrew) a form of Abigail.
Abbeygale, Abbygale, Abbygayl, Abbygayle

Abegail (Hebrew) a form of Abigail.
Abegale, Abegaile, Abegayle

Abel **B** (Hebrew) breath. (Assyrian) meadow. (German) a short form of Abelard (see Boys' Names).

Abelina (American) a combination of Abbey + Lina.
Abilana, Abilene

Abha (Indian) beautiful.

Abhaya, Abhitha (Indian) fearless.

Abhilasha (Indian) wish, desire.

Abia (Arabic) great.
Abbia, Abbiah, Abiah, Abya

Abianne (American) a combination of Abbey + Ann.
Abena, Abeni, Abian, Abinaya

Abida (Arabic) worshiper.
Abedah, Abidah

Abigail ✿ (Hebrew) father's joy. Bible: one of the wives of King David. See also Gail.
Abagail, Abbagail, Abbey, Abbiegail, Abbiegayle, Abbigael, Abbigal, Abbigale, Abbigayl, Abbigayle, Abbygail, Abegail, Abgail, Abgale, Abgayle, Abigael, Abigaile, Abigaill, Abigal, Abigale, Abigayil, Abigayl, Abigayle, Abigel, Abigial, Abugail, Abygail, Avigail

Abigaíl (Spanish) a form of Abigail.

Abinaya (American) a form of Abiann.
Abenaa, Abenaya, Abinaa, Abinaiya, Abinayan

Abira (Hebrew) my strength.
Abbira, Abeer, Abeerah, Abeir, Abera, Aberah, Abhira, Abiir, Abir

Abishta (Indian) lady of the house.

Ablaa (Indian) perfectly formed.

Aboli (Indian) a kind of flower.

Abra (Hebrew) mother of many nations.
Abree, Abri, Abria

Abria (Hebrew) a form of Abra.
Abréa, Abrea, Abreia, Abriah, Abriéa, Abrya

Abrial (French) open; secure, protected.
Abrail, Abreal, Abreale, Abriale, Abrielle

Abriana (Italian) a form of Abra.
Abbrienna, Abbryana, Abreana, Abreanna, Abreanne, Abreeana, Abreona, Abreonia, Abriann, Abrianna, Abriannah, Abrieana, Abrien, Abrienna, Abrienne, Abrietta, Abrion, Abrionée, Abrionne, Abriunna, Abryann, Abryanna, Abryona

Abrielle (French) a form of Abrial.
Aabriella, Abriel, Abriell, Abryell

Abrienda (Spanish) opening.

Abril (French) a form of Abrial.
Abrilla, Abrille

Abundancia (Spanish) a form of Hilda.

Abygail (Hebrew) a form of Abigail.
Abygael, Abygale, Abygayle

Acacia (Greek) thorny. Mythology: the acacia tree symbolizes immortality and resurrection. See also Casey.
Acasha, Acatia, Accassia, Acey, Acie, Akacia, Cacia, Casia, Kasia

Acalia (Latin) adoptive mother of Romulus and Remus.

Achala (Indian) earth; steady.

Achina (Chuukese) good.

Achla (Indian) constant.

Acmahugo (Chamorro) to be squeezed together.

Acmaurig (Chamorro) good for each other.

Ada (German) a short form of Adelaide. (English) prosperous; happy.
Adabelle, Adah, Adan, Adaya, Adda, Auda

Adabella (Spanish) a combination of Ada and Bella.

Adagi (Chamorro) to guard, protect.

Adah (Hebrew) ornament.
Ada, Addah

Adair ☒ (Greek) a form of Adara.
Adaire

Adalene (Spanish) a form of Adalia.
Adalane, Adalena, Adalin, Adalina, Adaline, Adalinn, Adalyn, Adalynn, Adalynne, Addalyn, Addalynn

Adalgisa (German) noble hostage.

Adalia (German, Spanish) noble.
Adal, Adala, Adalea, Adaleah, Adalee, Adalene, Adali, Adalie, Adaly, Addal, Addala, Addaly

Adaluz (Spanish) a combination of Ada and Luz.

Adam ☒ (Phoenician) man; mankind. (Hebrew) earth; of the red earth.

Adama (Phoenician, Hebrew) a form of Adam.

Adamma (Ibo) child of beauty.

Adana (Spanish) a form of Adama.

Adanna (Nigerian) her father's daughter.
Adanya

Adara (Greek) beauty. (Arabic) virgin.
Adair, Adaira, Adaora, Adar, Adarah, Adare, Adaria, Adarra, Adasha, Adauré, Adra

Adaya (American) a form of Ada.
Adaija, Adaijah, Adaja, Adajah, Adayja, Adayjah, Adejah

Addie (Greek, German) a familiar form of Adelaide, Adrienne.
Aday, Adde, Addee, Addey, Addi, Addia, Addy, Ade, Adee, Adei, Adey, Adeye, Adi, Adie, Ady, Atti, Attie, Atty

Addison ☒☒ (English) child of Adam.
Addis, Addisen, Addisson, Adison

Addyson (English) a form of Addison.

Adela (English) a short form of Adelaide.
Adelae, Adelia, Adelista, Adella

Adelaide (German) noble and serene. See also Ada, Adela, Adeline, Adelle, Ailis, Delia, Della, Ela, Elke, Heidi.
Adelade, Adelaid, Adelaida, Adelei, Adelheid, Adeliade, Adelka, Aley, Laidey, Laidy

Adele (English) a form of Adelle.
Adel, Adelie, Adile

Adelfa (Spanish) adelfa flower.

Adelina (English) a form of Adeline.
Adalina, Adeleana, Adelena, Adellyna, Adeliana, Adellena, Adileena, Adlena

Adeline (English) a form of Adelaide.
Adaline, Adelaine, Adelin, Adelina, Adelind, Adelita, Adeliya, Adelle, Adelyn, Adelynn, Adelynne, Adilene, Adlin, Adline, Adlyn, Adlynn, Aline

Adelle (German, English) a short form of Adelaide, Adeline.
Adele, Adell

Adelma (Teutonic) protector of the needy.

Adena (Hebrew) noble; adorned.
Adeana, Adeen, Adeena, Aden, Adene, Adenia, Adenna, Adina

Adhara (Arabic) name of a star in the Canis constellation.

Adia (Swahili) gift.
Addia, Adéa, Adea, Adiah

Adiani (French) a form of Adrianne.

Adila (Arabic) equal.
Adeala, Adeela, Adela, Adelah, Adeola, Adilah, Adileh, Adilia, Adyla

Adilene (English) a form of Adeline.
Adilen, Adileni, Adilenne, Adlen, Adlene

Adina (Hebrew) a form of Adena. See also Dina.
Adeana, Adiana, Adiena, Adinah, Adine, Adinna, Adyna

Adira (Hebrew) strong.
Ader, Adera, Aderah, Aderra, Adhira, Adirah, Adirana

Adishree (Indian) exalted.

Adison, Adyson (English) forms of Addison, Addyson.
Adis, Adisa, Adisen, Adisynne, Adysen

Aditi (Hindi) unbound. Religion: the mother of the Hindu sun gods.
Adithi, Aditti

Aditri (Indian) highest honor.

Adiya (Indian) God's treasure.

Adleigh (Hebrew) my ornament.
Adla, Adleni

Adlihna (Pohnpeian) a form of Esther.

Adoncia (Spanish) sweet.

Adonia (Spanish) beautiful.
Adonica, Ádonis, Adonna, Adonnica, Adonya

Adora (Latin) beloved. See also Dora.
Adore, Adoree, Adoria

Adoración (Latin) action of venerating the magical gods.

Adra (Arabic) virgin.
Adara

Adreana, Adreanna (Latin) forms of Adrienne.
Adrean, Adreanne, Adreauna, Adreeanna, Adreen, Adreena, Adreeyana, Adrena, Adrene, Adrenea, Adréona, Adreonia, Adreonna

Adria (English) a short form of Adriana, Adriene.
Adrea, Adriani, Adrya

Adriadna (Greek) she who is very holy, who doesn't yield.

Adrian **B** (English) a form of Adriane.

Adriana **G** (Italian) a form of Adrienne.
Adreiana, Adreinna, Adria

Adriane, Adrianne (English) forms of Adrienne.
Addrian, Adranne, Adria, Adrian, Adreinne, Adriann, Adriayon, Adrion

Adrianna (Italian) a form of Adriana.
Addrianna, Addriyanna, Adriannea, Adriannia, Adrionna

Adrielle (Hebrew) member of God's flock.
Adriel, Adrielli, Adryelle

Adrien, Adriene **B** (English) forms of Adrienne.

Adrienna (Italian) a form of Adrienne. See also Edrianna.
Adreana, Adrieanna, Adrieaunna, Adriena, Adrienia, Adriennah, Adrieunna

Adrienne **G** (Greek) rich. (Latin) dark. See also Hadriane.
Addie, Adrien, Adriana, Adriane, Adrianna, Adrianne, Adrie, Adrieanne, Adrien, Adrienna, Adriyanna

Adrika (Indian) celestial.

Adrina (English) a short form of
Adriana.
Adrinah, Adrinne

Adriyanna (American) a form of
Adrienne.
Adrieyana, Adriyana, Adryan,
Adryana, Adryane, Adryanna,
Adryanne

Adwita, Adwiteya (Indian) unique.

Adwitiya (Indian) matchless.

Adya (Hindi) Sunday.
Adia

Ae (Korean) distant moon.

Aeoma (Hawaiian) a kind of bird.

Aerial, Aeriel (Hebrew) forms of
Ariel.
Aeriale, Aeriela, Aerielle, Aeril, Aerile,
Aeryal

Afaf (Indian) chastity.

Afi (African) born on Friday.
Affi, Afia, Efi, Efia

Afra (Hebrew) young doe. (Arabic)
earth color. See also Aphra.
Affery, Affrey, Affrie, Afraa

Africa (Latin, Greek) sunny; not
cold. Geography: one of the seven
continents.
Affrica, Afric, Africah, Africaya, Africia,
Africiana, Afrika, Aifric

Afrika (Irish) a form of Africa.
Afrikah

Afrodite, Aphrodite (Greek)
Mythology: the goddess of love
and beauty.
Afrodita

Afton ☐ (English) from Afton,
England.
Aftan, Aftine, Aftinn, Aftyn

Agacia (Greek) kind.

Agalia (Spanish) bright, joy.

Agamya (Indian) knowledge,
wisdom.

Agapita (Greek) she who is beloved
and wanted.

Agar (Hebrew) she who fled.

Agate (English) a semiprecious stone.
Aggie

Agatha (Greek) good, kind.
Literature: Agatha Christie was a
British writer of more than seventy
detective novels. See also Gasha.
Agace, Agaisha, Agasha, Agata,
Agatah, Agathe, Agathi, Agatka,
Agetha, Aggie, Agota, Agotha,
Agueda, Atka

Agathe (Greek) a form of Agatha.

Aggie (Greek) a short form of
Agatha, Agnes.
Ag, Aggy, Agi

Aghanashini (Indian) destroyer of
sins.

Aglaia (Greek) splendorous one;
beautiful; resplendent.

Agmagof (Chamorro) being happy
together.

Agñasiña (Chamorro) mighty for
each other.

Agnes (Greek) pure. See also
Aneesa, Anessa, Anice, Anisha, Ina,
Inez, Necha, Nessa, Nessie, Neza,
Nyusha, Una, Ynez.
Aganetha, Aggie, Agna, Agne, Agneis,
Agnelia, Agnella, Agnés, Agnesa,
Agnesca, Agnese, Agnesina, Agness,
Agnessa, Agnesse, Agneta, Agneti,
Agnetta, Agnies, Agnieszka, Agniya,
Agnola, Agnus, Aignéis, Aneska, Anka

Agnishikha (Indian) flames of fire.

Agostina (Spanish) a form of Agustina.
Agostiña

Agot (Chamorro) embrace each other.

Agrata (Indian) leadership.

Agripina (Greek) from the Agripa family.

Agua (Chamorro) milkfish.

Agüeda (Greek) having many virtues.

Águeda (Spanish) a form of Agatha.

Aguilina (Spanish) a form of Justina.

Aguon (Chamorro) food, bread, taro.

Agustina (Latin) a form of Augustine.

Ah (Chinese) from a Chinese character.

Ah Kum (Chinese) treasure.

Ahalya (Indian) wife of Rishi Gautam.

Ahanti (Indian) gift.

Ahava (Hebrew) beloved.
Ahivia

Ahd (Indian) pledge; knowledge.

Ahilya (Indian) wife of a rishi (divinely inspired poet or sage).

Ahladita (Indian) in a happy and nice mood.

Ahlani (Hawaiian) a form of Alani.

Ahliya (Hebrew) a form of Aliya.
Ahlai, Ahlaia, Ahlaya, Ahleah, Ahleeyah, Ahley, Ahleya, Ahlia, Ahliah, Ahliyah

Ahmed **B** (Swahili) praiseworthy.

Ah-Rum (Korean) torch light.

Aida (Latin) helpful. (English) a form of Ada.
Aída, Aidah, Aidan, Aide, Aidee

Aidan, Aiden **B** (Latin) forms of Aida.

Aidia (Spanish) help.

Aiesha (Swahili, Arabic) a form of Aisha.
Aeisha, Aeshia, Aieshia, Aieysha, Aiiesha

Aiisha (Arabic) a form of Aisha.

Aiko (Japanese) beloved.

Ailani (Hawaiian) chief.
Aelani, Ailana

Aileen (Scottish) light bearer. (Irish) a form of Helen. See also Eileen.
Ailean, Aileena, Ailen, Ailene, Aili, Ailina, Ailinn, Aillen

Ailén (Mapuche) ember.

Aili (Scottish) a form of Alice. (Finnish) a form of Helen.
Aila, Ailee, Ailey, Ailie, Aily

Ailín (Mapuche) transparent, very clear.

Ailis (Irish) a form of Adelaide.
Ailesh, Ailish, Ailyse, Eilis

Ailsa (Scottish) island dweller. Geography: Ailsa Craig is an island in Scotland.
Ailsha

Ailya (Hebrew) a form of Aliya.
Ailiyah

Aimee (Latin) a form of Amy. (French) loved.
Aime, Aimée, Aimey, Aimi, Aimia, Aimie, Aimy

Ain (Arabic) eye; the name of an orange star in the constellation of Taurus.

Ainara (Basque) swallow.

Ainhoa (Basque) allusion to the Virgin Mary.

Ainoa (Basque) she who has fertile soil.

Ainsley ☀ (Scottish) my own meadow.
Ainslee, Ainsleigh, Ainslie, Ainsly, Ansley, Aynslee, Aynsley, Aynslie

Airiana (English) a form of Ariana, Arianna.
Airana, Airanna, Aireana, Aireanah, Aireanna, Aireona, Aireonna, Aireyonna, Airianna, Airianne, Airiona, Airriana, Airrion, Airryon, Airyana, Airyanna

Airiél (Hebrew) a form of Ariel.
Aieral, Aierel, Aiiryel, Aire, Aireal, Aireale, Aireel, Airel, Airele, Airelle, Airi, Airial, Airiale, Airrel

Aisha (Swahili) life. (Arabic) woman. See also Asha, Asia, Iesha, Isha, Keisha, Yiesha.
Aaisha, Aaishah, Aesha, Aeshah, Aheesha, Aiasha, Aiesha, Aieshah, Aisa, Aischa, Aish, Aishah, Aisheh, Aishia, Aishiah, Aiysha, Aiyesha, Ayesha, Aysa, Ayse, Aytza

Aishwarya (Indian) wealth, prosperity.

Aislinn, Aislynn (Irish) forms of Ashlyn.
Aishellyn, Aishlinn, Aislee, Aisley, Aislin, Aisling, Aislyn, Aislynne

Aivi (Chuukese) intravenous.

Aiyana (Native American) forever flowering.
Aiyhana, Aiyona, Aiyonia, Ayana

Aiyanna (Hindi) a form of Ayanna.
Aianna, Aiyannah, Aiyonna, Aiyunna

Aja ☀ (Hindi) goat.
Ahjah, Aija, Aijah, Ajá, Ajada, Ajah, Ajara, Ajaran, Ajare, Ajaree, Ajha, Ajia

Ajala (Indian) the Earth.

Ajanae (American) a combination of the letter A + Janae.
Ajahnae, Ajahne, Ajana, Ajanaé, Ajane, Ajané, Ajanee, Ajanique, Ajena, Ajenae, Ajené

Ajanta (Indian) a famous Buddhist cave.

Ajia (Hindi) a form of Aja.
Aijia, Ajhia, Aji, Ajjia

Ajita (Indian) a winner.

Akako (Japanese) red.

Akanisi (Fijian) a form of Agnes.

Akanksha (Indian) wish; desire; hope.

Akasuki (Japanese) bright; helper.

Akata (Fijian) a form of Agueda.

Akayla (American) a combination of the letter A + Kayla.
Akaela, Akaelia, Akaila, Akailah, Akala, Akaylah, Akaylia

Akeisha (American) a combination of the letter A + Keisha.
Akaesha, Akaisha, Akasha, Akasia, Akeecia, Akeesha, Akeishia, Akeshia, Akisha

Akela (Hawaiian) noble.
Ahkayla, Ahkeelah, Akelah, Akelia, Akeliah, Akeya, Akeyla, Akeylah

Akemi (Japanese) the dawn of a beautiful day.

Akeneta (Fijian) a form of Agnes.

Akeria (American) a form of Akira.
Akera, Akerah, Akeri, Akerra, Akerra

Akhila (Indian) complete.

Aki (Japanese) born in autumn.
Akeeye

Akia (American) a combination of
the letter A + Kia.
*Akaja, Akeia, Akeya, Akiá, Akiah,
Akiane, Akiaya, Akiea, Akiya, Akiyah,
Akya, Akyan, Akyia, Akyiah*

Akiha (Japanese) autumn leaves.

Akiho (Japanese) autumn crops.

Akiko (Japanese) bright light.

Akilah (Arabic) intelligent.
*Aikiela, Aikilah, Akeela, Akeelah,
Akeila, Akeilah, Akeiyla, Akiela,
Akielah, Akila, Akilaih, Akilia, Akilka,
Akillah, Akkila, Akyla, Akylah*

Akili (Tanzanian) wisdom.

Akimi (Japanese) the truth of autumn.

Akina (Japanese) spring flower.

Akira **G** (American) a combination
of the letter A + Kira.
*Akeria, Akiera, Akierra, Akirah, Akire,
Akiria, Akirrah, Akyra*

Akiye (Japanese) glitter; inlet; blessed.

Akiyo (Japanese) bright fourth-born
child; life like a poem.

Akriti (Indian) diagram.

Akshadha (Indian) God's blessings.

Akshara (Indian) letter.

Akshata (Indian) rice.

Akshaya (Indian) indestructible.

Akshi (Indian) existence.

Akshita (Indian) wonder girl.

Akuti (Indian) princess.

Alabhya (Indian) unique, difficult to
acquire.

Alago (Chamorro) rice soup.

Alai (Chinese) wheat.

Alaina, Alayna (Irish) forms of
Alana.
*Aalaina, Alainah, Alaine, Alainna,
Alainnah, Alane, Alaynah, Alayne,
Alaynna, Aleine, Alleyna, Alleynah,
Alleyne*

Alair (French) a form of Hilary.
Alaira, Ali, Allaire

Alak, Alaka (Indian) world;
beautiful tresses.

Alaknanda (Indian) a river.

Alamea (Hawaiian) ripe; precious.

Alameda (Spanish) poplar tree.

Alan **B** (Irish) beautiful; peaceful.

Alana (Irish) a form of Alan.
(Hawaiian) offering. See also Lana.
*Alaana, Alaina, Alanae, Alanah, Alane,
Alanea, Alani, Alania, Alanis, Alanna,
Alawna, Alayna, Allana, Allanah, Allyn,
Alonna*

Alandra, Alandria (Spanish) forms
of Alexandra, Alexandria.
Alandrea, Alantra, Aleandra, Aleandrea

Alani (Hawaiian) orange tree. (Irish)
a form of Alana.
*Alaini, Alainie, Alania, Alanie, Alaney,
Alannie*

Alankrita (Indian) decorated lady.

Alanna (Irish) a form of Alana.
Alannah

Alanza (Spanish) noble and eager.

Alas (Chamorro) shell money.

Alasña (Chamorro) her shell money.

Alaysha, Alaysia (American) forms
of Alicia.
Alaysh, Alayshia

Alba (Latin) from Alba Longa, an ancient city near Rome, Italy.
Albana, Albani, Albanie, Albany, Albeni, Albina, Albine, Albinia, Albinka

Albert 🄱 (German, French) noble and bright.

Alberta (German, French) a form of Albert. See also Auberte, Bertha, Elberta.
Albertina, Albertine, Albertyna, Albertyne, Alverta

Albreanna (American) a combination of Alberta + Breanna (see Breana).
Albré, Albrea, Albreona, Albreonna, Albreyon

Alcina (Greek) strong-minded.
Alceena, Alcine, Alcinia, Alseena, Alsinia, Alsyna, Alzina

Alcira (German) adornment of nobility.

Alda (German) old; elder.
Aldina, Aldine

Aldana (Spanish) a combination of Alda and Ana.

Alden 🄱 (English) old; wise protector.
Aldan, Aldon, Aldyn

Aldina, Aldine (Hebrew) forms of Alda.
Aldeana, Aldene, Aldona, Aldyna, Aldyne

Aldonsa, Aldonza (Spanish) nice.

Alea, Aleah (Arabic) high, exalted. (Persian) God's being.
Aileah, Aleea, Aleeah, Aleia, Aleiah, Allea, Alleah, Alleea, Alleeah

Aleasha, Aleesha (Greek) forms of Alisha.
Aleashae, Aleashea, Aleashia, Aleassa, Aleeshia

Alec, Alek 🄱 (Greek) short forms of Alexander.

Alecia (Greek) a form of Alicia.
Aalecia, Ahlasia, Aleacia, Aleacya, Aleasia, Alecea, Aleceea, Aleceia, Aleciya, Aleciyah, Alecy, Alecya, Aleeceia, Aleecia, Aleesia, Aleesiya, Aleicia, Alesha, Alesia, Allecia, Alleecia

Aleela (Swahili) she cries.
Aleelah, Alila, Alile

Aleena (Dutch) a form of Aleene.
Ahleena, Aleana, Aleeanna

Aleene (Dutch) alone.
Aleen, Aleena, Alene, Alleen

Aleeya (Hebrew) a form of Aliya.
Alee, Aleea, Aleeyah, Aleiya, Aleiyah

Aleeza (Hebrew) a form of Aliza. See also Leeza.
Aleiza

Alegria (Spanish) cheerful.
Aleggra, Alegra, Alegría, Allegra, Allegria

Aleisha, Alesha (Greek) forms of Alecia, Alisha.
Aleasha, Aleashea, Aleasia, Aleesha, Aleeshah, Aleeshia, Aleeshya, Aleisa, Alesa, Alesah, Aleisha, Aleshia, Aleshya, Alesia, Alessia

Alejandra 🄶 (Spanish) a form of Alexandra.
Aleiandra, Alejanda, Alejandr, Alejandrea, Alejandria, Alejandrina, Alejandro

Alejandro 🄱 (Spanish) a form of Alejandra.

Aleka (Hawaiian) a form of Alice.
Aleeka, Alekah

Alekhya (Indian) that which cannot be written.

Aleksandra (Greek) a form of
Alexandra.
*Alecsandra, Aleksasha, Aleksandrija,
Aleksandriya*

Alena (Russian) a form of Helen.
*Alenah, Alene, Alenea, Aleni, Alenia,
Alenka, Alenna, Alennah, Alenya, Alyna*

Alesia, Alessia (Greek) forms of
Alice, Alicia, Alisha.
Alessea, Alesya, Allesia

Alessa (Greek) a form of Alice.
Alessi, Allessa

Alessandra (Italian) a form of
Alexandra.
*Alesandra, Alesandrea, Alissandra,
Alissondra, Allesand, Allessandra*

Alessandro **B** (Italian) a form of
Alexander.

Aleta (Greek) a form of Alida. See
also Leta.
Aletta, Alletta

Alethea (Greek) truth.
*Alathea, Alathia, Aletea, Aletha, Aletheia,
Alethia, Aletia, Alithea, Alithia*

Alette (Latin) wing.

Alex **B** (Greek) a short form of
Alexander, Alexandra.
Aleix, Aleks, Alexe, Alexx, Allex, Allexx

Alexa ✫ **G** (Greek) a short form of
Alexandra.
*Aleixa, Alekia, Aleksa, Aleksha, Aleksi,
Alexah, Alexsa, Alexssa, Alexxa, Allexa,
Alyxa*

Alexander **B** (Greek) defender of
humankind.

Alexandra ✫ **G** (Greek) a form of
Alexander. History: the last czarina
of Russia. See also Lexia, Lexie,
Olesia, Ritsa, Sandra, Sandrine, Sasha,
Shura, Sondra, Xandra, Zandra.
Alandra, Alaxandra, Aleczandra,

*Alejandra, Aleksandra, Alessandra,
Alex, Alexa, Alexande, Alexandera,
Alexandre, Alexas, Alexi, Alexina,
Alexine, Alexis, Alexsandra, Alexius,
Alexsis, Alexus, Alexxandra, Alexys,
Alexzandra, Alix, Alixandra, Aljexi, Alla,
Alyx, Alyxandra, Lexandra*

Alexandre **B** (Greek) a form of
Alexandra.

Alexandrea (Greek) a form of
Alexandria.
*Alexandreana, Alexandreia,
Alexandriea, Alexandrieah, Alexanndrea*

Alexandria **G** (Greek) a form of
Alexandra. See also Drinka, Xandra,
Zandra.
*Alaxandria, Alecsandria, Aleczandria,
Alexanderia, Alexanderine, Alexandrea,
Alexandrena, Alexandrie, Alexandrina,
Alexandrine, Alexanndria, Alexandrya,
Alexendria, Alexendrine, Alexia,
Alixandrea, Alyxandria*

Alexandrine (Greek) a form of
Alexandra.
Alexandrina

Alexanne (American) a combination
of Alex + Anne.
*Alexan, Alexanna, Alexane, Alexann,
Alexanna, Alexian, Alexiana*

Alexas, Alexes (Greek) short forms
of Alexandra.
Alexess

Alexe **G** (Greek) a form of Alex.

Alexi, Alexie **G** (Greek) short
forms of Alexandra.
Aleksey, Aleksi, Alexey, Alexy

Alexia (Greek) a short form of
Alexandria. See also Lexia.
*Aleksia, Aleska, Alexcia, Alexea,
Alexsia, Alexsiya, Allexia, Alyxia*

Alexis ☆ **G** (Greek) a short form of Alexandra.
Aalexis, Ahlexis, Alaxis, Alecsis, Alecxis, Aleexis, Aleksis, Alexcis, Alexias, Alexiou, Alexiss, Alexiz, Alexxis, Alixis, Allexis, Elexis, Lexis

Alexius (Greek) a short form of Alexandra.
Allexius

Alexsandra (Greek) a form of Alexandra.
Alexsandria, Alexsandro, Alixsandra

Alexsis, Alexxis (Greek) short forms of Alexandra.
Alexxiz

Alexus **G** (Greek) a short form of Alexandra.
Aalexus, Aalexxus, Aelexus, Ahlexus, Alecsus, Alexsus, Alexuss, Alexxus, Alixus, Allexus, Elexus, Lexus

Alexys (Greek) a short form of Alexandra.
Alexsys, Alexyes, Alexyis, Alexyss, Allexys

Alexzandra (Greek) a form of Alexandra.
Alexzand, Alexzandrea, Alexzandriah, Alexzandrya, Alixzandria

Aleya, Aleyah (Hebrew) forms of Aliya.
Alayah, Aleayah; Aleeya, Aléyah, Aleyia, Aleyiah

Alfa (Greek) symbolizes the beginning of all.

Alfie **B** (English) a familiar form of Alfreda.
Alfi, Alfy

Alfonsa (Spanish) noble.

Alfonsina (German) noble and ready for battle.

Alfreda (English) elf counselor; wise counselor. See also Effie, Elfrida, Freda, Frederica.
Alfie, Alfredda, Alfredia, Alfreeda, Alfreida, Alfrieda

Alhertina (Spanish) noble.

Ali, Aly **B** (Greek) familiar forms of Alice, Alicia, Alisha, Alison.
Allea, Alli, Allie, Ally

Alia, Aliah (Hebrew) forms of Aliya. See also Aaliyah, Alea.
Aelia, Allia, Alya

Alice **G** (Greek) truthful. (German) noble. See also Aili, Aleka, Alie, Alisa, Alison, Alli, Alysa, Alyssa, Alysse, Elke.
Adelice, Alecia, Aleece, Alesia, Alicie, Aliece, Alise, Alix, Alize, Alla, Alleece, Allice, Allis, Allise, Allix

Alicia **G** (English) a form of Alice. See also Elicia, Licia.
Aelicia, Alaysha, Alecea, Alecia, Aleecia, Ali, Alicea, Alicha, Alichia, Aliciah, Alician, Alicja, Alicya, Aliecia, Alisha, Allicea, Allicia, Alycia, Ilysa

Alida (Latin) small and winged. (Spanish) noble. See also Aleta, Lida, Oleda.
Aleda, Aleida, Alidia, Alita, Alleda, Allida, Allidah, Alyda, Alydia, Elida, Elidia

Alie (Greek) a familiar form of Alice.

Aliesha (Greek) a form of Alisha.
Alieshai, Alieshia, Alliesha

Ali'i (Hawaiian) queen, noble, royal.

Alika (Hawaiian) truthful. (Swahili) most beautiful.
Aleka, Alica, Alikah, Alike, Alikee, Aliki

Aliksa (Kosraean) forever.

Alima (Arabic) sea maiden; musical.

Alina, Alyna (Slavic) bright.
(Scottish) fair. (English) short forms
of Adeline. See also Alena.
Aliana, Alianna, Alinah, Aline, Alinna,
Allyna, Alynna, Alyona

Aline (Scottish) a form of Alina.
Alianne, Allene, Alline, Allyn, Allyne,
Alyne, Alynne

Alisa (Greek) a form of Alice. See
also Elisa, Ilisa.
Aalissah, Aaliysah, Aleessa, Alisah,
Alisea, Alisia, Alisza, Alisza, Aliysa,
Allissa, Alyssa

Alise, Allise (Greek) forms of Alice.
Alics, Aliese, Alis, Aliss, Alisse, Alisse,
Alles, Allesse, Allis, Allisse

Alisha G (Greek) truthful. (German)
noble. (English) a form of Alicia. See
also Elisha, Ilisha, Lisha.
Aalisha, Aleasha, Aleesha, Aleisha,
Alesha, Ali, Aliesha, Aliscia, Alishah,
Alishay, Alishaye, Alishia, Alishya,
Alitsha, Allisha, Allysha, Alysha

Alishia, Alisia, Alissia (English)
forms of Alisha.
Alishea, Alisheia, Alishiana, Alyssaya,
Alisea, Alissya, Alisyia, Allissia

Alison G (English) a form of Alice.
Ali, Alicen, Alicyn, Alisan, Alisann,
Alisanne, Alisen, Alisenne, Alisin,
Alision, Alisonn, Alisson, Alisun

Alissa G (Greek) a form of Alice.
See also Elisa, Ilisa.
Aelicia, Alaysha, Alecea, Alecia,
Aleecia, Ali, Alicea, Alicha, Alichia,
Aliciah, Alician, Alicja, Alicya, Aliecia,
Alisha, Allicea, Allicia, Alycia, Ilysa

Alita (Spanish) a form of Alida.
Allita

Alivia (Latin) a form of Olivia.
Alivah

Alix G (Greek) a short form of
Alexandra, Alice.
Alixe, Alixia, Allix, Alyx

Alixandra, Alixandria (Greek)
forms of Alexandria.
Alixandriya, Allixandra, Allixandria,
Allixandrya

Aliya (Hebrew) ascender.
Aaleyah, Aaliyah, Aeliyah, Ahliya,
Ailya, Alea, Aleya, Alia, Alieya, Alieyah,
Aliyah, Aliyiah, Aliyyah, Allia, Alliyah,
Aly, Alyah

Aliye (Arabic) noble.
Aliyeh

Aliza (Hebrew) joyful. See also
Aleeza, Eliza.
Alieza, Aliezah, Alitza, Aliz, Alizah,
Alize, Alizee

Alizabeth (Hebrew) a form of
Elizabeth.
Alyzabeth

Alka (Indian) beauty.

Allan B (Irish) a form of Alan.

Allana, Allanah (Irish) forms of
Alana.
Allanie, Allanna, Allauna

Allegra (Latin) cheerful.
Legra

Allen B (Irish) a form of Alan.

Allena (Irish) a form of Alana.
Alleen, Alleyna, Alleynah

Alli, Ally (Greek) familiar forms of
Alice.
Ali, Alley

Allia, Alliah (Hebrew) forms of
Aliya.

Allie G (Greek) familiar forms of
Alice.

Allison ❦ **G** (English) a form of
Alice. See also Lissie.
Alles, Allesse, Alleyson, Allie, Allisson,
Allisyn, Allix, Allsun

Allissa (Greek) a form of Alyssa.
Allisa

Alliyah (Hebrew) a form of Aliya.
Alliya, Alliyha, Alliyia, Alliyyah, Allya,
Allyah

Allysa, Allyssa (Greek) a form of
Alyssa.
Allissa, Allyisa, Allysa, Allysah, Allyssah

Allysha (English) a form of Alisha.
Alishia, Allysia

Allyson, Alyson (English) forms of
Alison.
Allysen, Allyson, Allysonn, Allysson,
Allysun, Alyson

Alma **G** (Arabic) learned. (Latin)
soul.
Almah

Almas (Indian) diamond.

Almeda (Arabic) ambitious.
Allmeda, Allmedah, Allmeta, Allmita,
Almea, Almedah, Almeta, Almida,
Almita

Almira (Arabic) aristocratic, princess;
exalted. (Spanish) from Almeíra,
Spain. See also Elmira, Mira.
Allmeera, Allmeria, Allmira, Almeera,
Almeeria, Almeira, Almeria, Almire

Almudena (Spanish) city.

Almunda (Spanish) refers to the
Virgin Mary.

Almundena, Almundina (Spanish)
forms of Almunda.

Alo (Chamorro) a form of Alu.

Aloha (Hawaiian) loving,
kindhearted, charitable.
Alohi

Alohilani (Hawaiian) bright sky.

Aloisa (German) famous warrior.
Aloisia, Aloysia

Aloki (Indian) brightness.

Alola (Chamorro) a form of Alula.

Aloma (Latin) a short form of Paloma.

Alondra **G** (Spanish) a form of
Alexandra.
Allandra, Alonda

Alonna (Irish) a form of Alana.
Alona, Alonnah, Alonya, Alonyah

Alonsa (English) eager for battle.

Alonza (English) noble and eager.

Alopa (Indian) faultless.

Alora (American) a combination of
the letter A + Lora.
Alorah, Alorha, Alorie, Aloura, Alouria

Alos (Chamorro) a form of Alas.

Alpa (Indian) small.

Alpana (Indian) beautiful.

Alpha (Greek) first-born. Linguistics:
the first letter of the Greek alphabet.
Alphia

Alta (Latin) high; tall.
Allta, Altah, Altana, Altanna, Altea, Alto

Altagracia (Spanish) refers to the
high grace of the Virgin Mary.

Althea (Greek) wholesome; healer.
History: Althea Gibson was the
first African American to win a
major tennis title. See also Thea.
Altha, Altheda, Altheya, Althia, Elthea,
Eltheya, Elthia

Alu (Chamorro) barracuda; shark.

Alula (Chamorro) hurry.

Aluminé (Mapuche) she who shines.

Alva **BG** (Latin, Spanish) white; light skinned. See also Elva.
Alvana, Alvanna, Alvannah

Alvarita, Alvera (Spanish) speaker of truth.

Alvina (English) friend to all; noble friend; friend to elves. See also Elva, Vina.
Alveanea, Alveen, Alveena, Alveenia, Alvenea, Alvie, Alvinae, Alvincia, Alvine, Alvinea, Alvinesha, Alvinia, Alvinna, Alvita, Alvona, Alvyna, Alwin, Alwina, Alwyn

Alyah, Alyiah (Hebrew) forms of Aliya.
Aly, Alya, Aleah, Alyia

Alycia, Alyssia (English) forms of Alicia.
Allyce, Alycea, Alyciah, Alyse, Lycia

Alysa, Alyse (Greek) forms of Alice.
Allys, Allyse, Allyss, Alys, Alyss

Alysha, Alysia (Greek) forms of Alisha.
Allysea, Allyscia, Alysea, Alyshia, Alyssha, Alyssia

Alyssa ✿ **G** (Greek) rational. Botany: alyssum is a flowering herb. See also Alice, Elissa.
Ahlyssa, Alissa, Allissa, Allyssa, Alyesa, Alyessa, Alyissa, Alysah, Ilyssa, Lyssa, Lyssah

Alysse (Greek) a form of Alice.
Allyce, Allys, Allyse, Allyss, Alys, Alyss

Alyx, Alyxis (Greek) short forms of Alexandra.

Alyxandra, Alyxandria (Greek) forms of Alexandria.
Alyxandrea, Alyxzandrya

Am (Vietnamese) lunar; female.

Ama (African) born on Saturday.

Amabel (Latin) lovable. See also Bel, Mabel.

Amada (Spanish) beloved.
Amadea, Amadi, Amadia, Amadita

Amadis (Latin) great love, the most beloved.

Amai (Chamorro) rain.

Amairani (Greek) a form of Amara.
Amairaine, Amairane, Amairanie, Amairany

Amako (Japanese) child of God.

Amal **G** (Hebrew) worker. (Arabic) hopeful.
Amala

Amaldeepti (Indian) camphor.

Amaleperka (Pohnpeian) royal.

Amalia (German) a form of Amelia.
Ahmalia, Amalea, Amaleah, Amaleta, Amalija, Amalina, Amalisa, Amalita, Amaliya, Amalya, Amalyn

Amalie (German) a form of Amelia.
Amalee, Amali, Amaly

Amalsinda (German) one that God points to.

Amami (Japanese) sky; sea.

Aman, Amani (Arabic) forms of Imani.
Aamani, Ahmani, Amane, Amanee, Amaney, Amanie, Ammanu

Amanada (Latin) a form of Amanda.

Amancái, Amancay (Quechua) voice that gives a name to a beautiful yellow flower streaked with red.

Amanda ✿ **G** (Latin) lovable. See also Manda.
Amada, Amanada, Amandah, Amandalee, Amandalyn, Amandi, Amandie, Amandine, Amandy

Amandeep 🄱🄶 (Punjabi) peaceful light.

Amannie (Arabic) a form of Amani.

Amapola (Arabic) poppy.

Amara (Greek) eternally beautiful. See also Mara.
Amar, Amaira, Amairani, Amarah, Amari, Amaria, Amariah

Amaranta (Spanish) a flower that never fades.

Amarante (Japanese) flower that never fades.

Amari (Greek) a form of Amara.
Amaree, Amarie, Amarii, Amarri

Amarilia, Amarilla (Greek) she who shines.

Amarinda (Greek) she who shines.

Amaris (Hebrew) promised by God.
Amarissa, Amarys, Maris

Amarú (Quechua) snake, boa.

Amaryllis (Greek) fresh; flower.
Amarillis, Amarylis

Amatullah (Indian) female servant of Allah.

Amaui (Hawaiian) thrush.

Amay (Chamorro) a form of Amai.

Amaya (Japanese) night rain.

Ambalika (Indian) mother.

Ambar 🄶 (French) a form of Amber.

Amber 🄶 (French) amber.
Aamber, Ahmber, Amberia, Amberise, Amberly, Ambria, Ambur, Ambyr, Ambyre, Ammber, Ember

Amberly (American) a familiar form of Amber.
Amberle, Amberlea, Amberlee, Amberleigh, Amberley, Amberli, Amberlie, Amberlly, Amberlye

Amberlyn, Amberlynn (American) combinations of Amber + Lynn.
Amberlin, Amberlina, Amberlyne, Amberlynne

Ambhom (Tai) a form of Jingjing.

Ambria (American) a form of Amber.
Ambrea, Ambra, Ambriah

Ambrosia (Greek) she who is immortal.

Ambu (Indian) water.

Ambuda (Indian) cloud.

Amedia (Spanish) beloved.

Amelia ☆ (German) hard working. (Latin) a form of Emily. History: Amelia Earhart, an American aviator, was the first woman to fly solo across the Atlantic Ocean. See also Ima, Melia, Millie, Nuela, Yamelia.
Aemilia, Aimilia, Amalia, Amalie, Amaliya, Ameila, Ameilia, Amelie, Amelina, Ameline, Amelisa, Amelita, Amella, Amilia, Amilina, Amilisa, Amilita, Amilyn, Amylia

Amélia (Portuguese) a form of Amelia.

Amelie (German) a familiar form of Amelia.
Amaley, Amalie, Amelee, Ameleigh, Ameley, Amélie, Amely, Amilie

Amena (Arabic) a form of Amina.

America (Teutonic) industrious.
América, Americana, Amerika

Ami, Amie (French) forms of Amy.
Aami, Amiee, Amii, Amiiee, Ammee, Ammie, Ammiee

Amihan (Tagalog) abundance.

Amilia, Amilie (Latin, German) forms of Amelia.
Amilee, Amili, Amillia, Amily, Amilya

Amina (Arabic) trustworthy, faithful. History: the mother of the prophet Muhammad.
Aamena, Aamina, Aaminah, Ameena, Ameenah, Aminah, Aminda, Amindah, Aminta, Amintah

Amir **G** (Hebrew) proclaimed. (Punjabi) wealthy; king's minister. (Arabic) prince.

Amira (Hebrew) speech; utterance. (Arabic) princess. See also Mira.
Ameera, Ameerah, Amirah

Amisha (Indian) beautiful.

Amishi, Amla (Indian) pure.

Amissa (Hebrew) truth.
Amissah

Amista (Chamorro) fidelity, loyalty.

Amita (Hebrew) truth.
Amitha

Amithi (Indian) unique.

Amitjyoti (Indian) bright.

Amity (Latin) friendship.
Amitie

Amiya (Indian) delightful.

Amlika (Hindi) mother.
Amlikah

Amma (Hindi) god, godlike. Religion: another name for the Hindu goddess Shakti.

Ammei, Ammey (Chamorro) forms of Amai.

Amoda (Indian) happiness.

Amodini (Indian) pleasurable.

Amog (Chamorro) medicine.

Amolika (Indian) priceless.

Amor (German) a form of Amorie.

Amora (Spanish) a form of Amor.

Amorie (German) industrious leader.

Amorina (Spanish) she who falls in love easily.

Amparo (Spanish) protected.

Amrapali (Indian) disciple of Buddha.

Amrit **BG** (Sanskrit) nectar.
Amrita

Amritambu (Indian) moon.

Amritkala (Indian) nectarine art.

Amritrashmi (Indian) moonlight.

Amrusha (Indian) sudden.

Amshula, Anshula (Indian) sunny.

Amti (Chamorro) a form of Aorta.

Amuillan (Mapuche) useful, helpful; enthusiastic woman who does all that she can to serve those around her.

Amvi (Indian) a goddess.

Amy **G** (Latin) beloved. See also Aimee, Emma, Esmé.
Amata, Ame, Amey, Ami, Amia, Amie, Amio, Ammy, Amye, Amylyn

An **B** (Chinese) peaceful.

Ana (Hawaiian, Spanish) a form of Hannah.
Anai, Anaia

Aña (Chamorro) to overpower; to punish.

Anaan (Indian) clouds.

Anaba (Native American) she returns from battle.

Anabel, Anabelle (English) forms of Annabel.
Anabela, Anabele, Anabell, Anabella

Anaclara (Spanish) a combination of Ana and Clara.

Anacleta (Greek) she who has been called on; the required one.

Anagha (Indian) without sin.

Anahí, Anahid (Guarani) alluding to the flower of the Ceibo plant.

Anahita (Persian) a river and water goddess.
Anahai, Anahi, Anahit, Anahy

Anais (Hebrew) gracious.
Anaise, Anaïse

Anala (Hindi) fine.

Analena (Spanish) a form of Ana.

Analía (Spanish) a combination of Ana and Lía.

Analilia (Indian) full of grace.

Analisa, Analise (English) combinations of Ana + Lisa.
Analice, Analicia, Analis, Analisha, Analisia, Analissa

Anam (Indian) blessing.

Anamaria (English) a combination of Ana + Maria.
Anamarie, Anamary

Anamika (Indian) ring finger.

Anamitra (Indian) the sun.

Anana (Chamorro) she punishes.

Ananda (Hindi) blissful.

Anandamayi (Indian) full of joy.

Anandani, Anandini (Indian) joyful.

Anandi (Indian) joyful; unending.

Anandita (Indian) happy.

Anandmayee (Indian) full of happiness.

Ananti (Indian) gift.

Ananya (Indian) without a second, endless; unique.

Anarghya (Indian) priceless.

Anarosa (English) a form of Ana.

Anasdasia (Pohnpeian) a form of Adela.

Anaseini (Fijian) a combination of Ana + Jane.

Anastacia (Greek) a form of Anastasia.
Anastace, Anastacie

Anastasia (Greek) resurrection. See also Nastasia, Stacey, Stacia, Stasya.
Anastacia, Anastase, Anastascia, Anastasha, Anastashia, Anastasie, Anastasija, Anastassia, Anastassya, Anastasya, Anastatia, Anastaysia, Anastazia, Anastice, Annastasia, Annastasija, Annastaysia, Annastazia, Annstás

Anasua (Indian) one who is not jealous of anyone.

Anatilde (Spanish) a combination of Ana and Matilde.

Anatola (Greek) from the east.

Anatolia (Greek) east.

Anay (Chamorro) when.

Anbar (Indian) perfume.

Ancarla (Spanish) a combination of Ana and Carla.

Ancelín (Latin) single woman.

Anchita (Indian) honored, worshipped.

Anci (Hungarian) a form of Hannah.
Annus, Annushka

Anda (Japanese) meet at the field.

Andeana (Spanish) leaving.

Andee, Andi, Andie (American) short forms of Andrea, Fernanda.
Ande, Andea, Andy

Andere (Greek) valiant, courageous.

Anderson **B** (Swedish) child of Andrew.

Anding (Tagalog) like an eagle.

Andre, André **B** (French) forms of Andrew.

Andrea 🌟 **G** (Greek) strong; courageous. See also Ondrea.
Aindrea, Andee, Andera, Anderea, Andra, Andrah, Andraia, Andraya, Andreah, Andreaka, Andreana, Andreane, Andree, Andrée, Andreea, Andreia, Andreja, Andreka, Andrel, Andrell, Andrelle, Andreo, Andressa, Andrette, Andreya, Andria, Andriana, Andrieka, Andrietta, Andris, Aundrea

Andréa, Andréia (Portuguese) valiant, courageous.

Andreana, Andreanna (Greek) forms of Andrea.
Ahndrianna, Andreina, Andrena, Andreyana, Andreyonna, Andrina, Andriona, Andrionna

Andreane, Andreanne (Greek) forms of Andrea.
Andrean, Andreeanne, Andree Anne, Andrene, Andrian, Andrienne

Andreas **B** (Greek) a form of Andrew.

Andreína (Spanish) a form of Andrea.

Andres **B** (Spanish) a form of Andrew.

Andresa (Spanish) a form of Andrea.

Andrew **B** (Greek) strong; courageous.

Andria (Greek) a form of Andrea.
Andri, Andriea

Andriana, Andrianna (Greek) forms of Andrea.

Andromaca (Greek) she who battles with a man.

Andromeda (Greek) in Greek mythology, the daughter of Cassiopeia and Cepheus.

Andy **B** (American) a form of Andee.

Aneesa, Aneesha (Greek) forms of Agnes.
Ahnesha, Ahnesia, Ahnesshia, Anee, Aneesah, Aneese, Aneeshah, Aneesia, Aneisa, Aneisha, Anessa, Anessia

Aneko (Japanese) older sister.

Anela (Hawaiian) angel.
Anel, Anelle

Anelida, Anelina (Spanish) combinations of Ana and Elida.

Anesin (Chuukese) name derived from the brand name for aspirin.

Anessa (Greek) a form of Agnes.
Anesha, Aneshia, Anesia, Anessia, Annessa

Anetra (American) a form of Annette.
Anitra

Anezka (Czech) a form of Hannah.

Angana (Indian) one with a beautiful body.

Angarika (Indian) flower.

Angel 🅑 (Greek) a short form of Angela.
Angele, Angéle, Angell, Angelle, Angil, Anjel

Angela 🅖 (Greek) angel; messenger.
Angala, Anganita, Angel, Angelanell, Angelanette, Angelee, Angeleigh, Angeles, Angeli, Angelia, Angelica, Angelina, Angelique, Angelita, Angella, Angellita, Angie, Anglea, Anjela, Anjelica

Ángela (Spanish) a form of Angela.

Ángeles (Catalonian) angels.

Angelia (Greek) a form of Angela.
Angelea, Angeleah, Angelie

Angélica (Spanish) a form of Angela.

Angelica, Angelika (Greek) forms of Angela.
Angalic, Angelic, Angelici, Angelicia, Angelike, Angeliki, Angellica, Angilica

Angelina ✵ 🅖 (Russian) a form of Angela.
Angalena, Angalina, Angelena, Angeliana, Angeleana, Angellina, Angelyna, Anhelina, Anjelina

Angeline (Russian) a form of Angela.
Angeleen, Angelene, Angelyn, Angelyna, Angelyne, Angelynn, Angelynne

Angelique (French) a form of Angela.
Angeliqua, Angélique, Angilique, Anjelique

Angeni (Native American) spirit.

Angha (Indian) beauty.

Angie (Greek) a familiar form of Angela.
Ange, Angee, Angey, Angi, Angy

Anginis (Chuukese) a form of ángeles.

Angkelina (Pohnpeian) a form of Anastasia.

Angoco (Chamorro) trust, rely on.

Angocog, Angog (Chamorro) forms of Angoco.

Angoori (Indian) grape.

Angustias (Latin) she who suffers from grief or sorrow.

Ani (Hawaiian) beautiful.
Aany, Aanye

Ania (Polish) a form of Hannah.
Ahnia, Anaya, Aniah

Anica, Anika (Czech) familiar forms of Anna.
Aanika, Anaka, Aneeky, Aneka, Anekah, Anicka, Anik, Anikah, Anike, Anikka, Anikke, Aniko, Anneka, Annik, Annika, Anouska, Anuska

Anice (English) a form of Agnes.
Anesse, Anis, Anise, Annes, Annice, Annis, Annus

Aniceta (Spanish) she who is invincible because of her great strength.

Anik 🅖 (Czech) a form of Anica.

Anila (Hindi) Religion: an attendant of the Hindu god Vishnu.
Anilla

Anillang (Mapuche) stable altar; decisive and courageously noble woman.

Anima (Indian) the power of becoming minute.

Anindita (Indian) beautiful.

Anisa, Anisah (Arabic) friendly.
Annissah

Anisha G (English) a form of Agnes, Ann.
Aanisha, Aeniesha, Annisha

Anissa (English) a form of Agnes, Ann.
Anis, Anisa, Anissah, Anise, Annisa, Annissa, Anyssa

Anita G (Spanish) a form of Ann, Anna. See also Nita.
Aneeta, Aneetah, Aneethah, Anetha, Anitha, Anithah, Anitia, Anitra, Anitte

Anjana, Anjini (Indian) mother of Hanuman.

Anjelica (Greek) a form of Angela.
Anjelika

Anjelita (Spanish) heavenly messenger.

Anjika (Indian) blessed.

Anju (Indian) blessings; unconquerable.

Anjushree, Anjushri (Indian) dear to one's heart.

Anka G (Polish) a familiar form of Hannah.
Anke

Ankal (Indian) whole.

Ankita (Indian) distinguished, marked by the Lord; dedicate.

Ann (English) gracious. See also Anne.
Anissa, Anita, Annchen, Annette, Annie, Annik, Annika, Annze, Anouche

Anna ★ G (German, Italian, Czech, Swedish) gracious. Culture: Anna Pavlova was a famous Russian ballerina. See also Anica, Anissa, Nina.
Ahnna, Ana, Anah, Anica, Anita, Annah, Annina, Annora, Anona, Anya, Anyu, Aska

Annabel (English) a combination of Anna + Bel.
Amabel, Anabel, Annabal, Annabelle

Annabelle (English) a form of Annabel.
Anabelle, Annabell, Annabella

Annalie (Finnish) a form of Hannah.
Analee, Annalea, Annaleah, Annalee, Annaleigh, Annaleigha, Annali, Anneli, Annelie

Annalisa, Annalise (English) combinations of Anna + Lisa.
Analisa, Analise, Annaliesa, Annaliese, Annalissa, Annalisse

Annamarie, Annemarie, Annmarie, Anne-Marie (English) combinations of Anne + Marie.
Annamaria, Anna-Maria, Anna-Marie, Annmaria

Annapoorna (Indian) goddess of grains.

Annapurna (Indian) goddess of food.

Anne G (English) gracious.

Anneka (Swedish) a form of Hannah.
Annaka, Anneke, Annika, Anniki, Annikki

Annelisa (English) a combination of Ann + Lisa.
Analiese, Anelisa, Anelise, Anneliese, Annelise

Annette (French) a form of Ann. See also Anetra, Nettie.
Anet, Aneta, Anetra, Anett, Anetta, Anette, Anneth, Annett, Annetta

Annie (English) a familiar form of Ann.
Anni, Anny

Annik, Annika (Russian) forms of Ann.
Aneka, Anekah, Annick, Annicka, Annike, Annikka, Anninka, Anouk

Annjanette (American) a combination of Ann + Janette.
Angen, Angenett, Angenette, Anjane, Anjanetta, Anjani

Anokhi (Indian) different.

Anona (English) pineapple.

Anouhea (Hawaiian) cool, soft fragrance.

Anouka (Indian) spirit of God.

Anoushka, Anushka (Indian) a term of endearment.

Anselma (German, Dutch, Italian, Spanish) helmet; protection.

Ansha (Indian) portion.

Anshika (Indian) minute particle.

Anshumali (Indian) sun.

Ansina (Chuukese) a form of Angela.

Ansley ☷ (Scottish) forms of Ainsley.
Anslea, Anslee, Ansleigh, Anslie

Ansuya (Indian) learned woman.

Antara (Indian) beauty.

Antariksha (Indian) space; sky.

Anthea (Greek) flower.
Antha, Anthe, Anthia, Thia

Anthony ☷ (Latin) praiseworthy. (Greek) flourishing.

Anti (Chamorro) soul.

Antía (Galician) priceless; flourishing; flower.

Antígona (Greek) distinguished by her brothers.

Antione ☷ (French) a form of Anthony.

Antionette (French) a form of Antonia.
Antionet, Antionett, Anntionett

Antoinette (French) a form of Antonia. See also Netti, Toinette, Toni.
Anta, Antanette, Antoinella, Antoinet, Antonella, Antonetta, Antonette, Antonice, Antonieta, Antonietta, Antonique

Antolina (Spanish) flourishing, beautiful as a flower.

Antonia ☷ (Greek) flourishing. (Latin) praiseworthy. See also Toni, Tonya, Tosha.
Ansonia, Ansonya, Antania, Antinia, Antionette, Antoinette, Antona, Antoñía, Antonice, Antonie, Antonina, Antonine, Antoniya, Antonnea, Antonnia, Antonya

Antónia (Portuguese) a form of Antonia.

Antonice (Latin) a form of Antonia.
Antanise, Antanisha, Antonesha, Antoneshia, Antonise, Antonisha

Antoniña (Latin) she who confronts or is the adversary.

Antonio ☷ (Italian) a form of Anthony.

Antti (Chamorro) a form of Anti.

Anubhuti (Indian) feelings.

Anugraha (Indian) divine blessing.

Anugya (Indian) permission.

Anuhea (Hawaiian) sweet fragrance of the rain forest.

Anuhya (Indian) something pleasantly unexpected.

Anuja (Indian) younger sister.

Anukeertana (Indian) praising God's virtues.

Anula (Indian) not wild, agreeable.

Anulata (Indian) one with very slim figure.

Anumati, Anurati (Indian) consent.

Anuncia (Latin) announcer, messenger.

Anunciación (Spanish) annunciation.

Anunciada (Spanish) a form of Anunciación.

Anunciata (Italian) a form of Anunciación.

Anupama (Indian) beautiful.

Anuprabha (Indian) brightness.

Anupriya (Indian) beloved daughter.

Anuradha (Indian) Lord Krishna's consort.

Anuragini (Indian) beloved.

Anusha (Indian) following desires.

Anushri (Indian) pretty; prosperous.

Anusuya (Indian) not jealous.

Anuva (Indian) knowledge.

Anwaar (Indian) rays of light.

Anwesha (Indian) quest.

Anya (Russian) a form of Anna.
Aaniyah, Aniya, Aniyah, Anja

Anyssa (English) a form of Anissa.
Anysa, Anysha

Anzu (Japanese) an apricot.

Aoi (Japanese) hollyhock.

'Aolani (Hawaiian) heavenly cloud.

Aorta (Chamorro) heal.

Aosgi (Chamorro) to resemble one another.

Aosgui (Chamorro) a form of Aosgi.

Apala (Indian) most beautiful.

Aparajita (Indian) undefeated; the name of a flower.

Aparijita (Indian) a form of Aparajita.

Apeksha, Apekshaa (Indian) expectation.

Aphra (Hebrew) young doe. See also Afra.

Apia (Latin) devout woman.

Apolinaria (Spanish) sun goddess.

Apolinia (Latin) sun goddess.

Apolonia (Greek) devoted to the god, Apollo.

Appa (Chamorro) to place one's hand on someone's shoulder.

April **G** (Latin) opening. See also Avril.
Aprele, Aprelle, Apriell, Aprielle, Aprila, Aprile, Aprilette, Aprili, Aprill, Apryl

Apryl (Latin) a form of April.
Apryle

Apsara (Indian) angel; the beautiful dancers of Lord Indra.

Apurba (Indian) never seen before.

Aqilah (Indian) intelligent woman.

Aquene (Native American) peaceful.

Aquilina (Latin) eagle.

Aquilinia (Spanish) eagle.

Ara (Arabic) opinionated.
Ahraya, Aira, Arae, Arah, Araya, Arayah

Arabel (Latin) beautiful altar.

Arabella (Latin) beautiful altar. See also Belle, Orabella.
Arabela, Arabele, Arabelle

Araceli, Aracely (Latin) heavenly altar.
Aracele, Aracelia, Aracelli, Araseli, Arasely, Arcelia, Arceli

Aracelis (Spanish) altar of heaven.

Aradhana (Indian) prayer.

Arama (Spanish) reference to the Virgin Mary.

Arán (Catalonian) she is a conflicted virgin.

Aránzazu (Basque) you in the thorn.

Aranzuru (Spanish) a form of Aránzazu.

Arati (Indian) hymns sung in praise of God with lamp in hand.

Arcadia (Latin) adventurous.

Arcángela (Greek) archangel.

Archa, Archan, Archana (Indian) worship.

Archini, Archisha (Indian) ray of light.

Archita (Indian) one who is worshipped.

Arcilla (Latin) altar of heaven.

Ardelle (Latin) warm; enthusiastic.
Ardelia, Ardelis, Ardella

Arden 🄶 (English) valley of the eagle. Literature: in Shakespeare, a romantic place of refuge.
Ardeen, Ardeena, Ardena, Ardene, Ardenia, Ardi, Ardin, Ardina, Ardine

Ardi (Hebrew) a short form of Arden, Ardice, Ardith.
Ardie, Arti, Artie

Ardice (Hebrew) a form of Ardith.
Ardis, Artis, Ardiss, Ardyce, Ardys

Ardith (Hebrew) flowering field.
Ardath, Ardi, Ardice, Ardyth

Ardra (Indian) the sixth nakshatra (star constellation).

Arebela (Latin) beautiful altar.

Areebah (Indian) witty and smart.

Areej (Indian) pleasant smell.

Arejab (Marshallese) a personality like a lamb or goat.

Areli 🄶 (American) a form of Oralee.
Areil, Areile, Arelee, Arelis, Arelli, Arellia

Arella (Hebrew) angel; messenger.
Arela, Arelle, Orella, Orelle

Arely (American) a form of Oralee.
Arelly

Ares (Catalonian) virgin of the Pyrenees mountains.

Aretha (Greek) virtuous. See also Oretha.
Areatha, Areetha, Areta, Aretina, Aretta, Arette, Arita, Aritha, Retha, Ritha

Aretusa (Greek) Mythology: one of Artemis's companions.

Argelia (Latin) jewelry boxes full of treasures.

Argentina (Latin) she who shines like gold.

Ari 🄶 (Hebrew) a short form of Ariel.

Aria (Hebrew) a short form of Ariel.
Ariah, Ariea, Aryia

Ariadna (Spanish) most holy.

Ariadne (Greek) holy. Mythology: the daughter of King Minos of Crete.

Ariana ✾ **G** (Greek) holy.
Aeriana, Ahriana, Airiana, Arieana, Ariona

Ariane, Arianne **G** (French, English) forms of Ariana, Arianna.
Aerian, Aeriann, Aerion, Aerionne, Airiann, Ari, Arianie, Ariann, Ariannie, Arieann, Arien, Ariene, Arienne, Arieon, Arionne, Aryane, Aryann, Aryanne

Arianna ✾ (Greek) a form of Ariana.
Aerianna, Aerionna, Ahreanna, Ahrianna, Arionna, Aryonna

Arica (Scandinavian) a form of Erica.
Aerica, Aericka, Aeryka, Aricca, Aricka, Arika, Arike, Arikka

Aricela (Latin) altar of heaven.

Arie (Hebrew) a short form of Ariel.

Ariel **G** (Hebrew) lion of God.
Aerial, Aeriale, Aeriel, Aeriela, Aeryal, Ahriel, Aire, Aireal, Airial, Ari, Aria, Arial, Ariale, Arieal, Ariela, Arielle, Arrieal, Arriel, Aryel, Auriel

Arielle (French) a form of Ariel.
Aeriell, Ariella, Arriele, Arriell, Arrielle, Aryelle, Aurielle

Arin (Hebrew) enlightened. (Arabic) messenger. See also Erin.
Aaren, Aerin, Aieron, Aieren, Arinn, Aryn

Arista (Greek) best.
Aris, Arissa, Aristana, Aristen

Arjuni (Indian) dawn; white cow.

Arkita (Indian) plentiful.

Arla (German) a form of Carla.

Arleigh (English) a form of Harley.
Arlea, Arlee, Arley, Arlie, Arly

Arlene (Irish) pledge. See also Lena, Lina.
Airlen, Arlana, Arleen, Arleene, Arlen, Arlena, Arlenis, Arlette, Arleyne, Arliene, Arlina, Arlinda, Arline, Arlis

Arlette (English) a form of Arlene.
Arleta, Arletta, Arletty

Arlynn (American) a combination of Arlene + Lynn.
Arlyn, Arlyne, Arlynne

Armanda (Latin) noble.

Armani **B** (Persian) desire, goal.
Armahni, Arman, Armanee, Armanii

Armentaria (Latin) pastor of older livestock.

Armida (Spanish) a form of Arminda.

Arminda (German) warrior.

Armine (Latin) noble. (German) soldier. (French) a form of Herman (see Boys' Names).
Armina

Armonía (Spanish) balance, harmony.

Arna (Indian) dewdrops.

Arnalda (Spanish) strong as an eagle.

Arnelle (German) eagle.
Arnell, Arnella

Arni, Aruna (Indian) sun.

Aroa (German) good person.

Aroma (Indian) fragrance.

Aron, Arron **B** (Hebrew) forms of Aaron.

Aroob (Indian) she who is loving to her husband.

Arpana (Indian) offering.

Arpita (Indian) a dedication.

Arshia (Indian) divine.

Arte (Tagalog) north.

Artemia (Greek) Greek goddess of the moon and hunt.

Artemisa (Spanish) Greek goddess of the hunt.

Artemisia (Greek) perfection.

Artha (Hindi) wealthy, prosperous.
Arthi, Arti, Artie

Arthur 🅱 (Irish) noble; lofty hill. (Scottish) bear. (English) rock. (Icelandic) follower of Thor.

Artis (Irish, Scottish, English, Icelandic) a form of Arthur.
Arthea, Arthelia, Arthene, Arthette, Arthurette, Arthurina, Arthurine, Artina, Artice

Artura (Celtic) noble, follower of Thor.

Arundhati (Indian) a small star near the Great Bear constellation.

Aruni (Indian) dawn.

Arunima (Indian) red glow of dawn.

Arwa (Indian) female mountain goat.

Aryahi (Indian) another name for the goddess Durga.

Aryana, Aryanna (Italian) forms of Ariana.
Aryan, Aryanah, Aryannah

Aryn (Hebrew) a form of Arin.
Aerryn, Aeryn, Airyn, Aryne, Arynn, Arynne

Arzo (Turkish) a form of Jingjing.

Asa 🅱 (Japanese) born in the morning.

Asako (Japanese) child of the morning.

Asalah (Indian) purity.

Asami (Japanese) morning birth.

Asansa (Chuukese) toward the east.

Asawari (Indian) raga in Hindustani classical music.

Asayo (Japanese) morning; flax; generation.

Ascención (Spanish) ascension.

Ascharya (Indian) surprise.

Aseelah (Indian) one belonging to a great heritage and family.

Aseema, Ashima (Indian) limitless.

Asgari (Indian) devotee.

Asha (Arabic, Swahili) a form of Aisha, Ashia.

Ashakiran (Indian) ray of hope.

Ashalata (Indian) hope.

Ashanti 🅶 (Swahili) from a tribe in West Africa.
Achante, Achanti, Asante, Ashanta, Ashantae, Ashante, Ashanté, Ashantee, Ashantie, Ashaunta, Ashauntae, Ashauntee, Ashaunti, Ashonti, Ashuntae, Ashunti

Ashely (English) form of Ashley.
Ashelee, Ashelei, Asheley, Ashelie, Ashelley, Ashelly

Ashia (Arabic) life.
Asha, Ashya, Ashyah, Ashyia, Ayshia

Ashika (Indian) one without sorrow; mercury.

Ashis (Indian) benediction.

Ashita, Asita (Indian) the Yamuna River.

Ashlee 🅶 (English) a form of Ashley.
Ashle, Ashlea, Ashleah, Ashleeh

Ashleigh **G** (English) a form of
Ashley.
Ahsleigh, Asheleigh, Ashlei, Ashliegh

Ashlesha (Indian) a star.

Ashley ☀ **G** (English) ash-tree
meadow. See also Lee.
*Ahslee, Aishlee, Ashala, Ashalee,
Ashalei, Ashaley, Ashely, Ashla, Ashlay,
Ashleay, Ashlee, Ashleigh, Ashleye,
Ashli, Ashlie, Ashly, Ashlye*

Ashli, Ashlie, Ashly (English)
forms of Ashley.
Ashliee

Ashlin (English) a form of Ashlyn.
Ashlean, Ashliann, Ashlianne, Ashline

Ashlyn, Ashlynn **G** (English) ash-
tree pool. (Irish) vision, dream.
*Ashlan, Ashleann, Ashleen, Ashleene,
Ashlen, Ashlene, Ashlin, Ashling,
Ashlyne, Ashlynne*

Ashmita (Indian) born of the rock,
very hard and strong.

Ashna (Indian) a friend.

Ashten, Ashtin (English) forms of
Ashton.
Ashtine

Ashton **BG** (English) ash-tree
settlement.
Ashten, Ashtyn

Ashtyn **G** (English) a form of
Ashton.
Ashtynne

Ashwina (Indian) child of the star.

Asi (Chamorro) pity.

Asia (Greek) resurrection. (English)
eastern sunrise. (Swahili) a form of
Aisha.
*Ahsia, Aisia, Aisian, Asiah, Asian,
Asianae, Asya, Aysia, Aysiah, Aysian,
Ayzia*

Asin (Chamorro) salt.

Aslesha (Indian) a star.

Asmita, Asmitha (Indian) pride.

Asonn (Chamorro) lie down.

Asonna (Chamorro) she lies down.

Aspasia (Greek) follower of the
philosopher Aristotle.

Aspen **G** (English) aspen tree.
Aspin, Aspyn

Assa (Chamorro) a form of Asa.

Assi (Chamorro) a form of Asi.

Asson (Chamorro) a form of Asonn.

Assunção (Portuguese) Assumption.

Aster (English) a form of Astra.
Astera, Asteria, Astyr

Astha (Indian) faith.

Astra (Greek) star.
Asta, Astara, Aster, Astraea, Astrea

Astrid (Scandinavian) divine strength.
Astri, Astrida, Astrik, Astrud, Atti, Estrid

Astriz (German) of the stars.

Astryd (German) beloved one of the
gods.

Asuka (Japanese) the scent of
tomorrow.

Asunción (Spanish) Assumption.

Asunta (Spanish) to go up, to ascend.

Atagui (Chamorro) alternate.

Atala (Greek) youthful one.

Atalanta (Greek) mighty huntress.
Mythology: an athletic young
woman who refused to marry any
man who could not outrun her in a
footrace. See also Lani.
Atalaya, Atlanta, Atlante, Atlee

Atalía (Spanish) guard tower.

Atanasia (Spanish) one who will be reborn; immortal.

Atara (Hebrew) crown.
Atarah, Ataree

Atasi (Indian) a blue flower.

Atenea (Greek) evokes the figure of Palas Atenea, goddess protectorate of the Athenians.

Athana (Mycenaean) promise.

Athena (Greek) wise. Mythology: the goddess of wisdom.
Athenea, Athene, Athina, Atina

Ati, Atie (Chamorro) forms of Atti.

Ática (Greek) city of Athens.

Atira (Hebrew) prayer.

Atisa (Chamorro) increase; brighten.

Atmikha (Indian) light of God.

Atreyi (Indian) a river.

Atsuko (Japanese) child with profound emotions.

Atsushi (Japanese) rich.

Attau (Chamorro) hides herself.

Attiya (Indian) gift.

Atula (Indian) incomparable.

Au (Japanese) meeting.

Auberte (French) a form of Alberta.
Auberta, Aubertha, Auberthe, Aubine

Aubree, Aubrie 🄖 (French) forms of Aubrey.
Auberi, Aubre, Aubrei, Aubreigh, Aubri, Aubrielle

Aubrey 🄖 (German) noble; bearlike. (French) blond ruler; elf ruler.
Aubary, Aubery, Aubray, Aubrea, Aubreah, Aubree, Aubrette, Aubria, Aubrie, Aubry, Aubury, Avery

Aubriana, Aubrianna (English) combinations of Aubrey + Anna.
Aubreyana, Aubreyanna, Aubreyanne, Aubreyena, Aubrianne

Auchon (Chamorro) torch.

Audelina (German) nobility, strength.

Audey (English) a familiar form of Audrey.
Aude, Audi, Audie

Audra 🄖 (French) a form of Audrey.
Audria, Audriea

Audreanne (English) a combination of Audrey + Anne.
Audrea, Audreen, Audrianne, Audrienne

Audree, Audrie (English) forms of Audrey.
Audre, Audri

Audrey ☀ 🄖 (English) noble strength.
Adrey, Audey, Audra, Audray, Audree, Audrie, Audrin, Audriya, Audry, Audrye

Audriana, Audrianna (English) combinations of Audrey + Anna.
Audreanna, Audrienna, Audrina

Audris (German) fortunate, wealthy.
Audrys

August 🄑 (Latin) a form of Augusta.

Augusta (Latin) a short form of Augustine. See also Gusta.
Agusta, August, Auguste, Augustia, Augustus, Austina

Augustine **B** (Latin) majestic.
Religion: Saint Augustine was the
first archbishop of Canterbury. See
also Tina.
*Augusta, Augustina, Augustyna,
Augustyne, Austin*

'Aulani (Hawaiian) royal messenger.
Lani, Lanie

Aulii (Hawaiian) dainty; perfect.

Aundrea (Greek) a form of Andrea.
Aundreah

Aura (Greek) soft breeze. (Latin)
golden. See also Ora.

Aurelia (Latin) golden. See also Oralia.
*Auralea, Auralia, Aurea, Aureal, Aurel,
Aurele, Aurelea, Aureliana, Aurelie,
Auria, Aurie, Aurilia, Aurita*

Aurelie (Latin) a form of Aurelia.
*Auralee, Auralei, Aurelee, Aurelei,
Aurelle*

Auristela (Latin) golden star.

Aurora (Latin) dawn. Mythology:
Aurora was the goddess of dawn.
Aurore, Ora, Ori, Orie, Rora

Austen **B** (Latin) a form of Austin.

Austin (Latin) a short form of
Augustine.

Austyn (Latin) a form of Austin.
Austynn

Autumn ☆ **G** (Latin) autumn.
Autum

Ava ☆ (Greek) a form of Eva.
Avada, Avae, Ave, Aveen

Avalon (Latin) island.
Avallon

Avani (Indian) earth.

Avanti (Indian) modest.

Avantika (Indian) the princess of
Ujjain.

Avelina (Latin) she who was born in
Avella.

Avery ☆ **B** (English) a form of
Aubrey.
Aivree, Averi, Averie, Avry

Avinashi (Indian) indestructible.

Avis (Latin) bird.
*Avais, Avi, Avia, Aviana, Avianca,
Aviance, Avianna*

Avishi (Indian) earth; river.

Aviva (Hebrew) springtime. See also
Viva.
*Aviv, Avivah, Avivi, Avivice, Avni, Avnit,
Avri, Avrit, Avy*

Avneet **G** (Hebrew) a form of
Avner (see Boys' Names).

Avnita (Indian) earth.

Avril (French) a form of April.
*Averil, Averyl, Avra, Avri, Avrilia, Avrill,
Avrille, Avrillia, Avy*

Axelle (Latin) axe. (German) small
oak tree; source of life.
Aixa

Aya (Hebrew) bird; fly swiftly.
Aia, Aiah, Aiya, Aiyah

Ayaka (Japanese) she who reminds
you of summer.

Ayako (Japanese) damask pattern.

Ayalga (Asturian) treasure.

Ayame (Japanese) iris.

Ayanna (Hindi) innocent.
*Ahyana, Aiyanna, Ayan, Ayana,
Ayania, Ayannica, Ayna*

Ayano (Japanese) twill cloth.

Ayati (Indian) royal.

Ayeh (Indian) sun; distinct.

Ayelen (Mapuche) she who represents joy; smiling.

Ayelén (Araucanian) joy.

Ayesha (Persian) a form of Aisha.
Ayasha, Ayeshah, Ayessa, Ayisha, Ayishah, Aysha, Ayshah, Ayshe, Ayshea, Aysia

Ayig (Chamorro) choose.

Ayinhual (Mapuche) beloved, darling, generous and preferred huala (Great Grebe).

Ayinleo (Mapuche) deep, inextinguishable love.

Ayiqueo (Mapuche) soft-spoken; pleasant.

Ayita (Cherokee) first in the dance.

Ayla (Hebrew) oak tree.
Aylana, Aylee, Ayleen, Aylene, Aylie, Aylin

Aymara (Spanish) people and language of the south Andes.

Ayme (Mapuche) significant.

Ayshalynn (Arabic) a form of Aisha.

Ayumi (Japanese) step; beautiful.

Ayushi (Indian) long life.

Ayushmati (Indian) one who has a long life.

Aza (Arabic) comfort.
Aiza, Aizha, Aizia, Azia

Azaad (Persian) dam to stop the flow.

Azad (Persian) a form of Grace.

Azalea (Latin) desert flower.

Azami (Japanese) defiant.

Azari (Japanese) thistle flower.

Azeeza (Indian) esteemed, precious, cherished.

Azhaar (Indian) flowers; blossoms.

Azima (Arabic) resolute, determined.

Aziza (Swahili) precious.
Azize

Azucena (Arabic) admirable mother.

Azura (Spanish) sky blue.

Azusa (Japanese) the catalpa tree.

Azza (Indian) young female gazelle.

B

B 🅱🅶 (American) an initial used as a first name.

Baasima, Baseema (Indian) smiling.

Baba (African) born on Thursday.
Aba

Babe (Latin) a familiar form of Barbara. (American) a form of Baby.
Babby

Babette (French, German) a familiar form of Barbara.
Babita, Barbette

Babs (American) a familiar form of Barbara.
Bab

Baby (American) baby.
Babby, Babe, Bebe

Bach, Bach Yen (Vietnamese) forms of Kasinda.

Bachtuyet (Vietnamese) white; clear.

Bada (Korean) beautiful.

Badriya (Indian) resembling the full moon.

Bae (Vietnamese) white.

Baek (Korean) a form of Ah-Rum.

Bagya (Indian) lucky.

Baheera (Indian) dazzling, brilliant.

Bahiyaa (Indian) beautiful, radiant.

Bahugandha (Indian) very fragrant; the bud of the champa flower.

Bahula (Indian) cow.

Bai (Chinese) outgoing.

Baijanti (Indian) Lord Vishnu's favorite flower.

Baijayanthi (Indian) garland of Lord Vishnu.

Bailee **G** (English) a form of Bailey.
Baelee, Bailea, Bailei, Baillee

Baileigh, Baleigh (English) forms of Bailey.
Baeleigh

Bailey ☀ **G** (English) bailiff.
Baeley, Bailee, Baileigh, Bailley, Bailly, Baily, Bali, Balley, Baylee, Bayley

Bailie (English) a form of Bailey.
Baeli, Baillie, Bailli

Bairavi (Indian) music, melody.

Baisakhi (Indian) of the month Baishakh.

Baishali (Indian) an ancient city.

Baka (Hindi) crane.

Bakul (Indian) the name of a flower.

Bakula (Hindi) flower.

Balbina (Latin) she who mutters.

Baldomera (Spanish) bold, brave; famous.

Balic (Chamorro) worth, value.

Ballari (Indian) creeper.

Balqis (Indian) the name of the Queen of Sheba.

Baltasalisa, Baltasara, Batasara (Assyrian) forms of Baltazara.

Baltazara (Assyrian) may Baal protect the king.

Bambi (Italian) child.
Bambee, Bambie, Bamby

Bambing (Filipino) baby.

Banamala, Banani (Indian) forests.

Banan (Indian) fingertips.

Bandana (Indian) worship.

Bandhula (Indian) charming.

Bandhura (Indian) pretty.

Bandi **BG** (Punjabi) prisoner.
Banda, Bandy

Banhi (Indian) fire.

Banhishikha (Indian) flame.

Banita (Indian) woman.

Banmala (Indian) a garland of five types of flowers.

Banni (Indian) maiden.

Bansari (Indian) flute; the instrument played by Lord Krishna.

Bansuri (Indian) flute.

Bao-Jin (Chinese) precious gold.

Bao-Yo (Chinese) jade; pretty.

Baptista (Latin) baptizer.
Baptiste, Batista, Battista, Bautista

Bara, Barra (Hebrew) chosen.
Bára, Bari

Baraa'a (Indian) excelling.

Barb (Latin) a short form of Barbara.
Barba, Barbe

Barbara (Latin) stranger, foreigner.
See also Bebe, Varvara, Wava.
*Babara, Babb, Babbie, Babe, Babette,
Babina, Babs, Barb, Barbara-Ann,
Barbarit, Barbarita, Barbary, Barbeeleen,
Barbera, Barbie, Barbora, Barborah,
Barborka, Barbra, Barbraann, Barbro,
Barùska, Basha, Bebe, Bobbi, Bobbie*

Bárbara (Greek) a form of Barbara.

Barbie (American) a familiar form of
Barbara.
Barbee, Barbey, Barbi, Barby, Baubie

Barbra (American) a form of Barbara.
Barbro

Barisha (Indian) pure.

Barkha, Barsha (Indian) rain.

Barnali (Indian) dispersion of seven
colors.

Barrett ☒ (German) strong as a
bear.

Barrie (Irish) spear; markswoman.
Bari, Barri, Berri, Berrie, Berry

Barry ☒ (Welsh) child of Harry.
(Irish) spear, marksman. (French)
gate, fence.

Bartolomea (Spanish) daughter of
Talmai.

Baruna (Indian) wife of the lord·of
the sea.

Basabi (Indian) wife of Lord Indra.

Basanti (Indian) spring.

Basheera (Indian) bringer of good
tidings.

Basia (Hebrew) daughter of God.
Basya, Bathia, Batia, Batya, Bitya, Bithia

Basiana (Spanish) having acute
judgment.

Basilia (Greek) queen, princess;
governor.

Basma (Indian) a smile.

Batbara (Chamorro) a form of
Barbara.

Bathsheba (Hebrew) daughter of
the oath; seventh daughter. Bible: a
wife of King David. See also Sheba.
*Bathshua, Batsheva, Bersaba,
Bethsabee, Bethsheba*

Batilde (German) she who battles.

Batini (Swahili) inner thoughts.

Batool (Indian) ascetic virgin.

Baudilia (Teutonic) audacious and
brave.

Bay (Vietnamese) white as snow.

Baye, Be, Bich (Vietnamese)
Saturday's child; patient; unique.

Baylee ☒ (English) a form of
Bailey.
*Bayla, Bayle, Baylea, Bayleah, Baylei,
Bayli, Bayliee*

Bayleigh, Baylie (English) forms of
Bailey.
Bayliegh

Bayley ☒ (English) a form of
Bailey.
Bayly

Bayo (Yoruba) joy is found.

Bea, Bee (American) short forms of
Beatrice.

Beata (Latin) a short form of
Beatrice.
Beatta

Beatrice (Latin) blessed; happy;
bringer of joy. See also Trish, Trixie.
*Bea, Beata, Beatrica, Béatrice,
Beatricia, Beatriks, Beatrisa, Beatrise,
Beatrissa, Beatriz, Beattie, Beatty, Bebe,
Bee, Trice*

Beatriz **G** (Latin) a form of
Beatrice.
Beatris, Beatriss, Beatrix, Beitris

Beau **B** (French) beautiful.

Bebe **BG** (Spanish) a form of
Barbara, Beatrice.
BB, Beebee, Bibi

Becca (Hebrew) a short form of
Rebecca.
Beca, Becka, Bekah, Bekka

Bechekldil (Palauan) a form of
Athena.

Becky (American) a familiar form of
Rebecca.
Beckey, Becki, Beckie

Bedebii (Palauan) a form of Athena.

Bedelia (Irish) a form of Bridget.
Bedeelia, Biddy, Bidelia

Beena (Indian) a musical instrument.

Beetna (Korean) sea.

Begoña (Basque) place of the
dominant hill.

Begonia (Spanish) begonia flower.

Behsel (Pohnpeian) a form of
Antonia.

Bei (Chinese) shellfish.

Bel (Hindi) sacred wood of apple
trees. A short form of Amabel,
Belinda, Isabel.

Bela **BG** (Czech) white. (Hungarian)
bright.
Belah, Biela

Belarmina (Spanish) having
beautiful armor.

Belen **G** (Greek) arrow. (Spanish)
Bethlehem.
Belina

Belicia (Spanish) dedicated to God.
Beli, Belia, Belica

Belinda (Spanish) beautiful.
Literature: a name coined by
English poet Alexander Pope in *The
Rape of the Lock*. See also Blinda,
Linda.
Bel, Belindra, Belle, Belynda

Belisa (Latin) most slender.

Belisaria (Greek) right-handed
archer; she who shoots arrows
skillfully.

Bella ※ (Latin) beautiful.
Bellah

Belle (French) beautiful. A short
form of Arabella, Belinda, Isabel.
See also Billie.
Belita, Bell, Belli, Bellina

Belva (Latin) beautiful view.
Belvia

Bena (Native American) pheasant.
See also Bina.
Benea

Benazir (Indian) incomparable.

Benecia (Latin) a short form of
Benedicta.
*Beneisha, Benicia, Benish, Benisha,
Benishia, Bennicia*

Benedicta (Latin) blessed.
*Bendite, Benecia, Benedetta, Benedicte,
Benedikta, Bengta, Benita, Benna, Benni,
Bennicia, Benoîte, Binney*

Benedicte (Latin) a form of
Benedicta.

Benedita (Portuguese) blessed.

Benicio (Spanish) benevolent one.

Benigna (Spanish) kind.

Benilda (German) she who fights with the bears.

Benilde (Spanish) a form of Benilda.

Benita (Spanish) a form of Benedicta.
Beneta, Benetta, Benitta, Bennita, Neeta

Benjamin 🅱 (Hebrew) child of my right hand.

Benjamina (Spanish) preferred daughter.

Bennett 🅱 (Latin) little blessed one.
Bennet, Bennetta

Benni (Latin) a familiar form of Benedicta.
Bennie, Binni, Binnie, Binny

Bente (Latin) blessed.

Berar (Fijian) slow.

Berenice (Greek) a form of Bernice.
Berenise, Berenisse, Bereniz, Berenize

Berget (Irish) a form of Bridget.
Bergette, Bergit

Berit (German) glorious.
Beret, Berette

Berkley (Scottish, English) birch-tree meadow.
Berkeley, Berkly

Berlynn (English) a combination of Bertha + Lynn.
Berla, Berlin, Berlinda, Berline, Berling, Berlyn, Berlyne, Berlynne

Bernabela (Hebrew) child of prophecy.

Bernabella (Spanish) a form of Bernabela.

Bernadette 🅖 (French) a form of Bernadine. See also Nadette.
Bera, Beradette, Berna, Bernadet, Bernadete, Bernadett, Bernadetta, Bernarda, Bernardette, Bernedet, Bernedette, Bernessa, Berneta

Bernadine (English, German) brave as a bear.
Bernadene, Bernadette, Bernadin, Bernadina, Bernardina, Bernardine, Berni

Berneta (French) a short form of Bernadette.
Bernatta, Bernetta, Bernette, Bernita

Berni (English) a familiar form of Bernadine, Bernice.
Bernie, Berny

Bernice (Greek) bringer of victory. See also Bunny, Vernice.
Berenice, Berenike, Bernessa, Berni, Bernicia, Bernise, Nixie

Berta (German) a form of Berit.

Bertha (German) bright; illustrious; brilliant ruler. A short form of Alberta. See also Birdie, Peke.
Barta, Bartha, Berta, Berthe, Bertille, Bertita, Bertrona, Bertus, Birtha

Berti (German, English) a familiar form of Gilberte, Bertina.
Berte, Bertie, Berty

Bertilda (German) she who fights; the distinguished one.

Bertilia (German, Latin) a form of Berta.

Bertille (French) a form of Bertha.

Bertina (English) bright, shining.
Bertine

Beryl (Greek) sea green jewel.
Beryle

Besichel (Palauan) new woman.

Bess, Bessie (Hebrew) familiar forms of Elizabeth.
Bessi, Bessy

Betania (Hebrew) name of a village in ancient Palestine.

Beth (Hebrew, Aramaic) house of God. A short form of Bethany, Elizabeth.
Betha, Bethe, Bethia

Bethani, Bethanie (Aramaic) forms of Bethany.
Bethanee, Bethania, Bethannie, Bethni, Bethnie

Bethann (English) a combination of Beth + Ann.
Beth-Ann, Bethan, Bethane, Bethanne, Beth-Anne

Bethany (Aramaic) house of figs. Bible: the site of Lazarus's resurrection.
Beth, Bethaney, Bethani, Bethanney, Bethanny, Bethena, Betheny, Bethia, Bethina, Bethney, Bethny, Betthany

Betikerarengul (Palauan) let us divide and share.

Betra (Marshallese) love.

Betsabe (Hebrew) daughter of an oath or pact.
Betsabé

Betsy (American) a familiar form of Elizabeth.
Betsey, Betsi, Betsie

Bette (French) a form of Betty.
Beta, Beti, Betka, Bett, Betta

Bettina (American) a combination of Beth + Tina.
Betina, Betine, Betti, Bettine

Betty (Hebrew) consecrated to God. (English) a familiar form of Elizabeth.
Bette, Bettey, Betti, Bettie, Bettye, Bettyjean, Betty-Jean, Bettyjo, Betty-Jo, Bettylou, Betty-Lou, Bety, Boski, Bözsi

Betula (Hebrew) girl, maiden.

Beulah (Hebrew) married. Bible: Beulah is a name for Israel.
Beula, Beulla, Beullah

Bev (English) a short form of Beverly.

Bevanne (Welsh) child of Evan.
Bevan, Bevann, Bevany

Beverly G (English) beaver field. See also Buffy.
Bev, Bevalee, Beverle, Beverlee, Beverley, Beverlie, Beverlly, Bevlyn, Bevlynn, Bevlynne, Bevvy, Verly

Beverlyann (American) a combination of Beverly + Ann.
Beverliann, Beverlianne, Beverlyanne

Bhadra (Indian) good.

Bhagirathi (Indian) the Ganges River.

Bhagwanti, Bhagya, Bhagyashri, Bhagyawati (Indian) lucky.

Bhagyalakshmi (Indian) goddess of wealth.

Bhagyashree (Indian) fortunate.

Bhairavi (Indian) musical notes.

Bhakti (Indian) prayer.

Bhamini (Indian) a beautiful, short-tempered lady.

Bhanuja (Indian) the Yamuna River.

Bhanumati (Indian) famous.

Bhanuni (Indian) charming woman.

Bhanupriya (Indian) the sun's beloved.

Bharani (Indian) a star.

Bharavi (Indian) tulsi plant.

Bhavana (Indian) feelings, sentiments.

Bhavi, Bhavini (Indian) emotional.

Bhavika (Indian) cheerful expression.

Bhavna (Indian) good feelings.

Bhawna (Indian) feelings.

Bhilangana (Indian) a river.

Bhini (Indian) mild.

Bhoomi, Bhoomika, Boomika (Indian) the Earth.

Bhrithi (Indian) strengthened, nourished.

Bhumika (Indian) earth.

Bhuvana (Indian) goddess of Earth.

Bhuvi (Indian) heaven.

Bi, Bik (Chinese) jade.

Bian (Vietnamese) hidden; secretive.

Bianca 🄶 (Italian) white. See also Blanca, Vianca.
Biancca, Biancha, Biancia, Bianco, Bianey, Bianica, Bianka, Biannca, Binney, Bionca, Blanca, Blanche, Byanca

Bianka (Italian) a form of Bianca.
Beyanka, Biannka

Biao (Chinese) example.

Bibi (Latin) a short form of Bibiana. (Arabic) lady. (Spanish) a form of Bebe.

Bibiana (Latin) lively.
Bibi

Biblis (Latin) swallow.

Biddy (Irish) a familiar form of Bedelia.
Biddie

Bienvenida (Spanish) welcome.

Bijal, Bijli (Indian) lightning.

Billi (English) a form of Billie.

Billie 🄶 (English) strong willed. (German, French) a familiar form of Belle, Wilhelmina.
Bilee, Bileigh, Bili, Bilie, Billee, Billi, Billy, Billye

Billie-Jean (American) a combination of Billie + Jean.
Billiejean, Billyjean, Billy-Jean

Billie-Jo (American) a combination of Billie + Jo.
Billiejo, Billyjo, Billy-Jo

Billy 🄱 (English) a form of Billie.
Billye

Bilomena (Pohnpeian) a form of Angelina.

Bilomina (Pohnpeian) a form of Bethel.

Bimala (Indian) pure.

Bimbi (Indian) glorious.

Bin (Chinese) refined and courteous.

Bina (Hebrew) wise; understanding. (Swahili) dancer. (Latin) a short form of Sabina. See also Bena.
Binah, Binney, Binta, Bintah

Binata (Indian) the wife of sage Kashyap.

Bindhu, Bindiya (Indian) a drop.

Bindu (Indian) point.

Bing (Chinese) ice.

Bing Qing (Chinese) clear as ice.

Bing-Qing (Chinese) ice; crystal clear.

Binita (Indian) modest.

Binney (English) a familiar form of Benedicta, Bianca, Bina.
Binnee, Binni, Binnie, Binny

Binodini (Indian) handsome.

Biola (Kosraean) young; clear, pure; request; understand; court.

Bionca (Italian) a form of Bianca.
Beonca, Beyonca, Beyonka, Bioncha, Bionica, Bionka, Bionnca

Bipasha (Indian) a river.

Birdie (English) bird. (German) a familiar form of Bertha.
Bird, Birdee, Birdella, Birdena, Birdey, Birdi, Birdy, Byrd, Byrdey, Byrdie, Byrdy

Birgitte (Swedish) a form of Bridget.
Birgit, Birgita, Birgitta

Birte (German) a form of Bertha.

Bishakha (Indian) star.

Blaine **B** (Irish) thin.
Blane, Blayne

Blair **BG** (Scottish) plains dweller.
Blaire

Blaire (Scottish) a form of Blair.
Blare, Blayre

Blaise **B** (French) one who stammers.
Blaize, Blasha, Blasia, Blaza, Blaze, Blazena

Blake **B** (English) dark.
Blaque, Blayke

Blakely **BG** (English) dark meadow.
Blakelea, Blakelee, Blakeleigh, Blakeley, Blakeli, Blakelyn, Blakelynn, Blakesley, Blakley, Blakli

Blanca **G** (Italian) a form of Bianca.
Bellanca, Blancka, Blanka

Blanche (French) a form of Bianca.
Blanch, Blancha, Blinney

Blandina (Latin) flattering.

Blandinas, Blindina (Chamorro) forms of Blandina.

Blasa (French) stammerer.

Blessy (Indian) blessing.

Blinda (American) a short form of Belinda.
Blynda

Bliss **G** (English) blissful, joyful.
Blisse, Blyss, Blysse

Blodwyn (Welsh) flower. See also Wynne.
Blodwen, Blodwynne, Blodyn

Blondelle (French) blond, fair haired.
Blondell, Blondie

Blondie (American) a familiar form of Blondell.
Blondee, Blondey, Blondy

Blossom (English) flower.

Blum (Yiddish) flower.
Bluma

Blythe **G** (English) happy, cheerful.
Blithe, Blyss, Blyth

Bo **B** (Chinese) precious.

Bo Mee (Korean) white; senior, esteemed.

Boacha (Hebrew) blessed.

Bo-Bae (Korean) shining.

Bobbette (American) a familiar form of Roberta.
Bobbet, Bobbetta

Bobbi, Bobbie **G** (American) familiar forms of Barbara, Roberta.
Baubie, Bobbe, Bobbey, Bobbisue, Bobby, Bobbye, Bobi, Bobie, Bobina, Bobbie-Jean, Bobbie-Lynn, Bobbie-Sue

Bobbi-Ann, Bobbie-Ann
(American) combinations of Bobbi
+ Ann.
*Bobbiann, Bobbi-Anne, Bobbianne,
Bobbie-Anne, Bobby-Ann, Bobbyann,
Bobby-Anne, Bobbyanne*

Bobbi-Jo (American) a combination
of Bobbi + Jo.
*Bobbiejo, Bobbie-Jo, Bobbijo, Bobby-
Jo, Bobijo*

Bobbi-Lee (American) a
combination of Bobbi + Lee.
*Bobbie-Lee, Bobbilee, Bobbylee, Bobby-
Leigh, Bobile*

Bobby 🅱 (American) a form of
Bobbi.

Bomy (Korean) a form of Bomy.

Bon (Korean) treasure; precious.

Bonfila, Bonfilia (Italian) good
daughter.

Bong-Cha (Korean) like spring.

Bonifacia (Italian) benefactor.

Bonita (Spanish) pretty.
*Bonesha, Bonetta, Bonnetta, Bonnie,
Bonny*

Bonnie, Bonny (English, Scottish)
beautiful, pretty. (Spanish) familiar
forms of Bonita.
*Boni, Bonie, Bonne, Bonnee, Bonnell,
Bonney, Bonni, Bonnin*

Bonnie-Bell (American) a
combination of Bonnie + Belle.
*Bonnebell, Bonnebelle, Bonnibell,
Bonnibelle, Bonniebell, Bonniebelle,
Bonnybell, Bonnybelle*

Boo (Korean) origin; essential.

Boon (Korean) excellent daughter.

Boram (Korean) sage; help, support;
wealth; class; written charm; give,
bestow.

Boulej (Marshallese) on the lagoon
beach side of the atoll.

Boupha (Vietnamese) baby; doll.

Brad 🅱 (English) a short form of
Bradley.

Braden 🅱 (English) broad valley.

Bradley 🅱 (English) broad
meadow.
Bradlee, Bradleigh, Bradlie

Brady 🅱 (Irish) spirited.
*Bradee, Bradey, Bradi, Bradie, Braedi,
Braidee, Braidi, Braidie, Braidey,
Braidy, Braydee*

Braeden 🅱 (English) broad hill.
*Bradyn, Bradynn, Braedan, Braedean,
Braedyn, Braidan, Braidyn, Braydn*

Braelyn (American) a combination
of Braeden + Lynn.
*Braelee, Braeleigh, Braelin, Braelle,
Braelon, Braelynn, Braelynne, Brailee,
Brailenn, Brailey, Braili, Brailyn, Braylee,
Brayley, Braylin, Braylon, Braylyn,
Braylynn*

Braiden 🅱 (English) a form of
Braeden.

Branca (Portuguese) white.

Branda (Hebrew) blessing.

Brandan 🅱 (English) a form of
Branden.

Brandee (Dutch) a form of Brandy.
Brande, Brandea, Brendee

Branden 🅱 (English) beacon valley.
Brendan, Brandyn, Brennan

Brandi, Brandie 🅶 (Dutch) forms
of Brandy.
*Brandei, Brandice, Brandiee, Brandii,
Brandily, Brandin, Brandis, Brandise,
Brani, Branndie, Brendi*

Brandon 🅱 (English) a form of
Branden.

Brandy **G** (Dutch) an after-dinner drink made from distilled wine.
Brand, Brandace, Brandaise, Brandala, Brandee, Brandeli, Brandell, Brandi, Brandye, Brandylee, Brandy-Lee, Brandy-Leigh, Brann, Branyell, Brendy

Brandy-Lynn (American) a combination of Brandy + Lynn.
Brandalyn, Brandalynn, Brandelyn, Brandelynn, Brandelynne, Brandilyn, Brandilynn, Brandilynne, Brandlin, Brandlyn, Brandlynn, Brandlynne, Brandolyn, Brandolynn, Brandolynne, Brandylyn, Brandy-Lyn, Brandylynne, Brandy-Lynne

Brantley **B** (Dutch) a form of Brandy.

Bratati (Indian) creeper.

Braulia (Teutonic) gleaming.

Braxton **B** (English) Brock's town.
Braxten, Braxtyn

Brayden **B** (English) a form of Braeden.

Braydon (English) a form of Braeden.

Brea, Bria (Irish) short forms of Breana, Briana.
Breah, Breea, Briah, Brya

Breana (Irish) a form of Briana.
Brea, Breanah, Breanda, Bre-Anna, Breasha, Breawna, Breila

Breann (Irish) a short form of Briana.
Breane, Bree, Breean, Breelyn, Breeon, Brieon

Breanna **G** (Irish) a form of Briana.
Bre-Anna, Breannah, Breannea, Breannia, Breeanna

Breanne **G** (Irish) a short form of Brianna.
Bre-Anne, Breaunne, Breeann, Breeanne, Breiann, Breighann, Breyenne, Brieann

Breasha (Russian) a familiar form of Breana.

Breauna, Breunna, Briauna (Irish) forms of Briana.
Breaunna, Breeauna, Breuna, Breuna, Briaunna

Breck **BG** (Irish) freckled.
Brecken

Bree (English) broth. (Irish) a short form of Breann. See also Brie.
Breay, Brei, Breigh

Breeana, Breeanna (Irish) forms of Briana.
Breeanah, Breeannah

Breena (Irish) fairy palace. A form of Brina.
Breenea, Breene, Breina, Brina

Breiana, Breianna (Irish) forms of Briana.
Breiane, Breiann, Breianne

Brenda **G** (Irish) little raven. (English) sword.
Brendell, Brendelle, Brendette, Brendie, Brendyl, Brenna

Brenda-Lee (American) a combination of Brenda + Lee.
Brendalee, Brendaleigh, Brendali, Brendaly, Brendalys, Brenlee, Brenley

Brendan **B** (Irish) little raven. (English) sword.

Brenden **B** (Irish) a form of Brendan.

Brenna **G** (Irish) a form of Brenda.
Bren, Brenie, Brenin, Brenn, Brennah, Brennaugh, Brenne

Brennan **B** (English) a form of Brendan.
Brennea, Brennon, Brennyn

Brennen **B** (English) a form of Brennan.

Brenton 🅱 (English) steep hill.

Breon 🅱 (Irish, Scottish) a form of Brian.

Breona, Breonna (Irish) forms of Briana.
Breeona, Breiona, Breionna, Breonah, Breonia, Breonie, Breonne

Bret 🅱 (Irish) a form of Brett.

Brett 🅱 (Irish) a short form of Britany. See also Brita.
Bret, Brette, Brettin, Bretton

Breyana, Breyann, Breyanna (Irish) forms of Briana.
Breyan, Breyane, Breyannah, Breyanne

Breyona, Breyonna (Irish) forms of Briana.
Breyonia

Brian 🅱 (Irish, Scottish) strong; virtuous; honorable.

Briana 🅶 (Irish) a form of Brian.
Brana, Brea, Breana, Breauna, Breeana, Breiana, Breona, Breyana, Breyona, Bria, Briahna, Brianah, Briand, Brianda, Brina, Briona, Briyana, Bryona

Brianna ☀ 🅶 (Irish) a form of Brian.
Bhrianna, Breann, Briannah, Brianne, Brianni, Briannon, Brienna, Bryanna

Brianne 🅶 (Irish) a form of Briana.
Briane, Briann, Brienne, Bryanne

Briar (French) heather.
Brear, Brier, Bryar

Brice 🅱 (Welsh) alert; ambitious. (English) child of Rice.

Bricia (Spanish) represents strength.

Bridey (Irish) a familiar form of Bridget.
Bridi, Bridie, Brydie

Bridget 🅶 (Irish) strong. See also Bedelia, Bryga, Gitta.
Berget, Birgitte, Bride, Bridey, Bridger, Bridgete, Bridgett, Bridgette, Bridgid, Bridgot, Brietta, Brigada, Briget, Brigid, Brigida, Brigitte, Brita

Bridgett, Bridgette (Irish) forms of Bridget.
Bridgitte, Brigette, Bridggett, Briggitte, Bridgitt, Brigitta

Brie (French) a type of cheese. Geography: a region in France known for its cheese. See also Bree.
Briea, Brielle, Briena, Brieon, Brietta, Briette

Brieana, Brieanna (American) combinations of Brie + Anna.
Brieannah

Brieann, Brieanne (American) combinations of Brie + Ann. See also Briana.
Brie-Ann, Brie-Anne

Brielle 🅶 (French) a form of Brie.
Briel, Briele, Briell, Briella

Brienna (Irish) a form of Briana.
Briene, Brieon, Brieona, Brieonna

Brienne (French) a form of Briana.
Brienn

Brigette (French) a form of Bridget.
Briget, Brigett, Brigetta, Brigettee, Brigget

Brígida (Celtic) strong, victorious.

Brigidia (Celtic) strong.

Brigitte (French) a form of Bridget.
Briggitte, Brigit, Brigita

Brina (Latin) a short form of Sabrina. (Irish) a familiar form of Briana.
Brin, Brinan, Brinda, Brindi, Brindy, Briney, Brinia, Brinlee, Brinly, Brinn, Brinna, Brinnan, Briona, Bryn, Bryna

Brindha (Indian) the basil plant.

Briona (Irish) a form of Briana.
Brione, Brionna, Brionne, Briony,
Briunna, Bryony

Brisa (Spanish) beloved. Mythology:
Briseis was the Greek name of
Achilles's beloved.
Breezy, Breza, Brisha, Brishia, Brissa,
Bryssa

Briselda (Spanish) a form of
Briselda.

Brisia, Briza (Greek) beloved.

Brita (Irish) a form of Bridget.
(English) a short form of Britany.
Bretta, Brieta, Brietta, Brit, Britta

Britaney, Brittaney (English) forms
of Britany, Brittany.
Britanee, Britanny, Britenee, Briteny,
Britianey, British, Britkney, Britley, Britlyn,
Britney, Briton

Britani, Brittani, Brittanie
(English) forms of Britany.
Brit, Britania, Britanica, Britanie, Britanii,
Britanni, Britannia, Britatani, Britia, Britini,
Brittane, Brittanee, Brittanni, Brittannia,
Brittannie, Brittenie, Brittiani, Brittianni

Britany, Brittany G (English)
from Britain. See also Brett.
Brita, Britana, Britaney, Britani,
Britanna, Britlyn, Britney, Britt, Brittainny,
Brittainy, Brittamy, Brittana, Brittaney,
Brittani, Brittania, Brittanica, Brittanny,
Britany-Ann, Brittanyne, Brittell, Britteny,
Brittiany, Brittini, Brittlin, Brittlynn,
Brittnee, Brittony, Bryttany

Britin, Brittin (English) from Britain.
Britann, Brittan, Brittin, Brittina, Brittine,
Brittini, Brittiny

Britney, Brittny (English) forms of
Britany.
Bittney, Bridnee, Bridney, Britnay, Britne,
Britnee, Britnei, Britni, Britny, Britnye,
Brittnay, Brittnaye, Brytnea, Brytni

Britni, Brittni, Brittnie (English)
forms of Britney, Brittny.
Britnie

Briton (English) a form of Britin.
Britton

Britt, Britta (Latin) short forms of
Britany, Brittany. (Swedish) strong.
Brett, Briet, Brit, Brita, Britte

Britteny (English) a form of Britany,
Brittany.
Britten, Brittenay, Brittenee, Britteney,
Brittenie

Brittini, Brittiny (English) forms of
Britany, Brittany.
Brittinee, Brittiney, Brittinie, Brittiny

Brittnee (English) a form of Britany,
Brittany.
Brittne, Brittnea, Brittnei, Brittneigh

Brittney G (English) a form of
Britany.

Briyana, Briyanna (Irish) forms of
Briana.

Brock B (English) badger.

Brodie B (Irish) ditch; canal
builder.
Brodee, Brodi

Brody B (Irish) a form of Brodie.

Bronnie (Welsh) a familiar form of
Bronwyn.
Bron, Bronia, Bronney, Bronny, Bronya

Bronwyn G (Welsh) white
breasted.
Bronnie, Bronwen, Bronwin, Bronwynn,
Bronwynne

Brook G (English) brook, stream.
Bhrooke, Brookelle, Brookie, Brooky

Brooke ✹ G (English) brook,
stream.

Brooklyn ☀ **G** (American) a
combination of Brook + Lynn.
*Brookellen, Brookelyn, Brookelyne,
Brookelynn, Brooklen, Brooklin,
Brooklyne, Brooklynne*

Brooklynn **G** (American) a form of
Brooklyn.

Brooks **B** (English) a form of Brook.

Bruce **B** (French) brushwood
thicket; woods.

Bruna (German) a short form of
Brunhilda.
Brona

Brunela (Italian) a form of Bruna.

Brunhilda (German) armored warrior.
*Brinhilda, Brinhilde, Bruna, Brunhilde,
Brünnhilde, Brynhild, Brynhilda,
Brynhilde, Hilda*

Brunilda (German) line of defense in
battle.

Bryan **B** (Irish) a form of Brian.

Bryana **G** (Irish) a form of Bryan.

Bryanna, Bryanne (Irish) short
forms of Bryana.
Bryann, Bryanni

Bryce **B** (Welsh) alert; ambitious.

Bryden **B** (English) a form of
Braden.

Bryga (Polish) a form of Bridget.
Brygid, Brygida, Brygitka

Brylee **G** (American) a form of
Brylie.

Brylie (American) a combination of
the letter B + Riley.
Brylei, Bryley, Bryli

Bryn, Brynn **G** (Latin) from the
boundary line. (Welsh) mound.
Brinn, Brynee, Brynne

Bryna (Latin, Irish) a form of Brina.
Brynan, Brynna, Brynnan

Bryona, Bryonna (Irish) forms of
Briana.
Bryonia, Bryony

Bryson **B** (Welsh) child of Brice.
Brysan, Brysen, Brysun, Brysyn

Bryton **B** (English) a form of
Bryttani.

Bryttani, Bryttany (English) forms
of Britany.
*Brytani, Brytanie, Brytanny, Brytany,
Brytnee, Brytnie, Bryttanee, Bryttanie,
Bryttine, Bryttney, Bryttnie, Brytton*

Bsibs (Palauan) adornment,
decoration.

Bu (Vietnamese) jade.

Bua (Vietnamese) flower girl.

Bubby (Indian) my beloved.

Buena (Spanish) good.

Buenaventura (Castilian) she who
wishes good fortune and joy to
those around her.

Buffy (American) buffalo; from the
plains.
Buffee, Buffey, Buffie, Buffye

Bujen (Marshallese) a form of Petra.

Bulbul (Indian) nightingale.

Bulbuli (Indian) a songbird.

Bum (Korean) duty; fragrance;
impetuous.

Bunny (Greek) a familiar form of
Bernice. (English) little rabbit. See
also Bonnie.
Bunni, Bunnie

Burgundy (French) Geography: a region of France known for its Burgundy wine.
Burgandi, Burgandie, Burgandy, Burgunde

Buthayna (Indian) she who has a beautiful and tender body.

Byung (Korean) worth.

C

C BG (American) an initial used as a first name.

Caca (Chamorro) crack, crevice.

Cacac (Chamorro) type of bird.

Cachet (French) prestigious; desirous.
Cachae, Cache, Cachea, Cachee, Cachée

Cade B (English) a form of Cady.

Caden B (American) a form of Kadin (see Boys' Names).

Cadence (Latin) rhythm.
Cadena, Cadenza, Kadena

Cadhna, Chadna (Indian) love.

Cadmi (Chamorro) calm, no breeze.

Cady (English) a form of Kady.
Cade, Cadee, Cadey, Cadi, Cadie, Cadine, Cadye

Caeley, Cailey, Cayley (American) forms of Kaylee, Kelly.
Caela, Caelee, Caeleigh, Caeley, Caeli, Caelie, Caelly, Caely, Cailee, Caileigh, Caili, Cailie, Cailley, Caillie, Caily, Caylee

Caelin, Caelyn (American) forms of Kaelyn.
Caelan, Caelinn, Caelynn, Cailan, Caylan

Cai (Vietnamese) feminine.
Cae, Cay, Caye

Caija (Chamorro) to take a long time.

Cailida (Spanish) adoring.
Kailida

Cailin, Cailyn (American) forms of Caitlin.
Caileen, Cailene, Cailine, Cailynn, Cailynne, Calen, Cayleen, Caylen, Caylene, Caylin, Cayline, Caylyn, Caylyne, Caylynne

Cais (Vietnamese) fortunate.

Caitlan (Irish) a form of Caitlin.
Caitland, Caitlandt

Caitlin G (Irish) pure. See also Kaitlin, Katalina, Katelin, Katelyn, Kaytlin.
Caetlin, Cailin, Caitlan, Caitleen, Caitlen, Caitlene, Caitlenn, Caitline, Caitlinn, Caitlon, Caitlyn, Catlee, Catleen, Catleene, Catlin

Caitlyn, Caitlynn (Irish) forms of Caitlin. See also Kaitlyn.
Caitlyne, Caitlynne, Catelyn, Catlyn, Catlynn, Catlynne

Cala (Arabic) castle, fortress. See also Callie, Kala.
Calah, Calan, Calla, Callah

Calachuchi (Tagalog) aunt.

Calandra (Greek) lark.
Calan, Calandrea, Calandria, Caleida, Calendra, Calendre, Kalandra, Kalandria

Calanthe (Greek) beautiful flower.

Caleb B (Hebrew) dog; faithful. (Arabic) bold, brave.

Caledonia (Spanish) native of Caledonia.

Caleigh ◧ (American) a form of Caeley.
Caileigh, Caleah

Caley (American) a form of Caeley.

Calfuray (Mapuche) blue or violet flower.

Cali, Calli (Greek) forms of Callie. See also Kali.
Calee

Calida (Spanish) warm; ardent.
Calina, Calinda, Callida, Callinda, Kalida

Calíope (Greek) a form of Calliope.

Calisto (Spanish, Portuguese) most beautiful.

Callie (Greek, Arabic) a familiar form of Cala, Callista. See also Kalli.
Cal, Cali, Calie, Callee, Calley, Calli, Cally, Caly

Calliope (Greek) beautiful voice. Mythology: the Muse of epic poetry.

Callista (Greek) most beautiful. See also Kallista.
Calesta, Calista, Callie, Calysta

Callum ◧ (Irish) dove.

Caltha (Latin) yellow flower.

Calvina (Latin) bald.
Calvine, Calvinetta, Calvinette

Calypso (Greek) concealer. Botany: a pink orchid native to northern regions. Mythology: the sea nymph who held Odysseus captive for seven years.
Caly, Lypsie, Lypsy

Cam ◧ (Vietnamese) sweet citrus.
Kam

Camara (American) a form of Cameron.
Camera, Cameri, Cameria, Camira, Camry

Camberly (American) a form of Kimberly.
Camber, Camberlee, Camberleigh

Cambria (Latin) from Wales. See also Kambria.
Camberry, Cambreia, Cambie, Cambrea, Cambree, Cambrie, Cambrina, Cambry, Cambrya, Cami

Camden ◨ (Scottish) winding valley.
Camdyn

Camellia (Italian) Botany: a camellia is an evergreen tree or shrub with fragrant roselike flowers.
Camala, Camalia, Camallia, Camela, Camelia, Camelita, Camella, Camellita, Cami, Kamelia, Kamellia

Cameo (Latin) gem or shell on which a portrait is carved.
Cami, Kameo

Cameron ◨ (Scottish) crooked nose. See also Kameron, Kamryn.
Camara, Cameran, Cameren, Camira, Camiran, Camiron, Camryn

Cami (French) a short form of Camille. See also Kami.
Camey, Camie, Cammi, Cammie, Cammy, Cammye, Camy

Camila ☆ (Italian) a form of Camille. See also Kamila, Mila.
Camia, Camilia, Camillia, Camilya, Cammilla, Chamelea, Chamelia, Chamika, Chamila, Chamilia

Camilla (Italian) a form of Camille.

Camille ◧ (French) young ceremonial attendant. See also Millie.
Cam, Cami, Camiel, Camielle, Camil, Camila, Camile, Camill, Cammille, Cammillie, Cammilyn, Cammyl, Cammyll, Camylle, Chamelle, Chamille, Kamille

Camisha (American) a combination
of Cami + Aisha.
*Cameasha, Cameesha, Cameisha,
Camesa, Camesha, Cameshaa,
Cameshia, Camiesha, Camyeshia*

Camri, Camrie (American) short
forms of Camryn. See also Kamri.
Camrea, Camree, Camrey, Camry

Camron **B** (American) a form of
Camryn.

Camryn (American) a form of
Cameron. See also Kamryn.
Camri, Camrin, Camron, Camrynn

Camylle (French) a form of Camille.
Camyle, Camyll

Can (Chinese) bright.

Cancia (Spanish) native of the city of
Anzio.

Canciana, Cancianila (Spanish)
forms of Cancia.

Candace (Greek) glittering white;
glowing. History: the title of the
queens of ancient Ethiopia. See also
Dacey, Kandace.
*Cace, Canace, Canda, Candas,
Candece, Candelle, Candi, Candiace,
Candice, Candyce*

Candela (Spanish) candle; fire.

Candelaria (Latin) Candlemas; she
who shines brightly.

Candelas (Spanish) a form of
Candela.

Candi, Candy (American) familiar
forms of Candace, Candice,
Candida. See also Kandi.
Candee, Candie

Candice **G** (Greek) a form of
Candace.
Candise, Candiss

Candida (Latin) bright white.
*Candeea, Candi, Candia, Candide,
Candita*

Cándida (Latin) a form of Candida.

Candis (Greek) a form of Candace.
*Candes, Candi, Candias, Candies,
Candus*

Candra (Latin) glowing. See also
Kandra.
Candrea, Candria

Candyce (Greek) a form of Candace.
Candys, Candyse, Cyndyss

Canela (Latin) name of an aromatic
plant and the color of its dry bark.

Cang (Chinese) sea blue.

Canh (Vietnamese) fortunate.

Cantara (Arabic) small crossing.
Cantarah

Cantrelle (French) song.
Cantrella

Capitolina (Latin) she who lives
with the gods.

Capri (Italian) a short form of
Caprice. Geography: an island off
the west coast of Italy. See also
Kapri.
Capria, Caprie, Capry

Caprice (Italian) fanciful.
*Cappi, Caprece, Caprecia, Capresha,
Capricia, Capriese, Caprina, Capris,
Caprise, Caprisha, Capritta*

Cara (Latin) dear. (Irish) friend.
See also Karah.
*Caira, Caragh, Carah, Caralee,
Caranda, Carey, Carra*

Caralee (Irish) a form of Cara.
*Caralea, Caraleigh, Caralia, Caralie,
Carely*

Caralyn (English) a form of Caroline.
Caralin, Caraline, Caralynn, Caralynna, Caralynne

Carem (Spanish) a form of Karen.

Caressa (French) a form of Carissa.
Caresa, Carese, Caresse, Carissa, Charessa, Charesse, Karessa

Carey 🆖 (Welsh) a familiar form of Cara, Caroline, Karen, Katherine. See also Carrie, Kari.
Caree, Cari, Carrey, Cary

Cari, Carie (Welsh) forms of Carey, Kari.

Caridad (Latin) she who gives love, affection, and tenderness to those around her.

Carina 🆖 (Italian) dear little one. (Swedish) a form of Karen. (Greek) a familiar form of Cora.
Carena, Carinah, Carine, Carinna

Carine (Italian) a form of Carina.
Carin, Carinn, Carinne

Carisa, Carrisa (Greek) forms of Carissa.
Carise, Carisha, Carisia, Charisa

Carissa (Greek) beloved. See also Karissa.
Caressa, Carisa, Carrissa, Charissa

Carita (Latin) charitable.
Caritta, Karita, Karitta

Caritina (Latin) grace, graceful.

Carl 🅱 (German, English) a short form of Carlton. A form of Charles. See also Carroll, Kale, Kalle, Karl.

Carla (German) farmer. (English) strong. (Latin) a form of Carol, Caroline.
Carila, Carilla, Carleta, Carlia, Carliqua, Carliyle, Carlonda, Carlyjo, Carlyle, Carlysle

Carlee, Carley 🆖 (English) forms of Carly. See also Karlee.
Carle, Carlea, Carleah, Carleh

Carleen, Carlene (English) forms of Caroline. See also Karlene.
Carlaen, Carlaena, Carleena, Carlen, Carlena, Carlenna, Carline, Carlyn, Carlyne

Carleigh (English) a form of Carly.
Carli, Carlie 🆖 *(English) forms of Carly. See also Karli.*

Carlin 🆖 (Irish) little champion. (Latin) a short form of Caroline.
Carlan, Carlana, Carlandra, Carlina, Carlinda, Carline, Carling, Carllan, Carlyn, Carllen, Carrlin

Carlisa (American) a form of Carlissa.
Carilis, Carilise, Carilyse, Carleesia, Carlesia, Carletha, Carlethe, Carlicia, Carlis, Carlise, Carlisha, Carlisia, Carlyse

Carlissa (American) a combination of Carla + Lissa.
Carleeza, Carlisa, Carliss, Carlissah, Carlisse, Carlissia, Carlista

Carlos 🅱 (Spanish) a form of Carl, Charles.

Carlotta (Italian) a form of Charlotte.
Carletta, Carlita, Carlota

Carlton 🅱 (English) Carl's town.

Carly 🆖 (English) a familiar form of Caroline, Charlotte. See also Karli.
Carlye

Carlyn, Carlynn (Irish) forms of Carlin.
Carlyna, Carlynne

Carme (Galician) garden.

Carmela, Carmella (Hebrew) garden; vineyard. Bible: Mount Carmel in Israel is often thought of as paradise. See also Karmel.
Carma, Carmalla, Carmarit, Carmel, Carmeli, Carmelia, Carmelina, Carmelit, Carmelle, Carmellia, Carmellina, Carmesa, Carmesha, Carmi, Carmie, Carmiel, Carmil, Carmila, Carmile, Carmilla, Carmille, Carmisha, Leeta, Lita

Carmelit (Hebrew) a form of Carmela.
Carmaletta, Carmalit, Carmalita, Carmelita, Carmelitha, Carmelitia, Carmellit, Carmellita, Carmellitha, Carmellitia

Carmen **G** (Latin) song. Religion: Nuestra Señora del Carmen-Our Lady of Mount Carmel-is one of the titles of the Virgin Mary. See also Karmen.
Carma, Carmaine, Carman, Carmelina, Carmencita, Carmene, Carmi, Carmia, Carmin, Carmina, Carmine, Carmita, Carmon, Carmynn, Charmaine

Carmiña (Spanish) a form of Carmen.

Carminda (Spanish) beautiful song.

Carmo (Portuguese) garden.

Carnelian (Latin) precious, red rock.

Carol **G** (German) farmer. (French) song of joy. (English) strong. See also Charlene, Kalle, Karoll.
Carel, Cariel, Caro, Carola, Carole, Carolenia, Carolinda, Caroline, Caroll, Carrie, Carrol, Carroll, Caryl

Carolane, Carolann, Carolanne (American) combinations of Carol + Ann. Forms of Caroline.
Carolan, Carol Ann, Carole-Anne

Carole (English) a form of Carol.
Carolee, Karole, Karrole

Carolina **G** (Italian) a form of Caroline. See also Karolina.
Carilena, Carlena, Carlina, Caroleena, Caroleina, Carolena, Carrolena

Caroline ✶ **G** (French) little and strong. See also Carla, Carleen, Carlin, Karolina.
Caralin, Caraline, Carileen, Carilene, Carilin, Cariline, Carling, Carly, Caro, Carolann, Caroleen, Carolin, Carolina, Carolyn, Carrie, Carroleen, Carrolene, Carrolin, Carroline, Cary, Charlene

Carolyn **G** (English) a form of Caroline. See also Karolyn.
Carilyn, Carilynn, Carilynne, Carlyn, Carlynn, Carlynne, Carolyne, Carolynn, Carolynne, Carrolyn, Carrolynn, Carrolynne

Caron (Welsh) loving, kindhearted, charitable.
Caronne, Carron, Carrone

Carona (Spanish) crown.

Carra (Irish) a form of Cara.
Carrah

Carrie **G** (English) a familiar form of Carol, Caroline. See also Carey, Kari, Karri.
Carree, Carrey, Carri, Carria, Carry, Cary

Carrola (French) song of joy.

Carson **B** (English) child of Carr.
Carsen, Carsyn

Carter **B** (English) cart driver.

Caryl (Latin) a form of Carol.
Caryle, Caryll, Carylle

Caryn (Danish) a form of Karen.
Caren, Carren, Carrin, Carryn, Caryna, Caryne, Carynn

Carys (Welsh) love.
Caris, Caryse, Ceris, Cerys

Casandra (Greek) a form of
Cassandra.
Casandera, Casandre, Casandrea,
Casandrey, Casandri, Casandria,
Casanndra, Casaundra, Casaundre,
Casaundri, Casaundria, Casondra,
Casondre, Casondri, Casondria

Casey 🇧🇬 (Irish) brave. (Greek) a
familiar form of Acacia. See also
Kasey.
Cacy, Cascy, Casie, Casse, Cassee,
Cassey, Cassye, Casy, Cayce, Cayse,
Caysee, Caysy

Casiana (Latin) empty, vain.

Casidy (Irish) a form of Cassidy.
Casidee, Casidi

Casie (Irish) a form of Casey.
Caci, Caesi, Caisie, Casci, Cascie, Casi,
Cayci, Caysi, Caysie, Cazzi

Casiel (Latin) mother of the earth.

Casilda (Arabic) virgin carrier of the
lance.

Casimira (Polish) predicts peace.

Cass 🇧 (Greek) a short form of
Cassandra.

Cassady (Irish) a form of Cassidy.
Casadee, Casadi, Casadie, Cassaday,
Cassadee, Cassadey, Cassadi,
Cassadie, Cassadina

Cassandra 🇬 (Greek) helper of
men. Mythology: a prophetess of
ancient Greece whose prophesies
were not believed. See also
Kassandra, Sandra, Sandy, Zandra.
Casandra, Cass, Cassandre, Cassandri,
Cassandry, Cassaundra, Cassie,
Cassondra

Cassaundra (Greek) a form of
Cassandra.
Cassaundre, Cassaundri, Cassundra,
Cassundre, Cassundri, Cassundria

Cassey, Cassi (Greek) familiar
forms of Cassandra, Catherine.
Cassee, Cassii, Cassy, Casy

Cassia (Greek) a cinnamon-like
spice. See also Kasia.
Casia, Cass, Casya

Cassidy 🇬 (Irish) clever. See also
Kassidy.
Casidy, Cassady, Casseday, Cassiddy,
Cassidee, Cassidi, Cassidie, Cassity

Cassie 🇬 (Greek) a familiar form of
Cassandra, Catherine. See also
Kassie.

Cassiopeia (Greek) clever.
Mythology: the wife of the Ethiopian
king Cepheus; the mother of
Andromeda.
Cassio

Cassondra (Greek) a form of
Cassandra.
Cassondre, Cassondri, Cassondria

Casta (Greek) pure.

Castalia (Greek) fountain of purity.

Castel (Spanish) to the castle.

Castora (Spanish) brilliant.

Catalina (Spanish) a form of
Catherine. See also Katalina.
Cataleen, Catalena, Catalene, Catalin,
Catalyn, Catalyna, Cateline

Catarina (German) a form of
Catherine.
Catarena, Catarin, Catarine, Caterin,
Caterina, Caterine

Catelyn (Irish) a form of Caitlin.
Catelin, Cateline, Catelyne, Catelynn

Catharine (Greek) a form of
Catherine.
Catharen, Catharin, Catharina,
Catharyn

Catherine **G** (Greek) pure.
(English) a form of Katherine.
*Cat, Catalina, Catarina, Cate, Cathann,
Cathanne, Catharine, Cathenne,
Catheren, Catherene, Catheria,
Catherin, Catherina, Catheryn,
Catheryne, Cathi, Cathleen, Cathrine,
Cathryn, Cathy, Catlaina, Catreeka,
Catrelle, Catrice, Catricia, Catrika,
Catrina*

Cathi, Cathy (Greek) familiar forms
of Catherine, Cathleen. See also
Kathy.
Catha, Cathe, Cathee, Cathey, Cathie

Cathleen (Irish) a form of Catherine.
See also Caitlin, Kathleen.
*Caithlyn, Cathaleen, Cathelin,
Cathelina, Cathelyn, Cathi, Cathleana,
Cathleene, Cathlene, Cathleyn, Cathlin,
Cathline, Cathlyn, Cathlyne, Cathlynn,
Cathy*

Cathrine (Greek) a form of
Catherine.

Cathryn (Greek) a form of
Catherine.
Cathryne, Cathrynn, Catryn

Catrina (Slavic) a form of Catherine,
Katrina.
*Caitriana, Caitriona, Catina, Catreen,
Catreena, Catrene, Catrenia, Catrin,
Catrine, Catrinia, Catriona, Catroina*

Cauvery, Cavery (Indian) the name
of a river in India.

Cayetana (Spanish) native of the
city of Gaeta.

Cayfutray (Mapuche) noise from the
bluish sky; blue thread; crystalline,
celestial waterfall from heaven.

Cayla (Hebrew) a form of Kayla.
Caylea, Caylia

Caylee, Caylie (American) forms of
Caeley, Cailey, Cayley.
Cayle, Cayleigh, Cayli, Cayly

Ceara (Irish) a form of Ciara.
*Ceaira, Ceairah, Ceairra, Cearaa,
Cearie, Cearah, Cearra, Cera*

Cecelia (Latin) a form of Cecilia.
See also Sheila.
*Caceli, Cacelia, Cece, Ceceilia, Ceceli,
Cecelia, Cecelie, Cecely, Cecelyn,
Cecette, Cescelia, Cescelie*

Cecil **B** (Latin) a short form of
Cecilia.

Cecilia (Latin) blind. See also Cicely,
Cissy, Secilia, Selia, Sissy.
*Cacilia, Caecilia, Cecelia, Cecil, Cecila,
Cecile, Cecilea, Cecilija, Cecilla,
Cecille, Cecillia, Cecily, Cecilya, Ceclia,
Cecylia, Cee, Ceil, Ceila, Ceilagh,
Ceileh, Ceileigh, Ceilena, Celia, Cesilia,
Cicelia*

Cecília (Portuguese) a form of
Cecilia.

Cecily (Latin) a form of Cecilia.
*Cacilie, Cecilee, Ceciley, Cecilie,
Cescily, Cicely, Cilley*

Ceferina (German) caresses like a
soft wind.

Ceil (Latin) a short form of Cecilia.
Ceel, Ciel

Ceira, Ceirra (Irish) forms of Ciara.
Ceire

Celedonia (German) like the
celedonia flower.

Celena (Greek) a form of Selena.
Celeena, Celene, Celenia, Celine, Cena

Celene (Greek) a form of Celena.
Celeen

Celerina (Spanish) quick.

Celeste (Latin) celestial, heavenly.
Cele, Celeeste, Celense, Celes, Celesia, Celesley, Celest, Celesta, Celestia, Celestial, Celestin, Celestina, Celestine, Celestinia, Celestyn, Celestyna, Cellest, Celleste, Selestina

Celia (Latin) a short form of Cecilia.
Ceilia, Celie

Célia (Portuguese) a form of Celia.

Celidonia (Greek) a certain type of herbal medicine.

Celina (Greek) a form of Celena. See also Selina.
Caleena, Calena, Calina, Celena, Celinda, Celinka, Celinna, Celka, Cellina

Celine G (Greek) a form of Celena.
Caline, Celeen, Celene, Céline, Cellinn

Celmira (Arabic) brilliant one.

Celsa (Latin) very spiritual.

Cemelia (Punic) she has God present.

Cenobia (Greek) stranger.

Centola (Arabic) light of knowledge.

Cera (French) a short form of Cerise.
Cerea, Ceri, Ceria, Cerra

Cercira (Greek) she who is from the island of Circe.

Cerella (Latin) springtime.
Cerelisa, Ceres

Cerise (French) cherry; cherry red.
Cera, Cerese, Cerice, Cericia, Cerissa, Cerria, Cerrice, Cerrina, Cerrita, Cerryce, Ceryce, Cherise

Cesar B (Spanish) a form of Caesar (see Boys' Names).

Cesara (Latin) longhaired.

Cesare, Cesaria, Cesarina, Cesira (Latin) she who was forcibly separated from her mother.

Cesilia (Latin) a form of Cecilia.
Cesia, Cesya

Chaaya, Chhaya (Indian) shadow.

Chabe (Chamorro) chop; pepper.

Chabela (Hebrew) a form of Isabel.

Chabi (Indian) picture.

Chablis (French) a dry, white wine. Geography: a region in France where wine grapes are grown.
Chabeli, Chabelly, Chabely, Chablee, Chabley, Chabli

Chaca (Chamorro) mouse.

Chad B (English) warrior. A short form of Chadwick (see Boys' Names). Geography: a country in north-central Africa.

Chadee (French) from Chad, a country in north-central Africa. See also Sade.
Chaday, Chadday, Chade, Chadea, Chadi

Chadfaulus, Charfaulos (Chamorro) forms of Charfaulus.

Chaguna, Changuna (Indian) a good woman.

Chai (Hebrew) life.
Chae, Chaela, Chaeli, Chaella, Chaena, Chaia

Chairavali (Indian) full moon of Chaitra month.

Chaitalee (Indian) girl born in the Chaitra month.

Chaitali (Indian) a season; born in the Chaitra month.

Chaitaly (Indian) name of an ancient city.

Chaitan (Indian) consciousness.

Chaka (Sanskrit) a form of Chakra. See also Shaka.
Chakai, Chakia, Chakka, Chakkah

Chakori (Indian) alert.

Chakra (Sanskrit) circle of energy.
Chaka, Chakara, Chakaria, Chakena, Chakina, Chakira, Chakrah, Chakria, Chakriya, Chakyra

Chalan (Chamorro) way, path.

Chalana (Chamorro) her way.

Chalice (French) goblet.
Chalace, Chalcie, Chalece, Chalicea, Chalie, Chaliese, Chalis, Chalisa, Chalise, Chalisk, Chalissa, Chalisse, Challa, Challaine, Challis, Challisse, Challysse, Chalsey, Chalyce, Chalyn, Chalyse, Chalyssa, Chalysse

Chalina (Spanish) a form of Rose.
Chaline, Chalini

Chalonna (American) a combination of the prefix Cha + Lona.
Chalon, Chalona, Chalonda, Chalonn, Chalonne, Chalonte, Shalon

Chambray (French) a lightweight fabric.
Chambrae, Chambre, Chambree, Chambrée, Chambrey, Chambria, Chambrie

Chameli (Indian) a flower.

Chamiyu (Chamorro) not enough of you.

Chamorra (Chamorro) a woman of the Chamorro people.

Champa (Indian) a flower.

Champabati (Indian) the capital.

Champakali (Indian) a bud of champa.

Champakmala (Indian) a garland made of champa flowers.

Chan **B** (Cambodian) sweet-smelling tree.

Chan Juan, Chang-Juan (Chinese) the moon; graceful, ladylike.

Chana (Hebrew) a form of Hannah.
Chanae, Chanai, Chanay, Chanea, Chanie

Chance **B** (English) a short form of Chancey.

Chancey (English) chancellor; church official.
Chance, Chancee, Chancie, Chancy

Chanchala (Indian) unsteady; lightening.

Chanchari (Indian) bird.

Chanda (Sanskrit) short tempered. Religion: the demon defeated by the Hindu goddess Chamunda. See also Shanda.
Chandee, Chandey, Chandi, Chandie, Chandin

Chandana (Indian) sandal.

Chandanika (Indian) diminutive.

Chandelle (French) candle.
Chandal, Chandel, Shandal, Shandel

Chandini, Chandrabha, Chandrajyoti, Chandrakanti (Indian) moonlight.

Chandler **B** (Hindi) moon. (Old English) candlemaker.
Chandlar, Chandlier, Chandlor, Chandlyr

Chandni (Indian) moonlit.

Chandra (Sanskrit) moon. Religion: the Hindu god of the moon. See also Shandra.
Chandrae, Chandray, Chandre, Chandrea, Chandrelle, Chandria

Chandrabali (Indian) Krishna's girlfriend.

Chandrabhaga (Indian) the Chenab River.

Chandrakala (Indian) phases of the moon.

Chandraki, Chandrakin (Indian) peacock.

Chandralekha (Indian) the phase of moon two nights after new moon; a moon ray.

Chandraleksha (Indian) a moon ray.

Chandramukhi (Indian) one with a round face.

Chandrani (Indian) wife of the moon.

Chandraprabha (Indian) star; moonlight.

Chandrapushpa (Indian) star.

Chandrika, Chandrima (Indian) moon.

Chanel (English) channel. See also Shanel.
Chanal, Chaneel, Chaneil, Chanele, Chanell, Channal, Channel, Chenelle

Chanell, Chanelle (English) forms of Chanel.
Channell, Shanell

Chang (Chinese) free, uninhibited.

Chang-O (Chinese) moon goddess, keeper of the ambrosia of immortality.

Chanise (American) a form of Shanice.
Chanisse, Chenice, Chenise

Channa (Hindi) chickpea.
Channah

Channary (Vietnamese) one who rejoices.

Chantal G (French) song.
Chandal, Chantaal, Chantael, Chantala, Chantale, Chantall, Chantalle, Chantara, Chantarai, Chantasia, Chante, Chanteau, Chantel, Chantle, Chantoya, Chantrill, Chauntel

Chante BG (French) a short form of Chantal.
Chanta, Chantae, Chantai, Chantay, Chantaye, Chanté, Chantéa, Chantee, Chanti, Chantia, Chaunte, Chauntea, Chauntéa, Chauntee

Chantel, G (French) a form of Chantal. See also Shantel.

Chantell, Chantelle (French) forms of Chantel.
Chanteese, Chantela, Chantele, Chantella, Chanter, Chantey, Chantez, Chantrel, Chantrell, Chantrelle, Chatell

Chantilly (French) fine lace. See also Shantille.
Chantiel, Chantielle, Chantil, Chantila, Chantilée, Chantill, Chantille

Chantrea (Cambodian) moon; moonbeam.
Chantra, Chantrey, Chantri, Chantria

Chantrice (French) singer. See also Shantrice.
Chantreese, Chantress

Chao (Chinese) great one.

Chapala (Indian) quick.

Charani (Chamorro) lead, guide.

Chardae, Charde (Punjabi)
charitable. (French) short forms of
Chardonnay. See also Shardae.
*Charda, Chardai, Charday, Chardea,
Chardee, Chardée, Chardese,
Chardey, Chardie*

Chardonnay (French) a dry white
wine.
*Char, Chardae, Chardnay, Chardney,
Chardon, Chardonae, Chardonai,
Chardonay, Chardonaye, Chardonee,
Chardonna, Chardonnae, Chardonnai,
Chardonnee, Chardonnée,
Chardonney, Shardonay, Shardonnay*

Charfaulus (Chamorro) one with a
rough appearance.

Charge (Chamorro) to laugh at.

Chargi, Chargui (Chamorro) forms
of Charge.

Charis (Greek) grace; kindness.
*Charece, Chareece, Chareeze,
Charese, Chari, Charice, Charie,
Charish, Charisse*

Charissa, Charisse (Greek) forms
of Charity.
*Charesa, Charese, Charessa, Charesse,
Charis, Charisa, Charise, Charisha,
Charissee, Charista, Charyssa*

Charitha (Indian) good.

Charity **G** (Latin) charity, kindness.
*Chariety, Charis, Charissa, Charisse,
Charista, Charita, Chariti, Charitie,
Sharity*

Charla (French, English) a short
form of Charlene, Charlotte.
Char, Charlea

Charlaine (English) a form of
Charlene.
*Charlaina, Charlane, Charlanna,
Charlayna, Charlayne*

Charlee, Charley (German,
English) forms of Charlie.
Charle, Charleigh

Charlene (English) a form of
Caroline. See also Carol, Karla,
Sharlene.
*Charla, Charlaine, Charlean, Charleen,
Charleene, Charleesa, Charlena,
Charlenae, Charlesena, Charline,
Charlyn, Charlyne, Charlynn,
Charlynne, Charlzina, Charoline*

Charles **B** (German) farmer.
(English) strong.

Charlie **B** (German, English) a
familiar form of Charles.
*Charlee, Charley, Charli, Charyl,
Chatty, Sharli, Sharlie*

Charlotte 🌱 (French) a form of
Caroline. Literature: Charlotte
Brontë was a British novelist and
poet best known for her novel *Jane
Eyre.* See also Karlotte, Lotte,
Sharlotte, Tottie.
*Carlotta, Carly, Chara, Charil, Charl,
Charla, Charlet, Charlett, Charletta,
Charlette, Charlisa, Charlita, Charlott,
Charlotta, Charlottie, Charlotty, Charolet,
Charolette, Charolot, Charolotte*

Charmaine (French) a form of
Carmen. See also Sharmaine.
*Charamy, Charma, Charmae,
Charmagne, Charmaigne, Charmain,
Chamaine, Charmalique, Charman,
Charmane, Charmar, Charmara,
Charmayane, Charmayne, Charmeen,
Charmeine, Charmene, Charmese,
Charmian, Charmin, Charmine,
Charmion, Charmisa, Charmon,
Charmyn, Charmyne, Charmynne*

Charnette (American) a
combination of Charo + Annette.
Charnetta, Charnita

Charnika (American) a combination
of Charo + Nika.
Charneka, Charniqua, Charnique

Charo (Spanish) a familiar form of
Rosa.

Charsaga, Chartsagua
(Chamorro) forms of Chatsaga.

Charu, Charuprabha (Indian)
beautiful.

Charulata (Indian) beautiful; like a
creeper.

Charulekha (Indian) beautiful; like
a picture.

Charumati, Charvi (Indian) a
beautiful lady.

Charusheela (Indian) beautiful jewel.

Charushila (Indian) a diamond.

Charusmita (Indian) one with a
beautiful smile.

Charyanna (American) a
combination of Charo + Anna.
Charian, Charyian, Cheryn

Chase 🅱 (French) hunter.

Chashmum (Indian) my eyes.

Chasidy, Chassidy (Latin) forms of
Chastity.
*Chasa Dee, Chasadie, Chasady,
Chasidee, Chasidey, Chasidie,
Chassedi, Chassidi, Chasydi*

Chasity (Latin) a form of Chastity.
*Chasiti, Chasitie, Chasitty, Chassey,
Chassie, Chassiti, Chassity, Chassy*

Chastain (French) chestnut-colored
hair.

Chastity (Latin) pure.
*Chasidy, Chasity, Chasta, Chastady,
Chastidy, Chastin, Chastitie, Chastney,
Chasty*

Chata (Chamorro) not enough.

Chateria (Vietnamese) scenery.

Chathanum (Chamorro) not
enough water.

Chatsaga (Chamorro) not enough
to live on, poor.

Chau, Cuc (Vietnamese) moon girl.

Chauncey 🅱 (English) chancellor;
church official.

Chauntel (French) a form of
Chantal.
*Chaunta, Chauntae, Chauntay,
Chaunte, Chauntell, Chauntelle,
Chawntel, Chawntell, Chawntelle,
Chontelle*

Chava (Hebrew) life. (Yiddish) bird.
Religion: the original name of Eve.
*Chabah, Chavae, Chavah, Chavalah,
Chavarra, Chavarria, Chave, Chavé,
Chavette, Chaviva, Chavvis, Hava,
Kaòa*

Chavela (Spanish) consecrated to
God.

Chavella (Spanish) a form of Isabel.
*Chavel, Chaveli, Chavell, Chavelle,
Chevelle, Chavely, Chevie*

Chavi (Gypsy) girl.
Chavali

Chavon (Hebrew) a form of Jane.
*Chavona, Chavonda, Chavonn,
Chavonne, Shavon*

Chavonne (Hebrew) a form of
Chavon. (American) a combination
of the prefix Cha + Yvonne.
*Chavondria, Chavonna, Chevon,
Chevonn, Chevonna*

Chaya (Hebrew) life; living.
*Chaike, Chaye, Chayka, Chayla,
Chaylah, Chaylea, Chaylee, Chaylene,
Chayra*

Chaz **B** (English) a familiar form of Charles.

Cheboc (Chamorro) fat, plump.

Chein (Chuukese) a form of Jane.

Chela (Spanish) consolation.

Chelci, Chelcie (English) forms of Chelsea.
Chelce, Chelcee, Chelcey, Chelcy

Chelo (Spanish) a form of Consuelo.

Chelsea **G** (English) seaport. See also Kelsi, Shelsea.
Chelci, Chelese, Chelesia, Chelsa, Chelsae, Chelsah, Chelse, Chelseah, Chelsee, Chelsey, Chelsia, Chelsie, Chesea, Cheslee, Chessea

Chelsee (English) a form of Chelsea.
Chelsei, Chelseigh

Chelsey **G** (English) a form of Chelsea. See also Kelsey.
Chelsay, Chelssey, Chesley

Chelsie (English) a form of Chelsea.
Chelli, Chellie, Chellise, Chellsie, Chelsi, Chelssie, Cheslie, Chessie

Chelsy (English) a form of Chelsea.
Chelcy, Chelssy, Chelsye

Chen (Chinese) dawn.

Chenelle (English) a form of Chanel.
Chenel, Chenell

Cheng (Chinese) succeed; capable.

Chenoa (Native American) white dove.
Chenee, Chenika, Chenita, Chenna, Chenoah

Cher (French) beloved, dearest. (English) a short form of Cherilyn.
Chere, Cheri, Cherie, Sher

Cherelle, Cherrelle (French) forms of Cheryl. See also Sherelle.
Charell, Charelle, Cherell, Cherrel, Cherrell

Cherese (Greek) a form of Cherish.
Chereese, Cheresa, Cheresse, Cherice

Cheri, Cherie (French) familiar forms of Cher.
Cheree, Chérie, Cheriee, Cherri, Cherrie

Cherilyn (English) a combination of Cheryl + Lynn.
Cher, Cheralyn, Chereen, Chereena, Cherilynn, Cherlyn, Cherlynn, Cherralyn, Cherrilyn, Cherrylyn, Cherylene, Cherylin, Cheryline, Cheryl-Lyn, Cheryl-Lynn, Cheryl-Lynne, Cherylyn, Cherylynn, Cherylynne, Sherilyn

Cherise (French) a form of Cherish. See also Sharice, Sherice.
Charisa, Charise, Cherece, Chereese, Cheresa, Cherice, Cheriss, Cherissa, Cherisse, Cherrise

Cherish (English) dearly held, precious.
Charish, Charisha, Cheerish, Cherise, Cherishe, Cherrish, Sherish

Cherokee **G** (Native American) a tribal name.
Cherika, Cherkita, Cherrokee, Sherokee

Cherry (Latin) a familiar form of Charity. (French) cherry; cherry red.
Chere, Cheree, Cherey, Cherida, Cherita, Cherrey, Cherrita, Cherry-Ann, Cherry-Anne, Cherrye, Chery, Cherye

Cheryl (French) beloved. See also Sheryl.
Charel, Charil, Charyl, Cherelle, Cherrelle, Cheryl-Ann, Cheryl-Anne, Cheryle, Cherylee, Cheryll, Cherylle, Cheryl-Lee

Chesarey (American) a form of Desiree.
Chesarae, Chessa

Cheshta (Indian) to try.

Chesna (Slavic) peaceful.
Chesnee, Chesney, Chesnie, Chesny

Chessa (American) a short form of Chesarey.
Chessi, Chessie, Chessy

Chetna (Indian) power of intellect; alert.

Cheyanne (Cheyenne) a form of Cheyenne.
Cheyan, Cheyana, Cheyane, Cheyann, Cheyanna, Cheyeana, Cheyeannna, Cheyeannne

Cheyenne 🅖 (Cheyenne) a tribal name. See also Shaianne, Sheyenne, Shianne, Shyann.
Cheyanne, Cheyeene, Cheyena, Cheyene, Cheyenna, Cheyna, Chi, Chi-Anna, Chie, Chyanne

Cheyla (American) a form of Sheila.
Cheylan, Cheyleigh, Cheylo

Cheyna (American) a short form of Cheyenne.
Chey, Cheye, Cheyne, Cheynee, Cheyney, Cheynna

Chhavi (Indian) reflection.

Chi 🅱🅖 (Chinese) younger generation. (Nigerian) personal guardian angel.

Chia (Chinese) home, family; addition; armor.

Chiaki (Japanese) a thousand autumns.

Chiako (Pohnpeian) a form of Filomena.

Chiara (Italian) a form of Clara.
Cheara, Chiarra

Chiharu (Japanese) a thousand; clear weather.

Chihiro (Japanese) she who is very curious.

Chih-Nii (Chinese) goddess of spinners, weavers, and clouds.

Chiho (Japanese) a thousand plants.

Chika (Japanese) near and dear.
Chikaka, Chikako, Chikara, Chikona

Chiko (Japanese) arrow; pledge.

Chiku (Swahili) chatterer.

Chimayi (Indian) blissful.

Chin (Chinese) a form of Jin.

China 🅖 (Chinese) fine porcelain. Geography: a country in eastern Asia. See also Ciana, Shina.
Chinaetta, Chinah, Chinasa, Chinda, Chinea, Chinesia, Chinita, Chinna, Chinwa, Chyna, Chynna

Chinami (Japanese) cause.

Chinatsu (Japanese) she who is as beautiful as the summer.

Chinira (Swahili) God receives.
Chinara, Chinarah, Chinirah

Chinmayi (Indian) happy, blissful.

Chintana, Chintanika (Indian) meditation.

Chinue (Ibo) God's own blessing.

Chioko (Japanese) child.

Chionen (Chuukese) their companion.

Chiquita (Spanish) little one. See also Shiquita.
Chaqueta, Chaquita, Chica, Chickie, Chicky, Chikata, Chikita, Chiqueta, Chiquila, Chiquite, Chiquitha, Chiquithe, Chiquitia, Chiquitta

Chirika (Chamorro) the name of a bird.

Chisa (Japanese) torch.

Chisako (Japanese) torch child.

Chisa-Rae (Japanese) child of Yutso.

Chisato (Japanese) a thousand; knowledge; village.

Chiti (Indian) love.

Chitkala (Indian) knowledge.

Chitose (Japanese) a thousand years.

Chitra (Indian) drawing.

Chitragandha (Indian) a fragrant material.

Chitralekha (Indian) portrait.

Chitrali (Indian) a line of pictures.

Chitramala (Indian) series of pictures.

Chitrangada (Indian) wife of Arjun.

Chitrani (Indian) the Ganges River.

Chitrarekha (Indian) picture.

Chitrita (Indian) beautiful; decorated.

Chiyako (Japanese) thousand valley child.

Chiye (Japanese) a thousand; knowledge; blessed; branch.

Chiyeko (Japanese) prospering child.

Chiyemi (Japanese) wisdom; blessed; beautiful.

Chiyo (Japanese) eternal.
Chiya

Chiyoko (Japanese) wise child of the world.

Chiyoye (Japanese) a thousand blessed generations.

Chizu, Chizue (Japanese) a thousand storks; longevity.

Chizuko (Japanese) a form of Chizue.

Chloe ✿ **G** (Greek) blooming, verdant. Mythology: another name for Demeter, the goddess of agriculture.
Chloé, Chlöe, Chloee, Chloie, Cloe, Kloe

Chloris (Greek) pale. Mythology: the only daughter of Niobe to escape the vengeful arrows of Apollo and Artemis. See also Loris.
Cloris, Clorissa

Cho (Korean) beautiful.
Choe

Chocholage (Chamorro) eat a little more.

Choda (Chamorro) green banana.

Choko (Japanese) butterfly child.

Cholena (Native American) bird.

Chomay (Chamorro) spill, pour.

Chomma (Chamorro) forbid.

Chong, Cong (Chinese) intelligent, clever.

Chow (Chinese) summer.

Chriki (Swahili) blessing.

Chris **B** (Greek) a short form of Christina. See also Kris.
Chrys, Cris

Chrissa (Greek) a short form of Christina. See also Khrissa.
Chrysa, Chryssa, Crissa, Cryssa

Chrissy (English) a familiar form of Christina.
Chrisie, Chrissee, Chrissie, Crissie, Khrissy

Christa 🅖 (German) a short form
of Christina. History: Christa
McAuliffe, an American school
teacher, was the first civilian on a
U.S. space flight. See also Krista.
Chrysta, Crista, Crysta

Christabel (Latin, French) beautiful
Christian.
*Christabell, Christabella, Christabelle,
Christable, Cristabel, Kristabel*

Christain 🅑 (Greek) a form of
Christina.
Christana, Christann, Christanna

Christal (Latin) a form of Crystal.
(Scottish) a form of Christina.
*Christalene, Christalin, Christaline,
Christall, Christalle, Christalyn,
Christelle, Christle, Chrystal*

Christelle (French) a form of Christal.
*Christel, Christele, Christell, Chrystel,
Chrystelle*

Christen 🅖 (Greek) a form of
Christin. See also Kristen.
*Christan, Christyn, Chrystan, Chrysten,
Chrystyn, Crestienne*

Christena (Greek) a form of
Christina.

Christi (Greek) a short form of
Christina, Christine. See also Kristi.
Christy, Chrysti, Chrysty

Christian 🅑 (Greek) a form of
Christina.

Christiana, Christianna (Greek)
forms of Christina. See also
Kristian, Krystian.
*Christiane, Christiann, Christi-Ann,
Christianne, Christi-Anne, Christianni,
Christiaun, Christiean, Christien,
Christiena, Christienne, Christinan,
Christy-Ann, Christy-Anne, Crystian,
Chrystyann, Chrystyanne, Crystiann,
Crystianne*

Christie 🅖 (Greek) a short form of
Christina, Christine.
Christy, Chrysti, Chrysty

Christin 🅖 (Greek) a short form of
Christina.
Chrystin

Christina 🅖 (Greek) Christian;
anointed. See also Khristina,
Kristina, Stina, Tina.
*Chris, Chrissa, Chrissy, Christa,
Christain, Christal, Christeena,
Christella, Christen, Christena, Christi,
Christian, Christie, Christin, Christinaa,
Christine, Christinea, Christinia,
Christinna, Christinnah, Christna,
Christy, Christyn, Christyna, Christynna,
Chrystina, Chrystyna, Cristeena,
Cristena, Cristina, Crystina, Chrystena,
Cristena*

Christine 🅖 (French, English) a
form of Christina. See also Kirsten,
Kristen, Kristine.
*Chrisa, Christeen, Christen, Christene,
Christi, Christie, Christy, Chrystine,
Cristeen, Cristene, Cristine, Crystine*

Christophe 🅑 (Greek) a form of
Christopher.

Christopher 🅑 (Greek) Christ-
bearer.

Christy 🅖 (English) a short form of
Christina, Christine.
Cristy

Christyn (Greek) a form of
Christina.
Christyne

Chrys (English) a form of Chris.
Krys

Chrystal (Latin) a form of Christal.
*Chrystale, Chrystalla, Chrystallina,
Chrystallynn*

Chu (Chinese) neat.

Chu Hua (Chinese) chrysanthemum.

Chuan (Chinese) river.

Chubasca (Chamorro) storm at sea.

Chul (Korean) law, rule; pattern, model.

Chumani (Lakota) dewdrops.
Chumany

Chun **B** (Burmese) nature's renewal.

Chung (Korean) lotus; lovely.

Chunni (Indian) a star.

Chuo (Chinese) ample.

Chyanne, Chyenne (Cheyenne) forms of Cheyenne.
Chyan, Chyana, Chyane, Chyann, Chyanna, Chyeana, Chyenn, Chyenna, Chyennee

Chyna, Chynna (Chinese) forms of China.

Chyou (Chinese) autumn.

Ci (Chinese) tenderhearted.

Ciana (Chinese) a form of China. (Italian) a form of Jane.
Cian, Ciandra, Ciann, Cianna

Ciara, Ciarra **G** (Irish) black. See also Sierra.
Ceara, Chiairah, Ciaara, Ciaera, Ciaira, Ciarah, Ciaria, Ciarrah, Cieara, Ciearra, Ciearria, Ciera, Cierra, Cioria, Cyarra

Cibeles (Greek) mythological goddess.

Cicely (English) a form of Cecilia. See also Sissy.
Cicelia, Cicelie, Ciciley, Cicilia, Cicilie, Cicily, Cile, Cilka, Cilla, Cilli, Cillie, Cilly

Cidney (French) a form of Sydney.
Cidnee, Cidni, Cidnie

Cielo (Latin) she who is celestial.

Ciera, Cierra (Irish) forms of Ciara.
Ceira, Cierah, Ciere, Cieria, Cierrah, Cierre, Cierria, Cierro

Cilji (Indian) lovely girl.

Cinderella (French, English) little cinder girl. Literature: a fairy tale heroine.
Cindella

Cindy **G** (Greek) moon. (Latin) a familiar form of Cynthia. See also Sindy.
Cindee, Cindi, Cindie, Cyndi

Cinthia, Cinthya (Greek) forms of Cynthia.
Cinthiya, Cintia

Cíntia (Portuguese) a form of Cynthia.

Cipriana (Greek) from Cyprus.

Ciprina (Spanish) blessed by the goddess of love.

Cira (Spanish) a form of Cyrilla.

Circe (Greek) from Greek mythology.

Cirenia, Cirinea (Greek) native of Cyrene, Libya.

Ciri (Greek) lady-like.

Ciríaca (Spanish) she who is the property of the Lord; belonging to God.

Cirila (Greek) great king or Almighty One.

Cissy (American) a familiar form of Cecelia, Cicely.
Cissey, Cissi, Cissie

Citlali (Nahuatl) star.

Claire ✿ **G** (French) a form of Clara.
Clair, Klaire, Klarye

Clairissa (Greek) a form of Clarissa.
Clairisa, Clairisse, Claraissa

Clara 🅖 (Latin) clear; bright.
Music: Clara Shumann was a
famous nineteenth-century German
composer. See also Chiara, Klara.
*Claira, Claire, Clarabelle, Clare,
Claresta, Clarice, Clarie, Clarina,
Clarinda, Clarine, Clarissa, Clarita*

Clarabelle (Latin) bright and
beautiful.
Clarabella, Claribel, Claribell

Clare 🅖 (English) a form of Clara.

Clarence 🅑 (Latin) clear;
victorious.

Clarice (Italian) a form of Clara.
*Claris, Clarise, Clarisse, Claryce,
Cleriese, Klarice, Klarise*

Clarie (Latin) a familiar form of Clara.
Clarey, Clari, Clary

Clarisa (Greek) a form of Clarissa.
Claresa, Clarise, Clarisia

Clarissa 🅖 (Greek) brilliant. (Italian)
a form of Clara. See also Klarissa.
*Clairissa, Clarecia, Claressa, Claresta,
Clarisa, Clarissia, Claritza, Clarizza,
Clarrisa, Clarrissa, Clerissa*

Clarita (Spanish) a form of Clara.
*Clairette, Clareta, Claretta, Clarette,
Claritza*

Clark 🅑 (French) cleric; scholar.

Claude 🅑 (Latin, French) lame.

Claudette (French) a form of Claudia.
Clauddetta

Claudia (Latin) lame. See also
Gladys, Klaudia.
*Claudeen, Claudel, Claudelle,
Claudette, Claudex, Claudiana,
Claudiane, Claudie, Claudie-Anne,
Claudina, Claudine*

Claudie 🅖 (Latin) a form of
Claudia.
Claudee

Claudio 🅑 (Italian) a form of
Claude.

Clayton 🅑 (English) town built on
clay.

Clea (Greek) a form of Cleo, Clio.

Clementine (Latin) merciful.
*Clemence, Clemencia, Clemencie,
Clemency, Clementia, Clementina,
Clemenza, Clemette*

Clemira (Arabic) illuminated,
brilliant princess.

Clena (Marshallese) to arrive at the
burial ground.

Cleo (Greek) a short form of
Cleopatra.
Chleo, Clea

Cleodora (Greek) she who
represents the gift of God.

Cleofe (Greek) she who shows signs
of glory.

Cleone (Greek) famous.
Cleonie, Cleonna, Cliona

Cleopatra (Greek) her father's fame.
History: a great Egyptian queen.
Cleo

Cleta (Greek) illustrious.

Clidia (Greek) agitated in the sea.

Clifton 🅑 (English) cliff town.

Clio (Greek) proclaimer; glorifier.
Mythology: the Muse of history.
Clea

Clío (Greek) a form of Clio.

Clitemestra (Greek) Mythology: a
form of Clytemnestra, the daughter
of Tyndareus and Leda.

Cloe (Greek) a form of Chloe.
Clo, Cloei, Cloey, Cloie

Clorinda (Greek) fresh, healthy-looking, and vital.

Clotilda (German) heroine.

Clotilde (Teutonic) illustrious warrior full of wisdom.

Clovis (Teutonic) illustrious warrior full of wisdom.

Coco **G** (Spanish) coconut. See also Koko.

Codey **B** (English) a form of Codi, Cody.

Codi **BG** (English) cushion. See also Kodi.
Coady, Codee, Codey, Codia, Codie

Codie **B** (English) a form of Codi, Cody.

Cody **B** (English) cushion.

Colby **B** (English) coal town. Geography: a region in England known for cheese-making.
Cobi, Cobie, Colbi, Colbie

Cole **B** (Irish) a short form of Colleen.

Coleman **B** (Latin) cabbage farmer. (English) coal miner.

Coleta (French) victory of the people.

Colette (Greek, French) a familiar form of Nicole.
Coe, Coetta, Coletta, Collet, Collete, Collett, Colletta, Collette, Kolette, Kollette

Colin **B** (Irish) young cub. (Greek) a short form of Nicholas (see Boys' Names).

Colleen (Irish) girl. See also Kolina.
Coe, Coel, Cole, Coleen, Colene, Coley, Coline, Colleene, Collen, Collene, Collie, Collina, Colline, Colly

Collin **B** (Scottish) a form of Colin.

Collina (Irish) a form of Colleen.
Colena, Colina, Colinda

Collipal (Mapuche) colored star.

Coloma, Columbia (Spanish) forms of Colomba.

Colomba (Latin) dove.

Colt **B** (English) young horse; frisky. A short form of Colton.

Colton **B** (English) coal town.

Comemaulig (Chamorro) getting better.

Concepción (Latin) she who conceives; related to the virginal miracle of Jesus' mother.

Concetta (Italian) pure.
Concettina, Conchetta

Conchita (Spanish) conception.
Chita, Conceptia, Concha, Conciana

Concordia (Latin) harmonious. Mythology: the goddess governing the peace after war.
Con, Cordae, Cordaye

Conejo (Chamorro) what was caught.

Conexo (Chamorro) a form of Conejo.

Conner **B** (Scottish, Irish) a form of Connor.

Connie **G** (Latin) a familiar form of Constance.
Con, Connee, Conni, Conny, Konnie, Konny

Connie-Kim (Vietnamese) pearls.

Connor **B** (Scottish) wise. (Irish) praised; exhalted.
Connar, Conner, Connery, Conor

Conor ☒ (Scottish, Irish) a form of Connor.

Consolación (Latin) consolation.

Constance (Latin) constant; firm. History: Constance Motley was the first African-American woman to be appointed as a U.S. federal judge. See also Konstance, Kosta.
Connie, Constancia, Constancy, Constanta, Constantia, Constantina, Constantine, Constanza, Constynse

Constanza (Spanish) a form of Constance.
Constanz, Constanze

Consuelo (Spanish) consolation. Religion: Nuestra Señora del Consuelo Our Lady of Consolation
is a name for the Virgin Mary.
Consolata, Consuela, Consuella, Consula, Conzuelo, Konsuela, Konsuelo

Cooper ☒ (English) barrel maker.

Cora (Greek) maiden. Mythology: Kore is another name for Persephone, the goddess of the underworld. See also Kora.
Corah, Coralee, Coretta, Corissa, Corey, Corra

Corabelle (American) a combination of Cora + Belle.
Corabel, Corabella

Coral (Latin) coral. See also Koral.
Coraal, Corral

Coralee (American) a combination of Cora + Lee.
Coralea, Cora-Lee, Coralena, Coralene, Coraley, Coralie, Coraline, Coraly, Coralyn, Corella, Corilee, Koralie

Coralie (American) a form of Coralee.
Corali, Coralia, Coralina, Coralynn, Coralynne

Corazon (Spanish) heart.

Corbin ☒ (Latin) raven.
Corbe, Corbi, Corby, Corbyn, Corbynn

Cordasha (American) a combination of Cora + Dasha.

Cordelia (Latin) warm-hearted. (Welsh) sea jewel. See also Delia, Della.
Cordae, Cordelie, Cordett, Cordette, Cordi, Cordilia, Cordilla, Cordula, Kordelia, Kordula

Cordi (Welsh) a short form of Cordelia.
Cordey, Cordia, Cordie, Cordy

Coretta (Greek) a familiar form of Cora.
Coreta, Corette, Correta, Corretta, Corrette, Koretta, Korretta

Corey, Cory ☒ (Irish) from the hollow. (Greek) familiar forms of Cora. See also Kori.
Coree, Cori, Correy, Correye, Corry

Cori ☒ (Irish) a form of Corey.

Coriann, Corianne (American) combinations of Cori + Ann, Cori + Anne.
Corian, Coriane, Cori-Ann, Corri, Corrie-Ann, Corrianne, Corrie-Anne

Corie, Corrie (Irish) forms of Corey.

Corina, Corinna (Greek) familiar forms of Corinne. See also Korina.
Coreena, Coriana, Corianna, Corinda, Correna, Corrinna, Coryna

Corinne (Greek) maiden.
Coreen, Coren, Corin, Corina, Corine, Corinee, Corinn, Corinna, Corrina, Coryn, Corynn, Corynne

Corissa (Greek) a familiar form of Cora.
Coresa, Coressa, Corisa, Coryssa, Korissa

Corliss (English) cheerful; goodhearted.
Corlisa, Corlise, Corlissa, Corly, Korliss

Cornelia (Latin) horn colored. See also Kornelia, Nelia, Nellie.
Carna, Carniella, Corneilla, Cornela, Cornelie, Cornella, Cornelle, Cornie, Cornilear, Cornisha, Corny

Cornelius **B** (Greek) cornel tree. (Latin) horn colored.

Corrina, Corrine (Greek) forms of Corinne.
Correen, Corren, Corrin, Corrinn, Corrinna, Corrinne, Corrinne, Corryn

Cortney **G** (English) a form of Courtney.
Cortne, Cortnea, Cortnee, Cortneia, Cortni, Cortnie, Cortny, Cortnye, Corttney

Cosette (French) a familiar form of Nicole.
Cosetta, Cossetta, Cossette, Cozette

Coty **B** (French) slope, hillside.

Courtenay (English) a form of Courtney.
Courtaney, Courtany, Courteney, Courteny

Courtnee, Courtnie (English) forms of Courtney.
Courtne, Courtnée, Courtnei, Courtneigh, Courtni, Courtnii

Courtney **G** (English) from the court. See also Kortney, Kourtney.
Cortney, Courtena, Courtenay, Courtene, Courtnae, Courtnay, Courtnee, Courtny, Courtonie

Covadonga (Spanish) large cave that is close to Asturias, which is the scene of the Spanish avocation of the Virgin Mary.

Craig **B** (Irish, Scottish) crag; steep rock.

Crescencia (Spanish) growth.

Crimilda (German) she fights wearing a helmet.

Crisanta (Spanish) golden flower.

Crisbell (American) a combination of Crista + Belle.
Crisbel, Cristabel

Crispina (Latin) having curly locks of hair.

Crista, Crysta (Italian) forms of Christa.
Cristah

Cristal **G** (Latin) a form of Crystal.
Cristalie, Cristalina, Cristalle, Cristel, Cristela, Cristelia, Cristella, Cristelle, Cristhie, Cristle

Cristen, Cristin (Irish) forms of Christen, Christin. See also Kristin.
Cristan, Cristyn, Crystan, Crysten, Crystin, Crystyn

Cristian **B** (Greek) a form of Christian.

Cristiana (Spanish) Christian, follower of Christ.

Cristina, Cristine (Greek) forms of Christina. See also Kristina.
Cristiona, Cristy

Cristy (English) a familiar form of Cristina. A form of Christy. See also Kristy.
Cristey, Cristi, Cristie, Crysti, Crystie, Crysty

Cruz **B** (Portuguese, Spanish) cross.

Cruzita (Spanish) a form of Cruz.

Crystal 🄶 (Latin) clear, brilliant
glass. See also Kristal, Krystal.
Christal, Chrystal, Chrystal-Lynn,
Chrystel, Cristal, Crystala, Crystale,
Crystalee, Crystalin, Crystall, Crystalle,
Crystaly, Crystel, Crystela, Crystelia,
Crystelle, Crysthelle, Crystl, Crystle,
Crystol, Crystole, Crystyl

Crystalin (Latin) crystal pool.
Crystal-Ann, Cristalanna, Crystal-Anne,
Cristalina, Cristallina, Cristalyn,
Crystallynn, Crystallynne, Cristilyn,
Crystalina, Crystal-Lee, Crystal-Lynn,
Crystalyn, Crystalynn

Crystina (Greek) a form of Christina.
Crystin, Crystine, Crystyn, Crystyna,
Crystyne

Cui (Chinese) resplendent.

Cullen 🄱 (Irish) beautiful.

Curipán (Mapuche) brave lioness;
black mountain; valorous soul.

Curran 🄱 (Irish) heroine.
Cura, Curin, Curina, Curinna

Curtis 🄱 (Latin) enclosure.
(French) courteous.

Custodia (Latin) guardian angel.

Cuyen (Mapuche) moon.

Cybele (Greek) a form of Sybil.
Cybel, Cybil, Cybill, Cybille

Cydney (French) a form of Sydney.
Cydne, Cydnee, Cydnei, Cydni, Cydnie

Cyerra (Irish) a form of Ciara.
Cyera, Cyerria

Cyndi (Greek) a form of Cindy.
Cynda, Cyndal, Cyndale, Cyndall,
Cyndee, Cyndel, Cyndia, Cyndie,
Cyndle, Cyndy

Cynthia 🄶 (Greek) moon.
Mythology: another name for

Artemis, the moon goddess. See
also Hyacinth, Kynthia.
Cindy, Cinthia, Cyneria, Cynethia,
Cynithia, Cynthea, Cynthiana,
Cynthiann, Cynthie, Cynthria, Cynthy,
Cynthya, Cyntia, Cyntreia, Cythia,
Synthia

Cyrilla (Greek) noble.
Cerelia, Cerella, Cira, Cirilla, Cyrella,
Cyrille

Cyteria (Greek) goddess of love.

Czaee (Indian) name of a flower.

D

D 🄱 (American) an initial used as a
first name.

Da (Chinese) eldest.

Dabria (Latin) name of an angel.

Dacey 🄶 (Irish) southerner.
(Greek) a familiar form of Candace.
Dacee, Dacei, Daci, Dacia, Dacie,
Dacy, Daicee, Daici, Daicie, Daicy,
Daycee, Daycie, Daycy

Dacia (Irish) a form of Dacey.
Daciah

Dadau (Chamorro) fierce, ferocious.

Daddi (Chamorro) young coconut.

Dae (English) day. See also Dai.

Daeja (French) a form of Déja.
Daejah, Daejia

Daelynn (American) a combination
of Dae + Lynn.
Daeleen, Daelena, Daelin, Daelyn,
Daelynne

Daeshandra (American) a combination of Dae + Shandra.
Daeshandria, Daeshaundra, Daeshaundria, Daeshawndra, Daeshawndria, Daeshondra, Daeshondria

Daeshawna (American) a combination of Dae + Shawna.
Daeshan, Daeshaun, Daeshauna, Daeshavon, Daeshawn, Daeshawntia, Daeshon, Daeshona

Daeshonda (American) a combination of Dae + Shonda.
Daeshanda, Daeshawnda

Dafny (American) a form of Daphne.
Dafany, Daffany, Daffie, Daffy, Dafna, Dafne, Dafney, Dafnie

Dagmar (German) glorious.
Dagmara

Dagny (Scandinavian) day.
Dagna, Dagnanna, Dagne, Dagney, Dagnie

Dago (Chamorro) a type of plant.

Dahlia (Scandinavian) valley. Botany: a perennial flower. See also Daliah.
Dahliah, Dahlya, Dahlye

Dai **G** (Japanese) great. See also Dae.
Day, Daye

Daija, Daijah (French) forms of Déja.
Daijaah, Daijea, Daijha, Daijhah, Dayja

Daila (Latin) beautiful like a flower.

Daisha (American) a form of Dasha.
Daesha, Daishae, Daishia, Daishya, Daisia

Daisy (English) day's eye. Botany: a white and yellow flower.
Daisee, Daisey, Daisi, Daisia, Daisie, Dasey, Dasi, Dasie, Dasy, Daysi, Deisy

Daja, Dajah (French) forms of Déja.
Dajae, Dajai, Daje, Dajha, Dajia

Dakayla (American) a combination of the prefix Da + Kayla.
Dakala, Dakila

Dakira (American) a combination of the prefix Da + Kira.
Dakara, Dakaria, Dakarra, Dakirah, Dakyra

Dakota **B** (Native American) a tribal name.
Dakkota, Dakoda, Dakotah, Dakotha, Dakotta, Dekoda, Dekota, Dekotah, Dekotha

Dakotah **B** (Native American) a form of Dakota.

Daksha (Indian) the Earth; wife of Lord Shiva.

Dakshata (Indian) skill.

Dalaja (Indian) honey.

Dale **B** (English) valley.
Dael, Dahl, Daile, Daleleana, Dalena, Dalina, Dayle

Dalia, Daliah (Hebrew) branch. See also Dahlia.
Daelia, Dailia, Daleah, Daleia, Dalialah, Daliyah

Dalila (Swahili) gentle.
Dalela, Dalida, Dalilah, Dalilia

Dalisha (American) a form of Dallas.
Dalisa, Dalishea, Dalishia, Dalishya, Dalisia, Dalissia

Dallas **B** (Irish) wise.
Dalis, Dalise, Dalisha, Dalisse, Dallace, Dallis, Dallise, Dallus, Dallys, Dalyce, Dalys

Dallen **B** (English) a form of Dallan (see Boys' Names).

Dallyn **B** (English) pride's people.

Dalma (Spanish) a form of Dalmacia.

Dalmacia (Latin) native of Dalmacia.

Dalmira (Teutonic) illustrious; respected for her noble ancestry.

Dalton 🅱 (English) town in the valley.

Damaris 🅶 (Greek) gentle girl. See also Maris.
Dama, Damar, Damara, Damarius, Damary, Damarylis, Damarys, Dameress, Dameris, Damiris, Dammaris, Dammeris, Damris, Demaras, Demaris

Damasia (Spanish) a form of Dalmacia.

Damayanti (Indian) wife of Nala.

Damian 🅱 (Greek) tamer; soother.

Damiana (Greek) a form of Damian.
Daimenia, Daimiona, Damia, Damiann, Damianna, Damianne, Damien, Damienne, Damiona, Damon, Demion

Damica (French) friendly.
Damee, Dameeka, Dameka, Damekah, Damicah, Damicia, Damicka, Damie, Damieka, Damika, Damikah, Damyka, Demeeka, Demeka, Demekah, Demica, Demicah

Damien 🅱 (Greek) a form of Damian.

Damini (Indian) lightning.

Damita (Spanish) small noblewoman.
Damee, Damesha, Dameshia, Damesia, Dametia, Dametra, Dametrah

Damon 🅱 (Greek) a form of Damian.

Damonica (American) a combination of the prefix Da + Monica.
Damonec, Damoneke, Damonik, Damonika, Damonique, Diamoniqua, Diamonique

Damyanti (Indian) beautiful.

Dan 🅱 (Vietnamese) yes. (Hebrew) a short form of Daniel.

Dana 🅶 (English) from Denmark; bright as day.
Daina, Dainna, Danah, Danaia, Danan, Danarra, Dane, Danean, Danna, Dayna

Danae (Greek) Mythology: the mother of Perseus.
Danaë, Danay, Danayla, Danays, Danai, Danea, Danee, Dannae, Denae, Denee

Dánae (Greek) a form of Danae.

Danalyn (American) a combination of Dana + Lynn.
Danalee, Donaleen

Danas (Spanish) a form of Dana.

D'andre 🅱 (French) a form of Deandre.

Dane 🅱 (English) a form of Dana.

Daneil (Hebrew) a form of Danielle.
Daneal, Daneala, Daneale, Daneel, Daneela, Daneila

Danella (American) a form of Danielle.
Danayla, Danela, Danelia, Danelle, Danna, Donella, Donnella

Danelle (Hebrew) a form of Danielle.
Danael, Danalle, Danel, Danele, Danell, Danella, Donelle, Donnelle

Danesha, Danisha (American) forms of Danessa.
Daneisha, Daneshia, Daniesha, Danishia

Danessa (American) a combination of Danielle + Vanessa. See also Doneshia.
Danasia, Danesa, Danesha, Danessia, Daniesa, Danisa, Danissa

Danessia (American) a form of
Danessa.
Danesia, Danieshia, Danisia, Danissia

Danette (American) a form of
Danielle.
Danetra, Danett, Danetta, Donnita

Dani (Hebrew) a familiar form of
Danielle.
*Danee, Danie, Danne, Dannee, Danni,
Dannie, Danny, Dannye, Dany*

Dania, Danya (Hebrew) short forms
of Danielle.
Daniah, Danja, Dannia, Danyae

Danica, Danika ᴳ (Slavic) morning
star. (Hebrew) forms of Danielle.
*Daneca, Daneeka, Daneekah, Danicah,
Danicka, Danieka, Danikah, Danikla,
Danneeka, Dannica, Dannika,
Dannikah, Danyka, Denica, Donica,
Donika, Donnaica, Donnica, Donnika*

Danice (American) a combination of
Danielle + Janice.
Donice

Daniel ᴮ (Hebrew, French) God is
my judge.

Daniela (Italian) a form of Danielle.
Daniellah, Dannilla, Danijela

Danielan (Spanish) a form of
Danielle.

Daniella (English) a form of Dana.
Danka, Danniella, Danyella

Danielle ᴳ (Hebrew, French) a
form of Daniel.
*Daneen, Daneil, Daneille, Danelle,
Dani, Danial, Danialle, Danica, Daniel,
Daniela, Danielan, Daniele, Danielka,
Daniell, Daniella, Danilka, Danille,
Danit, Dannielle, Danyel, Donniella*

Danille (American) a form of Danielle.
Danila, Danile, Danilla, Dannille

Danit (Hebrew) a form of Danielle.
*Danett, Danis, Danisha, Daniss, Danita,
Danitra, Danitrea, Danitria, Danitza,
Daniz*

Danna (Hebrew) a short form of
Danella.
Dannah

Dannielle (Hebrew, French) a form
of Danielle.
Danniel, Danniele, Danniell

Danny ᴮ (Hebrew) a form of Dani.

Dante, Danté ᴮ (Latin) lasting,
enduring.

Dany ᴮ (Hebrew) a form of Dani.

Danyel ᴳ (American) a form of
Danielle.
*Daniyel, Danyae, Danyail, Danyaile,
Danyal, Danyale, Danyea, Danyele,
Danyiel, Danyle, Donnyale, Donyale*

Danyell, Danyelle (American)
forms of Danyel.
Danyielle, Donnyell, Donyell

Dao (Vietnamese) golden girl.

Daphne (Greek) laurel tree.
*Dafny, Daphane, Daphany, Dapheney,
Daphna, Daphnee, Daphnique,
Daphnit, Daphny*

Daphnee (Greek) a form of
Daphne.
*Daphaney, Daphanie, Daphney,
Daphni, Daphnie*

Dara ᴳ (Hebrew) compassionate.
*Dahra, Daira, Dairah, Darah, Daraka,
Daralea, Daralee, Daraleigh, Daralie,
Daravie, Darda, Darice, Darisa,
Darissa, Darja, Darra, Darrah*

Darby ᴳ (Irish) free. (Scandinavian)
deer estate.
*Darb, Darbe, Darbee, Darbi, Darbie,
Darbra, Darbye*

Darcelle (French) a form of Darci.
Darcel, Darcell, Darcella, Darselle

Darci, Darcy 🄶 (Irish) dark.
(French) fortress.
*Darcee, Darcelle, Darcey, Darcie,
Darsey, Darsi, Darsie*

Daria (Greek) wealthy.
*Dari, Daría, Dariya, Darria, Darya,
Daryia*

Darian, Darrian 🄱🄶 (Greek) forms
of Daron.
*Dariana, Dariane, Dariann, Darianna,
Darianne, Dariyan, Dariyanne,
Darriana, Darriane, Darriann,
Darrianna, Darrianne, Derrian, Driana*

Darielle (French) a form of Daryl.
*Dariel, Dariela, Dariell, Darriel,
Darrielle*

Darien, Darrien 🄱 (Greek) forms
of Daron.
Dariene, Darienne, Darriene

Darika (Indian) maiden.

Darilynn (American) a form of
Darlene.
*Daralin, Daralyn, Daralynn, Daralynne,
Darilin, Darilyn, Darilynne, Darlin,
Darlyn, Darlynn, Darlynne, Darylin,
Darylyn, Darylynn, Darylynne*

Darin 🄱 (Irish) a form of Darren.

Darion, Darrion 🄱 (Irish) forms
of Daron.
*Dariona, Darione, Darionna, Darionne,
Darriona, Darrionna*

Darius 🄱 (Greek) wealthy.

Darla (English) a short form of
Darlene.
*Darlecia, Darli, Darlice, Darlie, Darlis,
Darly, Darlys*

Darlene (French) little darling. See
also Daryl.
*Darilynn, Darla, Darlean, Darlee,
Darleen, Darleene, Darlena, Darlenia,*

*Darlenne, Darletha, Darlin, Darline,
Darling, Darlyn, Darlynn, Darlynne*

Darnee (Irish) a familiar form of
Darnelle.

Darnell 🄱 (English) a form of
Darnelle.

Darnelle (English) hidden place.
*Darnee, Darnel, Darnell, Darnella,
Darnesha, Darnetta, Darnette, Darnice,
Darniece, Darnita, Darnyell*

Darnesha, Darnisha (American)
forms of Darnelle.
*Darneisha, Darneishia, Darneshea,
Darneshia, Darnesia, Darniesha,
Darnishia, Darnisia, Darrenisha*

Daron (Irish) great.
*Darian, Darien, Darion, Daronica,
Daronice, Darron, Daryn*

Darpana (Indian) mirror.

Darrell (English, French) a form of
Daryl.

Darren 🄱 (Irish) great. (English)
small; rocky hill.

Darryl 🄱 (English, French) a form
of Daryl.

Darselle (French) a form of
Darcelle.
Darsel, Darsell, Darsella

Darshana (Indian) observation.

Darshwana (Indian) pure of heart.

Daru (Hindi) pine tree.

Daryl 🄱 (English) beloved.
(French) a short form of Darlene.
*Darelle, Darielle, Daril, Darilynn,
Darrel, Darrell, Darrelle, Darreshia,
Darryl, Darryll, Daryll, Darylle*

Daryn (Greek) gifts. (Irish) great.
*Daron, Daryan, Daryne, Darynn,
Darynne*

Dasha, Dasia (Russian) forms of Dorothy.
Daisha, Dashae, Dashenka, Dashia, Dashiah, Dasiah, Daysha

Dashawn **B** (American) a form of Dashawna.

Dashawna (American) a combination of the prefix Da + Shawna.
Dashawnna, Dashay, Dashell, Dayshana, Dayshawnna, Dayshona, Deshawna

Dashiki (Swahili) loose-fitting shirt worn in Africa.
Dashi, Dashika, Dashka, Desheka, Deshiki

Dashonda (American) a combination of the prefix Da + Shonda.
Dashawnda, Dishante

Davalinda (American) a combination of Davida + Linda.
Davalynda, Davelinda, Davilinda, Davylinda

Davalynda (American) a form of Davalinda.
Davelynda, Davilynda, Davylynda

Davalynn (American) a combination of Davida + Lynn.
Davalin, Davalyn, Davalynne, Davelin, Davelyn, Davelynn, Davelynne, Davilin, Davilyn, Davilynn, Davilynne, Dayleen, Devlyn

Dave **B** (Hebrew) a short form of David, Davis.

David **B** (Hebrew) beloved.

Davida (Hebrew) a form of David. See also Vida.
Daveta, Davetta, Davette, Davika, Davita

Davin **B** (Scottish) a form of Davina.

Davina (Scottish) a form of Davida. See also Vina.
Dava, Davannah, Davean, Davee, Daveen, Daveena, Davene, Daveon,

Davey, Davi, Daviana, Davie, Davin, Davinder, Davine, Davineen, Davinia, Davinna, Davonna, Davria, Devean, Deveen, Devene, Devina

Davion **B** (Scottish, English) a form of Davonna.

Davis **B** (American) a form of Davisha.

Davisha (American) a combination of the prefix Da + Aisha.
Daveisha, Davesia, Davis, Davisa

Davon **B** (Scottish, English) a short form of Davonna.

Davonna (Scottish, English) a form of Davina, Devonna.
Davion, Daviona, Davionna, Davon, Davona, Davonda, Davone, Davonia, Davonne, Davonnia

Davonte **B** (American) a combination of Davon + the suffix Te.

Dawn **G** (English) sunrise, dawn.
Dawana, Dawandrea, Dawanna, Dawin, Dawna, Dawne, Dawnee, Dawnetta, Dawnisha, Dawnlynn, Dawnn, Dawnrae

Dawna (English) a form of Dawn.
Dawnna, Dawnya

Dawnisha (American) a form of Dawn.
Dawnesha, Dawni, Dawniell, Dawnielle, Dawnisia, Dawniss, Dawnita, Dawnnisha, Dawnysha, Dawnysia

Dawnyelle (American) a combination of Dawn + Danielle.
Dawnele, Dawnell, Dawnelle, Dawnyel, Dawnyella

Dawson **B** (English) child of David.

Da-Xia (Chinese) big hero.

Dayamayee (Indian) kind.

Dayamayi, Dayanita (Indian) merciful.

Dayana (Latin) a form of Diana.
Dayanara, Dayani, Dayanna, Dayanne, Dayanni, Deyanaira, Dyani, Dyanna, Dyia

Dayanira (Greek) she stirs up great passions.

Dayita (Indian) beloved.

Dayle (English) a form of Dale.
Dayla, Daylan, Daylea, Daylee

Dayna (Scandinavian) a form of Dana.
Daynah, Dayne, Daynna, Deyna

Daysha (American) a form of Dasha.
Daysa, Dayshalie, Daysia, Deisha

Daysi, Deysi (English) forms of Daisy.
Daysee, Daysia, Daysie, Daysy, Deysia, Deysy

Dayton 🅱 (English) day town; bright, sunny town.

Daytona (English) a form of Dayton.
Daytonia

De 🅱 (Chinese) virtuous.

Dean 🅱 (French) leader. (English) valley.

Deana 🅶 (Latin) divine. (English) a form of Dean.
Deanah, Deane, Deanielle, Deanisha, Deanna, Deeana, Deeann, Deeanna, Deena

Deandra (American) a combination of Dee + Andrea.
Dandrea, Deandre, Deandré, Deandrea, Deandree, Deandreia, Deandria, Deanndra, Deaundra, Deaundria, Deeandra, Deyaneira, Deondra, Diandra, Diandre, Diandrea, Diondria, Dyandra

Deandre 🅱 (American) a form of Deandra, Deanna.

Deangela (Italian) a combination of the prefix De + Angela.
Deangala, Deangalique, Deangle

Deanna 🅶 (Latin) a form of Deana, Diana.
Deaana, Deahana, Deandra, Deandre, Déanna, Deannia, Deeanna, Deena

Deanne (Latin) a form of Diane.
Deahanne, Deane, Deann, Déanne, Deeann, Dee-Ann, Deeanne

Debbie (Hebrew) a short form of Deborah.
Debbee, Debbey, Debbi, Debby, Debee, Debi, Debie

Débora, Déborah (Hebrew) forms of Deborah.

Deborah 🅶 (Hebrew) bee. Bible: a great Hebrew prophetess.
Deb, Debbie, Debbora, Debborah, Deberah, Debor, Debora, Deboran, Deborha, Deborrah, Debra, Debrena, Debrina, Debroah, Devora, Dobra

Debra (American) a form of Deborah.
Debbra, Debbrah, Debrah, Debrea, Debria

Dedra (American) a form of Deirdre.
Deeddra, Deedra, Deedrea, Deedrie

Dedriana (American) a combination of Dedra + Adriana.
Dedranae

Dee (Welsh) black, dark.
De, Dea, Deah, Dede, Dedie, Deea, Deedee, Dee Dee, Didi

Deeba (Indian) silk.

Deena (American) a form of Deana, Dena, Dinah.

Deepa, Deepal (Indian) light.

Deepabali, Deepamala, Deepavali (Indian) row of lamps.

Deepakala (Indian) evening time; the time to light lamps.

Deepali (Indian) collection of lamps.

Deepanwita (Indian) lit by lamps.

Deepaprabha (Indian) light of lamps.

Deepashikha (Indian) the flame of a lamp.

Deepjyoti (Indian) the light of the lamp.

Deepshika, Deepika, Dipashri (Indian) lamp.

Deepta (Indian) luminous, glowing, bright.

Deepti (Indian) full of light.

Deeptikana (Indian) a beam of light.

Deeptimoyee (Indian) lustrous.

Deidamia (Greek) she who is patient in battle.

Deidra, Deidre (Irish) forms of Deirdre.
Deidrah, Deidrea, Deidrie, Diedra, Diedre, Dierdra

Deina (Spanish) religious holiday.

Deion **B** (Greek) a form of Dion.

Deirdre (Irish) sorrowful; wanderer.
Dedra, Deerdra, Deerdre, Deidra, Deidre, Deirdree, Didi, Diedra, Dierdre, Diérdre, Dierdrie

Deisy (English) a form of Daisy.
Deisi, Deissy

Deitra (Greek) a short form of Demetria.
Deetra, Detria

Deja **G** (French) a form of Déja.

Déja (French) before.
Daeja, Daija, Deejay, Dejae, Déjah, Dejai, Dejanae, Dejanelle, Dejon

Dejanae (French) a form of Déja.
Dajahnae, Dajona, Dejana, Dejanah, Dejanae, Dejanai, Dejanay, Dejane, Dejanea, Dejanee, Dejanna, Dejannaye, Dejena, Dejonae

Dejanira (Greek) destroyer of men.

Dejon (French) a form of Déja.
Daijon, Dajan, Dejone, Dejonee, Dejonelle, Dejonna

Deka (Somali) pleasing.
Dekah

Delacy (American) a combination of the prefix De + Lacy.
Delaceya

Delainey (Irish) a form of Delaney
Delaine, Delainee, Delaini, Delainie, Delainy

Delana (German) noble protector.
Dalanna, Dalayna, Daleena, Dalena, Dalenna, Dalina, Dalinda, Dalinna, Delaina, Delania, Delanya, Delayna, Deleena, Delena, Delenya, Delina, Dellaina

Delaney **G** (Irish) descendant of the challenger. (English) a form of Adeline.
Dalaney, Dalania, Dalene, Daleney, Daline, Del, Delainey, Delane, Delanee, Delanie, Delany, Delayne, Delayney, Delaynie, Deleani, Déline, Della, Dellaney

Delanie (Irish) a form of Delaney.
Delani

Delfina (Greek) a form of Delphine. (Spanish) dolphin.
Delfeena, Delfine

Delia (Greek) visible; from Delos, Greece. (German, Welsh) a short form of Adelaide, Cordelia. Mythology: a festival of Apollo held in ancient Greece.
Dehlia, Delea, Deli, Deliah, Deliana, Delianne, Delinda, Dellia, Dellya, Delya

Delicia (English) delightful.
Delecia, Delesha, Delice, Delisa, Delise, Delisha, Delishia, Delisiah, Delya, Delys, Delyse, Delysia, Doleesha

Delilah (Hebrew) brooder. Bible: the companion of Samson. See also Lila.
Dalialah, Dalila, Daliliah, Delila, Delilia

Della (English) a short form of Adelaide, Cordelia, Delaney.
Del, Dela, Dell, Delle, Delli, Dellie, Dells

Delma (German) noble protector.

Delmara (Latin) of the sea.

Delmira (Spanish) a form of Dalmira.

Delores (Spanish) a form of Dolores.
Delora, Delore, Deloria, Delories, Deloris, Delorise, Delorita, Delsie

Delphine ☆ (Greek) from Delphi, Greece. See also Delfina.
Delpha, Delphe, Delphi, Delphia, Delphina, Delphinia, Delvina

Delsie (English) a familiar form of Delores.
Delsa, Delsey, Delza

Delta (Greek) door. Linguistics: the fourth letter in the Greek alphabet. Geography: a triangular land mass at the mouth of a river.
Delte, Deltora, Deltoria, Deltra

Demetria ☆ (Greek) cover of the earth. Mythology: Demeter was the Greek goddess of the harvest.
Deitra, Demeta, Demeteria, Demetra, Demetriana, Demetrianna, Demetrias, Demetrice, Demetriona, Demetris, Demetrish, Demetrius, Demi, Demita, Demitra, Demitria, Dymitra

Demetrius ☒ (Greek) a form of Demetria.

Demi (French) half. (Greek) a short form of Demetria.
Demia, Demiah, Demii, Demmi, Demmie, Demy

Demofila (Greek) friend of the village.

Den (Japanese) bequest from ancestors.

Dena (English, Native American) valley. (Hebrew) a form of Dinah. See also Deana.
Deane, Deena, Deeyn, Denae, Denah, Dene, Denea, Deney, Denna, Deonna

Denae (Hebrew) a form of Dena.
Denaé, Denay, Denee, Deneé

Deng (Chinese) light.

Deni (French) a short form of Denise.
Deney, Denie, Denni, Dennie, Denny, Dinnie, Dinny

Denica, Denika (Slavic) forms of Danica.
Denikah, Denikia

Denis ☒ (Greek) a form of Dennis.

Denisa (Spanish) god of wine.

Denise ☆ (French) Mythology: follower of Dionysus, the god of wine.
Danice, Danise, Denese, Deni, Denice, Denicy, Deniece, Denisha, Denisse, Denize, Dennise, Dennys, Denyce, Denys, Denyse

Denisha (American) a form of Denise.
Deneesha, Deneichia, Deneisha, Deneishea, Denesha, Deneshia, Deniesha, Denishia

Denisse (French) a form of Denise.
Denesse, Denissa

Dennis **B** (Greek) Mythology: a follower of Dionysus, the god of wine.

Denver **B** (English) green valley. Geography: the capital of Colorado.

Denzel **B** (Cornish) a form of Denzell (see Boys' Names).

Deon **B** (English) a short form of Deonna.

Deonilde (German) she who fights.

Deonna (English) a form of Dena. *Deona, Deonah, Deondra, Deonne*

Deonte **B** (American) a form of Deontae (see Boys' Names).

Dep (Vietnamese) chrysanthemum.

Derek **B** (German) a short form of Theodoric (see Boys' Names).

Derika (German) ruler of the people. *Dereka, Derekia, Derica, Dericka, Derrica, Derricka, Derrika*

Derrick **B** (German) ruler of the people. A form of Derek.

Derry **BG** (Irish) redhead. *Deri, Derie*

Deryn (Welsh) bird. *Derien, Derienne, Derion, Derin, Deron, Derren, Derrin, Derrine, Derrion, Derriona, Deryne*

Desarae (French) a form of Desiree. *Desara, Desarai, Desaraie, Desaray, Desare, Desaré, Desarea, Desaree, Desarie, Dezarae*

Desdemona (Greek) she who is very unfortunate; unhappy one.

Deserae, Desirae (French) forms of Desiree. *Desera, Deserai, Deseray, Desere, Deseree, Deseret, Deseri, Deserie, Deserrae, Deserray, Deserré, Dessirae,*

Dezeray, Dezere, Dezerea, Dezrae, Dezyrae

Deshawn **B** (American) a form of Deshawna.

Deshawna (American) a combination of the prefix De + Shawna. *Dashawna, Deshan, Deshane, Deshaun, Deshawn, Desheania, Deshona, Deshonna*

Deshawnda (American) a combination of the prefix De + Shawnda. *Deshanda, Deshandra, Deshaundra, Deshawndra, Deshonda*

Desi (French) a short form of Desiree. *Désir, Desira, Dezi, Dezia, Dezzia, Dezzie*

Desideria (French) desired or longed for.

Desiha (Indian) happy; lemon.

Desiree (French) desired, longed for. See also Dessa. *Chesarey, Desarae, Deserae, Desi, Desirae, Desirah, Desirai, Desiray, Desire, Desirea, Desireah, Desirée, Désirée, Desirey, Desiri, Desray, Desree, Dessie, Dessire, Dezarae, Dezirae, Deziree*

Dessa (Greek) wanderer. (French) a form of Desiree.

Desta (Ethiopian) happy. (French) a short form of Destiny. *Desti, Destie, Desty*

Destany (French) a form of Destiny. *Destanee, Destaney, Destani, Destanie, Destannee, Destannie*

Destin **B** (French) a form of Destiny.

Destina (Spanish) fate.

Destinee, Destini, Destinie
(French) forms of Destiny.
Desteni, Destiana, Destine, Destinée,
Destnie

Destiney (French) a form of Destiny.

Destiny ☆ **G** (French) fate.
Desnine, Desta, Destany, Destenee,
Destenie, Desteny, Destin, Destinee,
Destiney, Destini, Destinie, Destonie,
Destynee, Dezstany

Destynee, Destyni (French) forms
of Destiny.
Desty, Desfyn, Destyne, Destyne,
Destynie

Deva (Hindi) divine.
Deeva

Devahuti (Indian) daughter of
Manu.

Devaki, Devki (Indian) the mother
of Lord Krishna.

Devan **B** (Irish) a form of Devin.
Devana, Devane, Devanee, Devaney,
Devani, Devanie, Devann, Devanna,
Devannae, Devanne, Devany

Devangana (Indian) celestial
maiden.

Devangi, Devyani (Indian) like a
goddess.

Devanshi (Indian) divine.

Devashri, Devasree (Indian) divine
beauty.

Deven **B** (Irish) a form of Devin.

Devera (Spanish) task.

Devi (Hindi) goddess. Religion: the
Hindu goddess of power and
destruction.

Devin **B** (Irish) poet.
Devan, Deven, Devena, Devenje,
Deveny, Devine, Devinn, Devinne, Devyn

Devishi (Indian) chief of the
goddesses.

Devkanya (Indian) divine damsel.

Devmani (Indian) divine gift.

Devon **B** (English) a short form of
Devonna. (Irish) a form of Devin.
Deaven, Devion, Devione, Devionne,
Devone, Devoni, Devonne

Devonna (English) from
Devonshire.
Davonna, Devon, Devona, Devonda,
Devondra, Devonia

Devonta **B** (American) a
combination of Devon + the suffix
Ta.

Devonte **B** (American) a combination of Devon + the suffix Te.

Devora (Hebrew) a form of
Deborah.
Deva, Devorah, Devra, Devrah

Devota (Latin) faithful to God.

Devyn **BG** (Irish) a form of Devin.
Deveyn, Devyne, Devynn, Devynne

Dewi (Indonesian) goddess.

Dextra (Latin) adroit, skillful.
Dekstra, Dextria

Deyanira (Latin) destroyer of men.

Dezarae, Dezirae, Deziree
(French) forms of Desiree.
Dezaraee, Dezarai, Dezaray, Dezare,
Dezaree, Dezarey, Dezerie, Deziray,
Dezirea, Dezirée, Dezorae, Dezra

Dhanishta (Indian) the name of a
nakshatra, a star constellation.

Dhanvanti (Indian) holding wealth.

Dhanya (Indian) thankful; lucky.

Dhanyata (Indian) success;
fulfillment.

Dharani, Dharitri (Indian) the Earth.

Dharini, Dharti, Dhatri (Indian) earth.

Dhriti (Indian) patience.

Dhruti (Indian) motion.

Dhruvi (Indian) firm.

Dhuha (Indian) forenoon.

Dhvani (Indian) sound, voice.

Dhyana (Indian) meditation.

Di (Latin) a short form of Diana, Diane.
Dy

Dia (Latin) a short form of Diana, Diane.

Diamond **G** (Latin) precious gem.
Diamantina, Diamon, Diamonda, Diamonde, Diamonia, Diamonique, Diamonte, Diamontina, Dyamond

Diamondra (English) diamond. .

Diana 🌿 **G** (Latin) divine. Mythology: the goddess of the hunt, the moon, and fertility. See also Deanna, Deanne, Dyan.
Daiana, Daianna, Dayana, Dayanna, Di, Dia, Dianah, Dianalyn, Dianarose, Dianatris, Dianca, Diandra, Diane, Dianelis, Diania, Dianielle, Dianita, Dianna, Dianys, Didi

Diane, Dianne (Latin) short forms of Diana.
Deane, Deanne, Deeane, Deeanne, Di, Dia, Diahann, Dian, Diani, Dianie, Diann

Dianna (Latin) a form of Diana.
Diahanna, Diannah

Diantha (Greek) divine flower.
Diandre, Dianthe

Dibech (Palauan) one's beloved.

Die (Chinese) butterfly.

Diedra (Irish) a form of Deirdre.
Didra, Diedre

Diega (Spanish) supplanter.

Diella (Latin) she who adores God.

Diep (Vietnamese) peach blossom.

Digna (Latin) worthy.

Di'isha (Arabic) a form of Aisha.

Diksha (Indian) initiation.

Dilan (Indian) son of the sea.

Dilbelau (Palauan) termite.

Dilber (Indian) lover.

Dilchur (Palauan) to create.

Dillan **B** (Irish) loyal, faithful.
Dillon, Dillyn

Dillon **B** (Irish) a form of Dillan.

Dilngas (Palauan) woman of Palau.

Dilshad (Indian) happy.

Dilsubed (Palauan) laughing girl.

Dilys (Welsh) perfect; true.

Dimitri **B** (Russian) a form of Demetrius.

Dimple (Indian) dimples.

Dina (Hebrew) a form of Dinah.
Dinna, Dyna

Dinah (Hebrew) vindicated. Bible: a daughter of Jacob and Leah.
Dina, Dinnah, Dynah

Ding (Chinese) calm, stable.

Dinka (Swahili) people.

Dinora (Hebrew) avenged or vindicated.

Dinorah (Aramic) she who personifies light.

Diomira (Spanish) a form of Teodomira.

Dion 🅱 (Greek) a form of Dionne.

Dionisa (Greek) divine.

Dionisia (Greek) lover of wine; blessed by God in face of adversity.

Dionna (Greek) a form of Dionne.
Deona, Deondra, Deonia, Deonna, Deonyia, Diona, Diondra, Diondrea

Dionne (Greek) divine queen. Mythology: Dione was the mother of Aphrodite, the goddess of love.
Deonne, Dion, Dione, Dionee, Dionís, Dionna, Dionte

Dior (French) golden.
Diora, Diore, Diorra, Diorre

Dipali (Indian) lamps.

Dipti (Indian) brightness.

Dirngas (Palauan) ironwood woman.

Disha (Indian) direction.

Dishita (Indian) focus.

Dita (Spanish) a form of Edith.
Ditka, Ditta

Diti (Indian) idea.

Diu (Vietnamese) beautiful.

Diva (Latin) divine.

Divija (Indian) born to perform great things.

Divinia (Latin) divine.
Devina, Devinae, Devinia, Devinie, Devinna, Diveena, Divina, Divine, Diviniea, Divya

Divyata (Indian) divine lights.

Dixie (French) tenth. (English) wall; dike. Geography: a nickname for the American South.
Dix, Dixee, Dixi, Dixy

Diza (Hebrew) joyful.
Ditza, Ditzah, Dizah

Doan Vien (Vietnamese) leaves; type of trees that have red flowers.

Dodie (Hebrew) beloved. (Greek) a familiar form of Dorothy.
Doda, Dode, Dodee, Dodi, Dody

Dolly (American) a short form of Dolores, Dorothy.
Dol, Doll, Dollee, Dolley, Dolli, Dollie, Dollina

Dolon (Indian) scent of a beautiful white flower.

Dolores 🅶 (Spanish) sorrowful. Religion: Nuestra Señora de los Dolores

Our Lady of Sorrows is a name for the Virgin Mary. See also Lola.
Delores, Deloria, Dolly, Dolorcitas, Dolorita, Doloritas

Domenic 🅱 (Latin) an alternate form of Dominic.

Domicia (Greek) she who loves her house.

Domiciana (Spanish) a form of Domicia.

Dominga (Latin) a form of Dominica.

Dominic 🅱 (Latin) belonging to the Lord.

Domínica (Latin) a form of Dominica.

Dominica, Dominika (Latin) a form of Dominic. See also Mika.
Domenica, Domenika, Domineca, Domineka, Domini, Dominick,

Dominicka, Dominique, Dominixe, Domino, Dominyika, Domka, Domnicka, Domonica, Domonice, Domonika

Dominick **B** (Latin) a form of Dominica.

Dominique, Domonique **G** (French) forms of Dominica, Dominika.
Domanique, Domeneque, Domenique, Domineque, Dominiqua, Domino, Dominoque, Dominque, Dominuque, Domique, Domminique, Domoniqua

Domino (English) a short form of Dominica, Dominique.

Dominque **BG** (French) a form of Dominique.

Domítica (Spanish) a form of Dominga.

Domitila (Latin) she who loves her house.

Domoko (Pohnpeian) a form of Filomena.

Don **B** (Scottish) a short form of Donald (see Boys' Names).

Dona (English) world leader; proud ruler. (Italian) a form of Donna.
Donae, Donah, Donalda, Donaldina, Donelda, Donellia, Doni

Doña (Italian) a form of Donna.
Donail, Donalea, Donalisa, Donay, Doni, Donia, Donie, Donise, Donitrae

Donata (Latin) gift.
Donatha, Donato, Donatta, Donetta, Donette, Donita, Donnette, Donnita, Donte

Dondi (American) a familiar form of Donna.
Dondra, Dondrea, Dondria

Doneshia, Donisha (American) forms of Danessa.
Donasha, Donashay, Doneisha, Doneishia, Donesha, Donisa, Donisha, Donishia, Donneshia, Donnisha

Dong (Chinese) east; winter.

Donina (Latin) gift of God.

Donna (Italian) lady.
Doña, Dondi, Donnae, Donnalee, Donnalen, Donnay, Donne, Donnell, Donni, Donnie, Donnise, Donny, Dontia, Donya

Donnell **B** (Italian) a form of Donna.

Donnie **B** (Italian) a familiar form of Donna.

Donniella (American) a form of Danielle.
Donella, Doniele, Doniell, Doniella, Donielle, Donnella, Donnielle, Donnyella, Donyelle

Donosa (Latin) she who has grace and charm.

Donte **B** (Latin) a form of Donata.

Dontrell **B** (American) a form of Dantrell (see Boys' Names).

Dora (Greek) gift. A short form of Adora, Eudora, Pandora, Theodora.
Dorah, Doralia, Doralie, Doralisa, Doraly, Doralynn, Doran, Dorchen, Dore, Dorece, Doree, Doreece, Doreen, Dorelia, Dorella, Dorelle, Doresha, Doressa, Doretta, Dori, Dorielle, Dorika, Doriley, Dorilis, Dorinda, Dorion, Dorita, Doro, Dory

Doralynn (English) a combination of Dora + Lynn.
Doralin, Doralyn, Doralynne, Dorlin

Dorana (Spanish) a form of Dorotea.

Dorbeta (Spanish) reference to the Virgin Mary.

Dorcas (Greek) gazelle.

Doreen (Irish) moody, sullen. (French) golden. (Greek) a form of Dora.
Doreena, Dorena, Dorene, Dorina, Dorine

Dores (Portuguese) a form of Dolores.

Doretta (American) a form of Dora, Dorothy.
Doretha, Dorette, Dorettie

Dori, Dory (American) familiar forms of Dora, Doria, Doris, Dorothy.
Dore, Dorey, Dorie, Dorree, Dorri, Dorrie, Dorry

Doria (Greek) a form of Dorian.
Dori

Dorian 🅱 (Greek) from Doris, Greece.
Dorean, Doriana, Doriane, Doriann, Dorianna, Dorianne, Dorin, Dorina, Dorriane

Dorinda (Spanish) a form of Dora.

Doris (Greek) sea. Mythology: wife of Nereus and mother of the Nereids or sea nymphs.
Dori, Dorice, Dorisa, Dorise, Dorris, Dorrise, Dorrys, Dory, Dorys

Dorotea (Greek) a form of Dorothea.

Doroteia (Spanish) gift of God.

Dorotéia (Portuguese) a form of Doroteia.

Dorothea (Greek) a form of Dorothy. See also Thea.
Dorethea, Doroteya, Dorotha, Dorothia, Dorotthea, Dorthea, Dorthia

Dorothy (Greek) gift of God. See also Dasha, Dodie, Lolotea, Theodora.
Dasya, Do, Doa, Doe, Dolly, Doortje, Dorathy, Dordei, Dordi, Doretta, Dori, Dorika, Doritha, Dorka, Dorle, Dorlisa, Doro, Dorolice, Dorosia, Dorota, Dorothea, Dorothee, Dorothi, Dorothie, Dorottya, Dorte, Dortha, Dorthy, Dory, Dosi, Dossie, Dosya, Dottie

Dorrit (Greek) dwelling. (Hebrew) generation.
Dorit, Dorita, Doritt

Dottie, Dotty (Greek) familiar forms of Dorothy.
Dot, Dottee

Douglas 🅱 (Scottish) dark river, dark stream.

Doyel (Indian) a songbird.

Drake 🅱 (English) dragon; owner of the inn with the dragon trademark.

Draupadi (Indian) the wife of Pandavas.

Draven 🅱 (American) a combination of the letter D + Raven.

Drew 🅱 (Greek) courageous; strong. (Latin) a short form of Drusilla.
Dru, Drue

Drinka (Spanish) a form of Alexandria.
Dreena, Drena, Drina

Drishti, Drishya, Dristi (Indian) sight.

Drusi (Latin) a short form of Drusilla.
Drucey, Druci, Drucie, Drucy, Drusey, Drusie, Drusy

Drusihla (Pohnpeian) a form of Chiyako.

Drusilla (Latin) descendant of Drusus, the strong one. See also Drew.
Drewsila, Drucella, Drucill, Drucilla, Druscilla, Druscille, Drusi

Du (Chinese) sincere.

Duan (Chinese) upright, proper.

Duane B (Irish) a form of Dwayne.

Duda (Chamorro) doubtful, dubious.

Duk (Korean) third; soldier; protection.

Dulari (Indian) dear.

Dulce (Latin) sweet.
Delcina, Delcine, Douce, Doucie, Dulcea, Dulcey, Dulci, Dulcia, Dulciana, Dulcibel, Dulcibella, Dulcie, Dulcine, Dulcinea, Dulcy, Dulse, Dulsea

Dulcina, Dulcinia (Spanish) sweet.

Dulcinea (Spanish) sweet. Literature: Don Quixote's love interest.

Dung (Vietnamese) tender, gentle; mellow.

Dunia (Hebrew) life.

Duo (Chinese) much, more, many.

Durba, Durva (Indian) sacred grass.

Durga (Indian) a goddess.

Duscha (Russian) soul; sweetheart; term of endearment.
Duschah, Dusha, Dushenka

Dusti (English) a familiar form of Dustine.
Dustee, Dustie

Dustin B (German, English) a form of Dustine.

Dustine (German) valiant fighter. (English) brown rock quarry.
Dusteena, Dusti, Dustin, Dustina, Dustyn

Dusty B (English) a familiar form of Dustine.

Duyen (Vietnamese) happy reunion.

Dvita (Indian) existing in two forms; spiritual.

Dwayne B (Irish) dark.

Dwipavati (Indian) river.

Dyamond, Dymond (Latin) forms of Diamond.
Dyamin, Dyamon, Dyamone, Dymin, Dymon, Dymonde, Dymone, Dymonn

Dyana (Latin) a form of Diana. (Native American) deer.
Dyan, Dyane, Dyani, Dyann, Dyanna, Dyanne

Dylan B (Welsh) sea.
Dylaan, Dylaina, Dylana, Dylane, Dylanee, Dylanie, Dylann, Dylanna, Dylen, Dylin, Dyllan, Dylynn

Dyllis (Welsh) sincere.
Dilys, Dylis, Dylys

Dynasty (Latin) powerful ruler.
Dynastee, Dynasti, Dynastie

Dyshawna (American) a combination of the prefix Dy + Shawna.
Dyshanta, Dyshawn, Dyshonda, Dyshonna

Dyumna (Indian) glorious.

Dyuti (Indian) light.

E

E G (American) an initial used as a first name.

Ealani (Hawaiian) a form of Ewelani.

Earlene (Irish) pledge. (English)
noblewoman.
*Earla, Earlean, Earlecia, Earleen,
Earlena, Earlina, Earlinda, Earline, Erla,
Erlana, Erlene, Erlenne, Erlina, Erlinda,
Erline, Erlisha*

Eartha (English) earthy.
Ertha

Easter (English) Easter time.
History: a name for a child born on
Easter.
Eastan, Eastlyn, Easton

Ebe (Greek) youthful like a flower.

Ebil (Palauan) announcement,
message.

Ebone, Ebonee (Greek) forms of
Ebony.
*Abonée, Ebanee, Eboné, Ebonea,
Ebonne, Ebonnee*

Eboni, Ebonie (Greek) forms of
Ebony.
Ebanie, Ebeni, Ebonni, Ebonnie

Ebony ☑ (Greek) a hard, dark wood.
*Abony, Eban, Ebanie, Ebany, Ebbony,
Ebone, Eboney, Eboni, Ebonie,
Ebonique, Ebonisha, Ebonye, Ebonyi*

Ecchumati (Indian) a river.

Echa (Chamorro) to give blessing.

Echo (Greek) repeated sound.
Mythology: the nymph who pined
for the love of Narcissus until only
her voice remained.
Echoe, Ecko, Ekko, Ekkoe

Eda (Irish, English) a short form of
Edana, Edith.

Edana (Irish) ardent; flame.
Eda, Edan, Edanna

Edda (German) a form of Hedda.
Etta

Eddy ☑ (American) a familiar form
of Edwina.
Eady, Eddi, Eddie, Edy

Edelia (Greek) remains young.

Edeline (English) noble; kind.
Adeline, Edelyne, Ediline, Edilyne

Edelma, Edelmira (Teutonic) of
noble heritage; known for her noble
heritage.

Eden ☑ (Babylonian) a plain.
(Hebrew) delightful. Bible: the
earthly paradise.
*Eaden, Ede, Edena, Edene, Edenia,
Edin, Edyn*

Edén (Hebrew) a form of Eden.

Edgar ☑ (English) successful
spearman.

Edgarda (Teutonic) defends her
homes and land with a lance.

Edha (Indian) sacred.

Edie (English) a familiar form of
Edith.
Eadie, Edi, Edy, Edye, Eyde, Eydie

Edilia, Edilma (Greek) remains young.

Edith (English) rich gift. See also Dita.
*Eadith, Eda, Ede, Edetta, Edette, Edie,
Edit, Edita, Edite, Editha, Edithe, Editta,
Ediva, Edyta, Edyth, Edytha, Edythe*

Edna (Hebrew) rejuvenation.
Religion: the wife of Enoch,
according to the Book of Enoch.
*Adna, Adnisha, Ednah, Edneisha,
Edneshia, Ednisha, Ednita, Edona*

Edrianna (Greek) a form of Adrienne.
Edria, Edriana, Edrina

Eduarda (Teutonic) attentive
guardian of her domain.

Eduardo ☑ (Spanish) a form of
Edward (see Boys' Names).

Edurne (Basque) snow.

Eduviges (Teutonic) fighting woman.

Eduvijis (German) fortunate in battle.

Edwin 🅑 (English) prosperous friend.

Edwina (English) a form of Edwin. See also Winnie.
Eddy, Edina, Edweena, Edwena, Edwine, Edwyna, Edwynn

Eesha (Indian) purity.

Effia (Ghanaian) born on Friday.

Effie (Greek) spoken well of. (English) a short form of Alfreda, Euphemia.
Effi, Effia, Effy, Ephie

Efigenia (Greek) woman of strong heritage.

Efigênia (Portuguese) a form of Efigenia.

Egda (Greek) shield-bearer.

Egege (Chamorro) cardinal honey-eating bird.

Egeria (Greek) she who gives encouragement.

Egida (Spanish) born or having lived in Elade, Greece.

Egidia (Greek) warrior with a shield of goatskin.

Egigi (Chamorro) a form of Egege.

Ei (Japanese) flourishing; excellent.

Eiga (Japanese) long river.

Eiko (Japanese) flourishing child.

Eila (Indian) the Earth.

Eileen 🅖 (Irish) a form of Helen. See also Aileen, Ilene.
Eilean, Eileena, Eileene, Eilena, Eilene, Eiley, Eilie, Eilieh, Eilina, Eiline, Eilleen, Eillen, Eilyn, Eleen, Elene

Eira (Scandinavian) goddess-protectorate of health.

Eiravati (Indian) the Ravi River.

Ekaja (Indian) only child.

Ekanta (Indian) devoted girl.

Ekantika (Indian) singly focused.

Ekaparana (Indian) wife of Himalaya.

Ekata, Ekta, Ektaa (Indian) unity.

Ekaterina (Russian) a form of Katherine.
Ekaterine, Ekaterini

Ekavali (Indian) single string.

Ela (Polish) a form of Adelaide.

Eladia (Greek) born or having lived in Elade, Greece.

Elaina (French) a form of Helen.
Elainea, Elainia, Elainna

Elaine (French) a form of Helen. See also Lainey, Laine.
Eilane, Elain, Elaina, Elaini, Elan, Elana, Elane, Elania, Elanie, Elanit, Elauna, Elayna, Ellaine

Elaís (Spanish) a form of Elam.

Elam (Hebrew) highlands.

Elana (Greek) a short form of Eleanor. See also Ilana, Lana.
Elan, Elanee, Elaney, Elani, Elania, Elanie, Elanna, Elanni

Elata (Latin) elevated.

Elavarasi (Indian) princess.

Elayna (French) a form of Elaina.
Elayn, Elaynah, Elayne, Elayni

Elba (Latin) a form of Alba.

Elberta (English) a form of Alberta.
Elbertha, Elberthina, Elberthine, Elbertina, Elbertine

Elbia (Spanish) a form of Elba.

Elcira (Teutonic) noble adornment.

Elda (German) she who battles.

Eldora (Spanish) golden, gilded.
Eldoree, Eldorey, Eldori, Eldoria, Eldorie, Eldory

Eleadora (Spanish) gift of the sun.

Eleanor G (Greek) light. History: Anna Eleanor Roosevelt was a U.S. delegate to the United Nations, a writer, and the thirty-second First Lady of the United States. See also Elana, Ella, Ellen, Leanore, Lena, Lenore, Leonore, Leora, Nellie, Nora, Noreen.
Elana, Elanor, Elanore, Eleanora, Eleanore, Elena, Eleni, Elenor, Elenorah, Elenore, Eleonor, Eleonore, Elianore, Elinor, Elinore, Elladine, Ellenor, Ellie, Elliner, Ellinor, Ellinore, Elna, Elnore, Elynor, Elynore

Eleanora (Greek) a form of Eleanor. See also Lena.
Elenora, Eleonora, Elianora, Ellenora, Ellenorah, Elnora, Elynora

Electa (Greek) blonde like the sun.

Electra (Greek) shining; brilliant. Mythology: the daughter of Agamemnon, leader of the Greeks in the Trojan War.
Elektra

Elena (Greek) a form of Eleanor. (Italian) a form of Helen.
Eleana, Eleen, Eleena, Elen, Elene, Elenitsa, Elenka, Elenna, Elenoa, Elenola, Ellena, Lena

Eleni (Greek) a familiar form of Eleanor.
Elenie, Eleny

Eleodora (Greek) she who came from the sun.

Eleora (Hebrew) the Lord is my light.
Eliora, Elira, Elora

Eleutería (Spanish) free.

Elevuka (Fijian) from Levuka.

Elexis (Greek) a form of Alexis.
Elexas, Elexes, Elexess, Elexeya, Elexia, Elexiah

Elexus (Greek) a form of Alexius, Alexus.
Elexius, Elexsus, Elexxus, Elexys

Elfrida (German) peaceful. See also Freda.
Elfrea, Elfreda, Elfredda, Elfreeda, Elfreyda, Elfrieda, Elfryda

Elga (Norwegian) pious. (German) a form of Helga.
Elgiva

Eli B (Hebrew) uplifted. A short form of Elijah, Elisha.

Elia G (Hebrew) a short form of Eliana.
Eliah

Eliana (Hebrew) my God has answered me. See also Iliana.
Elia, Eliane, Elianna, Ellianna, Liana, Liane

Eliane (Hebrew) a form of Eliana.
Elianne, Elliane, Ellianne

Elicia (Hebrew) a form of Elisha. See also Alicia.
Elecia, Elica, Elicea, Elicet, Elichia, Eliscia, Elisia, Elissia, Ellecia, Ellicia

Elida, Elide (Latin) forms of Alida.
Elidee, Elidia, Elidy

Eligia (Italian, Spanish) chosen one.

Elihna (Pohnpeian) a form of Tomoko.

Elijah **B** (Hebrew) a form of Eliyahu (see Boys' Names).

Elina (Greek, Italian) a form of Elena.

Elisa (Spanish, Italian, English) a short form of Elizabeth. See also Alisa, Ilisa.
Elecea, Eleesa, Elesa, Elesia, Elisia, Elisya, Ellisa, Ellisia, Ellissa, Ellissia, Ellissya, Ellisya, Elysa, Elysia, Elyssia, Elyssya, Elysya, Lisa

Elisabete (Portuguese) consecrated to God.

Elisabeth **G** (Hebrew) a form of Elizabeth.
Elisabet, Elisabeta, Elisabethe, Elisabetta, Elisabette, Elisabith, Elisebet, Elisheba, Elisheva

Elisapeci, Eliseva (Fijian) forms of Elizabeth.

Elise (French, English) a short form of Elizabeth, Elysia. See also Ilise, Liese, Lisette, Lissie.
Eilis, Eilise, Elese, Elise, Elisee, Elisie, Elisse, Elizé, Ellice, Ellise, Ellyce, Ellyse, Ellyze, Elsey, Elsie, Elsy, Elyce, Elyci, Elyse, Elyze, Lisel, Lisl, Lison

Elisea (Hebrew) God is salvation, protect my health.

Elisha **BG** (Hebrew) consecrated to God. (Greek) a form of Alisha. See also Ilisha, Lisha.
Eleacia, Eleasha, Eleesha, Eleisha, Elesha, Eleshia, Eleticia, Elicia, Elishah, Elisheva, Elishia, Elishua, Eliska, Ellesha, Ellexia, Ellisha, Elsha, Elysha, Elyshia

Elissa (Greek, English) a form of Elizabeth. A short form of Melissa. See also Alissa, Alyssa, Lissa.
Elissah, Ellissa, Ellyssa, Ilissa, Ilyssa

Elita (Latin, French) chosen. See also Lida, Lita.
Elitia, Elitia, Elitie, Ellita, Ellitia, Ellitie, Ilida, Ilita, Litia

Eliza (Hebrew) a short form of Elizabeth. See also Aliza.
Eliz, Elizaida, Elizalina, Elize, Elizea

Elizabet (Hebrew) a form of Elizabeth.
Elizabete, Elizabette

Elizabeth ✡ **G** (Hebrew) consecrated to God. Bible: the mother of John the Baptist. See also Bess, Beth, Betsy, Betty, Elsa, Ilse, Libby, Liese, Liesel, Lisa, Lisbeth, Lisette, Lissa, Lissie, Liz, Liza, Lizabeta, Lizabeth, Lizbeth, Lizina, Lizzy, Veta, Yelisabeta, Zizi.
Alizabeth, Eliabeth, Elisa, Elisabeth, Elise, Elissa, Eliza, Elizabee, Elizabet, Elizaveta, Elizebeth, Elka, Elsabeth, Elsbeth, Elschen, Elspeth, Elysabeth, Elzbieta, Elzsébet, Helsa, Ilizzabet, Lusa

Elizapet (Pohnpeian) a form of Drusilla.

Elizaveta (Polish, English) a form of Elizabeth.
Elisavet, Elisaveta, Elisavetta, Elisveta, Elizavet, Elizavetta, Elizveta, Elsveta, Elzveta

Elka (Polish) a form of Elizabeth.
Ilka

Elke (German) a form of Adelaide, Alice.
Elki, Ilki

Ella ✡ **G** (English) elfin; beautiful fairy-woman. (Greek) a short form of Eleanor.
Ellah, Ellamae, Ellia, Ellie

Elle (Greek) a short form of Eleanor. (French) she.
El, Ele, Ell

Ellen (English) a form of Eleanor, Helen.
Elen, Elenee, Eleny, Elin, Elina, Elinda, Ellan, Ellena, Ellene, Ellie, Ellin, Ellon, Ellyn, Ellynn, Ellynne, Elyn

Ellice (English) a form of Elise.
Ellecia, Ellyce, Elyce

Ellie G (English) a short form of Eleanor, Ella, Ellen.
Ele, Elie, Ellee, Elleigh, Elli

Elliot, Elliott B (English) forms of Eli, Elijah.

Ellis B (English) a form of Elias.

Elly (English) a short form of Eleanor, Ella, Ellen.

Elma (Turkish) sweet fruit.

Elmira (Arabic, Spanish) a form of Almira.
Elmeera, Elmera, Elmeria, Elmyra

Elnohra (Pohnpeian) a form of Elena.

Elnora (American) a combination of Ella + Nora.

Elodie (American) a form of Melody. (English) a form of Alodie.
Elodee, Elodia, Elody

Eloísa (German) a form of Louise.

Eloise (French) a form of Louise.
Elois, Eloisa, Eloisia

Elora (American) a short form of Elnora.
Ellora, Elloree, Elorie

Elpidia (Greek) she who waits faithfully, who lives her life waiting.

Elsa (German) noble. (Hebrew) a short form of Elizabeth. See also Ilse.
Ellsa, Ellse, Else, Elsia, Elsie, Elsje

Elsbeth (German) a form of Elizabeth.
Elsbet, Elzbet, Elzbieta

Elsie (German) a familiar form of Elsa, Helsa.
Ellsie, Ellsie, Ellsy, Elsi, Elsy

Elspeth (Scottish) a form of Elizabeth.
Elspet, Elspie

Elva (English) elfin. See also Alva, Alvina.
Elvia, Elvie

Elvina (English) a form of Alvina.
Elvenea, Elvinea, Elvinia, Elvinna

Elvira (Latin) white; blond. (German) closed up. (Spanish) elfin. Geography: the town in Spain that hosted a Catholic synod in 300 A. D.
Elva, Elvera, Elvire, Elwira, Vira

Elvisa (Teutonic) famous warrior.

Elvita (Spanish) truth.

Elyse (Latin) a form of Elysia.
Ellysa, Ellyse, Elyce, Elys, Elysee, Elysse

Elysia (Greek) sweet; blissful. Mythology: Elysium was the dwelling place of happy souls.
Elise, Elishia, Ellicia, Elycia, Elyssa, Ilysha, Ilysia

Elyssa (Latin) a form of Elysia.
Ellyssa

Emalee (Latin) a form of Emily.
Emaili, Emalea, Emaleigh, Emali, Emalia, Emalie

Emani (Arabic) a form of Iman.
Eman, Emane, Emaneé, Emanie, Emann

Emanuel B (Hebrew) a form of Emanuelle.

Emanuelle (Hebrew) a form of
Emmanuelle.
*Emanual, Emanuel, Emanuela,
Emanuella*

Ember (French) a form of Amber.
Emberlee, Emberly

Emelia, Emelie (Latin) forms of
Emily.
Emellie

Emelinda (Teutonic) hard-working
and kind.

Emely (Latin) a form of Emily.
Emelly

Emerald (French) bright green
gemstone.
Emelda, Esmeralda

Emerenciana (Latin) she who will
be rewarded.

Emerita (Latin) she who God
rewards for her virtues.

Emerson **B** (German, English)
child of Emery.

Emery **B** (German) industrious
leader.
Emeri, Emerie

Emesta (Spanish) serious.

Emiko (Japanese) blessed and
beautiful child.

Emile **B** (English) a form of Emilee.

Emilee, Emilie (English) forms of
Emily.
*Emile, Emilea, Emileigh, Émilie, Emiliee,
Emillee, Emillie, Emmélie, Emmilee,
Emylee*

Emilia (Italian) a form of Amelia,
Emily.
Emalia, Emelia, Emila

Emilio **B** (Italian, Spanish) a form
of Emil (see Boys' Names).

Emily ✿ **G** (Latin) flatterer.
(German) industrious. See also
Amelia, Emma, Millie.
*Eimile, Em, Emaily, Emalee, Emeli,
Emelia, Emelie, Emelita, Emely, Emilee,
Emiley, Emili, Emilia, Emilie, Émilie,
Emilis, Emilka, Emillie, Emilly, Emmaline,
Emmaly, Emmélie, Emmey, Emmi, Emmie,
Emmilly, Emmily, Emmy, Emmye, Emyle*

Emilyann (American) a combination
of Emily + Ann.
*Emileane, Emileann, Emileanna,
Emileanne, Emiliana, Emiliann,
Emilianna, Emilianne, Emillyane,
Emillyann, Emillyanna, Emillyanne,
Emliana, Emliann, Emlianna, Emlianne*

Emma ✿ **G** (German) a short
form of Emily. See also Amy.
Em, Ema, Emmah, Emmy

Emmalee (American) a combination
of Emma + Lee. A form of Emily.
*Emalea, Emalee, Emilee, Emmalea,
Emmalei, Emmaleigh, Emmaley, Emmali,
Emmalia, Emmalie, Emmaliese,
Emmalyse, Emylee*

Emmaline (French) a form of Emily.
*Emalina, Emaline, Emelina, Emeline,
Emilienne, Emilina, Emiline, Emmalina,
Emmalene, Emmeline, Emmiline*

Emmalynn (American) a combi-
nation of Emma + Lynn.
*Emelyn, Emelyne, Emelynne, Emilyn,
Emilynn, Emilynne, Emlyn, Emlynn,
Emlynne, Emmalyn, Emmalynne*

Emmanuel **B** (Hebrew) God is
with us.

Emmanuela (Hebrew) a form of
Emmanuelle.

Emmanuelle **G** (Hebrew) a form
of Emmanuel.
Emanuelle, Emmanuella

Emmy (German) a familiar form of
Emma.
*Emi, Emie, Emiy, Emmi, Emmie, Emmye,
Emy*

Emmylou (American) a combination
of Emmy + Lou.
*Emlou, Emmalou, Emmelou, Emmilou,
Emylou*

Emna (Teutonic) hard-working and
kind.

Emory 🅱 (German) a form of
Emery.

Emperatriz (Latin) she who is the
sovereign leader.

En (Chinese) favor, grace.

Ena (Irish) a form of Helen.
Enna

Enakshi (Indian) one with eyes like a
deer.

Enara (Basque) name given to a
swallow.

Encarna, Encarnita (Spanish)
forms of Encarnación.

Encarnación (Latin) alluding to the
incarnation of Jesus in his mother,
Mary.

Enedina (Greek) warm or indulgent.

Enerika (Pohnpeian) a form of
Elizabeth.

Enerita (Chuukese) a form of
Hilaria.

Enid (Welsh) life; spirit.

Enisa (Chuukese) a form of
Elizabeth.

Enma (Hebrew) a form of
Emmanuela.

Enrica (Spanish) a form of Henrietta.
See also Rica.
*Enrieta, Enrietta, Enrika, Enriqua,
Enriqueta, Enriquetta, Enriquette*

Epifanía (Spanish) epiphany.

Eppie (English) a familiar form of
Euphemia.
Effie, Effy, Eppy

Er (Chinese) jade or pearl earring.

Ercilia (Greek) she who is delicate,
tender, kind.

Erendira, Erendiria (Spanish) one
with a smile.

Erensia (Chamorro) heritage.

Eria (Indian) cat.

Eriahna (Pohnpeian) a form of
Eleanor.

Eric 🅱 (Scandinavian) ruler of all.
(English) brave ruler. (German) a
short form of Frederick (see Boys'
Names).

Erica 🅶 (Scandinavian) ruler of all.
(English) brave ruler. See also Arica,
Rica, Ricki.
Érica, Ericca, Ericha, Ericka, Errica

Ericka (Scandinavian) a form of Erica.
Erickah, Erricka

Erik 🅱 (Scandinavian) a form of
Eric.

Erika 🅶 (Scandinavian) a form of
Erica.
*Erikaa, Erikah, Erikka, Errika, Eyka,
Erykka, Eyrika*

Eriko (Japanese) child with a collar.

Erin 🄶 (Irish) peace. History: another name for Ireland. See also Arin.
Earin, Earrin, Eran, Eren, Erena, Erene, Ereni, Eri, Erian, , Erine, Erinetta, Erinn, Errin, Eryn

Erina (Irish) a form of Erin.

Erinda (Spanish) a form of Erina.

Erinn (Irish) a form of Erin.
Erinna, Erinne

Erma (Latin) a short form of Ermine, Hermina. See also Irma.
Ermelinda

Ermenilda (German) powerful warrior.

Ermine (Latin) a form of Hermina.
Erma, Ermin, Ermina, Erminda, Erminie

Erminia (Latin) a form of Ermine.

Erna (English) a short form of Ernestine.

Ernestine (English) earnest, sincere.
Erna, Ernaline, Ernesia, Ernesta, Ernestina, Ernesztina

Eryn 🄶 (Irish) a form of Erin.
Eiryn, Eryne, Erynn, Erynne

Escolástica (Latin) she who knows much and teaches.

Eshana (Indian) search.

Eshe (Swahili) life.
Eisha, Esha

Eshita (Indian) one who desires.

Esisihna (Pohnpeian) a form of Enriqueta.

Esiteri (Fijian) a form of Esther.

Esiuch (Palauan) a form of Dilngas.

Eskolastika (Pohnpeian) a form of Ariana.

Esmé (French) a familiar form of Esmeralda. A form of Amy.
Esma, Esme, Esmëe

Esmerada (Latin) shining, standing out. radiates purity and hope.

Esmeralda (Greek, Spanish) a form of Emerald.
Emelda, Esmé, Esmerelda, Esmerilda, Esmiralda, Ezmerelda, Ezmirilda

Esperanza (Spanish) hope. See also Speranza.
Esparanza, Espe, Esperance, Esperans, Esperansa, Esperanta, Esperanz, Esperenza

Essence (Latin) life; existence.
Essa, Essenc, Essencee, Essences, Essenes, Essense, Essynce

Essie (English) a short form of Estelle, Esther.
Essa, Essey, Essie, Essy

Estaquia (Spanish) possessor of a head of wheat.

Estebana (Spanish) crowned with laurels.

Ested (Chamorro) a form of Esther.

Estee (English) a short form of Estelle, Esther.
Esta, Estée, Esti

Estefani, Estefania, Estefany (Spanish) forms of Stephanie.
Estafania, Estefana, Estefane, Estefanía, Estefanie

Estela (French) a form of Estelle.

Estelinda (Teutonic) she who is noble and protects the village.

Estelle (French) a form of Esther. See also Stella, Trella.
Essie, Estee, Estel, Estele, Esteley, Estelina, Estelita, Estell, Estella, Estellina, Estellita, Esthella

Estephanie (Spanish) a form of
Stephanie.
Estephania, Estephani, Estephany

Esterina (Greek) she who is strong
and vital.

Esterlaine (Persian) a form of Azad.

Esteva (Greek) crowned with laurels.

Esther (Persian) star. Bible: the
Jewish captive whom Ahasuerus
made his queen. See also Hester.
Essie, Estee, Ester, Esthur, Eszter, Eszti

Estherlita (Persian) noble.

Esthermae (Persian) a form of Esther.

Estralita (Spanish) a form of
Estrella.

Estrella (French) star.
*Estrela, Estrelinha, Estrell, Estrelle,
Estrellita*

Eta (Indian) luminous.

Etel (Spanish) a short form of
Etelvina.

Etelinda (German) noble one that
protects her village.

Etelvina (German) she who is a loyal
and noble friend.

Ethan 🅱 (Hebrew) strong; firm.

Ethana (Hebrew) a form of Ethan.

Ethel (English) noble.
*Ethelda, Ethelin, Etheline, Ethelle,
Ethelyn, Ethelynn, Ethelynne, Ethyl*

Etienne 🅱 (French) a form of
Stephen.

Étoile (French) star.

Etor (Palauan) woman.

Etsu (Japanese) delight.

Etsuko (Japanese) blessed child.

Etta (German) little. (English) a
short form of Henrietta.
Etka, Etke, Etti, Ettie, Etty, Itke, Itta

Eudocia, Eudosia, Eudoxia
(Greek) famous one, very
knowledgeable.

Eudora (Greek) honored gift. See
also Dora.

Eufrasia (Greek) she who is full of joy.

Eugene 🅱 (Greek) born to nobility.

Eugenia (Greek) a form of Eugene.
See also Gina.
Eugenie, Eugenina, Eugina, Evgenia

Eugània (Portuguese) a form of
Eugenia.

Eugenie (Greek) a form of Eugenia.
Eugenee, Eugénie

Eulalia (Greek) well spoken. See also
Ula.
Eula, Eulalee, Eulalie, Eulalya, Eulia

Eulália (Portuguese) a form of
Eulalia.

Eulogia (Greek) she who speaks
eloquently.

Eumelia (Greek) she who sings well,
the melodious one.

Eun (Korean) silver.

Eunice (Greek) happy; victorious.
Bible: the mother of Saint Timothy.
See also Unice.
Euna, Eunique, Eunise, Euniss

Eunomia (Greek) good order.

Euphemia (Greek) spoken well of, in
good repute. History: a fourth-
century Christian martyr.
*Effam, Effie, Eppie, Eufemia, Euphan,
Euphemie, Euphie*

Eurídice (Greek) a form of Eurydice.

Eva ☆ **G** (Greek) a short form of
Evangelina. (Hebrew) a form of
Eve. See also Ava, Chava.
Éva, Evah, Evalea, Evalee, Evike

Evalani, Evalonni, Evelanie
(Hawaiian) forms of Ewelani.

Evaline (French) a form of Evelyn.
*Evalin, Evalina, Evalyn, Evalynn,
Eveleen, Evelene, Evelina, Eveline*

Evan **B** (Irish) young warrior.

Evangelina (Greek) bearer of good
news.
*Eva, Evangelene, Evangelia, Evangelica,
Evangeline, Evangelique, Evangelyn,
Evangelynn*

Evangelina Eny (Irish) fire.

Evania (Irish) a form of Evan.
*Evana, Evanka, Evann, Evanna, Evanne,
Evany, Eveania, Evvanne, Evvunea,
Evyan*

Evarista (Greek) excellent one.

Eve (Hebrew) life. Bible: the first
woman created by God. (French) a
short form of Evonne. See also
Chava, Hava, Naeva, Vica, Yeva.
Eva, Evie, Evita, Evuska, Evyn, Ewa, Yeva

Evelia (Hebrew) she who generates
life.

Evelin (English) a form of Evelyn.
Evelina, Eveline

Evelyn ☆ **G** (English) hazelnut.
*Avalyn, Aveline, Evaleen, Evalene,
Evaline, Evalyn, Evalynn, Evalynne,
Eveleen, Evelin, Evelyna, Evelyne,
Evelynn, Evelynne, Evline, Ewalina*

Everett **B** (German) courageous as
a boar.

Everilda (German) she who fought
with the wild boar.

Evette (French) a form of Yvette. A
familiar form of Evonne. See also
Ivette.
Evett

Evie (Hungarian) a form of Eve.
*Evey, Evi, Evicka, Evike, Evka, Evuska,
Evvie, Evvy, Evy, Ewa*

Evita (Spanish) a form of Eve.

Evline (English) a form of Evelyn.
*Evleen, Evlene, Evlin, Evlina, Evlyn,
Evlynn, Evlynne*

Evodia (Greek) she who always
wants others to have a good trip.

Evonne (French) a form of Yvonne.
See also Ivonne.
*Evanne, Eve, Evenie, Evenne, Eveny,
Evette, Evin, Evon, Evona, Evone, Evoni,
Evonna, Evonnie, Evony, Evyn, Evynn,
Eyona, Eyvone*

Ewalani (Hawaiian) a form of
Ewelani.

Ewelani (Hawaiian) chief of divine
descent.

Exal (Spanish) diminutive form of
Exaltación.

Exaltación (Spanish) lifted up.

Ezmeralda (Spanish) emerald.

Ezra 🅱 (Hebrew) a form of Ezri.

Ezri (Hebrew) helper; strong.
Ezra, Ezria

Faasi (Chamorro) clean.

Faatin, Faatina (Indian) captivating.

Fabia (Latin) bean grower.
Fabiana, Fabienne, Fabiola, Fabra,
Fabria

Fabian 🅱 (Latin) a form of
Fabienne.

Fabiana (Latin) a form of Fabia.
Fabyana

Fabienne (Latin) a form of Fabia.
Fabian, Fabiann, Fabianne, Fabiene,
Fabreanne

Fabiola, Faviola (Latin) forms of
Fabia.
Fabiole, Fabyola, Faviana, Faviolha

Fabricia (Latin) artisan, daughter of
artisans.

Fachalang (Chamorro) make a path.

Fachalig (Chamorro) she who laughs
a lot; she who pretends to laugh.

Facunda (Latin) eloquent speaker.

Fadheela (Indian) virtue.

Fadwa (Indian) name derived from
self-sacrifice.

Faedeng (Chamorro) federico palm.

Faith ☀ 🅶 (English) faithful;
fidelity. See also Faye, Fidelity.
Fayth, Faythe

Faizah (Arabic) victorious.

Fajyaz (Indian) artistic.

Falda (Icelandic) folded wings.
Faida, Fayda

Faline (Latin) catlike.
Faleen, Falena, Falene, Falin, Falina,
Fallyn, Fallyne, Faylina, Fayline, Faylyn,
Faylynn, Faylynne, Felenia, Felina

Fallon 🅶 (Irish) grandchild of the
ruler.
Falan, Falen, Fallan, Fallen, Fallonne,
Falon, Falyn, Falynn, Falynne, Phalon

Falviana (Spanish) she who has
blonde locks of hair.

Fancy (French) betrothed. (English)
whimsical; decorative.
Fanchette, Fanchon, Fanci, Fancia,
Fancie

Fang (Chinese) fragrant, sweet
smelling.

Fang Yin, Fang-Yin (Chinese)
fragrant carpet of grass; the scent of
flowers.

Fannie, Fanny (American) familiar
forms of Frances.
Fan, Fanette, Fani, Fania, Fannee,
Fanney, Fanni, Fannia, Fany, Fanya

Fantasia (Greek) imagination.
Fantasy, Fantasya, Fantaysia, Fantazia,
Fiantasi

Farah, Farrah (English) beautiful;
pleasant.
Fara, Farra, Fayre

Fareeda (Indian) unique.

Fareeha (Indian) happy, joyful.

Faren, Farren (English) wanderer.
Faran, Fare, Farin, Faron, Farrahn,
Farran, Farrand, Farrin, Farron, Farryn,
Farye, Faryn, Feran, Ferin, Feron,
Ferran, Ferren, Ferrin, Ferron, Ferryn

Farha (Indian) happiness.

Farhana (Indian) beautiful.

Farzana (Indian) intelligence.

Fatangisña (Chamorro) she who cries a lot.

Fátim (Arabic) only daughter of Mahoma.

Fatima (Arabic) daughter of the Prophet. History: the daughter of Muhammad.
Fatema, Fathma, Fatimah, Fatime, Fatma, Fatmah, Fatme, Fattim

Fátima (Arabic) a form of Fatima.

Fausta, Faustina (Latin) fortunate or lucky.

Favia (Latin) she who raises beans.

Fawiza (Indian) successful.

Fawn (French) young deer.
Faun, Fawna, Fawne

Fawna (French) a form of Fawn.
Fauna, Fawnia, Fawnna

Fawziya (Indian) successful; victorious.

Faye (French) fairy; elf. (English) a form of Faith.
Fae, Fay, Fayann, Fayanna, Fayette, Fayina, Fey

Fayola (Nigerian) lucky.
Fayla, Feyla

Fe (Latin) trust or belief.

Febe (Greek) shining one.

Fedra (Greek) splendid one.

Fegorgor (Chamorro) one who gossips a lot.

Fegurgur (Chamorro) a form of Fegorgor.

Felecia (Latin) a form of Felicia.
Flecia

Felecidade (Portuguese) happiness.

Felica (Spanish) a short form of Felicia.
Falisa, Felisa, Felisca, Felissa, Feliza

Felice (Latin) a short form of Felicia.
Felece, Felicie, Felise, Felize, Felyce, Felysse

Felicia (Latin) fortunate; happy. See also Lecia, Phylicia.
Falecia, Faleshia, Falicia, Fela, Felecia, Felica, Felice, Felicidad, Feliciona, Felicity, Felicya, Felisea, Felisha, Felisia, Felisiana, Felissya, Felita, Felixia, Felizia, Felka, Fellcia, Felycia, Felysia, Felyssia, Fleasia, Fleichia, Fleishia, Flichia

Feliciana (Spanish, Italian, Ancient Roman) a form of Felix.

Felicity (English) a form of Felicia.
Falicity, Felicita, Felicitas, Félicité, Feliciti, Felisita, Felisity

Felipe **B** (Spanish) a form of Philip.

Felisha (Latin) a form of Felicia.
Faleisha, Falesha, Falisha, Falleshia, Feleasha, Feleisha, Felesha, Felishia, Fellishia, Felysha, Flisha

Felix (Latin) fortunate; happy.

Femi (French) woman. (Nigerian) love me.
Femie, Femmi, Femmie, Femy

Fen (Chinese) fragrant, sweet-smelling.

Feng (Chinese) maple.

Feng-Po-Po (Chinese) goddess of winds.

Feodora (Greek) gift of God.
Fedora, Fedoria

Fermina (Spanish) strong.

Fern (English) fern. (German) a short form of Fernanda.
Ferne, Ferni, Fernlee, Fernleigh, Fernley, Fernly

Fernanda (German) daring, adventurous. See also Andee, Nan.
Ferdie, Ferdinanda, Ferdinande, Fern, Fernande, Fernandette, Fernandina, Nanda

Feronia (Latin) goddess of the forest and fountains.

Fersita (Palauan) pearl.

Fesamay (Chamorro) serious child.

Fetangis (Chamorro) one who cries a lot.

Fhoolwathi (Indian) dedicated as a flower.

Fiala (Czech) violet.

Fidelia (Latin) a form of Fidelity.
Fidela, Fidele, Fidelina

Fidelity (Latin) faithful, true. See also Faith.
Fidelia, Fidelita

Fifi 🅖 (French) a familiar form of Josephine.
Feef, Feefee, Fifine

Figan (Chamorro) red hot.

Fiho, Fihon (Chamorro) forms of Fihu.

Fihu (Chamorro) often.

Filippa (Italian) a form of Philippa.
Felipa, Filipa, Filippina, Filpina

Filis (Greek) adorned with leaves.

Filomena (Italian) a form of Philomena.
Fila, Filah, Filemon

Filotea (Greek) she who loves God.

Filza (Indian) light.

Fiona (Irish) fair, white.
Fionna

Fionnula (Irish) white shouldered. See also Nola, Nuala.
Fenella, Fenula, Finella, Finola, Finula

Fiorel (Latin) a form of Flor.

Fiorela (Italian) small flower.

Fiorella (Spanish) a form of Fiorela.

Firdoos (Indian) paradise.

Firoza, Phiroza (Indian) turquoise.

Fiza (Indian) breeze.

Fizza (Indian) nature.

Flair (English) style; verve.
Flaire, Flare

Flaminia (Latin) alluding to one who belongs to a religious order.

Flannery (Irish) redhead. Literature: Flannery O'Connor was a renowned American writer.
Flan, Flann, Flanna

Flavia (Latin) blond, golden haired.
Flavere, Flaviar, Flavie, Flavien, Flavienne, Flaviere, Flavio, Flavyere, Fulvia

Flávia (Portuguese) a form of Flavia.

Flavie (Latin) a form of Flavia.
Flavi

Fleur (French) flower.
Fleure, Fleuree, Fleurette

Flo (American) a short form of Florence.

Flor (Latin) a short form of Flora.

Flora (Latin) flower. A short form of Florence. See also Lore.
Fiora, Fiore, Fiorenza, Florann, Florella, Florelle, Floren, Floria, Floriana, Florianna, Florica, Florimel

Floramaría (Spanish) flower of Mary.

Florehna (Pohnpeian) a form of
Efigenia.

Florence (Latin) blooming; flowery;
prosperous. History: Florence
Nightingale, a British nurse, is
considered the founder of modern
nursing. See also Florida.
*Fiorenza, Flo, Flora, Florance, Florencia,
Florency, Florendra, Florentia,
Florentina, Florentyna, Florenza,
Floretta, Florette, Florie, Florina, Florine,
Floris, Flossie*

Floria (Basque) a form of Flora.
Flori, Florria

Florida (Spanish) a form of
Florence.
Floridia, Florinda, Florita

Florie (English) a familiar form of
Florence.
Flore, Flori, Florri, Florrie, Florry, Flory

Florinia (Latin) blooming or flowering.

Floris (English) a form of Florence.
Florisa, Florise

Florisel (Spanish) a form of Flora.

Flossie (English) a familiar form of
Florence.
Floss, Flossi, Flossy

Floyd **B** (English) a form of Lloyd.

Fo (Chinese) Buddhist.

Fola (Yoruba) honorable.

Fonda (Latin) foundation. (Spanish)
inn.
Fondea, Fonta

Fontanna (French) fountain.
*Fontaine, Fontana, Fontane, Fontanne,
Fontayne*

Foolan, Phoolan (Indian)
flowering.

Foolwati, Phoolwati (Indian)
delicate as a flower.

Foram, Forum (Indian) fragrance.

Forest **B** (French) a form of Forrest.

Forrest **B** (French) forest;
woodsman.

Fortuna (Latin) fortune; fortunate.
Fortoona, Fortune

Fortunata (Latin) fortunate one.

Fran **G** (Latin) a short form of
Frances.
Frain, Frann

Frances **G** (Latin) a form of
Francis. See also Paquita.
*Fanny, Fran, Franca, France, Francee,
Francena, Francesca, Francess,
Francesta, Franceta, Francetta,
Francette, Francine, Francisca,
Françoise, Frankie, Frannie, Franny*

Francesca **G** (Italian) a form of
Frances.
*Franceska, Francessca, Francesta,
Franchesca, Franzetta*

Franchesca (Italian) a form of
Francesca.
*Cheka, Chekka, Chesca, Cheska,
Francheca, Francheka, Franchelle,
Franchesa, Francheska, Franchessca,
Franchesska*

Franci (Hungarian) a familiar form
of Francine.
Francey, Francie, Francy

Francine (French) a form of Frances.
*Franceen, Franceine, Franceline,
Francene, Francenia, Franci, Francin,
Francina, Francyne*

Francis **B** (Latin) free; from France.
Francise, Franncia, Francys

Francisca (Italian) a form of Frances.
*Franciska, Franciszka, Frantiska,
Franziska*

Françoise (French) a form of Frances.

Frankie 🅱 (American) a familiar form of Frances.
Francka, Francki, Franka, Frankey, Franki, Frankia, Franky, Frankye

Franklin 🅱 (English) free landowner.

Frannie, Franny (English) familiar forms of Frances.
Frani, Frania, Franney, Franni, Frany

Fraser 🅱 (French) strawberry. (English) curly haired.

Freda, Freida, Frida (German) short forms of Alfreda, Elfrida, Frederica, Sigfreda.
Frayda, Fredda, Fredella, Fredia, Fredra, Freeda, Freeha, Freia, Frida, Frideborg, Frieda

Freddi (English) familiar forms of Frederica, Winifred.
Fredda, Freddy, Fredi, Fredia, Fredy, Frici

Freddie 🅱 (English) a form of Freddi.

Fredel (Nahuatl) forever you.

Frederica (German) peaceful ruler. See also Alfreda, Rica, Ricki.
Farica, Federica, Freda, Fredalena, Fredaline, Freddi, Freddie, Frederickina, Frederika, Frederike, Frederina, Frederine, Frederique, Fredith, Fredora, Fredreca, Fredrica, Fredricah, Fredricia, Freida, Fritzi, Fryderica

Frederika (German) a form of Frederica.
Fredericka, Fredreka, Fredricka, Fredrika, Fryderyka

Frederike (German) a form of Frederica.
Fredericke, Friederike

Frederique 🅶 (French) a form of Frederica.
Frédérique, Rike

Fredrick 🅱 (German) a form of Frederick (see Boys' Names).

Freja (Scandinavian) a form of Freya.

Frescura (Spanish) freshness.

Freya (Scandinavian) noblewoman. Mythology: the Norse goddess of love.
Fraya, Freya

Freyra (Slavic) goddess of love.

Frine (Spanish) female toad.

Fritzi (German) a familiar form of Frederica.
Friezi, Fritze, Fritzie, Fritzinn, Fritzline, Fritzy

Fronde (Latin) leafy branch.

Fructuosa (Spanish) fruitful.

Fu (Chinese) lotus.

Fu'una (Chamorro) her place.

Fuasyo (Japanese) whole; room; generation.

Fuji (Japanese) wisteria.

Fujiko (Japanese) wisteria child.

Fujita (Japanese) field.

Fujiye (Japanese) wisteria branch.

Fuka (Japanese) she who stays beautiful even in difficult times.

Fukiko (Japanese) wealthy; precious child.

Fukuko (Japanese) child of good fortune.

Fukuyo (Japanese) a lifetime of good fortune.

Fulgencia (Spanish) she who excels because of her great kindness.

Fulki (Indian) spark.

Fullan (Indian) blooming.

Fullara (Indian) wife of Kalketu.

Fulmala (Indian) garland.

Fumi (Japanese) beautiful helper; writings, letter.

Fumie (Kosraean) a form of Alexa.

Fumii (Japanese) that one is a chronicle.

Fumiko (Japanese) beautiful, wealthy child; born to be a writer.

Fumiye (Japanese) born to be a writer; she who chronicles through painting.

Fumiyo (Japanese) she who writes for a lifetime.

Fusa (Japanese) tassel; cluster; room.

Fusae (Japanese) wealthy; clever.

Fusako (Japanese) lotus; gaze; help; child.

Fuyu (Japanese) born in winter.

Fuyuko (Japanese) child of reason.

Fuyumi (Japanese) beautiful winter.

G

G **B** (American) an initial used as a first name.

Gabina (Latin) she who is a native of Gabio, an ancient city close to Rome where Romulus was raised.

Gabriel **B** (French) devoted to God.

Gabriela **G** (Italian) a form of Gabrielle.
Gabriala, Gabrielia, Gabrila

Gabriele (French) forms of Gabrielle.
Gabbriel, Gabbryel, Gabreal, Gabreale, Gabreil, Gabrial, Gabryel

Gabriella 🌟 **G** (Italian) a form of Gabrielle.
Gabrialla, Gabriellia, Gabrilla, Gabryella

Gabrielle 🌟 **G** (French) a form of Gabriel.
Gabbrielle, Gabielle, Gabrealle, Gabriana, Gabriel, Gabriela, Gabriele, Gabriell, Gabriella, Gabrille, Gabrina, Gabriylle, Gabryell, Gabryelle, Gaby, Gavriella

Gabryel **B** (French) a form of Gabriel.

Gaby (French) a familiar form of Gabrielle.
Gabbey, Gabbi, Gabbie, Gabby, Gabey, Gabi, Gabie, Gavi, Gavy

Gada (Hebrew) lucky.
Gadah

Gaea (Greek) planet Earth. Mythology: the Greek goddess of Earth.
Gaia, Gaiea, Gaya

Gaetana (Italian) from Gaeta. Geography: Gaeta is a city in southern Italy.
Gaetan, Gaétane, Gaetanne

Gafahongoc (Chamorro) cutting off coconuts.

Gafo (Chamorro) coconut.

Gaga (Chamorro) a type of fish.

Gagandeep **B** (Sikh) sky's light.
Gagandip, Gagnadeep, Gagndeep

Gage **B** (French) pledge.

Gago (Chamorro) lazy; ironwood tree.

Gaho (Chamorro) bamboo joint.

Gail (Hebrew) a short form of
Abigail. (English) merry, lively.
*Gael, Gaela, Gaelle, Gaila, Gaile,
Gale, Gayla, Gayle*

Gajagamini (Indian) majestic.

Gajara (Indian) garland of flowers.

Gajra (Indian) flowers.

Gala (Norwegian) singer.
Galla

Galatea (Greek) she with skin as
white as milk.

Galen 🅱 (Greek) healer; calm.
(Irish) little and lively.
*Gaelen, Gaellen, Galyn, Gaylaine,
Gayleen, Gaylen, Gaylene, Gaylyn*

Galena (Greek) healer; calm.

Galenia (Greek) healer.

Gali (Hebrew) hill; fountain; spring.
Galice, Galie

Galilah (Hebrew) important, exalted.

Galina (Russian) a form of Helen.
*Gailya, Galayna, Galenka, Galia,
Galiana, Galiena, Galinka, Galochka,
Galya, Galyna*

Gamami (Chamorro) we love.

Gamomo (Chamorro) she who loves
a battle.

Gamumu (Chamorro) a form of
Gamomo.

Gamumus (Chamorro) a form of
Gamomo.

Gan (Chinese) sweet.

Gandhali (Indian) sweet scent.

Ganesa (Hindi) fortunate. Religion:
Ganesha was the Hindu god of
wisdom.

Ganga (Indian) sacred river.

Gangika (Indian) river.

Gangotri (Indian) sacred river of
India.

Ganika (Indian) flower.

Ganjan (Indian) exceeding.

Ganya 🅱🅶 (Hebrew) garden of the
Lord. (Zulu) clever.
Gana, Gani, Gania, Ganice, Ganit

Gao (Chinese) tall.

Garabina, Garabine (Spanish)
purification.

Garaitz (Basque) victory.

Garati (Indian) virtuous woman.

Garbina, Garbine (Spanish)
purification.

García (Latin) she who demon-
strates her charm and grace.

Gardenia (English) Botany: a sweet-
smelling flower.
Deeni, Denia, Gardena, Gardinia

Garett 🅱 (Irish) a form of Garrett.

Gargi (Indian) wise woman.

Garima (Indian) warmth.

Garland 🅱 (French) wreath of
flowers.

Garnet (English) dark red gem.
Garnetta, Garnette

Garoa (Basque) fern.

Garrett 🅱 (Irish) brave spear carrier.

Garrison 🅱 (French) troops
stationed at a fort; garrison.

Gary 🅱 (German) mighty spear
carrier. (English) a familiar form of
Gerald.

Garyn (English) spear carrier.
Garan, Garen, Garra, Garryn

Gasha (Russian) a familiar form of Agatha.
Gashka

Gaspara (Spanish) treasurer.

Gatita (Indian) a river.

Gaudencia (Spanish) happy, content.

Gauhar (Indian) a pearl.

Gaurika (Indian) pretty young girl.

Gautami (Indian) the Guava River.

Gavin B (Welsh) white hawk.

Gavriella (Hebrew) a form of Gabrielle.
Gavila, Gavilla, Gavrid, Gavrieela, Gavriela, Gavrielle, Gavrila, Gavrilla

Gay (French) merry.
Gae, Gai, Gaye

Gayle (English) a form of Gail.
Gayla

Gayna (English) a familiar form of Guinevere.
Gaynah, Gayner, Gaynor

Gazala (Indian) a deer.

Ge (Chinese) pattern.

Gea (Greek) old name given to the earth.

Gechina (Basque) grace.

Geela (Hebrew) joyful.
Gela, Gila

Geena (American) a form of Gena.
Geania, Geeana, Geeanna

Geeta (Indian) holy book of the Hindus.

Geeti (Indian) melody.

Geetika (Indian) a little song.

Gehna (Indian) ornament.

Gelya (Russian) angelic.

Gema, Gemma (Latin, Italian) jewel, precious stone. See also Jemma.
Gem, Gemmey, Gemmie, Gemmy

Gemini (Greek) twin.
Gemelle, Gemima, Gemina, Geminine, Gemmina

Gen (Japanese) spring. A short form of names beginning with "Gen."

Gena G (French) a form of Gina. A short form of Geneva, Genevieve, Iphigenia.
Geanna, Geena, Geenah, Gen, Genae, Genah, Genai, Genea, Geneja, Geni, Genia, Genie

Gene (Chamorro) a type of plant.

Geneen (Scottish) a form of Jeanine.
Geanine, Geannine, Gen, Genene, Genine, Gineen, Ginene

Genell (American) a form of Jenelle.

Generosa (Spanish) generous.

Genesis ☀ ★ **G** (Latin) origin; birth.
Genes, Genese, Genesha, Genesia, Genesiss, Genessa, Genesse, Genessie, Genessis, Genicis, Genises, Genysis, Yenesis

Geneva (French) juniper tree. A short form of Genevieve. Geography: a city in Switzerland.
Geena, Gen, Gena, Geneieve, Geneiva, Geneive, Geneve, Ginneva, Janeva, Jeaneva, Jeneva

Genevieve ☐ (German, French) a form of Guinevere. See also Gwendolyn.
Gen, Genaveeve, Genaveve, Genavie, Genavieve, Genavive, Geneva, Geneveve, Genevie, Geneviéve, Genevieve, Genevive, Genovieve, Genvieve, Ginette, Gineveve, Ginevieve, Ginevive, Guinieveve, Guinivive, Gwenevieve, Gwenivive, Jennavieve

Genevra (French, Welsh) a form of Guinevere.
Gen, Genever, Genevera, Ginevra

Geng (Chinese) honest.

Genice (American) a form of Janice.
Gen, Genece, Geneice, Genesa, Genesee, Genessia, Genis, Genise

Genita (American) a form of Janita.
Gen, Genet, Geneta

Genji (Chinese) gold.

Genna (English) a form of Jenna.
Gen, Gennae, Gennay, Genni, Gennie, Genny

Gennifer (American) a form of Jennifer.
Gen, Genifer, Ginnifer

Genovieve (French) a form of Genevieve.
Genoveva, Genoveve, Genovive

Georgeanna (English) a combination of Georgia + Anna.
Georgana, Georganna, Georgeana, Georgiana, Georgianna, Georgyanna, Giorgianna

Georgeanne (English) a combination of Georgia + Anne.
Georgann, Georganne, Georgean, Georgeann, Georgie, Georgyann, Georgyanne

Georgene (English) a familiar form of Georgia.
Georgeena, Georgeina, Georgena, Georgenia, Georgiena, Georgienne, Georgina, Georgine

Georgette (French) a form of Georgia.
Georgeta, Georgett, Georgetta, Georjetta

Georgia ☐ (Greek) farmer. Art: Georgia O'Keeffe was an American painter known especially for her paintings of flowers. Geography: a southern American state; a country in Eastern Europe. See also Jirina, Jorja.
Georgene, Georgette, Georgie, Giorgia

Georgianna (English) a form of Georgeanna.
Georgiana, Georgiann, Georgianne, Georgie, Georgieann, Georgionna

Georgie (English) a familiar form of Georgeanne, Georgia, Georgianna.
Georgi, Georgy, Giorgi

Georgina (English) a form of Georgia.
Georgena, Georgene, Georgine, Giorgina, Jorgina

Gerald ☐ (German) mighty spear carrier.

Geraldine (German) a form of Gerald. See also Dena, Jeraldine.
Geralda, Geraldina, Geraldyna, Geraldyne, Gerhardine, Geri, Gerianna, Gerianne, Gerrilee, Giralda

Geralyn (American) a combination of Geraldine + Lynn.
Geralisha, Geralynn, Gerilyn, Gerrilyn

Geranio (Greek) she is as beautiful as a geranium.

Gerardo **B** (English) brave with a spear.
Gerardine

Gerda (Norwegian) protector. (German) a familiar form of Gertrude.
Gerta

Geri (American) a familiar form of Geraldine. See also Jeri.
Gerri, Gerrie, Gerry

Germaine (French) from Germany. See also Jermaine.
Germain, Germana, Germanee, Germani, Germanie, Germaya, Germine

Gertie (German) a familiar form of Gertrude.
Gert, Gertey, Gerti, Gerty

Gertrude (German) beloved warrior. See also Trudy.
Gerda, Gerta, Gertie, Gertina, Gertraud, Gertrud, Gertruda

Gertrudes, Gertrudis (Spanish) beloved warrior.

Gervaise **BG** (French) skilled with a spear.

Gervasi (Spanish) having to do with spears.

Gessica (Italian) a form of Jessica.
Gesica, Gesika, Gess, Gesse, Gessy

Geva (Hebrew) hill.
Gevah

Gezana, Gezane (Spanish) reference to the Incarnation.

Ghaada (Indian) beautiful.

Ghaaliya (Indian) fragrant.

Ghada (Arabic) young; tender.
Gada

Ghaydaa (Indian) young and delicate.

Ghita (Italian) pearly.
Gita

Ghusoon (Indian) branches.

Giang (Vietnamese) brave, courageous.

Gianira (Greek) nymph from the sea.

Gianna (Italian) a short form of Giovanna. See also Jianna, Johana.
Geona, Geonna, Giana, Gianella, Gianetta, Gianina, Gianinna, Gianne, Giannee, Giannella, Giannetta, Gianni, Giannie, Giannina, Gianny, Gianoula

Giao (Vietnamese) charm and grace.

Gigi (French) a familiar form of Gilberte.
Geegee, G. G., Giggi

Gilana (Hebrew) joyful.
Gila, Gilah

Gilberte (German) brilliant; pledge; trustworthy. See also Berti.
Gigi, Gilberta, Gilbertina, Gilbertine, Gill

Gilda (English) covered with gold.
Gilde, Gildi, Gildie, Gildy

Gill (Latin, German) a short form of Gilberte, Gillian.
Gili, Gilli, Gillie, Gilly

Gillian **G** (Latin) a form of Jillian.
Gila, Gilana, Gilenia, Gili, Gilian, Gill, Gilliana, Gilliane, Gilliann, Gillianna, Gillianne, Gillie, Gilly, Gillyan, Gillyane, Gillyann, Gillyanne, Gyllian, Lian

Gin (Japanese) silver. A short form of names beginning with "Gin."

Gina (Italian) a short form of Angelina, Eugenia, Regina, Virginia. See also Jina.
Gena, Gin, Ginah, Ginai, Ginna

Giña (Chamorro) silversides fish.

Ginebra (Celtic) white as foam.

Gines (Greek) she who engenders life.

Ginette (English) a form of Genevieve.
Gin, Ginata, Ginett, Ginetta, Ginnetta, Ginnette

Ging Ging (Tagalog) one who puts on an act to be noticed.

Ginger (Latin) flower; spice. A familiar form of Virginia.
Gin, Ginja, Ginjer, Ginny

Ginia (Latin) a familiar form of Virginia.
Gin

Ginnifer (English) white; smooth; soft. (Welsh) a form of Jennifer.
Gin, Ginifer

Ginny (English) a familiar form of Ginger, Virginia. See also Jin, Jinny.
Gin, Gini, Ginney, Ginni, Ginnie, Giny, Gionni, Gionny

Gioconda (Latin) she who engenders life.

Giordana (Italian) a form of Jordana.

Giorgianna (English) a form of Georgeanna.
Giorgina

Giovanna (Italian) a form of Jane.
Geovana, Geovanna, Geovonna, Giavanna, Giavonna, Giovana, Giovanne, Giovannica, Giovonna, Givonnie, Jeveny

Giovanni B (Italian) a form of Giovanna.

Gira (Indian) language.

Girija (Indian) daughter of the mountain.

Gisa (Hebrew) carved stone.
Gazit, Gissa

Gisela (German) a form of Giselle.
Gisella, Gissela, Gissella

Giselda (German, Teutonic) arrow; ray; token of happiness.

Giselle G (German) pledge; hostage. See also Jizelle.
Ghisele, Gisel, Gisela, Gisele, Geséle, Giseli, Gisell, Gissell, Gisselle, Gizela, Gysell

Gissel, Gisselle (German) forms of Giselle.
Gissell

Gita (Yiddish) good. (Polish) a short form of Margaret.
Gitka, Gitta, Gituska

Gitali (Indian) melodious.

Gitana (Spanish) gypsy; wanderer.

Gitanjali (Indian) melodious tribute.

Gitika (Indian) a small song.

Gitta (Irish) a short form of Bridget.
Getta

Giulia (Italian) a form of Julia.
Giulana, Giuliana, Giulianna, Giulliana, Guila, Guiliana, Guilietta

Giunia (Latin) she who was born in June.

Gizela (Czech) a form of Giselle.
Gizel, Gizele, Gizella, Gizelle, Gizi, Giziki, Gizus

Gladis (Irish) a form of Gladys.
Gladi, Gladiz

Gladys (Latin) small sword. (Irish) princess. (Welsh) a form of Claudia.
Glad, Gladis, Gladness, Gladwys, Glady, Gwladys

Glaucia (Portuguese) brave gift.

Glen B (Irish) a form of Glenn.

Glenda (Welsh) a form of Glenna.
Glanda, Glennda, Glynda

Glenn B (Irish) valley, glen.

Glenna (Irish) a form of Glenn. See also Glynnis.
Glenda, Glenetta, Glenina, Glenine, Glenne, Glennesha, Glennia, Glennie, Glenora, Gleny, Glyn

Glennesha (American) a form of Glenna.
Glenesha, Glenisha, Glennisha, Glennishia

Gloria G (Latin) glory. History: Gloria Steinem, a leading American feminist, founded *Ms.* magazine.
Gloresha, Gloriah, Gloribel, Gloriela, Gloriella, Glorielle, Gloris, Glorisha, Glorvina, Glory

Glorianne (American) a combination of Gloria + Anne.
Gloriana, Gloriane, Gloriann, Glorianna

Glory (Latin) a form of Gloria.

Glynnis (Welsh) a form of Glenna.
Glenice, Glenis, Glenise, Glenyse, Glennis, Glennys, Glenwys, Glenys, Glenyss, Glinnis, Glinys, Glynesha, Glynice, Glynis, Glynisha, Glyniss, Glynitra, Glynys, Glynyss

Godalupe (Spanish) reference to the Virgin Mary.

Godavari (Indian) the Godavari River.

Godavri (Indian) a river.

Godongña (Chamorro) she is entrapped.

Gofaras (Chamorro) a lot of shell money.

Gofhenum (Chamorro) lots of water.

Gofmatanmiyu (Chamorro) your face.

Gofnaam (Chamorro) very great name.

Gofsaina (Chamorro) very supreme, godlike.

Goftalu (Chamorro) very central.

Goftaotao (Chamorro) many people.

Gogo (Chamorro) a form of Gogui.

Gogui (Chamorro) protect; save, rescue.

Golda (English) gold. History: Golda Meir was a Russian-born politician who served as prime minister of Israel.
Goldarina, Golden, Goldie, Goldina

Goldie (English) a familiar form of Golda.
Goldi, Goldy

Goma (Swahili) joyful dance.

Gomathi, Gomti (Indian) a river.

Gomati (Indian) the Gomati River.

Gong (Chinese) respectful.

Gool (Indian) a flower.

Gopa (Indian) wife of Gautama.

Gopi (Indian) milkmaid friends of Lord Krishna.

Gopika (Indian) cowherd girls.

Goptoña (Chamorro) his or her party.

Gourangi (Indian) fair complexion.

Govindi (Indian) a devotee of Lord Krishna.

Graça (Portuguese) a form of Grace.

Grace ☀ (Latin) graceful.
*Engracia, Graca, Gracia, Gracie,
Graciela, Graciella, Gracinha, Graice,
Grata, Gratia, Gray, Grayce, Grecia*

Graceanne (English) a combination
of Grace + Anne.
*Graceann, Graceanna, Gracen,
Graciana, Gracianna, Gracin, Gratiana*

Gracia (Spanish) a form of Grace.
Gracea, Grecia

Gracie (English) a familiar form of
Grace.
*Gracee, Gracey, Graci, Gracy,
Graecie, Graysie*

Graham B (English) grand home.

Grant B (English) great; giving.

Granthana (Indian) book.

Grayson B (English) bailiff's child.
*Graison, Graisyn, Grasien, Grasyn,
Graysen*

Grazia (Latin) a form of Grace.
*Graziella, Grazielle, Graziosa,
Grazyna*

Greashma (Indian) summer.

Grecia (Latin) a form of Grace.

Greer (Scottish) vigilant.
Grear, Grier

Gregoria (Spanish) vigilant watchman.

Gregoriana (Spanish) a form of
Gregoria.

Gregorina (Latin) watches over her
group of people.

Gregory B (Latin) vigilant watch
guard.

Greta (German) a short form of
Gretchen, Margaret.
*Greatal, Greatel, Greeta, Gretal, Grete,
Gretel, Gretha, Grethal, Grethe, Grethel,
Gretta, Grette, Grieta, Gryta, Grytta*

Gretchen (German) a form of
Margaret.
Greta, Gretchin, Gretchyn

Gricelda (German) a form of Griselda.
Gricelle

Griffin B (Latin) hooked nose.

Grisel (German) a short form of
Griselda.
*Grisell, Griselle, Grissel, Grissele,
Grissell, Grizel*

Grisela (Spanish) a form of Griselda.

Griselda (German) gray woman
warrior. See also Selda, Zelda.
*Gricelda, Grisel, Griseldis, Griseldys,
Griselys, Grishilda, Grishilde, Grisselda,
Grissely, Grizelda*

Grishma (Indian) warmth.

Gu (Chinese) valley.

Guadalupe G (Arabic) river of
black stones. See also Lupe.
*Guadalup, Guadelupe, Guadlupe,
Guadulupe, Gudalupe*

Guan (Chinese) the best.

Guang (Chinese) light, brightness.

Guan-yin (Chinese) the goddess of
mercy.

Gudrun (Scandinavian) battler. See
also Runa.
Gudren, Gudrin, Gudrinn, Gudruna

Gui (Chinese) precious.

Guía (Spanish) guide.

Guillelmina (Italian, Spanish)
resolute protector.

Guillerma (Spanish) a short form of
Guillermina.
Guilla, Guillermina

Guinevere (French, Welsh) white wave; white phantom. Literature: the wife of King Arthur. See also Gayna, Genevieve, Genevra, Jennifer, Winifred, Wynne.
Generva, Genn, Ginette, Guenevere, Guenna, Guinivere, Guinna, Gwen, Gwenevere, Gwenivere, Gwynnevere

Guioma (Spanish) a form of Giuomar.

Guiomar (German) famous in combat.

Gulika (Indian) a pearl.

Gunavati, Gunita, Gunwanti (Indian) virtuous.

Gunda (Norwegian) female warrior.
Gundala, Gunta

Gundelina (Teutonic) she who helps in battle.

Gundelinda (German) pious one in the battle.

Gundenia (German) fighter.

Guneet (Indian) full of talent.

Gunjana (Indian) buzzing of a bee.

Gunjita (Indian) the humming of bee.

Gunnika (Indian) garland.

Guo (Chinese) result.

Gurbani (Indian) Sikh's religious prayer.

Gurit (Hebrew) innocent baby.

Gurjot **BG** (Sikh) light of the guru.

Gurleen (Sikh) follower of the guru.

Gurpreet **BG** (Punjabi) religion.
Gurprit

Gurvir **B** (Sikh) guru's warrior.

Gusta (Latin) a short form of Augusta.
Gus, Gussi, Gussie, Gussy, Gusti, Gustie, Gusty

Gustava (Scandinavian) staff of the Goths.

Guy **B** (Hebrew) valley. (German) warrior. (French) guide.

Gwen (Welsh) a short form of Guinevere, Gwendolyn.
Gwenesha, Gweness, Gweneta, Gwenetta, Gwenette, Gweni, Gwenisha, Gwenita, Gwenn, Gwenna, Gwennie, Gwenny

Gwenda (Welsh) a familiar form of Gwendolyn.
Gwinda, Gwynda, Gwynedd

Gwendolyn (Welsh) white wave; white browed; new moon. Literature: Gwendoloena was the wife of Merlin, the magician. See also Genevieve, Gwyneth, Wendy.
Guendolen, Gwen, Gwendalin, Gwenda, Gwendalee, Gwendaline, Gwendalyn, Gwendalynn, Gwendela, Gwendelyn, Gwendelynn, Gwendilyn, Gwendolen, Gwendolene, Gwendolin, Gwendoline, Gwendolyne, Gwendolynn, Gwendolynne, Gwendylan, Gwyndolyn, Gwynndolen

Gwyn **G** (Welsh) a short form of Gwyneth.
Gwinn, Gwinne, Gwynn, Gwynne

Gwyneth (Welsh) a form of Gwendolyn. See also Winnie, Wynne.
Gweneth, Gwenith, Gwenneth, Gwennyth, Gwenyth, Gwyn, Gwynneth

Gypsy (English) wanderer.
Gipsy, Gypsie, Jipsi

H 🅖 (American) an initial used as a first name.

Ha (Vietnamese) river.

Ha'ane, Haane, Haani (Chamorro) forms of Ha'ani.

Ha'ani (Chamorro) day.

Haadiya (Indian) guide to righteousness.

Haala (Indian) aureole.

Habiba (Arabic) beloved.
Habibah, Habibeh

Hachi (Japanese) eight; good luck.
Hachiko, Hachiyo

Hada (Hebrew) she who radiates joy.

Hadara (Hebrew) adorned with beauty.
Hadarah

Hadasa (Hebrew) myrtle.

Hadassah (Hebrew) myrtle tree.
Hadas, Hadasah, Hadassa, Haddasa, Haddasah

Hadiya (Swahili) gift.
Hadaya, Hadia, Hadiyah, Hadiyyah

Hadley 🅖 (English) field of heather.
Hadlea, Hadlee, Hadleigh, Hadli, Hadlie, Hadly

Hadriane (Greek, Latin) a form of Adrienne.
Hadriana, Hadrianna, Hadrianne, Hadriene, Hadrienne

Haeley (English) a form of Hailey.
Haelee, Haeleigh, Haeli, Haelie, Haelleigh, Haelli, Haellie, Haely

Hafiza (Indian) protected.

Hagar (Hebrew) forsaken; stranger. Bible: Sarah's handmaiden, the mother of Ishmael.
Haggar

Hai (Vietnamese) happy; kiss of life.

Haidee (Greek) modest.
Hady, Haide, Haidi, Haidy, Haydee, Haydy

Haiden 🅑 (English) heather-covered hill.
Haden, Hadyn, Haeden, Haidn, Haidyn

Hailee (English) a form of Hayley.
Haile, Hailei, Haileigh, Haillee

Hailey ⚘ 🅖 (English) a form of Hayley.
Haeley, Haiely, Hailea, Hailley, Hailly, Haily

Haili, Hailie (English) forms of Hayley.
Haille, Hailli, Haillie

Haima (Indian) snow.

Haimavati (Indian) Parvati, a consort of Lord Shiva.

Haimi (Indian) golden.

Haisha (Arabic) a form of Aisha.

Hakeem 🅑 (Arabic) a form of Hakim (see Boys' Names).

Haldana (Norwegian) half-Danish.

Halee 🅖 (English) a form of Haley.
Hale, Halea, Haleah, Haleh, Halei

Haleigh (English) a form of Haley.

Haley 🅖 (Scandinavian) heroine. See also Hailey, Hayley.
Halee, Haleigh, Hali, Halley, Hallie, Haly, Halye

Hali 🅖 (English) a form of Haley.

Halia (Hawaiian) in loving memory.

Halie (English) a form of Haley.
Haliegh

Halimah (Arabic) gentle; patient.
Halima, Halime

Halina (Hawaiian) likeness.
(Russian) a form of Helen.
Haleen, Haleena, Halena, Halinka

Halla (African) unexpected gift.
Hala, Hallah, Halle

Halley **G** (English) a form of
Haley.
Hally, Hallye

Hallie **G** (Scandinavian) a form of
Haley.
Hallee, Hallei, Halleigh, Halli

Halona (Native American) fortunate.
Halonah, Haloona, Haona

Halsey **G** (English) Hall's island.
Halsea, Halsie

Hama (Japanese) shore.

Hamako (Japanese) a form of Hama.

Hameeda (Indian) praiseworthy.

Hamsini (Indian) one who rides a
swan.

Han (Vietnamese) good.

Hana, Hanah (Japanese) flower.
(Arabic) happiness. (Slavic) forms
of Hannah.
*Hanae, Hanan, Haneen, Hanicka,
Hanin, Hanita, Hanka*

Hanako (Japanese) flower child.

Hang (Vietnamese) old name for shoe.

Hang Man (Korean) iron, firm; wise,
knowing.

Hanh (Vietnamese) moral.

Hanh Phuc (Vietnamese) moon.

Hania (Hebrew) resting place.
Haniya, Hanja, Hannia, Hanniah, Hanya

Hanima (Indian) a wave.

Hanna **G** (Hebrew) a form of
Hannah.

Hannah ✺ **G** (Hebrew) gracious.
Bible: the mother of Samuel. See
also Anci, Anezka, Ania, Anka,
Ann, Anna, Annalie, Anneka,
Chana, Nina, Nusi.
*Hana, Hanna, Hanneke, Hannele,
Hanni, Hannon, Honna*

Hanni (Hebrew) a familiar form of
Hannah.
Hani, Hanne, Hannie, Hanny

Hano (Hawaiian) glorious, honored,
dignified.

Hansa, Hansika (Indian) swan.

Hansamala (Indian) a line of swans.

Hansini (Indian) swan; very pretty
lady.

Hansuja (Indian) another name for
Laxmi, goddess of wealth.

Hanumta (Chamorro) our water.

Hao (Vietnamese) moral.

Happy (English) happy.
Happi

Hara **G** (Hindi) tawny. Religion:
another name for the Hindu god
Shiva, the destroyer.

Harathi (Indian) divine fire in the
puja ritual.

Haribala (Indian) daughter of Lord
Vishnu.

Harimanti, Hemanti (Indian) born
in the Hemant season.

Harinakshi (Indian) one with eyes like a deer.

Harini (Indian) a deer.

Harita (Indian) green.

Harlee, Harleigh, Harlie (English) forms of Harley.
Harlei, Harli

Harley BG (English) meadow of the hare. See also Arleigh.
Harlee, Harleey, Harly

Harleyann (English) a combination of Harley + Ann.
Harlann, Harlanna, Harlanne, Harleen, Harlene, Harleyanna, Harleyanne, Harliann, Harlianna, Harlianne, Harlina, Harline

Harmony (Latin) harmonious.
Harmene, Harmeni, Harmon, Harmonee, Harmonei, Harmoni, Harmonia, Harmonie

Harpreet G (Punjabi) devoted to God.
Harprit

Harriet (French) ruler of the household. (English) a form of Henrietta. Literature: Harriet Beecher Stowe was an American writer noted for her novel *Uncle Tom's Cabin*.
Harri, Harrie, Harriett, Harrietta, Harriette, Harriot, Harriott, Hattie

Harrison B (English) child of Harry.

Harshada (Indian) giver of joy.

Harshi, Harshini (Indian) joyous.

Harsika (Indian) laugh.

Haru (Japanese) spring.

Harue (Japanese) springtime bay.

Haruka (Japanese) distant fragrance.

Haruna (Japanese) she who blossoms in the spring.

Haruye (Japanese) blessed spring season.

Haruyo (Japanese) healing generation.

Harvir B (Sikh) God's warrior.

Hasana (Swahili) she arrived first. Culture: a name used for the first-born female twin. See also Huseina.
Hasanna, Hasna, Hassana, Hassna, Hassona

Hasina (Swahili) good.
Haseena, Hasena, Hassina

Hasita (Indian) full of laughter.

Hassuyi (Chamorro) to remember.

Hasumati (Indian) happy.

Hateya (Moquelumnan) footprints.

Hatsu (Japanese) first born.

Hatsuko (Japanese) first daughter.

Hatsumi (Japanese) beautiful beginning.

Hatsuye (Japanese) blessed beginning.

Hattie (English) familiar forms of Harriet, Henrietta.
Hatti, Hatty, Hetti, Hettie, Hetty

Haulani (Hawaiian) royal ruler.

Hauoli (Hawaiian) joy, happiness.

Hausu (Moquelumnan) like a bear yawning upon awakening.

Hava (Hebrew) a form of Chava. See also Eve.
Havah, Havvah

Haven G (English) a form of Heaven.
Havan, Havana, Havanna, Havannah, Havyn

Haviva (Hebrew) beloved.
Havalee, Havelah, Havi, Hayah

Hayaam (Indian) deliriously in love.

Hayato (Japanese) prompt person.

Hayden B (English) a form of
Haiden.
Hayde, Haydin, Haydn, Haydon

Hayfa (Arabic) shapely.

Haylee, Hayleigh, Haylie
(English) forms of Hayley.
*Hayle, Haylea, Haylei, Hayli, Haylle,
Hayllie*

Hayley G (English) hay meadow.
See also Hailey, Haley.
Hailee, Haili, Haylee, Hayly

Hazel (English) hazelnut tree;
commanding authority.
*Hazal, Hazaline, Haze, Hazeline,
Hazell, Hazelle, Hazen, Hazyl*

Hazuki (Japanese) the eighth lunar
month.

He (Chinese) harmony.

Hea (Korean) virtue, goodness;
power.

Heath B (English) a form of
Heather.

Heather G (English) flowering
heather.
Heatherlee, Heatherly

Heaven G (English) place of
beauty and happiness. Bible: where
God and angels are said to dwell.
*Haven, Heavan, Heavenly, Heavin,
Heavon, Heavyn, Hevean, Heven, Hevin*

Hebe (Greek) youthful like a flower.

Hecuba (Greek) wife of Priam, king
of Troy.

Hedda (German) battler. See also
Edda, Hedy.
*Heda, Hedaya, Hedia, Hedvick,
Hedvig, Hedvika, Hedwig, Hedwiga,
Heida, Hetta*

Hedy (Greek) delightful; sweet.
(German) a familiar form of Hedda.
*Heddey, Heddi, Heddie, Heddy, Hede,
Hedi*

Heera (Indian) diamond.

Heerkani, Hirkani (Indian) small
diamond.

Hei (Korean) harbor.

Heidi, Heidy (German) short forms
of Adelaide.
*Heida, Heide, Heidee, Heidie, Heydy,
Hidee, Hidi, Hidie, Hidy, Hiede, Hiedi,
Hydi*

Heija (Korean) grace.

Helda (German) she who battles.

Helen G (Greek) light. See also
Aileen, Aili, Alena, Eileen, Elaina,
Elaine, Eleanor, Ellen, Galina, Ila,
Ilene, Ilona, Jelena, Leanore, Leena,
Lelya, Lenci, Lene, Liolya, Nellie,
Nitsa, Olena, Onella, Yalena,
Yelena.
*Elana, Ena, Halina, Hela, Hele, Helena,
Helene, Helle, Hellen, Helli, Hellin,
Hellon, Hellyn, Helon*

Helena (Greek) a form of Helen. See
also Ilena.
*Halena, Halina, Helaina, Helana,
Helania, Helayna, Heleana, Heleena,
Helenia, Helenka, Helenna, Helina,
Hellanna, Hellena, Hellenna, Helona,
Helonna*

Helene (French) a form of Helen.
*Helaine, Helanie, Helayne, Heleen,
Heleine, Hèléne, Helenor, Heline,
Hellenor*

Helga (German) pious.
(Scandinavian) a form of Olga. See
also Elga.

Heli (Spanish) a form of Heliana.

Helia (Greek) as if she were the sun.

Heliana (Greek) she who offers
herself to God.

Heliena (Greek) sun.

Helki 🎌 (Native American)
touched.
Helkey, Helkie, Helky

Helma (German) a short form of
Wilhelmina.
Halma, Helme, Helmi, Helmine, Hilma

Heloísa (German) a form of Eloísa.

Heloise (French) a form of Louise.
Héloïse, Hlois

Helsa (Danish) a form of Elizabeth.
Helse, Helsey, Helsi, Helsie, Helsy

Heltu (Moquelumnan) like a bear
reaching out.

Helvecia (Latin) member of the
Helvetians, ancient inhabitants of
Switzerland; happy friend.

Helvia (Latin) she who has blonde
locks of hair.

Helya (Chuukese) a form of Helia.

Hema (Indian) gold.

Hemakshi (Indian) golden eyes.

Hemalata (Indian) golden creeper.

Hemali (Indian) to bring wealth.

Hemangi (Indian) golden body.

Hemangini (Indian) girl with a
golden body.

Hemaprabha (Indian) golden light.

Hemashri (Indian) one with a
golden body.

Hemkanta (Indian) golden girl.

Hemlata (Indian) golden flower.

Heng (Chinese) constant.

Henna (English) a familiar form of
Henrietta.
*Hena, Henaa, Henah, Heni, Henia,
Henny, Henya*

Henrietta (English) ruler of the
household. See also Enrica, Etta,
Yetta.
*Harriet, Hattie, Hatty, Hendrika,
Heneretta, Henka, Henna, Hennrietta,
Hennriette, Henretta, Henrica, Henrie,
Henrieta, Henriete, Henriette, Henrika,
Henrique, Henriquetta, Henryetta,
Hetta, Hettie*

Hera (Greek) queen; jealous.
Mythology: the queen of heaven
and the wife of Zeus.

Hercilia, Hersilia (Greek) she who
is delicate, tender, kind.

Hermelinda (German) she who is
the shield of strength.

Hermenegilda (Spanish) she who
offers sacrifices to God.

Hermia (Greek) messenger.

Hermilda (German) battle of force.

Hermina (Latin) noble. (German)
soldier. See also Erma, Ermine,
Irma.
Herma, Hermenia, Hermia, Herminna

Herminda (Greek) announcer.

Hermínia (Portuguese) a form of
Hermina.

Hermione (Greek) earthy.
*Hermalina, Hermia, Hermina, Hermine,
Herminia*

Hermosa (Spanish) beautiful.

Hernanda (Spanish) bold voyager.

Hertha (English) child of the earth.
Heartha, Hirtha

Herundina (Latin) like a swallow.

Hessa (Indian) destiny.

Hester (Dutch) a form of Esther.
Hessi, Hessie, Hessye, Hesther, Hettie

Hestia (Persian) star. Mythology: the
Greek goddess of the hearth and
home.
Hestea, Hesti, Hestie, Hesty

Heta (Native American) racer.

Heti (Indian) sunray.

Hetta (German) a form of Hedda.
(English) a familiar form of
Henrietta.

Hettie (German) a familiar form of
Henrietta, Hester.
Hetti, Hetty

Hia (Korean) grace.

Hiah (Korean) bright.

Hidako (Japanese) beautiful child.

Hide (Japanese) excellent.

Hideko (Japanese) excellent child.

Hidemi (Japanese) beautiful; excellent.

Hideyo (Japanese) superior
generations.

Hien (Vietnamese) blessing from
above.

Higa (Japanese) evil.

Highly (Chuukese) high.

Higinia (Greek) she who has and
enjoys good health.

Hikaru (Japanese) generation of
excellence.

Hilary, Hillary **G** (Greek) cheerful,
merry. See also Alair.
*Hilaree, Hilari, Hilaria, Hilarie, Hilery,
Hiliary, Hillaree, Hillari, Hillarie,
Hilleary, Hilleree, Hilleri, Hillerie,
Hillery, Hillianne, Hilliary, Hillory*

Hilda (German) a short form of
Brunhilda, Hildegarde.
*Helle, Hilde, Hildey, Hildie, Hildur,
Hildy, Hulda, Hylda*

Hildegarda (German) she who
hopes to fight.

Hildegarde (German) fortress.
*Hilda, Hildagard, Hildagarde,
Hildegard, Hildred*

Hildegunda (German) heroic
fighter.

Hili (Indian) dancer.

Hilla (Indian) timid.

Hima (Indian) snow.

Himani (Indian) cold.

Himeko (Japanese) princess child.

Hina (Indian) a shrub.

Hinako (Japanese) child named for
the sun.

Hind (Indian) proper name.

Hinda (Hebrew) hind; doe.
Hindey, Hindie, Hindy, Hynda

Hipatia (Greek) best.

Hipólita (Greek) she who unties her
horse and readies herself for battle.

Hiral (Indian) wealthy.

Hiranmayi (Indian) like a deer.

Hiro (Japanese) broad.

Hiroe (Japanese) large branch.

Hiromi (Japanese) the beautiful ocean.

Hisa (Japanese) long lasting.
Hisae, Hisako, Hisay

Hisano (Japanese) open plain.

Hita (Indian) lovable.

Hitaishi (Indian) well wisher.

Hitee (Indian) love and care.

Hiti (Eskimo) hyena.
Hitty

Hiya (Indian) heart; happiness.

Hoa (Vietnamese) flower; peace.
Ho, Hoai

Hogolina (Teutonic) having clear thoughts and great intelligence.

Hokulani (Hawaiian) star of the heavens.

Hola (Hopi) seed-filled club.

Holden 🅑 (English) hollow in the valley.

Holley (English) a form of Hólly.
Holleah, Hollee

Holli (English) a form of Holly.

Hollie 🅖 (English) a form of Holly.
Holeigh, Holleigh

Hollis 🅑🅖 (English) near the holly bushes.
Hollise, Hollyce, Holyce

Holly 🅖 (English) holly tree.
Holley, Hollye

Hollyann (English) a combination of Holly + Ann.
Holliann, Hollianna, Hollianne, Hollyanne, Hollyn

Hollyn (English) a short form of Hollyann.
Holin, Holeena, Hollina, Hollynn

Holo (Hawaiian) fleet.

Honami (Japanese) sail; a type of red apple; beautiful.

Honey (English) sweet. (Latin) a familiar form of Honora.
Honalee, Hunney, Hunny

Hong (Vietnamese) pink.

Hong Hoa (Vietnamese) perfect.

Hong Yen (Vietnamese) meek and gentle.

Hongminh (Vietnamese) rose.

Honnesha (Indian) rich person.

Honora (Latin) honorable. See also Nora, Onora.
Honey, Honner, Honnor, Honnour, Honor, Honorah, Honorata, Honore, Honoree, Honoria, Honorina, Honorine, Honour, Honoure

Honoratas (Spanish) honor.

Hoon (Korean) bright.

Hoor (Indian) celestial.

Hooriya (Indian) angel.

Hop (Vietnamese) pink swallow bird.

Hope 🅖 (English) hope.
Hopey, Hopi, Hopie

Hopoe (Hawaiian) in full bloom.

Hortense (Latin) gardener. See also Ortensia.
Hortencia, Hortensia

Hoshi (Japanese) star.
Hoshie, Hoshiko, Hoshiyo

Hoshimi (Japanese) beautiful, shining star.

Houston **B** (English) hill town. Geography: a city in Texas.

Hradini (Indian) lightening.

Hridyesha (Indian) heart.

Hsia (Chinese) summer.

Hsiang (Chinese) incense; village; enjoy; image.

Hsiao (Chinese) dawn; tiny; smile.

Hsiu (Chinese) pretty.

Hsun (Chinese) to teach.

Hu (Chinese) lake.

Hua (Chinese) flower.

Huai (Chinese) bosom.

Huan (Chinese) happiness.

Huan Yue, Huan-Yue (Chinese) joyful, happy.

Huang (Chinese) yellow.

Huanquyi (Mapuche) announcer; she who has a loud voice, shouted.

Huata (Moquelumnan) basket carrier.

Hudaña (Chamorro) she is mute.

Hue (Vietnamese) bright red.

Hugo **B** (Latin) a form of Hugh (see Boys' Names).

Hugolina (Teutonic) having clear thoughts and great intelligence.

Hui (Chinese) orchid.

Hui Ying, Hui-Ying (Chinese) bright, intelligent.

Huilen, Huillen, Hullen (Araucanian) spring.

Huma (Indian) bird of paradise.

Humaila (Indian) golden necklace.

Humiko (Palauan) large red ant.

Humildad (Latin) humility.

Hung (Vietnamese) consistent.

Hunter **B** (English) hunter.
Hunta, Huntar, Huntter

Huo (Chinese) fire.

Huong (Vietnamese) flower.

Huseina (Swahili) a form of Hasana.

Husn, Husna (Indian) beauty.

Hu-Tu (Chinese) female deity that represents Earth.

Huyen (Vietnamese) lily flower; intelligence, mental brilliance.

Hwan (Korean) a form of Heija.

Hy (Korean) instruct.

Hya (Korean) joyful; ring.

Hyacinth (Greek) Botany: a plant with colorful, fragrant flowers. See also Cynthia, Jacinda.
Giacinta, Hyacintha, Hyacinthe, Hyacinthia, Hyacinthie, Hycinth, Hycynth

Hyang (Korean) a form of Heija.

Hydi, Hydeia (German) forms of Heidi.
Hyde, Hydea, Hydee, Hydia, Hydie, Hydiea

Hye (Korean) graceful.

Hyun (Korean) bright.

Hyun Ah (Korean) fragrance, incense; village; enjoy.

Hyun Mee (Korean) worth; wise; dark; subtle; bowstring, musical string.

Hyun Mi (Korean) she who has wisdom.

Hyung (Korean) a form of Hyun Mi.

Hyunh (Vietnamese) pink rose.

Hyunsook (Korean) unpolished; rice.

I Wei (Chinese) a form of Iwei.

Iaesha, Ieeshia (Arabic) forms of Aisha.

Ian ☒ (Hebrew) God is gracious.
Iaian, Iain, Iana, Iann, Ianna, Iannel, Iyana

Ianthe (Greek) violet flower.
Iantha, Ianthia, Ianthina

Iara (Tupi) she is a lady.

Iberia (Latin) she who is a native of Iberia or comes from the Iberian peninsula.

Ibtihaaj (Indian) joy.

Ibtisam (Arabic) smiling.

Ibuuch (Palauan) a form of Evarista.

Icess (Egyptian) a form of Isis.
Ices, Icesis, Icesse, Icey, Icia, Icis, Icy

Ichieko (Chuukese) a form of Ichiko.

Ichiko (Japanese) first daughter.

Ida (German) hard working. (English) prosperous.
Idah, Idaia, Idalia, Idalis, Idaly, Idamae, Idania, Idarina, Idarine, Idaya, Ide, Idelle, Idette, Idys

Idalina (English) a combination of Ida + Lina.
Idaleena, Idaleene, Idalena, Idalene, Idaline

Idalis (English) a form of Ida.
Idalesse, Idalise, Idaliz, Idallas, Idallis, Idelis, Idelys, Idialis

Idara (Latin) well-organized woman.

Ideashia (American) a combination of Ida + Iesha.
Idasha, Idaysha, Ideesha, Idesha

Idelgunda (German) combative when fighting.

Idelia, Idelina (German) she who is noble.

Idelle (Welsh) a form of Ida.
Idell, Idella, Idil

Idha (Indian) insight.

Idika (Indian) the Earth.

Iditri (Indian) complimentary.

Idoia (Spanish) reference to the Virgin Mary.

Idoshi (Kosraean) a form of Violeta.

Idoya (Spanish) pond, an important place of worship of the Virgin Mary.

Idub (Palauan) a form of Yumiko.

Idumea (Latin) red.

Idurre (Spanish) reference to the Virgin Mary.

Ieko (Japanese) house child.

Iesha (American) a form of Aisha.
Ieachia, Ieaisha, Ieasha, Ieashe, Ieesha, Ieeshia, Ieisha, Ieishia, Iescha, Ieshah, Ieshea, Iesheia, Ieshia, Iiesha, Iisha

Ifigenia (Greek) having great strength and vitality; woman of strong, vital roots.

Ifiginia (Spanish) a form of Ifigenia.

Ignacia (Latin) fiery, ardent.
Ignacie, Ignasha, Ignashia, Ignatia, Ignatzia

Iha (Indian) wish.

Ihina (Indian) enthusiasm.

Ihita (Indian) desire.

Ijaya (Indian) sacrifice.

Ikia (Hebrew) God is my salvation. (Hawaiian) a form of Isaiah.
Ikaisha, Ikea, Ikeea, Ikeia, Ikeisha, Ikeishi, Ikeishia, Ikesha, Ikeshia, Ikeya, Ikeyia, Ikiea, Ikiia

Ikraam (Indian) honor; hospitality, generosity.

Iksha (Indian) sight.

Ikshita (Indian) visible.

Ikshula (Indian) holy river.

Iku (Japanese) nourishing.

Ikuko (Japanese) flourishing child.

Ikuku (Japanese) perfume child.

Ikumi (Japanese) drinking well.

Ikuye (Japanese) blessed cultural flourishing.

Ila (Hungarian) a form of Helen.

Ilana (Hebrew) tree.
Ikaina, Ilane, Ilani, Ilania, Ilainie, Illana, Illane, Illani, Ilania, Illanie, Ilanit

Ilchahueque (Mapuche) young, virginal woman.

Ilda (German) heroine in battle.

Ildegunda (German) she who knows how to fight.

Ileana (Hebrew) a form of Iliana.
Ilea, Ileah, Ileane, Ileanna, Ileanne, Illeana

Ilebed (Palauan) betel nut.

Ilena (Greek) a form of Helena.
Ileana, Ileena, Ileina, Ilina, Ilyna

Ilene (Irish) a form of Helen. See also Aileen, Eileen.
Ileen, Ileene, Iline, Ilyne

Ileseva (Fijian) a form of Elizabeth.

Ilhaam (Indian) intuition.

Iliana (Greek) from Troy.
Ileana, Ili, Ilia, Iliani, Illiana, Illiani, Illianna, Illyana, Illyanna

Ilima (Hawaiian) flower of Oahu.

Ilisa (Scottish, English) a form of Alisa, Elisa.
Ilicia, Ilissa, Iliza, Illisa, Illissa, Illysa, Illyssa, Ilycia, Ilysa, Ilysia, Ilyssa, Ilyza

Ilisapeci (Fijian) a form of Elizabeth.

Ilise (German) a form of Elise.
Ilese, Illytse, Ilyce, Ilyse

Ilisha (Hebrew) a form of Alisha, Elisha. See also Lisha.
Ileshia, Ilishia, Ilysha, Ilyshia

Ilka (Hungarian) a familiar form of Ilona.
Ilke, Milka, Milke

Ilona (Hungarian) a form of Helen.
Ilka, Illona, Illonia, Illonya, Ilonka, Ilyona

Ilse (German) a form of Elizabeth. See also Elsa.
Ilsa, Ilsey, Ilsie, Ilsy

Iluminada (Spanish) illuminated.

Iluochel (Palauan) something used to kill fish.

Im (Korean) wise and virtuous woman.

Ima (Japanese) presently. (German) a familiar form of Amelia.

Imaculada (Portuguese) immaculate.

Imala (Native American) strong-minded.

Iman 🄶 (Arabic) believer.
Aman, Imana, Imane, Imani

Imani 🄶 (Arabic) a form of Iman.
Amani, Emani, Imahni, Imanie, Imanii, Imonee, Imoni

Imelda (German) warrior.
Imalda, Irmhilde, Melda

Imena (African) dream.
Imee, Imene

Imogene (Latin) image, likeness.
Emogen, Emogene, Imogen, Imogenia, Imojean, Imojeen, Innogen, Innogene

Imperia (Latin) imperial.

Imperio (Latin) head of state, ruler.

Imtithal (Indian) obedience.

In (Korean) two; different; finished.

Ina (Irish) a form of Agnes.
Ena, Inanna, Inanne

Inaam (Indian) act of kindness, bestowal.

Inagangta (Chamorro) our noise.

Inaganta (Chamorro) a form of Inagangta.

Inah (Chamorro) a form of Ina.

Inara, Inaria (Chuukese) forms of Hilaria.

Inaya (Indian) concern.

Inayat (Indian) kindness.

Inayic (Chamorro) choice.

Indali (Indian) powerful.

Indamira, Indemira (Arabic) guest of the princess.

India (Hindi) from India.
Indea, Indeah, Indee, Indeia, Indeya, Indi, Indiah, Indian, Indiana, Indianna, Indie, Indieya, Indiya, Indy, Indya

Indigo (Latin) dark blue color.
Indiga, Indygo

Indira (Hindi) splendid. History: Indira Nehru Gandhi was an Indian politician and prime minister.
Indiara, Indra, Indre, Indria

Indrakshi (Indian) one having beautiful eyes.

Indrani (Indian) wife of Indra.

Indrayani (Indian) a holy river.

Indu, Induleksh (Indian) the moon.

Induja (Indian) the moon's daughter.

Indukala (Indian) phases of the moon.

Indulala (Indian) moonlight.

Indulekha (Indian) moon.

Induma (Indian) moon.

Indumati (Indian) full moon.

Indumukhi (Indian) one with a face like the moon.

Induprabha (Indian) moon rays.

Ine (Japanese) rice plant; clothes; sound.

Inàs (Portuguese) a form of Ines.

Ines, Inés, Inez (Spanish) forms of Agnes. See also Ynez.
Inesa, Inesita, Inésita, Inessa

Inga (Scandinavian) a short form of Ingrid.
Ingaberg, Ingaborg, Inge, Ingeberg, Ingeborg, Ingela

Ingrid (Scandinavian) hero's daughter; beautiful daughter.
Inga, Inger

Inika (Indian) small earth.

Inina (Chuukese) a glimmer of light.

Inmaculada (Latin) she who is pure and clean, without blemishes.

Inoa (Hawaiian) name.

Inocencia, Inoceneia, Inocenta (Spanish) innocence.

Inseng (Tagalog) the plumeria flower.

Insinani (Kosraean) a form of Fumii.

Intisaar (Indian) triumph.

Inu (Indian) attractive.

Invención (Latin) invention.

Ioana (Romanian) a form of Joan.
Ioani, Ioanna

Iola (Greek) dawn; violet colored. (Welsh) worthy of the Lord.
Iole, Iolee, Iolia

Iolana (Hawaiian) soaring like a hawk.

Iolani (Hawaiian) royal hawk.

Iolanthe (English) a form of Yolanda. See also Jolanda.
Iolanda, Iolande

Iona (Greek) violet flower.
Ione, Ioney, Ioni, Ionia, Iyona, Iyonna

Iosefa (Fijian) a form of Josefa.

Iphigenia (Greek) sacrifice. Mythology: the daughter of the Greek leader Agamemnon. See also Gena.

Ipi (Mapuche) harvester; careful.

Ipo (Hawaiian) sweetheart lover.

Ipsa (Indian) ambition; desire.

Ipsita (Indian) desire.

Iraja (Indian) wind's daughter.

Iratze (Basque) reference to the Virgin Mary.

Iravati (Indian) the Ravi River.

Irene 🅶 (Greek) peaceful. Mythology: the goddess of peace. See also Orina, Rena, Rene, Yarina.
Irén, Irien, Irina, Jereni

Iridia (Latin) belonging to Iris.

Iriel (Hebrew) a form of Uriel.

Irimia (Spanish) name of the place where the Miño river starts.

Irina (Russian) a form of Irene.
Eirena, Erena, Ira, Irana, Iranda, Iranna, Irena, Irenea, Irenka, Iriana, Irin, Irinia, Irinka, Irona, Ironka, Irusya, Iryna, Irynka, Rina

Iris 🅶 (Greek) rainbow. Mythology: the goddess of the rainbow and messenger of the gods.
Irisa, Irisha, Irissa, Irita, Irys, Iryssa

Irma (Latin) a form of Erma.
Irmina, Irminia

Irmã (Portuguese) a form of Irma.

Irma de la Paz (Spanish) peaceful Irma.

Irta (Greek) pearl.

Irune (Basque) reference to the holy trinity.

Irupe (Guarani) like the flower of the same name.

Irupé (Guarani) refers to the aquatic plant of the same name.

Isabeau (French) a form of Isabel.

Isabel 🄶 (Spanish) conse-crated to God. See also Bel, Belle, Chavella, Ysabel.
Isabal, Isabeau, Isabeli, Isabelita, Isabella, Isabelle, Ishbel, Isobel, Issie, Izabel, Izabele, Izabella

Isabelina (Hebrew) she who loves God.

Isabella ☀ 🄶 (Italian) a form of Isabel.
Isabela, Isabelia, Isabello

Isabelle ☀🄶 (French) a form of Isabel.
Isabele, Isabell

Isadora (Latin) gift of Isis.
Isidora

Isaiah 🄱 (Hebrew) God is my salvation.

Isako (Japanese) helpful child.

Isaldina (German) powerful warrior, she who controls harshly.

Isamar 🄶 (Hebrew) a form of Itamar.

Isamu (Japanese) rock.

Isano (Japanese) helpful.

Isapela (Fijian) a form of Isabel.

Isaura (Greek) native of Isauria, ancient region in Asia Minor.

Isaye (Japanese) help; branch; inlet.

Isberga (German) she who protects, sword in hand.

Isela (Scottish) a form of Isla.
Isel

Iselda (German) she who remains faithful.

Iseult (Welsh) fair lady. Literature: Also known as Isolde, a princess in the Arthurian legends; a heroine in the medieval romance *Tristan and Isolde*. See also Yseult.

Isha (American) a form of Aisha.
Ishae, Ishana, Ishanaa, Ishanda, Ishanee, Ishaney, Ishani, Ishanna, Ishaun, Ishawna, Ishaya, Ishenda, Ishia, Iysha

Ishi (Japanese) rock.
Ishiko, Ishiyo, Shiko, Shiyo

Ishie (Japanese) a form of Ishi.

Ishika (Indian) paintbrush.

Ishita (Indian) superior.

Ishwari (Indian) goddess.

Ishwarya (Indian) wealth, prosperity.

Ishya (Indian) spring.

Isis (Egyptian) supreme goddess. Mythology: the goddess of nature and fertility.
Icess, Issis, Isys

Isla (Scottish) Geography: the River Isla is in Scotland.
Isela

Isleta (Spanish) small island.

Ismelda (German) she who uses the sword in battle.

Ismenia (Greek) she who words anxiously.

Isobel (Spanish) a form of Isabel.
Isobell, Isobella, Isobelle

Isoka (Benin) gift from god.
Soka

Isoko (Japanese) child of the beach.

Isolde (Welsh) fair lady. Literature: Also known as Iseult, a princess in the Arthurian legends; a heroine in the medieval romance *Tristan and Isolde*. See also Yseult.
Isolda, Isolt, Izolde

Isolina (German) powerful warrior, she who controls harshly.

Isono (Japanese) shore; field, plain.

Issie (Spanish) a familiar form of Isabel.
Isa, Issi, Issy, Iza

Ister (Persian) a form of Esther.

Ita (Irish) thirsty.

Italia (Italian) from Italy.
Itali, Italie, Italy, Italya

Italina (Italian) native of the land between two seas.

Itamar (Hebrew) palm island.
Isamar, Isamari, Isamaria, Ithamar, Ittamar

Itatay (Guarani) hand bell.

Itati (Guarani) refers to the dedication of the virgin of Itatí.

Itatí (Guarani) white rock; refers to the dedication of the virgin of Itatí.

Itkila (Indian) fragrant.

Ito (Japanese) thread.

Itsaso (Basque) sea.

Itsuko (Japanese) fifth daughter.

Itzel (Spanish) protected.
Itcel, Itchel, Itesel, Itsel, Itssel, Itza, Itzallana, Itzayana, Itzell, Ixchel

Iva (Slavic) a short form of Ivana.
Ivah

Ivalani (Hawaiian) a form of Ewelani.

Ivan **B** (Russian) a form of John.

Ivana (Slavic) God is gracious. See also Yvanna.
Iva, Ivanah, Ivania, Ivanka, Ivanna, Ivannia, Ivany

Iverem (Tiv) good fortune; blessing.

Iverna (Latin) from Ireland.
Ivernah

Ivette (French) a form of Yvette. See also Evette.
Ivet, Ivete, Iveth, Ivetha, Ivett, Ivetta

Ivey **G** (English) a form of Ivy.

Ivón (Spanish) a form of Ivonne.

Ivonne (French) a form of Yvonne. See also Evonne.
Ivon, Ivona, Ivone, Ivonna, Iwona, Iwonka, Iwonna, Iwonne

Ivory (Latin) made of ivory.
Ivoory, Ivori, Ivorie, Ivorine, Ivree

Ivria (Hebrew) from the land of Abraham.
Ivriah, Ivrit

Ivy **G** (English) ivy tree.
Ivey, Ivie

Iwa (Japanese) rock.

Iwalani (Hawaiian) heavenly frigate bird.

Iwei (Chinese) consider, think.

Iyabo (Yoruba) mother has returned.

Iyana, Iyanna (Hebrew) forms of Ian.
Iyanah, Iyannah, Iyannia

Izabella (Spanish) a form of Isabel.
Izabela, Izabell, Izabellah, Izabelle, Izobella

Izanami (Japanese) she who invites you to enter.

Izar (Basque) star.

Izarbe (Aragonese) Virgin Mary of the Pyrenees mountains.

Izarra, Izarre (Basque) star.

Izazkun (Basque) reference to the Virgin Mary.

Izdihaar (Indian) flourishing, blossoming.

Izna (Indian) light.

Izora (Arabic) dawn.

Izusa (Native American) white stone.

J

J B (American) an initial used as a first name.

Jaba (Indian) hibiscus.

Jabeen (Indian) forehead.

Jabel (Hebrew) flowing stream.

Jabrea, Jabria (American) combinations of the prefix Ja + Brea.
Jabreal, Jabree, Jabreea, Jabreena, Jabrelle, Jabreona, Jabri, Jabriah, Jabriana, Jabrie, Jabriel, Jabrielle, Jabrienna, Jabrina

Jacalyn (American) a form of Jacqueline.
Jacalynn, Jacolyn, Jacolyne, Jacolynn

Jace B (Greek) a form of Jacey.

Jacelyn (American) a form of Jocelyn.
Jaceline, Jacelyne, Jacelynn, Jacilyn, Jacilyne, Jacilynn, Jacylyn, Jacylyne, Jacylynn

Jacey G (Greek) a familiar form of Jacinda. (American) a combination of the initials J. + C.

Jaci, Jacie (Greek) forms of Jacey.
Jacci, Jacia, Jacie, Jaciel, Jaici, Jaicie

Jacinda, Jacinta (Greek) beautiful, attractive. (Spanish) forms of Hyacinth.
Jacenda, Jacenta, Jacey, Jacinthe, Jacintia, Jacynthe, Jakinda, Jaxine

Jacinthe (Spanish) a form of Jacinda.
Jacinte, Jacinth, Jacintha

Jackalyn (American) a form of Jacqueline.
Jackalene, Jackalin, Jackaline, Jackalynn, Jackalynne, Jackelin, Jackeline, Jackelyn, Jackelynn, Jackelynne, Jackilin, Jackilyn, Jackilynn, Jackilynne, Jackolin, Jackoline, Jackolyn, Jackolynn, Jackolynne

Jackeline, Jackelyn (American) forms of Jacqueline.
Jackelin, Jackelline, Jackellyn, Jockeline

Jacki (American) a familiar form of Jacqueline.

Jackie BG (American) a familiar form of Jacqueline.
Jackee, Jackey, Jackia, Jackielee, Jacky, Jackye

Jacklyn (American) a form of Jacqueline.
Jacklin, Jackline, Jacklyne, Jacklynn, Jacklynne

Jackquel (French) a short form of Jacqueline.
Jackqueline, Jackquetta, Jackquiline, Jackquilyn, Jackquilynn, Jackquilynne

Jackson B (English) child of Jack.

Jaclyn G (American) a short form of Jacqueline.
Jacleen, Jaclin, Jacline, Jaclyne, Jaclynn

Jacob B (Hebrew) supplanter, substitute.

Jacobi (Hebrew) a form of Jacob.
Coby, Jacoba, Jacobee, Jacobette, Jacobia, Jacobina, Jacoby, Jacolbi, Jacolbia, Jacolby

Jacoby **B** (Hebrew) a form of Jacobi.

Jacqualine (French) a form of Jacqueline.
Jacqualin, Jacqualine, Jacqualyn, Jacqualyne, Jacqualynn

Jacquelin (French) a form of Jacqueline.
Jacquelina

Jacqueline (French) supplanter, substitute; little Jacqui.
Jacalyn, Jackalyn, Jackeline, Jacki, Jacklyn, Jackquel, Jaclyn, Jacqueena, Jacqueine, Jacquel, Jacqueleen, Jacquelene, Jacquelin, Jacquelyn, Jacquelynn, Jacquena, Jacquene, Jacquenetta, Jacquenette, Jacqui, Jacquiline, Jacquine, Jakelin, Jaquelin, Jaqueline, Jaquelyn, Jocqueline

Jacquelyn, Jacquelynn (French) forms of Jacqueline.
Jackquelyn, Jackquelynn, Jacquelyne, Jacquelynne

Jacques **B** (French) a form of Jacob, James.

Jacqui (French) a short form of Jacqueline.
Jacquay, Jacqué, Jacquee, Jacqueta, Jacquete, Jacquetta, Jacquette, Jacquie, Jacquise, Jacquita, Jaquay, Jaqui, Jaquie, Jaquiese, Jaquina, Jaquita

Jacquiline (French) a form of Jacqueline.
Jacquil, Jacquilin, Jacquilyn, Jacquilyne, Jacquilynn

Jacqulin, Jacqulyn (American) forms of Jacqueline.
Jackquilin, Jacqul, Jacqulin, Jacqulyne, Jacqulynn, Jacqulynne, Jacquoline

Jacy (Greek) a familiar form of Jacinda. (American) a combination of the initials J. + C.
Jace, Jac-E, Jacee, Jaci, Jacie, Jacylin, Jaice, Jaicee

Jacynthe (Spanish) a form of Jacinda.
Jacynda, Jacynta, Jacynth, Jacyntha

Jada **G** (Spanish) a form of Jade.
Jadah, Jadda, Jadae, Jadzia, Jadziah, Jaeda, Jaedra, Jayda

Jade **G** (Spanish) jade.
Jadea, Jadeann, Jadee, Jaden, Jadera, Jadi, Jadie, Jadienne, Jady, Jadyn, Jaedra, Jaida, Jaide, Jaiden, Jayde, Jayden

Jadelyn (American) a combination of Jade + Lynn.
Jadalyn, Jadelaine, Jadeline, Jadelyne, Jadelynn, Jadielyn

Jaden **B** (Spanish) a form of Jade.
Jadeen, Jadena, Jadene, Jadeyn, Jadin, Jadine, Jaeden, Jaedine

Jadyn **G** (Spanish) a form of Jade.
Jadynn, Jaedyn, Jaedynn

Jae (Latin) jaybird. (French) a familiar form of Jacqueline.
Jaea, Jaey, Jaya

Jael **G** (Hebrew) mountain goat; climber. See also Yael.
Jaela, Jaelee, Jaeli, Jaelie, Jaelle, Jahla, Jahlea

Jaelyn, Jaelynn (American) combinations of Jae + Lynn.
Jaeleen, Jaelin, Jaelinn, Jaelyn, Jailyn, Jalyn, Jalynn, Jayleen, Jaylyn, Jaylynn, Jaylynne

Jaffa (Hebrew) a form of Yaffa.
Jaffice, Jaffit, Jafit, Jafra

Jagadamba, Jagamata (Indian) mother of the world.

Jagamohini (Indian) one who attracts the world.

Jagrati (Indian) awakening.

Jagravi (Indian) king.

Jagriti (Indian) vigilance.

Jagruti (Indian) awareness.

Jagvi (Indian) worldly.

Jaha (Swahili) dignified.
Jahaida, Jahaira, Jaharra, Jahayra, Jahida, Jahira, Jahitza

Jahanara (Indian) queen of the world.

Jaheel (Indian) a lake.

Jahnavi, Janhavi (Indian) the Ganga River.

Jai 🅱 (Tai) heart. (Latin) a form of Jaye.

Jaida, Jaide (Spanish) forms of Jade.
Jaidah, Jaidan

Jaiden 🅱 (Spanish) a form of Jade.
Jaidey, Jaidi, Jaidin, Jaidon

Jaidyn (Spanish) a form of Jade.

Jailyn (American) a form of Jaelyn.
Jaileen, Jailen, Jailene, Jailin, Jailine

Jaime 🅱 (French) I love.
Jaima, Jaimee, Jaimey, Jaimie, Jaimini, Jaimme, Jaimy, Jamee

Jaimee 🅶 (French) a form of Jaime.

Jaimie 🅶 (French) a form of Jaime.
Jaimi, Jaimmie

Jaira (Spanish) Jehovah teaches.
Jairah, Jairy

Jaishree (Indian) honor of victory.

Jaisudha (Indian) nectar of victory.

Jaiwanthi, Jaiwanti (Indian) victory.

Jakeisha (American) a combination of Jakki + Aisha.
Jakeisia, Jakesha, Jakisha

Jakelin (American) a form of Jacqueline.
Jakeline, Jakelyn, Jakelynn, Jakelynne

Jakki (American) a form of Jacki.
Jakala, Jakea, Jakeela, Jakeida, Jakeita, Jakela, Jakelia, Jakell, Jakena, Jaketta, Jakevia, Jaki, Jakia, Jakiah, Jakira, Jakita, Jakiya, Jakiyah, Jakke, Jakkia

Jalabala (Indian) a river.

Jalaja (Indian) goddess of wealth; lotus.

Jalbala (Indian) lotus flower.

Jaleel 🅱 (Hindi) a form of Jalil (see Boys' Names).

Jaleesa (American) a form of Jalisa.
Jaleasa, Jalece, Jalecea, Jaleesah, Jaleese, Jaleesia, Jaleisa, Jaleisha, Jaleisya

Jalen 🅱 (American) a form of Jalena.

Jalena (American) a combination of Jane + Lena.
Jalaina, Jalana, Jalani, Jalanie, Jalayna, Jalean, Jaleen, Jaleena, Jaleene, Jalen, Jalene, Jalina, Jaline, Jallena, Jalyna, Jelayna, Jelena, Jelina, Jelyna

Jalesa, Jalessa (American) forms of Jalisa.
Jalese, Jalesha, Jaleshia, Jalesia

Jalia, Jalea (American) combinations of Jae + Leah.
Jaleah, Jalee, Jaleea, Jaleeya, Jaleia, Jalitza

Jalila (Arabic) great.
Jalile

Jalisa, Jalissa (American) combinations of Jae + Lisa.
Jaleesa, Jalesa, Jalise, Jalisha, Jalisia, Jalysa

Jalsa (Indian) celebration.

Jalyn, Jalynn (American) combinations of Jae + Lynn. See also Jaylyn.
Jaelin, Jaeline, Jaelyn, Jaelyne, Jaelynn, Jaelynne, Jalin, Jaline, Jalyne, Jalynne

Jalysa (American) a form of Jalisa.
Jalyse, Jalyssa, Jalyssia

Jamaal B (Arabic) a form of Jamal.

Jamaica (Spanish) Geography: an island in the Caribbean.
Jameca, Jamecia, Jameica, Jameika, Jameka, Jamica, Jamika, Jamoka, Jemaica, Jemika, Jemyka

Jamal B (Arabic) beautiful.

Jamani (American) a form of Jami.
Jamana

Jamar B (American) a form of Jamaria.

Jamarcus B (American) a combination of the prefix Ja + Marcus.

Jamaria (American) combinations of Jae + Maria.
Jamar, Jamara, Jamarea, Jamaree, Jamari, Jamarie, Jameira, Jamerial, Jamira

Jamecia (Spanish) a form of Jamaica.

Jamee (French) a form of Jaime.

Jameerah (Indian) beautiful one.

Jameika, Jameka (Spanish) forms of Jamaica.
Jamaika, Jamaka, Jamecka, Jamekia, Jamekka

James B (Hebrew) supplanter, substitute. (English) a form of Jacob.

Jamesha (American) a form of Jami.
Jameisha, Jamese, Jameshia, Jameshyia, Jamesia, Jamesica, Jamesika, Jamesina, Jamessa, Jameta, Jametta, Jamiesha, Jamisha, Jammesha, Jammisha

Jameson B (English) son of James.

Jamey (English) a form of Jami, Jamie.

Jami, Jamie G (Hebrew, English) supplanter, substitute.
Jama, Jamani, Jamay, Jamesha, Jamey,

Jamia, Jamii, Jamis, Jamise, Jammie, Jamy, Jamye, Jayme, Jaymee, Jaymie

Jamia (English) a form of Jami, Jamie.
Jamea, Jamiah, Jamiea, Jamiya, Jamiyah, Jamya, Jamyah

Jamica (Spanish) a form of Jamaica.
Jamika

Jamil B (Arabic) a form of Jamal.

Jamila (Arabic) beautiful. See also Yamila.
Jahmela, Jahmelia, Jahmil, Jahmilla, Jameela, Jameelah, Jameeliah, Jameila, Jamela, Jamelia, Jameliah, Jamell, Jamella, Jamelle, Jamely, Jamelya, Jamiela, Jamielee, Jamilah, Jamilee, Jamilia, Jamiliah, Jamilla, Jamillah, Jamille, Jamillia, Jamilya, Jamyla, Jemeela, Jemelia, Jemila, Jemilla

Jamilam (Arabic) a form of Jamilah.

Jamilynn (English) a combination of Jami + Lynn.
Jamielin, Jamieline, Jamielyn, Jamielyne, Jamielynn, Jamielynne, Jamilin, Jamiline, Jamilyn, Jamilyne, Jamilynne

Jamini (Indian) night.

Jaminie (Indian) flower.

Jamison B (English) child of James.

Jammie (American) a form of Jami.
Jammi, Jammice, Jammise

Jamonica (American) a combination of Jami + Monica.
Jamoni

Jamuna (Indian) holy river.

Jamylin (American) a form of Jamilynn.
Jamylin, Jamyline, Jamylyn, Jamylyne, Jamylynn, Jamylynne, Jaymylin, Jaymyline, Jaymylyn, Jaymylyne, Jaymylynn, Jaymylynne

Jan 🅱 (Dutch, Slavic) a form of John. (English) a short form of Jane, Janet, Janice.
Jania, Jandy

Jana 🄶 (Hebrew) gracious, merciful. (Slavic) a form of Jane. See also Yana.
Janalee, Janalisa, Janna, Janne

Janaan (Indian) heart; soul.

Janae 🄶 (American) a form of Jane.
Janaé, Janaea, Janaeh, Janah, Janai, Janea, Janee, Janée, Jannae, Jenae, Jennae

Janai (American) a form of Janae.
Janaiah, Janaira, Janaiya

Janaknandini (Indian) daughter of King Janak.

Janalynn (American) a combination of Jana + Lynn.
Janalin, Janaline, Janalyn, Janalyne, Janalynne

Janan (Arabic) heart; soul.
Jananee, Janani, Jananie, Janann, Jananni

Janay (American) a form of Jane.
Janaya, Janaye, Jannay, Jenay, Jenaya, Jennay, Jennaya, Jennaye

Jane 🄶 (Hebrew) God is gracious. See also Chavon, Jean, Joan, Juanita, Seana, Shana, Shawna, Sheena, Shona, Shunta, Sinead, Zaneta, Zanna, Zhana.
Jaine, Jan, Jana, Janae, Janay, Janelle, Janessa, Janet, Jania, Janice, Janie, Janika, Janine, Janis, Janka, Jannie, Jasia, Jayna, Jayne, Jenica

Janel (French) a form of Janelle.
Janiel, Jannel, Jaynel

Janell 🄶 (French) a form of Janelle.
Jannell, Janyll, Jaynell

Janelle 🄶 (French) a form of Jane.
Janel, Janela, Janele, Janelis, Janell, Janella, Janelli, Janellie, Janelly, Janely, Janelys, Janielle, Janille, Jannelle, Jannellies, Jaynelle

Janesha (American) a form of Janessa.
Janeisha, Janeshia, Janiesha, Janisha, Janishia, Jannesha, Jannisha, Janysha, Jenesha, Jenisha, Jennisha

Janessa 🄶 (American) a form of Jane.
Janeesa, Janesa, Janesea, Janesha, Janesia, Janeska, Janessi, Janessia, Janiesa, Janissa, Jannesa, Jannessa, Jannisa, Jannissa, Janyssa, Jenesa, Jenessa, Jenissa, Jennisa, Jennissa

Janet (English) a form of Jane. See also Jessie, Yanet.
Jan, Janeta, Janete, Janeth, Janett, Janette, Jannet, Janot, Jante, Janyte

Janeth (English) a form of Janet.
Janetha, Janith, Janneth

Janette 🄶 (French) a form of Janet.
Janett, Janetta

Janice (Hebrew) God is gracious. (English) a familiar form of Jane. See also Genice.
Jan, Janece, Janecia, Janeice, Janiece, Janizzette, Jannice, Janniece, Janyce, Jenice, Jhanice, Jynice

Janie (English) a familiar form of Jane.
Janey, Jani, Janiyh, Jannie, Janny, Jany

Janika (Slavic) a form of Jane.
Janaca, Janeca, Janecka, Janeika, Janeka, Janica, Janick, Janicka, Janieka, Janikka, Janikke, Janique, Janka, Jankia, Jannica, Jannick, Jannika, Janyca, Jenica, Jenicka, Jenika, Jeniqua, Jenique, Jennica, Jennika, Jonika

Janine 🄶 (French) a form of Jane.
Janean, Janeann, Janeanne, Janeen, Janenan, Janene, Janina, Jannen, Jannina, Jannine, Jannyne, Janyne, Jeannine, Jeneen, Jenine

Janis 🄶 (English) a form of Jane.
Janees, Janese, Janesey, Janess,

Janesse, Janise, Jannis, Jannise, Janys, Jenesse, Jenis, Jennise, Jennisse

Janita (American) a form of Juanita. See also Genita.
Janitra, Janitza, Janneta, Jaynita, Jenita, Jennita

Janna (Arabic) harvest of fruit. (Hebrew) a short form of Johana.
Janaya, Janaye, Jannae, Jannah, Jannai

Jannette (French) a form of Janet.
Jannett, Jannetta

Jannie (English) a familiar form of Jan, Jane.
Janney, Janny

Januja (Indian) female offspring.

Jaquan **B** (American) a combination of the prefix Ja + Quan (see Boys' Names).

Jaquana (American) a combination of Jacqueline + Anna.
Jaqua, Jaquai, Jaquanda, Jaquania, Jaquanna

Jaquelen (American) a form of Jacqueline.
Jaquala, Jaquera, Jaqulene, Jaquonna

Jaquelin, Jaqueline (French) forms of Jacqueline.
Jaqualin, Jaqualine, Jaquelina, Jaquline, Jaquella

Jaquelyn (French) a form of Jacqueline.
Jaquelyne, Jaquelynn, Jaquelynne

Jardena (Hebrew) a form of Jordan. (French, Spanish) garden.
Jardan, Jardana, Jardane, Jarden, Jardenia, Jardin, Jardine, Jardyn, Jardyne

Jared **B** (Hebrew) a form of Jordan.

Jarian (American) a combination of Jane + Marian.

Jarita (Arabic) earthen water jug.
Jara, Jaretta, Jari, Jaria, Jarica, Jarida, Jarietta, Jarika, Jarina, Jaritta, Jaritza, Jarixa, Jarnita, Jarrika, Jarrine

Jarod **B** (Hebrew) a form of Jared.

Jarred **B** (Hebrew) a form of Jared.

Jarrett **B** (English) a form of Garrett, Jared.

Jarul (Indian) flower queen.

Jas **BG** (American) a short form of Jasmine.
Jase, Jass, Jaz, Jazz, Jazze, Jazzi

Jasia (Polish) a form of Jane.
Jaisha, Jasa, Jasea, Jasha, Jashae, Jashala, Jashona, Jashonte, Jasie, Jassie, Jaysa

Jaskaran **B** (Sikh) sings praises to the Lord.

Jaskarn **B** (Sikh) a form of Jaskaran.

Jasleen **G** (Latin) a form of Jocelyn.
Jaslene, Jaslien, Jaslin, Jasline

Jaslyn (Latin) a form of Jocelyn.
Jaslynn, Jaslynne

Jasmain (Persian) a short form of Jasmine.
Jasmaine, Jasmane, Jassmain, Jassmaine

Jasmarie (American) a combination of Jasmine + Marie.
Jasmari

Jasmeet **BG** (Persian) a form of Jasmine.

Jasmin **G** (Persian) a form of Jasmine.
Jasimin, Jasman, Jasmeen, Jasmen, Jasmon, Jassmin, Jassminn

Jasmine ☀ **G** (Persian) jasmine
flower. See also Jessamine, Yasmin.
*Jas, Jasma, Jasmain, Jasme, Jasmeet,
Jasmene, Jasmin, Jasmina, Jasminne,
Jasmira, Jasmit, Jasmyn, Jassma,
Jassmin, Jassmine, Jassmit, Jassmon,
Jassmyn, Jazmin, Jazmyn, Jazzmin*

Jasmyn, Jasmyne (Persian) forms of
Jasmine.
Jasmynn, Jasmynne, Jassmyn

Jasoda (Indian) mother of Lord
Krishna.

Jasodhara (Indian) mother of Lord
Buddha.

Jasone (Basque) assumption.

Jasper **B** (Punjabi) a form of
Jaspreet.

Jaspreet **BG** (Punjabi) virtuous.
*Jaspar, Jasparit, Jasparita, Jasper,
Jasprit, Jasprita, Jasprite*

Jasum (Indian) hibiscus.

Jasweer (Indian) victorious.

Jatara (American) a combination of
Jane + Tara.
Jataria, Jatarra, Jatori, Jatoria

Jauria (Arabic) jewel, gem.

Javana (Malayan) from Java.
*Javán, Javanna, Javanne, Javona,
Javonna, Jawana, Jawanna, Jawn*

Javiera (Spanish) owner of a new
house. See also Xaviera.
Javeera, Viera

Javon **B** (Malayan) a form of
Javona.

Javona, Javonna (Malayan) forms of
Javana.
*Javon, Javonda, Javone, Javoni,
Javonne, Javonni, Javonya*

Javonte **B** (American) a form of
Javan (see Boys' Names).

Jay **B** (French) blue jay.

Jaya (Hindi) victory.
Jaea, Jaia

Jayalakshmi, Jayashri (Indian) the
goddess of victory.

Jayamala (Indian) a garland of
flowers given to the one who wins.

Jayani (Indian) a Shakti (consort) of
Ganesha.

Jayaprabha (Indian) the light of
victory.

Jayaprada (Indian) one who gives
victory.

Jayashree (Indian) victorious
woman.

Jayasudha (Indian) the nectar of
victory.

Jayati, Jayavanti, Jayita (Indian)
victorious.

Jayavardhini (Indian) goddess who
increases victory.

Jaycee (American) a combination of
the initials J. + C.
*Jacee, Jacey, Jaci, Jacie, Jacy, Jayce,
Jaycey, Jayci, Jaycie, Jaycy*

Jayda (Spanish) a form of Jada.
Jaydah, Jeyda

Jayde **G** (Spanish) a form of Jade.
Jayd

Jaydee (American) a combination of
the initials J. + D.
*Jadee, Jadey, Jadi, Jadie, Jady, Jaydey,
Jaydi, Jaydie, Jaydy*

Jayden **B** (Spanish) a form of Jade.
*Jaydeen, Jaydene, Jaydin, Jaydn,
Jaydon*

Jaye (Latin) jaybird.
Jae, Jay

Jayla **G** (American) a short form of
Jaylene.
*Jaylaa, Jaylah, Jayli, Jaylia, Jayliah,
Jaylie*

Jaylen **B** (American) a form of
Jaylene.

Jaylene (American) forms of Jaylyn.
*Jayelene, Jayla, Jaylan, Jayleana,
Jaylee, Jayleen, Jayleene, Jaylen,
Jaylenne*

Jaylin **B** (American) a form of Jaylyn.
Jayline, Jaylinn

Jaylon **B** (American) a form of Jaylen.

Jaylyn **BG** (American) a combination
of Jaye + Lynn. See also Jalyn.
Jaylene, Jaylin, Jaylyne

Jaylynn (American) a form of Jaylyn.
Jaylynne

Jayme **G** (English) a form of Jami.

Jaymee, Jaymi (English) forms of
Jami.

Jaymie (English) a form of Jami.
Jaymi, Jaymia, Jaymine, Jaymini

Jayna (Hebrew) a form of Jane.
Jaynae, Jaynah, Jaynna

Jayne (Hindi) victorious. (English) a
form of Jane.
Jayn, Jaynie, Jaynne

Jaynie (English) a familiar form of
Jayne.
Jaynee, Jayni

Jazlyn (American) a combination of
Jazmin + Lynn.
*Jasleen, Jazaline, Jazalyn, Jazleen,
Jazlene, Jazlin, Jazline, Jazlon, Jazlynn,
Jazlynne, Jazzalyn, Jazzleen, Jazzlene,
Jazzlin, Jazzline, Jazzlyn, Jazzlynn,
Jazzlynne*

Jazmin (Persian) a form of Jasmine.
*Jazmaine, Jazman, Jazmen, Jazmín,
Jazminn, Jazmon, Jazzmit*

Jazmine **G** (Persian) a form of
Jasmine.

Jazmyn, Jazmyne (Persian) forms of
Jasmine.
*Jazmynn, Jazmynne, Jazzmyn,
Jazzmyne*

Jazzmin, Jazzmine (Persian) forms
of Jasmine.
*Jazzman, Jazzmeen, Jazzmen,
Jazzmene, Jazzmenn, Jazzmon*

Jean **B** (Scottish) a form of Jeanne.

Jeana, Jeanna (Scottish) forms of
Jean.
Jeanae, Jeannae, Jeannia

Jeanette **G** (French) a form of Jean.
*Jeanet, Jeanete, Jeanett, Jeanetta,
Jeanita, Jenet, Jenett, Jenette, Jinetta,
Jinette*

Jeanie, Jeannie (Scottish) familiar
forms of Jean.
Jeannee, Jeanney, Jeani, Jeanny, Jeany

Jeanine, Jenine (Scottish) forms of
Jean. See also Geneen.
*Jeaneane, Jeaneen, Jeanene, Jeanina,
Jeannina, Jeannine, Jennine*

Jeanne (Scottish) God is gracious.
See also Kini.
*Jeana, Jeanann, Jeancie, Jeane,
Jeaneia, Jeanette, Jeaneva, Jeanice,
Jeanie, Jeanine, Jeanmaria, Jeanmarie,
Jeanna, Jeanné, Jeannie, Jeannita,
Jeannot, Jeantelle*

Jeannett (French) a form of Jean.
*Jeannete, Jeannetta, Jeannette,
Jeannita, Jennet, Jennett, Jennetta,
Jennette, Jennita*

Jedidiah **B** (Hebrew) friend of
God, beloved of God.

Jeeval (Indian) full of life.

Jeevana (Indian) life.

Jeevankala (Indian) art of life.

Jeevika (Indian) water.

Jefferson Ⓑ (English) child of Jeff.

Jeffery Ⓑ (English) a form of Jeffrey.

Jeffrey Ⓑ (English) divinely peaceful.

Jehannaz (Indian) pride of the universe.

Jelena (Russian) a form of Helen. See also Yelena.
Jalaine, Jalane, Jalani, Jalanna, Jalayna, Jalayne, Jaleen, Jaleena, Jaleene, Jalena, Jalene, Jelaina, Jelaine, Jelana, Jelane, Jelani, Jelanni, Jelayna, Jelayne, Jelean, Jeleana, Jeleen, Jeleena, Jelene

Jelisa (American) a combination of Jean + Lisa.
Jalissa, Jelesha, Jelessa, Jelise, Jelissa, Jellese, Jellice, Jelysa, Jelyssa, Jillisa, Jillissa, Julissa

Jem Ⓖ (Hebrew) a short form of Jemima.
Gem, Jemi, Jemia, Jemiah, Jemie, Jemm, Jemmi, Jemmy

Jemima (Hebrew) dove.
Jamim, Jamima, Jem, Jemimah, Jemma

Jemina, Jenima (Hebrew) dove.

Jemma (Hebrew) a short form of Jemima. (English) a form of Gemma.
Jemmia, Jemmiah, Jemmie, Jemmy

Jena, Jenae (Arabic) forms of Jenna.
Jenah, Jenai, Jenal, Jenay, Jenaya, Jenea

Jenara (Latin) dedicated to the god, Janus.

Jendaya (Zimbabwean) thankful.
Daya, Jenda, Jendayah

Jenelle (American) a combination of Jenny + Nelle.
Genell, Jeanell, Jeanelle, Jenall, Jenalle, Jenel, Jenela, Jenele, Jenell, Jenella, Jenille, Jennel, Jennell, Jennella, Jennelle, Jennielle, Jennille, Jinelle, Jinnell

Jenessa (American) a form of Jenisa.
Jenesa, Jenese, Jenesia, Jenessia, Jennesa, Jennese, Jennessa, Jinessa

Jenica (Romanian) a form of Jane.
Jeneca, Jenika, Jenikka, Jennica, Jennika

Jenifer, Jeniffer (Welsh) forms of Jennifer.
Jenefer

Jenilee (American) a combination of Jennifer + Lee.
Jenalea, Jenalee, Jenaleigh, Jenaly, Jenelea, Jenelee, Jeneleigh, Jenely, Jenelly, Jenileigh, Jenily, Jennalee, Jennely, Jennielee, Jennilea, Jennilee, Jennilie

Jenisa (American) a combination of Jennifer + Nisa.
Jenessa, Jenisha, Jenissa, Jenisse, Jennisa, Jennise, Jennisha, Jennissa, Jennisse, Jennysa, Jennyssa, Jenysa, Jenyse, Jenyssa, Jenysse

Jenka (Czech) a form of Jane.

Jenna Ⓖ (Arabic) small bird. (Welsh) a short form of Jennifer. See also Gen.
Jena, Jennae, Jennah, Jennai, Jennat, Jennay, Jennaya, Jennaye, Jhenna

Jenni, Jennie (Welsh) familiar forms of Jennifer.
Jeni, Jenne, Jenné, Jennee, Jenney, Jennia, Jennier, Jennita, Jennora, Jensine

Jennifer Ⓖ (Welsh) white wave; white phantom. A form of Guinevere. See also Gennifer, Ginnifer, Yenifer.
Jen, Jenifer, Jeniffer, Jenipher, Jenna,

Jennafer, Jenni, Jenniferanne,
Jenniferlee, Jenniffe, Jenniffer, Jenniffier,
Jennifier, Jennilee, Jenniphe, Jennipher,
Jenny, Jennyfer

Jennilee (American) a combination
of Jenny + Lee.
Jennalea, Jennalee, Jennielee, Jennilea,
Jennilie, Jinnalee

Jennilyn, Jennilynn (American)
combinations of Jenni + Lynn.
Jennalin, Jennaline, Jennalyn,
Jenalynann, Jenelyn, Jenilyn, Jennalyne,
Jennalynn, Jennalynne, Jennilin,
Jenniline, Jennilyne, Jennilynne

Jenny **G** (Welsh) a familiar form of
Jennifer.
Jenney, Jenni, Jennie, Jeny, Jinny

Jennyfer (Welsh) a form of Jennifer.
Jenyfer

Jeraldine (English) a form of
Geraldine.
Jeraldeen, Jeraldene, Jeraldina,
Jeraldyne, Jeralee, Jeri

Jeremiah **B** (Hebrew) God will
uplift.

Jeremy **B** (English) a form of
Jeremiah.

Jereni (Russian) a form of Irene.
Jerena, Jerenae, Jerina

Jeri, Jerri, Jerrie (American) short
forms of Jeraldine. See also Geri.
Jera, Jerae, JeRae, Jeree, Jeriel, Jerilee,
Jerinda, Jerra, Jerrah, Jerrece, Jerree,
Jerriann, Jerrilee, Jerrine, Jerry,
Jerrylee, Jerryne, Jerzy

Jerica (American) a combination of
Jeri + Erica.
Jereca, Jerecka, Jerice, Jericka, Jerika,
Jerrica, Jerrice, Jeryka

Jerilyn (American) a combination of
Jeri + Lynn.
Jeralin, Jeraline, Jeralyn, Jeralyne,
Jeralynn, Jeralynne, Jerelin, Jereline,
Jerelyn, Jerelyne, Jerelynn, Jerelynne,
Jerilin, Jeriline, Jerilyne, Jerilynn,
Jerilynne, Jerrilin, Jerriline, Jerrilyn,
Jerrilyne, Jerrilynn, Jerrilynne, Jerrylea

Jermaine **B** (French) a form of
Germaine.
Jermain, Jerman, Jermanay, Jermanaye,
Jermane, Jermanee, Jermani, Jermanique,
Jermany, Jermayne, Jermecia, Jermia,
Jermice, Jermicia, Jermika, Jermila

Jerónima (Greek) she who has a
sacred name.

Jerrica (American) a form of Jerica.
Jerreka, Jerricah, Jerricca, Jerricha,
Jerricka, Jerrieka, Jerrika

Jerry **B** (American) a form of Jeri.

Jerusalén (Hebrew) vision of peace.

Jerusha (Hebrew) inheritance.
Jerushah, Yerusha

Jesabel (Hebrew) God's oath.

Jesenia, Jessenia **G** (Arabic) flower.
Jescenia, Jessennia, Jessenya

Jeshna (Indian) victory.

Jésica (Slavic) a form of Jessica.

Jesica, Jesika (Hebrew) forms of
Jessica.
Jesicca, Jesikah, Jesikkah

Jess **B** (Hebrew) a short form of
Jessie.

Jessa (American) a short form of
Jessalyn, Jessamine, Jessica.
Jesa, Jesha, Jessah

Jessalyn (American) a combination
of Jessica + Lynn.
*Jesalin, Jesaline, Jesalyn, Jesalyne,
Jesalynn, Jesalynne, Jesilin, Jesiline,
Jesilyn, Jesilyne, Jesilynn, Jesilynne,
Jessa, Jessalin, Jessaline, Jessalyne,
Jessalynn, Jessalynne, Jesselin, Jesseline,
Jesselyn, Jesselyne, Jesselynn,
Jesselynne, Jesslyn*

Jessamine (French) a form of
Jasmine.
*Jessa, Jessamin, Jessamon, Jessamy,
Jessamyn, Jessemin, Jessemine, Jessimin,
Jessimine, Jessmin, Jessmine, Jessmon,
Jessmy, Jessmyn*

Jesse 🅱 (Hebrew) a form of Jessie.
Jese, Jesi, Jesie

Jesseca (Hebrew) a form of Jessica.

Jessi 🇬 (Hebrew) a form of Jessie.

Jessica ☀ 🇬 (Hebrew) wealthy.
Literature: a name perhaps invented
by Shakespeare for a character in his
play *The Merchant of Venice*. See
also Gessica, Yessica.
*Jesica, Jesika, Jessa, Jessaca, Jessca,
Jesscia, Jesseca, Jessia, Jessicah, Jessicca,
Jessicia, Jessicka, Jessika, Jessiqua, Jessy,
Jessyca, Jessyka, Jezeca, Jezica, Jezika,
Jezyca*

Jessie 🅱🇬 (Hebrew) a short form of
Jessica. (Scottish) a form of Janet.
*Jescie, Jesey, Jessé, Jessee, Jessey, Jessi,
Jessia, Jessiya, Jessye*

Jessika 🇬 (Hebrew) a form of Jessica.
Jessieka

Jesslyn (American) a short form of
Jessalyn.
*Jessilyn, Jessilynn, Jesslin, Jesslynn,
Jesslynne*

Jessy 🅱 (Hebrew, Scottish) a form
of Jessie.

Jessyca, Jessyka (Hebrew) forms of
Jessica.

Jesus 🅱 (Hebrew) a form of Joshua.

Jesusa (Spanish) Jehovah is salvation.

Jésusa (Hebrew, Spanish) God is my
salvation.

Jetta (English) jet black mineral.
(American) a familiar form of
Jevette.
Jeta, Jetia, Jetje, Jette, Jettie

Jevette (American) a combination of
Jean + Yvette.
Jetta, Jeva, Jeveta, Jevetta

Jewel (French) precious gem.
*Jewelann, Jewelia, Jeweliana,
Jeweliann, Jewelie, Jewell, Jewelle,
Jewellee, Jewellene, Jewellie, Juel, Jule*

Jezebel (Hebrew) unexalted; impure.
Bible: the wife of King Ahab.
*Jesibel, Jessabel, Jessebel, Jez, Jezabel,
Jezabella, Jezabelle, Jezebell,
Jezebella, Jezebelle*

Jhalak (Indian) glimpse; spark.

Jharna (Indian) a spring.

Jheel (Indian) lake.

Jhilmil (Indian) sparkling.

Jhinuk (Indian) oyster.

Ji (Chinese) lucky.

Ji Hye (Korean) the ninth of the ten
heavenly stems; official.

Ji Won (Korean) mankind; to lead;
cause; enduring; tiger; bride.

Jia (Chinese) beautiful.

Jia Hui (Chinese) excellent flower.

Jia Li (Chinese) good and beautiful.

Jian (Chinese) strong.

Jiang (Chinese) river.

Jiang Li, Jiang-Li (Chinese) beautiful river.

Jianna (Italian) a form of Giana.
Jiana, Jianina, Jianine, Jianni, Jiannini

Jiao (Chinese) beautiful, handsome, lovely; tender; charming.

Jibon (Hindi) life.

Jie (Chinese) pure.

Jigisha (Indian) superior.

Jigna, Jignasa (Indian) intellectual curiosity.

Jigya, Jigyasa (Indian) curiosity.

Jill **G** (English) a short form of Jillian.
Jil, Jilli, Jillie, Jilly

Jillaine (Latin) a form of Jillian.
Jilaine, Jilane, Jilayne, Jillana, Jillane, Jillann, Jillanne, Jillayne

Jilleen (Irish) a form of Jillian.
Jileen, Jilene, Jiline, Jillene, Jillenne, Jilline, Jillyn

Jillian **G** (Latin) youthful. See also Gillian.
Jilian, Jiliana, Jiliann, Jilianna, Jilianne, Jilienna, Jilienne, Jill, Jillaine, Jilliana, Jilliane, Jilliann, Jillianne, Jileen, Jillien, Jillienne, Jillion, Jillyn

Jilpa (Indian) life-giving.

Jimi (Hebrew) supplanter, substitute.
Jimae, Jimaria, Jimee, Jimella, Jimena, Jimia, Jimiah, Jimie, Jimiyah, Jimmeka, Jimmet, Jimmi, Jimmia, Jimmie

Jimisha (American) a combination of Jimi + Aisha.
Jimica, Jimicia, Jimmicia, Jimysha

Jimmie **B** (Hebrew) a form of Jimi.

Jimmy **B** (English) a familiar form of Jim (see Boys' Names).

Jin **B** (Japanese) tender. (American) a short form of Ginny, Jinny.

Jina (Swahili) baby with a name. (Italian) a form of Gina.
Jena, Jinae, Jinan, Jinda, Jinna, Jinnae

Jing (Chinese) crystal; sparkly.

Jingjing (Tagalog) a form of Jingjing.

Jinky (Tagalog) term of respect for an elder sister.

Jinny (Scottish) a familiar form of Jenny. (American) a familiar form of Virginia. See also Ginny.
Jin, Jinnee, Jinney, Jinni, Jinnie

Jiong (Chinese) shining.

Jirina (Czech) a form of Georgia.
Jirah, Jireh

Jivantika (Indian) one who gives life.

Jiyoung (Korean) wisdom, intelligence.

Jizelle (American) a form of Giselle.
Jessel, Jezel, Jezell, Jezella, Jezelle, Jisel, Jisela, Jisell, Jisella, Jiselle, Jissel, Jissell, Jissella, Jisselle, Jizel, Jizella, Joselle

Jlu (Chinese) for a long time.

Jo **G** (American) a short form of Joanna, Jolene, Josephine.
Joangie, Joetta, Joette, Joey

Joan (Hebrew) God is gracious. History: Joan of Arc was a fifteenth-century heroine and resistance fighter. See also Ioana, Jean, Juanita, Siobhan.
Joane, Joaneil, Joanel, Joanelle, Joanie, Joanmarie, Joann, Joannanette, Joanne, Joannel, Joanny, Jonni

Joana (English) a form of Joanna.

Joanie, Joannie (Hebrew) familiar forms of Joan.
Joanee, Joani, Joanni, Joenie, Johanie, Johnnie, Joni

Joanna ☀ (English) a form of Joan. See also Yoanna.
Janka, Jhoana, Jo, Jo-Ana, Joandra, Joanka, Joananna, Jo-Anie, Joanka, Jo-Anna, Joannah, Jo-Annie, Joeana, Joeanna, Johana, Johanna, Johannah

Joanne (English) a form of Joan.
Joanann, Joananne, Joann, Jo-Ann, Jo-Anne, Joayn, Joeann, Joeanne

Joanny (Hebrew) a familiar form of Joan.
Joany

Joaquina (Hebrew) God will establish.
Joaquine

Jobeth (English) a combination of Jo + Beth.

Joby 🄱 (Hebrew) afflicted. (English) a familiar form of Jobeth.
Jobey, Jobi, Jobie, Jobina, Jobita, Jobrina, Jobye, Jobyna

Jocacia (American) a combination of Joy + Acacia.

Jocelín (Latin) a form of Jocelin.

Jocelin, Joceline (Latin) forms of Jocelyn.
Jocelina, Jocelinn

Jocelyn ☀ 🄶 (Latin) joyous. See also Yocelin, Yoselin.
Jacelyn, Jasleen, Jocelin, Jocelle, Jocelyne, Jocelynn, Joci, Jocia, Jocilyn, Jocilynn, Jocinta, Joclyn, Joclynn, Josalyn, Joscelin, Joselin, Joselyn, Joshlyn, Josilin, Jossalin, Josselyn, Joycelyn

Jocelyne (Latin) a form of Jocelyn.
Joceline, Jocelynne, Joclynne

Jocosa, Jocose (Latin) jubilant.

Jodi, Jodie 🄶 (American) familiar forms of Judith.

Jodiann (American) a combination of Jodi + Ann.
Jodene, Jodi-Ann, Jodianna, Jodi-Anna, Jodianne, Jodi-Anne, Jodine, Jodyann, Jody-Ann, Jodyanna, Jody-Anna, Jodyanne, Jody-Anne, Jodyne

Jody 🄱🄶 (American) a familiar form of Judith.
Jodee, Jodele, Jodell, Jodelle, Jodevea, Jodey, Jodia, Jodiee, Jodilee, Jodi-Lee, Jodilynn, Jodi-Lynn, Joedi, Joedy

Joe 🄱 (Latin) a form of Joy.

Joel 🄱 (Hebrew) God is willing.

Joelle 🄱🄶 (Hebrew) a form of Joel.
Joela, Joele, Joelee, Joeli, Joelia, Joelie, Joell, Joella, Joëlle, Joelli, Joelly, Joely, Joyelle

Joelynn (American) a combination of Joelle + Lynn.
Joeleen, Joelene, Joeline, Joellen, Joellyn, Joelyn, Joelyne

Joey 🄱 (French) a familiar form of Josephine. (American) a form of Jo.

Johana, Johanna, Johannah (German) forms of Joana.
Janna, Joahna, Johanah, Johanka, Johanne, Johnna, Johonna, Jonna, Joyhanna, Joyhannah

Johanie, Johannie (Hebrew) forms of Joanie.
Johani, Johanni, Johanny, Johany

John 🄱 (Hebrew) God is gracious.

Johnna, Jonna (American) forms of Johana, Joanna.
Jahna, Jahnaya, Jhona, Jhonna, Johna, Johnda, Johnnielynn, Johnnie-Lynn, Johnnquia, Joncie, Jonda, Jondrea, Jontel, Jutta

Johnnessa (American) a combination of Johnna + Nessa.
Jahnessa, Johneatha, Johnecia, Johnesha, Johnetra, Johnisha, Johnishi, Johnnise, Jonyssa

Johnnie B (Hebrew) a form of Joanie.
Johni, Johnie, Johnni, Johnny

Johnny B (Hebrew) a form of Johnnie.

Joi G (Latin) a form of Joy.
Joia, Joie

Jojiana (Fijian) a form of Georgia.

Jokla (Swahili) beautiful robe.

Jolanda (Greek) a form of Yolanda. See also Iolanthe.
Jola, Jolan, Jolán, Jolande, Jolander, Jolanka, Jolánta, Jolantha, Jolanthe

Joleen, Joline (English) forms of Jolene.
Joleena, Joleene, Jolleen, Jollene

Jolene G (Hebrew) God will add, God will increase. (English) a form of Josephine.
Jo, Jolaine, Jolana, Jolane, Jolanna, Jolanne, Jolanta, Jolayne, Jole, Jolean, Joleane, Joleen, Jolena, Joléne, Jolenna, Jolin, Jolina, Jolinda, Joline, Jolinn, Jolinna, Jolleane, Jolleen, Jolline

Jolie (French) pretty.
Jole, Jolea, Jolee, Joleigh, Joley, Joli, Jolibeth, Jollee, Jollie, Jolly, Joly, Jolye

Jolisa (American) a combination of Jo + Lisa.
Joleesa, Joleisha, Joleishia, Jolieasa, Jolise, Jolisha, Jolisia, Jolissa, Jolysa, Jolyssa, Julissa

Jolynn (American) a combination of Jo + Lynn.
Jolyn, Jolyne, Jolynne

Jon B (Hebrew) a form of John. A short form of Jonathan.

Jonah B (Hebrew) dove.

Jonatan B (Hebrew) a form of Jonathan.

Jonatha (Hebrew) gift of God.
Johnasha, Johnasia, Jonesha, Jonisha

Jonathan B (Hebrew) gift of God.

Jonelle (American) a combination of Joan + Elle.
Jahnel, Jahnell, Jahnelle, Johnel, Johnell, Johnella, Johnelle, Jonel, Jonell, Jonella, Jonyelle, Jynell, Jynelle

Jonesha, Jonisha (American) forms of Jonatha.
Joneisha, Jonesa, Joneshia, Jonessa, Jonisa, Jonishia, Jonneisha, Jonnesha, Jonnessia

Jong (Tagalog) little girl.

Joni (American) a familiar form of Joan.
Jona, Jonae, Jonai, Jonann, Jonati, Joncey, Jonci, Joncie, Jonice, Jonie, Jonilee, Joni-lee, Jonis, Jony

Jonika (American) a form of Janika.
Johnica, Johnique, Johnquia, Johnnica, Johnnika, Joneeka, Joneika, Jonica, Joniqua, Jonique

Jonina (Hebrew) dove. See also Yonina.
Jona, Jonita, Jonnina

Jonita (Hebrew) a form of Jonina. See also Yonita.
Johnetta, Johnette, Johnita, Johnittia, Jonati, Jonetia, Jonetta, Jonette, Jonit, Jonnita, Jonta, Jontae, Jontaé, Jontaya

Jonni, Jonnie (American) familiar forms of Joan.
Jonny

Jonquil (Latin, English) Botany: an
ornamental plant with fragrant
yellow flowers.
Jonquelle, Jonquie, Jonquill, Jonquille

Jontel (American) a form of Johnna.
*Jontaya, Jontell, Jontelle, Jontia, Jontila,
Jontrice*

Joo (Korean) aspiring; volunteering.

Joo-Eun (Korean) wisdom and
courage.

Joon (Korean) master, ruler; red;
eternity; daytime; boat; tree trunk;
pillar.

Jora 🄶 (Hebrew) autumn rain.
Jorah

Jordan 🄱 (Hebrew) descending.
See also Jardena.
*Jordain, Jordaine, Jordana, Jordane,
Jordann, Jordanna, Jordanne, Jordany,
Jordea, Jordee, Jorden, Jordi, Jordian,
Jordie, Jordin, Jordon, Jordyn, Jori,
Jorie, Jourdan*

Jordana, Jordanna (Hebrew) forms
of Jordan. See also Giordana,
Yordana.
*Jordannah, Jordina, Jordonna,
Jourdana, Jourdanna*

Jorden 🄱 (Hebrew) a form of Jordan.
Jordenne

Jordin (Hebrew) a form of Jordan.
Jordine

Jordon 🄱 (Hebrew) a form of
Jordan.

Jordyn 🄶 (Hebrew) a form of
Jordan.
Jordyne, Jordynn, Jordynne

Jorge 🄱 (Spanish) a form of George
(see Boys' Names).

Jorgelina (Greek) she who works
well in the countryside.

Jori, Jorie (Hebrew) familiar forms
of Jordan.
*Jorai, Jorea, Joree, Jorée, Jorey, Jorian,
Jorin, Jorina, Jorine, Jorita, Jorre,
Jorrey, Jorri, Jorrian, Jorrie, Jorry, Jory*

Joriann (American) a combination of
Jori + Ann.
*Jori-Ann, Jorianna, Jori-Anna, Jorianne,
Jori-Anne, Jorriann, Jorrianna,
Jorrianne, Jorryann, Jorryanna,
Jorryanne, Joryann, Joryanna,
Joryanne*

Jorja (American) a form of Georgia.
*Jeorgi, Jeorgia, Jorgana, Jorgi, Jorgia,
Jorgina, Jorjana, Jorji*

Josalyn (Latin) a form of Jocelyn.
*Josalene, Josalin, Josalind, Josaline,
Josalynn, Joshalyne*

Joscelin, Joscelyn (Latin) forms of
Jocelyn.
*Josceline, Joscelyne, Joscelynn,
Joscelynne, Joselin, Joseline, Joselyn,
Joselyne, Joselynn, Joselynne, Joshlyn*

Jose 🄱 (Spanish) a form of Joseph.

Josee 🄶 (American) a familiar form
of Josephine.
Joesee, Josey, Josi, Josina, Josy, Jozee

Josée (American) a familiar form of
Josephine.

Josefina (Spanish) a form of Josephine.
Josefa, Josefena, Joseffa, Josefine

Joselín (Latin) a form of Joselin.

Joselin, Joseline (Latin) forms of
Jocelyn.
Joselina, Joselinne, Josielina

Joselle (American) a form of Jizelle.
Joesell, Jozelle

Joselyn, Joslyn (Latin) forms of
Jocelyn.
*Joselene, Joselyne, Joselynn, Joshely,
Josiline, Josilyn*

Joseph B (Hebrew) God will add, God will increase.

Josephine G (French) a form of Joseph. See also Fifi, Pepita, Yosepha.
Fina, Jo, Joey, Josee, Josée, Josefina, Josepha, Josephe, Josephene, Josephin, Josephina, Josephyna, Josephyne, Josette, Josey, Josie, Jozephine, Jozie, Sefa

Josette (French) a familiar form of Josephine.
Joesette, Josetta, Joshetta, Jozette

Josevini (Fijian) a form of Josephine.

Josey (Hebrew) a familiar form of Josephine.
Josi, Josse, Jossee, Jossie, Josy, Josye

Joshann (American) a combination of Joshlyn + Ann.
Joshana, Joshanna, Joshanne

Joshika (Indian) young maiden.

Joshita, Joshitha (Indian) pleased.

Joshlyn (Latin) a form of Jocelyn. (Hebrew) God is my salvation.
Joshalin, Joshalyn, Joshalynn, Joshalynne, Joshelle, Joshleen, Joshlene, Joshlin, Joshline, Joshlyne, Joshlynn, Joshlynne

Joshua B (Hebrew) God is my salvation.

Josiah B (Hebrew) fire of the Lord.

Josiane, Josianne (American) combinations of Josie + Anne.
Josian, Josie-Ann, Josieann

Josie (Hebrew) a familiar form of Josephine.

Josilin, Joslin (Latin) forms of Jocelyn.
Josielina, Josiline, Josilyn, Josilyne, Josilynn, Josilynne, Joslin, Josline, Joslyn, Joslyne, Joslynn, Joslynne

Josivini (Fijian) a form of Josefa.

Jossalin (Latin) a form of Jocelyn.
Jossaline, Jossalyn, Jossalynn, Jossalynne, Josselyn, Josslin, Jossline

Josselyn (Latin) a form of Jocelyn.
Josselen, Josselin, Josseline, Jossellen, Jossellin, Jossellyn, Josselyne, Josselynn, Josselynne, Josslyn, Josslyne, Josslynne

Josune (Spanish) named for Jesus.

Jourdan (Hebrew) a form of Jordan.
Jourdain, Jourdann, Jourdanne, Jourden, Jourdian, Jourdon, Jourdyn

Jovana (Latin) a form of Jovanna.
Jeovana, Jouvan, Jovan, Jovanah, Jovena, Jovian, Jowan, Jowana

Jovani B (Italian) a form of Jovannie.

Jovanna (Latin) majestic. (Italian) a form of Giovanna. Mythology: Jove, also known as Jupiter, was the supreme Roman god.
Jeovanna, Jovado, Joval, Jovana, Jovann, Jovannie, Jovena, Jovina, Jovon, Jovonda, Jovonia, Jovonna, Jovonnah, Jovonne, Jowanna

Jovanni B (Italian) a form of Jovannie.

Jovannie (Italian) a familiar form of Jovanna.
Jovanee, Jovani, Jovanie, Jovanne, Jovanni, Jovanny, Jovonnie

Jovita (Latin) jovial.
Joveda, Joveta, Jovetta, Jovida, Jovitta

Jowaki (Indian) a firefly.

Joy G (Latin) joyous.
Joya, Joye, Joyeeta, Joyella, Joyia, Joyous, Joyvina

Joyanne (American) a combination of Joy + Anne.
Joyan, Joyann, Joyanna

Joyce (Latin) joyous. A short form of Joycelyn.
Joice, Joycey, Joycie, Joyous, Joysel

Joycelyn (American) a form of Jocelyn.
Joycelin, Joyceline, Joycelyne, Joycelynn, Joycelynne

Joyceta (Spanish) a form of Joyce.

Joylyn (American) a combination of Joy + Lynn.
Joyleen, Joylene, Joylin, Joyline, Joylyne, Joylynn, Joy-Lynn, Joylynne

Jozie (Hebrew) a familiar form of Josephine.
Jozee, Jozée, Jozi, Jozy

Ju (Chinese) chrysanthemum.

Juan (Chinese) beautiful.

Juana (Spanish) a short form of Juanita.
Juanell, Juaney, Juanika, Juanit, Juanna, Juannia

Juana del Pilar (Spanish) a form of Juana.

Juandalyn (Spanish) a form of Juanita.
Jualinn, Juandalin, Juandaline, Juandalyne, Juandalynn, Juandalynne

Juaneta (Spanish) God is gracious.

Juanita (Spanish) a form of Jane, Joan. See also Kwanita, Nita, Waneta, Wanika.
Juana, Juandalyn, Juaneice, Juanequa, Juanesha, Juanice, Juanicia, Juaniqua, Juanisha, Juanishia

Juci (Hungarian) a form of Judy.
Jucika

Judith (Hebrew) praised. Mythology: the slayer of Holofernes, according to ancient Jewish legend. See also Yehudit, Yudita.
Giuditta, Ioudith, Jodi, Jodie, Jody, Jude, Judine, Judit, Judita, Judite, Juditha, Judithe, Judy, Judyta, Jutka

Judy ☐ (Hebrew) a familiar form of Judith.
Juci, Judi, Judie, Judye

Judyann (American) a combination of Judy + Ann.
Judana, Judiann, Judianna, Judianne, Judyanna, Judyanne

Jue (Chinese) two pieces of jade.

Juhi, Jui (Indian) flower.

Juichi (Japanese) long-lived first-born.

Juily (Indian) a flower.

Jui-Ying (Chinese) beautiful flower; lucky flower.

Jula (Polish) a form of Julia.
Julca, Julcia, Juliska, Julka

Julene (Basque) a form of Julia. See also Yulene.
Julena, Julina, Juline, Julinka, Juliska, Julleen, Jullena, Jullene, Julyne

Julia ☀ ☐ (Latin) youthful. See also Giulia, Jill, Jillian, Sulia, Yulia.
Iulia, Jula, Julea, Juleah, Julene, Juliah, Juliana, Juliann, Julica, Julie, Juliea, Juliet, Julija, Julina, Juline, Julisa, Julissa, Julita, Juliya, Julka, Julyssa

Julian ☐ (English) a form of Juliann.

Juliana (Czech, Spanish, Hungarian) a form of Julia.
Julieana, Juliena, Julliana, Julyana, Yuliana

Juliann (English) a form of Julia.
Julean, Julian, Juliane, Julien, Juliene, Jullian

Julianna ☐ (Czech, Spanish, Hungarian) a form of Julia.
Julieanna, Jullianna, Julyanna

Julianne ☐ (English) a form of Julia.
Juleann, Julieann, Julie-Ann, Julieanne, Julie-Anne, Julienn, Julienne

Julie **G** (English) a form of Julia.
Juel, Jule, Julee, Juli, Julie-Lynn, Julie-
Mae, Julle, Jullee, Jullie, Jully, July

Julien **B** (English) a form of
Juliann.

Juliet **G** (French) a form of Julia.
Julet, Julieta, Jullet, Julliet

Juliette (French) a form of Julia.
Juliett, Julietta, Jullietta

Julio **B** (Hispanic) a form of Julius.

Julisa, Julissa (Latin) forms of Julia.
Julis, Julisha, Julysa, Julyssa

Julita (Spanish) a form of Julia.
Julitta, Julyta

Julius **B** (Greek, Latin) youthful,
downy bearded.

Jum (Korean) silver pearl.

Jumaana (Indian) silver pearl.

Jumaris (American) a combination
of Julie + Maris.

Jun **B** (Chinese) truthful.

June (Latin) born in the sixth month.
Juna, Junea, Junel, Junell, Junella, Junelle,
Junette, Juney, Junia, Junie, Juniet, Junieta,
Junietta, Juniette, Junina, Junita

Jung Sook (Korean) true; heroic;
handsome; obey, honor.

Junko (Japanese) obedient.

Juno (Latin) queen. Mythology: the
supreme Roman goddess.

Juong (Korean) foretell.

Juri (Japanese) scarlet; hometown.

Justa (Latin) she who lives for and
according to the law of God.

Justice **G** (Latin) just, righteous.
Justis, Justise, Justiss, Justisse, Justus,
Justyce, Justys

Justin **B** (Latin) just, righteous.

Justina **G** (Italian) a form of Justine.
Jestena, Jestina, Justinna, Justyna

Justine **G** (Latin) just, righteous.
Giustina, Jestine, Juste, Justi, Justice,
Justie, Justina, Justinn, Justy, Justyn,
Justyne, Justynn, Justynne

Justiniana (Spanish) just, fair.

Justyn **B** (Latin) a form of Justine.

Juvencia, Juventina (Latin) youth.

Juwan **B** (American) a form of
Jajuan (see Boys' Names).

Jwala (Indian) flame.

Jyeshtha (Indian) biggest.

Jyothi, Jyotika (Indian) light.

Jyoti (Indian) light; brilliant.

Jyotibala (Indian) splendor.

Jyotirmoyee (Indian) lustrous.

Jyotishmati (Indian) luminous,
bright, glowing.

K

K **G** (American) an initial used as a
first name.

Ka (Korean) chaste, virtuous; quiet,
silent.

Kaamla (Indian) perfect.

Kaapuni (Hawaiian) to travel; a hula
step.

Kaasni (Indian) flower.

Kacey, Kacy G (Irish) brave.
(American) forms of Casey.
Combinations of the initials K. + C.
*K. C., Kace, Kacee, Kaci, Kacie, Kaicee,
Kaicey, Kasey, Kasie, Kaycee, Kayci,
Kaycie*

Kachina (Native American) sacred
dancer.
Kachine

Kaci, Kacie G (American) forms of
Kacey, Kacy.
Kasci, Kaycie, Kaysie

Kacia (Greek) a short form of Acacia.
Kaycia, Kaysia

Kadalina (Pohnpeian) a form of Flora.

Kadambari (Indian) novel;
nightingale bird.

Kadambhari (Indian) goddess.

Kadambini (Indian) clouds.

Kade B (Scottish) wetlands.
(American) a combination of the
initials K. + D.

Kadedra (American) a combination
of Kady + Dedra.
*Kadeadra, Kadedrah, Kadedria,
Kadeedra, Kadeidra, Kadeidre,
Kadeidria*

Kadeem B (Arabic) servant.

Kadejah (Arabic) a form of Kadijah.
Kadeija, Kadeijah, Kadejá, Kadejia

Kadelyn (American) a combination
of Kady + Lynn.

Kaden B (Arabic) a form of Kadin
(see Boys' Names).

Kadesha (American) a combination
of Kady + Aisha.
*Kadeesha, Kadeeshia, Kadeesia,
Kadeesiah, Kadeezia, Kadesa,
Kadesheia, Kadeshia, Kadesia,
Kadessa, Kadezia*

Kadie (English) a form of Kady.
Kadi, Kadia, Kadiah

Kadijah (Arabic) trustworthy.
Kadajah, Kadeeja, Kadeejah, Kadija

Kadisha (American) a form of
Kadesha.
*Kadiesha, Kadieshia, Kadishia, Kadisia,
Kadysha, Kadyshia*

Kady (English) a form of Katy. A
combination of the initials K. + D.
See also Cady.
*K. D., Kade, Kadee, Kadey, Kadie,
Kadya, Kadyn, Kaidi, Kaidy, Kayde,
Kaydee, Kaydey, Kaydi, Kaydie, Kaydy*

Kae (Greek, Teutonic, Latin) a form
of Kay.

Kaede (Japanese) maple leaf.

Kaedé (Japanese) maple leaf.

Kaela (Hebrew, Arabic) beloved,
sweetheart. A short form of Kalila,
Kelila.
*Kaelah, Kaelea, Kaeleah, Kaelee, Kaeli,
Kayla*

Kaelee, Kaeli (American) forms of
Kaela.
*Kaelei, Kaeleigh, Kaeley, Kaelia, Kaelie,
Kaelii, Kaelly, Kaely, Kaelye*

Kaelin (American) a form of Kaelyn.
*Kaeleen, Kaelene, Kaelina, Kaelinn,
Kalan*

Kaelyn G (American) a combi-
nation of Kae + Lynn. See also
Caelin, Kaylyn.
*Kaelan, Kaelen, Kaelin, Kaelynn,
Kaelynne*

Kaetlyn (Irish) a form of Kaitlin.
Kaetlin, Kaetlynn

Kagami (Japanese) mirror.

Kahawi (Hawaiian) river.

Kahekili (Hawaiian) thunder.

Kahkashan (Indian) stars.

Kahlil **B** (Arabic) a form of Khalíl (see Boys' Names).

Kaho (Japanese) fragrance; sail.

Kahsha (Native American) fur robe.
Kasha, Kashae, Kashia

Kai **B** (Hawaiian) sea. (Hopi, Navajo) willow tree.
Kae, Kaie

Kaia (Greek) earth. Mythology: Gaea was the earth goddess.
Kaiah, Kaija

Kaida (Japanese) little dragon.

Kaila (Hebrew) laurel; crown.
Kailah, Kailea, Kaileah, Kailee, Kailey, Kayla

Kailee, Kailey (American) familiar forms of Kaila. Forms of Kaylee.
Kaile, Kaileh, Kaileigh, Kaili, Kailia, Kailie, Kailli, Kaillie, Kaily, Kailya

Kailyn **G** (American) a form of Kaitlin.
Kailan, Kaileen, Kaileena, Kailen, Kailena, Kailene, Kaileyne, Kailin, Kailina, Kailon

Kailynn (American) a form of Kailyn.
Kailynne

Kaiolohia (Hawaiian) calm sea; peace of mind.

Kaipo (Hawaiian) the sweetheart.

Kairos (Greek) last, final, complete. Mythology: the last goddess born to Jupiter.
Kaira, Kairra

Kaishawn (American) a combination of Kai + Shawna.
Kaeshun, Kaisha, Kaishala, Kaishon

Kaitlin **G** (Irish) pure. See also Katelin.
Kaetlyn, Kailyn, Kailynn, Kaitlan, Kaitland, Kaitleen, Kaitlen, Kaitlind, Kaitlinn, Kaitlinne, Kaitlon, Kaytlin

Kaitlyn ☆ (Irish) a form of Caitlyn.

Kaitlynn (Irish) a form of Caitlyn.
Kaitelynne, Kaitlynne

Kaiulani (Hawaiian) the zenith, the highest point of the heavens.

Kaiya (Japanese) forgiveness.
Kaiyah, Kaiyia

Kaiyo (Japanese) forgiveness.

Kajal, Kajjali (Indian) eyeliner.

Kajri (Indian) light as a cloud.

Kakali (Indian) the chirping of birds.

Kako (Japanese) summer; rainbow.

Kala **G** (Arabic) a short form of Kalila. A form of Cala.
Kalah, Kalla, Kallah

Kalama **BG** (Hawaiian) torch.

Kalani **G** (Hawaiian) chieftain; sky.
Kailani, Kalanie, Kaloni

Kalapi (Indian) peacock; nightingale.

Kalapini (Indian) peacock; night.

Kalare (Latin, Basque) bright; clear.

Kalavati (Indian) artist.

Kalea (Hawaiian) bright; clear.
Kahlea, Kahleah, Kailea, Kaileah, Kaleah, Kaleea, Kaleeia, Kaleia, Kalia, Kallea, Kalleah, Kaylea, Kayleah, Khalea, Khaleah

Kaleb **B** (Hebrew) a form of Caleb.

Kalee, Kalie (American) forms of Caley, Kaylee.
Kalei

Kalei (Hawaiian) flower wreath.
Kahlei, Kailei, Kallei, Kaylei, Khalei

Kaleigh, Kaley ☼ (American) forms of Caley, Kaylee.
Kalley, Kalleigh, Kally, Kaly

Kaleinani (Hawaiian) the beautiful lei.

Kaleipunani (Hawaiian) the leis of beautiful flowers.

Kalena (Hawaiian) pure. See also Kalina.
Kaleen, Kaleena, Kalene, Kalenea, Kalenna

Kalere (Swahili) short woman.
Kaleer

Kali ☼ (Hindi) the black one. (Hawaiian) hesitating. Religion: a form of the Hindu goddess Devi. See also Cali.
Kalee, Kaleigh, Kaley, Kalie, Kallee, Kalley, Kalli, Kallie, Kally, Kallye, Kaly

Kalia (Hawaiian) a form of Kalea.
Kaliah, Kaliea, Kalieya

Kalifa (Somali) chaste; holy.

Kalila (Arabic) beloved, sweetheart. See also Kaela.
Kahlila, Kala, Kaleela, Kalilla, Kaylil, Kaylila, Kelila, Khalila, Khalilah, Khalillah, Kylila, Kylilah, Kylillah

Kalima (Indian) blackish.

Kalina (Slavic) flower. (Hawaiian) a form of Karen. See also Kalena.
Kalin, Kalinna, Kalyna, Kalynah, Kalynna

Kalinda (Hindi) sun.
Kaleenda, Kalindi, Kalynda, Kalyndi

Kalini (Indian) flower.

Kalisa (American) a combination of Kate + Lisa.
Kalise, Kalissa, Kalysa, Kalyssa

Kalisha (American) a combination of Kate + Aisha.
Kaleesha, Kaleisha, Kalishia

Kaliska (Moquelumnan) coyote chasing deer.

Kallan (Slavic) stream, river.
Kalahn, Kalan, Kalen, Kallen, Kallon, Kalon

Kalle ☼☼ (Finnish) a form of Carol.
Kaille, Kaylle

Kalli, Kallie (Greek) forms of Callie. Familiar forms of Kalliope, Kallista, Kalliyan.
Kalle, Kallee, Kalley, Kallita, Kally

Kalliope (Greek) a form of Calliope.
Kalli, Kallie, Kallyope

Kallista (Greek) a form of Callista.
Kalesta, Kalista, Kallesta, Kalli, Kallie, Kallysta, Kaysta

Kalliyan (Cambodian) best.
Kalli, Kallie

Kallol (Indian) large waves; gurgling of water.

Kalpana (Indian) imagination.

Kalpita (Indian) imaginary.

Kaltha (English) marigold, yellow flower.

Kaluwa (Swahili) forgotten one.
Kalua

Kalyani (Indian) fortunate.

Kalyca (Greek) rosebud.
Kalica, Kalika, Kaly

Kalyn ☼ (American) a form of Kaylyn.
Kalin, Kallen, Kallin, Kallon, Kallyn, Kalyne

Kalynn ☼ (American) a forms of Kalyn.
Kalynne

Kama (Sanskrit) loved one. Religion: the Hindu god of love.

Kamaka (Hawaiian) the favorite one.

Kamako (Japanese) kettle child; cattail child; scythe child.

Kamala (Hindi) lotus.
Kamalah, Kammala

Kamalakshi (Indian) one with eyes like a lotus.

Kamali (Mahona) spirit guide; protector.
Kamalie

Kamalika, Kamalini (Indian) lotus.

Kamalkali (Indian) the bud of a lotus.

Kamana (Indian) desire.

Kamaria (Swahili) moonlight.
Kamar, Kamara, Kamarae, Kamaree, Kamari, Kamariah, Kamarie, Kamariya, Kamariyah, Kamarya

Kamata (Moquelumnan) gambler.

Kambria (Latin) a form of Cambria.
Kambra, Kambrie, Kambriea, Kambry

Kamea (Hawaiian) one and only; precious.
Kameah, Kameo, Kamiya

Kamehameha (Hawaiian) the solitary.

Kameke (Swahili) blind.

Kameko (Japanese) turtle child. Mythology: the turtle symbolizes longevity.

Kameron **B** (American) a form of Cameron.
Kameran, Kamri

Kameyo (Japanese) generations of the tortoise.

Kami **G** (Japanese) divine aura. (Italian, North African) a short form of Kamila, Kamilah. See also Cami.
Kamie, Kammi, Kammie, Kammy, Kammye, Kamy

Kamil **B** (Arabic) a form of Kamal (see Boys' Names).

Kamila (Slavic) a form of Camila. See also Millie.
Kameela, Kamela, Kamelia, Kamella, Kami, Kamilah, Kamilia, Kamilka, Kamilla, Kamille, Kamma, Kammilla, Kamyla

Kamilah (North African) perfect.
Kameela, Kameelah, Kami, Kamillah, Kammilah

Kamini (Indian) beautiful woman.

Kamiya (Hawaiian) a form of Kamea.
Kamia, Kamiah, Kamiyah

Kamna (Indian) wish.

Kamri (American) a short form of Kameron. See also Camri.
Kamree, Kamrey, Kamrie, Kamry, Kamrye

Kamryn (American) a short form of Kameron. See also Camryn.
Kameryn, Kamren, Kamrin, Kamron, Kamrynn

Kanaka, Kanchana (Indian) gold.

Kanakabati (Indian) a fairytale.

Kanaklata (Indian) gold climber plant.

Kanakpriya (Indian) one who loves gold.

Kananbala (Indian) daughter of the forest.

Kanani (Hawaiian) beautiful.
Kana, Kanae, Kanan

Kanchanprabha (Indian) golden light.

Kanchi (Indian) a waistband.

Kanda (Native American) magical power.

Kandace, Kandice 🄶 (Greek) glittering white; glowing. (American) forms of Candace, Candice.
Kandas, Kandess, Kandi, Kandis, Kandise, Kandiss, Kandus, Kandyce, Kandys, Kandyse

Kandi (American) a familiar form of Kandace, Kandice. See also Candi.
Kandhi, Kandia, Kandie, Kandy, Kendi, Kendie, Kendy, Kenndi, Kenndie, Kenndy

Kandra (American) a form of Kendra. See also Candra.
Kandrea, Kandree, Kandria

Kane 🄱 (Japanese) two right hands.

Kaneisha, Kanisha (American) forms of Keneisha.
Kaneasha, Kanecia, Kaneesha, Kanesah, Kanesha, Kaneshea, Kaneshia, Kanessa, Kaneysha, Kaniece, Kanishia

Kanene (Swahili) a little important thing.

Kaneru (Japanese) bronze.

Kang (Chinese) fervent; generous.

Kani (Hawaiian) sound.

Kanika (Mwera) black cloth.
Kanica, Kanicka

Kanira (Indian) grain.

Kanista (Chuukese) a form of Calista.

Kanjri (Indian) bird.

Kankana (Indian) a bracelet.

Kannitha (Cambodian) angel.

Kanoa 🄱 (Hawaiian) free.

Kanoe (Hawaiian) mist.

Kanon (Japanese) flower; sound.

Kanta (Indian) beauty.

Kanthi (Indian) luster; loveliness.

Kanti (Indian) light.

Kanya (Hindi) virgin. (Tai) young lady. Religion: a form of the Hindu goddess Devi.
Kanea, Kania, Kaniya, Kanyia

Kaohinani (Hawaiian) gatherer of beauty.

Kaopua (Hawaiian) the rain clouds.

Kaori (Japanese) strong.

Kaoru (Japanese) fragrant.

Kapelani (Hawaiian) a form of Kapiolani.

Kapila (Indian) sacred cow.

Kapiolani (Hawaiian) sacred arch of heaven.

Kapotakshi (Indian) one with eyes like a dove.

Kapri (American) a form of Capri.
Kapre, Kapree, Kapria, Kaprice, Kapricia, Kaprisha, Kaprisia

Kapua (Hawaiian) blossom.

Kapuki (Swahili) first-born daughter.

Kara 🄶 (Greek, Danish) pure.
Kaira, Kairah, Karah, Karalea, Karaleah, Karalee, Karalie, Kari, Karra

Karabi (Indian) flower.

Karah (Greek, Danish) a form of Kara. (Irish, Italian) a form of Cara.
Karrah

Karalaini (Fijian) a form of Caroline.

Karalynn (English) a combination of Kara + Lynn.
Karalin, Karaline, Karalyn, Karalyne, Karalynne

Kareem **B** (Arabic) noble; distinguished.

Karel **BG** (American) a form of Karelle.

Karelle (American) a form of Carol.
Karel, Kareli, Karell, Karely

Karen **G** (Greek) pure. See also Carey, Carina, Caryn.
Kaaren, Kalina, Karaina, Karan, Karena, Karin, Karina, Karine, Karna, Karon, Karren, Karron, Karyn, Kerron, Koren

Karena (Scandinavian) a form of Karen.
Kareen, Kareena, Kareina, Karenah, Karene, Karreen, Karreena, Karrena, Karrene

Karessa (French) a form of Caressa.

Kari **G** (Greek) pure. (Danish) a form of Caroline, Katherine. See also Carey, Cari, Carrie.
Karee, Karey, Karia, Kariah, Karie, Karrey, Karri, Karrie, Karry, Kary

Kariane, Karianne (American) combinations of Kari + Ann.
Karian, Kariana, Kariann, Karianna

Karida (Arabic) untouched, pure.
Kareeda, Karita

Karilynn (American) a combination of Kari + Lynn.
Kareelin, Kareeline, Kareelinn, Kareelyn, Kareelyne, Kareelynn, Kareelynne, Karilin, Kariline, Karilinn, Karilyn, Karilyne, Karilynne, Karylin, Karyline, Karylinn, Karylyn, Karylyne, Karylynn, Karylynne

Karimah (Arabic) generous.
Kareema, Kareemah, Karima, Karime

Karin (Scandinavian) a form of Karen.
Kaarin, Kareen, Karina, Karine, Karinne, Karrin, Kerrin

Karina **G** (Russian) a form of Karen.
Kaarina, Karinna, Karrina, Karryna, Karyna, Karynna

Karine (Russian) a form of Karen.
Karrine, Karryne, Karyne

Karis (Greek) graceful.
Karess, Karice, Karise, Karisse, Karris, Karys, Karyss

Karissa (Greek) a form of Carissa.
Karese, Karesse, Karisa, Karisha, Karishma, Karisma, Karissimia, Kariza, Karrisa, Karrissa, Karysa, Karyssa, Kerisa

Karla **G** (German) a form of Carla. (Slavic) a short form of Karoline.
Karila, Karilla, Karle, Karlene, Karlicka, Karlinka, Karlisha, Karlisia, Karlitha, Karlla, Karlon, Karlyn

Karlee, Karleigh (American) forms of Karley, Karly. See also Carlee.
Karlea, Karleah, Karlei

Karlene, Karlyn (American) forms of Karla. See also Carleen.
Karleen, Karlen, Karlena, Karlign, Karlin, Karlina, Karlinna, Karlyan, Karlynn, Karlynne

Karley, Karly **G** (Latin) little and strong. (American) forms of Carly.
Karlee, Karley, Karlie, Karlyan, Karlye

Karli, Karlie (American) forms of Karley, Karly. See also Carli.

Karlotte (American) a form of Charlotte.
Karlita, Karletta, Karlette, Karlotta

Karma (Hindi) fate, destiny; action.

Karmel 🅱🅶 (Hebrew) a form of Carmela.
Karmeita, Karmela, Karmelina, Karmella, Karmelle, Karmiella, Karmielle, Karmyla

Karmen (Latin) song.
Karman, Karmencita, Karmin, Karmina, Karmine, Karmita, Karmon, Karmyn, Karmyne

Karolane (American) a combination of Karoll + Anne.
Karolan, Karolann, Karolanne, Karol-Anne

Karolina, Karoline (Slavic) forms of Caroline. See also Carolina.
Karaleen, Karalena, Karalene, Karalin, Karaline, Karileen, Karilena, Karilene, Karilin, Karilina, Kariline, Karleen, Karlen, Karlena, Karlene, Karling, Karoleena, Karolena, Karolinka, Karroleen, Karrolena, Karrolene, Karrolin, Karroline

Karoll (Slavic) a form of Carol.
Karel, Karilla, Karily, Karol, Karola, Karole, Karoly, Karrol, Karyl, Kerril

Karolyn (American) a form of Carolyn.
Karalyn, Karalyna, Karalynn, Karalynne, Karilyn, Karilyna, Karilynn, Karilynne, Karlyn, Karlynn, Karlynne, Karolyna, Karolynn, Karolynne, Karrolyn, Karrolyna, Karrolynn, Karrolynne

Karri, Karrie (American) forms of Carrie.
Kari, Karie, Karry, Kary

Karsen, Karsyn (English) child of Kar. Forms of Carson.
Karson

Karuka (Indian) heavenly piece of art.

Karuli (Indian) innocent.

Karuna (Hindi) merciful.

Karunamayee (Indian) full of pity for others.

Karunamayi (Indian) merciful.

Karunya (Indian) compassionate.

Karyn (American) a form of Karen.
Karyne, Karynn, Karynna, Kerrynn, Kerrynne

Kasa (Hopi) fur robe.

Kasandra (Greek) a form of Kassandra.
Kasander, Kasandria, Kasandra, Kasaundra, Kasondra, Kasoundra

Kasanita (Fijian) strike wood together to make fire.

Kasey, Kasie 🅶 (Irish) brave. (American) forms of Casey, Kacey.
Kaisee, Kaisie, Kasci, Kascy, Kasee, Kasi, Kassee, Kassey, Kasy, Kasya, Kaysci, Kaysea, Kaysee, Kaysey, Kaysi, Kaysie, Kaysy

Kashawna (American) a combination of Kate + Shawna.
Kasha, Kashae, Kashana, Kashanna, Kashauna, Kashawn, Kasheana, Kasheanna, Kasheena, Kashena, Kashonda, Kashonna

Kashika (Indian) the shiny one.

Kashmir (Sanskrit) Geography: a region located between India and Pakistan.
Cashmere, Kashmear, Kashmere, Kashmia, Kashmira, Kasmir, Kasmira, Kazmir, Kazmira

Kashvi (Indian) shining.

Kashyapi (Indian) earth.

Kasi (Hindi) from the holy city.

Kasia (Polish) a form of Katherine. See also Cassia.
Kashia, Kasiah, Kasian, Kasienka, Kasja, Kaska, Kassa, Kassia, Kassya, Kasya

Kasind (Umbundu) sky.

Kasinda (Umbundu) our last baby.

Kasinta (Umbundu) wish.

Kassandra **G** (Greek) a form of
Cassandra.
*Kassandr, Kassandre, Kassandré,
Kassaundra, Kassi, Kassondra,
Kassondria, Kassundra, Kazandra,
Khrisandra, Krisandra, Krissandra*

Kassi, Kassie (American) familiar
forms of Kassandra, Kassidy. See
also Cassie.
Kassey, Kassia, Kassy

Kassidy **G** (Irish) clever.
(American) a form of Cassidy.
*Kassadee, Kassadi, Kassadie,
Kassadina, Kassady, Kasseday,
Kassedee, Kassi, Kassiddy, Kassidee,
Kassidi, Kassidie, Kassity, Kassydi*

Kasturi (Indian) scented.

Kasuga (Japanese) a child of spring.

Kat'min (Chamorro) a form of
Carmen.

Katalina (Irish) a form of Caitlin.
See also Catalina.
*Kataleen, Kataleena, Katalena, Katalin,
Katalyn, Katalynn*

Katarina (Czech) a form of
Katherine.
*Kata, Katareena, Katarena, Katarin,
Katarine, Katarinna, Katarinne,
Katarrina, Kataryna, Katarzyna,
Katinka, Katrika, Katrinka*

Kate **G** (Greek) pure. (English) a
short form of Katherine.
*Kait, Kata, Katee, Kati, Katica, Katie,
Katka, Katy, Katya*

Katee, Katey (English) familiar
forms of Kate, Katherine.

Katelin (Irish) a form of Caitlin. See
also Kaitlin.
*Kaetlin, Katalin, Katelan, Kateland,
Kateleen, Katelen, Katelene, Katelind,
Kateline, Katelinn, Katelun, Kaytlin*

Katelyn ⭐ **G** (Irish) a form of
Caitlin.
Kaetlyn, Katelyne, Kaytlyn

Katelynn (Irish) a forms of Katelyn.
*Kaetlynn, Kaetlynne, Katelynne,
Kaytlynn, Kaytlynne*

Katerina **G** (Slavic) a form of
Katherine.
Katenka, Katerine, Katerini, Katerinka

Katharine (Greek) a form of
Katherine.
*Katharaine, Katharin, Katharina,
Katharyn*

Katherine ⭐ **G** (Greek) pure. See
also Carey, Catherine, Ekaterina,
Kara, Karen, Kari, Kasia, Katerina,
Yekaterina.
*Ekaterina, Ekatrinna, Kasienka, Kasin,
Kat, Katarina, Katchen, Kate, Katee,
Kathann, Kathanne, Katharine,
Kathereen, Katheren, Katherene,
Katherenne, Katherin, Katherina,
Katheryn, Katheryne, Kathi, Kathleen,
Kathrine, Kathryn, Kathy, Kathyrine,
Katia, Katina, Katlaina, Katoka,
Katreeka, Katrina, Kay, Kitty*

Kathi (English) a form of Kathy. See
also Cathi.

Kathleen (Irish) a form of
Katherine. See also Cathleen.
*Katheleen, Kathelene, Kathi, Kathileen,
Kathlean, Kathleena, Kathleene, Kathlene,
Kathlin, Kathlina, Kathlyn, Kathlyne,
Kathlynn, Kathy, Katleen*

Kathrine **G** (Greek) a form of
Katherine.
*Kathreen, Kathreena, Kathrene, Kathrin,
Kathrina*

Kathryn 🄶 (English) a form of
Katherine.
Kathren, Kathryne, Kathrynn, Kathrynne

Kathy 🄶 (English) familiar forms of
Katherine, Kathleen. See also Cathi.
*Kaethe, Katha, Kathe, Kathee, Kathey,
Kathie, Katka, Katla, Kató*

Kati (Estonian) a familiar form of
Kate.
Katja, Katya, Katye

Katia 🄶 (Russian) a form of
Katherine.
Cattiah, Katiya, Kattia, Kattiah

Katie ⚝ (English) a familiar form of
Kate.
*Katee, Kati, Kātia, Katti, Kattie, Katy,
Kayte, Kaytee, Kaytie*

Katilyn (Irish) a form of Katlyn.
Katilin, Katilynn

Katlin 🄶 (Irish) a form of Katlyn.
Katlina, Katline

Katlyn (Greek) pure. (Irish) a form
of Katelin.
*Kaatlain, Katilyn, Katland, Katlin,
Katlynd, Katlyne, Katlynn, Katlynne*

Katriel (Hebrew) God is my crown.
Katrelle, Katri, Katrie, Katry, Katryel

Katrina (German) a form of
Katherine. See also Catrina, Trina.
*Katreen, Katreena, Katrene, Katri,
Katrice, Katricia, Katrien, Katrin,
Katrine, Katrinia, Katriona, Katryn,
Katryna, Kattrina, Kattryna, Katus,
Katuska*

Katsu (Japanese) victorious.

Katsuki (Japanese) season of victory.

Katsuko (Japanese) fragrant harbor
child.

Katsuye (Japanese) blessed victory.

Katy (English) a familiar form of
Kate. See also Cady.
Kady, Katey, Katty, Kayte

Katya (Russian) a form of Katia
Katyah

Kaud (Palauan) ensnared.

Kaulana (Hawaiian) famous.
Kaula, Kauna, Kahuna

Kaulani, Kauleen (Hawaiian) forms
of Kaulana.

Kaumudi (Indian) full moon.

Kauser, Kawthar (Indian) a river in
paradise.

Kaushalya (Indian) Lord Ram's
mother.

Kaushey (Indian) silken.

Kaveri (Hindi) Geography: a sacred
river in India.

Kavika (Indian) poetess.

Kavindra (Hindi) poet.

Kawa (Japanese) river.

Kawehi (Hawaiian) the ornament.

Kawena (Hawaiian) glow.
Kawana, Kawona

Kawkab (Indian) satellite.

Kay 🄶 (Greek) rejoicer. (Teutonic) a
fortified place. (Latin) merry. A
short form of Katherine.
Caye, Kae, Kai, Kaye, Kayla

Kaya (Hopi) wise child. (Japanese)
resting place.
Kaja, Kayah, Kayia

Kayani (Persian) a form of Esther.

Kaycee 🄶 (American) a
combination of the initials K. + C.
*Kayce, Kaysee, Kaysey, Kaysi, Kaysie,
Kaysii*

Kaydee (American) a combination of the initials K. + D.
Kayda, Kayde, Kayden, Kaydi, Kaydie

Kayden B (American) a form of Kaydee.

Kayla ✵ **G** (Arabic, Hebrew) laurel; crown. A form of Kaela, Kaila. See also Cayla.
Kaylah, Kaylea, Kaylee, Kayleen, Kaylene, Kaylia, Keila, Keyla

Kaylah (Arabic, Hebrew) a form of Kayla.
Kayleah, Kaylia, Keylah

Kaylan G (Hebrew) a form of Kayleen.
Kaylana, Kayland, Kaylani, Kaylann

Kaylee ✵ **G** (American) a form of Kayla. See also Caeley, Kalee.
Kailee, Kayle, Kayleigh, Kayley, Kayli, Kaylie

Kayleen, Kaylene (Hebrew) beloved, sweetheart. Forms of Kayla.
Kaylan, Kayleena, Kayleene, Kaylen, Kaylena

Kayleigh (American) a form of Kaylee.
Kaylei

Kaylen (Hebrew) a form of Kayleen.
Kaylean, Kayleana, Kayleanna, Kaylenn

Kayley, Kayli, Kaylie (American) forms of Kaylee.

Kaylin G (American) a form of Kaylyn.
Kaylon B (American) a form of Kaylin.

Kaylyn G (American) a combination of Kay + Lynn. See also Kaelyn.
Kalyn, Kayleen, Kaylene, Kaylin, Kaylyna, Kaylyne

Kaylynn (American) a combination of Kay + Lynn.
Kalynn, Kaylynne

Kaytlin, Kaytlyn (Irish) forms of Kaitlin.
Kaytlan, Kaytlann, Kaytlen, Kaytlyne, Kaytlynn, Kaytlynne

Kazahi (Japanese) hair ornament.

Kazu (Japanese) first; obedient.

Kazuki (Japanese) the fragrance of the moon.

Kazuko (Japanese) a form of Kazu.

Kazuno (Japanese) to bring peace.

Kazuye (Japanese) blessed, peaceful first daughter.

Ke (Chinese) a jade-like stone.

Ke'ala (Hawaiian) a form of Keala.

Keahi (Hawaiian) the fire.

Keaira (Irish) a form of Keara.
Keair, Keairah, Keairra, Keairre, Keairrea

Keala (Hawaiian) path.

Keana, Keanna G (German) bold; sharp. (Irish) beautiful.
Keanah, Keanne, Keanu, Keenan, Keeyana, Keeyanah, Keeyanna, Keeyona, Keeyonna, Keiana, Keianna, Keona, Keonna

Keandra, Keondra (American) forms of Kenda.
Keandrah, Keandre, Keandrea, Keandria, Kedeana, Kedia, Keonda, Keondre, Keondria

Keanu B (German, Irish) a form of Keana.

Keara (Irish) dark; black. Religion: an Irish saint.
Keaira, Kearah, Kearia, Kearra, Keera, Keerra, Keiara, Keiarah, Keiarra, Keira, Kera

Kearsten, Keirsten (Greek) forms of Kirstin.
Kearstin, Kearston, Kearstyn, Keirstan, Keirstein, Keirstin, Keirston, Keirstyn, Keirstynne

Keaton B (English) where hawks fly.

Keegan B (Irish) little; fiery.

Keeley, Keely G (Irish) forms of Kelly.
Kealee, Kealey, Keali, Kealie, Keallie, Kealy, Keela, Keelan, Keele, Keelee, Keeleigh, Keeli, Keelia, Keelie, Keellie, Keelye, Keighla, Keilee, Keileigh, Keiley, Keilly, Kiela, Kiele, Kieley, Kielly, Kiely

Keelyn (Irish) a form of Kellyn.
Kealyn, Keelin, Keilan, Kielyn

Keena (Irish) brave.
Keenya, Kina

Keenan B (German, Irish) a form of Keana.

Keertana (Indian) song.

Keerthana (Indian) devotional song.

Keesha (American) a form of Keisha.
Keesa, Keeshae, Keeshana, Keeshanne, Keeshawna, Keeshonna, Keeshya, Keiosha

Kehau (Hawaiian) the dew.

Kehaulani (Hawaiian) the dew of heaven.

Kei (Japanese) reverent.

Keiana, Keianna (Irish) forms of Keana. (American) forms of Kiana.
Keiann, Keiannah, Keionna

Keiki (Hawaiian) child.
Keikana, Keikann, Keikanna, Keikanne

Keikilani (Hawaiian) the child of heaven.

Keiko (Japanese) happy child.

Keila (Arabic, Hebrew) a form of Kayla.
Keilah, Kela, Kelah

Keilani (Hawaiian) glorious chief.
Kaylani, Keilan, Keilana, Keilany, Kelana, Kelanah, Kelane, Kelani, Kelanie

Keilanylyn (Hawaiian) a form of Keilani.

Keira (Irish) a form of Keara.
Keiara, Keiarra, Keirra, Keirrah, Kera, Keyeira

Keisha (American) a short form of Keneisha.
Keasha, Keashia, Keesha, Keishaun, Keishauna, Keishawn, Kesha, Keysha, Kiesha, Kisha, Kishanda

Keita (Scottish) woods; enclosed place.
Keiti

Keiyona (Indian) morning star.

Kekoe (Hawaiian) the courageous soldier.

Kekona (Hawaiian) second-born child.

Kelcey, Kelci, Kelcie (Scottish) forms of Kelsey.
Kelse, Kelcee, Kelcy

Kelila (Hebrew) crown, laurel. See also Kaela, Kayla, Kalila.
Kelilah, Kelula

Kellen B (Irish) a form of Kellyn.

Kelley G (Irish) a form of Kelly.

Kelli, Kellie G (Irish) familiar forms of Kelly.
Keleigh, Keli, Kelia, Keliah, Kelie, Kellee, Kelleigh, Kellia, Kellisa

Kelly **G** (Irish) brave warrior. See also Caeley.
Keeley, Keely, Kelley, Kelley, Kelli, Kellie, Kellye

Kellyanne (Irish) a combination of Kelly + Anne.
Kelliann, Kellianne, Kellyann

Kellyn (Irish) a combination of Kelly + Lynn.
Keelyn, Kelleen, Kellen, Kellene, Kellina, Kelline, Kellynn, Kellynne

Kelsea **G** (Scottish) a form of Kelsey.
Kelcea, Kelcia, Kelsa, Kelsae, Kelsay, Kelse

Kelsey **G** (Scandinavian, Scottish) ship island. (English) a form of Chelsea.
Kelcey, Kelda, Kellsee, Kellsei, Kellsey, Kellsie, Kellsy, Kelsea, Kelsei, Kelsey, Kelsi, Kelsie, Kelsy, Kelsye

Kelsi, Kelsie, Kelsy **G** (Scottish) forms of Chelsea.
Kalsie, Kelci, Kelcie, Kellsi

Kelton **B** (English) keel town; port.

Kelvin **B** (Irish, English) narrow river. Geography: a river in Scotland.

Ken (Chinese) earnestly, sincerely.

Kenda (English) water baby. (Dakota) magical power.
Keandra, Kendra, Kennda

Kendal **G** (English) a form of Kendall.
Kendahl, Kendale, Kendalie, Kendalin, Kendalyn, Kendalynn, Kendel, Kendele, Kendil, Kindal

Kendall **G** (English) ruler of the valley.
Kendal, Kendalla, Kendalle, Kendell, Kendelle, Kendera, Kendia, Kendyl,

Kinda, Kindall, Kindi, Kindle, Kynda, Kyndal, Kyndall, Kyndel

Kendra **G** (English) a form of Kenda.
Kandra, Kendrah, Kendre, Kendrea, Kendreah, Kendria, Kenndra, Kentra, Kentrae, Kindra, Kyndra

Kendrick **B** (Irish) child of Henry. (Scottish) royal chieftain.

Kendyl (English) a form of Kendall.
Kendyle, Kendyll

Keneisha (American) a combination of the prefix Ken + Aisha.
Kaneisha, Keisha, Keneesha, Kenesha, Keneshia, Kenisha, Kenneisha, Kennesha, Kenneshia, Keosha, Kineisha

Kenenza (English) a form of Kennice.
Kenza

Kenia **G** (Hebrew) a form of Kenya.
Keniya, Kennia

Kenisha (American) a form of Keneisha.
Kenisa, Kenise, Kenishia, Kenissa, Kennisa, Kennisha, Kennysha

Kenna **G** (Irish) a short form of Kennice.

Kennedy **G** (Irish) helmeted chief. History: John F. Kennedy was the thirty-fifth U.S. president.
Kenedee, Kenedey, Kenedi, Kenedie, Kenedy, Kenidee, Kenidi, Kenidie, Kenidy, Kennadee, Kennadi, Kennadie, Kennady, Kennedee, Kennedey, Kennedi, Kennedie, Kennidee, Kennidi, Kennidy, Kynnedi

Kenneth **B** (Irish) beautiful. (English) royal oath.

Kennice (English) beautiful.
Kanice, Keneese, Kenenza, Kenese, Kennise

Kenny 🅑 (Scottish) a familiar form of Kenneth.

Kent 🅑 (Welsh) white; bright.
Geography: a region in England.

Kentrell 🅑 (English) king's estate.

Kenya 🅖 (Hebrew) animal horn.
Geography: a country in Africa.
Keenya, Kenia, Kenja, Kenyah, Kenyana, Kenyatta, Kenyia

Kenyatta (American) a form of Kenya.
Kenyata, Kenyatah, Kenyatte, Kenyattia, Kenyatta, Kenyette

Kenzie 🅖 (Scottish) light skinned. (Irish) a short form of Mackenzie.
Kenzea, Kenzee, Kenzey, Kenzi, Kenzia, Kenzy, Kinzie

Keoki, Keokia (Hawaiian) forms of Georgia.

Keon 🅑 (Irish) a form of Ewan (see Boys' Names).

Keona, Keonna (Irish) forms of Keana.
Keiona, Keionna, Keoana, Keoni, Keonia, Keonnah, Keonni, Keonnia

Keosha (American) a short form of Keneisha.
Keoshae, Keoshi, Keoshia, Keosia

Kerani (Hindi) sacred bells. See also Rani.
Kera, Kerah, Keran, Kerana

Keren (Hebrew) animal's horn.
Kerrin, Keryn

Kerensa (Cornish) a form of Karenza.
Karensa, Karenza, Kerenza

Keri, Kerri, Kerrie 🅖 (Irish) forms of Kerry.
Keriann, Kerianne, Kerriann, Kerrianne

Kerry 🅖 (Irish) dark haired.
Geography: a county in Ireland.
Keary, Keiry, Keree, Kerey, Keri, Kerri, Kerrie, Kerryann, Kerryanne, Kery, Kiera, Kierra

Kerstin (Scandinavian) a form of Kirsten.
Kerstan, Kerste, Kerstein, Kersten, Kerstie, Kerstien, Kerston, Kerstyn, Kerstynn

Kesare (Latin) long haired. (Russian) a form of Caesar (see Boys' Names).

Kesari (Indian) saffron; a lion.

Kesha (American) a form of Keisha.
Keshah, Keshal, Keshala, Keshan, Keshana, Keshara, Keshawn, Keshawna, Keshawnna

Keshi, Keshika (Indian) a woman with beautiful hair.

Keshia (American) a form of Keisha. A short form of Keneisha.
Kecia, Keishia, Keschia, Keshea, Kesia, Kesiah, Kessia, Kessiah

Keshini (Indian) one with beautiful hair.

Kesi (Swahili) born during difficult times.

Kesse 🅖 (Ashanti) a form of Kessie.

Kessie (Ashanti) chubby baby.
Kess, Kessa, Kessey, Kessi

Ket Nien (Vietnamese) jet black.

Ketaki (Indian) a cream-colored flower.

Ketana, Kethana (Indian) home.

Ketki (Indian) flower.

Keven 🅑 (Irish) a form of Kevyn.

Kevin 🅑 (Irish) beautiful.

Kevon 🅑 (Irish) a form of Kevyn.

Kevyn **B** (Irish) beautiful.
*Keva, Kevan, Keven, Kevia, Keviana,
Kevinna, Kevina, Kevion, Kevionna,
Kevon, Kevona, Kevone, Kevonia,
Kevonna, Kevonne, Kevonya, Kevynn*

Keyana **G** (American) a form of
Kiana.
Keya, Keyanah, Keyanda, Keyandra

Keyanna (American) a form of Kiana.
Keyannah

Keyara (Irish) a form of Kiara.
*Keyarah, Keyari, Keyarra, Keyera,
Keyerah, Keyerra*

Keyona (American) a form of Kiana.
Keyonda, Keyondra

Keyonna **G** (American) a form of
Kiana.
Keyonnia, Keyonnie

Keysha (American) a form of Keisha.
*Keyosha, Keyoshia, Keyshana,
Keyshanna, Keyshawn, Keyshawna,
Keyshia, Keyshla, Keyshona, Keyshonna*

Keyuri (Indian) armlet.

Keziah (Hebrew) cinnamon-like
spice. Bible: one of the daughters of
Job.
*Kazia, Kaziah, Ketzi, Ketzia, Ketziah,
Kezi, Kezia, Kizzy*

Khadijah **G** (Arabic) trustworthy.
History: Muhammed's first wife.
*Khadaja, Khadajah, Khadeeja,
Khadeejah, Khadeja, Khadejah,
Khadejha, Khadija, Khadije, Khadijia,
Khadijiah*

Khairiya (Indian) charitable.

Khalida (Arabic) immortal, everlasting.
Khali, Khalia, Khaliah, Khalidda, Khalita

Khanh (Vietnamese) yellow.

Khawlah (Indian) proper name.

Khloe ☆ (Greek) a form of Chloe.

Khrissa (American) a form of
Chrissa. (Czech) a form of Krista.
*Khrishia, Khryssa, Krisha, Krisia, Krissa,
Krysha, Kryssa*

Khristina (Russian, Scandinavian) a
form of Kristina, Christina.
*Khristeen, Khristen, Khristin, Khristine,
Khyristya, Khristyana, Khristyna,
Khrystyne*

Khulood (Indian) immortality.

Khushboo (Indian) fragrance.

Khushi, Khusi (Indian) happiness.

Khuyen (Vietnamese) year of unity.

Khyati (Indian) fame.

Ki (Korean) arisen.

Kia **G** (African) season's beginning.
(American) a short form of Kiana.
Kiah

Kiana **G** (American) a combination
of the prefix Ki + Ana.
*Keanna, Keiana, Keyana, Keyona,
Khiana, Khianah, Khianna, Ki, Kiahna,
Kiane, Kiani, Kiania, Kianna, Kiandra,
Kiandria, Kiauna, Kiaundra, Kiyana,
Kyana*

Kianna (American) a form of Kiana.
Kiannah, Kianne, Kianni

Kiara **G** (Irish) little and dark.
*Keyara, Kiarra, Kieara, Kiearah,
Kiearra, Kyara*

Kiaria, Kiarra, Kichi (Japanese)
fortunate.

Kiele **G** (Hawaiian) gardenia;
fragrant blossom.
Kiela, Kieley, Kieli, Kielli, Kielly

Kiera, Kierra (Irish) forms of Kerry.
Kierana, Kieranna, Kierea

Kieran **B** (Irish) little and dark;
little Keir.

Kiersten 🅖 (Scandinavian) a form
of Kirsten.
Keirstan, Kerstin, Kierstan, Kierston,
Kierstyn, Kierstynn

Kierstin (Scandinavian) a form of
Kirsten.

Kieu (Vietnamese) precious stone.

Kik (Japanese) chrysanthemum.

Kiki 🅖 (Spanish) a familiar form of
names ending in "queta."

Kiku (Japanese) chrysanthemum.
Kiko

Kikue (Japanese) chrysanthemum
branch.

Kikuko (Japanese) chrysanthemum
child.

Kikuno (Japanese) chrysanthemum
field.

Kikuye (Japanese) she who ushers in
a long period of joy.

Kikuyo (Japanese) long period of joy.

Kilani (Hawaiian) a form of Kalani.

Kiley 🅖 (Irish) attractive; from the
straits.
Kilea, Kilee, Kileigh, Kili, Kilie, Kylee,
Kyli, Kylie

Kim 🅖 (Vietnamese) needle.
(English) a short form of Kimberly.
Kima, Kimette, Kym

Kim Cuc (Vietnamese) advise.

Kimana (Shoshone) butterfly.
Kiman, Kimani

Kimaya (Indian) divine.

Kimber (English) a short form of
Kimberly.
Kimbra

Kimberlee, Kimberley (English)
forms of Kimberly.
Kimbalee, Kimberlea, Kimberlei,
Kimberleigh, Kimbley

Kimberly ☀ 🅖 (English) chief,
ruler.
Cymberly, Cymbre, Kim, Kimba,
Kimbely, Kimber, Kimbereley,
Kimberely, Kimberlee, Kimberli,
Kimberlie, Kimberlyn, Kimbery, Kimbria,
Kimbrie, Kimbry, Kimmie, Kymberly

Kimberlyn (English) a form of
Kimberly.
Kimberlin, Kimberlynn

Kimi (Japanese) righteous.
Kimia, Kimika, Kimiko, Kimiyo, Kimmi,
Kimmie, Kimmy

Kimiye (Japanese) she who is a
blessed and beautiful delight.

Kim-Ly (Vietnamese) graceful;
beloved; legend name.

Kimmie (English) a familiar form of
Kimberly.
Kimee, Kimme, Kimmee, Kimmi, Kimmy,
Kimy

Kin (Japanese) golden.

Kina (Hawaiian) from China.

Kinaari (Indian) shore.

Kineisha (American) a form of
Keneisha.
Kineesha, Kinesha, Kineshia, Kinisha,
Kinishia

Kineta (Greek) energetic.
Kinetta

Kini 🅖 (Hawaiian) a form of Jean.
Kina

Kinjal (Indian) river bank.

Kinnari (Indian) musical instrument.

Kinsey **G** (English) offspring;
relative.
*Kinsee, Kinsley, Kinza, Kinze, Kinzee,
Kinzey, Kinzi, Kinzie, Kinzy*

Kinsley (American) a form of
Kinsey.
Kinslee, Kinslie, Kinslyn

Kintuben (Indian) a beautiful
athlete.

Kinu (Japanese) silk cloth.

Kinuye (Japanese) blessed silk.

Kioko (Japanese) happy child.
Kiyo, Kiyoko

Kiona (Native American) brown
hills.
Kionah, Kioni, Kionna

Kioshi (Japanese) clear, bright.

Kira **G** (Persian) sun. (Latin) light.
*Kirah, Kiri, Kiria, Kiro, Kirra, Kirrah,
Kirri*

Kiran **G** (Hindi) ray of light.

Kiranmala (Indian) garland.

Kirby **B** (Scandinavian) church
village. (English) cottage by the
water.
Kirbee, Kirbi

Kirima (Eskimo) hill.

Kirsi (Hindi) amaranth blossoms.
Kirsie

Kirsta (Scandinavian) a form of
Kirsten.

Kirsten **G** (Greek) Christian;
anointed. (Scandinavian) a form of
Christine.
*Karsten, Kearsten, Keirstan, Kerstin,
Kiersten, Kirsteni, Kirsta, Kirstan,
Kirstene, Kirstie, Kirstin, Kirston, Kirsty,
Kirstyn, Kjersten, Kursten, Kyersten,
Kyrsten, Kyrstin*

Kirstie, Kirsty (Scandinavian)
familiar forms of Kirsten.
*Kerstie, Kirsta, Kirste, Kirstee, Kirstey,
Kirsti, Kjersti, Kyrsty*

Kirstin (Scandinavian) a form of
Kirsten.
Karstin, Kirsteen, Kirstien, Kirstine

Kirstyn (Greek) a form of Kirsten.
Kirstynn

Kirtana (Indian) hymn, a song sung
in praise of God.

Kisa (Russian) kitten.
Kisha, Kiska, Kissa, Kiza

Kishi (Japanese) long and happy life.

Kishori (Indian) young damsel.

Kissa (Ugandan) born after twins.

Kita (Japanese) north.

Kitra (Hebrew) crowned.

Kitty (Greek) a familiar form of
Katherine.
*Ketter, Ketti, Ketty, Kit, Kittee, Kitteen,
Kittey, Kitti, Kittie*

Kiwa (Japanese) borderline.

Kiyana (American) a form of Kiana.
*Kiya, Kiyah, Kiyan, Kiyani, Kiyanna,
Kiyenna*

Kiyomi (Japanese) precious and
beautiful girl.

Kiyono (Japanese) clean and clear
field.

Kiyoshi (Japanese) quiet child.

Kiyoye (Japanese) blessedly clean
girl.

Kizzy (American) a familiar form of
Keziah.
Kezi, Kissie, Kizzi, Kizzie

Klara (Hungarian) a form of Clara.
Klára, Klari, Klarika

Klarise (German) a form of Klarissa.
Klarice, Kláris, Klaryce

Klarissa (German) clear, bright.
(Italian) a form of Clarissa.
*Klarisa, Klarise, Klarrisa, Klarrissa,
Klarrissia, Klarisza, Klarysa, Klaryssa,
Kleresa*

Klaudia (American) a form of
Claudia.
Klaudija

Kloe (American) a form of Chloe.
Khloe, Kloee, Kloey, Klohe, Kloie

Ko (Japanese) filial piety.

Kodi 🅱🅶 (American) a form of Codi.
*Kodee, Kodey, Kodie, Kody, Kodye,
Koedi*

Kody 🅱 (American) a form of
Kodi.

Koffi (Swahili) born on Friday.
Kaffe, Kaffi, Koffe, Koffie

Kohana (Japanese) little flower.

Kokila (Indian) a singer.

Koko (Japanese) stork. See also
Coco.

Kolby 🅱 (American) a form of
Colby.
*Kobie, Koby, Kolbee, Kolbey, Kolbi,
Kolbie*

Kolina (Swedish) a form of
Katherine. See also Colleen.
*Koleen, Koleena, Kolena, Kolene, Koli,
Kolleen, Kollena, Kollene, Kolyn, Kolyna*

Koma (Japanese) filly.

Komali (Indian) tender.

Kome (Japanese) rice.

Kona 🅱 (Hawaiian) lady. (Hindi)
angular.
Koni, Konia

Konami (Japanese) she who makes
things happen.

Kong (Chinese) glorious.

Konomi (Japanese) nuts.

Konstance (Latin) a form of
Constance.
*Konstantina, Konstantine, Konstanza,
Konstanze*

Kora (Greek) a form of Cora.
*Korah, Kore, Koren, Koressa, Koretta,
Korra*

Koral (American) a form of Coral.
*Korel, Korele, Korella, Korilla, Korral,
Korrel, Korrell, Korrelle*

Korey 🅱 (American) a form of
Kori.

Kori 🅶 (American) a short form of
Korina. See also Corey, Cori.
*Koree, Korey, Koria, Korie, Korri,
Korrie, Korry, Kory*

Korina (Greek) a form of Corina.
*Koreena, Korena, Koriana, Korianna,
Korine, Korinna, Korreena, Korrina,
Korrinna, Koryna, Korynna*

Korine (Greek) a form of Korina.
*Koreen, Korene, Koriane, Korianne,
Korin, Korinn, Korinne, Korrin, Korrine,
Korrinne, Korryn, Korrynne, Koryn,
Koryne, Korynn*

Kornelia (Latin) a form of Cornelia.
*Karniela, Karniella, Karnis, Kornelija,
Kornelis, Kornelya, Korny*

Kortney 🅶 (English) a form of
Courtney.
Kortnay, Kortnee, Kortni, Kortnie, Kortny

Kory 🅱 (American) a form of Kori.

Kosha (Indian) origin; the name of a
river.

Kosma (Greek) order; universe.
Cosma

Kosta (Latin) a short form of
Constance.
Kostia, Kostusha, Kostya

Koto (Japanese) harp.

Kotone (Japanese) the sound of the
koto.

Kotose (Japanese) star.

Kotoyo (Japanese) she who plays the
koto for a lifetime.

Koume (Japanese) little plum.

Kourtney **G** (American) a form of
Courtney.
*Kourtnay, Kourtne, Kourtnee, Kourtnei,
Kourtneigh, Kourtni, Kourtny, Kourtynie*

Kouther (Indian) a river in paradise.

Koyel (Indian) the cuckoo.

Koyuki (Japanese) small snowfall.

Kozakura (Japanese) little cherry
tree.

Kozue (Japanese) tree branches.

Kozuye (Japanese) twig.

Krandasi (Indian) the sky and the
earth.

Kranti (Indian) revolution.

Krasia (Palauan) whimsical.

Kripa (Indian) compassion.

Kripi (Indian) beautiful.

Kris **B** (American) a short form of
Kristine. A form of Chris.
Khris, Krissy

Krisha (Indian) divine.

Krishnakali (Indian) a flower.

Krissy (American) a familiar form of
Kris.
Krissey, Krissi, Krissie

Krista **G** (Czech) a form of
Christina. See also Christa.
*Khrissa, Khrista, Khryssa, Khrysta,
Krissa, Kryssa, Krysta*

Kristal (Latin) a form of Crystal.
*Kristale, Kristall, Kristill, Kristl, Kristle,
Kristy*

Kristan (Greek) a form of Kristen.
*Kristana, Kristanna, Kristanne, Kriston,
Krystan, Krystane*

Kristen **G** (Greek) Christian;
anointed. (Scandinavian) a form of
Christine.
*Christen, Kristan, Kristene, Kristien,
Kristin, Kristyn, Krysten*

Kristi, Kristie (Scandinavian) short
forms of Kristine.
Christi

Kristian **B** (Greek) Christian;
anointed. Forms of Christian.
*Khristian, Kristian, Kristiane, Kristiann,
Kristi-Ann, Kristianna, Kristianne, Kristi-
Anne, Kristienne, Kristyan, Kristyana,
Kristy-Ann, Kristy-Anne*

Kristiana (Greek) a form of
Kristian.

Kristin **G** (Scandinavian) a form of
Kristen. See also Cristen.
Kristiin, Krystin

Kristina **G** (Greek) Christian;
anointed. (Scandinavian) a form of
Christina. See also Cristina.
*Khristina, Kristena, Kristeena, Kristina,
Kristinka, Krystina*

Kristine **G** (Scandinavian) a form
of Christine.
*Kris, Kristeen, Kristene, Kristi, Kristie,
Kristy, Krystine, Krystyne*

Kristopher **B** (Greek) a form of
Christopher.

Kristy 🅖 (American) a familiar form of Kristine, Krystal. See also Cristy.
Kristi, Kristia, Kristie, Krysia, Krysti

Kristyn 🅖 (Greek) a form of Kristen.
Kristyne, Kristynn

Kriti (Indian) work of art.

Krittika (Indian) the third nakshatra (star constellation).

Krupa (Indian) God's forgiveness.

Krupali (Indian) she who always forgives.

Kruthika (Indian) name of a star.

Kruti (Indian) creation.

Krysta (Polish) a form of Krista.
Krystah, Krystka

Krystal 🅖 (American) clear, brilliant glass.
Kristabel, Kristal, Krystalann, Krystalanne, Krystale, Krystall, Krystalle, Krystel, Krystil, Krystle, Krystol

Krystalee (American) a combination of Krystal + Lee.
Kristalea, Kristaleah, Kristalee, Krystalea, Krystaleah, Krystlea, Krystleah, Krystlee, Krystlelea, Krystleleah, Krystlelee

Krystalynn (American) a combination of Krystal + Lynn.
Kristaline, Kristalyn, Kristalynn, Kristilyn, Kristilynn, Kristlyn, Krystaleen, Krystalene, Krystalin, Krystalina, Krystallyn, Krystalyn, Krystalynne

Krystel (Latin) a form of Krystal.
Kristel, Kristell, Kristelle, Krystelle

Krysten (Greek) a form of Kristen.
Krystene, Krystyn, Krystyne

Krystian 🅑🅖 (Greek) a form of Christian.
Krystianne, Krysty-Ann, Krystyan, Krystyanne, Krysty-Anne, Krystyen

Krystiana (Greek) a form of Krystian.
Krystiana, Krystianna, Kristyana, Krystyanna

Krystin (Czech) a form of Kristin.

Krystina (Greek) a form of Kristina.
Krysteena, Krystena, Krystyna, Krystynka

Krystle (American) a form of Krystal.
Krystl, Krystyl

Kshama (Indian) forgiveness, mercy.

Kshamya, Kshiti (Indian) earth.

Kshanaprabha, Kshanika (Indian) lightning.

Kshipa (Indian) night.

Kshipra (Indian) the name of a river in India.

Kshipva (Indian) elasticized.

Kshirin (Indian) flower.

Kuan (Chinese) happy.

Kuan-Yin (Chinese) Buddhist deity of mercy.

Kudio (Swahili) born on Monday.

Kuhu (Indian) the sweet note of the bird.

Kui (Chinese) sunflower.

Kulthoom (Indian) daughter of the prophet Mohammed.

Kuma (Japanese) bear. (Tongan) mouse.

Kumiko (Japanese) girl with braids.
Kumi

Kumkum (Indian) sacred powder.

Kumud, Kumudini (Indian) lotus.

Kumuda (Sanskrit) lotus flower.

Kun (Chinese) female.

Kundanika (Indian) flower.

Kuni (Japanese) born in the country.

Kuniko (Japanese) child from the country.

Kuniye (Japanese) country, nation; branch.

Kunjal (Indian) cuckoo; nightingale.

Kunjalata (Indian) wild climber plant.

Kunjana (Indian) forest girl.

Kunshi (Indian) shining.

Kuntala (Indian) one with beautiful hair.

Kunti (Indian) mother of the five brothers, the Pandavas.

Kunto (Twi) third-born.

Kura (Japanese) treasure house.

Kurangi (Indian) deer.

Kuri (Japanese) chestnut.

Kurva (Japanese) mulberry tree.

Kusa (Hindi) God's grass.

Kushala (Indian) safe; happy; expert.

Kusum, Kusuma (Indian) flower.

Kusumanjali (Indian) flower offering.

Kusumavati (Indian) flowering.

Kusumita (Indian) flowers in bloom.

Kusumlata (Indian) flowering creeper.

Kuvira (Indian) courageous woman.

Kwanita (Zuni) a form of Juanita.

Kwashi (Swahili) born on Sunday.

Kwau (Swahili) born on Thursday.

Kyana (American) a form of Kiana.
Kyanah, Kyani, Kyann, Kyanna, Kyanne, Kyanni, Kyeana, Kyeanna

Kyara (Irish) a form of Kiara.
Kiyara, Kiyera, Kiyerra, Kyarah, Kyaria, Kyarie, Kyarra, Kyera, Kyerra

Kyla **G** (Irish) attractive. (Yiddish) crown; laurel.
Khyla, Kylah, Kylea, Kyleah, Kylia

Kyle **B** (Irish) attractive.
Kial, Kiele, Kylee, Kyleigh, Kylene, Kylie

Kylee **G** (Irish) a familiar form of Kyle.
Kylea, Kyleah, Kylie, Kyliee

Kyleigh (Irish) a form of Kyle.
Kyliegh

Kylene (Irish) a form of Kyle.
Kyleen, Kylen, Kylyn, Kylynn

Kyler **B** (English) a form of Kyle.

Kylie ✨ **G** (West Australian Aboriginal) curled stick; boomerang. (Irish) a familiar form of Kyle.
Keiley, Keilley, Keilly, Keily, Kiley, Kye, Kylee, Kyley, Kyli, Kyllie

Kym **G** (English, Vietnamese) a form of Kim.

Kymberly (English) a form of Kimberly.
Kymber, Kymberlee, Kymberleigh, Kymberley, Kymberli, Kymberlie, Kymberlyn, Kymberlynn, Kymberlynne

Kyndal (English) a form of Kendall.
Kyndahl, Kyndel, Kyndle, Kyndol

Kyndall **G** (English) a form of Kendall.
Kyndalle, Kyndell, Kyndelle

Kynthia (Greek) a form of Cynthia.
Kyndi

Kyoko (Japanese) mirror.

Kyon (Korean) increase; important.

Kyra (Greek) ladylike. A form of Cyrilla.
Keera, Keira, Kira, Kyrah, Kyrene, Kyria, Kyriah, Kyriann, Kyrie

L

L 🆎 (American) an initial used as a first name.

Laabha (Indian) profit.

Laalamani (Indian) ruby.

Laasya (Indian) name of a dance.

Labangalata (Indian) a flowering creeper.

Laboni (Indian) graceful.

Labuki (Indian) musical instrument.

Lacey, Lacy 🅖 (Latin) cheerful. (Greek) familiar forms of Larissa.
Lacee, Laci, Lacie, Lacye

Lachandra (American) a combination of the prefix La + Chandra.
Lachanda, Lachandice

Laci, Lacie (Latin) forms of Lacey.
Lacia, Laciann, Lacianne

Lacrecia (Latin) a form of Lucretia.
Lacrasha, Lacreash, Lacreasha, Lacreashia, Lacreisha, Lacresha, Lacreshia, Lacresia, Lacretia, Lacricia, Lacriesha, Lacrisah, Lacrisha, Lacrishia, Lacrissa

Lada (Russian) Mythology: the Slavic goddess of beauty.

Ladasha (American) a combination of the prefix La + Dasha.
Ladaesha, Ladaisa, Ladaisha, Ladaishea, Ladaishia, Ladashiah, Ladaseha, Ladashia, Ladasia, Ladassa, Ladaysha, Ladesha, Ladisha, Ladosha

Ladeidra (American) a combination of the prefix La + Deidra.
Ladedra, Ladiedra

Ladli (Indian) loved one.

Ladonna (American) a combination of the prefix La + Donna.
Ladan, Ladana, Ladon, Ladona, Ladonne, Ladonya

Laela (Arabic, Hebrew) a form of Leila.
Lael, Laelle

Laelia (Latin) she who is talkative.

Laghuvi (Indian) tender.

Lahela (Hawaiian) a form of Rachel.

Lai (Chinese) arrive.

Laiba (Indian) female of the haven.

Laica (Greek) pure, secular.

Laila (Arabic) a form of Leila.
Lailah, Laili, Lailie

Laine, Layne 🅑 (French) short forms of Elaine.
Lain, Laina, Lainah, Lainee, Lainna, Layna

Lainey, Layney (French) familiar forms of Elaine.
Laini, Lainie, Laynee, Layni, Laynie

Lajila (Hindi) shy, coy.

Lajita, Lajwati (Indian) modest.

Lajja (Indian) modesty.

Lajjawati (Indian) a sensitive plant; modest woman.

Lajuana (American) a combination of the prefix La + Juana.
Lajuanna, Lawana, Lawanna, Lawanza, Lawanze, Laweania

Lajvanti (Indian) the touch-me-not plant.

Lajvati (Indian) shy.

Lajwanti (Indian) modest, humble.

Laka (Hawaiian) attractive; seductive; tame. Mythology: the goddess of the hula.

Lakayla (American) a combination of the prefix La + Kayla.
Lakala, Lakaya, Lakeila, Lakela, Lakella

Lakeisha (American) a combination of the prefix La + Keisha. See also Lekasha.
Lakaiesha, Lakaisha, Lakasha, Lakashia, Lakaysha, Lakaysia, Lakeasha, Lakecia, Lakeesh, Lakeesha, Lakeeshia, Lakesha, Lakeshia, Lakeysha, Lakezia, Lakicia, Lakieshia, Lakisha

Laken **G** (American) a short form of Lakendra.
Lakena

Lakendra (American) a combination of the prefix La + Kendra.
Lakanda, Lakedra, Laken, Lakenda

Lakenya (American) a combination of the prefix La + Kenya.
Lakeena, Lakeenna, Lakeenya, Lakena, Lakenia, Lakinja, Lakinya, Lakwanya, Lekenia, Lekenya

Lakesha, Lakeshia, Lakisha (American) forms of Lakeisha.
Lakecia, Lakeesha, Lakesa, Lakese, Lakeseia, Lakeshya, Lakesi, Lakesia, Lakeyshia, Lakiesha

Laketa (American) a combination of the prefix La + Keita.
Lakeeta, Lakeetah, Lokeita, Lakeitha, Lakeithia, Laketha, Laketia, Laketta, Lakieta, Lakietha, Lakita, Lakitia, Lakitra, Lakitri, Lakitta

Lakia (Arabic) found treasure.
Lakiea, Lakkia

Lakin, Lakyn (American) short forms of Lakendra.
Lakyna, Lakynn

Lakota **BG** (Dakota) a tribal name.
Lakoda, Lakohta, Lakotah

Lakresha (American) a form of Lucretia.
Lacresha, Lacreshia, Lacresia, Lacretia, Lacrisha, Lakreshia, Lakrisha, Lekresha, Lekresia

Laksha, Lakshya (Indian) aim.

Lakshaki (Indian) another name for the goddess Sita.

Lakshana (Indian) one with auspicious signs on her.

Lakshanya (Indian) one who achieves.

Lakshita (Indian) distinguished.

Lakshmi (Indian) the goddess of wealth.

Lakshmishree (Indian) fortunate.

Lakya (Hindi) born on Thursday.
Lakeya, Lakeyah, Lakieya, Lakiya, Lakyia

Lala (Slavic) tulip.
Lalah, Lalla

Lalan (Indian) nurturing.

Lalana (Indian) a girl.

Lalasa (Hindi) love.

Laleh (Persian) tulip.
Lalah

Lali (Spanish) a form of Lulani.
Lalia, Lalli, Lally

Lalima (Indian) beauty.

Lalita (Greek) talkative. (Sanskrit) charming; candid.

Lalitamohana (Indian) attractive, beautiful.

Lalitha (Indian) elegant; beautiful.

Lallie (English) babbler.
Lalli, Lally

Lam (Chinese) jungle or dense forest.

Lamar 🅱 (German) famous throughout the land. (French) sea, ocean.

Lamesha (American) a combination of the prefix La + Mesha.
Lamees, Lameesha, Lameise, Lameisha, Lameshia, Lamisha, Lamishia, Lemisha

Lamia (German) bright land.
Lama, Lamiah

Lamis (Arabic) soft to the touch.
Lamese, Lamise

Lamonica (American) a combination of the prefix La + Monica.
Lamoni, Lamonika

Lamont 🅱 (Scandinavian) lawyer.

Lamya (Arabic) dark lipped.
Lama

Lan (Vietnamese) flower.

Lana (Latin) woolly. (Irish) attractive, peaceful. A short form of Alana, Elana. (Hawaiian) floating; bouyant.
Lanae, Lanai, Lanata, Lanay, Laneah, Laneetra, Lanette, Lanna, Lannah

Lanca (Latin) blessed, fortunate one.

Lance 🅱 (German) a short form of Lancelot (see Boys' Names).

Landa (Basque) another name for the Virgin Mary.

Landin 🅱 (English) a form of Landon.

Landon 🅱 (English) open, grassy meadow.
Landan, Landen, Landin, Landyn, Landynne

Landra (German, Spanish) counselor.
Landrea

Landrada (Spanish) counselor.

Lane 🅱 (English) narrow road.
Laina, Laney, Layne

Laneisha (American) a combination of the prefix La + Keneisha.
Laneasha, Lanecia, Laneesha, Laneise, Laneishia, Lanesha, Laneshe, Laneshea, Laneshia, Lanesia, Lanessa, Lanesse, Lanisha, Lanishia

Laney (English) a familiar form of Lane.
Lanie, Lanni, Lanny, Lany

Lang (Vietnamese) yellow chrysanthemum.

Langging (Tagalog) a form of Jingjing.

Lanh (Vietnamese) golden lion.

Lani 🅖 (Hawaiian) sky; heaven. A short form of Atalanta, 'Aulani, Leilani.
Lanee, Lanei, Lania, Lanie, Lanita, Lanney, Lanni, Lannie

Laporsha (American) a combination of the prefix La + Porsha.
Laporcha, Laporche, Laporscha, Laporsche, Laporschia, Laporshe, Laporshia, Laportia

Laqueena (American) a combination of the prefix La + Queenie.
Laqueen, Laquena, Laquenetta, Laquinna

Laquinta (American) a combination of the prefix La + Quintana.
Laquanta, Laqueinta, Laquenda, Laquenta, Laquinda

Laquisha (American) a combination of the prefix La + Queisha.
Laquasha, Laquaysha, Laqueisha, Laquesha, Laquiesha

Laquita (American) a combination of the prefix La + Queta.
Laqeita, Laqueta, Laquetta, Laquia, Laquiata, Laquieta, Laquitta, Lequita

Lara **G** (Greek) cheerful. (Latin) shining; famous. Mythology: a Roman nymph. A short form of Laraine, Larissa, Laura.
Larae, Larah, Laretta, Larette

Laraine (Latin) a form of Lorraine.
Lara, Laraene, Larain, Larane, Larayn, Larayne, Laraynna, Larein, Lareina, Lareine, Laren, Larenn, Larenya, Lauraine, Laurraine

Laranya (Indian) graceful.

Larina (Greek) seagull.
Larena, Larine

Larisa (Greek) a form of Larissa.
Lareesa, Lareese, Laresa, Laris, Larise, Larisha, Larrisa, Larysa, Laurisa

Larissa (Greek) cheerful. See also Lacey.
Lara, Laressa, Larisa, Larissah, Larrissa, Larryssa, Laryssa, Laurissa, Laurissah

Lark (English) skylark.

Larry **B** (Latin) a familiar form of Lawrence.

Lashae, Lashay (American) combinations of the prefix La + Shay.
Lasha, Lashai, Lashaia, Lashaya, Lashaye, Lashea

Lashana (American) a combination of the prefix La + Shana.
Lashanay, Lashane, Lashanna, Lashannon, Lashona, Lashonna

Lashanda (American) a combination of the prefix La + Shanda.
Lashandra, Lashanta, Lashante

Lashawna (American) a combination of the prefix La + Shawna.
Lashaun, Lashauna, Lashaune, Lashaunna, Lashaunta, Lashawn, Lashawnd, Lashawnda, Lashawndra, Lashawne, Lashawnia, Leshawn, Leshawna

Lashonda (American) a combination of the prefix La + Shonda.
Lachonda, Lashaunda, Lashaundra, Lashon, Lashond, Lashonde, Lashondia, Lashondra, Lashonta, Lashunda, Lashundra, Lashunta, Lashunte, Leshande, Leshandra, Leshondra, Leshundra

Lata (Indian) creeper.

Latakara (Indian) mass of creepers.

Latangi (Indian) slim girl.

Latanya (American) a combination of the prefix La + Tanya.
Latana, Latandra, Latania, Latanja, Latanna, Latanua, Latonshia

Latara (American) a combination of the prefix La + Tara.

Latasha (American) a combination of the prefix La + Tasha.
Latacha, Latacia, Latai, Lataisha, Latashia, Latasia, Lataysha, Letasha, Letashia, Letasiah

Latavia (American) a combination of the prefix La + Tavia.

Lateefah (Arabic) pleasant. (Hebrew) pat, caress.
Lateefa, Latifa, Latifah, Latipha

Latesha (American) a form of Leticia.
Lataeasha, Lateasha, Lateashia, Latecia, Lateicia, Lateisha, Latesa, Lateshia, Latessa, Lateysha, Latisa, Latissa, Leteisha, Leteshia

Latha (Indian) a creeper.

Latia (American) a combination of
the prefix La + Tia.
Latea, Lateia, Lateka

Latika (Hindi) elegant.
Lateeka, Lateka

Latisha (Latin) joy. (American) a
combination of the prefix La +
Tisha.
Laetitia, Laetizia, Latashia, Lateasha,
Lateashia, Latecia, Lateesha, Lateicia,
Lateisha, Latice, Laticia, Latiesha,
Latishia, Latishya, Latissha, Latitia,
Latysha

Latona (Latin) Mythology: the
powerful goddess who bore Apollo
and Diana.
Latonna, Latonnah

Latonya (American) a combination
of the prefix La + Tonya. (Latin) a
form of Latona.
Latoni, Latonia

Latoria (American) a combination of
the prefix La + Tori.
Latoira, Latorio, Latorja, Latorray,
Latorreia, Latory, Latorya, Latoyra,
Latoyria

Latosha (American) a combination
of the prefix La + Tosha.
Latoshia, Latoshya, Latosia

Latoya (American) a combination of
the prefix La + Toya.
Latoia, Latoiya, LaToya, Latoye, Latoyia,
Latoyita, Latoyo

Latrice (American) a combination of
the prefix La + Trice.
Latrece, Latreece, Latreese, Latresa,
Latrese, Latressa, Letreece, Letrice

Latricia (American) a combination
of the prefix La + Tricia.
Latrecia, Latresh, Latresha, Latreshia,
Latrica, Latrisha, Latrishia

Laura ☀ 🅖 (Latin) crowned with laurel.
Lara, Laurah, Lauralee, Laurelen,
Laurella, Lauren, Lauricia, Laurie,
Laurka, Laury, Lauryn, Lavra, Lolly,
Lora, Loretta, Lori, Lorinda, Lorna,
Loura

Laurel (Latin) laurel tree.
Laural, Laurell, Laurelle, Lorel, Lorelle

Lauren ☀ 🅖 (English) a form of
Laura.
Lauran, Laureen, Laurena, Laurene,
Laurien, Laurin, Laurine, Lawren, Loren,
Lorena

Laurence 🅖 (Latin) crowned with
laurel.
Laurencia, Laurens, Laurent,
Laurentana, Laurentina, Lawrencia

Laurianna (English) a combination
of Laurie + Anna.
Laurana, Laurann, Laureana,
Laureanne, Laureen, Laureena, Laurian,
Lauriana, Lauriane, Laurianna, Laurie
Ann, Laurie Anne, Laurina

Laurie 🅖 (English) a familiar form
of Laura.
Lari, Larilia, Laure, Lauré, Lauri, Lawrie

Laurinda, Laurita (Spanish)
crowned with laurels.

Laury 🅖 (English) a familiar form
of Laura.

Lauryn (English) a familiar form of
Laura.
Laurynn

Lavali (Indian) clove.

Laveda (Latin) cleansed, purified.
Lavare, Lavetta, Lavette

Lavelle (Latin) cleansing.
Lavella

Lavena (Irish, French) joy. (Latin) a
form of Lavina.

Laverne (Latin) springtime. (French) grove of alder trees. See also Verna.
Laverine, Lavern, Laverna, La Verne

Laviana (Latin) native of Rome.

Lavina (Latin) purified; woman of Rome. See also Vina.
Lavena, Lavenia, Lavinia, Lavinie, Levenia, Levinia, Livinia, Louvinia, Lovina, Lovinia

Lavonna (American) a combination of the prefix La + Yvonne.
Lavon, Lavonda, Lavonder, Lavondria, Lavone, Lavonia, Lavonica, Lavonn, Lavonne, Lavonnie, Lavonya

Lawan (Tai) pretty.
Lawanne

Lawanda (American) a combination of the prefix La + Wanda.
Lawonda, Lawynda

Lawrence **B** (Latin) crowned with laurel.

Laxmi (Indian) goddess of wealth.

Layce (American) a form of Lacey.
Laycee, Layci, Laycia, Laycie, Laysa, Laysea, Laysie

Layla (Hebrew, Arabic) a form of Leila.
Laylah, Layli, Laylie

Layton **B** (English) a form of Leighton (see Boys' Names).

Le (Vietnamese) pearl.

Lea (Hawaiian) Mythology: the goddess of canoe makers. (Hebrew) a form of Leah.

Leah ☆ **G** (Hebrew) weary. Bible: the first wife of Jacob. See also Lia.
Lea, Léa, Lee, Leea, Leeah, Leia

Leala (French) faithful, loyal.
Lealia, Lealie, Leial

Lean, Leann (English) forms of Leeann, Lian.
Leane

Leandra (Latin) like a lioness.
Leanda, Leandre, Leandrea, Leandria, Leeanda, Leeandra

Leanna, Leeanna (English) forms of Liana.
Leana, Leeana, Leianna

Leanne **G** (English) a form of Leeann, Lian.

Leanore (Greek) a form of Eleanor. (English) a form of Helen.
Leanora, Lanore

Lecia (Latin) a short form of Felecia.
Leasia, Leecia, Leesha, Leesia, Lesha, Leshia, Lesia

Leda (Greek) lady. Mythology: the queen of Sparta and the mother of Helen of Troy.
Ledah, Lyda, Lydah

Ledicia (Latin) great joy.

Lee **B** (Chinese) plum. (Irish) poetic. (English) meadow. A short form of Ashley, Leah.
Lea, Leigh

Leeann, Leeanne (English) combinations of Lee + Ann. Forms of Lian.
Leane, Leean, Leian, Leiann, Leianne

Leelamayee (Indian) playful.

Leena (Estonian) a form of Helen. (Greek, Latin, Arabic) a form of Lina.

Leeza (Hebrew) a short form of Aleeza. (English) a form of Lisa, Liza.
Leesa

Lefitray (Mapuche) sound, the speed of sound, rapid sound.

Leflay (Mapuche) lethargic woman without energies, lacking in curiosity.

Lei 🔠 (Hawaiian) a familiar form of Leilani.

Leigh 🄖 (English) a form of Leah.
Leighann, Leighanne

Leigha (English) a form of Leigh.
Leighanna

Leiko (Japanese) arrogant.

Leila (Hebrew) dark beauty; night. (Arabic) born at night. See also Laela, Layla, Lila.
Laila, Leela, Leelah, Leilah, Leilia, Lela, Lelah, Leland, Lelia, Leyla

Leilani (Hawaiian) heavenly flower; heavenly child.
Lailanee, Lailani, Lailanie, Lailany, Lailoni, Lani, Lei, Leilany, Leiloni, Leilony, Lelani, Lelania

Leira (Basque) reference to the Virgin Mary.

Lekasha (American) a form of Lakeisha.
Lekeesha, Lekeisha, Lekesha, Lekeshia, Lekesia, Lekicia, Lekisha

Lekha (Indian) writing.

Leland 🄱 (Hebrew) a form of Leila.

Leli (Swiss) a form of Magdalen.
Lelie

Lelia (Greek) fair speech. (Hebrew, Arabic) a form of Leila.
Leliah, Lelika, Lelita, Lellia

Lelica (Latin) talkative.

Lelya (Russian) a form of Helen.

Lemmie (Indian) devoted to the Lord.

Lena (Hebrew) dwelling or lodging. (Latin) temptress. (Norwegian) illustrious. (Greek) a short form of Eleanor. Music: Lena Horne, a well-known African American singer and actress.
Lenah, Lene, Lenee, Leni, Lenka, Lenna, Lennah, Lina, Linah

Lenci (Hungarian) a form of Helen.
Lency

Lene (German) a form of Helen.
Leni, Line

Leneisha (American) a combination of the prefix Le + Keneisha.
Lenece, Lenesha, Leniesha, Lenieshia, Leniesia, Leniessia, Lenisa, Lenise, Lenisha, Lennise, Lennisha, Lynesha

Lenia (German) a form of Leona.
Lenayah, Lenda, Lenea, Leneen, Lenna, Lennah, Lennea, Leny

Lenis (Latin) half, soft, silky.

Lenita (Latin) gentle.
Leneta, Lenette, Lennette

Lenore (Greek, Russian) a form of Eleanor.
Lenni, Lenor, Lenora, Lenorah

Leocadia (Greek) she who shines because of her whiteness.

Leocricia (Greek) she who judges her village well.

Leona (German) brave as a lioness. See also Lona.
Lenia, Leoine, Leola, Leolah, Leonae, Leonah, Leondra, Leone, Leonelle, Leonia, Leonice, Leonicia, Leonie, Leonissa, Leonna, Leonne, Liona

Leonarda, Leoncia Leonela (Latin) strong and fierce as a lion.

Leonie (German) a familiar form of Leona.
Leoni, Léonie, Leony

Leonilda (German) fighter.

Leonore (Greek) a form of Eleanor.
See also Nora.
Leonor, Leonora, Leonorah, Léonore

Leontina (German) strong as a lion.

Leontine (Latin) like a lioness.
Leona, Leonine, Leontyne, Léontyne

Leopolda (German) princess of the
village.

Leopoldina (Spanish) a form of
Leopoldo.

Leopoldo (Italian) a form of
Leopold (see Boys' Names).

Leora (Hebrew) light. (Greek) a
familiar form of Eleanor. See also
Liora.
Leorah, Leorit

Leotie (Native American) prairie
flower.

Lera (Russian) a short form of Valera.
Lerka

Lesbia (Greek) native of the Greek
island of Lesbos.

Lesley **G** (Scottish) gray fortress.
*Leslea, Leslee, Leslie, Lesly, Lezlee,
Lezley*

Leslie **G** (Scottish) a form of Lesley.
Leslei, Lesleigh, Lesli, Lesslie, Lezli

Lesly **G** (Scottish) a form of Lesley.
Leslye, Lessly, Lezly

Lester **B** (Latin) chosen camp.
(English) from Leicester, England.

Leta (Latin) glad. (Swahili) bringer.
(Greek) a short form of Aleta.
Lita, Lyta

Leticia (Latin) joy. See also Latisha,
Tisha.
Laticia, Leisha, Leshia, Let, Leta, Letesa,
Letesha, Leteshia, Letha, Lethia, Letice,
Letichia, Letisha, Letishia, Letisia, Letissa,
Letita, Letitia, Letiticia, Letiza, Letizia,
Letty, Letycia, Loutitia

Letty (English) a familiar form of
Leticia.
Letta, Letti, Lettie

Levana (Hebrew) moon; white.
(Latin) risen. Mythology: the
goddess of newborn babies.
Lévana, Levania, Levanna, Levenia,
Lewana, Livana

Levani (Fijian) anointed with oil.

Levi **B** (Hebrew) a form of Levia.

Levia (Hebrew) joined, attached.
Leevya, Levi, Levie

Levina (Latin) flash of lightning.
Levene

Levona (Hebrew) spice; incense.
Leavonia, Levonat, Levonna, Levonne,
Livona

Lewana (Hebrew) a form of Levana.
Lebhanah, Lewanna

Lewis **B** (Welsh) a form of
Llewellyn. (English) a form of
Louis (see Boys' Names).

Lexandra (Greek) a short form of
Alexandra.
Lisandra

Lexi (Greek) a familiar form of
Alexandra.

Lexia (Greek) a familiar form of
Alexandra.
Leska, Lesya, Lexa, Lexane, Lexina,
Lexine

Lexie **G** (Greek) a familiar form of
Alexandra.
Leksi, Lexey, Lexy

Lexis (Greek) a short form of Alexius, Alexus.
Laexis, Lexius, Lexsis, Lexxis

Lexus **G** (Greek) a short form of Alexis.
Lexuss, Lexxus, Lexyss

Leya (Spanish) loyal. (Tamil) the constellation Leo.
Leyah, Leyla

Li (Chinese) strength; beautiful.

Li Hua (Chinese) pear blossom.

Li Mei (Chinese) beautiful plum blossom.

Li Ming (Chinese) beautiful and bright.

Li Na (Chinese) beautiful and graceful.

Li Qin, Li-Qin (Chinese) beautiful stringed musical instrument.

Li Wei (Chinese) beautiful rose.

Lia **G** (Greek) bringer of good news. (Hebrew, Dutch, Italian) dependent. See also Leah.
Lía, Liah

Liam **B** (Irish) a form of William.

Lian (Chinese) graceful willow. (Latin) a short form of Gillian, Lillian.
Lean, Leeann, Liane, Liann, Lianne

Liana, Lianna **G** (Latin) youth. (French) bound, wrapped up; tree covered with vines. (English) meadow. (Hebrew) short forms of Eliana.
Leanna

Liane, Lianne (Hebrew) short forms of Eliane. (English) forms of Lian.
Leeanne

Liang (Chinese) good.

Liao (Chinese) faraway, vast.

Liban **B** (Hawaiian) a form of Laban (see Boys' Names).

Libby (Hebrew) a familiar form of Elizabeth.
Ibby, Lib, Libbee, Libbey, Libbie

Libera, Líbera (Latin) she who bestows abundance.

Liberada (Latin) liberated.

Liberata (Latin) she who loves liberty.

Liberia, Liberta (Spanish) freedom.

Libertad (Latin) she who has the skills to act in good faith.

Liberty (Latin) free.
Liberti, Libertie

Libia (Latin) comes from the desert.

Libitina (Latin) she who is wanted.

Libna (Latin) whiteness.

Libni, Lipi (Indian) manuscripts of God.

Liboria (Latin) she who was born in Libor, the name of several ancient cities in Spain and Portugal.

Librada (Latin) liberated.

Lican (Mapuche) flint stone.

Licia (Greek) a short form of Alicia.
Licha, Lishia, Lisia, Lycia

Lida (Greek) happy. (Slavic) loved by people. (Latin) a short form of Alida, Elita.
Leeda, Lidah, Lidochka, Lyda

Lide (Latin, Basque) life.

Lidia (Greek) a form of Lydia.
Lidea, Lidi, Lidija, Lidiya, Lidka, Lidya

Lídia (Portuguese) a form of Lidia.

Lien (Chinese) lotus.
Lienne

Liesabet (German) a short form of
Elizabeth.
Liesbeth, Lisbete

Liese (German) a familiar form of
Elise, Elizabeth.
Liesa, Lieschen, Lise

Liesel (German) a familiar form of
Elizabeth.
*Leesel, Leesl, Leezel, Leezl, Liesl, Liezel,
Liezl, Lisel*

Lieu (Vietnamese) sweet potato.

Ligia (Greek) Mythology: name of a
mermaid.

Lígia (Portuguese) a form of Ligia.

Likhitha (Indian) writing.

Lila (Arabic) night. (Hindi) free will
of God. (Persian) lilac. A short form
of Dalila, Delilah, Lillian.
Lilah, Lilia, Lyla, Lylah

Lilac (Sanskrit) lilac; blue purple.

Lilia (Persian) a form of Lila.
Lili

Lilian (Latin) a form of Lillian.
Liliane, Liliann, Lilianne

Lilián (Spanish) a form of Lilian.

Lílian (Portuguese) a form of Lilian.

Liliana (Latin) a form of Lillian.
*Lileana, Lilliana, Lilianna, Lilliana,
Lillianna*

Lilibeth (English) a combination of
Lily + Beth.
Lilibet, Lillibeth, Lillybeth, Lilybet, Lilybeth

Lilith (Arabic) of the night; night
demon. Mythology: the first wife of

Adam, according to ancient Jewish
legends.
Lillis, Lily

Lillian ✿ (Latin) lily flower.
*Lian, Lil, Lila, Lilas, Lileane, Lilia, Lilian,
Liliana, Lilias, Liliha, Lilja, Lilla, Lilli, Lillia,
Lilliane, Lilliann, Lillianne, Lillyann, Lis,
Liuka*

Lillyann (English) a combination of
Lily + Ann. (Latin) a form of
Lillian.
*Lillyan, Lillyanne, Lily, Lilyan, Lilyana,
Lilyann, Lilyanna, Lilyanne*

Lilvina (Latin, German) friend of the
Iris.

Lily ✿ (Latin, Arabic) a familiar
form of Lilith, Lillian, Lillyann.
*Lil, Lile, Lili, Lilie, Lilijana, Lilika, Lilike,
Liliosa, Lilium, Lilka, Lille, Lilli, Lillie, Lilly*

Lim (Chinese) a form of Lin.

Limber (Tiv) joyful.

Lin **G** (Chinese) beautiful jade.
(English) a form of Lynn.
Linh, Linn

Lin Yao (Chinese) beautiful jade
treasure.

Lina (Greek) light. (Arabic) tender.
(Latin) a form of Lena.

Lincoln **B** (English) settlement by
the pool.

Linda **G** (Spanish) pretty.
Lind, Lindy, Linita, Lynda

Lindsay **G** (English) a form of
Lindsey.
Lindsi, Linsay, Lyndsay

Lindsey **G** (English) linden tree
island; camp near the stream.
*Lind, Lindsea, Lindsee, Lindsi, Linsey,
Lyndsey, Lynsey*

Lindsi (American) a familiar form of Lindsay, Lindsey.
Lindsie, Lindsy, Lindze, Lindzee, Lindzey, Lindzy

Lindy (Spanish) a familiar form of Linda.
Linde, Lindee, Lindey, Lindi, Lindie

Linette (Welsh) idol. (French) bird.
Lanette, Linet, Linnet, Linnetta, Linnette, Lyannette, Lynette

Ling (Chinese) delicate, dainty.

Lin-Lin (Chinese) beauty of a tinkling bell.

Linnea (Scandinavian) lime tree. Botany: the national flower of Sweden.
Lin, Linae, Linea, Linnae, Linnaea, Linneah, Lynea, Lynnea

Linsey (English) a form of Lindsey.
Linsea, Linsee, Linsi, Linsie, Linsy, Linzee, Linzey, Linzi, Linzie, Linzy, Linzzi, Lynsey

Liolya (Russian) a form of Helen.

Lionela (Greek) little lion.

Liora (Hebrew) light. See also Leora.

Lipika (Indian) alphabets.

Lirit (Hebrew) poetic; lyrical, musical.

Liron 🅱🅶 (Hebrew) my song.
Leron, Lerone, Lirone

Li-Rong (Chinese) beautiful lotus.

Lisa 🅶 (Hebrew) consecrated to God. (English) a short form of Elizabeth.
Leeza, Liesa, Liisa, Lise, Lisenka, Lisette, Liszka, Litsa, Lysa

Lisbeth (English) a short form of Elizabeth.
Lisbet

Lise 🅶 (German) a form of Lisa.

Lisette 🅶 (French) a form of Lisa. (English) a familiar form of Elise, Elizabeth.
Liset, Liseta, Lisete, Liseth, Lisett, Lisetta, Lisettina, Lizet, Lizette, Lysette

Lisha (Arabic) darkness before midnight. (Hebrew) a short form of Alisha, Elisha, Ilisha.
Lishe

Lissa (Greek) honey bee. A short form of Elissa, Elizabeth, Melissa, Millicent.
Lyssa

Lissette (French) a form of Lisa. (English) a familiar form of Elise, Elizabeth.
Lisset, Lissete, Lissett

Lissie (American) a familiar form of Allison, Elise, Elizabeth.
Lissee, Lissey, Lissi, Lissy, Lissye

Lita (Latin) a familiar form of names ending in "lita."
Leta, Litah, Litta

Litonya (Moquelumnan) darting hummingbird.

Liu (Chinese) willow.

Liv (Latin) a short form of Livia, Olivia.

Livana (Hebrew) a form of Levana.
Livna, Livnat

Livia (Hebrew) crown. A familiar form of Olivia. (Latin) olive.
Levia, Liv, Livie, Livy, Livya, Livye

Liviya (Hebrew) brave lioness; royal crown.
Leviya, Levya, Livya

Livona (Hebrew) a form of Levona.

Lixue (Chinese) pretty snow.

Liz (English) a short form of Elizabeth.

Liza (American) a short form of Elizabeth.
Leeza, Lizela, Lizka, Lyza

Lizabeta (Russian) a form of Elizabeth.
Lizabetah, Lizaveta, Lizonka

Lizabeth (English) a short form of Elizabeth.
Lisabet, Lisabeth, Lisabette, Lizabette

Lizbeth **G** (English) a short form of Elizabeth.
Lizbet, Lizbett

Lizet, Lizette (French) forms of Lisette.
Lizet, Lizete, Lizeth, Lizett, Lizzet, Lizzeth, Lizzette

Lizina (Latvian) a familiar form of Elizabeth.

Lizzy (American) a familiar form of Elizabeth.
Lizzie, Lizy

Llanquipan (Mapuche) fallen branch; solitary lioness; retiring soul; lady who distances herself from the noise of the world.

Llanquiray (Mapuche) flowered pearl; fallen flower, fallen petals.

Llesenia (Spanish) gypsy female lead in a 1970s soap opera.

Lloyd **B** (Welsh) gray haired; holy.

Lluvia (Spanish) rain.

Lochana (Indian) eye.

Logan **B** (Irish) meadow.
Logann, Loganne, Logen, Loghan, Logun, Logyn, Logynn

Lohini (Indian) red skinned.

Loida, Loída (Greek) example of faith and piousness.

Lois (German) famous warrior.

Lok (Chinese) happy.

Lola (Spanish) a familiar form of Carlotta, Dolores, Louise.
Lolah, Lolita

Lolida (Pohnpeian) a form of Jacinta.

Lolita (Spanish) sorrowful. A familiar form of Lola.
Lita, Lulita

Lolly (English) sweet; candy. A familiar form of Laura.

Lolotea (Zuni) a form of Dorothy.

Lomasi (Native American) pretty flower.

Lona (Latin) lioness. (English) solitary. (German) a short form of Leona.
Loni, Lonna

London **BG** (English) fortress of the moon. Geography: the capital of the United Kingdom.
Landyn, Londen, Londun, Londyn

Loni (American) a form of Lona.
Lonee, Lonie, Lonni, Lonnie

Lonoris (Chuukese) a form of Dolores.

Lopa (Indian) learned.

Lopamudra (Indian) learned woman.

Lora (Latin) crowned with laurel. (American) a form of Laura.
Lorah, Lorane, Lorann, Lorra, Lorrah, Lorrane

Lorda (Spanish) shrine of the Virgin Mary.

Lore (Basque) flower. (Latin) a short
form of Flora.
Lor

Lorelei (German) alluring.
Mythology: the siren of the Rhine
River who lured sailors to their
deaths. See also Lurleen.
Loralee, Loralei, Lorali, Loralie, Loralyn,
Loreal, Lorelea, Loreley, Loreli, Lorilee,
Lorilyn

Lorelle (American) a form of Laurel.

Loren 🔠 (American) a form of
Lauren.
Loreen, Lorena, Lorin, Lorne, Lorren,
Lorrin, Lorryn, Loryn, Lorynn, Lorynne

Lorena 🔠 (English) a form of
Lauren.
Lorene, Lorenea, Lorenia, Lorenna,
Lorina, Lorrina, Lorrine, Lurana

Lorenza (Latin) a form of Laura.
Laurencia, Laurentia, Laurentina

Loreta (Spanish) a form of Loreto.

Loreto (Italian) a form of Loretta.

Loretta (English) a familiar form of
Laura.
Larretta, Lauretta, Laurette, Loretah,
Lorette, Lorita, Lorretta, Lorrette

Lori 🔠 (Latin) crowned with laurel.
(French) a short form of Lorraine.
(American) a familiar form of
Laura.
Loree, Lorey, Loria, Lorianna, Lorianne,
Lorie, Lorree, Lorri, Lorrie, Lory

Lorin (American) a form of Loren.
Lorine

Lorinda (Spanish) a form of Laura.

Loris 🔠🔠 (Latin) thong. (Dutch)
clown. (Greek) a short form of
Chloris.
Laurice, Laurys, Lorice

Lorna (Latin) crowned with laurel.
Literature: probably coined by
Richard Blackmore in his novel
Lorna Doone.
Lorrna

Lorraine (Latin) sorrowful. (French)
from Lorraine, a former province of
France. See also Rayna.
Laraine, Lorain, Loraine, Lorayne,
Lorein, Loreine, Lori, Lorine, Lorrain,
Lorraina, Lorrayne, Lorreine

Lo-Shen (Chinese) goddess of rivers.

Lotte (German) a short form of
Charlotte.
Lotie, Lotta, Lottchen, Lottey, Lottie, Lotty,
Loty

Lotus (Greek) lotus.

Lou 🔠 (American) a short form of
Louise, Luella.
Lu

Louam (Ethiopian) sleep well.

Louisa (English) a familiar form of
Louise. Literature: Louisa May
Alcott was an American writer and
reformer best known for her novel
Little Women.
Aloisa, Eloisa, Heloisa, Lou, Louisian,
Louisane, Louisina, Louiza, Lovisa, Luisa,
Luiza, Lujza, Lujzika

Louise 🔠 (German) famous warrior.
See also Alison, Eloise, Heloise,
Lois, Lola, Ludovica, Luella, Lulu.
Loise, Lou, Louisa, Louisette, Louisiane,
Louisine, Lowise, Loyce, Loyise, Luise

Lourdes 🔠 (French) from Lourdes,
France. Religion: a place where the
Virgin Mary was said to have
appeared.

Louredes (Spanish) shrine of the
Virgin Mary.

Love (English) love, kindness, charity.
*Lovely, Lovewell, Lovey, Lovie, Lovy, Luv,
Luvvy*

Lovisa (German) a form of Louisa.

Lúa (Latin) moon.

Luann (Hebrew, German) graceful
woman warrior. (Hawaiian) happy;
relaxed. (American) a combination
of Louise + Ann.
*Louann, Louanne, Lu, Lua, Luan, Luane,
Luanna, Luanne, Luanni, Luannie*

Luanna (German) a form of Luann.
Lewanna, Louanna, Luana, Luwana

Lubaaba (Indian) the innermost
essence.

Lubov (Russian) love.
Luba, Lubna, Lubochka, Lyuba, Lyubov

Luca **B** (Latin) a form of Lucy.

Lucas **B** (German, Irish, Danish,
Dutch) a form of Lucius (see Boys'
Names).

Lucelia (Spanish) a combination of
Luz and Celia.

Lucena (Spanish) bringer of light.

Lucerne (Latin) lamp; circle of light.
Geography: the Lake of Lucerne is
in Switzerland.
Lucerna, Lucero

Lucero (Latin) a form of Lucerne.

Lucetta (English) a familiar form of
Lucy.
Lucette

Lucia (Italian, Spanish) a form of
Lucy.
Lúcia, Lucía, Luciana, Lucianna

Lucie (French) a familiar form of
Lucy.

Lucille (English) a familiar form of
Lucy.
Lucila, Lucile, Lucilla

Lucinda (Latin) a form of Lucy. See
also Cindy.

Lucine (Arabic) moon. (Basque) a
form of Lucy.
*Lucienne, Lucina, Lucyna, Lukene,
Lusine, Luzine*

Lucita (Spanish) a form of Lucy.
Lusita

Lucretia (Latin) rich; rewarded.
*Lacrecia, Lucrece, Lucréce, Lucrecia,
Lucreecia, Lucresha, Lucreshia, Lucrezia,
Lucrisha, Lucrishia*

Lucrezia (Italian) a form of Lucretia.
History: Lucrezia Borgia was the
Duchess of Ferrara and a patron of
learning and the arts.

Lucy (Latin) light; bringer of light.
*Luca, Luce, Lucetta, Luci, Lucia, Lucida,
Lucie, Lucija, Lucika, Lucille, Lucinda,
Lucine, Lucita, Luciya, Lucya, Luzca, Luzi*

Ludmilla (Slavic) loved by the
people. See also Mila.
Ludie, Ludka, Ludmila, Lyuba, Lyudmila

Ludovica (German) a form of
Louise.
Ludovika, Ludwiga

Luella (English) elf. (German) a
familiar form of Louise.
*Loella, Lou, Louella, Ludella, Luelle,
Lula, Lulu*

Luis **B** (Spanish) a form of Louis
(see Boys' Names).

Luisa **G** (Spanish) a form of Louisa.

Luisina (Teutonic) celebrated warrior;
celebrated; very well known.

Luke **B** (Latin) a form of Lucius
(see Boys' Names).

Lulani 🆑🆖 (Polynesian) highest point of heaven.

Lulu (Arabic) pearl. (English) soothing, comforting. (Native American) hare. (German) a familiar form of Louise, Luella.
Loulou, Lula, Lulie

Luna (Latin) moon.
Lunetta, Lunette, Lunneta, Lunnete

Luo (Chinese) name of a river.

Lupa (Latin) wolf.

Lupe (Latin) wolf. (Spanish) a short form of Guadalupe.
Lupi, Lupita, Luppi

Lupita (Latin) a form of Lupe.

Lurdes (Portuguese, Spanish) a form of Lourdes.

Lurleen, Lurlene (Scandinavian) war horn. (German) forms of Lorelei.
Lura, Lurette, Lurline

Lusa (Finnish) a form of Elizabeth.

Lusela (Moquelumnan) like a bear swinging its foot when licking it.

Lutgarda (German) she who protects her village.

Luvena (Latin, English) little; beloved.
Lovena, Lovina, Luvenia, Luvina

Luyu 🆑🆖 (Moquelumnan) like a pecking bird.

Luz 🆖 (Spanish) light. Religion: Nuestra Señora de Luz—Our Lady of the Light—is another name for the Virgin Mary.
Luzi, Luzija

Luzia (Portuguese) a form of Lucia.

Lycoris (Greek) twilight.

Lyda (Greek) a short form of Lidia, Lydia.

Lydia 🆖 (Greek) from Lydia, an ancient land in Asia. (Arabic) strife.
Lidia, Lidija, Lidiya, Lyda, Lydie, Lydië

Lyla (French) island. (English) a form of Lyle (see Boys' Names). (Arabic, Hindi, Persian) a form of Lila.
Lila, Lilah

Lynda (Spanish) pretty. (American) a form of Linda.
Lyndah, Lynde, Lyndi, Lynnda

Lyndell (English) a form of Lynelle.
Lyndall, Lyndel, Lyndella

Lyndi (Spanish) a familiar form of Lynda.
Lyndee, Lindie, Lyndy, Lynndie, Lynndy

Lyndsay 🆖 (American) a form of Lindsay.
Lyndsaye

Lyndsey (English) linden tree island; camp near the stream. (American) a form of Lindsey.
Lyndsea, Lyndsee, Lyndsi, Lyndsie, Lyndsy, Lyndzee, Lyndzey, Lyndzi, Lyndzie, Lynndsie

Lynelle (English) pretty.
Linel, Linell, Linnell, Lyndell, Lynel, Lynell, Lynella, Lynnell

Lynette (Welsh) idol. (English) a form of Linette.
Lynett, Lynetta, Lynnet, Lynnette

Lynn, Lynne 🆖 (English) waterfall; pool below a waterfall.
Lin, Lina, Linley, Linn, Lyn, Lynlee, Lynley, Lynna, Lynnae, Lynnea

Lynnell (English) a form of Lynelle.
Linnell, Lynnelle

Lynsey (American) a form of Lyndsey.
Lynnsey, Lynnzey, Lynsie, Lynsy, Lynzee, Lynzey, Lynzi, Lynzie, Lynzy

Lyra (Greek) lyre player.
Lyre, Lyric, Lyrica, Lyrie, Lyris

Lysandra (Greek) liberator.
Lisandra, Lysandre, Lytle

Lysanne (American) a combination of Lysandra + Anne.
Lisanne, Lizanne

M **G** (American) an initial used as a first name.

Ma (Chinese) agate.

Maanasa (Indian) mind.

Maanika (Indian) ruby.

Mab (Irish) joyous. (Welsh) baby. Literature: queen of the fairies.
Mabry

Mabel (Latin) lovable. A short form of Amabel.
Mabelle, Mable, Mabyn, Maible, Maybel, Maybeline, Maybelle, Maybull

Macarena (Spanish) she who carries the sword; name for the Virgin Mary.

Macaria (Greek) having a long life.

Macawi (Dakota) generous; motherly.

Macayla (American) a form of Michaela.
Macaela, Macaila, Macala, Macalah, Macaylah, Macayle, Macayli, Mackayla

Macey (Polish) a familiar form of Macia.
Macee

Machaela (Hebrew) a form of Michaela.
Machael, Machaelah, Machaelie, Machaila, Machala, Macheala

Machiko (Japanese) fortunate child.
Machi

Macia (Polish) a form of Miriam.
Macelia, Macey, Machia, Macie, Macy, Masha, Mashia

Macie, Macy **G** (Polish) familiar forms of Macia.
Maci, Macye

Maciela (Latin) very slender, skeletal.

Mackenna (American) a form of Mackenzie.
Mackena, Makenna, Mckenna

Mackenzie ☆ **G** (Irish) child of the wise leader. See also Kenzie.
Macenzie, Mackenna, Mackensi, Mackensie, Mackenzee, Mackenzee, Mackenzey, Mackenzi, Mackenzia, Mackenzy, Mackenzye, Mackinsey, Mackynze, Makenzie, McKenzie, Mckinzie, Mekenzie, Mykenzie

Mackinsey (Irish) a form of Mackenzie.
Mackinsie, Mackinze, Mackinzee, Mackinzey, Mackinzi, Mackinzie

Macra (Greek) she who grows.

Mada (English) a short form of Madaline, Magdalen.
Madda, Mahda

Madaline (English) a form of Madeline.
Mada, Madailéin, Madaleen, Madaleine, Madalene, Madalin, Madaline

Madalyn (Greek) a form of Madeline.
Madalyne, Madalynn, Madalynne

Maddie (English) a familiar form of
Madeline.
*Maddi, Maddy, Mady, Maidie,
Maydey*

Maddison 🄶 (English) a form of
Madison.
*Maddisan, Maddisen, Maddisson,
Maddisyn, Maddyson*

Madeeha (Indian) praiseworthy.

Madelaine (French) a form of
Madeline.
Madelane, Madelayne

Madeleine (French) a form of
Madeline.
*Madalaine, Madalayne, Madelaine,
Madelein, Madeliene*

Madelena (English) a form of
Madeline.
*Madalaina, Madalena, Madalina,
Maddalena, Madelaina, Madeleina,
Madelina, Madelyna*

Madeline ⚝ 🄶 (Greek) high
tower. See also Lena, Lina, Maud.
*Madaline, Madalyn, Maddie, Madel,
Madelaine, Madeleine, Madelena,
Madelene, Madelia, Madella,
Madelle, Madelon, Madelyn, Madge,
Madilyn, Madlen, Madlin, Madline,
Madlyn, Madolyn, Maida*

Madelón (Spanish) a form of
Magdalen.

Madelyn ⚝ (Greek) a form of
Madeline.
*Madelyne, Madelynn, Madelynne,
Madilyn, Madlyn, Madolyn*

Madena, Madia, Madina (Greek)
from the high tower.

Madge (Greek) a familiar form of
Madeline, Margaret.
Madgi, Madgie, Mady

Madhavi (Indian) honey.

Madhavilata (Indian) a flowering
creeper.

Madhuchanda (Indian) pleasing
composition.

Madhuksara (Indian) one who
showers honey.

Madhul, Madhura, Madhuri
(Indian) sweet.

Madhulata (Indian) lovely creeper.

Madhulekha (Indian) beautiful.

Madhulika (Indian) nectar.

Madhumalati (Indian) flowering
creeper.

Madhumathi (Indian) delight;
moon.

Madhumati, Mahabhadra
(Indian) the Ganga River.

Madhumita (Indian) sweet girl.

Madhumitha (Indian) sweet person.

Madhunisha (Indian) pleasant
night.

Madhurima (Indian) charming.

Madhusha (Indian) beauty.

Madhushri (Indian) beauty of the
spring season.

Madhuvanthi (Indian) one who is
sweet like honey.

Madilyn (Greek) a form of
Madeline.
*Madilen, Madiline, Madilyne,
Madilynn*

Madirakshi (Indian) woman with
intoxicating eyes.

Madisen 🄶 (English) a form of
Madison.
Madisan, Madisin, Madissen, Madisun

Madison ☀ ❄ **G** (English) good; child of Maud.
Maddison, Madisen, Madisson, Madisyn, Madyson, Mattison

Madisyn (English) a form of Madison.
Madissyn, Madisynn, Madisynne

Madolyn (Greek) a form of Madeline.
Madoline, Madolyne, Madolynn, Madolynne

Madonna (Latin) my lady.
Madona

Madrona (Spanish) mother.
Madre, Madrena

Madyson (English) a form of Madison.
Madysen, Madysun

Mae (English) a form of May. History: Mae Jemison was the first African American woman in space.
Maelea, Maeleah, Maelen, Maelle, Maeona

Maegan (Irish) a form of Megan.
Maegen, Maeghan, Maegin

Maeko (Japanese) honest child.
Mae, Maemi

Maeve (Irish) joyous. Mythology: a legendary Celtic queen. See also Mavis.
Maevi, Maevy, Maive, Mayve

Mafalda (Spanish) a form of Matilde.

Magadhi (Indian) flower.

Magalí (French) a form of Magali.

Magali, Magaly (Hebrew) from the high tower.
Magalie, Magally

Magan, Magen (Greek) forms of Megan.
Maggen, Maggin

Magda (Czech, Polish, Russian) a form of Magdalen.
Mahda, Makda

Magdalen (Greek) high tower. Bible: Magdala was the home of Saint Mary Magdalen. See also Madeline, Malena, Marlene.
Mada, Magda, Magdala, Magdaleen, Magdalena, Magdalene, Magdaline, Magdalyn, Magdalynn, Magdelane, Magdelene, Magdeline, Magdelyn, Magdlen, Magdolna, Maggie, Magola, Maighdlin, Mala, Malaine

Magdalena (Greek) a form of Magdalen.
Magdalina, Magdelana, Magdelena, Magdelina

Magena (Native American) coming moon.

Maggie (Greek) pearl. (English) a familiar form of Magdalen, Margaret.
Mag, Magge, Maggee, Maggi, Maggia, Maggie, Maggiemae, Maggy, Magi, Magie, Mags

Maggy, Meggy (English) forms of Maggie.
Maggey, Magy

Magnolia (Latin) flowering tree. See also Nollie.
Nola

Mahajabeen (Indian) beautiful.

Mahakanta, Mahika (Indian) earth.

Mahal (Filipino) love.

Mahala (Arabic) fat, marrow; tender. (Native American) powerful woman.
Mahalah, Mahalar, Mahalla, Mahela, Mahila, Mahlah, Mahlaha, Mehala, Mehalah

Mahalia (American) a form of Mahala.
Mahaley, Mahaliah, Mahalie, Mahayla, Mahaylah, Mahaylia, Mahelea, Maheleah, Mahelia, Mahilia, Mehalia

Maharene (Ethiopian) forgive us.

Mahati (Indian) great.

Mahek (Indian) smell.

Mahendi (Indian) leaves.

Mahesa (Hindi) great lord. Religion: a name for the Hindu god Shiva.
Maheesa, Mahisa

Mahi (Indian) the world.

Mahijuba (Indian) a hostess.

Mahila (Sanskrit) woman.

Mahima (Indian) glorious.

Mahina (Hawaiian) moon glow.

Mahira (Hebrew) energetic.
Mahri

Mahiya (Indian) joy.

Maho (Japanese) truth; sail.

Mahogony (Spanish) rich; strong.
Mahogany, Mahoganey, Mahogani, Mahoganie, Mahogany, Mahogney, Mahogny, Mohogany, Mohogony

Mahua (Indian) an intoxicating flower.

Mahuya (Indian) the name of a beautiful flower.

Mai (Japanese) brightness. (Vietnamese) flower. (Navajo) coyote.

Maia (Greek) mother; nurse. (English) kinswoman; maiden. Mythology: the loveliest of the Pleiades, the seven daughters of Atlas, and the mother of Hermes. See also Maya.
Maiah, Maie, Maiya

Maiara (Tupi) wise.

Maida (English) maiden. (Greek) a short form of Madeline.
Maidel, Mayda, Maydena

Maija (Finnish) a form of Mary.
Maiji, Maikki

Maika (Hebrew) a familiar form of Michaela.
Maikala, Maikka, Maiko

Maimoona (Indian) auspicious; blessed.

Maina (Indian) a bird.

Maira ☐ (Irish) a form of Mary.
Maairah, Mair, Mairi, Mairim, Mairin, Mairona, Mairwen

Maire (Irish) a form of Mary.

Maisie (Scottish) familiar forms of Margaret.
Maisa, Maise, Maisey, Maisi, Maisy, Maizie, Maycee, Maysie, Mayzie, Mazey, Mazie, Mazy, Mazzy, Mysie, Myzie

Maita (Spanish) a form of Martha.
Maitia

Maite (Spanish) a form of Maita.

Maitea (Spanish) dearly loved.

Maiten (Spanish) a form of Malen.

Maitena (Spanish) a form of Maite.

Maitlyn (American) a combination of Maita + Lynn.
Maitlan, Maitland, Maitlynn, Mattilyn

Maitreyi (Indian) a wise woman.

Maitri (Indian) friendship.

Maiya (Greek) a form of Maia.
Maiyah

Maja (Arabic) a short form of
   Majidah.
   Majal, Majalisa, Majalyn, Majalynn

Majeeda (Indian) glorious.

Majesta (Latin) majesty.

Majidah (Arabic) splendid.
   Maja, Majida

Makaarim (Indian) of good and
   honorable character.

Makaela, Makaila (American)
   forms of Michaela.
   *Makaelah, Makaelee, Makaella,
   Makaely, Makail, Makailah, Makailee,
   Makailla, Makaillah, Makealah,
   Makell*

Makala (Hawaiian) myrtle. (Hebrew)
   a form of Michaela.
   *Makalae, Makalah, Makalai, Makalea,
   Makalee, Makaleh, Makaleigh,
   Makaley, Makalia, Makalie, Makalya,
   Makela, Makelah, Makell, Makella*

Makana (Hawaiian) gift, present.

Makani **B** (Hawaiian) wind.

Makara (Hindi) Astrology: another
   name for the zodiac sign Capricorn.

Makayla ✼ (American) a form of
   Michaela.
   *Macayla, Makaylah, Makaylee,
   Makayleigh, Makayli, Makaylia,
   Makaylla, Makell, Makyla, Makylah,
   Mckayla, Mekayla, Mikayla*

Makell **G** (American) a short form
   of Makaela, Makala, Makayla.
   Makele, Makelle, Mckell, Mekel

Makenna **G** (American) a form of
   Mackenna.
   Makena, Makennah, Mikenna

Makenzie **G** (Irish) a form of
   Mackenzie.
   *Makense, Makensey, Makensie,
   Makenze, Makenzee, Makenzey,*
   *Makenzi, Makenzy, Makenzye,
   Makinzey, Makynzey, Mekenzie,
   Mykenzie*

Maki (Japanese) she who prays for
   the truth.

Makiko (Japanese) child of Maki.

Makshi (Indian) honeybee.

Ma-Ku (Chinese) goddess of
   springtime.

Mala (Greek) a short form of
   Magdalen.
   Malana, Malee, Mali

Malana (Hawaiian) bouyant, light.

Malarvizhi (Indian) cute eyes.

Malashree (Indian) an early evening
   melody.

Malati (Indian) jasmine; moonlight.

Malavika (Indian) princess of the
   kingdom of Malava.

Malaya (Filipino) free.
   *Malayaa, Malayah, Malayna, Malea,
   Maleah*

Malen (Swedish) a form of Malena.

Malena (Swedish) a familiar form of
   Magdalen.
   *Malenna, Malin, Malina, Maline,
   Malini, Malinna*

Malha (Hebrew) queen.
   *Maliah, Malkah, Malkia, Malkiah,
   Malkie, Malkiya, Malkiyah, Miliah*

Mali (Tai) jasmine flower. (Tongan)
   sweet. (Hungarian) a short form of
   Malika.
   Malea, Malee, Maley

Malia (Hawaiian, Zuni) a form of
   Mary. (Spanish) a form of Maria.
   *Malea, Maleah, Maleeya, Maleeyah,
   Maleia, Maliah, Maliasha, Malie,
   Maliea, Maliya, Maliyah, Malli, Mally*

Malik 🅱 (Hungarian, Arabic) a form of Malika.

Malika (Hungarian) industrious. (Arabic) queen.
Malak, Maleeka, Maleka, Mali, Maliaka, Malik, Malikah, Malikee, Maliki, Malikia, Malky

Malina (Hebrew) tower. (Native American) soothing. (Russian) raspberry.
Malin, Maline, Malina, Malinna, Mallie

Malinda (Greek) a form of Melinda.
Malinde, Malinna, Malynda

Malini (Hindi) gardener.
Maliny

Malissa (Greek) a form of Melissa.
Malisa, Malisah, Malyssa

Maljumana (Indian) beautiful.

Mallalai (Pashto) beautiful.

Malley (American) a familiar form of Mallory.
Mallee, Malli, Mallie, Mally, Maly

Mallika (Indian) queen; a creeper plant.

Mallorie (French) a form of Mallory.
Malerie, Mallari, Mallerie, Malloreigh, Mallori

Mallory 🅶 (German) army counselor. (French) unlucky.
Maliri, Mallary, Mallauri, Mallery, Malley, Malloree, Mallorey, Mallorie, Malorie, Malory, Malorym, Malree, Malrie, Mellory

Malorie, Malory (German) forms of Mallory.
Malarie, Maloree, Malori, Melorie, Melory

Malti (Indian) moonlight.

Malva (English) a form of Melba.
Malvi, Malvy

Malvina (Scottish) a form of Melvina. Literature: a name created by the eighteenth-century Romantic poet James Macpherson.
Malvane, Malvi

Mamata (Indian) love, affection.

Mamie (American) a familiar form of Margaret.
Mame, Mamee, Mami, Mammie, Mamy, Mamye

Mamiko (Japanese) child of Mami.

Mamo 🅱🅶 (Hawaiian) saffron flower; yellow bird.

Mamta (Indian) motherly love.

Man (Chinese) trailing plant.

Mana (Hawaiian) psychic; sensitive.
Manal, Manali, Manna, Mannah

Manaal (Indian) attainment, achievement.

Manaar (Indian) guiding light.

Manami (Japanese) beautiful love and affection.

Manana (Indian) meditation.

Manar (Arabic) guiding light.
Manayra

Manchu (Chinese) pure.

Manda (Spanish) woman warrior. (Latin) a short form of Amanda.
Mandy

Mandakini (Indian) a river.

Mandakranta (Indian) a Sanskrit meter.

Mandara (Hindi) calm.

Mandaraa (Indian) coral tree.

Mandarmalika (Indian) a garland of celestial.

Mandavi (Indian) wife of Bharat.

Mandeep BG (Punjabi) enlightened.

Mandira (Indian) melody.

Mandisa (Xhosa) sweet.

Mandodari (Indian) one with narrow abdomen.

Mandy G (Latin) lovable. A familiar form of Amanda, Manda, Melinda.
Mandee, Mandi, Mandie

Manela (Catalonian) a form of Manuela.

Manette (French) a form of Mary.

Mang (Chinese) rays of light.

Mangala (Indian) auspicious; bliss.

Mangena (Hebrew) song, melody.
Mangina

Mangla (Indian) auspicious.

Mani (Chinese) a mantra repeated in Tibetan Buddhist prayer to impart understanding.
Manee

Manideepa (Indian) a lamp of precious stones.

Manika (Indian) jewel.

Manikuntala (Indian) one whose hair is like gems.

Manila (Latin) woman with small hands.

Manimala (Indian) a string of pearls.

Manimekhala (Indian) a girdle of gems.

Manini (Indian) self-respected.

Maniratna (Indian) diamond.

Manishika (Indian) intelligence.

Manjari (Indian) bud of a mango tree.

Manjira (Indian) ankle bells.

Manjistha (Indian) extremely.

Manjot BG (Indian) light of the mind.

Manju (Indian) pleasant.

Manjubala (Indian) beautiful girl.

Manjula (Indian) lovely, charming.

Manjulika (Indian) a sweet girl.

Manjusha (Indian) lady with a sweet voice.

Manka (Polish, Russian) a form of Mary.

Manmayi (Indian) jealous.

Manoela (Hebrew) God is with us.

Manola (Spanish) a form of Manuela.

Manon (French) a familiar form of Marie.
Mannon

Manón (Spanish) a form of Manon.

Manorama (Indian) beautiful.

Manoranjana (Indian) entertaining; pleasing.

Manpreet G (Punjabi) mind full of love.
Manprit

Manque (Mapuche) condor; the main woman; woman of unyielding character.

Mansha (Indian) wish.

Mansi (Hopi) plucked flower.
Mancey, Manci, Mancie, Mansey, Mansie, Mansy

Manuela (Spanish) a form of
Emmanuelle.
*Manuala, Manuelita, Manuella,
Manuelle*

Manya (Russian) a form of Mary.

Mao (Chinese) luxuriant.

Mar (Spanish) sea.

Mara (Hebrew) melody. (Greek) a
short form of Amara. (Slavic) a
form of Mary.
*Mahra, Marae, Marah, Maralina,
Maraline, Marra*

Maraam (Indian) aspiration.

Marabel (English) a form of
Mirabel.
Marabella, Marabelle

Marala (Indian) swan.

Maranda (Latin) a form of Miranda.

Maraya (Hebrew) a form of Mariah.
Mareya

Marcel 🅱 (French) a form of
Marcellus (see Boys' Names).

Marcela (Latin) a form of Marcella.
*Marcele, Marcelen, Marcelia,
Marcelina, Marceline, Maricela*

Marcelen (English) a form of
Marcella.
*Marcelen, Marcelin, Marcelina,
Marceline, Marcellin, Marcellina,
Marcelline, Marcelyn, Marcilen*

Marceliana (Latin) a form of
Marcela.

Marcella (Latin) martial, warlike.
Mythology: Mars was the god of
war.
*Mairsil, Marca, Marce, Marceil,
Marcela, Marcelen, Marcell, Marcelle,
Marcello, Marcena, Marchella,
Marchelle, Marci, Marcia, Marcie,*

*Marciella, Marcile, Marcilla, Marcille,
Marella, Marsella, Marselle, Marsiella*

Marcena (Latin) a form of Marcella,
Marcia.
*Maracena, Marceen, Marcene,
Marcenia, Marceyne, Marcina*

Marci, Marcie (English) familiar
forms of Marcella, Marcia.
*Marca, Marcee, Marcita, Marcy,
Marsi, Marsie*

Marcia (Latin) martial, warlike. See
also Marquita.
*Marcena, Marchia, Marci, Marciale,
Marcie, Marcsa, Marsha, Martia*

Márcia (Portuguese) a form of
Marcia.

Marciann (American) a combination
of Marci + Ann.
*Marciane, Marcianna, Marcianne,
Marcyane, Marcyanna, Marcyanne*

Marcilynn (American) a
combination of Marci + Lynn.
*Marcilen, Marcilin, Marciline, Marcilyn,
Marcilyne, Marcilynne, Marcylen,
Marcylin, Marcyline, Marcylyn,
Marcylyne, Marcylynn, Marcylynne*

Marco 🅱 (Italian) a form of Marcus.

Marcus 🅱 (Latin) martial, warlike.

Marcy (English) a form of Marci.
Marsey, Marsy

Mardi (French) born on Tuesday.
(Aramaic) a familiar form of
Martha.

Mare (Irish) a form of Mary.
Mair, Maire

Marelda (German) renowned warrior.
Marella, Marilda

Maren 🅶 (Latin) sea. (Aramaic) a
form of Mary. See also Marina.
Marin, Marine, Marinn, Miren

Maresa, Maressa (Latin) forms of
Marisa.
Maresha, Meresa

Maretta (English) a familiar form of
Margaret.
Maret, Marette

Margaret G (Greek) pearl. History:
Margaret Hilda Thatcher served as
British prime minister. See also Gita,
Greta, Gretchen, Marjorie, Markita,
Meg, Megan, Peggy, Reet, Rita.
*Madge, Maergrethe, Maggie, Maisie,
Mamie, Maretta, Marga, Margalo,
Marganit, Margara, Maretha,
Margarett, Margarette, Margarida,
Margarit, Margarita, Margaro,
Margaux, Marge, Margeret, Margeretta,
Margerette, Margery, Margetta,
Margiad, Margie, Margisia, Margit,
Margo, Margot, Margret, Marguerite,
Meta*

Margarit (Greek) a form of Margaret.
*Margalide, Margalit, Margalith,
Margarid, Margaritt, Margerit*

Margarita (Italian, Spanish) a form
of Margaret.
*Margareta, Margaretta, Margarida,
Margaritis, Margaritta, Margeretta,
Margharita, Margherita, Margrieta,
Margrita, Marguarita, Marguerita,
Margurita*

Margaux (French) a form of Margaret.
Margeaux

Marge (English) a short form of
Margaret, Marjorie.
Margie

Margery (English) a form of
Margaret.
Margerie, Margorie

Margie (English) a familiar form of
Marge, Margaret.
Margey, Margi, Margy

Margit (Hungarian) a form of
Margaret.
Marget, Margette, Margita

Margo, Margot (French) forms of
Margaret.
Mago, Margaro

Margret (German) a form of
Margaret.
*Margreta, Margrete, Margreth,
Margrett, Margretta, Margrette,
Margrieta, Margrita*

Marguerite (French) a form of
Margaret.
*Margarete, Margaretha, Margarethe,
Margarite, Margerite, Marguaretta,
Marguarette, Marguarite, Marguerette,
Margurite*

Mari (Japanese) ball. (Spanish) a
form of Mary.

Maria ⭐ **G** (Hebrew) bitter; sea of
bitterness. (Italian, Spanish) a form
of Mary.
*Maie, Malia, Marea, Mareah,
Mariabella, Mariae, Mariesa,
Mariessa, Mariha, Marija, Mariya,
Mariyah, Marja, Marya*

María (Hebrew) a form of Maria.

María de la Concepción (Spanish)
Mary of the conception.

María de la Paz (Spanish) Mary of
peace.

María de las Nieves (Spanish)
Mary of the snows.

María de las Victorias (Spanish)
victorious Mary.

María de los Angeles (Spanish)
angelic Mary.

María de los Milagros (Spanish)
miraculous Mary.

María del Mar (Spanish) Mary of the sea.

María Inmaculada (Spanish) immaculate Mary.

María José (Latin) name composed of María and José.

María Noel (Latin) name composed of María and Noel.

Mariah ☀ 🅖 (Hebrew) a form of Mary. See also Moriah.
Maraia, Maraya, Mariyah, Marriah, Meriah

Mariam 🅖 (Hebrew) a form of Miriam.
Mariama, Mariame, Mariem, Meryam

Marian 🅖 (English) a form of Maryann.
Mariana, Mariane, Mariann, Marianne, Mariene, Marion, Marrian, Marriann

Marián (Spanish) a short form of Mariana.

Mariana, Marianna (Spanish) forms of Marian.
Marriana, Marrianna, Maryana, Maryanna

Mariane, Marianne 🅖 (English) forms of Marian.
Marrianne, Maryanne

Marianela (Spanish) a combination of Mariana and Estela.

Mariángeles (Spanish) a combination of María and Ángeles.

Maribel (French) beautiful. (English) a combination of Maria + Bell.
Marabel, Marbelle, Mariabella, Maribella, Maribelle, Maridel, Marybel, Marybella, Marybelle

Marice (Italian) a form of Mary. See also Maris.
Marica, Marise, Marisse

Maricela (Latin) a form of Marcella.
Maricel, Mariceli, Maricelia, Maricella, Maricely

Marichi (Indian) name of a star.

Marichika (Indian) mirage; ray.

Maricruz (Spanish) a combination of María and Cruz.

Maridel (English) a form of Maribel.

Marie 🅖 (French) a form of Mary.
Maree, Marietta, Marrie

Mariel, Marielle (German, Dutch) forms of Mary.
Marial, Marieke, Marielana, Mariele, Marieli, Marielie, Marieline, Mariell, Mariellen, Marielsie, Mariely, Marielys

Mariela, Mariella (German, Dutch) forms of Mary.

Marieta (Hebrew) a form of María.

Marietta (Italian) a familiar form of Marie.
Maretta, Marette, Mariet, Mariette, Marrietta

Marieve (American) a combination of Mary + Eve.

Marigold (English) Mary's gold. Botany: a plant with yellow or orange flowers.
Marygold

Marika (Dutch, Slavic) a form of Mary.
Marica, Marieke, Marija, Marijke, Marikah, Marike, Marikia, Marikka, Mariska, Mariske, Marrika, Maryk, Maryka, Merica, Merika

Mariko (Japanese) circle.

Marilee (American) a combination of Mary + Lee.
Marili, Marilie, Marily, Marrilee, Marylea, Marylee, Merrilee, Merrili, Merrily

Marilena (Spanish) a combination of María and Elena.

Marilina (Latin) a combination of María and Elina.

Marilla (Hebrew, German) a form of Mary.
Marella, Marelle

Marilou (American) a form of Marylou.
Marilu, Mariluz

Marilú (Spanish) a combination of María and Luz.

Marilyn (Hebrew) Mary's line of descendants. See also Merilyn.
Maralin, Maralyn, Maralyne, Maralynn, Maralynne, Marelyn, Marilin, Marillyn, Marilyne, Marilynn, Marilynne, Marlyn, Marolyn, Marralynn, Marrilin, Marrilyn, Marrilynn, Marrilynne, Marylin, Marylinn, Marylyn, Marylyne, Marylynn, Marylynne

Marina **G** (Latin) sea. See also Maren.
Mareena, Marena, Marenka, Marinae, Marinah, Marinda, Marindi, Marinka, Marinna, Marrina, Maryna, Merina, Mirena

Mariña (Latin) a form of Marina.

Marinés (Spanish) a combination of María and Inés.

Marini (Swahili) healthy; pretty.

Mario **B** (Italian) a form of Marino (see Boys' Names).

Mariola (Italian) a form of María.

Marion **G** (French) a form of Mary.
Marrian, Marrion, Maryon, Maryonn

Marión (Spanish) a form of María.

Maris (Latin) sea. (Greek) a short form of Amaris, Damaris. See also Marice.
Maries, Marise, Marris, Marys, Maryse, Meris

Marisa (Latin) sea.
Maresa, Mariesa, Mariessa, Marisela, Marissa, Marita, Mariza, Marrisa, Marrissa, Marysa, Maryse, Maryssa, Merisa

Marisabel (Spanish) a combination of María and Isabel.

Marisabela (Spanish) a form of Marisabel.

Marisel (Spanish) a combination of María and Isabel.

Marisela **G** (Latin) a form of Marisa.
Mariseli, Marisella, Marishelle, Marissela

Marisha (Russian) a familiar form of Mary.
Mareshah, Marishenka, Marishka, Mariska

Marisol (Spanish) sunny sea.
Marise, Marizol, Marysol

Marissa ☆ **G** (Latin) a form of Maris, Marisa.
Maressa, Marisa, Marisha, Marissah, Marisse, Marizza, Marrissa, Marrissia, Maryssa, Merissa, Morissa

Marit (Aramaic) lady.
Marita, Marite

Marita (Spanish) a form of Marisa. (Aramaic) a form of Marit.
Marité, Maritha

Maritza (Arabic) blessed.
Maritsa, Maritssa

Mariyan (Arabic) purity.
Mariya, Mariyah, Mariyana,
Mariyanna

Marja (Finnish) a form of Mary.
Marjae, Marjatta, Marjie

Marjan (Persian) coral. (Polish) a
form of Mary.
Marjaneh, Marjanna

Marjie (Scottish) a familiar form of
Marjorie.
Marje, Marjey, Marji, Marjy

Marjolaine 🄶 (French) marjoram.

Marjorie (Greek) a familiar form of
Margaret. (Scottish) a form of Mary.
Majorie, Marge, Margeree, Margerey,
Margerie, Margery, Margorie, Margory,
Marjarie, Marjary, Marjerie, Marjery,
Marjie, Marjorey, Marjori, Marjory

Mark 🄱 (Latin) a form of Marcus.

Markayla (American) a combination
or Mary + Kayla.
Marka, Markaiah, Markaya,
Markayel, Markeela, Markel

Markeisha (English) a combination
of Mary + Keisha.
Markasha, Markeisa, Markeisia,
Markesha, Markeshia, Markesia,
Markiesha, Markisha, Markishia,
Marquesha

Markell 🄱 (Latin) a form of Mark.

Markita (Czech) a form of Margaret.
Marka, Markeah, Markeda, Markee,
Markeeta, Marketa, Marketta, Marki,
Markia, Markie, Markieta, Markita,
Markitha, Markketta, Merkate

Marla (English) a short form of
Marlena, Marlene.
Marlah, Marlea, Marleah

Marlana (English) a form of Marlena.
Marlaena, Marlaina, Marlainna,
Marlania, Marlanna, Marlayna,
Marleana

Marlee (English) a form of Marlene.
Marlea, Marleah, Marleigh

Marlen 🄶 (Greek, Slavic) a form of
Marlene.

Marlena (German) a form of Marlene.
Marla, Marlaina, Marlana, Marlanna,
Marleena, Marlina, Marlinda,
Marlyna, Marna

Marlene (Greek) high tower. (Slavic)
a form of Magdalen.
Marla, Marlaine, Marlane, Marlayne,
Marlee, Marleen, Marleene, Marlen,
Marlena, Marlenne, Marley, Marlin,
Marline, Marlyne

Marley 🄶 (English) a familiar form
of Marlene.
Marlee, Marli, Marlie, Marly

Marlis (English) a combination of
Maria + Lisa.
Marles, Marlisa, Marlise, Marlys,
Marlyse, Marlyssa

Marlo (English) a form of Mary.
Marlow, Marlowe

Marlon 🄱 (English) a form of Marlo.

Marlyn 🄶 (Hebrew) a short form of
Marilyn. (Greek, Slavic) a form of
Marlene.
Marlynn, Marlynne

Marmara (Greek) sparkling, shining.
Marmee

Marni (Hebrew) a form of Marnie.
Marnia, Marnique

Marnie (Hebrew) a short form of
Marnina.
Marna, Marnay, Marne, Marnee,
Marney, Marni, Marnisha, Marnja,
Marny, Marnya, Marnye

Marnina (Hebrew) rejoice.

Maro (Japanese) myself.

Maromisa (Japanese) a combination of Maro+ Misa.

Maroula (Greek) a form of Mary.

Marquesa (Spanish) she who works with a hammer.

Marquez **B** (Portuguese) a form of Marques (see Boys' Names).

Marquilla (Spanish) bitter.

Marquis **B** (French) a form of Marquise.

Marquise **B** (French) noblewoman.
Markese, Marquees, Marquese, Marquice, Marquies, Marquiese, Marquis, Marquisa, Marquisee, Marquisha, Marquisse, Marquiste

Marquisha (American) a form of Marquise.
Marquiesha, Marquisia

Marquita (Spanish) a form of Marcia.
Marquatte, Marqueda, Marquedia, Marquee, Marqueita, Marquet, Marqueta, Marquetta, Marquette, Marquia, Marquida, Marquietta, Marquitra, Marquitia, Marquitta

Marrim (Chinese) tribal name in Manpur state.

Marsala (Italian) from Marseilles, France.
Marsali, Marseilles

Marsha (English) a form of Marcia.
Marcha, Marshae, Marshay, Marshel, Marshele, Marshell, Marshia, Marshiela

Marshall **B** (French) caretaker of the horses; military title.

Marta (English) a short form of Martha, Martina.
Martá, Martä, Marte, Martia, Marttaha, Merta

Martha (Aramaic) lady; sorrowful. Bible: a friend of Jesus. See also Mardi.
Maita, Marta, Martaha, Marth, Marthan, Marthe, Marthy, Marti, Marticka, Martita, Mattie, Matty, Martus, Martuska, Masia

Marti **G** (English) a familiar form of Martha, Martina.
Martie, Marty

Martin **B** (Latin, French) a form of Martinus (see Boys' Names).

Martina **G** (Latin) martial, warlike. See also Tina.
Marta, Martel, Martella, Martelle, Martene, Marthena, Marthina, Marthine, Marti, Martine, Martinia, Martino, Martisha, Martosia, Martoya, Martricia, Martrina, Martyna, Martyne, Martynne

Martine **G** (Latin) a form of Martina.

Martiniana (Latin) she who was consecrated to the god Mars; born in May.

Martirio (Spanish) martyrdom.

Martiza (Arabic) blessed.

Maru (Japanese) round.

Maruca (Spanish) a form of Mary.
Maruja, Maruska

Marvella (French) marvelous.
Marva, Marvel, Marvela, Marvele, Marvelle, Marvely, Marvetta, Marvette, Marvia, Marvina

Mary 🄶 (Hebrew) bitter; sea of bitterness. Bible: the mother of Jesus. See also Maija, Malia, Maren, Mariah, Marjorie, Maura, Maureen, Miriam, Mitzi, Moira, Mollie, Muriel.
Maira, Maire, Manette, Manka, Manon, Manya, Mara, Mare, Maree, Maren, Marella, Marelle, Mari, Maria, Maricara, Marice, Marie, Mariel, Mariela, Marika, Marilla, Marilyn, Marion, Mariquilla, Mariquita, Marisha, Marja, Marjan, Marlo, Maroula, Maruca, Marye, Maryla, Marynia, Masha, Mavra, Mendi, Mérane, Meridel, Mhairie, Mirja, Molara, Morag, Moya

Marya (Arabic) purity; bright whiteness.
Maryah

Maryam (Hebrew) a form of Miriam.
Maryama

Maryann, Maryanne (English) combinations of Mary + Ann.
Marian, Marryann, Maryan, Meryem

Marybeth (American) a combination of Mary + Beth.
Maribeth, Maribette

Maryellen (American) a combination of Mary + Ellen.
Mariellen

Maryjane (American) a combination of Mary + Jane.

Maryjo (American) a combination of Mary + Jo.
Marijo, Maryjoe

Marykate (American) a combination of Mary + Kate.
Mary-Kate

Marylou (American) a combination of Mary + Lou.
Marilou, Marylu

Maryssa (Latin) a form of Marissa.
Maryse, Marysia

Masa (Japanese) good and straightforward.

Masago (Japanese) sands of time.

Masako (Japanese) justice.

Masani (Luganda) gap toothed.

Masaye (Japanese) blessedly proper.

Masayo (Japanese) she who thrives for a lifetime.

Masha (Russian) a form of Mary.
Mashka, Mashenka

Mashika (Swahili) born during the rainy season.
Masika

Mason 🄱 (French) stone worker.

Massimo 🄱 (Italian) greatest.

Masu (Japanese) increase.

Masumi (Indian) innocence.

Matana (Hebrew) gift.
Matat

Mat-Chinoi (Chinese) serpent goddess, mother of the Chinese.

Mathena (Hebrew) gift of God.

Mathew 🄱 (Hebrew) a form of Matthew.

Mathieu 🄱 (French) a form of Matthew.

Mathilde (German) a form of Matilda.
Mathilda

Matilda (German) powerful battler. See also Maud, Tilda, Tillie.
Máda, Mahaut, Maitilde, Malkin, Mat, Matelda, Mathilde, , Mattie, Matty, Matusha, Matylda

Matilde (German) a form of
Matilda.

Matrika (Hindi) mother. Religion: a
name for the Hindu goddess Shakti
in the form of the letters of the
alphabet.
Matrica

Matsuko (Japanese) pine tree.

Matsuyo (Japanese) she who is as
strong as a pine tree.

Mattea (Hebrew) gift of God.
*Matea, Mathea, Mathia, Matia, Matte,
Matthea, Matthia, Mattia, Matya*

Matthew **B** (Hebrew) gift of God.

Mattie, Matty (English) familiar
forms of Martha, Matilda.
Matte, Mattey, Matti, Mattye

Matusha (Spanish) a form of
Matilda.
Matuja, Matuxa

Maud, Maude (English) short
forms of Madeline, Matilda. See
also Madison.
Maudie, Maudine, Maudlin

Maura (Irish) dark. A form of Mary,
Maureen. See also Moira.
*Maurah, Maure, Maurette, Mauricette,
Maurita*

Maureen (French) dark. (Irish) a
form of Mary.
*Maura, Maurene, Maurine, Mo,
Moreen, Morena, Morene, Morine,
Morreen, Moureen*

Maurelle (French) dark; elfin.
Mauriel, Mauriell, Maurielle

Mauricia (Spanish) a form of Mauro.

Mauricio **B** (Spanish) a form of
Maurice (see Boys' Names).

Maurise (French) dark skinned;
moor; marshland.
Maurisa, Maurissa, Maurita, Maurizia

Mauro (Latin) a short form of
Maurice (see Boys' Names).

Mausam (Indian) season.

Mausami (Indian) seasonal.

Maushmi (Indian) monsoon wind.

Mausi (Native American) plucked
flower.

Mausumi (Indian) beauty; monsoon
wind.

Mauve (French) violet colored.

Maverick **B** (American)
independent.

Mavis (French) thrush, songbird. See
also Maeve.
*Mavies, Mavin, Mavine, Mavon,
Mavra*

Max **B** (Latin) a short form of
Maxine.

Maxie (English) a familiar form of
Maxine.
Maxi, Maxy

Máxima (Latin) great one.

Maxime **B** (Latin) a form of
Maxine.

Maximiana (Spanish) a form of
Máxima.

Maximiliana (Latin) eldest of all.

Maxine **G** (Latin) greatest.
*Max, Maxa, Maxeen, Maxena, Maxene,
Maxie, Maxima, Maxime, Maximiliane,
Maxina, Maxna, Maxyne*

Maxwell **B** (English) great spring.

May (Latin) great. (Arabic) discerning. (English) flower; month of May. See also Mae, Maia.
Maj, Mayberry, Maybeth, Mayday, Maydee, Maydena, Maye, Mayela, Mayella, Mayetta, Mayrene

Maya ☀ (Hindi) God's creative power. (Greek) mother; grandmother. (Latin) great. A form of Maia.
Mayam, Mya

Mayako (Japanese) child of Maya.

Maybeline (Latin) a familiar form of Mabel.

Maygan, Maygen (Irish) forms of Megan.
Mayghan, Maygon

Maylyn (American) a combination of May + Lynn.
Mayelene, Mayleen, Maylen, Maylene, Maylin, Maylon, Maylynn, Maylynne

Mayoko (Japanese) child of Mayo.

Mayoree (Tai) beautiful.
Mayra, Mayree, Mayariya

Mayra (Tai) a form of Mayoree.

Maysa (Arabic) walks with a proud stride.

Maysaa, Mayyada (Indian) to walk with a swinging gait.

Maysoon (Indian) of beautiful face and body.

Maysun (Arabic) beautiful.

Mayte (Spanish) a combination of María and Teresa.

Mayu (Japanese) she who possesses truth and reason.

Mayuka, Mayukhi (Indian) peahen.

Mayuko (Japanese) child of Mayu.

Mayumi (Japanese) beautiful truth.

Mayura (Indian) illusion.

Mayurakhsi (Indian) eye of the peacock.

Mayuri (Indian) peahen.

Mayurika (Indian) baby peahen.

Mazel (Hebrew) lucky.
Mazal, Mazala, Mazella

Mc Kenna 🅖 (American) a form of Mackenna.

Mc Kenzie 🅖 (Irish) a form of Mackenzie.

Mckay 🅱 (Scottish) child of Kay.

Mckayla 🅖 (American) a form of Makayla.
Mckaela, Mckaila, Mckala, Mckaylah, Mckayle, Mckaylee, Mckayleh, Mckayleigh, Mckayli, Mckaylia, Mckaylie

Mckell 🅖 (American) a form of Makell.
Mckelle

Mckenna 🅖 (American) a form of Mackenna.
Mckena, Mckennah, Mckinna, Mckinnah

Mckenzie 🅖 (Scottish) a form of Mackenzie.
Mckennzie, Mckensee, Mckensey, McKensi, Mckensi, Mckensie, Mckensy, Mckenze, Mckenzee, Mckenzey, Mckenzi, Mckenzy, Mckenzye, Mekensie, Mekenzi, Mekenzie

Mckinley 🅱 (Irish) daughter of the learned ruler.
Mckinlee, Mckinleigh, Mckinlie, Mckinnley

Mckinzie (American) a form of Mackenzie.
Mckinsey, Mckinze, Mckinzea, Mckinzee, Mckinzi, Mckinzy, Mckynze, Mckynzie

Me (Japanese) triple branch.

Mead, Meade **B** (Greek) honey wine.

Meagan (Irish) a form of Megan.
Maegan, Meagain, Meagann, Meagen, Meagin, Meagnah, Meagon

Meaghan **G** (Welsh) a form of Megan.
Maeghan, Meaghann, Meaghen, Meahgan

Meara (Irish) mirthful.

Mecha (Latin) a form of Mercedes.

Meda (Native American) prophet; priestess.

Medea (Greek) ruling. (Latin) middle. Mythology: a sorceress who helped Jason get the Golden Fleece.
Medeia

Medha (Indian) wisdom, intellect.

Medina (Arabic) History: the site of Muhammed's tomb.
Medinah

Medini (Indian) earth.

Medora (Greek) mother's gift. Literature: a character in Lord Byron's poem *The Corsair*.

Mee (Chinese) beautiful.

Meena (Hindi) blue semiprecious stone; bird. (Greek, German, Dutch) a form of Mena.

Meenakshi (Indian) eye.

Meenal (Indian) precious gem.

Meg (English) a short form of Margaret, Megan.

Megan **G** (Greek) pearl; great. (Irish) a form of Margaret.
Maegan, Magan, Magen, Meagan, Meaghan, Magen, Maygan, Maygen,
Meg, Megane, Megann, Megean, Megen, Meggan, Meggen, Meggie, Meghan, Megyn, Meygan

Megane (Irish) a form of Megan.
Magana, Meganna, Meganne

Megara (Greek) first. Mythology: Heracles's first wife.

Meggie (English) a familiar form of Margaret, Megan.
Meggi, Meggy

Meghamala (Indian) an array of clouds.

Meghan **G** (Welsh) a form of Megan.
Meeghan, Meehan, Megha, Meghana, Meghane, Meghann, Meghanne, Meghean, Meghen, Mehgan, Mehgen

Meghna (Indian) the Ganges River.

Megumi (Japanese) blessing; merry; charity.

Meha (Indian) intelligent; rain.

Mehadi (Hindi) flower.

Mehak (Indian) sweet smell, fragrance.

Mehbooba (Indian) beloved.

Meher (Indian) grace.

Mehira (Hebrew) speedy; energetic.
Mahira

Mehitabel (Hebrew) benefited by trusting God.
Mehetabel, Mehitabelle, Hetty, Hitty

Mehri (Persian) kind; lovable; sunny.

Mehrunissa (Indian) benevolent.

Mei (Hawaiian) great. (Chinese) a short form of Meiying.
Meiko

Meira (Hebrew) light.
Meera

Meit (Burmese) affectionate.

Meiying (Chinese) beautiful flower.
Mei

Meka 🄶 (Hebrew) a familiar form of Michaela.

Mekayla (American) a form of Michaela.
Mekaela, Mekaila, Mekayela, Mekaylia

Mekhala (Indian) girdle.

Mel 🄱🄶 (Portuguese, Spanish) sweet as honey.

Mela (Hindi) religious service. (Polish) a form of Melanie.

Melana (Russian) a form of Melanie.
Melanna, Melashka, Melenka, Milana

Melanie ☆ 🄶 (Greek) dark skinned.
Malania, Malanie, Meila, Meilani, Meilin, Melaine, Melainie, Melana, Melane, Melanee, Melaney, Melani, Melania, Mélanie, Melanka, Melanney, Melannie, Melany, Melanya, Melasya, Melayne, Melenia, Mella, Mellanie, Melonie, Melya, Milena, Milya

Melantha (Greek) dark flower.

Melba (Greek) soft; slender. (Latin) mallow flower.
Malva, Melva

Mele (Hawaiian) song; poem.

Melesse (Ethiopian) eternal.
Mellesse

Melia (German) a short form of Amelia.
Melcia, Melea, Meleah, Meleia, Meleisha, Meli, Meliah, Melida, Melika, Mema

Melina (Latin) canary yellow. (Greek) a short form of Melinda.
Melaina, Meleana, Meleena, Melena, Meline, Melinia, Melinna, Melynna

Melinda (Greek) honey. See also Linda, Melina, Mindy.
Maillie, Malinda, Melinde, Melinder, Mellinda, Melynda, Melyne, Milinda, Milynda, Mylenda, Mylinda, Mylynda

Meliora (Latin) better.
Melior, Meliori, Mellear, Melyor, Melyora

Melisa (Greek) a form of Melissa.
Melesa, Mélisa, Melise, Melisha, Melishia, Melisia, Meliza, Melizah, Mellisa, Melosa, Milisa, Mylisa, Mylisia

Melisande (French) a form of Melissa, Millicent.
Lisandra, Malisande, Malissande, Malyssandre, Melesande, Melisandra, Melisandre, Mélisandré, Melisenda, Melissande, Melissandre, Mellisande, Melond, Melysande, Melyssandre

Melissa 🄶 (Greek) honey bee. See also Elissa, Lissa, Melisande, Millicent.
Malissa, Mallissa, Melessa, Meleta, Melisa, Mélissa, Melisse, Melissia, Mellie, Mellissa, Melly, Melyssa, Milissa, Millie, Milly, Missy, Molissia, Mollissa, Mylissa, Mylissia

Melita (Greek) a form of Melissa. (Spanish) a short form of Carmelita (see Carmelit).
Malita, Meleeta, Melitta, Melitza, Melletta, Molita

Melitona (Greek) she who was born in Malta.

Melly (American) a familiar form of names beginning with "Mel." See also Millie.
Meli, Melie, Melli, Mellie

Melody (Greek) melody. See also
Elodie.
*Meladia, Melodee, Melodey, Melodi,
Melodia, Melodie, Melodyann,
Melodye*

Melonie (American) a form of
Melanie.
*Melloney, Mellonie, Mellony, Melonee,
Meloney, Meloni, Melonie, Melonnie,
Melony*

Melosa (Spanish) sweet; tender.

Melosia (Spanish) sweet.

Melusina (Greek) she who is sweet
as honey.

Melvina (Irish) armored chief. See
also Malvina.
*Melevine, Melva, Melveen, Melvena,
Melvene, Melvonna*

Melyne (Greek) a short form of
Melinda.
Melyn, Melynn, Melynne

Melyssa (Greek) a form of Melissa.

Mena (German, Dutch) strong.
(Greek) a short form of Philomena.
History: Menes is believed to be the
first king of Egypt.
Menah

Menaha (Indian) celestial damsel.

Menaka (Indian) celestial damsel;
heavenly beauty.

Mendi (Basque) a form of Mary.
Menda, Mendy

Meng (Chinese) dream.

Meranda (Latin) a form of Miranda.
*Merana, Merandah, Merandia,
Merannda*

Mérane (French) a form of Mary.
Meraine, Merrane

Mercé (Spanish) a form of Mercedes.

Mercedes (Latin) reward, payment.
(Spanish) merciful.
*Mercades, Mercadez, Mercadie,
Meceades, Merced, Mercede,
Mercedees, Mercedeez, Mercedez,
Mercedies, Mercedis, Mersade,
Mersades*

Merces (Latin) favors, graces; skills.

Mercia (English) a form of Marcia.
History: an ancient British
kingdom.

Mercy (English) compassionate,
merciful. See also Merry.
*Mercey, Merci, Mercie, Mercille,
Mersey*

Meredith **G** (Welsh) protector of
the sea.
*Meredeth, Meredithe, Meredy,
Meredyth, Meredythe, Meridath,
Merideth, Meridie, Meridith, Merridie,
Merridith, Merry*

Meri (Finnish) sea. (Irish) a short
form of Meriel.

Meriel (Irish) shining sea.
Meri, Merial, Meriol, Meryl

Merilyn (English) a combination of
Merry + Lynn. See also Marilyn.
*Merelyn, Merlyn, Merralyn, Merrelyn,
Merrilyn*

Merissa (Latin) a form of Marissa.
Merisa, Merisha

Merle **B** (Latin, French) blackbird.
*Merl, Merla, Merlina, Merline, Merola,
Murle, Myrle, Myrleen, Myrlene,
Myrline*

Merry (English) cheerful, happy. A
familiar form of Mercy, Meredith.
*Merie, Merree, Merri, Merrie,
Merrielle, Merrilee, Merrili, Merrilyn,
Merris, Merrita*

Meryl (German) famous. (Irish) shining sea. A form of Meriel, Muriel.
Meral, Merel, Merrall, Merrell, Merril, Merrile, Merrill, Merryl, Meryle, Meryll

Mesha (Hindi) another name for the zodiac sign Aries.
Meshal

Meta (German) a short form of Margaret.
Metta, Mette, Metti

Mhairie (Scottish) a form of Mary.
Mhaire, Mhairi, Mhari, Mhary

Mi, Mye (Chinese) obsessive.

Mia ❀ (Italian) mine. A familiar form of Michaela, Michelle.
Mea, Meah, Miah

Miaka (Japanese) influential.

Mian (Chinese) continuous, unbroken.

Miao (Chinese) wonderful.

Micaela (Hebrew) a form of Michaela.
Macaela, Micaella, Micaila, Micala, Miceala

Micah 🅱 (Hebrew) a short form of Michael. Bible: one of the Old Testament prophets.
Meecah, Mica, Micha, Mika, Myca, Mycah

Micayla, Michayla (Hebrew) forms of Michaela.
Micayle, Micaylee, Michaylah

Michael 🅱 (Hebrew) who is like God?

Michaela 🅶 (Hebrew) a form of Michael.
Machaela, Maika, Makaela, Makaila, Makala, Makayla, Mia, Micaela, Micayla, Michael, Michaelann,
Michala, Michayla, Michealia, Michaelina, Michaeline, Michaell, Michaella, Michaelyn, Michaila, Michal, Michala, Micheal, Micheala, Michelia, Michelina, Michelle, Michely, Michelyn, Micheyla, Micheline, Micki, Miguela, Mikaela, Mikala, Misha, Mycala, Mychael, Mychal

Michal 🅱 (Hebrew) a form of Michaela, Michele.

Michala (Hebrew) a form of Michaela.
Michalann, Michale, Michalene, Michalin, Mchalina, Michalisha, Michalla, Michalle, Michayla, Michayle, Michela

Micheal 🅱 (Hebrew) a form of Michael.

Michel 🅱 (French) a form of Michelle.

Michele 🅶 (Italian) a form of Michaela.
Michaelle, Michal, Michela

Michelle 🅶 (French) a form of Michael. See also Shelley.
Machealle, Machele, Machell, Machella, Machelle, Mechelle, Meichelle, Meschell, Meshell, Meshelle, Mia, Michel, Michéle, Michell, Michella, Michellene, Michellyn, Mischel, Mischelle, Mishael, Mishaela, Mishayla, Mishell, Mishelle, Mitchele, Mitchelle

Michi (Japanese) righteous way.
Miche, Michee, Michiko

Michiye (Japanese) beautiful, blessed knowledge.

Michiyo (Japanese) a lifetime of beautiful wisdom.

Mickael 🅱 (Hebrew) a form of Mikaela.

Micki (American) a familiar form of
Michaela.
*Mickee, Mickeeya, Mickia, Mickie,
Micky, Mickya, Miquia*

Micol (Hebrew) she who is queen.

Midori (Japanese) green.

Mieko (Japanese) prosperous.
Mieke

Mielikki (Finnish) pleasing.

Miette (French) small; sweet.

Migina (Omaha) new moon.

Mignon (French) dainty, petite;
graceful.
*Mignonette, Minnionette, Minnonette,
Minyonette, Minyonne*

Miguel **B** (Portuguese, Spanish) a
form of Michael.

Miguela (Spanish) a form of
Michaela.
*Micquel, Miguelina, Miguelita, Miquel,
Miquela, Miquella*

Mihika (Indian) dewdrop.

Miho (Japanese) beautiful; keep; step.

Mihoko (Japanese) child of Mihoko.

Mika **G** (Japanese) new moon.
(Russian) God's child. (Native
American) wise racoon. (Hebrew) a
form of Micah. (Latin) a form of
Dominica.
Mikah, Mikka

Mikael **B** (Hebrew) a form of
Mikaela.

Mikaela (Hebrew) a form of
Michaela.
*Mekaela, Mekala, Mickael, Mickaela,
Mickala, Mickalla, Mickeel, Mickell,
Mickelle, Mikael, Mikail, Mikaila,
Mikal, Mikalene, Mikalovna, Mikalyn,
Mikayla, Mikea, Mikeisha, Mikeita,*
*Mikel, Mikela, Mikele, Mikell, Mikella,
Mikesha, Mikeya, Mikhaela, Mikie,
Mikiela, Mikkel, Mikyla, Mykaela*

Mikako (Japanese) beautiful girl.

Mikala (Hebrew) a form of
Michaela.
*Mickala, Mikalah, Mikale, Mikalea,
Mikalee, Mikaleh*

Mikayla (American) a form of
Mikaela.
*Mekayla, Mickayla, Mikala, Mikayle,
Mikyla*

Mikayo (Japanese) a lifetime of
beauty.

Mikazuki (Japanese) moon of the
third night.

Mikel **B** (Hebrew) a form of
Mikaela.

Mikhaela (American) a form of
Mikaela.
*Mikhail, Mikhaila, Mikhala, Mikhalea,
Mikhayla, Mikhelle*

Miki **G** (Japanese) flower stem.
*Mikia, Mikiala, Mikie, Mikita, Mikiyo,
Mikki, Mikkie, Mikkiya, Mikko, Miko*

Mikiko (Japanese) beautiful and
precious child.

Mikino (Japanese) a beautiful
beginning.

Mila (Russian) dear one. (Italian,
Slavic) a short form of Camila,
Ludmilla.
Milah, Milla

Milada (Czech) my love.
Mila, Milady

Milagres (Latin) wonder, miracle;
prodigy.

Milagros (Spanish) miracle.
*Mila, Milagritos, Milagro, Milagrosa,
Mirari*

Milana (Italian) from Milan, Italy.
(Russian) a form of Melana.
*Milan, Milane, Milani, Milanka,
Milanna, Milanne*

Milba, Milburga (German) kind
protector.

Milca, Milcal (Hebrew) queen.

Mildereda (German) she who
speaks soft, kind words.

Mildred (English) gentle counselor.
*Mil, Mila, Mildrene, Mildrid, Millie,
Milly*

Mildreda (German) counselor.

Milena (Greek, Hebrew, Russian) a
form of Ludmilla, Magdalen,
Melanie.
*Mila, Milène, Milenia, Milenny, Milini,
Millini*

Mileta (German) generous, merciful.

Milia (German) industrious. A short
form of Amelia, Emily.
Mila, Milka, Milla, Milya

Miliani (Hawaiian) caress.
Milanni, Miliany

Mililani ☆ (Hawaiian) heavenly
caress.
Milliani

Milissa (Greek) a form of Melissa.
Milessa, Milisa, Millisa, Millissa

Milka (Czech) a form of Amelia.
Milica, Milika

Millaray (Mapuche) golden or silver
flower; fragrant, pleasant flower;
subtle essence of fragrance.

Millicent (English) industrious.
(Greek) a form of Melissa. See also
Lissa, Melisande.
*Melicent, Meliscent, Mellicent,
Mellisent, Melly, Milicent, Milisent,
Millie, Milliestone, Millisent, Milly,
Milzie, Missy*

Millie, Milly (English) familiar forms
of Amelia, Camille, Emily, Kamila,
Melissa, Mildred, Millicent.
Mili, Milla, Millee, Milley, Millie, Mylie

Milva (German) kind protector.

Mima (Burmese) woman.
Mimma

Mimi (French) a familiar form of
Miriam.

Mina ☖ (German) love. (Persian)
blue sky. (Arabic) harbor. (Japanese)
south. A short form of names
ending in "mina."
Meena, Mena, Min

Minako (Japanese) child of Mina.

Minakshi (Indian) fish eyes.

Minal (Native American) fruit.

Minati (Indian) prayer.

Minda (Hindi) knowledge.

Mindy (Greek) a familiar form of
Melinda.
*Mindee, Mindi, Mindie, Mindyanne,
Mindylee, Myndy*

Mine (Japanese) peak; mountain
range.
Mineko

Minerva (Latin) wise. Mythology:
the goddess of wisdom.
Merva, Minivera, Minnie, Myna

Minette (French) faithful defender.
Minnette, Minnita

Mineyo (Japanese) she who reaches
the summit.

Ming (Chinese) shiny; hope of
tomorrow.

Ming Ue, Ming Yue, Ming-Yue
(Chinese) bright moon.

Mingmei (Chinese) smart; beautiful.

Minia (German) great, strong.

Miniami (Japanese) a form of Mina.

Minka (Polish) a short form of
Wilhelmina.

Minna (German) a short form of
Wilhelmina.
Mina, Minka, Minnie, Minta

Minnie (American) a familiar form
of Mina, Minerva, Minna,
Wilhelmina.
Mini, Minie, Minne, Minni, Minny

Minori (Japanese) truth; pear.

Minowa (Native American) singer.
Minowah

Minta (English) Literature: originally
coined by playwright Sir John
Vanbrugh in his comedy *The
Confederacy*.
Minty

Minu (Indian) a gem, precious stone.

Minya (Osage) older sister.

Mio (Japanese) three times as strong.

Mira (Latin) wonderful. (Spanish)
look, gaze. A short form of Almira,
Amira, Marabel, Mirabel, Miranda.
Mirae, Mirra, Mirah

Mirabel (Latin) beautiful.
*Mira, Mirabell, Mirabella, Mirabelle,
Mirable*

Miracle **G** (Latin) wonder, marvel.

Mirai (Japanese) future.

Mirana (Spanish) a form of Miranda.

Miranda **G** (Latin) strange;
wonderful; admirable. Literature:

the heroine of Shakespeare's *The
Tempest*. See also Randi.
*Maranda, Marenda, Meranda, Mira,
Miran, Miranada, Mirandia, Mirinda,
Mirindé, Mironda, Mirranda,
Muranda, Myranda*

Miraya (Indian) Lord Krishna's
devotee.

Mireille (Hebrew) God spoke.
(Latin) wonderful.
*Mireil, Mirel, Mirella, Mirelle, Mirelys,
Mireya, Mireyda, Mirielle, Mirilla,
Myrella, Myrilla*

Mireya (Hebrew) a form of Mireille.
Mireea, Miriah, Miryah

Miri (Gypsy) a short form of Miriam.
Miria, Miriah

Miriam **G** (Hebrew) bitter; sea of
bitterness. Bible: the original form
of Mary. See also Macia, Mimi,
Mitzi.
*Mairwen, Mariam, Maryam, Miram,
Mirham, Miri, Miriain, Miriama,
Miriame, Mirian, Mirit, Mirjam,
Mirjana, Mirriam, Mirrian, Miryam,
Miryan, Myriam*

Mirium (Indian) wished-for child.

Mirta, Mirtha (Greek) crown of
myrtle.

Mirya (French) she who has earned
everyone's admiration.

Misa, Misaye (Japanese) beautiful
helper.

Misael **B** (Hebrew) a form of
Michael.

Misaki (Japanese) she who blooms
beautifully.

Misako (Japanese) child of Misa.

Misao (Japanese) fidelity.

Misayo (Japanese) a lifelong beauty.

Misha G (Russian) a form of
Michaela.
Mischa, Mishae

Mishka (Indian) gift of love.

Mishti (Indian) sweet person.

Misora (Japanese) beautiful sky.

Misri (Indian) sweet.

Missy (English) a familiar form of
Melissa, Millicent.
Missi, Missie

Misty G (English) shrouded by
mist.
*Missty, Mistee, Mistey, Misti, Mistie,
Mistin, Mistina, Mistral, Mistylynn,
Mystee, Mysti, Mystie*

Mitali (Indian) friendly.

Mitchell B (English) a form of
Michael.

Mitra (Hindi) Religion: god of
daylight. (Persian) angel.
Mita

Mitsu (Japanese) shine, reflect.

Mitsuki (Japanese) beautiful month.

Mitsuko (Japanese) child of Mitsu.

Mitsuye (Japanese) blessed beauty.

Mitsuyo (Japanese) beautiful third
daughter.

Mituna (Moquelumnan) like a fish
wrapped up in leaves.

Mitzi (German) a form of Mary,
Miriam.
Mieze, Mitzee, Mitzie, Mitzy

Miwa (Japanese) wise eyes.
Miwako

Miya (Japanese) temple.
Miyah, Miyana, Miyanna

Miyabi (Japanese) elegant.

Miyako (Japanese) she who is a
beautiful girl.

Miye (Japanese) beautiful inlet.

Miyeko (Japanese) beautiful and
blessed girl.

Miyo (Japanese) beautiful generation.
Miyoko, Miyuko

Miyuki (Japanese) snow.

Moana (Hawaiian) ocean; fragrance.

Mocha (Arabic) chocolate-flavored
coffee.
Moka

Modesty (Latin) modest.
*Modesta, Modeste, Modestia,
Modestie, Modestina, Modestine,
Modestus*

Moe (Japanese) bud, sprout.

Moeka (Japanese) sprouting flower.

Moema (Tupi) sweet.

Moena (Japanese) bud; vegetable.

Moesha (American) a short form of
Monisha.
Myesha

Mohala (Hawaiian) flowers in
bloom.
Moala

Mohamed B (Arabic) a form of
Muhammad (see Boys' Names).

Mohana (Indian) attractive;
charming.

Moira (Irish) great. A form of Mary.
See also Maura.
*Moirae, Moirah, Moire, Moya, Moyra,
Moyrah*

Molara (Basque) a form of Mary.

Mollie (Irish) a form of Molly.
Moli, Molie, Molli

Molly ✿ **G** (Irish) a familiar form of Mary.
Moll, Mollee, Molley, Mollissa

Momiji (Japanese) a Japanese maple tree.

Momo (Japanese) peaches.

Momoka (Japanese) the scent of a peach.

Momoko (Japanese) child of Momo.

Momone (Japanese) she whose life is made of many great deeds.

Momose (Japanese) one hundred stars.

Momoye (Japanese) a hundred blessings.

Momoyo (Japanese) one hundred; world; lifetime.

Mon (Japanese) gate.

Mona **G** (Irish) noble. (Greek) a short form of Monica, Ramona, Rimona.
Moina, Monah, Mone, Monea, Monna, Moyna

Monal (Indian) bird.

Monalisa (Indian) noble.

Monet (French) Art: Claude Monet was a leading French impressionist remembered for his paintings of water lilies.
Monae, Monay, Monee

Monica **G** (Greek) solitary. (Latin) advisor.
Mona, Monca, Monee, Monia, Monic, Mónica, Monice, Monicia, Monicka, Monika, Monique, Monise, Monn, Monnica, Monnie, Monya

Monifa (Yoruba) I have my luck.

Monika (German) a form of Monica.
Moneka, Monieka, Monike, Monnika

Monique (French) a form of Monica.
Moneeke, Moneik, Moniqua, Moniquea, Moniquie, Munique

Monisha (American) a combination of Monica + Aisha.
Moesha, Moneisha, Monishia

Monita (Spanish) noble.

Montana **G** (Spanish) mountain. Geography: a U.S. state.
Montanna

Montrell **B** (French) a form of Montreal (see Boys' Names).

Moon (Korean) beautiful; song; able; family; professional; add.

Mora (Spanish) blueberry.
Morae, Morea, Moria, Morita

Morela (Polish) apricot.
Morelia, Morelle

Morena (Irish) a form of Maureen.

Morgan ✿ **G** (Welsh) seashore. Literature: Morgan le Fay was the half-sister of King Arthur.
Morgance, Morgane, Morganetta, Morganette, Morganica, Morgann, Morganne, Morgen, Morghan, Morgyn, Morrigan

Morgana (Welsh) a form of Morgan.
Morganna

Morganda (Spanish) a form of Morgana.

Morghan (Welsh) a form of Morgan.
Morghen, Morghin, Morghyn

Moriah 🅖 (Hebrew) God is my teacher. (French) dark skinned. Bible: the mountain on which the Temple of Solomon was built. See also Mariah.
Moria, Moriel, Morit, Morria, Morriah

Morie (Japanese) bay.

Morowa (Akan) queen.

Morrisa (Latin) dark skinned; moor; marshland.
Morisa, Morissa, Morrissa

Moselle (Hebrew) drawn from the water. (French) a white wine.
Mozelle

Moses 🅑 (Hebrew) drawn out of the water. (Egyptian) child.

Mosi 🅑 (Swahili) first-born.

Moswen 🅑🅖 (Tswana) white.

Motoko (Japanese) beginning child.

Motoye (Japanese) origin; branch.

Motoyo (Japanese) the beginning of a new generation.

Moubani (Indian) a flower.

Mouna (Arabic) wish, desire.
Moona, Moonia, Mounia, Muna, Munia

Mrena (Slavic) white eyes.
Mren

Mridu (Indian) gentle.

Mridula (Indian) an ideal woman.

Mrigakshi, Mriganayani (Indian) one with beautiful eyes.

Mrinali (Indian) lotus.

Mrinalika (Indian) stem of the lotus.

Mrinalini (Indian) lotus.

Mrinmayee (Indian) a deer's eye.

Mrinmayi (Indian) of the earth.

Mritsa (Indian) the good earth.

Mrittika (Indian) Mother Earth.

Mrunali (Indian) lotus stalk.

Mu (Chinese) wood.

Mubarak (Indian) blessed.

Mudra (Indian) healing hand movement.

Mudrika (Indian) ring.

Mufeeda (Indian) useful.

Mugdha (Indian) innocent young girl.

Muhja (Indian) heart's blood; soul.

Mukta (Indian) pearl.

Mukti (Indian) liberation.

Mukula, Mukulita (Indian) bud.

Mulan (Chinese) magnolia blossom.

Mumtaz (Arabic) distinguished.

Muneera (Indian) illuminating; shedding light.

Munira (Arabic) she who is the source of light.

Muniya (Indian) name of a bird.

Mura (Japanese) village.

Muracaki (Japanese) purple.

Muriel (Arabic) myrrh. (Irish) shining sea. A form of Mary. See also Meryl.
Merial, Meriel, Meriol, Merrial, Merriel, Muire, Murial, Muriell, Murielle

Musetta (French) little bagpipe.
Musette

Musheera (Indian) giving counsel.

Muskaan (Indian) smile; happiness.

Muslimah (Arabic) devout believer.

Musu (Indian) beautiful.

Mutsuko (Japanese) child of Mutsu.

Mya ☆ **G** (Burmese) emerald.
(Italian) a form of Mia.
My, Myah, Myia, Myiah

My-duyen (Vietnamese) gentle.

Myesha (American) a form of
Moesha.
Myeisha, Myeshia, Myiesha, Myisha

Mykaela, Mykayla (American)
forms of Mikaela.
*Mykael, Mykaila, Mykal, Mykala,
Mykaleen, Mykel, Mykela, Mykyla*

Myla (English) merciful.

Mylene (Greek) dark.
Mylaine, Mylana, Mylee, Myleen

Myles **B** (Latin) soldier. (German) a
form of Miles (see Boys' Names).

Myra (Latin) fragrant ointment.
Mayra, Myrena, Myria

Myranda (Latin) a form of Miranda.
Myrandah, Myrandia, Myrannda

Myriam **G** (American) a form of
Miriam.
Myriame, Myryam

Myrna (Irish) beloved.
Merna, Mirna, Morna, Muirna

Myrtle (Greek) dark green shrub.
*Mertis, Mertle, Mirtle, Myrta, Myrtia,
Myrtias, Myrtice, Myrtie, Myrtilla,
Myrtis*

Mythili (Indian) another name for
the goddess Sita.

Mythri (Indian) friendship.

N

N **B** (American) an initial used as a
first name.

Na (Chinese) graceful.

Naaz (Indian) pride.

Nabeeha (Indian) intelligent.

Nabila (Arabic) born to nobility.
Nabeela, Nabiha, Nabilah

Nachni (Indian) dancer; suggestive
look.

Nadal (Catalonian) a form of
Natividad.

Nadda (Arabic) generous; dewy.
Nada

Nadeeda (Indian) equal to another
person; rival.

Nadette (French) a short form of
Bernadette.

Nadia (French, Slavic) hopeful.
*Nadea, Nadenka, Nadezhda, Nadiah,
Nadie, Nadija, Nadijah, Nadine,
Nadiya, Nadiyah, Nadja, Nadjae,
Nadjah, Nadka, Nadusha, Nady,
Nadya*

Nadine **G** (French, Slavic) a form
of Nadia.
*Nadean, Nadeana, Nadeen, Nadena,
Nadene, Nadien, Nadin, Nadina,
Nadyne, Naidene, Naidine*

Nadira (Arabic) rare, precious.
Naadirah, Nadirah

Nadwa (Indian) council.

Naeema (Indian) blessing; living an
enjoyable life.

Naeva (French) a form of Eve.
Nahvon

Nafuna (Luganda) born feet first.

Nagida (Hebrew) noble; prosperous.
Nagda, Nageeda

Nagina (Indian) jewel.

Nagisa (Japanese) from the shore.

Nahid (Persian) Mythology: another name for Venus, the goddess of love and beauty.

Nahimana (Dakota) mystic.

Nahla (Indian) a drink of water.

Naho (Japanese) a type of red apple; shore.

Nahoko (Japanese) child of Naho.

Naiara (Spanish) reference to the Virgin Mary.

Naida (Greek) water nymph.
Naiad, Naiya, Nayad, Nyad

Naigisa (Japanese) beach, shore.

Naija (Indian) daughter of wisdom.

Naila (Arabic) successful.
Nailah

Naina (Indian) eyes.

Nairi (Armenian) land of rivers. History: a name for ancient Armenia.
Naira, Naire, Nayra

Naís (Spanish) a form of Inés.

Naisha (Indian) special.

Naishadha (Indian) poetry.

Naiya (Greek) a form of Naida.
Naia, Naiyana, Naja, Najah, Naya

Najaah (Indian) success.

Najam (Arabic) star.
Naja, Najma

Najat (Indian) safety.

Najeeba (Indian) of noble birth.

Najila (Arabic) brilliant eyes.
Naja, Najah, Najia, Najja, Najla

Najiya (Indian) safe.

Najwa (Indian) confidential talk, secret conversation.

Najya (Indian) victorious.

Nakeisha (American) a combination of the prefix Na + Keisha.
Nakeesha, Nakesha, Nakeshea, Nakeshia, Nakeysha, Nakiesha, Nakisha, Nekeisha

Nakeita (American) a form of Nikita.
Nakeeta, Nakeitha, Nakeithra, Nakeitra, Nakeitress, Nakeitta, Nakeittia, Naketta, Nakieta, Nakitha, Nakitia, Nakitta, Nakyta

Nakia 🄶 (Arabic) pure.
Nakea, Nakeia, Nakeya, Nakeyah, Nakeyia, Nakiah, Nakiaya, Nakiea, Nakiya, Nakiyah, Nekia

Nakita (American) a form of Nikita.
Nakkita, Naquita

Nakula (Indian) another name for the goddess Parvati.

Nalani (Hawaiian) calm as the heavens.
Nalanie, Nalany

Nalika (Indian) lotus.

Nalini (Indian) lotus; sweet nectar.

Nam Ha (Vietnamese) willow tree.

Namaha (Indian) respect; pray.

Ñambi (Guarani) curative herb.

Nami (Japanese) wave.
Namika, Namiko

Namita (Indian) humble.

Namrata (Indian) politeness.

Namya (Indian) worthy of honor.

Nan (German) a short form of
Fernanda. (English) a form of Ann.
Nana, Nanice, Nanine, Nanna, Nanon

Nana (Hawaiian) spring.

Naná (Greek) she who is very young.

Nanako (Japanese) child of Nana.

Nanami (Japanese) beautiful
vegetable.

Nanase (Japanese) seven stars.

Nanci (English) a form of Nancy.
Nancie, Nancsi, Nansi

Nancy **G** (English) gracious. A
familiar form of Nan.
*Nainsi, Nance, Nancee, Nancey,
Nanci, Nancine, Nancye, Nanette,
Nanice, Nanncey, Nanncy, Nanouk,
Nansee, Nansey, Nanuk*

Nandika (Indian) water vessel made
of clay.

Nandita (Indian) cheerful.

Nanette (French) a form of Nancy.
*Nan, Nanete, Nannette, Nettie, Nineta,
Ninete, Ninetta, Ninette, Nini, Ninita,
Ninnetta, Ninnette, Nynette*

Nani (Greek) charming. (Hawaiian)
beautiful.
Nanni, Nannie, Nanny

Nantilde (German) daring in
combat.

Nao (Japanese) truthful; pleasing.

Naoki (Japanese) straight tree.

Naoko (Japanese) child of Nao.

Naolin (Spanish) sun god of the
Mexican people.

Naomi (Hebrew) pleasant, beautiful.
Bible: Ruth's mother-in-law.
*Naoma, Naomia, Naomie, Naomy,
Navit, Neoma, Neomi, Noami, Noemi,
Noma, Nomi, Nyomi*

Naomí (Hebrew) a form of Naomi.

Naomie (Hebrew) a form of Naomi.
Naome, Naomee, Noemie

Napea (Latin) from the valleys.

Nara (Greek) happy. (English) north.
(Japanese) oak.
Narah

Narcissa (Greek) daffodil.
Mythology: Narcissus was the youth
who fell in love with his own
reflection.
*Narcessa, Narcisa, Narcisse, Narcyssa,
Narissa, Narkissa*

Narda (Latin) fervently devoted.

Narelle (Australian) woman from
the sea.
Narel

Nari (Japanese) thunder.
Narie, Nariko

Narmada (Hindi) pleasure giver.

Naroa (Basque) tranquil, peaceful.

Narois (Indian) flower.

Narpendyah (Indian) queen.

Naseen (Indian) cool breeze.

Nashawna (American) a combi-
nation of the prefix Na + Shawna.
*Nashan, Nashana, Nashanda,
Nashaun, Nashauna, Nashaunda,
Nashauwna, Nashawn, Nasheena,
Nashounda, Nashuana*

Nashida (Indian) student.

Nashita (Indian) energetic and full of life.

Nashota (Native American) double; second-born twin.

Nasiha (Indian) one who gives valuable advice.

Nasira (Indian) victorious; helper.

Nastasia (Greek) a form of Anastasia.
Nastasha, Nastashia, Nastasja, Nastassa, Nastassia, Nastassiya, Nastassja, Nastassya, Nastasya, Nastazia, Nastisija, Nastka, Nastusya, Nastya

Nasya (Hebrew) miracle.
Nasia, Nasyah

Nata (Sanskrit) dancer. (Latin) swimmer. (Native American) speaker; creator. (Polish, Russian) a form of Natalie. See also Nadia.
Natia, Natka, Natya

Natacha (Russian) a form of Natasha.
Natachia, Natacia, Naticha

Natalee, Natali (Latin) forms of Natalie.
Natale, Nataleh, Nataleigh, Nattlee

Natalí (Spanish) a form of Natalia.

Natalia (Russian) a form of Natalie. See also Talia.
Nacia, Natala, Natalea, Nataliia, Natalija, Natalina, Nataliya, Nataliyah, Natalja, Natalka, Natallea, Natallia, Natalya, Nathalia, Natka

Natália (Hungarian, Portuguese) a form of Natalie.

Natalie ☀ 🅖 (Latin) born on Christmas day. See also Nata, Natasha, Noel, Talia.
Nat, Natalee, Natali, Natalia, Nataliee, Nataline, Natalle, Natallie, Nataly, Natelie, Nathalie, Nathaly, Natie, Natilie, Natlie, Nattalie, Nattilie

Nataline (Latin) a form of Natalie.
Natalene, Nataléne, Natalyn

Natalle (French) a form of Natalie.
Natale

Nataly (Latin) a form of Natalie.
Nathaly, Natally, Natallye

Natane (Arapaho) daughter.
Natanne

Natania (Hebrew) gift of God.
Natanya, Natée, Nathania, Nathenia, Netania, Nethania

Natara (Arabic) sacrifice.
Natori, Natoria

Natasha 🅖 (Russian) a form of Natalie. See also Stacey, Tasha.
Nahtasha, Natacha, Natasa, Natascha, Natashah, Natashea, Natashenka, Natashia, Natashiea, Natashja, Natashka, Natasia, Natassia, Natassija, Natassja, Natasza, Natausha, Natawsha, Natesha, Nateshia, Nathasha, Nathassha, Natisha, Natishia, Natosha, Netasha, Notosha

Natesa (Hindi) cosmic dancer. Religion: another name for the Hindu god Shiva.
Natisa, Natissa

Nathália (Portuguese) a form of Natalie.

Nathalie, Nathaly (Latin) forms of Natalie.
Nathalee, Nathali, Nathalia, Nathalya

Nathan 🅑 (Hebrew) a short form of Nathaniel.

Nathaniel 🅑 (Hebrew) gift of God.

Natie (English) a familiar form of Natalie.
Nati, Natti, Nattie, Natty

Natividad (Spanish) nativity.

Natori **G** (Arabic) a form of Natara.

Natosha (Russian) a form of Natasha.
Natoshia, Natoshya, Netosha, Notosha

Natsu, Natsuyo (Japanese) summer's child.

Natsuki (Japanese) vegetable month.

Natsuko (Japanese) summer child.

Natsumi (Japanese) she who is like the sea in summer.

Natsuye (Japanese) summer harbor.

Natun, Navami, Navashree, Navdha, Naveta (Indian) new.

Nauka (Indian) boat.

Nava (Hebrew) beautiful; pleasant.
Navah, Naveh, Navit

Navaneeta (Indian) butter.

Navdeep **BG** (Sikh) new light.

Navneeta (Indian) like butter.

Navya (Indian) young.

Nawar (Indian) flower.

Nayana (Indian) one with attractive eyes.

Nayantara (Indian) star of the eyes.

Nayara (Basque) swallow.

Nayeli (Zapotec) I love you.

Nayely (Irish) a form of Neila.
Naeyli, Nayelia, Nayelli, Nayelly, Nayla

Nayoko (Japanese) child of Nayo.

Nazaaha (Indian) purity; righteousness; honesty.

Nazarena (Hebrew) native of Nazareth.

Nazarha (Indian) a sight.

Nazaria (Spanish) dedicated to God.

Nazeeha (Indian) honest.

Nazeera (Indian) like; equal; matching.

Nazeeya (Indian) optimistic and full of hope.

Nazima (Indian) song.

Neala (Irish) a form of Neila.
Nayela, Naylea, Naylia, Nealia, Neela, Neelia, Neila

Necha (Spanish) a form of Agnes.
Necho

Neci **BG** (Hungarian) fiery, intense.
Necia, Necie

Neda (Slavic) born on Sunday.
Nedah, Nedi, Nedia, Neida

Nedda (English) prosperous guardian.
Neddi, Neddie, Neddy

Neeharika, Neharika (Indian) dewdrops.

Neelabja (Indian) blue lotus.

Neelaja (Indian) river starting from the blue mountain.

Neelakshi (Indian) blue-eyed girl.

Neelanjana (Indian) blue.

Neelima (Indian) blue sky.

Neely (Irish) a familiar form of Neila, Nelia.
Nealee, Nealie, Nealy, Neelee, Neeley, Neeli, Neelie, Neili, Neilie

Neema (Swahili) born during prosperous times.

Neena (Spanish) a form of Nina.
  Neenah, Nena

Neepa (Indian) a flower.

Neeraja (Indian) lotus.

Neeru (Indian) light.

Neeti (Indian) good behavior.

Neftali (Hebrew) she who fights and
  ends up victorious.

Nehal (Indian) rainy; beautiful.

Neila (Irish) champion. See also
  Neala, Neely.
  *Nayely, Neilah, Neile, Neilia, Neilla,
  Neille*

Nekeisha (American) a form of
  Nakeisha.
  *Nechesa, Neikeishia, Nekesha,
  Nekeshia, Nekiesha, Nekisha, Nekysha*

Nekia (Arabic) a form of Nakia.
  *Nekeya, Nekiya, Nekiyah, Nekya,
  Nekiya*

Nelia (Spanish) yellow. (Latin) a
  familiar form of Cornelia.
  *Neelia, Neely, Neelya, Nela, Neli,
  Nelka, Nila*

Nélida (Greek) compassionate,
  merciful.

Nelle (Greek) stone.

Nellie, Nelly 🅖 (English) familiar
  forms of Cornelia, Eleanor, Helen,
  Prunella.
  *Nel, Neli, Nell, Nella, Nelley, Nelli,
  Nellianne, Nellice, Nellis, Nelma*

Nelson 🅱 (English) child of Neil
  (see Boys' Names).

Nemesia (Greek) she who
  administers justice.

Nene (Japanese) she who is peaceful
  and tranquil.

Nenet (Egyptian) born near the sea.
  Mythology: Nunet was the goddess
  of the sea.

Neng (Chinese) ability.

Neola (Greek) youthful.
  Neolla

Neona (Greek) new moon.

Nereida (Greek) a form of Nerine.
  Nereyda, Nereyida, Nerida

Nerine (Greek) sea nymph.
  Nereida, Nerina, Nerita, Nerline

Nerissa (Greek) sea nymph. See also
  Rissa.
  *Narice, Narissa, Nerice, Nerisa,
  Nerisse, Nerrisa, Nerys, Neryssa*

Nesayem (Indian) flower.

Nesipa (Fijian) a form of Elizabeth.

Nessa (Scandinavian) promontory.
  (Greek) a short form of Agnes. See
  also Nessie.
  *Nesa, Nesha, Neshia, Nesiah, Nessia,
  Nesta, Nevsa, Neysa, Neysha, Neyshia*

Nessie (Greek) a familiar form of
  Agnes, Nessa, Vanessa.
  *Nese, Neshie, Nesho, Nesi, Ness,
  Nessi, Nessy, Nest, Neys*

Nestor 🅱 (Greek) traveler; wise.

Neta (Hebrew) plant, shrub. See also
  Nettie.
  Netia, Netta, Nettia

Netis (Native American) trustworthy.

Netra (Indian) eyes.

Netravati (Indian) one with
  beautiful eyes.

Nettie (French) a familiar form of
  Annette, Nanette, Antoinette.
  Neti, Netie, Netta, Netti, Netty, Nety

Neva (Spanish) snow. (English) new. Geography: a river in Russia.
Neiva, Neve, Nevia, Neyva, Nieve, Niva, Nivea, Nivia

Nevada **G** (Spanish) snow. Geography: a western U.S. state.
Neiva, Neva

Nevaeh ☆ (American) the word *heaven* spelled backward.

Neves (Portuguese) a form of Nieves.

Nevina (Irish) worshipper of the saint.
Neveen, Nevein, Nevena, Neveyan, Nevin, Nivena

Neylan (Turkish) fulfilled wish.
Neya, Neyla

Neza (Slavic) a form of Agnes.

Ngoc **G** (Vietnamese) jade.

Ngoc Bich (Vietnamese) beautiful, pretty.

Ngu (Vietnamese) the South River.

Nguyet (Vietnamese) sapphire jade.

Nhi (Vietnamese) stupid; to sleep; fisherman; fifth number; written language.

Nhu (Vietnamese) moon child.

Nhung (Vietnamese) little one.

Ni, Niu (Chinese) girl.

Nia **G** (Irish) a familiar form of Neila. Mythology: Nia Ben Aur was a legendary Welsh woman.
Neya, Niah, Niajia, Niya, Nya

Niabi (Osage) fawn.

Nian (Chinese) a period of life.

Nibaal (Indian) arrows.

Nicanora (Spanish) victorious army.

Niceta (Spanish) victorious one.

Nichelle (American) a combination of Nicole + Michelle. Culture: Nichelle Nichols was the first African American woman featured in a television drama (*Star Trek*).
Nichele, Nichell, Nishelle

Nichole (French) a form of Nicole.
Nichol, Nichola, Nicholle

Nicki (French) a familiar form of Nicole.
Nicci, Nickey, Nickeya, Nickia, Nickie, Nickiya, Nicky, Niki

Nickolas **B** (Greek) a form of Nicholas (see Boys' Names).

Nickole (French) a form of Nicole.
Nickol

Nico **B** (Greek) a short form of Nicholas (see Boys' Names).

Nicola **G** (Italian) a form of Nicole.
Nacola, Necola, Nichola, Nickola, Nicolea, Nicolla, Nikkola, Nikola, Nikolia, Nykola

Nicolas **B** (Italian) a form of Nicholas (see Boys' Names).

Nicolasa (Spanish) victorious people.

Nicole **G** (French) a form of Nicholas (see Boys' Names). See also Colette, Cosette, Nikita.
Nacole, Necole, Nica, Nichole, Nicia, Nicki, Nickole, Nicol, Nicola, Nicolette, Nicoli, Nicolie, Nicoline, Nicolle, Nikayla, Nikelle, Nikki, Niquole, Nocole, Nycole

Nicoleta (Greek) winner over all.

Nicolette **G** (French) a form of Nicole.
Nicholette, Nicoletta, Nicollete, Nicollette, Nikkolette, Nikoleta, Nikoletta, Nikolette

Nicoline (French) a familiar form of Nicole.
Nicholine, Nicholyn, Nicoleen, Nicolene, Nicolina, Nicolyn, Nicolyne, Nicolynn, Nicolynne, Nikolene, Nikolina, Nikoline

Nicolle (French) a form of Nicole.
Nicholle

Nida (Omaha) Mythology: an elflike creature.
Nidda

Nidhi (Indian) wealth.

Nidia (Latin) nest.
Nidi, Nidya

Nidra (Indian) sleep.

Niesha (American) pure. (Scandinavian) a form of Nissa.
Neisha, Neishia, Neissia, Nesha, Neshia, Nesia, Nessia, Niessia, Nisha, Nyesha

Nieves (Latin) refers to the blessed Virgin Mary.

Nige (Latin) dark night.
Nigea, Nigela, Nija, Nijae, Nijah

Nigel 🅱 (Latin) dark night.

Niharika (Indian) nebula.

Nika (Russian) belonging to God.
Nikka

Nikayla, Nikelle (American) forms of Nicole.
Nikeille, Nikel, Nikela, Nikelie

Nike 🅱🅶 (Greek) victorious. Mythology: the goddess of victory.

Nikhita (Indian) sharp; earth.

Niki 🅶 (Russian) a short form of Nikita. (American) a familiar form of Nicole.
Nikia, Nikiah

Nikita 🅶 (Russian) victorious people.
Nakeita, Nakita, Niki, Nikitah, Nikitia, Nikitta, Nikki, Nikkita, Niquita, Niquitta

Nikki 🅶 (American) a familiar form of Nicole, Nikita.
Nicki, Nikia, Nikkea, Nikkey, Nikkia, Nikkiah, Nikkie, Nikko, Nikky

Nikko 🅱 (American) a form of Nikki.

Niko 🅱 (Hungarian) a form of Nicholas (see Boys' Names).

Nikola 🅱 (French) a form of Nikole. (Italian) a form of Nicola.

Nikole (French) a form of Nicole.
Nikkole, Nikkolie, Nikola, Nikole, Nikolena, Nicolia, Nikolina, Nikolle

Nila 🅶 (Latin) Geography: the Nile River is in Africa. (Irish) a form of Neila.
Nilah, Nilesia, Nyla

Nilakshi (Indian) blue eyed.

Nilambari (Indian) clothed in blue.

Nilanjana (Indian) one with blue eyes.

Nilasha (Indian) blueness.

Nilaya (Indian) abode, house.

Nilda (Spanish) a short form of Brunilda.

Nileen, Nivedita (Indian) surrendered.

Nili (Hebrew) Botany: a pea plant that yields indigo.

Nilima (Indian) blue.

Niloufer (Indian) celestial.

Nilutha (Indian) providing water.

Nima (Hebrew) thread. (Arabic) blessing.
Nema, Niama, Nimali

Nimaat (Indian) blessings; loans.

Nimia (Latin) she who has a lot of ambition.

Nimisha (Indian) momentary.

Nina **G** (Hebrew) a familiar form of Hannah. (Spanish) girl. (Native American) mighty.
Neena, Ninah, Ninacska, Ninja, Ninna, Ninon, Ninosca, Ninoshka

Ninarika (Indian) misty.

Ninfa (Greek) young wife.

Ning (Chinese) peace, rest, tranquility.

Ninon (French) a form of Nina.

Niobe (Greek) she who rejuvenates.

Nipa (Indian) one who watches over.

Niral (Indian) calm.

Niramayee (Indian) pure, clean, spotless.

Nirel (Hebrew) light of God.
Nirali, Nirelle

Nirmala (Indian) clean.

Nirmayi (Indian) without blemish.

Nirosha (Indian) pious.

Nirupa (Indian) a decree.

Nirupama (Indian) matchless.

Nirveli (Hindi) water child.

Nisa (Arabic) woman.

Nisha (American) a form of Niesha, Nissa.
Niasha, Nishay

Nishi (Japanese) west.

Nishita (Indian) alert.

Nishithini (Indian) night.

Nishka (Indian) honest.

Nishtha (Indian) faith.

Nissa (Hebrew) sign, emblem. (Scandinavian) friendly elf; brownie. See also Nyssa.
Nisha, Nisse, Nissie, Nissy

Nita (Hebrew) planter. (Choctaw) bear. (Spanish) a short form of Anita, Juanita.
Nitai, Nitha, Nithai, Nitika

Nitara (Hindi) deeply rooted.

Nitasha (American) a form of Natasha.
Nitasia, Niteisha, Nitisha, Nitishia

Niti (Indian) ethics.

Nitsa (Greek) a form of Helen.

Nituna (Native American) daughter.

Nitya (Indian) eternal.

Nityapriya (Indian) ever-pleasing.

Nitza (Hebrew) flower bud.
Nitzah, Nitzana, Nitzanit, Niza, Nizah

Niveditha (Indian) offered to God.

Nivriti (Indian) bliss.

Nivritti (Indian) nonattachment.

Nixie (German) water sprite.

Niya (Irish) a form of Nia.
Niyah, Niyana, Niyia, Nyia

Niyati (Indian) destiny.

Nizana (Hebrew) a form of Nitza.
Nitzana, Nitzania, Zana

Noah **B** (Hebrew) peaceful, restful.

Nobuko (Japanese) the girl who reaches out to others.

Nobuye (Japanese) blessed belief.

Noe ◼ (Czech, French) a form of Noah.

Noel ◼ (Latin) Christmas. See also Natalie.
Noël, Noela, Noelani, Noele, Noeleen, Noelene, Noelia, Noeline, Noelle, Noelyn, Noelynn, Nohely, Noleen, Novelenn, Novelia, Nowel, Noweleen, Nowell

Noelani (Hawaiian) beautiful one from heaven.
Noela

Noelle (French) Christmas.
Noell, Noella, Noelleen, Noelly, Noellyn

Noemi (Hebrew) a form of Naomi.
Noam, Noemie, Noemy, Nohemi, Nomi

Noemí (Hebrew) a form of Noemi.

Noemie (Hebrew) a form of Noemi.

Noemy (Hebrew) a form of Noemi.
Noamy

Noga (Hebrew) morning light.

Nohely (Latin) a form of Noel.
Noeli, Noelie, Noely, Nohal, Noheli

Nokomis (Dakota) moon daughter.

Nola (Latin) small bell. (Irish) famous; noble. A short form of Fionnula.
Nuala

Nolan ◼ (Irish) famous; noble.

Noleta (Latin) unwilling.
Nolita

Nollie ◼ (English) a familiar form of Magnolia.
Nolia, Nolle, Nolley, Nolli, Nolly

Noma (Hawaiian) a form of Norma.

Nominanda (Latin) she who will be elected.

Nona (Latin) ninth.
Nonah, Noni, Nonia, Nonie, Nonna, Nonnah, Nonya

Noopur, Nupoor, Nupura (Indian) anklet.

Noor (Aramaic) a form of Nura.
Noorie, Nour, Nur

Noorjehan (Indian) light of the world.

Nora ◧ (Greek) light. A familiar form of Eleanor, Honora, Leonore.
Norah, Noreen

Noreen (Irish) a form of Eleanor, Nora. (Latin) a familiar form of Norma.
Noorin, Noreena, Noreene, Noren, Norena, Norene, Norina, Norine, Nureen

Norell (Scandinavian) from the north.
Narell, Narelle, Norela, Norelle, Norely

Nori (Japanese) law, tradition.
Noria, Norico, Noriko, Norita

Norika, Norike (Japanese) athletic.

Norma (Latin) rule, precept.
Noma, Noreen, Normi, Normie

Norman ◼ (French) Norseman.

Nouf (Indian) highest point on a mountain.

Nova (Latin) new. A short form of Novella, Novia. (Hopi) butterfly chaser. Astronomy: a star that releases bright bursts of energy.

Novella (Latin) newcomer.
Nova, Novela

Novia (Spanish) sweetheart.
Nova, Novka, Nuvia

Nozomi (Japanese) hope.

Nu (Burmese) tender. (Vietnamese) girl.
Nue

Nuala (Irish) a short form of Fionnula.
Nola, Nula

Nuan (Chinese) genial.

Nubia (Latin) cloud.

Nudhar (Indian) gold.

Nuela (Spanish) a form of Amelia.

Nuha (Indian) intelligence; mind.

Numa, Numas (Greek) she who lays down rules and establishes laws.

Numeria (Latin) she who elaborates, who enumerates.

Nuna (Native American) land.

Nuncia (Latin) she who leaves messages, who informs.

Nunciata (Latin) messenger.
Nunzia

Nunila (Spanish) ninth daughter.

Nunu (Vietnamese) gentle, peaceful.

Nuo (Chinese) graceful.

Nura (Aramaic) light.
Noor, Noora, Noorah, Noura, Nurah

Nuria (Aramaic) the Lord's light.
Nuri, Nuriel, Nurin

Nurita (Hebrew) Botany: a flower with red and yellow blossoms.
Nurit

Nuru **BG** (Swahili) daylight.

Nusayba (Indian) proper name.

Nusi (Hungarian) a form of Hannah.

Nusrat (Indian) help.

Nutan (Indian) new; fresh.

Nuwa (Chinese) mother goddess. Mythology: another name for Nü-gua, the creator of mankind.

Nuzha (Indian) pleasure trip; excursion spot.

Nya (Irish) a form of Nia.
Nyaa, Nyah, Nyia

Nycole (French) a form of Nicole.
Nychelle, Nycolette, Nycolle

Nydia (Latin) nest.
Nyda

Nyesha (American) a form of Niesha.
Nyeisha, Nyeshia

Nyla (Latin, Irish) a form of Nila.
Nylah

Nyoko (Japanese) gem, treasure.

Nyomi (Hebrew) a form of Naomi.
Nyome, Nyomee, Nyomie

Nyree (Maori) sea.
Nyra, Nyrie

Nyssa (Greek) beginning. See also Nissa.
Nisha, Nissi, Nissy, Nyasia, Nysa

Nyusha (Russian) a form of Agnes.
Nyushenka, Nyushka

Oba **BG** (Yoruba) chief, ruler.

Obdulia (Latin) she who takes away sadness and pain.

Obelia (Greek) needle.

Oceana (Greek) ocean. Mythology: Oceanus was the god of the ocean.
Ocean, Oceananna, Oceane, Oceania, Oceanna, Oceanne, Oceaonna, Oceon

Octavia 🄶 (Latin) eighth. See also Tavia.
Octabia, Octaviah, Octaviais, Octavice, Octavie, Octavienne, Octavio, Octavious, Octavise, Octavya, Octivia, Otavia, Ottavia

Octaviana (Spanish) a form of Octavia.

Octavio 🄱 (Latin) a form of Octavia.

Odalis, Odalys (Spanish) a form of Odilia.

Odeda (Hebrew) strong; courageous.

Odele (Greek) melody, song.
Odelet, Odelette, Odell, Odelle

Odelia (Greek) ode; melodic. (Hebrew) I will praise God. (French) wealthy. See also Odetta.
Oda, Odeelia, Odeleya, Odelina, Odelinda, Odelyn, Odila, Odile

Odella (English) wood hill.
Odela, Odelle, Odelyn

Odera (Hebrew) plough.

Odessa (Greek) odyssey, long voyage.
Adesha, Adeshia, Adessa, Adessia, Odessia

Odetta (German, French) a form of Odelia.
Oddetta, Odette

Odilia (Greek, Hebrew, French) a form of Odelia.

Odina (Algonquin) mountain.

Oditi (Indian) dawn.

Ofelia (Greek) a form of Ophelia.
Ofeelia, Ofilia

Ofélia (Portuguese) a form of Ophelia.

Ofira (Hebrew) gold.
Ofarrah, Ophira

Ofra (Hebrew) a form of Aphra.
Ofrat

Ogin (Native American) wild rose.

Oh, Ohara (Japanese) meditative.

Ohanna (Hebrew) God's gracious gift.

Oja (Indian) vitality.

Ojal (Indian) vision.

Ojasvi (Indian) bright.

Ojaswini (Indian) lustrous.

Oka (Japanese) flowering cherry blossom.

Okalani (Hawaiian) heaven.
Okilani

Okei (Japanese) from Oki; ocean.

Oki (Japanese) middle of the ocean.
Okie

Oksana (Latin) a form of Osanna.
Oksanna

Ola 🄶 (Greek) a short form of Olesia. (Scandinavian) ancestor.

Olalla (Spanish) well-spoken one.

Olathe (Native American) beautiful.
Olathia

Olaya (Greek) she who speaks well.

Oleda (Spanish) a form of Alida. See also Leda.
Oleta, Olida, Olita

Olena (Russian) a form of Helen.
Oleena, Olenka, Olenna, Olenya, Olya

Olesia (Greek) a form of Alexandra.
Cesya, Ola, Olecia, Oleesha, Oleishia, Olesha, Olesya, Olexa, Olice, Olicia, Olisha, Olishia, Ollicia

Oletha (Scandinavian) nimble.
Oleta, Yaletha

Olethea (Latin) truthful. See also Alethea.
Oleta

Olga (Scandinavian) holy. See also Helga, Olivia.
Olenka, Olia, Olja, Ollya, Olva, Olya

Oliana (Polynesian) oleander.

Olina (Hawaiian) filled with happiness.

Olinda (Latin) scented. (Spanish) protector of property. (Greek) a form of Yolanda.

Olisa (Ibo) God.

Olive (Latin) olive tree.
Oliff, Oliffe, Olivet, Olivette

Oliver **B** (Latin) olive tree. (Scandinavian) kind; affectionate.

Oliveria (Latin) affectionate.

Olivia ❀ **G** (Latin) a form of Olive. (English) a form of Olga. See also Liv, Livia.
Alivia, Alyvia, Olevia, Oliva, Olivea, Oliveia, Olivetta, Olivi, Olivianne, Olivya, Oliwia, Ollie, Olva, Olyvia

Olívia (Portuguese) a form of Olivia.

Olivier **B** (French) a form of Oliver.

Ollie **Bg** (English) a familiar form of Olivia.
Olla, Olly, Ollye

Olwen (Welsh) white footprint.
Olwenn, Olwin, Olwyn, Olwyne, Olwynne

Olympia (Greek) heavenly.
Olimpia, Olympe, Olympie

Olyvia (Latin) a form of Olivia.

Oma (Hebrew) reverent. (German) grandmother. (Arabic) highest.

Omaira (Arabic) red.
Omar, Omara, Omarah, Omari, Omaria, Omarra

Omaja (Indian) result of spiritual unity.

Omana (Indian) a woman.

Omar **B** (Arabic) a form of Omaira.

Omega (Greek) last, final, end. Linguistics: the last letter in the Greek alphabet.

Omisha (Indian) goddess of birth and death.

Ona (Latin, Irish) a form of Oona, Una. (English) river.

Onatah (Iroquois) daughter of the earth and the corn spirit.

Onawa (Native American) wide awake.
Onaja, Onajah

Ondine (Latin) a form of Undine.
Ondene, Ondina, Ondyne

Ondrea (Czech) a form of Andrea.
Ohndrea, Ohndreea, Ohndreya, Ohndria, Ondraya, Ondreana, Ondreea, Ondreya, Ondria, Ondrianna, Ondriea

Oneida (Native American) eagerly awaited.
Onida, Onyda

Onella (Hungarian) a form of Helen.

Onesha (American) a combination
of Ondrea + Aisha.
*Oneshia, Onesia, Onessa, Onessia,
Onethia, Oniesha, Onisha*

Oni (Yoruba) born on holy ground.
Onnie

Onora (Latin) a form of Honora.
Onoria, Onorine, Ornora

Oona (Latin, Irish) a form of Una.
Ona, Onna, Onnie, Oonagh, Oonie

Oorja (Indian) energy.

Opa (Choctaw) owl. (German)
grandfather.

Opal (Hindi) precious stone.
Opale, Opalina, Opaline

Ophelia (Greek) helper. Literature:
Hamlet's love interest in the
Shakespearean play *Hamlet.*
Filia, Ofelia, Ophélie, Ophilia, Phelia

Oprah (Hebrew) a form of Orpah.
Ophra, Ophrah, Opra

Ora (Latin) prayer. (Spanish) gold.
(English) seacoast. (Greek) a form
of Aura.
Orah, Orlice, Orra

Orabella (Latin) a form of Arabella.
Orabel, Orabela, Orabelle

Oraida (Arabic) eloquent; she who
speaks well.

Oralee (Hebrew) the Lord is my
light. See also Yareli.
*Areli, Orali, Oralit, Orelie, Orlee, Orli,
Orly*

Oralia (French) a form of Aurelia.
See also Oriana.
*Oralis, Oriel, Orielda, Orielle, Oriena,
Orlena, Orlene*

Orea (Greek) mountains.
Oreal, Oria, Oriah

Orela (Latin) announcement from
the gods; oracle.
Oreal, Orella, Orelle, Oriel, Orielle

Orenda (Iroquois) magical power.

Oretha (Greek) a form of Aretha.
Oreta, Oretta, Orette

Orfilia (German) female wolf.

Oriana (Latin) dawn, sunrise. (Irish)
golden.
*Orane, Orania, Orelda, Orelle, Ori,
Oria, Orian, Oriane, Orianna,
Orieana, Oryan*

Orieta (Spanish) a form of Oriana.

Orina (Russian) a form of Irene.
Orya, Oryna

Orinda (Hebrew) pine tree. (Irish)
light skinned, white.
Orenda

Orino (Japanese) worker's field.
Ori

Oriole (Latin) golden; black-and-
orange bird.
Auriel, Oriel, Oriell, Oriella, Oriola

Orion 🅱 (Greek) child of fire.
Mythology: a giant hunter who was
killed by Artemis.

Orisha (Greek) a form of Aura.

Orla (Irish) golden woman.
Orlagh, Orlie, Orly

Orlanda (German) famous
throughout the land.
Orlandia, Orlantha, Orlenda, Orlinda

Orlenda (Russian) eagle.

Orli (Hebrew) light.
Orlice, Orlie, Orly

Ormanda (Latin) noble. (German)
mariner.
Orma

Ornella (Latin) she who is like a flowery ash tree.

Ornice (Hebrew) cedar tree. (Irish) pale; olive colored.
Orna, Ornah, Ornat, Ornette, Ornit

Orpah (Hebrew) runaway. See also Oprah.
Orpa, Orpha, Orphie

Orquidea (Spanish) orchid.
Orquidia

Orquídea (Italian) a form of Orquidea.

Orsa (Latin) a short form of Orseline. See also Ursa.
Orsaline, Orse, Orsel, Orselina, Orseline, Orsola

Ortensia (Italian) a form of Hortense.

Orva (French) golden; worthy. (English) brave friend.

Osaka (Japanese) a commercial and cultural city center.

Osanna (Latin) praise the Lord.
Oksana, Osana

Oscar **B** (Scandinavian) divine spear carrier.

Osen (Japanese) one thousand.

Oseye (Benin) merry.

Oshma (Indian) summer season.

Osma (English) divine protector.
Ozma

Otilde (Spanish) a form of Otilia.

Otilia (Czech) a form of Otilie.

Otilie (Czech) lucky heroine.
Otila, Otka, Ottili, Otylia

Ova (Latin) egg.

Ovia (Latin, Danish) egg.

Ovidia (German) she who takes care of the sheep.

Owen **B** (Irish) born to nobility; young warrior. (Welsh) a form of Evan.

Owena (Welsh) a form of Owen.

Oya **B** (Moquelumnan) called forth.

Oz **BG** (Hebrew) strength.

Ozara (Hebrew) treasure, wealth.

P

P **BG** (American) an initial used as a first name.

Pa (Chinese) flower.

Paasi (Chamorro) a form of Faasi.

Pabla (Spanish) little.

Paca (Spanish) a short form of Pancha. See also Paka.

Pacífica (Spanish) derived from the name of the Pacific Ocean.

Padget **BG** (French) a form of Page.
Padgett, Paget, Pagett

Padma (Hindi) lotus.

Padmakali (Indian) lotus bud.

Padmakshi (Indian) one with eyes like lotuses.

Padmal, Padnuni (Indian) lotus.

Padmalaya (Indian) lake of lotuses.

Padmalochana (Indian) lotus-eyed.

Padmavasa (Indian) one who resided in a lotus.

Padmini (Indian) lotus flower.

Page G (French) young assistant.
Pagen, Pagi, Payge

Pahal (Indian) the start.

Paige ☆ G (English) young child.
Payge

Paisley (Scottish) patterned fabric
first made in Paisley, Scotland.
Paislay, Paislee, Paisleyann, Paisleyanne,
Paizlei, Paizleigh, Paizley, Pasley, Pazley

Paiton (English) warrior's town.
Paiten, Paityn, Paityne, Paiyton, Paten,
Patton

Paka (Swahili) kitten. See also Paca.

Pakhi, Pakshi (Indian) bird.

Pakuna (Moquelumnan) deer
bounding while running downhill.

Palaciada, Palaciata (Greek) she
who has a sumptuous mansion.

Paladia (Spanish) a form of Pallas.

Palas (Greek) goddess of wisdom
and war.

Palba (Basque) blond.

Palila (Polynesian) bird.

Palixena (Greek) she who returns
from the foreign land.

Pallas (Greek) wise. Mythology:
another name for Athena, the
goddess of wisdom.

Pallavi (Indian) bud.

Pallavini (Indian) with new leaves.

Palma (Latin) palm tree.
Pallma, Palmira

Palmera (Spanish) palm tree.

Palmira (Spanish) a form of Palma.
Pallmirah, Pallmyra, Palmer, Palmyra

Paloma G (Spanish) dove. See also
Aloma.
Palloma, Palometa, Palomita, Paluma,
Peloma

Pamela (Greek) honey.
Pam, Pama, Pamala, Pamalla, Pamelia,
Pamelina, Pamella, Pamila, Pamilla,
Pammela, Pammi, Pammie, Pammy,
Pamula

Pampa (Indian) river.

Panambi (Guarani) butterfly.

Pancha (Spanish) free; from France.
Paca, Panchita

Pancracia (Greek) she who has all
the power.

Pandita (Hindi) scholar.

Pandora (Greek) all-gifted.
Mythology: a woman who opened a
box out of curiosity and released evil
into the world. See also Dora.
Pandi, Pandorah, Pandora, Pandorrah,
Pandy, Panndora, Panndorah,
Panndorra, Panndorrah

Pang (Chinese) innovative.

Pankaja (Indian) lotus.

Pankhadi (Indian) petal.

Pankti (Indian) sentence.

Pansy (Greek) flower; fragrant.
(French) thoughtful.
Pansey, Pansie

Panthea (Greek) all the gods.
Pantheia, Pantheya

Panya (Swahili) mouse; tiny baby.
(Russian) a familiar form of
Stephanie.
Panyia

Panyin (Fante) older twin.

Paola G (Italian) a form of Paula.
Paoli, Paolina

Papiha (Indian) a sweet singing bird.

Papina (Moquelumnan) vine growing on an oak tree.

Paquita (Spanish) a form of Frances.
Paqua

Parama (Indian) the best.

Paravi, Parnavi (Indian) bird.

Parbarti (Indian) surrender.

Pardeep **B** (Sikh) mystic light.

Pari (Persian) fairy eagle.

Paridhi (Indian) limit.

Parinita (Indian) complete.

Paris **G** (French) Geography: the capital of France. Mythology: the Trojan prince who started the Trojan War by abducting Helen.
Parice, Paries, Parisa, Parise, Parish, Parisha, Pariss, Parissa, Parisse, Parris, Parys, Parysse

Parishi (Indian) like a fairy.

Pariyat (Indian) flower.

Parker **B** (English) park keeper.
Park, Parke

Parmenia (Greek) constant, faithful.

Parmenias (Spanish) a form of Parmenia.

Parmita (Indian) wisdom.

Parnal, Parni (Indian) leafy.

Parnashri (Indian) leafy beauty.

Parnik (Indian) creeper.

Parnika (Indian) a small leaf.

Parris (French) a form of Paris.
Parrise, Parrish, Parrisha, Parrys, Parrysh

Partenia (Greek) she who is as pure as a virgin.

Parthenia (Greek) virginal.
Partheenia, Parthenie, Parthinia, Pathina

Parthivi (Indian) another name for the goddess Sita.

Parul (Indian) graceful; flow of water.

Parvani (Indian) full moon; a festival or a special day.

Parveneh (Persian) butterfly.

Pascal **B** (French) born on Easter or Passover.
Pascalette, Pascaline, Pascalle, Paschale, Paskel

Pascale **G** (French) a form of Pascal.

Pascua, Pascualina (Hebrew) she who was born during the Easter festivities.

Pascuala (Spanish) born during the Easter season.

Pascuas (Hebrew) sacrificed for the good of the village.

Pasha **BG** (Greek) sea.
Palasha, Pascha, Pasche, Pashae, Pashe, Pashel, Pashka, Pasia, Passia

Passion (Latin) passion.
Pashion, Pashonne, Pasion, Passionaé, Passionate, Passionette

Pastora (German) shepherdess.

Pasua (Swahili) born by cesarean section.

Pat **BG** (Latin) a short form of Patricia, Patsy.

Pati (Moquelumnan) fish baskets made of willow branches.

Patia (Gypsy, Spanish) leaf. (Latin, English) a familiar form of Patience, Patricia.

Patience (English) patient.
Paciencia, Patia, Patiance, Patient, Patince, Patishia

Patra (Greek, Latin) a form of Petra.

Patralekha (Indian) a name from ancient epics.

Patrice 🄶 (French) a form of Patricia.
Patrease, Patrece, Patreece, Patreese, Patreice, Patriece, Patryce, Pattrice

Patricia 🄶 (Latin) noblewoman. See also Payton, Peyton, Tricia, Trisha, Trissa.
Pat, Patia, Patresa, Patrica, Patrice, Patricea, Patriceia, Patrichea, Patriciana, Patricianna, Patricja, Patricka, Patrickia, Patrisha, Patrishia, Patrisia, Patrissa, Patrizia, Patrizzia, Patrycia, Patrycja, Patsy, Patty

Patrick 🄱 (Latin) noble. Religion: the patron saint of Ireland.

Patsy (Latin) a familiar form of Patricia.
Pat, Patsey, Patsi

Patty (English) a familiar form of Patricia.
Patte, Pattee, Patti, Pattie

Paul 🄱 (Latin) small.

Paula (Latin) a form of Paul. See also Pavla, Polly.
Paliki, Paola, Paulane, Paulann, Paule, Paulette, Paulina, Pauline, Paulla, Pavia

Paulette (Latin) a familiar form of Paula.
Paulet, Paulett, Pauletta, Paulita, Paullett, Paulletta, Paullette

Paulina (Slavic) a form of Paula.
Paulena, Paulene, Paulenia, Pauliana, Paulianne, Paullena, Paulyna, Pawlina, Polena, Polina, Polinia

Pauline (French) a form of Paula.
Pauleen, Paulene, Paulien, Paulin, Paulyne, Paulynn, Pouline

Pausha (Hindi) lunar month of Capricorn.

Pavana (Indian) sacred.

Paveena (Indian) freshness, purity.

Pavla (Czech, Russian) a form of Paula.
Pavlina, Pavlinka

Paxton 🄱🄶 (Latin) peaceful town.
Paxtin, Paxtynn

Payge (English) a form of Paige.

Payoja (Indian) lotus.

Payton ☀ 🄶 (Irish) a form of Patricia.
Paydon, Paytan, Payten, Paytin, Paytn, Paytton

Paz 🄶 (Spanish) peace.

Pazi (Ponca) yellow bird.

Pazia (Hebrew) golden.
Paza, Pazice, Pazit

Peace (English) peaceful.

Pearl (Latin) jewel.
Pearle, Pearleen, Pearlena, Pearlene, Pearlette, Pearlina, Pearline, Pearlisha, Pearlyn, Perl, Perla, Perle, Perlette, Perlie, Perline, Perlline

Pedra (Portuguese) rock.

Peggy (Greek) a familiar form of Margaret.
Peg, Pegeen, Pegg, Peggey, Peggi, Peggie, Pegi

Pei (Chinese) abundant.

Peke (Hawaiian) a form of Bertha.

Pela (Polish) a short form of Penelope.
Pele

Pelagia (Greek) sea.
Pelage, Pelageia, Pelagie, Pelga,
Pelgia, Pellagia

Pelipa (Zuni) a form of Philippa.

Pemba (Bambara) the power that
controls all life.

Penda (Swahili) loved.

Penelope (Greek) weaver.
Mythology: the clever and loyal wife
of Odysseus, a Greek hero.
Pela, Pen, Penelopa, Penna, Pennelope,
Penny, Pinelopi

Penélope (Greek) a form of Penelope.

Peng (Chinese) friend.

Peni (Carrier) mind.

Peninah (Hebrew) pearl.
Penina, Peninit, Peninnah, Penny

Penny (Greek) a familiar form of
Penelope, Peninah.
Penee, Peni, Penney, Penni, Pennie

Peony (Greek) flower.
Peonie

Pepita (Spanish) a familiar form of
Josephine.
Pepa, Pepi, Peppy, Peta

Pepper (Latin) condiment from the
pepper plant.

Perah (Hebrew) flower.

Perdita (Latin) lost. Literature: a
character in Shakespeare's play *The
Winter's Tale*.
Perdida, Perdy

Peregrina (Latin) pilgrim, traveler.

Perfecta (Spanish) flawless.

Peri (Greek) mountain dweller
(Persian) fairy or elf.
Perita

Perla (Latin) a form of Pearl.
Pearla

Perlie (Latin) a familiar form of Pearl.
Pearley, Pearlie, Pearly, Perley, Perli,
Perly, Purley, Purly

Perlita (Spanish) a form of Perla.

Pernella (Greek, French) rock.
(Latin) a short form of Petronella.
Parnella, Pernel, Pernell, Pernelle

Pernita (Indian) answered prayer

Perpetua (Spanish) continuous.

Perri (Greek, Latin) small rock;
traveler. (French) pear tree. (Welsh)
child of Harry.
Perre, Perrey, Perriann, Perrie, Perrin,
Perrine, Perry

Perry **B** (Greek, French, Welsh) a
form of Perri.

Persephone (Greek) Mythology:
the goddess of the underworld.
Persephanie, Persephany, Persephonie

Perseveranda (Latin) she who
perseveres on the good road.

Persis (Latin) from Persia.
Perssis, Persy

Peta (Blackfoot) golden eagle.

Peter **B** (Greek, Latin) small rock.

Petra (Greek, Latin) small rock. A
short form of Petronella.
Patra, Pet, Peta, Petena, Peterina,
Petraann, Petrice, Petrina, Petrine,
Petrova, Petrovna, Pier, Pierce, Pietra

Petronella (Greek) small rock. (Latin) of the Roman clan Petronius.
Pernella, Peternella, Petra, Petrona, Petronela, Petronella, Petronelle, Petronia, Petronija, Petronilla, Petronille

Petula (Latin) seeker.
Petulah

Petunia (Native American) flower.

Peyeche (Mapuche) unforgettable woman, remembered; popular, sought-after.

Peyton ☀ **BG** (Irish) a form of Patricia.
Peyden, Peydon, Peyten, Peytyn

Phaedra (Greek) bright.
Faydra, Phae, Phaidra, Phe, Phedre

Phallon (Irish) a form of Fallon.
Phalaine, Phalen, Phallan, Phallie, Phalon, Phalyn

Pheakkley (Vietnamese) velvet.

Phebe (Greek) a form of Phoebe.
Pheba, Pheby

Pheodora (Greek, Russian) a form of Feodora.
Phedora, Phedorah, Pheodorah, Pheydora, Pheydorah

Philana (Greek) lover of mankind.
Phila, Philanna, Philene, Philiane, Philina, Philine

Philantha (Greek) lover of flowers.

Philicia (Latin) a form of Phylicia.
Philecia, Philesha, Philica, Philicha, Philycia

Philip **B** (Greek) lover of horses.

Philippa (Greek) a form of Philip. See also Filippa.
Phil, Philipa, Philippe, Phillipina, Phillippine, Phillie, Philly, Pippa, Pippy

Philomena (Greek) love song; loved one. Bible: a first-century saint. See also Filomena, Mena.
Philoméne, Philomina

Phoebe (Greek) shining.
Phaebe, Phebe, Pheobe, Phoebey

Phuong (Vietnamese) friendly.

Phylicia (Latin) fortunate; happy. (Greek) a form of Felicia.
Philicia, Phylecia, Phylesha, Phylesia, Phylica, Phylisha, Phylisia, Phylissa, Phyllecia, Phyllicia, Phyllisha, Phyllisia, Phyllissa, Phyllyza

Phyllida (Greek) a form of Phyllis.
Fillida, Philida, Phillida, Phillyda

Phyllis (Greek) green bough.
Filise, Fillys, Fyllis, Philis, Phillis, Philliss, Philys, Philyss, Phylis, Phyllida, Phyllis, Phylliss, Phyllys

Pi (Chinese) stringed musical instrument.

Pia (Latin, Italian) devout.
Pía

Piedad (Spanish) devoted; pious.

Pier (French) a form of Petra.
Pierette, Pierrette, Pierra, Pierre

Pierce **B** (English) a form of Petra.

Pierre **B** (French) a form of Pier.

Piki (Indian) cuckoo.

Pilar (Spanish) pillar, column.
Peelar, Pilár, Pillar

Pili (Spanish) a form of Pilar.

Pilmayquen (Araucanian) swallow.

Pimpinela (Latin) fickle one.

Ping (Chinese) duckweed. (Vietnamese) peaceful.

Pinga (Eskimo) Mythology: the goddess of game and the hunt.

Piper (English) pipe player.

Pippa (English) a short form of Phillipa.

Pippi (French) rosy cheeked.
Pippen, Pippie, Pippin, Pippy

Piro (Mapuche) snows.

Pita (African) fourth daughter.

Pitrel (Mapuche) very small woman.

Pival, Piyali (Indian) a tree.

Plácida (Latin) she who is gentle and peaceful.

Placidia (Latin) serene.
Placida

Pleasance (French) pleasant.
Pleasence

Plorine (Pohnpeian) a form of Catalina.

Polimnia (Greek) a form of Polyhymnia, one of the nine Muses; she who inspires hymns.

Polixena (Greek) welcoming one.

Polla (Arabic) poppy.
Pola

Polly (Latin) a familiar form of Paula.
Paili, Pali, Pauli, Paulie, Pauly, Poll, Pollee, Polley, Polli, Pollie

Pollyam (Hindi) goddess of the plague. Religion: the Hindu name invoked to ward off bad spirits.

Pollyanna (English) a combination of Polly + Anna. Literature: an overly optimistic heroine created by Eleanor Porter.

Poloma (Choctaw) bow.

Pomona (Latin) apple. Mythology: the goddess of fruit and fruit trees.

Poni (African) second daughter.

Poorbi (Indian) eastern.

Poornima, Purnima (Indian) full moon.

Poorva (Indian) earlier one, elder; east.

Poorvaganga (Indian) the Narmada River.

Poorvaja (Indian) elder sister.

Poorvi (Indian) a classical melody.

Popea (Greek) venerable mother.

Poppy (Latin) poppy flower.
Popi, Poppey, Poppi, Poppie

Pora, Poria (Hebrew) fruitful.

Porcha (Latin) a form of Portia.
Porchae, Porchai, Porche, Porchia, Porcia

Porscha, Porsche (German) forms of Portia.
Porcsha, Porcshe, Porschah, Porsché, Porschea, Porschia, Pourche

Porsha (Latin) a form of Portia.
Porshai, Porshay, Porshe, Porshea, Porshia

Portia (Latin) offering. Literature: the heroine of Shakespeare's play *The Merchant of Venice*.
Porcha, Porscha, Porsche, Porsha, Portiea

Poulomi (Indian) Indra's second wife.

Poushali (Indian) of the month Poush.

Prabha (Indian) light.

Prabhada (Indian) lady.

Prabhati (Indian) of the morning.

Prabhavati (Indian) wife of Sun.

Prabhjot 🅱 (Sikh) the light of God.

Pracheeta, Prasheetha (Indian) origin, starting point.

Prachi (Indian) east.

Pradeepta (Indian) glowing.

Pradnya, Pragya, Pramiti (Indian) wisdom.

Prafula (Indian) in bloom.

Pragati (Indian) progress.

Pragyaparamita (Indian) wise.

Pragyawati (Indian) a wise woman.

Prajakta (Indian) fragrant flower.

Prakriti (Indian) nature; beautiful.

Prakruthi (Indian) weather.

Prakruti (Indian) nature.

Prama (Indian) knowledge of truth.

Pramada (Indian) beautiful lady.

Pramila (Indian) sleep.

Pranali (Indian) organization.

Pranati (Indian) greeting elders with respect.

Pranjal (Indian) honest and dignified.

Prapti (Indian) advantage.

Prarthana (Indian) prayer.

Prashanti (Indian) complete peace.

Prasheila (Indian) ancient time.

Pratibha (Indian) splendor; intelligence.

Pratichi (Indian) west.

Pratigya (Indian) pledge, vow.

Pratima (Indian) idol.

Pratishtha (Indian) preeminence.

Pratiti (Indian) faith.

Pratyusha (Indian) early morning.

Praveena (Indian) skilled.

Praxedes (Greek) she who has firm intentions.

Práxedes (Greek) a form of Praxedes.

Prayerna (Indian) worship.

Preciosa (Latin) she who possesses great valor and is invaluable.

Precious (French) precious; dear.
Pracious, Preciouse, Precisha, Prescious, Preshious, Presious

Preeti (Indian) happiness.

Preksha (Indian) viewing.

Premala (Indian) loving.

Prerana, Prerna (Indian) inspiration.

Presencia (Spanish) presence.

Presentación (Latin) she who expresses herself.

Presley 🇬 (English) priest's meadow.
Preslea, Preslee, Preslei, Presli, Preslie, Presly, Preslye, Pressley, Presslie, Pressly

Presta (Spanish) hurry, quick.

Preston 🅱 (English) priest's estate.

Preyasi (Indian) beloved.

Prianka (Indian) favorite.

Prima (Latin) first, beginning; first child.
Prema, Primalia, Primetta, Primina, Priminia

Primavera (Italian, Spanish) spring.

Primitiva (Latin) first of all.

Primrose (English) primrose flower.
Primula

Prina (Indian) content.

Princess (English) daughter of royalty.
Princcess, Princes, Princesa, Princessa, Princetta, Princie, Princilla

Priscilla (Latin) ancient.
Cilla, Piri, Precila, Precilla, Prescilla, Presilla, Pressilia, Pricila, Pricilla, Pris, Prisca, Priscela, Priscella, Priscila, Priscilia, Priscill, Priscille, Priscillia, Prisella, Prisila, Prisilla, Prissila, Prissilla, Prissy, Pryscylla, Prysilla

Prisha (Indian) beloved; God's gift.

Prissy (Latin) a familiar form of Priscilla.
Prisi, Priss, Prissi, Prissie

Prita (Indian) dear one.

Prital, Pritika (Indian) loved one.

Prithika (Indian) flower.

Prithuloma (Indian) fish.

Priti (Indian) love.

Pritikana (Indian) an atom of love.

Pritilata (Indian) a creeper of love.

Priya (Hindi) beloved; sweet natured.
Pria

Priyadarshini (Indian) dear.

Priyadutta (Indian) earth.

Priyal (Indian) beloved.

Priyamvada (Indian) one who speaks with love.

Priyanvada (Indian) one who speaks nicely.

Procopia (Latin) declared leader.

Promise (Latin) promise, pledge.
Promis, Promiss, Promys, Promyse

Proserpina (Greek) she who wants to annihilate.

Próspera (Greek) prosperous.

Pru (Latin) a short form of Prudence.
Prue

Prudence (Latin) cautious; discreet.
Pru, Prudencia, Prudens, Prudy

Prudenciana (Spanish) modest and honest.

Prudy (Latin) a familiar form of Prudence.
Prudee, Prudi, Prudie

Prunella (Latin) brown; little plum. See also Nellie.
Prunela

Psyche (Greek) soul. Mythology: a beautiful mortal loved by Eros, the Greek god of love.

Pu (Chinese) uncut jade.

Pua (Hawaiian) flower.

Pualani (Hawaiian) heavenly flower.
Puni

Puebla (Spanish) taken from the name of the Mexican city.

Puji (Indian) gentle.

Pujita (Indian) worshipped.

Pulak (Indian) a gem; smile.

Puloma (Indian) wife of the sage Bhrigu.

Punarnava (Indian) a star.

Punita (Indian) holy.

Punthali (Indian) doll.

Punya (Indian) virtuous.

Pura (English) a form of Purity.

Purificación (Spanish) a form of Pura.

Purity (English) purity.
Pureza, Purisima

Purva (Indian) elder; breeze.

Purvaja (Indian) elder sister.

Purvi (Indian) from the east.

Pusha (Indian) nourishing.

Pushpa (Indian) flower.

Pushpagandha (Indian) juhi flower.

Pushpalata (Indian) flower creeper.

Pushpanjali (Indian) flower offering.

Pushpita, Pushpitha (Indian) decorated with flowers.

Pusti (Indian) nourishment.

Putul (Indian) doll.

Pyralis (Greek) fire. Pyrene.

Qadira (Arabic) powerful.
Kadira

Qamra (Arabic) moon.
Kamra

Qi (Chinese) fine jade; outstanding; distinguished.

Qian (Chinese) courteous.

Qiao (Chinese) handsome; pretty.

Qin (Chinese) celery.

Qing (Chinese) greenish blue.

Qing Yuan, Qing-Yuan (Chinese) clear spring.

Qiong (Chinese) fine jade.

Qitarah (Arabic) fragrant.

Qiu (Chinese) autumn.

Qu (Chinese) delight.

Quaashie 🔠 (Ewe) born on Sunday.

Quadeisha (American) a combination of Qadira + Aisha.
Qudaisha, Quadaishia, Quadajah, Quadasha, Quadasia, Quadayshia, Quadaza, Quadejah, Quadesha, Quadeshia, Quadiasha, Quaesha

Quan (Chinese) goddess of compassion.

Quaneisha (American) a combination of the prefix Qu + Niesha.
Quaneasa, Quanece, Quanecia, Quaneice, Quanesha, Quanisha, Quansha, Quarnisha, Queisha, Qwanisha, Qynisha

Quanesha (American) a form of Quaneisha.
Quamesha, Quaneesha, Quaneshia, Quanesia, Quanessa, Quanessia, Quannesha, Quanneshia, Quannezia, Quayneshia, Quinesha

Quanika (American) a combination of the prefix Qu + Nika.
Quanikka, Quanikki, Quaniqua, Quanique, Quantenique, Quawanica, Queenika, Queenique

Quanisha (American) a form of Quaneisha.
Quaniesha, Quanishia, Quaynisha, Queenisha, Quenisha, Quenishia

Quarrtulain (Indian) God's mercy.

Quartilla (Latin) fourth.
Quantilla

Quasar (Indian) meteor.

Qubilah (Arabic) agreeable.

Que (Chinese) true; reliable.

Queagon (Chamorro) striving for food.

Queen (English) queen. See also Quinn.
Queena, Queenie, Quenna

Queenie (English) a form of Queen.
Queenation, Queeneste, Queeny

Queisha (American) a short form of Quaneisha.
Qeysha, Queshia, Queysha

Quenby BG (Scandinavian) feminine.

Quenisha (American) a combination of Queen + Aisha.
Queneesha, Quenesha, Quennisha, Quensha, Quinesha, Quinisha

Quenna (English) a form of Queen.
Quenell, Quenessa

Quentin B (Latin) fifth. (English) queen's town.

Querida (Spanish) dear; beloved.

Querima, Querina (Arabic) generous one.

Quesara (Latin) youthful.

Questa (French) searcher.

Queta (Spanish) a short form of names ending in "queta" or "quetta."
Quenetta, Quetta

Quetaca (Chamorro) striving to achieve, attain.

Quetogua (Chamorro) striving to conquer or strike down.

Quetromán (Mapuche) mute condor; restrained soul; prudence.

Quiana (American) a combination of the prefix Qu + Anna.
Quian, Quianah, Quianda, Quiane, Quiani, Quianita, Quianna, Quianne, Quionna

Quíbele (Turkish) goddess mother.

Quidilis (Chamorro) striving to surpass.

Quiliana (Spanish) substantial; productive.

Quillen (Spanish) woman of the heights.

Quimey (Mapuche) beautiful.

Quinby (Scandinavian) queen's estate.

Quincy B (Irish) fifth.
Quincee, Quincey, Quinci, Quincia, Quincie

Quinella (Latin) a form of Quintana.

Quinesburga (Anglo-Saxon) royal strength.

Quinesha, Quinisha (American) forms of Quenisha.
Quineshia, Quinessa, Quinessia, Quinisa, Quinishia, Quinnesha, Quinneshia, Quinnisha, Quneasha, Quonesha, Quonisha, Quonnisha

Quinetta (Latin) a form of Quintana.
Queenetta, Queenette, Quinette, Quinita, Quinnette

Quinn B (German, English) queen. See also Queen.
Quin, Quinna, Quinne, Quynn

Quinshawna (American) a combination of Quinn + Shauna.
Quinshea

Quintana (Latin) fifth. (English) queen's lawn. See also Quinella, Quinetta.
Quinntina, Quinta, Quintanna, Quintara, Quintarah, Quintia, Quintila, Quintilla, Quintina, Quintona, Quintonice

Quintessa (Latin) essence. See also Tess.
Quintaysha, Quintesa, Quintesha, Quintessia, Quintice, Quinticia, Quintisha, Quintosha

Quintiliana (Spanish) born in the fifth month of the year.

Quinton B (Latin) a form of Quentin.

Quintrell (American) a combination of Quinn + Trella.
Quintela, Quintella, Quintrelle

Quintruy (Mapuche) investigator; woman of initiative and curiosity; leader.

Quintuqueo (Mapuche) she who searches for wisdom; woman of experience, having the gifts of knowledge, counseling, and perfection.

Quinturay (Mapuche) she who has a flower; she whose goal is to find the nectar and the essence of the flower.

Quionia (Greek) she who is fertile.

Quipuha (Chamorro) striving to capsize.

Quirina (Latin) she who carries the lance.

Quirita (Latin) citizen.

Quiterie (Latin, French) tranquil.
Quita

Qun (Chinese) the masses.

Quon (Chinese) bright.

Quy (Vietnamese) faithful.

Quyen (Vietnamese) destiny, direction.

Quynh (Vietnamese) precious.

Qwanisha (American) a form of Quaneisha.
Qwanechia, Qwanesha, Qwanessia, Qwantasha

R

R BG (American) an initial used as a first name.

Raaida (Indian) leader.

Raawiya (Indian) transmitter of ancient Arabic poetry.

Rabab (Indian) white cloud.

Rabani (Indian) divine.

Rabecca (Hebrew) a form of Rebecca.
Rabecka, Rabeca, Rabekah

Rabeea (Indian) garden.

Rabhya (Indian) worshipped.

Rabi BG (Arabic) breeze.
Rabia, Rabiah

Rachael (Hebrew) a form of Rachel.
Rachaele, Rachaell, Rachail, Rachalle

Rachana, Rachna (Indian) creation.

Racheal (Hebrew) a form of Rachel.

Rachel ★ G (Hebrew) female sheep. Bible: the second wife of Jacob. See also Lahela, Rae, Rochelle.
Racha, Rachael, Rachal, Racheal, Rachela, Rachelann, Rachele, Rachelle, Racquel, Raechel, Rahel, Rahela, Rahil, Raiche, Raquel, Rashel, Rashelle, Ray, Raycene, Raychel, Raychelle, Rey, Ruchel

Rachelle (French) a form of Rachel.
See also Shelley.
*Rachalle, Rachell, Rachella, Raechell,
Raechelle, Raeshelle, Rashel, Rashele,
Rashell, Rashelle, Raychell, Rayshell,
Ruchelle*

Rachita (Indian) created.

Racquel (French) a form of Rachel.
Rackel, Racquell, Racquella, Racquelle

Radegunda (German) she who
counsels regarding battling.

Radella (German) counselor.

Radeyah (Arabic) content, satisfied.
Radeeyah, Radhiya, Radiah, Radiyah

Radha (Indian) Lord Krishna's lover.

Radhiyaa (Indian) content, satisfied.

Radhwa (Indian) the name of a
mountain in Medina.

Radinka (Slavic) full of life; happy,
glad.

Radmilla (Slavic) worker for the
people.

Rae (English) doe. (Hebrew) a short
form of Rachel.
*Raeh, Raeneice, Raeneisha, Raesha,
Ray, Raye, Rayetta, Rayette, Rayma, Rey*

Raeann (American) a combination
of Rae + Ann. See also Rayanne.
*Raea, Raean, Raeanna, Raeannah,
Raeona, Reanna, Raeanne*

Raechel (Hebrew) a form of Rachel.
*Raechael, Raechal, Raechele, Raechell,
Raechyl*

Raeden (Japanese) Mythology:
Raiden was the god of thunder and
lightning.
Raeda, Raedeen

Raegan **G** (Irish) a form of Reagan.
Raegen, Raegene, Raegine, Raegyn

Raelene (American) a combination
of Rae + Lee.
*Rael, Raela, Raelani, Raele, Raeleah,
Raelee, Raeleen, Raeleia, Raeleigh,
Raeleigha, Raelein, Raelene, Raelennia,
Raelesha, Raelin, Raelina, Raelle,
Raelyn, Raelynn*

Raelyn, Raelynn (American) forms
of Raelene.
Raelynda, Raelyne, Raelynne

Raena (German) a form of Raina.
*Raenah, Raenia, Raenie, Raenna,
Raeonna, Raeyauna, Raeyn, Raeyonna*

Raeven (English) a form of Raven.
*Raevin, Raevion, Raevon, Raevonna,
Raevyn, Raevynne, Raewyn, Raewynne,
Raivan, Raiven, Raivin, Raivyn*

Rafa (Arabic) happy; prosperous.

Rafael **B** (Spanish) a form of
Raphael.

Rafaela (Hebrew) a form of
Raphaela.
Rafaelia, Rafaella

Ragan (Irish) a form of Reagan.
*Ragean, Rageane, Rageen, Ragen,
Ragene, Rageni, Ragenna, Raggan,
Raygan, Raygen, Raygene, Rayghan,
Raygin*

Raghd (Indian) pleasant.

Ragi (Indian) loving.

Ragine (English) a form of Regina.
Raegina, Ragin, Ragina, Raginee

Ragini (Indian) melody.

Ragnild (Scandinavian) battle
counsel.
*Ragna, Ragnell, Ragnhild, Rainell,
Renilda, Renilde*

Rahat (Indian) relief.

Raheem **B** (Punjabi)
compassionate God.
Raheema, Rahima

Ráidah (Arabic) leader.

Raimunda (Spanish) wise defender.

Raina (German) mighty. (English) a short form of Regina. See also Rayna.
Raeinna, Raena, Raheena, Rain, Rainah, Rainai, Raine, Rainea, Rainna, Reanna

Rainbow (English) rainbow.
Rainbeau, Rainbeaux, Rainbo, Raynbow

Raine 🅖 (Latin) a short form of Regina. A form of Raina, Rane.
Rainee, Rainey, Raini, Rainie, Rainy, Reyne

Raingarda (German) prudent defender.

Raisa (Russian) a form of Rose.
Raisah, Raissa, Raiza, Raysa, Rayza, Razia

Raizel (Yiddish) a form of Rose.
Rayzil, Razil, Reizel, Resel

Raja (Arabic) hopeful.
Raia, Rajaah, Rajae, Rajah, Rajai

Rajanigandha (Indian) scented flower.

Rajashri (Indian) king's pride; ornament.

Rajasi (Indian) worthy of a king.

Rajata (Indian) silver.

Rajeshri (Indian) queen.

Rajeshwari (Indian) the goddess of a state.

Rajhans (Indian) swan.

Raji (Indian) shining.

Rajika (Indian) lamp.

Rajkumari, Rajnandhini, Rajnandini (Indian) princess.

Rajni (Indian) night.

Rajrita (Indian) prince of living.

Rajshri (Indian) sage-like king.

Rajul (Indian) brilliant.

Raka (Indian) full moon.

Rakhi (Indian) bond of protection.

Rakti (Indian) pleasing.

Raku (Japanese) pleasure.

Raleigh 🅑 (Irish) a form of Riley.
Ralea, Raleiah, Raley

Ralph 🅑 (English) wolf counselor.

Rama (Hebrew) lofty, exalted. (Hindi) godlike. Religion: an incarnation of the Hindu god Vishnu.
Ramah

Raman 🅖 (Spanish) a form of Ramona.

Ramandeep (Sikh) covered by the light of the Lord's love.

Ramani (Indian) a beautiful girl.

Rambha (Indian) name of an apsaras (female spirit).

Ramira (Spanish) judicious.

Ramita (Indian) pleasing.

Ramla (Swahili) fortuneteller.
Ramlah

Ramona (Spanish) mighty; wise protector. See also Mona.
Raman, Ramonda, Raymona, Romona, Romonda

Ramra (Indian) splendor.

Ramsey 🅑 (English) ram's island.
Ramsha, Ramsi, Ramsie, Ramza

Ran (Japanese) water lily. (Scandinavian) destroyer. Mythology: the Norse sea goddess who destroys.

Rana (Sanskrit) royal. (Arabic) gaze, look.
Rahna, Rahni, Rani

Ranait (Irish) graceful; prosperous.
Rane, Renny

Rand (Indian) tree of good scent.

Randall **B** (English) protected.
Randa, Randah, Randal, Randalee, Randel, Randell, Randelle, Randi, Randilee, Randilynn, Randlyn, Randy, Randyl

Randi **G** (English) a familiar form of Miranda, Randall.
Rande, Randee, Randeen, Randene, Randey, Randie, Randii

Randy **B** (English) a form of Randi.

Rane (Scandinavian) queen.
Raine

Rangana (Indian) happy.

Ranhita (Indian) quick.

Rani **G** (Sanskrit) queen. (Hebrew) joyful. A short form of Kerani.
Rahni, Ranee, Raney, Rania, Ranie, Ranice, Ranique, Ranni, Rannie

Ranita (Hebrew) song; joyful.
Ranata, Ranice, Ranit, Ranite, Ranitta, Ronita

Raniyah (Arabic) gazing.
Ranya, Ranyah

Ranjana (Indian) pleasing; exciting.

Ranjini (Indian) pleasing.

Ranjita (Indian) amusing; decorated.

Rapa (Hawaiian) moonbeam.

Raphael **B** (Hebrew) God has healed.

Raphaela (Hebrew) healed by God.
Rafaella, Raphaella, Raphaelle

Raphaelle (French) a form of Raphaela.
Rafaelle, Raphael, Raphaele

Raquel **G** (French) a form of Rachel.
Rakel, Rakhil, Rakhila, Raqueal, Raquela, Raquella, Raquelle, Rickelle, Rickquel, Ricquel, Ricquelle, Rikell, Rikelle, Rockell

Raquildis (German) fighting princess.

Rasha (Arabic) young gazelle.
Rahshea, Rahshia, Rashae, Rashai, Rashea, Rashi, Rashia

Rashawn **B** (American) a form of Rashawna.

Rashawna (American) a combination of the prefix Ra + Shawna.
Rashana, Rashanae, Rashanah, Rashanda, Rashane, Rashani, Rashanna, Rashanta, Rashaun, Rashauna, Rashaunda, Rashaundra, Rashaune, Rashawn, Rashawnda, Rashawnna, Rashon, Rashona, Rashonda, Rashunda

Rasheed **B** (Arabic) a form of Rashad (see Boys' Names).

Rashel, Rashelle (American) forms of Rachel.
Rashele, Rashell, Rashella

Rashida **G** (Swahili, Turkish) righteous.
Rahshea, Rahsheda, Rahsheita, Rashdah, Rasheda, Rashedah, Rasheeda, Rasheedah, Rasheeta, Rasheida, Rashidah, Rashidi

Rashieka (Arabic) descended from royalty.
Rasheeka, Rasheika, Rasheka, Rashika, Rasika

Rashmika (Indian) a ray of light.

Rasia (Greek) rose.

Rasna (Indian) ray.

Ratana (Tai) crystal.
*Ratania, Ratanya, Ratna, Rattan,
Rattana*

Ratanjali (Indian) red sandalwood.

Rathna (Indian) pearl.

Rati (Indian) joy.

Ratnabala (Indian) jeweled.

Ratnabali (Indian) string of pearls.

Ratnajyoti (Indian) light from a
jewel.

Ratnajyouti (Indian) lustrous jewel.

Ratnalekha (Indian) beauty of
jewels.

Ratnali (Indian) a jewel.

Ratnamala (Indian) a jeweled
necklace.

Ratnangi (Indian) whole body
adorned with jewels.

Ratnaprabha (Indian) earth; light
from a jewel.

Ratnapriya (Indian) one who likes
jewels.

Ratnavali (Indian) a bunch of gems;
earth.

Ratri (Hindi) night. Religion: the
goddess of the night.

Ratrudis (German) faithful
counselor.

Raula (French) wolf counselor.
Raoula, Raulla, Raulle

Raven 🄶 (English) blackbird.
*Raeven, Raveen, Raveena, Raveenn,
Ravena, Ravene, Ravenn, Ravenna,
Ravennah, Ravenne, Raveon, Ravin,
Ravon, Ravyn, Rayven, Revena*

Ravin (English) a form of Raven.
Ravi, Ravina, Ravine, Ravinne, Ravion

Raviprabha (Indian) light of the
sun.

Ravyn (English) a form of Raven.
Ravynn

Rawdha (Indian) garden.

Rawnie (Gypsy) fine lady.
Rawan, Rawna, Rhawnie

Ray 🄱 (Hebrew) a short form of
Raya.

Raya (Hebrew) friend.
Raia, Raiah, Raiya, Ray, Rayah

Rayanne (American) a form of
Raeann.
*Rayane, Ray-Ann, Rayan, Rayana,
Rayann, Rayanna, Rayeanna, Rayona,
Rayonna, Reyan, Reyana, Reyann,
Reyanna, Reyanne*

Raychel, Raychelle (Hebrew) forms
of Rachel.
Raychael, Raychele, Raychell, Raychil

Rayén (Araucanian, Mapuche)
flower.

Raylene (American) forms of
Raylyn.
*Ralina, Rayel, Rayele, Rayelle,
Rayleana, Raylee, Rayleen, Rayleigh,
Raylena, Raylin, Raylinn, Raylona,
Raylyn, Raylynn, Raylynne*

Raymonde (German) wise protector.
Rayma, Raymae, Raymie

Rayna (Scandinavian) mighty.
(Yiddish) pure, clean. (English)
king's advisor. (French) a familiar
form of Lorraine. See also Raina.
*Raynah, Rayne, Raynell, Raynelle,
Raynette, Rayona, Rayonna, Reyna*

Rayven (English) a form of Raven.
*Rayvan, Rayvana, Rayvein, Rayvenne,
Rayveona, Rayvin, Rayvon, Rayvonia*

Rayya (Arabic) thirsty no longer.

Razi **B** (Aramaic) secretive.
Rayzil, Rayzilee, Raz, Razia, Raziah, Raziela, Razilee, Razili

Raziya (Swahili) agreeable.

Rea (Greek) poppy flower.
Reah

Reagan **G** (Irish) little ruler.
Reagen, Reaghan, Reagine

Reanna (German, English) a form of Raina. (American) a form of Raeann.
Reannah

Reanne (American) a form of Raeann, Reanna.
Reana, Reane, Rearin, Reannan, Reanne, Reannen, Reannon, Reeana

Reba (Hebrew) fourth-born child. A short form of Rebecca. See also Reva, Riva.
Rabah, Reeba, Rheba

Rebeca (Hebrew) an alernate form of Rebecca.
Rebbeca, Rebecah

Rebecca **G** (Hebrew) tied, bound. Bible: the wife of Isaac. See also Becca, Becky.
Rabecca, Reba, Rebbecca, Rebeca, Rebeccah, Rebeccea, Rebeccka, Rebecha, Rebecka, Rebeckah, Rebeckia, Rebecky, Rebekah, Rebeque, Rebi, Reveca, Riva, Rivka

Rebekah **G** (Hebrew) a form of Rebecca.
Rebeka, Rebekha, Rebekka, Rebekkah, Rebekke, Revecca, Reveka, Revekka, Rifka

Rebha (Indian) sings praises.

Rebi (Hebrew) a familiar form of Rebecca.
Rebbie, Rebe, Rebie, Reby, Ree, Reebie

Reece **B** (Welsh) a form of Rhys.

Reed **B** (English) a form of Reid.

Reena (Greek) peaceful. (English) a form of Rina. (Hebrew) a form of Rinah.
Reen, Reenie, Rena, Reyna

Reese **G** (Welsh) a form of Reece.

Reet (Estonian) a form of Margaret.
Reatha, Reta, Retha

Regan **G** (Irish) a form of Reagan.
Regane, Reghan

Reganne (Irish) a form of Reagan.
Raegan, Ragan, Reagan, Regin

Reggie **B** (English) a familiar form of Regina.
Reggi, Reggy, Regi, Regia, Regie

Regina (Latin) queen. (English) king's advisor. Geography: the capital of Saskatchewan. See also Gina.
Ragine, Raina, Raine, Rega, Regena, Regennia, Reggie, Regiena, Regine, Reginia, Regis, Reina, Rena

Reginald **B** (English) king's advisor.

Regine (Latin) a form of Regina.
Regin

Rehana (Indian) sweet-smelling plant.

Rei **G** (Japanese) polite, well behaved.
Reiko

Reia (Spanish) a form of Reina.

Reid **B** (English) redhead.

Reika (Japanese) summit; scent.

Reilly **B** (Irish) a form of Riley.
Reilee, Reileigh, Reiley, Reili, Reilley, Reily

Reina (Spanish) a short form of
Regina. See also Reyna.
*Reinah, Reine, Reinette, Reinie, Reinna,
Reiny, Reiona, Renia, Rina*

Rekha (Hindi) thin line.
Reka, Rekia, Rekiah, Rekiya

Relinda (German) kind-hearted
princess.

Remedios (Spanish) remedy.

Remi 🅑 (French) from Rheims,
France.
Raymi, Remee, Remie, Remy

Remington 🅑 (English) raven
estate.
Remmington

Ren (Japanese) arranger; water lily;
lotus.

Rena (Hebrew) song; joy. A familiar
form of Irene, Regina, Renata,
Sabrina, Serena.
Reena, Rina, Rinna, Rinnah

Renae (French) a form of Renée.
Renay

Renata (French) a form of Renée.
*Ranata, Rena, Renada, Renatta, Renita,
Rennie, Renyatta, Rinada, Rinata*

Rene 🅑 (Greek) a short form of
Irene, Renée.
Reen, Reenie, Reney, Rennie

Renee 🅖 (French) a form of René.

Renée (French) born again.
*Renae, Renata, Renay, Rene, Renea,
Reneigh, Renell, Renelle, Renne*

Renita (French) a form of Renata.
Reneeta, Renetta, Renitza

Rennie (English) a familiar form of
Renata.
Reni, Renie, Renni

Renu (Indian) particle, grain; sand.

Reseda (Spanish) fragrant
mignonette blossom.

Resha (Indian) line.

Resham (Indian) silk.

Reshawna (American) a combi-
nation of the prefix Re + Shawna.
*Resaunna, Reshana, Reshaunda,
Reshawnda, Reshawnna, Reshonda,
Reshonn, Reshonta*

Reshma (Indian) silky.

Reshmi (Indian) silken.

Resi (German) a familiar form of
Theresa.
*Resia, Ressa, Resse, Ressie, Reza,
Rezka, Rezi*

Reta (African) shaken.
Reeta, Retta, Rheta, Rhetta

Reubena (Hebrew) behold a child.
*Reubina, Reuvena, Rubena, Rubenia,
Rubina, Rubine, Rubyna*

Reva (Latin) revived. (Hebrew) rain;
one-fourth. A form of Reba, Riva.
Ree, Reeva, Revia, Revida

Revati (Indian) prosperity.

Reveca, Reveka (Slavic) forms of
Rebecca, Rebekah.
Reve, Revecca, Revekka, Rivka

Rewa (Indian) swift.

Rexanne (American) queen.
Rexan, Rexana, Rexann, Rexanna

Reya (Spanish) a form of Reina.

Reyes (Spanish) a form of Reyna.

Reyhan 🅑 (Turkish) sweet-smelling
flower.

Reyna (Greek) peaceful. (English) a
form of Reina.
Reyana, Reyanna, Reyni, Reynna

Reynalda (German) king's advisor.

Réz **BG** (Latin, Hungarian) copper-colored hair.

Reza (Czech) a form of Theresa.
Rezi, Rezka

Rhea (Greek) brook, stream. Mythology: the mother of Zeus.
Rheá, Rhéa, Rhealyn, Rheanna, Rhia, Rhianna

Rheanna, Rhianna (Greek) forms of Rhea.
Rheana, Rheann, Rheanne, Rhiana, Rhiauna

Rhett **B** (Welsh) a form of Rhys.

Rhian (Welsh) a short form of Rhiannon.
Rhianne, Rhyan, Rhyann, Rhyanne, Rian, Riane, Riann, Rianne, Riayn

Rhiannon (Welsh) witch; nymph; goddess.
Rheannan, Rheannin, Rheannon, Rheanon, Rhian, Rhianen, Rhianna, Rhiannan, Rhiannen, Rhianon, Rhianwen, Rhinnon, Rhyanna, Riana, Riannon, Rianon

Rhoda (Greek) from Rhodes, Greece.
Rhode, Rhodeia, Rhodie, Rhody, Roda, Rodi, Rodie, Rodina

Rhona (Scottish) powerful, mighty. (English) king's advisor.
Rhonae, Rhonnie

Rhonda (Welsh) grand.
Rhondene, Rhondiesha, Ronda, Ronelle, Ronnette

Rhys **B** (Welsh) enthusiastic; stream.

Ria (Spanish) river.
Riah

Riana, Rianna (Irish) short forms of Briana. (Arabic) forms of Rihana.
Reana, Reanna, Rhianna, Rhyanna, Riana, Rianah

Rica (Spanish) a short form of Erica, Frederica, Ricarda. See also Enrica, Sandrica, Terrica, Ulrica.
Ricca, Rieca, Riecka, Rieka, Rikka, Riqua, Rycca

Ricarda (Spanish) rich and powerful ruler.
Rica, Richanda, Richarda, Richi, Ricki

Ricardo **B** (Portuguese, Spanish) a form of Richard.

Richael (Irish) saint.

Richard **B** (English) a form of Richart (see Boys' Names).

Richelle (German, French) a form of Ricarda.
Richel, Richela, Richele, Richell, Richella, Richia

Rickelle (American) a form of Raquel.
Rickel, Rickela, Rickell

Rickey **B** (English) a familiar form of Richard.

Ricki, Rikki **G** (American) familiar forms of Erica, Frederica, Ricarda.
Rica, Ricci, Riccy, Rici, Rickee, Rickia, Rickie, Rickilee, Rickina, Rickita, Ricky, Ricquie, Riki, Rikia, Rikita, Rikka, Rikke, Rikkia, Rikkie, Rikky, Riko

Ricky **B** (American) a form of Ricki.

Rico **B** (Spanish) a familiar form of Richard. (Italian) a short form of Enrico (see Boys' Names).

Ricquel (American) a form of Raquel.
Rickquell, Ricquelle, Rikell, Rikelle

Rida **BG** (Arabic) favored by God.

Riddhi (Indian) fortunate.

Rieko (Japanese) child of Rie.

Rigel (Spanish) most brilliant star in the sky.

Rihana (Arabic) sweet basil.
Rhiana, Rhianna, Riana, Rianna

Riju (Indian) innocent.

Rijuta (Indian) innocence.

Rika (Swedish) ruler.
Ricka

Rikako (Japanese) child of Rika.

Riku (Japanese) land.

Rilee (Irish) a form of Riley.
Rielee, Rielle

Riley ☀ **B** (Irish) valiant.
Raleigh, Reilly, Rieley, Rielly, Riely, Rilee, Rileigh, Rilie

Rilla (German) small brook.

Rima (Arabic) white antelope.
Reem, Reema, Reemah, Rema, Remah, Rhymia, Rim, Ryma

Rimona (Hebrew) pomegranate. See also Mona.

Rimpy (Indian) pretty.

Rin (Japanese) park. Geography: a Japanese village.
Rini, Rynn

Rina (English) a short form of names ending in "rina." (Hebrew) a form of Rena, Rinah.
Reena, Rena

Rinah (Hebrew) joyful.
Rina

Rinako (Japanese) child of Rina.

Río (Spanish) river.

Riona (Irish) saint.

Risa (Latin) laughter.
Reesa, Resa

Risako (Japanese) child of Risa.

Risha (Hindi) born during the lunar month of Taurus.
Rishah, Rishay

Rishika (Indian) saintly.

Rishima (Indian) moonbeam.

Rishita (Indian) the best.

Rishona (Hebrew) first.
Rishina, Rishon

Rissa (Greek) a short form of Nerissa.
Risa, Rissah, Ryssa, Ryssah

Rita (Sanskrit) brave; honest. (Greek) a short form of Margarita.
Reatha, Reda, Reeta, Reida, Reitha, Rheta, Riet, Ritah, Ritamae, Ritamarie

Riti (Indian) memory; well being.

Ritika (Indian) movement.

Ritsa (Greek) a familiar form of Alexandra.
Ritsah, Ritsi, Ritsie, Ritsy

Ritsuko (Japanese) child of Ritsu.

Ritu (Indian) season.

Riva (French) river bank. (Hebrew) a short form of Rebecca. See also Reba, Reva.
Rivalee, Rivi, Rivvy

River **B** (Latin, French) stream, water.
Rivana, Rivanna, Rivers, Riviane

Rivka (Hebrew) a short form of Rebecca.
Rivca, Rivcah, Rivkah

Riya (Indian) flower.

Riye (Japanese) blessed truth.

Riyeko (Japanese) flourishing child of reason.

Riza (Greek) a form of Theresa.
Riesa, Rizus, Rizza

Roanna (American) a form of
Rosanna.
Ranna, Roana, Roanda, Roanne

Robbi (English) a familiar form of
Roberta.
*Robby, Robbye, Robey, Robi, Robia,
Roby*

Robbie **B** (English) a form of Robbi.

Robert **B** (English) famous
brilliance.

Roberta (English) a form of Robert.
*Roba, Robbi, Robbie, Robena,
Robertena, Robertina*

Roberto **B** (Italian, Portuguese,
Spanish) a form of Robert.

Robin **G** (English) robin. A form of
Roberta.
*Robann, Robbin, Robeen, Roben,
Robena, Robian, Robina, Robine,
Robinette, Robinia, Robinn, Robinta,
Robyn*

Robinette (English) a familiar form
of Robin.
Robernetta, Robinet, Robinett, Robinita

Robyn **G** (English) a form of Robin.
*Robbyn, Robbynn, Robyne, Robynn,
Robynne*

Rochelle **G** (French) large stone.
(Hebrew) a form of Rachel. See also
Shelley.
*Reshelle, Roch, Rocheal, Rochealle,
Rochel, Rochele, Rochell, Rochella,
Rochette, Rockelle, Roshele, Roshell,
Roshelle*

Rochely (Latin) goddess of the earth.

Rochi (Indian) light.

Rocio (Spanish) dewdrops.
Rocío

Roderica (German) famous ruler.
*Rica, Rika, Rodericka, Roderika,
Rodreicka, Rodricka, Rodrika*

Roderiga (Spanish) notable leader.

Rodnae (English) island clearing.
Rodna, Rodnetta, Rodnicka

Rodneisha (American) a
combination of Rodnae + Aisha.
*Rodesha, Rodisha, Rodishah, Rodnecia,
Rodnesha, Rodneshia, Rodneycia,
Rodneysha, Rodnisha*

Rodney **B** (English) island clearing.

Rogelia (Teutonic) beautiful one.

Rogelio **B** (Spanish) famous warrior.

Rohana (Hindi) sandalwood.
(American) a combination of Rose
+ Hannah.
Rochana, Rohena

Rohini (Hindi) woman.

Rohita (Indian) Brahma's daughter.

Roja (Spanish) red.

Roku (Japanese) emolument.

Rolanda (German) a form of Rolando.
*Ralna, Rolande, Rolando, Rolaunda,
Roleesha, Rolene, Rolinda, Rollande,
Rolonda*

Rolando **B** (German) famous
throughout the land.

Rolene (German) a form of Rolanda.
Rolaine, Rolena, Rolleen, Rollene

Roma (Latin) from Rome.
*Romai, Rome, Romeise, Romeka,
Romelle, Romesha, Rometta, Romia,
Romilda, Romilla, Romina, Romini,
Romma, Romonia*

Romaine (French) from Rome.
*Romana, Romanda, Romanelle,
Romania, Romanique, Romany,
Romayne, Romona, Romy*

Romanela (Latin) native of Rome.

Romelia (Hebrew) God's beloved or
preferred one.

Romola (Latin) Roman woman.

Rómula (Spanish) possessor of great strength.

Romy ☀ (French) a familiar form of Romaine. (English) a familiar form of Rosemary.
Romi, Romie

Rona (Scandinavian) a short form of Ronalda.
Rhona, Roana, Ronalda, Ronna, Ronnae, Ronnay, Ronne, Ronni, Ronsy

Ronaele (Greek) the name Eleanor spelled backwards.
Ronalee, Ronni, Ronnie, Ronny

Ronald ☐ (Scottish) a form of Reginald.

Ronda (Welsh) a form of Rhonda.
Rondai, Rondesia, Rondi, Rondie, Ronelle, Ronnette, Ronni, Ronnie, Ronny

Rondelle (French) short poem.
Rhondelle, Rondel, Ronndelle

Roneisha (American) a combination of Rhonda + Aisha.
Roneasha, Ronecia, Ronee, Roneeka, Roneesha, Roneice, Ronese, Ronesha, Roneshia, Ronesia, Ronessa, Ronessia, Ronichia, Ronicia, Roniesha, Ronisha, Ronneisha, Ronnesa, Ronnesha, Ronneshia, Ronni, Ronnie, Ronniesha, Ronny

Ronelle (Welsh) a form of Rhonda, Ronda.
Ranell, Ranelle, Ronel, Ronella, Ronielle, Ronnella, Ronnelle

Rong (Chinese) lotus; beautiful; elegant.

Ronisha (American) a form of Roneisha.
Ronise, Ronnise, Ronnisha, Ronnishia

Ronli (Hebrew) joyful.
Ronia, Ronice, Ronit, Ronlee, Ronlie, Ronni, Ronnie, Ronny

Ronnette (Welsh) a familiar form of Rhonda, Ronda.
Ronetta, Ronette, Ronit, Ronita, Ronnetta, Ronni, Ronnie, Ronny

Ronni (American) a familiar form of Veronica and names beginning with "Ron."
Rone, Ronee, Roni, Ronnee, Ronney

Ronnie, Ronny ☐ (American) forms of Ronni.

Roopa (Indian) blessed with beauty.

Roquelina (Latin) strong as a rock.

Rori (Irish) famous brilliance; famous ruler.
Rorie

Rory ☐ (Irish) a form of Rori.

Ros, Roz (English) short forms of Rosalind, Rosalyn.
Rozz, Rozzey, Rozzi, Rozzie, Rozzy

Rosa ☀ (Italian, Spanish) a form of Rose. History: Rosa Parks inspired the American Civil Rights movement by refusing to give up her bus seat to a white man in Montgomery, Alabama. See also Charo, Roza.

Rosa de Lima (Spanish) a form of Rosa.

Rosabel (French) beautiful rose
Rosabelia, Rosabella, Rosabelle, Rosebelle

Rosalba (Latin) white rose.
Rosalva, Roselba

Rosalía (Spanish) a combination of Rosa and Lía.

Rosalie (English) a form of Rosalind.
*Rosalea, Rosalee, Rosaleen, Rosaleigh,
Rosalene, Rosalia, Rosealee, Rosealie,
Roselee, Roseli, Roselia, Roselie,
Roseley, Rosely, Rosilee, Rosli, Rozali,
Rozália, Rozalie, Rozele*

Rosalín, Roselín (Spanish) a
combination of Rosa and Linda.

Rosalind (Spanish) fair rose.
*Ros, Rosalie, Rosalinda, Rosalinde,
Rosalyn, Rosalynd, Rosalynde, Roselind,
Roselyn, Rosie, Roz, Rozalind, Rozland*

Rosalinda (Spanish) a form of
Rosalind.
Rosalina

Rosalyn (Spanish) a form of
Rosalind.
*Ros, Rosaleen, Rosalin, Rosaline,
Rosalyne, Rosalynn, Rosalynne, Rosilyn,
Roslin, Roslyn, Roslyne, Roslynn, Roz,
Rozalyn, Rozlyn*

Rosamond (German) famous
guardian.
*Rosamund, Rosamunda, Rosemonde,
Rozamond*

Rosanna, Roseanna (English)
combinations of Rose + Anna.
*Ranna, Roanna, Rosana, Rosannah,
Roseana, Roseannah, Rosehanah,
Rosehannah, Rosie, Rossana, Rossanna,
Rozana, Rozanna*

Rosanne, Roseanne (English)
combinations of Rose + Ann.
*Roanne, Rosan, Rosann, Roseann, Rose
Ann, Rose Anne, Rossann, Rossanne,
Rozann, Rozanne*

Rosario **G** (Filipino, Spanish) rosary.
*Rosarah, Rosaria, Rosarie, Rosary,
Rosaura*

Rose (Latin) rose. See also Chalina,
Raisa, Raizel, Roza.
*Rada, Rasia, Rasine, Rois, Róise, Rosa,
Rosea, Rosella, Roselle, Roses, Rosetta,
Rosie, Rosina, Rosita, Rosse*

Roselani (Hawaiian) heavenly rose.

Roselyn (Spanish) a form of Rosalind.
*Roseleen, Roselene, Roselin, Roseline,
Roselyne, Roselynn, Roselynne*

Rosemarie (English) a combination
of Rose + Marie.
*Rosamaria, Rosamarie, Rosemari,
Rosemaria, Rose Marie*

Rosemary (English) a combination
of Rose + Mary.
Romi, Romy

Rosenda (German) excellent lady.

Rosetta (Italian) a form of Rose.
Roseta, Rosette

Roshan (Sanskrit) shining light.

Roshawna (American) a
combination of Rose + Shawna.
*Roshan, Roshana, Roshanda, Roshani,
Roshann, Roshanna, Roshanta,
Roshaun, Roshauna, Roshaunda,
Roshawn, Roshawnda, Roshawnna,
Roshona, Roshonda, Roshowna,
Roshunda*

Rosie (English) a familiar form of
Rosalind, Rosanna, Rose.
*Rosey, Rosi, Rosio, Rosse, Rosy, Rozsi,
Rozy*

Rosilda (German) horse-riding
warrior.

Rosina (English) a familiar form of
Rose.
*Rosena, Rosenah, Rosene, Rosheen,
Rozena, Rozina*

Rosinda (Teutonic) famous warrior.

Rosine (Latin) little rose.

Rosita (Spanish) a familiar form of
Rose.
Roseeta, Roseta, Rozeta, Rozita, Rozyte

Roslyn (Scottish) a form of Rossalyn.
Roslin, Roslynn, Rosslyn, Rosslynn

Rosmarí (Spanish) a combination of Rosa and María.

Rosmira (German) celebrated horse-riding warrior.

Ross ☒ (Latin) rose. (Scottish) peninsula. (French) red.

Rossalyn (Scottish) cape; promontory.
Roslyn, Rosselyn, Rosylin, Roszaliyn

Rosura (Latin) golden rose.

Rou (Chinese) soft; tender.

Rouble (Indian) money.

Rowan ☒ (English) tree with red berries. (Welsh) a form of Rowena.
Rowana

Rowena (Welsh) fair-haired. (English) famous friend. Literature: Ivanhoe's love interest in Sir Walter Scott's novel *Ivanhoe*.
Ranna, Ronni, Row, Rowan, Rowe, Roweena, Rowen, Rowina

Roxana, Roxanna (Persian) forms of Roxann.
Rocsana, Roxannah

Roxann, Roxanne (Persian) sunrise. Literature: Roxanne is the heroine of Edmond Rostand's play *Cyrano de Bergerac*.
Rocxann, Roxan, Roxana, Roxane, Roxanna, Roxianne, Roxy

Roxy (Persian) a familiar form of Roxann.
Roxi, Roxie

Royale (English) royal.
Royal, Royalene, Royalle, Roylee, Roylene, Ryal, Ryale

Royanna (English) queenly, royal.
Roya

Royce ☒ (English) child of Roy.

Roza (Slavic) a form of Rosa.
Roz, Rozalia, Roze, Rozel, Rozele, Rozell, Rozella, Rozelli, Rozia, Rozsa, Rozsi, Rozyte, Rozza, Rozzie

Rozene (Native American) rose blossom.
Rozena, Rozina, Rozine, Ruzena

Rozmin (Indian) rose.

Ruana (Hindi) stringed musical instrument.
Ruan, Ruon

Rubaina (Indian) bright.

Ruben ☒ (Hebrew) a form of Reuben (see Boys' Names).

Rubena (Hebrew) a form of Reubena.
Rubenia, Rubina, Rubine, Rubinia, Rubyn, Rubyna

Rubi (French) a form of Ruby.
Ruba, Rubbie, Rubee, Rubí, Rubia, Rubie

Ruby ☒ (French) precious stone.
Rubby, Rubetta, Rubette, Rubey, Rubi, Rubiann, Rubyann, Rubye

Ruchi (Hindi) one who wishes to please.

Ruchika (Indian) shining; beautiful; desirous.

Ruchira (Indian) saffron; tasty.

Ruchita (Indian) splendorous.

Rudecinda (Spanish) a form of Rosenda.

Rudee (German) famous wolf.
Rudeline, Rudell, Rudella, Rudi, Rudie, Rudina, Rudy

Rudra (Hindi) seeds of the rudraksha plant.

Rudrapriya (Indian) beloved of Rudra.

Rudy **B** (German) a form of Rudee.

Rue (German) famous. (French) street. (English) regretful; strong-scented herbs.
Ru, Ruey

Rufa (Latin) red-haired.

Ruffina (Italian) redhead.
Rufeena, Rufeine, Rufina, Ruphyna

Ruhani (Indian) spiritual; sacred, divine.

Ruhi (Indian) soul.

Ruhin (Indian) spiritual.

Rui (Japanese) affectionate.

Rujula (Indian) she who endows wealth; soft.

Rujuta (Indian) polite.

Ruka (Japanese) flower.

Rukan (Arabic) steady; confident.

Rukma (Indian) gold.

Rukmini (Indian) wife of Krishna.

Ruksana (Indian) brilliant.

Rula (Latin, English) ruler.

Rumi (Japanese) beautiful perch.

Rumiko (Japanese) child of Rumi.

Run (Chinese) moist; smooth, sleek.

Run zhun (Indian) sweet sound.

Runa (Norwegian) secret; flowing.
Runna

Ruo (Chinese) to seem like.

Rupa (Indian) silver.

Rupal (Indian) made of silver.

Rupali (Indian) beautiful, pretty.

Rupashi (Indian) beautiful.

Rupasi (Indian) beautiful lady.

Ruperta (Spanish) a form of Roberta.

Rupeshwari (Indian) the goddess of beauty.

Rupi (Indian) beauty.

Rupika (Indian) gold coin.

Rupinder **G** (Sanskrit) beautiful.

Ruqaya (Indian) name of the prophet's daughter.

Rure, Rurrie, Ruru (Japanese) emerald.

Ruri (Japanese) emerald.
Ruriko

Rusalka (Czech) wood nymph. (Russian) mermaid.

Rusham (Indian) peaceful.

Russhell (French) redhead; fox colored.
Rushell, Rushelle, Russellynn, Russhelle

Rusti (English) redhead.
Russet, Rustie, Rusty

Rute (Portuguese) a form of Ruth.

Ruth (Hebrew) friendship. Bible: daughter-in-law of Naomi.
Rutha, Ruthalma, Ruthe, Ruthella, Ruthetta, Ruthie, Ruthven

Ruthann (American) a combination of Ruth + Ann.
Ruthan, Ruthanna, Ruthannah, Ruthanne, Ruthina, Ruthine

Ruthie (Hebrew) a familiar form of Ruth.
Ruthey, Ruthi, Ruthy

Rutilda (German) strong because of her fame.

Rutuja (Indian) the queen of seasons.

Rutva (Indian) speech.

Ruwayda (Indian) walking gently.

Ruza (Czech) rose.
Ruzena, Ruzenka, Ruzha, Ruzsa

Ryan 🄱 (Irish) little ruler.
*Raiann, Raianne, Rhyann, Riana, Riane,
Ryana, Ryane, Ryanna, Ryanne, Rye,
Ryen, Ryenne*

Ryann 🄶 (Irish) a form of Ryan.

Ryba (Czech) fish.

Rylan 🄱 (English) land where rye is
grown.

Rylee 🄶 (Irish) valiant.
*Rye, Ryelee, Rylea, Ryleigh, Ryley, Rylie,
Rylina, Rylyn*

Ryleigh, Rylie (Irish) forms of
Rylee.
Ryelie, Ryli, Rylleigh, Ryllie

Ryley 🄱 (Irish) a form of Rylee.
Ryeley, Rylly, Ryly

Ryo (Japanese) dragon.
Ryoko

S

S 🄶 (American) an initial used as a
first name.

Saabira (Indian) patient.

Saachee (Indian) beloved.

Saachi (Indian) truth.

Saaliha (Indian) good; useful.

Saalima (Indian) safe.

Saamiya (Indian) elevated.

Saarah (Arabic) princess.

Saashi (Indian) moon.

Saatvika (Indian) calm.

Saba (Arabic) morning. (Greek) a
form of Sheba.
Sabaah, Sabah, Sabba, Sabbah

Sabana (Latin) from the open plain.

Sabelia (Spanish) a form of Sabina.

Sabi (Arabic) young girl.

Sabiha (Indian) beautiful.

Sabina (Latin) History: the Sabine
were a tribe in ancient Italy. See also
Bina.
*Sabeen, Sabena, Sabienne, Sabin,
Sabine, Sabinka, Sabinna, Sabiny,
Saby, Sabyne, Savina, Sebina, Sebinah*

Sabiya (Arabic) morning; eastern
wind.
Saba, Sabaya, Sabiyah

Sable (English) sable; sleek.
Sabel, Sabela, Sabella

Sabra (Hebrew) thorny cactus fruit.
(Arabic) resting. History: a name for
native-born Israelis, who were said
to be hard on the outside and soft
and sweet on the inside.
*Sabera, Sabira, Sabrah, Sabre,
Sabrea, Sabreah, Sabree, Sabreea,
Sabri, Sabria, Sabriah, Sabriya, Sebra*

Sabreena (English) a form of
Sabrina.
Sabreen, Sabrena, Sabrene

Sabrina 🄶 (Latin) boundary line.
(English) princess. (Hebrew) a
familiar form of Sabra. See also
Bree, Brina, Rena, Zabrina.
*Sabre, Sabreena, Sabrinas, Sabrinah,
Sabrine, Sabrinia, Sabrinna, Sabryna,
Sebree, Sebrina, Subrina*

Sabryna (English) a form of
Sabrina.
Sabrynna

Sacha **BG** (Russian) a form of Sasha.
Sache, Sachia

Sachee, Sachey, Sachy, Shashie
(Japanese) girl.

Sachi (Japanese) blessed; lucky.
Saatchi, Sachie, Sachiko

Sachita (Indian) wise.

Sachiye (Japanese) blessed
happiness.

Sachiyo (Japanese) she who
possesses happiness and knowledge
for a lifetime.

Sacnite (Mayan) white flower.

Sada (Japanese) chaste. (English) a
form of Sadie.
Sadá, Sadah, Sadako

Sadayo (Japanese) she who is
decisive throughout her life.

Sade **G** (Hebrew) a form of
Chadee, Sarah, Shardae, Sharday.
Sáde, Sadé, Sadea, Sadee, Shaday

Sadella (American) a combination of
Sade + Ella.
Sadelle, Sydel, Sydell, Sydella, Sydelle

Sadgata (Indian) she who moves in
the right direction.

Sadgati (Indian) liberation.

Sadguna (Indian) good virtues.

Sadhan (Indian) fulfillment.

Sadhana (Hindi) devoted.

Sadhna (Indian) worship.

Sadhvi (Indian) virtuous woman.

Sadie (Hebrew) a familiar form of
Sarah. See also Sada.
*Saddie, Sadee, Sadey, Sadi, Sadiey,
Sady, Sadye, Saide, Saidee, Saidey,
Saidi, Saidia, Saidie, Saidy, Sayde,
Saydee, Seidy*

Sadiqua (Indian) kindly.

Sadira (Persian) lotus tree. (Arabic)
star.
Sadra

Sadiya (Arabic) lucky, fortunate.
*Sadi, Sadia, Sadiah, Sadiyah,
Sadiyyah, Sadya*

Sadvita (Indian) combination.

Sadzi (Carrier) sunny disposition.

Saee (Indian) female friend.

Saeeda (Indian) priestly.

Saeko (Japanese) child of Sae.

Saffron (English) Botany: a plant with
purple or white flowers whose orange
stigmas are used as a spice.
Safron

Safiya (Arabic) pure; serene; best
friend.
Safa, Safeya, Saffa, Safia, Safiyah

Safo (Greek) she who sees with
clarity.

Sagara (Hindi) ocean.

Sagarika (Indian) wave.

Sage **BG** (English) wise. Botany: an
herb used as a seasoning.
Sagia, Saige, Salvia

Saguna (Indian) virtuous.

Sahana (Indian) patience.

Sahara (Arabic) desert; wilderness.
*Sahar, Saharah, Sahari, Saheer, Saher,
Sahira, Sahra, Sahrah*

Saheli (Indian) friend.

Sahiba (Indian) the lady.

Sahila (Indian) guide.

Sahima (Indian) snowed.

Sahithi (Indian) literature.

Sahla (Indian) smooth; soft ground; fluent.

Sahoj (Indian) strong.

Sai (Japanese) talented.
Saiko

Saida (Hebrew) a form of Sarah. (Arabic) happy; fortunate.
Saidah

Saige (English) a form of Sage.

Saima (Indian) the mother of flowers.

Saira (Hebrew) a form of Sara.
Sairah, Sairi

Saisha (Indian) God.

Sajala (Indian) cloud.

Sajani (Indian) beloved, well loved.

Sajili (Indian) decorated.

Sajni (Indian) beloved.

Sakae (Japanese) prosperity.

Sakaë (Japanese) prosperous.

Sakari (Hindi) sweet.
Sakkara

Sakaye (Japanese) prosper, flourish.

Sakeena (Indian) tranquility inspired by God.

Sakhi (Indian) friend.

Saki (Japanese) cloak; rice wine.

Sakiko (Japanese) child of Saki.

Sakshi (Indian) witness.

Sakti (Hindi) energy, power.

Saku (Japanese) remembrance of the Lord.

Sakuko (Japanese) child of Saku.

Sakuna (Native American) bird.

Sakura (Japanese) cherry blossom; wealthy; prosperous.

Sakurako (Japanese) child of Sakura.

Sala (Hindi) sala tree. Religion: the sacred tree under which Buddha died.

Salaberga (German) she who defends the sacrifice.

Salali (Cherokee) squirrel.

Salama (Arabic) peaceful. See also Zulima.

Salbatora (Spanish) savior.

Salena (French) a form of Salina.
Saleana, Saleen, Saleena, Salene, Salenna, Sallene

Saleta (French) location in the French Alps where there was a sighting of the Virgin Mary.

Salila (Indian) water.

Salima (Arabic) safe and sound; healthy.
Saleema, Salema, Salim, Salimah, Salma

Salina (French) solemn, dignified.
Salena, Salin, Salinah, Salinda, Saline

Salliann (English) a combination of Sally + Ann.
Sallian, Sallianne, Sallyann, Sally-Ann, Sallyanne, Sally-Anne

Sally G (English) princess. History: Sally Ride, an American astronaut, became the first U.S. woman in space.
Sal, Salaid, Sallee, Salletta, Sallette, Salley, Salli, Sallie

Salome (Hebrew) peaceful. History: Salome Alexandra was a ruler of ancient Judea. Bible: the niece of King Herod.
Saloma, Salomé, Salomey, Salomi

Saloni (Indian) beautiful.

Salud (Spanish) health.

Salvadora (Spanish) savior.

Salvatora (Italian) savior.

Salvia (Spanish) healthy; saved. (Latin) a form of Sage.
Sallvia, Salviana, Salviane, Salvina, Salvine

Salwa (Indian) quail; solace.

Sam B (Aramaic, Hebrew) a short form of Samantha.

Samaah (Indian) generosity.

Samala (Hebrew) asked of God.
Samale, Sammala

Samali (Indian) bouquet.

Samanta (Hebrew) a form of Samantha.
Samantah, Smanta

Samantha ☀ G (Aramaic) listener. (Hebrew) told by God.
Sam, Samana, Samanath, Samanatha, Samanitha, Samanithia, Samanta, Samanth, Samanthe, Samanthi, Samanthia, Samatha, Sami, Sammanth, Sammantha, Semantha, Simantha, Smantha, Symantha

Samapti, Sampatti (Indian) wealth.

Samara (Latin) elm-tree seed.
Saimara, Samaira, Samar, Samarah, Samari, Samaria, Samariah, Samarie, Samarra, Samarrea, Samary, Samera, Sameria, Samira, Sammar, Sammara, Samora

Samata (Indian) equality.

Samatha (Hebrew) a form of Samantha.
Sammatha

Sameeha (Indian) generous.

Sameeksha (Indian) abstract.

Sameena (Indian) happy.

Sameh (Hebrew) listener. (Arabic) forgiving.
Samaiya, Samaya

Samhita (Indian) a Vedic composition.

Sami B (Arabic) praised. (Hebrew) a short form of Samantha, Samuela.
Samia, Samiah, Samiha, Samina, Sammey, Sammi, Sammie, Sammijo, Sammy, Sammyjo, Samya, Samye

Samidha (Indian) an offering for a sacred fire.

Samika (Indian) peaceful.

Samiksha (Indian) close inspection, analysis.

Samira (Arabic) entertaining.
Samirah, Samire, Samiria, Samirra, Samyra

Samita (Indian) collected.

Sammy B (Arabic, Hebrew) a form of Sami.

Samone (Hebrew) a form of Simone.
Samoan, Samoane, Samon, Samona, Samoné, Samonia

Sampada (Indian) blessing.

Sampriti (Indian) attachment.

Samuel 🅱 (Hebrew) heard God; asked of God.

Samuela (Hebrew) a form of Samuel.
Samala, Samelia, Samella, Sami, Samielle, Samille, Sammile, Samuelle

Samuelle 🅖 (Hebrew) a form of Samuela.
Samuella

Samyuktheswari (Indian) a princess.

San (Chinese) three.

Sana (Arabic) mountaintop; splendid; brilliant.
Sanaa, Sanáa, Sanaah, Sane, Sanah

Sanako (Japanese) child of Sana.

Sananda (Indian) pleasure.

Sanaya (Indian) eminent.

Sanaye (Japanese) girl who grows quickly.

Sanchala (Indian) Sanskrit synonym for water.

Sanchali (Indian) movement.

Sanchaya, Sanchita, Sandhaya (Indian) collection.

Sancia (Spanish) holy, sacred.
Sanceska, Sancha, Sancharia, Sanchia, Sancie, Santsia, Sanzia

Sandeep 🅱 (Punjabi) enlightened.
Sandip

Sandhya (Indian) dusk; perfection.

Sandi (Greek) a familiar form of Sandra.
Sandee, Sandia, Sandie, Sandiey, Sandine, Sanndie

Sandra (Greek) defender of mankind. A short form of Cassandra. History: Sandra Day O'Connor was the first woman appointed to the U.S. Supreme Court. See also Zandra.
Sahndra, Sandi, Sandira, Sandrea, Sandria, Sandrica, Sandy, Sanndra, Saundra

Sandrea (Greek) a form of Sandra.
Sandreea, Sandreia, Sandrell, Sandria, Sanndria

Sandrica (Greek) a form of Sandra. See also Rica.
Sandricka, Sandrika

Sandrine (Greek) a form of Alexandra.
Sandreana, Sandrene, Sandrenna, Sandrianna, Sandrina

Sandy 🅖 (Greek) a familiar form of Cassandra, Sandra.
Sandya, Sandye

Sanemi (Indian) perfect.

Sang (Vietnamese) bird.

Sangeeta, Sangita (Indian) musical.

Sangeetha (Indian) music.

Sangria (Indian) music.

Sani (Indian) gift.

Sanika (Indian) flute.

Saniya (Indian) wisdom.

Sanjana (Indian) in harmony.

Sanjeevani, Sanjivani (Indian) immortality.

Sanjita (Indian) triumphant.

Sanjoli (Indian) period of twilight.

Sanjukta (Indian) connection.

Sanjula, Sanjushree (Indian) beautiful.

Sanne (Hebrew, Dutch) lily.
Sanea, Saneh, Sanna, Sanneen

Sannidhi (Indian) nearness.

Sanoja (Indian) eternal.

Sansita (Indian) praise.

Sanskriti (Indian) heritage.

Sanskruti (Indian) culture.

Santana **G** (Spanish) Saint Anne.
Santa, Santaniata, Santanna, Santanne, Santena, Santenna, Shantana

Santawana (Indian) consolation.

Santayani (Indian) of the evening.

Santina (Spanish) little saint.
Santinia

Santoshi (Indian) the name of a goddess.

Santushti (Indian) complete satisfaction.

Sanura (Swahili) kitten.
Sanora

Sanuye (Moquelumnan) red clouds at sunset.

Sanvali, Sanwari (Indian) dusky.

Sanya (Sanskrit) born on Saturday.
Saneiya, Sania, Sanyia

Sanyakta (Indian) joined, united.

Sanyu **BG** (Luganda) happiness.

Sanyukta (Indian) union.

Saparna (Indian) leafy.

Sapata (Native American) dancing bear.

Saphala (Indian) successful.

Sapna (Indian) dream.

Sapphira (Hebrew) a form of Sapphire.
Safira, Sapheria, Saphira, Saphyra, Sephira

Sapphire (Greek) blue gemstone.
Saffire, Saphire, Saphyre, Sapphira

Saqui (Mapuche) preferred one, chosen one; kind soul.

Sara **G** (Hebrew) a form of Sarah.
Saira, Sarae, Saralee, Sarra, Sera

Sarah ☆ **G** (Hebrew) princess. Bible: the wife of Abraham and mother of Isaac. See also Sadie, Saida, Sally, Saree, Sharai, Shari, Zara, Zarita.
Sahra, Sara, Saraha, Sarahann, Sarahi, Sarai, Sarann, Saray, Sarha, Sariah, Sarina, Sarita, Sarolta, Sarotte, Sarrah, Sasa, Sayra, Sorcha

Sarai, Saray (Hebrew) forms of Sarah.
Saraya

Sarakshi (Indian) good sight.

Sarala (Indian) simple, black tulsi (a plant).

Saralyn (American) a combination of Sarah + Lynn.
Saralena, Saraly, Saralynn

Sarama (Indian) wife of Bibhisan.

Saranya (Indian) surrendered.

Sarasa (Indian) swan.

Sarasi (Indian) jolly, happy.

Sarasvati, Saraswati (Indian) the goddess of learning.

Saravati (Indian) a river.

Sarayu (Indian) wind.

Saree (Arabic) noble. (Hebrew) a familiar form of Sarah.

Saree (Arabic) noble. (Hebrew) a familiar form of Sarah.
Sareeka, Sareka, Sari, Sarika, Sarka, Sarri, Sarrie, Sary

Sariah (Hebrew) forms of Sarah.
Saria, Sarie

Sarila (Turkish) waterfall.

Sarina (Hebrew) a familiar form of Sarah.
Sareen, Sareena, Saren, Sarena, Sarene, Sarenna, Sarin, Sarine, Sarinna, Sarinne

Sarita (Hebrew) a familiar form of Sarah.
Saretta, Sarette, Sarit, Saritia, Saritta

Sarjana (Indian) creative.

Sarla (Indian) straight-forward.

Saroj, Saroja (Indian) lotus.

Sarojini (Indian) in the lotus.

Sarolta (Hungarian) a form of Sarah.

Sarotte (French) a form of Sarah.

Sarrah (Hebrew) a form of Sarah.
Sarra

Saruchi (Indian) wonderful.

Sarupa (Indian) beautiful.

Saruprani (Indian) beautiful woman.

Saryu (Indian) the Sharayu River.

Sasa (Japanese) assistant. (Hungarian) a form of Sarah, Sasha.

Sasha ◨ (Russian) defender of mankind. See also Zasha.
Sacha, Sahsha, Sasa, Sascha, Saschae, Sashae, Sashah, Sashai, Sashana, Sashay, Sashea, Sashel, Sashenka, Sashey, Sashi, Sashia, Sashira, Sashsha, Sashya, Sasjara, Sauscha, Sausha, Shasha, Shashi, Shashia

Sasmita (Indian) always laughing.

Sasquia (Teutonic) she who carries a knife.

Sass (Irish) Saxon.
Sassie, Sassoon, Sassy

Satara (American) a combination of Sarah + Tara.
Sataria, Satarra, Sateriaa, Saterra, Saterria

Sati (Indian) wife of Shiva.

Satin (French) smooth, shiny.
Satinder

Satinka (Native American) sacred dancer.

Sato (Japanese) sugar.
Satu

Satoko (Japanese) child of Sato.

Satomi (Japanese) wise and beautiful girl.

Satoyo (Japanese) she who stays in her hometown for a lifetime.

Satsuki (Japanese) the fifth month.

Saturia (Latin) she who has it all.

Saturnina (Spanish) gift of Saturn.

Satvari (Indian) night.

Satvi (Indian) existence.

Satyaki (Indian) one who is truthful.

Satyarupa (Indian) truth.

Satyavati (Indian) one who speaks the truth.

Saudamini (Indian) lightning.

Saul ◧ (Hebrew) asked for, borrowed.

Saumyi (Indian) moonlight.

Saundra (English) a form of Sandra, Sondra.
Saundee, Saundi, Saundie, Saundy

Saura (Hindi) sun worshiper.

Savana, Savanna (Spanish) forms of Savannah.
Saveena, Savhana, Savhanna, Savina, Savine, Savona, Savonna

Savanah (Spanish) a form of Savannah.
Savhannah

Savannah ☆ **G** (Spanish) treeless plain.
Sahvannah, Savana, Savanah, Savanha, Savanna, Savannha, Savauna, Savonnah, Savonne, Sevan, Sevanah, Sevanh, Sevann, Sevanna, Svannah

Savarna (Indian) daughter of the ocean; wife of the sun.

Saveria (Teutonic) from the new house.

Savita (Indian) sun.

Savitashri (Indian) luster of the sun.

Savitri (Indian) mother.

Savon **B** (Spanish) a treeless plain.

Sawa (Japanese) swamp. (Moquelumnan) stone.

Sawda (Indian) proper name.

Sawini (Indian) a river.

Sawyer **B** (English) wood worker.
Sawyar, Sawyor

Sayantini (Indian) evening.

Sayde, Saydee (Hebrew) forms of Sadie.
Saydi, Saydia, Saydie, Saydy

Sayeeda (Indian) leader.

Sayeko (Japanese) blessed and helpful child.

Sayén (Mapuche) sweet, lovable, warm; openhearted woman.

Sayo (Japanese) born at night.

Sayoko (Japanese) child of Sayo.

Sayra (Hebrew) a form of Sarah.
Sayrah, Sayre, Sayri

Sayuri (Japanese) small; quick; lily.

Scarlett (English) bright red. Literature: Scarlett O'Hara is the heroine of Margaret Mitchell's novel *Gone with the Wind*.
Scarlet, Scarlette, Scarlotte, Skarlette

Schyler **G** (Dutch) sheltering.
Schuyla, Schuyler, Schuylia, Schylar

Scott **B** (English) from Scotland.

Scotti (Scottish) from Scotland.
Scota, Scotia, Scottie, Scotty

Se (Chinese) a musical instrument.

Sean **B** (Irish) a form of John.

Seana, Seanna (Irish) forms of Sean. See also Shauna, Shawna.
Seaana, Sean, Seane, Seann, Seannae, Seannah, Seannalisa, Seanté, Sianna, Sina

Sebastian **B** (Greek) venerable. (Latin) revered. (French) a form of Sebastian.

Sebastiane (Greek, Latin, French) a form of Sebastian.
Sebastene, Sebastia, Sebastian, Sebastiana, Sebastien, Sebastienne

Sebastien **B** (Greek, Latin, French) a form of Sebastian.

Seble (Ethiopian) autumn.

Sebrina (English) a form of Sabrina.
Sebrena, Sebrenna, Sebria, Sebriana

Secilia (Latin) a form of Cecilia.
Saselia, Sasilia, Sesilia, Sileas

Secunda (Latin) second.

Secundina (Latin) family's second daughter.

Seda (Armenian) forest voices.

Sedna (Eskimo) well-fed. Mythology: the goddess of sea animals.

Seelia (English) a form of Sheila.

Seema (Greek) sprout. (Afghan) sky; profile.
Seemah, Sima, Simah

Seemanti (Indian) parting line.

Seemantini (Indian) woman.

Seerat (Indian) inner beauty; fame.

Sefa (Swiss) a familiar form of Josefina.

Séfora (Hebrew) like a small bird.

Segismunda (German) victorious protector.

Segunda (Spanish) second-born.

Sei, Seiko (Japanese) force; truth.

Seika (Japanese) she who is famous for her songs.

Seiki (Japanese) star; beginning.

Seina (Basque) innocent.

Seirra (Irish) a form of Sierra.
Seiara, Seiarra, Seira, Seirria

Seki (Japanese) wonderful.
Seka

Sela (English) a short form of Selena.
Seeley, Selah

Selam (Ethiopian) peaceful.

Selda (German) a short form of Griselda. (Yiddish) a form of Zelda.
Seldah, Selde, Sellda, Selldah

Selena G (Greek) moon. Mythology: Selene was the goddess of the moon. See also Celena.
Saleena, Sela, Selana, Seleana, Seleena, Selen, Selenah, Selene, Séléné, Selenia, Selenna, Selina, Sena, Syleena, Sylena

Selene (Greek) a form of Selena.
Seleni, Selenie, Seleny

Selia (Latin) a short form of Cecilia.
Seel, Seil, Sela, Silia

Selima (Hebrew) peaceful.
Selema, Selemah, Šelimah

Selina (Greek) a form of Celina, Selena.
Selie, Selin, Selinda, Seline, Selinia, Selinka, Sellina, Selyna, Selyne, Selynne, Sylina

Selma (German) divine protector. (Irish) fair, just. (Scandinavian) divinely protected. (Arabic) secure. See also Zelma.
Sellma, Sellmah, Selmah

Selva (Latin) she who was born in the jungle.

Selvi (Indian) happy, prosperous daughter.

Sema (Turkish) heaven; divine omen.
Semaj

Semanti (Indian) a white rose.

Semele (Latin) once.

Seminaris, Semíramis (Assyrian) she who lives harmoniously with the doves.

Sempronia (Spanish) prudent and measured.

Sen BG (Japanese) Mythology: a magical forest elf that lives for thousands of years.

Senalda (Spanish) sign.
Sena, Senda, Senna

Seneca (Iroquois) a tribal name.
*Senaka, Seneka, Senequa, Senequae,
Senequai, Seneque*

Seni (Fijian) a form of Jane.

Senona (Spanish) lively.

Septima (Latin) seventh.

Sequoia (Cherokee) giant redwood
tree.
*Seqoiyia, Seqouyia, Seqoya, Sequoi,
Sequoiah, Sequora, Sequoya,
Sequoyah, Sikoya*

Serafina (Hebrew) burning; ardent.
Bible: seraphim are an order of
angels.
*Sarafina, Serafine, Seraphe, Seraphin,
Seraphina, Seraphine, Seraphita,
Serapia, Serofina*

Serena (Latin) peaceful. See also Rena.
*Sarina, Saryna, Seraina, Serana,
Sereen, Sereina, Seren, Serenah,
Serene, Serenea, Serenia, Serenna,
Serina, Serreana, Serrena, Serrenna*

Serenela (Spanish) a form of
Serena.

Serenity 🌱 (Latin) peaceful.
*Serenidy, Serenitee, Serenitey, Sereniti,
Serenitiy, Serinity, Serrennity*

Sergia (Greek) attendant.

Serilda (Greek) armed warrior woman.

Serina (Latin) a form of Serena.
*Sereena, Serin, Serine, Serreena, Serrin,
Serrina, Seryna*

Servanda (Latin) she who must be
saved and protected.

Servia (Latin) daughter of those who
serve the Lord.

Seth **B** (Hebrew) appointed.

Setsu (Japanese) fidelity.

Setsuko (Japanese) a form of Setsu.

Seva (Indian) worship.

Sevanda (Latin) she who deserves to
be saved and guarded.

Sevati (Indian) white rose.

Severa (Spanish) severe.

Severina (Italian, Portuguese, Croatian,
German, Ancient Roman) severe.

Sevilla (Spanish) from Seville.
Seville

Sevita (Indian) cherished.

Sha (Chinese) a type of grass.

Shaadiya (Indian) singer.

Shaba (Spanish) rose.
Shabana, Shabina

Shabab (Indian) beauty.

Shabalini (Indian) mossy.

Shabari (Indian) a tribal devotee of
Lord Rama.

Shabnam, Shabnum (Indian) dew.

Shachi (Indian) intelligence.

Shada (Native American) pelican.
*Shadae, Shadea, Shadeana, Shadee,
Shadi, Shadia, Shadiah, Shadie,
Shadiya, Shaida*

Shaday (American) a form of Sade.
*Shadai, Shadaia, Shadaya, Shadayna,
Shadei, Shadeziah, Shaiday*

Shadrika (American) a combination
of the prefix Sha + Rika.
*Shadreeka, Shadreka, Shadrica,
Shadricka, Shadrieka*

Shae **G** (Irish) a form of Shea
Shaenel, Shaeya, Shai, Shaia

Shaelee (Irish) a form of Shea.
Shaeleigh, Shaeley, Shaelie, Shaely

Shaelyn (Irish) a form of Shea.
*Shael, Shaelaine, Shaelan, Shaelanie,
Shaelanna, Shaeleen, Shaelene,
Shaelin, Shaeline, Shaelyne, Shaelynn,
Shae-Lynn, Shaelynne*

Shafira (Swahili) distinguished.
Shaffira

Shagufta (Indian) flowering.

Shagun (Indian) auspicious moment.

Shahar (Arabic) moonlit.
Shahara

Shaheda (Indian) whiteness.

Shahina (Arabic) falcon.
Shaheen, Shaheena, Shahi, Shahin

Shahla (Afghani) beautiful eyes.
Shaila, Shailah, Shalah

Shahzeela (Indian) beautiful.

Shaianne (Cheyenne) a form of
Cheyenne.
*Shaeen, Shaeine, Shaian, Shaiana,
Shaiandra, Shaiane, Shaiann, Shaianna*

Shaila (Latin) a form of Sheila.
*Shaela, Shaelea, Shaeyla, Shailah,
Shailee, Shailey, Shaili, Shailie, Shailla,
Shaily, Shailyn, Shailynn*

Shaiming (Chinese) sunshine.

Shaina ☐ (Yiddish) beautiful.
*Shaena, Shainah, Shaine, Shainna,
Shajna, Shanie, Shayna, Shayndel,
Sheina, Sheindel*

Shaista (Indian) well behaved.

Shaivi (Indian) prosperity.

Shajuana (American) a combination
of the prefix Sha + Juanita. See also
Shawanna.
*Shajuan, Shajuanda, Shajuanita,
Shajuanna, Shajuanza*

Shaka ☐ (Hindi) a form of Shakti.
A short form of names beginning
with "Shak. " See also Chaka.
Shakah, Shakha

Shakarah (American) a combi-
nation of the prefix Sha + Kara.
*Shacara, Shacari, Shaccara, Shaka,
Shakari, Shakkara, Shikara*

Shakayla (Arabic) a form of Shakila.
Shakaela, Shakail, Shakaila, Shakala

Shakeel (Indian) handsome.

Shakeena (American) a combi-
nation of the prefix Sha + Keena.
*Shaka, Shakeina, Shakeyna, Shakina,
Shakyna*

Shakeita (American) a combination
of the prefix Sha + Keita. See also
Shaqueita.
*Shaka, Shakeeta, Shakeitha, Shakeithia,
Shaketa, Shaketha, Shakethia, Shaketia,
Shakita, Shakitra, Sheketa, Shekita,
Shikita, Shikitha*

Shakera (Arabic) a form of Shakira.
*Chakeria, Shakeira, Shakeirra, Shakerah,
Shakeria, Shakeriah, Shakeriay, Shakerra,
Shakerri, Shakerria, Shakerya, Shakeryia,
Shakeyra*

Shakia (American) a combination of
the prefix Sha + Kia.
*Shakeeia, Shakeeyah, Shakeia,
Shakeya, Shakiya, Shekeia, Shekia,
Shekiah, Shikia*

Shakila (Arabic) pretty.
*Chakila, Shaka, Shakayla, Shakeela,
Shakeena, Shakela, Shakelah, Shakilah,
Shakyla, Shekila, Shekilla, Shikeela*

Shakira (Arabic) thankful.
*Shaakira, Shacora, Shaka, Shakeera,
Shakeerah, Shakeeria, Shakera,
Shakiera, Shakierra, Shakir, Shakirah,
Shakirat, Shakirea, Shakirra, Shakora,
Shakuria, Shakyra, Shaquira, Shekiera,
Shekira, Shikira*

Shakti (Hindi) energy, power.
Religion: a form of the Hindu
goddess Devi.
Sakti, Shaka, Sita

Shakuntala (Indian) the wife of
Dushyant.

Shakyra (Arabic) a form of Shakira.
Shakyria

Shalaka (Indian) another name for
the goddess Parvati.

Shalalu (Indian) perfume.

Shalana (American) a combination
of the prefix Sha + Lana.
*Shalaana, Shalain, Shalaina, Shalaine,
Shaland, Shalanda, Shalane, Shalann,
Shalaun, Shalauna, Shalayna,
Shalayne, Shalaynna, Shallan, Shelan,
Shelanda*

Shaleah (American) a combination
of the prefix Sha + Leah.
*Shalea, Shalee, Shaleea, Shalia,
Shaliah*

Shaleisha (American) a combination
of the prefix Sha + Aisha.
Shalesha, Shalesia, Shalicia, Shalisha

Shalena (American) a combination
of the prefix Sha + Lena.
*Shaleana, Shaleen, Shaleena, Shalen,
Shálena, Shalene, Shalené, Shalenna,
Shalina, Shalinda, Shaline, Shalini,
Shalinna, Shelayna, Shelayne, Shelena*

Shalika (Indian) flute.

Shalisa (American) a combination of
the prefix Sha + Lisa.
*Shalesa, Shalese, Shalessa, Shalice,
Shalicia, Shaliece, Shalise, Shalisha,
Shalishea, Shalisia, Shalissa, Shalisse,
Shalyce, Shalys, Shalyse*

Shalita (American) a combination of
the prefix Sha + Lita.
Shaleta, Shaletta, Shalida, Shalitta

Shalona (American) a combination
of the prefix Sha + Lona.
Shalon, Shalone, Shálonna, Shalonne

Shalonda (American) a combination
of the prefix Sha + Ondine.
*Shalonde, Shalondine, Shalondra,
Shalondria*

Shalyn (American) a combination of
the prefix Sha + Lynn.
*Shalin, Shalina, Shalinda, Shaline,
Shalyna, Shalynda, Shalyne, Shalynn,
Shalynne*

Shamara (Arabic) ready for battle.
*Shamar, Shamarah, Shamare,
Shamarea, Shamaree, Shamari,
Shamaria, Shamariah, Shamarra,
Shamarri, Shammara, Shamora,
Shamori, Shamorra, Shamorria,
Shamorriah*

Shambari (Indian) illusion.

Shambhukanta (Indian) wife of
Shambhu.

Shameena (Indian) beautiful.

Shameka (American) a combination
of the prefix Sha + Meka.
*Shameaka, Shameakah, Shameca,
Shamecca, Shamecha, Shamecia,
Shameika, Shameke, Shamekia*

Shamika (American) a combination
of the prefix Sha + Mika.
*Shameeca, Shameeka, Shamica,
Shamicia, Shamicka, Shamieka,
Shamikia*

Shamim (Indian) fire.

Shamira (Hebrew) precious stone.
Shamir, Shamiran, Shamiria, Shamyra

Shamita (Indian) peacemaker.

Shamitha (Indian) she who is calm
and disciplined.

Shamiya (American) a combination of the prefix Sha + Mia.
Shamea, Shamia, Shamiah, Shamiyah, Shamyia, Shamyiah, Shamyne

Shampa (Indian) lightning.

Shana (Hebrew) a form of Shane. (Irish) a form of Jane.
Shaana, Shan, Shanae, Shanda, Shandi, Shane, Shania, Shanna, Shannah, Shauna, Shawna

Shanae (Irish) a form of Shana.
Shanay, Shanea

Shanda (American) a form of Chanda, Shana.
Shandae, Shandah, Shandra, Shannda

Shandi (English) a familiar form of Shana.
Shandee, Shandeigh, Shandey, Shandice, Shandie

Shandra (American) a form of Shanda. See also Chandra.
Shandrea, Shandreka, Shandri, Shandria, Shandriah, Shandrice, Shandrie, Shandry

Shane ☒ (Irish) God is gracious.
Shanea, Shaneah, Shanee, Shanée, Shanie

Shaneisha (American) a combination of the prefix Sha + Aisha.
Shanesha, Shaneshia, Shanessa, Shanisha, Shanissa

Shaneka (American) a form of Shanika.
Shanecka, Shaneeka, Shaneekah, Shaneequa, Shaneeque, Shaneika, Shaneikah, Shanekia, Shanequa, Shaneyka, Shonneka

Shanel, Shanell, Shanelle (American) forms of Chanel.
Schanel, Schanell, Shanella, Shanelly, Shannel, Shannell, Shannelle, Shenel, Shenela, Shenell, Shenelle, Shenelly, Shinelle, Shonelle, Shynelle

Shaneta (American) a combination of the prefix Sha + Neta.
Seanette, Shaneeta, Shanetha, Shanethis, Shanetta, Shanette, Shineta, Shonetta

Shang (Chinese) esteem.

Shani (Swahili) a form of Shany.

Shania (American) a form of Shana
Shanasia, Shanaya, Shaniah, Shaniya, Shanya, Shenia

Shanice (American) a form of Janice. See also Chanise.
Chenise, Shanece, Shaneese, Shaneice, Shanese, Shanicea, Shaniece, Shanise, Shanneice, Shannice, Shanyce, Sheneice

Shanida (American) a combination of the prefix Sha + Ida.
Shaneeda, Shannida

Shanika (American) a combination of the prefix Sha + Nika.
Shaneka, Shanica, Shanicca, Shanicka, Shanieka, Shanike, Shanikia, Shanikka, Shanikqua, Shanikwa, Shaniqua, Shenika, Shineeca, Shonnika

Shaniqua (American) a form of Shanika.
Shaniqa, Shaniquah, Shanique, Shaniquia, Shaniquwa, Shaniqwa, Shenequa, Sheniqua, Shinequa, Shiniqua

Shanise (American) a form of Shanice.
Shanisa, Shanisha, Shanisia, Shanissa, Shanisse, Shineese

Shanita (American) a combination of the prefix Sha + Nita.
Shanitha, Shanitra, Shanitta, Shinita

Shankari (Indian) the wife of Lord Shiva.

Shankhamala (Indian) a fairytale princess.

Shanley G (Irish) hero's child.
Shanlee, Shanleigh, Shanlie, Shanly

Shanna (Irish) a form of Shana, Shannon.
Shanea, Shannah, Shannea

Shannen (Irish) a form of Shannon.
Shanen, Shanena, Shanene

Shannon G (Irish) small and wise.
Shanan, Shanadoah, Shann, Shanna, Shannan, Shanneen, Shannen, Shannie, Shannin, Shannyn, Shanon

Shansa (Indian) praise.

Shanta, Shante (French) forms of Chantal.
Shantai, Shantay, Shantaya, Shantaye, Shanté, Shantea, Shantee, Shantée, Shanteia

Shantae G (French) a form of Chantal.

Shantal (American) a form of Shantel.
Shantall, Shontal

Shantana (American) a form of Santana.
Shantan, Shantanae, Shantanell, Shantanickia, Shantanika, Shantanna

Shantara (American) a combination of the prefix Sha + Tara.
Shantaria, Shantarra, Shantera, Shanteria, Shanterra, Shantira, Shontara, Shuntara

Shanteca (American) a combination of the prefix Sha + Teca.
Shantecca, Shanteka, Shantika, Shantikia

Shantel, Shantell G (American) song.
Seantelle, Shanntell, Shanta, Shantal, Shantae, Shantale, Shante, Shanteal, Shanteil, Shantele, Shantella, Shantelle, Shantrell, Shantyl, Shantyle, Shauntel, Shauntell, Shauntelle, Shauntrel,

Shauntrell, Shauntrella, Shentel, Shentelle, Shontal, Shontalla, Shontalle, Shontel, Shontelle

Shanteria (American) a form of Shantara.
Shanterica, Shanterria, Shanterrie, Shantieria, Shantirea, Shonteria

Shantesa (American) a combination of the prefix Sha + Tess.
Shantese, Shantice, Shantise, Shantisha, Shontecia, Shontessia

Shantia (American) a combination of the prefix Sha + Tia.
Shanteya, Shanti, Shantida, Shantie, Shaunteya, Shauntia, Shontia

Shantille (American) a form of Chantilly.
Shanteil, Shantil, Shantilli, Shantillie, Shantilly, Shantyl, Shantyle

Shantina (American) a combination of the prefix Sha + Tina.
Shanteena, Shontina

Shantora (American) a combination of the prefix Sha + Tory.
Shantoia, Shantori, Shantoria, Shantory, Shantorya, Shantoya, Shanttoria

Shantrice (American) a combination of the prefix Sha + Trice. See also Chantrice.
Shantrece, Shantrecia, Shantreece, Shantreese, Shantrese, Shantress, Shantrezia, Shantricia, Shantriece, Shantris, Shantrisse, Shontrice

Shany (Swahili) marvelous, wonderful.
Shaney, Shannai, Shannea, Shanni, Shannia, Shannie, Shanny, Shanya

Shao (Chinese) beautiful springtime.

Shappa (Native American) red thunder.

Shaquanda (American) a combination of the prefix Sha + Wanda.
Shaquan, Shaquana, Shaquand, Shaquandey, Shaquandra, Shaquandria, Shaquanera, Shaquani, Shaquania, Shaquanna, Shaquanta, Shaquantae, Shaquantay, Shaquante, Shaquantia, Shaquona, Shaquonda, Shaquondra, Shaquondria

Shaqueita, Shaquita (American) forms of Shakeita.
Shaqueta, Shaquetta, Shaquette, Shaquitta, Shequida, Shequita, Shequittia

Shaquila, Shaquilla (American) forms of Shakila.
Shaquail, Shaquia, Shaquil, Shaquilah, Shaquile, Shaquill, Shaquillah, Shaquille, Shaquillia, Shequela, Shequele, Shequila, Shquiyla

Shaquille ■ (American) a form of Shaquila.

Shaquira (American) a form of Shakira.
Shaquirah, Shaquire, Shaquirra, Shaqura, Shaqurah, Shaquri

Shara (Hebrew) a short form of Sharon.
Shaara, Sharah, Sharal, Sharala, Sharalee, Sharlyn, Sharlynn, Sharra, Sharrah

Sharadini (Indian) autumn.

Sharai (Hebrew) princess. See also Sharon.
Sharae, Sharaé, Sharah, Sharaiah, Sharay, Sharaya, Sharayah

Sharan (Hindi) protector.
Sharaine, Sharanda, Sharanjeet

Shardae, Sharday (Punjabi) charity. (Yoruba) honored by royalty. (Arabic) runaway. A form of Chardae.
Sade, Shadae, Sharda, Shar-Dae, Shardai, Shar-Day, Sharde, Shardea, Shardee, Shardée, Shardei, Shardeia, Shardey

Sharee (English) a form of Shari.
Shareen, Shareena, Sharine

Shareefa (Indian) noble.

Shari (French) beloved, dearest. (Hungarian) a form of Sarah. See also Sharita, Sheree, Sherry.
Shara, Share, Sharee, Sharia, Shariah, Sharian, Shariann, Sharianne, Sharie, Sharra, Sharree, Sharri, Sharrie, Sharry, Shary

Sharice (French) a form of Cherice.
Shareese, Sharesse, Sharese, Sharica, Sharicka, Shariece, Sharis, Sharise, Sharish, Shariss, Sharissa, Sharisse, Sharyse

Sharik (African) child of God.

Sharini (Indian) earth.

Sharissa (American) a form of Sharice.
Sharesa, Saressia, Sharisa, Sharisha, Shereeza, Shericia, Sherisa, Sherissa

Sharita (French) a familiar form of Shari. (American) a form of Charity. See also Sherita.
Shareeta, Sharrita

Sharla (French) a short form of Sharlene, Sharlotte.

Sharlene (French) little and strong.
Scharlane, Scharlene, Shar, Sharla, Sharlaina, Sharlaine, Sharlane, Sharlanna, Sharlee, Sharleen, Sharleine, Sharlena, Sharleyne, Sharline, Sharlyn, Sharlyne, Sharlynn, Sharlynne, Sherlean, Sherleen, Sherlene, Sherline

Sharlotte (American) a form of Charlotte.
Sharlet, Sharlett, Sharlott, Sharlotta

Sharma (American) a short form of Sharmaine.
Sharmae, Sharme

Sharmaine (American) a form of Charmaine.
Sharma, Sharmain, Sharman, Sharmane, Sharmanta, Sharmayne, Sharmeen, Sharmene, Sharmese, Sharmin, Sharmine, Sharmon, Sharmyn

Sharmila (Indian) shy.

Sharmistha (Indian) wife of Yayati.

Sharna (Hebrew) a form of Sharon.
Sharnae, Sharnay, Sharne, Sharnea, Sharnease, Sharnee, Sharneese, Sharnell, Sharnelle, Sharnese, Sharnett, Sharnetta, Sharnise

Sharon **G** (Hebrew) desert plain. A form of Sharai.
Shaaron, Shara, Sharai, Sharan, Shareen, Sharen, Shari, Sharin, Sharna, Sharonda, Sharone, Sharran, Sharren, Sharrin, Sharron, Sharrona, Sharyn, Sharyon, Sheren, Sheron, Sherryn

Sharonda (Hebrew) a form of Sharon.
Sharronda, Sheronda, Sherrhonda

Sharrona (Hebrew) a form of Sharon.
Sharona, Sharone, Sharonia, Sharonna, Sharony, Sharronne, Sheron, Sherona, Sheronna, Sherron, Sherronna, Sherronne, Shirona

Sharvari (Indian) twilight.

Shashibala (Indian) a girl with a round face.

Shashikala (Indian) phases of the moon.

Shashini (Indian) moon.

Shashiprabha (Indian) moonlight.

Shashirekha (Indian) moon ray.

Shaswati (Indian) eternal.

Shatara (Hindi) umbrella. (Arabic) good; industrious. (American) a combination of Sharon + Tara.
Shatarea, Shatari, Shataria, Shatarra, Shataura, Shateira, Shatera, Shaterah,
Shateria, Shaterra, Shaterri, Shaterria, Shatherian, Shatierra, Shatiria

Shatha (Indian) aromatic.

Shatoria (American) a combination of the prefix Sha + Tory.
Shatora, Shatorea, Shatori, Shatorri, Shatorria, Shatory, Shatorya, Shatoya

Shaun **B** (Hebrew, Irish) God is gracious.

Shauna (Hebrew) a form of Shaun. (Irish) a form of Shana. See also Seana, Shona.
Shaun, Shaunah, Shaunda, Shaune, Shaunee, Shauneen, Shaunelle, Shaunette, Shauni, Shaunice, Shaunicy, Shaunie, Shaunika, Shaunisha, Shaunna, Shaunnea, Shaunta, Shaunua, Shaunya

Shaunda (Irish) a form of Shauna. See also Shanda, Shawnda, Shonda.
Shaundal, Shaundala, Shaundel, Shaundela, Shaundell, Shaundelle, Shaundra, Shaundrea, Shaundree, Shaundria, Shaundrice

Shaunta (Irish) a form of Shauna. See also Shawnta, Shonta.
Schunta, Shauntae, Shauntay, Shaunte, Shauntea, Shauntee, Shauntée, Shaunteena, Shauntei, Shauntia, Shauntier, Shauntrel, Shauntrell, Shauntrella

Shavon **G** (American) a form of Shavonne.
Schavon, Schevon, Shavan, Shavana, Shavaun, Shavona, Shavonda, Shavone, Shavonia, Shivon

Shavonne (American) a combination of the prefix Sha + Yvonne. See also Siobhan.
Shavanna, Shavon, Shavondra, Shavonn, Shavonna, Shavonni, Shavonnia, Shavonnie, Shavontae, Shavonte, Shavonté, Shavoun, Shivaun, Shivawn, Shivonne, Shyvon, Shyvonne

Shawanna (American) a combination of the prefix Sha + Wanda. See also Shajuana, Shawna.
Shawan, Shawana, Shawanda, Shawante, Shiwani

Shawn 🅱 (Hebrew, Irish) God is gracious.

Shawna (Hebrew) a form of Shawn. (Irish) a form of Jane. A form of Shana, Shauna. See also Seana, Shona.
Sawna, Shaw, Shawn, Shawnae, Shawnai, Shawnea, Shawnee, Shawneen, Shawneena, Shawnell, Shawnette, Shawnna, Shawnra, Shawnta, Sheona, Siân, Siana, Sianna

Shawnda (Irish) a form of Shawna. See also Shanda, Shaunda, Shonda.
Shawndal, Shawndala, Shawndan, Shawndel, Shawndra, Shawndrea, Shawndree, Shawndreel, Shawndrell, Shawndria

Shawnee (Irish) a form of Shawna.
Shawne, Shawneea, Shawney, Shawni, Shawnie

Shawnika (American) a combination of Shawna + Nika.
Shawnaka, Shawnequa, Shawneika, Shawnicka

Shawnta 🅖 (Irish) a form of Shawna. See also Shaunta, Shonta.
Shawntae, Shawntay, Shawnte, Shawnté, Shawntee, Shawntell, Shawntelle, Shawnteria, Shawntia, Shawntil, Shawntile, Shawntill, Shawntille, Shawntina, Shawntish, Shawntrese, Shawntriece

Shay 🅱🅖 (Irish) a form of Shea.
Shaya, Shayah, Shayda, Shayha, Shayia, Shayla, Shey, Sheye

Shaye (Irish) a form of Shay.

Shayla (Irish) a form of Shay.
Shaylagh, Shaylah, Shaylain, Shaylan, Shaylea, Shayleah, Shaylla, Shaylyn, Sheyla

Shaylee (Irish) a form of Shea.
Shaylei, Shayleigh, Shayley, Shayli, Shaylie, Shayly, Shealy

Shaylyn (Irish) a form of Shea.
Shaylin, Shaylina, Shaylinn, Shaylynn, Shaylynne, Shealyn, Sheylyn

Shayna (Hebrew) beautiful.
Shaynae, Shaynah, Shayne, Shaynee, Shayney, Shayni, Shaynie, Shaynna, Shaynne, Shayny, Sheana, Sheanna

Shayne 🅱 (Hebrew) a form of Shayna.

Shea 🅖 (Irish) fairy palace.
Shae, Shay, Shaylee, Shaylyn, Shealy, Shaelee, Shaelyn, Shealyn, Sheann, Sheannon, Sheanta, Sheaon, Shearra, Sheatara, Sheaunna, Sheavon

Sheba (Hebrew) a short form of Bathsheba. Geography: an ancient country of south Arabia.
Saba, Sabah, Shebah, Sheeba

Sheena (Hebrew) God is gracious. (Irish) a form of Jane.
Sheenagh, Sheenah, Sheenan, Sheeneal, Sheenika, Sheenna, Sheina, Shena, Shiona

Sheetal (Indian) cool.

Shefali (Indian) fragrant.

Shefalika (Indian) a flower.

Shehla (Indian) dark brown, almost black.

Sheila (Latin) blind. (Irish) a form of Cecelia. See also Cheyla, Zelizi.
Seelia, Seila, Selia, Shaila, Sheela, Sheelagh, Sheelah, Sheilagh, Sheilah, Sheileen, Sheiletta, Sheilia, Sheillynn, Sheilya, Shela, Shelagh, Shelah, Shelia, Shiela, Shila, Shilah, Shilea, Shyla

Shejali (Indian) a fruit.

Shelbi, Shelbie (English) forms of Shelby.
Shelbbie, Shellbi, Shelbbie

Shelby **G** (English) ledge estate.
Chelby, Schelby, Shel, Shelbe, Shelbee, Shelbey, Shelbi, Shelbie, Shelbye, Shellby

Sheldon **B** (English) farm on the ledge.
Sheldina, Sheldine, Sheldrina, Sheldyn, Shelton

Shelee (English) a form of Shelley.
Shelee, Sheleen, Shelena, Sheley, Sheli, Shelia, Shelina, Shelinda, Shelita

Shelisa (American) a combination of Shelley + Lisa.
Sheleza, Shelica, Shelicia, Shelise, Shelisse, Sheliza

Shelley, Shelly **G** (English) meadow on the ledge. (French) familiar forms of Michelle. See also Rochelle.
Shelee, Shell, Shella, Shellaine, Shellana, Shellany, Shellee, Shellene, Shelli, Shellian, Shelliann, Shellie, Shellina

Shelsea (American) a form of Chelsea.
Shellsea, Shellsey, Shelsey, Shelsie, Shelsy

Shelton **B** (English) a form of Sheldon.

Shen (Chinese) spiritual, deep-thinking.

Shena (Irish) a form of Sheena.
Shenada, Shenae, Shenah, Shenay, Shenda, Shene, Shenea, Sheneda, Shenee, Sheneena, Shenica, Shenika, Shenina, Sheniqua, Shenita, Shenna, Shennae, Shennah, Shenoa

Sheng (Chinese) holy, sage.

Shera (Aramaic) light.
Sheera, Sheerah, Sherae, Sherah, Sheralee, Sheralle, Sheralyn, Sheralynn, Sheralynne, Sheray, Sheraya

Sheree (French) beloved, dearest.
Scherie, Sheeree, Shere, Shereé, Sherrelle, Shereen, Shereena

Sherelle (French) a form of Cherelle, Sheryl.
Sherel, Sherell, Sheriel, Sherrel, Sherrell, Sherrelle, Shirelle

Sheri, Sherri (French) forms of Sherry.
Sheria, Sheriah, Sherie, Sherrie

Sherian (American) a combination of Sheri + Ann.
Sherianne, Sherrina

Sherice (French) a form of Cherice.
Scherise, Sherece, Shereece, Sherees, Shereese, Sherese, Shericia, Sherise, Sherisse, Sherrish, Sherryse, Sheryce

Sheridan **G** (Irish) wild.
Sherida, Sheridane, Sherideen, Sheriden, Sheridian, Sheridon, Sherridan, Sherridon

Sherika (Punjabi) relative. (Arabic) easterner.
Shereka, Sherica, Shericka, Sherrica, Sherricka, Sherrika

Sherissa (French) a form of Sherry, Sheryl.
Shereeza, Sheresa, Shericia, Sherrish

Sherita (French) a form of Sherry, Sheryl. See also Sharita.
Shereta, Sheretta, Sherette, Sherrita

Sherleen (French, English) a form of Sheryl, Shirley.
Sherileen, Sherlene, Sherlin, Sherlina, Sherline, Sherlyn, Sherlyne, Sherlynne, Shirlena, Shirlene, Shirlina, Shirlyn

Sherry 🄶 (French) beloved, dearest. A familiar form of Sheryl. See also Sheree.
Sherey, Sheri, Sherissa, Sherrey, Sherri, Sherria, Sherriah, Sherrie, Sherye, Sheryy

Sheryl (French) beloved. A familiar form of Shirley. See also Sherry.
Sharel, Sharil, Sharilyn, Sharyl, Sharyll, Sheral, Sherell, Sheriel, Sheril, Sherill, Sherily, Sherilyn, Sherissa, Sherita, Sherleen, Sherral, Sherrelle, Sherril, Sherrill, Sherryl, Sherylly

Sherylyn (American) a combination of Sheryl + Lynn. See also Cherilyn.
Sharolin, Sharolyn, Sharyl-Lynn, Sheralyn, Sherilyn, Sherilynn, Sherilynne, Sherralyn, Sherralynn, Sherrilyn, Sherrilynn, Sherrilynne, Sherrylyn, Sherryn, Sherylanne

Shevalini (Indian) a river.

Shevanti (Indian) a flower.

Shevonne (American) a combination of the prefix She + Yvonne.
Shevaun, Shevon, Shevonda, Shevone

Sheyenne (Cheyenne) a form of Cheyenne. See also Shyann, Shyanne.
Shayhan, Sheyan, Sheyane, Sheyann, Sheyanna, Sheyannah, Sheyanne, Sheyen, Sheyene, Shiante, Shyanne

Shezreen (Indian) particle of gold.

Shianne (Cheyenne) a form of Cheyenne.
She, Shian, Shiana, Shianah, Shianda, Shiane, Shiann, Shianna, Shiannah, Shiany, Shieana, Shieann, Shieanne, Shiena, Shiene, Shienna

Shichi (Indian) glow.

Shielawatti (Indian) river.

Shiesta (Indian) modest; disciplined; cultured.

Shifa (Indian) friend; truthful.

Shifra (Hebrew) beautiful.
Schifra, Shifrah

Shigeko (Japanese) luxuriant child.

Shigemi (Japanese) luxuriant truth.

Shiho (Japanese) to maintain original intention.

Shihobu (Japanese) perseverance.

Shika (Japanese) gentle deer.
Shi, Shikah, Shikha

Shikhi (Indian) peacock; flame.

Shilavati (Indian) a river.

Shilo (Hebrew) God's gift. Bible: a sanctuary for the Israelites where the Ark of the Covenant was kept.
Shiloh

Shilpita (Indian) well proportioned.

Shin (Korean) brightness.

Shina (Japanese) virtuous, good; wealthy. (Chinese) a form of China.
Shinae, Shinay, Shine, Shinna

Shing (Chinese) victory.

Shinjini (Indian) ankle bells.

Shin-Mu (Chinese) mother of perfect intelligence; China's holy virgin.

Shino (Japanese) bamboo stalk.

Shiomi (Japanese) the beautiful tide.

Shione (Japanese) the noise made by the tide.

Shiori (Japanese) she who guides through poetry.

Shipra (Indian) the name of a river.

Shiquita (American) a form of
Chiquita.
Shiquata, Shiquitta

Shira (Hebrew) song.
Shirah, Shiray, Shire, Shiree, Shiri, Shirit, Shyra

Shirina, Shrina (Indian) night.

Shirlene (English) a form of Shirley.
Shirleen, Shirline, Shirlynn

Shirley (English) bright meadow. See
also Sheryl.
*Sherlee, Sherleen, Sherley, Sherli,
Sherlie, Shir, Shirl, Shirlee, Shirlie, Shirly,
Shirlly, Shurlee, Shurley*

Shishirkana (Indian) particles of
dew.

Shiuli (Indian) flower.

Shivangi (Indian) beautiful.

Shivani (Hindi) life and death.
Shiva, Shivana, Shivanie, Shivanna

Shivapriya (Indian) liked by Shiva.

Shivasundari (Indian) the goddess
Durga.

Shivika (Indian) a palanquin.

Shizu (Japanese) silent.
Shizue, Shizuka, Shizuko, Shizuyo

Shizuye (Japanese) blessed and
ambitious girl.

Shobhita (Indian) splendid.

Shobhna (Indian) ornamental;
shining; beautiful.

Shoka (Japanese) fly up; beautiful.

Shoko (Japanese) child of Sho.

Shona (Irish) a form of Jane. A form
of Shana, Shauna, Shawna.
*Shiona, Shonagh, Shonah, Shonalee,
Shonda, Shone, Shonee, Shonette,*
*Shoni, Shonie, Shonna, Shonnah,
Shonta*

Shonda (Irish) a form of Shona. See
also Shanda, Shaunda, Shawnda.
*Shondalette, Shondalyn, Shondel,
Shondelle, Shondi, Shondia, Shondie,
Shondra, Shondreka, Shounda*

Shonima (Indian) redness.

Shonta (Irish) a form of Shona. See
also Shaunta, Shawnta.
*Shontá, Shontae, Shontai, Shontalea,
Shontasia, Shontavia, Shontaviea,
Shontay, Shontaya, Shonte, Shonté,
Shontedra, Shontee, Shonteral, Shonti,
Shontol, Shontoy, Shontrail, Shountáe*

Shorashi (Indian) young woman.

Shoshana (Hebrew) a form of
Susan.
*Shosha, Shoshan, Shoshanah,
Shoshane, Shoshanha, Shoshann,
Shoshanna, Shoshannah, Shoshauna,
Shoshaunah, Shoshawna, Shoshona,
Shoshone, Shoshonee, Shoshoney,
Shoshoni, Shoushan, Shushana, Sosha,
Soshana*

Shou (Chinese) teacher.

Shoumo (Indian) the quiet one; the
learned one.

Shrabana, Shravana (Indian) the
name of a star.

Shraddha (Indian) faith; very
attentive person.

Shradhdha (Indian) faith.

Shramidhi (Indian) girl who likes to
work hard and earn.

Shravani (Indian) full moon of
Shravan month.

Shravanti (Indian) a name in
Buddhist literature.

Shravasti (Indian) an ancient city.

Shravya (Indian) musical tone.

Shreedevi (Indian) goddess.

Shreela, Shrila (Indian) beautiful.

Shreema (Indian) prosperous.

Shreemayi, Shrimati, Shrimayi (Indian) fortunate.

Shreeparna (Indian) a tree adorned with leaves.

Shresta (Indian) foremost.

Shreyashi (Indian) good.

Shreyasi (Indian) one who is most beautiful.

Shri (Indian) luster.

Shridevi (Indian) the goddess of wealth.

Shridula, Shridulla (Indian) blessing.

Shrijani (Indian) creative.

Shrika (Indian) fortune.

Shrikirti (Indian) lustrous fame.

Shrikumari (Indian) lustrous.

Shrilata (Indian) lustrous creeper.

Shristhi (Indian) creation; remembrance.

Shriya (Indian) prosperity.

Shriyadita (Indian) sun.

Shrusti (Indian) world.

Shruti (Indian) knowledge of the Vedas; musical pitch.

Shu (Chinese) kind, gentle.

Shu Fang, Shu-Fang (Chinese) gentle and sweet.

Shuang (Chinese) bright; openhearted.

Shubha (Indian) lucky for everybody.

Shubhada (Indian) one who brings goodness.

Shubhangi (Indian) beautiful.

Shubhi (Indian) good luck.

Shubhra (Indian) white; the Ganga River in mountain stage.

Shuchi (Indian) pure.

Shuchismita (Indian) one who has a pure smile.

Shuchita (Indian) purity.

Shug (American) a short form of Sugar.

Shui (Chinese) water.

Shukti (Indian) pearl oyster.

Shula (Arabic) flaming, bright.
Shulah

Shulamith (Hebrew) peaceful. See also Sula.
Shulamit, Sulamith

Shun (Chinese) smooth.

Shunka (Japanese) high; flower.

Shunta (Irish) a form of Shonta.
Shuntae, Shunté, Shuntel, Shuntell, Shuntelle, Shuntia

Shuo (Chinese) twinkle.

Shura (Russian) a form of Alexandra.
Schura, Shurah, Shuree, Shureen, Shurelle, Shuritta, Shurka, Shurlana

Shushma (Indian) fragrant.

Shveni, Shveta, Shweta, Shwetha (Indian) white.

Shwiti (Indian) fairness.

Shyamali, Shyamalika, Shyamalima, Shyamari, Shyamasri (Indian) dusky.

Shyamangi (Indian) dark complexioned.

Shyamlata (Indian) a creeper with dusky leaves.

Shyann, Shyanne (Cheyenne) forms of Cheyenne. See also Sheyenne.
Shyan, Shyana, Shyandra, Shyane, Shynee, Shyanna, Shyannah, Shye, Shyene, Shyenna, Shyenne

Shyla **G** (English) a form of Sheila.
Shya, Shyah, Shylah, Shylan, Shylayah, Shylana, Shylane, Shyle, Shyleah, Shylee, Shyley, Shyli, Shylia, Shylie, Shylo, Shyloe, Shyloh, Shylon, Shylyn

Shyma (Indian) sister of the prophet Mohammed.

Shyra (Hebrew) a form of Shira.
Shyrae, Shyrah, Shyrai, Shyrie, Shyro

Si (Chinese) silk.

Sianna (Irish) a form of Seana.
Sian, Siana, Sianae, Sianai, Sianey, Siannah, Sianne, Sianni, Sianny, Siany

Siara (Irish) a form of Sierra.
Siarah, Siarra, Siarrah, Sieara

Sibeta (Moquelumnan) finding a fish under a rock.

Sibila (Greek) she who prophesizes.

Sibley (English) sibling; friendly. (Greek) a form of Sybil.
Sybley

Siddhangana (Indian) accomplished; female saint; divine.

Siddhani (Indian) blessed.

Siddheshwari (Indian) Lord Shiva.

Siddhi, Siddhima (Indian) achievement.

Sidney **G** (French) a form of Sydney.
Sidne, Sidnee, Sidnei, Sidneya, Sidni, Sidnie, Sidny, Sidnye

Sidonia (Hebrew) enticing.
Sydania, Syndonia

Sidonie (French) from Saint-Denis, France. See also Sydney.
Sedona, Sidaine, Sidanni, Sidelle, Sidoine, Sidona, Sidonae, Sidonia, Sidony

Sidra (Latin) star child.
Sidrah, Sidras

Sienna (American) a form of Ciana.
Seini, Siena

Siera (Irish) a form of Sierra.
Sierah, Sieria

Sierra **G** (Irish) black. (Spanish) saw toothed. Geography: any rugged range of mountains that, when viewed from a distance, has a jagged profile. See also Ciara.
Seara, Searria, Seera, Seirra, Siara, Siearra, Siera, Sierrah, Sierre, Sierrea, Sierriah, Syerra

Sigfreda (German) victorious peace. See also Freda.
Sigfreida, Sigfrida, Sigfrieda, Sigfryda

Sigmunda (German) victorious protector.
Sigmonda

Signe (Latin) sign, signal. (Scandinavian) a short form of Sigourney.
Sig, Signa, Signy, Singna, Singne

Sigourney (English) victorious conquerer.
Signe, Sigournee, Sigourny

Sigrid (Scandinavian) victorious counselor.
Siegrid, Siegrida, Sigritt

Sihaam (Indian) arrows.

Sihu (Native American) flower; bush.

Sikata (Indian) sand.

Siko (African) crying baby.

Sikta (Indian) wet.

Silas 🄱 (Latin) a short form of Silvan (see Boys' Names).

Silvana (Latin) a form of Sylvana.
Silvaine, Silvanna, Silviane

Silveria (Spanish) she who was born in the jungle.

Silvia (Latin) a form of Sylvia.
Silivia, Silva, Silvya

Silvina (Spanish) a form of Silvana.

Simbala (Indian) pond.

Simcha 🄱 (Hebrew) joyful.

Simi (Indian) limit.

Simon 🄱 (Hebrew) he heard. Bible: one of the Twelve Disciples.

Simone 🄖 (Hebrew, French) a form of Simon.
Samone, Siminie, Simmi, Simmie, Simmona, Simmone, Simoane, Simona, Simonetta, Simonette, Simonia, Simonina, Simonne, Somone, Symone

Simran 🄖 (Sikh) absorbed in God.
Simren, Simrin, Simrun

Simrit (Indian) remembered.

Sina (Irish) a form of Seana.
Seena, Sinai, Sinaia, Sinan, Sinay

Sinclaire (French) prayer.
Sinclair

Sinclética (Greek) she who is invited.

Sindy (American) a form of Cindy.
Sinda, Sindal, Sindee, Sindi, Sindia, Sindie, Sinnedy, Synda, Syndal, Syndee, Syndey, Syndi, Syndia, Syndie, Syndy

Sinead (Irish) a form of Jane.
Seonaid, Sine, Sinéad

Sinforosa (Latin) full of misfortunes.

Sinjini (Indian) the sound of an anklet.

Sinsapa (Indian) ashok tree.

Sintiques (Greek) she who arrives on a special occasion.

Siobhan 🄖 (Irish) a form of Joan.
See also Shavonne.
Shibahn, Shibani, Shibhan, Shioban, Shobana, Shobha, Shobhana, Siobahn, Siobhana, Siobhann, Siobhon, Siovaun, Siovhan

Sira (Latin) she who comes from Syria.

Sirena (Greek) enchanter.
Mythology: Sirens were sea nymphs whose singing enchanted sailors and made them crash their ships into nearby rocks.
Sireena, Sirene, Sirine, Syrena, Syrenia, Syrenna, Syrina

Siria (Persian) brilliant as the sun.

Sisika (Native American) songbird.

Sissy (American) a familiar form of Cecelia.
Sisi, Sisie, Sissey, Sissie

Sita (Hindi) a form of Shakti.
Sitah, Sitarah, Sitha, Sithara

Siteri (Fijian) a form of Esther.

Siti (Swahili) respected woman.

Skye 🄖 (Arabic) water giver.
(Dutch) a short form of Skyler.

Geography: an island in the
Hebrides, Scotland.
Ski, Skie, Skii, Skky, Sky, Skya, Skyy

Skylar **BG** (Dutch) a form of Skyler.
Skyela, Skyelar, Skyla, Skylair, Skyylar

Skyler **B** (Dutch) sheltering.
*Skila, Skilah, Skye, Skyeler, Skyelur,
Skyla, Skylar, Skylee, Skylena, Skyli,
Skylia, Skylie, Skylin, Skyllar, Skylor,
Skylyn, Skylynn, Skylyr, Skyra*

Sloane (Irish) warrior.
Sloan, Sloanne

Socorro (Spanish) helper.

Sofia ✹ **G** (Greek) a form of
Sophia. See also Zofia, Zsofia.
*Sofeea, Sofeeia, Soffi, Sofi, Soficita,
Sofie, Sofija, Sofiya, Sofka, Sofya*

Sofía (Greek) a form of Sofia.

Sol (Latin) she who possesses
brightness.

Solada (Tai) listener.

Solana (Spanish) sunshine.
*Solande, Solanna, Soleil, Solena, Soley,
Solina, Solinda*

Solange (French) dignified.

Soledad (Spanish) solitary.
Sole, Soleda

Soledada (Spanish) solitary.

Solenne (French) solemn, dignified.
*Solaine, Solene, Soléne, Solenna,
Solina, Soline, Solonez, Souline, Soulle*

Solita (Latin) solitary.

Solomon **B** (Hebrew) peaceful.

Soma (Hindi) lunar.

Sommer (English) summer;
summoner. (Arabic) black. See also
Summer.
*Somara, Somer, Sommar, Sommara,
Sommers*

Somoche (Mapuche) distinguished
woman, woman of her word.

Sondra (Greek) defender of
mankind.
Saundra, Sondre, Sonndra, Sonndre

Song (Chinese) independent.

Sonia (Russian, Slavic) a form of
Sonya.
*Sonica, Sonida, Sonita, Sonna, Sonni,
Sonnia, Sonnie, Sonny*

Sonja (Scandinavian) a form of
Sonya.
Sonjae, Sonjia

Sonny **B** (Russian, Slavic) a form of
Sonia.

Sonoko (Japanese) child of the
garden.

Sonora (Spanish) pleasant sounding.

Sonya **G** (Greek) wise. (Russian,
Slavic) a form of Sophia.
Sonia, Sonja, Sonnya, Sonyae, Sunya

Soo (Korean) letters.

Sook (Korean) pure.

Soon-Vi (Chinese) delightful.

Sopheary (Cambodian) beautiful
girl.

Sophia ✹ **G** (Greek) wise. See
also Sonya, Zofia.
Sofia, Sophie

Sophie ✹ **G** (Greek) a familiar
form of Sophia. See also Zocha.
Sophey, Sophi, Sophy

Sophronia (Greek) wise; sensible.
Soffrona, Sofronia

Sora (Native American) chirping
songbird.

Sorami (Japanese) a form of Sorano.

Sorano (Japanese) space; truth.

Soraya (Persian) princess.
Suraya

Sorrel 🅖 (French) reddish brown. Botany: a plant whose leaves are used as salad greens.

Sorya (Spanish) she who is eloquent.

Sosefina (Chuukese) a form of Josefa.

Soso (Native American) tree squirrel dining on pine nuts; chubby-cheeked baby.

Souzan (Persian) burning fire.
Sousan, Souzanne

Spencer 🅑 (English) dispenser of provisions.
Spenser

Speranza (Italian) a form of Esperanza.
Speranca

Spica (Latin) star's name.

Spring (English) springtime.
Spryng

Stacey, Stacy 🅖 (Greek) resurrection. (Irish) a short form of Anastasia, Eustacia, Natasha.
Stace, Stacee, Staceyan, Staceyann, Staicy, Stasey, Stasya, Stayce, Staycee, Staci, Steacy

Staci, Stacie (Greek) forms of Stacey.
Stacci, Stacia, Stayci

Stacia (English) a short form of Anastasia.
Stasia, Staysha

Stanley 🅑 (English) stony meadow.

Starla (English) a form of Starr.
Starrla

Starleen (English) a form of Starr.
Starleena, Starlena, Starlene, Starlin, Starlyn, Starlynn, Starrlen

Starley (English) a familiar form of Starr.
Starle, Starlee, Staly

Starling 🅑🅖 (English) bird.

Starr 🅖 (English) star.
Star, Staria, Starisha, Starla, Starleen, Starlet, Starlette, Starley, Starlight, Starre, Starri, Starria, Starrika, Starrsha, Starsha, Starshanna, Startish

Stasya (Greek) a familiar form of Anastasia. (Russian) a form of Stacey.
Stasa, Stasha, Stashia, Stasia, Stasja, Staska

Stefani, Steffani (Greek) forms of Stephanie.
Stafani, Stefanni, Steffane, Steffanee, Stefini, Stefoni

Stefanía (Greek) a form of Stefanie.

Stefanie (Greek) a form of Stephanie.
Stafanie, Staffany, Stefane, Stefanee, Stefaney, Stefania, Stefanié, Stefanija, Stefannie, Stefcia, Stefenie, Steffanie, Steffi, Stefinie, Stefka

Stefany, Steffany (Greek) forms of Stephanie.
Stefanny, Stefanya, Steffaney

Steffi (Greek) a familiar form of Stefanie, Stephanie.
Stefa, Stefcia, Steffee, Steffie, Steffy, Stefi, Stefka, Stefy, Stepha, Stephi, Stephie, Stephy

Stella 🅖 (Latin) star. (French) a familiar form of Estelle.
Steile, Stellina

Stepania (Russian) a form of Stephanie.
Stepa, Stepahny, Stepanida, Stepanie, Stepanyda, Stepfanie, Stephana

Stephane B (Greek) a form of
Stephanie.

Stephani (Greek) a form of
Stephanie.
Stephania, Stephanni

Stephanie G (Greek) a form of
Stephen. See also Estefani,
Estephanie, Panya, Stevie,
Zephania.
*Stamatios, Stefani, Stefanie, Stefany,
Steffie, Stepania, Stephaija, Stephaine,
Stephanas, Stephane, Stephanee,
Stephani, Stephanida, Stéphanie,
Stephanine, Stephann, Stephannie,
Stephany, Stephene, Stephenie,
Stephianie, Stephney, Stesha, Steshka,
Stevanee*

Stephany G (Greek) a form of
Stephanie.
Stephaney, Stephanye

Stephen B (Greek) crowned.

Stephene (Greek) a form of
Stephanie.
Stephina, Stephine, Stephyne

Stephenie (Greek) a form of
Stephanie.
*Stephena, Stephenee, Stepheney,
Stepheni, Stephenny, Stepheny,
Stephine, Stephinie*

Stephney (Greek) a form of
Stephanie.
Stephne, Stephni, Stephnie, Stephny

Sterling B (English) valuable; silver
penny.

Stetson B (Danish) stepchild.

Steven B (Greek) a form of
Stephen.

Stevie G (Greek) a familiar form of
Stephanie.
*Steva, Stevana, Stevanee, Stevee,
Stevena, Stevey, Stevi, Stevy, Stevye*

Stewart B (English) a form of
Stuart.

Stina (German) a short form of
Christina.
Steena, Stena, Stine, Stinna

Stockard (English) stockyard.

Storm B (English) a short form of
Stormy.

Stormie (English) a form of Stormy.
Stormee, Stormi, Stormii

Stormy G (English) impetuous by
nature.
*Storm, Storme, Stormey, Stormie,
Stormm*

Stuart B (English) caretaker,
steward.

Suchin (Tai) beautiful thought.

Sue (Hebrew) a short form of Susan,
Susanna.

Sueann, Sueanna (American)
combinations of Sue + Ann, Sue +
Anna.
*Suann, Suanna, Suannah, Suanne,
Sueanne*

Suela (Spanish) consolation.
Suelita

Sugako (Japanese) of the sky.

Sugar (American) sweet as sugar.
Shug

Sugi (Japanese) cedar tree.

Sui (Chinese) peaceful.

Suke (Hawaiian) a form of Susan.

Sukey (Hawaiian) a familiar form of
Susan.
Suka, Sukee, Suki, Sukie, Suky

Sukhdeep G (Sikh) light of peace
and bliss.
Sukhdip

Suki (Japanese) loved one.
(Moquelumnan) eagle-eyed.
Sukie

Sula (Icelandic) large sea bird.
(Greek, Hebrew) a short form of
Shulamith, Ursula.

Sulamita (Hebrew) gentle, peaceful
woman.

Suletu (Moquelumnan) soaring bird.

Suli (Fijian) a form of Julia.

Sulia (Latin) a form of Julia.
Suliana

Sulwen (Welsh) bright as the sun.

Sumalee (Tai) beautiful flower.

Sumati (Hindi) unity.

Sumaya (American) a combination
of Sue + Maya.
Sumayah, Sumayya, Sumayyah

Sumi (Japanese) elegant, refined.
Sumiko

Sumiye (Japanese) child who knows
how to give thanks to others.

Summer ☐ (English) summertime.
See also Sommer.
*Sumer, Summar, Summerann,
Summerbreeze, Summerhaze,
Summerine, Summerlee, Summerlin,
Summerlyn, Summerlynn, Summers,
Sumrah, Summyr, Sumyr*

Sun (Korean) obedient.
*Suncance, Sundee, Sundeep, Sundi,
Sundip, Sundrenea, Sunta, Sunya*

Suna (Korean) belief.

Sunee (Tai) good.
Suni

Sun-Hi (Korean) good; joyful.

Suni (Zuni) native; member of our
tribe.
*Sunita, Sunitha, Suniti, Sunne, Sunni,
Sunnie, Sunnilei*

Sunki (Hopi) swift.
Sunkia

Sunny ☐☐ (English) bright, cheerful.
Sunni, Sunnie

Sunshine (English) sunshine.
Sunshyn, Sunshyne

Suong (Vietnamese) looking or
behaving like people of the upper
classes.

Surata (Pakistani) blessed joy.

Suri (Todas) pointy nose.
Suree, Surena, Surenia

Surya (Sanskrit) Mythology: a sun
god.
Suria, Suriya, Surra

Susammi (French) a combination of
Susan + Aimee.
Suzami, Suzamie, Suzamy

Susan ☐ (Hebrew) lily. See also
Shoshana, Sukey, Zsa Zsa, Zusa.
*Sawsan, Siusan, Sosan, Sosana, Sue,
Suesan, Sueva, Suisan, Suke, Susana,
Susann, Susanna, Suse, Susen, Susette,
Susie, Suson, Suzan, Suzanna,
Suzannah, Suzanne, Suzette*

Susana ☐ (Hebrew) a form of Susan.
Susanah, Susane

Susanita (Spanish) a form of Susana.

Susanna, Susannah (Hebrew)
forms of Susan. See also Xuxa,
Zanna, Zsuzsanna.
*Sonel, Sosana, Sue, Suesanna, Susana,
Susanah, Susanka, Susette, Susie,
Suzanna*

Suse (Hawaiian) a form of Susan.

Susette (French) a familiar form of Susan, Susanna.
Susetta

Susie, Suzie (American) familiar forms of Susan, Susanna.
Suse, Susey, Susi, Sussi, Sussy, Susy, Suze, Suzi, Suzy, Suzzie

Sute (Japanese) blessed purity.

Suzanna, Suzannah (Hebrew) forms of Susan.
Suzana, Suzenna, Suzzanna

Suzanne **G** (English) a form of Susan.
Susanne, Suszanne, Suzane, Suzann, Suzzane, Suzzann, Suzzanne

Suzette (French) a form of Susan.
Suzetta, Suzzette

Suzu (Japanese) little bell.
Suzue, Suzuko

Suzuha (Japanese) orphan.

Suzuki (Japanese) bell tree.

Svetlana (Russian) bright light.
Sveta, Svetochka

Syá (Chinese) summer.

Sybella (English) a form of Sybil.
Sebila, Sibbella, Sibeal, Sibel, Sibell, Sibella, Sibelle, Sibilla, Sibylla, Sybel, Sybelle, Sybila, Sybilla

Sybil (Greek) prophet. Mythology: sibyls were oracles who relayed the messages of the gods. See also Cybele, Sibley.
Sib, Sibbel, Sibbie, Sibbill, Sibby, Sibeal, Sibel, Sibyl, Sibylle, Sibylline, Sybella, Sybille, Syble

Sydnee **G** (French) a form of Sydney.
Sydne, Sydnea, Sydnei

Sydney 🌟 **G** (French) from Saint-Denis, France. See also Sidonie.
Cidney, Cydney, Sidney, Sy, Syd, Sydel, Sydelle, Sydna, Sydnee, Sydni, Sydnie, Sydny, Sydnye, Syndona, Syndonah

Sydni, Sydnie (French) forms of Sydney.

Syed **B** (Arabic) happy.

Sying **BG** (Chinese) star.

Sylvana (Latin) forest.
Sylva, Sylvaine, Sylvanah, Sylvania, Sylvanna, Sylvie, Sylvina, Sylvinnia, Sylvonah, Sylvonia, Sylvonna

Sylvia (Latin) forest. Literature: Sylvia Plath was a well-known American poet. See also Silvia, Xylia.
Sylvette, Sylvie, Sylwia

Sylvianne (American) a combination of Sylvia + Anne.
Sylvian

Sylvie (Latin) a familiar form of Sylvia.
Silvi, Silvie, Silvy, Sylvi

Symone (Hebrew) a form of Simone.
Symmeon, Symmone, Symona, Symoné, Symonne

Symphony (Greek) symphony, harmonious sound.
Symfoni, Symphanie, Symphany, Symphanée, Symphoni, Symphoni

Syreeta (Hindi) good traditions. (Arabic) companion.
Syretta, Syrrita

T

T 🅱🅶 (American) an initial used as a first name.

Tabatha 🅶 (Greek, Aramaic) a form of Tabitha.
Tabathe, Tabathia, Tabbatha

Tabby (English) a familiar form of Tabitha.
Tabbi

Tabetha (Greek, Aramaic) a form of Tabitha.

Tabia (Swahili) talented.
Tabea

Tabina (Arabic) follower of Muhammad.

Tabitha (Greek, Aramaic) gazelle.
Tabatha, Tabbee, Tabbetha, Tabbey, Tabbi, Tabbie, Tabbitha, Tabby, Tabetha, Tabiatha, Tabita, Tabithia, Tabotha, Tabtha, Tabytha

Tabora (Arabic) plays a small drum.

Tabytha (Greek, Aramaic) a form of Tabitha.
Tabbytha

Tacey (English) a familiar form of Tacita.
Tace, Tacee, Taci, Tacy, Tacye

Taci (Zuni) washtub. (English) a form of Tacey.
Tacia, Taciana, Tacie

Tacita (Latin) silent.
Tacey

Tadako (Japanese) bell; leaf.

Tadita (Omaha) runner.
Tadeta, Tadra

Taelor (English) a form of Taylor.
Taelar, Taeler, Taellor, Taelore, Taelyr

Taesha (Latin) a form of Tisha. (American) a combination of the prefix Ta + Aisha.
Tadasha, Taeshayla, Taeshia, Taheisha, Tahisha, Taiesha, Taisha, Taishae, Teasha, Teashia, Teisha, Tesha

Taffy 🅶 (Welsh) beloved.
Taffia, Taffine, Taffye, Tafia, Tafisa, Tafoya

Tahira (Arabic) virginal, pure.
Taheera, Taheerah, Tahera, Tahere, Taheria, Taherri, Tahiara, Tahirah, Tahireh

Tahlia (Greek, Hebrew) a form of Talia.
Tahleah, Tahleia

Tailor (English) a form of Taylor.
Tailar, Tailer, Taillor, Tailyr

Taima 🅶 (Native American) clash of thunder.
Taimi, Taimia, Taimy

Taipa (Moquelumnan) flying quail.

Tais (Greek) she who is beautiful.

Taite (English) cheerful.
Tate, Tayte, Tayten

Taja (Hindi) crown.
Taiajára, Taija, Tajae, Tajah, Tahai, Tehya, Teja, Tejah, Tejal

Taji (Japanese) child of Tada.

Taka (Japanese) honored.

Takako (Japanese) silver and yellow color.

Takala (Hopi) corn tassel.

Takara (Japanese) treasure.
Takarah, Takaria, Takarra, Takra

Takayla (American) a combination of the prefix Ta + Kayla.
Takayler, Takeyli

Take (Japanese) child of Taka.

Takeisha (American) a combination
of the prefix Ta + Keisha.
*Takecia, Takesha, Takeshia, Takesia,
Takisha, Takishea, Takishia, Tekeesha,
Tekeisha, Tekeshi, Tekeysia, Tekisha,
Tikesha, Tikisha, Tokesia, Tykeisha*

Takeko (Japanese) bamboo.

Takenya (Hebrew) animal horn.
(Moquelumnan) falcon. (American)
a combination of the prefix Ta +
Kenya.
Takenia, Takenja

Takeria (American) a form of
Takira.
*Takera, Takeri, Takerian, Takerra,
Takerria, Takirria, Takoria*

Taki (Japanese) waterfall.
Tiki

Takia (Arabic) worshiper.
*Takeia, Takeiyah, Takeya, Takeyah,
Takhiya, Takiah, Tokija, Takiya, Takiyah,
Takkia, Takya, Takyah, Takyia, Taqiyya,
Taquaia, Taquaya, Taquiia, Tekeiya,
Tekeiyah, Tekeyia, Tekiya, Tekiyah, Tikia,
Tykeia, Tykia*

Takiko (Japanese) child of the
bamboo.

Takila (American) a form of Tequila.
*Takayla, Takeika, Takela, Takelia,
Takella, Takeyla, Takiela, Takilah,
Takilla, Takilya, Takyla, Takylia,
Tatakyla, Tehilla, Tekeila, Tekela,
Tekelia, Tekilaa, Tekilia, Tekilla, Tekilyah,
Tekla*

Takira (American) a combination of
the prefix Ta + Kira.
*Takara, Takarra, Takeara, Takeera,
Takeira, Takeirah, Takera, Takiara,
Takiera, Takierah, Takierra, Takirah,
Takiria, Takirra, Takora, Tokyra, Tokyrra,
Taquera, Taquira, Tekeria, Tikara, Tikira,
Tykera*

Tala (Native American) stalking wolf.

Talasi (Hopi) corn tassel.
Talasea, Talasia

Taleah (American) a form of Talia.
*Talaya, Talayah, Talayia, Talea,
Taleana, Taleea, Taleéi, Talei, Taleia,
Taleiya, Tylea, Tyleah, Tylee*

Taleisha (American) a combination
of Talia + Aisha.
*Taileisha, Taleise, Tolesha, Talicia,
Taliesha, Talisa, Talisha, Talysha, Telisha,
Tilisha, Tyleasha, Tyleisha, Tylicia,
Tylisha, Tylishia*

Talena (American) a combination of
the prefix Ta + Lena.
*Talayna, Talihna, Taline, Tallenia, Talná,
Tilena, Tilene, Tylena*

Talesha (American) a form of
Taleisha.
*Taleesha, Talesa, Talese, Taleshia,
Talesia, Tallese, Tallesia, Tylesha,
Tyleshia, Tylesia*

Talia (Greek) blooming. (Hebrew)
dew from heaven. (Latin, French)
birthday. A short form of Natalie.
See also Thalia.
*Tahlia, Taleah, Taliah, Taliatha, Taliea,
Taliyah, Talley, Tallia, Tallya, Talya, Tylia*

Talía (Greek) a form of Talia.

Talina (American) a combination of
Talia + Lina.
*Talin, Talinda, Taline, Tallyn, Talyn,
Talynn, Tylina, Tyline*

Talisa (English) a form of Tallis.
*Talisha, Talishia, Talisia, Talissa, Talysa,
Talysha, Talysia, Talyssa*

Talitha (Arabic) young girl.
*Taleetha, Taletha, Talethia, Taliatha,
Talita, Talithia, Taliya, Telita, Tiletha*

Taliyah (Greek) a form of Talia.
*Taleya, Taleyah, Talieya, Talliyah, Talya,
Talyah, Talyia*

Talley (French) a familiar form of
Talia.
Tali, Talle, Tallie, Tally, Taly, Talye

Tallis (French, English) forest.
Talice, Talisa, Talise, Tallys

Tallulah (Choctaw) leaping water.
Tallou, Talula

Talon 🄱 (French, English) claw,
nail.

Tam 🄱 (Vietnamese) heart.

Tama (Japanese) jewel.
Tamaa, Tamah, Tamaiah, Tamala, Tema

Tamae (Japanese) very noble child.

Tamaka (Japanese) bracelet.
Tamaki, Tamako, Timaka

Tamar 🄶 (Hebrew) a short form of
Tamara. (Russian) History: a
twelfth-century Georgian queen.
(Hebrew) a short form of Tamara.
Tamer, Tamor, Tamour

Tamara (Hebrew) palm tree. See also
Tammy.
*Tamar, Tamará, Tamarae, Tamarah,
Tamaria, Tamarin, Tamarla, Tamarra,
Tamarria, Tamarrian, Tamarsha,
Tamary, Tamera, Tamira, Tamma,
Tammara, Tamora, Tamoya, Tamra,
Tamura, Tamyra, Temara, Temarian,
Thama, Thamar, Thamara, Thamarra,
Timara, Tomara, Tymara*

Tamassa (Hebrew) a form of
Thomasina.
*Tamasin, Tamasine, Tamsen, Tamsin,
Tamzen, Tamzin*

Tamaya (Quechua) in the center.

Tamayo (Japanese) ball; bell.

Tame (Japanese) a form of Tamaki.

Tameea (Japanese) unselfish.

Tameka (Aramaic) twin.
*Tameca, Tamecia, Tamecka, Tameeka,
Tamekia, Tamiecka, Tamieka, Temeka,
Timeeka, Timeka, Tomeka, Tomekia,
Trameika, Tymeka, Tymmeeka, Tymmeka*

Tamera (Hebrew) a form of Tamara.
*Tamer, Tamerai, Tameran, Tameria,
Tamerra, Tammera, Thamer, Timera*

Tamesha (American) a combination
of the prefix Ta + Mesha.
*Tameesha, Tameisha, Tameshia,
Tameshkia, Tameshya, Tamisha,
Tamishia, Tamnesha, Temisha, Timesha,
Timisha, Tomesha, Tomiese, Tomise,
Tomisha, Tramesha, Tramisha, Tymesha*

Tamico (Japanese) little gem.

Tamika (Japanese) a form of Tamiko.
*Tamica, Tamieka, Tamikah, Tamikia,
Tamikka, Tammika, Tamyka, Timika,
Timikia, Tomika, Tymika, Tymmicka*

Tamiko (Japanese) child of the people.
*Tami, Tamika, Tamike, Tamiqua, Tamiyo,
Tammiko*

Tamila (American) a combination of
the prefix Ta + Mila.
*Tamala, Tamela, Tamelia, Tamilla,
Tamille, Tamillia, Tamilya*

Tamira (Hebrew) a form of Tamara.
*Tamir, Tamirae, Tamirah, Tamiria,
Tamirra, Tamyra, Tamyria, Tamyrra*

Tammi, Tammie (English) forms of
Tammy.
*Tameia, Tami, Tamia, Tamiah, Tamie,
Tamijo, Tamiya*

Tammy 🄶 (English) twin. (Hebrew)
a familiar form of Tamara.
*Tamilyn, Tamlyn, Tammee, Tammey,
Tammi, Tammie, Tamy, Tamya*

Tamra (Hebrew) a short form of
Tamara.
Tammra, Tamrah

Tamsin (English) a short form of
Thomasina.

Tan (Vietnamese) lotus flower.

Tana (Slavic) a short form of Tanya.
Taina, Tanae, Tanaeah, Tanah, Tanairi, Tanairy, Tanalia, Tanara, Tanavia, Tanaya, Tanaz, Tanna, Tannah

Tanak (Japanese) the people's child.

Tanaka (Japanese) a form of Tamika.

Tandy (English) team.
Tanda, Tandalaya, Tandi, Tandie, Tandis, Tandra, Tandrea, Tandria

Tane (Japanese) dweller.

Taneisha (American) a combination of the prefix Ta + Nesha.
Tahniesha, Taineshia, Tanasha, Tanashia, Tanaysia, Tanniecia, Tanniesha, Tantashea

Tanesha **G** (American) a combination of the prefix Ta + Nesha.
Taneshea, Taneshia, Taneshya, Tanesia, Tanesian, Tanessa, Tanessia, Taniesha, Tannesha, Tanneshia, Tantashea

Taneya (Russian, Slavic) a form of Tanya.
Tanea, Taneah, Tanee, Taneé, Taneia

Tang (Chinese) stately, dignified.

Tangia (American) a combination of the prefix Ta + Angela.
Tangela, Tangi, Tangie, Tanja, Tanji, Tanjia, Tanjie

Tani **G** (Japanese) valley. (Slavic) stand of glory. A familiar form of Tania.
Tahnee, Tahni, Tahnie, Tanee, Taney, Tanie, Tany

Tania (Russian, Slavic) fairy queen.
Taneea, Tani, Taniah, Tanija, Tanika, Tanis, Taniya, Tannia, Tannis, Tanniya, Tannya, Tarnia

Taniel (American) a combination of Tania + Danielle.
Taniele, Tanielle, Teniel, Teniele, Tenielle

Tanika (American) a form of Tania.
Tanikka, Tanikqua, Taniqua, Tanique, Tannica, Tianeka, Tianika

Tanis **G** (Slavic) a form of Tania, Tanya.
Tanas, Tanese, Taniese, Tanise, Tanisia, Tanka, Tenice, Tenise, Tenyse, Tiannis, Tonise, Tranice, Tranise, Tynice, Tyniece, Tyniese, Tynise

Tanisha (American) a combination of the prefix Ta + Nisha.
Tahnisciah, Tahnisha, Tanasha, Tanashea, Tanicha, Taniesha, Tanish, Tanishah, Tanishia, Tanitia, Tannicia, Tannisha, Tenisha, Tenishka, Tinisha, Tonisha, Tonnisha, Tynisha

Tanissa (American) a combination of the prefix Tania + Nissa.
Tanesa, Tanisa, Tannesa, Tannisa, Tennessa, Tranissa

Tanita (American) a combination of the prefix Ta + Nita.
Taneta, Tonetta, Tanitra, Tanitta, Teneta, Tenetta, Tenita, Tenitta, Tyneta, Tynetta, Tynette, Tynita, Tynitra, Tynitta

Tanith (Phoenician) Mythology: Tanit is the goddess of love.
Tanitha

Tanner **B** (English) leather worker, tanner.
Tannor

Tannis (Slavic) a form of Tania, Tanya.
Tannese, Tanniece, Tanniese, Tannis, Tannise, Tannus, Tannyce, Tiannis

Tansy (Greek) immortal. (Latin) tenacious, persistent.
Tancy, Tansee, Tansey, Tanshay, Tanzey

Tanya (Russian, Slavic) fairy queen.
Tahnee, Tahnya, Tana, Tanaya, Taneya, Tania, Tanis, Taniya, Tanka, Tannis, Tannya, Tanoya, Tany, Tanyia, Taunya, Tawnya, Thanya

Tao (Chinese, Vietnamese) peach.

Tara 🅖 (Aramaic) throw; carry. (Irish) rocky hill. (Arabic) a measurement.
Taira, Tairra, Taraea, Tarah, Taráh, Tarai, Taralee, Tarali, Tarasa, Tarasha, Taraya, Tarha, Tari, Tarra, Taryn, Tayra, Tehra

Taraneh (Persian) melody.

Taree (Japanese) arching branch.
Tarea, Tareya, Tari, Taria

Tari (Irish) a familiar form of Tara.
Taria, Tarika, Tarila, Tarilyn, Tarin, Tarina, Tarita

Tarissa (American) a combination of Tara + Rissa.
Taris, Tarisa, Tarise, Tarisha

Tarra (Irish) a form of Tara.
Tarrah

Tarsicia (Greek) valiant.

Tarsilia (Greek) basket weaver.

Taru (Japanese) dweller.

Taryn 🅖 (Irish) a form of Tara.
Taran, Tareen, Tareena, Taren, Tarene, Tarin, Tarina, Tarren, Tarrena, Tarrin, Tarrina, Tarron, Tarryn, Taryna

Tasarla (Gypsy) dawn.

Tasha 🅖 (Greek) born on Christmas day. (Russian) a short form of Natasha. See also Tashi, Tosha.
Tacha, Tachiana, Tahsha, Tasenka, Tashae, Tashana, Tashay, Tashe, Tashee, Tasheka, Tashka, Tasia, Taska, Taysha, Thasha, Tiaisha, Tysha

Tashana (American) a combination of the prefix Ta + Shana.
Tashan, Tashanda, Tashani, Tashanika, Tashanna, Tashiana, Tashianna, Tashina, Tishana, Tishani, Tishanna, Tishanne, Toshanna, Toshanti, Tyshana

Tashara (American) a combination of the prefix Ta + Shara.
Tashar, Tasharah, Tasharia, Tasharna, Tasharra, Tashera, Tasherey, Tasheri, Tasherra, Tashira, Tashirah

Tashawna (American) a combination of the prefix Ta + Shawna.
Tashauna, Tashauni, Tashaunie, Tashaunna, Tashawanna, Tashawn, Tashawnda, Tashawnna, Tashawnnia, Tashonda, Tashondra, Tiashauna, Tishawn, Tishunda, Tishunta, Toshauna, Toshawna, Tyshauna, Tyshawna

Tasheena (American) a combination of the prefix Ta + Sheena.
Tasheana, Tasheeana, Tasheeni, Tashena, Tashenna, Tashennia, Tasheona, Tashina, Tisheena, Tosheena, Tysheana, Tysheena, Tyshyna

Tashelle (American) a combination of the prefix Ta + Shelley.
Tachell, Tashell, Techell, Techelle, Teshell, Teshelle, Tochell, Tochelle, Toshelle, Tychell, Tychelle, Tyshell, Tyshelle

Tashi (Hausa) a bird in flight. (Slavic) a form of Tasha.
Tashia, Tashie, Tashika, Tashima, Tashiya

Tasia (Slavic) a familiar form of Tasha.
Tachia, Tashea, Tasiya, Tassi, Tassia, Tassiana, Tassie, Tasya

Tassos (Greek) a form of Theresa.

Tata (Russian) a familiar form of Tatiana.
Tatia

Tate **B** (English) a short form of
Tatum. A form of Taite, Tata.

Tatiana (Slavic) fairy queen. See also
Tanya, Tiana.
Tata, Tatania, Tatanya, Tateana, Tati,
Tatia, Tatianna, Tatie, Tatihana,
Tatiyana, Tatjana, Tatyana, Tiatiana

Tatianna (Slavic) a form of Tatiana.
Taitiann, Taitianna, Tateanna, Tateonna,
Tationna

Tatiyana (Slavic) a form of Tatiana.
Tateyana, Tatiayana, Tatiyanna,
Tatiyona, Tatiyonna

Tatsu (Japanese) seed.

Tatum **G** (English) cheerful.
Tate, Tatumn

Tatyana (Slavic) a form of Tatiana.
Tatyanah, Tatyani, Tatyanna, Tatyannah,
Tatyona, Tatyonna

Taura (Latin) bull. Astrology: Taurus
is a sign of the zodiac.
Taurae, Tauria, Taurina

Tauri (English) a form of Tory.
Taure, Taurie, Taury

Tavia (Latin) a short form of Octavia.
See also Tawia.
Taiva, Tauvia, Tava, Tavah, Tavita

Tavie (Scottish) twin.
Tavey, Tavi

Tawanna (American) a combination
of the prefix Ta + Wanda.
Taiwana, Taiwanna, Taquana,
Taquanna, Tawan, Tawana, Tawanda,
Tawanne, Tequana, Tequanna,
Tequawna, Tewanna, Tewauna,
Tiquana, Tiwanna, Tiwena, Towanda,
Towanna, Tywania, Tywanna

Tawia (African) born after twins.
(Polish) a form of Tavia.

Tawni (English) a form of Tawny.
Tauni, Taunia, Tawnia, Tawnie, Tawnnie,
Tiawni

Tawny (Gypsy) little one. (English)
brownish yellow, tan.
Tahnee, Tany, Tauna, Tauné, Taunisha,
Tawnee, Tawnesha, Tawney, Tawni,
Tawnyell, Tiawna

Tawnya (American) a combination of
Tawny + Tonya.
Tawna

Taya, Taye (English) short forms of
Taylor.
Tay, Tayah, Tayana, Tayiah, Tayna,
Tayra, Taysha, Taysia, Tayva, Tayvonne,
Teya, Teyanna, Teyona, Teyuna, Tiaya,
Tiya, Tiyah, Tiyana, Tye

Tayla (English) a short form of
Taylor.
Taylah, Tayleah, Taylee, Tayleigh,
Taylie, Teila

Taylar (English) a form of Taylor.
Talar, Tayla, Taylah, Taylare, Tayllar

Tayler **G** (English) a form of
Taylor.
Tayller

Taylor ☆ **G** (English) tailor.
Taelor, Tailor, Taiylor, Talor, Talora,
Taya, Taye, Tayla, Taylar, Tayler, Tayllor,
Tayllore, Tayloir, Taylorann, Taylore,
Taylorr, Taylour, Taylur, Teylor

Tazu (Japanese) stork; longevity.
Taz, Tazi, Tazia

Te (Chinese) special.

Tea (Spanish) a short form of
Dorothy.

Teagan **G** (Welsh) beautiful,
attractive.
Taegen, Teage, Teagen, Teaghan,
Teaghanne, Teaghen, Teagin, Teague,
Teegan, Teeghan, Tegan, Tegwen,
Teigan, Tejan, Tiegan, Tigan, Tijan,
Tijana

Teaira (Latin) a form of Tiara.
Teairra, Teairre, Teairria, Teara, Tearah, Teareya, Teari, Tearia, Teariea, Tearra, Tearria

Teal (English) river duck; blue green.
Teala, Teale, Tealia, Tealisha

Teanna (American) a combination of the prefix Te + Anna. A form of Tiana.
Tean, Teana, Teanah, Teann, Teannah, Teanne, Teaunna, Teena, Teuana

Teca (Hungarian) a form of Theresa.
Techa, Teka, Tica, Tika

Tecla (Greek) God's fame.
Tekla, Theckla

Teddi (Greek) a familiar form of Theodora.
Tedde, Teddey, Teddie, Teddy, Tedi, Tediah, Tedy

Tedra (Greek) a short form of Theodora.
Teddra, Teddreya, Tedera, Teedra, Teidra

Tegan ◪ (Welsh) a form of Teagan.
Tega, Tegen, Teggan, Teghan, Tegin, Tegyn, Teigen

Telisha (American) a form of Taleisha.
Teleesha, Teleisia, Telesa, Telesha, Teleshia, Telesia, Telicia, Telisa, Telishia, Telisia, Telissa, Telisse, Tellisa, Tellisha, Telsa, Telysa

Telma (Spanish) will.

Telmao (Greek) loving with her fellow people.

Temira (Hebrew) tall.
Temora, Timora

Temis (Greek) she who establishes order and justice.

Tempest ◪ (French) stormy.
Tempesta, Tempeste, Tempestt, Tempist, Tempistt, Tempress, Tempteste

Tenesha, Tenisha (American) combinations of the prefix Te + Niesha.
Tenecia, Teneesha, Teneisha, Teneshia, Tenesia, Tenessa, Teneusa, Teniesha, Tenishia

Tennille (American) a combination of the prefix Te + Nellie.
Taniel, Tanille, Teneal, Teneil, Teneille, Teniel, Tenille, Tenneal, Tenneill, Tenneille, Tennia, Tennie, Tennielle, Tennile, Tineal, Tiniel, Tonielle, Tonille

Teodelina, Teodolinda (German) she who is loving with the people in her village; she loves her village.

Teodequilda (German) warrior of her village.

Teodomira (Spanish) an important woman in the village.

Teodora (Czech) a form of Theodora.
Teadora

Teofania, Teofanía (Greek) manifestation of God.

Teofila, Teófila (Greek) friend of God, loved by God.

Teolinda (German) a form of Teodelina.

Teona, Teonna (Greek) forms of Tiana, Tianna.
Teon, Teoni, Teonia, Teonie, Teonney, Teonnia, Teonnie

Tequila (Spanish) a kind of liquor. See also Takila.
Taquela, Taquella, Taquila, Taquilla, Tequilia, Tequilla, Tiquila, Tiquilia

Tera, Terra **G** (Latin) earth.
(Japanese) swift arrow. (American)
forms of Tara.
*Terah, Terai, Teria, Terrae, Terrah,
Terria, Tierra*

Teralyn (American) a combination of
Terri + Lynn.
*Taralyn, Teralyn, Teralynn, Terralin,
Terralyn*

Tercera (Spanish) third-born.

Terence **B** (Latin) a form of
Terrence (see Boys' Names).

Teresa (Greek) a form of Theresa.
See also Tressa.
*Taresa, Taressa, Tarissa, Terasa, Tercza,
Tereasa, Tereatha, Terese, Teresea,
Teresha, Teresia, Teresina, Teresita,
Tereska, Tereson, Teressa, Teretha,
Tereza, Terezia, Terezie, Terezilya,
Terezinha, Terezka, Terezsa, Terisa,
Terisha, Teriza, Terrasa, Terresa,
Terresha, Terresia, Terressa, Terrosina,
Tersa, Tersea, Teruska, Terza, Teté,
Tyresa, Tyresia*

Terese (Greek) a form of Teresa.
*Tarese, Taress, Taris, Tarise, Tereece,
Tereese, Teress, Terez, Teris, Terrise*

Teresinha (Portuguese) a form of
Theresa.

Teri **G** (Greek) reaper. A familiar
form of Theresa.
Terie

Terpsícore (Greek) she who enjoys
dancing.

Terrance **B** (Latin) a form of
Terrence (see Boys' Names).

Terrell **B** (Greek) a form of
Terrelle.

Terrelle (Greek) a form of Theresa.
*Tarrell, Teral, Terall, Terel, Terell, Teriel,
Terral, Terrall, Terrell, Terrella, Terriel,*

*Terriell, Terrielle, Terrill, Terryelle, Terryl,
Terryll, Terrylle, Teryl, Tyrell, Tyrelle*

Terrene (Latin) smooth.
*Tareena, Tarena, Teran, Teranee,
Tereena, Terena, Terencia, Terene,
Terenia, Terentia, Terina, Terran, Terren,
Terrena, Terrin, Terrina, Terron,
Terrosina, Terryn, Terun, Teryn, Teryna,
Terynn, Tyreen, Tyrene*

Terri **G** (Greek) reaper. A familiar
form of Theresa.
Terree, Terria, Terrie

Terriann (American) a combination
of Terri + Ann.
*Teran, Terian, Teriann, Terianne, Teriyan,
Terria, Terrian, Terrianne, Terryann*

Terrianna (American) a combination
of Terri + Anna.
*Teriana, Terianna, Terriana, Terriauna,
Terrina, Terriona, Terrionna, Terriyana,
Terriyanna, Terryana, Terryauna, Tyrina*

Terrica (American) a combination of
Terri + Erica. See also Rica.
*Tereka, Terica, Tericka, Terika, Terreka,
Terricka, Terrika, Tyrica, Tyricka, Tyrika,
Tyrikka, Tyronica*

Terry **B** (Greek) a short form of
Theresa.
*Tere, Teree, Terelle, Terene, Teri, Terie,
Terrey, Terri, Terrie, Terrye, Tery*

Terry-Lynn (American) a
combination of Terry + Lynn.
*Terelyn, Terelynn, Terri-Lynn, Terrilynn,
Terrylynn*

Tertia (Latin) third.
*Tercia, Tercina, Tercine, Terecena,
Tersia, Terza*

Teruko (Japanese) barrel.

Tesira (Greek) founder.

Tess **G** (Greek) a short form of
Quintessa, Theresa.
Tes, Tese

Tessa 🄖 (Greek) reaper.
Tesa, Tesah, Tesha, Tesia, Tessah, Tessia, Tezia

Tessie (Greek) a familiar form of
Theresa.
Tesi, Tessey, Tessi, Tessy, Tezi

Tetis (Greek) wet nurse; nursemaid.

Tetsu (Japanese) strong as iron.

Tetty (English) a familiar form of
Elizabeth.

Tevin 🄱 (American) a combination
of the prefix Te + Kevin.

Tevy (Cambodian) angel.
Teva

Teylor (English) a form of Taylor.
Teighlor, Teylar

Thaddea (Greek) courageous.
(Latin) praiser.
Thada, Thadda

Thalassa (Greek) sea, ocean.

Thalia (Greek) a form of Talia.
Mythology: the Muse of comedy.
Thaleia, Thalie, Thalya

Tham (Vietnamese) fog.

Than (Vietnamese) new.

Thana (Arabic) happy occasion.
Thaina, Thania, Thanie

Thanh (Vietnamese) bright blue.
(Punjabi) good place.
Thantra, Thanya

Thanh Ha (Vietnamese) discreet
grace.

Thao (Vietnamese) respectful of
parents.

The (Vietnamese) death; brilliant.

Thea (Greek) goddess. A short form
of Althea.
Theo

Thelma (Greek) willful.
Thelmalina

Thema (African) queen.

Thena (Mycenaean) a form of
Glenna.

Theodora (Greek) a form of
Theodore. See also Dora, Dorothy,
Feodora.
*Taedra, Teddi, Tedra, Teodora,
Teodory, Teodosia, Theda, Thedorsha,
Thedrica, Theo, Theodore, Theodoria,
Theodorian, Theodosia, Theodra*

Theodore 🄱 (Greek) gift of God.

Theone (Greek) a form of
Theodore.
Theondra, Theoni, Theonie

Theophania (Greek) God's
appearance. See also Tiffany.
Theo, Theophanie

Theophila (Greek) loved by God.
Theo

Theresa 🄖 (Greek) reaper. See also
Resi, Reza, Riza, Tassos, Teca,
Terrelle, Tracey, Tracy, Zilya.
*Teresa, Teri, Terri, Terry, Tersea, Tess,
Tessa, Tessie, Theresia, Theresina,
Theresita, Theressa, Thereza, Therisa,
Therissie, Thersa, Thersea, Tresha,
Tressa, Trice*

Therese (Greek) a form of Theresa.
*Terese, Thérése, Theresia, Theressa,
Therra, Therressa, Thersa*

Theta (Greek) Linguistics: a letter in
the Greek alphabet.

Thetis (Greek) disposed. Mythology:
the mother of Achilles.

Thi (Vietnamese) poem.
Thia, Thy, Thya

Thirza (Hebrew) pleasant.
Therza, Thirsa, Thirzah, Thursa, Thurza, Thyrza, Tirshka, Tirza

Thom (Vietnamese) teal river.

Thomas **B** (Greek, Aramaic) twin.

Thomasina (Hebrew) twin. See also Tamassa.
Tamsin, Thomasa, Thomasia, Thomasin, Thomasine, Thomazine, Thomencia, Thomethia, Thomisha, Thomsina, Toma, Tomasa, Tomasina, Tomasine, Tomina, Tommie, Tommina

Thora (Scandinavian) thunder.
Thordia, Thordis, Thorri, Thyra, Tyra

Thuong (Vietnamese) pledged.

Thuy (Vietnamese) gentle.

Tia (Greek) princess. (Spanish) aunt.
Téa, Teah, Teeya, Teia, Ti, Tiakeisha, Tialeigh, Tiamarie, Tianda, Tiandria, Tiante, Tiia, Tiye, Tyja

Tiana, Tianna (Greek) princess. (Latin) short forms of Tatiana.
Teana, Teanna, Tiahna, Tianah, Tiane, Tianea, Tianee, Tiani, Tiann, Tiannah, Tianne, Tianni, Tiaon, Tiauna, Tiena, Tiona, Tionna, Tiyana

Tiara (Latin) crowned.
Teair, Teaira, Teara, Téare, Tearia, Tearria, Teeaira, Teira, Teirra, Tiaira, Tiare, Tiarea, Tiareah, Tiari, Tiaria, Tiarra, Tiera, Tierra, Tyara

Tiarra **G** (Latin) a form of Tiara.
Tiairra, Tiarrah, Tyarra

Tiauna (Greek) a form of Tiana.
Tiaunah, Tiaunia, Tiaunna

Tiberia (Latin) Geography: the Tiber River in Italy.
Tib, Tibbie, Tibby

Tiburcia (Spanish) born in the place of pleasures.

Tichina (American) a combination of the prefix Ti + China.
Tichian, Tichin, Tichinia

Ticiana (Latin) valiant defender.

Tida (Tai) daughter.

Tien (Vietnamese) sweet smelling; pineapple.

Tien-Hou (Chinese) protector of sailors and others in times of danger.

Tien-Mu (Chinese) goddess of lightning.

Tiera, Tierra (Latin) forms of Tiara.
Tieara, Tiéra, Tierah, Tierre, Tierrea, Tierria

Tierney **G** (Irish) noble.
Tieranae, Tierani, Tieranie, Tieranni, Tierany, Tiernan, Tiernee, Tierny

Tiff (Latin) a short form of Tiffani, Tiffanie, Tiffany.

Tiffani, Tiffanie (Latin) forms of Tiffany.
Tephanie, Tifanee, Tifani, Tifanie, Tiff, Tiffanee, Tiffayne, Tiffeni, Tiffenie, Tiffennie, Tiffiani, Tiffianie, Tiffine, Tiffini, Tiffinie, Tiffni, Tiffy, Tiffynie, Tifni

Tiffany **G** (Latin) trinity. (Greek) a short form of Theophania. See also Tyfany.
Taffanay, Taffany, Tifaney, Tifany, Tiff, Tiffaney, Tiffani, Tiffanie, Tiffanny, Tiffeney, Tiffiany, Tiffiney, Tiffiny, Tiffnay, Tiffney, Tiffny, Tiffy, Tiphanie, Triffany

Tiffy (Latin) a familiar form of Tiffani, Tiffany.
Tiffey, Tiffi, Tiffie

Tijuana (Spanish) Geography: a border town in Mexico.
Tajuana, Tajuanna, Thejuana, Tiajuana, Tiajuanna, Tiawanna

Tilda (German) a short form of
Matilda.
Tilde, Tildie, Tildy, Tylda, Tyldy

Tillie (German) a familiar form of
Matilda.
Tilia, Tilley, Tilli, Tillia, Tilly, Tillye

Timi (English) a familiar form of
Timothea.
Timia, Timie, Timmi, Timmie

Timotea (Greek) she who honors
and praises God.

Timothea (English) honoring God.
Thea, Timi

Timothy 🄑 (Greek) honoring God.

Tina 🄖 (Spanish, American) a short
form of Augustine, Martina,
Christina, Valentina.
*Teanna, Teena, Teina, Tena, Tenae,
Tinai, Tine, Tinea, Tinia, Tiniah, Tinna,
Tinnia, Tyna, Tynka*

Tinble (English) sound bells make.
Tynble

Tinesha (American) a combination
of the prefix Ti + Niesha.
*Timnesha, Tinecia, Tineisha, Tinesa,
Tineshia, Tinessa, Tinisha, Tinsia*

Ting, Ting-Ting (Chinese) slim and
graceful.

Tinisha (American) a form of
Tenisha.
Tiniesha, Tinieshia, Tinishia, Tinishya

Tiona, Tionna (American) forms of
Tiana.
*Teona, Teonna, Tionda, Tiondra,
Tiondre, Tioné, Tionette, Tioni, Tionia,
Tionie, Tionja, Tionnah, Tionne, Tionya,
Tyonna*

Tiphanie (Latin) a form of Tiffany.
Tiphanee, Tiphani, Tiphany

Tiponya (Native American) great
horned owl.
Tipper

Tipper (Irish) water pourer. (Native
American) a short form of Tiponya.

Tira (Hindi) arrow.
Tirah, Tirea, Tirena

Tirtha (Hindi) ford.

Tirza (Hebrew) pleasant.
*Thersa, Thirza, Tierza, Tirsa, Tirzah,
Tirzha, Tyrzah*

Tisa (Swahili) ninth-born.
Tisah, Tysa, Tyssa

Tish (Latin) a short form of Tisha.

Tisha 🄖 (Latin) joy. A short form of
Leticia.
*Taesha, Tesha, Teisha, Tiesha, Tieshia,
Tish, Tishal, Tishia, Tysha, Tyshia*

Tita (Greek) giant. (Spanish) a short
form of names ending in "tita."

Titania (Greek) giant. Mythology:
the Titans were a race of giants.
*Tania, Teata, Titanna, Titanya, Titiana,
Tiziana, Tytan, Tytania, Tytiana*

Titiana (Greek) a form of Titania.
*Titianay, Titiania, Titianna, Titiayana,
Titionia, Titiyana, Titiyanna, Tityana*

Tivona (Hebrew) nature lover.

Tiwa (Zuni) onion.

Tiyana (Greek) a form of Tiana.
Tiyan, Tiyani, Tiyania, Tiyanna, Tiyonna

Toan (Vietnamese) love tenderly; in
pursuit.

Tobi 🄖 (Hebrew) God is good.
*Tobe, Tobee, Tobey, Tobie, Tobit, Toby,
Tobye, Tova, Tovah, Tove, Tovi, Tybi,
Tybie*

Toby 🄑 (Hebrew) a form of Tobi.

Tocarra (American) a combination of the prefix To + Cara.
Tocara, Toccara

Todd **B** (English) fox.

Toinette (French) a short form of Antoinette.
Toinetta, Tola, Tonetta, Tonette, Toni, Toniette, Twanette

Toki (Japanese) hopeful.
Toko, Tokoya, Tokyo

Tokiko (Japanese) dragon.

Tokiwa (Japanese) the girl who shines.

Tola (Polish) a form of Toinette.
Tolsia

Tomi **G** (Japanese) rich.
Tomie, Tomiju

Tommie **B** (Hebrew) a short form of Thomasina.
Tomme, Tommi, Tommia, Tommy

Tommy **B** (Hebrew) a form of Tommie.

Tomo (Japanese) intelligent.
Tomoko

Tomomi (Japanese) child of Toki.

Tonesha (American) a combination of the prefix To + Niesha.
Toneisha, Toneisheia, Tonesha, Tonesia, Toniece, Tonisha, Tonneshia

Tong (Chinese) phoenix tree.

Toni **G** (Greek) flourishing. (Latin) praiseworthy.
Tonee, Toney, Tonia, Tonie, Toniee, Tonni, Tonnie, Tony, Tonye

Tonia (Latin, Slavic) a form of Toni, Tonya.
Tonea, Toniah, Toniea, Tonja, Tonje, Tonna, Tonni, Tonnia, Tonnie, Tonnja

Tonisha (American) a form of Toneisha.
Toniesha, Tonisa, Tonise, Tonisia, Tonnisha

Tony **B** (Greek, Latin) a form of Toni.

Tonya (Slavic) fairy queen.
Tonia, Tonnya, Tonyea, Tonyetta, Tonyia

Tooka (Japanese) steady.

Topaz (Latin) golden yellow gem.

Topsy (English) on top. Literature: a slave in Harriet Beecher Stowe's novel *Uncle Tom's Cabin*.
Toppsy, Topsey, Topsie

Tora (Japanese) tiger.

Tori **G** (Japanese) bird. (English) a form of Tory.
Toria, Toriana, Torie, Torri, Torrie, Torrita

Toria (English) a form of Tori, Tory.
Toriah, Torria

Toriana (English) a form of Tori.
Torian, Toriane, Toriann, Torianna, Torianne, Toriauna, Torin, Torina, Torine, Torinne, Torion, Torionna, Torionne, Toriyanna, Torrina

Toribia (Latin) she who moves on to another life.

Torie, Torrie (English) forms of Tori.
Tore, Toree, Torei, Torre, Torree

Torilyn (English) a combination of Tori + Lynn.
Torilynn, Torrilyn, Torrilynn

Torri (English) a form of Tori.

Tory **G** (English) victorious. (Latin) a short form of Victoria.
Tauri, Torey, Tori, Torrey, Torreya, Torry, Torrye, Torya, Torye, Toya

Tosca (Latin) native of Toscana, Italy.

Toscana (Latin) she who was born in Etruria, Tuscany.

Tosha (Punjabi) armaments. (Polish) a familiar form of Antonia. (Russian) a form of Tasha.
Toshea, Toshia, Toshiea, Toshke, Tosia, Toska

Toshi (Japanese) mirror image.
Toshie, Toshiko, Toshikyo

Toshio (Japanese) she who is a beautiful companion.

Toski (Hopi) squashed bug.

Totsi (Hopi) moccasins.

Tottie (English) a familiar form of Charlotte.
Tota, Totti, Totty

Tou-Mou (Chinese) goddess of the polestar.

Tovah (Hebrew) good.
Tova, Tovia

Toya (Spanish) a form of Tory.
Toia, Toyanika, Toyanna, Toyea, Toylea, Toyleah, Toylenn, Toylin, Toylyn

Toyo (Japanese) ten days.

Tracey 🄶 (Greek) a familiar form of Theresa. (Latin) warrior.
Trace, Tracee, Tracell, Traci, Tracie, Tracy, Traice, Trasey, Treesy

Traci, Tracie 🄶 (Latin) forms of Tracey.
Tracia, Tracilee, Tracilyn, Tracilynn, Tracina, Traeci

Tracy 🄶 (Greek) a familiar form of Theresa. (Latin) warrior.
Treacy

Tralena (Latin) a combination of Tracy + Lena.
Traleen, Tralene, Tralin, Tralinda, Tralyn, Tralynn, Tralynne

Tranesha (American) a combination of the prefix Tra + Niesha.
Traneice, Traneis, Traneise, Traneisha, Tranese, Traneshia, Tranice, Traniece, Traniesha, Tranisha, Tranishia

Tranquila (Spanish) calm, tranquil.

Tránsito (Latin) she who moves on to another life.

Trashawn 🄱 (American) a combination of the prefix Tra + Shawn.
Trashan, Trashana, Trashauna, Trashon, Trayshauna

Trava (Czech) spring grasses.

Travis 🄱 (English) a form of Travers (see Boys' Names).

Travon 🄱 (American) a form of Trevon.

Treasure (Latin) treasure, wealth; valuable.
Treasa, Treasur, Treasuré, Treasury

Trella (Spanish) a familiar form of Estelle.

Tremaine 🄱 (Scottish) house of stone.

Trent 🄱 (Latin) torrent, rapid stream. (French) thirty. Geography: a city in northern Italy.

Tresha (Greek) a form of Theresa.
Trescha, Trescia, Treshana, Treshia

Tressa (Greek) a short form of Theresa. See also Teresa.
Treaser, Tresa, Tresca, Trese, Treska, Tressia, Tressie, Trez, Treza, Trisa

Trevina (Irish) prudent. (Welsh) homestead.
Treva, Trevanna, Trevena, Trevenia, Treveon, Trevia, Treviana, Trevien, Trevin, Trevona

Trevon 🄱 (Irish) a form of Trevona.

Trevona (Irish) a form of Trevina.
Trevion, Trevon, Trevonia, Trevonna, Trevonne, Trevonye

Trevor B (Irish) prudent. (Welsh) homestead.

Triana (Latin) third. (Greek) a form of Trina.
Tria, Triann, Trianna, Trianne

Trice (Greek) a short form of Theresa.
Treece

Tricia (Latin) a form of Trisha.
Trica, Tricha, Trichelle, Tricina, Trickia

Trilby (English) soft hat.
Tribi, Trilbie, Trillby

Trina G (Greek) pure.
Treena, Treina, Trenna, Triana, Trinia, Trinchen, Trind, Trinda, Trine, Trinette, Trini, Trinica, Trinice, Triniece, Trinika, Trinique, Trinisa, Tryna

Trinh (Vietnamese) fairy; spirit; angel.

Trini (Greek) a form of Trina.
Trinia, Trinie

Trinidad (Latin) three people in one God.

Trinity ★ G (Latin) triad. Religion: the Father, the Son, and the Holy Spirit.
Trinita, Trinite, Trinitee, Triniti, Trinnette, Trinty

Tripaileo (Mapuche) explosion of flames, explosive bomb; explosive, impulsive, passionate, and vehement woman.

Trish (Latin) a short form of Beatrice, Trisha.
Trishell, Trishelle

Trisha (Latin) noblewoman. (Hindi) thirsty. See also Tricia.
Treasha, Trish, Trishann, Trishanna, Trishanne, Trishara, Trishia, Trishna, Trissha, Trycia

Trissa (Latin) a familiar form of Patricia.
Trisa, Trisanne, Trisia, Trisina, Trissi, Trissie, Trissy, Tryssa

Trista (Latin) a short form of Tristen.
Trisatal, Tristess, Tristia, Trysta, Trystia

Tristan B (Latin) bold.
Trista, Tristane, Tristanni, Tristany, Tristen, Tristian, Tristiana, Tristin, Triston, Trystan, Trystyn

Tristana (Latin) she who carries sadness with her.

Tristen B (Latin) a form of Tristan.
Tristene, Trysten

Tristin B (Latin) a form of Tristan.
Tristina, Tristine, Tristinye, Tristn, Trystin

Triston B (Latin) a form of Tristan.
Tristony

Trixie (American) a familiar form of Beatrice.
Tris, Trissie, Trissina, Trix, Trixi, Trixy

Troy B (Irish) foot soldier.

Troya (Irish) a form of Troy.
Troi, Troia, Troiana, Troiya

Truc (Vietnamese) safe, secure.

Trudel (Dutch) a form of Trudy.

Trudy (German) a familiar form of Gertrude.
Truda, Trude, Trudel, Trudessa, Trudey, Trudi, Trudie

Trung (Vietnamese) pure.

Trycia (Latin) a form of Trisha.

Tryna (Greek) a form of Trina.
Tryane, Tryanna, Trynee

Tryne (Dutch) pure.
Trine

Trystyn (Latin) a form of Tristan.

Tsigana (Hungarian) a form of Zigana.
Tsigane, Tzigana, Tzigane

Tsi-Ku (Chinese) goddess of the outhouse.

Tsuhgi (Japanese) a one-year-old child.

Tsukiko (Japanese) plentiful.

Tsukina (Japanese) second daughter.

Tsuna (Japanese) moon child.

Tsuneko (Japanese) moon; a type of red apple.

Tsuru (Japanese) bond.

Tsuyu (Japanese) a child forever.

Tu 🅱 (Chinese) jade.

Tuan (Chinese) round, circular.

Tucker 🅱 (English) fuller, tucker of cloth.

Tuesday (English) born on the third day of the week.
Tuesdae, Tuesdea, Tuesdee, Tuesdey, Tusdai

Tuki (Japanese) stork; hope for long life.

Tula (Hindi) born in the lunar month of Capricorn.
Tulah, Tulla, Tullah, Tuula

Tullia (Irish) peaceful, quiet.
Tulia, Tulliah

Tulsi (Hindi) basil, a sacred Hindi herb.
Tulsia

Tuo (Chinese) proper, appropriate.

Turner 🅱 (Latin) lathe worker; wood worker.

Turquoise (French) blue-green semi-precious stone.
Turkois, Turkoise, Turkoys, Turkoyse

Tusa (Zuni) prairie dog.

Tusnelda (German) she who fights giants.

Tuyen (Vietnamese) angel.

Tuyet (Vietnamese) snow.

Twyla (English) woven of double thread.
Twila, Twilla

Ty 🅱 (English) a short form of Tyler, Tyson.

Tyanna (American) a combination of the prefix Ty + Anna.
Tya, Tyana, Tyann, Tyannah, Tyanne, Tyannia

Tyeisha (American) a form of Tyesha.
Tyeesha, Tyeishia, Tyieshia, Tyisha, Tyishea, Tyishia

Tyesha (American) a combination of Ty + Aisha.
Tyasha, Tyashia, Tyasia, Tyasiah, Tyeisha, Tyeshia, Tyeyshia, Tyisha

Tyfany (American) a short form of Tiffany.
Tyfani, Tyfanny, Tyffani, Tyffanni, Tyffany, Tyffini, Typhanie, Typhany

Tykeisha (American) a form of Takeisha.
Tkeesha, Tykeisa, Tykeishia, Tykesha, Tykeshia, Tykeysha, Tykeza, Tykisha

Tykera (American) a form of Takira.
Tykeira, Tykeirah, Tykereiah, Tykeria, Tykeriah, Tykerria, Tykiera, Tykierra, Tykira, Tykiria, Tykirra

Tyler 🅱 (English) tailor.
Tyller, Tylor

Tylor 🅱 (English) a form of Tyler.

Tyna (Czech) a short form of Kristina.
Tynae, Tynea, Tynia

Tyne (English) river.
Tine, Tyna, Tynelle, Tynessa, Tynetta

Tynesha (American) a combination of Ty + Niesha.
Tynaise, Tynece, Tyneicia, Tynesa, Tynesha, Tyneshia, Tynessia, Tyniesha, Tynisha, Tyseisha

Tynisha (American) a form of Tynesha.
Tyneisha, Tyneisia, Tynisa, Tynise, Tynishi

Tyra **G** (Scandinavian) battler. Mythology: Tyr was the god of war. A form of Thora. (Hindi) a form of Tira.
Tyraa, Tyrah, Tyran, Tyree, Tyria

Tyree **B** (Scandinavian) a form of Tyra.

Tyrell **B** (Greek) a form of Terrelle.

Tyshanna (American) a combination of Ty + Shawna.
Tyshana, Tyshanae, Tyshane, Tyshaun, Tyshaunda, Tyshawn, Tyshawna, Tyshawnah, Tyshawnda, Tyshawnna, Tysheann, Tysheanna, Tyshonia, Tyshonna, Tyshonya

Tyson **B** (French) child of Ty.

Tytiana (Greek) a form of Titania.
Tytana, Tytanna, Tyteana, Tyteanna, Tytianna, Tytianni, Tytionna, Tytiyana, Tytiyanna, Tytyana, Tytyauna

U (Korean) gentle.

Ubaldina (Teutonic) audacious, daring; intelligent.

Udele (English) prosperous.
Uda, Udella, Udelle, Yudelle

Ukara (Japanese) morning dew.

Uki (Japanese) moon.

Ula (Irish) sea jewel. (Scandinavian) wealthy. (Spanish) a short form of Eulalia.
Uli, Ulla

Ulani (Polynesian) cheerful.
Ulana, Ulane

Ulima (Arabic) astute; wise.
Ullima

Ulla (German, Swedish) willful. (Latin) a short form of Ursula.
Ulli

Ulrica (German) wolf ruler; ruler of all. See also Rica.
Ulka, Ullrica, Ullricka, Ullrika, Ulrika, Ulrike

Ultima (Latin) last, endmost, farthest.

Ululani (Hawaiian) heavenly inspiration.

Ulva (German) wolf.

Uma (Hindi) mother. Religion: another name for the Hindu goddess Devi.

Umay (Turkish) hopeful.
Umai

Umbelina (Latin) she who gives protective shade.

Umeko (Japanese) plum-blossom child; patient.
Ume, Umeyo

Umeno (Japanese) beautiful and serene.

Una (Latin) one; united. (Hopi) good memory. (Irish) a form of Agnes. See also Oona.
Unna, Uny

Undine (Latin) little wave. Mythology: the undines were water spirits. See also Ondine.
Undeen, Undene

Unice (English) a form of Eunice.

Unika 🄶 (American) a form of Unique.
Unica, Unicka, Unik, Unikqua, Unikue

Unique 🄶 (Latin) only one.
Unika, Uniqia, Uniqua, Uniquia

Unity (English) unity.
Uinita, Unita, Unitee

Unn (Norwegian) she who is loved.

Unna (German) woman.

Uoc (Vietnamese) bamboo; wish.

Urania (Greek) heavenly. Mythology: the Muse of astronomy.
Urainia, Uranie, Uraniya, Uranya

Urano (Japanese) air; hope, pray.

Urbana (Latin) city dweller.
Urbanah, Urbanna

Uriel 🄱 (Hebrew) God is my light.

Urika (Omaha) useful to everyone.
Ureka

Urit (Hebrew) bright.
Urice

Urraca (German) magpie.

Ursa (Greek) a short form of Ursula. (Latin) a form of Orsa.
Ursey, Ursi, Ursie, Ursy

Ursina (Latin) little bear.

Ursula (Greek) little bear. See also Sula, Ulla, Vorsila.
Irsaline, Ursa, Ursala, Ursel, Ursela, Ursella, Ursely, Ursilla, Ursillane, Ursola, Ursule, Ursulina, Ursuline, Urszula, Urszuli, Urzula

Úrsula (Portuguese) a form of Ursula.

Usagi (Japanese) plum tree field.

Usha (Hindi) sunrise.

Ushi (Chinese) ox. Astrology: a sign of the Chinese zodiac.

Uta (German) rich. (Japanese) poem.
Utako

Utina (Native American) woman of my country.
Utahna, Utona, Utonna

V 🄶 (American) an initial used as a first name.

Vail 🄱 (English) valley.
Vale, Vayle

Val 🄱 (Latin) a short form of Valentina, Valerie.

Vala (German) singled out.
Valla

Valarie (Latin) a form of Valerie.
Valarae, Valaree, Valarey, Valari, Valaria, Vallarie

Valburga (German) she who defends on the battlefield.

Valda (German) famous ruler.
Valida, Velda

Valdrada (German) she who gives advice.

Valencia (Spanish) strong. Geography: a region in eastern Spain.
Valecia, Valence, Valenica, Valentia, Valenzia

Valene (Latin) a short form of Valentina.
Valaine, Valean, Valeda, Valeen, Valen, Valena, Valeney, Valien, Valina, Valine, Vallan, Vallen

Valentina (Latin) strong. History:
Valentina Tereshkova, a Soviet
cosmonaut, was the first woman in
space. See also Tina, Valene, Valli.
*Val, Valantina, Vale, Valenteen,
Valentena, Valentijn, Valentin, Valentine,
Valiaka, Valtina, Valyn, Valynn*

Valera (Russian) a form of Valerie.
See also Lera.

Valeria (Latin) a form of Valerie.
Valaria, Valeriana, Valeriane, Veleria

Valéria (Hungarian, Portuguese) a
form of Valerie.

Valerie **G** (Latin) strong.
*Vairy, Val, Valarie, Vale, Valera,
Valeree, Valeri, Valeria, Valérie, Valery,
Valka, Valleree, Valleri, Vallerie, Valli,
Vallirie, Valora, Valorie, Valry, Valya,
Velerie, Waleria*

Valery (Latin) a form of Valerie.
Valerye, Vallary, Vallery

Valeska (Slavic) glorious ruler.
*Valesca, Valese, Valeshia, Valeshka,
Valezka, Valisha*

Valli (Latin) a familiar form of
Valentina, Valerie. Botany: a plant
native to India.
Vallie, Vally

Valma (Finnish) loyal defender.

Valonia (Latin) shadow valley.
Vallon, Valona

Valora (Latin) a form of Valerie.
Valoria, Valorya, Velora

Valorie (Latin) a form of Valerie.
Vallori, Vallory, Valori, Valory

Vance **B** (English) thresher.

Vanda **G** (German) a form of Wanda.
*Vandana, Vandella, Vandetta, Vandi,
Vannda*

Vanesa (Greek) a form of Vanessa.
Vanesha, Vaneshah, Vanesia, Vanisa

Vanessa ☆ **G** (Greek) butterfly.
Literature: a name invented by
Jonathan Swift as a nickname for
Esther Vanhomrigh. See also Nessie.
*Van, Vanassa, Vanesa, Vaneshia,
Vanesse, Vanessia, Vanessica, Vanetta,
Vaneza, Vaniece, Vaniessa, Vanija,
Vanika, Vanissa, Vanita, Vanna,
Vannesa, Vannessa, Vanni, Vannie,
Vanny, Varnessa, Venessa*

Vanetta (English) a form of Vanessa.
*Vaneta, Vanita, Vanneta, Vannetta,
Vannita, Venetta*

Vania, Vanya (Russian) familiar
forms of Anna.
*Vanija, Vanina, Vaniya, Vanja, Vanka,
Vannia*

Vanity (English) vain.
Vaniti, Vanitty

Vanna (Cambodian) golden. (Greek)
a short form of Vanessa.
*Vana, Vanoe, Vanelly, Vannah,
Vannalee, Vannaleigh, Vannie, Vanny*

Vannesa, Vannessa (Greek) forms
of Vanessa.
Vannesha, Vanneza

Vanora (Welsh) white wave.
Vannora

Vantrice (American) a combination
of the prefix Van + Trice.
Vantrece, Vantricia, Vantrisa, Vantrissa

Varda (Hebrew) rose.
*Vadit, Vardia, Vardice, Vardina, Vardis,
Vardit*

Varinia (Ancient Roman, Spanish)
versatile.

Varvara (Slavic) a form of Barbara.
*Vara, Varenka, Varina, Varinka, Varya,
Varyusha, Vava, Vavka*

Vashti (Persian) lovely. Bible: the wife
of Ahasuerus, king of Persia.
Vashtee, Vashtie, Vashty

Vaughn B (Welsh) small.

Veanna (American) a combination of
the prefix Ve + Anna.
Veeana, Veena, Veenaya, Veeona

Veda (Sanskrit) sacred lore;
knowledge. Religion: the Vedas are
the sacred writings of Hinduism.
*Vedad, Vedis, Veeda, Veida, Veleda,
Vida*

Vedette (Italian) sentry; scout.
(French) movie star.
Vedetta

Vega (Arabic) falling star.

Velda (German) a form of Valda.

Velika (Slavic) great, wondrous.

Velma (German) a familiar form of
Vilhelmina.
Valma, Vellma, Vilma, Vilna

Velvet (English) velvety.

Venancia (Latin) hunter; she likes to
hunt deer.

Venecia (Italian) from Venice, Italy.
*Vanecia, Vanetia, Veneise, Venesa,
Venesha, Venesher, Venesse, Venessia,
Venetia, Venette, Venezia, Venice,
Venicia, Veniece, Veniesa, Venise,
Venisha, Venishia, Venita, Venitia,
Venize, Vennesa, Vennice, Vennisa,
Vennise, Vonitia, Vonizia*

Venessa (Latin) a form of Vanessa.
*Veneese, Venesa, Venese, Veneshia,
Venesia, Venisa, Venissa, Vennessa*

Ventana (Spanish) window.

Ventura (Spanish) good fortune.

Venus (Latin) love. Mythology: the
goddess of love and beauty.
Venis, Venusa, Venusina, Vinny

Vera (Latin) true. (Slavic) faith. A
short form of Elvera, Veronica. See
also Verena, Wera.
*Vara, Veera, Veira, Veradis, Verasha,
Vere, Verka, Verla, Viera, Vira*

Verbena (Latin) sacred plants.
Verbeena, Verbina

Verda (Latin) young, fresh.
Verdi, Verdie, Viridiana, Viridis

Verdad (Spanish) truthful.

Veredigna (Latin) she who has
earned great honors for her dignity.

Verena (Latin) truthful. A familiar
form of Vera, Verna.
*Verene, Verenis, Vereniz, Verina, Verine,
Verinka, Veroshka, Verunka, Verusya,
Virna*

Verenice (Latin) a form of Veronica.
Verenis, Verenise, Vereniz

Verity (Latin) truthful.
Verita, Veritie

Verlene (Latin) a combination of
Veronica + Lena.
*Verleen, Verlena, Verlin, Verlina,
Verlinda, Verline, Verlyn*

Verna (Latin) springtime. (French) a
familiar form of Laverne. See also
Verena, Wera.
*Verasha, Verla, Verne, Vernetia, Vernetta,
Vernette, Vernia, Vernice, Vernita,
Verusya, Viera, Virida, Virna, Virnell*

Vernice (Latin) a form of Bernice,
Verna.
*Vernese, Vernesha, Verneshia, Vernessa,
Vernica, Vernicca, Verniece, Vernika,
Vernique, Vernis, Vernise, Vernisha,
Vernisheia, Vernissia*

Veronica (Latin) true image. See also
Ronni, Weronika.
*Varonica, Vera, Veranique, Verenice,
Verhonica, Verinica, Verohnica, Veron,
Verona, Verone, Veronic, Véronic,*

Veronice, Veronika, Veronique,
Véronique, Veronne, Veronnica,
Veruszhka, Vironica, Vron, Vronica

Verónica (Spanish) a form of
Veronica.

Verônica (Portuguese) a form of
Veronica.

Veronika (Latin) a form of Veronica.
Varonika, Veronick, Véronick, Veronik,
Veronike, Veronka, Veronkia, Veruka

Veronique, Véronique (French)
forms of Veronica.

Vespera (Latin) evening star.

Vesta (Latin) keeper of the house.
Mythology: the goddess of the
home.
Vessy, Vest, Vesteria

Veta (Slavic) a familiar form of
Elizabeth.
Veeta, Vita

Vi (Latin, French) a short form of
Viola, Violet.
Vye

Vianca (Spanish) a form of Bianca.
Vianeca, Vianica

Vianey (American) a familiar form of
Vianna.
Vianney, Viany

Vianna (American) a combination of
Vi + Anna.
Viana, Vianey, Viann, Vianne

Vica (Hungarian) a form of Eve.

Vicente **B** (Spanish) a form of
Vincent.

Vicki, Vickie (Latin) familiar forms
of Victoria.
Vic, Vicci, Vicke, Vickee, Vickiana,
Vickilyn, Vickki, Vicky, Vika, Viki, Vikie,
Vikki, Vikky

Vicky **G** (Latin) a familiar form of
Victoria.
Viccy, Vickey, Viky, Vikkey, Vikky

Victoria ☀ **G** (Latin) victorious.
See also Tory, Wicktoria, Wisia.
Vicki, Vicky, Victoire, Victoriana,
Victorianna, Victorie, Victoriana, Victorine,
Victoriya, Victorria, Victorriah, Victory,
Victorya, Viktoria, Vitoria, Vyctoria

Vida (Sanskrit) a form of Veda.
(Hebrew) a short form of Davida.
Vidamarie

Vidonia (Portuguese) branch of a vine.
Vedonia, Vidonya

Vienna (Latin) Geography: the
capital of Austria.
Veena, Vena, Venna, Vienette, Vienne,
Vina

Viktoria (Latin) a form of Victoria.
Viktorie, Viktorija, Viktorina, Viktorine,
Viktorka

Vilhelmina (German) a form of
Wilhelmina.
Velma, Vilhelmine, Vilma

Villette (French) small town.
Vietta

Vilma (German) a short form of
Vilhemina.

Vina (Hindi) Religion: a musical
instrument played by the Hindu
goddess of wisdom. (Spanish)
vineyard. (Hebrew) a short form of
Davina. (English) a short form of
Alvina. See also Lavina.
Veena, Vena, Viña, Vinesha, Vinessa,
Vinia, Viniece, Vinique, Vinisha, Viñita,
Vinna, Vinni, Vinnie, Vinny, Vinora, Vyna

Vincent **B** (Latin) victor,
conqueror.

Vincentia (Latin) a form of Vincent.
Vicenta, Vincenta, Vincentena, Vincentina,
Vincentine, Vincenza, Vincy, Vinnie

Viñita (Spanish) a form of Vina.
Viñeet, Viñeeta, Viñetta, Viñette, Viñitha, Viñta, Viñti, Viñtia, Vyñetta, Vyñette

Viola (Latin) violet; stringed instrument in the violin family. Literature: the heroine of Shakespeare's play *Twelfth Night*.
Vi, Violaine, Violanta, Violante, Viole, Violeine

Violet (French) Botany: a plant with purplish blue flowers.
Vi, Violeta, Violette, Vyolet, Vyoletta, Vyolette

Violeta (French) a form of Violet.
Violetta

Virgilia (Latin) rod bearer, staff bearer.
Virgillia

Virginia (Latin) pure, virginal. Literature: Virginia Woolf was a well-known British writer. See also Gina, Ginger, Ginny, Jinny.
Verginia, Verginya, Virge, Virgen, Virgenia, Virgenya, Virgie, Virgine, Virginie, Virginië, Virginio, Virginnia, Virgy, Virjeana

Virginie (French) a form of Virginia.

Viridiana (Latin) a form of Viridis.

Viridis (Latin) green.
Virdis, Virida, Viridia, Viridiana

Virtudes (Latin) blessed spirit.

Virtue (Latin) virtuous.

Visitación (Latin) refers to the Virgin Mary visiting Saint Isabel, who was her cousin.

Vita (Latin) life.
Veeta, Veta, Vitaliana, Vitalina, Vitel, Vitella, Vitia, Vitka, Vitke

Vitalia (Latin) she who is full of life.

Vitoria (Spanish) a form of Victoria.
Vittoria

Vitória (Portuguese) a form of Victoria.

Viv (Latin) a short form of Vivian.

Viva (Latin) a short form of Aviva, Vivian.
Vica, Vivan, Vivva

Viveca (Scandinavian) a form of Vivian.
Viv, Vivecca, Vivecka, Viveka, Vivica, Vivieca, Vyveca

Vivian ⬛ (Latin) full of life.
Vevay, Vevey, Viv, Viva, Viveca, Vivee, Vivi, Vivia, Viviana, Viviane, Viviann, Vivianne, Vivie, Vivien, Vivienne, Vivina, Vivion, Vivyan, Vivyann, Vivyanne, Vyvyan, Vyvyann, Vyvyanne

Viviana (Latin) a form of Vivian.
Viv, Vivianna, Vivyana, Vyvyana

Vondra (Czech) loving woman.
Vonda, Vondrea

Voneisha (American) a combination of Yvonne + Aisha.
Voneishia, Vonesha, Voneshia

Vonna (French) a form of Yvonne.
Vona

Vonny (French) a familiar form of Yvonne.
Vonney, Vonni, Vonnie

Vontricia (American) a combination of Yvonne + Tricia.
Vontrece, Vontrese, Vontrice, Vontriece

Vorsila (Greek) a form of Ursula.
Vorsilla, Vorsula, Vorsulla, Vorsyla

Vui (Vietnamese) medium; loyalty.

W **B** (American) an initial used as a first name.

Wadd (Arabic) beloved.

Waheeda (Arabic) one and only.

Wainani (Hawaiian) beautiful water.

Wakaba (Japanese) coast.

Wakako (Japanese) rabbit.

Wakana (Japanese) plant.

Wakanda (Dakota) magical power.
Wakenda

Wakeisha (American) a combination of the prefix Wa + Keisha.
Wakeishia, Wakesha, Wakeshia, Wakesia

Walad (Arabic) newborn.
Waladah, Walidah

Walda (German) powerful; famous.
Waldina, Waldine, Walida, Wallda, Welda

Waleria (Polish) a form of Valerie.
Wala

Walker **B** (English) cloth; walker.
Wallker

Wallis (English) from Wales.
Wallie, Walliss, Wally, Wallys

Wan (Chinese) gentle; gracious.

Wanda (German) wanderer. See also Wendy.
Vanda, Wahnda, Wandah, Wandely, Wandie, Wandis, Wandja, Wandzia, Wannda, Wonda, Wonnda

Wandie (German) a familiar form of Wanda.
Wandi, Wandy

Waneta (Native American) charger. See also Juanita.
Waneeta, Wanita, Wanite, Wanneta, Waunita, Wonita, Wonnita, Wynita

Wanetta (English) pale face.
Wanette, Wannetta, Wannette

Wang (Chinese) flourishing.

Wang-Mu (Chinese) highest goddess of ancient China.

Wanida (Pohnpeian) a form of Dolores.

Wanika (Hawaiian) a form of Juanita.
Wanicka

Wanya **B** (Russian) a form of Vania.

Warda (German) guardian.
Wardah, Wardeh, Wardena, Wardenia, Wardia, Wardine

Washi (Japanese) eagle.

Wattan (Japanese) homeland.

Wauna (Moquelumnan) snow geese honking.
Waunakee

Wava (Slavic) a form of Barbara.

Waverly **G** (English) quaking aspen-tree meadow.
Waverley, Waverli, Wavierlee

Wayna (Quechua) young.

Waynesha (American) a combination of Waynette + Niesha.
Wayneesha, Wayneisha, Waynie, Waynisha

Waynette (English) wagon maker.
Waynel, Waynelle, Waynetta, Waynlyn

Weeko (Dakota) pretty girl.

Wehilani (Hawaiian) heavenly adornment.

Wei (Chinese) valuable.

Wen (Chinese) cultured, refined.

Wenda (Welsh) a form of Wendy.
Wendaine, Wendayne

Wendelle (English) wanderer.
Wendaline, Wendall, Wendalyn, Wendeline, Wendella, Wendelline, Wendelly

Wendi (Welsh) a form of Wendy.
Wendie

Wendy (Welsh) white; light skinned. A familiar form of Gwendolyn, Wanda.
Wenda, Wende, Wendee, Wendey, Wendi, Wendye, Wuendy

Wera (Polish) a form of Vera. See also Verna.
Wiera, Wiercia, Wierka

Weronika (Polish) a form of Veronica.
Weronikra

Wesisa (Musoga) foolish.

Weslee (English) western meadow.
Weslea, Wesleigh, Weslene, Wesley, Wesli, Weslia, Weslie, Weslyn

Wesley 🅱 (English) a form of Weslee.

Weston 🅱 (English) western town.

Whitley 🅶 (English) white field.
Whitely, Whitlee, Whitleigh, Whitlie, Whittley

Whitney 🅶 (English) white island.
Whiteney, Whitne, Whitné, Whitnee, Whitneigh, Whitnie, Whitny, Whitnye, Whytne, Whytney, Witney

Whitnie (English) a form of Whitney.
Whitani, Whitnei, Whitni, Whytni, Whytnie

Whittney (English) a form of Whitney.
Whittaney, Whittanie, Whittany, Whitteny, Whittnay, Whittnee, Whittney, Whittni, Whittnie

Whoopi (English) happy; excited.
Whoopie, Whoopy

Wicktoria (Polish) a form of Victoria.
Wicktorja, Wiktoria, Wiktorja

Wilda (German) untamed. (English) willow.
Willda, Wylda

Wileen (English) a short form of Wilhelmina.
Wilene, Willeen, Willene

Wilhelmina (German) a form of Wilhelm (see Boys' Names). See also Billie, Guillerma, Helma, Minka, Minna, Minnie.
Vilhelmina, Wileen, Wilhelmine, Willa, Willamina, Willamine, Willemina, Willette, Williamina, Willie, Willmina, Willmine, Wilma, Wimina

Wilikinia (Hawaiian) a form of Virginia.

Willa (German) a short form of Wilhelmina.
Willabella, Willette, Williabelle

Willette (English) a familiar form of Wilhelmina, Willa.
Wiletta, Wilette, Willetta, Williette

William 🅱 (English) a form of Wilhelm (see Boys' Names).

Willie 🅱 (English) a familiar form of Wilhelmina.
Willi, Willina, Willisha, Willishia, Willy

Willow (English) willow tree.
Willough

Wilma (German) a short form of
Wilhelmina.
*Williemae, Wilmanie, Wilmayra,
Wilmetta, Wilmette, Wilmina, Wilmyne,
Wylma*

Wilona (English) desired.
Willona, Willone, Wilone

Wilson **B** (English) child of Will.

Win **B** (German) a short form of
Winifred. See also Edwina.
Wyn

Winda (Swahili) hunter.

Windy (English) windy.
*Windee, Windey, Windi, Windie,
Wyndee, Wyndy*

Winema (Moquelumnan) woman
chief.

Winifred (German) peaceful friend.
(Welsh) a form of Guinevere. See
also Freddi, Una, Winnie.
*Win, Winafred, Winefred, Winefride,
Winfreda, Winfrieda, Winiefrida,
Winifrid, Winifryd, Winnafred,
Winnefred, Winniefred, Winnifred,
Winnifrid, Wynafred, Wynifred,
Wynnifred*

Winna (African) friend.
Winnah

Winnie (English) a familiar form of
Edwina, Gwyneth, Winnifred,
Winona, Wynne. History: Winnie
Mandela kept the anti-apartheid
movement alive in South Africa
while her then-husband, Nelson
Mandela, was imprisoned.
Literature: the lovable bear in A. A.
Milne's children's story *Winnie-the-
Pooh*.
*Wina, Winne, Winney, Winni, Winny,
Wynnie*

Winola (German) charming friend.
Wynola

Winona (Lakota) oldest daughter.
*Wanona, Wenona, Wenonah, Winnie,
Winonah, Wynonna*

Winter **G** (English) winter.
Wintr, Wynter

Wira (Polish) a form of Elvira.
Wiria, Wirke

Wisia (Polish) a form of Victoria.
Wicia, Wikta

Wo (Chinese) fertile.

Wren (English) wren, songbird.

Wu (Chinese) a parasol.

Wyanet (Native American)
legendary beauty.
Wyaneta, Wyanita, Wynette

Wyatt **B** (French) little warrior.

Wynne (Welsh) white, light skinned.
A short form of Blodwyn,
Guinivere, Gwyneth.
Winnie, Wyn, Wynn

Wynonna (Lakota) a form of
Winona.
Wynnona, Wynona

Wynter (English) a form of Winter.
Wynteria

Wyoming (Native American)
Geography: a western U.S. state.
Wy, Wye, Wyoh, Wyomia

Xandra (Greek) a form of Zandra.
(Spanish) a short form of
Alexandra.
Xander, Xandrea, Xandria

Xanthe (Greek) yellow, blond. See also Zanthe.
Xanne, Xantha, Xanthia, Xanthippe

Xanthippe (Greek) a form of Xanthe. History: Socrates's wife.
Xantippie

Xavier ▣ (Arabic) bright. (Basque) owner of the new house.

Xaviera (Arabic, Basque) a form of Xavier. See also Javiera, Zaviera.
Xavia, Xaviére, Xavyera, Xiveria

Xela (Quiché) my mountain home.

Xena (Greek) a form of Xenia.

Xenia (Greek) hospitable. See also Zena, Zina.
Xeenia, Xena, Xenea, Xenya, Xinia

Xi (Chinese) rare, uncommon.

Xia (Chinese) glow of the sunrise or sunset.

Xia He, Xia-He (Chinese) summer lotus; pure and elegant.

Xian (Chinese) refined, elegant.

Xiang (Chinese) fragrant.

Xiao (Chinese) dawn.

Xiao Hong, Xiao-Hong (Chinese) morning rainbow.

Xiao-Chen, Xiao Chen (Chinese) early morning.

Xie (Chinese) harmonious.

Xin (Chinese) star.

Xin Qian, Xin-Qian (Chinese) happy and beautiful.

Xing (Chinese) apricot; almond.

Xiomara (Teutonic) glorious forest.
Xiomaris, Xiomayra

Xiu (Chinese) elegant; beautiful.

Xiu Juan, Xiu-Juan (Chinese) elegant, graceful.

Xiu Mei (Chinese) beautiful plum.

Xochitl (Aztec) place of many flowers.
Xochil, Xochilt, Xochilth, Xochiti

Xu (Chinese) brilliance of the rising sun.

Xuan (Vietnamese) spring.

Xue (Chinese) snow.

Xue Fang, Xue-Fang (Chinese) snow; fragrant.

Xun (Chinese) swift.

Xuxa (Portuguese) a familiar form of Susanna.

Xylia (Greek) a form of Sylvia.
Xylina, Xylona

Ya (Chinese) proper, correct.

Yachi (Japanese) young leaf.

Yachiko (Japanese) peaceful and beautiful child.

Yachiyo (Japanese) eight thousand.

Yachne (Hebrew) hospitable.

Yadira ▣ (Hebrew) friend.
Yadirah, Yadirha, Yadyra

Yael ▣ (Hebrew) strength of God. See also Jael.
Yaeli, Yaella, Yeala

Yaffa (Hebrew) beautiful. See also Jaffa.
Yafeal, Yaffit, Yafit

Yahaira (Hebrew) a form of Yakira.
Yahara, Yahayra, Yahira

Yaíza (Guanche) rainbow.

Yajaira (Hebrew) a form of Yakira.
Yahaira, Yajara, Yajayra, Yajhaira

Yaki, Yama (Japanese) forms of
Yachi.

Yakira (Hebrew) precious; dear.
Yahaira, Yajaira

Yalanda (Greek) a form of Yolanda.
Yalando, Yalonda, Ylana, Ylanda

Yalena (Greek, Russian) a form of
Helen. See also Lena, Yclena.

Yaletha (American) a form of
Oletha.
Yelitsa

Yamary (American) a combination
of the prefix Ya + Mary.
Yamairy, Yamarie, Yamaris, Yamayra

Yamelia (American) a form of
Amelia.
Yameily, Yamelya, Yamelys

Yamila (Arabic) a form of Jamila.
*Yamela, Yamely, Yamil, Yamile, Yamilet,
Yamiley, Yamilla, Yamille*

Yaminah (Arabic) right, proper.
*Yamina, Yamini, Yemina, Yeminah,
Yemini*

Yamka (Hopi) blossom.

Yamuna (Hindi) sacred river.

Yan (Chinese) bright red.

Yan Yan, Yan-Yan (Chinese) two
swallow birds; elegant.

Yana (Slavic) a form of Jana.
*Yanae, Yanah, Yanay, Yanaye, Yanesi,
Yanet, Yaneth, Yaney, Yani, Yanik,
Yanina, Yanis, Yanisha, Yanitza, Yanixia,
Yanna, Yannah, Yanni, Yannica,
Yannick, Yannina*

Yanaba (Navajo) brave.

Yanamaría (Slavic) bitter grace.

Yaneli (American) a combination of
the prefix Ya + Nellie.
*Yanela, Yanelis, Yaneliz, Yanelle, Yanelli,
Yanely, Yanelys*

Yanet (American) a form of Janet.
*Yanete, Yaneth, Yanethe, Yanette,
Yannet, Yanneth, Yannette*

Yang (Chinese) ocean.

Yáng (Chinese) sun.

Yao (Chinese) gentle and graceful.

Yara (Tupi) she is a lady.

Yareli (American) a form of Oralee.
Yarely, Yaresly

Yarina (Slavic) a form of Irene.
Yaryna

Yaritza (American) a combination of
Yana + Ritsa.
Yaritsa, Yaritsa

Yarkona (Hebrew) green.

Yarmilla (Slavic) market trader.

Yashira (Afghan) humble; takes it
easy. (Arabic) wealthy.

Yasinda (Pohnpeian) a form of Flora.

Yasmeen (Persian) a form of Yasmin.
*Yasemeen, Yasemin, Yasmeena,
Yasmen, Yasmene, Yasmeni, Yasmenne,
Yassmeen, Yassmen*

Yasmín (Persian) a form of Yasmin.

Yasmin, Yasmine (Persian) jasmine
flower.
*Yashmine, Yasiman, Yasimine, Yasma,
Yasmain, Yasmaine, Yasmina, Yasminda,
Yasmon, Yasmyn, Yazmin, Yesmean,
Yesmeen, Yesmin, Yesmina, Yesmine,
Yesmyn*

Yasu (Japanese) resting, calm.
Yasuko, Yasuyo

Yazmin (Persian) a form of Yasmin.
Yazmeen, Yazmen, Yazmene, Yazmina, Yazmine, Yazmyn, Yazmyne, Yazzmien, Yazzmine, Yazzmine, Yazzmyn

Ye (Chinese) leaf.

Yecenia (Arabic) a form of Yesenia.

Yehudit (Hebrew) a form of Judith.
Yudit, Yudita, Yuta

Yei (Japanese) flourishing.

Yeira (Hebrew) light.

Yekaterina (Russian) a form of Katherine.

Yelena (Russian) a form of Helen, Jelena. See also Lena, Yalena.
Yeleana, Yelen, Yelenna, Yelenne, Yelina, Ylena, Ylenia, Ylenna

Yelisabeta (Russian) a form of Elizabeth.
Yelizaveta

Yemena (Arabic) from Yemen.
Yemina

Yen (Chinese) yearning; desirous.
Yeni, Yenih, Yenny

Yenay (Chino) she who loves.

Yenene (Native American) shaman.

Yenifer (Welsh) a form of Jennifer.
Yenefer, Yennifer

Yeo (Korean) mild.
Yee

Yepa (Native American) snow girl.

Yeruti (Guarani) turtledove.

Yesenia (Arabic) flower.
Yasenya, Yecenia, Yesinia, Yesnia, Yessenia

Yesica (Hebrew) a form of Jessica.
Yesika, Yesiko

Yésica (Hebrew) a form of Yesica.

Yessenia (Arabic) a form of Yesenia.
Yessena, Yessenya, Yissenia

Yessica (Hebrew) a form of Jessica.
Yessika, Yesyka

Yetta (English) a short form of Henrietta.
Yette, Yitta, Yitty

Yeva (Ukrainian) a form of Eve.

Yhlda (Pohnpeian) a form of Juana.

Yi Jie, Yi-Jie (Chinese) happy and pure.

Yi Min, Yi-Min (Chinese) happy and smart.

Yi Ze, Yi-Ze (Chinese) happy and shiny like a pearl.

Yiesha (Arabic, Swahili) a form of Aisha.
Yiasha

Yin (Chinese) silver; polite; sound.

Yín (Chinese) silver.

Ying (Chinese) cherry.

Ynaganta (Chamorro) a form of Inagangta.

Ynez (Spanish) a form of Agnes. See also Inez.
Ynes, Ynesita

Yoanna (Hebrew) a form of Joanna.
Yoana, Yohana, Yohanka, Yohanna, Yohannah

Yocasta (Greek) violet.

Yocelin, Yocelyn (Latin) forms of Jocelyn.
Yoceline, Yocelyne, Yuceli

Yoconda (Italian) happy and jovial.

Yoi (Japanese) born in the evening.

Yoki (Hopi) bluebird.
Yokie

Yoko (Japanese) good girl.
Yo

Yokoh (Japanese) mountain.

Yolanda (Greek) violet flower. See also Iolanthe, Jolanda, Olinda.
Yalanda, Yolie, Yolaine, Yolana, Yoland, Yolande, Yolane, Yolanna, Yolantha, Yolanthe, Yolette, Yolonda, Yorlanda, Youlanda, Yulanda, Yulonda

Yole, Yone (Greek) beautiful as a violet.

Yolie (Greek) a familiar form of Yolanda.
Yola, Yoley, Yoli, Yoly

Yoluta (Native American) summer flower.

Yomara (American) a combination of Yolanda + Tamara.
Yomaira, Yomarie, Yomira

Yon (Burmese) rabbit. (Korean) lotus blossom.
Yona, Yonna

Yoné (Japanese) wealth; rice.

Yong (Chinese) elegant and poised.

Yonina (Hebrew) a form of Jonina.
Yona, Yonah

Yonita (Hebrew) a form of Jonita.
Yonat, Yonati, Yonit

Yonn (Korean) a long life.

Yoomee (Coos) star.
Yoome

Yordana (Basque) descendant. See also Jordana.

Yoree (Japanese) the scent of the sun.

Yorey (Japanese) good; striving.

Yori (Japanese) reliable.
Yoriko, Yoriyo

Yorie, Yory (Japanese) dependable.

Yoselin **G** (Latin) a form of Jocelyn.
Yoseline, Yoselyn, Yosselin, Yosseline, Yosselyn

Yosepha (Hebrew) a form of Josephine.
Yoseta, Yosifa, Yuseffa

Yoshe, Yoshimi (Japanese) dependable.

Yoshi (Japanese) good; respectful.
Yoshie, Yoshiko, Yoshiyo

Yoshino (Japanese) beauty.

You (Chinese) excellence.

Young (Korean) obedient girl.

Yovela (Hebrew) joyful heart; rejoicer.

Ysa (Chamorro) a form of Isa.

Ysabel (Spanish) a form of Isabel.
Ysabell, Ysabella, Ysabelle, Ysbel, Ysbella, Ysobel

Ysanne (American) a combination of Ysabel + Ann.
Ysande, Ysann, Ysanna

Yseult (German) ice rule. (Irish) fair; light skinned. (Welsh) a form of Isolde.
Yseulte, Ysolt

Yu Jie (Chinese) pure beautiful jade.

Yuana (Spanish) a form of Juana.
Yuan, Yuanna

Yudelle (English) a form of Udele.
Yudela, Yudell, Yudella

Yudita (Russian) a form of Judith.
Yudit, Yudith, Yuditt

Yue Wan, Yue-Wan (Chinese) happy and gentle.

Yue Yan, Yue-Yan (Chinese) happy and beautiful.

Yue Ying, Yue-Ying (Chinese) happy and smart; kind.

Yue You, Yue-You (Chinese) happy and friendly.

Yui (Japanese) she who is a fine and beautiful girl.

Yu-Jie (Chinese) jade; pure.

Yuka (Japanese) respectful.

Yukako (Japanese) she who wears her clothing well.

Yukari (Japanese) she who is as beautiful as a flower.

Yuki 🄑🄖 (Japanese) snow.
Yukie, Yukiko, Yukiyo

Yukino, Yumiko (Japanese) child of Yuka.

Yuko (Japanese) beautiful and truthful friend.

Yulene (Basque) a form of Julia.
Yuleen

Yulia (Russian) a form of Julia.
Yula, Yulenka, Yulinka, Yulka, Yulya

Yuliana (Spanish) a form of Juliana.
Yulenia, Yuliani

Yumako (Japanese) snow.

Yumi (Japanese) gracious child.

Yun (Chinese) clouds.

Yuna (Japanese) beauty.

Yuri 🄖 (Japanese) lily.
Yuree, Yuriko, Yuriyo

Yuriye (Japanese) arrow child.

Yustina (Pohnpeian) a form of Jacinta.

Yutsuko (Japanese) gentle as a red apple.

Yuzuki (Japanese) she who paints for the benefit of others.

Yvanna (Slavic) a form of Ivana.
Yvan, Yvana, Yvannia

Yvette (French) a familiar form of Yvonne. See also Evette, Ivette.
Yavette, Yevett, Yevette, Yevetta, Yvet, Yveta, Yvett, Yvetta

Yvonne 🄖 (French) young archer. (Scandinavian) yew wood; bow wood. See also Evonne, Ivonne, Vonna, Vonny, Yvette.
Yavanda, Yavanna, Yavanne, Yavonda, Yavonna, Yavonne, Yveline, Yvon, Yvone, Yvonna, Yvonnah, Yvonnia, Yvonnie, Yvonny

Z

Z 🄑 (American) an initial used as a first name.

Zaba (Hebrew) she who offers a sacrifice to God.

Zabrina (American) a form of Sabrina.
Zabreena, Zabrinia, Zabrinna, Zabryna

Zachariah 🄑 (Hebrew) God remembered.

Zacharie 🄑 (Hebrew) God remembered.
Zacari, Zacceaus, Zacchaea, Zachary, Zachoia, Zackaria, Zackeisha, Zackeria, Zakaria, Zakaya, Zakeshia, Zakiah, Zakiria, Zakiya, Zakiyah, Zechari

Zachary **B** (Hebrew) a form of Zacharie.
Zackery, Zakary

Zada (Arabic) fortunate, prosperous.
Zaida, Zayda, Zayeda

Zafina (Arabic) victorious.

Zafirah (Arabic) successful; victorious.

Zahar (Hebrew) daybreak; dawn.
Zahara, Zaharra, Zahera, Zahira, Zahirah, Zeeherah

Zahavah (Hebrew) golden.
Zachava, Zachavah, Zechava, Zechavah, Zehava, Zehavi, Zehavit, Zeheva, Zehuva

Zahra (Swahili) flower. (Arabic) white.
Zahara, Zahraa, Zahrah, Zahreh, Zahria

Zai (Chinese) to be living.

Zaira (Hebrew) a form of Zara.
Zaire, Zairea, Zirrea

Zakia **BG** (Swahili) smart. (Arabic) chaste.
Zakea, Zakeia, Zakiah, Zakiya

Zakira (Hebrew) a form of Zacharie.
Zaakira, Zakiera, Zakierra, Zakir, Zakirah, Zakiria, Zakiriya, Zykarah, Zykera, Zykeria, Zykerria, Zykira, Zykuria

Zakiya (Arabic) a form of Zakia.
Zakeya, Zakeyia, Zakiyaa, Zakiyah, Zakiyya, Zakiyyah, Zakkiyya, Zakkiyyah, Zakkyyah

Zalika (Swahili) born to royalty.
Zuleika

Zaltana (Native American) high mountain.

Zan (Chinese) praise; support.

Zana **G** (Spanish) a form of Zanna.

Zandra (Greek) a form of Sandra.
Zahndra, Zandrea, Zandria, Zandy, Zanndra, Zondra

Zane **B** (English) a form of John.

Zaneta (Spanish) a form of Jane.
Zanita, Zanitra

Zanna (Spanish) a form of Jane. (English) a short form of Susanna.
Zaina, Zainah, Zainna, Zana, Zanae, Zanah, Zanella, Zanette, Zannah, Zannette, Zannia, Zannie

Zanthe (Greek) a form of Xanthe.
Zanth, Zantha

Zara (Hebrew) a form of Sarah, Zora.
Zaira, Zarah, Zarea, Zaree, Zareea, Zareen, Zareena, Zareh, Zareya, Zari, Zaria, Zariya, Zarria

Zarifa (Arabic) successful.

Zarina (Slavic) empress.

Zarita (Spanish) a form of Sarah.

Zasha (Russian) a form of Sasha.
Zascha, Zashenka, Zashka, Zasho

Zaviera (Spanish) a form of Xaviera.
Zavera, Zavirah

Zawati (Swahili) gift.

Zayit **BG** (Hebrew) olive.

Zaynah (Arabic) beautiful.
Zayn, Zayna

Ze (Chinese) moist, glossy.

Zea (Latin) grain.

Zechariah **B** (Hebrew) a form of Zachariah.

Zelda (Yiddish) gray haired. (German) a short form of Griselda. See also Selda.
Zelde, Zella, Zellda

Zelene (English) sunshine.
 Zeleen, Zelena, Zeline

Zelia (Spanish) sunshine.
 Zele, Zelene, Zelie, Zélie, Zelina

Zelizi (Basque) a form of Sheila.

Zelma (German) a form of Selma.

Zelmira (Arabic) brilliant one.

Zemirah (Hebrew) song of joy.

Zena (Greek) a form of Xenia.
 (Ethiopian) news. (Persian) woman.
 See also Zina.
 Zanae, Zanah, Zeena, Zeenat, Zeenet,
 Zeenia, Zeenya, Zein, Zeina, Zenah,
 Zenana, Zenea, Zenia, Zenna, Zennah,
 Zennia, Zenya

Zenadia (Greek) she who is
 dedicated to God.

Zenaida (Greek) white-winged
 dove.
 Zenaide, Zenaïde, Zenayda, Zenochka

Zenda 🄶 (Persian) sacred; feminine.

Zeng (Chinese) increase, gain.

Zenobia (Greek) sign, symbol.
 History: a queen who ruled the city
 of Palmyra in ancient Syria.
 Zeba, Zeeba, Zenobie, Zenovia

Zephania, Zephanie (Greek)
 forms of Stephanie.
 Zepania, Zephanas, Zephany

Zephyr 🄱🄶 (Greek) west wind.
 Zefiryn, Zephra, Zephria, Zephyer,
 Zephyrine

Zera (Hebrew) seeds.
 Zerah, Zeriah

Zerdali (Turkish) wild apricot.

Zerlina (Latin, Spanish) beautiful
 dawn. Music: a character in
 Mozart's opera *Don Giovanni*.
 Zerla, Zerlinda

Zerrin (Turkish) golden.
 Zerren

Zeta (English) rose. Linguistics: a
 letter in the Greek alphabet.
 Zayit, Zetana, Zetta

Zetta (Portuguese) rose.

Zhan (Chinese) spread the wings.

Zhana (Slavic) a form of Zhane.
 Zhanay, Zhanaya, Zhaniah, Zhanna

Zhane 🄶 (Slavic) a form of Jane.
 Zhanae, Zhané, Zhanea, Zhanee,
 Zhaney, Zhani

Zhao (Chinese) spirit, vigor.

Zhen (Chinese) chaste.

Zhen Juan, Zhen-Juan (Chinese)
 precious and beautiful.

Zheng (Chinese) honest.

Zhi (Chinese) irises; orchids; noble
 character; true friendship.

Zho (Chinese) character.

Zhong (Chinese) honorable.

Zhu (Chinese) pearl, jewel.

Zhuan (Chinese) expert.

Zhuang (Chinese) serious, grave.

Zhuo (Chinese) smart; wonderful.

Zia 🄶 (Latin) grain. (Arabic) light.
 Zea

Zidanelia (Greek) she who is God's
 judge; bluish lotus flower.

Zigana (Hungarian) gypsy girl. See
 also Tsigana.
 Zigane

Zihna (Hopi) one who spins tops.

Zilla (Hebrew) shadow.
 Zila, Zillah, Zylla

Zilpah (Hebrew) dignified. Bible:
Jacob's wife.
Zilpha, Zylpha

Zilya (Russian) a form of Theresa.

Zimra (Hebrew) song of praise.
Zamora, Zemira, Zemora, Zimria

Zina (African) secret spirit. (English)
hospitable. (Greek) a form of Zena.
Zinah, Zine

Zinnia (Latin) Botany: a plant with
beautiful, rayed, colorful flowers.
Zinia, Zinny, Zinnya, Zinya

Zipporah (Hebrew) bird. Bible:
Moses' wife.
Zipora, Ziporah, Zipporia, Ziproh

Zita (Spanish) rose. (Arabic) mistress.
A short form of names ending in
"sita" or "zita."
Zeeta, Zyta, Zytka

Ziva (Hebrew) bright; radiant.
Zeeva, Ziv, Zivanka, Zivi, Zivit

Zizi (Hungarian) a familiar form of
Elizabeth.
Zsi Zsi

Zobeida (Arabic) pleasant as cream.

Zocha (Polish) a form of Sophie.

Zoe ☀ **G** (Greek) life.
*Zoé, Zoë, Zoee, Zoelie, Zoeline, Zoelle,
Zoey, Zoi, Zoie, Zowe, Zowey, Zowie,
Zoya*

Zoey ☀ **G** (Greek) a form of Zoe.
Zooey

Zofia (Slavic) a form of Sophia. See
also Sofia.
Zofka, Zsofia

Zohar **B** (Hebrew) shining, brilliant.
Zoheret

Zohra (Hebrew) blossom.

Zohreh (Persian) happy.
Zahreh, Zohrah

Zola (Italian) piece of earth.
Zoela, Zoila

Zona (Latin) belt, sash.
Zonia

Zondra (Greek) a form of Zandra.
Zohndra

Zong (Chinese) palm.

Zora (Slavic) aurora; dawn. See also
Zara.
*Zorah, Zorana, Zoreen, Zoreena,
Zorna, Zorra, Zorrah, Zorya*

Zoraida (Arabic) she who is
eloquent.

Zorina (Slavic) golden.
Zorana, Zori, Zorie, Zorine, Zorna, Zory

Zoya (Slavic) a form of Zoe.
*Zoia, Zoyara, Zoyechka, Zoyenka,
Zoyya*

Zsa Zsa (Hungarian) a familiar form
of Susan.
Zhazha

Zsofia (Hungarian) a form of Sofia.
Zofia, Zsofi, Zsofika

Zsuzsanna (Hungarian) a form of
Susanna.
*Zsuska, Zsuzsa, Zsuzsi, Zsuzsika,
Zsuzska*

Zu (Chinese) earliest ancestor.

Zudora (Sanskrit) laborer.

Zuleica (Arabic) beautiful and
plump.

Zuleika (Arabic) brilliant.
Zeleeka, Zul, Zulay, Zulekha, Zuleyka

Zulima (Arabic) a form of Salama.
Zuleima, Zulema, Zulemah, Zulimah

Zulma (Arabic) healthy and vigorous
woman.

Zulmara (Spanish) a form of Zulma.

Zuo (Chinese) smart; wonderful.

Zurafa (Arabic) lovely.
  Ziraf, Zuruf

Zuri (Basque) white; light skinned.
  (Swahili) beautiful.
  Zuria, Zurie, Zurisha, Zury

Zurina, Zurine (Basque) white.

Zurisaday (Arabic) over the earth.

Zusa (Czech, Polish) a form of
  Susan.
  Zuzana, Zuzanka, Zuzia, Zuzka, Zuzu

Zuwena (Swahili) good.
  Zwena

Zyanya (Zapotec) always.

Zytka (Polish) rose.

Boys

A G (American) an initial used as a first name.

Aakash (Hindi) a form of Akash.

Aaliyah G (Hebrew) a form of Aliya (see Girls' Names).

Aaron ☀ B (Hebrew) enlightened. (Arabic) messenger. Bible: the brother of Moses and the first high priest. See also Ron.
Aahron, Aaran, Aaren, Aareon, Aarin, Aaronn, Aarron, Aarronn, Aaryn, Aarynn, Aeron, Aharon, Ahran, Ahren, Aranne, Arek, Aren, Ari, Arin, Aron, Aronek, Aronne, Aronos, Arran, Arron

Aaronjames (American) a combination of Aaron + James.
Aaron James, Aaron-James

Aarronn (Hebrew) enlightened. (Arabic) messenger.
Aarynn

Aasiña (Chamorro) each other's mercy.

Abad (Hebrew) unique man.

Abag (Chamorro) lost.

Aban (Persian) Mythology: a figure associated with water and the arts.

Abaramo (Fijian) a form of Abram.

Abasi (Swahili) stern.
Abasee, Abasey, Abasie, Abasy

Abay (Arabic) descendant.

Abban (Latin) white.
Abben, Abbin, Abbine, Abbon

Abbas (Arabic) lion.

Abbau (Chamorro) to clear land.

Abbertus (Spanish) a form of Alberto.

Abbey G (Hebrew) a familiar form of Abe.
Abbee, Abbie, Abby, Abey, Aby

Abbie G (Hebrew) a form of Abbey.

Abbigail G (Hebrew) a form of Abigail (see Girls' Names).

Abbott (Hebrew) father; abbot.
Ab, Abba, Abbah, Abbán, Abbé, Abboid, Abbot, Abot, Abott

Abbu (Arabic) a form of Abu.

Abbud (Arabic) devoted.

Abby G (Hebrew) a form of Abbey.

Abdi (African) my servant.

Abdías (Hebrew) God's servant.

Abdirahman (Arabic) a form of Abdulrahman.
Abdirehman

Abdón (Hebrew) servant of God; the very helpful man.

Abdul (Arabic) servant.
Abdal, Abdeel, Abdel, Abdoul, Abdual, Abdull, Abul

Abdulaziz (Arabic) servant of the Mighty.
Abdelazim, Abdelaziz, Abdulazaz, Abdulazeez

Abdullah (Arabic) servant of Allah.
Abdala, Abdalah, Abdalla, Abdallah, Abdela, Abduala, Abdualla, Abduallah, Abdula, Abdulah, Abdulahi, Abdulha, Abdulla, Abdullahi

Abdulmalik (Arabic) servant of the Master.

Abdulrahman (Arabic) servant of the Merciful.
Abdelrahim, Abdelrahman, Abdirahman, Abdolrahem, Abdularahman, Abdurrahman, Abdurram

Abe (Hebrew) a short form of Abel, Abraham.
Abb, Abbe

Abel **B** (Hebrew) breath. (Assyrian) meadow. (German) a short form of Abelard. Bible: Adam and Eve's second son.
Abe, Abele, Abell, Able, Adal, Avel

Abelard (German) noble; resolute.
Ab, Abalard, Abel, Abelarde, Abelardo, Abelhard, Abilard, Adalard, Adelard

Abelino (Spanish) a form of Avelino.

Abercio (Greek) first son.

Abernethy (Scottish) river's beginning.
Abernathie, Abernethi

Abet (Chamorro) a form of Javier.

Abhinash (Sanskrit) indestructible.

Abi (Turkish) older brother.
Abee, Abbi

Abiah (Hebrew) God is my father.
Abia, Abiel, Abija, Abijah, Abisha, Abishai, Aviya, Aviyah

Abid (Arabic) one who worships God.

Abidan (Hebrew) father of judgment.
Abiden, Abidin, Abidon, Abydan, Abyden, Abydin, Abydon, Abydyn

Abie (Hebrew) a familiar form of Abraham.

Abiel (Hebrew) a form of Abiah.

Abiner (Pohnpeian) a form of Abner.

Abir (Hebrew) strong.
Abyr

Abisha (Hebrew) gift of God.
Abijah, Abishai, Abishal, Abysha, Abyshah

Abner (Hebrew) father of light. Bible: the commander of Saul's army.
Ab, Avner, Ebner

Abo (Hebrew) father.

Abraham (Hebrew) father of many nations. Bible: the first Hebrew patriarch. See also Avram, Bram, Ibrahim.
Abarran, Abe, Aberham, Abey, Abhiram, Abie, Abrahaim, Abrahame, Abrahamo, Abrahan, Abrahán, Abraheem, Abrahem, Abrahim, Abrahm, Abram, Abramo, Abrán, Abrao, Arram, Avram

Abrahan (Spanish) a form of Abraham.
Abrahin, Abrahon

Abram (Hebrew) a short form of Abraham. See also Bram.
Abrama, Abramo, Abrams, Avram

Absalom (Hebrew) father of peace. Bible: the rebellious third son of King David. See also Avshalom, Axel.
Absalaam, Absalon, Abselon, Absolam, Absolom, Absolum

Absalón (Hebrew) a form of Absalom.

Abu (Arabic) father.

Abug (Chamorro) friend.

Abundancio (Latin) rich, affluent.

Abundio (Latin) he who has a lot of property.

Acab (Hebrew) uncle.

Acacio (Greek) is not evil and is honorable.

Acañir (Mapuche) liberated fox.

Acapana (Quechua) lightning; small hurricane.

Acar (Turkish) bright.

Ace (Latin) unity.
Acer, Acey, Acie

Acfaye (Chamorro) wise together.

Achachic (Aymara) ancestor; grandfather.

Achaigua (Chamorro) similar, a likeness.

Achei (Chamorro) chin.

Achic (Quechua) luminous; resplendent.

Achilles (Greek) Mythology: a hero of the Trojan War. Literature: the hero of Homer's epic poem *Iliad*.
Achil, Achill, Achille, Achillea, Achilleus, Achillios, Achyl, Achyll, Achylle, Achylleus, Akil, Akili, Akilles

Achina (Sanskrit) free from worry.

Achudan (Sanskrit) the hunt, the chase.

Achuga (Chamorro) end together; to give pleasure to each other.

Acisclo (Latin) a pick used to work on rocks.

Ackerley (English) meadow of oak trees.
Accerlee, Accerleigh, Accerley, Ackerlea, Ackerlee, Ackerleigh, Ackerli, Ackerlie, Ackersley, Acklea, Ackleigh, Ackley, Acklie, Akerlea, Akerlee, Akerleigh, Akerley, Akerli, Akerlie, Akerly

Acklee (English) a short form of Ackerley.
Ackli, Ackly

Aconcauac (Quechua) stone sentinel.

Actassi (Chamorro) share the sea.

Acton (English) oak-tree settlement.
Actan, Acten, Actin, Actun, Actyn

Acursio (Latin) he who heads towards God.

Adahy (Cherokee) in the woods.
Adahi

Adai (Chamorro) friend.

Adair 🄶 (Scottish) oak-tree ford.
Adaire, Adare, Adayr, Adayre, Addair, Addaire, Addar, Addare, Addayr, Addyre

Adalbaro (Greek) combatant of nobility.

Adalberto (Germanic) belonging to nobility.

Adalgiso, Adalvino (Greek) lance of nobility.

Adalrico (Greek) noble chief of his lineage.

Adam ☆ 🄱 (Phoenician) man; mankind. (Hebrew) earth; man of the red earth. Bible: the first man created by God. See also Adamson, Addison, Damek, Keddy, Macadam.
Ad, Adama, Adamec, Adamo, Adāo, Adas, Addam, Addams, Addis, Addy, Adem, Adham, Adhamh, Adim, Adné, Adok, Adomas, Adym

Adamec (Czech) a form of Adam.
Adamek, Adamik, Adamka, Adamko, Adamok

Adamson (Hebrew) son of Adam.
Adams, Adamsson, Addamson

Adan (Irish) a form of Aidan.
Aden, Adian, Adin, Adun

Adán (Hebrew) a form of Adam.

Adao (Chamorro) the sun.

Adaoña (Chamorro) his sun.

Adar (Syrian) ruler; prince. (Hebrew) noble; exalted.
Addar

Adarius (American) a combination of Adam + Darius.
Adareus, Adarias, Adarrius, Adarro, Adarruis, Adaruis, Adauris

Adaucto (Latin) increase.

Addel (German) a short form of Adelard.
Adell

Addison **BG** (English) son of Adam.
Addis, Addisen, Addisun, Addoson, Addyson, Adison, Adisson, Adyson

Addy (Hebrew) a familiar form of Adam, Adlai. (German) a familiar form of Adelard.
Addey, Addi, Addie, Ade, Adi

Ade (Yoruba) royal.

Adelard (German) noble; courageous.
Adal, Adalar, Adalard, Adalarde, Addy, Adel, Adél, Adelar, Adelarde, Adelhard

Adelardo, Adelino (Greek) daring prince.

Adelbai (Palauan) the men's community house.

Adelfo (Greek) male friend.

Adelio (Germanic) father of the noble prince.

Adelmaro (Greek) distinguished because of his lineage.

Adelmo (Germanic) noble protector.

Adelric (German) noble ruler.
Adalric, Adelrich, Adelrick, Adelrik, Adelryc, Adelryck, Adelryk

Ademar, Ademaro, Adhemar, Adimar (German) he whose battles have made him distinguished; celebrated and famous combatant.

Aden (Arabic) Geography: a region in southern Yemen. (Irish) a form of Aidan, Aiden.

Ader (Palauan) the remainder.

Adham (Arabic) black.

Adhelmar (Greek) ennobled by his battles.

Adiel (Hebrew) he was adorned by God.

Adil (Arabic) just; wise.
Adeel, Adeele, Adill, Adyl, Adyll

Adin (Hebrew) pleasant.
Addin, Addyn, Adyn

Adir (Hebrew) majestic; noble.
Adeer

Adirán (Latin) from the Adriatic Sea.

Aditya (Hindi) sun.

Adiv (Hebrew) pleasant; gentle.
Adeev, Adev

Adlai (Hebrew) my ornament.
Ad, Addlai, Addlay, Addy, Adlay, Adley

Adler (German) eagle.
Ad, Addlar, Addler, Adlar

Adli (Turkish) just; wise.
Adlea, Adlee, Adleigh, Adlie, Adly

Admon (Hebrew) peony.

Adnan (Arabic) pleasant.
Adnaan, Adnane

Adney (English) noble's island.
Adnee, Adni, Adnie, Adny

Adolf (German) noble wolf. History: Adolf Hitler's German army was defeated in World War II. See also Dolf.
Ad, Addof, Addoff, Adof, Adolfo, Adolfus, Adolph

Adolfo (Spanish) a form of Adolf.
Addofo, Adolffo, Adolpho, Andolffo, Andolfo, Andolpho

Adolph (German) a form of Adolf.
Adolphe, Adolpho, Adolphus, Adulphus

Adolphus (French) a form of Adolf.
Adolphius

Adom (Akan) help from God.

Adon (Hebrew) Lord. (Greek) a short form of Adonis.

Adonai (Hebrew) my Lord.

Adonías (Hebrew) God is my Lord.

Adonis (Greek) highly attractive. Mythology: the attractive youth loved by Aphrodite.
Adon, Adonise, Adonnis, Adonys, Adonyse

Adren (Spanish) a form of Adriano.

Adri (Indo-Pakistani) rock.
Adree, Adrey, Adrie, Adry

Adrian ☀ 🅱 (Greek) rich. (Latin) dark. (Swedish) a short form of Hadrian.
Adarian, Ade, Adorjan, Adrain, Adreian, Adreyan, Adri, Adriaan, Adriane, Adriann, Adrianne, Adriano, Adrianus, Adriean, Adrien, Adrik, Adrin, Adrion, Adrionn, Adrionne, Adron, Adryan, Adryn, Adryon

Adrián (Latin) a form of Adrian.

Adriana, Adrianna 🅶 (Italian) forms of Adrienne.

Adriano (Italian) a form of Adrian.
Adrianno

Adriel (Hebrew) member of God's flock.
Adrial, Adriall, Adriell, Adryel, Adryell

Adrien 🅱 (French) a form of Adrian.
Adriene, Adrienne, Adryen

Adrienne 🅶 (French) a form of Adrien.

Adrik (Russian) a form of Adrian.
Adric

Adulfo (Germanic) of noble heritage.

Adwin (Ghanian) creative.
Adwyn

Aeneas (Greek) praised. (Scottish) a form of Angus. Literature: the Trojan hero of Vergil's epic poem *Aeneid*. See also Eneas.

Afaisin (Chamorro) asking each other.

Afi (Chamorro) fire.

Afif (Arabic) chaste, modest.

Afram (African) Geography: a river in Ghana, Africa.

Afton 🅶 (English) from Afton, England.
Affton, Aftan, Aften, Aftin, Aftyn

Afzal (Arabic) the best.

Aga (Chamorro) a kind of bird, the Marianas crow.

Agada, Agga (Chamorro) forms of Aga.

Agagan (Chamorro) redness.

Agamemnon (Greek) resolute. Mythology: the king of Mycenae who led the Greeks in the Trojan War.

Agamenón (Greek) he who moves slowly down the path.

Agapito (Hebrew) beloved one.

Agar (Hebrew) he who escaped.

Agaton (Greek) good.

Agatón (Greek) victor; good.

Age (Danish) ancestor.

Agenor (Greek) strong man.

Ageo (Hebrew) having a festive character.

Agesislao (Greek) leader of villages.

Agila (Teutonic) he who possesses combat support.

Agnasina (Chamorro) mighty.

Agnelo (Latin) reference to the lamb of God.

Agni (Hindi) Religion: the Hindu fire god.

Agon (Chamorro) a form of Aguon.

Agostine (Italian) a form of Augustine.
Agostyne

Agostiño (Latin) a form of Augusto.

Agrippa (Latin) born feet first. History: the commander of the Roman fleet that defeated Mark Antony and Cleopatra at Actium.
Agripa, Agripah, Agrippah, Agrypa, Agrypah, Agryppa, Agryppah

Agtano (Chamorro) land.

Agu (Ibo) leopard.

Agua (Chamorro) milkfish.

Aguaguat (Chamorro) stubborn; mischievous.

Agua'lin (Chamorro) a form of Aguarin.

Aguan (Chamorro) a form of Aguon.

Aguarin (Chamorro) one who overdresses.

Aguas (Chamorro) baby mullet fish.

Agui (Chamorro) ghost crab.

Aguigan (Chamorro) fish.

Aguon (Chamorro) food, bread.

Agupa (Chamorro) tomorrow.

Agús (Spanish) a form of Agustín.

Agusteen (Latin) a form of Augustine.
Agustyne

Agustin (Latin) a form of Augustine.
Agostino, Agoston, Aguistin, Agustein, Agusteyne, Agustine, Agustis, Agusto, Agustus, Agustyn

Agustín (Latin) a form of Augustine.

Ah (Chinese) from a Chinese character.

Ahab (Hebrew) father's brother. Literature: the captain of the Pequod in Herman Melville's novel *Moby-Dick*.

Ahanu (Native American) laughter.

Ahdik (Native American) caribou; reindeer.
Ahdic, Ahdick, Ahdyc, Ahdyck, Ahdyk

Ahearn (Scottish) lord of the horses. (English) heron.
Ahearne, Aherin, Ahern, Aherne, Aheron, Aheryn, Hearn

Ahgao (Chamorro) a kind of tree.

Ahir (Turkish) last.

Ahkeem (Hebrew) a form of Akeem.
Ahkiem, Ahkyem, Ahkyeme

Ahmad (Arabic) most highly praised.
See also Muhammad.
Achmad, Achmed, Ahamad, Ahamada, Ahamed, Ahmaad, Ahmaud, Amad, Amahd, Amed

Ahmed 🅱 (Swahili) praiseworthy.

Ahpel (Pohnpeian) a form of Abel.

Ahsan (Arabic) charitable.

Ai (Japanese) love.

Aian (Chuukese) an exclamation of surprise.

Aichi (Japanese) love; wisdom.

Aichy (Chuukese) a form of Aichi.

Aidan ✵ 🅱 (Irish) fiery.
Adan, Aden, Aiden, Aidun, Aydan, Ayden, Aydin

Aidano (Teutonic) he who distinguishes himself.

Aiden ✵ 🅱 (Irish) a form of Aidan.
Aden, Aidon, Aidwin, Aidwyn, Aidyn

Aiichiro (Japanese) favorite; first son.

Aiken (English) made of oak.
Aicken, Aikin, Ayken, Aykin

Ailwan (English) noble friends.
Ailwen, Ailwin

Aimery (French) a form of Emery.
Aime, Aimeree, Aimerey, Aimeri, Aimeric, Aimerie, Amerey, Aymeric, Aymery

Aimon (French) house. (Irish) a form of Eamon.

Aindrea (Irish) a form of Andrew.
Aindreas

Ainsley 🅶 (Scottish) my own meadow.
Ainslea, Ainslee, Ainslei, Ainsleigh, Ainsli, Ainslie, Ainsly, Ansley, Aynslee, Aynsley, Aynslie

Aisake (Fijian) a form of Isaac.

Aisea (Fijian) a form of Isaias.

Aisek (Pohnpeian) a form of Isaac.

Aisen (Chuukese) my cry.

Aito (Japanese) he who is very affectionate.

Aiyaz (Turkish) frosty winter night.

Aiyub (Arabic) a form of Ayub.

Aizik (Russian) a form of Isaac.

Aja 🅶 (Punjabi) a form of Ajay.

Ajala (Yoruba) potter.
Ajalah

Ajay (Punjabi) victorious; undefeatable. (American) a combination of the initials A. + J.
Aj, Aja, Ajae, Ajai, Ajaye, Ajaz, Ajé, Ajee, Ajit

Ajesh (Sanskrit) lord of illusion.

Ajit (Sanskrit) unconquerable.
Ajeet, Ajith

Akako (Japanese) red; a charm to cure disease.

Akar (Turkish) flowing stream.
Akara, Akare

Akash (Hindi) sky.
Aakash, Akasha, Akshay

Akbar (Arabic) great.
Akbara, Akbare

Akecheta (Sioux) warrior.
Akechetah

Akeem, Akim (Hebrew) short forms of Joachim.
Achim, Achym, Ackeem, Ackim, Ackime, Ackym, Ackyme, Ahkieme, Akeam, Akee, Akiem, Akima, Akym, Arkeem

Akeke (Marshallese) having a stomachache from eating too much.

Akemi (Japanese) dawn.
Akemee, Akemie, Akemy

Akeno (Japanese) in the morning; bright, shining field.

Akhtar (Persian) star, constellation; good omen.

Akifumi (Japanese) he who writes clear, historical chronicles.

Akihiko (Japanese) bright boy.

Akihiro (Japanese) glittering expansiveness.

Akiki (Chuukese) tickle.

Akil (Arabic) intelligent. (Greek) a form of Achilles.
Ahkeel, Akeel, Akeil, Akeyla, Akhil, Akiel, Akila, Akilah, Akile, Akili, Akyl, Akyle

Akimichi (Japanese) clear duty; bright and clear.

Akimitsu (Japanese) glittering adornment.

Akinino (Pohnpeian) a form of Joaquin.

Akinobu (Japanese) distinct beliefs.

Akinori (Japanese) clear ruling.

Akinory (Japanese) a form of Akinori.

Akins (Yoruba) brave.
Akin, Akyn, Akyns

Akioshi (Japanese) large, complete art.

Akioshy (Chuukese) a form of Akioshi.

Akir (Japanese) intelligent.

Akira **G** (Japanese) intelligent.
Akihito, Akio, Akirah, Akiyo, Akyra, Akyrah

Akito (Japanese) luxuriant result.

Akiva (Hebrew) a form of Jacob.
Akiba, Kiva

Akiwo (Kosraean) a form of Akio.

Akiyama (Japanese) autumn; mountain.

Akiyoshi (Japanese) clear justice.

Akiyuki (Japanese) this spirit; famous journey.

Aklea (English) a short form of Ackerley.
Aklee, Akleigh, Akley, Akli, Aklie, Akly

Aklesh (Sanskrit) swift lord.

Akmal (Arabic) perfect.
Ackmal

Akram (Arabic) most generous.

Aksel (Norwegian) father of peace.
Aksell

Akshat (Sanskrit) uninjurable.

Akshay (American) a form of Akash.
Akshaj, Akshaya

Aktar (Persian) a form of Akhtar.

Akuila (Fijian) a form of Aquila.

Akule (Native American) he looks up.
Akul

Akuo (Chuukese) a form of Akio.

Akyo (Japanese) bright.

Al (Irish) a short form of Alan, Albert, Alexander.

Aladdin (Arabic) height of faith. Literature: the hero of a story in the *Arabian Nights*.
Ala, Alaa, Alaaddin, Aladan, Aladdan, Aladden, Aladdyn, Aladean, Aladen, Aladin, Aladino, Aladyn

Alain (French) a form of Alan.
Alaen, Alaine, Alainn, Alayn, Alein,
Aleine, Aleyn, Aleyne, Allain, Allayn

Alaire (French) joyful.
Alayr, Alayre

Alam (Arabic) universe.
Alame

Alan ☙ (Irish) handsome; peaceful.
Ailan, Ailin, Al, Alaan, Alain, Alair,
Aland, Alande, Alando, Alane, Alani,
Alann, Alano, Alanson, Alante, Alao,
Allan, Allen, Alon, Alun, Alune, Alyn,
Alyne

Alanso (Chuukese) a form of
Alfonso.

Alardo (Greek) courageous prince.

Alaric (German) ruler of all. See also
Ulrich.
Alarich, Alarick, Alarico, Alarik,
Alaryc, Alaryck, Alaryk, Aleric,
Allaric, Allarick, Alric, Alrick, Alrik

Alastair (Scottish) a form of
Alexander.
Alaisdair, Alaistair, Alaister, Alasdair,
Alasteir, Alaster, Alastor, Aleister,
Alester, Alistair, Allaistar, Allastair,
Allaster, Allastir, Allysdair, Alystair

Alba (Latin) town on the white hill.

Alban (Latin) from Alba, Italy.
Albain, Albany, Albean, Albein, Alby,
Auban, Auben

Albano (Germanic) belonging to the
house of Alba.

Alberic (German) smart; wise ruler.
Alberich, Alberick, Alberyc, Alberyck,
Alberyk

Albern (German) noble; courageous.
Alberne, Alburn, Alburne

Albert ☙ (German, French) noble
and bright. See also Elbert, Ulbrecht.
Adelbert, Ailbert, Al, Albertik,
Alberto, Alberts, Albertus, Albie,
Albrecht, Albret, Alby, Albyrt, Albyrte,
Alvertos, Aubert

Alberto (Italian) a form of Albert.
Albertino, Berto

Albet (Chamorro) a form of Alberto.

Albie, Alby (German, French)
familiar forms of Albert.
Albee, Albey, Albi

Albin (Latin) a form of Alvin.
Alben, Albeno, Albinek, Albino,
Albins, Albinson, Albun, Alby, Albyn,
Auben

Albion (Latin) white cliffs.
Geography: a reference to the white
cliffs in Dover, England.
Albon, Albyon, Allbion, Allbyon

Alcandor (Greek) manly; strong.

Alceo (Greek) man of great strength
and vigor.

Alcibiades (Greek) generous and
violent.

Alcibíades (Greek) strong and valiant
man.

Alcides (Greek) strong and vigorous.

Alcott (English) old cottage.
Alcot, Alkot, Alkott, Allcot, Allcott,
Allkot, Allkott

Alcuino (Teutonic) friend of sacred
places, friend of the temple.

Aldair (German, English) a form of
Alder.
Aldahir, Aldayr

Aldano, Aldino (Celtic) noble;
experienced man.

Alden **B** (English) old; wise protector.
Aldan, Aldean, Aldin, Aldous, Aldyn,
Elden

Alder (German, English) alder tree.
Aldair, Aldar, Aldare, Aldyr

Alderidge (English) alder ridge.
Alderige, Aldrydge, Aldryge

Aldise (English) old house. (German)
a form of Aldous.
Aldiss, Aldys

Aldo (Italian) old; elder. (German) a
short form of Aldous.
Alda

Aldous (German) a form of Alden.
Aldis, Aldo, Aldon, Aldos, Aldus,
Elden

Aldred (English) old; wise counselor.
Alldred, Eldred

Aldrich (English) wise.
Aldric, Aldrick, Aldridge, Aldrige,
Aldritch, Aldryc, Aldryck, Aldryk,
Alldric, Alldrick, Alldridge,
Eldridge

Aldrin (English) old.

Aldwin (English) old friend.
Aldwan, Aldwen, Aldwon, Aldwyn,
Eldwin

Alec, Alek **B** (Greek) short forms of
Alexander.
Aleck, Aleik, Alekko, Aleko, Elek

Aleczander (Greek) a form of
Alexander.
Alecander, Aleckxander, Alecsander,
Alecxander

Aleem (Arabic) learned, wise.

Alejandra **G** (Spanish) a form of
Alexandra.

Alejandrino (Greek) he is the
protector and defender of men.

Alejandro **B** (Spanish) a form of
Alexander.

Alejándro (Spanish) a form of
Alexander.
Alejándra, Aléjo, Alexjandro,
Alexjándro

Alejo (Greek) he who protects and
defends.

Aleksandar, Aleksander (Greek)
forms of Alexander.
Aleksandor, Aleksandr, Aleksandras,
Aleksandur

Aleksei (Russian) a short form of
Alexander.
Aleks, Aleksey, Aleksi, Aleksis, Aleksy,
Alexei, Alexey

Alekzander, Alexzander (Greek)
forms of Alexander.
Alekxander, Alekxzander,
Alexkzandr, Alexzandr, Alexzandyr

Alem (Arabic) wise.

Aleric (German) a form of Alaric.
Alerick, Alerik, Alleric, Allerick,
Alleryc, Alleryck, Alleryk

Aleron (Latin) winged.
Aleronn

Alesio (Italian) a form of Alejo.

Alessandro **B** (Italian) a form of
Alexander.
Alessand, Alessander, Alessandre,
Allessandro

Alex ✶ **B** (Greek) a short form of
Alexander.
Alax, Alexx, Allax, Allex, Allyx, Allyxx,
Alyx, Elek

Alexa **G** (Greek) a short form of
Alexandra.

Alexander ☀ **B** (Greek) defender of mankind. History: Alexander the Great was the conqueror of the civilized world. See also Alastair, Alistair, Iskander, Jando, Leks, Lex, Lexus, Macallister, Oleksandr, Olés, Sander, Sándor, Sandro, Sandy, Sasha, Xan, Xander, Zander, Zindel.
Al, Alec, Alecsandar, Alejándro, Alek, Alekos, Aleksandar, Aleksander, Aleksei, Alekzander, Alessandro, Alex, Alexandar, Alexandor, Alexandr, Alexandre, Alexandro, Alexandròs, Alexi, Alexis, Alexxander, Alexzander, Alic, Alick, Alisander, Alixander

Alexandra **G** (Greek) defender of humankind.

Alexandre **B** (French) a form of Alexander.

Alexandria **G** (Greek) a form of Alexandra.

Alexandro (Greek) a form of Alexander.
Alexandras, Alexandros, Alexandru

Alexe **G** (Russian) a form of Alexi. (Greek) a form of Alex.

Alexi **G** (Russian) a form of Aleksei. (Greek) a short form of Alexander.
Alexe, Alexee, Alexey, Alexie, Alexio, Alexy, Alezio

Alexie **G** (Russian, Greek) a form of Alexi.

Alexis **G** (Greek) a short form of Alexander.
Alexei, Alexes, Alexey, Alexios, Alexius, Alexiz, Alexsis, Alexsus, Alexus, Alexys

Alexsander (Greek) a form of Alexander.

Alexus **G** (Greek) a form of Alexis.

Aleydis (Teutonic) born into a noble family.

Alfie **B** (English) a familiar form of Alfred.
Alfy

Alfio (Greek) he who has a white complexion.

Alfonso (Italian, Spanish) a form of Alphonse.
Affonso, Alfons, Alfonse, Alfonsus, Alfonza, Alfonzo, Alfonzus

Alford (English) old river ford.
Allford

Alfred (English) elf counselor; wise counselor. See also Fred.
Ailfrid, Ailfryd, Alf, Alfeo, Alfie, Alfredo, Alfredus, Alfrid, Alfried, Alfryd, Alured

Alfredo (Italian, Spanish) a form of Alfred.
Alfrido

Alger (German) noble spearman. (English) a short form of Algernon. See also Elger.
Aelfar, Algar, Algor, Allgar

Algernon (English) bearded, wearing a moustache.
Aelgernon, Algenon, Alger, Algie, Algin, Algon

Algie (English) a familiar form of Algernon.
Algee, Algia, Algy

Algis (German) spear.
Algiss

Algiso (Greek) lance of nobility.

Ali **B** (Arabic) greatest. (Swahili) exalted.
Aly

Alí (Arabic) a form of Ali.

Alic (Greek) a short form of
Alexander.
*Alick, Aliek, Alik, Aliko, Alyc, Alyck,
Alyk, Alyko*

Alice **G** (Greek) truthful. (German)
noble.

Alicia **G** (English) a form of Alice.

Aligao (Chamorro) to search for.

Alijah (Hebrew) a form of Elijah.

Alilim (Chamorro) cateye shell.

Alim (Arabic) scholar. (Arabic) a
form of Alem.
Alym

Alipate (Fijian) a form of Alberto.

Alipio (Greek) he who is not affected
by suffering.

Alisander (Greek) a form of
Alexander.
*Alisandre, Alisaunder, Alissander,
Alissandre, Alsandair, Alsandare,
Alsander*

Alisha **G** (Greek) truthful.
(German) noble. (English) a form
of Alicia.

Alison, Allison **G** (English) Alice's
son.
*Allisan, Allisen, Allisun, Allisyn,
Allysan, Allysen, Allysin, Allyson,
Allysun, Allysyn*

Alissa **G** (Greek) a form of Alice.

Alistair (English) a form of Alexander.
*Alisdair, Alistaire, Alistar, Alister,
Allistair, Allistar, Allister, Allistir,
Alstair, Alystayr, Alystyre*

Alivereti (Fijian) a form of Alfredo.

Alix **G** (Greek) a short form of Alex.
Alixx, Allix, Allixx, Allyx, Allyxx

Alixander (Greek) a form of Alexander.
*Alixandre, Alixandru, Alixsander,
Alixxander, Alixxzander, Alixzander,
Alyxxander, Alyxxsander,
Alyxxzander, Alyxzander*

Allah (Arabic) God.

Allambee (Australian) quiet place.
*Alambee, Alambey, Alambi, Alambie,
Alamby, Allambey, Allambi, Allambie,
Allamby*

Allan **B** (Irish) a form of Alan.
Allane, Allayne

Allante, Allanté (Spanish) forms of
Alan.

Allard (English) noble, brave.
Alard, Ellard

Allen **B** (Irish) a form of Alan.
*Alen, Allene, Alley, Alleyn, Alleyne,
Allie, Allin, Alline, Allon, Allyn, Allyne*

Allie **G** (Irish) a form of Allen.

Alma **G** (Arabic) learned. (Latin)
soul.

Almeric (German) powerful ruler.
*Almauric, Amaurick, Amaurik,
Amauryc, Amauryck, Amauryk,
Americk, Amerik, Ameryc, Ameryck,
Ameryk*

Almon (Hebrew) widower.
Alman, Almen, Almin, Almyn

Alo (Chamorro) a form of Alu.

Alois (German) a short form of
Aloysius.
Aloys

Aloisio (Spanish) a form of Louis.

Alok (Sanskrit) victorious cry.

Alon (Hebrew) oak.
Alonn

Alondra **G** (Spanish) a form of
Alexandra.

Alonso, Alonzo (Spanish) forms of
Alphonse.
*Alano, Alanzo, Alon, Alonz, Alonza,
Alonze, Allonza, Allonzo, Elonzo,
Lon, Lonnie, Lonso, Lonżo*

Aloysius (German) a form of Louis.
Alaois, Alois, Aloisius, Aloisio

Alpert (Pohnpeian) a form of
Alberto.

Alphonse (German) noble and eager.
*Alf, Alfie, Alfonso, Alonzo, Alphons,
Alphonsa, Alphonso, Alphonsus,
Alphonza, Alphonzus, Fonzie*

Alphonso (Italian) a form of
Alphonse.
Alphanso, Alphonzo, Fonso

Alpin (Irish) attractive.
Alpine, Alpyn, Alpyne

Alpino (Pohnpeian) a form of Albino.

Alroy (Spanish) king.
Alroi

Alsantry (Pohnpeian) a form of
Alejandro.

Alston (English) noble's settlement.
*Allston, Alstan, Alsten, Alstin, Alstun,
Alstyn*

Altair (Greek) star. (Arabic) flying.
Altayr, Altayre

Alterio (Greek) like a starry night.

Altman (German) old man.
Altmann, Altmen, Atman

Alton (English) old town.
Alten

Alu (Chamorro) barracuda; shark.

Alucio (Latin) he is lucid and
illustrious.

Alula (Latin) winged; swift.

Alva 🄱🄶 (Hebrew) sublime.
Alvah

Alvan (German) a form of Alvin.
Alvand, Alvun

Alvar (English) army of elves.
Alvara

Alvaro (Spanish) just; wise.

Alvern (Latin) spring.
Alverne, Elvern

Alvero (Germanic) completely
prudent.

Alvin (Latin) white; light skinned.
(German) friend to all; noble friend;
friend of elves. See also Albin,
Elvin.
*Aloin, Aluin, Aluino, Alvan, Alven,
Alvie, Alvino, Alvon, Alvy, Alvyn,
Alwin, Elwin*

Alvis (Scandinavian) all-knowing.

Alwin (German) a form of Alvin.
*Ailwyn, Alwan, Alwen, Alwon, Alwun,
Alwyn, Alwynn, Aylwin*

Alyssa 🄶 (Greek) rational. Botany:
alyssum is a flowering herb.

Ama, Amay (Chamorro) forms of
Amai.

Amactus (Chamorro) breaking off.

Amadeo (Italian) a form of
Amadeus.

Amadeus (Latin) loves God. Music:
Wolfgang Amadeus Mozart was a
famous eighteenth-century Austrian
composer.
*Amad, Amadeaus, Amadée,
Amadeo, Amadei, Amadio, Amadis,
Amado, Amador, Amadou, Amando,
Amedeo, Amodaos*

Amai (Chamorro) rain.

Amal 🄶 (Hebrew) worker. (Arabic)
hopeful.
Amahl

Amalio (Greek) a man who is carefree.

Amam (Chamorro) flattering.

Aman (Hebrew) magnificent one.

Amancio (Latin) he who loves God.

Amanda G (Latin) lovable.

Amandeep BG (Punjabi) light of peace.
Amandip, Amanjit, Amanjot, Amanpreet

Amando (French) a form of Amadeus.
Amand, Amandio, Amaniel, Amato

Amani (Arabic) believer. (Yoruba) strength; builder.
Amanee

Amar (Punjabi) immortal. (Arabic) builder.
Amare, Amaree, Amari, Amario, Amaris, Amarjit, Amaro, Amarpreet, Amarri, Ammar, Ammer

Amaranto (Greek) he who does not slow down.

Amaruquispe (Quechua) free, like the sacred Amaru.

Amarutopac (Quechua) glorious, majestic Amaru.

Amaruyupanqui (Quechua) he who honors Amaru; memorable Amaru.

Amato (French) loved.
Amat, Amatto

Ambar G (Sanskrit) sky.

Amber G (French) amber.

Ambrois (French) a form of Ambrose.

Ambrose (Greek) immortal.
Ambie, Ambrogio, Ambroise, Ambroisius, Ambros, Ambrosi, Ambrosio, Ambrosios, Ambrosius, Ambrossye, Ambrosye, Ambrotos, Ambroz, Ambrus, Amby

Ameen (Hebrew, Arabic, Hindi) a form of Amin.

Ameer (Hebrew) a form of Amir.
Ameir, Amer, Amere

Amelio (Teutonic) very hard worker, energetic.

Americ (French) a form of Emery.

Américo (Germanic) prince in action.

Amerigo (Teutonic) industrious. History: Amerigo Vespucci was the Italian explorer for whom America is named.
Americo, Americus, Amerygo

Amérigo (Italian) a form of Amerigo.

Ames (French) friend.
Amess

Ami (Hebrew) builder.

Amicus (English, Latin) beloved friend.
Amic, Amick, Amicko, Amico, Amik, Amiko, Amyc, Amyck, Amycko, Amyk, Amyko

Amid (Arabic) academic dean.

Amida (Japanese) the name of a Buddha.

Amiel (Hebrew) God of my people.
Amiell, Ammiel, Amyel, Amyell

Amílcar (Punic) he who governs the city.

Amin (Hebrew, Arabic) trustworthy; honest. (Hindi) faithful.
Amen, Amine, Ammen, Ammin, Ammyn, Amyn, Amynn

Amín (Arabic) a form of Amin.

Aminiasi (Fijian) a kind of tree.

Amintor (Greek) protector.

Amir 🅖 (Hebrew) proclaimed.
(Punjabi) wealthy; king's minister.
(Arabic) prince.
*Aamer, Aamir, Ameer, Amire, Amiri,
Amyr*

Amish (Sanskrit) honest.

Amit (Punjabi) unfriendly. (Arabic)
highly praised.
Amita, Amitan, Amreet

Ammei, Ammey (Chamorro) forms
of Amai.

Ammon (Egyptian) hidden.
Mythology: the ancient god
associated with reproduction.
Amman

Amol (Hindi) priceless, valuable.
Amul

Amoldo (Spanish) power of an eagle.

Amon (Hebrew) trustworthy; faithful.
Amun

Amón (Hebrew) a form of Amon.

Amory (German) a form of Emory.
*Ameree, Ameri, Amerie, Amery,
Ammeree, Ammerey, Ammeri, Ammerie,
Ammery, Ammoree, Ammorey, Ammori,
Ammorie, Ammory, Amor, Amoree,
Amorey, Amori, Amorie*

Amos (Hebrew) burdened, troubled.
Bible: an Old Testament prophet.
Amose, Amous

Amós (Hebrew) a form of Amos.

Amotho (Chamorro) medicine.

Ampelio (Greek) he who makes wine
from his own grapes.

Ampelo (Greek) son of a satyr and a
nymph, who died while trying to
pick grapes from a grapevine.

Amram (Hebrew) mighty nation.
Amarien, Amran, Amren, Amryn

Amrat (Arabic) handsome.

Amrit 🅑🅖 (Sanskrit) nectar. (Punjabi,
Arabic) a form of Amit.
Amryt

Amritpal (Sikh) protector of the
Lord's nectar.

Amuillan (Mapuche) movement
from the altar; he who warmly
serves others.

Amy 🅖 (Latin) beloved.

An 🅑 (Chinese, Vietnamese)
peaceful.
Ana

Aña (Chamorro) to overpower; to
punish.

Anacario (Greek) not without grace.

Anacleto (Greek) he who was called
upon.

Añaho (Chamorro) I punish; I
overcome.

Anaías (Hebrew) Lord answers.

Anand (Hindi) blissful.
Ananda, Anant, Ananth

Anandan (Sanskrit) a form of Anand.

Ananías (Hebrew) he who has the
grace of God.

Añao (Chamorro) to conquer.

Anastasius (Greek) resurrection.
*Anas, Anastacio, Anastacios,
Anastagio, Anastas, Anastase,
Anastasi, Anastasio, Anastasios,
Anastatius, Anastice, Anastisis,
Anaztáz, Athanasius*

Anatole (Greek) east.
*Anatol, Anatoley, Anatoli, Anatolie,
Anatolijus, Anatolio, Anatolis,
Anatoliy, Anatoly, Anitoly, Antoly*

Anbesa (Spanish) a Saracen governor of Spain.

Anca (Quechua) eagle; black eagle.

Ancasmayu (Quechua) blue like the river.

Ancaspoma, Ancaspuma (Quechua) bluish puma.

Ancavil (Mapuche) identical mythological being.

Ancavilo (Mapuche) snake's body; a body that is half snake.

Anchali (Taos) painter.
Anchalee, Anchaley, Anchalie, Anchaly

Ancuguiyca (Quechua) having sacred resistance.

Andero (Pohnpeian) a form of Andres.

Anders (Swedish) a form of Andrew.
Andar, Ander

Anderson **B** (Swedish) son of Andrew.
Andersen

Andolin (Pohnpeian) a form of Antonio.

Andon (Chuukese) a form of Antonio.

Andonios (Greek) a form of Anthony.
Andoni, Andonis, Andonny

Andor (Hungarian) a form of Andrew.

András (Hungarian) a form of Andrew.
Andraes, Andri, Andris, Andrius, Andriy, Aundras, Aundreas

Andre, André **B** (French) forms of Andrew.
Andra, Andrae, Andrecito, Andree, Andrei, Aundre, Aundré

Andrea **G** (Greek) a form of Andrew.
Andrean, Andreani, Andrian

Andreas **B** (Greek) a form of Andrew.
Andres, Andries

Andrei (Bulgarian, Romanian, Russian) a form of Andrew.
Andreian, Andrej, Andrey, Andreyan, Andrie, Aundrei

Andreo (Greek) manly.

Andres **B** (Spanish) a form of Andrew.
Andras, Andrés, Andrez

Andrew ✿ **B** (Greek) strong; manly; courageous. Bible: one of the Twelve Apostles. See also Bandi, Drew, Endre, Evangelos, Kendrew, Ondro.
Aindrea, Anders, Andery, Andonis, Andor, András, Andre, André, Andrea, Andreas, Andrei, Andres, Andrews, Andru, Andrue, Andrus, Andy, Anker, Anndra, Antal, Audrew

Andrike (Marshallese) something disliked.

Androcles (Greek) man covered with glory.

Andrónico (German) victorious man.

Andros (Polish) sea. Mythology: the god of the sea.
Andris, Andrius, Andrus

Andrzej (Polish) a form of Andrew.

Andy **B** (Greek) a short form of Andrew.
Ande, Andee, Andey, Andi, Andie, Andino, Andis, Andje

Aneurin (Welsh) honorable; gold. See also Nye.
Aneirin

Anfernee (Greek) a form of Anthony.
Anferney, Anfernie, Anferny, Anfranee, Anfrene, Anfrenee, Anpherne

Anfión (Greek) mythological son of Antiope and Jupiter.

Anfonee (Greek) a form of Anthony.
Anfoney, Anfoni, Anfonie, Anfony

Ang (Chinese) high spirited.

Angel ☀ **B** (Greek) angel. (Latin) messenger. See also Gotzon.
Ange, Angell, Angelo, Angie, Angy, Anjel, Anjell

Ángel (Greek) a form of Angel.

Angela **G** (Greek) angel; messenger.

Angelina **G** (Russian) forms of Angela.

Angeline (Russian) forms of Angela.

Angelino (Latin) messenger.

Angelo (Italian) a form of Angel.
Angeleo, Angelito, Angello, Angelos, Angelous, Angiolo, Anglo, Anjello, Anjolo

Anghet (Chamorro) angel.

Angilberto (Teutonic) he who shines with the power of God. A combination of Ángel and Alberto.

Angit (Chamorro) a form of Anghet.

Angkel (Pohnpeian) a form of Angel.

Angoco (Chamorro) to trust, to rely on.

Angocog, Angog (Chamorro) forms of Angoco.

Angus (Scottish) exceptional; outstanding. Mythology: Angus Og was the Celtic god of youth, love, and beauty. See also Ennis, Gus.
Aeneas, Aonghas

Anh (Vietnamese) peace; safety.

Anh Dung (Vietnamese) heroism; strength.

Aniano (Greek) he who is sad and upset.

Anías (Hebrew) God answers.

Anibal (Phoenician) a form of Hannibal.

Aníbal (Punic) he who has the grace of God.

Anicet, Aniceto (Greek) invincible man of great strength.

Anidreb (Marshallese) juggling ball made of pandanus fiber.

Anik **G** (Czech) a form of Anica (see Girls' Names).

Anil (Hindi) wind god.
Aneal, Aneel, Anel, Aniel, Aniello, Anielo, Anyl, Anyll

Anisha **G** (English) a form of Agnes (see Girls' Names).

Anita (Sanskrit) free.

Anitti (Chamorro) spirit.

Anjua (Marshallese) proud.

Anka **G** (Turkish) phoenix.

Anker (Danish) a form of Andrew.
Ankor, Ankur

Anna **G** (Greek) a form of Annas.

Annan (Scottish) brook. (Swahili) fourth-born son.
Annen, Annin, Annon, Annun, Annyn

Annas (Greek) gift from God.
Anis, Anish, Anna, Annais

Anne **G** (English) gracious.

Anno (German) a familiar form of Johann.
Ano

Anoki (Native American) actor.
Anokee, Anokey, Anokie, Anoky

Anoop (Sikh) beauty.

Ansaldo (German) he who represents God; God is with him.

Ansel (French) follower of a nobleman.
Ancell, Ansa, Anselino, Ansell, Ansellus, Anselyno, Ansyl

Anselm (German) divine protector. See also Elmo.
Anse, Anselme, Anselmi, Anselmo

Ansis (Latvian) a form of Janis.

Ansley **G** (Scottish) a form of Ainsley.
Anslea, Anslee, Ansleigh, Ansli, Anslie, Ansly, Ansy

Anson (German) divine. (English) Anne's son.
Ansan, Ansen, Ansin, Ansun, Ansyn

Answer (English) a response.

Anta, Antay (Quechua) copper, copperish.

Antal (Hungarian) a form of Anthony.
Antek, Anti, Antos

Antares (Greek) giant, red star. Astronomy: the brightest star in the constellation Scorpio.
Antar, Antario, Antarious, Antarius, Antarr, Antarus

Antauaya (Quechua) copper-colored meadow; copper-colored grass.

Antavas (Lithuanian) a form of Anthony.
Antae, Antaeus, Antavious, Antavius, Ante, Anteo

Antelmo (Germanic) protector of the homeland.

Antenor (Greek) he who is a fighter.

Anthany (Latin, Greek) a form of Anthony.
Antanas, Antanee, Antanie, Antenee, Anthan, Antheny, Anthine, Anthney

Anthonie (Latin, Greek) a form of Anthony.
Anthone, Anthonee, Anthoni, Anthonia

Anthony ☼ **B** (Latin) praiseworthy. (Greek) flourishing. See also Tony.
Anathony, Andonios, Andor, András, Anothony, Antal, Antavas, Anfernee, Anthany, Anthawn, Anthey, Anthian, Anthino, Anthone, Anthoney, Anthonie, Anthonio, Anthonu, Anthonysha, Anthoy, Anthyoine, Anthyonny, Antione, Antjuan, Antoine, Anton, Antonio, Antony, Antwan, Antwon

Antígono (Greek) he who stands out amongst all of his fellow men.

Antilaf (Mapuche) happy day, joyous day.

Antininan (Quechua) copperish like fire.

Antioco (Greek) he who commands the chariot in the fight against the enemy.

Antione **B** (French) a form of Anthony.
Antion, Antionio, Antionne, Antiono

Antipan (Mapuche) sunny branch of a clear brown color.

Antipas (Greek) he is the enemy of all, in opposition to everyone.

Antivil (Mapuche) sunny snake.

Antjuan (Spanish) a form of Anthony.
Antajuan, Anthjuan, Antuan, Antuane

Antoan (Vietnamese) safe, secure.

An-Toan (Vietnamese) safe, secure.

Antoine (French) a form of Anthony.
Anntoin, Anthoine, Antoiné, Antoinne, Atoine

Antolín (Greek) flourishing, beautiful like a flower.

Anton (Slavic) a form of Anthony.
Anthon, Antone, Antonn, Antonne, Antons, Antos

Antón (Spanish) a form of Antonio.

Antonia Ⓖ (Greek) flourishing. (Latin) praiseworthy.

Antonio Ⓑ (Italian) a form of Anthony. See also Tino, Tonio.
Anthonio, Antinio, Antoinio, Antoino, Antonello, Antoneo, Antonin, Antonín, Antonino, Antonnio, Antonios, Antonius, Antonyia, Antonyio, Antonyo

Antony (Latin) a form of Anthony.
Antin, Antini, Antius, Antonee, Antoney, Antoni, Antonie, Antonin, Antonios, Antonius, Antonyia, Antonyio, Antonyo, Anty

Antreas (Pohnpeian) a form of Andrés.

Antti (Finnish) manly.
Anthey, Anthi, Anthie, Anthy, Anti, Antty

Antu (Indigenous) salt.

Antwan (Arabic) a form of Anthony.
Antaw, Antawan, Antawn, Anthawn, Antowan, Antowaun, Antowine, Antowne, Antowyn, Antuwan, Antwain, Antwaina, Antwaine, Antwainn, Antwaion, Antwane, Antwann, Antwanne, Antwarn, Antwaun, Antwen, Antwian, Antwine, Antwuan, Antwun, Antwyné

Antwon (Arabic) a form of Anthony.
Antown, Antuwon, Antwion, Antwione, Antwoan, Antwoin, Antwoine, Antwone, Antwonn, Antwonne, Antwoun, Antwyon, Antwyone, Antyon, Antyonne, Antywon

Anukal (Chuukese) alone.

Anukul (Sanskrit) suitable.

Anwar (Arabic) luminous.
Anour, Anouar, Anwi

Anyaypoma, Anyaypuma (Quechua) he who roars and becomes angry like the puma.

Aparama (Fijian) a form of Abraham.

Aparicio (Latin) he who refers to the appearances of the Virgin in different stages.

Apeles (Greek) he who is in a sacred place.

Apenisa (Fijian) a form of Ebenezer.

Api (Indonesian) fire.

Apiatan (Kiowa) wooden lance.

Apiner (Pohnpeian) a form of Abner.

Apisai (Fijian) a form of Abishai.

Apisalome (Fijian) a form of Apisalome.

Apo' (Chamorro) to lean against.

Apo, Apu (Quechua) chief, Lord God; he who moves forward.

Apólito (Latin) dedicated to the god Apollo.

Apollo (Greek) manly. Mythology: the god of prophecy, healing, music, poetry, and light. See also Polo.
Apolinar, Apolinario, Apollos, Apolo, Apolonio, Appollo, Appolo, Appolonio

Apolodoro (Griego) skill of Apollo.

Apono (Chuukese) a form of Apollo.

Appa (Chamorro) to place one's hand on someone's shoulder.

April Ⓖ (Latin) opening.

Apucachi (Quechua) lord of salt, salty.

Apucatequil, Apucatiquil (Quechua) god of lightning.

Apumaita (Quechua) where are you, master?

Apurimac (Quechua) eloquent master.

Apuyurac (Quechua) white chief.

Aquila (Latin, Spanish) eagle.
Acquilla, Aquil, Aquilas, Aquileo, Aquiles, Aquilino, Aquill, Aquilla, Aquille, Aquillino, Aquyl, Aquyla, Aquyll, Aquylla

Arafat (Arabic) mountain of recognition. History: Yasir Arafat led Al Fatah, an Arab guerilla group, and the Palestine Liberation Organization, advocating an independent Palestinian state.

Araldo (Spanish) a form of Harold.
Aralodo, Aralt, Aroldo, Arry

Aram (Syrian) high, exalted.
Ara, Aramia, Arem, Arim, Arra, Arram, Arum, Arym

Aramis (French) Literature: one of the title characters in Alexandre Dumas's novel *The Three Musketeers*.
Airamis, Aramith, Aramys

Aran (Tai) forest. (Danish) a form of Aren. (Hebrew, Scottish) a form of Arran.
Arane

Arata (Japanese) new.

Arbedul (Palauan) the leaders.

Arcángel (Greek) prince of all angels.

Archer (English) bowman.
Archar, Archie, Archor

Archibald (German) bold. See also Arkady.
Arch, Archaimbaud, Archambault, Archibaldes, Archibaldo, Archibold, Archie, Archybald, Archybalde, Archybaldes, Archybauld, Archybaulde

Archie (German, English) a familiar form of Archer, Archibald.
Arche, Archee, Archey, Archi, Archy

Ardal (Irish) a form of Arnold.
Ardale, Ardall

Ardell (Latin) eager; industrious.
Ardel

Arden **G** (Latin) ardent; fiery.
Ard, Ardan, Ardene, Ardent, Ardian, Ardie, Ardin, Ardint, Ardn, Arduino, Ardyn, Ardynt

Ardley (English) ardent meadow.
Ardlea, Ardlee, Ardleigh, Ardli, Ardlie, Ardly

Ardon (Hebrew) bronzed.
Ardun

Ardur (Chuukese) a form of Arthur.

Areli **G** (American) a form of Oralee (see Girls' names).

Aren (Danish) eagle; ruler. (Hebrew, Arabic) a form of Aaron.

Aretas (Arabic) metal forger.

Aretino (Greek, Italian) victorious.
Aretin, Aretine, Artyn, Artyno

Argenis (Greek) he who has a great whiteness.

Argentino, Argento (Latin) shines like silver.

Argimiro (Greek) careful; vigilant.

Argus (Danish) watchful, vigilant.
Agos, Arguss

Argyle (Irish) from Ireland.
Argile, Argiles, Argyles

Ari ☗ (Hebrew) a short form of
Ariel. (Greek) a short form of
Aristotle.
*Aree, Arey, Arias, Arie, Arieh, Arih,
Arij, Ario, Arri, Ary, Arye*

Aria (Hebrew) a form of Ariel.

Arian (Greek) a form of Arion.
Ariann, Arrian, Aryan

Ariana ☗ (Greek) a form of Arian.

Ariane ☗ (Greek) a form of Arian.

Arianne ☗ (Greek) a form of Arian.

Aric (German) a form of Richard.
(Scandinavian) a form of Eric.
*Aaric, Aarick, Aarik, Arec, Areck,
Arich, Arick, Ariek, Arik, Arrek, Arric,
Arrick, Arrik, Aryc, Aryck, Aryk*

Ariel ☗ (Hebrew) lion of God.
Bible: another name for Jerusalem.
Literature: the name of a sprite in
the Shakespearean play *The
Tempest.*
*Airal, Airel, Arel, Areli, Ari, Ariele,
Ariell, Arielle, Ariya, Ariyel, Arrial,
Arriel, Aryel, Aryell, Aryl, Aryll, Arylle*

Aries (Latin) ram. Astrology: the first
sign of the zodiac.
Arees, Ares, Arie, Ariez, Aryes

Arif (Arabic) knowledgeable.
Areef, Aryf

Arion (Greek) enchanted. (Hebrew)
melodious.
Arian, Arien, Ario, Arione, Aryon

Aristarco (Greek) best of the princes.

Aristeo (Greek) outstanding one.

Aristides (Greek) son of the best.
*Aris, Aristede, Aristedes, Aristeed,
Aristide, Aristides, Aristidis, Arystides,
Arystydes*

Arístides (Greek) a form of
Aristides.

Aristóbulo (Greek) greatest and best
counselor; he who gives very good
advice.

Aristofanes (Greek) best, the
optimum.

Aristóteles (Greek) best; the most
renowned; the most optimistic; he
who has noble intentions.

Aristotle (Greek) best; wise. History:
a third-century b.c. philosopher who
tutored Alexander the Great.
*Ari, Aris, Aristito, Aristo, Aristokles,
Aristotal, Aristotel, Aristotelis,
Aristotol, Aristott, Aristotyl, Arystotle*

Arjun (Hindi) white; milk colored.
Arjen, Arjiin, Arju, Arjuna, Arjune

Arkady (Russian) a form of
Archibald.
*Arcadio, Arkadee, Arkadey, Arkadi,
Arkadie, Arkadij, Arkadiy*

Arkin (Norwegian) son of the eternal
king.
Aricin, Arkeen, Arkyn

Arledge (English) lake with the
hares.
Arlege, Arlidge, Arlledge, Arllege

Arlen (Irish) pledge.
*Arlan, Arland, Arlend, Arlin, Arlinn,
Arlon, Arlyn, Arlynn*

Arley (English) a short form of Harley.
Arleigh, Arlie, Arly

Arlo (Spanish) barberry. (English)
fortified hill. A form of Harlow.
(German) a form of Charles.
Arlow

Arman (Persian) desire, goal.
Armaan, Armahn, Armaine

Armand (Latin, German) a form of
Herman. See also Mandek.
*Armad, Arman, Armanda, Armando,
Armands, Armanno, Armaude,
Armenta, Armond*

Armando (Spanish) a form of
Armand.
Armondo

Armani **B** (Hungarian) sly.
(Hebrew) a form of Armon.
*Arman, Armanee, Armaney, Armanie,
Armann, Armany, Armoni, Armonie,
Armonio, Armonni, Armony*

Armentario (Greek) herder of
livestock.

Armon (Hebrew) high fortress,
stronghold.
*Armani, Armen, Armin, Armino,
Armonn, Armons, Armyn*

Armstrong (English) strong arm.
History: astronaut Neil Armstrong
was the commander of Apollo 11
and the first person to walk on the
moon.
Armstron, Armstronge

Arnaud (French) a form of Arnold.
Arnaude, Arnauld, Arnault, Arnoll

Arne (German) a form of Arnold.
*Arna, Arnay, Arnel, Arnele, Arnell,
Arnelle*

Arnette (English) little eagle.
*Arnat, Arnatt, Arnet, Arnett, Arnetta,
Arnot, Arnott*

Arnie (German) a familiar form of
Arnold.
Arnee, Arney, Arni, Arnny, Arny

Arno (German) a short form of
Arnold. (Czech) a short form of
Ernest.
Arnou, Arnoux

Arnold (German) eagle ruler.
*Ardal, Arnald, Arnaldo, Arnaud,
Arndt, Arne, Arnhold, Arnie, Arno,
Arnol, Arnoldas, Arnolde, Arnoldo,
Arnoll, Arnolt, Arnoud, Arnulfo,
Arnyld*

Arnon (Hebrew) rushing river.
Arnan, Arnen, Arnin, Arnyn

Arnulfo (German) a form of Arnold.

Aron, Arron **B** (Hebrew) forms of
Aaron. (Danish) forms of Aren.
Arrion

Aroon (Tai) dawn.
Aroone

Arquelao (Greek) governor of his
village.

Arquimedes (Greek) he who has
profound thoughts.

Arquímedes (Greek) deep thinker.

Arquipo (Greek) horse breaker.

Arran (Scottish) island dweller.
Geography: an island off the west
coast of Scotland. (Hebrew) a form
of Aaron.
Aeran, Arren, Arrin, Arryn, Aryn

Arrigo (Italian) a form of Harry.
Alrigo, Arrighetto

Arrio (Spanish) warlike.
Ario, Arrow, Arryo, Aryo

Arsenio (Greek) masculine; virile.
History: Saint Arsenius was a
teacher in the Roman Empire.
*Arsen, Arsène, Arseneo, Arsenius,
Arseny, Arsenyo, Arsinio, Arsinyo,
Arsynio, Arsynyo*

Arsha (Persian) venerable.
Arshah

Art (English) a short form of Arthur.

Artemus (Greek) gift of Artemis.
Mythology: Artemis was the
goddess of the hunt and the moon.
*Artemas, Artemio, Artemis, Artimas,
Artimis, Artimus*

Arthur 🄱 (Irish) noble; lofty hill.
(Scottish) bear. (English) rock.
(Icelandic) follower of Thor. See
also Turi.
*Art, Artair, Artek, Arth, Arther,
Arthor, Arthyr, Artie, Artor, Arturo,
Artus, Aurthar, Aurther, Aurthur*

Artie (English) a familiar form of
Arthur.
Arte, Artee, Artian, Artis, Arty, Atty

Artjuni (Sanskrit) white; silvery.

Arturo (Italian) a form of Arthur.
Arthuro, Artur

Arun (Cambodian, Hindi) sun.
Aruns

Arundel (English) eagle valley.

Arurang (Palauan) he who is timid or
ashamed.

Arve (Norwegian) heir, inheritor.

Arvel (Welsh) wept over.
*Arval, Arvell, Arvelle, Arvil, Arvol,
Arvyn*

Arvid (Hebrew) wanderer.
(Norwegian) eagle tree. See also
Ravid.
*Arv, Arvad, Arve, Arvie, Arvind,
Arvinder, Arvyd, Arvydas*

Arvin (German) friend of the people;
friend of the army.
*Arv, Arvan, Arven, Arvie, Arvind,
Arvinder, Arvon, Arvy, Arvyn, Arwan,
Arwen, Arwin, Arwon, Arwyn*

Arya (Hebrew) a form of Aria.

Aryeh (Hebrew) lion.

Asa 🄱 (Hebrew) physician, healer.
(Yoruba) falcon.
Asaa, Asah, Ase

Asád (Arabic) lion.
Asaad, Asad, Asid, Assad, Azad

Asadel (Arabic) prosperous.
Asadour, Asadul, Asadyl, Asael

Asaf (Hebrew) one chosen by God.

Asaichi (Japanese) first dawn.

Asao (Japanese) morning man.

Ascensión (Spanish) mystical name
that alludes to the ascension of Jesus
Christ to heaven.

Ascot (English) eastern cottage; style
of necktie. Geography: a village near
London and the site of the Royal
Ascot horseraces.
Ascott

Asdrúbal (Punic) he who is protected
by God.

Asgar (Arabic) the smallest;
repetitions of names and praises.

Asgard (Scandinavian) court of the
gods.

Ash (Hebrew) ash tree.
Ashby

Ashad (Arabic) most vehement.

Ashanti 🄶 (Swahili) from a tribe in
West Africa.
*Ashan, Ashani, Ashante, Ashantee,
Ashaunte*

Ashburn (English) from the ash-tree
stream.
*Ashbern, Ashberne, Ashbirn,
Ashbirne, Ashborn, Ashborne,
Ashbourn, Ashbourne, Ashburne,
Ashbyrn, Ashbyrne*

Ashby (Scandinavian) ash-tree farm.
(Hebrew) a form of Ash.
Ashbee, Ashbey, Ashbi, Ashbie

Asher (Hebrew) happy; blessed.
Ashar, Ashir, Ashor, Ashur, Ashyr

Ashford (English) ash-tree ford.
Ash, Ashforde, Ashtin

Ashlee **G** (English) a form of Ashley.

Ashleigh **G** (English) a form of Ashley.

Ashley **G** (English) ash-tree meadow.
Ash, Asheley, Ashelie, Ashely, Ashlan, Ashlea, Ashlen, Ashli, Ashlie, Ashlin, Ashling, Ashlinn, Ashlone, Ashly, Ashlynn, Aslan

Ashlyn **G** (English) a form of Ashley.

Ashon (Swahili) seventh-born son.

Ashraf (Arabic) most honorable.

Ashton **BG** (English) ash-tree settlement.
Ashtan, Ashten, Ashtian, Ashtin, Ashtion, Ashtonn, Ashtown, Ashtun

Ashtyn **G** (English) a form of Ashton.

Ashur (Swahili) Mythology: the principal Assyrian deity.

Ashwani (Hindi) first. Religion: the first of the twenty-seven galaxies revolving around the moon.
Ashwan

Ashwin (Hindi) star.
Ashwen, Ashwon, Ashwyn

Asi (Chamorro) pity.

Asiel (Hebrew) created by God.
Asyel

Asif (Arabic) forgiveness.

Asker (Turkish) soldier.

Aslam (Arabic) safer; freer.

Asou (Chuukese) further out; awaited.

Aspen **G** (English) aspen tree.

Asraf (Arabic) a form of Ashraf.

Assi (Chamorro) a form of Asi.

Asterio (Greek) mythical figure that was thrown into the sea because of his escape from Zeus.

Astley (Greek) starry field.
Asterlea, Asterlee, Asterleigh, Asterley, Asterli, Asterlie, Asterly, Astlea, Astlee, Astleigh, Astli, Astlie, Astly

Asto, Astu (Quechua) bird of the Andes.

Astolfo (Greek) he who helps with his lance.

Aston (English) eastern town.
Astan, Asten, Astin, Astown, Astyn

Astuguaraca (Quechua) he who hunts astus with a sling.

Asuka (Japanese) flying bird.

Aswad (Arabic) dark skinned, black.
Aswald

Ata (Fante) twin.
Atah

Atahualpa (Quechua) bird of fortune.

Atake (Chuukese) farming; gardening.

Atalig (Chamorro) staring.

Atanasio (Greek) immortal.

Atao (Chamorro) sun.

Atau (Quechua) fortunate.

Atauaipa (Quechua) bird of fortune; creator of fortune.

Atauanca (Quechua) fortunate eagle.

Atauchi (Quechua) he who makes us good fortunes.

Atchiro (Kosraean) a form of Ichiro.

Atek (Polish) a form of Tanek.

Atenodoro (Greek) gift of wisdom.

Athan (Greek) immortal.
Athen, Athens, Athin, Athon, Athons, Athyn, Athyns

Atherton (English) town by a spring.
Atharton, Athorton

Athol (Scottish) from Ireland.
Affol, Athal, Athel, Athil, Atholton, Athyl

Atid (Tai) sun.
Atyd

Atif (Arabic) caring.
Ateef, Atef, Atyf

Atik (Chuukese) the name of a fish.

Atila (Gothic) a form of Attila.

Atilano (Spanish) a form of Atila.

Atiniui (Chuukese) man of the sea.

Atirek (Sanskrit) surpassing.

Atish (Sanskrit) great ruler.

Atkins (English) from the home of the relatives.
Atkin, Atkyn, Atkyns

Atlas (Greek) lifted; carried. Mythology: Atlas was forced by Zeus to carry the heavens on his shoulders as a punishment for his share of the war of the Titans.

Atley (English) meadow.
Atlea, Atlee, Atleigh, Atli, Atlie, Atly, Attlea, Attlee, Attleigh, Attley, Attli, Attlie, Attly

Atma (Sanskrit) the soul.

Ato (Japanese) myself; gift; copper.

Atoc, Atuc (Quechua) sly as a fox; wolf.

Atocuaman (Quechua) he who possesses the strength of a falcon and the shrewdness of a fox.

Atogor, Atogot (Chamorro) forms of Atugud.

Atong (Chuukese) pity.

Atsuhiro (Japanese) developing kindliness.

Atsuo (Japanese) affectionate man.

Atsuyoshi (Japanese) virtuous intentions; affectionate and rare.

Atti (Chamorro) a form of Atti.

Atticus (Latin) from Attica, a region outside Athens.

Attila (Gothic) little father. History: the Hun leader who invaded the Roman Empire.
Atalik, Atila, Atilio, Atilla, Atiya, Attal, Attilah, Attilio, Attyla, Attylah

Atugud (Chamorro) to prop up each other.

Atuguit, Atugus, Atugut (Chamorro) forms of Atugud.

Atwater (English) at the water's edge.
Attwater

Atwell (English) at the well.
Attwel, Atwel

Atwood (English) at the forest.
Attwood

Atworth (English) at the farmstead.
Attworth

Auberon (German) a form of Oberon.
Auberron, Aubrey

Auberto (French) a form of Alberto.

Aubree **G** (German, French) a form of Aubrey.

Aubrey **G** (German) noble; bearlike. (French) a familiar form of Auberon.
Aubary, Aube, Aubery, Aubie, Aubré, Aubreii, Aubri, Aubry, Aubury

Aubrie **G** (German, French) a form of Aubrey.

Auburn (Latin) reddish brown.
Abern, Aberne, Abirn, Abirne, Aburn, Aburne, Abyrn, Abyrne, Aubern, Auberne, Aubin, Aubirn, Aubirne, Aubun, Auburne, Aubyrn, Aubyrne

Auden (English) old friend.
Audan, Audin, Audyn

Audie (German) noble; strong. (English) a familiar form of Edward.
Audee, Audey, Audi, Audiel, Audley, Audy

Audomaro (Greek) famous because of his riches.

Audon (French) old; rich.
Audelon

Audra **G** (English) a form of Audrey.

Audrey **G** (English) noble strength.
Audre, Audrea, Audri, Audrius, Audry

Audric (English) wise ruler.
Audrick, Audrik, Audryc, Audryck, Audryk

Audun (Scandinavian) deserted, desolate.

Augie (Latin) a familiar form of August.
Auggie, Augy

August **B** (Latin) a short form of Augustine, Augustus.
Agosto, Augie, Auguste, Augusto

Augustín (Spanish) a form of Augustine.

Augustine **B** (Latin) majestic. Religion: Saint Augustine was the first archbishop of Canterbury. See also Austin, Gus, Tino.
Agustin, August, Augusteen, Augustein, Augusteyn, Augusteyne, Augustin, Augustinas, Augustino, Augustyn, Augustyne, Austen, Austin, Auston, Austyn

Augusto (Latin) a form of August.

Augustus (Latin) majestic; venerable. History: an honorary title given to the first Roman emperor, Octavius Caesar.
Agustas, Agustys, August

Aukai (Hawaiian) seafarer.
Aukay

Aundre (Greek) a form of Andre.
Aundrae, Aundray, Aundrea, Aundrey, Aundry

Auqui (Quechua) master; prince.

Auquipuma (Quechua) a prince who is as strong as a puma.

Auquitupac (Quechua) glorious prince.

Auquiyupanqui (Quechua) he who honors his masters.

Aurek (Polish) golden haired.
Aurec

Aurelia (Latin) gold.

Aurelio (Latin) a short form of Aurelius.
Aurel, Aurele, Aureli, Aurellio

Aurelius (Latin) golden. History: Marcus Aurelius was a second-century A.D. philosopher and emperor of Rome.
Arelian, Areliano, Aurèle, Aureliano, Aurelien, Aurélien, Aurelio, Aurelyus, Aurey, Auriel, Aury

Aurick (German) protecting ruler.
Auric, Aurik, Auryc, Auryck, Auryk

Auseto (Chuukese) come to me.

Austen, Auston, Austyn 🅱 (Latin)
short forms of Augustine.
Austan, Austun, Austyne

Austin 🌟 🅱 (Latin) a short form of
Augustine.
Astin, Austine, Oistin, Ostin

Austín (Spanish) a form of Augustín.

Autumn 🅶 (Latin) autumn.

Auxilio (Latin) he who saves, who
brings help.

Avel (Greek) breath.
Avell

Avelino (Latin) he who was born in
Avella, Italy.

Avent (French) born during Advent.
Advent, Aventin, Aventino, Aventyno

Averill (French) born in April.
*Ave, Averal, Averall, Averel, Averell,
Averiel, Averil, Averyl, Averyll, Avrel,
Avrell, Avrill, Avryll*

Avery 🅱 (English) a form of Aubrey.
*Avary, Aveary, Avere, Averee,
Averey, Averi, Averie, Avrey, Avry*

Avi (Hebrew) God is my father.
*Avian, Avidan, Avidor, Avie, Aviel,
Avion, Avy*

Avito (Latin) he who is from the
grandfather.

Aviv (Hebrew) youth; springtime.

Avneet 🅶 (Hebrew) a form of Avner.

Avner (Hebrew) a form of Abner.
Avniel

Avram (Hebrew) a form of Abraham,
Abram.
*Arram, Avraam, Avraham, Avrohom,
Avrohom, Avrom, Avrum*

Avshalom (Hebrew) father of peace.
See also Absalom.
Avsalom

Awan (Native American) somebody.

Awes (Chuukese) to call over; finish,
end.

Awesh (Sanskrit) excitement.

Axel (Latin) axe. (German) small oak
tree; source of life. (Scandinavian) a
form of Absalom.
*Aksel, Ax, Axe, Axell, Axil, Axill, Axl,
Axle, Axyle*

Ayar (Quechua) wild quinoa.

Ayden 🌟 (Irish) a form of Aidan.
Aydean

Aydin (Turkish) intelligent.

Ayers (English) heir to a fortune.

Ayhi (Chamorro) a form of Ayuhi.

Ayig (Chamorro) to choose.

Ayinde (Yoruba) we gave praise and
he came.

Aylmer (English) a form of Elmer.
Aillmer, Ailmer, Allmer, Ayllmer

Aymil (Greek) a form of Emil.
Aimil, Aimyl

Aymon (French) a form of Raymond.
Aiman, Aimen, Aimin, Aimyn

Ayo (Yoruba) happiness.

Ayu (Chamorro) that one.

Ayumi (Japanese) walk, step.

Ayumu (Japanese) step, walk; dream.

Ayuyu (Chamorro) coconut crab.

Azaad (Persian) a form of Azad.

Azad (Turkish) free.

Azam (Arabic) the greatest.

Azanías (Hebrew) God hears him.

Azarias (Hebrew) Lord sustains me; divine salvation; God is my soul.

Azarías (Hebrew) Lord sustains and guides me.

Azariel (Hebrew) he who has control over the waters.

Azeem (Arabic) a form of Azim. *Aseem, Asim*

Azi (Nigerian) youth.

Azim (Arabic) defender. *Azeem*

Aziz (Arabic) strong.

Azizi (Swahili) precious.

Azriel (Hebrew) God is my aid.

Azuriah (Hebrew) aided by God. *Azaria, Azariah, Azuria*

Azusa (Japanese) catalpa tree.

B

B **BG** (American) an initial used as a first name.

Baal (Chaldean) he who dominates a territory; owner and lord.

Babang (Chamorro) butterfly.

Babao (Chamorro) battle flag.

Babaoña (Chamorro) his battle flag.

Babaota (Chamorro) our battle flag.

Babela (Chamorro) moth.

Babeldaob (Palauan) the upper sea; the big island of Palau.

Babul (Sanskrit) relative of the bride.

Bacar (Chamorro) a type of spiny tree.

Bach (Vietnamese) white; clear.

Baco (Greek) he who creates disturbances.

Bada (Korean) sea.

Badahur (Persian) courage, valor; heroism.

Baden (German) bather. *Baeden, Bayden, Baydon*

Baek (Korean) white; senior; esteemed; one.

Bahadur (Arabic) brave, bold.

Bahir (Arabic) brilliant, dazzling.

Bahram (Persian) ancient king.

Baiei (Palauan) guest house.

Bailee **G** (French) a form of Bailey.

Bailey **G** (French) bailiff, steward. *Bail, Bailie, Bailio, Baillie, Baily, Bailye, Baley, Bayley*

Bain (Irish) a short form of Bainbridge. *Baine, Bayne, Baynn*

Bainbridge (Irish) fair bridge. *Bain, Baynbridge, Bayne, Baynebridge*

Baird (Irish) traveling minstrel, bard; poet. *Bairde, Bard*

Bakar (Arabic) a young camel.

Bakari (Swahili) noble promise. *Bacari, Baccari, Bakarie*

Baker (English) baker. See also Baxter. *Bakir, Bakory, Bakr*

Bakin, Bakusui (Japanese) literary figures.

Baklai (Maranao) a form of Baklay.

Baklay (Maranao) walking, strolling; traveling.

Bal (Sanskrit) child born with lots of hair.

Balasi (Basque) flat footed.

Balbino (Latin) he who mumbles, who speaks in a stammering manner.

Balbo (Latin) stammerer.
Bailby, Balbi, Ballbo

Baldemar (German) bold; famous.
Baldemer, Baldomero, Baumar, Baumer

Balder (Scandinavian) bald. Mythology: the Norse god of light, summer, purity, and innocence.
Baldier, Baldur, Baudier

Baldesar (Pohnpeian) a form of Baltazar.

Baldovín (Spanish) a form of Balduino.

Baldric (German) brave ruler.
Baldrick, Baudric

Balduino (Germanic) valiant friend.

Baldwin (German) bold friend.
Bald, Baldovino, Balduin, Baldwinn, Baldwyn, Baldwynn, Balldwin, Baudoin

Balfour (Scottish) pastureland.
Balfor, Balfore

Balin (Hindi) mighty soldier.
Bali, Baylen, Baylin, Baylon, Valin

Ballard (German) brave; strong.
Balard

Balraj (Hindi) strongest.

Baltazar (Greek) a form of Balthasar.
Baltasar

Balthasar (Greek) God save the king. Bible: one of the three wise men who bore gifts for the infant Jesus.
Badassare, Baldassare, Baltazar, Balthasaar, Balthazar, Balthazzar, Baltsaros, Belshazar, Belshazzar, Boldizsár

Balu (Sanskrit) child, baby; boy; strength.

Bancroft (English) bean field.
Ban, Bancrofft, Bank, Bankroft, Banky, Binky

Bandemar (Chuukese) a form of Baldemar.

Bandi 🆎 (Hungarian) a form of Andrew.
Bandit

Bandrik (Marshallese) too small to do it.

Bane (Hawaiian) a form of Bartholomew.

Bang (Chinese) nation; state.

Bangoña (Chamorro) he wakes up.

Banner (Scottish, English) flag bearer.
Bannor, Banny

Banning (Irish) small and fair.
Bannie, Banny

Baplo (Chuukese) a form of Pablo.

Barak (Hebrew) lightning bolt. Bible: the valiant warrior who helped Deborah.
Barrak

Baran (Russian) ram.
Baren

Barasa (Kikuyu) meeting place.

Barclay (Scottish, English) birch-tree meadow.
Bar, Barcley, Barklay, Barkley, Barklie, Barrclay, Berkeley

Bard (Irish) a form of Baird.
Bar, Barde, Bardia, Bardiya, Barr

Bardolf (German) bright wolf.
Bardo, Bardolph, Bardou, Bardoul, Bardulf, Bardulph

Bardrick (Teutonic) axe ruler.
Bardric, Bardrik

Baris (Turkish) peaceful.

Barkat (Persian) blessing; abundance; prosperity.

Barker (English) lumberjack; advertiser at a carnival.

Barlow (English) bare hillside.
Barlowe, Barrlow, Barrlowe

Barnabas (Greek, Hebrew, Aramaic, Latin) son of the missionary. Bible: Christian apostle and companion of Paul on his first missionary journey.
Bane, Barna, Barnaba, Barnabus, Barnaby, Barnebas, Barnebus, Barney

Barnaby (English) a form of Barnabas.
Barnabe, Barnabé, Barnabee, Barnabey, Barnabi, Barnabie, Bernabé, Burnaby

Barnard (French) a form of Bernard.
Barn, Barnard, Barnhard, Barnhardo

Barnes (English) bear; son of Barnett.

Barnett (English) nobleman; leader.
Barn, Barnet, Barney, Baronet, Baronett, Barrie, Barron, Barry

Barney (English) a familiar form of Barnabas, Barnett.
Barnie, Barny

Barnum (German) barn; storage place. (English) baron's home.
Barnham

Baron (German, English) nobleman, baron.
Baaron, Barion, Baronie, Barrin, Barrion, Barron, Baryn, Bayron, Berron

Barrett **B** (German) strong as a bear.
Bar, Baret, Barrat, Barret, Barretta, Barrette, Barry, Berrett, Berrit

Barric (English) grain farm.
Barrick, Beric, Berric, Berrick, Berrik

Barrington (English) fenced town. Geography: a town in England.

Barry **B** (Welsh) son of Harry. (Irish) spear, marksman. (French) gate, fence.
Baris, Barri, Barrie, Barris, Bary

Bart (Hebrew) a short form of Bartholomew, Barton.
Barrt, Bartel, Bartie, Barty

Bartholomew (Hebrew) son of Talmaí. Bible: one of the Twelve Apostles. See also Jerney, Parlan, Parthalán.
Balta, Bane, Bart, Bartek, Barth, Barthel, Barthelemy, Barthélemy, Barthélmy, Bartho, Bartholo, Bartholomaus, Bartholome, Bartholomeo, Bartholomeus, Bartholomieu, Bartimous, Bartlet, Barto, Bartolome, Bartolomé, Bartolomeo, Bartolomeô, Bartolommeo, Bartome, Bartz, Bat

Bartlet (English) a form of Bartholomew.
Bartlett, Bartley

Barto (Spanish) a form of Bartholomew.
Bardo, Bardol, Bartol, Bartoli, Bartolo, Bartos

Barton (English) barley town; Bart's town.
Barrton, Bart

Bartram (English) a form of Bertram.
Barthram

Baruc (Hebrew) he who is blessed by God.

Baruch (Hebrew) blessed.
Boruch

Basaant (Sanskrit) spring; garland of yellow flowers.

Basam (Arabic) smiling.
Basem, Basim, Bassam

Basho (Japanese) literary figure.

Basil (Greek, Latin) royal, kingly. Religion: a saint and founder of monasteries. Botany: an herb often used in cooking. See also Vasilis, Wasili.
Bas, Basal, Base, Baseal, Basel, Basle, Basile, Basilio, Basilios, Basilius, Bassel, Bazek, Bazel, Bazil, Bazyli

Basir (Turkish) intelligent, discerning.
Bashar, Basheer, Bashir, Bashiyr, Bechir, Bhasheer

Bassett (English) little person.
Basett, Basit, Basset, Bassit

Bastien (German) a short form of Sebastian.
Baste, Bastiaan, Bastian, Bastion

Basudeo (Sanskrit) lord of the earth.

Bat (English) a short form of Bartholomew.

Baudilio (Teutonic) he who is brave and valiant.

Baul (Gypsy) snail.

Baulis (Tagalog) one with the power of the evil eye.

Bautista (Greek) he who baptizes.

Bavol (Gypsy) wind; air.

Baxter (English) a form of Baker.
Bax, Baxie, Baxty, Baxy

Bay (Vietnamese) seventh son. (French) chestnut brown color; evergreen tree. (English) howler.

Bayani (Tagalog) hero.

Bayard (English) reddish brown hair.
Baiardo, Bay, Bayardo, Bayerd, Bayrd

Baylee ☰ (French) a form of Bayley.

Bayley ☰ (French) a form of Bailey.
Bayleigh, Baylie, Bayly

Beacan (Irish) small.
Beacán, Becan

Beacher (English) beech trees.
Beach, Beachy, Beech, Beecher, Beechy

Beagan (Irish) small.
Beagen, Beagin

Beale (French) a form of Beau.
Beal, Beall, Bealle, Beals

Beaman (English) beekeeper.
Beamann, Beamen, Beeman, Beman

Beamer (English) trumpet player.

Beasley (English) field of peas.

Beatriz ☰ (Latin) a form of Beatrice (see Girls' Names).

Beattie (Latin) blessed; happy; bringer of joy.
Beatie, Beatty, Beaty

Beau ☐ (French) handsome.
Beale, Beaux, Bo

Beaufort (French) beautiful fort.

Beaumont (French) beautiful mountain.

Beauregard (French) handsome; beautiful; well regarded.

Beaver (English) beaver.
Beav, Beavo, Beve, Bevo

Bebe ☐☐ (Spanish) baby.

Beches (Palauan) new, clean; straight.

Beck (English, Scandinavian) brook.
Beckett

Beda (Teutonic) he who orders and provides for.

Bede (English) prayer. Religion: the patron saint of lectors.

Bedinin (Marshallese) to stay on this island.

Bedro (Pohnpeian) a form of Pedro.

Bei (Chinese) north.

Bekebekmad (Palauan) one who is pleasing to the eye.

Beketaut (Palauan) good at shooting.

Bela **BG** (Czech) white. (Hungarian) bright.
Béla, Belaal, Belal, Belall, Belay, Bellal

Belarmino (Germanic) having beautiful armor.

Belau (Palauan) the island of Palau.

Belden (French, English) pretty valley.
Beldin, Beldon, Bellden, Belldon

Belechel (Palauan) good with a slingshot.

Belen **G** (Greek) arrow.

Belengel (Palauan) middle.

Belisario (Greek) he who shoots arrows skillfully.

Bell (French) handsome. (English) bell ringer.

Bellamy (French) beautiful friend.
Belamy, Bell, Bellamey, Bellamie

Bello (African) helper or promoter of Islam.

Belmiro (Portuguese) good-looking; attractive.

Bem (Tiv) peace.
Behm

Ben (Hebrew) a short form of Benjamin.
Behn, Benio, Benn, Benne, Benno

Ben Zion (Hebrew) son of Zion.
Benson, Benzi

Ben-ami (Hebrew) son of my people.
Baram, Barami

Bendicion, Benedicion (Chamorro) forms of Bendision.

Bendision (Chamorro) blessed.

Benedict (Latin) blessed. See also Venedictos, Venya.
Benci, Bendick, Bendict, Bendino, Bendix, Bendrick, Benedetto, Benedick, Benedicto, Benedictus, Benedikt, Bengt, Benito, Benoit

Benedikt (German, Slavic) a form of Benedict.
Bendek, Bendik, Benedek, Benedik

Bengt (Scandinavian) a form of Benedict.
Beng, Benke, Bent

Beniam (Ethiopian) a form of Benjamin.
Beneyam, Beniamin, Beniamino

Benicio (Latin) riding friend.

Benido (Pohnpeian) a form of Bonito.

Benigno (Latin) prodigal son; he who does good deeds.

Benijamini (Fijian) a form of Benjamin.

Benildo (Teutonic) fights against bears.

Benito (Italian) a form of Benedict. History: Benito Mussolini led Italy during World War II.
Benedo, Benino, Benno, Beno, Betto, Beto

Benjamen (Hebrew) a form of
Benjamin.
Benejamen, Benjermen, Benjjmen

Benjamin ☀ **B** (Hebrew) son of
my right hand. See also Peniamina,
Veniamin.
*Behnjamin, Bejamin, Bemjiman, Ben,
Benejaminas, Bengamin, Beniam,
Benja, Benjahmin, Benjaim, Benjam,
Benjamaim, Benjaman, Benjamen,
Benjamine, Benjaminn, Benjamino,
Benjamon, Benjamyn, Benjamynn,
Benjemin, Benjermain, Benjermin,
Benji, Benjie, Benjiman, Benjy,
Benkamin, Bennjamin, Benny,
Benyamin, Benyamino, Binyamin,
Mincho*

Benjamín (Hebrew) a form of
Benjamin.

Benjiman (Hebrew) a form of
Benjamin.
*Benjimen, Benjimin, Benjimon,
Benjmain*

Benjir (Japanese) peaceful, to enjoy
peace.

Benjiro (Japanese) enjoys peace.

Bennett **B** (Latin) little blessed one.
*Benet, Benett, Bennet, Benette,
Bennete, Bennette*

Benny (Hebrew) a familiar form of
Benjamin.
Bennie

Beno (Hebrew) son. (Mwera) band
member.

Benoit (French) a form of Benedict.
Benoît

Benoni (Hebrew) son of my sorrow.
Bible: Ben-oni was the son of Jacob
and Rachel.
Ben-Oni

Benson (Hebrew) son of Ben.
A short form of Ben Zion.
Bensan, Bensen, Benssen, Bensson

Bentley (English) moor; coarse grass
meadow.
Bent, Bentlea, Bentlee, Bentlie, Lee

Benton (English) Ben's town; town
on the moors.
Bent

Benzi (Hebrew) a familiar form of
Ben Zion.

Beouch (Palauan) title of chiefs in
Ngardmau.

Beppe (Italian) a form of Joseph.
Beppy

Ber (English) boundary. (Yiddish)
bear.

Berardo (Germanic) a form of
Bernard.

Bercy (Pohnpeian) a form of Percy.

Beredei (Russian) a form of Hubert.
Berdry, Berdy, Beredej, Beredy

Berenguer (Teutonic) bear that is
prepared for battle.

Berg (German) mountain.
Berdj, Berge, Bergh, Berje

Bergen (German, Scandinavian) hill
dweller.
Bergin, Birgin

Berger (French) shepherd.

Bergren (Scandinavian) mountain
stream.
Berg

Berk (Turkish) solid, rugged.

Berkeley (English) a form of Barclay.
*Berk, Berkely, Berkie, Berkley, Berklie,
Berkly, Berky*

Berl (German) a form of Burl.
Berle, Berlie, Berlin, Berlyn

Berlyn (German) boundary line. See also Burl.
Berlin, Burlin

Bern (German) a short form of Bernard.
Berne

Bernadette **G** (French) a form of Bernadine (see Girls' Names).

Bernal (German) strong as a bear.
Bernald, Bernaldo, Bernel, Bernhald, Bernhold, Bernold

Bernaldino (German) strong bear.

Bernard (German) brave as a bear. See also Bjorn.
Barnard, Bear, Bearnard, Benek, Ber, Berend, Bern, Bernabé, Bernadas, Bernardel, Bernardin, Bernardo, Bernardus, Bernardyn, Bernarr, Bernat, Bernek, Bernal, Bernel, Bernerd, Berngards, Bernhard, Bernhards, Bernhardt, Bernie, Bjorn, Burnard

Bernardo (Spanish) a form of Bernard.
Barnardino, Barnardo, Barnhardo, Beñardo, Bernardino, Bernhardo, Berno, Burnardo, Nardo

Bernie (German) a familiar form of Bernard.
Berney, Berni, Berny, Birney, Birnie, Birny, Burney

Berry (English) berry; grape.
Berrie

Bersh (Gypsy) one year.

Bert (German, English) bright, shining. A short form of Berthold, Berton, Bertram, Bertrand, Egbert, Filbert.
Bertie, Bertus, Birt, Burt

Berthold (German) bright; illustrious; brilliant ruler.
Bert, Berthoud, Bertold, Bertolde

Bertie (English) a familiar form of Bert, Egbert.
Berty, Birt, Birtie, Birty

Bertín (Spanish) distinguished friend.
Berti

Berto (Spanish) a short form of Alberto.

Bertoldo (Germanic) splendid boss.

Berton (English) bright settlement; fortified town.
Bert

Bertram (German) bright; illustrious. (English) bright raven. See also Bartram.
Beltran, Beltrán, Beltrano, Bert, Berton, Bertrae, Bertraim, Bertraum, Bertron

Bertrand (German) bright shield.
Bert, Bertran, Bertrando, Bertranno

Bertulfo (Teutonic) warrior who shines.

Berwyn (Welsh) white head.
Berwin, Berwynn, Berwynne

Besarión (Greek) walker.

Besebes (Palauan) vine used for tying and binding.

Betsabé (Hebrew) oath of God.

Bevan (Welsh) son of Evan.
Beavan, Beaven, Beavin, Bev, Beve, Beven, Bevin, Bevo, Bevon

Beverly **G** (English) beaver meadow.
Beverlea, Beverleigh, Beverley, Beverlie

Bevis (French) from Beauvais, France; bull.
Beauvais, Bevys

Bhag (Sanskrit) fate, divine power; glory.

Bhagwandas (Hindi) servant of God.

Bhagwanjee (Sanskrit) God; fortunate, prosperous.

Bhagwanji (Sanskrit) a form of Bhagwanjee.

Bhai (Sanskrit) brother, kinsman.

Bhan (Sanskrit) brightness; sun; master; planet.

Bharkat (Persian) a form of Barkat.

Bhisham (Sanskrit) valiant; superlative.

Bhup (Sanskrit) earth guardian.

Bi (Chinese) green jade.

Bian (Chinese) discriminating.

Bianca 🄶 (Italian) white.

Biao (Chinese) young tiger.

Bibi (Fijian) heavy.

Bibiano (Spanish) small man.

Bich (Vietnamese) a jewel.

Bickford (English) axe-man's ford.

Bien (Vietnamese) ocean, sea.

Bienvenido (Filipino) welcome.

Bijan (Persian) ancient hero.
Bihjan, Bijann, Bijhan, Bijhon, Bijon

Bilal (Arabic) chosen.
Bila, Bilaal, Bilale, Bile, Bilel, Billaal, Billal

Bill (German) a short form of William.
Bil, Billee, Billijo, Billye, Byll, Will

Billie 🄶 (German) a form of Billy.

Billiem (Pohnpeian) a form of William.

Billy 🄱 (German) a familiar form of Bill, William.
Bille, Billey, Billie, Billy, Bily, Willie

Binah (Hebrew) understanding; wise.
Bina

Bing (German) kettle-shaped hollow.

Bingo (Chamorro) to bud.

Bing-Qing (Chinese) ice; crystal clear.

Binh (Vietnamese) peaceful.

Binkentios (Greek) a form of Vincent.

Binky (English) a familiar form of Bancroft, Vincent.
Bink, Binkentios, Binkie

Birch (English) white; shining; birch tree.
Birk, Burch

Birger (Norwegian) rescued.

Birkey (English) island with birch trees.
Birk, Birkie, Birky

Birkitt (English) birch-tree coast.
Birk, Birket, Birkit, Burket, Burkett, Burkitt

Birley (English) meadow with the cow barn.
Birlee, Birlie, Birly

Birney (English) island with a brook.
Birne, Birnie, Birny, Burney, Burnie, Burny

Birtle (English) hill with birds.

Bishamon (Japanese) god of war.

Bishop (Greek) overseer. (English)
bishop.
Bish, Bishup

Bitang (Palauan) one half.

Bjorn (Scandinavian) a form of
Bernard.
Bjarne

Blacheos (Palauan) a kind of tree in
the verbena family.

Blackburn (Scottish) black brook.

Blade (English) knife, sword.
*Bladen, Bladon, Bladyn, Blae, Blaed,
Blayde*

Bladimir (Russian) a form of
Vladimir.
Bladimer

Bladimiro (Slavic) prince of peace.

Blaine **B** (Irish) thin, lean. (English)
river source.
Blain, Blane, Blayne

Blair **BG** (Irish) plain, field. (Welsh)
place.
Blaire, Blare, Blayr, Blayre

Blaise, Blaize **B** (French) forms of
Blaze.
*Ballas, Balyse, Blais, Blaisot, Blas,
Blase, Blasi, Blasien, Blasius, Blass,
Blaz, Blaze, Blayz, Blayze, Blayzz*

Blake ✵ **B** (English) attractive;
dark.
*Blaik, Blaike, Blakely, Blakeman,
Blakey, Blayke*

Blakely **BG** (English) dark meadow.
*Blakelee, Blakeleigh, Blakeley,
Blakelie, Blakelin, Blakelyn, Blakeny,
Blakley, Blakney*

Blanca **G** (Italian) a form of Bianca.

Blanco (Spanish) light skinned;
white; blond.

Blandino (Latin) he who is flattered.

Blane (Irish) a form of Blaine.
Blaney, Blanne

Blasco (Latin) of a pale color.

Blayne (Irish) a form of Blaine.
Blayn, Blayney

Blaze (Latin) stammerer. (English)
flame; trail mark made on a tree.
*Balázs, Biaggio, Biagio, Blaise,
Blaize, Blazen, Blazer*

Blekeu (Palauan) courage.

Bliss **G** (English) blissful; joyful.

Blodk (Palauan) cut, slit.

Blosech (Palauan) unusual, strange.

Bloyang (Palauan) he who has been
split or cracked.

Blu (Chuukese) blue.

Bly (Native American) high.

Blythe **G** (English) carefree; merry,
joyful.
Blithe, Blyth

Bo **B** (English) a form of Beau,
Beauregard. (German) a form of
Bogart.
Boe

Boaz (Hebrew) swift; strong.
Bo, Boas, Booz, Bos, Boz

Bob (English) a short form of
Robert.
Bobb, Bobby, Bobek, Rob

Bobbi, Bobbie **G** (English) a form
of Bobby.

Bobby **B** (English) a familiar form
of Bob, Robert.
Bobbey, Bobbie, Bobbye, Boby

Bobek (Czech) a form of Bob,
Robert.

Bobi (English) a form of Bobby.

Bobong, Bong (Tagalog) forms of Bongbong.

Bobot, Boboy (Tagalog) forms of Bongbong.

Boden (Scandinavian) sheltered. (French) messenger, herald.
Bodie, Bodin, Bodine, Bodyne, Boe

Bodie (Scandinavian) a familiar form of Boden.
Boddie, Bode, Bodee, Bodey, Bodhi, Bodi, Boedee, Boedi, Boedy

Bodil (Norwegian) mighty ruler.

Bodua (Akan) animal's tail.

Boecio (Greek) he who helps; the defender, who goes into battle ready.

Bogart (German) strong as a bow. (Irish, Welsh) bog, marshland.
Bo, Bogey, Bogie, Bogy

Bohdan (Ukrainian) a form of Donald.
Bogdan, Bogdashka, Bogdon, Bohden, Bohdon

Bokusui, Bokuyo (Japanese) literary figures.

Boleslao (Slavic) most glorious of the glorious.

Bonaro (Italian, Spanish) friend.
Bona, Bonar

Bonaventure (Italian) good luck.

Bond (English) tiller of the soil.
Bondie, Bondon, Bonds, Bondy

Bongbong (Tagalog) boy; junior.

Bon-Hwa (Korean) glorious.

Bonie (Tagalog) a form of Bongbong.

Boniface (Latin) do-gooder.
Bonifacio, Bonifacius, Bonifacy

Boo (Korean) help, support; father; wealth.

Booker (English) bookmaker; book lover; Bible lover.
Bookie, Books, Booky

Boone (Latin, French) good. History: Daniel Boone was an American pioneer.
Bon, Bone, Bonne, Boonie, Boony

Booth (English) hut. (Scandinavian) temporary dwelling.
Boot, Boote, Boothe

Borak (Arabic) lightning. Mythology: the horse that carried Muhammad to seventh heaven.

Boram (Korean) worth.

Borden (French) cottage. (English) valley of the boar; boar's den.
Bord, Bordie, Bordy

Boreas (Greek) north wind.

Borg (Scandinavian) castle.

Boris (Slavic) battler, warrior. Religion: the patron saint of Moscow, princes, and Russia.
Boriss, Borja, Borris, Borya, Boryenka, Borys

Borka (Russian) fighter.
Borkinka

Boromeo (Italian) a good Roman.

Boseda (Tiv) born on Saturday.

Bosley (English) grove of trees.

Botan (Japanese) blossom, bud.

Bourey (Cambodian) country.

Bourne (Latin, French) boundary. (English) brook, stream.

Boutros (Arabic) a form of Peter.

Bowen (Welsh) son of Owen.
Bow, Bowe, Bowie

Bowie (Irish) yellow haired. History:
James Bowie was an American-born
Mexican colonist who died during
the defense of the Alamo.
Bow, Bowen

Boyce (French) woods, forest.
Boice, Boise, Boy, Boycey, Boycie

Boyd (Scottish) yellow haired.
Boid, Boyde

Brad **B** (English) a short form of
Bradford, Bradley.
Bradd, Brade

Bradburn (English) broad stream.

Braden **B** (English) broad valley.
*Bradan, Bradden, Bradeon, Bradin,
Bradine, Bradyn, Braeden, Braiden,
Brayden, Bredan, Bredon*

Bradford (English) broad river
crossing.
Brad, Braddford, Ford

Bradlee (English) a form of Bradley.
Bradlea, Bradleigh, Bradlie

Bradley **B** (English) broad meadow.
*Brad, Braddly, Bradlay, Bradlee,
Bradly, Bradlyn, Bradney*

Bradly (English) a form of Bradley.

Bradon (English) broad hill.
Braedon, Braidon, Braydon

Bradshaw (English) broad forest.

Brady **B** (Irish) spirited. (English)
broad island.
Bradey, Bradi, Bradie, Bradye, Braidy

Bradyn (English) a form of Braden.
Bradynne, Breidyn

Braedan (English) a form of
Braeden.

Braeden, Braiden **B** (English)
forms of Braden.
Braedin, Braedyn, Braidyn

Braedon (English) a form of Bradon.
Breadon

Bragi (Scandinavian) poet.
Mythology: the god of poetry,
eloquence, and song.
Brage

Braham (Hindi) creator.
*Braheem, Braheim, Brahiem,
Brahima, Brahm*

Brainard (English) bold raven; prince.
Brainerd

Bram (Scottish) bramble, brushwood.
(Hebrew) a short form of Abraham,
Abram.
Brame, Bramm, Bramdon

Bramwell (English) bramble spring.
*Brammel, Brammell, Bramwel,
Bramwyll*

Branch (Latin) paw; claw; tree
branch.

Brand (English) firebrand; sword. A
short form of Brandon.
*Brandall, Brande, Brandel, Brandell,
Brander, Brandley, Brandol, Brandt,
Brandy, Brann*

Brandan **B** (English) a form of
Brandon.

Brandeis (Czech) dweller on a
burned clearing.
Brandis

Branden (English) beacon valley.
*Brandden, Brandene, Brandin,
Brandine, Brandyn, Breandan*

Brandi **G** (Dutch, English) a form
of Brandy.

Brandon ☆ **B** (English) beacon hill.
Bran, Brand, Branddon, Brandone, Brandonn, Brandyn, Branndan, Branndon, Brannon, Breandon, Brendon

Brandt (English) a form of Brant.

Brandy **G** (Dutch) brandy. (English) a familiar form of Brand.
Branddy, Brandey, Brandi, Brandie

Brandyn (English) a form of Branden, Brandon.
Brandynn

Brannon (Irish) a form of Brandon.
Branen, Brannan, Brannen, Branon

Branson (English) son of Brandon, Brant. A form of Bronson.
Bransen, Bransin, Brantson

Brant (English) proud.
Brandt, Brannt, Brante, Brantley, Branton

Brantley **B** (English) a form of Brant.
Brantlie, Brantly, Brentlee, Brentley, Brently

Braulio (Italian) a form of Brawley.
Brauli, Brauliuo

Brawley (English) meadow on the hillside.
Braulio, Brawlee, Brawly

Braxton **B** (English) Brock's town.
Brax, Braxdon, Braxston, Braxten, Braxtin, Braxxton

Brayan (Irish, Scottish) a form of Brian.
Brayn, Brayon

Brayden ☆ **B** (English) a form of Braden.
Braydan, Braydn, Bradyn, Breydan, Breyden, Brydan, Bryden

Braydon **B** (English) a form of Bradon.
Braydoon, Brydon, Breydon

Breana, Breanna **G** (Irish) forms of Briana.

Breann, Breanne **G** (Irish) short forms of Briana.

Breck **BG** (Irish) freckled.
Brec, Breckan, Brecken, Breckie, Breckin, Breckke, Breckyn, Brek, Brexton

Brede (Scandinavian) iceberg, glacier.

Brencis (Latvian) a form of Lawrence.
Brence

Brenda **G** (Irish) little raven. (English) sword.

Brendan **B** (Irish) little raven. (English) sword.
Breandan, Bren, Brenden, Brendis, Brendon, Brendyn, Brenn, Brennan, Brennen, Brenndan, Brenyan, Bryn

Brenden **B** (Irish) a form of Brendan.
Bren, Brendene, Brendin, Brendine, Brennden

Brendon (English) a form of Brandon. (Irish, English) a form of Brendan.
Brenndon

Brenna **G** (English, Irish) a form of Brennan.

Brennan, Brennen **B** (English, Irish) forms of Brendan.
Bren, Brenan, Brenen, Brenin, Brenn, Brennann, Brenner, Brennin, Brennon, Brennor, Brennyn, Brenon

Brent (English) a short form of Brenton.
Brendt, Brente, Brentson, Brentt

Brenton **B** (English) steep hill.
Brent, Brentan, Brenten, Brentin, Brentten, Brentton, Brentyn

Breogán (Spanish) indicative of family or origin.

Breon **B** (Irish, Scottish) a form of Brian.

Bret, Brett **B** (Scottish) from Great Britain. See also Britton.
Bhrett, Braten, Braton, Brayton, Bretin, Bretley, Bretlin, Breton, Brettan, Brette, Bretten, Bretton, Brit, Britt

Brewster (English) brewer.
Brew, Brewer, Bruwster

Breyon (Irish, Scottish) a form of Brian.
Breyan

Brian 🌿 **B** (Irish, Scottish) strong; virtuous; honorable. History: Brian Boru was an eleventh-century Irish king and national hero. See also Palaina.
Brayan, Breyon, Briann, Briano, Briant, Briante, Briaun, Briayan, Brien, Brience, Brient, Brin, Briny, Brion, Bryan, Bryen

Briana **G** (Irish, Scottish) a form of Brian.

Brianna **G** (Irish, Scottish) a form of Brian.

Brianne **G** (Irish, Scottish) a form of Brian.

Briar (French) heather.
Brier, Brierly, Bryar, Bryer, Bryor

Brice **B** (Welsh) alert; ambitious. (English) son of Rice.
Bricen, Briceton, Bryce

Bricio (Celtic) represents strength.

Brick (English) bridge.
Bricker, Bricklen, Brickman, Brik

Bridger (English) bridge builder.
Bridd, Bridge, Bridgeley, Bridgely

Bridget **G** (Irish) strong.

Brielle **G** (French) a form of Brie (see Girls' Names).

Brigham (English) covered bridge. (French) troops, brigade.
Brig, Brigg, Briggs, Brighton

Brighton (English) bright town.
Breighton, Bright, Brightin, Bryton

Brigido (Celtic) the high one; strength.

Brij (Sanskrit) cattle shed.

Brion (Irish, Scottish) a form of Brian.
Brieon, Brione, Brionn, Brionne

Brit, Britt (Scottish) forms of Bret, Brett. See also Britton.
Brit, Brityce

Britany, Brittany **G** (English) from Britain.

Britney, Brittney, Brittny **G** (English) forms of Britany.

Britton (Scottish) from Great Britain. See also Bret, Brett, Brit, Britt.
Britain, Briten, Britian, Britin, Briton, Brittain, Brittan, Britten, Brittian, Brittin, Britton

Brock **B** (English) badger.
Broc, Brocke, Brockett, Brockie, Brockley, Brockton, Brocky, Brok, Broque

Brod (English) a short form of Broderick.
Brode, Broden

Broderick (Welsh) son of the famous ruler. (English) broad ridge. See also Roderick.
Brod, Broddie, Brodderick, Brodderrick, Broddy, Broderic, Broderrick, Brodrick

Brodie 🅱 (Irish) a form of Brody.
Brodi, Broedi

Brodrick (Welsh, English) a form of
Broderick.
Broddrick, Brodric, Brodryck

Brody ☆ 🅱 (Irish) ditch; canal
builder.
*Brodee, Broden, Brodey, Brodie,
Broedy*

Brogan (Irish) a heavy work shoe.
Brogen, Broghan, Broghen

Bromley (English) brushwood
meadow.

Bron (Afrikaans) source.

Bronislaw (Polish) weapon of glory.

Bronson (English) son of Brown.
*Bransen, Bransin, Branson, Bron,
Bronnie, Bronnson, Bronny, Bronsan,
Bronsen, Bronsin, Bronsonn, Bronsson,
Bronsun, Bronsyn, Brunson*

Bronwyn 🅶 (Welsh) white breasted.

Brook 🅶 (English) brook, stream.
Brooker, Brookin

Brooke 🅶 (English) a form of
Brook.

Brooklyn, Brooklynn 🅶
(American) combinations of Brook
+ Lynn.

Brooks 🅱 (English) son of Brook.
Brookes, Broox

Brown (English) brown; bear.

Bruce 🅱 (French) brushwood
thicket; woods.
Brucey, Brucy, Brue, Bruis

Bruno (German, Italian) brown
haired; brown skinned.
Brunon, Bruns

Bryan ☆ (Irish) a form of Brian.
Brayan, Bryann, Bryant, Bryen

Bryana, Bryanna 🅶 (Irish) forms of
Bryan.

Bryanne (Irish) a form of Bryan.

Bryant (Irish) a form of Bryan.
Bryent

Bryce 🅱 (Welsh) a form of Brice.
Brycen, Bryceton, Bryson, Bryston

Bryden 🅱 (English) a form of
Brayden.

Brylee 🅶 (American) a combination
of the letter B + Riley.

Brynn 🅶 (German) a form of
Bryon.

Bryon (German) cottage. (English)
bear.
Bryeon, Bryn, Bryne, Brynne, Bryone

Bryson 🅱 (Welsh) child of Brice.

Bryton 🅱 (English) a form of
Brighton.
*Brayten, Brayton, Breyton, Bryeton,
Brytan, Bryten, Brytin, Brytten, Brytton*

Bu (Vietnamese) leader.

Bubba (German) a boy.
Babba, Babe, Bebba

Buck (German, English) male deer.
*Buckie, Buckley, Buckner, Bucko,
Bucky*

Buckley (English) deer meadow.
Bucklea, Bucklee

Buckminster (English) preacher.

Bud (English) herald, messenger.
Budd, Buddy

Buddy (American) a familiar form of
Bud.
Budde, Buddey, Buddie

Buell (German) hill dweller. (English)
bull.

Buenaventura (Latin) he who predicts happiness.

Buford (English) ford near the castle.
Burford

Bujen (Marshallese) promise.

Bum (Korean) law, rule; pattern, model.

Burcardo (Germanic) daring protector; the defender of the fortress.

Burgess (English) town dweller; shopkeeper.
Burg, Burges, Burgh, Burgiss, Burr

Burian (Ukrainian) lives near weeds.

Burke (German, French) fortress, castle.
Berk, Berke, Birk, Bourke, Burk, Burkley

Burl (English) cup bearer; wine servant; knot in a tree. (German) a short form of Berlyn.
Berl, Burley, Burlie, Byrle

Burleigh (English) meadow with knotted tree trunks.
Burlee, Burley, Burlie, Byrleigh, Byrlee

Burne (English) brook.
Beirne, Burn, Burnell, Burnett, Burney, Byrn, Byrne

Burney (English) island with a brook. A familiar form of Rayburn.

Burr (Swedish) youth. (English) prickly plant.

Burris (English) town dweller.

Burt (English) a form of Bert. A short form of Burton.
Burrt, Burtt, Burty

Burton (English) fortified town.
Berton, Burt

Busby (Scottish) village in the thicket; tall military hat made of fur.
Busbee, Buzby, Buzz

Buster (American) hitter, puncher.

Butch (American) a short form of Butcher.

Butcher (English) butcher.
Butch

Buuch (Palauan) betel nut.

Buyugo (Chamorro) coaxing; flattering.

Buzz (Scottish) a short form of Busby.
Buzzy

Bwijtak (Marshallese) school of needlefish.

Byford (English) by the ford.

Byochel (Palauan) to be sifted, winnowed.

Byong (Korean) brilliant.

Byram (English) cattle yard.

Byrd (English) birdlike.
Bird, Birdie, Byrdie

Byrne (English) a form of Burne.
Byrn, Byrnes

Byron (French) cottage. (English) barn.
Beyren, Beyron, Biren, Biron, Buiron, Byram, Byran, Byrann, Byren, Byrom, Byrone

Byung (Korean) third; soldier; protection.

C 🄱🄶 (American) an initial used as a first name.

Cable (French, English) rope maker.
Cabell

Caca (Chamorro) crack, crevice.

Cachayauri (Quechua) hard as a shard of copper; sharp as a spine or needle.

Cadao (Vietnamese) folksong.

Cadassi (Chamorro) to have something of the sea.

Cadby (English) warrior's settlement.

Caddock (Welsh) eager for war.

Cade 🄱 (Welsh) a short form of Cadell.
Cady

Cadell (Welsh) battler.
Cade, Cadel, Cedell

Caden 🄱 (American) a form of Kadin.
Cadan, Caddon, Cadian, Cadien, Cadin, Cadon, Cadyn, Caeden, Caedon, Caid, Caiden, Cayden

Cadeo (Vietnamese) folk song.

Cadmus (Greek) from the east. Mythology: a Phoenician prince who founded Thebes and introduced writing to the Greeks.

Caelan (Scottish) a form of Nicholas.
Cael, Caelon, Caelyn, Cailan, Cailean, Caillan, Cailun, Cailyn, Calan, Calen, Caleon, Caley, Calin, Callan, Callon, Callyn, Calon, Calyn, Caylan, Cayley

Caesar (Latin) long-haired. History: a title for Roman emperors. See also Kaiser, Kesar, Sarito.
Caesarae, Caesear, Caeser, Caezar, Caseare, Ceasar, Cesar, Ceseare, Cezar, Cézar, Czar, Seasar

Cahil (Turkish) young, naive.

Cai (Welsh) a form of Gaius.
Caio, Caius, Caw

Caifas (Assyrian) man of little energy.

Cain (Hebrew) spear; gatherer. Bible: Adam and Eve's oldest son. See also Kabil, Kane, Kayne.
Cainaen, Cainan, Caine, Cainen, Caineth, Cayn, Cayne

Caín (Hebrew) a form of Cain.

Cairn (Welsh) landmark made of a mound of stones.
Cairne, Carn, Carne

Cairo (Arabic) Geography: the capital of Egypt.
Kairo

Cais (Vietnamese) one who rejoices.

Caitlin 🄶 (Irish) pure.

Caiya (Quechua) close, nearby; unique.

Calder (Welsh, English) brook, stream.

Caldwell (English) cold well.

Cale (Hebrew) a short form of Caleb.

Caleb ☆ 🄱 (Hebrew) dog; faithful. (Arabic) bold, brave. Bible: one of the twelve spies sent by Moses. See also Kaleb, Kayleb.
Caeleb, Calab, Calabe, Cale, Caley, Calib, Calieb, Callob, Calob, Calyb, Cayleb, Caylebb, Caylib, Caylob

Caleigh 🄶 (Irish) a form of Caley.

Calen, Calin (Scottish) forms of Caelan.
Caelen, Caelin, Caellin, Cailen, Cailin, Caillin, Calean, Callen, Caylin

Calepodio (Greek) he who has beautiful feet.

Calen, Calin (Scottish) forms of Caelan.
Caelen, Caelin, Caellin, Cailen, Cailin, Caillin, Calean, Callen, Caylin

Calepodio (Greek) he who has beautiful feet.

Caley (Irish) a familiar form of Caleb.
Calee, Caleigh

Calfumil (Mapuche) glazed ceramic tile; brilliant blue.

Calhoun (Irish) narrow woods. (Scottish) warrior.
Colhoun, Colhoune, Colquhoun

Calígula (Latin) he who wears sandals.

Calimaco (Greek) excellent fighter.

Calímaco (Greek) good fighter.

Calimerio (Greek) he who ushers in a beautiful day.

Calinico (Greek) he who secures a beautiful victory.

Calistenes (Greek) beautiful and strong.

Calisto, Calixto (Greek) best and the most beautiful.

Calistrato (Greek) he who commands a great army.

Calístrato (Greek) chief of a great army.

Callahan (Irish) descendant of Ceallachen.
Calahan, Callaghan

Callum B (Irish) dove.
Callam, Calum, Calym

Calogero (Greek) wise one; the beautiful man; he who is going to age well.

Calvert (English) calf herder.
Cal, Calbert, Calvirt

Calvin (Latin) bald. See also Kalvin, Vinny.
Cal, Calv, Calvien, Calvon, Calvyn

Calvino (Latin) bald.

Calvucura (Mapuche) blue stone.

Cam B (Gypsy) beloved. (Scottish) a short form of Cameron. (Latin, French, Scottish) a short form of Campbell.
Camm, Cammie, Cammy, Camy

Cama (Chamorro) resting place.

Camaron (Scottish) a form of Cameron.
Camar, Camari, Camaran, Camaren

Camden B (Scottish) winding valley.
Kamden

Cameron ☆ **B** (Scottish) crooked nose. See also Kameron.
Cam, Camaron, Cameran, Cameren, Camerin, Cameroun, Cameron, Camerson, Camerun, Cameryn, Camiren, Camiron, Cammeron, Camron

Camille G (French) young ceremonial attendant.
Camile

Camilo (Latin) child born to freedom; noble.
Camiel, Camillo, Camillus

Campbell (Latin, French) beautiful field. (Scottish) crooked mouth.
Cam, Camp, Campy

Camron B (Scottish) a short form of Cameron.
Camren, Cammrin, Cammron, Camran, Camreon, Camrin, Camryn, Camrynn

Can (Vietnamese) advice, counsel.

Canaan (French) a form of Cannon.
History: an ancient region between
the Jordan River and the
Mediterranean.
Canan, Canen, Caynan

Canaho (Chamorro) I am suspended.

Canai (Chamorro) a form of Cannai.

Cancio (Latin) founder of the city of
Anzio.

Candice 🌐 (Greek) a form of
Candace (see Girls' Names).

Candide (Latin) pure; sincere.
Candid, Candido, Candonino

Cándido (Latin) a form of Candide.

Cang (Chinese) dark green pines.

Canh (Vietnamese) scenery;
environment.

Cannai (Chamorro) hand; arm.

Cannon (French) church official;
large gun. See also Kannon.
*Canaan, Cannan, Cannen, Cannin,
Canning, Canon*

Canute (Latin) white haired.
(Scandinavian) knot. History: a
Danish king who became king of
England after 1016. See also Knute.
Cnut, Cnute

Canuto (Latin) wise man with
abundant white hair.

Cao (Chinese) conduct.

Capac, Capah (Quechua) Lord; rich
in kindness; great, powerful, just,
correct.

Capacuari (Quechua) kind-hearted
master and untamable like the
vicuna.

Capaquiupanqui (Quechua) he who
honors his master; memorable
master.

Cappi (Gypsy) good fortune.

Caquia (Quechua) thunder; bolt of
lightning.

Car (Irish) a short form of Carney.

Caraca (Chamorro) a type of shell.

Carey 🌐🌐 (Greek) pure. (Welsh)
castle; rocky island. See also Karey.
*Care, Caree, Cari, Carre, Carree,
Carrie, Cary*

Carim (Arabic) generous.

Carina 🌐 (Italian) dear little one.
(Swedish) a form of Karen. (Greek)
a familiar form of Cora (see Girls'
Names).

Carl 🌐 (German, English) a short
form of Carlton. A form of Charles.
See also Carroll, Kale, Kalle, Karl,
Karlen, Karol.
*Carle, Carles, Carless, Carlis, Carll,
Carlo, Carlos, Carlson, Carlston,
Carlus, Carolos*

Carlee 🌐 (English) a form of Carly.

Carley 🌐 (English) a familiar form
of Carlin.

Carli 🌐 (English) a form of Carly.

Carlie 🌐 (English) a familiar form
of Carlin.

Carlin 🌐🌐 (Irish) little champion.
*Carlan, Carlen, Carley, Carlie,
Carling, Carlino, Carly*

Carlisle (English) Carl's island.
Carlyle, Carlysle

Carlito (Spanish) a familiar form of
Carlos.
Carlitos

Carlo (Italian) a form of Carl, Charles.
Carolo

Carlomagno (Spanish) Charles the great.

Carlos ✵ **B** (Spanish) a form of Carl, Charles.
Carlito

Carlton **B** (English) Carl's town.
Carl, Carleton, Carllton, Carlston, Carltonn, Carltton, Charlton

Carly **G** (English) a familiar form of Carlin.

Carmel (Hebrew) vineyard, garden. See also Carmine.
Carmello, Carmelo, Karmel

Carmen **G** (Latin) a form of Carmine.

Carmichael (Scottish) follower of Michael.

Carmine (Latin) song; crimson. (Italian) a form of Carmel.
Carmain, Carmaine, Carman, Carmen, Carmon

Carnelius (Greek, Latin) a form of Cornelius.
Carnealius, Carneilius, Carnellius, Carnilious

Carnell (English) defender of the castle. (French) a form of Cornell.

Carney (Irish) victorious. (Scottish) fighter. See also Kearney.
Car, Carny, Karney

Carol **G** (Irish, German) a form of Carroll.

Carolina **G** (Italian) a form of Caroline.

Caroline **G** (French) little and strong.

Carolyn **G** (English) a form of Caroline.

Carpo (Greek) valuable fruit.

Carr (Scandinavian) marsh. See also Kerr.
Karr

Carrick (Irish) rock.
Carooq, Carricko

Carrie **G** (Greek, Welsh) a form of Carey.

Carrington (Welsh) rocky town.

Carroll (Irish) champion. (German) a form of Carl.
Carel, Carell, Cariel, Cariell, Carol, Carole, Carolo, Carols, Carollan, Carolus, Carrol, Cary, Caryl

Carson ✵ **B** (English) son of Carr.
Carsen, Carsino, Carrson, Karson

Carsten (Greek) a form of Karsten.
Carston

Carter ✵ **B** (English) cart driver.
Cart

Cartwright (English) cart builder.

Caruamayu (Quechua) yellow river.

Carvell (French, English) village on the marsh.
Carvel, Carvelle, Carvellius

Carver (English) wood-carver; sculptor.

Cary (Welsh) a form of Carey. (German, Irish) a form of Carroll.
Carray, Carry

Casandro (Greek) hero's brother.

Case (Irish) a short form of Casey. (English) a short form of Casimir.

Casey **BG** (Irish) brave.
Case, Casie, Casy, Cayse, Caysey, Kacey, Kasey

Cash (Latin) vain. (Slavic) a short form of Casimir.
Cashe

Casiano (Latin) he who is equipped with a helmet.

Casildo (Arabic) youth that carries the lance.

Casimir (Slavic) peacemaker.
Cachi, Cas, Case, Cash, Cashemere, Cashi, Cashmeire, Cashmere, Casimere, Casimire, Casimiro, Castimer, Kasimir, Kazio

Casiodoro (Greek) gift from a friend.

Casper (Persian) treasurer. (German) imperial. See also Gaspar, Jasper, Kasper.
Caspar, Cass

Cass 🅱 (Irish, Persian) a short form of Casper, Cassidy.

Cassandra 🅶 (Greek) helper.

Cassidy 🅶 (Irish) clever; curly haired.
Casidy, Cass, Cassady, Cassie, Kassidy

Cassie (Irish) a familiar form of Cassidy.
Casi, Casie, Casio, Cassey, Cassy, Casy

Cassius (Latin, French) box; protective cover.
Cassia, Cassio, Cazzie

Casta (Spanish) pure.

Castle (Latin) castle.
Cassle, Castel

Casto (Greek) pure, honest, clean.

Castor (Greek) beaver. Astrology: one of the twins in the constellation Gemini. Mythology: one of the patron saints of mariners.
Caster, Caston

Cástor (Greek) a form of Castor.

Cataldo (Greek) outstanding in war.

Catari (Aymara) serpent.

Catequil, Catiquil, Catuilla (Quechua) ray of light.

Cater (English) caterer.

Catherine 🅶 (Greek) pure. (English) a form of Katherine.

Catlahi (Chamorro) a form of Chatlahe.

Cato (Latin) knowledgeable, wise.
Caton

Catón (Latin) a form of Cato.
Caton, Catón

Catricura (Mapuche) cut stone.

Catulo (Latin) puppy; soft.

Cátulo (Spanish) a form of Catulo.

Cauac (Quechua) sentinel; he who guards.

Cauachi (Quechua) he who makes us attentive, vigilant.

Cauana (Quechua) he who is in a place where all can be seen.

Cautaro (Araucanian) daring and enterprising.

Cavan (Irish) handsome. See also Kevin.
Caven, Cavin, Cavan, Cawoun

Cayden (American) a form of Caden.
Cayde, Caydin

Cayetano (Latin) he who is from Gaeta, an ancient city in the Lacio region.

Caylan (Scottish) a form of Caelan.
Caylans, Caylen, Caylon

Cayo (Latin) happy and fun.

Cayua (Quechua) he who follows, follower; faithful.

Cazzie (American) a familiar form of Cassius.
Caz, Cazz, Cazzy

Ce (Chinese) to plan, scheme.

Cear (Irish) black.

Ceasar (Latin) a form of Caesar.
Ceaser

Cecil **B** (Latin) blind.
Cece, Cecile, Cecilio, Cecilius, Cecill, Celio, Siseal

Cedric (English) battle chieftain. See also Kedrick, Rick.
Cad, Caddaric, Ced, Cederic, Cedrec, Cédric, Cedrick, Cedryche, Sedric

Cedrick (English) a form of Cedric.
Ceddrick, Cederick, Cederrick, Cedirick, Cedrik

Cedro (Spanish) strong gift.

Ceejay (American) a combination of the initials C. + J.
Cejay, C.J.

Ceferino (Greek) he who caresses like the wind.

Celedonio (Latin) he is like the swallow.

Celestino (Latin) resident of the celestial reign.

Celine **G** (Greek) a form of Celena (see Girls' Names).

Celso (Latin) tall, elevated; noble.

Cemal (Arabic) attractive.

Cencio (Italian) a form of Vicente.

Cenobio (Latin) he who rejects the strangers; God gives him protection and good health.

Cephas (Latin) small rock. Bible: the term used by Jesus to describe Peter.
Cepheus, Cephus

Cerdic (Welsh) beloved.
Caradoc, Caradog, Ceredig, Ceretic

Cerek (Polish) lordly. (Greek) a form of Cyril.

Cesar **B** (Spanish) a form of Caesar.
Casar, César, Cesare, Cesareo, Cesario, Cesaro, Cessar

Cesáreo (Latin) relating to Caesar.

Cesarión (Latin) Caesar's follower.

Cestmir (Czech) fortress.

Cezar (Slavic) a form of Caesar.
Cézar, Cezary, Cezek, Chezrae, Sezar

Chace (French) a form of Chase.
Chayce

Chad **B** (English) warrior. A short form of Chadwick. Geography: a country in north-central Africa.
Ceadd, Chaad, Chadd, Chaddie, Chaddy, Chade, Chadleigh, Chadler, Chadley, Chadlin, Chadlyn, Chadmen, Chado, Chadron, Chady

Chadfaulus, Charfaulos (Chamorro) forms of Charfaulus.

Chadi (Chamorro) fast, quick.

Chadrick (German) mighty warrior.
Chaddrick, Chaderic, Chaderick, Chadrack, Chadric

Chadwick (English) warrior's town.
Chad, Chaddwick, Chadvic, Chadwyck

Chae (Korean) decorated, ornamented.

Chaggi (Chamorro) to attempt.

Chago (Spanish) a form of Jacob.
Chango, Chanti

Chaguina (Chamorro) his attempt.

Chaicu (Aymara) he who has great strength in order to fling stones, is skillful with the sling.

Cha'ife (Chamorro) not fiery.

Chaim (Hebrew) life. See also Hyman.
Chai, Chaimek, Haim, Khaim

Chaise (French) a form of Chase.
Chais, Chaisen, Chaison

Chal (Gypsy) boy; son.
Chalie, Chalin

Chale (Spanish) strong and youthful.

Chalmers (Scottish) son of the lord.
Chalmer, Chalmr, Chamar, Chamarr

Chalten (Tehuelchean) bluish.

Cham (Vietnamese) hard worker.
Chams

Chambi, Champi (Aymara) halberd, lance; he who brings good news.

Chambigüiyca, Champigüiyca (Aymara) beam of sunlight; sent from the gods.

Chammangro (Chamorro) not enough wind.

Champacco (Chamorro) not burnt enough.

Champaklal (Sanskrit) caress of the champion's fragrant yellow flowers.

Chan 🅑 (Sanskrit) shining. (English) a form of Chauncey. (Spanish) a form of Juan.
Chann, Chano, Chayo

Chanan (Hebrew) cloud.

Chance 🅑 (English) a short form of Chancellor, Chauncey.
Chanc, Chancee, Chancey, Chancie, Chancy, Chanse, Chansy, Chants, Chantz, Chanze, Chanz, Chaynce

Chancellor (English) record keeper.
Chance, Chancelar, Chancelen, Chanceleor, Chanceler, Chanceller, Chancelor, Chanselor, Chanslor

Chandar (Sanskrit) a form of Chandra.

Chander (Hindi) moon.
Chand, Chandan, Chandany, Chandara, Chandon

Chandler 🅑 (English) candle maker.
Chandelar, Chandlan, Chandlar, Chandlier, Chandlor, Chandlyr

Chane (Swahili) dependable.

Chaney (French) oak.
Chayne, Cheaney, Cheney, Cheyn, Cheyne, Cheyney

Chang (Chinese) smooth.

Chankrisna (Cambodian) sweet smelling tree.

Channing (English) wise. (French) canon; church official.
Chane, Chann

Chanse (English) a form of Chance.
Chans, Chansey

Chantal 🅖 (French) song.

Chante 🅑🅖 (French) singer.
Chant, Chantha, Chanthar, Chantra, Chantry, Shantae

Chantel 🅖 (French) a form of Chantal.

Chao (Chinese) surpassing.

Chapman (English) merchant.
Chap, Chappie, Chappy

Charfaulus (Chamorro) one with a rough appearance.

Chargadi, Chargati (Chamorro) forms of Chatgadi.

Chargiya (Chamorro) a form of Charguiya.

Chargualaf (Chamorro) a form of Chatguaraf.

Charguiya (Chamorro) not enough of him.

Charity **G** (Latin) charity, kindness.

Charles 🌟 **B** (German) farmer. (English) strong and manly. See also Carl, Searlas, Tearlach, Xarles. *Arlo, Chareles, Charels, Charlese, Carlo, Carlos, Charl, Charle, Charlen, Charlie, Charlot, Charlz, Charlzell, Chaz, Chick, Chip, Chuck*

Charlie **B** (German, English) a familiar form of Charles. *Charle, Charlee, Charley, Charli, Charly*

Charlton (English) a form of Carlton. *Charlesten, Charleston, Charleton, Charlotin*

Charro (Spanish) cowboy.

Charsaga, Chartsagua (Chamorro) forms of Chatsaga.

Chase 🌟 **B** (French) hunter. *Chace, Chaise, Chasen, Chason, Chass, Chasse, Chastan, Chasten, Chastin, Chastinn, Chaston, Chasyn, Chayse*

Chaska (Sioux) first-born son.

Chataam (Chamorro) a form of Chataan.

Chataan (Chamorro) rainy season.

Chataga (Chamorro) not enough chopping.

Chatam (Chamorro) choosy.

Chatgadi (Chamorro) not catching enough fish.

Chatgaia (Chamorro) disliked.

Chatguaraf (Chamorro) not enough like a full moon.

Chatguemangro (Chamorro) he who doesn't have enough wind.

Chatguiot (Chamorro) not enough support.

Chatguma (Chamorro) not enough of a house.

Chathigam, Chathigem, Chatigam (Chamorro) forms of Chatigan.

Chathigan (Chamorro) a form of Chatigan.

Chatigan (Chamorro) not enough fish.

Chatlahe (Chamorro) not enough of a man.

Chatongo (Chamorro) not knowing enough.

Chatpagat (Chamorro) not preaching enough.

Chatpangon (Chamorro) not awake enough.

Chatsaga (Chamorro) poor.

Chattai (Chamorro) barely enough.

Chau (Vietnamese) pearl.

Chauar (Quechua) fiber, rope.

Chauncey **B** (English) chancellor; church official. *Chan, Chance, Chancey, Chaunce, Chauncei, Chauncy, Chaunecy, Chaunesy, Chaunszi*

Chaupi (Quechua) he who is in the middle of everything.

Chavey (Portuguese) a form of Chaves.

Chavez (Hispanic) a surname used as a first name.
Chavaz, Chaves, Chaveze, Chavies, Chavis, Chavius, Chevez, Cheveze, Cheviez, Chevious, Chevis, Chivass, Chivez

Chayse (French) a form of Chase.
Chaysea, Chaysen, Chayson, Chaysten

Chayton (Lakota) falcon.

Chaz 🅑 (English) a familiar form of Charles.
Chas, Chasz, Chaze, Chazwick, Chazy, Chazz, Chez

Che (Spanish) God will add or multiply.

Ché (Spanish) a familiar form of José. History: Ernesto "Che" Guevara was a revolutionary who fought at Fidel Castro's side in Cuba.
Chay

Cheban (Chamorro) chop off.

Cheboc (Chamorro) fat, plump.

Checha (Spanish) a familiar form of Jacob.

Cheche (Spanish) a familiar form of Joseph.

Chelsea 🅖 (English) seaport.

Chelsey 🅖 (English) a form of Chelsea.

Chelsie 🅖 (English) a form of Chelsea.

Chen (Chinese) great, tremendous.

Chencho (Spanish) a familiar form of Lawrence.

Cheng (Chinese) accomplished.

Cheng-Gong (Chinese) success.

Chepe (Spanish) a familiar form of Joseph.
Cepito

Cherokee 🅖 (Cherokee) people of a different speech.
Cherrakee

Cherubin (Italian) little cherub.

Chesmu (Native American) gritty.

Chester (English) a short form of Rochester.
Ches, Cheslav, Cheston, Chet

Chet (English) a short form of Chester.
Chett, Chette

Cheung (Chinese) good luck.

Chevalier (French) horseman, knight.
Chev, Chevy

Chevy (French) a familiar form of Chevalier. Geography: Chevy Chase is a town in Maryland. Culture: a short form of Chevrolet, an American automobile company.
Chev, Chevey, Chevi, Chevie, Chevvy, Chewy

Chew (Chinese) mountain.

Cheyenne 🅖 (Cheyenne) a tribal name.
Chayann, Chayanne, Cheyeenne, Cheyene, Chyenne, Shayan

Chi 🅑🅖 (Chinese) younger generation. (Nigerian) personal guardian angel.

Chia (Chinese) home, family; addition.

Chibocta (Chamorro) our little one.

Chican (Quechua) unique, different from the rest.

Chick (English) a familiar form of Charles.
Chic, Chickie, Chicky

Chico (Spanish) boy.

Chien (Vietnamese) fight, battle, combat.

Chih Cheng (Chinese) one who controls the government.

Chiharu (Japanese) a thousand springtimes.

Chihiro (Japanese) a thousand measures; a thousand fathoms.

Chik (Gypsy) earth.

Chika (Japanese) near, close.

Chikaaki (Japanese) a form of Chika.

Chikafusa (Japanese) a form of Chika.

Chikai (Japanese) a thousand heads of grain.

Chikamusa (Japanese) close; good.

Chikao (Japanese) clever, wise.

Chikara (Japanese) tax; strength; energetic man; a thousand tree trunks.

Chike (Ibo) God's power.

Chiko (Japanese) arrow; pledge.

Chilo (Spanish) a familiar form of Francisco.

Chilton (English) farm by the spring.
Chil, Chill, Chillton, Chilt

Chim (Vietnamese) bird.

Chin (Chinese) a form of Jin.

China **G** (Chinese) fine porcelain. Geography: a country in eastern Asia.

Chinami (Japanese) cause.

Chincolef (Mapuche) swift squad; rapid.

Ching Cheng (Chinese) competition.

Chinh (Vietnamese) correctness; righteousness.

Chin-Hwa (Korean) the wealthiest.

Chin-Mae (Korean) truth.

Chinua (Ibo) God's blessing.
Chino, Chinou

Chioke (Ibo) gift of God.

Chip (English) a familiar form of Charles.
Chipman, Chipper

Chiram (Hebrew) exalted; noble.

Chiro (Chuukese) a form of Ichiro.

Chisato (Japanese) very wise.

Chishin (Japanese) historical figure.

Chitamag (Yapese) my father.

Chitaro (Chuukese) the speed of one thousand legs.

Chitose (Japanese) a thousand years.

Chloe **G** (Greek) blooming, verdant.

Cho (Korean) first; herbs; welcome; likeness; excel; foundation.

Chogua (Chamorro) to work.

Chokichi (Japanese) good fortune.

Chong (Chinese) intelligent, clever.

Chong Duy (Vietnamese) eats like a bird.

Chongwon (Korean) garden.

Choque, Chuqui (Quechua) lance; dancer.

Chorche (Aragonese) a form of George.

Chotaro (Japanese) chief son.

Chow (Chinese) everywhere.

Chris ⬛ (Greek) a short form of Christian, Christopher. See also Kris.
Chriss, Christ, Chrys, Cris, Crist

Christa 🄶 (Greek) a form of Christian.

Christain ⬛ (Greek) a form of Christian.
Christai, Christan, Christane, Christaun, Christein

Christen 🄶 (Greek) a form of Christian.

Christian ☀ ⬛ (Greek) follower of Christ; anointed. See also Jaan, Kerstan, Khristian, Kit, Krister, Kristian, Krystian.
Chretien, Chris, Christa, Christain, Christé, Christen, Christensen, Christiaan, Christiana, Christiane, Christiann, Christianna, Christianno, Christiano, Christianos, Christien, Christin, Christino, Christion, Christon, Christos, Christyan, Christyon, Chritian, Chrystian, Cristian, Crystek

Christie 🄶 (Greek) a short form of Christina, Christine.

Christien (Greek) a form of Christian.
Christienne, Christinne, Chrystien

Christin 🄶 (Greek) a form of Christian.

Christina 🄶 (Greek) Christian; anointed.

Christine 🄶 (French, English) a form of Christina.

Christofer (Greek) a form of Christopher.
Christafer, Christafur, Christefor, Christerfer, Christifer, Christoffer, Christofher, Christofper, Chrystofer

Christoff (Russian) a form of Christopher.
Chrisof, Christif, Christof, Cristofe

Christophe ⬛ (French) a form of Christopher.
Christoph

Christopher ☀ ⬛ (Greek) Christ-bearer. Religion: the patron saint of travelers. See also Cristopher, Kester, Kit, Kristopher, Risto, Stoffel, Tobal, Topher.
Chris, Chrisopherson, Christapher, Christepher, Christerpher, Christhoper, Christipher, Christobal, Christofer, Christoff, Christoforo, Christoher, Christopehr, Christoper, Christophe, Christopherr, Christophor, Christophoros, Christophr, Christophre, Christophyer, Christophyr, Christorpher, Christos, Christovao, Christpher, Christphere, Christphor, Christpor, Christrpher, Chrystopher, Cristobal

Christophoros (Greek) a form of Christopher.
Christoforo, Christoforos, Christophor, Christophorus, Christphor, Cristoforo, Cristopher

Christos (Greek) a form of Christopher. See also Khristos.

Christy 🄶 (English) a short form of Christina, Christine.

Chu (Chinese) the stone base of a column.

Chuan (Chinese) river.

Chuang (Chinese) achieve.

Chucho (Hebrew) a familiar form of Jesus.

Chuck (American) a familiar form of Charles.
Chuckey, Chuckie, Chucky

Chui (Swahili) leopard.

Chu-Jung (Chinese) the god of fire and executions.

Chul (Korean) firm.

Chula (Chamorro) to grasp.

Chul-Moo (Korean) iron weapon.

Chuma (Ibo) having many beads, wealthy. (Swahili) iron.

Chuminga (Spanish) a familiar form of Dominic.
Chumin

Chumo (Spanish) a familiar form of Thomas.

Chun **B** (Chinese) spring.

Chung (Chinese) intelligent.
Chungo, Chuong

Chung-Hee, Chung-Ho (Korean) righteous.

Chungi (Chamorro) gray haired.

Chupaho (Chamorro) my smoke.

Chuquigüaman (Quechua) dancing falcon; golden falcon.

Chuquigüiyca (Quechua) sacred dance.

Chuquilla (Quechua) ray of light; golden light.

Churchill (English) church on the hill. History: Sir Winston Churchill served as British prime minister and won a Nobel Prize for literature.

Chuscu (Quechua) fourth son.

Chu-Tak (Chinese) ancestor's virtue.

Chuya (Quechua) clear as water, pure.

Cian (Irish) ancient.
Céin, Cianán, Kian

Ciara **G** (Irish) black.

Cibrao (Latin) inhabitant of Cyprus.

Cicero (Latin) chickpea. History: a famous Roman orator, philosopher, and statesman.
Cicerón

Cid (Spanish) lord. History: title for Rodrigo Díaz de Vivar, an eleventh-century Spanish soldier and national hero.
Cyd

Cidro (Spanish) strong gift.

Cindy **G** (Greek) moon. (Latin) a familiar form of Cynthia.

Ciqala (Dakota) little.

Ciríaco (Greek) he who belongs to the Lord.

Cirineo (Greek) native of Cyrene (present-day Libya).

Cirrillo (Italian) a form of Cyril.
Cirilio, Cirillo, Cirilo, Ciro

Cisco (Spanish) a short form of Francisco.

Ciset (Spanish) a form of Narciso.

Citino (Latin) quick to act.

Claire **G** (French) a form of Clara.

Clancy (Irish) redheaded fighter.
Clancey, Claney

Clara **G** (Latin) clear; bright.

Clare **G** (Latin) a short form of Clarence.
Clair, Clarey, Clary

Clarence **B** (Latin) clear; victorious.
Clarance, Clare, Clarrance, Clarrence, Clearence

Clarissa **G** (Greek) brilliant. (Italian) a form of Clara.

Clark 🅱 (French) cleric; scholar.
Clarke, Clerc, Clerk

Claro (Latin) he who is clean and transparent.

Claude 🅱 (Latin, French) lame.
Claud, Claudan, Claudel, Claudell, Claudey, Claudi, Claudian, Claudianus, Claudie, Claudien, Claudin, Claudio, Claudis, Claudius, Claudy

Claudie 🅶 (Latin, French) a form of Claude.

Claudino (Latin) he who belongs to the ancient Roman family Claudios.

Claudio 🅱 (Italian) a form of Claude.

Claus (German) a short form of Nicholas. See also Klaus.
Claas, Claes, Clause

Clay (English) clay pit. A short form of Clayborne, Clayton.
Klay

Clayborne (English) brook near the clay pit.
Claibern, Claiborn, Claiborne, Claibrone, Clay, Claybon, Clayborn, Claybourn, Claybourne, Clayburn, Clebourn

Clayton 🅱 (English) town built on clay.
Clay, Clayten, Cleighton, Cleyton, Clyton, Klayton

Cleandro (Greek) glorious man.

Cleary (Irish) learned.

Cleavon (English) cliff.
Clavin, Clavion, Clavon, Clavone, Clayvon, Claywon, Clévon, Clevonn, Clyvon

Clem (Latin) a short form of Clement.
Cleme, Clemmy, Clim

Clement (Latin) merciful. Bible: a coworker of Paul. See also Klement, Menz.
Clem, Clemens, Clément, Clemente, Clementius, Clemmons

Clemente (Italian, Spanish) a form of Clement.
Clemento, Clemenza

Clenn (Marshallese) a form of Glenn.

Cleofas (Greek) he is the glory of his father.

Cleon (Greek) famous.
Kleon

Cleto (Greek) he was chosen to fight.

Cletus (Greek) illustrious. History: a Roman pope and martyr.
Cleatus, Cledis, Cleotis, Clete, Cletis

Cleveland (English) land of cliffs.
Cleaveland, Cleavland, Cleavon, Cleve, Clevelend, Clevelynn, Clevey, Clevie, Clevon

Cliff (English) a short form of Clifford, Clifton.
Clif, Clift, Clive, Clyff, Clyph, Kliff

Clifford (English) cliff at the river crossing.
Cliff, Cliford, Clyfford, Klifford

Clifton 🅱 (English) cliff town.
Cliff, Cliffton, Clift, Cliften, Clyfton

Climaco (Greek) he who climbs the ladder.

Clímaco (Greek) he who ascends.

Clímene (Greek) famous, celebrated.

Clint (English) a short form of Clinton.
Klint

Clinton (English) hill town.
Clenten, Clint, Clinten, Clintion, Clintton, Clynton, Klinton

Clive (English) a form of Cliff.
Cleve, Clivans, Clivens, Clyve, Klyve

Clodio (German) glorious.

Clodoaldo (Teutonic) prince that is the chosen and illustrious captain.

Clodomiro (Germanic) he of illustrious fame.

Clodulfo (Germanic) glory.

Clorindo (Greek) he who is like the grass.

Clotario (Gothic) a form of Lotario.

Cloud (English) cloud.

Clove (Spanish) nail.

Clovis (German) famous soldier. See also Louis.

Cluny (Irish) meadow.

Clyde (Welsh) warm. (Scottish) Geography: a river in Scotland.
Cly, Clywd, Klyde

Coby (Hebrew) a familiar form of Jacob.
Cob, Cobby, Cobe, Cobey, Cobi, Cobia, Cobie

Cochise (Apache) hardwood. History: a famous Chiricahua Apache leader.

Coco **G** (French) a familiar form of Jacques.
Coko, Koko

Codey **B** (English) a form of Cody.
Coday

Codi **BG** (English) a form of Cody.

Codie **B** (English) a form of Cody.
Coadi, Codea

Cody ⭐ **B** (English) cushion. History: William "Buffalo Bill" Cody was an American frontier scout who toured America and Europe with his Wild West show. See also Kody.
Coady, Coddy, Code, Codee, Codell, Codey, Codi, Codiak, Codie, Coedy

Coffie (Ewe) born on Friday.

Coique (Quechua) silver.

Coiquiyoc (Quechua) he who is rich with silver.

Coka (Fijian) running stomach.

Cola (Italian) a familiar form of Nicholas, Nicola.
Colas

Colar (French) a form of Nicholas.

Colbert (English) famous seafarer.
Cole, Colt, Colvert, Culbert

Colby **B** (English) dark; dark haired.
Colbey, Colbi, Colbie, Colbin, Colebee, Coleby, Collby, Kolby

Cole ⭐ **B** (Latin) cabbage farmer. (English) a short form of Coleman.
Colet, Coley, Colie, Kole

Coleman **B** (Latin) cabbage farmer. (English) coal miner.
Cole, Colemann, Colm, Colman, Koleman

Colin ⭐ **B** (Irish) young cub. (Greek) a short form of Nicholas.
Cailean, Colan, Cole, Colen, Coleon, Colinn, Collin, Colyn, Kolin

Colla, Culla (Quechua) from the village Colla; eminent, excellent.

Collacapac, Cullacapac (Quechua) Lord Colla, eminent and kind-hearted lord.

Collana, Cullana (Quechua) best; he who excels.

Collatupac, Cullatupac (Quechua) glorious, majestic Colla; royal eminence.

Colley (English) black haired; swarthy.
Colee, Collie, Collis

Collier (English) miner.
Colier, Collayer, Collie, Collyer, Colyer

Collin ☒ (Scottish) a form of Colin, Collins.
Collan, Collen, Collian, Collon, Collyn

Collins (Greek) son of Colin. (Irish) holly.
Collin, Collis

Colon (Latin) he has the beauty of a dove.

Colson (Greek, English) son of Nicholas.
Colsen, Coulson

Colt ☒ (English) young horse; frisky. A short form of Colter, Colton.
Colte

Colten (English) a form of Colton.

Colter (English) herd of colts.
Colt

Colton ☼ ☒ (English) coal town.
Colt, Coltan, Colten, Coltin, Coltinn, Coltn, Coltrane, Colttan, Coltton, Coltun, Coltyn, Coltyne, Kolton

Columba (Latin) dove.
Coim, Colum, Columbia, Columbus

Colwyn (Welsh) Geography: a river in Wales.
Colwin, Colwinn

Coman (Arabic) noble. (Irish) bent.
Comán

Coñalef (Mapuche) swift youngster; rapid, agile; well meaning.

Conall (Irish) high, mighty.
Conal, Connal, Connel, Connell, Connelly, Connolly

Conan (Irish) praised; exalted. (Scottish) wise.
Conant, Conary, Connen, Connie, Connon, Connor, Conon

Conary (Irish) a form of Conan.
Conaire

Cong (Chinese) intelligent.

Coni (Quechua) warm.

Coniraya (Quechua) heat from the sun; he who has heat from the sun.

Conlan (Irish) hero.
Conlen, Conley, Conlin, Conlyn

Conner ☒ (Irish) a form of Connor.
Connar, Connary, Conneer, Connery, Konner

Connie ☒ (English, Irish) a familiar form of Conan, Conrad, Constantine, Conway.
Con, Conn, Conney, Conny

Connor ☼ ☒ (Scottish) wise. (Irish) a form of Conan.
Conner, Connoer, Connory, Connyr, Conor, Konner, Konnor

Cono (Mapuche) ringdove.

Conor ☒ (Irish) a form of Connor.
Conar, Coner, Conour, Konner

Conrad (German) brave counselor.
Connie, Conrade, Conrado, Corrado, Konrad

Conroy (Irish) wise.
Conry, Roy

Constancio (Latin) perseverant one.

Constant (Latin) a short form of Constantine.

Constantine (Latin) firm, constant. History: Constantine the Great was

the Roman emperor who adopted the Christian faith. See also Dinos, Konstantin, Stancio.
Connie, Constadine, Constandine, Constandios, Constandine, Constant, Constantin, Constantino, Constantinos, Constantios, Costa

Contardo (Teutonic) he who is daring and valiant.

Conun-Huenu (Mapuche) entrance to the sky; elevated hill.

Conway (Irish) hound of the plain.
Connie, Conwy

Cook (English) cook.
Cooke

Cooper ✺ **B** (English) barrel maker. See also Keiffer.
Coop, Couper

Corbett (Latin) raven.
Corbbitt, Corbet, Corbette, Corbit, Corbitt

Corbin **B** (Latin) raven.
Corban, Corben, Corbey, Corbie, Corbon, Corby, Corbyn, Korbin

Corcoran (Irish) ruddy.

Cordaro (Spanish) a form of Cordero.
Coradaro, Cordairo, Cordara, Cordarel, Cordarell, Cordarelle, Cordareo, Cordarin, Cordario, Cordarion, Cordarious, Cordarius, Cordarrel, Cordarrell, Cordarris, Cordarrius, Cordarro, Cordarrol, Cordarus, Cordarryl, Cordaryal, Corddarro, Corrdarl

Cordell (French) rope maker.
Cord, Cordae, Cordale, Corday, Cordeal, Cordeil, Cordel, Cordele, Cordelle, Cordie, Cordy, Kordell

Cordero (Spanish) little lamb.
Cordaro, Cordeal, Cordeara, Cordearo, Cordeiro, Cordelro, Corder, Cordera, Corderall, Corderias, Corderious, Corderral,
Corderro, Corderryn, Corderun, Corderus, Cordiaro, Cordierre, Cordy, Corrderio

Corey **B** (Irish) hollow. See also Korey, Kory.
Core, Coreaa, Coree, Cori, Corian, Corie, Corio, Correy, Corria, Corrie, Corry, Corrye, Cory

Cori **G** (Irish) a form of Corey.

Coriguaman (Quechua) golden falcon.

Coriñaui (Quechua) he who has eyes that are the color and beauty of gold.

Coripoma (Quechua) golden puma.

Cormac (Irish) raven's son. History: a third-century king of Ireland who was a great lawmaker.
Cormack, Cormick

Cornelius **B** (Greek) cornel tree. (Latin) horn colored. See also Kornel, Kornelius, Nelek.
Carnelius, Conny, Cornealous, Corneili, Corneilius, Corneilus, Corneliaus, Cornelious, Cornelias, Cornelis, Corneliu, Cornell, Cornellious, Cornellis, Cornellius, Cornelous, Corneluis, Cornelus, Corney, Cornie, Cornielius, Corniellus, Corny, Cournelius, Cournelyous, Nelius, Nellie

Cornell (French) a form of Cornelius.
Carnell, Cornall, Corneil, Cornel, Cornelio, Corney, Cornie, Corny, Nellie

Cornwallis (English) from Cornwall.

Corona (Latin) crown.

Corrado (Italian) a form of Conrad.
Carrado

Corrigan (Irish) spearman.
Carrigan, Carrigen, Corrigon, Corrigun, Korrigan

Corrin (Irish) spear carrier.
Corin, Corion

Corry (Latin) a form of Corey.

Cort (German) bold. (Scandinavian) short. (English) a short form of Courtney.
Corte, Cortie, Corty, Kort

Cortez (Spanish) conqueror. History: Hernando Cortés was a Spanish conquistador who conquered Aztec Mexico.
Cartez, Cortes, Cortis, Cortize, Courtes, Courtez, Curtez, Kortez

Cortney 🅖 (English) a form of Courtney.

Corwin (English) heart's companion; heart's delight.
Corwinn, Corwyn, Corwynn, Corwynne

Cory 🅑 (Latin) a form of Corey. (French) a familiar form of Cornell. (Greek) a short form of Corydon.
Corye

Corydon (Greek) helmet, crest.
Coridon, Corradino, Cory, Coryden, Coryell

Cosgrove (Irish) victor, champion.

Cosimus (Italian) a form of Cosme.

Cosme (Greek) a form of Cosmo.

Cosmo (Greek) orderly; harmonious; universe.
Cos, Cosimo, Cosme, Cosmé, Cozmo, Kosmo

Costa (Greek) a short form of Constantine.
Costandinos, Costantinos, Costas, Costes

Coty 🅑 (French) slope, hillside.
Cote, Cotee, Cotey, Coti, Cotie, Cotty, Cotye

Courtland (English) court's land.
Court, Courtlan, Courtlana, Courtlandt, Courtlin, Courtlind, Courtlon, Courtlyn, Kourtland

Courtney 🅖 (English) court.
Cort, Cortnay, Cortne, Cortney, Court, Courten, Courtenay, Courteney, Courtnay, Courtnee, Curt, Kortney

Cowan (Irish) hillside hollow.
Coe, Coven, Covin, Cowen, Cowey, Cowie

Coy (English) woods.
Coye, Coyie, Coyt

Coyahue (Mapuche) meeting place for speaking and debating.

Coyle (Irish) leader in battle.

Coyne (French) modest.
Coyan

Craddock (Welsh) love.
Caradoc, Caradog

Craig 🅑 (Irish, Scottish) crag; steep rock.
Crag, Craige, Craigen, Craigery, Craigh, Craigon, Creag, Creg, Cregan, Cregg, Creig, Creigh, Criag, Kraig

Crandall (English) crane's valley.
Cran, Crandal, Crandel, Crandell, Crendal

Crandon (English) from the hill of cranes.

Crawford (English) ford where crows fly.
Craw, Crow, Ford

Creed (Latin) belief.
Creedon

Creighton (English) town near the rocks.
Cray, Crayton, Creighm, Creight, Creighto, Crichton

Crepin (French) a form of Crispin.

Crescencio (Latin) he who constantly increases his virtue.

Crescente (Latin) growing.

Cripín, Cripo (Latin) having curly hair.

Crisanto (Greek) golden flower.

Crisipo (Greek) golden horse.

Crisoforo (Greek) he who wears gold.

Crisóforo (Greek) he who gives advice that has value; his word is valuable.

Crisologo (Greek) he who says words that are like gold.

Crisólogo (Greek) he who gives advice that is as good as gold.

Crisostomo (Greek) mouth of gold.

Crisóstomo (Greek) he who gives valuable advice.

Crispin (Latin) curly haired.
Crepin, Cris, Crispian, Crispien, Crispino, Crispo, Krispin

Cristal **G** (Latin) a form of Crystal.

Cristian **B** (Greek) a form of Christian.
Crétien, Cristean, Cristhian, Cristiano, Cristien, Cristino, Cristle, Criston, Cristos, Cristy, Cristyan, Crystek, Crystian

Cristián (Latin) Christian, he who follows Christ.

Cristo (Greek) because of the Messiah.

Cristobal (Greek) a form of Christopher.
Cristóbal, Cristoval, Cristovao

Cristoforo (Italian) a form of Christopher.
Cristofor

Cristopher (Greek) a form of Christopher.
Cristaph, Cristhofer, Cristifer, Cristofer, Cristoph, Cristophe, Crystapher, Crystifer

Cristovo (Greek) Christ's servant.

Crofton (Irish) town with cottages.

Cromwell (English) crooked spring, winding spring.

Crosby (Scandinavian) shrine of the cross.
Crosbey, Crosbie, Cross

Crosley (English) meadow of the cross.
Cross

Crowther (English) fiddler.

Cruz **B** (Portuguese, Spanish) cross.
Cruze, Kruz

Crystal **G** (Latin) clear, brilliant glass.

Crystek (Polish) a form of Christian.

Cuarto (Spanish) born fourth.

Cuasimodo (Latin) he who is child-like.

Cui (Chinese) resplendent.

Cuirpuma (Quechua) golden puma.

Cuiycui (Quechua) silver.

Cullen **B** (Irish) handsome.
Cull, Cullan, Cullie, Cullin

Culley (Irish) woods.
Cullie, Cully

Culver (English) dove.
Colver, Cull, Cullie, Cully

Cuminao (Mapuche) crimson glow, the sun's last twinkle.

Cumya (Quechua) thunder, thundering; luminous.

Cunac (Quechua) he who counsels; counselor.

Cuñi (Quechua) warm.

Cunibaldo (Greek) of noble birth.

Cuniberto (Teutonic) he who stands apart from the other noble gentlemen because of his heritage.

Cuñiraya (Quechua) heat from the sun; he who has heat from the sun.

Cunningham (Irish) village of the milk pail.

Cuntur (Quechua) condor.

Cunturcanqui, Cunturchaua (Quechua) he who has all the virtues of a condor.

Cunturi (Aymara) representative of the gods; sent from the ancestral spirits.

Cunturpoma, Cunturpuma (Quechua) powerful as the puma and the condor.

Cunturuari (Quechua) untamable and savage like the vicuna and the condor.

Cunturumi (Quechua) strong as the stone and the condor.

Cuong (Vietnamese) healthy and prosperous.

Curamil (Mapuche) brilliant stone of gold and silver.

Curi (Quechua) golden.

Curiguaman (Quechua) golden falcon.

Curileo (Mapuche) black river.

Curiman (Mapuche) black condor.

Curiñaui (Quechua) he who has eyes that are the color and beauty of gold.

Curipan (Mapuche) leafy stinging nettle; furious puma.

Curran 🅑 (Irish) hero.
Curan, Curon, Curr, Curren, Currey, Curri, Currie, Currin, Curry

Currito (Spanish) a form of Curtis.
Curcio

Curro (Spanish) polite or courteous.

Curt (Latin) a short form of Courtney, Curtis. See also Kurt.

Curtis 🅑 (Latin) enclosure. (French) courteous. See also Kurtis.
Curio, Currito, Curt, Curtice, Curtiss, Curtus

Cusi (Quechua) happy, fortunate, prosperous man who is always lucky in all that he does.

Cusiguaman (Quechua) happy falcon.

Cusiguaypa (Quechua) happy rooster; creator of joyous things.

Cusiñaui (Quechua) smiling, with happy eyes.

Cusipoma, Cusipuma (Quechua) happy puma.

Cusirimachi (Quechua) he who fills us with happy words.

Cusiyupanqui (Quechua) honored and fortunate.

Custodio (Latin) guardian spirit, guardian angel.

Cuthbert (English) brilliant.

Cutler (English) knife maker.
Cut, Cuttie, Cutty

Cutmano (Anglo Saxon) man who is famous.

Cuycusi (Quechua) he who moves happily.

Cuyquiyuc (Quechua) he who is rich with silver.

Cuyuc (Quechua) he who moves; restless.

Cuyuchi (Quechua) he who makes us move.

Cy (Persian) a short form of Cyrus.

Cyle (Irish) a form of Kyle.

Cynthia **G** (Greek) moon.

Cyprian (Latin) from the island of Cyprus.
Ciprian, Cipriano, Ciprien, Cyprien

Cyrano (Greek) from Cyrene, an ancient city in North Africa. Literature: *Cyrano de Bergerac* is a play by Edmond Rostand about a great guardsman and poet whose large nose prevented him from pursuing the woman he loved.

Cyril (Greek) lordly. See also Kiril.
Cerek, Cerel, Ceril, Ciril, Cirillo, Cirrillo, Cyra, Cyrel, Cyrell, Cyrelle, Cyrill, Cyrille, Cyrillus, Syrell, Syril

Cyrus (Persian) sun. Historical: Cyrus the Great was a king in ancient Persia. See also Kir.
Ciro, Cy, Cyress, Cyris, Cyriss, Cyruss, Syris, Syrus

Czaren, Czarin (Russian) forms of Czar.

Czyz (Polish) greenfinch.

D

D **B** (American) an initial used as a first name.

Da (Chinese) attainment.

Dabi (Basque) a form of David.

Dabir (Arabic) tutor.

Dac Kien (Vietnamese) acquired view or knowledge.

Dacey **G** (Latin) from Dacia, an area now in Romania. (Irish) southerner.
Dace, Dache, Dacian, Dacias, Dacio, Dacy, Daicey, Daicy

Dachelbai (Palauan) skillful, clever.

Dada (Yoruba) curly haired.
Dadi

Daedalus (Greek) clever worker.

Daegel (English) from Daegel, England.

Daelen (English) a form of Dale.
Daelan, Daelin, Daelon, Daelyn, Daelyne

Daemon (Greek) a form of Damian. (Greek, Latin) a form of Damon.
Daemean, Daemeon, Daemien, Daemin, Daemion, Daemyen

Daequan (American) a form of Daquan.
Daequane, Daequon, Daequone, Daeqwan

Daeshawn (American) a combination of the prefix Da + Shawn.
Daesean, Daeshaun, Daeshon, Daeshun, Daisean, Daishaun, Daishawn, Daishon, Daishoun

Daevon (American) a form of Davon.
Daevion, Daevohn, Daevonne, Daevonte, Daevontey

Daeyong (Korean) substitution.

Dafi (Chamorro) weak.

Dafydd (Welsh) a form of David.
Dafyd

Dag (Scandinavian) day; bright.
Daeg, Daegan, Dagen, Dagny, Deegan

Dagan (Hebrew) corn; grain.
Daegan, Daegon, Dagen, Dageon, Dagon

Dagfel (Yapese) I am not good.

Dago (Chamorro) a type of plant.

Dagoberto (Germanic) he who shines like the sun.

Dagwood (English) shining forest.

Dahi (Chamorro) friend.

Dai 🄶 (Japanese) big.

Daichi (Japanese) large; grand.

Daigoro (Japanese) great fifth-born son.

Daijiro (Japanese) great second son.

Daimian (Greek) a form of Damian.
Daiman, Daimean, Daimen, Daimeon, Daimeyon, Daimien, Daimin, Daimion, Daimyan

Daimon (Greek, Latin) a form of Damon.
Daimone

Daiquan (American) a form of Dajuan.
Daekwaun, Daekwon, Daiqone, Daiqua, Daiquane, Daiquawn, Daiquon, Daiqwan, Daiqwon

Daishiro (Japanese) great fourth-born son.

Daisuke (Japanese) big help; voluminous writings.

Daitaro (Japanese) great first-born son.

Daivon (American) a form of Davon.
Daivain, Daivion, Daivonn, Daivonte, Daiwan

Dajon (American) a form of Dajuan.
Dajean, Dajiawn, Dajin, Dajion, Dajn, Dajohn, Dajonae

Dajuan (American) a combination of the prefix Da + Juan. See also Dejuan.
Daejon, Daejuan, Daiquan, Dajon, Da Jon, Da-Juan, Dajwan, Dajwoun, Dakuan, Dakwan, Dawan, Dawaun, Dawawn, Dawon, Dawoyan, Dijuan, Diuan, Dujuan, D'Juan, D'juan, Dwaun

Dakarai (Shona) happy.
Dakairi, Dakar, Dakaraia, Dakari, Dakarri

Dakasy (Pohnpeian) a form of Takashi.

Dak-Ho (Korean) deep lake.

Dakoda (Dakota) a form of Dakota.
Dacoda, Dacodah, Dakodah, Dakodas

Dakota 🄱 (Dakota) friend; partner; tribal name.
Dac, Dack, Dackota, Dacota, DaCota, Dak, Dakcota, Dakkota, Dakoata, Dakoda, Dakotah, Dakotha, Dakotta, Dekota

Dakotah 🄱 (Dakota) a form of Dakota.
Dakottah

Daksh (Hindi) efficient.

Dalal (Sanskrit) broker.

Dalbert (English) bright, shining. See also Delbert.

Dale **B** (English) dale, valley.
Dael, Daelen, Dal, Dalen, Daley,
Dalibor, Dallan, Dallin, Dallyn, Daly,
Dayl, Dayle

Dalen (English) a form of Dale.
Dailin, Dalaan, Dalan, Dalane,
Daleon, Dalian, Dalibor, Dalione,
Dallan, Dalon, Daylan, Daylen,
Daylin, Daylon

Daley (Irish) assembly. (English) a
familiar form of Dale.
Daily, Daly, Dawley

Dalip (Yapese) three.

Dallan (English) a form of Dale.
Dallen, Dallon

Dallas **B** (Scottish) valley of the
water; resting place. Geography: a
town in Scotland; a city in Texas.
Dal, Dalieass, Dall, Dalles, Dallis,
Dalys, Dellis

Dallen **B** (English) a form of Dallan.

Dallin, Dallyn **B** (English) pride's
people.
Dalin, Dalyn

Dalmacio (Latin) native of Dalmatia,
the western part of the Balkans.

Dalmazio (Italian) a form of Dalmacio.

Dalmiro (Germanic) illustrious one
because of his heritage.

Dalston (English) Daegel's place.
Dalis, Dallon

Dalton **B** (English) town in the valley.
Dal, Dalaton, Dallton, Dalt, Daltan,
Dalten, Daltin, Daltyn, Daulton,
Delton

Dalvin (English) a form of Delvin.
Dalven, Dalvon, Dalvyn

Dalziel (Scottish) small field.

Damar (American) a short form of
Damarcus, Damario.
Damare, Damari, Damarre, Damauri

Damarcus (American) a combination
of the prefix Da + Marcus.
Damacus, Damar, Damarco,
Damarcue, Damarick, Damark,
Damarkco, Damarkis, Damarko,
Damarkus, Damarques, Damarquez,
Damarquis, Damarrco

Damario (Greek) gentle. (American)
a combination of the prefix Da +
Mario.
Damar, Damarea, Damareus,
Damaria, Damarie, Damarino,
Damarion, Damarious, Damaris,
Damarius, Damarrea, Damarrion,
Damarrious, Damarrius, Damaryo,
Dameris, Damerius

Damaris **G** (Greek, American) a
form of Damario.

Damaso (Greek) skillful horse breaker.

Dámaso (Greek) skillful tamer.

Damek (Slavic) a form of Adam.
Damick, Damicke

Dameon (Greek) a form of Damian.
Damein, Dameion, Dameone

Dametrius (Greek) a form of
Demetrius.
Dametri, Dametries, Dametrious,
Damitri, Damitric, Damitrie,
Damitrious, Damitrus

Damian **B** (Greek) tamer; soother.
Daemon, Daimian, Damaiaon,
Damaian, Damaien, Damain,
Damaine, Damaion, Damani,
Damanni, Damaun, Damayon, Dame,
Damean, Dameon, Damián,
Damiane, Damiann, Damiano,
Damianos, Damien, Damion,
Damiyan, Damján, Damyan,
Daymian, Dema, Demyan

Damien 🅱 (Greek) a form of
Damian. Religion: Father Damien
ministered to the leper colony on
the Hawaiian island Molokai.
*Daemien, Daimien, Damie,
Damienne, Damyen*

Damion (Greek) a form of Damian.
*Damieon, Damiion, Damin, Damine,
Damionne, Damiyon, Dammion,
Damyon*

Damocles (Greek) gives glory to his
village.

Damon 🅱 (Greek) constant, loyal.
(Latin) spirit, demon.
*Daemen, Daemon, Daemond,
Daimon, Daman, Damen, Damond,
Damone, Damoni, Damonn,
Damonni, Damonta, Damontae,
Damonte, Damontez, Damontis,
Damyn, Daymon, Daymond*

Dan 🅱 (Vietnamese) yes.
(Hebrew) a short form of Daniel.
Dahn, Danh, Danne

Dana 🅶 (Scandinavian) from
Denmark.
Dain, Daina, Dayna

Dandin (Hindi) holy man.

D'andre 🅱 (French) a form of
Deandre.

Dandré (French) a combination of
the prefix De + André.
*D'André, Dandrae, D'andrea,
Dandras, Dandray, Dandre, Dondrea*

Dane 🅱 (English) from Denmark.
See also Halden.
Dain, Daine, Danie, Dayne, Dhane

Danek (Polish) a form of Daniel.

Danforth (English) a form of Daniel.

Danglon (Chamorro) cowfish.

Danial (Hebrew) a form of Daniel.
*Danal, Daneal, Danieal, Daniyal,
Dannial*

Danick, Dannick (Slavic) familiar
forms of Daniel.
*Danek, Danieko, Danik, Danika,
Danyck*

Daniel ☀ 🅱 (Hebrew) God is my
judge. Bible: a Hebrew prophet. See
also Danno, Kanaiela.
*Dacso, Dainel, Dan, Daneel, Daneil,
Danek, Danel, Danforth, Danial,
Danick, Dániel, Daniël, Daniele,
Danielius, Daniell, Daniels, Danielson,
Danilo, Daniyel, Dan'l, Dannel,
Dannick, Danniel, Dannil, Danno,
Danny, Dano, Danukas, Dany, Danyel,
Danyell, Daoud, Dasco, Dayne, Deniel,
Doneal, Doniel, Donois, Dusan, Nelo*

Daniele (Hebrew) a form of Daniel.
Danile, Danniele

Danielle 🅶 (Hebrew, French) a
form of Daniel

Danika 🅶 (Slavic) a form of Danick.

Danilo (Slavic) a form of Daniel.
*Danielo, Danil, Danila, Danilka,
Danylo*

Danior (Gypsy) born with teeth.

Danladi (Hausa) born on Sunday.

Danno (Hebrew) a familiar form of
Daniel. (Japanese) gathering in the
meadow.
Dannon, Dano

Dannon (American) a form of Danno.
*Daenan, Daenen, Dainon, Danaan,
Danen, Danon*

Danny, Dany 🅱 (Hebrew) familiar
forms of Daniel.
*Daney, Dani, Dannee, Danney,
Danni, Dannie, Dannye*

Dano (Czech) a form of Daniel.
Danko, Danno

Dante, Danté **B** (Latin) lasting, enduring.
Danatay, Danaté, Dant, Dantae, Dantay, Dantee, Dauntay, Dauntaye, Daunté, Dauntrae, Deante, Dontae, Donté

Dantel (Latin) enduring.

Dantrell (American) a combination of Dante + Darell.
Dantrel, Dantrey, Dantril, Dantyrell, Dontrell

Danyel **G** (Hebrew) a form of Daniel.
Danya, Danyal, Danyale, Danyele, Danyell, Danyiel, Danyl, Danyle, Danylets, Danylo, Donyell

Dao (Vietnamese) religions.

Daoud (Arabic) a form of David.
Daudi, Daudy, Dauod, Dawud

Daquan (American) a combination of the prefix Da + Quan.
Daequan, Daqon, Daquain, Daquaine, Da'quan, Daquandre, Daquandrey, Daquane, Daquann, Daquantae, Daquante, Daquarius, Daquaun, Daquawn, Daquin, Daquon, Daquone, Daquwon, Daqwain, Daqwan, Daqwane, Daqwann, Daqwon, Daqwone, Dayquan, Dequain, Dequan, Dequann, Dequaun

Dar (Hebrew) pearl.

Dara **G** (Cambodian) stars.

Daran (Irish) a form of Darren.
Darann, Darawn, Darian, Darran, Dayran, Deran

Darby **G** (Irish) free. (English) deer park.
Dar, Darb, Darbee, Darbey, Darbie, Derby

Darcy **G** (Irish) dark. (French) from Arcy, France.
Dar, Daray, D'Aray, Darce, Darcee, Darcel, Darcey, Darcio, D'Arcy, Darsey, Darsy

Dardo (Greek) astute and skillful.

Dareh (Persian) wealthy.

Darell (English) a form of Darrell.
Darall, Daralle, Dareal, Darel, Darelle, Darral, Darrall

Daren (Hausa) born at night. (Irish, English) a form of Darren.
Dare, Dayren, Dheren

Darian, Darrian **BG** (Irish) forms of Darren.
Daryan

Darick (German) a form of Derek.
Darek, Daric, Darico, Darieck, Dariek, Darik, Daryk

Darien, Darrien **B** (Irish) forms of Darren.

Darin **B** (Irish) a form of Darren.
Daryn, Darynn, Dayrin, Dearin, Dharin

Dario (Spanish) affluent.

Darío (Spanish) a form of Dario.

Darion, Darrion **B** (Irish) forms of Darren.
Dairean, Dairion, Darian, Darien, Darion, Darrian, Darrien, Darrione, Darriyun, Derrian, Derrion, Daryeon, Daryon

Darius **B** (Greek) wealthy.
Dairus, Dare, Darieus, Darioush, Dariuse, Dariush, Dariuss, Dariusz, Darrius

Darnell **B** (English) hidden place.
Dar, Darn, Darnall, Darneal, Darneil, Darnel, Darnelle, Darnyell, Darnyll

Daron B (Irish) a form of Darren.
*Daeron, Dairon, Darone, Daronn,
Darroun, Dayron, Dearon, Dharon,
Diron*

Darrell B (French) darling, beloved;
grove of oak trees.
*Dare, Darel, Darell, Darral, Darrel,
Darrill, Darrol, Darryl, Derrell*

Darren B (Irish) great. (English)
small; rocky hill.
*Daran, Dare, Daren, Darian, Darien,
Darin, Darion, Daron, Darran,
Darrian, Darrien, Darrience, Darrin,
Darrion, Darron, Darryn, Darun,
Daryn, Dearron, Deren, Dereon,
Derren, Derron*

Darrick (German) a form of Derek.
*Darrec, Darrek, Darric, Darrik,
Darryk*

Darrin (Irish) a form of Darren.

Darrius (Greek) a form of Darius.
*Darreus, Darrias, Darrious, Darris,
Darriuss, Darrus, Darryus, Derrious,
Derris, Derrius*

Darron (Irish) a form of Darren.
Darriun, Darroun

Darryl B (French) darling, beloved;
grove of oak trees. A form of
Darrell.
*Dahrll, Darryle, Darryll, Daryl,
Daryle, Daryll, Derryl*

Darshan (Hindi) god; godlike.
Religion: another name for the
Hindu god Shiva.
Darshaun, Darshon

Darton (English) deer town.
Dartel, Dartrel

Darwin (English) dear friend.
History: Charles Darwin was the
British naturalist who established
the theory of evolution.
*Darvin, Darvon, Darwyn, Derwin,
Derwynn, Durwin*

Daryl B (French) a form of Darryl.
*Darel, Daril, Darl, Darly, Daryell,
Daryle, Daryll, Darylle, Daroyl*

Dasan (Pomo) leader of the bird clan.
Dassan

Dashawn B (American) a
combination of the prefix Da +
Shawn.
*Dasean, Dashan, Dashane,
Dashante, Dashaun, Dashaunte,
Dashean, Dashon, Dashonnie,
Dashonte, Dashuan, Dashun,
Dashwan, Dayshawn*

Dativo (Latin) term from Roman
law, which is applied to educators.

Dato (Latin) a form of Donato.

Dauid (Swahili) a form of David.

Daulton (English) a form of Dalton.

Davante (American) a form of
Davonte.
Davanta, Davantay, Davinte

Davaris (American) a combination of
Dave + Darius.
*Davario, Davarious, Davarius,
Davarrius, Davarus*

Dave B (Hebrew) a short form of
David, Davis.

Davey (Hebrew) a familiar form of
David.
Davee, Davi, Davie, Davy

David ☆ B (Hebrew) beloved.
Bible: the second king of Israel. See
also Dov, Havika, Kawika, Taaveti,
Taffy, Tevel.
*Dabi, Daevid, Dafydd, Dai, Daivid,
Daoud, Dauid, Dav, Dave, Daved,
Daveed, Daven, Davey, Davidde,
Davide, Davidek, Davido, Davon,
Davoud, Davyd, Dawid, Dawit,
Dawud, Dayvid, Dodya, Dov*

Davin **B** (Scandinavian) brilliant
Finn.
*Daevin, Davion, Davon, Davyn,
Dawan, Dawin, Dawine, Dayvon,
Deavan, Deaven*

Davion **B** (American) a form of
Davin.
*Davione, Davionne, Daviyon,
Davyon, Deaveon*

Davis **B** (Welsh) son of David.
Dave, Davidson, Davies, Davison

Davon **B** (American) a form of
Davin.
*Daevon, Daivon, Davon, Davone,
Davonn, Davonne, Deavon, Deavone,
Devon*

Davonte **B** (American) a combi-
nation of Davon + the suffix Te.
*Davante, Davonnte, Davonta,
Davontae, Davontah, Davontai,
Davontay, Davontaye, Davontea,
Davontee, Davonti*

Dawan (American) a form of Davin.
*Dawann, Dawante, Dawaun,
Dawayne, Dawon, Dawone,
Dawoon, Dawyne, Dawyun*

Dawit (Ethiopian) a form of David.

Dawn **G** (English) sunrise, dawn.

Dawson **B**　(English) son of David.
Dawsyn

Dax (French, English) water.

Day (English) a form of Daniel.

Daylon (American) a form of Dillon.
*Daylan, Daylen, Daylin, Daylun,
Daylyn*

Daymian (Greek) a form of Damian.
*Daymayne, Daymen, Daymeon,
Daymiane, Daymien, Daymin,
Dayminn, Daymion, Daymn*

Dayne (Scandinavian) a form of Dane.
Dayn

Dayquan (American) a form of
Daquan.
*Dayquain, Dayquawane, Dayquin,
Dayqwan*

Dayshawn (American) a form of
Dashawn.
*Daysean, Daysen, Dayshaun,
Dayshon, Dayson*

Dayton **B** (English) day town;
bright, sunny town.
*Daeton, Daiton, Daythan, Daython,
Daytona, Daytonn, Deyton*

Dayvon (American) a form of Davin.
*Dayven, Dayveon, Dayvin, Dayvion,
Dayvonn*

De **B** (Chinese) virtuous.

Deacon (Greek) one who serves.
Deke

Dean **B** (French) leader. (English)
valley. See also Dino.
Deane, Deen, Dene, Deyn, Deyne

Deana **G** (Latin) divine. (English)
valley.

Deandre **B** (French) a combination
of the prefix De + André.
*D'andre, D'andré, D'André,
D'andrea, Deandra, Deandrae,
Déandre, Deandré, De André,
Deandrea, De Andrea, Deandres,
Deandrey, Deaundera, Deaundra,
Deaundray, Deaundre, De Aundre,
Deaundrey, Deaundry, Deondre,
Diandre, Dondre*

Deangelo (Italian) a combination of
the prefix De + Angelo.
*Dang, Dangelo, D'Angelo, Danglo,
Deaengelo, Deangelio, Deangello,
Déangelo, De Angelo, Deangilio,
Deangleo, Deanglo, Deangulo,
Diangelo, Di'angelo*

Deanna **G** (Latin) a form of Deana,
Diana.

Deante (Latin) a form of Dante.
*Deanta, Deantai, Deantay, Deanté,
De Anté, Deanteé, Deaunta, Diantae,
Diante, Diantey*

Deanthony (Italian) a combination
of the prefix De + Anthony.
D'anthony, Danton, Dianthony

Dearborn (English) deer brook.
*Dearbourn, Dearburne, Deaurburn,
Deerborn*

Debesol (Palauan) one who is to be
cut from the tree, like fruit before it
is ripe.

Deborah ☀ (Hebrew) bee.

Decarlos (Spanish) a combination of
the prefix De + Carlos.
Dacarlos, Decarlo, Di'carlos

Decha (Tai) strong.

Decherong (Palauan) just standing up.

Decimus (Latin) tenth.

Decio (Latin) tenth.

Declan (Irish) man of prayer.
Religion: Saint Declan was a fifth-
century Irish bishop.
Deklan

Decoroso (Latin) he is well; he is
practical.

Dédalo (Greek) industrious and
skillful artisan.

Dedrick (German) ruler of the
people. See also Derek, Theodoric.
*Deadrick, Deddrick, Dederick,
Dedrek, Dedreko, Dedric, Dedrix,
Dedrrick, Deedrick, Diedrich,
Diedrick, Dietrich, Detrick*

Deems (English) judge's child.

Deicola (Latin) he who cultivates a
relationship with God.

Deion ☀ (Greek) a form of Dion.
Deione, Deionta, Deionte

Deja ☀ (French) a form of Déja (see
Girls' Names).

Dejuan (American) a combination of
the prefix De + Juan. See also
Dajuan.
*Dejan, Dejon, Dejuane, Dejun,
Dewan, Dewaun, Dewon, Dijaun,
Djuan, D'Juan, Dujuan, Dujuane,
D'Won*

Dekel (Hebrew, Arabic) palm tree,
date tree.

Dekota (Dakota) a form of Dakota.
Decoda, Dekoda, Dekodda, Dekotes

Del (English) a short form of Delbert,
Delvin, Delwin.

Delaney ☀ (Irish) descendant of the
challenger.
*Delaine, Delainey, Delainy, Delan,
Delane, Delanny, Delany*

Delano (French) nut tree. (Irish)
dark.
Delanio, Delayno, Dellano

Delbert (English) bright as day. See
also Dalbert.
Bert, Del, Dilbert

Delfin (Greek) playful one with a
graceful and beautiful form.

Delfino (Latin) dolphin.
Delfine

Déli (Chinese) virtuous.

Dell (English) small valley. A short
form of Udell.

Delling (Scandinavian) scintillating.

Delmar (Latin) sea.
*Dalmar, Dalmer, Delmare, Delmario,
Delmarr, Delmer, Delmor, Delmore*

Delon (American) a form of Dillon.
Deloin, Delone, Deloni, Delonne

Delphine **G** (Greek) from Delphi, Greece.

Delroy (French) belonging to the king. See also Elroy, Leroy.
Delray, Delree, Delroi

Delshawn (American) a combination of Del + Shawn.
Delsean, Delshon, Delsin, Delson

Delsin (Native American) he is so.
Delsy

Delton (English) a form of Dalton.
Delten, Delfyn

Delvin (English) proud friend; friend from the valley.
Dalvin, Del, Delavan, Delvian, Delvon, Delvyn, Delwin

Delwin (English) a form of Delvin.
Dalwin, Dalwyn, Del, Dellwin, Dellwyn, Delwyn, Delwynn

Deman (Dutch) man.

Demarco (Italian) a combination of the prefix De + Marco.
Damarco, Demarcco, Demarceo, Demarcio, Demarkco, Demarkeo, Demarko, Demarquo, D'Marco

Demarcus (American) a combination of the prefix De + Marcus.
Damarcius, Damarcus, Demarces, Demarcis, Demarcius, Demarcos, Demarcuse, Demarkes, Demarkis, Demarkos, Demarkus, Demarqus, D'Marcus

Demario (Italian) a combination of the prefix De + Mario.
Demarea, Demaree, Demareo, Demari, Demaria, Demariea, Demarion, Demarreio, Demariez, Demarious, Demaris, Demariuz, Demarrio, Demerio, Demerrio

Demarius (American) a combination of the prefix De + Marius.

Demarquis (American) a combination of the prefix De + Marquis.
Demarques, Demarquez, Demarqui

Dembe (Luganda) peaceful.
Damba

Demetri, Demitri (Greek) short forms of Demetrius.
Dametri, Damitré, Demeter, Demetre, Demetrea, Demetriel, Demitre, Demitrie, Domotor

Demetria **G** (Greek) cover of the earth.

Demetris (Greek) a short form of Demetrius.
Demeatric, Demeatrice, Demeatris, Demetres, Demetress, Demetric, Demetrice, Demetrick, Demetrics, Demetricus, Demetrik, Demitrez, Demitries, Demitris

Demetrius **B** (Greek) lover of the earth. Mythology: a follower of Demeter, the goddess of the harvest. See also Dimitri, Mimis, Mitsos.
Dametrius, Demeitrius, Demeterious, Demetreus, Demetri, Demetrias, Demetrio, Demetrios, Demetrious, Demetris, Demetriu, Demetrium, Demetrois, Demetruis, Demetrus, Demitirus, Demitri, Demitrias, Demitriu, Demitrius, Demitrus, Demtrius, Demtrus, Dimitri, Dimitrios, Dimitrius, Dmetrius, Dymek

Demian (Greek) he who emerged from the village.

Demián (Spanish) a form of Demian.

Demichael (American) a combination of the prefix De + Michael.
Dumichael

Demócrito (Greek) chosen by the villagers to be judge; the arbiter of the village.

Demond (Irish) a short form of Desmond.
Demonde, Demonds, Demone, Dumonde

Demont (French) mountain.
Démont, Demonta, Demontae, Demontay, Demontaz, Demonte, Demontez, Demontre

Demorris (American) a combination of the prefix De + Morris.
Demoris, DeMorris, Demorus

Demos (Greek) people.
Demas, Demosthenes

Demóstenes (Greek) strength of the village.

Demothi (Native American) talks while walking.

Dempsey (Irish) proud.
Demp, Demps, Dempsie, Dempsy

Dempster (English) one who judges.
Demster

Denbei, Denji (Japanese) forms of Den.

Denby (Scandinavian) Geography: a Danish village.
Danby, Den, Denbey, Denney, Dennie, Denny

Deng (Chinese) to ascend.

Dengyo (Japanese) historical figure.

Denham (English) village in the valley.

Denholm (Scottish) Geography: a town in Scotland.

Denis 🅱 (Greek) a form of Dennis.
Deniz

Denise 🅶 (Greek) a form of Denis.

Denjiro (Japanese) good ancestors.

Denley (English) meadow; valley.
Denlie, Denly

Denman (English) man from the valley.

Dennis 🅱 (Greek) Mythology: a follower of Dionysus, the god of wine. See also Dion, Nicho.
Den, Dénes, Denies, Denis, Deniz, Dennes, Dennet, Dennez, Denny, Dennys, Denya, Denys, Deon, Dinis

Dennison (English) son of Dennis. See also Dyson, Tennyson.
Den, Denison, Denisson, Dennyson

Denny (Greek) a familiar form of Dennis.
Den, Denney, Dennie, Deny

Denton (English) happy home.
Dent, Denten, Dentin

Denver 🅱 (English) green valley. Geography: the capital of Colorado.

Denzel 🅱 (Cornish) a form of Denzell.
Danzel, Dennzel, Denzal, Denzale, Denzall, Denzell, Denzelle, Denzle, Denzsel

Denzell (Cornish) Geography: a location in Cornwall, England.
Dennzil, Dennzyl, Denzel, Denzial, Denziel, Denzil, Denzill, Denzyel, Denzyl, Donzell

Deodato (Latin) he who serves God.

Deon 🅱 (Greek) a form of Dennis. See also Dion.
Deion, Deone, Deonn, Deonno

Deondre (French) a form of Deandre.
Deiondray, Deiondre, Deondra, Deondrae, Deondray, Deondré, Deondrea, Deondree, Deondrei, Deondrey, Diondra, Diondrae, Diondre, Diondrey

Deontae (American) a combination
of the prefix De + Dontae.
*Deonta, Deontai, Deontay, Deontaye,
Deonte, Deonté, Deontea, Deonteya,
Deonteye, Deontia, Dionte*

Deonte, Deonté **B** (American)
forms of Deontae.
D'Ante, Deante, Deontée, Deontie

Deontre (American) a form of
Deontae.
*Deontrae, Deontrais, Deontray,
Deontrea, Deontrey, Deontrez,
Deontreze, Deontrus*

Dequan (American) a combination
of the prefix De + Quan.
*Dequain, Dequane, Dequann,
Dequante, Dequantez, Dequantis,
Dequaun, Dequavius, Dequawn,
Dequian, Dequin, Dequine, Dequinn,
Dequion, Dequoin, Dequon, Deqwan,
Deqwon, Deqwone*

Dereck, Derick (German) forms of
Derek.
*Derekk, Dericka, Derico, Deriek,
Derique, Deryck, Deryk, Deryke, Detrek*

Derek **B** (German) a short form of
Theodoric. See also Dedrick, Dirk.
*Darek, Darick, Darrick, Derak,
Dereck, Derecke, Derele, Deric,
Derick, Derik, Derk, Derke, Derrek,
Derrick, Deryek*

Deric, Derik (German) forms of
Derek.
Deriek, Derikk

Dermot (Irish) free from envy.
(English) free. (Hebrew) a short
form of Jeremiah. See also Kermit.
*Der, Dermod, Dermott, Diarmid,
Diarmuid*

Deron (Hebrew) bird; freedom.
(American) a combination of the
prefix De + Ron.
*Daaron, Daron, Da-Ron, Darone,
Darron, Dayron, Dereon, Deronn,*

*Deronne, Derrin, Derrion, Derron,
Derronn, Derronne, Derryn, Diron,
Duron, Durron, Dyron*

Deror (Hebrew) lover of freedom.
Derori, Derorie

Derrek (German) a form of Derek.
Derrec, Derreck

Derrell (French) a form of Darrell.
*Derel, Derele, Derell, Derelle, Derrel,
Dérrell, Derriel, Derril, Derrill, Deryl,
Deryll*

Derren (Irish, English) a form of
Darren.
*Deren, Derran, Derraun, Derreon,
Derrian, Derrien, Derrin, Derrion,
Derron, Derryn, Deryan, Deryn,
Deryon*

Derrick **B** (German) ruler of the
people. A form of Derek.
Derric, Derrik, Derryck, Derryk

Derry **BG** (Irish) redhead. Geography:
a city in Northern Ireland.
*Darrie, Darry, Derri, Derrie, Derrye,
Dery*

Derryl (French) a form of Darryl.
Deryl, Deryll

Derward (English) deer keeper.

Derwin (English) a form of Darwin.
Derwyn

Desean (American) a combination of
the prefix De + Sean.
Dasean, D'Sean, Dusean

Deshane (American) a combination
of the prefix De + Shane.
Deshan, Deshayne

Deshaun (American) a combination
of the prefix De + Shaun.
*Deshan, Deshane, Deshann,
Deshaon, Deshaune, D'shaun,
D'Shaun, Dushaun*

Deshawn 🅑 (American) a combination of the prefix De + Shawn.
Dashaun, Dashawn, Deshauwn, Deshawan, Deshawon, Deshon, D'shawn, D'Shawn, Dushan, Dushawn

Deshea (American) a combination of the prefix De + Shea.
Deshay

Deshi (Chinese) moral.

Déshì (Chinese) virtuous.

Deshon (American) a form of Deshawn.
Deshondre, Deshone, Deshonn, Deshonte, Deshun, Deshunn

Desiderato (Latin) he who is desired.

Desiderio (Spanish) desired.

Desiderius (German) a form of Desiderio.

Desmond (Irish) from south Munster.
Demond, Des, Desi, Desimon, Desman, Desmand, Desmane, Desmen, Desmine, Desmon, Desmound, Desmund, Desmyn, Dezmon, Dezmond

Destin 🅑 (French) destiny, fate.
Destan, Desten, Destine, Deston, Destry, Destyn

Destiny 🅖 (French) fate.

Destry (American) a form of Destin.
Destrey, Destrie

Detrick (German) a form of Dedrick.
Detrek, Detric, Detrich, Detrik, Detrix

Devan 🅑 (Irish) a form of Devin.
Devaan, Devain, Devane, Devann, Devean, Devun, Diwan

Devante (American) a combination of Devan + the suffix Te.
Devanta, Devantae, Devantay, Devanté, Devantée, Devantez, Devanty, Devaughntae, Devaughnte, Devaunte, Deventae, Deventay, Devente, Divante

Devaughn (American) a form of Devin.
Devaugh, Devaun

Devayne (American) a form of Dewayne.
Devain, Devaine, Devan, Devane, Devayn, Devein, Deveion

Deven 🅑 (Hindi) for God. (Irish) a form of Devin.
Deaven, Deivin, Devein, Devenn, Devven, Diven

Devender (Sanskrit) Indra, the greatest god.

Deverell (English) riverbank.

Devin 🅑 (Irish) poet.
Deavin, Deivin, Dev, Devan, Devaughn, Deven, Devlyn, Devon, Devvin, Devy, Devyn, Dyvon

Devine (Latin) divine. (Irish) ox.
Davon, Devinn, Devon, Devyn, Devyne, Dewine

Devlin (Irish) brave, fierce.
Dev, Devlan, Devland, Devlen, Devlon, Devlyn

Devon 🅑 (Irish) a form of Devin.
Deavon, Deivon, Deivone, Deivonne, Deveon, Deveone, Devion, Devoen, Devohn, Devonae, Devone, Devoni, Devonio, Devonn, Devonne, Devontaine, Devvon, Devvonne, Dewon, Dewone, Divon, Diwon

Devonta 🅑 (American) a combination of Devon + the suffix Ta.
Deveonta, Devonnta, Devonntae, Devontae, Devontai, Devontay, Devontaye

Devonte B (American) a combination of Devon + the suffix Te.
Deveonte, Devionte, Devonté, Devontea, Devontee, Devonti, Devontia, Devontre

Devyn BG (Irish) a form of Devin.
Devyin, Devynn, Devynne

Dewayne (Irish) a form of Dwayne. (American) a combination of the prefix De + Wayne.
Deuwayne, Devayne, Dewain, Dewaine, Dewan, Dewane, Dewaun, Dewaune, Dewayen, Dewean, Dewon, Dewune

Dewei (Chinese) highly virtuous.

Dewey (Welsh) prized.
Dew, Dewi, Dewie

DeWitt (Flemish) blond.
Dewitt, Dwight, Wit

Dexter (Latin) dexterous, adroit. (English) fabric dyer.
Daxter, Decca, Deck, Decka, Dekka, Dex, Dextar, Dextor, Dextrel, Dextron

Dezmon, Dezmond (Irish) forms of Desmond.
Dezman, Dezmand, Dezmen, Dezmin

Dhani (Sanskrit) a rich person.

Dhanpal (Sanskrit) property; riches.

Dharam (Sanskrit) that which is held fast or kept; law; custom.

Di (Chinese) to enlighten.

Diakelmad (Palauan) never die.

Diamond G (English) brilliant gem; bright guardian.
Diaman, Diamanta, Diamante, Diamend, Diamenn, Diamont, Diamonta, Diamonte, Diamund, Dimond, Dimonta, Dimontae, Dimonte

Dian (Chinese) model, type.

Diana G (Latin) divine. Mythology: the goddess of the hunt, the moon, and fertility.

Dick (German) a short form of Frederick, Richard.
Dic, Dicken, Dickens, Dickie, Dickon, Dicky, Dik

Dickran (Armenian) History: an ancient Armenian king.
Dicran, Dikran

Dickson (English) son of Dick.
Dickenson, Dickerson, Dikerson, Diksan

Diderot (Spanish) a form of Desiderio.

Didi (Hebrew) a familiar form of Jedidiah, Yedidyah.

Didier (French) desired, longed for.

Didimo (Greek) twin brother.

Dídimo (Greek) identical twin brother.

Didio (Spanish) given by God.

Diedrich (German) a form of Dedrick, Dietrich.
Didrich, Didrick, Didrik, Diederick

Diego ※ (Spanish) a form of Jacob, James.
Iago, Diaz, Jago

Dien (Vietnamese) farm, farming.

Dietbald (German) a form of Theobald.
Dietbalt, Dietbolt

Dieter (German) army of the people.
Deiter

Dietrich (German) a form of Dedrick.
Deitrich, Deitrick, Deke, Diedrich, Dietrick, Dierck, Dieter, Dieterich, Dieterick, Dietz

Dieu Hien (Vietnamese) amaryllis.

Digby (Irish) ditch town; dike town.

Dillan 🅱 (Irish) a form of Dillon.
Dilan, Dillian, Dilun, Dilyan

Dillon 🅱 (Irish) loyal, faithful. See also Dylan.
Daylon, Delon, Dil, Dill, Dillan, Dillen, Dillie, Dillin, Dillion, Dilly, Dillyn, Dilon, Dilyn, Dilynn

Dilwyn (Welsh) shady place.
Dillwyn

Dima (Russian) a familiar form of Vladimir.
Dimka

Dimas (Greek) loyal comrade; exemplary companion.

Dimitri 🅱 (Russian) a form of Demetrius.
Dimetra, Dimetri, Dimetric, Dimetrie, Dimitr, Dimitric, Dimitrie, Dimitrik, Dimitris, Dimitry, Dimmy, Dmitri, Dymitr, Dymitry

Dimitrios (Greek) a form of Demetrius.
Dhimitrios, Dimitrius, Dimos, Dmitrios

Dimitrius (Greek) a form of Demetrius.
Dimetrius, Dimitricus, Dimitrius, Dimetrus, Dmitrius

Ding (Chinese) able-bodied man.

Dingbang (Chinese) protector of the country.

Dinh (Vietnamese) calm, peaceful.
Din

Dinh Hoa (Vietnamese) flower at the peak.

Dinís (Greek) devoted to Dionysus.

Dino (German) little sword. (Italian) a form of Dean.
Deano

Dinos (Greek) a familiar form of Constantine, Konstantin.

Dinsmore (Irish) fortified hill.
Dinnie, Dinny, Dinse

Diodoro (Greek) Mythology: the grandson of Hercules who brought to submission many villages.

Diogenes (Greek) honest. History: an ancient philosopher who searched with a lantern in daylight for an honest man.
Diogenese

Diógenes (Greek) a form of Diogenes.

Diómedes (Greek) he who trusts in God's protection.

Dion 🅱 (Greek) a short form of Dennis, Dionysus.
Deion, Deon, Dio, Dione, Dionigi, Dionis, Dionn, Dionne, Diontae, Dionte, Diontray

Dionisio (Greek) a form of Dionysus.

Dionte (American) a form of Deontae.
Diante, Dionta, Diontae, Diontay, Diontaye, Dionté, Diontea

Dionysus (Greek) celebration. Mythology: the god of wine.
Dion, Dionesios, Dionicio, Dionisio, Dionisios, Dionusios, Dionysios, Dionysius, Dunixi

Dioscoro (Latin) he who is of the Lord.

Dióscoro (Greek) a form of Dioscoro.

Dip (Sanskrit) light.

Diquan (American) a combination of the prefix Di + Quan.
Diqawan, Diqawn, Diquane

Dirk (German) a short form of
Derek, Theodoric.
Derk, Dirck, Dirke, Durc, Durk, Dyrk

Dishi (Chinese) man of virtue.

Diven (Sanskrit) a form of Divendra.

Divendra (Sanskrit) divine Indra;
most divine.

Dixon (English) son of Dick.
Dickson, Dix

Dmitri (Russian) a form of Dimitri.
*Dmetriy, Dmitiri, Dmitri, Dmitrik,
Dmitriy*

Doami (Japanese) literary figure.

Doane (English) low, rolling hills.
Doan

Dob (English) a familiar form of
Robert.
Dobie

Dobry (Polish) good.

Doherty (Irish) harmful.
Docherty, Dougherty, Douherty

Doho (Japanese) literary figure.

Dohpi (Pohnpeian) a form of Toby.

Dolan (Irish) dark haired.
Dolin, Dolyn

Dolf, Dolph (German) short forms
of Adolf, Adolph, Rudolf, Rudolph.
Dolfe, Dolfi, Dolphe, Dolphus

Dolores **G** (Spanish) sorrowful.

Dom (Latin) a short form of
Dominic.
Dome, Domó

Domenic **B** (Latin) an alternate
form of Dominic.
Domanick, Domenick

Domenico (Italian) a form of
Dominic.
Domenic, Domicio, Dominico, Menico

Domiciano (Spanish) a form of
Domicio.

Domicio (Italian) a form of
Domenico.

Domigko, Domingko (Chuukese)
forms of Domingo.

Domingo (Spanish) born on Sunday.
See also Mingo.
Demingo, Domingos

Dominic 🌟 **B** (Latin) belonging to
the Lord. See also Chuminga.
*Deco, Demenico, Dom, Domanic,
Domeka, Domenic, Domenico,
Domini, Dominie, Dominik,
Dominique, Dominitric, Dominy,
Domminic, Domnenique, Domokos,
Domonic, Nick*

Dominick **B** (Latin) a form of
Dominic.
*Domiku, Domineck, Dominiick,
Dominicke, Dominiek, Dominik,
Dominnick, Dominyck, Domminick,
Dommonick, Domnick, Domokos,
Domonick, Donek, Dumin*

Dominik (Latin) a form of Dominic.
*Domenik, Dominiko, Dominyk,
Domonik*

Dominique **G** (French) a form of
Dominic.
*Domeniq, Domeniqu, Domenique,
Domenque, Diminiqu, Dominque,
Dominiqueia, Domnenique,
Domniqu, Domoniqu, Domonique,
Domunique*

Dominque **BG** (French) a form of
Dominique.

Domokos (Hungarian) a form of
Dominic.
*Dedo, Dome, Domek, Domok,
Domonkos*

Domonique **G** (French) a form of
Dominique.

Domotom (Chuukese) a form of Domingo.

Don B (Scottish) a short form of Donald. See also Kona.
Donn

Donado (Pohnpeian) a form of Donato.

Donahue (Irish) dark warrior.
Donohoe, Donohue

Donal (Irish) a form of Donald.

Donald (Scottish) world leader; proud ruler. See also Bohdan, Tauno.
Don, Donal, Dónal, Donaldo, Donall, Donalt, Donát, Donaugh, Donnie

Donardo (Celtic) he who governs boldly.

Donatien (French) gift.
Donathan, Donathon

Donato (Italian) gift.
Dodek, Donatello, Donati, Donatien, Donatus

Donavan (Irish) a form of Donovan.
Donaven, Donavin, Donavon, Donavyn

Dondre (French) a form of Deandre.
Dondra, Dondrae, Dondray, Dondré, Dondrea

Dong (Vietnamese) easterner.
Duong

Dong-Sun (Korean) eastern integrity.

Dong-Yul (Korean) eastern passion.

Donkor (Akan) humble.

Donnell B (Irish) brave; dark.
Doneal, Donel, Donele, Donell, Donelle, Doniel, Donielle, Donnel, Donnele, Donnelle, Donnelly, Donniel, Donyel, Donyell

Donnelly (Irish) a form of Donnell.
Donelly, Donlee, Donley

Donnie, Donny B (Irish) familiar forms of Donald.

Donovan (Irish) dark warrior.
Dohnovan, Donavan, Donevan, Donevon, Donivan, Donnivan, Donnovan, Donnoven, Donoven, Donovin, Donovon, Donvan

Dontae, Donté (American) forms of Dante.
Donta, Dontai, Dontao, Dontate, Dontavious, Dontavius, Dontay, Dontaye, Dontea, Dontee, Dontez

Donte B (Latin) a form of Donata (see Girls' Names).

Dontrell B (American) a form of Dantrell.
Dontral, Dontrall, Dontray, Dontre, Dontreal, Dontrel, Dontrelle, Dontriel, Dontriell

Donzell (Cornish) a form of Denzell.
Donzeil, Donzel, Donzelle, Donzello

Dooley (Irish) dark hero.
Dooly

Dopi (Pohnpeian) a form of Tobias.

Dopias (Pohnpeian) a form of Tobias.

Dor (Hebrew) generation.

Doran (Greek, Hebrew) gift. (Irish) stranger; exile.
Dore, Dorin, Dorran, Doron, Dorren, Dory

Dorian B (Greek) from Doris, Greece. See also Isidore.
Dore, Dorey, Dorie, Dorien, Dorin, Dorion, Dorján, Doron, Dorrian, Dorrien, Dorrin, Dorrion, Dorron, Dorryen, Dory

Doroteo (Greek) gift of God.

Dorrell (Scottish) king's doorkeeper. See also Durell.
Dorrel, Dorrelle

Dositeo (Greek) God's possession.

Dotan (Hebrew) law.
Dothan

Doug (Scottish) a short form of Dougal, Douglas.
Dougie, Dougy, Dugey, Dugie, Dugy

Dougal (Scottish) dark stranger. See also Doyle.
Doug, Dougall, Dugal, Dugald, Dugall, Dughall

Douglas **B** (Scottish) dark river, dark stream. See also Koukalaka.
Doug, Douglass, Dougles, Dugaid, Dughlas

Dov (Yiddish) bear. (Hebrew) a familiar form of David.
Dovid, Dovidas, Dowid

Dovev (Hebrew) whisper.

Dow (Irish) dark haired.

Doyle (Irish) a form of Dougal.
Doy, Doyal, Doyel

Drago (Italian) a form of Drake.

Drake **B** (English) dragon; owner of the inn with the dragon trademark.
Drago

Draper (English) fabric maker.
Dray, Draypr

Draven **B** (American) a combination of the letter D + Raven.
Dravian, Dravin, Dravion, Dravon, Dravone, Dravyn, Drayven, Drevon

Dreng (Norwegian) hired hand; brave.

Dreshawn (American) a combination of Drew + Shawn.
Dreshaun, Dreshon, Dreshown

Drevon (American) a form of Draven.
Drevan, Drevaun, Dreven, Drevin, Drevion, Drevone

Drew **B** (Welsh) wise. (English) a short form of Andrew.
Drewe, Dru

Dru (English) a form of Drew.
Druan, Drud, Drue, Drugi, Drui

Drummond (Scottish) druid's mountain.
Drummund, Drumond, Drumund

Drury (French) loving. Geography: Drury Lane is a street in London's theater district.

Dryden (English) dry valley.
Dry

Du (Vietnamese) play.

Duan (Chinese) upright.

Duane **B** (Irish) a form of Dwayne.
Deune, Duain, Duaine, Duana

Duardo (Spanish) prosperous guardian.

Duarte (Portuguese) rich guard. See also Edward.

Duc (Vietnamese) moral.
Duoc, Duy

Duck-Hwan (Korean) integrity returns.

Duck-Young (Korean) integrity lasts.

Dudd (English) a short form of Dudley.
Dud, Dudde, Duddy

Dudley (English) common field.
Dudd, Dudly

Dudus (Chamorro) flirtatious; handsome.

Due (Vietnamese) virtuous.

Duer (Scottish) heroic.

Duff (Scottish) dark.
Duffey, Duffie, Duffy

Dugan (Irish) dark.
Doogan, Dougan, Douggan, Duggan

Duilio (Latin) ready to fight.

Duke (French) leader; duke.
Dukey, Dukie, Duky

Dukker (Gypsy) fortuneteller.

Dulani (Nguni) cutting.

Dulcidio (Latin) sweet.

Dumaka (Ibo) helping hand.

Duman (Turkish) misty, smoky.

Duncan (Scottish) brown warrior.
Literature: King Duncan was
Macbeth's victim in Shakespeare's
play *Macbeth*.
Dunc, Dunn

Dung (Vietnamese) bravery.

Dunham (Scottish) brown.

Dunixi (Basque) a form of Dionysus.

Dunley (English) hilly meadow.

Dunlop (Scottish) muddy hill.

Dunmore (Scottish) fortress on the
hill.

Dunn (Scottish) a short form of
Duncan.
Dun, Dune, Dunne

Dunstan (English) brownstone
fortress.
Dun, Dunston

Dunton (English) hill town.

Duo (Chinese) much, many; more.

Dur (Hebrew) stacked up. (English) a
short form of Durwin.

Durand (Latin) a form of Durant.

Durant (Latin) enduring.
Duran, Durance, Durand, Durante,
Durontae, Durrant

Durell (Scottish, English) king's
doorkeeper. See also Dorrell.
Durel, Durial, Durreil, Durrell, Durrelle

Durko (Czech) a form of George.

Durriken (Gypsy) fortuneteller.

Durril (Gypsy) gooseberry.
Durrel, Durrell

Durward (English) gatekeeper.
Dur, Ward

Durwin (English) a form of Darwin.

Dushawn (American) a combination
of the prefix Du + Shawn.
Dusan, Dusean, Dushan, Dushane,
Dushaun, Dushon, Dushun

Dustin 🅱 (German) valiant fighter.
(English) brown rock quarry.
Dust, Dustain, Dustan, Dusten, Dustie,
Dustine, Dustion, Duston, Dusty,
Dustyn, Dustynn

Dusty 🅱 (English) a familiar form
of Dustin.

Dustyn (English) a form of Dustin.

Dutch (Dutch) from the
Netherlands; from Germany.

Duval (French) a combination of the
prefix Du + Val.
Duvall, Duveuil

Dwaun (American) a form of Dajuan.
Dwan, Dwaunn, Dwawn, Dwon,
Dwuann

Dwayne **B** (Irish) dark. See also
Dewayne.
*Dawayne, Dawyne, Duane, Duwain,
Duwan, Duwane, Duwayn, Duwayne,
Dwain, Dwaine, Dwan, Dwane,
Dwyane, Dywan, Dywane, Dywayne,
Dywone*

Dwight (English) a form of DeWitt.

Dyami (Native American) soaring
eagle.

Dyer (English) fabric dyer.

Dyke (English) dike; ditch.
Dike

Dylan ☆ **B** (Welsh) sea. See also
Dillon.
*Dylane, Dylann, Dylen, Dylian, Dylin,
Dyllan, Dyllen, Dyllian, Dyllin, Dyllyn,
Dylon, Dylyn*

Dylon (Welsh) a form of Dylan.
Dyllion, Dyllon

Dyonis (German) a form of Dionisio.

Dyre (Norwegian) dear heart.

Dyson (English) a short form of
Dennison.
Dysen, Dysonn

E

E **G** (American) an initial used as a
first name.

Ea (Irish) a form of Hugh.

Eachan (Irish) horseman.

Eadberto (Teutonic) outstanding for
his riches.

Eagan (Irish) very mighty.
Egan, Egon

Eamon (Irish) a form of Edmond,
Edmund.
Aimon, Eammon, Eamonn

Ean (English) a form of Ian.
*Eaen, Eann, Eayon, Eion, Eon, Eyan,
Eyon*

Earl (Irish) pledge. (English)
nobleman.
*Airle, Earld, Earle, Earlie, Earlson,
Early, Eorl, Erl, Erle, Errol*

Earnest (English) a form of Ernest.
Earn, Earnesto, Earnie, Eranest

Easton (English) eastern town.
Eason, Easten, Eastin, Eastton

Eaton (English) estate on the river.
Eatton, Eton, Eyton

Eb (Hebrew) a short form of Ebenezer.
Ebb, Ebbie, Ebby

Eben (Hebrew) rock.
Eban, Ebin, Ebon

Ebenezer (Hebrew) foundation
stone. Literature: Ebenezer Scrooge
is a miserly character in Charles
Dickens's *A Christmas Carol*.
*Eb, Ebbaneza, Eben, Ebeneezer,
Ebeneser, Ebenezar, Eveneser*

Eberhard (German) courageous as a
boar. See also Everett.
*Eber, Ebere, Eberardo, Eberhardt,
Evard, Everard, Everardo, Everhardt,
Everhart*

Ebisu (Japanese) god of labor and luck.

Ebner (English) a form of Abner.

Ebo (Fante) born on Tuesday.

Ebony **G** (Greek) a hard, dark wood.

Echa (Chamorro) to give blessing.

Echu (Chamorro) completed.

Ecio (Latin) possessor of great strength.

Eco (Greek) sound, resonance.

Ed (English) a short form of Edgar, Edsel, Edward.
Edd

Edan (Scottish) fire.
Edain

Edbert (English) wealthy; bright.
Ediberto

Edberto (Germanic) he whose blade makes him shine.

Edco (Greek) he who blows with force.

Eddie (English) a familiar form of Edgar, Edsel, Edward.
Eddee, Eddy, Edi, Edie

Eddy 🅱 (English) a form of Eddie.
Eddye, Edy

Edel (German) noble.
Adel, Edell, Edelmar, Edelweiss

Edelberto (Teutonic) descendant of nobles.

Edelio (Greek) person who always remains young.

Edelmiro (Germanic) celebrated for the nobility that he represents.

Eden 🅶 (Hebrew) delightful. Bible: the garden that was first home to Adam and Eve.
Eaden, Eadin, Edan, Edenson, Edin, Edyn, Eiden

Edeng (Palauan) shark.

Eder (Hebrew) flock.
Ederick, Edir

Edgar 🅱 (English) successful spearman. See also Garek, Gerik, Medgar.
Ed, Eddie, Edek, Edgard, Edgardo, Edgars

Edgardo (Spanish) a form of Edgar.

Edigar (Pohnpeian) a form of Edgardo.

Edilio (Greek) he who is like a statue.

Edipo (Greek) he who has swollen feet.

Edison (English) son of Edward.
Eddison, Edisen, Edson

Edmond (English) a form of Edmund.
Eamon, Edmon, Edmonde, Edmondo, Edmondson, Esmond

Edmund (English) prosperous protector.
Eadmund, Eamon, Edmand, Edmaund, Edmond, Edmun, Edmundo, Edmunds

Edmundo (Spanish) a form of Edmund.
Edmando, Mundo

Edo (Czech) a form of Edward.

Edoardo (Italian) a form of Edward.

Edorta (Basque) a form of Edward.

Edouard (French) a form of Edward.
Édoard, Édouard

Edric (English) prosperous ruler.
Eddric, Eddrick, Ederick, Edrek, Edrice, Edrick, Edrico

Edsel (English) rich man's house.
Ed, Eddie, Edsell

Edson (English) a short form of Edison.
Eddson, Edsen

Eduardo 🅱 (Spanish) a form of Edward.
Estuardo, Estvardo

Edur (Basque) snow.

Edward (English) prosperous guardian. See also Audie, Duarte, Ekewaka, Ned, Ted, Teddy.
Ed, Eddie, Edik, Edko, Edo, Edoardo, Edorta, Édouard, Eduard, Eduardo,

Edus, Edvard, Edvardo, Edwardo, Edwards, Edwy, Edzio, Ekewaka, Etzio, Ewart

Edwin B (English) prosperous friend. See also Ned, Ted.
Eadwinn, Edik, Edlin, Eduino, Edwan, Edwen, Edwon, Edwyn

Efrain (Hebrew) fruitful.
Efran, Efrane, Efrayin, Efren, Efrian, Eifraine

Efraín (Hebrew) a form of Efrain.

Efrat (Hebrew) honored.

Efreín, Efrén (Spanish) a form of Efraín.

Efrem (Hebrew) a short form of Ephraim.
Efe, Efraim, Efrim, Efrum

Efren (Hebrew) a form of Efrain, Ephraim.

Egan (Irish) ardent, fiery.
Egann, Egen, Egon

Egbert (English) bright sword. See also Bert, Bertie.

Egerton (English) Edgar's town.
Edgarton, Edgartown, Edgerton, Egeton

Egidio (Greek) he who, in battle, carries the goatskin sword.

Egil (Norwegian) awe inspiring.
Eigil

Eginhard (German) power of the sword.
Eginhardt, Einhard, Einhardt, Enno

Egisto (Greek) raised on goat's milk.

Egon (German) formidable.

Egor (Russian) a form of George. See also Igor, Yegor.

Ehnos (Pohnpeian) a form of Enos.

Ehpel (Pohnpeian) a form of Abel.

Ehren (German) honorable.

Eiichi (Japanese) excellent first son.

Eiji (Japanese) excellent second son.

Eijiro (Japanese) splendid next son.

Eikki (Finnish) ever powerful.

Eileen G (Irish) a form of Helen.

Einar (Scandinavian) individualist.
Ejnar, Inar

Eion (Irish) a form of Ean, Ian.
Eann, Eian, Ein, Eine, Einn

Eisaku (Japanese) eternal creation; witty creation; flourishing creation.

Eitan (Hebrew) a form of Ethan.
Eita, Eithan, Eiton

Eitaro (Japanese) big, tall man; witty big man; prosperous man.

Eito (Japanese) prosperous person.

Ejau (Ateso) we have received.

Ekewaka (Hawaiian) a form of Edward.

Ekit (Chuukese) a form of Ekitekit.

Ekitekit (Chuukese) to strive for.

Ekon (Nigerian) strong.

Eladio (Greek) he who came from Greece.

Elam (Hebrew) highlands.

Elan (Hebrew) tree. (Native American) friendly.
Elann

Elbert (English) a form of Albert.
Elberto

Elbio (Celtic) he who comes from the mountain.

Elchanan (Hebrew) a form of John.
Elchan, Elchonon, Elhanan, Elhannan

Elden (English) a form of Alden, Aldous.
Eldan, Eldin

Elder (English) dweller near the elder trees.

Eldon (English) holy hill.

Eldred (English) a form of Aldred.
Eldrid

Eldridge (English) a form of Aldrich.
El, Eldred, Eldredge, Eldrege, Eldrid, Eldrige, Elric

Eldwin (English) a form of Aldwin.
Eldwinn, Eldwyn, Eldwynn

Eleanor 🄶 (Greek) light.

Eleazar (Hebrew) God has helped. See also Lazarus.
Elazar, Elazaro, Eleasar, Eléazar, Eliazar, Eliezer

Eleazaro (Hebrew) God will help me.

Elek (Hungarian) a form of Alec, Alex.
Elec, Elic, Elik

Elenio (Greek) he who shines like the sun.

Eleno (Spanish) bright.

Eleodoro (Greek) he who comes from the sun.

Eleuterio (Greek) he who enjoys liberty for being honest.

Elevuka (Fijian) from Levuka.

Elger (German) a form of Alger.
Elger, Ellgar, Ellger

Elgin (English) noble; white.
Elgan, Elgen

Eli ☆ 🄱 (Hebrew) uplifted. A short form of Elijah, Elisha. Bible: the high priest who trained the prophet Samuel. See also Elliot.
Elie, Elier, Ellie, Eloi, Eloy, Ely

Elia 🄶 (Zuni) a short form of Elijah.
Eliah, Elio, Eliya, Elya

Elian (English) a form of Elijah. See also Trevelyan.
Elion

Elias (Greek) a form of Elijah.
Elia, Eliasz, Elice, Eliyas, Ellias, Ellice, Ellis, Elyas, Elyes

Elías (Hebrew) a form of Elias.

Eliazar (Hebrew) a form of Eleazar.
Eliasar, Eliazer, Elizar, Elizardo

Elido (Greek) native of Elida.

Elie (Hebrew) a form of Eli.

Eliecer (Hebrew) God is his constant aid.

Eliezer (Hebrew) a form of Eleazar.
Elieser

Eligio (Latin) he who has been elected by God.

Elihu (Hebrew) a short form of Eliyahu.
Elih, Eliu, Ellihu

Elijah ☆ 🄱 (Hebrew) a form of Eliyahu. Bible: a Hebrew prophet. See also Eli, Elisha, Elliot, Ilias, Ilya.
El, Elia, Elian, Elias, Elija, Elijha, Elijiah, Elijio, Elijuah, Elijuo, Elisjsha, Eliya, Eliyah, Ellis

Elika (Hawaiian) a form of Eric.

Eliki (Fijian) a form of Alejandro.

Elimas (Chuukese) crescent moon.

Elisabeth 🄶 (Hebrew) a form of Elizabeth.

Elisandro (Greek) liberator of men.

Eliseo (Hebrew) a form of Elisha.
Elisee, Elisée, Elisei, Elisiah, Elisio

Elisha **BG** (Hebrew) God is my salvation. Bible: a Hebrew prophet, successor to Elijah. See also Eli, Elijah.
Elijsha, Eliseo, Elish, Elishah, Elisher, Elishia, Elishua, Elysha, Lisha

Eliyahu (Hebrew) the Lord is my God.
Éliyahou, Elihu

Elizabeth **G** (Hebrew) consecrated to God

Elkan (Hebrew) God is jealous.
Elkana, Elkanah, Elkin, Elkins

Elki (Moquelumnan) hanging over the top.

Ella **G** (English) elfin; beautiful. (Greek) a short form of Eleanor.

Ellard (German) sacred; brave.
Allard, Ellerd

Ellery (English) from a surname derived from the name Hilary.
Ellary, Ellerey

Ellie **G** (Hebrew) a form of Eli.

Elliot, Elliott **B** (English) forms of Eli, Elijah.
Elio, Eliot, Eliott, Eliud, Eliut, Elliotte, Elyot, Elyott

Ellis **B** (English) a form of Elias (see Boys' Names).
Elis

Ellison (English) son of Ellis.
Elison, Ellson, Ellyson, Elson

Ellsworth (English) nobleman's estate.
Ellswerth, Elsworth

Elman (German) like an elm tree.
Elmen

Elmer (English) noble; famous.
Aylmer, Elemér, Ellmer, Elmir, Elmo

Elmo (Greek) lovable, friendly. (Italian) guardian. (Latin) a familiar form of Anselm. (English) a form of Elmer.

Elmore (English) moor where the elm trees grow.

Elong (Palauan) big talker, braggart.

Eloni (Fijian) oak.

Elonzo (Spanish) a form of Alonzo.
Elon, Élon, Elonso

Eloy (Latin) chosen.
Eloi

Elpidio (Greek) he who has hopes.

Elrad (Hebrew) God rules.
Rad, Radd

Elroy (French) a form of Delroy, Leroy.
Elroi

Elsdon (English) nobleman's hill.

Elston (English) noble's town.
Ellston

Elsu (Native American) swooping, soaring falcon.

Elsworth (English) noble's estate.

Elton (English) old town.
Alton, Eldon, Ellton, Elthon, Eltonia

Eluney (Mapuche) gift.

Elvern (Latin) a form of Alvern.
Elver, Elverne

Elvin (English) a form of Alvin.
El, Elvyn, Elwin, Elwyn, Elwynn

Elvio (Spanish) light skinned; blond.

Elvis (Scandinavian) wise.
El, Elviz, Elvys

Elvy (English) elfin warrior.

Elwell (English) old well.

Elwood (English) old forest. See also Wood, Woody.

Ely (Hebrew) a form of Eli. Geography: a region of England with extensive drained fens.
Elya, Elyie

Eman (Czech) a form of Emmanuel.
Emaney, Emani

Emanuel 🅱 (Hebrew) a form of Emmanuel.
Emaniel, Emannual, Emannuel, Emanual, Emanueal, Emanuele, Emanuell, Emanuelle

Emanueli (Fijian) a form of Manuel.

Emerenciano (Latin) to be deserving, to acquire the rights to something.

Emerson 🅱 (German, English) son of Emery.
Emmerson, Emreson

Emery 🅱 (German) industrious leader.
Aimery, Emari, Emarri, Emeri, Emerich, Emerio, Emmerich, Emmerie, Emmery, Emmo, Emory, Emrick, Emry, Inre, Imrich

Emesto (Spanish) serious.

Emeterio (Greek) he who deserves affection.

Emigdio (Greek) he who has brown skin.

Emiir, Emr (Arabic) forms of Amir.

Emil (Latin) flatterer. (German) industrious. See also Milko, Milo.
Aymil, Emiel, Émile, Emilek, Emiliano, Emilio, Emill, Emils, Emilyan, Emlyn

Emile 🅱 (French) a form of Émile.

Émile (French) a form of Emil.
Emiel, Emile, Emille

Emiliano (Italian) a form of Emil.
Emilian, Emilion

Emilien (Latin) friendly; industrious.

Emilio 🅱 (Italian, Spanish) a form of Emil.
Emielio, Emileo, Emilio, Emilios, Emillio, Emilo

Emillen (Latin) hard-working man.

Emily 🅶 (Latin) flatterer. (German) industrious.

Emir (Arabic) chief, commander.

Emlyn (Welsh) waterfall.
Emelen, Emlen, Emlin

Emma 🅶 (German) a short form of Emily.

Emmanuel 🅱 (Hebrew) God is with us. See also Immanuel, Maco, Mango, Manuel.
Eman, Emanuel, Emanuell, Emek, Emmahnuel, Emmanel, Emmaneuol, Emmanle, Emmanual, Emmanueal, Emmanuele, Emmanuell, Emmanuelle, Emmanuil, Enmanuel

Emmanuelle 🅶 (Hebrew) a form of Emmanuel.

Emmett (German) industrious; strong. (English) ant. History: Robert Emmett was an Irish patriot.
Em, Emet, Emett, Emitt, Emmet, Emmette, Emmitt, Emmot, Emmott, Emmy

Emmitt (German, English) a form of Emmett.
Emmit

Emory 🅱 (German) a form of Emery.
Amory, Emmory, Emorye

Emosi (Fijian) a form of Amos.

Emre (Turkish) brother.
Emra, Emrah, Emreson

Emrick (German) a form of Emery.
*Emeric, Emerick, Emric, Emrique,
Emryk*

Emul (Palauan) weeds.

En (Chinese) kindness.

Enap (Chuukese) powerful one.

Enapay (Sioux) brave appearance; he
appears.

Endre (Hungarian) a form of
Andrew.
Ender

Eneas (Greek) a form of Aeneas.
Eneias, Enné

Eneriko (Pohnpeian) a form of
Enrique.

Engelbert (German) bright as an
angel. See also Ingelbert.
Bert, Englebert

Engelberto (Germanic) shining of
the Anglos.

Enio (Spanish) second divinity of war.

Enlai (Chinese) thankful.

Enli (Dene) that dog over there.

Ennio (Italian) from the area of
Enna.

Ennis (Greek) mine. (Scottish) a form
of Angus.
Eni, Enni

Enoch (Hebrew) dedicated,
consecrated. Bible: the father of
Methuselah.
Enoc, Enock, Enok

Enol (Asturian) referring to lake
Enol.

Enon (Hebrew) very strong.

Enos (Hebrew) man.
Enosh

Enric (Romanian) a form of Henry.
Enrica

Enrick (Spanish) a form of Henry.
Enricky

Enrico (Italian) a form of Henry.
Enzio, Enzo, Rico

Enrikos (Greek) a form of Henry.

Enrique (Spanish) a form of Henry.
See also Quiqui.
Enrigué, Enriqué, Enriquez, Enrrique

Enunaurois (Palauan) facing a
mountain.

Enver (Turkish) bright; handsome.

Enyeto (Native American) walks like
a bear.

Enzi (Swahili) powerful.

Eoin (Welsh) a form of Evan.

Eparama (Fijian) a form of
Abraham.

Epel, Epeli (Chuukese) forms of
Abel.

Epenisa (Fijian) a form of Ebenezer.

Ephraim (Hebrew) fruitful. Bible: the
second son of Joseph.
*Efraim, Efrayim, Efrem, Efren,
Ephraen, Ephrain, Ephram, Ephrem,
Ephriam*

Epicuro (Greek) he who helps.

Epifanio (Greek) he who gives off
brilliance because of his form.

Epimachus (Palauan) a form of
Epimaco.

Epimaco (Greek) easy to attack, easy
to wipe out.

Epineri (Fijian) a form of Abner.

Epipanio (Pohnpeian) a form of
Epifanio.

Eponu (Chuukese) a navigator.

Epreim (Pohnpeian) a form of Efren.

Epulef (Mapuche) two races, two
quick trips.

Er (Chinese) son.

Eraclio (Spanish) a form of Heraclio.

Eradio (Chuukese) a form of Eladio.

Erardo (Greek) he who is the guest
of honor, to whom homage is paid.

Erasmus (Greek) lovable.
Érasme, Erasmo, Rasmus

Erastus (Greek) beloved.
Éraste, Erastious, Ras, Rastus

Erato (Greek) kind, pleasant.

Erbert (German) a short form of
Herbert.
Ebert, Erberto

Ercole (Italian) splendid gift.

Erek (Scandinavian) a form of Eric.
Erec

Erhard (German) strong; resolute.
Erhardt, Erhart

Eri (Teutonic) vigilant.

Eriberto (Italian) a form of Herbert.
Erberto, Heriberto

Eric ☀ **B** (Scandinavian) ruler of
all. (English) brave ruler. (German)
a short form of Frederick. History:
Eric the Red was a Norwegian
explorer who founded Greenland's
first colony.
*Aric, Ehrich, Elika, Erek, Éric, Ericc,
Erich, Erick, Erico, Erik, Erikur, Erric,
Eryc, Rick*

Erica **G** (Scandinavian) a form of
Eric.

Erich (Czech, German) a form of Eric.

Erick (English) a form of Eric.
Errick, Eryck

Erickson (English) son of Eric.
*Erickzon, Erics, Ericson, Ericsson,
Erikson, Erikzzon, Eriqson*

Erik **B** (Scandinavian) a form of
Eric.
*Erek, Erike, Eriks, Erikur, Errick, Errik,
Eryk*

Erika **G** (Scandanavian) a form of
Erica.

Eriki (Fijian) a form of Eric.

Erikur (Icelandic) a form of Eric,
Erik.

Erin **G** (Irish) peaceful. History: an
ancient name for Ireland.
*Erine, Erinn, Erino, Eron, Errin, Eryn,
Erynn*

Erland (English) nobleman's land.
Erlend

Erling (English) nobleman's son.

Ermanno (Italian) a form of Herman.
Erman

Ermano (Spanish) a form of
Herman.
Ermin, Ermine, Erminio, Ermon

Ermelindo (Teutonic) offers sacrifices
to God.

Ermino (Spanish) a form of Erminia
(see Girls' names).

Erminoldo (Germanic) government
of strength.

Ernest (English) earnest, sincere. See
also Arno.
*Earnest, Ernestino, Ernesto, Ernestus,
Ernie, Erno, Ernst*

Ernesto (Spanish) a form of Ernest.
Ernester, Neto

Ernie (English) a familiar form of
Ernest.
Earnie, Erney, Erny

Erno (Hungarian) a form of Ernest.
Ernö

Ernst (German) a form of Ernest.
Erns

Erol (Turkish) strong, courageous.
Eroll

Eron (Irish) a form of Erin.
Erran, Erren, Errion, Erron

Eros (Greek) love.

Errando (Basque) bold.

Errol (Latin) wanderer. (English) a
form of Earl.
Erol, Erold, Erroll, Erryl

Erroman (Basque) from Rome.

Erskine (Scottish) high cliff.
(English) from Ireland.
Ersin, Erskin, Kinny

Erungel (Palauan) for good.

Ervin, Erwin (English) sea friend.
Forms of Irving, Irwin.
*Earvin, Erv, Erven, Ervyn, Erwan,
Erwinek, Erwinn, Erwyn, Erwynn*

Ervine (English) a form of Irving.
Erv, Ervin, Ervince, Erving, Ervins

Ervino (Germanic) he who is
consistent with honors.

Eryn **G** (Irish) a form of Erin.

Esang (Palauan) spider conch; nosy.

Esau (Hebrew) rough; hairy. Bible:
Jacob's twin brother.
Esaw

Esaú (Hebrew) a form of Esau.

Escipión (Latin) man who uses a
cane.

Escolástico (Latin) man who teaches
all that he knows.

Esculapio (Greek) doctor.

Esdanis (Pohnpeian) a form of
Estanislao.

Esekaia (Fijian) a form of Hezekiah.

Esequiel (Hebrew) a form of Ezekiel.

Eshkol (Hebrew) grape clusters.

Esi (Chuukese) sliced to make
thinner.

Eskiel (Chuukese) a form of
Ezequiel.

Eskil (Norwegian) god vessel.

Esleban (Hebrew) bearer of children.

Esmond (English) rich protector.

Esopo (Greek) he who brings good
luck.

Espartaco (Greek) he who plants.

Espen (Danish) bear of the gods.

Esprancio (Spanish) hope.

Essien (Ochi) sixth-born son.

Estanislao (Slavic) glory of his
village.

Estanislau (Slavic) glory.

Este (Italian) east.
Estes

Esteban (Spanish) crowned.

Estéban (Spanish) a form of
Stephen.
*Estabon, Esteben, Estefan, Estefano,
Estefen, Estephan, Estephen*

Estebe (Basque) a form of Stephen.

Estepan (Pohnpeian) a form of Esteban.

Estevan (Spanish) a form of Stephen.
Esteven, Estevon, Estiven

Estevao (Spanish) a form of Stephen.
Estevez

Estraton (Greek) man of the army.

Etcaro (Pohnpeian) a form of Edgardo.

Etelberto (Spanish) a form of Adalberto.

Eterio (Greek) as clean and pure as heaven.

Ethan ☙ **B** (Hebrew) strong; firm.
Eathan, Eathen, Eathon, Eeathen, Eitan, Etan, Ethaen, Ethe, Ethen, Ethian

Etienne **B** (French) a form of Stephen.

Étienne (French) a form of Stephen.
Etian, Etien, Étienn, Ettien

Etmont (Pohnpeian) a form of Edmundo.

Etongo (Chamorro) to search for knowledge.

Etsuo (Japanese) rejoicing man.

Ettore (Italian) steadfast.
Etor, Etore

Etu (Native American) sunny.

Etuate (Fijian) a form of Eduardo.

Eubulo (Greek) good counselor.

Eucario (Greek) gracious, generous.

Eucarpo (Greek) he who bears good fruit.

Euclid (Greek) intelligent. History: the founder of Euclidean geometry.

Eudoro (Greek) beautiful gift.

Eudoxio (Greek) good thought, he who is famous.

Eufemio (Greek) he who has a good reputation.

Eufrasio (Greek) he who uses words well, who is full of happiness.

Eufronio (Greek) having a good mind; he who makes others happy, who gives pleasure.

Eugen (German) a form of Eugene.

Eugene **B** (Greek) born to nobility. See also Ewan, Gene, Gino, Iukini, Jenö, Yevgenyi, Zenda.
Eoghan, Eugen, Eugéne, Eugeni, Eugenio, Eugenius, Evgeny, Ezven

Eugenio (Spanish) a form of Eugene.

Eulalio (Greek) good speaker.

Eulises (Latin) a form of Ulysses.

Eulogio (Greek) he who speaks well.

Eumenio (Greek) opportune, favorable; the kind-hearted one.

Eungel (Palauan) underneath.

Euniciano (Spanish) happy victory.

Euno (Greek) intellect, reason, understanding.

Eupilo (Greek) warmly welcomed.

Euprepio (Greek) decent, comfortable.

Eupsiquio (Greek) having a good soul; valiant.

Euquerio (Greek) sure handed.

Eurico (Germanic) prince to whom all pay homage.

Eusebio (Greek) with good feelings.

Eusiquio (Greek) a form of Eupsiquio.

Eustace (Greek) productive. (Latin) stable, calm. See also Stacey.
Eustache, Eustachius, Eustachy, Eustashe, Eustasius, Eustatius, Eustazio, Eustis, Eustiss

Eustacio, Eustasio (Greek) healthy and strong.

Eustaquio (Greek) he who has many heads of wheat.

Eustoquio (Greek) good marksman; a skillful man.

Eustorgio (Greek) well-loved.

Eustrato (Greek) good soldier.

Eutiquio (Greek) fortunate.

Eutrapio (Greek) returning; changing, transforming.

Eva **G** (Greek) a short form of Evangelina. (Hebrew) a form of Eve (see Girls' Names).

Evan ☀ **B** (Irish) young warrior. (English) a form of John. See also Bevan, Owen.
Eavan, Eoin, Ev, Evaine, Evann, Evans, Even, Evens, Evin, Evon, Evyn, Ewan, Ewen

Evando (Greek) he is considered a good man.

Evangelino (Greek) he who brings glad tidings.

Evangelos (Greek) a form of Andrew.
Evagelos, Evaggelos, Evangelo

Evaristo (Greek) excellent one.

Evelio (Hebrew) he who gives life.

Evelyn **G** (English) hazelnut.
Evelin

Evencio (Latin) successful.

Everardo (German) strong as a boar.
Everado

Everett **B** (English) a form of Eberhard.
Ev, Evered, Everet, Everette, Everhett, Everit, Everitt, Everrett, Evert, Evrett

Everley (English) boar meadow.
Everlea, Everlee

Everton (English) boar town.

Evgeny (Russian) a form of Eugene. See also Zhek.
Evgeni, Evgenij, Evgenyi

Evin (Irish) a form of Evan.
Evian, Evinn, Evins

Evodio (Greek) he who follows a good road.

Ewald (German) always powerful. (English) powerful lawman.

Ewan (Scottish) a form of Eugene, Evan. See also Keon.
Euan, Euann, Euen, Ewen, Ewhen

Ewert (English) ewe herder, shepherd.
Ewart

Ewing (English) friend of the law.
Ewin, Ewynn

Exavier (Basque) a form of Xavier.
Exaviar, Exavior, Ezavier

Exequiel (Hebrew) God is my strength.

Expedito (Latin) unencumbered, free of hindrances.

Exuperancio (Latin) he who is outstanding, excellent, superior.

Exuperio (Latin) he who exceeds expectations.

Eyota (Native American) great.

Ezekiel (Hebrew) strength of God. Bible: a Hebrew prophet. See also Haskel, Zeke.
Esequiel, Ezakeil, Ezéchiel, Ezeck, Ezeckiel, Ezeeckel, Ezekeial, Ezekeil, Ezekeyial, Ezekial, Ezekielle, Ezell, Ezequiel, Eziakah, Eziechiele

Ezequias (Hebrew) Yahweh is my strength.

Ezequías (Hebrew) one to whom God gave powers; the one has divine power.

Ezequiel (Hebrew) a form of Ezekiel.
Esequiel, Eziequel

Ezer (Hebrew) a form of Ezra.

Ezio (Latin) he who has a nose like an eagle.

Ezra 🅱 (Hebrew) helper; strong. Bible: a Jewish priest who led the Jews back to Jerusalem.
Esdras, Esra, Ezer, Ezera, Ezrah, Ezri, Ezry

Ezven (Czech) a form of Eugene.
Esven, Esvin, Ezavin, Ezavine

F

Fa (Chinese) beginning.

Faber (German) a form of Fabian.

Fabian 🅱 (Latin) bean grower.
Fabain, Fabayan, Fabe, Fabein, Fabek, Fabeon, Faber, Fabert, Fabi, Fabiano, Fabien, Fabin, Fabio, Fabion, Fabius, Fabiyan, Fabiyus, Fabyan, Fabyen, Faybian, Faybien

Fabián (Spanish) a form of Fabio.

Fabiano (Italian) a form of Fabian.
Fabianno, Fabio

Fabio (Latin) a form of Fabian. (Italian) a short form of Fabiano.
Fabbio

Fabrizio (Italian) craftsman.
Fabrice, Fabricio, Fabrizius

Fabron (French) little blacksmith; apprentice.
Fabre, Fabroni

Facundo (Latin) he who puts forth arguments that convince people.

Fadey (Ukrainian) a form of Thaddeus.
Faday, Faddei, Faddey, Faddy, Fade, Fadeyka, Fadie, Fady

Fadi (Arabic) redeemer.
Fadhi

Fadil (Arabic) generous.
Fadeel, Fadel

Fadrique (Spanish) a form of Federico.

Fagan (Irish) little fiery one.
Fagin

Fahd (Arabic) lynx.
Fahaad, Fahad

Fai (Chinese) beginning.

Fairfax (English) blond.
Fair, Fax

Faisal (Arabic) decisive.
Faisel, Faisil, Faisl, Faiyaz, Faiz, Faizal, Faize, Faizel, Faizi, Fasel, Fasil, Faysal, Fayzal, Fayzel

Faith 🅶 (English) faithful; fidelity.

Fakhir (Arabic) excellent.
Fahkry, Fakher

Fakih (Arabic) thinker; reader of the Koran.

Falaninug (Yapese) my thoughts are good.

Falco (Latin) falconer.
Falcon, Falk, Falke, Falken

Falito (Italian) a familiar form of Rafael, Raphael.

Falkner (English) trainer of falcons. See also Falco.
Falconer, Falconner, Faulconer, Faulconner, Faulkner

Fallon **G** (Irish) grandchild of the ruler.

Falthin (Yapese) good word.

Fan (Chinese) sail.

Fanathin (Yapese) silent word, sign language.

Fane (English) joyful, glad.
Fanes, Faniel

Fang (Chinese) wind.

Fantino (Latin) infant-like; innocent.

Fanuel (Hebrew) vision of God.

Faraji (Swahili) consolation.

Faraón (Egyptian) pharaoh; inhabitant of the grand palace.

Farid (Arabic) unique.

Faris (Arabic) horseman.
Faraz, Fares, Farhaz, Farice, Fariez, Farris

Farley (English) bull meadow; sheep meadow. See also Lee.
Fairlay, Fairlee, Fairleigh, Fairley, Fairlie, Far, Farlay, Farlee, Farleigh, Farlie, Farly, Farrleigh, Farrley

Farnell (English) fern-covered hill.
Farnall, Fernald, Fernall, Furnald

Farnham (English) field of ferns.
Farnam, Farnum, Fernham

Farnley (English) fern meadow.
Farnlea, Farnlee, Farnleigh, Farnly, Fernlea, Fernlee, Fernleigh, Fernley

Faro (Spanish) reference to the card game faro.

Faroh (Latin) a form of Pharaoh.

Farold (English) mighty traveler.

Farquhar (Scottish) dear.
Fark, Farq, Farquar, Farquarson, Farque, Farquharson, Farquy, Farqy

Farr (English) traveler.
Faer, Farran, Farren, Farrin, Farrington, Farron

Farrell (Irish) heroic; courageous.
Farrel, Farrill, Farryll, Ferrell

Farrow (English) piglet.

Farruco (Spanish) a form of Francis, Francisco.
Frascuelo

Faruq (Arabic) honest.
Farook, Farooq, Faroque, Farouk, Faruqh

Faste (Norwegian) firm.

Fastino (Kosraean) a form of Faustino.

Fath (Arabic) victor.

Fatin (Arabic) clever.

Fauac (Quechua) he who flies.

Fauacuaipa (Quechua) rooster in flight.

Faust (Latin) lucky, fortunate. History: the sixteenth-century German necromancer who inspired many legends.
Faustino, Faustis, Fausto, Faustus

Faustiniano (Latin) a form of Faustinus.

Faustino (Italian) a form of Faust.

Fausto (Italian) a form of Faust.

Favian (Latin) understanding.
Favain, Favio, Favyen

Faxon (German) long-haired.

Febe, Febo (Latin) he who shines, who stands out.

Federico (Italian, Spanish) a form of Frederick.
Federic, Federigo, Federoquito

Fedro (Greek) splendid man.

Fegorgor (Chamorro) one who gossips a lot.

Fegurgur (Chamorro) a form of Fegorgor.

Fei (Chinese) striking.

Feivel (Yiddish) God aids.

Feliks (Russian) a form of Felix.

Felipe ☆ (Spanish) a form of Philip.
Feeleep, Felipino, Felo, Filip, Filippo, Filips, Fillip, Flip

Felippo (Italian) a form of Philip.
Felip, Filippo, Lipp, Lippo, Pip, Pippo

Felis (Chamorro) happy.

Felisardo (Latin) valiant and skillful man.

Felix (Latin) fortunate; happy. See also Pitin.
Fee, Felic, Félice, Feliciano, Felicio, Felike, Feliks, Felo, Félix, Felizio, Phelix

Félix (Latin) a form of Felix.

Felton (English) field town.
Felten, Feltin

Felu (Chamorro) blade.

Feng (Chinese) handsome.

Fenton (English) marshland farm.
Fen, Fennie, Fenny, Fintan, Finton

Feo (Spanish) ugly.

Feodor (Slavic) a form of Theodore.
Dorek, Fedar, Fedinka, Fedor, Fedya, Fyodor

Feoras (Greek) smooth rock.

Ferdinand (German) daring, adventurous. See also Hernando.
Feranado, Ferd, Ferda, Ferdie, Ferdinánd, Ferdy, Ferdynand, Fernando, Nando

Ferenc (Hungarian) a form of Francis.
Feri, Ferke, Ferko

Feres (Chuukese) a form of Fares.

Fereti (Fijian) a form of Fred.

Fergus (Irish) strong; manly.
Fearghas, Fearghus, Feargus, Ferghus, Fergie, Ferguson, Fergusson

Fermin (French, Spanish) firm, strong.
Ferman, Firmin, Furman

Fermín (Spanish) a form of Fermin.

Fernán (Spanish) a form of Fernando.

Fernando (Spanish) a form of Ferdinand.
Ferando, Ferdinando, Ferdnando, Ferdo, Fernand, Fernandez, Fernendo

Feroz (Persian) fortunate.

Ferran (Arabic) baker.
Feran, Feron, Ferrin, Ferron

Ferrand (French) iron gray hair.
Farand, Farrand, Farrant, Ferrant

Ferrell (Irish) a form of Farrell.
Ferrel, Ferrill, Ferryl

Ferris (Irish) a form of Peter.
Fares, Faris, Fariz, Farris, Farrish, Feris, Ferriss

Fesongao (Chamorro) burning a lot.

Feta-plom (Mapuche) high and large plain.

Fiacro (Latin) soldier, combatant.

Fico (Spanish) a familiar form of Frederick.

Fidel (Latin) faithful. History: Fidel Castro was the Cuban revolutionary who overthrew a dictatorship in 1959 and established a communist regime in Cuba.
Fidele, Fidèle, Fidelio, Fidelis, Fidell, Fido

Fidencio (Latin) trusting; fearless, self-assured.

Field (English) a short form of Fielding.
Fields

Fielding (English) field; field worker.
Field

Fife (Scottish) from Fife, Scotland.
Fyfe

Fifi **G** (Fante) born on Friday.

Fiir (Yapese) that person.

Fil (Polish) a form of Phil.
Filipek

Filadelfo, Filademo (Greek) man who loves his brothers.

Filbert (English) brilliant. See also Bert.
Filberte, Filberto, Filiberto, Philbert

Fileas (Greek) he who loves deeply.

Fileberto (Yapese) a form of Philbert.

Filelio (Latin) he who is trustworthy.

Filemón (Greek) horse-lover; he who is spirited and friendly.

Filiberto (Spanish) a form of Filbert.

Filip (Greek) a form of Philip.
Filip, Filippo

Fillipp (Russian) a form of Philip.
Filip, Filipe, Filipek, Filips, Fill, Fillip, Filya

Filmore (English) famous.
Fillmore, Filmer, Fyllmer, Fylmer, Philmore

Filón (Greek) philosophical friend.

Filya (Russian) a form of Philip.

Finata (Chuukese) to decide.

Fineas (Irish) a form of Phineas.
Finneas

Fineto (Chuukese) spinning.

Finian (Irish) light skinned; white.
Finnen, Finnian, Fionan, Fionn, Phinean

Finisongsong (Chamorro) language of the village.

Finlay (Irish) blond-haired soldier.
Findlay, Findley, Finlea, Finlee, Finley, Finn, Finnlea, Finnley

Finn (German) from Finland. (Irish) blond haired; light skinned. A short form of Finlay. (Norwegian) from the Lapland.
Fin, Finnie, Finnis, Finny

Finnegan (Irish) light skinned; white.
Finegan

Finoho (Chamorro) my language.

Finoña (Chamorro) his language.

Fiorello (Italian) little flower.
Fiore

Firas (Arabic) persistent.

Firipo (Fijian) a form of Felipe.

Firman (French) firm; strong.
Ferman, Firmin

Firmino (Latin) firm, sure.

Firmo (Latin) morally and physically firm.

Firth (English) woodland.

Fischel (Yiddish) a form of Phillip.

Fiske (English) fisherman.
Fisk

Fitch (English) weasel, ermine.
Fitche

Fitelis (Chuukese) a form of Fidel.

Fito (Spanish) a form of Adolfo.

Fitz (English) son.
Filz

Fitzgerald (English) son of Gerald.

Fitzhugh (English) son of Hugh.
Hugh

Fitzpatrick (English) son of Patrick.

Fitzroy (Irish) son of Roy.

Fiu (Chuukese) a form of Pío.

Fiz (Latin) happy, fertile.

Flaminio (Spanish) Religion:
Marcantonio Flaminio coauthored
one of the most important texts of
the Italian Reformation.

Flann (Irish) redhead.
Flainn, Flannan, Flannery

Flavian (Latin) blond, yellow haired.
*Flavel, Flavelle, Flavien, Flavio,
Flawiusz*

Flaviano (Latin) belonging to the old
Roman family, Flavia; one of the
blonde ones.

Flavio (Italian) a form of Flavian.
Flabio, Flavious, Flavius

Fleming (English) from Denmark;
from Flanders.
Flemming, Flemmyng, Flemyng

Fletcher (English) arrow featherer,
arrow maker.
Flecher, Fletch

Flint (English) stream; flint stone.
Flynt

Flip (Spanish) a short form of Felipe.
(American) a short form of Philip.

Floreal (Latin) alludes to the eighth
month of the French Revolution.

Florencio (Italian) a form of Florent.

Florent (French) flowering.
*Florenci, Florencio, Florentin,
Florentino, Florentyn, Florentz,
Florinio, Florino*

Florente (Latin) to bloom.

Florian (Latin) flowering, blooming.
Florien, Florrian, Flory, Floryan

Florián (Latin) a form of Florian.

Floriano (Spanish) a form of Florian.

Florio (Spanish) a form of Florián.

Floyd 🅱 (English) a form of Lloyd.

Flurry (English) flourishing,
blooming.

Flynn (Irish) son of the red-haired
man.
Flin, Flinn, Flyn

Fo (Chinese) Buddha.

Focio (Latin) illuminated, shining.

Folke (German) a form of Volker.
Folker

Foluke (Yoruba) given to God.

Foma (Bulgarian, Russian) a form of
Thomas.
Fomka

Fonso (German, Italian) a short form
of Alphonso.
Fonzo

Fontaine (French) fountain.

Fonzie (German) a familiar form of
Alphonse.
Fons, Fonsie, Fonsy, Fonz

Forbes (Irish) prosperous.
Forbe

Ford (English) a short form of names ending in "ford."

Fordel (Gypsy) forgiving.

Forest **B** (French) a form of Forrest.
Forestt, Foryst

Forester (English) forest guardian.
Forrester, Forrie, Forry, Forster, Foss, Foster

Formerio (Latin) beauty.

Forrest **B** (French) forest; woodsman.
Forest, Forester, Forrestar, Forrester, Forrestt, Forrie

Fortino (Italian) fortunate, lucky.

Fortune (French) fortunate, lucky.
Fortun, Fortunato, Fortuné, Fortunio

Foster (Latin) a short form of Forester.

Fowler (English) trapper of wildfowl.

Fran **G** (Latin) a short form of Francis.
Franh

Frances **G** (Latin) a form of Francis.

Francesca **G** (Italian) a form of Frances.

Francesco (Italian) a form of Francis.

Franchot (French) a form of Francis.

Francis **B** (Latin) free; from France. Religion: Saint Francis of Assisi was the founder of the Franciscan order. See also Farruco, Ferenc.
Fran, France, Frances, Francesco, Franchot, Francisco, Franciskus, Franco, François, Frang, Frank, Frannie, Franny, Frans, Franscis, Fransis, Franta, Frantisek, Frants, Franus, Frantisek, Franz, Frencis

Francisco (Portuguese, Spanish) a form of Francis. See also Chilo, Cisco, Farruco, Paco, Pancho.
Franco, Fransisco, Fransysco, Frasco, Frisco

Franco (Latin) a short form of Francis.
Franko

François (French) a form of Francis.
Francoise

Frank (English) a short form of Francis, Franklin. See also Palani, Pancho.
Franc, Franck, Franek, Frang, Franio, Franke, Frankie, Franko

Frankie **B** (English) a familiar form of Frank.
Francky, Franke, Frankey, Franki, Franky, Franqui

Franklin **B** (English) free landowner.
Fran, Francklen, Francklin, Francklyn, Francylen, Frank, Frankin, Franklen, Franklinn, Franklyn, Franquelin

Franklyn (English) a form of Franklin.
Franklynn

Frans (Swedish) a form of Francis.
Frants

Frantisek (Czech) a form of Francis.
Franta

Franz (German) a form of Francis.
Fransz, Frantz, Franzen, Franzie, Franzin, Franzl, Franzy

Fraser **B** (French) strawberry. (English) curly haired.
Fraizer, Frasier, Fraze, Frazer, Frazier

Fraterno (Latin) relating to the brother.

Frayne (French) dweller at the ash tree. (English) stranger.
Fraine, Frayn, Frean, Freen, Freyne

Fred (German) a short form of Alfred, Frederick, Manfred.
Fredd, Fredde, Fredo, Fredson

Freddie 🅱 (German) a familiar form of Frederick.
Freddi, Freddy, Fredi, Fredy

Freddy, Fredy (German) familiar forms of Frederick.

Frederic (German) a form of Frederick.
Frédéric, Frederich, Frederric, Fredric, Fredrich

Frederick (German) peaceful ruler. See also Dick, Eric, Fico, Peleke, Rick.
Federico, Fico, Fred, Fredderick, Freddie, Freddrick, Freddy, Fredek, Frederic, Fréderick, Frédérick, Frederik, Frederique, Frederrick, Fredo, Fredrick, Fredwick, Fredwyck, Fredy, Friedrich, Fritz

Frederico (Spanish) a form of Frederick.
Fredrico, Frederigo

Frederik (German) a form of Frederick.
Frédérik, Frederrik, Fredrik

Frederique 🅶 (French) a form of Frederick.

Fredo (Spanish) a form of Fred.

Fredrick 🅱 (German) a form of Frederick.
Fredric, Fredricka, Fredricks

Freeborn (English) child of freedom.
Free

Freeman (English) free.
Free, Freedman, Freemin, Freemon, Friedman, Friedmann

Fremont (German) free; noble protector.

Fresco (Spanish) fresh.

Frewin (English) free; noble friend.
Frewen

Frey (English) lord. (Scandinavian) Mythology: the Norse god who dispenses peace and prosperity.

Frick (English) bold.

Fridolf (English) peaceful wolf.
Freydolf, Freydulf, Fridulf

Fridolino (Teutonic) he who loves peace.

Friedrich (German) a form of Frederick.
Friedel, Friedrick, Fridrich, Fridrick, Friedrike, Friedryk, Fryderyk

Frisco (Spanish) a short form of Francisco.

Fritz (German) a familiar form of Frederick.
Fritson, Fritts, Fritzchen, Fritzl

Froberto (Spanish) a form of Roberto.

Frode (Norwegian) wise.

Froilan (Teutonic) rich and beloved young master.

Froilán (Germanic) a form of Froilan.

Fronton (Latin) he who thinks.

Fructuoso (Latin) he who bears much fruit.

Frumencio (Latin) he who provides wheat.

Fu (Chinese) wealthy.

Fudo (Japanese) the god of fire and wisdom.

Fu-Hsi (Chinese) god of happiness, symbolized by a bat.

Fujikawa (Japanese) fruitful earth stream.

Fujita (Japanese) field.

Fukuo (Japanese) blessing hero.

Fukutaro (Japanese) big son blessing.

Fulberto (Germanic) he who shines amongst all in the village.

Fulbright (German) very bright.
Fulbert

Fulco (Spanish) village.

Fulgencio (Latin) he who shines and stands out because of his goodness.

Fuller (English) cloth thickener.

Fulton (English) field near town.

Fulu (Chamorro) to wrestle.

Fulvio (Latin) he who has reddish hair.

Fumihiko, Fumito (Japanese) he who writes or is a historian.

Fumihiro (Japanese) he who writes abundantly.

Fumio (Japanese) a great man about whom much has been written.

Fumitaka (Japanese) dutiful historian.

Fumiya (Japanese) he who will be a writer or historian.

Funsoni (Nguni) requested.

Fusao (Japanese) cluster of men.

Fuyuki (Japanese) winter; noble; precious.

Fyfe (Scottish) a form of Fife.
Fyffe

Fynn (Ghanaian) Geography: another name for the Offin River in Ghana.

Fyodor (Russian) a form of Theodore.

G

G **B** (American) an initial used as a first name.

Gabby (American) a familiar form of Gabriel.
Gabbi, Gabbie, Gabi, Gabie, Gaby

Gabe (Hebrew) a short form of Gabriel.

Gabibic (Chamorro) a form of Gabibig.

Gabibig (Chamorro) he who likes to whistle.

Gabino (American) a form of Gabriel.
Gabin, Gabrino

Gábor (Hungarian) God is my strength.
Gabbo, Gabko, Gabo

Gabrial (Hebrew) a form of Gabriel.
Gaberial, Gabrael, Gabraiel, Gabrail, Gabreal, Gabriael, Gabrieal, Gabryalle

Gabriel ✳ **B** (Hebrew) devoted to God. Bible: the angel of the Annunciation.
Gab, Gabe, Gabby, Gabino, Gabis, Gábor, Gabreil, Gabrel, Gabrell, Gabrial, Gabriël, Gabriele, Gabriell, Gabrielle, Gabrielli, Gabrile, Gabris, Gabryel, Gabys, Gavril, Gebereal, Ghabriel, Riel

Gabriela, Gabriella **G** (Italian) forms of Gabrielle.

Gabrielle **G** (Hebrew) a form of Gabriel.

Gabrielli (Italian) a form of Gabriel.
Gabriello

Gabrio (Spanish) God is my strength.

Gabryel 🅱 (Hebrew) a form of Gabriel.

Gachi (Chamorro) ax.

Gadao (Chamorro) the grouper fish.

Gadi (Arabic) God is my fortune.
Gad, Gaddy, Gadiel

Gadiña (Chamorro) he is catching fish at night with palm leaves.

Gaetan (Italian) from Gaeta, a region in southern Italy.
Gaetano, Gaetono

Gagandeep 🅱 (Sikh) sky's light.

Gage 🅱 (French) pledge.
Gager, Gaige, Gaje

Gago (Chamorro) lazy; ironwood tree.

Gaige (French) a form of Gage.

Gair (Irish) small.
Gaer, Gearr, Geir

Gaius (Latin) rejoicer. See also Cai.

Gakuto (Japanese) he who is from the mountain.

Galbraith (Irish) Scotsman in Ireland.
Galbrait, Galbreath

Gale (Greek) a short form of Galen.
Gael, Gail, Gaile, Gayle

Galeaso (Latin) he who is protected by the helmet.

Galen 🅱 (Greek) healer; calm.
(Irish) little and lively.
Gaelan, Gaelen, Gaelin, Gaelyn, Gailen, Galan, Gale, Galeno, Galin, Galyn, Gaylen

Galeno (Spanish) illuminated child.
(Greek, Irish) a form of Galen.

Galileo (Hebrew) he who comes from Galilee.

Gallagher (Irish) eager helper.

Galloway (Irish) Scotsman in Ireland.
Gallway, Galway

Galo (Latin) native of Galilee.

Galt (Norwegian) high ground.

Galton (English) owner of a rented estate.
Gallton

Galvin (Irish) sparrow.
Gal, Gall, Gallven, Gallvin, Galvan, Galven

Gamal (Arabic) camel. See also Jamal.
Gamall, Gamel, Gamil

Gamaliel (Hebrew) God is your reward.

Gamble (Scandinavian) old.

Gamelberto (Germanic) distinguished because of his advancing age.

Gan (Chinese) daring, adventurous.
(Vietnamese) near.

Gaña (Chamorro) to prefer.

Ganchu (Chamorro) hook; gaff.

Gandolfo (Germanic) valiant warrior.

Gang (Chinese) firm; strong.

Ganimedes (Spanish) he was the most beautiful of the mortals.

Gannon (Irish) light skinned, white.
Gannan, Gannen, Gannie, Ganny

Ganya 🅱🅶 (Zulu) clever.

Gao (Chinese) tall, high.

Gar (English) a short form of Gareth,
  Garnett, Garrett, Garvin.
  Garr

Garcia (Spanish) mighty with a spear.

García (Spanish) a form of Garcia.

Garcilaso (Spanish) a form of García.

Gardner (English) gardener.
  Gard, Gardener, Gardie, Gardiner,
  Gardy

Garek (Polish) a form of Edgar.

Garen (English) a form of Garry.
  Garan, Garen, Garin, Garion,
  Garon, Garyn, Garyon

Gareth (Welsh) gentle.
  Gar, Garith, Garreth, Garrith, Garth,
  Garyth

Garett **B** (Irish) a form of Garrett.
  Gared, Garet, Garette, Garhett,
  Garit, Garitt, Garritt

Garfield (English) field of spears;
  battlefield.

Garibaldo (Germanic) he who is
  bold with a lance.

Garland **B** (French) wreath of
  flowers; prize. (English) land of
  spears; battleground.
  Garlan, Garlen, Garllan, Garlund,
  Garlyn

Garman (English) spearman.
  Garmann, Garrman

Garner (French) army guard, sentry.
  Garnier

Garnett (Latin) pomegranate seed;
  garnet stone. (English) armed with
  a spear.
  Gar, Garnet, Garnie, Garrnett

Garnock (Welsh) dweller by the
  alder river.

Garrad (English) a form of Garrett.
  Gared, Garrard, Garred, Garrod,
  Gerred, Gerrid, Gerrod, Garrode,
  Jared

Garren, Garrin (English) forms of
  Garry.
  Garran, Garrion, Garron, Garyn,
  Gerren, Gerron, Gerryn

Garret (Irish) a form of Garrett.
  Garrit, Garyt, Gerret, Garrid, Gerrit,
  Gerrot

Garrett **B** (Irish) brave spearman.
  See also Jarrett.
  Gar, Gareth, Garett, Garrad, Garret,
  Garrette, Gerrett, Gerritt, Gerrott

Garrick (English) oak spear.
  Gaerick, Garek, Garick, Garik,
  Garreck, Garrek, Garric, Garrik,
  Garryck, Garryk, Gerreck, Gerrick

Garrison **B** (French) troops
  stationed at a fort; garrison.
  Garison, Garisson, Garris

Garroway (English) spear fighter.
  Garraway

Garry (English) a form of Gary.
  Garen, Garrey, Garri, Garrie,
  Garren, Garrin

Garson (English) son of Gar.

Garth (Scandinavian) garden, gardener.
  (Welsh) a short form of Gareth.

Garvey (Irish) rough peace.
  Garbhán, Garrvey, Garrvie, Garv,
  Garvan, Garvie, Garvy

Garvin (English) comrade in battle.
  Gar, Garvan, Garven, Garvyn,
  Garwen, Garwin, Garwyn, Garwynn

Garwood (English) evergreen forest.
  See also Wood, Woody.
  Garrwood

Gary 🅱 (German) mighty spearman.
(English) a familiar form of Gerald.
See also Kali.
Gare, Garey, Gari, Garry

Gaspar (French) a form of Casper.
*Gáspár, Gaspard, Gaspare,
Gaspari, Gasparo, Gasper, Gazsi*

Gaston (French) from Gascony,
France.
Gascon, Gastaun

Gastón (Germanic) a form of Gaston.

Gaudencio (Latin) he who is happy
and content.

Gaudioso (Latin) happy, joyful.

Gausberto (Germanic) Gothic
brightness.

Gaute (Norwegian) great.

Gautier (French) a form of Walter.
*Galtero, Gaulterio, Gaultier,
Gaultiero, Gauthier*

Gavin ✹ 🅱 (Welsh) white hawk.
*Gav, Gavan, Gaven, Gavinn,
Gavino, Gavn, Gavohn, Gavon,
Gavyn, Gavynn, Gawain*

Gavriel (Hebrew) man of God.
Gav, Gavi, Gavrel, Gavril, Gavy

Gavril (Russian) a form of Gavriel.
Ganya, Gavrilo, Gavrilushka

Gawain (Welsh) a form of Gavin.
*Gawaine, Gawayn, Gawayne,
Gawen, Gwayne*

Gaylen (Greek) a form of Galen.
Gaylin, Gaylinn, Gaylon, Gaylyn

Gaylord (French) merry lord; jailer.
*Gaillard, Gallard, Gay, Gayelord,
Gayler, Gaylor*

Gaynor (Irish) son of the fair-
skinned man.
*Gainer, Gainor, Gay, Gayner,
Gaynnor*

Ge (Chinese) standard; pattern.

Geary (English) variable, changeable.
Gearey, Gery

Gedeon (Bulgarian, French) a form
of Gideon.

Gedeón (Hebrew) a form of Gideon.

Geffrey (English) a form of Geoffrey.
See also Jeffrey.
Gefery, Geff, Geffery, Geffrard

Gelasio (Greek) cheerful and happy,
enjoys having fun.

Gellert (Hungarian) a form of
Gerald.

Gemelo (Latin) fraternal twin.

Geminiano (Latin) identical twin.

Gen (Chinese) root; base.

Gena 🅶 (Russian) a short form of
Yevgenyi.
Genka, Genya, Gine

Genaro (Latin) consecrated to God.
Genereo, Genero, Gennaro

Gendo, Genji, Genku (Japanese)
literary figures.

Gene 🅱 (Greek) a short form of
Eugene.
Genek

Genek (Polish) a form of Gene.

Generos, Generoso (Spanish)
generous.

Genesis 🅶 (Latin) origin; birth.

Genevieve 🅶 (German, French) a
form of Guinevere (see Girls'
Names).

Geng (Chinese) honest, just.

Genjiro (Japanese) good source.

Genkei (Japanese) source of reverence.

Genkichi (Japanese) fortunate source.

Genmei (Japanese) historical figure.

Geno (Italian) a form of John. A short form of Genovese.
Genio, Jeno

Genovese (Italian) from Genoa, Italy.
Geno, Genovis

Gent (English) gentleman.
Gentle, Gentry

Genty (Irish, English) snow.

Geoff (English) a short form of Geoffrey.

Geoffery (English) a form of Geoffrey.
Geofery

Geoffrey (English) a form of Jeffrey. See also Giotto, Godfrey, Gottfried, Jeff.
Geffrey, Geoff, Geoffery, Geoffre, Geoffrie, Geoffroi, Geoffroy, Geoffry, Geofrey, Geofri, Gofery

Geordan (Scottish) a form of Gordon.
Geordann, Geordian, Geordin, Geordon

Geordie (Scottish) a form of George.
Geordi, Geordy

Georg (Scandinavian) a form of George.

George (Greek) farmer. See also Durko, Egor, Iorgos, Jerzy, Jiri, Joji, Jörg, Jorge, Jorgen, Joris, Jorrín, Jur, Jurgis, Keoki, Mahiái, Semer, Yegor, Yorgos, Yoyi, Yrjo, Yuri, Zhora.
Geordie, Georg, Georgas, Georges, Georget, Georgi, Georgii, Georgio, Georgios, Georgiy, Georgy, Gevork, Gheorghe, Giorgio, Giorgos, Goerge, Goran, Gordios, Gorge, Gorje, Gorya, Grzegorz, Gyorgy

Georges (French) a form of George.
Geórges

Georgia **G** (Greek) a form of George.

Georgio (Italian) a form of George.

Georgios (Greek) a form of George.
Georgious, Georgius

Georgy (Greek) a familiar form of George.
Georgie

Geovanni, Geovanny (Italian) forms of Giovanni.
Geovan, Geovani, Geovanne, Geovannee, Geovannhi, Geovany

Geraint (English) old.

Gerald **B** (German) mighty spearman. See also Fitzgerald, Jarell, Jarrell, Jerald, Jerry, Kharald.
Garald, Garold, Garolds, Gary, Gearalt, Gellert, Gérald, Geralde, Geraldo, Gerale, Geraud, Gerek, Gerick, Gerik, Gerold, Gerrald, Gerrell, Gérrick, Gerrild, Gerrin, Gerrit, Gerrold, Gerry, Geryld, Giraldo, Giraud, Girauld

Geraldo (Italian, Spanish) a form of Gerald.

Gerard (English) brave spearman. See also Jerard, Jerry.
Garrard, Garrat, Garratt, Gearard, Gerad, Gerar, Gérard, Gerardo, Geraro, Géraud, Gerd, Gerek, Gerhard, Gerrard, Gerrit, Gerry, Girard

Gerardo **B** (Spanish) a form of Gerard.
Gherardo

Gerasimo (Greek) award, recompense.

Géraud (French) a form of Gerard.
Gerrad, Gerraud

Gerbrando (Germanic) sword.

Gerek (Polish) a form of Gerard.

Geremia (Hebrew) exalted by God.
(Italian) a form of Jeremiah.

Geremiah (Italian) a form of
Jeremiah.
Geremia, Gerimiah, Geromiah

Gerhard (German) a form of Gerard.
*Garhard, Gerhardi, Gerhardt,
Gerhart, Gerhort*

Gerik (Polish) a form of Edgar.
Geric, Gerick

Germain (French) from Germany.
(English) sprout, bud. See also
Jermaine.
*Germaine, German, Germane,
Germano, Germayn, Germayne*

Germán (Germanic) male warrior.

Germinal (Latin) he who sprouts.

Geroldo (Germanic) commander of
the lance.

Gerome (English) a form of Jerome.

Geronimo (Greek, Italian) a form of
Jerome. History: a famous Apache
chief.
Geronemo

Gerónimo (Greek) a form of
Geronimo.

Gerrit (Dutch) a form of Gerald.

Gerry (English) a familiar form of
Gerald, Gerard. See also Jerry.
Geri, Gerre, Gerri, Gerrie, Gerryson

Gershom (Hebrew) exiled. (Yiddish)
stranger in exile.
*Gersham, Gersho, Gershon, Gerson,
Geurson, Gursham, Gurshan*

Gerson (English) son of Gar.
Gersan, Gershawn

Gert (German, Danish) fighter.

Gervaise 🆖 (French) honorable. See
also Jervis.
*Garvais, Garvaise, Garvey, Gervais,
Gervase, Gervasio, Gervaso,
Gervayse, Gervis, Gerwazy*

Gerwin (Welsh) fair love.

Gesualdo (Germanic) prisoner of the
king.

Gethin (Welsh) dusky.
Geth

Getulio (Latin) he who came from
Getulia in the northern region of
Africa.

Ghazi (Arabic) conqueror.

Ghilchrist (Irish) servant of Christ.
See also Gil.
*Gilchrist, Gilcrist, Gilie, Gill, Gilley,
Gilly*

Ghislain (French) pledge.

Gi (Korean) brave.

Gia (Vietnamese) family.

Giacinto (Portuguese, Spanish) a
form of Jacinto.
Giacintho

Giacomo (Italian) a form of Jacob.
*Gaimo, Giacamo, Giaco, Giacobbe,
Giacobo, Giacopo*

Gian (Italian) a form of Giovanni,
John.
*Gianetto, Giann, Gianne, Giannes,
Gianni, Giannis, Giannos, Ghian*

Giancarlo (Italian) a combination of
John + Charles.
Giancarlos, Gianncarlo

Giang (Vietnamese) river.

Gianluca (Italian) a combination of
John + Lucas.

Gianni (Italian) a form of Johnny.
Giani, Gionni

Gianpaolo (Italian) a combination of John + Paul.
Gianpaulo

Giao (Vietnamese) to pass.

Gib (English) a short form of Gilbert.
Gibb, Gibbie, Gibby

Gibor (Hebrew) powerful.

Gibson (English) son of Gilbert.
Gibbon, Gibbons, Gibbs, Gillson, Gilson

Gideon (Hebrew) tree cutter. Bible: the judge who defeated the Midianites.
Gedeon, Gideone, Gidon, Hedeon

Gidon (Hebrew) a form of Gideon.

Gifford (English) bold giver.
Giff, Giffard, Gifferd, Giffie, Giffy

Gig (English) horse-drawn carriage.

Giichi (Japanese) righteous first son.

Gil (Greek) shield bearer. (Hebrew) happy. (English) a short form of Ghilchrist, Gilbert.
Gili, Gill, Gilli, Gillie, Gillis, Gilly

Gilad (Arabic) camel hump; from Giladi, Saudi Arabia.
Giladi, Gilead

Gilamu (Basque) a form of William.
Gillen

Gilbert (English) brilliant pledge; trustworthy. See also Gil, Gillett.
Gib, Gilberto, Gilburt, Giselbert, Giselberto, Giselbertus, Guilbert

Gilberto (Spanish) a form of Gilbert.

Gilby (Scandinavian) hostage's estate. (Irish) blond boy.
Gilbey, Gillbey, Gillbie, Gillby

Gilchrist (Irish) a form of Ghilchrist.

Gildo (Spanish) a form of Hermenegildo.

Gilen (Basque, German) illustrious pledge.

Giles (French) goatskin shield.
Gide, Gilles, Gyles

Gillean (Irish) Bible: Saint John's servant.
Gillan, Gillen, Gillian

Gillermo (Spanish) resolute protector.

Gillespie (Irish) son of the bishop's servant.
Gillis

Gillett (French) young Gilbert.
Gelett, Gelette, Gillette

Gillian **G** (Irish) a form of Gillean.

Gilmer (English) famous hostage.
Gilmar

Gilmore (Irish) devoted to the Virgin Mary.
Gillmore, Gillmour, Gilmour

Gilon (Hebrew) circle.

Gilroy (Irish) devoted to the king.
Gilderoy, Gildray, Gildroy, Gillroy, Roy

Giltamag (Yapese) my two fathers.

Gines (Greek) he who produces life.

Ginjiro (Japanese) good silver.

Gino (Greek) a familiar form of Eugene. (Italian) a short form of names ending in "gene," "gino."
Ghino

Giona (Italian) a form of Jonah.

Giordano (Italian) a form of Jordan.
Giordan, Giordana, Giordin, Guordan

Giorgio (Italian) a form of George.

Giorgos (Greek) a form of George.
Georgos, Giorgios

Giosia (Italian) a form of Joshua.

Giotto (Italian) a form of Geoffrey.

Giovani (Italian) a form of Giovanni.
Giavani, Giovan, Giovane, Giovanie,
Giovon

Giovanni 🅱 (Italian) a form of John.
See also Jeovanni, Jiovanni.
Geovanni, Geovanny, Gian, Gianni,
Giannino, Giovani, Giovann,
Giovannie, Giovanno, Giovanny,
Giovonathon, Giovonni, Giovonnia,
Giovonnie, Givonni

Giovanny (Italian) a form of Giovanni.
Giovany

Gipsy (English) wanderer.
Gipson, Gypsy

Girvin (Irish) small; tough.
Girvan, Girven, Girvon

Gisberto (Germanic) he who shines
in battle with his sword.

Giselle 🅶 (German) pledge; hostage.

Gitano (Spanish) gypsy.

Giuliano (Italian) a form of Julius.
Giulano, Giulino, Giulliano

Giulio (Italian) a form of Julius.
Guilano

Giuseppe (Italian) a form of Joseph.
Giuseppi, Giuseppino, Giusseppe,
Guiseppe, Guiseppi, Guiseppie,
Guisseppe

Giustino (Italian) a form of Justin.
Giusto

Givon (Hebrew) hill; heights.
Givan, Givawn, Givyn

Gladwin (English) cheerful. See also
Win.
Glad, Gladdie, Gladdy, Gladwinn,
Gladwyn, Gladwynne

Glanville (English) village with oak
trees.

Glen 🅱 (Irish) a form of Glenn.
Glyn

Glendon (Scottish) fortress in the
glen.
Glenden, Glendin, Glenn, Glennden,
Glennton, Glenton

Glendower (Welsh) from Glyndwr,
Wales.

Glenn 🅱 (Irish) a short form of
Glendon.
Gleann, Glen, Glennie, Glennis,
Glennon, Glenny, Glynn

Glentworth (English) from Glenton,
England.

Glenville (Irish) village in the glen.

Gloria 🅶 (Latin) glory.

Glyn (Welsh) a form of Glen.
Glin, Glynn

Goana (Fijian) time.

Goddard (German) divinely firm.
Godard, Godart, Goddart,
Godhardt, Godhart, Gothart,
Gotthard, Gotthardt, Gotthart

Godfredo (Spanish) friend of God.

Godfrey (Irish) God's peace.
(German) a form of Jeffrey. See also
Geoffrey, Gottfried.
Giotto, Godefroi, Godfree, Godfry,
Godofredo, Godoired, Godrey,
Goffredo, Gofraidh, Gofredo, Gorry

Godo (Chamorro) entrapped.

Godwin (English) friend of God. See
also Win.
Godewyn, Godwinn, Godwyn,
Goodwin, Goodwyn, Goodwynn,
Goodwynne

Goel (Hebrew) redeemer.

Gofchegi (Chamorro) to try a lot.

Gofgualaf (Chamorro) very round, like a full moon.

Gofhigam, Gofhigen (Chamorro) forms of Gofhigan.

Gofhigan (Chamorro) lots of fish.

Gofhihos (Chamorro) very close.

Goflache (Chamorro) very wrong.

Gofmanglo (Chamorro) very windy.

Gofsagua (Chamorro) rich.

Gogui (Chamorro) to protect, save, or rescue.

Gokomatsu (Japanese) historical figure.

Goldwin (English) golden friend. See also Win.
Golden, Goldewin, Goldewinn, Goldewyn, Goldwyn, Goldwynn

Goliard (Spanish) rebel.

Goliat (Hebrew) he who lives his life making pilgrimages.

Goliath (Hebrew) exiled. Bible: the giant Philistine whom David slew with a slingshot.
Golliath

Gomda (Kiowa) wind.

Gomer (Hebrew) completed, finished. (English) famous battle.

Gong (Chinese) capable.

Gonza (Rutooro) love.

Gonzalo (Spanish) wolf.
Goncalve, Gonsalo, Gonsalve, Gonzales, Gonzelee, Gonzolo

Goptoña (Chamorro) his party.

Gordon (English) triangular-shaped hill.
Geordan, Gord, Gordain, Gordan, Gorden, Gordonn, Gordy

Gordy (English) a familiar form of Gordon.
Gordie

Gore (English) triangular-shaped land; wedge-shaped land.

Gorgonio (Greek) violent one.

Gorman (Irish) small; blue eyed.

Goro (Japanese) fifth.

Gosheven (Native American) great leaper.

Gosvino (Teutonic) friend of God.

Gotardo (Germanic) he who is valiant because of the strength that he receives from God.

Gottfried (German) a form of Geoffrey, Godfrey.
Gotfrid, Gotfrids, Gottfrid

Gotzon (German) a form of Angel.

Govert (Dutch) heavenly peace.

Gower (Welsh) pure.

Gowon (Tiv) rainmaker.
Gowan

Goyo (Spanish) a form of Gerardo.

Gozol (Hebrew) soaring bird.
Gozal

Gracián (Latin) possessor of grace.

Graciano (Latin) one recognized by God; he has love and divine blessing.

Graciliano (Latin) name comes from Gados, the useful martyr from Faleria, Italy.

Grady (Irish) noble; illustrious.
Gradea, Gradee, Gradey,
Gradleigh, Graidey, Graidy

Graeme (Scottish) a form of
Graham.
Graem

Graham ☆ (English) grand home.
Graeham, Graehame, Graehme,
Graeme, Grahamme, Grahm,
Grahame, Grahme, Gram, Grame,
Gramm, Grayeme, Grayham

Granger (French) farmer.
Grainger, Grange

Grant ☆ (English) a short form of
Grantland.
Grand, Grantham, Granthem,
Grantley

Grantland (English) great plains.
Grant

Granville (French) large village.
Gran, Granvel, Granvil, Granvile,
Granvill, Grenville, Greville

Grato (Latin) one recognized by
God; he has love and divine
blessing.

Grau (Spanish) a form of Gerardo.

Gray (English) gray haired.
Graye, Grey, Greye

Grayden (English) gray haired.
Graden, Graydan, Graydyn,
Greyden

Graydon (English) gray hill.
Gradon, Grayton, Greydon

Grayson ☆ (English) bailiff's son.
See also Sonny.
Graysen, Greyson

Grazián (Spanish) a form of
Graciano.

Greeley (English) gray meadow.
Greelea, Greeleigh, Greely

Greenwood (English) green forest.
Green, Greener

Greg, Gregg (Latin) short forms of
Gregory.
Graig, Greig, Gregson

Greggory (Latin) a form of Gregory.
Greggery

Gregor (Scottish) a form of Gregory.
Gregoor, Grégor, Gregore

Gregorio (Italian, Portuguese) a form
of Gregory.
Gregorios

Gregory ☆ (Latin) vigilant
watchman. See also Jörn, Krikor.
Gergely, Gergo, Greagoir,
Greagory, Greer, Greg, Gregary,
Greger, Gregery, Greggory,
Grégoire, Gregor, Gregorey,
Gregori, Grégorie, Gregorio,
Gregorius, Gregors, Gregos,
Gregrey, Gregroy, Gregry, Greogry,
Gries, Grisha, Grzegorz

Gresham (English) village in the
pasture.

Greyson (English) a form of
Grayson.
Greysen, Greysten, Greyston

Griffin ☆ (Latin) hooked nose.
Griff, Griffen, Griffie, Griffon, Griffy,
Gryphon

Griffith (Welsh) fierce chief; ruddy.
Grifen, Griff, Griffeth, Griffie, Griffy,
Griffyn, Griffynn, Gryphon

Grigori (Bulgarian) a form of
Gregory.
Grigoi, Grigor, Grigore, Grigorios,
Grigorov, Grigory

Grimoaldo (Spanish) confessor.

Grimshaw (English) dark woods.

Grisha (Russian) a form of Gregory.

Griswold (German, French) gray forest.
Gris, Griz, Grizwald

Grosvener (French) big hunter.

Grover (English) grove.
Grove

Gu, Guo (Chinese) resolute.

Guacraya (Quechua) strong and brave like a bull.

Guadalberto (Germanic) he is all-powerful and shines because of it.

Guadalupe **G** (Arabic) river of black stones.
Guadalope

Guaina (Quechua) young; friend.

Gualberto (Spanish) a form of Walter.
Gualterio

Gualtar (Spanish) a form of Gerardo.

Gualtiero (Italian) a form of Walter.
Gualterio

Guaman (Quechua) falcon.

Guamanachachi (Quechua) he who has valorous ancestors such as the falcon.

Guamancapac (Quechua) lord falcon.

Guamancaranca (Quechua) he who fights like a thousand falcons.

Guamanchaua (Quechua) cruel as a falcon.`

Guamanchuri (Quechua) son of the falcon.

Guamanpuma (Quechua) strong and powerful as a puma and a falcon.

Guamantiupac (Quechua) glorious falcon.

Guamanyana (Quechua) black falcon.

Guamanyurac (Quechua) white falcon.

Guamay (Quechua) young, fresh, new.

Guan (Chinese) champion.

Guanca, Guancar (Quechua) rock; summit; drum.

Guang (Chinese) light.

Guanpú (Aymara) born in a festive time; he who arrives in an opportune moment.

Guari (Quechua) savage, untamable, untiring; wild like the vicuna; protected by the gods.

Guarino (Teutonic) he who defends well.

Guariruna (Quechua) untamed and wild man.

Guarititu, Guartito (Quechua) untamed and difficult to deal with, like the vicuna.

Guascar (Quechua) he of the chain, rope of bindweed.

Guaual (Quechua) myrtle.

Guayasamin (Quechua) happy, white bird in flight.

Guayau (Quechua) royal willow.

Guaynacapac (Quechua) young master.

Guaynarimac (Quechua) young speaker.

Guaynay (Quechua) my youngster; my beloved.

Guaypa, Guaypaya (Quechua) rooster; creator, inventor.

Guayra (Quechua) wind, fast as the wind.

Guayua (Aymara) restless, mischievous; fast as the wind.

Guglielmo (Italian) a form of William.

Gui (Chinese) noble.

Guido (Italian) a form of Guy.

Guilford (English) ford with yellow flowers.
Guildford

Guilherme (Portuguese) a form of William.

Güillac (Quechua) he who warns.

Guillaume (French) a form of William.
Guillaums, Guilleaume, Guilem, Guyllaume

Guillermo (Spanish) a form of William.
Guillerrmo

Güiracocha, Güiracucha (Quechua) sea foam; the sea's vital energy.

Güisa (Quechua) prophet; he is a sorcerer for having been a twin.

Güiuyac (Quechua) brilliant, luminous.

Güiyca (Quechua) sacred.

Güiycauaman (Quechua) sacred falcon.

Gumaña (Chamorro) his house.

Gumaro (Germanic) army of men; disciplined man.

Gumersindo (Germanic) excellent man.

Gundelberto (Teutonic) he who shines in battle.

Gunnar (Scandinavian) a form of Gunther.
Guner, Gunner

Gunther (Scandinavian) battle army; warrior.
Guenter, Guenther, Gun, Gunnar, Guntar, Gunter, Guntero, Gunthar, Günther

Guotin (Chinese) polite; strong leader.

Gurion (Hebrew) young lion.
Gur, Guri, Guriel

Gurjot 🅱🅶 (Sikh) light of the guru.

Gurpreet 🅱🅶 (Sikh) devoted to the guru; devoted to the Prophet.
Gurjeet, Gurmeet, Guruprit

Gurvir 🅱 (Sikh) guru's warrior.
Gurveer

Gus (Scandinavian) a short form of Angus, Augustine, Gustave.
Guss, Gussie, Gussy, Gusti, Gustry, Gusty

Gustaf (Swedish) a form of Gustave.
Gustaaf, Gustaff

Gustave (Scandinavian) staff of the Goths. History: Gustavus Adolphus was a king of Sweden. See also Kosti, Tabo, Tavo.
Gus, Gustaf, Gustaff, Gustaof, Gustav, Gustáv, Gustava, Gustaves, Gustavo, Gustavs, Gustavus, Gustik, Gustus, Gusztav

Gustavo (Italian, Spanish) a form of Gustave.
Gustabo

Guthrie (German) war hero. (Irish) windy place.
Guthrey, Guthry

Gutierre (Spanish) a form of Walter.

Guy **B** (Hebrew) valley. (German) warrior. (French) guide. See also Guido.
Guyon

Guyapi (Native American) candid.

Guzman (Gothic) good man; man of God.

Guzmán (Teutonic) a form of Guzman.

Gwayne (Welsh) a form of Gawain.
Gwaine, Gwayn

Gwidon (Polish) life.

Gwilym (Welsh) a form of William.
Gwillym

Gwyn **G** (Welsh) fair; blessed.
Gwynn, Gwynne

Gyasi (Akan) marvelous baby.

Gyorgy (Russian) a form of George.
Gyoergy, György, Gyuri, Gyurka

Gyula (Hungarian) youth.
Gyala, Gyuszi

H **G** (American) an initial used as a first name.

Ha (Korean) summer; congratulate; river; lotus.

Habib (Arabic) beloved.

Habid (Arabic) appreciated one.

Hacan (Quechua) brilliant, splendorous.

Hacanpoma, Hacanpuma (Quechua) brilliant puma.

Hackett (German, French) little wood cutter.
Hacket, Hackit, Hackitt

Hackman (German, French) wood cutter.

Hadar (Hebrew) glory.

Haddad (Arabic) blacksmith.

Hadden (English) heather-covered hill.
Haddan, Haddon, Haden

Haden (English) a form of Hadden.
Hadin, Hadon, Hadyn, Haeden

Hadi (Arabic) guiding to the right.
Hadee, Hady

Hadley **G** (English) heather-covered meadow.
Had, Hadlea, Hadlee, Hadleigh, Hadly, Lee, Leigh

Hadrian (Latin, Swedish) dark.
Adrian, Hadrien

Hadrián (Latin) a form of Hadrian.

Hadulfo (Germanic) combat wolf.

Hadwin (English) friend in a time of war.
Hadwinn, Hadwyn, Hadwynn, Hadwynne

Hae (Korean) sun; sea; boar; release.

Hag'man (Chamorro) eel.

Hagan (German) strong defense.
Haggan

Hagen (Irish) young, youthful.

Hagley (English) enclosed meadow.

Hagos (Ethiopian) happy.

Hahnee (Native American) beggar.

Hai (Vietnamese) sea.

Haidar (Arabic) lion.
Haider

Haiden 🅱 (English) a form of
Hayden.
Haidyn

Haig (English) enclosed with hedges.

Hailey 🅖 (Irish) a form of Haley.
Haile, Haille, Haily, Halee

Haji (Swahili) born during the
pilgrimage to Mecca.

Hajime (Japanese) first son.

Hajin (Japanese) literary figure.

Hakan (Native American) fiery.

Hakeem 🅱 (Arabic) a form of
Hakim.
Hakam, Hakem

Hakik (Persian) truth; genuine, real.

Hakim (Arabic) wise. (Ethiopian)
doctor.
Hakeem, Hakiem

Hakon (Scandinavian) of Nordic
ancestry.
*Haaken, Haakin, Haakon, Haeo,
Hak, Hakan, Hako*

Hal (English) a short form of Halden,
Hall, Harold.

Halbert (English) shining hero.
Bert, Halburt

Halden (Scandinavian) half-Danish.
See also Dane.
*Hal, Haldan, Haldane, Halfdan,
Halvdan*

Hale (English) a short form of Haley.
(Hawaiian) a form of Harry.
Hayle, Heall

Halee 🅖 (Irish) a form of Hailey.

Halen (Swedish) hall.
Hale, Hallen, Haylan, Haylen

Haley 🅖 (Irish) ingenious.
*Hailey, Hale, Haleigh, Halley,
Hayleigh, Hayley, Hayli*

Halford (English) valley ford.

Hali 🅖 (Greek) sea.

Halian (Zuni) young.

Halil (Turkish) dear friend.
Halill

Halim (Arabic) mild, gentle.
Haleem

Hall (English) manor, hall.
Hal, Halstead, Halsted

Hallam (English) valley.

Hallan (English) dweller at the hall;
dweller at the manor.
Halin, Hallene, Hallin

Halley 🅖 (English) meadow near
the hall; holy.

Hallie 🅖 (English) a form of Halley.

Halliwell (English) holy well.
Hallewell, Hellewell, Helliwell

Hallward (English) hall guard.

Halomtano (Chamorro) jungle;
forest.

Halsey 🅖 (English) Hal's island.

Halstead (English) manor grounds.
Halsted

Halton (English) estate on the hill.

Halvor (Norwegian) rock; protector.
Halvard

Ham (Hebrew) hot. Bible: one of
Noah's sons.

Hama (Japanese) shore.

Hamal (Arabic) lamb. Astronomy: a
bright star in the constellation of
Aries.

Hamar (Scandinavian) hammer.

Hamid (Arabic) praised. See also Muhammad.
Haamid, Hamaad, Hamadi, Hamd, Hamdrem, Hamed, Hamedo, Hameed, Hamidi, Hammad, Hammed, Humayd

Hamill (English) scarred.
Hamel, Hamell, Hammill

Hamilton (English) proud estate.
Hamel, Hamelton, Hamil, Hamill, Tony

Hamish (Scottish) a form of Jacob, James.

Hamisi (Swahili) born on Thursday.

Hamlet (German, French) little village; home. Literature: one of Shakespeare's tragic heroes.

Hamlin (German, French) loves his home.
Hamblin, Hamelen, Hamelin, Hamlen, Hamlyn, Lin

Hammet (English, Scandinavian) village.
Hammett, Hamnet, Hamnett

Hammond (English) village.
Hamond

Hampton (English) Geography: a town in England.
Hamp

Hamza (Arabic) powerful.
Hamzah, Hamze, Hamzeh, Hamzia

Han (Chinese) self-restraint.

Han Min (Korean) the (Korean) people.

Hanale (Hawaiian) a form of Henry.
Haneke

Hanan (Hebrew) grace.
Hananel, Hananiah, Johanan

Hanbal (Arabic) pure. History: Ahmad Ibn Hanbal founded an Islamic school of thought.

Handel (German, English) a form of John. Music: George Frideric Handel was a German composer whose works include *Messiah* and *Water Music*.

Ha-Neul (Korean) sky.

Hanford (English) high ford.

Hang (Korean) constant; bay; navigate.

Hanif (Arabic) true believer.
Haneef, Hanef

Hank (American) a familiar form of Henry.

Hanley (English) high meadow.
Handlea, Handleigh, Handley, Hanlea, Hanlee, Hanleigh, Hanly, Henlea, Henlee, Henleigh, Henley

Hanna, Hannah **G** (German) forms of Hanno.

Hannes (Finnish) a form of John.

Hannibal (Phoenician) grace of God. History: a famous Carthaginian general who fought the Romans.
Anibal

Hanno (German) a short form of Johan.
Hannon, Hannu, Hanon

Hanomtano (Chamorro) water land.

Hans (Scandinavian) a form of John.
Hanschen, Hansel, Hants, Hanz

Hansel (Scandinavian) a form of Hans.
Haensel, Hansell, Hansl, Hanzel

Hansen (Scandinavian) son of Hans.
Hanson

Hansh (Hindi) god; godlike.

Hanson (Scandinavian) a form of Hansen.
Hansen, Hanssen, Hansson

Hansuke (Japanese) sail; mediation.

Hanus (Czech) a form of John.

Hao (Vietnamese) good; perfect.

Haoa (Hawaiian) a form of Howard.

Hara 🄖 (Hindi) seizer. Religion: another name for the Hindu god Shiva.

Harald (Scandinavian) a form of Harold.
Haraldo, Haralds, Haralpos

Harb (Arabic) warrior.

Harbin (German, French) little bright warrior.
Harben, Harbyn

Harcourt (French) fortified dwelling.
Court, Harcort

Hardeep (Punjabi) a form of Harpreet.

Harden (English) valley of the hares.
Hardian, Hardin

Harding (English) brave; hardy.
Hardin

Hardwin (English) brave friend.

Hardy (German) bold, daring.
Hardie

Harel (Hebrew) mountain of God.
Harell, Hariel, Harrell

Harford (English) ford of the hares.

Hargrove (English) grove of the hares.
Hargreave, Hargreaves

Hari (Hindi) tawny.
Hariel, Harin

Harith (Arabic) cultivator.

Harjot (Sikh) light of God.
Harjeet, Harjit, Harjodh

Harkin (Irish) dark red.
Harkan, Harken

Harlan (English) hare's land; army land.
Harland, Harlen, Harlenn, Harlin, Harlon, Harlyn, Harlynn

Harland (English) a form of Harlan.
Harlend

Harley 🄱🄖 (English) hare's meadow; army meadow.
Arley, Harlea, Harlee, Harleigh, Harly

Harlow (English) hare's hill; army hill. See also Arlo.

Harman, Harmon (English) forms of Herman.
Harm, Harmen, Harmond, Harms

Harold (Scandinavian) army ruler. See also Jindra.
Araldo, Garald, Garold, Hal, Harald, Haraldas, Haraldo, Haralds, Harry, Heraldo, Herold, Heronim, Herrick, Herryck

Haroldo (Germanic) he who dominates the region with his army.

Haroun (Arabic) lofty; exalted.
Haarun, Harin, Haron, Haroon, Harron, Harun

Harper (English) harp player.
Harp, Harpo

Harpreet 🄖 (Punjabi) loves God, devoted to God.
Hardeep

Harris (English) a short form of Harrison.
Haris, Hariss

Harrison 🄱 (English) son of Harry.
Harison, Harreson, Harris, Harrisen, Harrisson

Harrod (Hebrew) hero; conqueror.

Harry (English) a familiar form of Harold. See also Arrigo, Hale, Parry.
Harm, Harray, Harrey, Harri, Harrie

Hart (English) a short form of Hartley.

Hartley (English) deer meadow.
Hart, Hartlea, Hartlee, Hartleigh, Hartly

Hartman (German) hard; strong.

Hartwell (English) deer well.
Harwell, Harwill

Hartwig (German) strong advisor.

Hartwood (English) deer forest.
Harwood

Haru (Japanese) born in the spring.

Haruakira, Haruchika (Japanese) forms of Haru.

Harue (Japanese) springtime bay.

Harujiro (Japanese) spring-born second son.

Haruka (Japanese) tranquil.

Haruki (Japanese) shining brightly.

Haruko (Japanese) first born.

Haruto (Japanese) spring.

Harvey (German) army warrior.
Harv, Hervé, Hervey, Hervie, Hervy

Harvir **B** (Sikh) God's warrior.
Harvier

Hasad (Turkish) reaper, harvester.

Hasan (Arabic) a form of Hassan.
Hasaan, Hasain, Hasaun, Hashaan, Hason

Hasani (Swahili) handsome.
Hasan, Hasanni, Hassani, Heseny, Hassen, Hassian, Husani

Hashida (Japanese) from the bridge by the rice field.

Hashim (Arabic) destroyer of evil.
Haashim, Hasham, Hasheem, Hashem

Hasin (Hindi) laughing.
Haseen, Hasen, Hassin, Hazen, Hesen

Haskel (Hebrew) a form of Ezekiel.
Haskell

Haslett (English) hazel-tree land.
Haze, Hazel, Hazlett, Hazlitt

Hasrat (Arabic) grief; longing, desire.

Hassan (Arabic) handsome.
Hasan, Hassen, Hasson

Hassel (German, English) witches' corner.
Hassal, Hassall, Hassell, Hazael, Hazell

Hastin (Hindi) elephant.

Hastings (Latin) spear. (English) house council.
Hastie, Hasty

Hastu (Quechua) bird of the Andes.

Hatim (Arabic) judge.
Hateem, Hatem

Hatuntupac (Quechua) magnificent, great and majestic.

Hauk (Norwegian) hawk.
Haukeye

Havelock (Norwegian) sea battler.

Haven **G** (Dutch, English) harbor, port; safe place.
Haeven, Havin, Hevin, Hevon, Hovan

Havika (Hawaiian) a form of David.

Hawk (English) hawk.
Hawke, Hawkin, Hawkins

Hawley (English) hedged meadow.
Hawleigh, Hawly

Hawthorne (English) hawthorn tree.

Hayato (Japanese) fast person; brave person.

Hayden ☆ **B** (English) hedged valley.
Haiden, Haydan, Haydenn, Haydn, Haydon

Hayes (English) hedged valley.
Hayse

Hayley **G** (Irish) a form of Haley.

Hayward (English) guardian of the hedged area.
Haward, Heyvard, Heyward

Haywood (English) hedged forest.
Heywood, Woody

Haziel (Hebrew) vision of God.

He (Chinese) river.

Hearn (Scottish, English) a short form of Ahearn.
Hearne, Herin, Hern

Heath **B** (English) heath.
Heathe, Heith

Heathcliff (English) cliff near the heath. Literature: the hero of Emily Brontë's novel *Wuthering Heights*.

Heather **G** (English) flowering heather.

Heaton (English) high place.

Heaven **G** (English) place of beauty and happiness. Bible: where God and angels are said to dwell.

Heber (Hebrew) ally, partner.

Hector (Greek) steadfast. Mythology: the greatest hero of the Trojan War in Homer's epic poem *Iliad*.

Héctor (Greek) a form of Hector.

Hedley (English) heather-filled meadow.
Headley, Headly, Hedly

Hegesipo (Greek) horse rider.

Heiichi (Japanese) peaceful first-born son.

Heinrich (German) a form of Henry.
Heindrick, Heiner, Heinreich, Heinrick, Heinrik, Hinrich

Heinz (German) a familiar form of Henry.

Heladio (Greek) native of Halade, Greece.

Helaku (Native American) sunny day.

Heldrado (Germanic) counselor of warriors.

Helen **G** (Greek) light.

Helge (Russian) holy.

Heli (Hebrew) he who offers himself to God.

Helio (Spanish) gift of the sun god.

Heliodoro (Greek) gift of god.

Heliogabalo (Syrian) he who adores the sun.

Helki **BG** (Moquelumnan) touching.

Helmer (German) warrior's wrath.

Helmut (German) courageous.
Helmuth

Helvecio (Latin) ancient inhabitants of present-day Switzerland.

Heman (Hebrew) faithful.

Henderson (Scottish, English) son of Henry.
Hendrie, Hendries, Hendron, Henryson

Hendrick (Dutch) a form of Henry.
*Hendricks, Hendrickson, Hendrik,
Hendriks, Hendrikus, Hendrix,
Henning*

Heng (Chinese) eternal.

Heniek (Polish) a form of Henry.
Henier

Henley (English) high meadow.

Henning (German) a form of
Hendrick, Henry.

Henoch (Yiddish) initiator.
Enoch, Henock, Henok

Henri (French) a form of Henry.
Henrico, Henrri

Henrick (Dutch) a form of Henry.
*Heinrick, Henerik, Henrich, Henrik,
Henryk*

Henrique (Portuguese) a form of
Henry.

Henry (German) ruler of the
household. See also Arrigo, Enric,
Enrick, Enrico, Enrikos, Enrique,
Hanale, Honok, Kiki.
*Hagan, Hank, Harro, Harry, Heike,
Heinrich, Heinz, Hendrick, Henery,
Heniek, Henning, Henraoi, Henri,
Henrick, Henrim, Henrique, Henrry,
Heromin, Hersz*

Hentrick (Pohnpeian) a form of
Enrique.

Heracleos, Heraclio (Greek)
belonging to Hercules.

Heraclito, Heráclito (Greek) he who
is drawn to the sacred.

Heraldo (Spanish) a form of Harold.
Herald, Hiraldo

Herb (German) a short form of
Herbert.
Herbie, Herby

Herbert (German) glorious soldier.
*Bert, Erbert, Eriberto, Harbert,
Hebert, Hébert, Heberto, Herb,
Heriberto, Hurbert*

Herculano (Latin) belonging to
Hercules.

Hercules (Latin) glorious gift.
Mythology: a Greek hero of
fabulous strength, renowned for his
twelve labors.
Herakles, Herc, Hercule, Herculie

Hércules (Etruscan) a form of
Hercules.

Herfy (Chuukese) a form of Harvey.

Heriberto (Spanish) a form of
Herbert.
Heribert

Hermagoras (Greek) disciple of
Hermes.

Hermalindo, Hermelindo
(German) he who is like a shield of
strength.

Herman (Latin) noble. (German)
soldier. See also Armand, Ermanno,
Ermano, Mandek.
*Harmon, Hermaan, Hermann,
Hermie, Herminio, Hermino, Hermon,
Hermy, Heromin*

Hermán (Germanic) a form of
Herman.

Hermenegildo (Germanic) he who
offers sacrifices to God.

Hermes (Greek) messenger.
Mythology: the divine herald of
Greek mythology.

Hermógenes (Greek) sent from
Hermes.

Hernan (German) peacemaker.

Hernán (Germanic) a form of Herman.

Hernando (Spanish) a form of Ferdinand.
Hernandes, Hernandez

Herodes (Greek) fire dragon.

Herodoto (Greek) sacred talent.

Heródoto (Greek) divine talent; gift.

Herón, Heros (Latin) hero.

Herrick (German) war ruler.
Herrik, Herryck

Herschel (Hebrew) a form of Hershel.
Herchel, Hersch, Herschel, Herschell

Hersh (Hebrew) a short form of Hershel.
Hersch, Hirsch

Hershel (Hebrew) deer.
Herschel, Hersh, Hershal, Hershall, Hershell, Herzl, Hirschel, Hirshel

Hertz (Yiddish) my strife.
Herzel

Herve (Breton) active in combat.

Hervé (French) a form of Harvey.

Hesiquio (Greek) tranquil.

Hesperos (Greek) evening star.
Hespero

Hesutu (Moquelumnan) picking up a yellow jacket's nest.

Heung (Korean) prosperous; fun.

Hew (Welsh) a form of Hugh.
Hewe, Huw

Hewitt (German, French) little smart one.
Hewe, Hewet, Hewett, Hewie, Hewit, Hewlett, Hewlitt, Hugh

Hewson (English) son of Hugh.

Hezekiah (Hebrew) God gives strength.
Hezekyah, Hazikiah, Hezikyah

Hiamovi (Cheyenne) high chief.

Hibah (Arabic) gift.

Hibiki (Japanese) sound; echo, reverberation.

Hidalgo (Spanish) noble one.

Hidayat (Arabic) guidance, instruction.

Hideak (Japanese) smart, clever.

Hideaki (Japanese) smart, clever.
Hideo

Hideharu (Japanese) excellent peacemaker.

Hidehisa (Japanese) long-lasting excellence.

Hidekazu (Japanese) harmonious beauty.

Hideki (Japanese) excellent foundation.

Hidenori (Japanese) excellent writings.

Hidetaka (Japanese) excellent obedience; prosperous.

Hidetaro (Japanese) witty big son; excellent big son.

Hideto (Japanese) excellent talent.

Hidetsugu (Japanese) gifted second-born; beautiful next-born; life of excellence.

Hideuki (Japanese) a form of Hideyuki.

Hideyuki (Japanese) good fortune; excellent traveling.

Hien (Vietnamese) meek and gentle.

Hiep (Vietnamese) chivalrous.

Hieremias (Greek) God will uplift.

Hieronymos (Greek) a form of Jerome. Art: Hieronymus Bosch was a fifteenth-century Dutch painter.
Hierome, Hieronim, Hieronimo, Hieronimos, Hieronymo, Hieronymus

Hieu (Vietnamese) respectful.

Higinio (Greek) he who has good health.

Hikaru (Japanese) shine.

Hikokatsu (Japanese) doorway to victory.

Hila'an (Chamorro) a man of words.

Hilario (Spanish) a form of Hilary.

Hilary **G** (Latin) cheerful. See also Ilari.
Hi, Hilair, Hilaire, Hilarie, Hilario, Hilarion, Hilarius, Hil, Hill, Hillary, Hillery, Hilliary, Hillie, Hilly

Hildebrand (German) battle sword.
Hildebrando, Hildo

Hildemaro (Germanic) famous in combat.

Hilel (Arabic) new moon.

Hillary **G** (Latin) a form of Hilary.

Hillel (Hebrew) greatly praised. Religion: Rabbi Hillel originated the Talmud.

Hilliard (German) brave warrior.
Hillard, Hiller, Hillier, Hillierd, Hillyard, Hillyer, Hillyerd

Hilmar (Swedish) famous noble.

Hilton (English) town on a hill.
Hylton

Hineti (Chamorro) to brush against.

Hinto (Dakota) blue.

Hinun (Native American) spirit of the storm.

Hipacio (Spanish) confessor.

Hipócrates (Greek) powerful because of his cavalry.

Hipólito (Greek) a form of Hippolyte.

Hippolyte (Greek) horseman.
Hipolito, Hippolit, Hippolitos, Hippolytus, Ippolito

Hirabhai (Sanskrit) diamond brother.

Hiram (Hebrew) noblest; exalted.
Hi, Hirom, Huram, Hyrum

Hirao (Chamorro) emotion; attention; caring; heed.

Hiroaki (Japanese) abundant light.

Hirokazu (Japanese) abundant peace.

Hiroki (Japanese) air; space; noble.

Hiromasa (Japanese) fair, just.

Hiromichi (Japanese) wide street.

Hiromitsu (Japanese) extensive light.

Hironobu (Japanese) broad minded.

Hironori (Japanese) extensive writings.

Hiroshi (Japanese) generous.

Hiroto (Japanese) abundant.

Hiroyuki (Japanese) very fortunate.

Hisashi (Japanese) long period of time.

Hisoka (Japanese) secretive, reserved.

Hit (Chamorro) a form of Gil.

Hiteo (Kosraean) a form of Hideo.

Hiu (Hawaiian) a form of Hugh.

Ho (Chinese) good.

Hoa (Vietnamese) flower.

Hoai (Vietnamese) always, eternal.

Hoang (Vietnamese) finished.

Hobart (German) Bart's hill.
*Hobard, Hobbie, Hobby, Hobie,
Hoebart*

Hoben (Chamorro) youthful;
vigorous; fresh.

Hobert (German) Bert's hill.
Hobey

Hobson (English) son of Robert.
Hobbs, Hobs

Hoc (Vietnamese) studious.

Hocchocña (Chamorro) no more of
him.

Hochoc (Chamorro) no more.

Hochocguafiña (Chamorro) his fire
is no more.

Hochochinagu (Chamorro) no more
breath.

Hococnineti (Chamorro) no longer
sharp like the sword grass.

Hod (Hebrew) a short form of
Hodgson.

Hodaka (Japanese) tall plant.

Hodgson (English) son of Roger.
Hod

Hogan (Irish) youth.
Hogin

Holbrook (English) brook in the
hollow.
Brook, Holbrooke

Holden 🅱 (English) hollow in the
valley.
*Holdan, Holdin, Holdon, Holdun,
Holdyn*

Holic (Czech) barber.

Holland (French) Geography: a
former province of the Netherlands.

Holleb (Polish) dove.
Hollub, Holub

Hollie 🄶 (English) a form of Hollis.

Hollis 🄱🄶 (English) grove of holly
trees.

Holly 🄶 (English) a form of Hollis.

Holmes (English) river islands.

Holt (English) forest.
Holten, Holton

Homer (Greek) hostage; pledge;
security. Literature: a renowned
Greek epic poet.
*Homar, Homere, Homère, Homero,
Homeros, Homerus*

Hondo (Shona) warrior.

Honesto (Filipino) honest.

Hong (Chinese) magnificent.

Hongi (Chamorro) to believe, trust.

Hongminh (Vietnamese) bright red.

Honi (Hebrew) gracious.
Choni

Honok (Polish) a form of Henry.

Honon (Moquelumnan) bear.

Honorato (Spanish) honorable.

Honoré (Latin) honored.
*Honor, Honoratus, Honoray, Honorio,
Honorius*

Honovi (Native American) strong.

Honza (Czech) a form of John.

Hoon (Korean) instruct.

Hop (Chinese) agreeable.

Hope 🄶 (English) hope.

Horace (Latin) keeper of the hours.
Literature: a famous Roman lyric
poet and satirist.
Horacio, Horaz

Horacio (Latin) a form of Horace.

Horado (Spanish) timekeeper.

Horangel (Greek) messenger from
the heights or from the mountain.

Horatio (Latin) clan name. See also
Orris.
Horatius, Oratio

Horst (German) dense grove; thicket.
Hurst

Hortencio (Latin) he who has a
garden and loves it.

Hortensio (Latin) gardener.

Horton (English) garden estate.
Hort, Horten, Orton

Hosa (Arapaho) young crow.

Hosea (Hebrew) salvation. Bible: a
Hebrew prophet.
Hose, Hoseia, Hoshea, Hosheah

Hoshi (Japanese) star.

Hospicio (Spanish) he who is
accommodating.

Hotah (Lakota) white.

Hototo (Native American) whistler.

Hou (Chinese) nobleman.

Hou-Chi (Chinese) an ancient
harvest god.

Houghton (English) settlement on
the headland.

Houston **B** (English) hill town.
Geography: a city in Texas.
Housten, Houstin, Hustin, Huston

Howard (English) watchman. See
also Haoa.
Howie, Ward

Howe (German) high.
Howey, Howie

Howell (Welsh) remarkable.
Howel

Howi (Moquelumnan) turtledove.

Howie (English) a familiar form of
Howard, Howland.
Howey

Howin (Chinese) loyal swallow.

Howland (English) hilly land.
Howie, Howlan, Howlen

Hoyoung (Korean) vanity.

Hoyt (Irish) mind; spirit.

Hsia (Chinese) summer.

Hsiang (Chinese) incense; village;
enjoy; image.

Hsiao (Chinese) dawn; tiny; smile.

Hsin (Chinese) after an ancient
dynasty.

Hsun (Chinese) teach.

Hu (Chinese) tiger.

Hua (Chinese) the best part (the
cream).

Huai (Chinese) scholar.

Huaiquilaf (Mapuche) good, straight
lance.

Huan (Chinese) happiness.

Huang (Chinese) yellow.

Huan-Yue (Chinese) joyful, happy.

Huapi (Mapuche) island.

Hubbard (German) a form of
Hubert.

Hubert (German) bright mind; bright spirit. See also Beredei, Uberto.
Bert, Hobart, Hubbard, Hubbert, Huber, Hubertek, Huberto, Hubertson, Hubie, Huey, Hugh, Hugibert, Huibert, Humberto

Huberto (Spanish) a form of Hubert.
Humberto

Hubie (English) a familiar form of Hubert.
Hube, Hubi

Huc (Korean) earth, ground.

Hucsuncu (Quechua) he who has only one love; faithful.

Hud (Arabic) Religion: a Muslim prophet.

Hudson (English) son of Hud.

Huechacura (Mapuche) sharp rock; peak.

Huenchulaf (Mapuche) healthy man; happy, joyous, festive.

Huenchuleo (Mapuche) brave; handsome river; having grown up near the river.

Huenchuman (Mapuche) proud male condor.

Huenchumilla (Mapuche) ascending light; lucent point.

Huenchuñir (Mapuche) male fox.

Huentemil (Mapuche) light from above, beam of light; possessor of much silver and gold.

Huenuhueque (Mapuche) lamb from heaven.

Huenullan (Mapuche) heavenly altar.

Huenuman (Mapuche) condor from the sky; from heaven.

Huenupan (Mapuche) branch from heaven; lion from heaven.

Huey (English) a familiar form of Hugh.
Hughey, Hughie, Hughy, Hui

Hueypín (Mapuche) broken, odd land.

Hugh (English) a short form of Hubert. See also Ea, Hewitt, Huxley, Maccoy, Ugo.
Fitzhugh, Hew, Hiu, Hue, Huey, Hughes, Hugo, Hugues

Hugo ☀ (Latin) a form of Hugh.
Ugo

Hugolino (Germanic) he who has spirit and intelligence.

Hugua (Chamorro) two.

Huichacura (Mapuche) rock with just one ridge, just one side.

Huichahue (Mapuche) battlefield.

Huichalef (Mapuche) he who runs on just one side; one straight line.

Huichañir (Mapuche) fox from another region.

Huidaleo (Mapuche) branch in the river; the river separates.

Huinculche (Mapuche) people that live on the hill.

Huircalaf (Mapuche) cry of joy; healthy shout.

Huircaleo (Mapuche) whisper of the river, noise from the river.

Hui-Ying (Chinese) brilliant, intelligent.

Hulbert (German) brilliant grace.
Bert, Hulbard, Hulburd, Hulburt, Hull

Hullen (Mapuche) spring.

Humbaldo (Germanic) daring as a lion cub.

Humbert (German) brilliant strength. See also Umberto.
Hum, Humberto

Humberto (Portuguese) a form of Humbert.

Humio (Palauan) a form of Umio.

Humphrey (German) peaceful strength. See also Onofrio, Onufry.
Hum, Humfredo, Humfrey, Humfrid, Humfried, Humfry, Hump, Humph, Humphery, Humphry, Humphrys, Hunfredo

Huna (Chamorro) sand.

Hung (Vietnamese) brave.

Hunt (English) a short form of names beginning with "Hunt."

Hunter ✻ **B** (English) hunter.
Hunt, Huntur

Huntington (English) hunting estate.
Hunt, Huntingdon

Huntley (English) hunter's meadow.
Hunt, Huntlea, Huntlee, Huntleigh, Huntly

Huo (Chinese) fire.

Hurao (Chamorro) a form of Hirao.

Hurley (Irish) sea tide.
Hurlee, Hurleigh

Hurst (English) a form of Horst.
Hearst, Hirst

Husai (Hebrew) hurried one.

Husam (Arabic) sword.

Husamettin (Turkish) sharp sword.

Huslu (Native American) hairy bear.

Hussain (Arabic) a form of Hussein.
Hossain, Husain, Husani, Husayn, Hussan, Hussayn

Hussein (Arabic) little; handsome.
Hossein, Houssein, Houssin, Huiissien, Huossein, Husein, Husien, Hussain, Hussien

Hussien (Arabic) a form of Hussein.
Husian, Hussin

Husto (Chamorro) just, fair.

Hutchinson (English) son of the hutch dweller.
Hutcheson

Hute (Native American) star.

Hutton (English) house on the jutting ledge.
Hut, Hutt, Huttan

Huu (Vietnamese) very much so; amplifies the meaning of the first name.

Huxley (English) Hugh's meadow.
Hux, Huxlea, Huxlee, Huxleigh, Lee

Huy (Vietnamese) glorious.

Huyen (Vietnamese) black; mysterious; string of a musical instrument.

Huynh (Vietnamese) older brother.

Hwan (Korean) joyful; ring.

Hy (Vietnamese) hopeful. (English) a short form of Hyman.

Hyacinthe (French) hyacinth.

Hyang (Korean) fragrance, incense; village; enjoy.

Hyatt (English) high gate.
Hyat

Hyde (English) cache; measure of land equal to 120 acres; animal hide.

Hyder (English) tanner, preparer of animal hides for tanning.

Hye (Korean) favor, grace; kindness; wisdom, cleverness, wit.

Hyman (English) a form of Chaim.
Haim, Hayim, Hayvim, Hayyim, Hy, Hyam, Hymie

Hyosuke (Japanese) ice; mediation.

Hyota (Japanese) very icy.

Hyun (Korean) worth; wise; dark; subtle; bowstring, musical string.

Hyung (Korean) elder brother; successful; glowworm.

Hyun-Ki (Korean) wise.

Hyun-Shik (Korean) clever.

I (Korean) two; different; finished; extraordinary.

I Wei (Chinese) a form of Iwei.

Iacobus, Iocobus (Pohnpeian) forms of Jacob.

Iago (Spanish, Welsh) a form of Jacob, James. Literature: the villain in Shakespeare's *Othello*.
Jago

Iain (Scottish) a form of Ian.

Iakobos (Greek) a form of Jacob.
Iakov, Iakovos, Iakovs

Ian ☆ **B** (Scottish) a form of John. See also Ean, Eion.
Iain, Iane, Iann

Ianos (Czech) a form of John.
Iannis

Ib (Phoenician, Danish) oath of Baal.

Iban (Basque) a form of John.

Iber, Ibérico, Iberio, Ibero (Latin) native of Iberia or who comes from the Iberian peninsula.

Ibi (Latin) at another place.

Ibon (Basque) a form of Ivor.

Ibrahim (Hausa) my father is exalted.
Ibrahaim, Ibraham, Ibraheem, Ibrahem, Ibrahiem, Ibrahiim, Ibrahmim

Ichabod (Hebrew) glory is gone. Literature: Ichabod Crane is the main character of Washington Irving's story "The Legend of Sleepy Hollow."

Ichitaro (Japanese) first-born big son.

Idi (Swahili) born during the Idd festival.

Idris (Welsh) eager lord. (Arabic) Religion: a Muslim prophet.
Idrease, Idrees, Idres, Idress, Idreus, Idriece, Idriss, Idrissa, Idriys

Idumeo (Latin) red.

Iens (Pohnpeian) a form of Jens.

Iestyn (Welsh) a form of Justin.

Ietaka (Japanese) literary figure.

Iferemi (Fijian) a form of Efren.

Ifraim, Ifram (Chuukese) forms of Efren.

Igashu (Native American) wanderer; seeker.
Igasho

Igenansio, Igenasio (Fijian) forms of Ignacio.

Iggy (Latin) a familiar form of Ignatius.

Iginas (Chuukese) a form of Ignacio.

Ignacio (Italian) a form of Ignatius.
Ignazio

Ignado (Spanish) fiery or ardent.

Ignathio (Yapese) a form of Ignacio.

Ignatius (Latin) fiery, ardent. Religion: Saint Ignatius of Loyola founded the Jesuit order. See also Inigo, Neci.
Iggie, Iggy, Ignac, Ignác, Ignace, Ignacio, Ignacius, Ignatios, Ignatious, Ignatz, Ignaz, Ignazio

Igor (Russian) a form of Inger, Ingvar. See also Egor, Yegor.
Igoryok

Ihorangi (Maori) rain.

Ihsan (Turkish) compassionate.

Ike (Hebrew) a familiar form of Isaac. History: the nickname of the thirty-fourth U.S. president Dwight D. Eisenhower.
Ikee, Ikey

Ikeda (Japanese) from the rice field pool.

Iker (Basque) visitation.

Ikinas (Pohnpeian) a form of Ignacio.

Ikki (Japanese) tree.

Ikrebai (Palauan) in the back of the meeting house.

Iku (Japanese) nourishing.

Ikuo (Japanese) cultured man; conqueror.

Ikuya (Japanese) he who is cultured.

Il (Korean) one, first; best; sun; leisure.

Ilan (Hebrew) tree. (Basque) youth.

Ilari (Basque) a form of Hilary.
Ilario

Ilengelkei (Palauan) you are stopped from the side.

Ilias (Greek) a form of Elijah.
Illias, Illyas, Ilyas, Ilyes

Ilidio (Latin) troop.

Ilikena (Fijian) a form of Elkanah.

Illan (Basque, Latin) youth.

Illayuc (Quechua) luminous; fortunate, touched by the gods.

Ilom (Ibo) my enemies are many.

Ilsan (Korean) first-born child.

Iluminado (Latin) he who receives the inspiration of God.

Ilya (Russian) a form of Elijah.
Ilia, Ilie, Ilija, Iliya, Ilja, Illia, Illya

Imad (Arabic) supportive; mainstay.

Iman **G** (Hebrew) a short form of Immanuel.

Imani **G** (Hebrew) a form of Iman.
Imanni

Imetengel (Palauan) to come down.

Immanuel (Hebrew) a form of Emmanuel.
Iman, Imanol, Imanuel, Immanual, Immanuele, Immuneal

Imran (Arabic) host.
Imraan

Imre (Hungarian) a form of Emery.
Imri

Imrich (Czech) a form of Emery.
Imrus

In (Korean) mankind; lead, guide; humanity; cause, origin; end.

Inagangta (Chamorro) our noise, our loudness.

Inaganta (Chamorro) a form of Inagangta.

Inalef (Mapuche) swift reinforcement; he who follows behind.

Inapo (Chamorro) the wave.

Inario (Chuukese) a form of Hilario.

Inay (Hindi) god; godlike.

Inca (Quechua) king; prince or male-child of royal heritage.

Incaurco, Incaurcu (Quechua) hill; Incan god.

Ince (Hungarian) innocent.

Indalecio (Arabic) same as the master.

Inder (Hindi) god; godlike.
Inderbir, Inderdeep, Inderjeet, Inderjit, Inderpal, Inderpreet, Inderveer, Indervir, Indra, Indrajit

Indiana (American) land of Indians. Geography: name of a U.S. state.
Indi, Indy

Indíbil (Spanish) he who is very black.

Indro (Spanish) victor.

Inek (Welsh) a form of Irvin.

Ing (Scandinavian) a short form of Ingmar.
Inge

Ingelbert (German) a form of Engelbert.
Inglebert

Inger (Scandinavian) son's army.
Igor, Ingemar, Ingmar

Ingmar (Scandinavian) famous son.
Ing, Ingamar, Ingamur, Ingemar

Ingram (English) angel.
Inglis, Ingra, Ingraham, Ingrim

Ingvar (Scandinavian) Ing's soldier.
Igor, Ingevar

Inigo (Basque) a form of Ignatius.
Iñaki, Iniego, Iñigo

Iniko (Ibo) born during bad times.

Injung (Korean) acknowledged, recognized.

Inkem (Osage) red rabbit.

Innis (Irish) island.
Innes, Inness, Inniss

Innocenzio (Italian) innocent.
Innocenty, Inocenci, Inocencio, Inocente, Inosente

Inoke (Fijian) a form of Enoch.

Inos, Inosi (Fijian) forms of Enos.

Inriann (Chuukese) a form of Henry.

Inteus (Native American) proud; unashamed.

Intiauqui (Quechua) sun prince.

Intichurin (Quechua) child of the sun.

Intiguaman (Quechua) sun falcon.

Intiyafa (Quechua) ray of sunlight.

Inus (Kosraean) a form of Enos.

Ioakim (Russian) a form of Joachim.
Ioachime, Ioakimo, Iov

Ioan (Greek, Bulgarian, Romanian) a form of John.
Ioane, Ioann, Ioannes, Ioannikios, Ioannis, Ionel

Ioanis (Pohnpeian) a form of Johannes.

Iokepa (Hawaiian) a form of Joseph.
Keo

Iolo (Welsh) the Lord is worthy.
Iorwerth

Ionakana (Hawaiian) a form of Jonathan.

Ionis (Pohnpeian) a form of Juan.

Iop (Pohnpeian) a form of Job.

Iorgos (Greek) a form of George.

Iosefa (Fijian) a form of Jose.

Iosif (Greek, Russian) a form of Joseph.

Iosua (Romanian) a form of Joshua.

Iowahn (Pohnpeian) a form of Johannes.

Iowane (Fijian) a form of Johannes.

Iowanes, Iwanis (Chuukese) forms of Johannes.

Ipyana (Nyakyusa) graceful.

Ira (Hebrew) watchful.

Iram (English) bright.

Irasdos (Pohnpeian) a form of Irastos.

Irasema (Fijian) a form of Erasmo.

Irastos (Pohnpeian) a form of Erastus.

Irene **G** (Greek) peaceful.

Ireneo, Irineo (Greek) lover of peace.

Iris **G** (Greek) rainbow.

Irumba (Rutooro) born after twins.

Irv (Irish, Welsh, English) a short form of Irvin, Irving.

Irvin (Irish, Welsh, English) a short form of Irving. See also Ervine.
Inek, Irv, Irven, Irvine, Irvinn, Irvon

Irving (Irish) handsome. (Welsh) white river. (English) sea friend. See also Ervin, Ervine.
Irv, Irvin, Irvington, Irwin, Irwing

Irwin (English) a form of Irving. See also Ervin.
Irwinn, Irwyn

Isa (Arabic) a form of Jesus.
Isaah

Isaac ☆ (Hebrew) he will laugh. Bible: the son of Abraham and Sarah. See also Itzak, Izak, Yitzchak.
Aizik, Icek, Ike, Ikey, Ikie, Isaak, Isaakios, Isac, Isacc, Isacco, Isack, Isaic, Ishaq, Isiac, Isiacc, Issac, Issca, Itzak, Izak, Izzy

Isaak (Hebrew) a form of Isaac.
Isack, Isak, Isik, Issak

Isabel **G** (Spanish) consecrated to God.

Isabella **G** (Italian) a form of Isabel.

Isabelle **G** (French) a form of Isabel.

Isacar (Hebrew) he was given for a favor.

Isadoro (Spanish) gift of Isis.

Isaiah ☆ **B** (Hebrew) God is my salvation. Bible: a Hebrew prophet.
Isa, Isai, Isaia, Isaias, Isaid, Isaih, Isaish, Ishaq, Isia, Isiah, Isiash, Issia, Issiah, Izaiah, Izaiha, Izaya, Izayah, Izayaih, Izayiah, Izeyah, Izeyha

Isaias (Hebrew) a form of Isaiah.
Isaiahs, Isais, Izayus

Isaías (Hebrew) a form of Isaias.

Isake (Fijian) a form of Isaac.

Isam (Arabic) safeguard.

Isamar **G** (Hebrew) a form of Itamar.

Isaoshi (Japanese) honor.

Isaoshy (Chuukese) a form of Isaoshi.

Isas (Japanese) meritorious.

Iscay (Quechua) second child.

Iscaycuari (Quechua) doubly savage and untamable.

Isekemu (Native American) slow-moving creek.

Isham (English) home of the iron one.

Ishan (Hindi) direction.
Ishaan, Ishaun

Ishaq (Arabic) a form of Isaac.
Ishaac, Ishak

Ishi (Japanese) stone.

Ishio (Japanese) a form of Ishi.

Ishmael (Hebrew) God will hear. Literature: the narrator of Herman Melville's novel *Moby-Dick*.
Isamael, Isamail, Ishma, Ishmail, Ishmale, Ishmeal, Ishmeil, Ishmel, Ishmil, Ismael, Ismail

Isidore (Greek) gift of Isis. See also Dorian, Ysidro.
Isador, Isadore, Isadorios, Isidor, Isidro, Issy, Ixidor, Izadore, Izidor, Izidore, Izydor, Izzy

Isidro (Greek) a form of Isidore.
Isidoro, Isidoros

Isikel (Chuukese) a form of Ezequiel.

Isikeli (Fijian) a form of Ezequiel.

Isikia (Fijian) a form of Esekaia.

Isikio (Pohnpeian) a form of Ezequiel.

Isiler (Chuukese) I know them.

Isimeli (Fijian) a form of Ismael.

Isireli (Fijian) a form of Israel.

Iskander (Afghan) a form of Alexander.

Ismael (Arabic) a form of Ishmael.

Ismail (Arabic) a form of Ishmael.
Ismeil, Ismiel

Isocrates (Greek) he who can do as much as the next man.

Isod (Hebrew) God fights and prevails; the angel's antagonist.

Israel (Hebrew) prince of God; wrestled with God. History: the nation of Israel took its name from the name given Jacob after he wrestled with the angel of the Lord. See also Yisrael.
Iser, Isreal, Israhel, Isrell, Isrrael, Isser, Izrael, Izzy, Yisrael

Isreal (Hebrew) a form of Israel.
Isrieal

Issa (Swahili) God is our salvation.

Issac (Hebrew) a form of Isaac.
Issacc, Issaic, Issiac

Issiah (Hebrew) a form of Isaiah.
Issaiah, Issia

Istu (Native American) sugar pine.

István (Hungarian) a form of Stephen.
Isti, Istvan, Pista

Itaete (Guarani) blade.

Italo (Latin) he came from the land that is between the seas.

Itamar, Ittamar (Hebrew) island of palms.

Itchiro (Kosraean) a form of Ichiro.

Ithel (Welsh) generous lord.

Itoshi (Japanese) this thread.

Itsuo (Japanese) fifth son; man of leisure.

Ittu (Kosraean) first, winner.

Itzak (Hebrew) a form of Isaac, Yitzchak.
Itzik

Iuaiu (Palauan) calm, peaceful.

Iukini (Hawaiian) a form of Eugene.
Kini

Iul (Palauan) the freycinetia tree.

Iusful (Chuukese) useful.

Iustin (Bulgarian, Russian) a form of Justin.

Ivan (Russian) a form of John.
Iván, Ivanchik, Ivanichek, Ivann, Ivano, Ivas, Iven, Ivin, Ivon, Ivyn, Vanya

Ivar **B** (Scandinavian) a form of Ivor. See also Yves, Yvon.
Iv, Iva

Ives (English) young archer.
Ive, Iven, Ivey, Yves

Ivey **G** (English) a form of Ives.

Ivo (German) yew wood; bow wood.
Ibon, Ivar, Ives, Ivon, Ivonnie, Ivor, Yvo

Ivor (Scandinavian) a form of Ivo.
Ibon, Ifor, Ivar, Iver, Ivory, Ivry

Ivy **G** (English) ivy tree.

Iwan (Polish) a form of John.

Iwao (Japanese) rock of life; rugged.

Iwei (Chinese) to consider.

Iyafa, Iyapa (Quechua) lightning.

Iyapo (Yoruba) many trials; many obstacles.

Iyapoma, Iyapuma (Quechua) puma of light.

Iyapu (Quechua) lightning.

Iyatecsi, Iyaticsi (Quechua) eternal light; origin of light.

Iye (Native American) smoke.

Izak (Czech) a form of Isaac.
Itzhak, Ixaka, Izaac, Izaak, Izac, Izaic, Izak, Izec, Izeke, Izick, Izik, Izsak, Izsák, Izzak

Izzy (Hebrew) a familiar form of Isaac, Isidore, Israel.
Issy

J

J **B** (American) an initial used as a first name.
J.

Ja (Korean) attractive, magnetic.

Jaali (Swahili) powerful.

Jaan (Estonian) a form of Christian.

Jaap (Dutch) a form of Jim.

Jabari (Swahili) fearless, brave.
Jabaar, Jabahri, Jabar, Jabarae, Jabare, Jabaree, Jabarei, Jabarie, Jabarri, Jabarrie, Jabary, Jabbar, Jabbaree, Jabbari, Jaber, Jabiari, Jabier, Jabori, Jaborie

Jabel (Hebrew) like the arrow that flies.

Jabez (Hebrew) born in pain.
Jabe, Jabes, Jabesh

Jabin (Hebrew) God has created.
Jabain, Jabien, Jabon

Jabir (Arabic) consoler, comforter.
Jabiri, Jabori

Jabranne (Arabic) consolation; reward.

Jabril (Arabic) a form of Jibril.
Jabrail, Jabree, Jabreel, Jabrel, Jabrell, Jabrelle, Jabri, Jabrial, Jabrie, Jabriel, Jabrielle, Jabrille

Jabulani (Shona) happy.

Jabuwe (Marshallese) don't get on.

Jacan (Hebrew) trouble.
Jachin

Jacari (American) a form of Jacorey.
Jacarey, Jacaris, Jacarius, Jacarre,
Jacarri, Jacarrus, Jacarus, Jacary,
Jacaure, Jacauri, Jaccar, Jaccari

Jace B (American) a combination of
the initials J. + C.
JC, J.C., Jacee, Jacek, Jacey, Jacie,
Jaice, Jaicee

Jacen (Greek) a form of Jason.
Jaceon

Jacey G (American) a form of Jace.

Jacho (Korean) to bring on oneself.

Jacinto (Portuguese, Spanish)
hyacinth. See also Giacinto.
Jacindo, Jacint, Jacinta

Jack ☝ (American) a familiar form
of Jacob, John. See also Keaka.
Jackie, Jacko, Jackub, Jak, Jax, Jock,
Jocko

Jackie, Jacky BG (American) familiar
forms of Jack.
Jackey

Jackson ☝ B (English) son of Jack.
Jacksen, Jacksin, Jacson, Jakson,
Jaxon

Jaclyn G (American) a short form of
Jacqueline (see Girls' Names).

Jaco (Portuguese) a form of Jacob.

Jacob ☝ B (Hebrew) supplanter,
substitute. Bible: son of Isaac,
brother of Esau. See also Akiva,
Chago, Checha, Coby, Diego,
Giacomo, Hamish, Iago, Iakobos,
James, Kiva, Koby, Kuba, Tiago,
Yakov, Yasha, Yoakim.
Jaap, Jachob, Jack, Jackob, Jackub,
Jaco, Jacobb, Jacobe, Jacobi,
Jacobo, Jacoby, Jacolbi, Jacolby,
Jacque, Jacques, Jacub, Jaecob,
Jago, Jaicob, Jaime, Jake, Jakob,
Jalu, Jasha, Jaycob, Jecis, Jeks,

Jeska, Jim, Jocek, Jock, Jocob,
Jocobb, Jocoby, Jocolby, Jokubas

Jacobi, Jacoby B (Hebrew) forms
of Jacob.
Jachobi, Jacobbe, Jacobee, Jacobey,
Jacobie, Jacobii, Jacobis

Jacobo (Hebrew) a form of Jacob.

Jacobson (English) son of Jacob.
Jacobs, Jacobsen, Jacobsin, Jacobus

Jacorey (American) a combination of
Jacob + Corey.
Jacari, Jacori, Jacoria, Jacorie, Jacoris,
Jacorius, Jacorrey, Jacorrien, Jacorry,
Jacory, Jacouri, Jacourie, Jakari

Jacque (French) a form of Jacob.
Jacquay, Jacqui, Jocque, Jocqui

Jacques B (French) a form of Jacob,
James. See also Coco.
Jackque, Jackques, Jackquise, Jacot,
Jacquan, Jacquees, Jacquese,
Jacquess, Jacquet, Jacquett, Jacquez,
Jacquis, Jacquise, Jaquez, Jarques,
Jarquis

Jacquez, Jaquez (French) forms of
Jacques.
Jaques, Jaquese, Jaqueus, Jaqueze,
Jaquis, Jaquise, Jaquze, Jocquez

Jacy (Tupi-Guarani) moon.
Jaicy, Jaycee

Jada G (American) a short form of
Jadrien.

Jade G (Spanish) jade, precious
stone.
Jaeid, Jaid, Jaide

Jaden B (Hebrew) a form of Jadon.
Jadee, Jadeen, Jadenn, Jadeon,
Jadin, Jaeden

Jadon (Hebrew) God has heard.
Jaden, Jadyn, Jaedon, Jaiden,
Jaydon

Jadrien (American) a combination of
Jay + Adrien.
Jad, Jada, Jadd, Jader, Jadrian

Jadyn **G** (Hebrew) a form of Jadon.
Jadyne, Jaedyn

Jae Jik (Korean) to hold office, to be
in service.

Jaegar (German) hunter.
Jaager, Jaeger, Jagur

Jae-Hwa (Korean) rich, prosperous.

Jael **G** (Hebrew) mountain goat.
Yael

Jaelen (American) a form of Jalen.
*Jaelan, Jaelaun, Jaelin, Jaelon,
Jaelyn*

Ja'far (Sanskrit) little stream.
Jafar, Jafari, Jaffar, Jaffer, Jafur

Jage (Sanskrit) the world.

Jagger (English) carter.
Jagar, Jager, Jaggar

Jago (English) a form of James.

Jaguar (Spanish) jaguar.
Jagguar

Jahi (Swahili) dignified.

Jahlil (Hindi) a form of Jalil.
Jahlal, Jahlee, Jahleel, Jahliel

Jahmar (American) a form of Jamar.
Jahmare, Jahmari, Jahmarr, Jahmer

Jahvon (Hebrew) a form of Javan.
Jahvan, Jahvine, Jahwaan, Jahwon

Jai **B** (Tai) heart.
Jaie, Jaii

Jaiden **B** (Hebrew) a form of Jadon.
Jaidan, Jaidon, Jaidyn

Jailen (American) a form of Jalen.
*Jailan, Jailani, Jaileen, Jailen, Jailon,
Jailyn, Jailynn*

Jaime **B** (Spanish) a form of Jacob,
James.
*Jaimey, Iaimie, Jaimito, Jaimy, Jayme,
Jaymie*

Jaimee **G** (Spanish) a form of Jaime.

Jaimie **G** (English) a form of Jamie.
(Spanish) a form of Jaime.

Jair (Spanish) a form of Jairo.

Jairo (Spanish) God enlightens.
Jair, Jairay, Jaire, Jairus, Jarius

Jaison (Greek) a form of Jason.
Jaisan, Jaisen, Jaishon, Jaishun

Jaivon (Hebrew) a form of Javan.
Jaiven, Jaivion, Jaiwon

Jaiya (Sanskrit) a form of Jaya.

Jaja (Ibo) honored.

Jajuan (American) a combination of
the prefix Ja + Juan.
*Ja Juan, Jauan, Jawaun, Jejuan,
Jujuan, Juwan*

Jakari (American) a form of Jacorey.
*Jakaire, Jakar, Jakaray, Jakarie,
Jakarious, Jakarius, Jakarre, Jakarri,
Jakarus*

Jake (Hebrew) a short form of Jacob.
Jakie, Jayk, Jayke

Jakeem (Arabic) uplifted.

Jakob (Hebrew) a form of Jacob.
*Jaekob, Jaikab, Jaikob, Jakab, Jakeb,
Jakeob, Jakeub, Jakib, Jakiv, Jakobe,
Jakobi, Jakobus, Jakoby, Jakov,
Jakovian, Jakub, Jakubek, Jekebs*

Jakome (Basque) a form of James.
Xanti

Jal (Gypsy) wanderer.

Jalan (American) a form of Jalen.
*Jalaan, Jalaen, Jalain, Jaland,
Jalane, Jalani, Jalanie, Jalann,
Jalaun, Jalean, Jallan*

Jale (Fijian) a form of Charles.

Jaleel 🅱 (Hindi) a form of Jalil.
Jaleell, Jaleil, Jalel

Jalen 🅱 (American) a combination of the prefix Ja + Len.
Jaelen, Jailen, Jalan, Jaleen, Jalend, Jalene, Jalin, Jallen, Jalon, Jalyn

Jalil (Hindi) revered.
Jahlil, Jalaal, Jalal

Jalin, Jalyn (American) forms of Jalen.
Jalian, Jaline, Jalynn, Jalynne

Jalisat (Arabic) he who receives little, gives more.

Jalon (American) a form of Jalen.
Jalone, Jaloni, Jalun

Jam (American) a short form of Jamal, Jamar.
Jama

Jamaal 🅱 (Arabic) a form of Jamal.

Jamaine (Arabic) a form of Germain.

Jamal 🅱 (Arabic) handsome. See also Gamal.
Jahmal, Jahmall, Jahmalle, Jahmeal, Jahmeel, Jahmeil, Jahmel, Jahmelle, Jahmil, Jahmile, Jaimal, Jam, Jamaal, Jamael, Jamahl, Jamail, Jamaile, Jamala, Jamale, Jamall, Jamalle, Jamar, Jamaul, Jamel, Jamil, Jammal, Jamor, Jamual, Jarmal, Jaumal, Jemal, Jermal, Jomal, Jomall

Jamar 🅱 (American) a form of Jamal.
Jam, Jamaar, Jamaari, Jamahrae, Jamair, Jamara, Jamaras, Jamaraus, Jamarl, Jamarr, Jamarre, Jamarrea, Jamarree, Jamarri, Jamarvis, Jamaur, Jamir, Jamire, Jamiree, Jammar, Jarmar, Jarmarr, Jaumar, Jemaar, Jemar, Jimar, Jomar

Jamarcus 🅱 (American) a combination of the prefix Ja + Marcus.
Jamarco, Jamarkus, Jemarcus, Jimarcus

Jamari (American) a form of Jamario.
Jamare, Jamarea, Jamaree, Jamareh, Jamaria, Jamarie, Jamaul

Jamario (American) a combination of the prefix Ja + Mario.
Jamareo, Jamari, Jamariel, Jamarious, Jamaris, Jamarius, Jamariya, Jemario, Jemarus

Jamarquis (American) a combination of the prefix Ja + Marquis.
Jamarkees, Jamarkeus, Jamarkis, Jamarqese, Jamarqueis, Jamarques, Jamarquez, Jamarquios, Jamarqus

Jamel (Arabic) a form of Jamal.
Jameel, Jamele, Jamell, Jamelle, Jammel, Jamuel, Jamul, Jarmel, Jaumal, Jaumell, Je-Mell, Jimell

James ☆ 🅱 (Hebrew) supplanter, substitute. (English) a form of Jacob. Bible: James the Great and James the Less were two of the Twelve Apostles. See also Diego, Hamish, Iago, Kimo, Santiago, Seamus, Seumas, Yago, Yasha.
Jacques, Jago, Jaime, Jaimes, Jakome, Jamesie, Jamesy, Jamez, Jameze, Jamie, Jamies, Jamse, Jamyes, Jamze, Jas, Jasha, Jay, Jaymes, Jem, Jemes, Jim

Jamesa, Jemesa (Fijian) forms of James.

Jameson 🅱 (English) son of James.
Jamerson, Jamesian, Jamison, Jaymeson

Jami 🅶 (English) a form of Jamie.

Jamie 🅶 (English) a familiar form of James.
Jaime, Jaimey, Jaimie, Jame, Jamee, Jamey, Jameyel, Jami, Jamia, Jamiah, Jamian, Jamme, Jammie, Jamiee, Jammy, Jamy, Jamye, Jayme, Jaymee, Jaymie

Jamil B (Arabic) a form of Jamal.
Jamiel, Jamiell, Jamielle, Jamile,
Jamill, Jamille, Jamyl, Jarmil

Jamin (Hebrew) favored.
Jamen, Jamian, Jamien, Jamion,
Jamionn, Jamon, Jamun, Jamyn,
Jarmin, Jarmon, Jaymin

Jamison B (English) son of James.
Jamiesen, Jamieson, Jamis, Jamisen,
Jamyson, Jaymison

Jamon (Hebrew) a form of Jamin.
Jamohn, Jamone, Jamoni

Jamond (American) a combination of
James + Raymond.
Jamod, Jamont, Jamonta, Jamontae,
Jamontay, Jamonte, Jarmond

Jamor (American) a form of Jamal.
Jamoree, Jamori, Jamorie, Jamorius,
Jamorrio, Jamorris, Jamory, Jamour

Jamsheed (Persian) from Persia.
Jamshaid, Jamshed

Jan B (Dutch, Slavic) a form of John.
Jaan, Jona, Janae, Jann, Janne,
Jano, Janson, Jenda, Yan

Jana G (Dutch, Slavic) a form of Jan.

Janab (Sanskrit) kin, acquaintance.

Janae G (Dutch, Slavic) a form of
Jan.

Janco (Czech) a form of John.
Jancsi, Janke, Janko

Jando (Spanish) a form of Alexander.
Jandino

Jane G (Hebrew) God is gracious.

Janeil (American) a combination of
the prefix Ja + Neil.
Janal, Janel, Janell, Janelle, Janiel,
Janielle, Janile, Janille, Jarnail,
Jarneil, Jarnell

Janek (Polish) a form of John.
Janak, Janik, Janika, Janka, Jankiel,
Janko

Janell, Janelle G (American) forms
of Janeil.

Janessa G (American) a form of
Jane.

Janette G (French) a form of Janet
(see Girls' Names).

Jang (Persian) battle, war.

Janine G (French) a form of Jane.

Janis G (Latvian) a form of John.
Ansis, Jancis, Zanis

Janne (Finnish) a form of John.
Jann, Jannes

János (Hungarian) a form of John.
Jancsi, Jani, Jankia, Jano

Janson (Scandinavian) son of Jan.
Janse, Jansen, Jansin, Janssen,
Jansun, Jantzen, Janzen, Jensen,
Jenson

Jantzen (Scandinavian) a form of
Janson.
Janten, Jantsen, Jantson

Janus (Latin) gate, passageway; born
in January. Mythology: the Roman
god of beginnings and endings.
Jannese, Jannus, Januario, Janusz

Japheth (Hebrew) handsome.
(Arabic) abundant. Bible: a son of
Noah. See also Yaphet.
Japeth, Japhet

Jaquan B (American) a combi-
nation of the prefix Ja + Quan.
Jaequan, Jaiqaun, Jaiquan, Jaqaun,
Jaqawan, Jaquaan, Jaquain,
Ja'quan, Jaquane, Jaquann,
Jaquanne, Jaquavius, Jaquawn,
Jaquin, Jaquon, Jaqwan

Jaquarius (American) a combination of Jaquan + Darius.
Jaquari, Jaquarious, Jaquaris

Jaquavius (American) a form of Jaquan.
Jaquavas, Jaquaveis, Jaquaveius, Jaquaveon, Jaquaveous, Jaquavias, Jaquavious, Jaquavis, Jaquavus

Jaquon (American) a form of Jaquan.
Jaequon, Jaqoun, Jaquinn, Jaqune, Jaquoin, Jaquone, Jaqwon

Jarad (Hebrew) a form of Jared.
Jaraad, Jaraed

Jarah (Hebrew) sweet as honey.
Jerah

Jardan (Hebrew) a form of Jordan.
Jarden, Jardin, Jardon

Jareb (Hebrew) contending.
Jarib

Jared ☒ (Hebrew) a form of Jordan.
Jahred, Jaired, Jarad, Jaredd, Jareid, Jarid, Jarod, Jarred, Jarrett, Jarrod, Jarryd, Jerad, Jered, Jerod, Jerrad, Jerred, Jerrod, Jerryd, Jordan

Jarek (Slavic) born in January.
Janiuszck, Januarius, Janusz, Jarec, Jarrek, Jarric, Jarrick

Jarell (Scandinavian) a form of Gerald.
Jairell, Jarael, Jareil, Jarel, Jarelle, Jariel, Jarrell, Jarryl, Jayryl, Jerel, Jerell, Jerrell, Jharell

Jaren (Hebrew) a form of Jaron.
Jarian, Jarien, Jarin, Jarion

Jareth (American) a combination of Jared + Gareth.
Jarreth, Jereth, Jarreth

Jarett (English) a form of Jarrett.
Jaret, Jarette

Jarl (Scandinavian) earl, nobleman.

Jarlath (Latin) in control.
Jarl, Jarlen

Jarman (German) from Germany.
Jerman

Jarod ☒ (Hebrew) a form of Jared.
Jarodd, Jaroid

Jaron (Hebrew) he will sing; he will cry out.
Jaaron, Jairon, Jaren, Jarone, Jarren, Jarron, Jaryn, Jayron, Jayronn, Je Ronn, J'ron

Jaroslav (Czech) glory of spring.
Jarda

Jarred ☒ (Hebrew) a form of Jared.
Ja'red, Jarrad, Jarrayd, Jarrid, Jarrod, Jarryd, Jerrid

Jarrell (English) a form of Gerald.
Jarel, Jarell, Jarrel, Jerall, Jerel, Jerell

Jarren (Hebrew) a form of Jaron.
Jarrain, Jarran, Jarrian, Jarrin

Jarrett ☒ (English) a form of Garrett, Jared.
Jairett, Jareth, Jarett, Jaretté, Jarhett, Jarratt, Jarret, Jarrette, Jarrot, Jarrott, Jerrett

Jarrod (Hebrew) a form of Jared.
Jarod, Jerod, Jerrod

Jarryd (Hebrew) a form of Jared.
Jarrayd, Jaryd

Jarvis (German) skilled with a spear.
Jaravis, Jarv, Jarvaris, Jarvas, Jarvaska, Jarvey, Jarvez, Jarvie, Jarvios, Jarvious, Jarvius, Jarvorice, Jarvoris, Jarvous, Jarvus, Javaris, Jervey, Jervis

Jaryn (Hebrew) a form of Jaron.
Jarryn, Jarynn, Jaryon

Jas ☒ (Polish) a form of John. (English) a familiar form of James.
Jasio

Jasha (Russian) a familiar form of Jacob, James.
Jascha

Jashawn (American) a combination of the prefix Ja + Shawn.
Jasean, Jashan, Jashaun, Jashion, Jashon

Jaskaran **B** (Sikh) sings praises to the Lord.
Jaskaren, Jaskarn, Jaskiran

Jaskarn **B** (Sikh) a form of Jaskaran.

Jasleen **G** (Latin) a form of Jocelyn.

Jasmeet **BG** (Persian) a form of Jasmine.

Jasmin **G** (Persian) jasmine flower.
Jasman, Jasmanie, Jasmine, Jasmon, Jasmond

Jasmine **G** (Persian) a form of Jasmin.

Jason ☀ (Greek) healer. Mythology: the hero who led the Argonauts in search of the Golden Fleece.
Jacen, Jaeson, Jahson, Jaison, Jasan, Jasaun, Jase, Jasen, Jasin, Jasson, Jasten, Jasun, Jasyn, Jathan, Jathon, Jay, Jayson

Jasón (Greek) a form of Jason.

Jaspal (Punjabi) living a virtuous lifestyle.

Jasper **B** (French) brown, red, or yellow ornamental stone. (English) a form of Casper. See also Kasper.
Jaspar, Jazper, Jespar, Jesper

Jaspreet **BG** (Punjabi) virtuous.

Jasson (Greek) a form of Jason.
Jassen, Jassin

Jatinra (Hindi) great Brahmin sage.

Javan (Hebrew) Bible: son of Japheth.
Jaewan, Jahvaughan, Jahvon, Jaivon, Javante, Javaon, JaVaughn, Javen, Javian, Javien, Javin, Javine, Javoanta, Javon, Javona, Javone, Javonte, Jayvin, Jayvion, Jayvon, Jevan, Jevon

Javante (American) a form of Javan.
Javantae, Javantai, Javantée, Javanti

Javaris (English) a form of Jarvis.
Javaor, Javar, Javaras, Javare, Javares, Javari, Javarias, Javaries, Javario, Javarius, Javaro, Javaron, Javarous, Javarre, Javarreis, Javarri, Javarrious, Javarris, Javarro, Javarte, Javarus, Javorious, Javoris, Javorius, Javouris

Javas (Sanskrit) quick, swift.
Jayvas, Jayvis

Javid (Persian) eternal, immortal; perpetual.

Javier (Spanish) owner of a new house. See also Xavier.
Jabier, Javer, Javere, Javiar

Javiero (Spanish) born in January.

Javon **B** (Hebrew) a form of Javan.
Jaavon, Jaevin, Jaevon, Jaewon, Javeon, Javion, Javionne, Javohn, Javona, Javone, Javoney, Javoni, Javonn, Javonne, Javonni, Javonnie, Javonnte, Javoun, Jayvon

Javonte **B** (American) a form of Javan.
Javona, Javontae, Javontai, Javontay, Javontaye, Javonté, Javontee, Javonteh, Javontey

Jawaun (American) a form of Jajuan.
Jawaan, Jawan, Jawann, Jawn, Jawon, Jawuan

Jawhar (Arabic) jewel; essence.

Jaxon (English) a form of Jackson.
Jaxen, Jaxsen, Jaxson, Jaxsun, Jaxun

Jay 🅱 (French) blue jay. (English) a short form of James, Jason.
Jae, Jai, Jave, Jaye, Jeays, Jeyes

Jaya (Sanskrit) victory.

Jayantha (Sanskrit) victorious, triumphant.

Jayce (American) a combination of the initials J. + C.
JC, J.C., Jayc, Jaycee, Jay Cee, Jaycey, Jecie

Jaycob (Hebrew) a form of Jacob.
Jaycub, Jaykob

Jayde 🅖 (American) a combination of the initials J. + D.
JD, J.D., Jayd, Jaydee, Jayden

Jayden ☀ 🅱 (American) a form of Jayde.
Jaydan, Jaydin, Jaydn, Jaydon

Jayla 🅖 (American) a form of Jaylee.

Jaylee (American) a combination of Jay + Lee.
Jayla, Jayle, Jaylen

Jaylen 🅱 (American) a combination of Jay + Len.
Jaylaan, Jaylan, Jayland, Jayleen, Jaylend, Jaylin, Jayln, Jaylon, Jaylun, Jaylund, Jaylyn

Jaylin 🅱 (American) a form of Jaylen.
Jaylian, Jayline

Jaylon 🅱 (American) a form of Jaylen.
Jayleon

Jaylyn 🅱🅖 (American) a form of Jaylen.
Jaylynd, Jaylynn, Jaylynne

Jayme 🅖 (English) a form of Jamie.
Jaymie

Jaymes (English) a form of James.
Jaymis, Jayms, Jaymz

Jayquan (American) a combination of Jay + Quan.
Jaykwan, Jaykwon, Jayqon, Jayquawn, Jayqunn

Jayson (Greek) a form of Jason.
Jaycent, Jaysean, Jaysen, Jayshaun, Jayshawn, Jayshon, Jayshun, Jaysin, Jaysn, Jayssen, Jaysson, Jaysun

Jayvon (American) a form of Javon.
Jayvion, Jayvohn, Jayvone, Jayvonn, Jayvontay, Jayvonte, Jaywan, Jaywaun, Jaywin

Jaywant (Sanskrit) possessing victory.

Jazmine 🅖 (Persian) a form of Jasmine.

Jazz (American) jazz.
Jaz, Jazze, Jazzlee, Jazzman, Jazzmen, Jazzmin, Jazzmon, Jazztin, Jazzton, Jazzy

Jean 🅱 (French) a form of John.
Jéan, Jeane, Jeannah, Jeannie, Jeannot, Jeano, Jeanot, Jeanty, Jene

Jeanette 🅖 (French) a form of Jean.

Jeb (Hebrew) a short form of Jebediah.
Jebb, Jebi, Jeby

Jebediah (Hebrew) a form of Jedidiah.
Jeb, Jebadia, Jebadiah, Jebadieh, Jebidiah

Jed (Hebrew) a short form of Jedidiah. (Arabic) hand.
Jedd, Jeddy, Jedi

Jediah (Hebrew) hand of God.
Jedaia, Jedaiah, Jedeiah, Jedi, Yedaya

Jedidiah 🅱 (Hebrew) friend of God, beloved of God. See also Didi.
Jebediah, Jed, Jedadiah, Jeddediah, Jedediah, Jedediha, Jedidia, Jedidiah, Jedidiyah, Yedidya

Jedrek (Polish) strong; manly.
Jedric, Jedrik, Jedrus

Jeff (English) a short form of Jefferson, Jeffrey. A familiar form of Geoffrey.
Jef, Jefe, Jeffe, Jeffey, Jeffie, Jeffy, Jhef

Jefferson **B** (English) son of Jeff. History: Thomas Jefferson was the third U.S. president.
Jeferson, Jeff, Jeffers

Jeffery **B** (English) a form of Jeffrey.
Jefery, Jeffari, Jeffary, Jeffeory, Jefferay, Jeffereoy, Jefferey, Jefferie, Jeffory

Jefford (English) Jeff's ford.

Jeffrey **B** (English) divinely peaceful. See also Geffrey, Geoffrey, Godfrey.
Jeff, Jefferies, Jeffery, Jeffre, Jeffree, Jeffrery, Jeffrie, Jeffries, Jeffry, Jefre, Jefri, Jefry, Jeoffroi, Joffre, Joffrey

Jeffry (English) a form of Jeffrey.

Jehan (French) a form of John.
Jehann

Jehová (Hebrew) I am what I am.

Jehu (Hebrew) God lives. Bible: a military commander and king of Israel.
Yehu

Jeke (Fijian) a form of Jack.

Jekesoni (Fijian) a form of Jackson.

Jelani (Swahili) mighty.
Jel, Jelan, Jelanie, Jelaun

Jeltanbwij (Marshallese) someone who makes trouble in the family.

Jem **G** (English) a short form of James, Jeremiah.
Jemmie, Jemmy

Jemal (Arabic) a form of Jamal.
Jemaal, Jemael, Jemale, Jemel

Jemaluit (Marshallese) rainbow.

Jemel (Arabic) a form of Jemal.
Jemeal, Jemehl, Jemehyl, Jemell, Jemelle, Jemello, Jemeyle, Jemile, Jemmy

Jemond (French) worldly.
Jemon, Jémond, Jemonde, Jemone

Jenaro (Latin) born in January.

Jenkin (Flemish) little John.
Jenkins, Jenkyn, Jenkyns, Jennings

Jenna **G** (Arabic) small bird. (Welsh) a short form of Jennifer.

Jennifer **G** (Welsh) white wave; white phantom. A form of Guinevere (see Girls' Names).

Jenny **G** (Welsh) a familiar form of Jennifer.

Jenö (Hungarian) a form of Eugene.
Jenci, Jency, Jenoe, Jensi, Jensy

Jenofonte (Greek) he who comes from another country and is eloquent.

Jens (Danish) a form of John.
Jense, Jensen, Jenson, Jenssen, Jensy, Jentz

Jeovanni (Italian) a form of Giovanni.
Jeovahny, Jeovan, Jeovani, Jeovany

Jequan (American) a combination of the prefix Je + Quan.
Jeqaun, Jequann, Jequon

Jerad, Jerrad (Hebrew) forms of Jared.
Jeread, Jeredd

Jerahmy (Hebrew) a form of Jeremy.
Jerahmeel, Jerahmeil, Jerahmey

Jerald (English) a form of Gerald.
Jeraldo, Jerold, Jerral, Jerrald, Jerrold, Jerry

Jerall (English) a form of Jarrell.
Jerael, Jerai, Jerail, Jeraile, Jeral, Jerale, Jerall, Jerrail, Jerral, Jerrel, Jerrell, Jerrelle

Jeramie, Jeramy (Hebrew) forms of Jeremy.
Jerame, Jeramee, Jeramey, Jerami, Jerammie

Jerard (French) a form of Gerard.
Jarard, Jarrard, Jerardo, Jeraude, Jerrard

Jere (Hebrew) a short form of Jeremiah, Jeremy.
Jeré, Jeree

Jered, Jerred (Hebrew) forms of Jared.
Jereed, Jerid, Jerryd, Jeryd

Jerel, Jerell, Jerrell (English) forms of Jarell.
Jerelle, Jeriel, Jeril, Jerrail, Jerral, Jerrall, Jerrel, Jerrill, Jerrol, Jerroll, Jerryl, Jerryll, Jeryl, Jeryle

Jeremaia (Fijian) a form of Jeremy.

Jereme, Jeremey (Hebrew) forms of Jeremy.
Jarame

Jeremiah ☝ **B** (Hebrew) God will uplift. Bible: a Hebrew prophet. See also Dermot, Yeremey, Yirmaya.
Geremiah, Jaramia, Jem, Jemeriah, Jemiah, Jeramiah, Jeramiha, Jere, Jereias, Jeremaya, Jeremi, Jeremia, Jeremial, Jeremias, Jeremija, Jeremy, Jerimiah, Jerimiha, Jerimya, Jermiah, Jermija, Jerry

Jeremías (Hebrew) a form of Jeremiah.

Jeremie, Jérémie (Hebrew) forms of Jeremy.
Jeremi, Jérémie, Jeremii

Jeremy **B** (English) a form of Jeremiah.
Jaremay, Jaremi, Jaremy, Jem, Jemmy, Jerahmy, Jeramie, Jeramy, Jere, Jereamy, Jereme, Jeremee, Jeremey, Jeremie, Jérémie, Jeremry, Jérémy, Jeremye, Jereomy, Jeriemy, Jerime, Jerimy, Jermey, Jeromy, Jerremy

Jeriah (Hebrew) Jehovah has seen.

Jericho (Arabic) city of the moon. Bible: a city conquered by Joshua.
Jeric, Jerick, Jerico, Jerik, Jerric, Jerrick, Jerrico, Jerricoh, Jerryco

Jermaine **B** (French) a form of Germain. (English) sprout, bud.
Jarman, Jeremaine, Jeremane, Jerimane, Jermain, Jerman, Jermane, Jermanie, Jermanne, Jermany, Jermayn, Jermayne, Jermiane, Jermine, Jer-Mon, Jermone, Jermoney, Jhirmaine

Jermal (Arabic) a form of Jamal.
Jermael, Jermail, Jermall, Jermaul, Jermel, Jermell, Jermil, Jermol, Jermyll

Jermey (English) a form of Jeremy.
Jerme, Jermee, Jermere, Jermery, Jermie, Jermy, Jhermie

Jermiah (Hebrew) a form of Jeremiah.
Jermiha, Jermiya

Jerney (Slavic) a form of Bartholomew.

Jerod, Jerrod (Hebrew) forms of Jarrod.
Jerode, Jeroid

Jerolin (Basque, Latin) holy.

Jerome (Latin) holy. See also Geronimo, Hieronymos.
Gerome, Jere, Jeroen, Jerom, Jérome, Jérôme, Jeromo, Jeromy, Jeron, Jerónimo, Jerrome, Jerromy

Jeromy (Latin) a form of Jerome.
Jeromee, Jeromey, Jeromie

Jeron (English) a form of Jerome.
Jéron, Jerone, Jeronimo, Jerrin,
Jerrion, Jerron, Jerrone, J'ron

Jeronimwus (Pohnpeian) a form of
Jeronimo.

Jerrett (Hebrew) a form of Jarrett.
Jeret, Jerett, Jeritt, Jerret, Jerrette,
Jerriot, Jerritt, Jerrot, Jerrott

Jerrick (American) a combination of
Jerry + Derrick.
Jaric, Jarrick, Jerick, Jerrik

Jerry **B** (German) mighty spearman.
(English) a familiar form of Gerald,
Gerard. See also Gerry, Kele.
Jehri, Jere, Jeree, Jeris, Jerison, Jerri,
Jerrie, Jery

Jerusalén (Hebrew) peaceful place.

Jervis (English) a form of Gervaise,
Jarvis.

Jerzy (Polish) a form of George.
Jersey, Jerzey, Jurek

Jesabel, Jezabel (Hebrew) oath of
God.

Jeshua (Hebrew) a form of Joshua.
Jeshuah

Jess **B** (Hebrew) a short form of
Jesse.

Jesse 🌟 **B** (Hebrew) wealthy. Bible:
the father of David. See also Yishai.
Jese, Jesee, Jesi, Jess, Jessé, Jessee,
Jessie, Jessy

Jessenia **G** (Arabic) flower.

Jessi **G** (Hebrew) a form of Jessie.

Jessica **G** (Hebrew) wealthy.

Jessie **BG** (Hebrew) a form of Jesse.
Jesie

Jessika **G** (Hebrew) a form of Jessica.

Jessy **B** (Hebrew) a form of Jesse.
Jescey, Jessey, Jessye, Jessyie, Jesy

Jestin (Welsh) a form of Justin.
Jessten, Jesten, Jeston, Jesstin, Jesston

Jesualdo (Germanic) he who takes
the lead.

Jesus 🌟 **B** (Hebrew) a form of
Joshua. Bible: son of Mary and
Joseph, believed by Christians to be
the Son of God. See also Chucho,
Isa, Yosu.
Jecho, Jessus, Jesu, Jesús, Josu

Jesús (Hispanic) a form of Jesus.

Jethro (Hebrew) abundant. Bible: the
father-in-law of Moses. See also
Yitro.
Jeth, Jethroe, Jetro, Jett

Jett (English) hard, black mineral.
(Hebrew) a short form of Jethro.
Jet, Jetson, Jetter, Jetty

Jevan (Hebrew) a form of Javan.
Jevaun, Jeven, Jevin

Jevon (Hebrew) a form of Javan.
Jevion, Jevohn, Jevone, Jevonn,
Jevonne, Jevonnie

Jevonte (American) a form of Jevon.
Jevonta, Jevontae, Jevontaye, Jevonté

Ji Hye (Korean) wisdom, intelligence.

Jia (Chinese) increase.

Jiang-Li (Chinese) river; beautiful.

Jiao (Chinese) beautiful, handsome.

Jibade (Yoruba) born close to royalty.

Jibben (Gypsy) life.
Jibin

Jibril (Arabic) archangel of Allah.
Jabril, Jibreel, Jibriel

Jie (Chinese) pure.

Jien (Japanese) literary figure.

Jieri (Fijian) a form of Jerry.

Jill G (English) a short form of Jillian.

Jillian G (Latin) youthful.

Jilt (Dutch) money.

Jim (Hebrew, English) a short form of James. See also Jaap.
Jimbo, Jimm, Jimmy

Jimbo (American) a familiar form of Jim.
Jimboo

Jimell (Arabic) a form of Jamel.
Jimel, Jimelle, Jimill, Jimmell, Jimmelle, Jimmiel, Jimmil

Jimeno (Spanish) a form of Simeón.

Jimiyu (Abaluhya) born in the dry season.

Jimmie B (English) a form of Jimmy.
Jimi, Jimie, Jimmee, Jimmi

Jimmy B (English) a familiar form of Jim.
Jimmey, Jimmie, Jimmye, Jimmyjo, Jimy

Jimoh (Swahili) born on Friday.

Jin B (Chinese) gold.
Jinn

Jindra (Czech) a form of Harold.

Jing (Chinese) unblemished.

Jing-Quo (Chinese) ruler of the country.

Jioje, Jioji, Joiji (Fijian) forms of George.

Jione (Fijian) a form of John.

Jiong (Chinese) bright, shining.

Jiovanni (Italian) a form of Giovanni.
Jio, Jiovani, Jiovanie, Jiovann, Jiovannie, Jiovanny, Jiovany, Jiovoni, Jivan

Jirair (Armenian) strong; hard working.

Jiri (Czech) a form of George.
Jirka

Jiro (Japanese) second son.

Jivin (Hindi) life giver.
Jivanta

Jiyoung (Korean) wisdom and courage.

Jle (Chinese) wonderful.

Jln (Chinese) golden.

Jlu (Chinese) for a long time.

Jo G (Hebrew, Japanese) a form of Joe.

Joab (Hebrew) God is father. See also Yoav.
Joabe, Joaby

Joachim (Hebrew) God will establish. See also Akeem, Ioakim, Yehoyakem.
Joacheim, Joakim, Joaquim, Joaquín, Jokin, Jov

Joanes (Chuukese) a form of Johannes.

Joanis (Pohnpeian) a form of Johannes.

Joanna G (English) a form of Joan (see Girls' Names).

João (Portuguese) a form of John.

Joaquim (Portuguese) a form of Joachim.

Joaquín (Spanish) a form of Joachim, Yehoyakem.
Jehoichin, Joaquin, Jocquin, Jocquinn, Juaquin

Job (Hebrew) afflicted. Bible: a righteous man whose faith in God survived the test of many afflictions.
Jobe, Jobert, Jobey, Jobie, Joby

Joben (Japanese) enjoys cleanliness.
Joban, Jobin

Jobo (Spanish) a familiar form of Joseph.

Joby **B** (Hebrew) a familiar form of Job.
Jobie

Jocelyn **G** (Latin) joyous.

Jock (American) a familiar form of Jacob.
Jocko, Joco, Jocoby, Jocolby

Jocquez (French) a form of Jacquez.
Jocques, Jocquis, Jocquise

Jodan (Hebrew) a combination of Jo + Dan.
Jodahn, Joden, Jodhan, Jodian, Jodin, Jodon, Jodonnis

Jodi, Jodie **G** (Hebrew) forms of Jody.

Jody **BG** (Hebrew) a familiar form of Joseph.
Jodey, Jodi, Jodie, Jodiha, Joedy

Joe **B** (Hebrew) a short form of Joseph.
Jo, Joely, Joey

Joel **B** (Hebrew) God is willing. Bible: an Old Testament Hebrew prophet.
Jóel, Joël, Joell, Joelle, Joely, Jole, Yoel

Joelle **BG** (Hebrew) a form of Joel.

Joeseph (Hebrew) a form of Joseph.
Joesph

Joey **B** (Hebrew) a familiar form of Joe, Joseph.

Johan, Johann (German) forms of John. See also Anno, Hanno, Yoan, Yohan.
Joahan, Joannes, Johahn, Johan, Johanan, Johane, Johannan, Johannes, Johanthan, Johatan, Johathan, Johathon, Johaun, Johon

Johannes (German) a form of Johan, Johann.
Johanes, Johannas, Johannus, Johansen, Johanson, Johonson

John ☆ **B** (Hebrew) God is gracious. Bible: the name honoring John the Baptist and John the Evangelist. See also Elchanan, Evan, Geno, Gian, Giovanni, Handel, Hannes, Hans, Hanus, Honza, Ian, Ianos, Iban, Ioan, Ivan, Iwan, Keoni, Kwam, Ohannes, Sean, Ugutz, Yan, Yanka, Yanni, Yochanan, Yohance, Zane.
Jack, Jacsi, Jaenda, Jahn, Jan, Janak, Janco, Janek, Janis, Janne, János, Jansen, Jantje, Jantzen, Jas, Jean, Jehan, Jen, Jenkin, Jenkyn, Jens, Jhan, Jhanick, Jhon, Jian, Joáo, João, Jock, Joen, Johan, Johann, Johne, Johnl, Johnlee, Johnnie, Johnny, Johnson, Jon, Jonam, Jonas, Jone, Jones, Jonny, Jonté, Jovan, Juan, Juhana

Johnathan (Hebrew) a form of Jonathan.
Jhonathan, Johathe, Johnatan, Johnathann, Johnathaon, Johnathen, Johnathyne, Johnatten, Johniathin, Johnothan, Johnthan

Johnathon (Hebrew) a form of Jonathon. See also Yanton.
Johnaton

Johnnie **B** (Hebrew) a familiar form of John.
Johnie, Johnier, Johnni, Johnsie, Jonni, Jonnie

Johnny **B** (Hebrew) a familiar form of John. See also Gianni.
Jantje, Jhonny, Johney, Johnney, Johny, Jonny

Johnson (English) son of John.
Johnston, Jonson

Joi **G** (Latin) a form of Joy.

Joji (Japanese) a form of George.

Jojo (Fante) born on Monday.

Jokim (Basque) a form of Joachim.

Joklur (Marshallese) calm landing.

Jolene 🅖 (Hebrew) God will add, God will increase. (English) a form of Josephine.

Jolon (Native American) valley of the dead oaks.
Jolyon

Jomar (American) a form of Jamar.
Jomari, Jomarie, Jomarri

Jomei (Japanese) spreads light.

Jon 🅑 (Hebrew) a form of John. A short form of Jonathan.
J'on, Joni, Jonn, Jonnie, Jonny, Jony

Jonacani (Fijian) a form of Jonathan.

Jonah 🅑 (Hebrew) dove. Bible: an Old Testament prophet who was swallowed by a large fish.
Giona, Jona, Yonah, Yunus

Jonas (Hebrew) he accomplishes. (Lithuanian) a form of John.
Jonahs, Jonass, Jonaus, Jonelis, Jonukas, Jonus, Jonutis, Joonas

Jonás (Hebrew) a form of Jonas.

Jonasa (Fijian) a form of Jona.

Jonatan 🅑 (Hebrew) a form of Jonathan.
Jonatane, Jonate, Jonattan, Jonnattan

Jonathan ☀ 🅑 (Hebrew) gift of God. Bible: the son of King Saul who became a loyal friend of David. See also Ionakana, Yanton, Yonatan.
Janathan, Johnathan, Johnathon, Jon, Jonatan, Jonatha, Jonathen, Jonathin, Jonathon, Jonathun, Jonathyn, Jonethen, Jonnatha, Jonnathan, Jonnathun, Jonothan, Jonthan

Jonathon (Hebrew) a form of Jonathan.
Joanathon, Johnathon, Jonnathon, Jonothon, Jonthon, Jounathon, Yanaton

Jones (Welsh) son of John.
Joenns, Joness, Jonesy

Jonetani (Fijian) a form of Jonathan.

Jonny (Hebrew) a familiar form of John.
Jonhy, Joni, Jonnee, Jony

Jontae (French) a combination of Jon + the suffix Tae.
Johntae, Jontay, Jontea, Jonteau, Jontez

Jontay (American) a form of Jontae.
Johntay, Johnte, Johntez, Jontai, Jonte, Jonté, Jontez

Joo (Korean) jewel; lord, master, ruler; red; universe; eternity.

Joo-Chan (Korean) praise the Lord.

Joop (Dutch) a familiar form of Joseph.
Jopie

Joost (Dutch) just.

Jope (Indonesian) a form of Job.

Joquin (Spanish) a form of Joaquín.
Joquan, Joquawn, Joqunn, Joquon

Jora 🅖 (Hebrew) teacher.
Yora, Jorah

Joram (Hebrew) Jehovah is exalted.
Joran, Jorim

Jordan ☀ 🅑 (Hebrew) descending. See also Giordano, Yarden.
Jardan, Jared, Jordaan, Jordae, Jordain, Jordaine, Jordane, Jordani, Jordanio, Jordann, Jordanny, Jordano, Jordany, Jordáo, Jordayne, Jorden, Jordian, Jordin, Jordon, Jordun, Jordy, Jordyn, Jorrdan, Jory, Jourdan

Jordán (Hebrew) a form of Jordan.

Jorden **B** (Hebrew) a form of Jordan.
Jordenn

Jordon **B** (Hebrew) a form of Jordan.
Jeordon, Johordan

Jordy (Hebrew) a familiar form of Jordan.
Jordi, Jordie

Jordyn **G** (Hebrew) a form of Jordan.

Jorell (American) he saves. Literature: a name inspired by the fictional character Jor-El, Superman's father.
Jorel, Jor-El, Jorelle, Jorl, Jorrel, Jorrell

Jörg (German) a form of George.
Jeorg, Juergen, Jungen, Jürgen

Jorge **B** (Spanish) a form of George.
Jorrín

Jorgen (Danish) a form of George.
Joergen, Jorgan, Jörgen

Joribwij (Marshallese) broken family.

Joris (Dutch) a form of George.

Jorlikej (Marshallese) pillar on the windward side of the atoll.

Jörn (German) a familiar form of Gregory.

Jorrín (Spanish) a form of George.
Jorian, Jorje

Jory (Hebrew) a familiar form of Jordan.
Joar, Joary, Jorey, Jori, Jorie, Jorrie

Josafat (Hebrew) God's judgment.

Josaia (Fijian) a form of Josiah.

Jose ✲ **B** (Spanish) a form of Joseph.

José (Spanish) a form of Joseph. See also Ché, Pepe.
Josean, Josecito, Josee, Joseito, Joselito, Josey

Josee **G** (Spanish) a form of José.

Josef (German, Portuguese, Czech, Scandinavian) a form of Joseph.
Joosef, Joseff, Josif, Jozef, József, Juzef

Joseluis (Spanish) a combination of Jose + Luis.

Joseph ✲ **B** (Hebrew) God will add, God will increase. Bible: in the Old Testament, the son of Jacob who came to rule Egypt; in the New Testament, the husband of Mary. See also Beppe, Cheche, Chepe, Giuseppe, Iokepa, Iosif, Osip, Pepa, Peppe, Pino, Sepp, Yeska, Yosef, Yousef, Youssel, Yusif, Yusuf, Zeusef.
Jazeps, Jo, Jobo, Jody, Joe, Joeseph, Joey, Jojo, Joop, Joos, Jooseppi, Jopie, José, Joseba, Josef, Josep, Josephat, Josephe, Josephie, Josephus, Josheph, Josip, Jóska, Joza, Joze, Jozef, Jozeph, Jozhe, Jozio, Jozka, Jozsi, Jozzepi, Jupp, Juziu

Josephine **G** (French) a form of Joseph.

Josese (Fijian) a form of Jose.

Joseva (Fijian) a form of Jose.

Josh (Hebrew) a short form of Joshua.
Joshe

Josha (Hindi) satisfied.

Joshi (Swahili) galloping.

Joshua ☀ **B** (Hebrew) God is my salvation. Bible: led the Israelites into the Promised Land. See also Giosia, Iosua, Jesus, Yehoshua.
Jeshua, Johsua, Johusa, Josh, Joshau, Joshaua, Joshauh, Joshawa, Joshawah, Joshia, Joshu, Joshuaa, Joshuah, Joshuea, Joshuia, Joshula, Joshus, Joshusa, Joshuwa, Joshwa, Josue, Jousha, Jozshua, Jozsua, Jozua, Jushua

Josiah ☀ **B** (Hebrew) fire of the Lord. See also Yoshiyahu.
Joshiah, Josia, Josiahs, Josian, Josias, Josie

Josie **G** (Hebrew) a form of Josiah.

Joss (Chinese) luck; fate.
Josse, Jossy

Josue (Hebrew) a form of Joshua.
Joshue, Jossue, Josu, Josua, Josuha, Jozus

Josué (Hebrew) a form of Josue.

Jotama (Fijian) a form of Jotham.

Jotham (Hebrew) may God complete. Bible: a king of Judah.

Jourdan (Hebrew) a form of Jordan.
Jourdain, Jourden, Jourdin, Jourdon, Jourdyn

Jovan (Latin) Jove-like, majestic. (Slavic) a form of John. Mythology: Jove, also known as Jupiter, was the supreme Roman deity.
Johvan, Johvon, Jovaan, Jovane, Jovani, Jovanic, Jovann, Jovanni, Jovannis, Jovanny, Jovany, Jovaughn, Jovaun, Joven, Jovenal, Jovenel, Jovi, Jovian, Jovin, Jovito, Jovoan, Jovon, Jovone, Jovonn, Jovonne, Jowan, Jowaun, Yovan, Yovani

Jovani, Jovanni **B** (Latin) forms of Jovan.
Jovanie, Jovannie, Jovoni, Jovonie, Jovonni

Jovanny, Jovany (Latin) forms of Jovan.
Jovony

Joy **G** (Latin) joyous.

Jr (Latin) a short form of Junior.
Jr.

Ju (Chinese) to hold up.

Juan ☀ **B** (Spanish) a form of John. See also Chan.
Juanch, Juanchito, Juane, Juanito, Juann, Juaun

Juancarlos (Spanish) a combination of Juan + Carlos.

Juanelo (Spanish) a form of Juan.

Juanjo (Spanish) a combination of Juan and José.

Juanma (Spanish) a combination of Juan and Manuel.

Juaquin (Spanish) a form of Joaquín.
Juaqin, Juaqine, Juquan, Juaquine

Jubal (Hebrew) ram's horn. Bible: a musician and a descendant of Cain.

Jucundo (Latin) happy, joyous one.

Judah (Hebrew) praised. Bible: the fourth of Jacob's sons. See also Yehudi.
Juda, Judas, Judd, Jude

Judas (Latin) a form of Judah. Bible: Judas Iscariot was the disciple who betrayed Jesus.
Jude

Judd (Hebrew) a short form of Judah.
Jud, Judson

Jude (Latin) a short form of Judah, Judas. Bible: one of the Twelve Apostles, author of "The Epistle of Jude."

Judson (English) son of Judd.

Judy **G** (Hebrew) a familiar form of Judith (see Girls' Names).

Juhana (Finnish) a form of John.
Juha, Juho

Juku (Estonian) a form of Richard.
Jukka

Jules (French) a form of Julius.
Joles, Jule

Julia **G** (Latin) youthful.

Julian ☆ **B** (Greek, Latin) a form of Julius.
Jolyon, Julean, Juliaan, Julianne, Juliano, Julien, Jullian, Julyan

Julián (Spanish) a form of Julio.

Julianna **G** (Czech, Spanish, Hungarian) a form of Julia.

Julianne **G** (Greek, Latin) a form of Julian.

Julie **G** (Greek, Latin) a familiar form of Julius.

Julien **B** (Latin) a form of Julian.
Juliene, Julienn, Julienne, Jullien, Jullin

Juliet **G** (French) a form of Julia.

Julio **B** (Hispanic) a form of Julius.

Julius **B** (Greek, Latin) youthful, downy bearded. History: Julius Caesar was a great Roman dictator. See also Giuliano.
Jolyon, Julas, Jule, Jules, Julen, Jules, Julian, Julias, Julie, Julio, Juliusz, Jullius, Juluis

Ju-Long (Chinese) powerful.

Jum (Korean) foretell.

Jumaane (Swahili) born on Tuesday.

Jumah (Arabic, Swahili) born on Friday, a holy day in the Islamic religion.
Jimoh, Juma

Jumoke (Yoruba) loved by everyone.

Jun **B** (Chinese) truthful. (Japanese) obedient; pure.
Junnie

Jun'ichi (Japanese) first born; purity.

Jung (Korean) righteous.

Junior (Latin) young.
Jr, Junious, Junius, Junor

Junji (Japanese) pure peace; obedient listener.

Juong (Korean) increase; give; important; all; second born.

Júpiter (Latin) origin or source of light. *Jupiter*

Jupp (German) a form of Joseph.

Jur (Czech) a form of George.
Juraz, Jurek, Jurik, Jurko, Juro

Jurgis (Lithuanian) a form of George.
Jurgi, Juri

Juro (Japanese) best wishes; long life.

Jurrien (Dutch) God will uplift.
Jore, Jurian, Jurre

Justen (Latin) a form of Justin.
Jasten

Justice **G** (Latin) a form of Justis.
Justic, Justiz, Justyc, Justyce

Justin ☆ **B** (Latin) just, righteous. See also Giustino, Iestyn, Iustin, Tutu, Ustin, Yustyn.
Jastin, Jaston, Jestin, Jobst, Joost, Jost, Jusa, Just, Justain, Justan, Justas, Justek, Justen, Justian, Justinas, Justine, Justinian, Justinius, Justinn, Justino, Justins, Justinus, Justo, Juston, Justton, Justukas, Justun, Justyn

Justina **G** (Italian) a form of Justine.

Justine **G** (Latin) a form of Justin.

Justiniano (Spanish) a form of Justino.

Justino (Latin) a form of Justin.

Justis (French) just.
Justice, Justs, Justus, Justyse

Justyn 🅱 (Latin) a form of Justin.
Justn, Justyne, Justynn

Juven, Juvencio, Juventino (Latin) he is the one that represents youth.

Juvenal (Latin) young. Literature: a Roman satirist.
Juvon, Juvone

Juwan 🅱 (American) a form of Jajuan.
Juvon, Juvone, Juvaun, Juwaan, Juwain, Juwane, Juwann, Juwaun, Juwon, Juwonn, Juwuan, Juwuane, Juwvan, Jwan, Jwon

K

K 🅶 (American) an initial used as a first name.

Ka (Korean) beautiful; good; song; able; family; professional.

Kabiito (Rutooro) born while foreigners are visiting.

Kabil (Turkish) a form of Cain.
Kabel

Kabir (Hindi) History: an Indian mystic poet.
Kabar, Kabeer, Kabier

Kabonero (Runyankore) sign.

Kabonesa (Rutooro) difficult birth.

Kabua (Marshallese) uncle.

Kacani (Chuukese) a form of Kasani.

Kacey 🅶 (Irish) a form of Casey. (American) a combination of the initials K. + C. See also KC.
Kace, Kacee, Kaci, Kacy, Kaesy, Kase, Kasey, Kasie, Kasy, Kaycee

Kachio (Japanese) victor.

Kachumasa (Chuukese) a form of Katsumasa.

Kachuo (Chuukese) a form of Kachio.

Kachutoshi (Chuukese) a form of Katsutoshi.

Kaci 🅶 (Irish) a form of Kacey.

Kadar (Arabic) powerful.
Kader

Kadarius (American) a combination of Kade + Darius.
Kadairious, Kadarious, Kadaris, Kadarrius, Kadarus, Kaddarrius, Kaderious, Kaderius

Kade 🅱 (Scottish) wetlands. (American) a combination of the initials K. + D.
Kadee, Kady, Kaid, Kaide, Kaydee

Kadeem 🅱 (Arabic) servant.
Kadim, Khadeem

Kaden 🅱 (Arabic) a form of Kadin.
Kadeen, Kadein, Kaidan, Kaiden

Kadiasang (Palauan) big spear.

Kadin (Arabic) friend, companion.
Caden, Kaden, Kadyn, Kaeden, Kayden

Kadir (Arabic) spring greening.
Kadeer

Kado (Japanese) gateway.

Kaeden (Arabic) a form of Kadin.
Kaedin, Kaedon, Kaedyn

Kaelan, Kaelin (Irish) forms of Kellen.
Kael, Kaelen, Kaelon, Kaelyn

Kaeleb (Hebrew) a form of Kaleb.
Kaelib, Kaelob, Kaelyb, Kailab,
Kaileb

Kaelyn **G** (Irish) a form of Kaelan.

Kaemon (Japanese) joyful; right-
handed.
Kaeman, Kaemen, Kaemin

Kaenan (Irish) a form of Keenan.
Kaenen, Kaenin, Kaenyn

Ka'eo (Hawaiian) victorious.

Kafele (Nguni) worth dying for.

Kaga (Native American) writer.

Kagan (Irish) a form of Keegan.
Kage, Kagen, Kaghen, Kaigan

Kahale (Hawaiian) home.

Kahil (Turkish) young; inexperienced;
naive.
Cahil, Kaheel, Kale, Kayle

Kahlil **B** (Arabic) a form of Khalíl.
Kahleal, Kahlee, Kahleel, Kahleil,
Kahli, Kahliel, Kahlill, Kalel, Kalil

Kaholo (Hawaiian) runner.

Kahraman (Turkish) hero.

Kai **B** (Welsh) keeper of the keys.
(German) a form of Kay.
(Hawaiian) sea.
Kae, Kaie, Kaii

Kaikara (Runyoro) Religion: a
Banyoro deity.

Kailen (Irish) a form of Kellen.
Kail, Kailan, Kailey, Kailin, Kailon,
Kailyn

Kaili (Hawaiian) Religion: a
Hawaiian god.
Kailli

Kailyn **G** (Irish) a form of Kailen.

Kaimu (Japanese) sea; dream.

Kain (Welsh, Irish) a form of Kane.
Kainan, Kaine, Kainen, Kainin, Kainon

Kainoa (Hawaiian) name.

Kaipo (Hawaiian) sweetheart.

Kairo (Arabic) a form of Cairo.
Kaire, Kairee, Kairi

Kaiser (German) a form of Caesar.
Kaesar, Kaisar, Kaizer

Kaisho (Japanese) to fly to the sea.

Kaitlin **G** (Irish) pure.

Kaito (Japanese) sea.

Kaiven (American) a form of Kevin.
Kaivan, Kaiven, Kaivon, Kaiwan

Kaj (Danish) earth.
Kai, Kaje

Kakar (Hindi) grass.

Kala **G** (Hindi) black; phase.
(Hawaiian) sun.
Kalam

Kalama **BG** (Hawaiian) torch.
Kalam

Kalan (Irish) a form of Kalen.
Kalane, Kallan

Kalani **G** (Hawaiian) sky; chief.
Kalan

Kale (Arabic) a short form of Kahlil.
(Hawaiian) a familiar form of Carl.
Kalee, Kalen, Kaleu, Kaley, Kali,
Kalin, Kalle, Kayle

Kaleb **B** (Hebrew) a form of Caleb.
Kaeleb, Kal, Kalab, Kalabe, Kalb,
Kale, Kaleob, Kalev, Kalib, Kalieb,
Kallb, Kalleb, Kalob, Kaloeb, Kalub,
Kalyb, Kilab

Kaleigh **G** (American) a form of
Caley.

Kalen, Kalin (Arabic, Hawaiian) forms
of Kale. (Irish) forms of Kellen.
Kalan

Kalevi (Finnish) hero.

Kaley 🄶 (Arabic) a familiar form of Kale.

Kali 🄶 (Arabic) a short form of Kalil. (Hawaiian) a form of Gary.

Kalil (Arabic) a form of Khalíl.
Kaleel, Kalell, Kali, Kaliel, Kaliil

Kaliova (Fijian) a form of Caleb.

Kaliq (Arabic) a form of Khaliq.
Kalic, Kalique

Kalkin (Hindi) tenth. Religion: Kalki is the final incarnation of the Hindu god Vishnu.
Kalki

Kalle 🄱🄶 (Scandinavian) a form of Carl. (Arabic, Hawaiian) a form of Kale.

Kallen (Irish) a form of Kellen.
Kallan, Kallin, Kallion, Kallon, Kallun, Kalun

Kalon (Irish) forms of Kellen.
Kalone, Kalonn, Kalyen, Kalyne, Kalynn

Kaloosh (Armenian) blessed event.

Kalover (Chuukese) call over.

Kalvin (Latin) a form of Calvin.
Kal, Kalv, Kalvan, Kalven, Kalvon, Kalvyn, Vinny

Kalwin (Pohnpeian) a form of Calvin.

Kalyn 🄶 (Irish) a form of Kellen.

Kamaka (Hawaiian) face.

Kamakani (Hawaiian) wind.

Kamal (Hindi) lotus. (Arabic) perfect, perfection.
Kamaal, Kamel, Kamil

Kamau (Kikuyu) quiet warrior.

Kamden (Scottish) a form of Camden.
Kamdon

Kameron 🄱 (Scottish) a form of Cameron.
Kam, Kamaren, Kamaron, Kameran, Kameren, Kamerin, Kamerion, Kamerron, Kamerun, Kameryn, Kamey, Kammeren, Kammeron, Kammy, Kamoryn, Kamran, Kamron

Kami 🄶 (Hindi) loving.

Kamil 🄱 (Arabic) a form of Kamal.
Kameel

Kamlyn (Japanese) a form of Kami.

Kamran, Kamron (Scottish) forms of Kameron.
Kammron, Kamrein, Kamren, Kamrin, Kamrun, Kamryn

Kamuela (Hawaiian) a form of Samuel.

Kamuhanda (Runyankore) born on the way to the hospital.

Kamukama (Runyankore) protected by God.

Kamuzu (Nguni) medicine.

Kamya (Luganda) born after twin brothers.

Kana (Japanese) powerful; capable. (Hawaiian) Mythology: a demigod.

Kanae (Japanese) fragrant seedling.

Kanaiela (Hawaiian) a form of Daniel.
Kana, Kaneii

Kaname (Japanese) main point.

Kanaye (Japanese) zealous one.

Kandace 🄶 (Greek) glittering white; glowing. (American) a form of Candice.

Kane **B** (Welsh) beautiful. (Irish) tribute. (Japanese) golden. (Hawaiian) eastern sky. (English) a form of Keene. See Kahan, Kain, Kaney, Kayne.

Kange (Lakota) raven.
Kang, Kanga

Kaniel (Hebrew) stalk, reed.
Kan, Kani, Kannie, Kanny

Kanji (Japanese) generous second son; thorough administrator.

Kannan (Hindi) Religion: another name for the Hindu god Krishna.
Kanaan, Kanan, Kanen, Kanin, Kanine, Kannen

Kannon (Polynesian) free. (French) A form of Cannon.
Kanon

Kano (Japanese) one's masculine power; capability.

Kanoa **B** (Hawaiian) free.

Kantit (Chamorro) cliff.

Kantu (Hindi) happy.

Kanu (Swahili) wildcat.

Kaori (Japanese) strong.

Kap (Korean) first; armor.

Kapila (Hindi) ancient prophet.
Kapil

Kapono (Hawaiian) righteous.
Kapena

Kapriel (Pohnpeian) a form of Gabriel.

Kara **G** (Greek, Danish) pure.

Karaistiani (Fijian) a form of Christian.

Karavi (Fijian) poling a boat through mangroves.

Kardal (Arabic) mustard seed.
Karandal, Kardell

Kare (Norwegian) enormous.
Karee

Kareem **B** (Arabic) noble; distinguished.
Karee, Karem, Kareme, Karim, Karriem

Karel **BG** (Czech) a form of Carl.
Karell, Karil, Karrell

Karen **G** (Greek) pure.

Karey (Greek) a form of Carey.
Karee, Kari, Karry, Kary

Kari **G** (Greek) a form of Karey.

Karif (Arabic) born in autumn.
Kareef

Kariisa (Runyankore) herdsman.

Karim (Arabic) a form of Kareem.

Karina **G** (Russian) a form of Karen.

Karl (German) a form of Carl.
Kaarle, Kaarlo, Kale, Kalle, Kalman, Kálmán, Karcsi, Karel, Kari, Karlen, Karlitis, Karlo, Karlos, Karlton, Karlus, Karol, Kjell

Karla **G** (German) a form of Carla. (Slavic) a short form of Karoline (see Girls' Names).

Karlen (Latvian, Russian) a form of Carl.
Karlan, Karlens, Karlik, Karlin, Karlis, Karlon

Karly **G** (Latin) little and strong. (American) a form of Carly.

Karmel **BG** (Hebrew) a form of Carmel.

Karney (Irish) a form of Carney.

Karol (Czech, Polish) a form of Carl.
*Karal, Karolek, Karolis, Karalos,
Károly, Karrel, Karrol*

Karr (Scandinavian) a form of Carr.

Karson (English) a form of Carson.
Karrson, Karsen

Karsten (Greek) anointed.
Carsten, Karstan, Karston

Karu (Hindi) cousin.
Karun

Karutunda (Runyankore) little.

Karwana (Rutooro) born during
wartime.

Kasani (Chuukese) you like it.

Kasau (Chuukese) ashamed.

Kaseem (Arabic) divided.
*Kasceem, Kaseam, Kaseym, Kasim,
Kasseem, Kassem, Kazeem*

Kaseko (Rhodesian) mocked,
ridiculed.

Kasem (Tai) happiness.

Kasen (Basque) protected with a
helmet.
*Kasean, Kasene, Kaseon, Kasin,
Kason, Kassen*

Kasey 🅖 (Irish) a form of Casey.
Kaese, Kaesy, Kasay, Kassey

Kashawn (American) a combination
of the prefix Ka + Shawn.
*Kashain, Kashan, Kashaun, Kashen,
Kashon*

Kasib (Arabic) fertile.

Kasim (Arabic) a form of Kaseem.
Kassim

Kasimir (Arabic) peace. (Slavic) a
form of Casimir.
*Kasim, Kazimierz, Kazimir, Kazio,
Kazmer, Kazmér, Kázmér*

Kasiya (Nguni) separate.

Kasper (Persian) treasurer. (German)
a form of Casper.
Jasper, Kaspar, Kaspero

Kass (German) blackbird.
Kaese, Kasch, Kase

Kassandra 🅖 (Greek) a form of
Cassandra.

Kassidy 🅖 (Irish) a form of Cassidy.
Kassady, Kassie, Kassy

Kastino, Kasty (Chuukese) forms of
Kasto.

Kasto (Chuukese) pure; chaste.

Kasumi (Japanese) haze, mist.

Kate 🅖 (Greek) pure. (English) a
short form of Katherine.

Kateb (Arabic) writer.

Katelyn 🅖 (Irish) a form of Caitlin.

Katerina 🅖 (Slavic) a form of
Katherine.

Katherine 🅖 (Greek) pure.

Kathrine 🅖 (Greek) a form of
Katherine.

Kathryn 🅖 (English) a form of
Katherine.

Kathy 🅖 (English) a familiar form
of Katherine.

Katia 🅖 (Russian) a form of
Katherine.

Katie 🅖 (English) a familiar form of
Kate.

Katlin 🅖 (Irish) a form of Katlyn
(see Girls' Names).

Kato (Runyankore) second of twins.

Katsumasa (Japanese) flourishing victory; border man; righteous.

Katsumi (Japanese) beautiful winner; patient snake.

Katsunori (Japanese) patient lawmaker.

Katsutoshi (Japanese) kindly victory; victory age.

Katungi (Runyankore) rich.

Kaumerang (Palauan) trust each other.

Kavan (Irish) handsome.
Cavan, Kavanagh, Kavaugn, Kaven, Kavenaugh, Kavin, Kavon, Kayvan

Kaveh (Persian) ancient hero.

Kavi (Hindi) poet.

Kavin, Kavon (Irish) forms of Kavan.
Kaveon, Kavion, Kavone, Kayvon, Kaywon

Kawasio (Chuukese) a form of Jarvis.

Kawika (Hawaiian) a form of David.

Kay **G** (Greek) rejoicing. (German) fortified place. Literature: one of King Arthur's knights of the Round Table.
Kai, Kaycee, Kaye, Kayson

Kayako (Japanese) miscanthus reed.

Kaycee **G** (Greek, German) a form of Kay. (American, Irish) a form of Kacey.

Kayden **B** (Arabic) a form of Kadin.
Kayde, Kaydee, Kaydin, Kaydn, Kaydon

Kayin (Nigerian) celebrated. (Yoruba) long-hoped-for child.

Kayla **G** (Hebrew, Arabic) a form of Kayle.

Kaylan **G** (Irish) a form of Kaylen.

Kayle (Hebrew) faithful dog. (Arabic) a short form of Kahlil.
Kayl, Kayla, Kaylee

Kayleb (Hebrew) a form of Caleb.
Kaylib, Kaylob, Kaylub

Kaylee **G** (Hebrew, Arabic) a form of Kayle.

Kaylen (Irish) a form of Kellen.
Kaylan, Kaylin, Kaylon, Kaylyn, Kaylynn

Kaylin **G** (Irish) a form of Kaylen.

Kaylon **B** (Irish) a form of Kaylen.

Kaylyn, Kaylynn **G** (Irish) forms of Kaylen.

Kayne (Hebrew) a form of Cain.
Kaynan, Kaynen, Kaynon

Kayode (Yoruba) he brought joy.

Kayonga (Runyankore) ash.

Kazio (Polish) a form of Casimir, Kasimir. See also Cassidy.

Kazu (Japanese) first; obedient.

Kazuaki (Japanese) peaceful; brilliant light.

Kazujiro (Japanese) obedient second son.

Kazuki (Japanese) he who prays for peace.

Kazumi (Japanese) fruit of harmony.

Kazuo (Japanese) man of peace.

Kazushige (Japanese) harmonious luxury.

Kazuto (Japanese) harmonious person; the first to ascend.

Kazuyuki (Japanese) harmonious travel.

KC (American) a combination of the initials K. + C. See also Kacey.
Kc, K.C., Kcee, Kcey

Ke (Chinese) able.

Keagan (Irish) a form of Keegan.
Keagean, Keagen, Keaghan, Keagyn

Keahi (Hawaiian) flames.

Keaka (Hawaiian) a form of Jack.

Kealoha (Hawaiian) fragrant.
Ke'ala

Keanan (Irish) a form of Keenan.
Keanen, Keanna, Keannan, Keanon

Keandre (American) a combination of the prefix Ke + Andre.
Keandra, Keandray, Keandré, Keandree, Keandrell, Keondre

Keane (German) bold; sharp. (Irish) handsome. (English) a form of Keene.
Kean

Keanna 🄶 (Irish) a form of Keanan.

Keanu 🄱 (Irish) a form of Keenan.
Keaneu, Keani, Keanno, Keano, Keanue, Keeno, Keenu, Kianu

Kearn (Irish) a short form of Kearney.
Kearne

Kearney (Irish) a form of Carney.
Kar, Karney, Karny, Kearn, Kearny

Keary (Irish) a form of Kerry.
Kearie

Keaton 🄱 (English) where hawks fly.
Keatan, Keaten, Keatin, Keatton, Keatyn, Keeton, Keetun

Keaven (Irish) a form of Kevin.
Keavan, Keavon

Keawe (Hawaiian) strand.

Keb (Egyptian) earth. Mythology: an ancient earth god, also known as Geb.

Kebekol (Palauan) to go sailing together.

Keboech (Palauan) hurl spears together.

Ked (Palauan) hill.

Kedar (Hindi) mountain lord. (Arabic) powerful. Religion: another name for the Hindu god Shiva.
Kadar, Kedaar, Keder

Keddy (Scottish) a form of Adam.
Keddie

Kedem (Hebrew) ancient.

Kedrick (English) a form of Cedric.
Keddrick, Kederick, Kedrek, Kedric, Kiedric, Kiedrick

Keefe (Irish) handsome; loved.

Keegan 🄱 (Irish) little; fiery.
Kaegan, Kagan, Keagan, Keagen, Keeghan, Keegon, Keegun, Kegan, Keigan

Keelan (Irish) little; slender.
Keelen, Keelin, Keelyn, Keilan, Kelan

Keeley 🄶 (Irish) handsome.
Kealey, Kealy, Keeli, Keelian, Keelie

Keely 🄶 (Irish) a form of Keeley.

Keenan 🄱 (Irish) little Keene.
Kaenan, Keanan, Keanu, Keenen, Keennan, Keenon, Kenan, Keynan, Kienan, Kienon

Keene (German) bold; sharp. (English) smart. See also Kane.
Kaene, Keane, Keen, Keenan

Keenen (Irish) a form of Keenan.
Keenin, Kienen

Kees (Dutch) a form of Kornelius.
Keese, Keesee, Keyes

Keevon (Irish) a form of Kevin.
Keevan, Keeven, Keevin, Keewan, Keewin

Kegan (Irish) a form of Keegan.
Kegen, Keghan, Kegon, Kegun

Kehind (Yoruba) second-born twin.
Kehinde

Keichiro (Chuukese) a form of Kiichiro.

Keiffer (German) a form of Cooper.
Keefer, Keifer, Kiefer

Keigan (Irish) a form of Keegan.
Keighan, Keighen

Keigo (Japanese) corner; self.

Keiji (Japanese) cautious ruler.

Keilan (Irish) a form of Keelan.
Keilen, Keilin, Keillene, Keillyn, Keilon, Keilynn

Keir (Irish) a short form of Kieran.

Keitaro (Japanese) blessed.
Keita

Keith (Welsh) forest. (Scottish) battle place. See also Kika.
Keath, Keeth, Keithen

Keithen (Welsh, Scottish) a form of Keith.
Keithan, Keitheon, Keithon

Keivan (Irish) a form of Kevin.
Keiven, Keivn, Keivon, Keivone

Keizo (Japanese) respectful third son.

Kekapa (Hawaiian) tapa cloth.

Kekerelchad (Palauan) young man.

Kekipi (Hawaiian) rebel.

Kekoa (Hawaiian) bold, courageous.

Kelby (German) farm by the spring.
Keelby, Kelbee, Kelbey, Kelbi, Kellby

Kele (Hopi) sparrow hawk.
(Hawaiian) a form of Jerry.
Kelle

Kelemen (Hungarian) gentle; kind.
Kellman

Kelevi (Finnish) hero.

Keli (Hawaiian) a form of Terry.

Keli'i (Hawaiian) chief.

Kelile (Ethiopian) protected.

Kell (Scandinavian) spring.

Kellan (Irish) a form of Kellen.
Keillan

Kellen **B** (Irish) mighty warrior.
Kaelan, Kailen, Kakan, Kalen, Kalin, Kallen, Kalon, Kalyn, Kaylen, Keelan, Kelden, Kelin, Kellan, Kelle, Kellin, Kellyn, Kelyn, Kelynn

Keller (Irish) little companion.

Kelley **G** (Irish) a form of Kelly.

Kelli, Kellie **G** (Irish) forms of Kelly.

Kelly **G** (Irish) warrior.
Kelle, Kellen, Kelley, Kelli, Kellie, Kely

Kelmen (Basque) merciful.
Kelmin

Kelsea **G** (Scandinavian) a form of Kelsey.

Kelsey **G** (Scandinavian) island of ships.
Kelcy, Kelse, Kelsea, Kelsi, Kelsie, Kelso, Kelsy, Kesley, Kesly

Kelsi, Kelsy **G** (Scandinavian) forms of Kelsey.

Kelton **B** (English) keel town; port.
Kelden, Keldon, Kelson, Kelston, Kelten, Keltin, Keltonn, Keltyn

Kelulau (Palauan) confidential; a whisper.

Kelvin B (Irish, English) narrow river. Geography: a river in Scotland.
Kelvan, Kelven, Kelvon, Kelvyn, Kelwin, Kelwyn

Kemal (Turkish) highest honor.

Kemen (Basque) strong.

Kemp (English) fighter; champion.

Kempton (English) military town.

Ken (Japanese) one's own kind. (Scottish) a short form of Kendall, Kendrick, Kenneth.
Kena, Kenn, Keno

Ken'ichi (Japanese) healthy first born; modest first born.

Kenan (Irish) a form of Keenan.

Kenaz (Hebrew) bright.

Kenchy (Chuukese) a form of Ken'ichi.

Kendal G (English) a form of Kendall.
Kendale, Kendali, Kendel, Kendul, Kendyl

Kendall G (English) valley of the river Kent.
Ken, Kendal, Kendell, Kendrall, Kendryll, Kendyll, Kyndall

Kendarius (American) a combination of Ken + Darius.
Kendarious, Kendarrious, Kendarrius, Kenderious, Kenderius, Kenderyious

Kendell (English) a form of Kendall.
Kendelle, Kendrel, Kendrell

Kendra G (English) a form of Kenda (see Girls' Names).

Kendrew (Scottish) a form of Andrew.

Kendrick B (Irish) son of Henry. (Scottish) royal chieftain.
Ken, Kenderrick, Kendric, Kendrich, Kenedrick, Kendricks, Kendrik,
Kendrix, Kendryck, Kenndrick, Keondric, Keondrick

Kenia G (Hebrew) a form of Kenya.

Kenjiro (Japanese) second son who sees with insight.

Kenley (English) royal meadow.
Kenlea, Kenlee, Kenleigh, Kenlie, Kenly

Kenn (Scottish) a form of Ken.

Kenna G (Scottich) a form of Kennan.

Kennan (Scottish) little Ken.
Kenna, Kenan, Kenen, Kennen, Kennon

Kennard (Irish) brave chieftain.
Kenner

Kennedy G (Irish) helmeted chief. History: John F. Kennedy was the thirty-fifth U.S. president.
Kenedy, Kenidy, Kennady, Kennedey

Kenneth B (Irish) handsome. (English) royal oath.
Ken, Keneth, Kenneith, Kennet, Kennethen, Kennett, Kennieth, Kennith, Kennth, Kenny, Kennyth, Kenya

Kenny B (Scottish) a familiar form of Kenneth.
Keni, Kenney, Kenni, Kennie, Kinnie

Kenrick (English) bold ruler; royal ruler.
Kenric, Kenricks, Kenrik

Kent B (Welsh) white; bright. (English) a short form of Kenton. Geography: a region in England.

Kenta (Japanese) very healthy.

Kentaro (Japanese) big boy.

Kento (Japanese) he who has good health.

Kenton (English) from Kent, England.
Kent, Kenten, Kentin, Kentonn

Kentrell **B** (English) king's estate.
Kenreal, Kentrel, Kentrelle

Kenward (English) brave; royal guardian.

Kenya **G** (Hebrew) animal horn. (Russian) a form of Kenneth. Geography: a country in east-central Africa.
Kenyatta

Kenyatta (American) a form of Kenya.
Kenyata, Kenyatae, Kenyatee, Kenyatter, Kenyatti, Kenyotta

Kenyon (Irish) white haired, blond.
Kenyan, Kenynn, Keonyon

Kenzie **G** (Scottish) wise leader. See also Mackenzie.
Kensie

Keoki (Hawaiian) a form of George.

Keola (Hawaiian) life.

Keon **B** (Irish) a form of Ewan.
Keeon, Keion, Keionne, Keondre, Keone, Keonne, Keonte, Keony, Keyon, Kian, Kion

Keoni (Hawaiian) a form of John.

Keonte (American) a form of Keon.
Keonntay, Keonta, Keontae, Keontay, Keontaye, Keontez, Keontia, Keontis, Keontrae, Keontre, Keontrey, Keontrye

Kerbasi (Basque) warrior.

Kerel (Afrikaans) young.
Kerell

Kerem (Turkish) noble; kind.
Kereem

Keremes (Chuukese) a form of Jeremy.

Kerey (Gypsy) homeward bound.
Ker

Keri **G** (Irish) a form of Kerry.

Kerman (Basque) from Germany.

Kermit (Irish) a form of Dermot.
Kermey, Kermie, Kermitt, Kermy

Kern (Irish) a short form of Kieran.
Kearn, Kerne

Kerr (Scandinavian) a form of Carr.
Karr

Kerri (Irish) a form of Kerry.

Kerrick (English) king's rule.

Kerry (Irish) dark; dark haired.
Keary, Keri, Kerrey, Kerri, Kerrie

Kers (Todas) Botany: an Indian plant.

Kersen (Indonesian) cherry.

Kerstan (Dutch) a form of Christian.

Kerwin (Irish) little; dark. (English) friend of the marshlands.
Kervin, Kervyn, Kerwinn, Kerwyn, Kerwynn, Kirwin, Kirwyn

Kesar (Russian) a form of Caesar.
Kesare

Keshawn (American) a combination of the prefix Ke + Shawn.
Keeshaun, Keeshawn, Keeshon, Kesean, Keshan, Keshane, Keshaun, Keshayne, Keshion, Keshon, Keshone, Keshun, Kishan

Kesin (Hindi) long-haired beggar.

Kesse **G** (Ashanti, Fante) chubby baby.
Kessie

Kester (English) a form of Christopher.

Kestrel (English) falcon.
Kes

Keung (Chinese) universe.

Kevan (Irish) a form of Kevin.
Kavan, Kewan, Kewane, Kewaun, Keyvan, Kiwan, Kiwane

Keven 🅱 (Irish) a form of Kevin.
Keve, Keveen, Kiven

Kevin ✼ 🅱 (Irish) handsome. See also Cavan.
Kaiven, Keaven, Keevon, Keivan, Kev, Kevan, Keven, Keverne, Kevian, Kevien, Kévin, Kevinn, Kevins, Kevis, Kevn, Kevon, Kevvy, Kevyn, Kyven

Kevon 🅱 (Irish) a form of Kevin.
Keveon, Kevion, Kevone, Kevonne, Kevontae, Kevonte, Kevoyn, Kevron, Kewon, Kewone, Keyvon, Kivon

Kevyn 🅱 (Irish) a form of Kevin.
Kevyon

Key (English) key; protected.

Keyana 🅶 (American) a form of Kiana.

Keyon (Irish) a form of Keon.
Keyan, Keyen, Keyin, Keyion

Keyonna 🅶 (American) a form of Kiana.

Keyshawn (American) a combination of Key + Shawn.
Keyshan, Keyshaun, Keyshon, Keyshun

Khachig (Armenian) small cross.
Khachik

Khadijah 🅶 (Arabic) trustworthy.

Khaim (Russian) a form of Chaim.

Khaldun (Arabic) forever.
Khaldoon, Khaldoun

Khalfani (Swahili) born to lead.
Khalfan

Khälid (Arabic) eternal.
Khaled, Khallid, Khalyd

Khalîl (Arabic) friend.
Kahlil, Kaleel, Kalil, Khahlil, Khailil, Khailyl, Khalee, Khaleel, Khaleil, Khali, Khalial, Khaliel, Khalihl, Khalill, Khaliyl

Khaliq (Arabic) creative.
Kaliq, Khalique

Khamisi (Swahili) born on Thursday.
Kham

Khan (Turkish) prince.
Khanh

Kharald (Russian) a form of Gerald.

Khayru (Arabic) benevolent.
Khiri, Khiry, Kiry

Khoury (Arabic) priest.
Khory

Khristian (Greek) a form of Christian, Kristian.
Khris, Khristan, Khristin, Khriston, Khrystian

Khristopher (Greek) a form of Kristopher.
Khristofer, Khristophar, Khrystopher

Khristos (Greek) a form of Christos.
Khris, Khristophe, Kristo, Kristos

Khuyen (Vietnamese) advise.

Kia 🅶 (African) season's beginning. (American) a short form of Kiana.

Kiana 🅶 (American) a combination of the prefix Ki + Anna.

Kiara 🅶 (Irish) little and dark.

Kibo (Uset) worldly; wise.

Kibuuka (Luganda) brave warrior. History: a Ganda warrior deity.

Kidd (English) child; young goat.

Kiefer (German) a form of Keifer.
Kief, Kieffer, Kiefor, Kiffer, Kiiefer

Kiel (Irish) a form of Kyle.
Kiell

Kiele **G** (Hawaiian) gardenia.

Kieran **B** (Irish) little and dark;
little Keir.
*Keiran, Keiren, Keiron, Kiaron,
Kiarron, Kier, Kieren, Kierian, Kierien,
Kierin, Kiernan, Kieron, Kierr, Kierre,
Kierron, Kyran*

Kiernan (Irish) a form of Kieran.
Kern, Kernan, Kiernen

Kiersten **G** (Scandanavian) a form
of Kirsten.

Kiet (Tai) honor.

Kifeda (Luo) only boy among girls.

Kiho (Rutooro) born on a foggy day.

Kiichiro (Japanese) pleasing first son.

Kijika (Native American) quiet
walker.

Kika (Hawaiian) a form of Keith.

Kiki **G** (Spanish) a form of Henry.

Kile (Irish) a form of Kyle.
Kilee, Kilen, Kiley, Kiyl, Kiyle

Kiley **G** (Irish) a form of Kile, Kyle.

Killian (Irish) little Kelly.
*Kilean, Kilian, Kilien, Killie, Killien,
Killiean, Killion, Killy*

Kim **G** (English) a short form of
Kimball.
Kimie, Kimmy

Kimball (Greek) hollow vessel.
(English) warrior chief.
Kim, Kimbal, Kimbel, Kimbell, Kimble

Kimberly **G** (English) chief, ruler.

Kimo (Hawaiian) a form of James.

Kimokeo (Hawaiian) a form of
Timothy.

Kimy (Vietnamese) gold.

Kin (Japanese) golden.

Kincaid (Scottish) battle chief.
Kincade, Kinkaid

Kindin (Basque) fifth.

King (English) king. A short form of
names beginning with "King."

Kingsley (English) king's meadow.
*King, Kings, Kingslea, Kingslie,
Kingsly, Kingzlee, Kinslea, Kinslee,
Kinsley, Kinslie, Kinsly*

Kingston (English) king's estate.
King, Kinston

Kingswell (English) king's well.
King

Kini **G** (Hawaiian) a short form of
Iukini.

Kinjiro (Japanese) golden second son.

Kinnard (Irish) tall slope.

Kinsey **G** (English) victorious
royalty.
Kinze, Kinzie

Kinshiro (Japanese) golden fourth-
born son.

Kintaro (Japanese) golden boy.

Kinton (Hindi) crowned.

Kion (Irish) a form of Keon.
Kione, Kionie, Kionne

Kioshi (Japanese) quiet.

Kiosho (Japanese) clear, bright.

Kipp (English) pointed hill.
Kip, Kippar, Kipper, Kippie, Kippy

Kir (Bulgarian) a familiar form of
Cyrus.

Kira **G** (Persian) sun. (Latin) light.

Kiral (Turkish) king; supreme leader.

Kiran 🅖 (Sanskrit) beam of light.
Kyran

Kirby 🅑 (Scandinavian) church village. (English) cottage by the water.
Kerbey, Kerbie, Kerby, Kirbey, Kirbie, Kirkby

Kiri (Cambodian) mountain.

Kiril (Slavic) a form of Cyril.
Kirill, Kiryl, Kyrillos

Kirios (Greek) supreme being, the Lord.

Kiritan (Hindi) wearing a crown.

Kirk (Scandinavian) church.
Kerk

Kirkland (English) church land.
Kirklin, Kirklind, Kirklynd

Kirkley (English) church meadow.

Kirklin (English) a form of Kirkland.
Kirklan, Kirklen, Kirkline, Kirkloun, Kirklun, Kirklyn, Kirklynn

Kirkwell (English) church well; church spring.

Kirkwood (English) church forest.

Kirsten 🅖 (Greek) Christian; anointed. (Scandinavian) a form of Christine.

Kirton (English) church town.

Kishan (American) a form of Keshawn.
Kishaun, Kishawn, Kishen, Kishon, Kyshon, Kyshun

Kishi (Japanese) long and happy life.

Kisho (Japanese) one who knows his own mind.

Kistna (Hindi) sacred, holy. Geography: a sacred river in India.

Kistur (Gypsy) skillful rider.

Kit (Greek) a familiar form of Christian, Christopher, Kristopher.
Kitt, Kitts

Kito (Swahili) jewel; precious child.

Kitwana (Swahili) pledged to live.

Kiva (Hebrew) a short form of Akiva, Jacob.
Kiba, Kivi, Kiwa

Kiyoshi (Japanese) quiet; peaceful.

Kiyoto (Japanese) noble person.

Kizza (Luganda) born after twins.
Kizzy

Kjell (Swedish) a form of Karl.
Kjel

Klaudio (Pohnpeian) a form of Claudio.

Klaus (German) a short form of Nicholas. A form of Claus.
Klaas, Klaes, Klas, Klause

Klay (English) a form of Clay.

Klayton (English) a form of Clayton.

Kleef (Dutch) cliff.

Klement (Czech) a form of Clement.
Klema, Klemenis, Klemens, Klemet, Klemo, Klim, Klimek, Kliment, Klimka

Kleng (Norwegian) claw.

Knight (English) armored knight.
Knightly

Knoton (Native American) a form of Nodin.

Knowles (English) grassy slope.
Knolls, Nowles

Knox (English) hill.

Knute (Scandinavian) a form of Canute.
Knud, Knut

Koby (Polish) a familiar form of Jacob.
Kobby, Kobe, Kobey, Kobi, Kobia, Kobie

Kodi **BG** (English) a form of Kody.
Kode, Kodee, Kodie

Kody **B** (English) a form of Cody.
Kodey, Kodi, Kodye, Koty

Kofi (Twi) born on Friday.

Kohana (Lakota) swift.

Kohei (Japanese) peace.

Koi (Choctaw) panther. (Hawaiian) a form of Troy.

Koichi (Japanese) obedient first son.

Koji (Japanese) successful peacemaker.

Kojo (Akan) born on Monday.

Koka (Hawaiian) Scotsman.

Kokai (Japanese) he who crosses over the sea.

Kokayi (Shona) gathered together.

Koki (Japanese) shine; to be hopeful.

Kolby **B** (English) a form of Colby.
Kelby, Koalby, Koelby, Kohlbe, Kohlby, Kolbe, Kolbey, Kolbi, Kolbie, Kolebe, Koleby, Kollby

Kole (English) a form of Cole.
Kohl, Kohle

Koleman (English) a form of Coleman.
Kolemann, Kolemen

Kolin (English) a form of Colin.
Kolen, Kollen, Kollin, Kollyn, Kolyn

Kolton (English) a form of Colton.
Kolt, Koltan, Kolte, Kolten, Koltin, Koltn, Koltyn

Kolya (Russian) a familiar form of Nikolai, Nikolos.
Kola, Kolenka, Kolia, Kolja

Kona **B** (Hawaiian) a form of Don.
Konala

Konane (Hawaiian) bright moonlight.

Kondo (Swahili) war.

Kong (Chinese) glorious; sky.

Konner (Irish) a form of Conner, Connor.
Konar, Koner

Konnor (Irish) a form of Connor.
Kohner, Kohnor, Konor

Kono (Moquelumnan) squirrel eating a pine nut.

Konrad (German) a form of Conrad.
Khonrad, Koen, Koenraad, Kon, Konn, Konney, Konni, Konnie, Konny, Konrád, Konrade, Konrado, Kord, Kort, Kunz

Konstantin (German, Russian) a form of Constantine. See also Dinos.
Konstancji, Konstadine, Konstadino, Konstandinos, Konstantinas, Konstantine, Konstantinos, Konstantio, Konstanty, Konstantyn, Konstanz, Konstatino, Kostadino, Kostadinos, Kostandino, Kostandinos, Kostantin, Kostantino, Kostas, Kostenka, Kostya, Kotsos

Kontar (Akan) only child.

Korb (German) basket.

Korbin (English) a form of Corbin.
Korban, Korben, Korbyn

Kordell (English) a form of Cordell.
Kordel

Korey **B** (Irish) a form of Corey, Kory.
Kore, Koree, Korei, Korio, Korre, Korria, Korrye

Kori 🄶 (Irish) a form of Kory.

Kornel (Latin) a form of Cornelius, Kornelius.
Kees, Korneil, Kornél, Korneli, Kornelisz, Kornell, Krelis, Soma

Kornelius (Latin) a form of Cornelius. See also Kees, Kornel.
Karnelius, Korneilius, Korneliaus, Kornelious, Kornellius

Korrigan (Irish) a form of Corrigan.
Korigan, Korigan, Korrigon, Korrigun

Kort (German, Dutch) a form of Cort, Kurt.
Kourt

Kortney 🄶 (English) a form of Courtney.
Kortni, Kourtney

Korudon (Greek) helmeted one.

Kory 🄱 (Irish) a form of Corey.
Korey, Kori, Korie, Korrey, Korri, Korrie, Korry

Kosei (Japanese) he who navigates through life well.

Kosey (African) lion.
Kosse

Kositatino (Fijian) a form of Constantino.

Kosmo (Greek) a form of Cosmo.
Kosmy, Kozmo

Kostas (Greek) a short form of Konstantin.

Kosti (Finnish) a form of Gustave.

Kosuke (Japanese) inlet; clear; help.

Kosumi (Moquelumnan) spear fisher.

Kota (Japanese) very fortunate.

Koukalaka (Hawaiian) a form of Douglas.

Kourtland (English) a form of Courtland.
Kortlan, Kortland, Kortlend, Kortlon, Kourtlin

Kourtney 🄶 (American) a form of Courtney.

Kovit (Tai) expert.

Kozue (Japanese) tree branches.

Kraig (Irish, Scottish) a form of Craig.
Kraggie, Kraggy, Krayg, Kreg, Kreig, Kreigh

Krikor (Armenian) a form of Gregory.

Kris 🄱 (Greek) a form of Chris. A short form of Kristian, Kristofer, Kristopher.
Kriss, Krys

Krischan (German) a form of Christian.
Krishan, Krishaun, Krishawn, Krishon, Krishun

Krishna (Hindi) delightful, pleasurable. Religion: the eighth and principal avatar of the Hindu god Vishnu.
Kistna, Kistnah, Krisha, Krishnah

Krispin (Latin) a form of Crispin.
Krispian, Krispino, Krispo

Krista 🄶 (Czech) a form of Christina.

Kristen 🄶 (Greek) a form of Kristian, Kristyn. (French, English) a form of Christine.

Krister (Swedish) a form of Christian.
Krist, Kristar

Kristian 🄱 (Greek) a form of Christian, Khristian.
Kerstan, Khristos, Kit, Kris, Krischan, Krist, Kristan, Kristar, Kristek, Kristen,

Krister, Kristien, Kristin, Kristine,
Kristinn, Kristion, Kristjan, Kristo,
Kristos, Krists, Krystek, Krystian,
Khrystiyan

Kristin **G** (Greek) a form of
Kristian.

Kristina **G** (Greek) Christian;
anointed. (Scandinavian) a form of
Christina.

Kristine **G** (Greek) a form of
Kristian.

Kristo (Greek) a short form of
Khristos.

Kristofer (Swedish) a form of
Kristopher.
Kris, Kristafer, Kristef, Kristifer, Kristoff,
Kristoffer, Kristofo, Kristofor, Kristofyr,
Kristufer, Kristus, Krystofer

Kristoff (Greek) a short form of
Kristofer, Kristopher.
Kristof, Kristóf

Kristophe (French) a form of
Kristopher.

Kristopher **B** (Greek) a form of
Christopher. See also Topher.
Khristopher, Kit, Kris, Krisstopher,
Kristapher, Kristepher, Kristfer,
Kristfor, Kristo, Kristofer, Kristoff,
Kristoforo, Kristoph, Kristophe,
Kristophor, Kristos, Krists, Krisus,
Krystopher, Krystupas, Krzysztof

Kristy **G** (American) a familiar form
of Kristine, Krystal.

Kristyn **G** (Greek) a form of
Kristen.

Kruz (Spanish) a form of Cruz.
Kruise, Kruize, Kruse, Kruze

Krystal **G** (American) clear, brilliant
glass.

Krystian **BG** (Polish) a form of
Christian.
Krys, Krystek, Krystien, Krystin

Kuan (Chinese) well-off.

Kuan-Ti (Chinese) god of war and
fortunetelling.

Kuan-Yin (Chinese) Buddhist deity of
mercy.

Kuba (Czech) a form of Jacob.
Kubo, Kubus

Kueng (Chinese) universe.

Kugonza (Rutooro) love.

Kui (Chinese) stalwart.

Kuiril (Basque) lord.

Kulian (Pohnpeian) a form of Julio.

Kuma (Japanese) bear.

Kumar (Sanskrit) prince.

Kumi (Japanese) long, continued
beauty.

Kun (Chinese) universe; mountain
range.

Kunihide (Japanese) beautiful nation.

Kunihiro (Japanese) spacious nation.

Kuniyuki (Japanese) nation full of
good fortune.

Kunle (Yoruba) home filled with
honors.

Kuper (Yiddish) copper.

Kuri (Japanese) chestnut.

Kurt (Latin, German, French) a short
form of Kurtis. A form of Curt.
Kirt, Kort, Kuno, Kurtt

Kurtis (Latin, French) a form of Curtis.
Kirtis, Kirtus, Kurt, Kurtes, Kurtez, Kurtice, Kurties, Kurtiss, Kurtus, Kurtys

Kuruk (Pawnee) bear.

Kustin (Pohnpeian) a form of Justo.

Kustino (Fijian) a form of Justo.

Kuya (Japanese) sky.

Kuzih (Carrier) good speaker.

Kwabena (Akan) born on Tuesday.

Kwacha (Nguni) morning.

Kwako (Akan) born on Wednesday.
Kwaka, Kwaku

Kwam (Zuni) a form of John.

Kwame (Akan) born on Saturday.
Kwamen, Kwami, Kwamin

Kwan (Korean) strong.
Kwane

Kwasi (Akan) born on Sunday. (Swahili) wealthy.
Kwasie, Kwazzi, Kwesi

Kwayera (Nguni) dawn.

Kwende (Nguni) let's go.

Kyele (Irish) a form of Kyle.

Kyla 🄖 (Irish) attractive. (Yiddish) crown; laurel.

Kylan (Irish) a form of Kyle.
Kyelen, Kyleen, Kylen, Kylin, Kyline, Kylon, Kylun

Kyle ☼ 🄑 (Irish) narrow piece of land; place where cattle graze. (Yiddish) crowned with laurels.
Cyle, Kiel, Kilan, Kile, Kilen, Kiley, Ky, Kye, Kyel, Kyele, Kylan, Kylee, Kyler, Kyley, Kylie, Kyll, Kylle, Kyrell

Kylee 🄖 (Irish) a form of Kyle.

Kyler 🄑 (English) a form of Kyle.
Kylar, Kylor

Kylie 🄖 (West Australian Aboriginal) curled stick; boomerang. (Irish) a familiar form of Kyle.

Kym 🄖 (English, Vietnamese) a form of Kim.

Kynan (Welsh) chief.

Kyndall 🄖 (English) a form of Kendall.
Kyndal, Kyndel, Kyndell, Kyndle

Kyne (English) royal.

Kyoshi (Japanese) quiet.

Kyran (Sanskrit) a form of Kiran.
Kyren, Kyron, Kyrone

Kyros (Greek) master.

Kyven (American) a form of Kevin.
Kyvan, Kyvaun, Kyvon, Kywon, Kywynn

L

L 🄑🄖 (American) an initial used as a first name.

Laban (Hawaiian) white.
Labon, Lebaan, Leban, Liban

Labaron (American) a combination of the prefix La + Baron.
Labaren, Labarren, Labarron, Labearon, Labron

Labib (Arabic) sensible; intelligent.

Labrentsis (Russian) a form of Lawrence.
Labhras, Labhruinn, Labrencis

Lacey 🄖 (Latin) cheerful. (Greek) a familiar form of Larissa.

Lachlan (Scottish) land of lakes.
Lache, Lachlann, Lachunn, Lakelan, Lakeland

Lacy **G** (Latin) a form of Lacey.

Ladarian (American) a combination of the prefix La + Darian.
Ladarien, Ladarin, Ladarion, Ladarren, Ladarrian, Ladarrien, Ladarrin, Ladarrion, Laderion, Laderrian, Laderrion

Ladarius (American) a combination of the prefix La + Darius.
Ladarious, Ladaris, Ladarrius, Ladauris, Laderius, Ladirus

Ladarrius (American) a form of Ladarius.
Ladarrias, Ladarries, Ladarrious, Laderrious, Laderris

Ladd (English) attendant.
Lad, Laddey, Laddie, Laddy

Laderrick (American) a combination of the prefix La + Derrick.
Ladarrick, Ladereck, Laderic, Laderricks

Ladio (Slavic) he who governs with glory.

Ladislao (Slavic) he who governs with glory.

Ladislav (Czech) a form of Walter.
Laco, Lada, Ladislaus

Lado (Fante) second-born son.

Ladolfo, Landolfo (Germanic) skillful as a wolf in the city.

Laertes (Greek) rock-picker.

Lafayette (French) History: Marquis de Lafayette was a French soldier and politician who aided the American Revolution.
Lafaiete, Lafayett, Lafette, Laffyette

Lahual (Araucanian) larch tree.

Lai (Chinese) future.

Laijia (Fijian) a form of Elias.

Laine **B** (English) a form of Lane.
Lain

Laird (Scottish) wealthy landowner.

Lais (Arabic) lion.

Lajos (Hungarian) famous; holy.
Lajcsi, Laji, Lali

Lake (English) lake.
Lakan, Lakane, Lakee, Laken, Lakin

Laken **G** (English) a form of Lake.

Lakota **BG** (Dakota) a tribal name.
Lakoda

Lal (Hindi) beloved.

Lam (Vietnamese) full understanding, knowledge.

Lamar **B** (German) famous throughout the land. (French) sea, ocean.
Lamair, Lamario, Lamaris, Lamarr, Lamarre, Larmar, Lemar

Lambert (German) bright land.
Bert, Lambard, Lamberto, Lambirt, Lampard, Landbert

Lamond (French) world.
Lammond, Lamon, Lamonde, Lamondo, Lamondre, Lamund, Lemond

Lamont **B** (Scandinavian) lawyer.
Lamaunt, Lamonta, Lamonte, Lamontie, Lamonto, Lamount, Lemont

Lan (Vietnamese) fictitious four-legged animal with a single horn.

Lance **B** (German) a short form of Lancelot.
Lancy, Lantz, Lanz, Launce

Lancelot (French) attendant.
Literature: the knight who loved
King Arthur's wife, Queen
Guinevere.
Lance, Lancelott, Launcelet, Launcelot

Landelino (Teutonic) he who is a
friend of the earth.

Landen (English) a form of Landon.
Landenn

Lander (Basque) lion man. (English)
landowner.
Landers, Landor

Landerico (Teutonic) powerful in the
region; he who exercises power in
the region.

Landin 🅑 (English) a form of
Landon.

Lando (Portuguese, Spanish) a short
form of Orlando, Rolando.

Landon ☀ 🅑 (English) open,
grassy meadow.
Landan, Landen, Landin, Landyn

Landrada (Teutonic) counselor in his
village.

Landry (French, English) ruler.
Landre, Landré, Landrue

Lane 🅑 (English) narrow road.
Laine, Laney, Lanie, Layne

Lang (Scandinavian) tall man.
Lange

Langdon (English) long hill.
Landon, Langsdon, Langston

Langford (English) long ford.
Lanford, Lankford

Langley (English) long meadow.
Langlea, Langlee, Langleigh, Langly

Langston (English) long, narrow
town.
Langsden, Langsdon

Langundo (Native American) peaceful.

Lanh (Vietnamese) quick-minded,
smart; street smart.

Lani 🅖 (Hawaiian) heaven.

Lanny (American) a familiar form of
Lawrence, Laurence.
Lanney, Lannie, Lennie

Lanu (Moquelumnan) running
around the pole.

Lanz (Italian) a form of Lance.
Lanzo, Lonzo

Lao (Spanish) a short form of
Stanislaus.

Lap (Vietnamese) independent.

Lapidos (Hebrew) torches.
Lapidoth

Laquan (American) a combination of
the prefix La + Quan.
*Laquain, Laquann, Laquanta,
Laquantae, Laquante, Laquawn,
Laquawne, Laquin, Laquinn, Laqun,
Laquon, Laquone, Laqwan, Laqwon*

Laquintin (American) a combination
of the prefix La + Quintin.
*Laquentin, Laquenton, Laquintas,
Laquinten, Laquintiss, Laquinton*

Lara 🅖 (Greek) cheerful. (Latin)
shining; famous. Mythology: a
Roman nymph. A short form of
Laraine, Laura.

Laramie (French) tears of love.
Geography: a town in Wyoming on
the Overland Trail.
Larami, Laramy, Laremy

Larenzo (Italian, Spanish) a form of
Lorenzo.
Larenz, Larenza, Larinzo, Laurenzo

Larissa (Greek) cheerful.

Larkin (Irish) rough; fierce.
Larklin

Larnell (American) a combination of
Larry + Darnell.

Laron (French) thief.
*Laran, La'ron, La Ron, Larone,
Laronn, Larron, La Ruan*

Larrimore (French) armorer.
Larimore, Larmer, Larmor

Larry **B** (Latin) a familiar form of
Lawrence.
Larrie, Lary

Lars (Scandinavian) a form of
Lawrence.
*Laris, Larris, Larse, Larsen, Larson,
Larsson, Larz, Lasse, Laurans, Laurits,
Lavrans, Lorens*

LaSalle (French) hall.
Lasal, Lasalle, Lascell, Lascelles

Lasarusa (Fijian) a form of Eleazar.

Lash (Gypsy) a form of Louis.
Lashi, Lasho

Lashawn (American) a combination
of the prefix La + Shawn.
*Lasaun, Lasean, Lashajaun, Lashan,
Lashane, Lashaun, Lashon, Lashun*

Lashon (American) a form of
Lashawn.
Lashone, Lashonne

Lasse (Finnish) a form of Nicholas.

László (Hungarian) famous ruler.
Laci, Lacko, Laslo, Lazlo

Lateef (Arabic) gentle; pleasant.
Latif, Letif

Latham (Scandinavian) barn.
(English) district.
Laith, Lathe, Lay

Lathan (American) a combination of
the prefix La + Nathan.
Lathaniel, Lathen, Lathyn, Leathan

Lathrop (English) barn, farmstead.
Lathe, Lathrope, Lay

Latimer (English) interpreter.
Lat, Latimor, Lattie, Latty, Latymer

Latravis (American) a combination of
the prefix La + Travis.
*Latavious, Latavius, Latraveus,
Latraviaus, Latravious, Latravius,
Latrayvious, Latrayvous, Latrivis*

Latrell (American) a combination of
the prefix La + Kentrell.
*Latreal, Latreil, Latrel, Latrelle, Letreal,
Letrel, Letrell, Letrelle*

Laudalino (Portuguese) praised.
Lino

Laughlin (Irish) servant of Saint
Secundinus.
Lanty, Lauchlin, Leachlainn

Laura **G** (Latin) crowned with
laurel.

Laurelino, Laurentino (Latin)
winner; worthy of honors.

Lauren **G** (Latin) a form of
Laurence.

Laurence **G** (Latin) crowned with
laurel. A form of Lawrence. See also
Rance, Raulas, Raulo, Renzo.
*Lanny, Lauran, Laurance, Laureano,
Laurencho, Laurencio, Laurens,
Laurent, Laurentij, Laurentios,
Laurentiu, Laurentius, Laurentz,
Laurentzi, Laurie, Laurin, Lauris,
Laurits, Lauritz, Laurnet, Lauro,
Laurus, Lavrenti, Lurance*

Laurencio (Spanish) a form of
Laurence.

Laurens (Dutch) a form of Laurence.
Laurenz

Laurent (French) a form of Laurence.
Laurente

Laurie G (English) a familiar form of Laurence.
Lauri, Laury, Lorry

Lauris (Swedish) a form of Laurence.

Lauro (Filipino) a form of Laurence.

Laury G (English) a form of Laurie.

Lautaro (Araucanian) daring and enterprising.

LaValle (French) valley.
Lavail, Laval, Lavalei, Lavalle, Lavell

Lavan (Hebrew) white.
Lavane, Lavaughan, Laven, Lavon, Levan

Lavaughan (American) a form of Lavan.
Lavaughn, Levaughan, Levaughn

Lave (Italian) lava. (English) lord.

Lavell (French) a form of LaValle.
Lavel, Lavele, Lavelle, Levele, Levell, Levelle

Lavi (Hebrew) lion.

Lavon (American) a form of Lavan.
Lavion, Lavone, Lavonn, Lavonne, Lavont, Lavonte

Lavrenti (Russian) a form of Lawrence.
Larenti, Lavrentij, Lavrusha, Lavrik, Lavro

Lawerence (Latin) a form of Lawrence.
Lawerance

Lawford (English) ford on the hill.
Ford, Law

Lawler (Irish) soft-spoken.
Lawlor, Lollar, Loller

Lawrence B (Latin) crowned with laurel. See also Brencis, Chencho.
Labrentsis, Laiurenty, Lanny, Lanty, Larance, Laren, Larian, Larien, Laris, Larka, Larrance, Larrence, Larry, Lars, Larya, Laurence, Lavrenti, Law, Lawerence, Lawrance, Lawren, Lawrey,

Lawrie, Lawron, Lawry, Lencho, Lon, Lóránt, Loreca, Loren, Loretto, Lorenzo, Lorne, Lourenco, Lowrance

Lawson (English) son of Lawrence.
Lawsen, Layson

Lawton (English) town on the hill.
Laughton, Law

Layne B (English) a form of Lane.
Layn, Laynee

Layton B (English) a form of Leighton.
Laydon, Layten, Layth, Laythan, Laython

Lazaro, Lázaro (Italian) forms of Lazarus.
Lazarillo, Lazarito, Lazzaro

Lazarus (Greek) a form of Eleazar. Bible: Lazarus was raised from the dead by Jesus.
Lazar, Lázár, Lazare, Lazarius, Lazaro, Lazaros, Lazorus

Leah G (Hebrew) weary.

Leal (Spanish) loyal and faithful worker.

Leander (Greek) lion-man; brave as a lion.
Ander, Leandro

Leandre (Greek) calm, serene man.

Leandro (Spanish) a form of Leander.
Leandra, Léandre, Leandrew, Leandros

Leanne G (English) a form of Leeann, Lian (see Girls' Names).

Learco (Greek) judge of his village.

Leben (Yiddish) life.
Laben, Lebon

Lebna (Ethiopian) spirit; heart.

Ledarius (American) a combination of the prefix Le + Darius.
Ledarrious, Ledarrius, Lederious, Lederris

Lee **B** (English) a short form of Farley, Leonard, and names containing "lee."
Leigh

Leggett (French) one who is sent; delegate.
Legate, Legette, Leggitt, Liggett

Lei **BG** (Chinese) thunder. (Hawaiian) a form of Ray.

Leib (Yiddish) roaring lion.
Leibel

Leif (Scandinavian) beloved.
Laif, Leife, Lief

Leigh **G** (English) a form of Lee.

Leighton (English) meadow farm.
Lay, Layton, Leigh, Leyton

Leith (Scottish) broad river.

Lek (Tai) small.

Lekeke (Hawaiian) powerful ruler.

Leks (Estonian) a familiar form of Alexander.
Leksik, Lekso

Lel (Gypsy) taker.

Leland **B** (English) meadowland; protected land.
Lealand, Lee, Leeland, Leigh, Leighland, Lelan, Lelann, Lelend, Lelund, Leyland

Lelio (Latin) he who is talkative.

Lemar (French) a form of Lamar.
Lemario, Lemarr

Lemuel (Hebrew) devoted to God.
Lem, Lemmie, Lemmy

Len (Hopi) flute. (German) a short form of Leonard.

Lenard (German) a form of Leonard.
Lennard

Lencho (Spanish) a form of Lawrence.
Lenci, Lenzy

Lennart (Swedish) a form of Leonard.
Lennerd

Lenno (Native American) man.

Lennon (Irish) small cloak; cape.
Lenon

Lennor (Gypsy) spring; summer.

Lennox (Scottish) with many elms.
Lennix, Lenox

Lenny (German) a familiar form of Leonard.
Leni, Lennie, Leny

Leo (Latin) lion. (German) a short form of Leon, Leopold.
Lavi, Leão, Lee, Leib, Leibel, Léo, Léocadie, Leos, Leosko, Leosoko, Lev, Lio, Lion, Liutas, Lyon, Nardek

Leobardo (Italian) a form of Leonard.

Leocadio (Greek) he who shines because of his whiteness.

Leodoualdo (Teutonic) he who governs his village.

Leofrido (Teutonic) he who brings peace to his village.

Leon (Greek, German) a short form of Leonard, Napoleon.
Leo, Léon, Leonas, Léonce, Leoncio, Leondris, Leone, Leonek, Leonetti, Leoni, Leonid, Leonidas, Leonirez, Leonizio, Leonon, Leons, Leontes, Leontios, Leontrae, Liutas

León (Latin) a form of Leon.

Leonard (German) brave as a lion.
Leanard, Lee, Len, Lena, Lenard,
Lennart, Lenny, Leno, Leobardo, Leon,
Léonard, Leonardis, Leonardo,
Leonart, Leonerd, Leonhard,
Leonidas, Leonnard, Leontes, Lernard,
Lienard, Linek, Lnard, Lon, Londard,
Lonnard, Lonya, Lynnard

Leonardo (Italian) a form of Leonard.
Leonaldo, Lionardo

Leonel (English) little lion. See also
Lionel.
Leonell

Leonelo (Spanish) a form of Leonel.

Leonhard (German) a form of
Leonard.
Leonhards

Leonid (Russian) a form of Leonard.
Leonide, Lyonechka, Lyonya

Leonidas (Greek) a form of Leonard.
Leonida, Leonides

Leónidas (Spanish) a form of León.

Leontino (German) strong as a lion.

Leopold (German) brave people.
Leo, Leopoldo, Leorad, Lipót,
Lopolda, Luepold, Luitpold, Poldi

Leopoldo (Italian) a form of
Leopold.

Leor (Hebrew) my light.
Leory, Lior

Lequinton (American) a combination
of the prefix Le + Quinton.
Lequentin, Lequenton, Lequinn

Leron (French) round, circle.
(American) a combination of the
prefix Le + Ron.
Leeron, Le Ron, Lerone, Liron, Lyron

Leroy (French) king. See also Delroy,
Elroy.
Lee, Leeroy, LeeRoy, Leigh, Lerai,
Leroi, LeRoi, LeRoy, Roy

Les (Scottish, English) a short form
of Leslie, Lester.
Lessie

Lesharo (Pawnee) chief.

Leshawn (American) a combination
of the prefix Le + Shawn.
Lashan, Lesean, Leshaun, Leshon,
Leshun

Lesley ☐ (Scottish) a form of Leslie.

Leslie ☐ (Scottish) gray fortress.
Lee, Leigh, Les, Leslea, Leslee, Lesley,
Lesli, Lesly, Lezlie, Lezly

Lesly ☐ (Scottish) a form of Leslie.

Lesmes (Teutonic) he whose nobility
protects him.

Lester ☐ (Latin) chosen camp.
(English) from Leicester, England.
Leicester, Les

Leto (Latin) he who is always happy.

Leuco (Greek) luminous one.

Lev (Hebrew) heart. (Russian) a form of
Leo. A short form of Leverett, Levi.
Leb, Leva, Levka, Levko, Levushka

Leverett (French) young hare.
Lev, Leveret, Leverit, Leveritt

Levi ☆ ☐ (Hebrew) joined in
harmony. Bible: the third son of
Jacob; Levites are the priestly tribe
of the Israelites.
Leavi, Leevi, Leevie, Lev, Levey, Levie,
Levin, Levitis, Levy, Lewi, Leyvi

Levin (Hebrew) a form of Levi.
Levine, Levion

Levon (American) a form of Lavon.
Leevon, Levone, Levonn, Levonne,
Levonte, Lyvonne

Lew (English) a short form of Lewis.

Lewin (English) beloved friend.

Lewis **B** (Welsh) a form of Llewellyn. (English) a form of Louis.
Lew, Lewes, Lewie, Lewy

Lex (English) a short form of Alexander.
Lexi, Lexin

Lexie **G** (English) a form of Lex.

Lexus **G** (Greek) a short form of Alexander.
Lexis, Lexius, Lexxus

Leyati (Moquelumnan) shape of an abalone shell.

Li (Chinese) strength.

Lí (Chinese) strong.

Lia **G** (Greek) bringer of good news. (Hebrew, Dutch, Italian) dependent.

Liam **B** (Irish) a form of William.
Liem, Lliam, Lyam

Liana **G** (Latin) youth. (French) bound, wrapped up; tree covered with vines. (English) meadow. (Hebrew) short form of Eliana (see Girls' Names).

Liang (Chinese) good, excellent.

Liao (Chinese) faraway; vast.

Liban **B** (Hawaiian) a form of Laban.
Libaan, Lieban

Líbano (Latin) white.

Liber (Latin) he who spreads abundance.

Liberal (Latin) lover of liberty.

Liberato (Latin) liberated one.

Liberio (Portuguese) liberation.
Liberaratore, Liborio

Liberto (Latin) a form of Liberal.

Libiac, Llipiac (Quechua) ray of light; brilliant, glowing.

Libio, Livio (Latin) born in a dry place; comes from the desert.

Licas (Greek) wolf.

Licurgo (Greek) he who frightens off wolves.

Lidio (Greek, Portuguese) ancient.

Lie (Chinese) strong, raging fire.

Ligongo (Yao) who is this?

Likeke (Hawaiian) a form of Richard.

Liko (Chinese) protected by Buddha. (Hawaiian) bud.
Like

Lim (Chinese) a form of Lin.

Lin **G** (Burmese) bright. (English) a short form of Lyndon.
Linh, Linn, Linny, Lyn, Lynn

Linc (English) a short form of Lincoln.
Link

Lincoln **B** (English) settlement by the pool. History: Abraham Lincoln was the sixteenth U.S. president.
Linc, Lincon, Lyncoln

Linda **G** (Spanish) pretty.

Lindberg (German) mountain where linden grow.
Lindbergh, Lindburg, Lindy

Lindell (English) valley of the linden.
Lendall, Lendel, Lendell, Lindall, Lindel, Lyndale, Lyndall, Lyndel, Lyndell

Linden (English) a form of Lyndon.

Lindley (English) linden field.
Lindlea, Lindlee, Lindleigh, Lindly

Lindon (English) a form of Lyndon.
Lin, Lindan

Lindor (Latin) he who seduces, likes to seduce.

Lindsay G (English) a form of Lindsey.
Linsay

Lindsey G (English) linden-tree island.
Lind, Lindsay, Lindsee, Lindsie, Lindsy, Lindzy, Linsey, Linzie, Linzy, Lyndsay, Lyndsey, Lyndsie, Lynzie

Linford (English) linden ford.
Lynford

Linfred (German) peaceful, calm.

Ling (Chinese) quick, clever.

Linley (English) flax meadow.
Linlea, Linlee, Linleigh, Linly

Linton (English) flax town.
Lintonn, Lynton, Lyntonn

Linu (Hindi) lily.

Linus (Greek) flaxen haired.
Linas, Linux

Linwood (English) flax wood.

Lio (Hawaiian) a form of Leo.

Lionel (French) lion cub. See also Leonel.
Lional, Lionell, Lionello, Lynel, Lynell, Lyonel

Li-Qin (Chinese) beautiful stringed musical instrument.

Liron BG (Hebrew) my song.
Lyron

Lisa G (Hebrew) consecrated to God. (English) a short form of Elizabeth.

Lisandro, Lisias (Spanish) liberator.

Lisardo (Hebrew) defender of the faith, fights for God.

Lise G (Moquelumnan) salmon's head coming out of the water.

Lisette G (French) a form of Lisa. (English) a familiar form of Elise, Elizabeth.

Lisimba (Yao) lion.
Simba

Lisístrato (Greek) he who fights for the liberating army.

Lister (English) dyer.

Litton (English) town on the hill.
Liton

Liu (African) voice.

Liuz (Polish) light.
Lius

Livingston (English) Leif's town.
Livingstone

Liwanu (Moquelumnan) growling bear.

Lizbeth G (English) a short form of Elizabeth.

Llacsa (Quechua) he who is the color of bronze.

Llallaua (Aymara) magnificent.

Llancamil (Mapuche) shining stone, gold and silver pearl.

Llancañir (Mapuche) fox that is pearl-colored.

Llanqui (Quechua) potter's clay.

Llarico, Llaricu (Aymara) indomitable; he who does not allow himself to be humiliated nor does he to bow to anyone.

Llashapoma, Llashapuma (Quechua) heavy puma; slow.

Llewellyn (Welsh) lionlike.
Lewis, Llewelin, Llewellen, Llewelleyn, Llewellin, Llewlyn, Llywellyn, Llywellynn, Llywelyn

Lloque, Lluqui (Quechua) left-handed, from the left side.

Lloqueyupanqui, Lluquiyupanqui (Quechua) left-handed, memorable.

Lloyd B (Welsh) gray haired; holy. See also Floyd.
Loy, Loyd, Loyde, Loydie

Lobo (Spanish) wolf.

Lochlain (Irish, Scottish) land of lakes.
Laughlin, Lochlan, Lochlann, Lochlin, Locklynn

Locke (English) forest.
Lock, Lockwood

Loe (Hawaiian) a form of Roy.

Logan ☆ **B** (Irish) meadow.
Llogan, Loagan, Loagen, Loagon, Logann, Logen, Loggan, Loghan, Logon, Logn, Logun, Logunn, Logyn

Lok (Chinese) happy.

Lokela (Hawaiian) a form of Roger.

Lokni (Moquelumnan) raining through the roof.

Lomán (Irish) bare. (Slavic) sensitive.

Lombard (Latin) long bearded.
Bard, Barr

Lon (Irish) fierce. (Spanish) a short form of Alonso, Alonzo, Leonard, Lonnie.
Lonn

Lonan (Zuni) cloud.

Lonato (Native American) flint stone.

Loncopan (Mapuche) puma's head; leader of the pumas; principal branch or capitol.

London BG (English) fortress of the moon. Geography: the capital of the United Kingdom.
Londen, Londyn, Lunden, Lundon

Long (Chinese) dragon. (Vietnamese) hair.

Lonnie (German, Spanish) a familiar form of Alonso, Alonzo.
Lon, Loni, Lonie, Lonnell, Lonney, Lonni, Lonniel, Lonny

Lono (Hawaiian) Mythology: the god of learning and intellect.

Lonzo (German, Spanish) a short form of Alonso, Alonzo.
Lonso

Lootah (Lakota) red.

Lopaka (Hawaiian) a form of Robert.

Loránd (Hungarian) a form of Roland.

Lóránt (Hungarian) a form of Lawrence.
Lorant

Lorcan (Irish) little; fierce.

Lord (English) noble title.

Loren G (Latin) a short form of Lawrence.
Lorin, Lorren, Lorrin, Loryn

Lorena G (English) a form of Lauren.

Lorenzo (Italian, Spanish) a form of Lawrence.
Larenzo, Lerenzo, Lewrenzo, Lorenc, Lorence, Lorenco, Lorencz, Lorens, Lorenso, Lorentz, Lorenz, Lorenza, Loretto, Lorinc, Lörinc, Lorinzo, Loritz, Lorrenzo, Lorrie, Lorry, Lourenza, Lourenzo, Lowrenzo, Renzo, Zo

Loretto (Italian) a form of Lawrence.
Loreto

Lori 🄶 (English) a form of Lorry.

Lorién (Aragonese) a form of Lorenzo.

Lorimer (Latin) harness maker.
Lorrie, Lorrimer, Lorry

Loring (German) son of the famous warrior.
Lorrie, Lorring, Lorry

Loris 🄱🄶 (Dutch) clown.

Loritz (Latin, Danish) laurel.
Lauritz

Lorne (Latin) a short form of Lawrence.
Lorn, Lornie

Lorry (English) a form of Laurie.
Lori, Lorri, Lory

Lot (Hebrew) hidden, covered. Bible: Lot fled from Sodom, but his wife glanced back upon its destruction and was transformed into a pillar of salt.
Lott

Lotario (Germanic) distinguished warrior.

Lothar (German) a form of Luther.
Lotaire, Lotarrio, Lothair, Lothaire, Lothario, Lotharrio

Lou 🄱 (German) a short form of Louis.

Loudon (German) low valley.
Loudan, Louden, Loudin, Lowden

Louie (German) a familiar form of Louis.

Louis (German) famous warrior. See also Aloisio, Aloysius, Clovis, Luigi.
Lash, Lashi, Lasho, Lewis, Lou, Loudovicus, Louie, Louies, Louise, Lucho, Lude, Ludek, Ludirk, Ludis, Ludko, Ludwig, Lughaidh, Lui, Luigi, Luis, Luiz, Luki, Lutek

Louise 🄶 (German) famous warrior.

Lourdes 🄶 (French) from Lourdes, France. Religion: a place where the Virgin Mary was said to have appeared.

Louvain (English) Lou's vanity. Geography: a city in Belgium.
Louvin

Lovell (English) a form of Lowell.
Louvell, Lovel, Lovelle, Lovey

Lowell (French) young wolf. (English) beloved.
Lovell, Lowe, Lowel

Loyal (English) faithful, loyal.
Loy, Loyall, Loye, Lyall, Lyell

Loyola (Latin) has a wolf in his shield.

Lu (Chinese) land.

Luan (Chinese) mountain.

Luano (Latin) fountain.

Lubomir (Polish) lover of peace.

Luboslaw (Polish) lover of glory.
Lubs, Lubz

Luc (French) a form of Luke.
Luce

Luca 🄱 (Italian) a form of Lucius.
Lucca, Luka

Lucas ☀ 🄱 (German, Irish, Danish, Dutch) a form of Lucius.
Lucais, Lucassie, Lucaus, Luccas, Luccus, Luckas, Lucus

Lucero (Spanish) bringer of light.

Lucian (Latin) a form of Lucius.
Liuz, Lucan, Lucanus, Luciano, Lucianus, Lucias, Lucjan, Lukianos, Lukyan

Luciano (Italian) a form of Lucian.
Luca, Lucca, Lucino, Lucio

Lucien (French) a form of Lucius.

Lucila (Latin) bringer of light.

Lucio (Italian) a form of Lucius.

Lucius (Latin) light; bringer of light.
Loukas, Luc, Luca, Lucais, Lucanus,
Lucas, Luce, Lucian, Lucien, Lucio,
Lucious, Lucis, Luke, Lusio

Lucky (American) fortunate.
Luckee, Luckie, Luckson, Lucson

Lucrecio (Latin) twilight of dawn.

Ludlow (English) prince's hill.

Ludovic (German) a form of Ludwig.
Ludovick, Ludovico

Ludwig (German) a form of Louis.
Music: Ludwig van Beethoven was
a famous nineteenth-century
German composer.
Ludovic, Ludvig, Ludvik, Ludwik, Lutz

Lu-Hsing (Chinese) god of pay and
employees.

Lui (Hawaiian) a form of Louis.

Luigi (Italian) a form of Louis.
Lui, Luiggi, Luigino, Luigy

Luis ✯ **B** (Spanish) a form of Louis.
Luise

Luís (Spanish) a form of Luis.

Luisa **G** (Spanish) a form of Louisa
(see Girls' Names).

Luiz (Spanish) a form of Louis.

Lukas, Lukus (Greek, Czech,
Swedish) forms of Luke.
Loukas, Lukais, Lukash, Lukasha,
Lukass, Lukasz, Lukaus, Lukkas

Luke ✯ **B** (Latin) a form of
Lucius. Bible: companion of Saint
Paul and author of the third Gospel
of the New Testament.
Luc, Luchok, Luck, Lucky, Luk, Luka,
Lúkács, Lukas, Luken, Lukes, Lukus,
Lukyan, Lusio

Lukela (Hawaiian) a form of Russel.

Luken (Basque) bringer of light.
Lucan, Lucane, Lucano, Luk

Luki (Basque) famous warrior.

Lukman (Arabic) prophet.
Luqman

Lulani **BG** (Hawaiian) highest point
in heaven.

Lumo (Ewe) born facedown.

Lun (Chinese) logic; order.

Lundy (Scottish) grove by the island.

Lunn (Irish) warlike.
Lon, Lonn

Lunt (Swedish) grove.

Luo (Chinese) name of a river.

Luong (Vietnamese) from the land.

Lu-Pan (Chinese) god of carpenters
and masons.

Lupercio (Latin) name given to
people from Lupercus.

Luperco (Latin) he who frightens off
wolves.

Lusila (Hindi) leader.

Lusio (Zuni) a form of Lucius.

Lusorio (Latin) he enjoys games.

Lutalo (Luganda) warrior.

Lutardo (Teutonic) he who is valiant
in his village.

Lutfi (Arabic) kind, friendly.

Luther (German) famous warrior.
History: Martin Luther was one of
the central figures of the
Reformation.
Lothar, Lutero, Luthor

Lutherum (Gypsy) slumber.

Luyu ☆ (Moquelumnan) head shaker.

Luz ☆ (Spanish) light.

Lyall, Lyell (Scottish) loyal.

Lydia ☆ (Greek) from Lydia, an ancient land in Asia. (Arabic) strife.

Lyle (French) island.
Lisle, Ly, Lysle

Lyman (English) meadow.
Leaman, Leeman, Lymon

Lynch (Irish) mariner.
Linch

Lyndal (English) valley of lime trees.
Lyndale, Lyndall, Lyndel, Lyndell

Lyndon (English) linden hill.
History: Lyndon B. Johnson was the thirty-sixth U.S. president.
Lin, Linden, Lindon, Lyden, Lydon, Lyn, Lyndan, Lynden, Lynn

Lyndsay ☆ (English) a form of Lindsey.

Lynn ☆ (English) waterfall; brook.
Lyn, Lynell, Lynette, Lynnard, Lynoll

Lyron (Hebrew) a form of Leron, Liron.

Lysander (Greek) liberator.
Lyzander, Sander

M ☆ (American) an initial used as a first name.

Ma (Chinese) agate.

Maalik (Punjabi) a form of Malik.
Maalek, Maaliek

Mac (Scottish) son.
Macs

Macabeo (Hebrew) progressing.

Macadam (Scottish) son of Adam.
MacAdam, McAdam

Macallister (Irish) son of Alistair.
Macalaster, Macalister, MacAlister, McAlister, McAllister

Macario (Spanish) a form of Makarios.

Macarthur (Irish) son of Arthur.
MacArthur, McArthur

Macaulay (Scottish) son of righteousness.
Macaulee, Macauley, Macaully, Macauly, Maccauley, Mackauly, Macualay, McCauley

Macbride (Scottish) son of a follower of Saint Brigid.
Macbryde, Mcbride, McBride

Maccoy (Irish) son of Hugh, Coy.
MacCoy, Mccoy, McCoy

Maccrea (Irish) son of grace.
MacCrae, MacCray, MacCrea, Macrae, Macray, Makray, Mccrea, McCrea

Macdonald (Scottish) son of Donald.
MacDonald, Mcdonald, McDonald, Mcdonna, Mcdonnell, McDonnell

Macdougal (Scottish) son of Dougal.
MacDougal, Mcdougal, McDougal, McDougall, Dougal

Mace (French) club. (English) a short form of Macy, Mason.
Macean, Maceo, Macer, Macey, Macie, Macy

Macedonio (Greek) he who triumphs and grows in stature.

Macerio (Spanish) blessed.

Macgregor (Scottish) son of Gregor.
Macgreggor

Machas (Polish) a form of Michael.

Macías (Hebrew) a form of Matías.

Macie **G** (French, English) a form of Mace.

Maciel (Latin) very slender, skeleton-like.

Mack (Scottish) a short form of names beginning with "Mac" and "Mc."
Macke, Mackey, Mackie, Macklin, Macks, Macky

Mackenzie **G** (Irish) son of Kenzie.
Mackensy, Mackenxo, Mackenze, Mackenzey, Mackenzi, MacKenzie, Mackenzly, Mackenzy, Mackienzie, Mackinsey, Mackinzie, Makenzie, McKenzie, Mickenzie

Mackinnley (Irish) son of the learned ruler.
Mackinley, MacKinnley, Mackinnly, Mckinley

Macklain (Irish) a form of Maclean.
Macklaine, Macklane

Maclean (Irish) son of Leander.
Machlin, Macklain, MacLain, MacLean, Maclin, Maclyn, Makleen, McLaine, McLean

Macmahon (Irish) son of Mahon.
MacMahon, McMahon

Macmurray (Irish) son of Murray.
McMurray

Macnair (Scottish) son of the heir.
Macknair

Maco (Hungarian) a form of Emmanuel.

Macon (German, English) maker.

Macrobio (Greek) he who enjoys a long life.

Macy **G** (French) Matthew's estate.
Mace, Macey

Maddison **G** (English) a form of Madison.

Maddock (Welsh) generous.
Madoc, Madock, Madog

Maddox (Welsh, English) benefactor's son.
Maddux, Madox

Madeline **G** (Greek) high tower.

Madhar (Hindi) full of intoxication; relating to spring.

Madisen **G** (English) a form of Madison.

Madison **G** (English) son of Maude; good son.
Maddie, Maddison, Maddy, Madisen, Madisson, Madisyn, Madsen, Son, Sonny

Madongo (Luganda) uncircumcised.

Madu (Ibo) people.

Mael (Celtic) prince.

Maemi (Japanese) honest child.

Magar (Armenian) groom's attendant.
Magarious

Magee (Irish) son of Hugh.
MacGee, MacGhee, McGee

Magen (Hebrew) protector.

Magín (Latin) he who is imaginative.

Magnar (Norwegian) strong; warrior.
Magne

Magno (Latin) great, of great fame; magnificent.

Magnus (Latin) great.
Maghnus, Magnes, Manius, Mayer

Magomu (Luganda) younger of twins.

Maguire (Irish) son of the beige one.
MacGuire, McGuire, McGwire

Mahammed (Arabic) a form of
Muhammad.
Mahamad, Mahamed

Mahdi (Arabic) guided to the right
path.
Mahde, Mahdee, Mahdy

Mahesa (Hindi) great lord. Religion:
another name for the Hindu god
Shiva.

Mahi'ai (Hawaiian) a form of
George.

Mahir (Arabic, Hebrew) excellent;
industrious.
Maher

Mahkah (Lakota) earth.

Mahmoud (Arabic) a form of
Muhammad.
Mahamoud, Mahmmoud, Mahmuod

Mahmúd (Arabic) a form of
Muhammad.
Mahmed, Mahmood, Mahmut

Mahoma (Arabic) worthy of being
praised.

Mahomet (Arabic) a form of
Muhammad.
Mehemet, Mehmet

Mahon (Irish) bear.

Mahpee (Lakota) sky.

Mai (Chinese) to advance with big
strides.

Maicu (Quechua) eagle.

Maimun (Arabic) lucky.
Maimon

Maiqui (Quechua) tree.

Maira 🄶 (Irish) a form of Mary.

Mairtin (Irish) a form of Martin.
Martain, Martainn

Maitias (Irish) a form of Mathias.
Maithias

Maitiú (Irish) a form of Matthew.

Maitland (English) meadowland.

Majencio (Latin) he who becomes
more and more famous.

Majid (Arabic) great, glorious.
*Majd, Majde, Majdi, Majdy, Majed,
Majeed*

Major (Latin) greater; military rank.
Majar, Maje, Majer, Mayer, Mayor

Makaio (Hawaiian) a form of
Matthew.

Makalani (Mwera) writer.

Makani 🄱 (Hawaiian) wind.

Makarios (Greek) happy; blessed.
*Macario, Macarios, Maccario,
Maccarios*

Makell 🄶 (Hebrew) a form of
Michael.

Makenna 🄶 (American) a form of
Mackenna (see Girls' Names).

Makenzie 🄶 (Irish) a form of
Mackenzie.
Makensie, Makenzy

Makin (Arabic) strong.
Makeen

Makis (Greek) a form of Michael.

Makoto (Japanese) sincere.

Maks (Hungarian) a form of Max.
Makszi

Maksim (Russian) a form of
Maximilian.
Maksimka, Maksym, Maxim

Maksym (Polish) a form of Maximilian.
Makimus, Maksim, Maksymilian

Makyah (Hopi) eagle hunter.

Mal (Irish) a short form of names beginning with "Mal."

Malachi (Hebrew) angel of God. Bible: the last canonical Hebrew prophet.
Maeleachlainn, Mal, Malachai, Malachia, Malachie, Malachy, Malakai, Malake, Malaki, Malchija, Malechy, Málik

Malachy (Irish) a form of Malachi.

Malajitm (Sanskrit) garland of victory.

Malaquias, Malaquías (Hebrew) my messenger.

Malco, Malcon (Hebrew) he who is like a king.

Malcolm (Scottish) follower of Saint Columba who Christianized North Scotland. (Arabic) dove.
Mal, Malcalm, Malcohm, Malcolum, Malcom, Malkolm

Malcom (Scottish) a form of Malcolm.
Malcome, Malcum, Malkom, Malkum

Malden (English) meeting place in a pasture.
Mal, Maldon

Malek (Arabic) a form of Málik.
Maleak, Maleek, Maleik, Maleka, Maleke, Mallek

Maleko (Hawaiian) a form of Mark.

Malik **B** (Punjabi, Arabic) a form of Málik.

Málik (Punjabi) lord, master. (Arabic) a form of Malachi.
Maalik, Mailik, Malak, Malic, Malick, Malicke, Maliek, Maliik, Malik, Malike, Malikh, Maliq, Malique, Mallik, Malyk, Malyq

Malin (English) strong, little warrior.
Mal, Mallin, Mallon

Mallory **G** (German) army counselor. (French) wild duck.
Lory, Mal, Mallery, Mallori, Mallorie, Malory

Maloney (Irish) church going.
Malone, Malony

Malvern (Welsh) bare hill.
Malverne

Malvin (Irish, English) a form of Melvin.
Mal, Malvinn, Malvyn, Malvynn

Mamani (Aymara) falcon.

Mamertino (Latin) name given to inhabitants of Mesina in Sicily.

Mamerto (Latin) native of Mamertium, an ancient city in the south of Italy.

Mamo **BG** (Hawaiian) yellow flower; yellow bird.

Mamoru (Japanese) earth.

Manabu (Japanese) studious.

Manases (Hebrew) he who forgets everything.

Manchu (Chinese) pure.

Mancio (Latin) he who foretells the future.

Manco (Peruvian) supreme leader. History: a sixteenth-century Incan king.

Mandala (Yao) flowers.
Manda, Mandela

Mandeep 🄱🄶 (Punjabi) mind full of light.
Mandieep

Mandek (Polish) a form of Armand, Herman.
Mandie

Mandel (German) almond.
Mandell

Mander (Gypsy) from me.

Mandy 🄶 (Latin) lovable. A familiar form of Amanda.

Manford (English) small ford.

Manfred (English) man of peace. See also Fred.
Manfret, Manfrid, Manfried, Maniferd, Mannfred, Mannfryd

Manfredo (Germanic) he who has power to safeguard the peace.

Mang (Chinese) brilliant light.

Manger (French) stable.

Mango (Spanish) a familiar form of Emmanuel, Manuel.

Manheim (German) servant's home.

Manipi (Native American) living marvel.

Manius (Scottish) a form of Magnus.
Manus, Manyus

Manjot 🄱🄶 (Indian) light of the mind.

Manley (English) hero's meadow.
Manlea, Manleigh, Manly

Manlio (Latin) he who was born in the morning.

Mann (German) man.
Manin

Manning (English) son of the hero.

Mannix (Irish) monk.
Mainchin

Manny (German, Spanish) a familiar form of Manuel.
Mani, Manni, Mannie, Many

Mano (Hawaiian) shark. (Spanish) a short form of Manuel.
Manno, Manolo

Manoj (Sanskrit) cupid.

Manolito (Spanish) God is with us.

Manpreet 🄶 (Punjabi) mind full of love.

Manque (Mapuche) condor.

Manquecura (Mapuche) refuge from the condor; two-colored rock.

Manquepan (Mapuche) condor's branch; spotted puma.

Mansa (Swahili) king. History: a fourteenth-century king of Mali.

Mansel (English) manse; house occupied by a clergyman.
Mansell

Mansfield (English) field by the river; hero's field.

Man-Shik (Korean) deeply rooted.

Manso (Latin) delivered, trusted one.

Mansueto (Latin) he who is peaceful, docile.

Mansür (Arabic) divinely aided.
Mansoor, Mansour

Manton (English) man's town; hero's town.
Mannton, Manten

Manu (Hindi) lawmaker. History: the reputed writer of the Hindi compendium of sacred laws and customs. (Hawaiian) bird. (Ghanaian) second-born son.

Manuel (Hebrew) a short form of Emmanuel.
Maco, Mango, Mannuel, Manny, Mano, Manolón, Manual, Manuale, Manue, Manuelli, Manuelo, Manuil, Manyuil, Minel

Manville (French) worker's village. (English) hero's village.
Mandeville, Manvel, Manvil

Man-Young (Korean) ten thousand years of prosperity.

Manzo (Japanese) third son.

Manzur (Arabic) winner, he who defeats all.

Mao (Chinese) hair.

Maona (Winnebago) creator earth maker.

Mapira (Yao) millet.

Marc (French) a form of Mark.

Marcel **B** (French) a form of Marcellus.
Marcell, Marsale, Marsel

Marceliano (Spanish) a form of Marcelo.

Marcelino (Italian) a form of Marcellus.
Marceleno, Marcelin, Marcellin, Marcellino

Marcellus (Latin) a familiar form of Marcus.
Marceau, Marcel, Marceles, Marcelias, Marcelino, Marcelis, Marcelius, Marcellas, Marcelleous, Marcellis, Marcellous, Marcelluas, Marcelo, Marcelus, Marcely, Marciano, Marcilka, Marcsseau, Marquel, Marsalis

Marcelo, Marcello (Italian) forms of Marcellus.
Marchello, Marsello, Marselo

March (English) dweller by a boundary.

Marcial (Spanish) a form of Marcio.

Marciano (Italian) a form of Martin.
Marci, Marcio

Marcilka (Hungarian) a form of Marcellus.
Marci, Marcilki

Marcin (Polish) a form of Martin.

Marcio (Italian) a form of Marciano.

Marco **B** (Italian) a form of Marcus. History: Marco Polo was a thirteenth-century Venetian traveler who explored Asia.
Marcko, Marko

Marcos (Spanish) a form of Marcus.
Marckos, Marcous, Markos, Markose

Marcus **B** (Latin) martial, warlike.
Marc, Marcas, Marcellus, Marcio, Marckus, Marco, Marcos, Marcous, Marcuss, Marcuus, Marcux, Marek, Mark, Markov, Markus

Mardonio (Persian) male warrior.

Mardoqueo (Hebrew) he who adores the god of war.

Marek (Slavic) a form of Marcus.

Maren **G** (Basque) sea.

Mareo (Japanese) uncommon.

Margaret **G** (Greek) pearl.

Maria **G** (Hebrew) bitter; sea of bitterness. (Italian, Spanish) a form of Mary.

Mariah **G** (Hebrew) a form of Mary.

Mariam 🅖 (Hebrew) a form of Miriam.

Marian 🅖 (Polish) a form of Mark.

Marianne 🅖 (English) a form of Marian.

Mariano (Italian) a form of Mark.

Marid (Arabic) rebellious.

Marie 🅖 (French) a form of Mary.

Marin (French) sailor.
Marine, Mariner, Marino, Marius, Marriner

Marina 🅖 (Latin) sea.

Marino (Italian) a form of Marin.
Marinos, Marinus, Mario, Mariono

Mario 🅑 (Italian) a form of Marino.
Marios, Marrio

Marion 🅖 (French) bitter; sea of bitterness.
Mareon, Mariano

Marise (Japanese) infinite; endless.

Marisela 🅖 (Latin) a form of Marisa (see Girls' Names).

Marissa 🅖 (Latin) a form of Marisa (see Girls' Names).

Marius (Latin) a form of Marin.
Marious

Marjolaine 🅖 (French) marjoram.

Mark 🅑 (Latin) a form of Marcus. Bible: author of the second Gospel in the New Testament. See also Maleko.
Marc, Marek, Marian, Mariano, Marke, Markee, Markel, Markell, Markey, Marko, Markos, Márkus, Markusha, Marque, Martial, Marx

Markanthony (Italian) a combination of Mark + Anthony.

Marke (Polish) a form of Mark.

Markel, Markell 🅑 (Latin) forms of Mark.
Markelle, Markelo

Markes (Portuguese) a form of Marques.
Markess, Markest

Markese (French) a form of Marquis.
Markease, Markeece, Markees, Markeese, Markei, Markeice, Markeis, Markeise, Markes, Markez, Markeze, Markice

Markham (English) homestead on the boundary.

Markis (French) a form of Marquis.
Markies, Markiese, Markise, Markiss, Markist

Marko (Latin) a form of Marco, Mark.
Markco

Markus (Latin) a form of Marcus.
Markas, Markcus, Markcuss, Markys, Marqus

Marland (English) lake land.

Marlen 🅖 (English) a form of Marlin.

Marley 🅖 (English) lake meadow.
Marlea, Marleigh, Marly, Marrley

Marlin (English) deep-sea fish.
Marlion, Marlyn

Marlon 🅑 (French) a form of Merlin.

Marlow (English) hill by the lake.
Mar, Marlo, Marlowe

Marlyn 🅖 (English) a form of Marlin.

Marmion (French) small.
Marmyon

Marnin (Hebrew) singer; bringer of joy.

Maro (Japanese) myself.

Marón (Arabic) male saint.

Marquan (American) a combination of Mark + Quan.
Marquane, Marquante

Marquel (American) a form of Marcellus.
Marqueal, Marquelis, Marquell, Marquelle, Marquellis, Marquiel, Marquil, Marquiles, Marquill, Marquille, Marquillus, Marqwel, Marqwell

Marques (Portuguese) nobleman.
Markes, Markqes, Markques, Markquese, Marqese, Marqesse, Marqez, Marqeze, Marquees, Marquese, Marquess, Marquesse, Marquest, Markqueus, Marquez, Marqus

Marquez **B** (Portuguese) a form of Marques.
Marqueze, Marquiez

Marquice (American) a form of Marquis.
Marquaice, Marquece

Marquis, Marquise **B** (French) nobleman.
Marcquis, Marcuis, Markis, Markquis, Markquise, Markuis, Marqise, Marquee, Marqui, Marquice, Marquie, Marquies, Marquiss, Marquist, Marquiz, Marquize

Marquon (American) a combination of Mark + Quon.
Marquin, Marquinn, Marqwan, Marqwon, Marqwyn

Marr (Spanish) divine. (Arabic) forbidden.

Mars (Latin) bold warrior. Mythology: the Roman god of war.

Marsalis (Italian) a form of Marcellus.
Marsalius, Marsallis, Marsellis, Marsellius, Marsellus

Marsden (English) marsh valley.
Marsdon

Marsh (English) swamp land. (French) a short form of Marshall.

Marshal (French) a form of Marshall.
Marschal, Marshel

Marshall **B** (French) caretaker of the horses; military title.
Marsh, Marshal, Marshell

Marshawn (American) a combination of Mark + Shawn.
Marshaine, Marshaun, Marshauwn, Marshean, Marshon, Marshun

Marston (English) town by the marsh.

Martell (English) hammerer.
Martel, Martele, Martellis

Marten (Dutch) a form of Martin.
Maarten, Martein

Martez (Spanish) a form of Martin.
Martaz, Martaze, Martes, Martese, Marteze, Martice, Martiece, Marties, Martiese, Martiez, Martis, Martise, Martize

Marti **G** (Spanish) a form of Martin.
Martee, Martie

Martial (Latin) martial, warlike. (French) a form of Mark.

Martin 🅱 (Latin, French) a form of Martinus. History: Martin Luther King, Jr. led the Civil Rights movement and won the Nobel Peace Prize. See also Tynek.
Maartin, Mairtin, Marciano, Marcin, Marinos, Marius, Mart, Martan, Marten, Martez, Marti, Martijn, Martinas, Martine, Martinez, Martinho, Martiniano, Martinien, Martinka, Martino, Martins, Marto, Marton, Márton, Marts, Marty, Martyn, Mattin, Mertin, Morten, Moss

Martín (Latin) a form of Martin.

Martina 🅶 (Latin) a form of Martin.

Martine 🅶 (Latin, French) a form of Martin.

Martinez (Spanish) a form of Martin.
Martines

Martinho (Portuguese) a form of Martin.

Martino (Italian) a form of Martin.
Martinos

Martiño (Latin) a form of Martin.

Martins (Latvian) a form of Martin.

Martinus (Latin) martial, warlike.
Martin

Martir (Greek) he who gives a testament of faith.

Marty (Latin) a familiar form of Martin.
Martey, Marti, Martie

Marut (Hindi) Religion: the Hindu god of the wind.

Marv (English) a short form of Marvin.
Marve, Marvi, Marvis

Marvin (English) lover of the sea.
Marv, Marvein, Marven, Marvion, Marvn, Marvon, Marvyn, Marwin, Marwynn, Mervin

Marwan (Arabic) history personage.

Marwood (English) forest pond.

Mary 🅶 (Hebrew) bitter; sea of bitterness.

Masa (Japanese) good and straightforward.

Masaaki (Japanese) prosperous; brilliant.

Masaccio (Italian) twin.
Masaki

Masafumi (Japanese) prosperous writer.

Masahide (Japanese) prosperous commander.

Masahiro (Japanese) broad-minded.

Masaji, Masajiro (Japanese) integrity.

Masajun (Japanese) good; obedient.

Masakatsu (Japanese) patient; successful ruler.

Masakazu (Japanese) first son of Masa.

Masamba (Yao) leaves.

Masami (Japanese) beautiful ruler.

Masamitsu (Japanese) feeling.

Masanao (Japanese) good.

Masanobu (Japanese) elegant; trustworthy.

Masao (Japanese) righteous.

Masaru (Japanese) gentleness; intelligence.

Masashi (Japanese) ambitious truth-seeker.

Masataro (Japanese) good boy.

Masato (Japanese) just.

Masayuki (Japanese) problematic.

Mashama (Shona) surprising.

Mashiro (Japanese) broad minded.

Maska (Native American) powerful. (Russian) mask.

Maslin (French) little Thomas.
Maslen, Masling

Mason 🌱 **B** (French) stone worker.
Mace, Maison, Masson, Masun, Masyn, Sonny

Masou (Native American) fire god.

Massey (English) twin.
Massi

Massimo **B** (Italian) greatest.
Massimiliano

Masud (Arabic, Swahili) fortunate.
Masood, Masoud, Mhasood

Masura (Japanese) fated for a good life.

Matai (Basque, Bulgarian) a form of Matthew.
Máté, Matei

Matalino (Filipino) bright.

Mateo (Spanish) a form of Matthew.
Matías, Matteo

Mateos, Mathías (Hebrew) offered up to God.

Mateusz (Polish) a form of Matthew.
Matejs, Mateus

Mathe (German) a short form of Matthew.

Mather (English) powerful army.

Matheu (German) a form of Matthew.
Matheau, Matheus, Mathu

Mathew **B** (Hebrew) a form of Matthew.

Mathias, Matthias (German, Swedish) forms of Matthew.
Maitias, Mathi, Mathia, Mathis, Matías, Matthia, Matthieus, Mattia, Mattias, Matus

Mathieu, Matthieu **B** (French) forms of Matthew.
Mathie, Mathieux, Mathiew, Matthiew, Mattieu, Mattieux

Matías (Spanish) a form of Mathias.
Mattias

Mato (Native American) brave.

Matope (Rhodesian) our last child.

Matoskah (Lakota) white bear.

Mats (Swedish) a familiar form of Matthew.
Matts, Matz

Matson (Hebrew) son of Matt.
Matison, Matsen, Mattison, Mattson

Matsu (Japanese) pine.

Matt (Hebrew) a short form of Matthew.
Mat

Matteen (Afghan) disciplined; polite.

Matteus (Scandinavian) a form of Matthew.

Matthew ☀ **B** (Hebrew) gift of God. Bible: author of the first Gospel of the New Testament.
Mads, Makaio, Maitiú, Mata, Matai, Matek, Mateo, Mateusz, Matfei, Mathe, Matheson, Matheu, Mathew, Mathian, Mathias, Mathieson, Mathieu, Matro, Mats, Matt, Matteus, Matthaeus, Matthaios, Matthaus, Matthäus, Mattheus, Matthews, Mattmias, Matty, Matvey, Matyas, Mayhew

Matty (Hebrew) a familiar form of Matthew.
Mattie

Matus (Czech) a form of Mathias.

Matusalén (Hebrew) symbol of longevity.

Matvey (Russian) a form of Matthew.
Matviy, Matviyko, Matyash, Motka, Motya

Matyas (Polish) a form of Matthew.
Mátyás

Mauli (Hawaiian) a form of Maurice.

Maurice (Latin) dark skinned; moor; marshland. See also Seymour.
Mauli, Maur, Maurance, Maureo, Mauricio, Maurids, Mauriece, Maurikas, Maurin, Maurino, Maurise, Mauritz, Maurius, Maurizio, Mauro, Maurrel, Maurtel, Maury, Maurycy, Meurig, Moore, Morice, Moritz, Morrel, Morrice, Morrie, Morrill, Morris

Mauricio **B** (Spanish) a form of Maurice.
Mauriccio, Mauriceo, Maurico, Maurisio

Mauritz (German) a form of Maurice.

Maurizio (Italian) a form of Maurice.

Mauro (Latin) a short form of Maurice.
Maur, Maurio

Maury (Latin) a familiar form of Maurice.
Maurey, Maurie, Morrie

Maverick **B** (American) independent.
Maverik, Maveryke, Mavric, Mavrick

Mawuli (Ewe) there is a God.

Max **B** (Latin) a short form of Maximilian, Maxwell.
Mac, Mack, Maks, Maxe, Maxx, Maxy, Miksa

Maxfield (English) Mack's field.

Maxi (Czech, Hungarian, Spanish) a familiar form of Maximilian, Máximo.
Maksi, Maxey, Maxie, Maxis, Maxy

Maxim (Russian) a form of Maxime.

Maxime **B** (French) most excellent.
Maxim, Maxyme

Maximilian (Latin) greatest.
Mac, Mack, Maixim, Maksim, Maksym, Max, Maxamillion, Maxemilian, Maxemilion, Maxi, Maximalian, Maximili, Maximilia, Maximiliano, Maximilianus, Maximilien, Maximillian, Máximo, Maximos, Maxmilian, Maxmillion, Maxon, Maxymilian, Maxymillian, Mayhew, Miksa

Maximiliano (Italian) a form of Maximilian.
Massimiliano, Maximiano, Maximino

Maximillian (Latin) a form of Maximilian.
Maximillan, Maximillano, Maximillien, Maximillion, Maxmillian, Maxximillian, Maxximillion

Máximo (Spanish) a form of Maximilian.
Massimo, Maxi, Maximiano, Maximiliano, Maximino, Máximo

Maximos (Greek) a form of Maximilian.

Maxine **G** (Latin) greatest.

Maxwell **B** (English) great spring.
Max, Maxwel, Maxwill, Maxxwell,
Maxy

Maxy (English) a familiar form of
Max, Maxwell.
Maxi

Mayer (Hebrew) a form of Meir.
(Latin) a form of Magnus, Major.
Mahyar, Mayeer, Mayor, Mayur

Mayes (English) field.
Mayo, Mays

Mayhew (English) a form of
Matthew.

Maynard (English) powerful; brave.
See also Meinhard.
May, Mayne, Maynhard, Maynor,
Ménard

Mayo (Irish) yew-tree plain. (English)
a form of Mayes. Geography: a
county in Ireland.

Mayon (Indian) person of black
complexion. Religion: another name
for the Indian god Mal.

Mayonga (Luganda) lake sailor.

Mayta (Quechua) where are you?

Maytacuapac (Quechua) oh, Lord,
where are you?

Mayua (Quechua) violet, purple.

Mazi (Ibo) sir.
Mazzi

Mazin (Arabic) proper.
Mazen, Mazinn, Mazzin

Mbita (Swahili) born on a cold night.

Mbwana (Swahili) master.

Mc Kenna **G** (American) a form of
Mackenna (see Girls' Names).

Mc Kenzie **G** (Irish) a form of
Mackenzie.

McGeorge (Scottish) son of George.
MacGeorge

Mckade (Scottish) son of Kade.
Mccade

Mckay **B** (Scottish) son of Kay.
Mackay, MacKay, Mckae, Mckai,
McKay

Mckayla **G** (American) a form of
Makayla (see Girls' Names).

Mckell (American) a form of Makell.

Mckenna **G** (American) a form of
Mackenna (see Girls' Names).

McKenzie, Mckenzie **G** (Irish)
forms of Mackenzie.
Mccenzie, Mckennzie, Mckensey,
Mckensie, Mckenson, Mckensson,
Mckenzi, Mckenzy, Mckinzie

Mckinley **B** (Irish) a form of
Mackinnley.
Mckinely, Mckinnely, Mckinnlee,
Mckinnley, McKinnley

Mead **B** (English) meadow.
Meade, Meed

Meaghan **G** (Welsh) a form of
Megan.

Medardo (Germanic) boldly powerful;
he who is worthy of honors.

Medarno (Saxon) he who deserves to
be honored, distinguished, awarded.

Medgar (German) a form of Edgar.

Medwin (German) faithful friend.

Megan **G** (Greek) pearl; great.
(Irish) a form of Margaret.

Meghan **G** (Welsh) a form of
Megan.

Meginardo (Teutonic) he who is a strong leader.

Mehetabel (Hebrew) who God benefits.

Mehrdad (Persian) gift of the sun.

Mehtar (Sanskrit) prince.
Mehta

Meinhard (German) strong, firm. See also Maynard.
Meinhardt, Meinke, Meino, Mendar

Meinrad (German) strong counsel.

Meir (Hebrew) one who brightens, shines; enlightener. History: Golda Meir was the prime minister of Israel.
Mayer, Meyer, Muki, Myer

Meka 🄶 (Hawaiian) eyes.

Mel 🄱🄶 (English, Irish) a familiar form of Melvin.

Melanie 🄶 (Greek) dark skinned.

Melanio (Greek) having black skin.

Melbourne (English) mill stream.
Melborn, Melburn, Melby, Milborn, Milbourn, Milbourne, Milburn, Millburn, Millburne

Melchior (Hebrew) king.
Meilseoir, Melchor, Melker, Melkior

Meldon (English) mill hill.
Melden

Melecio (Greek) careful and attentive.

Melibeo (Greek) he who takes care of the mentally handicapped.

Melissa 🄶 (Greek) honey bee.

Meliton, Melitón (Greek) from the island of Malta.

Melivilu (Mapuche) four snakes.

Melquíades (Hebrew) king of God.

Melrone (Irish) servant of Saint Ruadhan.

Melvern (Native American) great chief.

Melville (French) mill town. Literature: Herman Melville was a well-known nineteenth-century American writer.
Milville

Melvin (Irish) armored chief. (English) mill friend; council friend. See also Vinny.
Malvin, Mel, Melvino, Melvon, Melvyn, Melwin, Melwyn, Melwynn

Menachem (Hebrew) comforter.
Menahem, Nachman

Menandro (Greek) he who remains a man.

Menas (Greek) related to the months.

Menassah (Hebrew) cause to forget.
Menashe, Menashi, Menashia, Menashiah, Menashya, Manasseh

Mendel (English) repairman.
Mendeley, Mendell, Mendie, Mendy

Mendo (Spanish) a form of Hermenegildo.

Menelao (Greek) he who goes to the village to fight.

Meng (Chinese) eldest brother.

Mengesha (Ethiopian) kingdom.

Menico (Spanish) a short form of Domenico.

Mensah (Ewe) third son.

Mentor (Greek) teacher.

Menz (German) a short form of Clement.

Mercer (English) storekeeper.
Merce

Mercurio (Latin) he who pays attention to business.

Mered (Hebrew) revolter.

Meredith G (Welsh) guardian from the sea.
Meredyth, Merideth, Meridith, Merry

Merion (Welsh) from Merion, Wales.
Merrion

Merle B (French) a short form of Merlin, Merrill.
Meryl

Merlin (English) falcon. Literature: the magician who served as counselor in King Arthur's court.
Marlon, Merle, Merlen, Merlinn, Merlyn, Merlynn

Merlín (Spanish) a form of Merlin.

Merlino (Spanish) a form of Merlín.

Merrick (English) ruler of the sea.
Merek, Meric, Merick, Merik, Merric, Merrik, Meryk, Meyrick, Myrucj

Merrill (Irish) bright sea. (French) famous.
Meril, Merill, Merle, Merrel, Merrell, Merril, Meryl

Merritt (Latin, Irish) valuable; deserving.
Merit, Meritt, Merrett

Merton (English) sea town.
Murton

Merulo (Latin) he who is fine as a blackbird.

Merv (Irish) a short form of Mervin.

Merville (French) sea village.

Mervin (Irish) a form of Marvin.
Merv, Mervyn, Mervynn, Merwin, Merwinn, Merwyn, Murvin, Murvyn, Myrvyn, Myrvynn, Myrwyn

Meshach (Hebrew) artist. Bible: one of Daniel's three friends who emerged unharmed from the fiery furnace of Babylon.

Mesut (Turkish) happy.

Metikla (Moquelumnan) reaching a hand underwater to catch a fish.

Metrenco (Mapuche) still water, without a current; stagnant.

Metrofanes (Greek) he who resembles his mother.

Mette (Greek, Danish) pearl.
Almeta, Mete

Meulén (Mapuche) whirlwind.

Meurig (Welsh) a form of Maurice.

Meyer (German) farmer.
Mayer, Meier, Myer

Mhina (Swahili) delightful.

Mi (Chinese) overflowing.

Mian (Chinese) continuous.

Miao (Chinese) young plant, seedling.

Micah B (Hebrew) a form of Michael. Bible: a Hebrew prophet.
Mic, Micaiah, Michiah, Mika, Mikah, Myca, Mycah

Micha (Hebrew) a short form of Michael.
Mica, Micha, Michah

Michael ☀ **B** (Hebrew) who is like God? See also Micah, Miguel, Mika, Miles.
Machael, Machas, Mahail, Maichail, Maikal, Makael, Makal, Makel, Makell, Makis, Meikel, Mekal, Mekhail, Mhichael, Micael, Micah, Micahel, Mical, Micha, Michaele, Michaell, Michail, Michak, Michal, Michale, Michalek, Michalel, Michau, Micheal, Micheil, Michel, Michele, Michelet, Michiel, Micho, Michoel, Mick, Mickael, Mickey, Mihail, Mihalje, Mihkel, Mika, Mikael, Mikáele, Mikal, Mike, Mikeal, Mikel, Mikelis, Mikell, Mikhail, Mikkel, Mikko, Miksa, Milko, Miquel, Misael, Misi, Miska, Mitchell, Mychael, Mychajlo, Mychal, Mykal, Mykhas

Michaela **G** (Hebrew) who is like God?

Michail (Russian) a form of Michael.
Mihas, Mikail, Mikale, Misha

Michal **B** (Polish) a form of Michael.
Michak, Michalek, Michall

Micheal **B** (Irish) a form of Michael.

Michel **B** (French) a form of Michael.
Michaud, Miche, Michee, Michell, Michelle, Michon

Michelangelo (Italian) a combination of Michael + Angelo. Art: Michelangelo Buonarroti was one of the greatest Renaissance painters.
Michelange, Miguelangelo

Michele **G** (Italian) a form of Michael.

Michelle **G** (French) a form of Michele.

Michinori (Japanese) he who leads by good example.

Michio (Japanese) man with the strength of three thousand.

Mick (English) a short form of Michael, Mickey.
Mickerson

Mickael **B** (English) a form of Michael.
Mickaele, Mickal, Mickale, Mickeal, Mickel, Mickell, Mickelle, Mickle

Mickenzie (Irish) a form of Mackenzie.
Mickenze, Mickenzy, Mikenzie

Mickey (Irish) a familiar form of Michael.
Mick, Micki, Mickie, Micky, Miki, Mique

Micu (Hungarian) a form of Nick.

Midas (Greek) fleeting and admirable business.

Mieko (Japanese) bright.

Miguel ☀ **B** (Portuguese, Spanish) a form of Michael.
Migeel, Migel, Miguelly, Migui

Miguelangel (Spanish) a combination of Miguel + Angel.

Mihail (Greek, Bulgarian, Romanian) a form of Michael.
Mihailo, Mihal, Mihalis, Mikail

Mijaíl (Russian) a form of Miguel.

Mika **G** (Ponca) raccoon. (Hebrew) a form of Micah. (Russian) a familiar form of Michael.
Miika, Mikah

Mikael **B** (Swedish) a form of Michael.
Mikaeel, Mikaele

Mikáele (Hawaiian) a form of Michael.
Mikele

Mikal (Hebrew) a form of Michael.
Mekal, Mikahl, Mikale

Mikasi (Omaha) coyote.

Mike (Hebrew) a short form of
Michael.
Mikey, Myk

Mikeal (Irish) a form of Michael.

Mikel **B** (Basque) a form of Michael.
*Mekel, Mikele, Mekell, Mikell,
Mikelle*

Mikelis (Latvian) a form of Michael.
Mikus, Milkins

Mikhail (Greek, Russian) a form of
Michael.
*Mekhail, Mihály, Mikhael, Mikhale,
Mikhalis, Mikhalka, Mikhall, Mikhel,
Mikhial, Mikhos*

Miki **G** (Japanese) tree.
Mikio

Mikkel (Norwegian) a form of Michael.
Mikkael, Mikle

Mikko (Finnish) a form of Michael.
*Mikk, Mikka, Mikkohl, Mikkol, Miko,
Mikol*

Mikolaj (Polish) a form of Nicholas.
Mikolai

Mikolas (Greek) a form of Nicholas.
Miklós, Milek

Miksa (Hungarian) a form of Max.
Miks

Milagro (Spanish) miracle.

Milan (Italian) northerner.
Geography: a city in northern Italy.
*Milaan, Milano, Milen, Millan, Millen,
Mylan, Mylen, Mylon, Mylynn*

Milap (Native American) giving.

Milborough (English) middle
borough.
Milbrough

Milcíades (Greek) he of reddish
complexion.

Milek (Polish) a familiar form of
Nicholas.

Miles (Greek) millstone. (Latin)
soldier. (German) merciful.
(English) a short form of Michael.
Milas, Milles, Milo, Milson, Myles

Milford (English) mill by the ford.

Mililani **BG** (Hawaiian) heavenly
caress.

Milko (Czech) a form of Michael.
(German) a familiar form of Emil.
Milkins

Millán (Latin) belonging to the
Emilia family.

Millañir (Mapuche) silver fox.

Millard (Latin) caretaker of the mill.
*Mill, Millar, Miller, Millward,
Milward, Myller*

Miller (English) miller; grain grinder.
Mellar, Millard, Millen

Mills (English) mills.

Milo (German) a form of Miles. A
familiar form of Emil.
Millo, Mylo

Milos (Greek, Slavic) pleasant.

Miloslav (Czech) lover of glory.
Milda

Milt (English) a short form of
Milton.

Milton (English) mill town.
Milt, Miltie, Milty, Mylton

Mimis (Greek) a familiar form of
Demetrius.

Min (Burmese) king.

Mina **G** (Burmese) a form of Min.

Mincho (Spanish) a form of
Benjamin.

Minel (Spanish) a form of Manuel.

Mineo, Mineto (Japanese) he who reaches the summit.

Miner (English) miner.

Ming (Chinese) comes from a dynasty.

Ming Yue, Ming-Yue (Chinese) bright moon.

Mingan (Native American) gray wolf.

Mingo (Spanish) a short form of Domingo.

Minh (Vietnamese) bright.
Minhao, Minhduc, Minhkhan, Minhtong, Minhy

Minkah (Akan) just, fair.

Minor (Latin) junior; younger.
Mynor

Minoru (Japanese) fruitful.

Mio (Spanish) mine.

Mique (Spanish) a form of Mickey.
Mequel, Mequelin, Miquel

Miracle 🄶 (Latin) wonder, marvel.

Miranda 🄶 (Latin) strange; wonderful; admirable.

Mirco (Spanish) he who assures the peace.

Miriam 🄶 (Hebrew) bitter; sea of bitterness.

Miron (Polish) peace.

Miroslav (Czech) peace; glory.
Mirek, Miroslaw, Miroslawy

Mirwais (Afghan) noble ruler.

Misael 🄱 (Hebrew) a form of Michael.
Mischael, Mishael, Missael

Misha 🄶 (Russian) a short form of Michail.
Misa, Mischa, Mishael, Mishal, Mishe, Mishenka, Mishka

Miska (Hungarian) a form of Michael.
Misi, Misik, Misko, Miso

Mister (English) mister.
Mistur

Misty 🄶 (English) shrouded by mist.

Misu (Moquelumnan) rippling water.

Mitch (English) a short form of Mitchell.

Mitchel (English) a form of Mitchell.
Mitchael, Mitchal, Mitcheal, Mitchele, Mitchil, Mytchel

Mitchell 🄱 (English) a form of Michael.
Mitch, Mitchall, Mitchel, Mitchelle, Mitchem, Mytch, Mytchell

Mitsos (Greek) a familiar form of Demetrius.

Mitsu (Japanese) light.

Mitsuaki (Japanese) he who shines brightly.

Mitsuhiro (Japanese) abundant shining light.

Mitsuho (Japanese) fullness; the blade of a plant.

Mitsunobu (Japanese) trustworthy light giver.

Mitsuo (Japanese) beautiful third son.

Mitsuru (Japanese) full; satisfactory.

Modesto (Latin) modest.

Moe (English) a short form of Moses.
Mo

Moeta (Japanese) sprout; luxury; large.

Mogens (Dutch) powerful.

Mohamad (Arabic) a form of
Muhammad.
Mohamid

Mohamed **B** (Arabic) a form of
Muhammad.
Mohamd, Mohameed

Mohamet (Arabic) a form of
Muhammad.
Mahomet, Mehemet, Mehmet

Mohammad (Arabic) a form of
Muhammad.
*Mahammad, Mohammadi,
Mohammd, Mohammid, Mohanad,
Mohmad*

Mohammed (Arabic) a form of
Muhammad.
*Mahammed, Mahomet, Mohammad,
Mohaned, Mouhamed, Muhammad*

Mohamud (Arabic) a form of
Muhammad.
Mohammud, Mohamoud

Mohan (Hindi) delightful.

Moises (Portuguese, Spanish) a form
of Moses.
*Moices, Moise, Moisés, Moisey,
Moisis*

Moishe (Yiddish) a form of Moses.
Moshe

Mojag (Native American) crying
baby.

Molimo (Moquelumnan) bear going
under shady trees.

Molly **G** (Irish) a familiar form of
Mary.

Momuso (Moquelumnan) yellow
jackets crowded in their nests for
the winter.

Mona **G** (Moquelumnan) gathering
jimsonweed seed.

Monahan (Irish) monk.
Monaghan, Monoghan

Mongo (Yoruba) famous.

Monica **G** (Greek) solitary. (Latin)
advisor.

Monitor (Latin) he who counsels.

Monroe (Irish) Geography: the
mouth of the Roe River.
Monro, Munro, Munroe

Montague (French) pointed
mountain.
Montagne, Montagu, Monte

Montana **G** (Spanish) mountain.
Geography: a U.S. state.
Montaine, Montanna

Montaro (Japanese) big boy.
Montario, Monterio, Montero

Monte (Spanish) a short form of
Montgomery.
*Montae, Montaé, Montay, Montea,
Montee, Monti, Montoya, Monty*

Montego (Spanish) mountainous.

Montel (American) a form of
Montreal.
Montele, Montell, Montelle

Montenegro (Spanish) black
mountain.

Montes (Spanish) mountains.

Montez (Spanish) dweller in the
mountains.
*Monteiz, Monteze, Montezz,
Montisze*

Montgomery (English) rich man's
mountain.
Monte, Montgomerie, Monty

Montre (French) show.
*Montra, Montrae, Montray,
Montraz, Montres, Montrey,
Montrez, Montreze*

Montreal (French) royal mountain.
Geography: a city in Quebec.
*Montel, Monterial, Monterrell,
Montrail, Montrale, Montrall,
Montreall, Montrell, Montrial*

Montrell 🄱 (French) a form of
Montreal.
*Montral, Montrel, Montrele,
Montrelle*

Montsho (Tswana) black.

Monty (English) a familiar form of
Montgomery.

Moore (French) dark; moor;
marshland.
Moor, Mooro, More

Mordecai (Hebrew) martial, warlike.
Mythology: Marduk was the
Babylonian god of war. Bible: wise
counselor to Queen Esther.
*Mord, Mordachai, Mordechai,
Mordie, Mordy, Mort*

Mordred (Latin) painful. Literature:
the bastard son of King Arthur.
Modred

Morel (French) an edible mushroom.
Morrel

Moreland (English) moor; marshland.
Moorland, Morland

Morell (French) dark; from Morocco.
*Moor, Moore, Morelle, Morelli,
Morill, Morrell, Morrill, Murrel,
Murrell*

Morey (Greek) a familiar form of
Moris. (Latin) a form of Morrie.
Morrey, Morry

Morfeo (Greek) he who makes you
see beautiful figures.

Morgan 🄶 (Scottish) sea warrior.
*Morgen, Morghan, Morgin,
Morgon, Morgun, Morgunn,
Morgwn, Morgyn, Morrgan*

Moriah 🄶 (Hebrew) God is my
teacher. (French) dark skinned.

Morio (Japanese) forest.

Moris (Greek) son of the dark one.
(English) a form of Morris.
Morey, Morisz, Moriz

Moritz (German) a form of Maurice,
Morris.
Morisz

Morley (English) meadow by the moor.
*Moorley, Moorly, Morlee, Morleigh,
Morlon, Morly, Morlyn, Morrley*

Morrie (Latin) a familiar form of
Maurice, Morse.
*Maury, Morey, Mori, Morie, Morry,
Mory, Morye*

Morris (Latin) dark skinned; moor;
marshland. (English) a form of
Maurice.
*Moris, Moriss, Moritz, Morrese,
Morrise, Morriss, Morry, Moss*

Morse (English) son of Maurice.
*Morresse, Morrie, Morrison,
Morrisson*

Mort (French, English) a short form
of Morten, Mortimer, Morton.
*Morte, Mortey, Mortie, Mortty,
Morty*

Morten (Norwegian) a form of Martin.
Mort

Mortimer (French) still water.
Mort, Mortymer

Morton (English) town near the moor.
Mort

Morven (Scottish) mariner.
Morvien, Morvin

Mose (Hebrew) a short form of
Moses.

Moses **B** (Hebrew) drawn out of the water. (Egyptian) son, child. Bible: the Hebrew lawgiver who brought the Ten Commandments down from Mount Sinai.
Moe, Moise, Moïse, Moisei, Moises, Moishe, Mose, Mosese, Moshe, Mosiah, Mosie, Moss, Mosses, Mosya, Mosze, Moszek, Mousa, Moyses, Moze

Moshe (Hebrew, Polish) a form of Moses.
Mosheh

Mosi **B** (Swahili) first-born.

Moss (Irish) a short form of Maurice, Morris. (English) a short form of Moses.

Moswen **BG** (African) light in color.

Motega (Native American) new arrow.

Mouhamed (Arabic) a form of Muhammad.
Mouhamad, Mouhamadou, Mouhammed, Mouhamoin

Mousa (Arabic) a form of Moses.
Moussa

Moze (Lithuanian) a form of Moses.
Mozes, Mózes

Mpasa (Nguni) mat.

Mposi (Nyakyusa) blacksmith.

Mpoza (Luganda) tax collector.

Msrah (Akan) sixth-born.

Mtima (Nguni) heart.

Mu (Chinese) wood.

Muata (Moquelumnan) yellow jackets in their nest.

Mucio (Latin) he who endures silence.

Mugamba (Runyoro) talks too much.

Mugisa (Rutooro) lucky.
Mugisha, Mukisa

Muhammad (Arabic) praised. History: the founder of the Islamic religion. See also Ahmad, Hamid, Yasin.
Mahmoud, Mahmúd, Mohamed, Mohamet, Mohamud, Mohammed, Mouhamed, Muhamad, Muhamed, Muhamet, Muhammadali, Muhammed

Muhannad (Arabic) sword.
Muhanad

Muhsin (Arabic) beneficent; charitable.

Muhtadi (Arabic) rightly guided.

Muir (Scottish) moor; marshland.

Mujahid (Arabic) fighter in the way of Allah.

Mukasa (Luganda) God's chief administrator.

Mukhtar (Arabic) chosen.
Mukhtaar

Mukul (Sanskrit) bud, blossom; soul.

Mullu (Quechua) coral, jewel.

Mulogo (Musoga) wizard.

Mundan (Rhodesian) garden.

Mundo (Spanish) a short form of Edmundo.

Mundy (Irish) from Reamonn.

Mungo (Scottish) amiable.

Mun-Hee (Korean) literate; shiny.

Munir (Arabic) brilliant; shining.

Munny (Cambodian) wise.

Muraco (Native American) white moon.

Murali (Hindi) flute. Religion: the instrument the Hindu god Krishna is usually depicted as playing.

Murat (Turkish) wish come true.

Murdock (Scottish) wealthy sailor.
Murdo, Murdoch, Murtagh

Murphy (Irish) sea warrior.
Murfey, Murfy

Murray (Scottish) sailor.
Macmurray, Moray, Murrey, Murry

Murtagh (Irish) a form of Murdock.
Murtaugh

Musa (Swahili) child.

Musád (Arabic) untied camel.

Musoke (Rukonjo) born while a rainbow was in the sky.

Mustafa (Arabic) chosen; royal.
Mostafa, Mostaffa, Moustafa, Mustafaa, Mustafah, Mustafe, Mustaffa, Mustafo, Mustapha, Mustoffa, Mustofo

Mustafá (Turkish) a form of Mustafa.

Mustapha (Arabic) a form of Mustafa.
Mostapha, Moustapha

Muti (Arabic) obedient.

Mwaka (Luganda) born on New Year's Eve.

Mwamba (Nyakyusa) strong.

Mwanje (Luganda) leopard.

Mwinyi (Swahili) king.

Mwita (Swahili) summoner.

Mya 🄶 (Burmese) emerald. (Italian) a form of Mia (see Girls' Names).

Mychajlo (Latvian) a form of Michael.
Mykhaltso, Mykhas

Mychal (American) a form of Michael.
Mychall, Mychalo, Mycheal

Myer (English) a form of Meir.
Myers, Myur

Mykal, Mykel (American) forms of Michael.
Mykael, Mikele, Mykell

Myles 🄱 (Latin) soldier. (German) a form of Miles.
Myels, Mylez, Mylles, Mylz

Mynor (Latin) a form of Minor.

Myo (Burmese) city.

Myriam 🄶 (American) a form of Miriam.

Myron (Greek) fragrant ointment.
Mehran, Mehrayan, My, Myran, Myrone, Ron

Myung-Dae (Korean) right; great.

Mzuzi (Swahili) inventive.

N

N 🄱 (American) an initial used as a first name.

Na (Chinese) graceful.

Naaman (Hebrew) pleasant.

Nabiha (Arabic) intelligent.

Nabil (Arabic) noble.
Nabeel, Nabiel

Nabor (Hebrew) prophet's light.

Nabucodonosor (Chaldean) God protects my reign.

Nachman (Hebrew) a short form of Menachem.
Nachum, Nahum

Nada (Arabic) generous.

Nadav (Hebrew) generous; noble.
Nadiv

Nadidah (Arabic) equal to anyone else.

Nadim (Arabic) friend.
Nadeem

Nadine **G** (French, Slavic) a form of Nadia (see Girls' Names).

Nadir (Afghan, Arabic) dear, rare.
Nader

Nadisu (Hindi) beautiful river.

Naeem (Arabic) benevolent.
Naem, Naim, Naiym, Nieem

Naftali (Hebrew) wreath.
Naftalie

Nagid (Hebrew) ruler; prince.

Nahele (Hawaiian) forest.

Nahma (Native American) sturgeon.

Nahuel (Araucanian) tiger.

Nai (Chinese) endurance.

Naiara (Spanish) reference to the Virgin Mary.

Nailah (Arabic) successful.

Nairn (Scottish) river with alder trees.
Nairne

Najee (Arabic) a form of Naji.
Najae, Najée, Najei, Najiee

Naji (Arabic) safe.
Najee, Najih

Najíb (Arabic) born to nobility.
Najib, Nejeeb

Najji (Muganda) second child.

Nakia **G** (Arabic) pure.
Nakai, Nakee, Nakeia, Naki, Nakiah, Nakii

Nakos (Arapaho) sage, wise.

Naldo (Spanish) a familiar form of Reginald.

Nalren (Dene) thawed out.

Nam (Vietnamese) scrape off.

Namaka (Hawaiian) eyes.

Namid (Ojibwa) star dancer.

Namir (Hebrew) leopard.
Namer

Namuncura (Mapuche) foot of stone, strong foot.

Nan (Chinese) man.

Ñancuvilu (Mapuche) snake that is the color of lead, off-white.

Nancy **G** (English) gracious. A familiar form of Nan (see Girls' Names).

Nandin (Hindi) Religion: a servant of the Hindu god Shiva.
Nandan

Nando (German) a familiar form of Ferdinand.
Nandor

Nangila (Abaluhya) born while parents traveled.

Nangwaya (Mwera) don't mess with me.

Nansen (Swedish) son of Nancy.

Nantai (Navajo) chief.

Nantan (Apache) spokesman.

Naoki (Japanese) repair; heal; tree.

Naoko (Japanese) straight, honest.

Naolin (Spanish) sun god of the Mexican people.

Naoya (Japanese) he who heals.

Napayshni (Lakota) he does not flee; courageous.

Napier (Spanish) new city.
Neper

Napoleon (Greek) lion of the woodland. (Italian) from Naples, Italy. History: Napoleon Bonaparte was a famous nineteenth-century French emperor.
Leon, Nap, Napolean, Napoléon, Napoleone, Nappie, Nappy

Napoleón (Greek) a form of Napoleon.

Naquan (American) a combination of the prefix Na + Quan.
Naqawn, Naquain, Naquen, Naquon

Narain (Hindi) protector. Religion: another name for the Hindu god Vishnu.
Narayan

Narciso (French) a form of Narcisse.

Narcisse (French) a form of Narcissus.
Narcis, Narciso, Narkis, Narkissos

Narcissus (Greek) daffodil. Mythology: the youth who fell in love with his own reflection.
Narcise

Nard (Persian) chess player.

Nardo (German) strong, hardy. (Spanish) a short form of Bernardo.

Narno (Latin) he who was born in the Italian city of Narnia.

Narses (Persian) what the two martyrs brought from Persia.

Narve (Dutch) healthy, strong.

Nashashuk (Fox, Sauk) loud thunder.

Nashoba (Choctaw) wolf.

Nasim (Persian) breeze; fresh air.
Naseem, Nassim

Nasser (Arabic) victorious.
Naseer, Naser, Nasier, Nasir, Nasr, Nassir, Nassor

Nat (English) a short form of Nathan, Nathaniel.
Natt, Natty

Natal (Spanish) a form of Noël.
Natale, Natalie, Natalino, Natalio, Nataly

Natalie 🄶 (Spanish) a form of Natal.

Natan (Hebrew, Hungarian, Polish, Russian, Spanish) God has given.
Naten

Natanael (Hebrew) a form of Nathaniel.
Natanel, Nataniel

Natasha 🄶 (Russian) a form of Natalie.

Nate (Hebrew) a short form of Nathan, Nathaniel.

Natesh (Hindi) destroyer. Religion: another name for the Hindu god Shiva.

Nathan ✨ 🄱 (Hebrew) a short form of Nathaniel. Bible: a prophet during the reigns of David and Solomon.
Naethan, Nat, Nate, Nathann, Nathean, Nathen, Nathian, Nathin, Nathon, Nathyn, Natthan, Naythan, Nethan

Nathanael (Hebrew) gift of God. Bible: one of the Twelve Apostles. Also known as Bartholomew.
Nathanae, Nathanal, Nathaneal, Nathaneil, Nathanel, Nathaneol

Nathanial (Hebrew) a form of Nathaniel.
Nathanyal, Nathanual

Nathanie (Hebrew) a familiar form
of Nathaniel.
Nathania, Nathanni

Nathaniel ✴ **B** (Hebrew) gift of
God.
*Nat, Natanael, Nate, Nathan,
Nathanael, Nathanial, Nathanie,
Nathanielle, Nathanil, Nathanile,
Nathanuel, Nathanyel, Nathanyl,
Natheal, Nathel, Nathinel, Nethaniel,
Thaniel*

Nathen (Hebrew) a form of Nathan.

Natividad (Spanish) nativity.

Natori **G** (Arabic) a form of Natara
(see Girls' Names).

Natsu (Japanese) born in summer.

Natsuhiko (Japanese) summer; boy.

Natsuki (Japanese) summer; tree.

Natsuo (Japanese) summer; birth.

Ñaupac (Quechua) first, principal,
first-born; before everyone.

Ñaupari (Quechua) ahead, first.

Ñauque, Ñauqui (Quechua) before
everyone.

Nav (Gypsy) name.

Naval (Latin) god of the sailing vessels.

Navarro (Spanish) plains.
Navarre

Navdeep **BG** (Sikh) new light.
Navdip

Navin (Hindi) new, novel.
Naveen, Naven

Nawat (Native American) left-handed.

Nawkaw (Winnebago) wood.

Nayati (Native American) wrestler.

Nayland (English) island dweller.

Nazareno (Hebrew) he who has
separated himself from the rest of
the people because he feels
constricted, because he has decided
to be solitary.

Nazareth (Hebrew) born in
Nazareth, Israel.
*Nazaire, Nazaret, Nazarie, Nazario,
Nazerene, Nazerine*

Nazih (Arabic) pure, chaste.
*Nazeeh, Nazeem, Nazeer, Nazieh,
Nazim, Nazir, Nazz*

Ndale (Nguni) trick.

Neal (Irish) a form of Neil.
Neale, Neall, Nealle, Nealon, Nealy

Neandro (Greek) young and manly.

Nebrido (Greek) graceful like the
fawn.

Neci **BG** (Latin) a familiar form of
Ignatius.

Nectario (Greek) he who sweetens
life with nectar.

Nectarios (Greek) saint. Religion: a
saint in the Greek Orthodox
Church.

Neculman (Mapuche) swift condor;
swift and rapid flight.

Neculqueo (Mapuche) rapid speaker,
good with words.

Ned (English) a familiar form of
Edward, Edwin.
Neddie, Neddym, Nedrick

Nehemiah (Hebrew) compassion of
Jehovah. Bible: a Jewish leader.
*Nahemiah, Nechemya, Nehemias,
Nehemie, Nehemyah, Nehimiah,
Nehmia, Nehmiah, Nemo, Neyamia*

Nehru (Hindi) canal.

Neil (Irish) champion.
*Neal, Neel, Neihl, Neile, Neill,
Neille, Nels, Niall, Niele, Niels,
Nigel, Nil, Niles, Nilo, Nils, Nyle*

Neka (Native American) wild goose.

Nelek (Polish) a form of Cornelius.

Nelius (Latin) a short form of
Cornelius.

Nellie ❑ (English) a familiar form
of Cornelius, Cornell, Nelson.
Nell, Nelly

Nelo (Spanish) a form of Daniel.
Nello, Nilo

Nels (Scandinavian) a form of Neil,
Nelson.
Nelse, Nelson, Nils

Nelson ❑ (English) son of Neil.
*Nealson, Neilsen, Neilson, Nellie,
Nels, Nelsen, Nilson, Nilsson*

Nemesio (Spanish) just.
Nemi

Nemo (Greek) glen, glade. (Hebrew)
a short form of Nehemiah.

Nen (Egyptian) ancient waters.

Neng (Chinese) capability.

Neofito (Greek) he who began
recently.

Neon (Greek) he who is strong.

Neopolo (Spanish) a form of
Napoleón.

Nepomuceno (Slavic) he who gives
his help.

Neptune (Latin) sea ruler. Mythology:
the Roman god of the sea.

Neptuno (Greek) god of the sea.

Nereo (Greek) he who is the captain
at sea.

Nerio (Greek) sea traveler.

Nero (Latin, Spanish) stern. History:
a cruel Roman emperor.
Neron, Nerone, Nerron

Nerón (Latin) very strong and intrepid.

Nesbit (English) nose-shaped bend
in a river.
*Naisbit, Naisbitt, Nesbitt, Nisbet,
Nisbett*

Nesto (Spanish) serious.

Nestor ❑ (Greek) traveler; wise.
Nester

Néstor (Greek) a form of Nestor.

Nestorio (Greek) a form of Nestor.

Nethaniel (Hebrew) a form of
Nathaniel.
*Netanel, Netania, Netaniah, Netaniel,
Netanya, Nethanel, Nethanial,
Nethaniel, Nethanyal, Nethanyel*

Neto (Spanish) a short form of
Ernesto.

Nevada ❑ (Spanish) covered in
snow. Geography: a U.S. state.
Navada, Nevade

Nevan (Irish) holy.
Nevean

Neville (French) new town.
Nev, Nevil, Nevile, Nevill, Nevyle

Nevin (Irish) worshiper of the saint.
(English) middle; herb.
*Nefen, Nev, Nevan, Neven, Nevins,
Nevyn, Niven*

Newbold (English) new tree.

Newell (English) new hall.
Newall, Newel, Newyle

Newland (English) new land.
Newlan

Newlin (Welsh) new lake.
Newlyn

Newman (English) newcomer.
Neiman, Neimann, Neimon,
Neuman, Numan, Numen

Newton (English) new town.
Newt

Ngai (Vietnamese) herb.

Nghia (Vietnamese) forever.

Ngoc **G** (Vietnamese) jade.

Ngozi (Ibo) blessing.

Ngu (Vietnamese) sleep.

Nguyen (Vietnamese) a form of Ngu.

Nhat (Vietnamese) long life; number one.

Nhean (Cambodian) self-knowledge.

Nhung (Vietnamese) velvet.

Nia **G** (Irish) a familiar form of Neila (see Girls' Names).

Niall (Irish) a form of Neil. History: Niall of the Nine Hostages was a famous Irish king.
Nial, Nialle

Nian (Chinese) year, age.

Nibal (Arabic) arrows.
Nibel

Nibaw (Native American) standing tall.

Nicabar (Gypsy) stealthy.

Nicandro (Greek) he who is victorious amongst men.

Nicasio, Niceto, Nicón (Greek) victorious one.

Níceas (Greek) he of the great victory.

Nicéforo (Greek) he who brings victory.

Nicho (Spanish) a form of Dennis.

Nicholas ♛ (Greek) victorious people. Religion: Nicholas of Myra is a patron saint of children. See also Caelan, Claus, Cola, Colar, Cole, Colin, Colson, Klaus, Lasse, Mikolaj, Mikolas, Milek.
Niccolas, Nichalas, Nichelas, Nichele, Nichlas, Nichlos, Nichola, Nicholaas, Nicholaes, Nicholase, Nicholaus, Nichole, Nicholias, Nicholl, Nichollas, Nicholos, Nichols, Nicholus, Nick, Nickalus, Nicklaus, Nickolas, Nicky, Niclas, Niclasse, Nico, Nicola, Nicolai, Nicolas, Nicoles, Nicolis, Nicoll, Nicolo, Nikhil, Niki, Nikili, Nikita, Nikko, Niklas, Niko, Nikolai, Nikolas, Nikolaus, Nikolos, Nils, Nioclás, Niocol, Nycholas

Nicholaus (Greek) a form of Nicholas.
Nichalaus, Nichalous, Nichaolas, Nichlaus, Nichloas, Nichlous, Nicholaos, Nicholous

Nichols, Nicholson (English) son of Nicholas.
Nicholes, Nicholis, Nicolls, Nickelson, Nickoles

Nick (English) a short form of Dominic, Nicholas. See also Micu.
Nic, Nik

Nickalus (Greek) a form of Nicholas.
Nickalas, Nickalis, Nickalos, Nickelas, Nickelus

Nicklaus, Nicklas (Greek) forms of Nicholas.
Nickalaus, Nickalous, Nickelous, Nicklauss, Nicklos, Nicklous, Nicklus, Nickolau, Nickolaus, Nicolaus, Niklaus, Nikolaus

Nickolas **B** (Greek) a form of Nicholas.
Nickolaos, Nickolis, Nickolos, Nickolus, Nickolys, Nickoulas

Nicky (Greek) a familiar form of
Nicholas.
Nickey, Nicki, Nickie, Niki, Nikki

Nico 🄑 (Greek) a short form of
Nicholas.
Nicco

Nicodemus (Greek) conqueror of the
people.
*Nicodem, Nicodemius, Nikodem,
Nikodema, Nikodemious, Nikodim*

Nicola 🄖 (Italian) a form of
Nicholas. See also Cola.
Nicolá, Nikolah

Nicolai (Norwegian, Russian) a form
of Nicholas.
*Nicholai, Nickolai, Nicolaj, Nicolau,
Nicolay, Nicoly, Nikalai*

Nicolas 🄑 (Italian) a form of
Nicholas.
*Nico, Nicolaas, Nicolás, Nicolaus,
Nicoles, Nicolis, Nicolus*

Nicole 🄖 (French) a form of
Nicholas.

Nicolette 🄖 (French) a form of
Nicole.

Nicolo (Italian) a form of Nicholas.
*Niccolo, Niccolò, Nicol, Nicolao,
Nicollo*

Nicomedes (Greek) he who prepares
the victories.

Nicostrato (Greek) general who
leads to victory.

Ñielol (Mapuche) eye of the
subterranean cavity, eye of the cave.

Niels (Danish) a form of Neil.
Niel, Nielsen, Nielson, Niles, Nils

Nien (Vietnamese) year.

Nigan (Native American) ahead.
Nigen

Nigel 🄑 (Latin) dark night.
*Niegel, Nigal, Nigale, Nigele, Nigell,
Nigiel, Nigil, Nigle, Nijel, Nye,
Nygel, Nyigel, Nyjil*

Nika (Yoruba) ferocious.

Nike 🄑🄖 (Greek) victorious.
Nikka

Niki 🄖 (Hungarian) a familiar form
of Nicholas.
*Nikia, Nikiah, Nikki, Nikkie, Nykei,
Nykey*

Nikita 🄖 (Russian) a form of
Nicholas.
Nakita, Nakitas, Nikula

Nikiti (Native American) round and
smooth like an abalone shell.

Nikki 🄖 (Greek) a form of Nicky.
(Hungarian) a form of Niki.

Nikko, Niko 🄑 (Hungarian) forms
of Nicholas.
Nikoe, Nyko

Niklas (Latvian, Swedish) a form of
Nicholas.
Niklaas, Niklaus

Nikola 🄑 (Greek) a short form of
Nicholas.
Nikolao, Nikolay, Nykola

Nikolai (Estonian, Russian) a form of
Nicholas.
*Kolya, Nikolais, Nikolaj, Nikolajs,
Nikolay, Nikoli, Nikolia, Nikula,
Nikulas*

Nikolas (Greek) a form of Nicholas.
*Nicanor, Nikalas, Nikalis, Nikalus,
Nikholas, Nikolaas, Nikolaos, Nikolis,
Nikolos, Nikos, Nilos, Nykolas,
Nykolus*

Nikolaus (Greek) a form of Nicholas.
Nikalous, Nikolaos

Nikolos (Greek) a form of Nicholas.
See also Kolya.
*Niklos, Nikolaos, Nikolò, Nikolous,
Nikolus, Nikos, Nilos*

Nil (Russian) a form of Neil.
Nilya

Nila **G** (Hindi) blue.

Niles (English) son of Neil.
Nilesh, Nyles

Nilo (Finnish) a form of Neil.

Nils (Swedish) a short form of
Nicholas.

Nimrod (Hebrew) rebel. Bible: a
great-grandson of Noah.

Nina **G** (Hebrew) a familiar form of
Hanna. (Native American) mighty.

Ninacolla (Quechua) flame of fire.

Ninacuyuchi (Quechua) he who
moves or stokes the fire; restless and
lively like fire.

Ninan (Quechua) fire; restless and
lively like fire.

Ninauari (Quechua) llama-like
animal of fire; he who is
uncontrollable like the vicuna.

Ninauíca (Quechua) sacred fire.

Ning (Chinese) peace, tranquility;
rest.

Nino (Chaldean) possessor of palaces.

Niño (Spanish) young child.

Niran (Tai) eternal.

Nishan (Armenian) cross, sign, mark.
Nishon

Nissan (Hebrew) sign, omen; miracle.
Nisan, Nissim, Nissin, Nisson

Nitis (Native American) friend.
Netis

Nixon (English) son of Nick.
Nixan, Nixson

Nizam (Arabic) leader.

Nkunda (Runyankore) loves those
who hate him.

N'namdi (Ibo) his father's name lives
on.

Noach (Hebrew) a form of Noah.

Noah ☆ **B** (Hebrew) peaceful,
restful. Bible: the patriarch who
built the ark to survive the Flood.
Noach, Noak, Noe, Noé, Noi

Noam (Hebrew) sweet; friend.

Noble (Latin) born to nobility.
Nobe, Nobie, Noby

Nodin (Native American) wind.
Knoton, Noton

Noe **B** (Czech, French) a form of
Noah.

Noé (Hebrew, Spanish) quiet,
peaceful. See also Noah.

Noel **B** (French) a form of Noël.

Noël (French) day of Christ's birth.
See also Natal.
*Noel, Noél, Noell, Nole, Noli,
Nowel, Nowell*

Noelino (Spanish) a form of Natal.

Nohea (Hawaiian) handsome.
Noha, Nohe

Nokonyu (Native American)
katydid's nose.
Noko, Nokoni

Nolan **B** (Irish) famous; noble.
*Noland, Nolande, Nolane, Nolen,
Nolin, Nollan, Nolyn*

Nolasco (Hebrew) he who departs
and forgets about promises.

Nolberto (Teutonic) a form of Norberto.

Nollie 🅱 (Latin, Scandinavian) a familiar form of Oliver.
Noll, Nolly

Nong (Chinese) farming.

Nora 🅖 (Greek) light.

Norbert (Scandinavian) brilliant hero.
Bert, Norberto, Norbie, Norby

Norberto (Spanish) a form of Norbert.

Nori (Japanese) belief.

Noriaki (Japanese) bright ruler.

Norio (Japanese) he who sets a good example as a husband.

Noriyuki (Japanese) he who governs with good fortune.

Norman 🅱 (French) Norseman. History: a name for the Scandinavians who settled in northern France in the tenth century, and who later conquered England in 1066.
Norm, Normand, Normen, Normie, Normy

Normando (Spanish) man from the north.

Norris (French) northerner. (English) Norman's horse.
Norice, Norie, Noris, Norreys, Norrie, Norry, Norrys

Northcliff (English) northern cliff.
Northcliffe, Northclyff, Northclyffe

Northrop (English) north farm.
North, Northup

Norton (English) northern town.

Norville (French, English) northern town.
Norval, Norvel, Norvell, Norvil, Norvill, Norvylle

Norvin (English) northern friend.
Norvyn, Norwin, Norwinn, Norwyn, Norwynn

Norward (English) protector of the north.
Norwerd

Norwood (English) northern woods.

Nostriano (Latin) he who is from our homeland.

Notaku (Moquelumnan) growing bear.

Notelmo (Teutonic) he who protects himself in combat with the helmet.

Nowles (English) a short form of Knowles.

Nsoah (Akan) seventh-born.

Numa (Arabic) pleasant.

Numair (Arabic) panther.

Nuncio (Italian) messenger.
Nunzi, Nunzio

Nuri (Hebrew, Arabic) my fire.
Nery, Noori, Nur, Nuris, Nurism, Nury

Nuriel (Hebrew, Arabic) fire of the Lord.
Nuria, Nuriah, Nuriya

Nuru 🅱🅖 (Swahili) born in daylight.

Nusair (Arabic) bird of prey.

Nwa (Nigerian) son.

Nwake (Nigerian) born on market day.

Nye (English) a familiar form of Aneurin, Nigel.

Nyle (English) island. (Irish) a form
of Neil.
Nyal, Nyll

Oakes (English) oak trees.
Oak, Oakie, Oaks, Ochs

Oakley (English) oak-tree field.
*Oak, Oakes, Oakie, Oaklee,
Oakleigh, Oakly, Oaks*

Oalo (Spanish) a form of Paul.

Oba **BG** (Yoruba) king.

Obadele (Yoruba) king arrives at the
house.

Obadiah (Hebrew) servant of God.
*Obadias, Obed, Obediah, Obie,
Ovadiach, Ovadiah, Ovadya*

Obdulio (Latin) he who calms in
sorrowful moments.

Obed (English) a short form of
Obadiah.

Oberon (German) noble; bearlike.
Literature: the king of the fairies in
the Shakespearean play *A
Midsummer Night's Dream.* See
also Auberon, Aubrey.
Oberen, Oberron, Oeberon

Obert (German) wealthy; bright.

Oberto (Germanic) a form of
Adalberto.

Obie (English) a familiar form of
Obadiah.
Obbie, Obe, Obey, Obi, Oby

Ocan (Luo) hard times.

Octavia **G** (Latin) a form of
Octavio.

Octavio **B** (Latin) eighth. See also
Tavey, Tavian.
*Octave, Octavia, Octavian,
Octaviano, Octavien, Octavious,
Octavius, Octavo, Octavous,
Octavus, Ottavio*

Octavious, Octavius (Latin) forms
of Octavio.
*Octavaius, Octaveous, Octaveus,
Octavias, Octaviaus, Octavis,
Octavous, Octavus*

Odakota (Lakota) friendly.
Oda

Odd (Norwegian) point.
Oddvar

Ode (Benin) born along the road.
(Irish, English) a short form of
Odell.
Odey, Odie, Ody

Odeberto (Teutonic) he who shines
because of his possessions.

Oded (Hebrew) encouraging.

Odell (Greek) ode, melody. (Irish)
otter. (English) forested hill.
Dell, Odall, Ode

Odilón (Teutonic) owner of a
bountiful inheritance.

Odin (Scandinavian) ruler.
Mythology: the Norse god of
wisdom and war.
Oden, Odín

Odion (Benin) first of twins.

Odo (Norwegian) a form of Otto.
Audo

Odoacro (German) he who watches
over his inheritance.

Odolf (German) prosperous wolf.
Odolff

Odom (Ghanaian) oak tree.

Odon (Hungarian) wealthy protector.
Odi

Odón (Latin) a form of Odon.

Odran (Irish) pale green.
Odhrán, Oran, Oren, Orin, Orran, Orren, Orrin

Odysseus (Greek) wrathful.
Literature: the hero of Homer's epic
poem *Odyssey*.

Ofer (Hebrew) young deer.

Ofir (Hebrew) ferocious.

Og (Aramaic) king. Bible: the king of
Basham.

Ogaleesha (Lakota) red shirt

Ogano (Japanese) wise.

Ogbay (Ethiopian) don't take him
from me.

Ogbonna (Ibo) image of his father.
Ogbonnia

Ogden (English) oak valley.
Literature: Ogden Nash was a
twentieth-century American writer
of light verse.
Ogdan, Ogdon

Ogima (Chippewa) chief.

Ogo, Ogu (Chamorro) forms of
Hochoc.

Ogun (Nigerian) Mythology: the god
of war.
Ogunkeye, Ogunsanwo, Ogunsheye

Ohanko (Native American) restless.

Ohannes (Turkish) a form of John.

Ohanzee (Lakota) comforting
shadow.

Ohin (African) chief.
Ohan

Ohitekah (Lakota) brave.

Ohln (Japanese) wanted child.

Oistin (Irish) a form of Austin.
Osten, Ostyn, Ostynn

OJ (American) a combination of the
initials O. + J.
O.J., Ojay

Ojo (Yoruba) difficult delivery.

Okapi (Swahili) an African animal
related to the giraffe but having a
short neck.

Oke (Hawaiian) a form of Oscar.

Okechuku (Ibo) God's gift.

Okeke (Ibo) born on market day.
Okorie

Okie (American) from Oklahoma.
Okee, Okey

Oko (Ghanaian) older twin. (Yoruba)
god of war.

Okon (Japanese) from the darkness.

Okorie (Ibo) a form of Okeke.

Okpara (Ibo) first son.

Okuth (Luo) born in a rain shower.

Ola ✿ (Yoruba) wealthy, rich.

Olaf (Scandinavian) ancestor. History:
a patron saint and king of Norway.
*Olaff, Olafur, Olav, Ole, Olef, Olof,
Oluf*

Olajuwon (Yoruba) wealth and honor
are God's gifts.
*Olajawon, Olajawun, Olajowuan,
Olajuan, Olajuanne, Olajuawon,
Olajuwa, Olajuwan, Olaujawon,
Oljuwoun*

Olamina (Yoruba) this is my wealth.

Olatunji (Yoruba) honor reawakens.

Olav (Scandinavian) a form of Olaf.
Ola, Olave, Olavus, Ole, Olen, Olin, Olle, Olov, Olyn

Ole (Scandinavian) a familiar form of Olaf, Olav.
Olay, Oleh, Olle

Oleg (Latvian, Russian) holy.
Olezka

Olegario (Germanic) he who dominates with his strength and his lance.

Oleksandr (Russian) a form of Alexander.
Olek, Olesandr, Olesko

Olés (Polish) a familiar form of Alexander.

Olimpo (Greek) party; sky; regarding Mount Olympus or the Olympus sanctuary.

Olin (English) holly.
Olen, Olney, Olyn

Olindo (Italian) from Olinthos, Greece.

Oliver 🌟 **B** (Latin) olive tree. (Scandinavian) kind; affectionate.
Nollie, Oilibhéar, Oliverio, Oliverios, Olivero, Olivier, Oliviero, Oliwa, Ollie, Olliver, Ollivor, Olvan

Olivia **G** (Latin) a form of Olive (see Girls' Names).

Olivier **B** (French) a form of Oliver.

Oliwa (Hawaiian) a form of Oliver.

Ollanta (Aymara) warrior who sees everything from his watchtower.

Ollantay (Quechua) lord Ollanta.

Ollie **BG** (English) a familiar form of Oliver.
Olie, Olle, Olley, Olly

Olo (Spanish) a short form of Orlando, Rolando.

Olubayo (Yoruba) highest joy.

Olufemi (Yoruba) wealth and honor favors me.

Olujimi (Yoruba) God gave me this.

Olushola (Yoruba) God has blessed me.

Omar **B** (Arabic) highest; follower of the Prophet. (Hebrew) reverent.
Omair, Omari, Omarr, Omer, Umar

Omari (Swahili) a form of Omar.
Omare, Omaree, Omarey

Omaro (Spanish) a form of Omar.

Omer (Arabic) a form of Omar.
Omeer, Omero

Omolara (Benin) child born at the right time.

On (Burmese) coconut. (Chinese) peace.

Onan (Turkish) prosperous.

Onaona (Hawaiian) pleasant fragrance.

Ondro (Czech) a form of Andrew.
Ondra, Ondre, Ondrea, Ondrey

O'neil (Irish) son of Neil.
Oneal, O'neal, Oneil, O'neill, Onel, Oniel, Onil

Onesíforo (Greek) he who bears much fruit.

Onésimo (Greek) he who is useful and worthwhile.

Onkar (Hindi) God in his entirety.

Onofrio (German) a form of Humphrey.
Oinfre, Onfre, Onfrio, Onofre, Onofredo

Onslow (English) enthusiast's hill.
Ounslow

Onufry (Polish) a form of Humphrey.

Onur (Turkish) honor.

Ophir (Hebrew) faithful. Bible: an Old Testament people and country.

Opio (Ateso) first of twin boys.

Optato (Latin) desired.

Oral (Latin) verbal; speaker.

Oran (Irish) green.
Odhran, Odran, Ora, Orane, Orran

Orangel (Greek) messenger from the heights or from the mountain.

Oratio (Latin) a form of Horatio.
Orazio

Orbán (Hungarian) born in the city.

Ordell (Latin) beginning.
Orde

Oren (Hebrew) pine tree. (Irish) light skinned, white.
Oran, Orin, Oris, Orono, Orren, Orrin

Orencio (Greek) examining judge.

Orestes (Greek) mountain man. Mythology: the son of the Greek leader Agamemnon.
Aresty, Oreste

Orfeo (Greek) he who has a good voice.

Ori (Hebrew) my light.
Oree, Orie, Orri, Ory

Orien (Latin) visitor from the east.
Orian, Orie, Orin, Oris, Oron, Orono, Orrin, Oryan

Orígenes (Greek) he who comes from Horus, the god of light; born into caring arms.

Oriol (Latin) golden oriole.

Orion ☐ (Greek) son of fire. Mythology: a giant hunter who was killed by Artemis. See also Zorion.

Orión (Greek) a form of Orion.

Orji (Ibo) mighty tree.

Orlando (German) famous throughout the land. (Spanish) a form of Roland.
Lando, Olando, Olo, Orlan, Orland, Orlanda, Orlandas, Orlandes, Orlandis, Orlandos, Orlandus, Orlo, Orlondo, Orlondon

Orleans (Latin) golden.
Orlean, Orlin

Orman (German) mariner, seaman. (Scandinavian) serpent, worm.
Ormand

Ormond (English) bear mountain; spear protector.
Ormande, Ormon, Ormonde

Oro (Spanish) golden.

Oroncio (Persian) runner.

Orono (Latin) a form of Oren.
Oron

Orosco (Greek) he who lives in the mountains.

Orrick (English) old oak tree.
Orric

Orrin (English) river.
Orin, Oryn, Orynn

Orris (Latin) a form of Horatio.
Oris, Orriss

Orry (Latin) from the Orient.
Oarrie, Orrey, Orrie

Orsino (Italian) a form of Orson.

Orson (Latin) bearlike.
Orscino, Orsen, Orsin, Orsini, Orsino, Son, Sonny, Urson

Orton (English) shore town.

Ortzi (Basque) sky.

Orunjan (Yoruba) born under the midday sun.

Orval (English) a form of Orville.
Orvel

Orville (French) golden village. History: Orville Wright and his brother Wilbur were the first men to fly an airplane.
Orv, Orval, Orvell, Orvie, Orvil

Orvin (English) spear friend.
Orwin, Owynn

Osahar (Benin) God hears.

Osakwe (Japanese) good destiny.

Osamu (Japanese) to study; to govern; peace.

Osanmwesr (Japanese) leaving.

Osayaba (Benin) God forgives.

Osaze (Benin) whom God likes.

Osbert (English) divine; bright.

Osborn (Scandinavian) divine bear. (English) warrior of God.
Osbern, Osbon, Osborne, Osbourn, Osbourne, Osburn, Osburne, Oz, Ozzie

Oscar **B** (Scandinavian) divine spearman.
Oke, Oskar, Osker, Oszkar

Óscar (Germanic) a form of Oscar.

Ose (Pohnpeian) a form of Jose.

Osea (Fijian) a form of Joshua.

Oseas, Osías, Ozias (Hebrew) Lord sustains me; divine salvation; God is my soul.

Osei (Fante) noble.
Osee

Osgood (English) divinely good.

O'Shea (Irish) son of Shea.
Oshae, Oshai, Oshane, O'Shane, Oshaun, Oshay, Oshaye, Oshe, Oshea, Osheon

Osip (Russian, Ukrainian) a form of Joseph, Yosef. See also Osya.

Osiris (Egyptian) he who possesses a powerful vision.

Oskar (Scandinavian) a form of Oscar.
Osker, Ozker

Osman (Turkish) ruler. (English) servant of God.
Osmanek, Osmen, Osmin, Otthmor, Ottmar

Osmán (Arabic) he who is as docile as a pigeon chick.

Osmar (English) divine; wonderful.

Osmaro (Germanic) he who shines like the glory of God.

Osmond (English) divine protector.
Osmand, Osmonde, Osmont, Osmund, Osmunde, Osmundo

Osorio (Slavic) killer of wolves.

Osric (English) divine ruler.
Osrick

Ostiano (Spanish) confessor.

Ostin (Latin) a form of Austin.
Ostan, Osten, Ostyn

Osvaldo (Spanish) a form of Oswald.
Osbaldo, Osbalto, Osvald, Osvalda

Oswald (English) God's power; God's crest. See also Waldo.
Osvaldo, Oswaldo, Oswall, Oswell, Oswold, Oz, Ozzie

Oswaldo (Spanish) a form of Oswald.

Oswin (English) divine friend.
Osvin, Oswinn, Oswyn, Oswynn

Osya (Russian) a familiar form of Osip.

Ota (Czech) prosperous.
Otik

Otadan (Native American) plentiful.

Otaktay (Lakota) kills many; strikes many.

Otek (Polish) a form of Otto.

Otello (Italian) a form of Othello.

Otelo (Spanish) a form of Otón.

Otem (Luo) born away from home.

Othello (Spanish) a form of Otto. Literature: the title character in the Shakespearean tragedy *Othello*.
Otello

Othman (German) wealthy.
Ottoman

Otilde (Teutonic) owner of a bountiful inheritance.

Otis (Greek) keen of hearing. (German) son of Otto.
Oates, Odis, Otes, Otess, Otez, Otise, Ottis, Otys

Otniel, Otoniel (Hebrew) God is my strength.

Otoronco (Quechua) jaguar; tiger; the bravest.

Ottah (Nigerian) thin baby.

Ottar (Norwegian) point warrior; fright warrior.

Ottmar (Turkish) a form of Osman.
Otomars, Ottomar

Otto (German) rich.
Odo, Otek, Otello, Otfried, Othello, Otho, Othon, Otik, Otilio, Otman, Oto, Otón, Otton, Ottone

Ottokar (German) happy warrior.
Otokars, Ottocar

Otu (Native American) collecting seashells in a basket.

Ouray (Ute) arrow. Astrology: born under the sign of Sagittarius.

Oved (Hebrew) worshiper, follower.

Ovid (Latin) having the shape of an egg.

Ovidio (Latin) he who takes care of sheep.

Owen ☀ **B** (Irish) born to nobility; young warrior. (Welsh) a form of Evan.
Owain, Owens, Owin, Uaine

Owney (Irish) elderly.
Oney

Oxford (English) place where oxen cross the river.
Ford

Oya **B** (Moquelumnan) speaking of the jacksnipe.

Oystein (Norwegian) rock of happiness.
Ostein, Osten, Ostin, _ystein

Oz **BG** (Hebrew) a short form of Osborn, Oswald.

Oziel (Hebrew) he who has divine strength.

Ozora (Japanese) big sky.

Ozturk (Turkish) pure; genuine Turk.

Ozzie (English) a familiar form of Osborn, Oswald.
Ossie, Ossy, Ozee, Ozi, Ozzi, Ozzy

P

P BG (American) an initial used as a first name.

Paavo (Finnish) a form of Paul.
Paaveli

Pabel (Russian) a form of Paul.

Pablo (Spanish) a form of Paul.
Pable, Paublo

Pace (English) a form of Pascal.
Payce

Pachacutec, Pachacutic (Quechua) he who changes the world, who helps bring about a new era.

Pacho (Spanish) free.

Paciano (Latin) he who belongs to the peace.

Paciente (Latin) he who knows how to be patient.

Pacifico (Filipino) peaceful.

Pacífico (Latin) he who searches for peace.

Paco (Italian) pack. (Spanish) a familiar form of Francisco. (Native American) bald eagle. See also Quico.
Pacorro, Panchito, Pancho, Paquito

Pacomio (Greek) he who is robust.

Paddy (Irish) a familiar form of Padraic, Patrick.
Paddey, Paddi, Paddie

Paden (English) a form of Patton.

Padget BG (English) a form of Page.
Padgett, Paget, Pagett

Padraic (Irish) a form of Patrick.
Paddrick, Paddy, Padhraig, Padrai, Pádraig, Padraigh, Padreic, Padriac, Padric, Padron, Padruig

Pafnucio (Greek) rich in merits.

Page G (French) youthful assistant.
Padget, Paggio, Paige, Payge

Paige G (English) a form of Page.

Paillalef (Mapuche) return quickly, go back.

Painecura (Mapuche) iridescent stone.

Painevilu (Mapuche) iridescent snake.

Pakelika (Hawaiian) a form of Patrick.

Paki (African) witness.

Pal (Swedish) a form of Paul.

Pál (Hungarian) a form of Paul.
Pali, Palika

Palaina (Hawaiian) a form of Brian.

Palani (Hawaiian) a form of Frank.

Palash (Hindi) flowery tree.

Palatino (Latin) he who comes from Mount Palatine.

Palben (Basque) blond.

Palladin (Native American) fighter.
Pallaton, Palleten

Palmacio (Latin) adorned with bordered palm leaves.

Palmer (English) palm-bearing pilgrim.
Pallmer, Palmar

Paloma G (Spanish) dove.

Palti (Hebrew) God liberates.
Palti-el

Pampín (Latin) he who has the vigor of a sprouting plant.

Pan (Chinese) huge rock.

Panapasa (Fijian) a form of Bernabe.

Panas (Russian) immortal.

Panayiotis (Greek) a form of Peter.
Panagiotis, Panajotis, Panayioti, Panayoti, Panayotis

Pancho (Spanish) a familiar form of Francisco, Frank.
Panchito

Pancracio (Greek) all-powerful one.

Panfilo (Greek) friend of all.

Pánfilo (Greek) a form of Panfilo.

Pang (Chinese) large.

Panos (Greek) a form of Peter.
Petros

Pantaleón (Greek) he who is all-merciful and has everything under control.

Panteno (Greek) he who is worthy of all praise.

Panti (Quechua) species of brush.

Paola G (Italian) a form of Paula (see Girls' Names).

Paolo (Italian) a form of Paul.

Papias (Greek) venerable father.

Paquito (Spanish) a familiar form of Paco.

Paramesh (Hindi) greatest. Religion: another name for the Hindu god Shiva.

Pardeep B (Sikh) mystic light.
Pardip

Pardulfo (Germanic) brave warrior, armed with an ax.

Paris G (Greek) lover. Geography: the capital of France. Mythology: the prince of Troy who started the Trojan War by abducting Helen.
Paras, Paree, Pares, Parese, Parie, Parris, Parys

París (Greek) a form of Paris.

Parisio (Spanish) a form of Paris.

Pariuana (Quechua) Andean flamingo.

Park (Chinese) cypress tree. (English) a short form of Parker.
Parke, Parkes, Parkey, Parks

Parker ♛ B (English) park keeper.
Park

Parkin (English) little Peter.
Perkin

Parlan (Scottish) a form of Bartholomew. See also Parthalán.

Parménides (Greek) he who is a constant presence.

Parmenio (Greek) he who is loyal and offers his constant presence.

Parnell (French) little Peter. History: Charles Stewart Parnell was a famous Irish politician.
Nell, Parle, Parnel, Parrnell, Pernell

Parodio (Greek) he who imitates the singing.

Parr (English) cattle enclosure, barn.

Parrish (English) church district.
Parish, Parrie, Parrisch, Parrysh

Parry (Welsh) son of Harry.
Parrey, Parrie, Pary

Partemio (Greek) having a pure and virginal appearance.

Parth (Irish) a short form of Parthalán.
Partha, Parthey

Parthalán (Irish) plowman. See also
Bartholomew.
Parlan, Parth

Parthenios (Greek) virgin. Religion:
a Greek Orthodox saint.

Partol (Chuukese) a form of
Bartolomé.

Pascal **B** (French) born on Easter or
Passover.
*Pace, Pascale, Pascalle, Paschal,
Paschalis, Pascoe, Pascow, Pascual,
Pasquale*

Pascale **G** (French) a form of
Pascal.

Pascasio (Spanish) a form of Pascual.

Pascua (Hebrew) in reference to
Easter, to the sacrifice of the village.

Pascual (Spanish) a form of Pascal.
Pascul

Pasha **BG** (Russian) a form of Paul.
Pashenka, Pashka

Pasicrates (Greek) he who dominates
everyone.

Pasquale (Italian) a form of Pascal.
Pascuale, Pasqual, Pasquali, Pasquel

Pastor (Latin) spiritual leader.

Pat **BG** (Native American) fish.
(English) a short form of Patrick.
Pattie, Patty

Patakusu (Moquelumnan) ant biting
a person.

Patamon (Native American) raging.

Patek (Polish) a form of Patrick.
Patick

Paterio (Greek) he who was born in
Pateria.

Paterno (Latin) belonging to the
father.

Patric (Latin) a form of Patrick.

Patrice **G** (French) a form of
Patrick.

Patricia **G** (Latin) noble.

Patricio (Spanish) a form of Patrick.
Patricius, Patrizio

Patrick **B** (Latin) nobleman.
Religion: the patron saint of
Ireland. See also Fitzpatrick, Ticho.
*Paddy, Padraic, Pakelika, Pat, Patek,
Patric, Patrice, Patricio, Patrickk,
Patrik, Patrique, Patrizius, Patryk,
Pats, Patsy, Pattrick*

Patrido (Latin) noble.

Patrin (Gypsy) leaf trail.

Patrocinio (Latin) patronage,
protection.

Patryk (Latin) a form of Patrick.
Patryck

Patterson (Irish) son of Pat.
Patteson

Pattin (Gypsy) leaf.

Patton (English) warrior's town.
*Paden, Paten, Patin, Paton, Patten,
Pattin, Patty, Payton, Peyton*

Patwin (Native American) man.

Patxi (Basque, Teutonic) free.

Paucar (Quechua) very refined,
excellent.

Paucartupac (Quechua) majestic and
excellent.

Paul **B** (Latin) small. Bible: Saul,
later renamed Paul, was the first to
bring the teachings of Christ to the
Gentiles.
*Oalo, Paavo, Pablo, Pal, Pál, Pall,
Paolo, Pasha, Pasko, Pauli, Paulia,
Paulin, Paulino, Paulis, Paulo, Pauls,
Paulus, Pavel, Pavlos, Pawel, Pol, Poul*

Pauli (Latin) a familiar form of Paul.
Pauley, Paulie, Pauly

Paulin (German, Polish) a form of Paul.

Paulino, Pauliño (Spanish) forms of Paul.

Paulo (Portuguese, Swedish, Hawaiian) a form of Paul.

Pausidio (Greek) deliberate, calm man.

Pauyu (Aymara) he who finishes, who brings to a happy ending all work that he undertakes.

Pavel (Russian) a form of Paul.
Paavel, Pasha, Pavils, Pavlik, Pavlo, Pavlusha, Pavlushenka, Pawl

Pavit (Hindi) pious, pure.

Pawel (Polish) a form of Paul.
Pawelek, Pawl

Pax (Latin) peaceful.

Paxton 🅱🅶 (Latin) peaceful town.
Packston, Pax, Paxon, Paxten, Paxtun

Payat (Native American) he is on his way.
Pay, Payatt

Payden (English) a form of Payton.
Paydon

Payne (Latin) from the country.
Paine, Paynn

Paytah (Lakota) fire.
Pay, Payta

Payton 🅶 (English) a form of Patton.
Paiton, Pate, Payden, Peaton, Peighton, Peyton

Paz 🅶 (Spanish) a form of Pax.

Pearce (English) a form of Pierce.
Pears, Pearse

Pearson (English) son of Peter. See also Pierson.
Pearsson, Pehrson, Peirson, Peterson

Peder (Scandinavian) a form of Peter.
Peadar, Pedey

Pedro (Spanish) a form of Peter.
Pedrin, Pedrín, Petronio

Peers (English) a form of Peter.
Peerus, Piers

Peeter (Estonian) a form of Peter.
Peet

Pegaso (Greek) born next to the fountain.

Pei (Chinese) abundant.

Peirce (English) a form of Peter.
Peirs

Pekelo (Hawaiian) a form of Peter.
Pekka

Pelagio, Pelayo (Greek) excellent sailor.

Peleke (Hawaiian) a form of Frederick.

Pelham (English) tannery town.

Pelí (Latin, Basque) happy.

Pelihpe, Pelipe (Pohnpeian) forms of Felipe.

Pell (English) parchment.
Pall

Pello (Greek, Basque) stone.
Peru, Piarres

Pelope (Greek) having a brown complexion.

Pelton (English) town by a pool.

Pembroke (Welsh) headland. (French) wine dealer. (English) broken fence.
Pembrook

Peng (Chinese) a bright future.

Peniame (Fijian) a form of Benjamin.

Peniamina (Hawaiian) a form of Benjamin.
Peni

Penley (English) enclosed meadow.

Penn (Latin) pen, quill. (English) enclosure. (German) a short form of Penrod.
Pen, Penna, Penney, Pennie, Penny

Penrod (German) famous commander.
Penn, Pennrod, Rod

Pepa (Czech) a familiar form of Joseph.
Pepek, Pepik

Pepe (Spanish) a familiar form of José.
Pepillo, Pepito, Pequin, Pipo

Pepin (German) determined; petitioner. History: Pepin the Short was an eighth-century king of the Franks.
Pepi, Peppie, Peppy

Peppe (Italian) a familiar form of Joseph.
Peppi, Peppo, Pino

Per (Swedish) a form of Peter.

Perben (Greek, Danish) stone.

Percival (French) pierce the valley. Literature: a knight of the Round Table who first appears in Chrétien de Troyes's poem about the quest for the Holy Grail.
Parsafal, Parsefal, Parsifal, Parzival, Perc, Perce, Perceval, Percevall, Percivall, Percy, Peredur, Purcell

Percy (French) a familiar form of Percival.
Pearcey, Pearcy, Percey, Percie, Piercey, Piercy

Perdinant (Pohnpeian) a form of Fernando.

Peregrine (Latin) traveler; pilgrim; falcon.
Peregrin, Peregryne, Perine, Perry

Peregrino (Latin) he who travels.

Perfecto (Latin) upright; errorless, without any defects.

Periandro (Greek) worries about men.

Pericles (Greek) just leader. History: an Athenian statesman.

Perico (Spanish) a form of Peter.
Pequin, Perequin

Perine (Latin) a short form of Peregrine.
Perino, Perion, Perrin, Perryn

Perkin (English) little Peter.
Perka, Perkins, Perkyn, Perrin

Pernell (French) a form of Parnell.
Perren, Perrnall

Perpetuo (Latin) having an unchanging goal, who remains faithful to his faith.

Perry **B** (English) a familiar form of Peregrine, Peter.
Parry, Perrie, Perrye

Perseo (Greek) destroyer, the destructive one.

Perth (Scottish) thorn-bush thicket. Geography: a burgh in Scotland; a city in Australia.

Pervis (Latin) passage.
Pervez

Pesach (Hebrew) spared. Religion: another name for Passover.
Pessach

Petar (Greek) a form of Peter.

Pete (English) a short form of Peter.
Peat, Peet, Petey, Peti, Petie, Piet, Pit

Peter ☿ (Greek, Latin) small rock. Bible: Simon, renamed Peter, was the leader of the Twelve Apostles. See also Boutros, Ferris, Takis.
Panayiotos, Panos, Peadair, Peder, Pedro, Peers, Peeter, Peirce, Pekelo, Per, Perico, Perion, Perkin, Perry, Petar, Pete, Péter, Peterke, Peterus, Petr, Petras, Petros, Petru, Petruno, Petter, Peyo, Piaras, Pierce, Piero, Pierre, Pieter, Pietrek, Pietro, Piotr, Piter, Piti, Pjeter, Pyotr

Peterson (English) son of Peter.
Peteris, Petersen

Petiri (Shona) where we are.
Petri

Petr (Bulgarian) a form of Peter.

Petras (Lithuanian) a form of Peter.
Petra, Petrelis

Petros (Greek) a form of Peter.
Petro

Petru (Romanian) a form of Peter.
Petrukas, Petrus, Petruso

Petter (Norwegian) a form of Peter.

Peverell (French) piper.
Peverall, Peverel, Peveril

Peyo (Spanish) a form of Peter.

Peyton ☿ (English) a form of Patton, Payton.
Peyt, Peyten, Peython, Peytonn

Pharaoh (Latin) ruler. History: a title for the ancient kings of Egypt.
Faroh, Pharo, Pharoah, Pharoh

Pharis (Chuukese) a form of Fares.

Phelan (Irish) wolf.

Phelipe (Spanish) a form of Philip.

Phelix (Latin) a form of Felix.

Phelps (English) son of Phillip.

Phil (Greek) a short form of Philip, Phillip.
Fil, Phill

Philander (Greek) lover of mankind.

Philbert (English) a form of Filbert.
Philibert, Phillbert

Philemon (Greek) kiss.
Phila, Philamina, Phileman, Philémon, Philmon

Philip ☿ (Greek) lover of horses. Bible: one of the Twelve Apostles. See also Felipe, Felippo, Filip, Fillipp, Filya, Fischel, Flip.
Phelps, Phelipe, Phil, Philipp, Philippe, Philippo, Phillip, Phillipos, Phillp, Philly, Philp, Phylip, Piers, Pilib, Pilipo, Pippo

Philipp (German) a form of Philip.
Phillipp

Philippe (French) a form of Philip.
Philipe, Phillepe, Phillipe, Phillippe, Phillippee, Phyllipe

Phillip (Greek) a form of Philip.
Phil, Phillipos, Phillipp, Phillips, Philly, Phyllip

Phillipos (Greek) a form of Phillip.

Philly (American) a familiar form of Philip, Phillip.
Phillie

Philo (Greek) love.

Phinean (Irish) a form of Finian.
Phinian

Phineas (English) a form of Pinchas.
Fineas, Phinehas, Phinny

Phirun (Cambodian) rain.

Phoenix (Latin) phoenix, a legendary bird.
Phenix, Pheonix, Phynix

Phong (Vietnamese) wind.

Phuc (Vietnamese) luck; blessings.

Phuok (Vietnamese) good.
Phuoc

Phuong (Vietnamese) destiny; direction.

Pias (Gypsy) fun.

Pichi (Araucanian) small.

Pichiu (Quechua) baby bird.

Pichulman (Mapuche) condor's feather.

Pichunlaf (Mapuche) lucky feather; virtue that brings health and happiness.

Pickford (English) ford at the peak.

Pickworth (English) wood cutter's estate.

Pierce **B** (English) a form of Peter.
Pearce, Peerce, Peers, Peirce, Piercy, Piers

Piero (Italian) a form of Peter.
Pero, Pierro

Pierre **B** (French) a form of Peter.
Peirre, Piere, Pierrot

Pierre-Luc (French) a combination of Pierre + Luc.
Piere Luc

Piers (English) a form of Philip.

Pierson (English) son of Peter. See also Pearson.
Pierrson, Piersen, Piersson, Piersun

Pieter (Dutch) a form of Peter.
Pietr

Pietro (Italian) a form of Peter.

Pigmalion (Spanish) sculptor.

Pihdelis (Pohnpeian) a form of Fidel.

Pilar (Spanish) pillar.

Pilato (Latin) soldier armed with a lance.

Pilatos (Latin) he who is armed with a pick.

Pili (Swahili) second born.

Pilipo (Hawaiian) a form of Philip.

Pillan (Native American) supreme essence.
Pilan

Pin (Vietnamese) faithful boy.

Pinchas (Hebrew) oracle. (Egyptian) dark skinned.
Phineas, Pincas, Pinchos, Pincus, Pinkas, Pinkus, Pinky

Ping (Chinese) peaceful.

Pinky (American) a familiar form of Pinchas.
Pink

Pino (Italian) a form of Joseph.

Piñon (Tupi-Guarani) Mythology: the hunter who became the constellation Orion.

Pio, Pío (Latin) pious.

Piotr (Bulgarian) a form of Peter.
Piotrek

Pipino (Latin) he who has a small stature.

Pippin (German) father.

Piquichaqui (Quechua) feet of a bug, light-footed.

Piran (Irish) prayer. Religion: the patron saint of miners.
Peran, Pieran

Pirro (Greek, Spanish) flaming hair.

Pista (Hungarian) a familiar form of István.
Pisti

Pitágoras (Greek) he who is like a divine oracle.

Piti (Spanish) a form of Peter.

Pitin (Spanish) a form of Felix.
Pito

Pitney (English) island of the strong-willed man.
Pittney

Pitt (English) pit, ditch.

Piyco, Piycu (Quechua) red bird.

Piycomayu, Piycumayu (Quechua) a river as red as a bright, red bird.

Placido (Spanish) serene.
Placide, Placidus, Placyd, Placydo

Plácido (Latin) a form of Placido.

Plato (Greek) broad shouldered. History: a famous Greek philosopher.
Platon

Platón (Greek) wide-shouldered.

Platt (French) flatland.
Platte

Plauto, Plotino (Greek) he who has flat feet.

Plinio (Latin) he who has many skills, gifts.

Plubio (Greek) man of the sea.

Plutarco (Greek) rich prince.

Plutón (Greek) owner of many riches.

Po Sin (Chinese) grandfather elephant.

Pol (Swedish) a form of Paul.
Pól, Pola, Poul

Poldi (German) a familiar form of Leopold.
Poldo

Poliano (Greek) he who suffers, the sorrowful one.

Policarpo (Greek) he who produces abundant fruit.

Policeto (Greek) he who caused much sorrow.

Polidoro (Greek) having virtues.

Poliecto (Greek) he who is very desired.

Polifemo (Greek) he who is spoken about a lot.

Polión (Greek) powerful Lord who protects.

Pollard (German) close-cropped head.
Poll, Pollerd, Pollyrd

Pollock (English) a form of Pollux. Art: American artist Jackson Pollock was a leader of abstract expressionism.
Pollack, Polloch

Pollux (Greek) crown. Astronomy: one of the stars in the constellation Gemini.
Pollock

Polo (Tibetan) brave wanderer. (Greek) a short form of Apollo. Culture: a game played on horseback. History: Marco Polo was a thirteenth-century Venetian explorer who traveled throughout Asia.

Poma, Pomacana (Quechua) strong and powerful puma.

Pomacaua (Quechua) he who guards with the quietness of a puma.

Pomagüiyca (Quechua) sacred like the puma.

Pomalloque (Quechua) left-handed puma.

Pomauari (Quechua) indomitable as a vicuna and strong as a puma.

Pomayauri (Quechua) copper-colored puma.

Pomeroy (French) apple orchard.
Pommeray, Pommeroy

Pompeyo (Greek) he who heads the procession.

Pomponio (Latin) lover of grandeur and the open plains.

Ponce (Spanish) fifth. History: Juan Ponce de León of Spain searched for the Fountain of Youth in Florida.

Poncio (Greek) having come from the sea.

Ponpey (English) a form of Pompeyo.

Pony (Scottish) small horse.
Poni

Porcio (Latin) he who earns his living raising pigs.

Porfirio (Greek, Spanish) purple stone.
Porphirios, Prophyrios

Porfiro (Greek) purple stone.

Porter (Latin) gatekeeper.
Port, Portie, Porty

Poseidón (Greek) owner of the waters.

Poshita (Sanskrit) cherished.

Posidio (Greek) he who is devoted to Poseidon.

Potenciano (Latin) he who dominates with his empire.

Poul (Danish) a form of Paul.
Poulos, Poulus

Pov (Gypsy) earth.

Powa (Native American) wealthy.

Powell (English) alert.
Powel

Prabhjot **B** (Sikh) the light of God.

Prácido (Latin) tranquil, calm.

Pragnacio (Greek) he who is skillful and practical in business.

Pramad (Hindi) rejoicing.

Pratyush (Indian) sun.

Pravan (Indian) bowed down; modest.

Pravar (Indian) chief.

Pravat (Tai) history.

Praveen (Indian) expert, skilled.

Praveer (Indian) an excellent warrior or king.

Prayadarshi (Indian) one who is liked by all.

Preetam (Indian) beloved; husband.

Preetidutt (Indian) gifted with love.

Preetish (Indian) god of love.

Preetiwardhan (Indian) one who increases love.

Prem (Hindi) love.

Premanand (Indian) joy of love.

Prentice (English) apprentice.
Prent, Prentis, Prentiss, Printes, Printiss

Prescott (English) priest's cottage. See also Scott.
Prescot, Prestcot, Prestcott

Presidio (Latin) he who gives pleasant shelter.

Presley G (English) priest's meadow. Music: Elvis Presley was an influential American rock 'n' roll singer.
Presleigh, Presly, Presslee, Pressley, Prestley, Priestley, Priestly

Preston B (English) priest's estate.
Prestan, Presten, Prestin, Prestyn

Pretextato (Latin) covered by a toga.

Prewitt (French) brave little one.
Preuet, Prewet, Prewett, Prewit, Pruit, Pruitt

Priamo (Greek) rescued one.

Príamo (Greek) a form of Priamo.

Price (Welsh) son of the ardent one.
Brice, Bryce, Pryce

Pricha (Tai) clever.

Prilidiano (Greek) he who remembers things from the past.

Primeiro (Italian) born first.

Primitivo (Latin) original.

Primo (Italian) first; premier quality.
Preemo, Premo

Prince (Latin) chief; prince.
Prence, Prinz, Prinze

Princeton (English) princely town.
Prenston, Princeston, Princton

Prithu (Indian) broad, spacious.

Prithvijaj (Indian) king of the earth.

Priyadarshan (Indian) nice to look at, handsome.

Priyam, Priyaranjan (Indian) beloved.

Priyanvad (Indian) sweet-talking person.

Probo (Latin) having moral conduct.

Proceso (Latin) he who moves forward.

Procopio (Greek) he who progresses.

Procoro (Greek) he who prospers.

Proctor (Latin) official, administrator.
Prockter, Procter

Proculo (Latin) he who was born far from home.

Prokopios (Greek) declared leader.

Promaco (Greek) he who prepares for battle.

Prometeo (Greek) he who resembles God.

Prosper (Latin) fortunate.
Prospero, Próspero

Protasio (Greek) he who is in front; the preferred one.

Proteo (Greek) lord of the sea's waves.

Proterio (Greek) he who precedes all the rest.

Proto (Greek) first.

Protólico (Greek) preferred one; he who deserves first place.

Prudenciano (Spanish) humble and honest.

Prudencio (Latin) he who works with sensitivity and modesty.

Pryor (Latin) head of the monastery; prior.
Prior, Pry

Pu (Chinese) uncut jade.

Publio (Latin) he who is popular.

Puchac (Quechua) leader; he who leads others down a good path.

Pueblo (Spanish) from the city.

Pujan (Indian) the ceremony of worshiping.

Pulkit (Indian) happy, thrilled, overjoyed.

Pulqueria (Latin) beautiful one.

Pulqui (Araucanian) arrow.

Puma, Pumacana (Quechua) strong and powerful puma.

Pumacaua (Quechua) he who guards with the quietness of a puma.

Pumagüiyca (Quechua) sacred like the puma.

Pumalluqui (Quechua) left-handed puma.

Pumasonjo, Pumasuncu (Quechua) courageous heart; heart of a puma.

Pumauari (Quechua) indomitable as a vicuna and strong as a puma.

Pumayauri (Quechua) copper-colored puma.

Pumeet (Sanskrit) pure.

Pundarik (Indian) white lotus.

Puneeth (Indian) pure.

Pupulo (Latin) little boy.

Purdy (Hindi) recluse.

Puric (Quechua) walker, fond of walking.

Purnendu (Indian) full moon.

Purujit (Indian) conqueror of the city.

Purumitra (Indian) friend of the city.

Purushottam (Indian) best among men.

Purvis (French, English) providing food.
Pervis, Purves, Purviss

Pushkara (Indian) blue lotus; fountain; lake.

Pushpad (Indian) he who gives flowers.

Pushpaj (Indian) born from a flower.

Pushpak (Indian) Kuber's plane taken away by Ravan.

Pushpakar (Indian) the spring season; flower season.

Pushpaketu (Indian) Kamdev, the love god.

Putnam (English) dweller by the pond.
Putnem

Putta (Indian) small baby.

Pyas (Indian) thirsty.

Pyotr (Russian) a form of Peter.
Petenka, Petinka, Petrusha, Petya, Pyatr

Qabil (Arabic) able.

Qadim (Arabic) ancient.

Qadir (Arabic) powerful.
Qaadir, Qadeer, Quaadir, Quadeer, Quadir

Qamar (Arabic) moon.
Quamar, Quamir

Qasim (Arabic) divider.
Quasim

Qatadah (Indian) a hardwood tree.

Qays (Indian) firm.

Qi (Chinese) fine jade; outstanding; distinguished.

Qian (Chinese) thousand.

Qiang (Chinese) powerful.

Qiao (Chinese) pretty, handsome.

Qimat (Hindi) valuable.

Qin (Chinese) industrious.

Qing (Chinese) stainless.

Qing Yuan, Qing-Yuan (Chinese) deep water; clear spring.

Qiong (Chinese) fine jade.

Qiu (Chinese) autumn.

Qu (Chinese) interest, delight.

Quaashie 🆖 (Ewe) born on Sunday.

Quadarius (American) a combination of Quan + Darius.
Quadara, Quadarious, Quadaris, Quandarious, Quandarius, Quandarrius, Qudarius, Qudaruis

Quade (Latin) fourth.
Quadell, Quaden, Quadon, Quadre, Quadrie, Quadrine, Quadrion, Quaid, Quayd, Quayde, Qwade

Quamaine (American) a combination of Quan + Jermaine.
Quamain, Quaman, Quamane, Quamayne, Quarmaine

Quan (Comanche) a short form of Quanah.

Quanah (Comanche) fragrant.
Quan

Quandre (American) a combination of Quan + Andre.
Quandrae, Quandré

Quang (Vietnamese) clear; brilliant; good reputation.

Quant (Greek) how much?
Quanta, Quantae, Quantai, Quantas, Quantay, Quante, Quantea, Quantey, Quantez, Quantu

Quantavius (American) a combination of Quan + Octavius.
Quantavian, Quantavin, Quantavion, Quantavious, Quantavis, Quantavous, Quatavious, Quatavius

Quashawn (American) a combination of Quan + Shawn.
Quasean, Quashaan, Quashan, Quashaun, Quashaunn, Quashon, Quashone, Quashun, Queshan, Queshon, Qweshawn, Qyshawn

Qudamah (Arabic) courage.

Que (Chinese) reliable.

Quenby 🆖 (Scandinavian) a form of Quimby.

Quennell (French) small oak.
Quenell, Quennel

Quenten (Latin) a form of Quentin.
Quienten

Quenti, Quinti (Quechua) hummingbird; shy, small.

Quentin 🅑 (Latin) fifth. (English) queen's town.
Qeuntin, Quantin, Quent, Quentan, Quenten, Quentine, Quenton, Quentyn, Quentynn, Quientin, Quinten, Quintin, Quinton, Qwentin

Quenton (Latin) a form of Quentin.
Quienton

Querubín (Hebrew) swift, young bull.

Quespi, Quispe, Quispi (Quechua) free, liberated; jewel, shiny like a diamond.

Queupulicán (Mapuche) white stone with a black stripe.

Queupumil (Mapuche) shining stone; brilliant, precious.

Quichuasamin (Quechua) he who brings fortune and happiness to the village.

Quico (Spanish) a familiar form of many names.
Paco

Quidequeo (Mapuche) brilliant; fiery tongue.

Quigley (Irish) maternal side.
Quigly

Quillan (Irish) cub.
Quill, Quillen, Quillin, Quillon

Quillinchu, Quilliyicu (Quechua) sparrow hawk.

Quimby (Scandinavian) woman's estate.
Quenby, Quinby

Quincy **B** (French) fifth son's estate.
Quenci, Quency, Quince, Quincee, Quincey, Quinci, Quinn, Quinncy, Quinnsy, Quinsey, Quinzy

Quindarius (American) a combination of Quinn + Darius.
Quindarious, Quindarrius, Quinderious, Quinderus, Quindrius

Quiñelef (Mapuche) a rapid trip, quick race.

Quinlan (Irish) strong; well shaped.
Quindlen, Quinlen, Quinlin, Quinn, Quinnlan, Quinnlin

Quinn **B** (Irish) a short form of Quincy, Quinlan, Quinton.
Quin

Quintavius (American) a combination of Quinn + Octavius.
Quintavious, Quintavis, Quintavus, Quintayvious

Quinten (Latin) a form of Quentin.
Quinnten

Quintilian (French) a form of Quintiliano.

Quintiliano (Spanish) a form of Quintilio.

Quintilio (Latin) he who was born in the fifth month.

Quintin (Latin) a form of Quentin.
Quinntin, Quintine, Quintyn

Quintín (Spanish) a form of Quinto.

Quinto (Latin) a form of Quinton.

Quinton **B** (Latin) a form of Quentin.
Quinn, Quinneton, Quinnton, Quint, Quintan, Quintann, Quintin, Quintion, Quintus, Quitin, Quito, Quiton, Qunton, Qwinton

Quintrilpe (Mapuche) place of organization.

Quintuillan (Mapuche) searching for the altar.

Quiqui (Spanish) a familiar form of Enrique.
Quinto, Quiquin

Quirino (Latin) he who carries a lance.

Quispiyupanqui (Quechua) he who honors his liberty.

Quisu (Aymara) he who appreciates the value of things.

Quitin (Latin) a short form of Quinton.
Quiten, Quito, Quiton

Quito (Spanish) a short form of
Quinton.

Qun (Chinese) the masses.

Quon (Chinese) bright.

Qutaybah (Indian) irritable,
impatient.

Quy (Vietnamese) precious.

R

R 🆖 (American) an initial used as a
first name.

Raakin (Indian) respectful.

Raamiz (Indian) symbol.

Raanan (Hebrew) fresh; luxuriant.

Raatib (Indian) arranger.

Rabi 🆖 (Arabic) breeze.
*Rabbi, Rabee, Rabeeh, Rabiah,
Rabie, Rabih*

Race (English) race.
Racel, Rayce

Racham (Hebrew) compassionate.
*Rachaman, Rachamim, Rachim,
Rachman, Rachmiel, Rachum, Raham,
Rahamim*

Rachel 🆖 (Hebrew) sheep.

Rad (English) advisor. (Slavic) happy.
*Raad, Radd, Raddie, Raddy, Rade,
Radee, Radell, Radey, Radi*

Radbert (English) brilliant advisor.

Radburn (English) red brook; brook
with reeds.
*Radborn, Radborne, Radbourn,
Radbourne, Radburne*

Radcliff (English) red cliff; cliff with
reeds.
Radcliffe, Radclyffe

Radford (English) red ford; ford with
reeds.

Radhakrishnan (Indian) the goddess
Radha.

Radley (English) red meadow;
meadow of reeds.
Radlea, Radlee, Radleigh, Radly

Radman (Slavic) joyful.
Radmen, Radusha

Radnor (English) red shore; shore
with reeds.

Radomil (Slavic) happy peace.

Radoslaw (Polish) happy glory.
Radik, Rado, Radzmir, Slawek

Ra'ed (Indian) leader.

Raegan 🆖 (Irish) a form of Reagan.

Raekwon (American) a form of
Raquan.
*Raekwan, Raikwan, Rakwane,
Rakwon*

Raequan (American) a form of
Raquan.
*Raequon, Raeqwon, Raiquan,
Raiquen, Raiqoun*

Raeshawn (American) a form of
Rashawn.
*Raesean, Raeshaun, Raeshon,
Raeshun*

Rafael 🅱 (Spanish) a form of
Raphael. See also Falito.
*Rafaelle, Rafaello, Rafaelo, Rafal,
Rafeal, Rafeé, Rafel, Rafello, Raffael,
Raffaelo, Raffeal, Raffel, Raffiel, Rafiel*

Rafaele (Italian) a form of Raphael.
Raffaele

Rafal (Polish) a form of Raphael.

Rafe (English) a short form of Rafferty, Ralph.
Raff

Rafee' (Indian) kind friend.

Rafer (Irish) a short form of Rafferty.
Raffer

Rafferty (Irish) rich, prosperous.
Rafe, Rafer, Raferty, Raffarty, Raffer

Rafi (Arabic) exalted. (Hebrew) a familiar form of Raphael.
Raffe, Raffee, Raffi, Raffy, Rafi

Rafiq (Arabic) friend.
Raafiq, Rafeeq, Rafic, Rafique

Rafu (Japanese) a net.

Ragesh (Indian) the man who sings sweet ragas.

Ragheb (Indian) desirous.

Raghib (Arabic) desirous.
Raquib

Raghnall (Irish) wise power.

Ragnar (Norwegian) powerful army.
Ragnor, Rainer, Rainier, Ranieri, Rayner, Raynor, Reinhold

Rago (Hausa) ram.

Raguel (Hebrew) everybody's friend.

Raheem **B** (Punjabi) compassionate God.
Rakeem

Rahim (Arabic) merciful.
Raaheim, Rahaeim, Raheam, Raheim, Rahiem, Rahiim, Rahime, Rahium, Rakim

Rahman (Arabic) compassionate.
Rahmatt, Rahmet

Rahul (Arabic) traveler.

Rai (Spanish) mighty protector.

Raíd (Arabic) leader.

Raiden (Japanese) Mythology: the thunder god.
Raidan, Rayden

Railef (Mapuche) a flower that is bedraggled because of a strong wind.

Raimi (Quechua) party, celebration.

Raimondo (Italian) a form of Raymond.
Raymondo, Reimundo

Raimund (German) a form of Raymond.
Rajmund

Raimundo (Portuguese, Spanish) a form of Raymond.
Mundo, Raimon, Raimond, Raimonds, Raymundo

Raine **G** (English) lord; wise.
Rain, Raines, Rayne

Rainer (German) counselor.
Rainar, Rainey, Rainier, Rainor, Raynier, Reinier

Rainero (Germanic) intelligence that guides.

Rainey (German) a familiar form of Rainer.
Raine, Rainee, Rainie, Rainney, Rainy, Reiny

Raini (Tupi-Guarani) Religion: the god who created the world.

Raishawn (American) a form of Rashawn.
Raishon, Raishun

Rajab (Indian) the seventh month of the Islamic calendar.

Rajabu (Swahili) born in the seventh month of the Islamic calendar.

Rajah (Hindi) prince; chief.
Raj, Raja, Rajaah, Rajae, Rajahe, Rajan, Raje, Rajeh, Raji

Rajak (Hindi) cleansing.

Rajan (Hindi) a form of Rajah.
Rajaahn, Rajain, Rajen, Rajin

Rajaneesh (Indian) the god of night;
god of the moon.

Rajani (Indian) night.

**Rajanikanta, Rajivlochan,
Rajivnayan** (Indian) king's sage.

Rajeet (Indian) decorated.

Rajiv (Indian) a blue lotus.

Rajkumar (Indian) prince.

Rajyeshwar (Indian) king.

Rakeem (Punjabi) a form of Raheem.
Rakeeme, Rakeim, Rakem

Rakim (Arabic) a form of Rahim.
Rakiim

Rakin (Arabic) respectable.
Rakeen

Rakishi (Indian) wide load.

Raksha (Indian) the moon; protection.

Rakshak (Indian) rescue.

Raktakamal (Indian) a red lotus.

Raktim (Hindi) bright red.

Raleigh 🅱 (English) a form of
Rawleigh.
Ralegh

Ralph 🅱 (English) wolf counselor.
*Radolphus, Rafe, Ralf, Ralpheal,
Ralphel, Ralphie, Ralston, Raoul, Raul,
Rolf*

Ralphie (English) a familiar form of
Ralph.
Ralphy

Ralston (English) Ralph's settlement.

Ram (Hindi) god; godlike. Religion:
another name for the Hindu god
Rama. (English) male sheep. A
short form of Ramsey.
Rami, Ramie, Ramy

Ramadan (Arabic) ninth month of
the Arabic year in the Islamic
calendar.
Rama

Ramakant (Indian) husband of
Rama.

Ramakrishna (Indian) a combination
of Rama + Krishna.

Raman 🅶 (Hindi) a short form of
Ramanan.

Ramanan (Hindi) god; godlike.
*Raman, Ramandeep, Ramanjit,
Ramanjot*

Ramanuja (Indian) born after Lord
Rama.

Ramavatar (Indian) reincarnation of
Lord Rama.

Ramdas (Indian) devotee of Rama.

Ramesh (Indian) the preserver.

Rami (Hindi, English) a form of
Ram. (Spanish) a short form of
Ramiro.
Rame, Ramee, Ramey, Ramih

Ramiro (Portuguese, Spanish)
supreme judge.
*Ramario, Rameer, Rameir, Ramere,
Rameriz, Ramero, Rami, Ramires,
Ramirez, Ramos*

Ramón (Spanish) a form of
Raymond.
Ramon, Remon, Remone, Romone

Ramone (Dutch) a form of
Raymond.
*Raemon, Raemonn, Ramond,
Ramonte, Remone*

Ramsden (English) valley of rams.

Ramsey B (English) ram's island.
Ram, Ramsay, Ramsee, Ramsie, Ramsy, Ramzee, Ramzey, Ramzi, Ramzy

Ran (Chinese) correct.

Ranajit (Indian) victorious.

Rance (English) a short form of Laurence. (American) a familiar form of Laurence.
Rancel, Rancell, Rances, Rancey, Rancie, Rancy, Ransel, Ransell

Rancul (Araucanian) plant from the grasslands whose leaves are used to make roofs for huts.

Rand (English) shield; warrior.
Randy

Randal (English) a form of Randall.
Randahl, Randale, Randel, Randl, Randle

Randall B (English) a form of Randolph.
Randal, Randell, Randy, Randyll

Randheer (Indian) one who shows bravery and boldness in war.

Randi G (English) a form of Randy.

Randolph (English) shield wolf.
Randall, Randol, Randolf, Randolfo, Randolpho, Randy, Ranolph

Randy B (English) a familiar form of Rand, Randall, Randolph.
Randdy, Randee, Randey, Randi, Randie, Ranndy

Rangan (Indian) a flower.

Ranger (French) forest keeper.
Rainger, Range

Rangle (American) cowboy.
Rangler, Wrangle

Rangsey (Cambodian) seven kinds of colors.

Rani G (Hebrew) my song; my joy.
Ranen, Ranie, Ranon, Roni

Ranieri (Italian) a form of Ragnar.
Raneir, Ranier, Rannier

Ranjan (Hindi) delighted; gladdened.

Ranjeet (Indian) victor in wars.

Rankin (English) small shield.
Randkin

Ransford (English) raven's ford.

Ransley (English) raven's field.

Ransom (Latin) redeemer. (English) son of the shield.
Rance, Ransome, Ranson

Ranveer (Indian) winner.

Raoul (French) a form of Ralph, Rudolph.
Raol, Raul, Raúl, Reuel

Raphael B (Hebrew) God has healed. Bible: one of the archangels. Art: a prominent painter of the Renaissance. See also Falito, Rafi.
Rafael, Rafaele, Rafal, Rafel, Raphaél, Raphale, Raphaello, Rapheal, Raphel, Raphello, Raphiel, Ray, Rephael

Rapheal (Hebrew) a form of Raphael.
Rafel, Raphiel

Rapier (French) blade-sharp.

Rapiman (Mapuche) condor's vomit; indigestion.

Raquan (American) a combination of the prefix Ra + Quan.
Raaquan, Rackwon, Racquan, Raekwon, Raequan, Rahquan, Raquané, Raquon, Raquwan, Raquwn, Raquwon, Raqwan, Raqwann

Raquel G (French) a form of Rachel.

Rashaad (Arabic) a form of Rashad.

Rashaan (American) a form of Rashawn.
Rasaan, Rashan, Rashann

Rashad (Arabic) wise counselor.
Raashad, Rachad, Rachard, Raeshad, Raishard, Rashaad, Rashadd, Rashade, Rashaud, Rasheed, Rashid, Rashod, Reshad, Rhashad, Rishad, Roshad

Rashard (American) a form of Richard.
Rasharrd

Rashaud (Arabic) a form of Rashad.
Rachaud, Rashaude

Rashaun (American) a form of Rashawn.

Rashawn ☐ (American) a combination of the prefix Ra + Shawn.
Raashawn, Raashen, Raeshawn, Rahshawn, Raishawn, Rasaun, Rasawn, Rashaan, Rashaun, Rashaw, Rashon, Rashun, Raushan, Raushawn, Rhashan, Rhashaun, Rhashawn

Rashean (American) a combination of the prefix Ra + Sean.
Rahsaan, Rahsean, Rahseen, Rasean, Rashane, Rasheen, Rashien, Rashiena

Rasheed ☐ (Arabic) a form of Rashad.
Rashead, Rashed, Rasheid, Rhasheed

Rashid (Arabic) a form of Rashad.
Rasheyd, Rashida, Rashidah, Rashied, Rashieda, Raushaid

Rashida ☐ (Swahili) righteous.

Rashidi (Swahili) wise counselor.

Rashod (Arabic) a form of Rashad.
Rashoda, Rashodd, Rashoud, Rayshod, Rhashod

Rashon (American) a form of Rashawn.
Rashion, Rashone, Rashonn, Rashuan, Rashun, Rashunn

Rasmus (Greek, Danish) a short form of Erasmus.

Rasraj (Indian) king of liquid; romance.

Ratan (Indian) gem.

Ratchell (Vietnamese) a form of Ritchell.

Rateesh (Indian) god and husband of Ratee.

Ratnakar (Indian) mine of jewels; sea.

Ratul (Indian) sweet.

Rauel (Hebrew) friend of God.

Raul (French) a form of Ralph.

Raulas (Lithuanian) a form of Laurence.

Raulo (Lithuanian) a form of Laurence.
Raulas

Raunak (Indian) pride, glory.

Raurac (Quechua) burning; ardent.

Raven ☐ (English) a short form of Ravenel.
Ravan, Ravean, Raveen, Ravin, Ravine, Ravon, Ravyn, Reven, Rhaven

Ravenel (English) raven.
Raven, Ravenell, Revenel

Ravi (Hindi) sun.
Ravee, Ravijot

Ravid (Hebrew) a form of Arvid.

Ravikiran (Indian) sun ray.

Ravinandan (Indian) son of the sun.

Ravindra (Indian) sun.

Ravinshu (Indian) Kamdev, the love god.

Raviv (Hebrew) rain, dew.

Ravon (English) a form of Raven.
Raveon, Ravion, Ravone, Ravonn, Ravonne, Rayvon, Revon

Rawdon (English) rough hill.

Rawleigh (English) deer meadow.
Raleigh, Rawle, Rawley, Rawling, Rawly, Rawylyn

Rawlins (French) a form of Roland.
Rawlings, Rawlinson, Rawson

Ray B (French) kingly, royal.
(English) a short form of Rayburn,
Raymond. See also Lei.
Rae, Raye

Rayan (Irish) a form of Ryan.
Rayaun

Rayburn (English) deer brook.
*Burney, Raeborn, Raeborne,
Raebourn, Ray, Raybourn,
Raybourne, Rayburne*

Rayce (English) a form of Race.

Rayden (Japanese) a form of Raiden.
Raidin, Raydun, Rayedon

Rayhan (Arabic) favored by God.
Rayhaan

Rayi (Hebrew) my friend, my
companion.

Raymon (English) a form of Raymond.
*Rayman, Raymann, Raymen,
Raymone, Raymun, Reamonn*

Raymond (English) mighty; wise
protector. See also Aymon.
*Radmond, Raemond, Raimondo,
Raimund, Raimundo, Ramón, Ramond,
Ramonde, Ramone, Ray, Raymand,
Rayment, Raymon, Raymont, Raymund,
Raymunde, Raymundo, Redmond,
Reymond, Reymundo*

Raymundo (Spanish) a form of
Raymond.
*Raemondo, Raimondo, Raimundo,
Raymondo*

Raynaldo (Spanish) a form of
Reynold.
Raynal, Raynald, Raynold

Raynard (French) a form of Renard,
Reynard.
Raynarde

Rayne (English) a form of Raine.
Raynee, Rayno

Raynor (Scandinavian) a form of
Ragnar.
*Rainer, Rainor, Ranier, Ranieri,
Raynar, Rayner*

Rayshawn (American) a combination
of Ray + Shawn.
*Raysean, Rayshaan, Rayshan,
Rayshaun, Raysheen, Rayshon,
Rayshone, Rayshonn, Rayshun,
Rayshunn*

Rayshod (American) a form of Rashad.
*Raychard, Rayshad, Rayshard,
Rayshaud*

Rayvon (American) a form of Ravon.
*Rayvan, Rayvaun, Rayven, Rayvone,
Reyven, Reyvon*

Razi B (Aramaic) my secret.
Raz, Raziel, Raziq

Read (English) a form of Reed, Reid.
Raed, Raede, Raeed, Reaad, Reade

Reading (English) son of the red
wanderer.
Redding, Reeding, Reiding

Reagan G (Irish) little king.
History: Ronald Wilson Reagan
was the fortieth U.S. president.
*Raegan, Reagen, Reaghan, Reegan,
Reegen, Regan, Reigan, Reighan,
Reign, Rheagan*

Rebecca G (Hebrew) tied, bound.

Rebekah G (Hebrew) a form of
Rebecca.

Rebel (American) rebel.
Reb

Recaredo (Teutonic) counsels his superiors.

Red (American) red, redhead.
Redd

Reda (Arabic) satisfied.
Ridha

Redford (English) red river crossing.
Ford, Radford, Reaford, Red, Redd

Redley (English) red meadow; meadow with reeds.
Radley, Redlea, Redleigh, Redly

Redmond (German) protecting counselor. (English) a form of Raymond.
Radmond, Radmund, Reddin, Redmund

Redpath (English) red path.

Reece 🅱 (Welsh) a form of Rhys.
Reace, Rece, Reice, Reyes, Rhys, Rice, Ryese

Reed 🅱 (English) a form of Reid.
Raeed, Read, Reyde, Rheed

Reese 🅱 (Welsh) a form of Reece.
Rease, Rees, Reis, Reise, Reiss, Riese, Riess

Reeve (English) steward.
Reave, Reaves, Reeves

Reg (English) a short form of Reginald.

Regan 🅶 (Irish) a form of Reagan.
Regen

Reggie 🅱 (English) a familiar form of Reginald.
Regi, Regie

Reginal (English) a form of Reginald.
Reginale, Reginel

Reginald 🅱 (English) king's advisor. A form of Reynold. See also Naldo.
Reg, Reggie, Regginald, Reggis, Reginal, Reginaldo, Reginalt, Reginauld, Reginault, Reginold, Reginuld, Regnauld, Ronald

Regis (Latin) regal.

Regulo, Régulo (Latin) forms of Rex.

Rehema (Swahili) second-born.

Rei 🅶 (Japanese) rule, law.

Reid 🅱 (English) redhead.
Read, Reed, Reide, Reyd, Ried

Reidar (Norwegian) nest warrior.

Reiji (Japanese) wise governor.

Reilly 🅱 (Irish) a form of Riley.
Reiley, Reilley, Reily, Rielly

Reinaldo (Spanish) a form of Reynold.

Reinardo (Teutonic) valiant counselor.

Reinhart (German) a form of Reynard.
Rainart, Rainhard, Rainhardt, Rainhart, Reinart, Reinhard, Reinhardt, Renke

Reinhold (Swedish) a form of Ragnar.
Reinold

Reizo (Japanese) cool, calm; well groomed.

Reku (Finnish) a form of Richard.

Remi, Rémi 🅱 (French) forms of Remy.
Remie, Remmie

Remigio (Latin) he who mans the oars.

Remington 🅱 (English) raven estate.
Rem, Reminton, Tony

Remo (Greek) strong one.

Remus (Latin) speedy, quick.
Mythology: Remus and his twin
brother, Romulus, founded Rome.

Remy (French) from Rheims, France.
Ramey, Remee, Remi, Rémi, Remmy

Renaldo (Spanish) a form of Reynold.
Raynaldo, Reynaldo, Rinaldo

Renán (Irish) seal.

Renard (French) a form of Reynard.
Ranard, Raynard, Reinard, Rennard

Renardo (Italian) a form of Reynard.

Renato (Italian) reborn.

Renaud (French) a form of Reynard,
Reynold.
Renauld, Renauldo, Renault, Renould

Rendor (Hungarian) policeman.

Rene **B** (Greek) a short form of
Irene, Renée.

René (French) reborn.
*Renat, Renato, Renatus, Renault,
Renay, Renee, Renny*

Renee **G** (French) a form of René.

Renfred (English) lasting peace.

Renfrew (Welsh) raven woods.

Renjiro (Japanese) virtuous.

Renny (Irish) small but strong.
(French) a familiar form of René.
Ren, Renn, Renne, Rennie

Reno (American) gambler.
Geography: a city in Nevada known
for gambling.
Renos, Rino

Renshaw (English) raven woods.
Renishaw

Renton (English) settlement of the
roe deer.

Renzo (Latin) a familiar form of
Laurence. (Italian) a short form of
Lorenzo.
Renz, Renzy, Renzzo

Repucura (Mapuche) jagged rock;
rocky road.

Reshad (American) a form of Rashad.
*Reshade, Reshard, Resharrd,
Reshaud, Reshawd, Reshead, Reshod*

Reshawn (American) a combination
of the prefix Re + Shawn.
Reshaun, Reshaw, Reshon, Reshun

Reshean (American) a combination
of the prefix Re + Sean.
*Resean, Reshae, Reshane, Reshay,
Reshayne, Reshea, Resheen, Reshey*

Restituto (Latin) he who returns to
God.

Reuben (Hebrew) behold a son.
*Reuban, Reubin, Reuven, Rheuben,
Rhuben, Rube, Ruben, Rubey, Rubin,
Ruby, Rueben*

Reuven (Hebrew) a form of Reuben.
Reuvin, Rouvin, Ruvim

Rex (Latin) king.
Rexx

Rexford (English) king's ford.

Rexton (English) king's town.

Rey (Spanish) a short form of
Reynaldo, Reynard, Reynold.

Reyes (English) a form of Reece.
Reyce

Reyhan **B** (Arabic) favored by God.
Reyham

Reymond (English) a form of
Raymond.
Reymon, Reymound, Reymund

Reymundo (Spanish) a form of
Raymond.
Reimond, Reimonde, Reimundo,
Reymon

Reynaldo (Spanish) a form of Reynold.
Renaldo, Rey, Reynauldo

Reynard (French) wise; bold,
courageous.
Raynard, Reinhard, Reinhardt, Reinhart,
Renard, Renardo, Renaud, Rennard,
Rey, Reynardo, Reynaud

Reynold (English) king's advisor. See
also Reginald.
Rainault, Rainhold, Ranald, Raynald,
Raynaldo, Reinald, Reinaldo,
Reinaldos, Reinhart, Reinhold, Reinold,
Reinwald, Renald, Renaldi, Renaldo,
Renaud, Renauld, Rennold, Renold,
Rey, Reynald, Reynaldo, Reynaldos,
Reynol, Reynolds, Rinaldo, Ronald

Réz 🄱🄶 (Hungarian) copper; redhead.
Rezsö

Rhett 🄱 (Welsh) a form of Rhys.
Literature: Rhett Butler was the
hero of Margaret Mitchell's novel
Gone with the Wind.
Rhet

Rhodes (Greek) where roses grow.
Geography: an island of southeast
Greece.
Rhoads, Rhodas, Rodas

Rhyan (Irish) a form of Rian.
Rhian

Rhys 🄱 (Welsh) enthusiastic; stream.
Rhett, Rhyce, Rhyse, Rice

Rian (Irish) little king.
Rhyan

Ric (Italian, Spanish) a short form of
Rico.
Ricca, Ricci, Ricco

Ricardo 🄱 (Portuguese, Spanish) a
form of Richard.
Racardo, Recard, Ricaldo, Ricard,
Ricardoe, Ricardos, Riccardo,
Riccarrdo, Ricciardo, Richardo

Rice (English) rich, noble. (Welsh) a
form of Reece.
Ryce

Rich (English) a short form of
Richard.
Ritch

Richard 🄱 (English) a form of
Richart. See also Aric, Dick, Juku,
Likeke.
Rashard, Reku, Ricardo, Rich, Richar,
Richards, Richardson, Richart,
Richaud, Richer, Richerd, Richie,
Richird, Richshard, Rick, Rickard,
Rickert, Rickey, Ricky, Rico, Rihardos,
Rihards, Rikard, Riocard, Riócard,
Risa, Risardas, Rishard, Ristéard,
Ritchard, Rostik, Rye, Rysio, Ryszard

Richart (German) rich and powerful
ruler.

Richie (English) a familiar form of
Richard.
Richey, Richi, Richy, Rishi, Ritchie

Richman (English) powerful.

Richmond (German) powerful
protector.
Richmon, Richmound

Rick (German, English) a short form
of Cedric, Frederick, Richard.
Ric, Ricke, Rickey, Ricks, Ricky, Rik,
Riki, Rykk

Rickard (Swedish) a form of Richard.

Ricker (English) powerful army.

Rickey 🄱 (English) a familiar form
of Richard, Rick, Riqui.

Ricki 🄶 (English) a form of Rickie.

Rickie (English) a form of Ricky.
Rickee, Ricki

Rickward (English) mighty guardian.
Rickwerd, Rickwood

Ricky **B** (English) a familiar form of
Richard, Rick.
*Ricci, Rickie, Riczi, Riki, Rikki, Rikky,
Riqui*

Rico **B** (Spanish) a familiar form of
Richard. (Italian) a short form of
Enrico.
Ric, Ricco

Rida **BG** (Arabic) favor.

Riddock (Irish) smooth field.
Riddick

Rider (English) horseman.
Ridder, Ryder

Ridge (English) ridge of a cliff.
Ridgy, Rig, Rigg

Ridgeley (English) meadow near the
ridge.
*Ridgeleigh, Ridglea, Ridglee,
Ridgleigh, Ridgley*

Ridgeway (English) path along the
ridge.

Ridhwan (Indian) acceptance; good
will.

Ridley (English) meadow of reeds.
*Rhidley, Riddley, Ridlea, Ridleigh,
Ridly*

Riel (Spanish) a short form of Gabriel.

Rigby (English) ruler's valley.

Rigel (Arabic) foot. Astronomy: one
of the stars in the constellation
Orion.

Rigg (English) ridge.
Rigo

Rigoberto (German) splendid; wealthy.
Rigobert

Riichi (Japanese) truthful first son.

Rijul (Indian) innocent.

Rikard (Scandinavian) a form of
Richard.
Rikárd

Rikhil (Indian) eternity.

Riki (Estonian) a form of Rick.
Rikkey, Rikki, Riks, Riky

Rikki **G** (English) a form of Ricky.
(Estonian) a form of Riki.

Riku, Rikuto (Japanese) land; shore.

Riley **B** (Irish) valiant.
*Reilly, Rhiley, Rhylee, Rhyley, Rieley,
Rielly, Riely, Rilee, Rilley, Rily, Rilye,
Rylee, Ryley*

Rimac (Quechua) speaker, eloquent.

Rimachi (Quechua) he who makes us
speak.

Rin (Japanese) park.

Rinaldo (Italian) a form of Reynold.
Rinald, Rinaldi

Ring (English) ring.
Ringo

Ringo (Japanese) apple. (English) a
familiar form of Ring.

Rinji (Japanese) peaceful forest.

Rio (Spanish) river. Geography: Rio
de Janeiro is a city in Brazil.

Riordan (Irish) bard, royal poet.
Rearden, Reardin, Reardon

Rip (Dutch) ripe; full grown.
(English) a short form of Ripley.
Ripp

Ripley (English) meadow near the
river.
Rip, Ripleigh, Ripply

Ripudaman (Indian) one who defeats his enemies.

Riqui (Spanish) a form of Rickey.

Rishabh (Indian) superior.

Rishad (American) a form of Rashad.
Rishaad

Rishawn (American) a combination of the prefix Ri + Shawn.
Rishan, Rishaun, Rishon, Rishone

Rishi (Hindi) sage.

Risley (English) meadow with shrubs.
Rislea, Rislee, Risleigh, Risly, Wrisley

Risto (Finnish) a short form of Christopher.

Riston (English) settlement near the shrubs.
Wriston

Ritchard (English) a form of Richard.
Ritcherd, Ritchyrd, Ritshard, Ritsherd

Ritchell (Vietnamese) nasty, gross.

Ritchie (English) a form of Richie.
Ritchy

Rithisak (Cambodian) powerful.

Rithwik (Indian) saint.

Ritter (German) knight; chivalrous.
Rittner

Ritujeet (Indian) conqueror of seasons.

River 🅑 (English) river; riverbank.
Rivers, Riviera, Rivor

Riyad (Arabic) gardens.
Riad, Riyaad, Riyadh, Riyaz, Riyod

Roald (Norwegian) famous ruler.

Roan (English) a short form of Rowan.
Rhoan

Roano (Spanish) reddish brown skin.

Roar (Norwegian) praised warrior.
Roary

Roarke (Irish) famous ruler.
Roark, Rorke, Rourke, Ruark

Rob (English) a short form of Robert.
Robb, Robe

Robbie 🅑 (English) a familiar form of Robert.
Robie, Robbi

Robby (English) a familiar form of Robert.
Rhobbie, Robbey, Robhy, Roby

Robert ☆ 🅑 (English) famous brilliance. See also Bobek, Dob, Lopaka.
Bob, Bobby, Rab, Rabbie, Raby, Riobard, Riobart, Rob, Robars, Robart, Robbie, Robby, Rober, Roberd, Robers, Roberte, Roberto, Roberts, Robin, Robinson, Roibeárd, Rosertas, Rubert, Ruberto, Rudbert, Rupert

Robertino (Spanish) a form of Roberto.

Roberto 🅑 (Italian, Portuguese, Spanish) a form of Robert.

Roberts, Robertson (English) son of Robert.
Roberson, Robertson, Robeson, Robinson, Robson

Robin 🅖 (English) a short form of Robert.
Robben, Robbin, Robbins, Robbyn, Roben, Robinet, Robinn, Robins, Robyn, Roibín

Robinson (English) a form of Roberts.
Robbinson, Robens, Robenson, Robson, Robynson

Robustiano (Latin) strong as the wood of an oak tree.

Robyn **G** (English) a form of
Robin.

Roca, Ruca (Aymara) principal, chief,
prince; strong.

Rocco (Italian) rock.
*Rocca, Rocio, Rocko, Rocky, Roko,
Roque*

Rochan (Indian) red lotus; bright.

Rochelle **G** (French) large stone.
(Hebrew) a form of Rachel.

Rochester (English) rocky fortress.
Chester, Chet

Rock (English) a short form of
Rockwell.
Roch, Rocky

Rockford (English) rocky ford.

Rockland (English) rocky land.

Rockledge (English) rocky ledge.

Rockley (English) rocky field.
Rockle

Rockwell (English) rocky spring. Art:
Norman Rockwell was a well-
known twentieth-century American
illustrator.
Rock

Rocky (American) a familiar form of
Rocco, Rock.
Rockey, Rockie

Rod (English) a short form of
Penrod, Roderick, Rodney.
Rodd

Rodas (Greek, Spanish) a form of
Rhodes.

Roddy (English) a familiar form of
Roderick.
Roddie, Rody

Rode (Greek) pink.

Roden (English) red valley. Art:
Auguste Rodin was an innovative
French sculptor.
Rodin

Roderich (German) a form of
Roderick.

Roderick (German) famous ruler. See
also Broderick.
*Rhoderick, Rod, Rodderick, Roddy,
Roderic, Roderich, Roderigo, Roderik,
Roderrick, Roderyck, Rodgrick,
Rodrick, Rodricki, Rodrigo, Rodrigue,
Rodrugue, Roodney, Rory, Rurik, Ruy*

Rodger (German) a form of Roger.
Rodge, Rodgy

Rodman (German) famous man, hero.
Rodmond

Rodney **B** (English) island clearing.
*Rhodney, Rod, Rodnee, Rodnei,
Rodni, Rodnie, Rodnne, Rodny*

Rodolfo (Spanish) a form of
Rudolph.
Rodolpho, Rodulfo

Rodrick (German) a form of Roderick.
*Roddrick, Rodric, Rodrich, Rodrik,
Rodrique, Rodryck, Rodryk*

Rodrigo (Italian, Spanish) a form of
Roderick.

Rodriguez (Spanish) son of Rodrigo.
Roddrigues, Rodrigues, Rodriquez

Rodrik (German) famous ruler.

Rodriquez (Spanish) a form of
Rodriguez.
Rodrigquez, Rodriques, Rodriquiez

Roe (English) roe deer.
Row, Rowe

Rogan (Irish) redhead.
Rogein, Rogen

Rogelio **B** (Spanish) famous warrior.
Rojelio

Roger (German) famous spearman.
See also Lokela.
*Rodger, Rog, Rogelio, Rogerick,
Rogerio, Rogers, Rogiero, Rojelio,
Rüdiger, Ruggerio, Rutger*

Rogerio (Portuguese, Spanish) a form
of Roger.
Rogerios

Rohan (Hindi) sandalwood.

Rohin (Hindi) upward path.

Rohiniraman (Indian) the enchanted
lord; Krishna.

Rohit (Hindi) big and beautiful fish.

Rohitashwa (Indian) one with red
horse; fire.

Roi (French) a form of Roy.

Roja (Spanish) red.
Rojay

Roka (Japanese) white crest of the
wave.

Rolán (Spanish) a form of Rolando.

Roland (German) famous throughout
the land.
*Loránd, Orlando, Rawlins, Rolan,
Rolanda, Rolando, Rolek, Rolland,
Rolle, Rollie, Rollin, Rollo, Rowe,
Rowland, Ruland*

Rolando 🅱 (Portuguese, Spanish) a
form of Roland.
Lando, Olo, Roldan, Roldán, Rolondo

Rolf (German) a form of Ralph. A
short form of Rudolph.
Rolfe, Rolle, Rolph, Rólphe

Rolle (Swedish) a familiar form of
Roland, Rolf.

Rollie (English) a familiar form of
Roland.
Roley, Rolle, Rolli, Rolly

Rollin (English) a form of Roland.
Rolin, Rollins

Rollo (English) a familiar form of
Roland.
Rolla, Rolo

Rolon (Spanish) famous wolf.

Romain (French) a form of Roman.
Romaine, Romane, Romanne

Roman, Román (Latin) from Rome,
Italy.
*Roma, Romain, Romann, Romanos,
Romman, Romochka, Romy*

Romanos (Greek) a form of Roman.
Romano

Romario (Italian) a form of Romeo.
Romar, Romarius, Romaro, Romarrio

Romel (Latin) a short form of
Romulus.
Romele, Romell, Romello, Rommel

Romelio (Hebrew) God's very
beloved one.

Romello (Italian) of Romel.
Romelo, Rommello

Romeo (Italian) pilgrim to Rome;
Roman. Literature: the title
character of the Shakespearean play
Romeo and Juliet.
Romario, Roméo, Romero

Romero (Latin) a form of Romeo.
*Romario, Romeiro, Romer, Romere,
Romerio, Romeris, Romeryo*

Romildo (Germanic) glorious hero.

Romney (Welsh) winding river.
Romoney

Romualdo (Germanic) glorious king.

Rómulo (Greek) he who is full of
strength.

Romulus (Latin) citizen of Rome. Mythology: Romulus and his twin brother, Remus, founded Rome.
Romel, Romolo, Romono, Romulo

Romy **G** (Italian) a familiar form of Roman.
Rommie, Rommy

Ron (Hebrew) a short form of Aaron, Ronald.
Ronn

Ronald **B** (Scottish) a form of Reginald.
Ranald, Ron, Ronal, Ronaldo, Ronnald, Ronney, Ronnie, Ronnold, Ronoldo

Ronaldo (Portuguese) a form of Ronald.

Rónán (Irish) seal.
Renan, Ronan, Ronat

Rondel (French) short poem.
Rondal, Rondale, Rondall, Rondeal, Rondell, Rondey, Rondie, Rondrell, Rondy, Ronel

Ronel (American) a form of Rondel.
Ronell, Ronelle, Ronnel, Ronnell, Ronyell

Rong (Chinese) martial.

Roni (Hebrew) my song; my joy.
Rani, Roneet, Roney, Ronit, Ronli, Rony

Ronin (Japanese) samurai without a master.

Ronnie **B** (Scottish) a familiar form of Ronald.
Roni, Ronie, Ronnie, Ronny

Ronny **B** (Scottish) a form of Ronnie.
Ronney

Ronson (Scottish) son of Ronald.
Ronaldson

Ronté (American) a combination of Ron + the suffix Te.
Rontae, Rontay, Ronte, Rontez

Rooney (Irish) redhead.

Roosevelt (Dutch) rose field. History: Theodore and Franklin D. Roosevelt were the twenty-sixth and thirty-second U.S. presidents, respectively.
Roosvelt, Rosevelt

Roper (English) rope maker.

Rory **B** (German) a familiar form of Roderick. (Irish) red king.
Rorey, Rori, Rorrie, Rorry

Rosa **G** (Italian, Spanish) a form of Rose (see Girls' Names).

Rosalio (Spanish) rose.
Rosalino

Rosario **G** (Portuguese) rosary.

Roscoe (Scandinavian) deer forest.
Rosco

Rosendo (Germanic) excellent master.

Roshad (American) a form of Rashad.
Roshard

Roshean (American) a combination of the prefix Ro + Sean.
Roshain, Roshan, Roshane, Roshaun, Roshawn, Roshay, Rosheen, Roshene

Rosito (Filipino) rose.

Ross **B** (Latin) rose. (Scottish) peninsula. (French) red.
Rosse, Rossell, Rossi, Rossie, Rossy

Rosswell (English) springtime of roses.
Rosvel

Rostislav (Czech) growing glory.
Rosta, Rostya

Roswald (English) field of roses.
Ross, Roswell

Roth (German) redhead.

Rothwell (Scandinavian) red spring.

Rover (English) traveler.

Rowan 🅖 (English) tree with red berries.
Roan, Rowe, Rowen, Rowney, Rowyn

Rowell (English) roe-deer well.

Rowland (English) rough land. (German) a form of Roland.
Rowlando, Rowlands, Rowlandson

Rowley (English) rough meadow.
Rowlea, Rowlee, Rowleigh, Rowly

Rowson (English) son of the redhead.

Roxbury (English) rook's town or fortress.
Roxburghe

Roy (French) king. A short form of Royal, Royce. See also Conroy, Delroy, Fitzroy, Leroy, Loe.
Rey, Roi, Roye, Ruy

Royal (French) kingly, royal.
Roy, Royale, Royall, Royell

Royce 🅑 (English) son of Roy.
Roice, Roy, Royz

Royden (English) rye hill.
Royd, Roydan

Ru (Chinese) scholar.

Ruben 🅑 (Hebrew) a form of Reuben.
Ruban, Rube, Rubean, Rubens, Rubin, Ruby

Rubén (Hebrew) a form of Ruben.

Rubert (Czech) a form of Robert.

Ruby 🅖 (Hebrew) a familiar form of Reuben, Ruben.

Rucahue (Mapuche) place of construction, field that is used for construction.

Rucalaf (Mapuche) sanitarium, resting home; house of joy.

Ruchir (Indian) radiant.

Ruchit (Indian) bright, shining; pleasant.

Ruda (Czech) a form of Rudolph.
Rude, Rudek

Rudd (English) a short form of Rudyard.

Rudecindo (Spanish) a form of Rosendo.

Rudesindo (Teutonic) excellent gentleman.

Rudi (Spanish) a familiar form of Rudolph.
Ruedi

Rudo (Shona) love.

Rudolf (German) a form of Rudolph.
Rodolf, Rodolfo, Rudolfo

Rudolph (German) famous wolf. See also Dolf.
Raoul, Rezsó, Rodolfo, Rodolph, Rodolphe, Rolf, Ruda, Rudek, Rudi, Rudolf, Rudolpho, Rudolphus, Rudy

Rudolpho (Italian) a form of Rudolph.

Rudy 🅑 (English) a familiar form of Rudolph.
Roody, Ruddy, Ruddie, Rudey, Rudi, Rudie

Rudyard (English) red enclosure.
Rudd

Rueben (Hebrew) a form of Reuben.
Rueban, Ruebin

Rufay (Quechua) warm.

Ruff (French) redhead.

Rufin (Polish) redhead.
Rufino

Rufio (Latin) red-haired.

Ruford (English) red ford; ford with reeds.
Rufford

Rufus (Latin) redhead.
Rayfus, Rufe, Ruffis, Ruffus, Rufino, Rufo, Rufous

Rugby (English) rook fortress. History: a famous British school after which the sport of Rugby was named,

Ruggerio (Italian) a form of Roger.
Rogero, Ruggero, Ruggiero

Ruhakana (Rukiga) argumentative.

Rujul (Indian) simple; honest.

Ruland (German) a form of Roland.
Rulan, Rulon, Rulondo

Rumford (English) wide river crossing.

Rumi (Quechua) strong and as eternal as a rock.

Rumimaqui, Rumiñaui (Quechua) he who has strong hands, hands of stone.

Rumisonjo, Rumisuncu (Quechua) hard-hearted, heart of stone.

Run (Chinese) sleek.

Runacatu, Runacoto (Quechua) short man, small man.

Runako (Shona) handsome.

Rune (German, Swedish) secret.

Runrot (Tai) prosperous.

Runto, Runtu (Quechua) hailstone.

Rupak (Indian) sign, feature; acting.

Rupang (Indian) beautiful.

Rupert (German) a form of Robert.
Ruperth, Ruperto, Ruprecht

Ruperto (Italian) a form of Rupert.

Rupin (Indian) embodied beauty.

Rupinder **G** (Sanskrit) handsome.

Ruprecht (German) a form of Rupert.

Rush (French) redhead. (English) a short form of Russell.
Rushi

Rushford (English) ford with rushes.

Rusk (Spanish) twisted bread.

Ruskin (French) redhead.
Rush, Russ

Russ (French) a short form of Russell.

Russel (French) a form of Russell.

Russell (French) redhead; fox colored. See also Lukela.
Roussell, Rush, Russ, Russel, Russelle, Rusty

Rusty (French) a familiar form of Russell.
Ruste, Rusten, Rustie, Rustin, Ruston, Rustyn

Rutajit (Indian) conqueror of truth.

Rutger (Scandinavian) a form of Roger.
Ruttger

Rutherford (English) cattle ford.
Rutherfurd

Ruthvik (Indian) saint.

Rutland (Scandinavian) red land.

Rutledge (English) red ledge.

Rutley (English) red meadow.

Rutujit (Indian) conqueror of seasons.

Rutveg (Indian) can travel in all climatic conditions.

Ruy (Spanish) a short form of Roderick.
Rui

Ruyan (Spanish) little king.

Ryan ★ **B** (Irish) little king.
Rayan, Rhyan, Rhyne, Ryane, Ryann, Ryen, Ryian, Ryiann, Ryin, Ryne, Ryon, Ryuan, Ryun, Ryyan

Ryann **G** (Irish) a form of Ryan.

Rycroft (English) rye field.
Ryecroft

Ryder (English) a form of Rider.
Rydder, Rye

Rye (English) a short form of Ryder. A grain used in cereal and whiskey. (Gypsy) gentleman.
Ry

Ryen (Irish) a form of Ryan.
Ryein, Ryien

Ryerson (English) son of Rider, Ryder.

Ryese (English) a form of Reece.
Reyse, Ryez, Ryse

Ryker (American) a surname used as a first name.
Riker, Ryk

Rylan **B** (English) land where rye is grown.
Ryland, Rylean, Rylen, Rylin, Rylon, Rylyn, Rylynn

Ryland (English) a form of Rylan.
Ryeland, Rylund

Ryle (English) rye hill.
Ryal, Ryel

Rylee **G** (Irish) a form of Riley.
Ryeleigh, Ryleigh, Rylie, Rillie

Ryley **B** (Irish) a form of Riley.
Ryely

Ryman (English) rye seller.

Ryne (Irish) a form of Ryan.
Rynn

Ryohei (Japanese) splendidly peaceful helper.

Ryoichi (Japanese) first son of Ryo.

Ryoji (Japanese) refreshingly splendid governor.

Ryoma (Japanese) dragon; horse.

Ryon (Irish) a form of Ryan.

Ryosuke (Japanese) cool; mediation.

Ryota (Japanese) very splendid.

Ryozo (Japanese) third son of Ryo.

Ryu (Japanese) dragon.

Ryuhei (Japanese) prosperous and peaceful.

Ryuichi (Japanese) first son of Ryu.

Ryuji (Japanese) dragon man.

Ryunosuke (Japanese) peaceful dragon.

S

S **G** (American) an initial used as a first name.

Saabir (Indian) patient.

Saahil (Indian) seashore.

Saahir (Indian) wakeful.

Saajid (Indian) he who worships God.

Saalih (Indian) good; righteous.

Saariyah (Indian) clouds at night.

Sabastian (Greek) a form of Sebastian.
Sabastain, Sabastiano, Sabastien,
Sabastin, Sabastion, Sabaston,
Sabbastiun, Sabestian

Sabeeh (Indian) beautiful.

Sabelio (Spanish) a form of Sabino.

Saber (French) sword.
Sabir, Sabre

Sabin (Basque) ancient tribe of
central Italy.
Saban, Saben, Sabian, Sabien, Sabino

Sabino (Basque) a form of Sabin.

Sabiti (Rutooro) born on Sunday.

Sabola (Nguni) pepper.

Sabrang (Indian) rainbow.

Sabrina **G** (Latin) boundary line.
(English) child of royalty. (Hebrew)
a familiar form of Sabra (see Girls'
Names).

Saburo (Japanese) third-born son.

Sacha **BG** (Russian) a form of Sasha.
Sascha

Sachar (Russian) a form of Zachary.

Sachidanandha (Indian) total bliss.

Sachio (Japanese) fortunately born.

Saddam (Arabic) powerful ruler.

Sade **G** (Hebrew) a form of Sarah.

Sadeeq (Indian) trustworthy.

Sadgun (Indian) virtues.

Sadiki (Swahili) faithful.
Saadiq, Sadeek, Sadek, Sadik,
Sadiq, Sadique

Sadiva (Indian) eternal.

Sadler (English) saddle maker.
Saddler

Sadoc (Hebrew) just one.

Safari (Swahili) born while traveling.
Safa, Safarian

Safford (English) willow river crossing.

Safiy (Indian) best friend.

Safwan (Indian) rocks.

Sagardutt (Indian) gift of the ocean.

Sage **BG** (English) wise. Botany: an
herb.
Sagen, Sager, Saige, Saje

Sahale (Native American) falcon.
Sael, Sahal, Sahel, Sahil

Sahar (Indian) sun; dawn.

Sahastrabahu (Indian) one with a
thousand arms.

Sahastrajit (Indian) a thousand times
victorious in battle.

Sahen (Hindi) above.
Sahan

Sahil (Native American) a form of
Sahale.
Saheel, Sahel

Sahir (Hindi) friend.

Sai (Indian) flower; everywhere.

Saiasi (Fijian) a form of Isaias.

Sa'id (Arabic) happy.
Sa'ad, Saaid, Saed, Sa'eed, Saeed,
Sahid, Saide, Sa'ied, Saied, Saiyed,
Saiyeed, Sajid, Sajjid, Sayed,
Sayeed, Sayid, Seyed, Shahid

Sairos (Pohnpeian) a form of Cyress.

Sairusi (Fijian) a form of Cyress.

Sajag (Hindi) watchful.

Saka (Swahili) hunter.

Sakeri (Danish) a form of Zachary.
Sakarai, Sakari

Sakima (Native American) king.

Saksham (Indian) capable.

Sakshik (Indian) witness.

Saku (Japanese) remembrance of the Lord.

Sakuruta (Pawnee) coming sun.

Sal (Italian) a short form of Salvatore.

Salah Udeen (Indian) the righteousness of the faith.

Salaj (Indian) water that flows from melted ice.

Salam (Arabic) lamb.
Salaam

Salamon (Spanish) a form of Solomon.
Saloman, Salomón

Salaun (French) a form of Solomon.

Sálih (Arabic) right, good.
Saleeh, Saleh, Salehe

Salim (Swahili) peaceful.

Salím (Arabic) peaceful, safe.
Saleem, Salem, Saliym, Salman

Sally 🄶 (Italian) a familiar form of Salvatore.

Salmalin (Hindi) taloned.

Salman (Czech) a form of Salím, Solomon.
Salmaan, Salmaine, Salmon

Salomon (French) a form of Solomon.
Salomone

Salton (English) manor town; willow town.

Salustio (Latin) he who offers salvation.

Salvador (Spanish) savior.
Salvadore

Salvatore (Italian) savior. See also Xavier.
Sal, Salbatore, Sallie, Sally, Salvator, Salvattore, Salvidor, Sauveur

Salviano (Spanish) a form of Salvo.

Salvio (Latin) cured, healthy; upright.

Salvo (Latin) healthy one.

Sam 🄱 (Hebrew) a short form of Samuel.
Samm, Sammy, Sem, Shem, Shmuel

Samantha 🄶 (Aramaic) listener. (Hebrew) told by God.

Samarjeet (Indian) winner of the battle.

Sambaran (Indian) restraint; name of an ancient king.

Sambathkrishna (Indian) a gift from Lord Krishna.

Sambha (Indian) shining.

Sambhav (Indian) born; manifested.

Sambhddha (Indian) wise.

Sambit (Indian) consciousness.

Sambo (American) a familiar form of Samuel.
Sambou

Sambodh (Indian) complete knowledge.

Sameen (Indian) valuable.

Sameer (Arabic) a form of Samír.

Samendra (Indian) winner of a war.

Sami, Samy 🄱 (Hebrew) forms of Sammy.
Sameeh, Sameh, Samie, Samih, Sammi

Samik (Indian) peaceful.

Samín (Quechua) fortunate, lucky; adventurous; successful; happy.

Samír (Arabic) entertaining companion.
Sameer

Samiran (Indian) breeze.

Samit (Indian) always making friends.

Sammad (Indian) joy.

Samman (Arabic) grocer.
Saman, Sammon

Sammy B (Hebrew) a familiar form of Samuel.
Saamy, Samey, Sami, Sammee, Sammey, Sammie, Samy

Samo (Czech) a form of Samuel.
Samho, Samko

Sampat (Indian) well to do.

Samrat (Indian) emperor.

Samrudh (Indian) the enriched one.

Samson (Hebrew) like the sun. Bible: a judge and powerful warrior betrayed by Delilah.
Sampson, Sansao, Sansom, Sansón, Shem, Shimshon

Samual (Hebrew) a form of Samuel.
Samuael, Samuail

Samudra (Indian) sea.

Samudragupta (Indian) a famous Gupta king.

Samuel ✿ **B** (Hebrew) heard God; asked of God. Bible: a famous Old Testament prophet and judge. See also Kamuela, Zamiel, Zanvil.
Sam, Samael, Samaru, Samauel, Samaul, Sambo, Sameul, Samiel, Sammail, Sammel, Sammuel, Sammy, Samo, Samouel, Samu, Samual, Samuele, Samuelis, Samuell, Samuello, Samuil, Samuka, Samule,

Samuru, Samvel, Sanko, Saumel, Schmuel, Shem, Shmuel, Simão, Simuel, Somhairle, Zamuel

Samuele (Italian) a form of Samuel.
Samulle

Samuelle G (Hebrew) a form of Samuela (see Girls' Names).

Samuru (Japanese) a form of Samuel.

Samvar (Indian) content.

Samyak (Indian) enough.

San (Chinese) three.

Sanabhi (Indian) related.

Sanam (Indian) beloved.

Sanat (Hindi) ancient.

Sanatan (Indian) eternal.

Sanborn (English) sandy brook.
Sanborne, Sanbourn, Sanbourne, Sanburn, Sanburne, Sandborn, Sandbourne

Sanchez (Latin) a form of Sancho.
Sanchaz, Sancheze

Sanchit (Indian) collection.

Sancho (Latin) sanctified; sincere. Literature: Sancho Panza was Don Quixote's squire.
Sanchez, Sauncho

Sandananda (Indian) eternal bliss.

Sandeep B (Punjabi) enlightened.
Sandip

Sandeepen (Indian) a sage.

Sander (English) a short form of Alexander, Lysander.
Sandor, Sándor, Saunder

Sanders (English) son of Sander.
Sanderson, Saunders, Saunderson

Sandesh (Indian) message.

Sándor (Hungarian) a short form of
Alexander.
Sanyi

Sandro (Greek, Italian) a short form
of Alexander.
*Sandero, Sandor, Sandre, Saundro,
Shandro*

Sandy 🅖 (English) a familiar form
of Alexander.
Sande, Sandey, Sandi, Sandie

Sanford (English) sandy river crossing.
Sandford

Sang (Vietnamese) looking or
behaving like people of upper classes.

Sani (Hindi) the planet Saturn.
(Navajo) old.

Saniiro (Japanese) praise; admirable.

Sanil (Indian) gifted, bestowed.

Sanjay (Sanskrit) triumphant.
(American) a combination of
Sanford + Jay.
Sanjaya, Sanje, Sanjey, Sanjo

Sanjiv (Hindi) long lived.
Sanjeev

Sanjivan (Indian) immortality.

Sanjog (Indian) coincidence.

Sankalp (Indian) aim.

Sankalpa (Indian) resolve.

Sankar (Hindi) a form of Shankara,
another name for the Hindu god
Shiva.

Sankarshan (Indian) a name of
Balaram, brother of Lord Krishna.

Sanket (Indian) signal.

Sannath (Indian) accompanied by a
protector.

Sanobar (Indian) palm tree.

Sansón (Spanish) a form of Samson.
Sanson, Sansone, Sansun

Santana 🅖 (Spanish) Saint Anne.
History: Antonio López de Santa
Anna was a Mexican general and
political leader.
Santanna

Santiago (Spanish) Saint James.

Santino (Spanish) a form of
Santonio.
Santion

Santo (Italian, Spanish) holy.
Santos

Santon (English) sandy town.

Santonio (Spanish) a short form of
San Antonio or Saint Anthony.
Santino, Santon, Santoni

Santos (Spanish) saint.
Santo

Santosh (Hindi) satisfied.

Sanurag (Indian) affectionate.

Sanyam (Indian) to have control.

Sanyu 🅱🅖 (Luganda) happy.

Sapan (Indian) dream.

Sapay (Quechua) unique; main.

Saqr (Arabic) falcon.

Saquan (American) a combination of
the prefix Sa + Quan.
*Saquané, Saquin, Saquon, Saqwan,
Saqwone*

Sara 🅖 (Hebrew) a form of Sarah.

Sarad (Hindi) born in the autumn.

Sarah 🅖 (Hebrew) child of royalty.

Sarang (Indian) musical instrument.

Saras, Sashank, Sasi (Indian) the
moon.

Sarasvat (Indian) learned.

Sargam (Indian) musical notes.

Sargent (French) army officer.
Sargant, Sarge, Sarjant, Sergeant, Sergent, Serjeant

Sarin (Indian) helpful.

Sarito (Spanish) a form of Caesar.
Sarit

Saritupac (Quechua) glorious prince.

Sariyah (Arabic) clouds at night.

Sarngin (Hindi) archer; protector.

Sarojin (Hindi) like a lotus.
Sarojun

Sarthak (Indian) to have its own importance.

Sarvbhanu (Indian) name of the sun.

Sarvendra, Sarvesh (Indian) god of all.

Sasha **G** (Russian) a short form of Alexander.
Sacha, Sash, Sashenka, Sashka, Sashok, Sausha

Sashang (Indian) connected.

Sashwat (Indian) eternal.

Sasmit (Indian) ever smiling.

Sasson (Hebrew) joyful.
Sason

Satadev (Indian) God.

Satchel (French) small bag.
Satch

Sathi (Indian) partner.

Satin (Indian) real.

Satordi (French) Saturn.
Satori

Satoru (Japanese) to enlighten; complete.

Satpal (Indian) protector.

Satu (Japanese) fairy tale.

Saturio (Latin) protector of the sown fields.

Saturnín (Spanish) gift of Saturn.

Saturnino (Spanish) a form of Saturno.

Saturno (Latin) he who is living an abundant life.

Satvik (Indian) virtuous.

Satwaki (Indian) fighter.

Satya (Indian) truth.

Satya Pramod (Indian) the true person.

Satyadarshi (Indian) one who can see the truth.

Satyamurty (Indian) statue of truth.

Satyaprakash (Indian) light of truth.

Satyavan (Indian) one who speaks truth.

Satyavrat (Indian) one who has taken the vow of truth.

Saul **B** (Hebrew) asked for, borrowed. Bible: in the Old Testament, a king of Israel and the father of Jonathan; in the New Testament, Saint Paul's original name was Saul.
Saül, Shaul, Sol, Solly

Saúl (Hebrew) a form of Saul.

Saulo (Greek) he who is tender and delicate.

Saumit (Indian) easy to get.

Saumya (Indian) handsome.

Saurabh (Indian) fragrant.

Saurav (Indian) melodious.

Saurjyesh (Indian) Kartikeya, the lord of valor.

Savannah ☗ (Spanish) treeless plain.

Saverio (Italian) a form of Xavier.

Saville (French) willow town.
Savelle, Savil, Savile, Savill, Savylle, Seville, Siville

Savio (Indian) saint's name.

Savitendra (Indian) the sun.

Savon ☗ (Spanish) a treeless plain.
Savan, Savaughn, Saveion, Saveon, Savhon, Saviahn, Savian, Savino, Savion, Savo, Savone, Sayvon, Sayvone

Saw (Burmese) early.

Sawyer ☗ (English) wood worker.
Sawyere

Sax (English) a short form of Saxon.
Saxe

Saxon (English) swordsman. History: the Roman name for the Teutonic raiders who ravaged the Roman British coasts.
Sax, Saxen, Saxsin, Saxxon

Sayani (Quechua) I stay on foot.

Sayarumi (Quechua) erect and strong as stone.

Sayer (Welsh) carpenter.
Say, Saye, Sayers, Sayr, Sayre, Sayres

Sayf Udeen (Indian) sword of the faith.

Sayri (Quechua) prince; he who is always helping those who ask for it.

Sayyid (Arabic) master.
Sayed, Sayid, Sayyad, Sayyed

Scanlon (Irish) little trapper.
Scanlan, Scanlen

Schafer (German) shepherd.
Schaefer, Schaffer, Schiffer, Shaffar, Shäffer

Schmidt (German) blacksmith.
Schmid, Schmit, Schmitt, Schmydt

Schneider (German) tailor.
Schnieder, Snider, Snyder

Schön (German) handsome.
Schoen, Schönn, Shon

Schuyler (Dutch) sheltering.
Schuylar, Schyler, Scoy, Scy, Skuyler, Sky, Skylar, Skyler, Skylor

Schyler ☗ (Dutch) a form of Schuyler.
Schylar, Schylre, Schylur

Scorpio (Latin) dangerous, deadly. Astronomy: a southern constellation near Libra and Sagittarius. Astrology: the eighth sign of the zodiac.
Scorpeo

Scott ☗ (English) from Scotland. A familiar form of Prescott.
Scot, Scottie, Scotto, Scotty

Scottie (English) a familiar form of Scott.
Scotie, Scotti

Scotty (English) a familiar form of Scott.
Scottey

Scoville (French) Scott's town.

Scully (Irish) town crier.

Seabert (English) shining sea.
Seabright, Sebert, Seibert

Seabrook (English) brook near the sea.

Seamus (Irish) a form of James.
Seamas, Seumas, Shamus

Sean ⭐ **B** (Irish) a form of John.
Seaghan, Séan, Seán, Seanán, Seane, Seann, Shaan, Shaine, Shane, Shaun, Shawn, Shayne, Shon, Sión

Searlas (Irish, French) a form of Charles.
Séarlas, Searles, Searlus

Searle (English) armor.

Seasar (Latin) a form of Caesar.
Seasare, Seazar, Sesar, Sesear, Sezar

Seaton (English) town near the sea.
Seeton, Seton

Sebastian ⭐ **B** (Greek) venerable. (Latin) revered.
Bastian, Sabastian, Sabastien, Sebashtian, Sebastain, Sebastiane, Sebastiano, Sebastien, Sébastien, Sebastin, Sebastine, Sebastion, Sebbie, Sebestyén, Sebo, Sepasetiano

Sebastián (Greek) a form of Sebastian.

Sebastien, Sébastien **B** (French) forms of Sebastian.
Sebasten, Sebastyen

Sebastion (Greek) a form of Sebastian.

Sedgely (English) sword meadow.
Sedgeley, Sedgly

Sedric (Irish) a form of Cedric.
Seddrick, Sederick, Sedrick, Sedrik, Sedriq

Seeley (English) blessed.
Sealey, Seely, Selig

Sef (Egyptian) yesterday. Mythology: one of the two lions that make up the Akeru, guardian of the gates of morning and night.

Sefton (English) village of rushes.

Sefu (Swahili) sword.

Seger (English) sea spear; sea warrior.
Seager, Seeger, Segar

Segismundo (Germanic) victorious protector.

Segun (Yoruba) conqueror.

Segundino (Latin) family's second son.

Segundo (Spanish) second.

Sehej (Indian) calm.

Seibert (English) bright sea.
Seabert, Sebert

Seif (Arabic) religion's sword.

Seifert (German) a form of Siegfried.

Seiichi (Japanese) first son of Sei.

Seiji (Japanese) lawful.

Seiko (Japanese) force; truth.

Sein (Basque) innocent.

Seito (Japanese) star.

Seiya (Japanese) he who is like a star.

Sekaye (Shona) laughter.

Sekove (Fijian) a form of Jacob.

Selby (English) village by the mansion.
Selbey, Shelby

Seldon (English) willow tree valley.
Selden, Sellden

Selemías (Hebrew) God rewards.

Selena **G** (Greek) moon.

Selig (German) a form of Seeley.
Seligman, Seligmann, Zelig

Selwyn (English) friend from the palace.
Selvin, Selwin, Selwinn, Selwynn, Selwynne, Wyn

Semanda (Luganda) cow clan.

Semarias (Hebrew) God guarded him.

Semer (Ethiopian) a form of George.
Semere, Semier

Semes (Chuukese) a form of James.

Semesa, Semisi (Fijian) forms of James.

Semon (Greek) a form of Simon.
Semion

Sempala (Luganda) born in prosperous times.

Sempronio (Latin) name of a Roman family based on male descent.

Sen ❦❦ (Japanese) wood fairy.
Senh

Senajit (Indian) conqueror of an army.

Séneca (Latin) venerable elderly man.

Sener (Turkish) bringer of joy.

Senichi (Japanese) first son of Sen.

Senín (Grego) god Jupiter.

Senior (French) lord.

Sennett (French) elderly.
Sennet

Senon (Spanish) living.

Senwe (African) dry as a grain stalk.

Sepp (German) a form of Joseph.
Seppi

Septimio (Latin) seventh child.

Séptimo (Latin) family's seventh son.

Septimus (Latin) seventh.

Serafin (Hebrew) a form of Seraphim.

Serafino (Portuguese) a form of Seraphim.

Seraphim (Hebrew) fiery, burning. Bible: the highest order of angels, known for their zeal and love.
Saraf, Saraph, Serafim, Serafin, Serafino, Seraphimus, Seraphin

Serapio (Latin) consecrated to Serapes, an Egyptian divinity.

Seremaia (Fijian) a form of Jeremy.

Seremesa (Chuukese) a form of Jeremy.

Sereno (Latin) calm, tranquil.

Serge (Latin) attendant.
Seargeoh, Serg, Sergei, Sergio, Sergios, Sergius, Sergiusz, Serguel, Sirgio, Sirgios

Sergei (Russian) a form of Serge.
Sergey, Sergeyuk, Serghey, Sergi, Sergie, Sergo, Sergunya, Serhiy, Serhiyko, Serjiro, Serzh

Sergio (Italian) a form of Serge.
Serginio, Serigo, Serjio

Servando (Spanish) to serve.
Servan, Servio

Sesario (Pohnpeian) a form of Cesar.

Sese (Kosraean) a form of Jesse.

Sesko (Pohnpeian) a form of Francisco.

Setefano (Fijian) a form of Esteban.

Seth ❦ ❂ (Hebrew) appointed. Bible: the third son of Adam.
Set, Sethan, Sethe, Shet

Setimba (Luganda) river dweller. Geography: a river in Uganda.

Setu (Indian) sacred symbol.

Seumas (Scottish) a form of James.
Seaumus

Seung (Korean) successor.

Severiano (Italian) a form of Séverin.

Séverin (French) severe.
Seve, Sevé, Severan, Severian,
Severiano, Severo, Sevien, Sevrin,
Sevryn

Severino (Spanish) a form of Severo.

Severn (English) boundary.
Sevearn, Sevren, Sevrnn

Severo (French) a form of Severin.

Sevilen (Turkish) beloved.

Seward (English) sea guardian.
Sewerd, Siward

Sewati (Moquelumnan) curved bear
claws.

Sexton (English) church official;
sexton.

Sextus (Latin) sixth.
Sixtus

Seymour (French) prayer. Religion:
name honoring Saint Maur. See
also Maurice.
Seamor, Seamore, Seamour, See

Shaady (Indian) singer.

Shabar (Indian) nectar.

Shabouh (Armenian) king, noble.
History: a fourth-century Persian
king.

Shad (Punjabi) happy-go-lucky.
Shadd

Shadi (Arabic) singer.
Shadde, Shaddi, Shaddy, Shade,
Shadee, Shadeed, Shadey, Shadie,
Shady, Shydee, Shydi

Shadrach (Babylonian) god; godlike.
Bible: one of three companions who
emerged unharmed from the fiery
furnace of Babylon.
Shad, Shadrack, Shadrick,
Sheddrach, Shedrach, Shedrick

Shadwell (English) shed by a well.

Shae **G** (Irish) a form of Shay.

Shafeeq (Indian) compassionate,
tender.

Shah (Persian) king. History: a title
for rulers of Iran.

Shaheem (American) a combination
of Shah + Raheem.
Shaheim, Shahiem, Shahm

Shahid (Arabic) a form of Sa'id.
Shahed, Shaheed

Shahnaaz (Indian) pride of a king.

Shai (Hebrew) a short form of Yeshaya.
Shaie

Shail, Sheil (Indian) mountain.

Shaildhar (Indian) he who holds
mountains.

Shaiming (Chinese) life; sunshine.

Shaina **G** (Yiddish) beautiful.

Shaine (Irish) a form of Sean.
Shain

Shaka **B** (Zulu) founder, first.
History: Shaka Zulu was the
founder of the Zulu empire.

Shaka-Nyorai (Chinese) historic
Buddha.

Shakeel (Arabic) a form of Shaquille.
Shakeil, Shakel, Shakell, Shakiel,
Shakil, Shakille, Shakyle

Shakir (Arabic) thankful.
Shaakir, Shakeer, Shakeir, Shakur

Shakti (Indian) power.

Shaktidhar (Indian) powerful one.

Shakunt (Indian) blue jay.

Shakur (Arabic) a form of Shakir.
Shakuur

Shalang (Indian) emperor.

Shalik (Indian) a sage.

Shalin (Indian) good manners.

Shalina (Indian) courteous.

Shaline (Indian) praiseworthy.

Shalmali (Indian) Lord Vishnu's power.

Shalom (Hebrew) peace.
Shalum, Shlomo, Sholem, Sholom

Shalya (Hindi) throne.

Shama (Indian) the sun.

Shaman (Sanskrit) holy man, mystic, medicine man.
Shamaine, Shamaun, Shamin, Shamine, Shammon, Shamon, Shamone

Shamar (Hebrew) a form of Shamir.
Shamaar, Shamare, Shamari

Shami (Indian) fire; name of a tree.

Shamir (Hebrew) precious stone.
Shahmeer, Shahmir, Shamar, Shameer, Shamyr

Shamun (Indian) name of a prophet.

Shamus (American) slang for detective.
Shamas, Shames, Shamos, Shemus

Shan (Irish) a form of Shane.
Shann, Shanne

Shanahan (Irish) wise, clever.

Shandy (English) rambunctious.
Shandey, Shandie

Shane ❚ (Irish) a form of Sean.
Shan, Shayn, Shayne

Shang (Chinese) to forge ahead.

Shangobunni (Yoruba) gift from Shango.

Shang-Ti (Chinese) the supreme God.

Shankhdhar (Indian) one who carries a conch shell.

Shankhi (Indian) the ocean; Lord Vishnu.

Shanley ☙ (Irish) small; ancient.
Shaneley, Shannley

Shannon ☙ (Irish) small and wise.
Shanan, Shannan, Shannen, Shannin, Shannone, Shanon

Shantae ☙ (French) a form of Chante.
Shant, Shanta, Shantai, Shante, Shantell, Shantelle, Shanti, Shantia, Shantie, Shanton, Shanty

Shante ☙ (French) a form of Shantae.

Shantell ☙ (American) song.

Shao (Chinese) glorious youth.

Shap (English) a form of Shep.

Shaquan (American) a combination of the prefix Sha + Quan.
Shaqaun, Shaqand, Shaquane, Shaquann, Shaquaunn, Shaquawn, Shaquen, Shaquian, Shaquin, Shaqwan

Shaquell (American) a form of Shaquille.
Shaqueal, Shaqueil, Shaquel, Shaquelle, Shaquiel, Shaquiell, Shaquielle

Shaquille 🅱 (Arabic) handsome.
Shakeel, Shaquell, Shaquil, Shaquile, Shaquill, Shaqul

Shaquon (American) a combination of the prefix Sha + Quon.
Shaikwon, Shaqon, Shaquoin, Shaquoné

Sharad (Pakistani) autumn.
Sharod

Sharif (Arabic) honest; noble.
Shareef, Sharef, Shareff, Shareif, Sharief, Sharife, Shariff, Shariyf, Sharrif, Sharyif

Sharod (Pakistani) a form of Sharad.
Sharrod

Sharon **G** (Hebrew) a form of Sharron.

Sharron (Hebrew) flat area, plain.
Sharon, Sharone, Sharonn, Sharonne

Sharvarish, Shashank, Shashee, Shashi, Shashin (Indian) moon.

Shashibhushan (Indian) one who wears the moon as an ornament.

Shashidhar (Indian) one who carries the moon.

Shashikant (Indian) moon stone.

Shashikar (Indian) moon ray.

Shashipushpa (Indian) lotus.

Shashishekhar (Indian) the one with the moon at the top of his head.

Shashvat (Indian) eternal, constant.

Shashwat (Indian) permanent; one who never dies; always present.

Shatrughna (Indian) destroyer of enemies; Lord Rama's brother.

Shatrunjay (Indian) he who defeats enemies.

Shattuck (English) little shad fish.

Shaun **B** (Irish) a form of Sean.
Shaughan, Shaughn, Shaugn, Shauna, Shaunahan, Shaune, Shaunn, Shaunne

Shavar (Hebrew) comet.
Shavit

Shavon **G** (American) a combination of the prefix Sha + Yvon.
Shauvan, Shauvon, Shavan, Shavaughn, Shaven, Shavin, Shavone, Shawan, Shawon, Shawun

Shaw (English) grove.

Shawn **B** (Irish) a form of Sean.
Shawen, Shawne, Shawnee, Shawnn, Shawon

Shawnta **G** (American) a combination of Shawn + the suffix Ta.
Shawntae, Shawntel, Shawnti

Shay **BG** (Irish) a form of Shea.
Shae, Shai, Shaya, Shaye, Shey

Shayan (Cheyenne) a form of Cheyenne.
Shayaan, Shayann, Shayon

Shayne **B** (Hebrew) a form of Sean.
Shayn, Shaynne, Shean

Shazad (Indian) prince.

Shea **G** (Irish) courteous.
Shay

Shedrick (Babylonian) a form of Shadrach.
Shadriq, Shederick, Shedric, Shedrique

Sheece (Indian) prophet's name.

Sheehan (Irish) little; peaceful.
Shean

Sheffield (English) crooked field.
Field, Shef, Sheff, Sheffie, Sheffy

Shel (English) a short form of Shelby, Sheldon, Shelton.

Shelby **G** (English) ledge estate.
Shel, Shelbe, Shelbey, Shelbie, Shell, Shellby, Shelley, Shelly

Sheldon **B** (English) farm on the ledge.
Shel, Sheldan, Shelden, Sheldin, Sheldyn, Shell, Shelley, Shelly, Shelton

Shelley **G** (English) a familiar form of Shelby, Sheldon, Shelton.
Literature: Percy Bysshe Shelley was a nineteenth-century British poet.
Shell, Shelly

Shelly G (English) a form of Shelby, Sheldon, Shelley.

Shelton B (English) town on a ledge.
Shel, Shelley, Shelten

Shem (Hebrew) name; reputation. (English) a short form of Samuel. Bible: Noah's oldest son.

Shen (Egyptian) sacred amulet. (Chinese) meditation.

Sheng (Chinese) winning.

Shen-Nung (Chinese) god of medicine, pharmacy, agriculture.

Shep (English) a short form of Shepherd.
Shap, Ship, Shipp

Shepherd (English) shepherd.
Shep, Shepard, Shephard, Shepp, Sheppard, Shepperd

Shepley (English) sheep meadow.
Sheplea, Sheplee, Shepply, Shipley

Sherborn (English) clear brook.
Sherborne, Sherbourn, Sherburn, Sherburne

Sheridan G (Irish) wild.
Dan, Sheredan, Sheriden, Sheridon, Sherridan

Sherill (English) shire on a hill.
Sheril, Sherril, Sherrill

Sherlock (English) light haired. Literature: Sherlock Holmes is a famous British detective character, created by Sir Arthur Conan Doyle.
Sherlocke, Shurlock, Shurlocke

Sherman (English) sheep shearer; resident of a shire.
Scherman, Schermann, Sherm, Shermain, Shermaine, Shermann, Shermie, Shermon, Shermy

Sherrod (English) clearer of the land.
Sherod, Sherrad, Sherrard, Sherrodd

Sherry G (French) beloved, dearest. A familiar form of Sheryl (see Girls' Names).

Sherwin (English) swift runner, one who cuts the wind.
Sherveen, Shervin, Sherwan, Sherwind, Sherwinn, Sherwyn, Sherwynd, Sherwynne, Win

Sherwood (English) bright forest.
Sherwoode, Shurwood, Woody

Sheshdhar (Indian) one who holds Shesha.

Shigekazu (Japanese) first son of Shige.

Shigeo (Japanese) luxuriant husband.

Shigeru (Japanese) luxuriant.

Shigeto (Japanese) luxuriant person.

Shihab (Arabic) blaze.

Shikhar (Indian) mountain; top of the mountain.

Shilang (Indian) virtuous.

Shilín (Chinese) intellectual.
Shilan

Shiloh (Hebrew) God's gift.
Shi, Shile, Shiley, Shilo, Shiloe, Shy, Shyle, Shylo, Shyloh

Shimon (Hebrew) a form of Simon.
Shymon

Shimshon (Hebrew) a form of Samson.
Shimson

Shin (Japanese) faithful.

Shinakio (Japanese) faithful boy.

Shing (Chinese) victory.
Shingae, Shingo

Shinichi (Japanese) first son of Shin.

Shinjiro (Japanese) faithful second son.

Shino (Japanese) stem of bamboo.

Shinshiro (Japanese) faithful fourth-born son.

Shipton (English) sheep village; ship village.

Shiquan (American) a combination of the prefix Shi + Quan.
Shiquane, Shiquann, Shiquawn, Shiquoin, Shiqwan

Shirish (Indian) name of a tree.

Shiro (Japanese) fourth-born son.

Shishul (Indian) baby.

Shiva (Hindi) life and death. Religion: the most common name for the Hindu god of destruction and reproduction.
Shiv, Shivan, Siva

Shivam (Indian) auspicious.

Shivanand (Indian) one who is happy in Lord Shiva's thoughts.

Shivang (Indian) part of Lord Shiva.

Shivank (Indian) mark of the Lord.

Shivendu (Indian) moon.

Shiveshvar (Indian) god of welfare.

Shivkumar (Indian) son of Lord Shiva.

Shivshekhar (Indian) one at the top of Shiva; moon.

Shlesh (Indian) physical bonding.

Shlomo (Hebrew) a form of Solomon.
Shelmu, Shelomo, Shelomoh, Shlomi, Shlomot

Shmuel (Hebrew) a form of Samuel.
Shem, Shemuel, Shmelke, Shmiel, Shmulka

Shneur (Yiddish) senior.
Shneiur

Sho (Japanese) commander; prosper; happiness.

Shoda (Japanese) a flat and level field.

Shogo (Japanese) a perceptive and prosperous person.

Shoichi (Japanese) first son of Sho.

Shoji (Japanese) he who governs properly.

Shon (German) a form of Schön. (American) a form of Sean.
Shoan, Shoen, Shondae, Shondale, Shondel, Shone, Shonn, Shonntay, Shontae, Shontarious, Shouan, Shoun

Shota (Japanese) great commander.

Shou (Chinese) leader.

Shou-Hsing (Chinese) god of longevity and old people.

Shravan (Indian) a Hindu month; the devoted son.

Shree (Indian) God.

Shreedhar (Indian) husband of Lakshmi.

Shreekant (Indian) husband of Shree; beautiful.

Shreekumar (Indian) beautiful.

Shreenivas (Indian) abode of Lakshmi.

Shrestajna (Indian) top knowledge.

Shresth, Shresthi (Indian) the best of all.

Shreyas (Indian) the best.

Shrikanth (Indian) Shiva.

Shrikrishna (Indian) Krishna.

Shrikumar (Indian) beautiful.

Shrinivas (Indian) abode of Lakshmi.

Shuang (Chinese) bright, clear; openhearted.

Shubh (Indian) fortunate.

Shubhankar (Indian) virtuous.

Shubhashis (Indian) blessings.

Shubhay (Indian) blessing.

Shubhojit (Indian) handsome.

Shubhranshu (Indian) moon; camphor.

Shu-Fang (Chinese) kind; gentle; sweet.

Shui (Chinese) water.

Shuichi (Japanese) first son of Shu.

Shui-Khan (Chinese) god who defends men against all evil and forgives.

Shulabh (Indian) easy.

Shun (Chinese) unhindered.

Shunichi (Japanese) first son of Shun.

Shunnar (Arabic) pheasant.

Shunsuke (Japanese) excellent mediator.

Shunya (Japanese) spring.

Shuo (Chinese) great achievements.

Shushil (Indian) pleasant.

Shusuke (Japanese) he who strives to help.

Shvant (Indian) placid.

Shvetang (Indian) fair complexion.

Shvetank (Indian) has a white mark.

Shvetanshu, Shwetanshu, Shwetbhanu (Indian) moon.

Shwetambar (Indian) one who wears white clothes.

Shyam (Indian) dark.

Shyamsundar (Indian) dark and handsome.

Shyla ☰ (English) a form of Sheila (see Girls' Names).

Si (Hebrew) a short form of Silas, Simon.
Sy

Siañu (Quechua) brown like the color of coffee.

Sid (French) a short form of Sidney.
Cyd, Siddie, Siddy, Sidey, Syd

Siddel (English) wide valley.
Siddell

Siddhanth (Indian) principle.

Siddhartha (Hindi) History: Siddhartha Gautama was the original name of Buddha, the founder of Buddhism.
Sida, Siddartha, Siddhaarth, Siddhart, Siddharth, Sidh, Sidharth, Sidhartha, Sidhdharth

Sidney ☰ (French) from Saint-Denis, France.
Cydney, Sid, Sidnee, Sidny, Sidon, Sidonio, Sydney, Sydny

Sidonio (Spanish) a form of Sidney.

Sidwell (English) wide stream.

Siegfried (German) victorious peace. See also Zigfrid, Ziggy.
Seifert, Seifried, Siegfred, Siffre, Sig, Sigfrid, Sigfried, Sigfroi, Sigfryd, Siggy, Sigifredo, Sigvard, Singefrid, Sygfried, Szygfrid

Sierra **G** (Irish) black. (Spanish)
saw-toothed.
Siera

Sig (German) a short form of
Siegfried, Sigmund.

Siggy (German) a familiar form of
Siegfried, Sigmund.

Sigifredo (German) a form of
Siegfried.
Sigefriedo, Sigfrido, Siguefredo

Sigmund (German) victorious
protector. See also Ziggy,
Zsigmond, Zygmunt.
*Siegmund, Sig, Siggy, Sigismond,
Sigismondo, Sigismund, Sigismundo,
Sigismundus, Sigmond, Sigsmond,
Szygmond*

Sigurd (German, Scandinavian)
victorious guardian.
Sigord, Sjure, Syver

Sigwald (German) victorious leader.

Sikander (Persian) a form of
Alejandro.

Silas **B** (Latin) a short form of
Silvan.
Si, Sias, Sylas

Silence (Japanese) thoughtful.

Silvan (Latin) forest dweller.
*Silas, Silvain, Silvano, Silvaon, Silvie,
Silvio, Sylvain, Sylvan, Sylvanus, Sylvio*

Silvano (Italian) a form of Silvan.
Silvanos, Silvanus, Silvino

Silverio (Spanish, Greek) god of trees.

Silvester (Latin) a form of Sylvester.
Silvestr, Silvestre, Silvestro, Silvy

Silvestro (Italian) a form of Sylvester.

Silvio (Italian) a form of Silvan.

Simão (Portuguese) a form of Samuel.

Simba (Swahili) lion. (Yao) a short
form of Lisimba.
Sim

Simcha **B** (Hebrew) joyful.
Simmy

Simeon (French) a form of Simon.
Simione, Simone

Simeón (Spanish) a form of Simón.

Simms (Hebrew) son of Simon.
Simm, Sims

Simmy (Hebrew) a familiar form of
Simcha, Simon.
Simmey, Simmi, Simmie, Symmy

Simon **B** (Hebrew) he heard. Bible:
one of the Twelve Disciples. See
also Symington, Ximenes.
*Saimon, Samien, Semon, Shimon, Si,
Sim, Simao, Simen, Simeon, Simion,
Simm, Simmon, Simmonds, Simmons,
Simms, Simmy, Simonas, Simone,
Simson, Simyon, Símón, Symon,
Szymon*

Simón (Hebrew) a form of Simon.

Simone **G** (French) a form of
Simeon.

Simplicio (Latin) simple.

Simpson (Hebrew) son of Simon.
Simonson, Simson

Simran **G** (Sikh) absorbed in God.

Sinche, Sinchi (Quechua) boss, leader;
strong, valorous, hard working.

Sinchipuma (Quechua) strong leader
and as valuable as a puma.

Sinchiroca (Quechua) strongest
prince amongst the strong ones.

Sinclair (French) prayer. Religion:
name honoring Saint Clair.
Sinclare, Synclair

Sinesio (Greek) intelligent one, the shrewd one.

Sinforiano (Spanish) a form of Sinforoso.

Sinforoso (Greek) he who is full of misfortune.

Singh (Hindi) lion.
Sing

Sinh (Vietnamese) birth; life.

Sinha (Hindi) hero.

Sinjon (English) saint, holy man. Religion: name honoring Saint John.
Sinjin, Sinjun, Sjohn, Syngen, Synjen, Synjon

Siobhan 🄶 (Irish) a form of Joan (see Girls' Names).

Sipatu (Moquelumnan) pulled out.

Sipho (Zulu) present.

Siraaj (Indian) lamp, light.

Siraj (Arabic) lamp, light.

Sirio (Latin) native of Syria; brilliant like the Syrian sun.

Siro (Latin) native of Syria.

Siseal (Irish) a form of Cecil.

Sisebuto (Teutonic) he who fulfills his leadership role whole-heartedly.

Sisi (Fante) born on Sunday.

Sitanshu (Indian) moon.

Siuca (Quechua) youngest son.

Siva (Hindi) a form of Shiva.
Siv

Sivan (Hebrew) ninth month of the Jewish year.

Siwatu (Swahili) born during a time of conflict.
Siwazuri

Siwili (Native American) long fox's tail.

Sixto (Greek) courteous one; he who has been treated well.

Skah (Lakota) white.
Skai

Skee (Scandinavian) projectile.
Ski, Skie

Skeeter (English) swift.
Skeat, Skeet, Skeets

Skelly (Irish) storyteller.
Shell, Skelley, Skellie

Skelton (Dutch) shell town.

Skerry (Scandinavian) stony island.

Skip (Scandinavian) a short form of Skipper.

Skipper (Scandinavian) shipmaster.
Skip, Skipp, Skippie, Skipton

Skiriki (Pawnee) coyote.

Skule (Norwegian) hidden.

Skye 🄶 (Dutch) a short form of Skylar, Skyler, Skylor.
Sky

Skylar 🄱🄶 (Dutch) a form of Schuyler.
Skilar, Skkylar, Skye, Skyelar, Skylaar, Skylare, Skylarr, Skylayr

Skyler 🄱 (Dutch) a form of Schuyler.
Skieler, Skiler, Skye, Skyeler, Skylee, Skyller

Skylor (Dutch) a form of Schuyler.
Skye, Skyelor, Skyloer, Skylore, Skylour, Skylur, Skylyr

Slade (English) child of the valley.
Slaide, Slayde

Slane (Czech) salty.
Slan

Slater (English) roof slater.
Slader, Slate, Slayter

Slava (Russian) a short form of
Stanislav, Vladislav, Vyacheslav.
Slavik, Slavoshka

Slawek (Polish) a short form of
Radoslaw.

Slevin (Irish) mountaineer.
Slaven, Slavin, Slawin

Sloan (Irish) warrior.
Sloane, Slone

Smaran (Indian) meditation.

Smedley (English) flat meadow.
Smedleigh, Smedly

Smith (English) blacksmith.
*Schmidt, Smid, Smidt, Smitt, Smitty,
Smyth, Smythe*

Snehakant (Indian) the lord of love.

Snehal (Indian) friendly.

Snowden (English) snowy hill.
Snowdon

So (Vietnamese) smart.

Soas, Sos (Chuukese) forms of
George.

Socorro (Spanish) helper.

Socrates (Greek) wise, learned.
History: a famous ancient Greek
philosopher.
Socratis, Sokrates, Sokratis

Sócrates (Greek) a form of Socrates.

Socso (Quechua) blackbird.

Sofanor (Greek) wise man.

Sofia **G** (Greek) a form of Sophia.

Sofian (Arabic) devoted.

Sofoclés, Sófocles (Greek) famous
for his wisdom.

Soham (Indian) I am.

Sohan (Hindi) handsome.

Sohil (Indian) beautiful.

Sohrab (Persian) ancient hero.

Sohse (Pohnpeian) a form of George.

Soja (Yoruba) soldier.

Soji (Japanese) he who loves to rule.

Sol (Hebrew) a short form of Saul,
Solomon.
Soll, Sollie, Solly

Solano (Latin) like the eastern wind.

Solly (Hebrew) a familiar form of
Saul, Solomon.
Sollie, Zollie, Zolly

Solomon **B** (Hebrew) peaceful.
Bible: a king of Israel famous for his
wisdom. See also Zalman.
*Salamen, Salamon, Salamun, Salaun,
Salman, Salomo, Salomon, Selim,
Shelomah, Shlomo, Sol, Solamh,
Solaman, Solly, Solmon, Soloman,
Solomonas, Sulaiman*

Solon (Greek) wise. History: a noted
ancient Athenian lawmaker.

Solón (Greek) a form of Solon.

Somac (Quechua) beautiful.

Somali (Indian) moon's love.

Somanshu (Indian) moonbeam.

Somerset (English) place of the
summer settlers. Literature: William
Somerset Maugham was a well-
known British writer.
Sommerset, Sumerset, Summerset

Somerville (English) summer village.
Somerton, Summerton, Summerville

Somesh (Indian) moon.

Somkar, Somprakash (Indian) moonlight.

Son (Vietnamese) mountain. (Native American) star. (English) son, boy. A short form of Madison, Orson. Sonny

Sonco, Sonjoc, Suncu (Quechua) heart; he who has a good and noble heart.

Soncoyoc, Sonjoyoc (Quechua) he who has a good heart.

Songan (Native American) strong. Song

Sonis (Pohnpeian) a form of Jona.

Sonny B (English) a familiar form of Grayson, Madison, Orson, Son. Soni, Sonnie, Sony

Sono (Akan) elephant.

Sonya G (Greek) wise. (Russian, Slavic) a form of Sophia.

Sophia G (Greek) wise.

Sophie G (Greek) a familiar form of Sophia.

Sora (Japanese) sky.

Sören (Danish) thunder; war. Sorren

Soroush (Persian) happy.

Sorrel G (French) reddish brown. Sorel, Sorell, Sorrell

Sosay (Pohnpeian) a form of Jose.

Sosef, Soses (Chuukese) forms of Jose.

Sota (Japanese) very gallant.

Soterios (Greek) savior. Soteris, Sotero

Soumil (Hindi) friend.

Southwell (English) south well.

Sovann (Cambodian) gold.

Sowande (Yoruba) wise healer sought me out.

Spalding (English) divided field. Spaulding

Spangler (German) tinsmith. Spengler

Spark (English) happy. Sparke, Sparkie, Sparky

Spear (English) spear carrier. Speare, Spears, Speer, Speers, Spiers

Speedy (English) quick; successful. Speed

Spence (English) a short form of Spencer. Spense

Spencer B (English) dispenser of provisions. Spence, Spencre, Spenser

Spenser (English) a form of Spencer. Literature: Edmund Spenser was the British poet who wrote *The Faerie Queene*. Spanser, Spense

Spike (English) ear of grain; long nail. Spyke

Spiro (Greek) round basket; breath. Spiridion, Spiridon, Spiros, Spyridon, Spyros

Spoor (English) spur maker. Spoors

Sproule (English) energetic. Sprowle

Spurgeon (English) shrub.

Spyros (Greek) a form of Spiro.

Squire (English) knight's assistant; large landholder.

Sravan (Indian) the devoted son.

Sridatta (Hindi) given by God.

Srikant (Indian) lover of wealth.

Stacey, Stacy **G** (English) familiar forms of Eustace.
Stace, Stacee

Stafford (English) riverbank landing.
Staffard, Stafforde, Staford

Stamford (English) a form of Stanford.

Stamos (Greek) a form of Stephen.
Stamatis, Stamatos

Stan (Latin, English) a short form of Stanley.

Stanbury (English) stone fortification.
Stanberry, Stanbery, Stanburghe, Stansbury

Stancio (Spanish) a form of Constantine.
Stancy

Stancliff (English) stony cliff.
Stanclife, Stancliffe

Standish (English) stony parkland. History: Miles Standish was a leader in colonial America.

Stane (Slavic) a short form of Stanislaus.

Stanfield (English) stony field.
Stansfield

Stanford (English) rocky ford.
Sandy, Stamford, Stan, Standford, Stanfield

Stanislaus (Latin) stand of glory. See also Lao, Tano.
Slavik, Stana, Standa, Stane, Stanislao, Stanislas, Stanislau, Stanislav, Stanislus, Stannes, Stano, Stasik, Stasio

Stanislav (Slavic) a form of Stanislaus. See also Slava.
Stanislaw

Stanley **B** (English) stony meadow.
Stan, Stanely, Stanlea, Stanlee, Stanleigh, Stanly

Stanmore (English) stony lake.

Stannard (English) hard as stone.

Stanton (English) stony farm.
Stan, Stanten, Staunton

Stanway (English) stony road.

Stanwick (English) stony village.
Stanwicke, Stanwyck

Stanwood (English) stony woods.

Starbuck (English) challenger of fate. Literature: a character in Herman Melville's novel *Moby-Dick*.

Stark (German) strong, vigorous.
Starke, Stärke, Starkie

Starling **BG** (English) bird.
Sterling

Starr **G** (English) star.
Star, Staret, Starlight, Starlon, Starwin

Stasik (Russian) a familiar form of Stanislaus.
Stas, Stash, Stashka, Stashko, Stasiek

Stasio (Polish) a form of Stanislaus.
Stas, Stasiek, Stasiu, Staska, Stasko

Stavros (Greek) a form of Stephen.

Steadman (English) owner of a farmstead.
Steadmann, Stedman, Stedmen, Steed

Steel (English) like steel.
Steele

Steen (German, Danish) stone.
Steenn, Stein

Steeve (Greek) a short form of
Steeven.

Steeven (Greek) a form of Steven.
*Steaven, Steavin, Steavon, Steevan,
Steeve, Steevn*

Stefan (German, Polish, Swedish) a
form of Stephen.
*Steafan, Steafeán, Stefaan, Stefane,
Stefanson, Stefaun, Stefawn, Steffan*

Stefano (Italian) a form of Stephen.
Stefanos, Steffano

Stefanos (Greek) a form of Stephen.
Stefans, Stefos, Stephano, Stephanos

Stefen (Norwegian) a form of
Stephen.
Steffen, Steffin, Stefin

Steffan (Swedish) a form of Stefan.
Staffan

Stefon (Polish) a form of Stephon.
*Staffon, Steffon, Steffone, Stefone,
Stefonne*

Stein (German) a form of Steen.
Steine, Steiner

Steinar (Norwegian) rock warrior.

Stella 🄶 (Latin) star. (French) a
familiar form of Estelle (see Girls'
Names).

Stepan (Russian) a form of Stephen.
*Stepa, Stepane, Stepanya, Stepka,
Stipan*

Steph (English) a short form of
Stephen.

Stephan (Greek) a form of Stephen.
*Stepfan, Stephanas, Stephano,
Stephanos, Stephanus, Stephaun*

Stephane 🄱 (Greek) a form of
Stephanie.

Stéphane (French) a form of
Stephen.
Stefane, Stepháne, Stephanne

Stephanie 🄶 (Greek) crowned.

Stephany 🄶 (Greek) a form of
Stephanie.

Stephen 🄱 (Greek) crowned. See
also Estéban, Estebe, Estevan,
Estevao, Étienne, István, Szczepan,
Tapani, Teb, Teppo, Tiennot.
*Stamos, Stavros, Stefan, Stefano,
Stefanos, Stefen, Stenya, Stepan,
Stepanos, Steph, Stephan, Stephanas,
Stéphane, Stephens, Stephenson,
Stephfan, Stephin, Stephon, Stepven,
Steve, Steven, Stevie*

Stephon (Greek) a form of Stephen.
*Stefon, Stepfon, Stepfone, Stephfon,
Stephion, Stephone, Stephonne*

Sterling 🄱 (English) valuable; silver
penny. A form of Starling.
Sterlen, Sterlin, Stirling

Stern (German) star.

Sterne (English) austere.
Stearn, Stearne, Stearns

Stetson 🄱 (Danish) stepson.
Steston, Steton, Stetsen, Stetzon

Stevan (Greek) a form of Steven.
*Stevano, Stevanoe, Stevaughn,
Stevean*

Steve (Greek) a short form of
Stephen, Steven.
Steave, Stevie, Stevy

Steven 🄱 (Greek) a form of Stephen.
*Steeven, Steiven, Stevan, Steve,
Stevens, Stevie, Stevin, Stevon, Stiven*

Stevens (English) son of Steven.
Stevenson, Stevinson

Stevie 🄶 (English) a familiar form
of Stephen, Steven.
Stevey, Stevy

Stevin, Stevon (Greek) forms of
Steven.
Stevieon, Stevion, Stevyn

Stewart **B** (English) a form of Stuart.
Steward, Stu

Sthir (Hindi) focused.

Stian (Norwegian) quick on his feet.

Stig (Swedish) mount.

Stiggur (Gypsy) gate.

Stillman (English) quiet.
Stillmann, Stillmon

Stimit (Indian) astonishing.

Sting (English) spike of grain.

Stockman (English) tree-stump remover.

Stockton (English) tree-stump town.

Stockwell (English) tree-stump well.

Stoddard (English) horse keeper.

Stoffel (German) a short form of Christopher.

Stoker (English) furnace tender.
Stoke, Stokes, Stroker

Stone (English) stone.
Stoen, Stoner, Stoney, Stonie, Stonie, Stoniy, Stony

Storm **B** (English) tempest, storm.
Storme, Stormey, Stormi, Stormmie, Stormy

Stormy **G** (English) a form of Storm.

Storr (Norwegian) great.
Story

Stover (English) stove tender.

Stowe (English) hidden; packed away.

Strahan (Irish) minstrel.
Strachan

Stratford (English) bridge over the river. Literature: Stratford-upon-Avon was Shakespeare's birthplace.
Stradford

Stratton (Scottish) river valley town.
Straten, Straton

Strephon (Greek) one who turns.

Strom (Greek) bed, mattress. (German) stream.

Strong (English) powerful.

Stroud (English) thicket.

Struthers (Irish) brook.

Stu (English) a short form of Stewart, Stuart.
Stew

Stuart **B** (English) caretaker, steward. History: a Scottish and English royal family.
Stewart, Stu, Stuarrt

Studs (English) rounded nail heads; shirt ornaments; male horses used for breeding. History: Louis "Studs" Terkel is a famous American journalist.
Stud, Studd

Styles (English) stairs put over a wall to help cross it.
Stiles, Style, Stylz

Su (Chinese) respectful.

Subali (Indian) strong.

Subaru (Japanese) rise.

Subeer (Indian) courageous.

Subhadr (Indian) gentleman.

Subhas (Indian) shining.

Subhash (Hindi) he who speaks good words.

Subhi (Arabic) early morning.

Subhy (Indian) early morning.

Subodh (Hindi) good lesson.

Suchet (Indian) attentive, alert.

Suchir (Indian) eternity.

Suck Chin (Korean) unshakable rock.

Sucsu (Quechua) blackbird.

Sudarsh (Indian) good-looking.

Sudarshan (Indian) good-looking.

Suday (Hindi) gift.

Sudeep (Indian) illuminated.

Sudeepta (Indian) bright.

Sudesh (Indian) strong; wise; skilled.

Sudesha (Indian) son of Lord Krishna.

Sudhakar (Indian) mine of nectar; moon.

Sudhang, Sudhanshu, Sudhanssu (Indian) moon.

Sudhir, Sumay, Sumed, Sunay (Hindi) wise.

Sudhit (Hindi) kind.

Sudi (Swahili) lucky.
Su'ud

Sudip, Sudir (Indian) bright.

Sued (Arabic) master, chief.
Suede

Suelita (Spanish) little lily.

Suffield (English) southern field.

Sugden (English) valley of sows.

Sughosh (Indian) one with a melodious voice.

Sugriva (Indian) one with a graceful neck; king of monkeys.

Suguru (Japanese) superiority; gentleness.

Suhail (Arabic) gentle.
Sohail, Sohayl, Souhail, Suhael, Sujal

Suhas (Indian) laughter.

Suhay (Quechua) he who is like yellow corn, fine and abundant; rock.

Suhayb (Indian) reddish hair or complexion.

Suhuba (Swahili) friend.

Sui (Chinese) peaceful.

Sujan (Indian) a good person.

Sujat (Indian) belonging to a good clan.

Sujit (Indian) great conqueror.

Suka (Indian) wind.

Sukanth (Indian) one with a sweet voice; one with a graceful neck.

Sukarma (Indian) one who does good deeds.

Sukhdeep 🄶 (Sikh) light of peace and bliss.

Sukhen (Indian) happy boy.

Sukhwant (Indian) full of happiness; pleasant.

Sukrant (Indian) extremely beautiful.

Sukru (Turkish) grateful.

Sukumar (Indian) very sensitive.

Sulabh (Indian) easy to get.

Sulaiman (Arabic) a form of Solomon.
Sulaman, Sulay, Sulaymaan, Sulayman, Suleiman, Suleman, Suleyman, Sulieman, Sulman, Sulomon, Sulyman

Sulalit (Indian) graceful.

Sulek (Hindi) sun.

Sullivan (Irish) black eyed.
Sullavan, Sullevan, Sully

Sully (Irish) a familiar form of
Sullivan. (French) stain, tarnish.
(English) south.
Sulleigh, Sulley

Sulochna (Indian) beautiful eyes.

Sultan (Swahili) ruler.
Sultaan

Sum (Tai) appropriate.

Sumainca (Quechua) beautiful Inca.

Sumant (Hindi) friendly.

Sumanyu (Indian) heaven.

Sumitr (Indian) good friend.

Sumitranandan (Indian) son of
Sumitra.

Summer **G** (English) a form of
Sumner.

Summit (English) peak, top.
Sumeet, Sumit, Summet, Summitt

Sumner (English) church officer;
summoner.
Summer

Sunam (Indian) good name; fame.

Sunandan (Indian) happy.

Sunar (Hindi) happy.

Suncuyuc (Quechua) he who has a
good heart.

Sundar (Indian) beautiful; pleasant to
the eyes and ears.

Sundaravathana (Indian) smart;
handsome.

Sundeep (Punjabi) light;
enlightened.
Sundip

Sunder (Indian) handsome.

Suneet (Indian) righteous.

Sunny **BG** (English) sunny, sunshine.
Sun, Sunni

Sunreep (Hindi) pure.
Sunrip

Suoud (Indian) good luck.

Suraj (Hindi) sun.

Suram (Indian) beautiful.

Suran (Indian) pleasant sound.

Suri (Quechua) fast like an ostrich.

Surjeet (Indian) conqueror of the
suras.

Surush (Hindi) shining.

Suryabhan (Indian) sun.

Suryadev (Indian) sun god.

Suryakant (Indian) loved by the sun;
a shining crystal.

Suryanshu (Hindi) sunbeam.

Suryaprakash (Indian) sunlight.

Suryesh (Indian) the sun is God.

Susan **G** (Hebrew) lily.

Susana **G** (Hebrew) a form of
Susan.

Sushant (Hindi) quiet.

Susher (Indian) kind.

Sushil (Indian) a man of good
character.

Sushim (Hindi) moonstone.

Sutcliff (English) southern cliff.
Sutcliffe

Sutherland (Scandinavian) southern land.
Southerland, Sutherlan

Sutosh (Indian) one who becomes happy easily.

Sutoya (Indian) a river.

Sutton (English) southern town.

Suvel (Indian) placid.

Suvidh (Indian) kind.

Suvit (Indian) good; wealth.

Suvrata (Indian) strict in religious vows.

Suyai, Suyay (Quechua) hope.

Suyash (Indian) good result, victory.

Suycauaman (Quechua) youngest son of the falcons.

Suzanne 🄶 (English) a form of Susan.

Suzu (Japanese) crane.

Svang (Indian) good looks.

Svanik (Indian) handsome.

Svarg (Indian) heaven.

Sven (Scandinavian) youth.
Svein, Svend, Svenn, Swen, Swenson

Swagat (Indian) welcome.

Swaggart (English) one who sways and staggers.
Swaggert

Swain (English) herdsman; knight's attendant.
Swaine, Swane, Swanson, Swayne

Swaley (English) winding stream.
Swail, Swailey, Swale, Swales

Swami (Hindi) a lord.

Swapnesh (Indian) king of dreams.

Swapnil (Indian) dreamy.

Swaraj (Indian) liberty, freedom.

Swarit (Hindi) toward heaven.

Swarup (Indian) figure.

Swastik (Indian) auspicious.

Sweeney (Irish) small hero.
Sweeny

Swinbourne (English) stream used by swine.
Swinborn, Swinborne, Swinburn, Swinburne, Swinbyrn, Swynborn

Swindel (English) valley of the swine.
Swindell

Swinfen (English) swine's mud.

Swinford (English) swine's crossing.
Swynford

Swinton (English) swine town.

Sy (Latin) a short form of Sylas, Symon.
Si

Sydnee 🄶 (French) a form of Sydney.

Sydney 🄶 (French) a form of Sidney.
Syd, Sydne, Sydnee, Syndey

Syed 🄱 (Arabic) happy.
Syeed, Syid

Sying 🄱🄶 (Chinese) star.

Sylas (Latin) a form of Silas.
Sy, Syles, Sylus

Sylvain (French) a form of Silvan, Sylvester.
Sylvan, Sylvian

Sylvester (Latin) forest dweller.
Silvester, Silvestro, Sly, Syl, Sylvain, Sylverster, Sylvestre

Symington (English) Simon's town, Simon's estate.

Symon (Greek) a form of Simon.
Sy, Syman, Symeon, Symion, Symms, Symon, Symone

Syon (Hindi) gentle.

Syum, Syun (Hindi) a ray.

Syuto (Japanese) holly.

Szczepan (Polish) a form of Stephen.

Szygfrid (Hungarian) a form of Siegfried.
Szigfrid

Szymon (Polish) a form of Simon.

T

T **BG** (American) an initial used as a first name.

Taahir (Indian) chaste, modest.

Taamir (Indian) one who knows dates.

Taaveti (Finnish) a form of David.
Taavi, Taavo

Tab (German) shining, brilliant. (English) drummer.
Tabb, Tabbie, Tabby

Tabaré (Tupi) man of the village.

Tabari (Arabic) he remembers.
Tabahri, Tabares, Tabarious, Tabarius, Tabarus, Tabur

Tabatha **G** (Greek, Aramaic) a form of Tabitha (see Girls' Names).

Tabib (Turkish) physician.
Tabeeb

Tabo (Spanish) a short form of Gustave.

Tabor (Persian) drummer. (Hungarian) encampment.
Tabber, Taber, Taboras, Taibor, Tayber, Taybor, Taver

Taciano, Tácito (Spanish) forms of Tacio.

Tacio (Latin) he who is quiet.

Tad (Welsh) father. (Greek, Latin) a short form of Thaddeus.
Tadd, Taddy, Tade, Tadek, Tadey

Tadaaki (Japanese) faithful; bright.

Tadahiro (Japanese) very loyal.

Tadan (Native American) plentiful.
Taden

Tadanori (Japanese) loyal ruler.

Tadao (Japanese) complacent, satisfied.

Tadarius (American) a combination of the prefix Ta + Darius.
Tadar, Tadarious, Tadaris, Tadarrius

Taddeo (Italian) a form of Thaddeus.
Tadeo

Taddeus (Greek, Latin) a form of Thaddeus.
Taddeous, Taddeusz, Taddius, Tadeas, Tades, Tadeusz, Tadio, Tadious

Tadi (Omaha) wind.

Tadzi (Carrier) loon.

Tadzio (Polish, Spanish) a form of Thaddeus.
Taddeusz

Taffy **G** (Welsh) a form of David. (English) a familiar form of Taft.

Taft (English) river.
Taffy, Tafton

Tage (Danish) day.
Tag

Taggart (Irish) son of the priest.
Tagart, Taggert

Tahír (Arabic) innocent, pure.
Taheer

Tai (Vietnamese) weather; prosperous; talented.

Taichi (Japanese) large first son.

Taiga (Japanese) big river.

Taiki (Japanese) big; noble; brilliant.

Taima 🄶 (Native American) born during a storm.

Taimu (Japanese) big dream.

Taishawn (American) a combination of Tai + Shawn.
Taisen, Taishaun, Taishon

Tait (Scandinavian) a form of Tate.
Taite, Taitt

Taiwan (Chinese) island; island dweller. Geography: a country off the coast of China.
Taewon, Tahwan, Taivon, Taiwain, Tawain, Tawan, Tawann, Tawaun, Tawon, Taywan, Tywan

Taiwo (Yoruba) first-born of twins.

Taiyo (Japanese) big sun.

Taj (Urdu) crown.
Taje, Tajee, Tajeh, Tajh, Taji

Tajo (Spanish) day.
Taio

Tajuan (American) a combination of the prefix Ta + Juan.
Taijuan, Taijun, Taijuon, Tájuan, Tajwan, Taquan, Tyjuan

Takahiro (Japanese) roof; heaven; air; space.

Takashi (Japanese) he who has dutiful ambitions.

Takayoshi (Japanese) obedient; righteousness.

Takeo (Japanese) strong as bamboo.
Takeyo

Takis (Greek) a familiar form of Peter.
Takias, Takius

Takoda (Lakota) friend to everyone.

Taksha (Indian) King Bharat's son.

Taksheel (Hindi) someone with a strong character.

Takuma (Japanese) the clear truth.

Takumi (Japanese) open; clear; truth; fruit.

Tal (Hebrew) dew; rain.
Tali, Talia, Talley, Talor, Talya

Talal (Indian) nice; admirable.

Talbert (German) bright valley.

Talbot (French) boot maker.
Talbott, Tallbot, Tallbott, Tallie, Tally

Talcott (English) cottage near the lake.

Tale (Tswana) green.

Talen (English) a form of Talon.
Talin, Tallen

Talha (Indian) a kind of tree.

Talib (Arabic) seeker.

Taliesin (Welsh) radiant brow.
Tallas, Tallis

Taliki (Hausa) fellow.

Talli (Delaware) legendary hero.

Talmadge (English) lake between two towns.
Talmage

Talmai (Aramaic) mound; furrow.
Telem

Talman (Aramaic) injured; oppressed.
Talmon

Talon **B** (French, English) claw, nail.
Taelon, Taelyn, Talen, Tallin, Tallon, Talyn

Talor (English) a form of Tal, Taylor.
Taelor, Taelur

Tam **B** (Vietnamese) number eight. (Hebrew) honest. (English) a short form of Thomas.
Tama, Tamas, Tamás, Tameas, Tamlane, Tammany, Tammas, Tammen, Tammy

Tamam (Indian) generous.

Taman (Slavic) dark, black.
Tama, Tamann, Tamin, Tamon, Tamone

Tamar **G** (Hebrew) date; palm tree.
Tamarie, Tamario, Tamarr, Timur

Tamasine (Japanese) twin.

Tambo (Swahili) vigorous.

Tamer (Arabic) he who makes way.

Tamir (Arabic) tall as a palm tree.
Tameer

Tamish (Indian) god of darkness.

Tammy **G** (English) a familiar form of Thomas.
Tammie

Tamson (Scandinavian) son of Thomas.
Tamsen

Tan (Burmese) million. (Vietnamese) new.
Than

Tanak (Hindi) prize.

Tanav (Hindi) flute.

Tancredo (Germanic) he who shrewdly gives advice.

Tanek (Greek) immortal. See also Atek.

Taneli (Finnish) God is my judge.
Taneil, Tanell, Tanella

Taner (English) a form of Tanner.
Tanar

Tanesha **G** (American) a combination of the prefix Ta + Nesha (see Girls' Names).

Tang (Chinese) dignified.

Tanguy (French) warrior.

Tanh (Vietnamese) having his way.

Tani **G** (Japanese) valley.

Tanis **G** (Slavic) a form of Tania (see Girls' Names).

Tanish (Hindi) ambition.

Tanjiro (Japanese) highly valued second son.

Tanmay (Sanskrit) engrossed.

Tanner **B** (English) leather worker; tanner.
Tan, Taner, Tanery, Tann, Tannar, Tannir, Tannor, Tanny

Tannin (English) tan colored; dark.
Tanin, Tannen, Tannon, Tanyen, Tanyon

Tanny (English) a familiar form of Tanner.
Tana, Tannee, Tanney, Tannie, Tany

Tano (Spanish) camp glory. (Ghanaian) Geography: a river in Ghana. (Russian) a short form of Stanislaus.
Tanno

Tanoj (Indian) son.

Tanton (English) town by the still river.

Tanvir (Hindi) strong.

Tao (Chinese) long life.

Tapan (Sanskrit) sun; summer.

Tapani (Finnish) a form of Stephen.
Tapamn, Teppo

Tapesh (Indian) the Holy Trinity.

Täpko (Kiowa) antelope.

Taporaj (Indian) moon.

Taquan (American) a combination of the prefix Ta + Quan.
Taquann, Taquawn, Taquon, Taqwan

Taquiri (Quechua) he who creates much music and dance.

Tara G (Aramaic) throw; carry. (Irish) rocky hill. (Arabic) a measurement.

Tarachandra (Indian) star; moon.

Tarak (Sanskrit) star; protector.

Taraksh (Hindi) mountain.

Taran (Sanskrit) heaven.
Tarran

Tarang (Hindi) wave.

Tarani (Indian) boat; sun.

Tarek (Arabic) a form of Táriq.
Tareek, Tareke

Tarell (German) a form of Terrell.
Tarelle, Tarrel, Tarrell, Taryl

Taren (American) a form of Taron.
Tarren, Tarrin

Tarendra (Hindi) prince of stars.

Taresh, Tarkesh (Indian) god of the stars.

Tarfah (Indian) a type of tree.

Tarif (Arabic) uncommon.
Tareef

Tarik (Arabic) a form of Táriq.
Taric, Tarick, Tariek, Tarikh, Tarrick, Tarrik, Taryk

Táriq (Arabic) conqueror. History: Tariq bin Ziyad was the Muslim general who conquered Spain.
Tareck, Tarek, Tarik, Tarique, Tarreq, Tereik

Tarius (Chuukese) a form of Dario.

Tarleton (English) Thor's settlement.
Tarlton

Taro (Japanese) first-born male.

Taron (American) a combination of Tad + Ron.
Taeron, Tahron, Taren, Tarone, Tarrion, Tarron, Taryn

Tarquino (Latin) he who was born in Tarquinia, an ancient Italian city.

Tarrant (Welsh) thunder.
Terrant

Tarsicio (Greek) valiant.

Taru (Hindi) small plant.

Tarun (Sanskrit) young, youth.
Taran

Tarver (English) tower; hill; leader.
Terver

Taryn G (American) a form of Taron.
Tarryn, Taryon

Tas (Gypsy) bird's nest.

Tasha G (Greek) born on Christmas day. (Russian) a short form of Natasha.

Tashawn (American) a combination of the prefix Ta + Shawn.
Tashaan, Tashan, Tashaun, Tashon, Tashun

Tass (Hungarian) ancient mythology name.

Tasunke (Dakota) horse.

Tate **B** (Scandinavian, English) cheerful. (Native American) long-winded talker.
Tait, Tayte

Tatharaj (Indian) Buddha.

Tatiano (Latin) he who is quiet.

Tatius (Latin) king, ruler. History: a Sabine king.
Tatianus, Tazio, Titus

Tatsuya (Japanese) like a dragon.

Tatum **G** (English) cheerful.

Tau (Tswana) lion.

Taua (Quechua) fourth child.

Tauacapac (Quechua) fourth lord; lord of the four regions.

Tauheed (Indian) victorious.

Tauno (Finnish) a form of Donald.

Taurean (Latin) strong; forceful. Astrology: born under the sign of Taurus.
Tauraun, Taurein, Taurin, Taurion, Taurone, Taurus

Taurino (Spanish) bull-like.

Tauro (Spanish) a form of Toro.

Taurus (Latin) Astrology: the second sign of the zodiac.
Taurice, Tauris

Tautik (Indian) pearl.

Tavares (Aramaic) a form of Tavor.
Tarvarres, Tavarres, Taveress

Tavaris (Aramaic) a form of Tavor.
Tarvaris, Tavar, Tavaras, Tavari, Tavarian, Tavarious, Tavarius, Tavarous, Tavarri, Tavarris, Tavars, Tavarse, Tavarus, Tevaris, Tevarius, Tevarus

Tavey (Latin) a familiar form of Octavio.

Tavi (Aramaic) good.

Tavian (Latin) a form of Octavio.
Taveon, Taviann, Tavien, Tavieon, Tavin, Tavio, Tavion, Tavionne, Tavon, Tayvon

Tavish (Scottish) a form of Thomas.
Tav, Tavi, Tavis

Tavo (Slavic) a short form of Gustave.

Tavon (American) a form of Tavian.
Tavonn, Tavonne, Tavonni

Tavor (Aramaic) misfortune.
Tarvoris, Tavares, Tavaris, Tavores, Tavorious, Tavoris, Tavorise, Tavorres, Tavorris, Tavuris

Tawfeeq (Indian) success; reconciliation.

Tawno (Gypsy) little one.
Tawn

Tayib (Hindi) good; delicate.

Tayler **G** (English) a form of Taylor.
Tailer, Taylar, Tayller, Teyler

Taylor **G** (English) tailor.
Tailor, Talor, Tayler, Tayllor, Taylour, Taylr, Teylor

Tayseer (Indian) facilitation.

Tayshawn (American) a combination of Taylor + Shawn.
Taysean, Tayshan, Tayshun, Tayson

Tayvon (American) a form of Tavian.
Tayvan, Tayvaughn, Tayven, Tayveon, Tayvin, Tayvohn, Taywon

Taz (Arabic) shallow ornamental cup.
Tazz

Tazio (Italian) a form of Tatius.

Te (Chinese) special.

Teagan **G** (Irish) a form of Teague.
Teagen, Teagun, Teegan

Teague (Irish) bard, poet.
Teag, Teagan, Teage, Teak, Tegan, Teige

Tearence (Latin) a form of Terrence.
Tearance, Tearnce, Tearrance

Tearlach (Scottish) a form of Charles.

Tearle (English) stern, severe.

Teasdale (English) river dweller. Geography: a river in England.

Teb (Spanish) a short form of Stephen.

Ted (English) a short form of Edward, Edwin, Theodore.
Tedd, Tedek, Tedik, Tedson

Teddy (English) a familiar form of Edward, Theodore.
Teddey, Teddie, Tedy

Tedmund (English) protector of the land.
Tedman, Tedmond

Tedorik (Polish) a form of Theodore.
Teodoor, Teodor, Teodorek

Tedrick (American) a combination of Ted + Rick.
Teddrick, Tederick, Tedric

Teerth (Indian) holy place; sacred water.

Teetonka (Lakota) big lodge.

Tefere (Ethiopian) seed.

Tegan ☀ (Irish) a form of Teague.
Teghan, Teigan, Tiegan

Teiji, Teijo (Japanese) righteous; well governed.

Teiljo (Japanese) established, regulated.

Tej (Sanskrit) light; lustrous.

Tejas (Sanskrit) sharp.

Tejeshwar (Indian) sun.

Tejomay (Indian) glorious.

Tekle (Ethiopian) plant.

Telek (Polish) a form of Telford.

Telem (Hebrew) mound; furrow.
Talmai, Tel

Telémaco (Greek) he who prepares for battle.

Telford (French) iron cutter.
Telek, Telfer, Telfor, Telfour

Teller (English) storyteller.
Tell, Telly

Telly (Greek) a familiar form of Teller, Theodore.

Telmo (English) tiller, cultivator.

Telutci (Moquelumnan) bear making dust as it runs.

Telvin (American) a combination of the prefix Te + Melvin.
Tellvin, Telvan

Tem (Gypsy) country.

Teman (Hebrew) on the right side; southward.

Tembo (Swahili) elephant.

Tempest ☀ (French) storm.

Temple (Latin) sanctuary.

Templeton (English) town near the temple.
Temp, Templeten

Teng (Chinese) gallop; prance.

Tenma (Japanese) sky; horse.

Tennant (English) tenant, renter.
Tenant, Tennent

Tennessee (Cherokee) mighty warrior. Geography: a southern U.S. state.
Tennessee, Tennesy, Tennysee

Tennyson (English) a form of
Dennison. Literature: Alfred, Lord
Tennyson was a nineteenth-century
British poet.
*Tenney, Tenneyson, Tennie, Tennis,
Tennison, Tenny, Tenson*

Teo (Vietnamese) a form of Tom.

Teobaldo (Italian, Spanish) a form of
Theobald.

Teócrito (Greek) God's chosen one.

Teodoro (Italian, Spanish) a form of
Theodore.
Teodore, Teodorico

Teodosio (Greek) he who gives to
God.

Teófano (Greek) friend of God;
loved by God.

Teófilo (Greek) loved by God.

Teppo (French) a familiar form of
Stephen.

Tequan (American) a combination of
the prefix Te + Quan.
Tequinn, Tequon

Terance (Latin) a form of Terrence.
Terriance

Tercio, Tertulio (Greek) third child
of the family.

Terell (German) a form of Terrell.
Tarell, Tereall, Terel, Terelle, Tyrel

Teremun (Tiv) father's acceptance.

Terence **B** (Latin) a form of
Terrence.
Teren, Teryn

Terencio (Spanish) a form of
Terrence.

Tereshan (Indian) solid redemption.

Teri **G** (Greek) reaper. A familiar
form of Theresa.

Terra **G** (Latin) earth. (Japanese)
swift arrow. (American) forms of
Tara.

Terran (Latin) a short form of
Terrance.
Teran, Teren, Terran, Terren

Terrance **B** (Latin) a form of
Terrence.
Tarrance, Terran

Terrell **B** (German) thunder ruler.
*Terell, Terrail, Terral, Terrale, Terrall,
Terreal, Terrel, Terrelle, Terrill, Terryal,
Terryel, Tirel, Tirrel, Tirrell, Turrell,
Tyrel, Tyrell*

Terrence (Latin) smooth.
*Tarrance, Tearence, Terance, Terence,
Terencio, Terrance, Terren, Terrin,
Terry, Torrence, Tyreese*

Terri **G** (English) a form of Terry.

Terrick (American) a combination of
the prefix Te + Derrick.
*Teric, Terick, Terik, Teriq, Terric, Terrik,
Tirek, Tirik*

Terrill (German) a form of Terrell.
*Teriel, Teriell, Terril, Terryl, Terryll,
Teryll, Teryl, Tyrill*

Terrin (Latin) a short form of
Terrence.
Terin, Terrien, Terryn, Teryn, Tiren

Terris (Latin) son of Terry.

Terron (American) a form of Tyrone.
*Tereon, Terion, Terione, Teron, Terone,
Terrion, Terrione, Terriyon, Terrone,
Terronn, Terryon, Tiron*

Terry **B** (English) a familiar form of
Terrence. See also Keli.
Tarry, Terrey, Terri, Terrie, Tery

Tertius (Latin) third.

Teru (Japanese) brilliant shine.

Teruaki (Japanese) brilliant autumn.

Teruyoshi (Japanese) brilliant justice.

Teseo (Greek) founder.

Teshawn (American) a combination of the prefix Te + Shawn.
Tesean, Teshaun, Teshon

Tess 🄶 (Greek) a short form of Theresa.

Tessa 🄶 (Greek) reaper.

Tet (Vietnamese) Vietnamese.

Tetsuo (Japanese) philosophical husband.

Teva (Hebrew) nature.

Tevan (American) a form of Tevin.
Tevaughan, Tevaughn, Teven, Tevvan

Tevel (Yiddish) a form of David.

Tevin 🄱 (American) a combination of the prefix Te + Kevin.
Teavin, Teivon, Tevan, Tevien, Tevinn, Tevon, Tevvin, Tevyn

Tevis (Scottish) a form of Thomas.
Tevish

Tevon (American) a form of Tevin.
Tevion, Tevohn, Tevone, Tevonne, Tevoun, Teyvon

Tewdor (German) a form of Theodore.

Tex (American) from Texas.
Tejas

Thaabit (Indian) firm.

Thabit (Arabic) firm, strong.

Thad (Greek, Latin) a short form of Thaddeus.
Thadd, Thade, Thadee, Thady

Thaddeus (Greek) courageous. (Latin) praiser. Bible: one of the Twelve Apostles. See also Fadey.
Tad, Taddeo, Taddeus, Thaddis, Thadeaus, Tadzio, Thad, Thaddaeus, Thaddaus, Thaddeau, Thaddeaus, Thaddeo, Thaddeous, Thaddiaus, Thaddius, Thadeaou, Thadeous, Thadeus, Thadieus, Thadious, Thadius, Thadus

Thady (Irish) praise.
Thaddy

Thai (Vietnamese) many, multiple.

Thakur (Indian) leader; God.

Thaman (Hindi) god; godlike.

Than (Burma) million.
Tan, Thanh

Thane (English) attendant warrior.
Thain, Thaine, Thayne

Thang (Vietnamese) victorious.

Thanh (Vietnamese) finished.

Thaniel (Hebrew) a short form of Nathaniel.

Thanos (Greek) nobleman; bear-man.
Athanasios, Thanasis

Thao (Vietnamese) courtesy.

Thaqib (Indian) shooting star.

Thatcher (English) roof thatcher, repairer of roofs.
Thacher, Thatch, Thaxter

Thaw (English) melting ice.

Thayer (French) nation's army.
Thay

Thel (English) upper story.

Thenga (Yao) bring him.

Theo (English) a short form of Theodore.

Theobald (German) people's prince;
bold people. See also Dietbald.
*Teobaldo, Thebault, Theòbault,
Thibault, Tibalt, Tibold, Tiebold,
Tiebout, Toiboid, Tybald, Tybalt,
Tybault*

Theodore **B** (Greek) gift of God.
See also Feodor, Fyodor.
*Téadóir, Teador, Ted, Teddy, Tedor,
Tedorek, Tedorik, Telly, Teodomiro,
Teodoro, Teodus, Teos, Tewdor, Theo,
Theodor, Theódor, Theodors,
Theodorus, Theodosios, Theodrekr,
Tivadar, Todor, Tolek, Tudor*

Theodoric (German) ruler of the
people. See also Dedrick, Derek,
Dirk.
*Teodorico, Thedric, Thedrick, Thierry,
Till*

Theophilus (Greek) loved by God.
*Teofil, Théophile, Theophlous,
Theopolis*

Theresa **G** (Greek) reaper.

Theron (Greek) hunter.
*Theran, Theren, Thereon, Therin,
Therion, Therrin, Therron, Theryn,
Theryon*

Thian (Vietnamese) smooth.
Thien

Thibault (French) a form of Theobald.
Thibaud, Thibaut

Thierry (French) a form of
Theodoric.
Theirry, Theory

Thinh (Vietnamese) prosperity.

Tho (Vietnamese) longevity.

Thom (English) a short form of
Thomas.
Thomy

Thoma (German) a form of Thomas.

Thomas ✹ **B** (Greek, Aramaic)
twin. Bible: one of the Twelve
Apostles. See also Chuma, Foma,
Maslin.
*Tam, Tammy, Tavish, Tevis, Thom,
Thoma, Thomason, Thomaz,
Thomeson, Thomison, Thommas,
Thompson, Thomson, Tom, Toma,
Tomas, Tomás, Tomasso, Tomcy,
Tomey, Tomey, Tomi, Tommy, Toomas*

Thompson (English) son of Thomas.
*Thomason, Thomison, Thomsen,
Thomson*

Thor (Scandinavian) thunder.
Mythology: the Norse god of
thunder.
Thorin, Tor, Tyrus

Thorald (Scandinavian) Thor's
follower.
Terrell, Terrill, Thorold, Torald

Thorbert (Scandinavian) Thor's
brightness.
Torbert

Thorbjorn (Scandinavian) Thor's
bear.
Thorburn, Thurborn, Thurburn

Thorgood (English) Thor is good.

Thorleif (Scandinavian) Thor's
beloved.
Thorlief

Thorley (English) Thor's meadow.
*Thorlea, Thorlee, Thorleigh, Thorly,
Torley*

Thorndike (English) thorny
embankment.
Thorn, Thorndyck, Thorndyke, Thorne

Thorne (English) a short form of
names beginning with "Thorn."
Thorn, Thornie, Thorny

Thornley (English) thorny meadow.
*Thorley, Thorne, Thornlea, Thornleigh,
Thornly*

Thornton (English) thorny town.
Thorne

Thorpe (English) village.
Thorp

Thorwald (Scandinavian) Thor's forest.
Thorvald

Thu (Vietnamese) autumn.

Thuan (Vietnamese) tamed, conforming.

Thuc (Vietnamese) aware.

Thuong (Vietnamese) to love tenderly; in pursuit.

Thurlow (English) Thor's hill.
Thurlo

Thurmond (English) defended by Thor.
Thormond, Thurmund

Thurston (Scandinavian) Thor's stone.
Thorstan, Thorstein, Thorsten, Thurstain, Thurstan, Thursten, Torsten, Torston

Thuyet (Vietnamese) theory.

Tiago (Spanish) a form of Jacob.

Tian (Chinese) heaven.

Tiarra 🅖 (Latin) a form of Tiara (see Girls' Names).

Tiberio (Italian) from the Tiber River region.
Tiberias, Tiberious, Tiberiu, Tiberius, Tibius, Tyberious, Tyberius, Tyberrius

Tibor (Hungarian) holy place.
Tiburcio

Tiburón (Spanish) shark.

Tichawanna (Shona) we shall see.

Ticho (Spanish) a short form of Patrick.

Ticiano (Spanish) a form of Tito.

Tico (Greek) adventurous one; happy, fortunate.

Tieler (English) a form of Tyler.
Tielar, Tielor, Tielyr

T'ien-Khuan (Chinese) god who bestows happiness.

Tiennot (French) a form of Stephen.
Tien

Tiernan (Irish) lord.

Tierney 🅖 (Irish) lordly.
Tiarnach, Tiernan

Tiffany 🅖 (Latin) trinity. (Greek) a short form of Theophania (see Girls' Names).

Tige (English) a short form of Tiger.
Ti, Tig, Tighe, Ty, Tyg, Tyge, Tygh, Tyghe

Tiger (American) tiger; powerful and energetic.
Tige, Tigger, Tyger

Tiimu (Moquelumnan) caterpillar coming out of the ground.

Tijil (Indian) moon.

Ti-Khuan (Chinese) god who grants remission of sins.

Tiktu (Moquelumnan) bird digging up potatoes.

Tilak (Indian) spot of vermillion or sandalwood paste on the forehead.

Tilden (English) tilled valley.
Tildon

Tilford (English) prosperous ford.

Till (German) a short form of Theodoric.
Thilo, Til, Tillman, Tilman, Tillmann, Tilson

Tilo (Teutonic) skillful and praises God.

Tilton (English) prosperous town.

Tim (Greek) a short form of Timothy.
Timmie, Timmy

Timin (Arabic) born near the sea.

Timirbaran (Indian) dark.

Timmothy (Greek) a form of Timothy.
Timmathy, Timmithy, Timmoty, Timmthy

Timmy (Greek) a familiar form of Timothy.
Timmie

Timo (Finnish) a form of Timothy.
Timio

Timofey (Russian) a form of Timothy.
Timofei, Timofej, Timofeo

Timon (Greek) honorable.

Timoteo (Portuguese, Spanish) a form of Timothy.

Timothy **B** (Greek) honoring God. See also Kimokeo.
Tadhg, Taidgh, Tiege, Tim, Tima, Timithy, Timka, Timkin, Timmothy, Timmy, Timo, Timofey, Timok, Timon, Timontheo, Timonthy, Timót, Timote, Timotei, Timoteo, Timoteus, Timothé, Timothée, Timotheo, Timotheos, Timotheus, Timothey, Timothie, Timthie, Tiomóid, Tisha, Tomothy, Tymon, Tymothy

Timur (Hebrew) a form of Tamar. (Russian) conqueror.
Timour

Tin (Vietnamese) thinker.

Tina **G** (Spanish, American) a short form of Augustine.

Tincupuma, Tinquipoma (Quechua) he who creates much music and dance.

Ting (Chinese) palace; pavilion.

Tinh (Vietnamese) mindful, aware.

Tino (Spanish) venerable, majestic. (Italian) small. A familiar form of Antonio. (Greek) a short form of Augustine.
Tion

Tinsley (English) fortified field.

Tiquan (American) a combination of the prefix Ti + Quan.
Tiquawn, Tiquine, Tiquon, Tiquwan, Tiqwan

Tíquico (Greek) very fortunate person.

Tirishaanth (Indian) king of the Surya dynasty.

Tirso (Greek) crowned with fig leaves.

Tirth (Indian) pilgrim.

Tirtha (Indian) holy place.

Tisha **G** (Russian) a form of Timothy.
Tishka

Tishawn (American) a combination of the prefix Ti + Shawn.
Tishaan, Tishaun, Tishean, Tishon, Tishun

Titir (Indian) a bird.

Tito (Italian) a form of Titus.
Titas, Titis, Titos

Titoatauchi, Tituatauchi (Quechua) he who brings luck in trying times.

Titu (Quechua) difficult, complicated.

Titus (Greek) giant. (Latin) hero. A form of Tatius. History: a Roman emperor.
Tite, Titek, Tito, Tytus

Tivon (Hebrew) nature lover.

TJ (American) a combination of the initials T. + J.
Teejay, Tj, T.J., T Jae, Tjayda

Toai (Vietnamese) satisfied.

Tobal (Spanish) a short form of Christopher.
Tabalito

Tobar (Gypsy) road.

Tobi 🅖 (Yoruba) great.

Tobias (Hebrew) God is good.
Tobia, Tobiah, Tobiás, Tobiath, Tobin, Tobit, Toby, Tobyas, Tuvya

Tobías (Hebrew) a form of Tobias.

Tobikuma (Japanese) cloud; misty.

Tobin (Hebrew) a form of Tobias.
Toben, Tobian, Tobyn, Tovin

Toby 🅑 (Hebrew) a familiar form of Tobias.
Tobbie, Tobby, Tobe, Tobee, Tobey, Tobie

Todd 🅑 (English) fox.
Tod, Toddie, Toddy

Todor (Basque, Russian) a form of Theodore.
Teodor, Todar, Todas, Todos

Toft (English) small farm.

Tohon (Native American) cougar.

Tokala (Dakota) fox.

Tokujiro (Japanese) virtuous second son.

Tokutaro (Japanese) virtuous son.

Toland (English) owner of taxed land.
Tolan

Tolbert (English) bright tax collector.

Toller (English) tax collector.

Tolomeo (Greek) powerful in battle.

Tom (English) a short form of Tomas, Thomas.
Teo, Thom, Tommey, Tommie, Tommy

Toma (Romanian) a form of Thomas.
Tomah

Tomas (German) a form of Thomas.
Tom, Tomaisin, Tomaz, Tomcio, Tome, Tomek, Tomelis, Tomico, Tomik, Tomislaw, Tommas, Tomo, Tomson

Tomás (Irish, Spanish) a form of Thomas.
Tomas, Tómas, Tomasz

Tomasso (Italian) a form of Thomas.
Tomaso, Tommaso

Tombe (Kakwa) northerners.

Tomé (Hebrew) identical twin brother.

Tomeo (Japanese) cautious man.

Tomey (Irish) a familiar form of Thomas.
Tome, Tomi, Tomie, Tomy

Tomi 🅖 (Japanese) rich. (Hungarian) a form of Thomas.

Tomlin (English) little Tom.
Tomkin, Tomlinson

Tommie 🅑 (Hebrew) a form of Tommy.
Tommi

Tommy 🅑 (Hebrew) a familiar form of Thomas.
Tommie, Tomy

Tomofumi (Japanese) wise writer.

Tomohiro (Japanese) very wise.

Tomoya (Japanese) he who is wise.

Tonda (Czech) a form of Tony.
Tonek

Tong (Vietnamese) fragrant.

Toni **G** (Greek, German, Slavic) a form of Tony.
Tonee, Tonie, Tonio, Tonis, Tonnie

Tonio (Portuguese) a form of Tony. (Italian) a short form of Antonio.
Tono, Tonyo

Tonto (Indian) indulgence; devotion.

Tony **B** (Greek) flourishing. (Latin) praiseworthy. (English) a short form of Anthony. A familiar form of Remington.
Tonda, Tonek, Toney, Toni, Tonik, Tonio, Tonny

Tooantuh (Cherokee) spring frog.

Toomas (Estonian) a form of Thomas.
Toomis, Tuomas, Tuomo

Topa, Tupa (Quechua) honorific title; royal, majestic, glorious, noble, honorable.

Topher (Greek) a short form of Christopher, Kristopher.
Tofer, Tophor

Topo (Spanish) gopher.

Topper (English) hill.

Tor (Norwegian) thunder. (Tiv) royalty, king.
Thor

Torao (Japanese) tiger; wild.

Torcuato (Latin) adorned with a collar or garland.

Tori **G** (English) a form of Tory.

Torian (Irish) a form of Torin.
Toran, Torean, Toriano, Toriaun, Torien, Torrian, Torrien, Torryan

Toribio (Greek) he who makes bows.

Torin (Irish) chief.
Thorfin, Thorstein, Torian, Torion, Torrin, Toryn

Torkel (Swedish) Thor's cauldron.

Tormey (Irish) thunder spirit.
Tormé, Tormee

Tormod (Scottish) north.

Torn (Irish) a short form of Torrence.
Toran

Toro (Spanish) bull.

Torquil (Danish) Thor's kettle.
Torkel

Torr (English) tower.
Tory

Torrance (Irish) a form of Torrence.
Torance

Torren (Irish) a short form of Torrence.
Torehn, Toren

Torrence (Irish) knolls. (Latin) a form of Terrence.
Tawrence, Toreence, Torence, Torenze, Torey, Torin, Torn, Torr, Torrance, Torren, Torreon, Torrin, Torry, Tory, Torynce, Tuarence, Turance

Torrey (English) a form of Tory.
Toreey, Torie, Torre, Torri, Torrie, Torry

Toru (Japanese) sea.

Tory **G** (English) familiar form of Torr, Torrence.
Torey, Tori, Torrey

Toshan (Indian) satisfaction.

Toshi (Japanese) mirror image.

Toshiharu (Japanese) excellent governor.

Toshihiro (Japanese) wise.

Toshiro (Japanese) talented; intelligent.

Toshi-Shita (Japanese) junior.

Toshiyuki (Japanese) excellent; auspicious; fortunate.

Tovi (Hebrew) good.
Tov

Townley (English) town meadow.
Townlea, Townlee, Townleigh, Townlie, Townly

Townsend (English) town's end.
Town, Townes, Towney, Townie, Townsen, Townshend, Towny

Toyo (Japanese) plentiful.

Trabunco (Mapuche) meeting at the marsh.

Trace (Irish) a form of Tracy.
Trayce

Tracey 🄶 (Irish) a form of Tracy.

Traci 🄶 (Irish) a form of Tracy.

Tracy 🄶 (Greek) harvester. (Latin) courageous. (Irish) battler.
Trace, Tracey, Tracie, Treacy

Trader (English) well-trodden path; skilled worker.

Trae (English) a form of Trey.
Trai, Traie, Tre, Trea

Traful (Araucanian) union.

Trahern (Welsh) strong as iron.
Traherne, Tray

Trailokva, Tribhuvan, Trilok (Indian) the three worlds (heaven, earth, hell).

Tramaine (Scottish) a form of Tremaine, Tremayne.
Tramain, Traman, Tramane, Tramayne, Traymain, Traymon

Tranamil (Mapuche) low, scattered light.

Trang (Vietnamese) decorated, honored.

Traquan (American) a combination of Travis + Quan.
Traequan, Traqon, Traquon, Traqwan, Traqwaun, Trayquan, Trayquane, Trayqwon

Trashawn 🄱 (American) a combination of Travis + Shawn.
Trasen, Trashaun, Trasean, Trashon, Trashone, Trashun, Trayshaun, Trayshawn

Traugott (German) God's truth.

Travaris (French) a form of Travers.
Travares, Travaress, Travarious, Travarius, Travarous, Travarus, Travauris, Traveress, Traverez, Traverus, Travoris, Travorus

Travell (English) traveler.
Travail, Travale, Travel, Travelis, Travelle, Trevel, Trevell, Trevelle

Traven (American) a form of Trevon.
Travin, Travine, Trayven

Travers (French) crossroads.
Travaris, Traver, Travis

Travion (American) a form of Trevon.
Traveon, Travian, Travien, Travione, Travioun

Travis 🄱 (English) a form of Travers.
Travais, Travees, Traves, Traveus, Travious, Traviss, Travius, Travous, Travus, Travys, Trayvis, Trevais, Trevis

Travon 🄱 (American) a form of Trevon.
Traevon, Traivon, Travone, Travonn, Travonne

Tray (English) a form of Trey.
Traye

Trayton (English) town full of trees.
Trayten

Trayvon (American) a combination of Tray + Von.
Trayveon, Trayvin, Trayvion, Trayvond, Trayvone, Trayvonne, Trayvyon

Treavon (American) a form of Trevon.
Treavan, Treavin, Treavion

Trecaman (Mapuche) majestic steps of the condor.

Tredway (English) well-worn road.
Treadway

Tremaine, Tremayne B (Scottish) house of stone.
Tramaine, Tremain, Tremane, Treymaine, Trimaine

Trent B (Latin) torrent, rapid stream. (French) thirty. Geography: a city in northern Italy.
Trente, Trentino, Trento, Trentonio

Trenton (Latin) town by the rapid stream. Geography: the capital of New Jersey.
Trendon, Trendun, Trenten, Trentin, Trentton, Trentyn, Trinten, Trintin, Trinton

Trequan (American) a combination of Trey + Quan.
Trequanne, Trequaun, Trequian, Trequon, Trequwon, Treyquane

Treshawn (American) a combination of Trey + Shawn.
Treshaun, Treshon, Treshun, Treysean, Treyshawn, Treyshon

Treston (Welsh) a form of Tristan.
Trestan, Trestin, Trestton, Trestyn

Trev (Irish, Welsh) a short form of Trevor.

Trevaughn (American) a combination of Trey + Vaughn.
Trevaughan, Trevaugn, Trevaun, Trevaune, Trevaunn, Treyvaughn

Trevelyan (English) Elian's homestead.

Trevin (American) a form of Trevon.
Trevian, Trevien, Trevine, Trevinne, Trevyn, Treyvin

Trevion (American) a form of Trevon.
Trevione, Trevionne, Trevyon, Treyveon, Treyvion

Trevis (English) a form of Travis.
Treves, Trevez, Treveze, Trevius

Trevon B (American) a combination of Trey + Von.
Traven, Travion, Travon, Tre, Treavon, Trévan, Treveyon, Trevin, Trevion, Trevohn, Trevoine, Trévon, Trevone, Trevonn, Trevonne, Treyvon

Trevor B (Irish) prudent. (Welsh) homestead.
Travor, Treavor, Trebor, Trefor, Trev, Trevar, Trevares, Trevarious, Trevaris, Trevarius, Trevaros, Trevarus, Trever, Trevore, Trevores, Trevoris, Trevorus, Trevour, Trevyr, Treyvor

Trey (English) three; third.
Trae, Trai, Tray, Treye, Tri, Trie

Treyvon (American) a form of Trevon.
Treyvan, Treyven, Treyvenn, Treyvone, Treyvonn, Treyvun

Tridev (Indian) the Hindu trinity (Brahma, Vishnu, and Mahesh).

Tridhaman, Trimurti (Indian) the Holy Trinity.

Tridib (Indian) heaven.

Trieu (Vietnamese) tide.

Trigg (Scandinavian) trusty.

Trigun (Indian) the three dimensions.

Trilokchand (Indian) moon of the three worlds.

Triman (Indian) ruler of three worlds; worshipped in three worlds.

Trina G (Greek) pure.

Trini (Latin) a short form of Trinity.

Trinity G (Latin) holy trinity.
Trenedy, Trini, Trinidy

Trip, Tripp (English) traveler.

Trishanku (Indian) a king of the Surya dynasty.

Trishar (Indian) pearl necklace.

Tristan 🅱 (Welsh) bold. Literature: a knight in the Arthurian legends who fell in love with his uncle's wife.
Treston, Tris, Trisan, Tristain, Tristán, Tristano, Tristen, Tristian, Tristin, Triston, Tristyn, Trystan

Tristano (Italian) a form of Tristan.

Tristen 🅱 (Welsh) a form of Tristan.
Trisden, Trissten

Tristin 🅱 (Welsh) a form of Tristan.
Tristian, Tristinn

Triston 🅱 (Welsh) a form of Tristan.

Tristram (Welsh) sorrowful. Literature: the title character in Laurence Sterne's eighteenth-century novel *Tristram Shandy*.
Tristam

Tristyn (Welsh) a form of Tristan.
Tristynne

Trivikram (Indian) a name of Vishnu.

Troilo (Egyptian) he who was born in Troy.

Trong (Vietnamese) respected.

Trong Tri (Vietnamese) not of small mind.

Trot (English) trickling stream.

Trowbridge (English) bridge by the tree.

Troy 🅱 (Irish) foot soldier. (French) curly haired. (English) water. See also Koi.
Troi, Troye, Troyton

Truc (Vietnamese) bamboo; wish.

True (English) faithful, loyal.
Tru

Truesdale (English) faithful one's homestead.

Truitt (English) little and honest.
Truett

Truman (English) honest. History: Harry S. Truman was the thirty-third U.S. president.
Trueman, Trumain, Trumaine, Trumann

Trumble (English) strong; bold.
Trumball, Trumbell, Trumbull

Trustin (English) trustworthy.
Trustan, Trusten, Truston

Trygve (Norwegian) brave victor.

Trystan (Welsh) a form of Tristan.
Tryistan, Trysten, Trystian, Trystin, Trystn, Tryston, Trystyn

Tsai-Shen (Chinese) god of wealth; most popular god.

Tsalani (Nguni) good-bye.

Tse (Ewe) younger of twins.

Tsubasa (Japanese) wing.

Tsukasa (Japanese) administrator.

Tsukiya (Japanese) he who is like the moon.

Tsutomu (Japanese) hard worker; diligent.

Tsuyoshi (Japanese) strong gentleman.

Tu 🅱 (Vietnamese) tree.

Tuaco (Ghanaian) eleventh-born.

Tuan (Vietnamese) goes smoothly.

Tubal (Hebrew) he who tills the soil.

Tucker **B** (English) fuller, tucker of cloth.
Tuck, Tuckie, Tucky, Tuckyr

Tudor (Welsh) a form of Theodore. History: an English ruling dynasty.
Todor

Tufan (Indian) storm.

Tug (Scandinavian) draw, pull.
Tugg

Tuhin (Indian) snow.

Tuhinsurra, Tusharsuvra (Indian) white as snow.

Tuka (Indian) young boy.

Tukaram (Indian) a poet saint.

Tuketu (Moquelumnan) bear making dust as it runs.

Tukuli (Moquelumnan) caterpillar crawling down a tree.

Tulasidas (Indian) servant of Tulsi.

Tulio (Italian, Spanish) lively.
Tullio

Tullis (Latin) title, rank.
Tullius, Tullos, Tully

Tully (Irish) at peace with God. (Latin) a familiar form of Tullis.
Tull, Tulley, Tullie, Tullio

Tulsidas (Indian) a famous saint.

Tumaini (Mwera) hope.

Tumu (Moquelumnan) deer thinking about eating wild onions.

Tung (Vietnamese) stately, dignified. (Chinese) everyone.

Tungar (Sanskrit) high; lofty.

Tungesh (Indian) moon.

Tuo (Chinese) appropriate.

Tuong (Vietnamese) everything.

Tupac (Quechua) Lord.

Tupacamaru (Quechua) glorious Amaru, an Incan lord.

Tupacapac (Quechua) glorious and kind-hearted lord.

Tupacusi (Quechua) happy and majestic.

Tupaquiupanqui, Tupayupanqui (Quechua) memorable and glorious lord.

Tupi (Moquelumnan) pulled up.

Tupper (English) ram raiser.

Turag (Hindi) a thought.

Turi (Spanish) a short form of Arthur.
Ture

Turk (English) from Turkey.

Turner **B** (Latin) lathe worker; wood worker.

Turpin (Scandinavian) Finn named after Thor.

Tushar (Hindi) winter.

Tut (Arabic) strong and courageous. History: a short form of Tutankhamen, an Egyptian king.
Tutt

Tutu (Spanish) a familiar form of Justin.

Tuvya (Hebrew) a form of Tobias.
Tevya, Tuvia, Tuviah

Tuwile (Mwera) death is inevitable.

Tuyen (Vietnamese) angel.

Twain (English) divided in two. Literature: Mark Twain (whose real name was Samuel Langhorne Clemens) was one of the most prominent nineteenth-century American writers.
Tawine, Twaine, Twan, Twane, Tway, Twayn, Twayne

Twen-Ch'ang (Chinese) god of literature and poetry.

Twia (Fante) born after twins.

Twitchell (English) narrow passage.
Twytchell

Twyford (English) double river crossing.

Txomin (Basque) like the Lord.

Ty B (English) a short form of Tyler, Tyrone, Tyrus.
Tye

Tyagraja (Indian) a famous poet.

Tyee (Native American) chief.

Tyger (English) a form of Tiger.
Tige, Tyg, Tygar

Tylar (English) a form of Tyler.
Tyelar, Tylarr

Tyler ☀ B (English) tile maker.
Tieler, Tiler, Ty, Tyel, Tyeler, Tyelor, Tyhler, Tylar, Tyle, Tylee, Tylere, Tyller, Tylor, Tylyr

Tylor B (English) a form of Tyler.
Tylour

Tymon (Polish) a form of Timothy. (Greek) a form of Timon.
Tymain, Tymaine, Tymane, Tymeik, Tymek, Tymen

Tymothy (English) a form of Timothy.
Tymithy, Tymmothy, Tymoteusz, Tymothee, Timothi

Tynan (Irish) dark.
Ty

Tynek (Czech) a form of Martin.
Tynko

Tyquan (American) a combination of Ty + Quan.
Tykwan, Tykwane, Tykwon, Tyquaan, Tyquane, Tyquann, Tyquine, Tyquinn, Tyquon, Tyquone, Tyquwon, Tyqwan

Tyra G (Scottish) a form of Tyree.

Tyran (American) a form of Tyrone.
Tyraine, Tyrane

Tyree B (Scottish) island dweller. Geography: Tiree is an island off the west coast of Scotland.
Tyra, Tyrae, Tyrai, Tyray, Tyre, Tyrea, Tyrée

Tyreese (American) a form of Terrence.
Tyreas, Tyrease, Tyrece, Tyreece, Tyreice, Tyres, Tyrese, Tyresse, Tyrez, Tyreze, Tyrice, Tyriece, Tyriese

Tyrel, Tyrell B (American) forms of Terrell.
Tyrelle, Tyrrel, Tyrrell

Tyrick (American) a combination of Ty + Rick.
Tyreck, Tyreek, Tyreik, Tyrek, Tyreke, Tyric, Tyriek, Tyrik, Tyriq, Tyrique

Tyrin (American) a form of Tyrone.
Tyrinn, Tyrion, Tyrrin, Tyryn

Tyron (American) a form of Tyrone.
Tyrohn, Tyronn, Tyronna, Tyronne

Tyrone (Greek) sovereign. (Irish) land of Owen.
Tayron, Tayrone, Teirone, Terron, Ty, Tyerone, Tyhrone, Tyran, Tyrin, Tyron, Tyroney, Tyronne, Tyroon, Tyroun

Tyrus (English) a form of Thor.
Ty, Tyruss, Tyryss

Tyshawn (American) a combination of Ty + Shawn.
Tyshan, Tyshaun, Tyshauwn, Tyshian, Tyshinn, Tyshion, Tyshon, Tyshone, Tyshonne, Tyshun, Tyshunn, Tyshyn

Tyson **B** (French) son of Ty.
Tison, Tiszon, Tyce, Tycen, Tyesn, Tyeson, Tysen, Tysie, Tysin, Tysne, Tysone

Tytus (Polish) a form of Titus.
Tyus

Tyvon (American) a combination of Ty + Von.
Tyvan, Tyvin, Tyvinn, Tyvone, Tyvonne

Tywan (Chinese) a form of Taiwan.
Tywain, Tywaine, Tywane, Tywann, Tywaun, Tywen, Tywon, Tywone, Tywonne

Tzadok (Hebrew) righteous.
Tzadik, Zadok

Tzion (Hebrew) sign from God.
Zion

Tzuriel (Hebrew) God is my rock.
Tzuriya

Tzvi (Hebrew) deer.
Tzevi, Zevi

Uaine (Irish) a form of Owen.

Ubadah (Arabic) serves God.

Ubaid (Arabic) faithful.

Ubaidah (Indian) servant of God.

Ubaldo (Germanic) he of daring thoughts.

Uberto (Italian) a form of Hubert.

Uche (Ibo) thought.

Uchit (Indian) correct.

Uchu (Quechua) hot like pepper.

Ucumari (Quechua) he who has the strength of a bear.

Udant (Hindi) correct message.

Udarsh (Hindi) brimming.

Uday (Sanskrit) to rise.

Udbal (Hindi) mighty.

Udbhav (Indian) creation; to arise from.

Uddip (Indian) giving light.

Uddiyan (Indian) flying speed.

Udeep (Indian) flood.

Udell (English) yew-tree valley.
Dell, Eudel, Udale, Udall, Yudell

Udit (Sanskrit) grown; shining.

Udo (Japanese) ginseng plant. (German) a short form of Udolf.

Udolf (English) prosperous wolf.
Udo, Udolfo, Udolph

Udu (Hindi) water.

Ugo (Italian) a form of Hugh, Hugo.

Ugutz (Basque) a form of John.

Uilliam (Irish) a form of William.
Uileog, Uilleam, Ulick

Uinseann (Irish) a form of Vincent.

Uistean (Irish) intelligent.
Uisdean

Uja (Sanskrit) growing.

Ujas (Indian) first light.

Ujendra (Indian) conqueror.

Ujesh (Indian) one who bestows light.

Ujjay (Indian) victorious.

Ujjwal, Ujval (Indian) splendorous.

Uku (Hawaiian) flea, insect; skilled ukulele player.

Ulan (African) first-born twin.

Ulbrecht (German) a form of Albert.

Ulf (German) wolf.

Ulfred (German) peaceful wolf.

Ulfrido (Teutonic) he imposes peace through force.

Ulger (German) warring wolf.

Ulises (Latin) a form of Ulysses.
Ulishes, Ulisse, Ulisses

Ullanta (Aymara) warrior who sees everything from his watchtower.

Ullantay (Quechua) lord Ollanta.

Ullas (Indian) light.

Ullock (German) sporting wolf.

Ulmer (English) famous wolf.
Ullmar, Ulmar

Ulmo (German) from Ulm, Germany.

Ulpiano, Ulpio (Latin) sly as a fox.

Ulric (German) a form of Ulrich.
Ullric

Ulrich (German) wolf ruler; ruler of all. See also Alaric.
Uli, Ull, Ulric, Ulrick, Ulrik, Ulrike, Ulu, Ulz, Uwe

Ulrico (Germanic) noble as a king.

Ultman (Hindi) god; godlike.

Ulyses (Latin) a form of Ulysses.
Ulysee, Ulysees

Ulysses (Latin) wrathful. A form of Odysseus.
Eulises, Ulick, Ulises, Ulyses, Ulysse, Ulyssees, Ulysses, Ulyssius

Umang (Sanskrit) enthusiastic.
Umanga

Umar (Arabic) a form of Omar.
Umair, Umarr, Umayr, Umer

Umberto (Italian) a form of Humbert.
Uberto

Umi (Yao) life.

Umio (Japanese) sea hero.

Umit (Turkish) hope.

Unai (Basque) shepherd.
Una

Unay (Quechua) previous; remote, underlying.

Uner (Turkish) famous.

Unika G (Lomwe) brighten.

Unique G (Latin) only, unique.
Uneek, Unek, Unikque, Uniqué, Unyque

Unnabh (Hindi) highest.

Unwin (English) nonfriend.
Unwinn, Unwyn

Upanshu (Indian) chanting of hymns or mantras in a low tone.

Uppas (Indian) gem.

Upshaw (English) upper wooded area.

Upton (English) upper town.

Upwood (English) upper forest.

Uqbah (Indian) the end of everything.

Urav (Indian) excitement.

Urban (Latin) city dweller; courteous.
Urbain, Urbaine, Urbane, Urbano, Urbanus, Urvan, Urvane

Urbane (English) a form of Urban.

Urbano (Italian) a form of Urban.

Urcucolla (Quechua) hill; the god Colla.

Uri (Hebrew) a short form of Uriah.
Urie

Uriah (Hebrew) my light. Bible: a soldier and the husband of Bathsheba. See also Yuri.
Uri, Uria, Urias, Urijah

Urian (Greek) heaven.
Urihaan

Urías (Greek) light of the lord.

Uriel **B** (Hebrew) God is my light.
Urie

Urso (Latin) bear.

Urson (French) a form of Orson.
Ursan, Ursus

Urtzi (Basque) sky.

Urvang (Indian) mountain.

Usaamah (Indian) description of a lion.

Usaku (Japanese) moonlit.

Usamah (Arabic) like a lion.
Usama

Usco, Uscu (Quechua) wild cat.

Uscouiyca, Uscuiyca (Quechua) sacred; wild cat.

Useni (Yao) tell me.
Usene, Usenet

Ushakanta (Indian) sun.

Ushapati (Indian) husband of dawn.

Ushi (Chinese) ox.

Usi (Yao) smoke.

Ustin (Russian) a form of Justin.

Usuy (Quechua) he who brings abundances.

Utanka (Indian) a disciple of the sage Veda.

Utatci (Moquelumnan) bear scratching itself.

Uthman (Arabic) companion of the Prophet.
Usman, Uthmaan

Utkarsh (Hindi) high quality.

Utkarsha (Indian) advancement.

Utpal (Indian) burst open.

Utsav (Indian) festival.

Uttam (Sanskrit) best.

Uttiya (Indian) a name in Buddhist literature.

Uturuncu (Quechua) jaguar; tiger; the bravest.

Uturuncu Achachi (Quechua) he who has brave ancestors, jaguar ancestors.

Uwe (German) a familiar form of Ulrich.

Uzi (Hebrew) my strength.
Uzzia

Uziel (Hebrew) God is my strength; mighty force.
Uzie, Uzziah, Uzziel

Uzoma (Nigerian) born during a journey.

Uzumati (Moquelumnan) grizzly bear.

V

V G (American) an initial used as a first name.

Vachel (French) small cow.
Vache, Vachell

Vaclav (Czech) wreath of glory.
Vasek

Vadin (Hindi) speaker.
Vaden

Vaijayi (Indian) victor.

Vaikartan (Indian) name of Karna.

Vaikunth (Indian) abode of Vishnu.

Vail B (English) valley.
Vaile, Vaill, Vale, Valle

Vairaj (Indian) spiritual glory.

Vairat (Indian) gem.

Vaishvik (Indian) belonging to the world.

Vajramani (Indian) diamond.

Val B (Latin) a short form of Valentin.

Valborg (Swedish) mighty mountain.

Valdemar (Swedish) famous ruler.

Valdo (Teutonic) he who governs, the monarch.

Valentin (Latin) strong; healthy.
Val, Valencio, Valenté, Valentijn, Valentine, Valentino, Valenton, Valentyn, Velentino

Valentín (Latin) a form of Valentin.

Valentino (Italian) a form of Valentin.

Valerian (Latin) strong; healthy.
Valeriano, Valerii, Valerio, Valeryn

Valerie G (Russian) a form of Valerii.

Valerii (Russian) a form of Valerian.
Valera, Valerie, Valerij, Valerik, Valeriy, Valery

Valfredo (Germanic) peaceful king.

Valfrid (Swedish) strong peace.

Valin (Hindi) a form of Balin. Mythology: a tyrannical monkey king.

Vallis (French) from Wales.
Valis

Valter (Lithuanian, Swedish) a form of Walter.
Valters, Valther, Valtr, Vanda

Van (Dutch) a short form of Vandyke.
Vander, Vane, Vann, Vanno

Vanad (Hindi) cloud.

Vance B (English) thresher.

Vanda G (Lithuanian) a form of Walter.
Vander

Vandyke (Dutch) dyke.
Van

Vanessa G (Greek) butterfly.

Vaninath (Indian) husband of goddess Saraswati.

Vansh (Indian) the coming generation.

Vanya (Russian) a familiar form of Ivan.
Vanechka, Vanek, Vanja, Vanka, Vanusha, Wanya

Varana (Indian) holy river.

Vardon (French) green knoll.
Vardaan, Varden, Verdan, Verdon, Verdun

Varian (Latin) variable.

Varick (German) protecting ruler.
Varak, Varek, Warrick

Vartan (Armenian) rose producer;
rose giver.

Varun (Hindi) rain god.
Varron

Vasant (Sanskrit) spring.
Vasanth

Vasavaj, Vasavi (Indian) son of Indra.

Vashawn (American) a combination
of the prefix Va + Shawn.
*Vashae, Vashan, Vashann, Vashaun,
Vashawnn, Vashon, Vashun, Vishon*

Vashita (Indian) one who hypnotizes
by her virtues.

Vasilis (Greek) a form of Basil.
*Vas, Vasaya, Vaselios, Vashon, Vasil,
Vasile, Vasileior, Vasileios, Vasilios,
Vasilius, Vasilos, Vasilus, Vasily,
Vassilios, Vasylko, Vasyltso, Vazul*

Vasily (Russian) a form of Vasilis.
*Vasilek, Vasili, Vasilii, Vasilije, Vasilik,
Vasiliy, Vassili, Vassilij, Vasya,
Vasyenka*

Vasin (Hindi) ruler, lord.

Vasu (Sanskrit) wealth.

Vasuman (Indian) born of fire.

Vasur (Hindi) precious.

Vasyl (German, Slavic) a form of
William.
*Vasos, Vassily, Vassos, Vasya,
Vasyuta, VaVaska, Wassily*

Vatsa (Hindi) son.

Vaughn **B** (Welsh) small.
*Vaughan, Vaughen, Vaun, Vaune,
Von, Voughn*

Vayun (Hindi) lively.

Vayya (Indian) friend.

Veasna (Cambodian) lucky.

Ved (Sanskrit) sacred knowledge.

Vedaant (Indian) the scriptures.

Vedang (Indian) from the Vedas.

Vedant (Indian) Hindu philosophy.

Vedbhushan (Indian) one adorned
with knowledge of the Vedas.

Vedie (Latin) sight.

Veer (Sanskrit) brave.

Veerbhadra (Indian) the
Ashwamedha horse.

Vegard (Norwegian) sanctuary;
protection.

Velvel (Yiddish) wolf.

Venancio (Latin) a fan of hunting.

Vencel (Hungarian) a short form of
Wenceslaus.
Venci, Vencie

Venceslao (Slavic) crowned with
glory.

Venedictos (Greek) a form of
Benedict.
Venedict, Venediktos, Venka, Venya

Veniamin (Bulgarian) a form of
Benjamin.
Venyamin, Verniamin

Venkat (Hindi) god; godlike.
Religion: another name for the
Hindu god Vishnu.

Ventura (Latin) he who will be happy.

Venturo (Spanish) food fortune.

Venya (Russian) a familiar form of
Benedict.
Venedict, Venka

Vere (Latin, French) true.

Vered (Hebrew) rose.

Vergil (Latin) a form of Virgil.
Literature: a Roman poet best
known for his epic poem *Aenid*.
Verge

Vern (Latin) a short form of Vernon.
Verna, Vernal, Verne, Verneal, Vernel,
Vernell, Vernelle, Vernial, Vernine,
Vernis, Vernol

Vernados (German) courage of the
bear.

Verner (German) defending army.
Varner

Verney (French) alder grove.
Vernie

Vernon (Latin) springlike; youthful.
Vern, Varnan, Vernen, Verney, Vernin

Vero (Latin) truthful, sincere,
credible.

Verrill (German) masculine. (French)
loyal.
Verill, Verrall, Verrell, Verroll, Veryl

Vespasiano (Latin) name of the
Roman emperor from the first
century.

Vian (English) full of life.

Vibhaas (Indian) shining.

Vibhakar (Indian) one emitting light.

Vibhas (Indian) luminous.

Vibhat (Indian) dawn.

Vibhishan (Indian) a character from
the epic Ramayana.

Vibhor (Indian) ecstatic.

Vibhu (Indian) all-pervading.

Vibhut (Indian) strong.

Vibodh (Hindi) wise.

Vic (Latin) a short form of Victor.
Vick, Vicken, Vickenson

Vicente 🇧 (Spanish) a form of
Vincent.
Vicent, Visente

Vicenzo (Italian) a form of Vincent.

Vicky 🇬 (Latin) a familiar form of
Victoria.

Victoir (French) a form of Victor.

Victor (Latin) victor, conqueror.
Vic, Victa, Victer, Victoir, Victoriano,
Victorien, Victorin, Victorio, Viktor,
Vitin, Vittorio, Vitya, Wikoli, Wiktor,
Witek

Víctor (Spanish) a form of Victor.

Victoria 🇬 (Latin) a form of Victor.

Victorio (Spanish) a form of Victor.
Victorino

Victoro (Latin) victor.

Vidal (Spanish) a form of Vitas.
Vida, Vidale, Vidall, Videll

Vidar (Norwegian) tree warrior.

Videl (Spanish) life.

Vidip (Indian) bright.

Vidor (Hungarian) cheerful.

Vidur (Hindi) wise.

Vidyacharan (Indian) learned.

Vidyadhar (Indian) demigod.

Vidyanand (Indian) one who enjoys
learning.

Vidyaranya (Indian) forest of
knowledge.

Vidyasagar (Indian) ocean of
knowledge.

Vidyut (Hindi) brilliant.

Vien (Vietnamese) completion, accomplishment; satisfaction.

Vihaan (Hindi) morning, dawn.

Vihang, Vihanga (Indian) a bird.

Viho (Cheyenne) chief.

Vijanyendra, Vijendra (Indian) victorious.

Vijay (Hindi) victorious.

Vijayendra (Indian) the god of victory.

Vijayketu (Indian) the flag of victory.

Vijval (Hindi) intelligent.

Vikas (Hindi) growing.
Vikash, Vikesh

Vikhyath (Indian) fame.

Vikram (Hindi) valorous.
Vikrum

Vikramaditya, Vikramajit (Indian) a famous king.

Vikramendra (Indian) king of prowess.

Vikrant (Hindi) powerful.
Vikran

Vikranta (Indian) brave.

Viktor (German, Hungarian, Russian) a form of Victor.
Viktoras, Viktors

Vilas (Hindi) coolness.

Vilfredo (Germanic) peaceful king.

Vilhelm (German) a form of William.
Vilhelms, Vilho, Vilis, Viljo, Villem

Vili (Hungarian) a short form of William.
Villy, Vilmos

Viliam (Czech) a form of William.
Vila, Vilek, Vilém, Viliami, Viliamu, Vilko, Vilous

Viljo (Finnish) a form of William.

Ville (Swedish) a short form of William.

Vilok (Indian) to see.

Vilokan (Indian) gaze.

Vimal (Hindi) pure.

Vimaladitya (Indian) clean sun.

Vimalmani (Indian) pure jewel.

Vin (Latin) a short form of Vincent.
Vinn

Vinay (Hindi) polite.

Vince (English) a short form of Vincent.
Vence, Vint

Vincent **B** (Latin) victor, conqueror. See also Binkentios, Binky.
Uinseann, Vencent, Vicente, Vicenzo, Vikent, Vikenti, Vikesha, Vin, Vince, Vincence, Vincens, Vincente, Vincentius, Vincents, Vincenty, Vincenzo, Vinci, Vincien, Vincient, Vinciente, Vincint, Vinny, Vinsent, Vinsint, Wincent

Vincente (Spanish) a form of Vincent.
Vencente

Vincenzo (Italian) a form of Vincent.
Vincenz, Vincenza, Vincenzio, Vinchenzo, Vinzenz

Vinci (Hungarian, Italian) a familiar form of Vincent.
Vinci, Vinco, Vincze

Vineet (Hindi) knowledgeable.

Vinesh (Hindi) godly.

Vinh (Vietnamese) bay, gulf.

Vinil (Indian) blue.

Vinny (English) a familiar form of Calvin, Melvin, Vincent.
Vinnee, Vinney, Vinni, Vinnie

Vinod (Hindi) happy, joyful.
Vinodh, Vinood

Vinoth (Indian) pleasing.

Vinson (English) son of Vincent.
Vinnis

Vipan (Indian) sail; small trade.

Vipin (Indian) forest.

Vipinbehari (Indian) forest wanderer.

Viplab (Indian) floating; revolution.

Viplav (Indian) drifting about; revolution.

Vipra (Indian) a priest.

Vipul (Hindi) plentiful.

Viraaj (Indian) king.

Viraj (Hindi) resplendent.

Viral (Hindi) precious.

Virat (Hindi) very big.

Virgil (Latin) rod bearer, staff bearer.
Vergil, Virge, Virgial, Virgie, Virgilio

Virgilio (Spanish) a form of Virgil.
Virjilio

Virginio (Latin) he is pure and simple.

Virote (Tai) strong, powerful.

Virurch, Vishresh (Indian) the Holy Trinity.

Vishal (Hindi) huge; great.
Vishaal

Vishesh (Hindi) special.

Vishnu (Hindi) protector.

Vishnudev (Indian) God.

Vishnudutt (Indian) gift of Vishnu.

Vishva (Indian) the universe.

Vishvajit (Indian) conqueror of the world.

Vishvakarma (Indian) architect of the universe.

Vishvamitra (Indian) a sage.

Vishvas (Indian) faith.

Vishvatma, Vishwatma (Indian) universal soul.

Vishwa (Indian) earth; universe.

Vishwajit (Indian) one who conquers the universe.

Vishwakarma (Indian) architect of the universe.

Vishwalochan (Indian) eyes of the universe.

Vishwambhar (Indian) the all-pervading one.

Vishwamitra (Indian) friend of the universe.

Vishwanath, Viswanath (Indian) god of the universe.

Vishwankar (Indian) creator of the universe.

Vishwas (Indian) faith; trust.

Vitaliano, Vitalicio (Latin) young and strong.

Vitas (Latin) alive, vital.
Vidal, Vitus

Vito (Latin) a short form of Vittorio.
Veit, Vidal, Vital, Vitale, Vitalis, Vitas, Vitin, Vitis, Vitus, Vitya, Vytas

Vitola (Indian) peaceful.

Vítor (Latin) victor.

Vittanath (Indian) owner of money.

Vittorio (Italian) a form of Victor.
Vito, Vitor, Vitorio, Vittore, Vittorios

Vitya (Russian) a form of Victor.
Vitenka, Vitka

Vivash (Hindi) bright.

Vivek (Hindi) wisdom.
Vivekinan

Vivekanand (Indian) joy of discrimination.

Vivian **G** (Latin) full of life.

Viviano (Spanish) small man.

Vladimir (Russian) famous prince. See also Dima, Waldemar, Walter.
Bladimir, Vimka, Vlad, Vladamir, Vladik, Vladimar, Vladimeer, Vladimer, Vladimere, Vladimire, Vladimyr, Vladjimir, Vladka, Vladko, Vladlen, Vladmir, Volodimir, Volodya, Volya, Vova, Wladimir

Vladimiro (Spanish) a form of Vladimir.

Vladislav (Slavic) glorious ruler. See also Slava.
Vladik, Vladya, Vlas, Vlasislava, Vyacheslav, Wladislav

Vlas (Russian) a short form of Vladislav.

Volker (German) people's guard.
Folke

Volney (German) national spirit.

Von (German) a short form of many German names.

Vova (Russian) a form of Walter.
Vovka

Vrishab (Hindi) excellent.

Vrishin (Indian) peacock.

Vrushket (Indian) son of Karna.

Vuai (Swahili) savior.

Vulpiano (Latin) sly as a fox.

Vuong (Vietnamese) prosperous, developed.

Vyacheslav (Russian) a form of Vladislav. See also Slava.

Vyan (Indian) air.

Vyas (Indian) sage who wrote *Mahabharat*.

Vyoman (Indian) sky.

W

W **B** (American) an initial used as a first name.

Waahid (Indian) single; exclusively; unequaled.

Waa'il (Indian) coming back for shelter.

Waban (Ojibwa) white.
Wabon

Wade (English) ford; river crossing.
Wad, Wadesworth, Wadi, Wadie, Waed, Waid, Waide, Wayde, Waydell, Whaid

Wadee' (Indian) calm, peaceful.

Wadley (English) ford meadow.
Wadleigh, Wadly

Wadsworth (English) village near the ford.
Waddsworth

Wafeeq (Indian) successful.

Wagner (German) wagoner, wagon maker. Music: Richard Wagner was a famous nineteenth-century German composer.
Waggoner

Wahid (Arabic) single; exclusively unequaled.
Waheed

Wahkan (Lakota) sacred.

Wahkoowah (Lakota) charging.

Wain (English) a short form of Wainwright. A form of Wayne.

Wainwright (English) wagon maker.
Wain, Wainright, Wayne, Wayneright, Waynewright, Waynright, Wright

Waite (English) watchman.
Waitman, Waiton, Waits, Wayte

Wajeeh (Indian) noble.

Wakaki (Japanese) young; life; brilliant.

Wakato (Japanese) youthful person.

Wakefield (English) wet field.
Field, Wake

Wakely (English) wet meadow.

Wakeman (English) watchman.
Wake

Wakin (Chuukese) a form of Joaquin.

Wakiza (Native American) determined warrior.

Walcott (English) cottage by the wall.
Wallcot, Wallcott, Wolcott

Waldemar (German) powerful; famous. See also Vladimir.
Valdemar, Waldermar, Waldo

Walden (English) wooded valley. Literature: Henry David Thoreau made Walden Pond famous with his book *Walden*.
Waldi, Waldo, Waldon, Welti

Waldino (Teutonic) having an open and bold spirit.

Waldo (German) a familiar form of Oswald, Waldemar, Walden.
Wald, Waldy

Waldron (English) ruler.

Waleed (Arabic) newborn.
Waled, Walid

Walerian (Polish) strong; brave.

Wales (English) from Wales.
Wael, Wail, Wali, Walie, Waly

Walford (English) Welshman's ford.

Walfred (German) peaceful ruler.
Walfredo, Walfried

Wali (Arabic) all-governing.

Waliyudeen (Indian) supporter of the faith.

Waliyullah (Indian) supporter of God.

Walker 🅱 (English) cloth walker; cloth cleaner.
Wallie, Wally

Wallace (English) from Wales.
Wallach, Wallas, Wallie, Wallis, Wally, Walsh, Welsh

Wallach (German) a form of Wallace.
Wallache

Waller (German) powerful. (English) wall maker.

Wally (English) a familiar form of Walter.
Walli, Wallie

Walmond (German) mighty ruler.

Walsh (English) a form of Wallace.
Welch, Welsh

Walt (English) a short form of
Walter, Walton.
Waltey, Waltli, Walty

Walter (German) army ruler, general.
(English) woodsman. See also
Gautier, Gualberto, Gualtiero,
Gutierre, Ladislav, Vladimir.
*Valter, Vanda, Vova, Walder, Wally,
Walt, Waltli, Walther, Waltr, Wat,
Waterio, Watkins, Watson, Wualter*

Walther (German) a form of Walter.

Walton (English) walled town.
Walt

Waltr (Czech) a form of Walter.

Walworth (English) fenced-in farm.

Walwyn (English) Welsh friend.
*Walwin, Walwinn, Walwynn,
Walwynne, Welwyn*

Wamblee (Lakota) eagle.

Wan (Chinese) ten thousand.

Wang (Chinese) hope; wish.

Wanikiya (Lakota) savior.

Wanya **B** (Russian) a form of
Vanya.
Wanyai

Wapi (Native American) lucky.

Warburton (English) fortified town.

Ward (English) watchman, guardian.
Warde, Warden, Worden

Wardell (English) watchman's hill.

Wardley (English) watchman's
meadow.
Wardlea, Wardleigh

Ware (English) wary, cautious.

Warfield (English) field near the weir
or fish trap.

Warford (English) ford near the weir
or fish trap.

Warley (English) meadow near the
weir or fish trap.

Warner (German) armed defender.
(French) park keeper.
Werner

Warren (German) general; warden;
rabbit hutch.
*Ware, Waring, Warrenson, Warrin,
Warriner, Worrin*

Warton (English) town near the weir
or fish trap.

Warwick (English) buildings near the
weir or fish trap.
Warick, Warrick

Washburn (English) overflowing
river.

Washi (Japanese) eagle.

Washington (English) town near
water. History: George Washington
was the first U.S. president.
Wash

Wasili (Russian) a form of Basil.
Wasyl

Wasim (Arabic) graceful; good-
looking.
Waseem, Wasseem, Wassim

Wataru (Japanese) he who reaches
out to others.

Watende (Nyakyusa) there will be
revenge.

Waterio (Spanish) a form of Walter.
Gualtiero

Watford (English) wattle ford; dam
made of twigs and sticks.

Watkins (English) son of Walter.
Watkin

Watson (English) son of Walter.
Wathson, Whatson

Waverly 🅖 (English) quaking aspen-
tree meadow.
Waverlee, Waverley

Wayland (English) a form of Waylon.
Weiland, Weyland

Waylon (English) land by the road.
*Wallen, Walon, Way, Waylan,
Wayland, Waylen, Waylin, Weylin*

Wayman (English) road man; traveler.
Waymon

Wayne (English) wagon maker. A
short form of Wainwright.
*Wain, Wanye, Wayn, Waynell,
Waynne, Wene, Whayne*

Wazir (Arabic) minister.

Webb (English) weaver.
Web, Weeb

Weber (German) weaver.
Webber, Webner

Webley (English) weaver's meadow.
Webbley, Webbly, Webly

Webster (English) weaver.

Weddel (English) valley near the
ford.

Wei-Quo (Chinese) ruler of the
country.
Wei

Welborne (English) spring-fed
stream.
*Welborn, Welbourne, Welburn,
Wellborn, Wellborne, Wellbourn,
Wellburn*

Welby (German) farm near the well.
Welbey, Welbie, Wellbey, Wellby

Weldon (English) hill near the well.
Weldan

Welfel (Yiddish) a form of William.
Welvel

Welford (English) ford near the well.

Wells (English) springs.
Welles

Welsh (English) a form of Wallace,
Walsh.
Welch

Welton (English) town near the well.

Wemilat (Native American) all give
to him.

Wemilo (Native American) all speak
to him.

Wen (Gypsy) born in winter.

Wenceslaus (Slavic) wreath of honor.
*Vencel, Wenceslao, Wenceslas,
Wenzel, Wenzell, Wiencyslaw*

Wendell (German) wanderer.
(English) good dale, good valley.
*Wandale, Wendall, Wendel, Wendle,
Wendy*

Wene (Hawaiian) a form of Wayne.

Wenford (English) white ford.
Wynford

Wentworth (English) pale man's
settlement.

Wenutu (Native American) clear sky.

Werner (English) a form of Warner.
Wernhar, Wernher

Wes (English) a short form of Wesley.
Wess

Wesh (Gypsy) woods.

Wesley 🅑 (English) western
meadow.
*Wes, Weseley, Wesle, Weslee,
Wesleyan, Weslie, Wesly, Wessley,
Westleigh, Westley, Wezley*

West (English) west.

Westbrook (English) western brook.
Brook, West, Westbrooke

Westby (English) western farmstead.

Westcott (English) western cottage.
Wescot, Wescott, Westcot

Westley (English) a form of Wesley.
Westlee, Westly

Weston B (English) western town.
West, Westen, Westin

Wetherby (English) wether-sheep
farm.
*Weatherbey, Weatherbie,
Weatherby, Wetherbey, Wetherbie*

Wetherell (English) wether-sheep
corner.

Wetherly (English) wether-sheep
meadow.

Weylin (English) a form of Waylon.
Weylan, Weylyn

Whalley (English) woods near a hill.
Whaley

Wharton (English) town on the bank
of a lake.
Warton

Wheatley (English) wheat field.
*Whatley, Wheatlea, Wheatleigh,
Wheatly*

Wheaton (English) wheat town.

Wheeler (English) wheel maker;
wagon driver.

Whistler (English) whistler, piper.

Whit (English) a short form of
Whitman, Whitney.
Whitt, Whyt, Whyte, Wit, Witt

Whitby (English) white house.

Whitcomb (English) white valley.
Whitcombe, Whitcumb

Whitelaw (English) small hill.
Whitlaw

Whitey (English) white skinned;
white haired.

Whitfield (English) white field.

Whitford (English) white ford.

Whitley G (English) white meadow.
Whitlea, Whitlee, Whitleigh

Whitman (English) white-haired man.
Whit

Whitmore (English) white moor.
*Whitmoor, Whittemore, Witmore,
Wittemore*

Whitney G (English) white island;
white water.
Whit, Whittney, Widney, Widny

Whittaker (English) white field.
Whitacker, Whitaker, Whitmaker

Wicasa (Dakota) man.

Wicent (Polish) a form of Vincent.
Wicek, Wicus

Wichado (Native American) willing.

Wickham (English) village enclosure.
Wick

Wickley (English) village meadow.
Wilcley

Wid (English) wide.

Wies (German) renowned warrior.

Wikoli (Hawaiian) a form of Victor.

Wiktor (Polish) a form of Victor.

Wilanu (Moquelumnan) pouring
water on flour.

Wilbert (German) brilliant; resolute.
Wilberto, Wilburt

Wilbur (English) wall fortification;
bright willows.
*Wilber, Wilburn, Wilburt, Willbur,
Wilver*

Wilder (English) wilderness, wild.
Wylder

Wildon (English) wooded hill.
Wilden, Willdon

Wile (Hawaiian) a form of Willie.

Wiley (English) willow meadow;
Will's meadow.
Whiley, Wildy, Willey, Wylie

Wilford (English) willow-tree ford.
Wilferd

Wilfred (German) determined
peacemaker.
*Wilferd, Wilfredo, Wilfrid, Wilfride,
Wilfried, Wilfryd, Will, Willfred,
Willfried, Willie, Willy*

Wilfredo (Spanish) a form of
Wilfred.
Fredo, Wifredo, Wilfrido, Willfredo

Wilhelm (German) determined
guardian.
Wilhelmus, Willem

Wiliama (Hawaiian) a form of
William.
Pila, Wile

Wilkie (English) a familiar form of
Wilkins.
Wikie, Wilke

Wilkins (English) William's kin.
*Wilkens, Wilkes, Wilkie, Wilkin, Wilks,
Willkes, Willkins*

Wilkinson (English) son of little
William.
Wilkenson, Willkinson

Will (English) a short form of
William.
Wil, Wilm, Wim

Willard (German) determined and
brave.
Williard

Willem (German) a form of William.
Willim

William ☼ **B** (English) a form
of Wilhelm. See also Gilamu,
Guglielmo, Guilherme, Guillaume,
Guillermo, Gwilym, Liam, Uilliam,
Wilhelm.
*Bill, Billy, Vasyl, Vilhelm, Vili, Viliam,
Viljo, Ville, Villiam, Welfel, Wilek,
Wiliam, Wiliama, Wiliame, Will,
Willaim, Willam, Willeam, Willem,
Williams, Willie, Willil, Willis, Willium,
Williw, Willyam, Wim*

Williams (German) son of William.
*Wilams, Willaims, Williamson,
Wuliams*

Willie **B** (German) a familiar form
of William.
Wile, Wille, Willi, Willia, Willy

Willis (German) son of Willie.
Willice, Wills, Willus, Wyllis

Willoughby (English) willow farm.
Willoughbey, Willoughbie

Wills (English) son of Will.

Willy (German) a form of Willie.
Willey, Wily

Wilmer (German) determined and
famous.
*Willimar, Willmer, Wilm, Wilmar,
Wylmar, Wylmer*

Wilmot (Teutonic) resolute spirit.
Willmont, Willmot, Wilm, Wilmont

Wilny (Native American) eagle
singing while flying.

Wilson **B** (English) son of Will.
Wilkinson, Willson, Wilsen, Wolson

Wilt (English) a short form of
Wilton.

Wilton (English) farm by the spring.
Will, Wilt

Wilu (Moquelumnan) chicken hawk squawking.

Win **B** (Cambodian) bright. (English) a short form of Winston and names ending in "win."
Winn, Winnie, Winny

Wincent (Polish) a form of Vincent.
Wicek, Wicenty, Wicus, Wince, Wincenty

Winchell (English) bend in the road; bend in the land.

Windsor (English) riverbank with a winch. History: the surname of the British royal family.
Wincer, Winsor, Wyndsor

Winfield (English) friendly field.
Field, Winfred, Winfrey, Winifield, Winnfield, Wynfield, Wynnfield

Winfried (German) friend of peace.

Wing (Chinese) glory.
Wing-Chiu, Wing-Kit

Wingate (English) winding gate.

Wingi (Native American) willing.

Winslow (English) friend's hill.

Winston (English) friendly town; victory town.
Win, Winsten, Winstin, Winstonn, Winton, Wynstan, Wynston

Winter **G** (English) born in winter.
Winterford, Wynter

Winthrop (English) victory at the crossroads.

Winton (English) a form of Winston.
Wynten, Wynton

Winward (English) friend's guardian; friend's forest.

Wit (Polish) life. (English) a form of Whit. (Flemish) a short form of DeWitt.
Witt, Wittie, Witty

Witek (Polish) a form of Victor.

Witha (Arabic) handsome.

Witter (English) wise warrior.

Witton (English) wise man's estate.

Wladislav (Polish) a form of Vladislav.
Wladislaw

Wo (Chinese) fertile.

Wolcott (English) cottage in the woods.

Wolf (German, English) a short form of Wolfe, Wolfgang.
Wolff, Wolfie, Wolfy

Wolfe (English) wolf.
Wolf, Woolf

Wolfgang (German) wolf quarrel. Music: Wolfgang Amadeus Mozart was a famous eighteenth-century Austrian composer.
Wolf, Wolfegang, Wolfgans

Wood (English) a short form of Elwood, Garwood, Woodrow.
Woody

Woodfield (English) forest meadow.

Woodford (English) ford through the forest.

Woodrow (English) passage in the woods. History: Thomas Woodrow Wilson was the twenty-eighth U.S. president.
Wood, Woodman, Woodroe, Woody

Woodruff (English) forest ranger.

Woodson (English) son of Wood.
Woods, Woodsen

Woodville (English) town at the edge of the woods.

Woodward (English) forest warden.
Woodard

Woody (American) a familiar form of Elwood, Garwood, Woodrow.
Wooddy, Woodie

Woolsey (English) victorious wolf.

Worcester (English) forest army camp.

Wordsworth (English) wolf-guardian's farm. Literature: William Wordsworth was a famous British poet.
Worth

Worie (Ibo) born on market day.

Worth (English) a short form of Wordsworth.
Worthey, Worthington, Worthy

Worton (English) farm town.

Wouter (German) powerful warrior.

Wrangle (American) a form of Rangle.
Wrangler

Wray (Scandinavian) corner property. (English) crooked.
Wreh

Wren (Welsh) chief, ruler. (English) wren.

Wright (English) a short form of Wainwright.

Wrisley (English) a form of Risley.
Wrisee, Wrislie, Wrisly

Wriston (English) a form of Riston.
Wryston

Wu (Chinese) army squad; crow; sorcerer.

Wuliton (Native American) will do well.

Wunand (Native American) God is good.

Wuyi (Moquelumnan) turkey vulture flying.

Wyatt ☝ **B** (French) little warrior.
Wiatt, Wyat, Wyatte, Wye, Wyeth, Wyett, Wyitt, Wytt

Wybert (English) battle bright.

Wyborn (Scandinavian) war bear.

Wyck (Scandinavian) village.

Wycliff (English) white cliff; village near the cliff.
Wyckliffe, Wycliffe

Wylie (English) charming.
Wiley, Wye, Wyley, Wyllie, Wyly

Wyman (English) fighter, warrior.

Wymer (English) famous in battle.

Wyn (Welsh) light skinned; white. (English) friend. A short form of Selwyn.
Win, Wyne, Wynn, Wynne

Wyndham (Scottish) village near the winding road.
Windham, Wynndham

Wynono (Native American) first-born son.

Wythe (English) willow tree.

X

Xabat (Basque) savior.

Xaiver (Basque) a form of Xavier.
Xajavier, Xzaiver

Xan (Greek) a short form of Alexander.
Xane

Xander (Greek) a short form of Alexander.
Xande, Xzander

Xanthus (Latin) golden haired.
Xanthos

Xarles (Basque) a form of Charles.

Xavier ☀ **B** (Arabic) bright. (Basque) owner of the new house. See also Exavier, Javier, Salvatore, Saverio.
Xabier, Xaiver, Xavaeir, Xaver, Xavian, Xaviar, Xavior, Xavon, Xavyer, Xever, Xizavier, Xxavier, Xzavier, Zavier

Xenophon (Greek) strange voice.
Xeno, Zennie

Xenos (Greek) stranger; guest.
Zenos

Xerxes (Persian) ruler. History: a king of Persia.
Zerk

Xi (Chinese) uncommon.

Xia (Chinese) the glow of sunrise or sunset.

Xiang (Chinese) to soar; auspicious; fragrant.

Xiao-Chen (Chinese) early morning.

Xiaoping (Chinese) brightest star.

Xie (Chinese) harmonious.

Ximenes (Spanish) a form of Simon.
Ximenez, Ximon, Ximun, Xymenes

Xing (Chinese) to rise, spring up.

Xing-Fu (Chinese) happy.

Xiong (Chinese) mighty; hero.

Xiu (Chinese) mastery.

Xi-Wang (Chinese) optimistic.

Xochiel, Xochtiel (Nahuatl) flower.

Xu (Chinese) open minded.

Xuan (Vietnamese) spring.

Xue (Chinese) snow; studious.

Xue-Fang (Chinese) snow; fragrant.

Xun (Chinese) fast.

Xylon (Greek) forest.

Xzavier (Basque) a form of Xavier.
Xzavaier, Xzaver, Xzavion, Xzavior, Xzvaier

Y

Ya (Chinese) refined; correct.

Yacu (Quechua) water.

Yadid (Hebrew) friend; beloved.
Yedid

Yadira **G** (Hebrew) friend.

Yadon (Hebrew) he will judge.
Yadean, Yadin, Yadun

Yael **G** (Hebrew) a form of Jael.

Yafeu (Ibo) bold.

Yagil (Hebrew) he will rejoice.

Yago (Spanish) a form of James.

Yaguatí (Guarani) leopard.

Yahto (Lakota) blue.

Yahya (Arabic) living.
Yahye

Yair (Hebrew) he will enlighten.
Yahir

Yajas (Indian) fame.

Yakecen (Dene) sky song.

Yakez (Carrier) heaven.

Yakov (Russian) a form of Jacob.
Yaacob, Yaacov, Yaakov, Yachov,
Yacoub, Yacov, Yakob, Yashko

Yale (German) productive. (English)
old.

Yamato (Japanese) mountain; scaling
heights.

Yamqui (Aymara) title of nobility,
master.

Yan, Yann 🅱 (Russian) forms of
John.
Yanichek, Yanick, Yanka, Yannick

Yana (Native American) bear.

Yanamayu (Quechua) black river.

Yancy (Native American)
Englishman, Yankee.
Yan, Yance, Yancey, Yanci, Yansey,
Yansy, Yantsey, Yauncey, Yauncy,
Yency

Yanick, Yannick (Russian) familiar
forms of Yan.
Yanic, Yanik, Yannic, Yannik, Yonic,
Yonnik

Yanka (Russian) a familiar form of
John.
Yanikm

Yanni (Greek) a form of John.
Ioannis, Yani, Yannakis, Yannis,
Yanny, Yiannis, Yoni

Yanton (Hebrew) a form of
Johnathon, Jonathon.

Yan-Yan (Chinese) swallow; elegant.

Yao (Ewe) born on Thursday.

Yao-Shih (Chinese) master of
healing.

Yaphet (Hebrew) a form of Japheth.
Yapheth, Yefat, Yephat

Yarb (Gypsy) herb.

Yardan (Arabic) king.

Yarden (Hebrew) a form of Jordan.

Yardley (English) enclosed meadow.
Lee, Yard, Yardlea, Yardlee,
Yardleigh, Yardly

Yarom (Hebrew) he will raise up.
Yarum

Yaron (Hebrew) he will sing; he will
cry out.
Jaron, Yairon

Yasashiku (Japanese) gentle; polite.

Yash (Hindi) victorious; glory.

Yasha (Russian) a form of Jacob,
James.
Yascha, Yashka, Yashko

Yashneil (Indian) famous; glorious;
successful.

Yashodhar (Indian) one who has
gained fame.

Yashwant (Hindi) glorious.

Yashwanth (Indian) always famous.

Yasin (Arabic) prophet.
Yasine, Yasseen, Yassin, Yassine,
Yazen

Yasir (Afghan) humble; takes it easy.
(Arabic) wealthy.
Yasar, Yaser, Yashar, Yasser

Yasuo (Japanese) restful.

Yasushi (Japanese) peace; historian.

Yasutaro (Japanese) peaceful.

Yates (English) gates.
Yeats

Yatin (Hindi) ascetic.

Yauar (Quechua) blood.

Yauarguacac (Quechua) he sheds tears of blood.

Yauarpuma (Quechua) puma blood.

Yauri (Quechua) lance, needle; copper.

Yavin (Hebrew) he will understand.
Jabin

Yawo (Akan) born on Thursday.

Yazid (Arabic) his power will increase.
Yazeed, Yazide

Ye (Chinese) professional work.

Yechiel (Hebrew) God lives.

Yedidya (Hebrew) a form of Jedidiah. See also Didi.
Yadai, Yedidia, Yedidiah, Yido

Yegor (Russian) a form of George. See also Egor, Igor.
Ygor

Yehoshua (Hebrew) a form of Joshua.
Yeshua, Yeshuah, Yoshua, Y'shua, Yushua

Yehoyakem (Hebrew) a form of Joachim, Joaquín.
Yakim, Yehayakim, Yokim, Yoyakim

Yehuai (Hebrew) a form of Judah.
Yechudi, Yechudit, Yehuda, Yehudah, Yehudit

Yelutci (Moquelumnan) bear walking silently.

Yemon (Japanese) guarding the palace.

Yen (Chinese) calming; capable.

Yeng-Wang-Yeh (Chinese) ruler of hell.

Yens (Vietnamese) calm.

Yeoman (English) attendant; retainer.
Yoeman, Youman

Yeremey (Russian) a form of Jeremiah.
Yarema, Yaremka, Yeremy, Yerik

Yervant (Armenian) king, ruler. History: an Armenian king.

Yeshaya (Hebrew) gift. See also Shai.

Yeshurun (Hebrew) right way.

Yeshwant (Indian) success.

Yeshwanth (Indian) a person who attains fame and glory.

Yeska (Russian) a form of Joseph.
Yesya

Yestin (Welsh) just.

Yevgenyi (Russian) a form of Eugene.
Gena, Yevgeni, Yevgenij, Yevgeniy

Yigal (Hebrew) he will redeem.
Yagel, Yigael

Yi-Jie (Chinese) happy; pure.

Yi-Min (Chinese) happy; smart.

Yin (Chinese) flourishing.

Ying (Chinese) hawk, eagle.

Yirmaya (Hebrew) a form of Jeremiah.
Yirmayahu

Yishai (Hebrew) a form of Jesse.

Yisrael (Hebrew) a form of Israel.
Yesarel, Yisroel

Yitro (Hebrew) a form of Jethro.

Yitzchak (Hebrew) a form of Isaac. See also Itzak.
Yitzak, Yitzchok, Yitzhak

Ynaganta (Chamorro) a form of Inagangta.

Yngve (Swedish) ancestor; lord, master.

Yo (Cambodian) honest.

Yoakim (Slavic) a form of Jacob.
Yoackim

Yoan (German) a form of Johan, Johann.
Yoann

Yoav (Hebrew) a form of Joab.

Yochanan (Hebrew) a form of John.
Yohanan

Yoel (Hebrew) a form of Joel.

Yog (Japanese) yoga practitioner.

Yoga (Japanese) he who makes things grow.

Yogendra (Indian) again; god of yoga.

Yogesh (Hindi) ascetic. Religion: another name for the Hindu god Shiva.

Yohan, Yohann (German) forms of Johan, Johann.
Yohane, Yohanes, Yohanne, Yohannes, Yohans, Yohn

Yohance (Hausa) a form of John.

Yohei (Japanese) calm ocean.

Yojiro (Japanese) hopes.

Yokuto (Japanese) wing.

Yonah (Hebrew) a form of Jonah.
Yona, Yonas

Yonatan (Hebrew) a form of Jonathan.
Yonathan, Yonathon, Yonaton, Yonattan

Yong (Chinese) courageous.
Yonge

Yong-Sun (Korean) dragon in the first position; courageous.

Yoni (Greek) a form of Yanni.
Yonis, Yonnas, Yonny, Yony

Yoofi (Akan) born on Friday.

Yooku (Fante) born on Wednesday.

Yoonus (Indian) a prophet's name.

Yoram (Hebrew) God is high.
Joram

Yorgos (Greek) a form of George.
Yiorgos, Yorgo

Yori (Japanese) dependence.

York (English) boar estate; yew-tree estate.
Yorick, Yorke, Yorker, Yorkie, Yorrick

Yorkoo (Fante) born on Thursday.

Yosef (Hebrew) a form of Joseph. See also Osip.
Yoceph, Yoosuf, Yoseff, Yoseph, Yosief, Yosif, Yosuf, Yosyf, Yousef, Yusif

Yoselin ☖ (Latin) a form of Jocelyn.

Yoshi (Japanese) good; respectful.

Yóshi (Japanese) adopted son.
Yoshiki, Yoshiuki

Yoshiaki (Japanese) attractive.

Yoshihiro (Japanese) very good and righteous.

Yoshikatsu (Japanese) good.

Yoshikazu (Japanese) joyous; harmonious.

Yoshinobu (Japanese) goodness.

Yoshio (Japanese) giving.

Yoshiro (Japanese) good son.

Yoshiyahu (Hebrew) a form of Josiah.
Yoshia, Yoshiah, Yoshiya, Yoshiyah, Yosiah

Yoskolo (Moquelumnan) breaking off pine cones.

Yosu (Hebrew) a form of Jesus.

Yosuke (Japanese) helper.

Yota (Japanese) big sun.

Yotimo (Moquelumnan) yellow jacket carrying food to its hive.

Yottoko (Native American) mud at the water's edge.

You (Chinese) first-rate.

Young (English) young.
Yung

Young-Jae (Korean) pile of prosperity.

Young-Soo (Korean) keeping the prosperity.

Youri (Russian) a form of Yuri.

Yousef (Yiddish) a form of Joseph.
Yousaf, Youseef, Yousef, Youseph, Yousif, Youssef, Yousseff, Yousuf

Youssel (Yiddish) a familiar form of Joseph.
Yussel

Yov (Russian) a short form of Yoakim.

Yovani (Slavic) a form of Jovan.
Yovan, Yovanni, Yovanny, Yovany, Yovni

Yoyi (Hebrew) a form of George.

Yrjo (Finnish) a form of George.

Ysaoahy (Chuukese) a form of Isaoshi.

Ysidro (Greek) a short form of Isidore.

Yu (Chinese) universe.
Yue

Yuan (Chinese) the original.

Yudell (English) a form of Udell.
Yudale, Yudel

Yudhajit (Indian) victor in war.

Yudhishthir (Indian) eldest Pandava brother.

Yudhisthir, Yudishtra (Indian) firm in battle.

Yue-Wan (Chinese) happy; gentle.

Yue-Yan (Chinese) happy; beautiful.

Yue-Ying (Chinese) happy; smart; kind.

Yue-You (Chinese) happy; friendly.

Yuga (Japanese) distant; long time; river.

Yugandhar (Indian) celestial god.

Yuji (Japanese) snow.

Yu-Jie (Chinese) jade; pure.

Yuki **BG** (Japanese) snow.
Yukiko, Yukio, Yuuki

Yukichi (Japanese) lucky snow.

Yukio (Japanese) gets what he wants.

Yul (Mongolian) beyond the horizon.

Yule (English) born at Christmas.

Yuli (Basque) youthful.

Yuma (Native American) son of a chief.

Yun (Chinese) fair, just.

Yunus (Turkish) a form of Jonah.

Yupanqui (Quechua) he who honors his ancestors.

Yurac (Quechua) white.

Yurcel (Turkish) sublime.

Yuri 🅖 (Russian, Ukrainian) a form
of George. (Hebrew) a familiar
form of Uriah.
*Yehor, Youri, Yura, Yure, Yuric, Yurii,
Yurij, Yurik, Yurko, Yurri, Yury, Yusha*

Yursa (Japanese) lily; delicate.

Yusif (Russian) a form of Joseph.
*Yuseph, Yusof, Yussof, Yusup, Yuzef,
Yuzep*

Yustyn (Russian) a form of Justin.
Yusts

Yusuf (Arabic, Swahili) a form of
Joseph.
Yusef, Yusuff

Yuta (Japanese) very gentle; a great
leader.

Yutaka (Japanese) abundant;
prosperity.

Yuto (Japanese) he who travels a lot.

Yutu (Moquelumnan) coyote out
hunting.

Yuval (Hebrew) rejoicing.

Yuvaraj, Yuvraj (Indian) prince, heir
apparent.

Yuya (Japanese) he who is superior
and gentle.

Yuyutsu (Indian) eager to fight.

Yuzuru (Japanese) he who is humble
and modest.

Yves (French) a form of Ivar, Ives.
Yvens, Yvon, Yyves

Yvon (French) a form of Ivar, Yves.
Ivon, Yuvon, Yvan, Yvonne

Yvonne 🅖 (French) a form of Yvon.

Z

Z 🅑 (American) an initial used as a
first name.

Zaafir (Indian) victorious.

Zaahid (Indian) abstemious; ascetic.

Zaahir (Indian) bright; shining.

Zac (Hebrew) a short form of
Zachariah, Zachary.
Zacc

Zacarias (Portuguese, Spanish) a
form of Zachariah.
Zacaria, Zacariah

Zacary (Hebrew) a form of Zachary.
*Zac, Zacaras, Zacari, Zacariah,
Zacarias, Zacarie, Zacarious, Zacery,
Zacory, Zacrye*

Zaccary (Hebrew) a form of
Zachary.
*Zac, Zaccaeus, Zaccari, Zaccaria,
Zaccariah, Zaccary, Zaccea,
Zaccharie, Zacchary, Zacchery,
Zaccury*

Zaccheus (Hebrew) innocent, pure.
Zacceus, Zacchaeus, Zacchious

Zach (Hebrew) a short form of
Zachariah, Zachary.

Zachari (Hebrew) a form of Zachary.
Zacheri

Zacharia (Hebrew) a form of
Zachary.
Zacharya

Zachariah 🅑 (Hebrew) God
remembered.
*Zac, Zacarias, Zacarius, Zacary,
Zaccary, Zach, Zacharias, Zachary,
Zacharyah, Zachory, Zachury, Zack,*

Zakaria, Zako, Zaquero, Zecharia, Zechariah, Zecharya, Zeggery, Zeke, Zhachory

Zacharias (German) a form of Zachariah.
Zacarías, Zacharais, Zachariaus, Zacharius, Zackarias, Zakarias, Zecharias, Zekarias

Zacharie **B** (Hebrew) a form of Zachary.
Zachare, Zacharee, Zachurie, Zecharie

Zachary 💥 **B** (Hebrew) a familiar form of Zachariah. History: Zachary Taylor was the twelfth U.S. president. See also Sachar, Sakeri.
Xachary, Zac, Zacary, Zaccary, Zach, Zacha, Zachaery, Zachaios, Zacharay, Zacharey, Zachari, Zacharia, Zacharias, Zacharie, Zacharry, Zachaury, Zachery, Zachory, Zachrey, Zachry, Zachuery, Zachury, Zack, Zackary, Zackery, Zackory, Zakaria, Zakary, Zakery, Zakkary, Zechary, Zechery, Zeke

Zachery (Hebrew) a form of Zachary.
Zacheray, Zacherey, Zacheria, Zacherias, Zacheriah, Zacherie, Zacherius, Zackery

Zachory (Hebrew) a form of Zachary.

Zachry (Hebrew) a form of Zachary.
Zachre, Zachrey, Zachri

Zack (Hebrew) a short form of Zachariah, Zachary.
Zach, Zak, Zaks

Zackary (Hebrew) a form of Zachary.
Zack, Zackari, Zacharia, Zackare, Zackaree, Zackariah, Zackarie, Zackery, Zackhary, Zackie, Zackree, Zackrey, Zackry

Zackery (Hebrew) a form of Zachery.
Zackere, Zackeree, Zackerey, Zackeri, Zackeria, Zackeriah, Zackerie, Zackerry

Zackory (Hebrew) a form of Zachary.
Zackoriah, Zackorie, Zacorey, Zacori, Zacory, Zacry, Zakory

Zadok (Hebrew) a short form of Tzadok.
Zaddik, Zadik, Zadoc, Zaydok

Zadornin (Basque) Saturn.

Zafir (Arabic) victorious.
Zafar, Zafeer, Zafer, Zaffar

Zahid (Arabic) self-denying, ascetic.
Zaheed

Zahir (Arabic) shining, bright.
Zahair, Zahar, Zaheer, Zahi, Zair, Zaire, Zayyir

Zahur (Swahili) flower.

Zaid (Arabic) increase, growth.
Zaied, Zaiid, Zayd

Zaide (Hebrew) older.

Zaim (Arabic) brigadier general.

Zain (English) a form of Zane.
Zaine

Zakaria (Hebrew) a form of Zachariah.
Zakaraiya, Zakareeya, Zakareeyah, Zakariah, Zakariya, Zakeria, Zakeriah

Zakariyya (Arabic) prophet.
Religion: an Islamic prophet.

Zakary (Hebrew) a form of Zachery.
Zak, Zakarai, Zakare, Zakaree, Zakari, Zakarias, Zakarie, Zakarius, Zakariye, Zake, Zakhar, Zaki, Zakir, Zakkai, Zako, Zakqary, Zakree, Zakri, Zakris, Zakry

Zakery (Hebrew) a form of Zachary.
Zakeri, Zakerie, Zakiry

Zaki (Arabic) bright; pure. (Hausa) lion.
Zakee, Zakia, Zakie, Zakiy, Zakki

Zakia 🎏 (Swahili) intelligent.

Zakkary (Hebrew) a form of Zachary.
Zakk, Zakkari, Zakkery, Zakkyre

Zako (Hungarian) a form of Zachariah.

Zale (Greek) sea strength.
Zayle

Zalmai (Afghan) young.

Zalman (Yiddish) a form of Solomon.
Zaloman

Zamiel (German) a form of Samuel.
Zamal, Zamuel

Zamir (Hebrew) song; bird.
Zameer

Zan (Italian) clown.
Zann, Zanni, Zannie, Zanny, Zhan

Zana 🎏 (Spanish) a form of Zanna (see Girls' Names).

Zander (Greek) a short form of Alexander.
Zandore, Zandra, Zandrae, Zandy

Zane 🎏 (English) a form of John.
Zain, Zayne, Zhane

Zanis (Latvian) a form of Janis.
Zannis

Zanvil (Hebrew) a form of Samuel.
Zanwill

Zapriel (Pohnpeian) a form of Gabriel.

Zaquan (American) a combination of the prefix Za + Quan.
Zaquain, Zaquon, Zaqwan

Zaqueo (Hebrew) pure, innocent.

Zareb (African) protector.

Zared (Hebrew) ambush.
Zaryd

Zarek (Polish) may God protect the king.
Zarik, Zarrick, Zerek, Zerick, Zerric, Zerrick

Zavier (Arabic) a form of Xavier.
Zavair, Zaverie, Zavery, Zavierre, Zavior, Zavyr, Zayvius, Zxavian

Zayit 🎏 (Hebrew) olive.

Zayne (English) a form of Zane.
Zayan, Zayin, Zayn

Zdenek (Czech) follower of Saint Denis.

Ze (Chinese) duty.

Zeb (Hebrew) a short form of Zebediah, Zebulon.
Zev

Zebedee (Hebrew) a familiar form of Zebediah.
Zebadee

Zebediah (Hebrew) God's gift.
Zeb, Zebadia, Zebadiah, Zebedee, Zebedia, Zebidiah, Zedidiah

Zebulon (Hebrew) exalted, honored; lofty house.
Zabulan, Zeb, Zebulan, Zebulen, Zebulin, Zebulun, Zebulyn, Zev, Zevulon, Zevulun, Zhebulon, Zubin

Zechariah 🎏 (Hebrew) a form of Zachariah.
Zecharia, Zecharian, Zecheriah, Zechuriah, Zekariah, Zekarias, Zeke, Zekeria, Zekeriah, Zekerya

Zed (Hebrew) a short form of
Zedekiah.

Zedekiah (Hebrew) God is mighty
and just.
Zed, Zedechiah, Zedekias, Zedikiah

Zedidiah (Hebrew) a form of
Zebediah.

Zeeman (Dutch) seaman.

Zeév (Hebrew) wolf.
Zeévi, Zeff, Zif

Zeheb (Turkish) gold.

Zeke (Hebrew) a short form of
Ezekiel, Zachariah, Zachary,
Zechariah.

Zeki (Turkish) clever, intelligent.
Zeky

Zelgai (Afghan) heart.

Zelig (Yiddish) a form of Selig.
Zeligman, Zelik

Zelimir (Slavic) wishes for peace.

Zemar (Afghan) lion.

Zen (Japanese) religious. Religion: a
form of Buddhism.

Zenda **G** (Czech) a form of Eugene.
Zhek

Zeng (Chinese) increase.

Zenjiro (Japanese) just second son.

Zeno (Greek) cart; harness. History:
a Greek philosopher.
Zenan, Zenas, Zenon, Zino, Zinon

Zenón (Greek) he who lives.

Zenshiro (Japanese) just fourth-born
son.

Zentaro (Japanese) just first-born
son.

Zenzo (Italian) a form of Lorenzo

Zephaniah (Hebrew) treasured by
God.
Zaph, Zaphania, Zeph, Zephan

Zephyr **BG** (Greek) west wind.
*Zeferino, Zeffrey, Zephery, Zephire,
Zephram, Zephran, Zephrin*

Zero (Arabic) empty, void.

Zeroun (Armenian) wise and
respected.

Zeshawn (American) a combination
of the prefix Ze + Shawn.
*Zeshan, Zeshaun, Zeshon, Zishaan,
Zishan, Zshawn*

Zesiro (Luganda) older of twins.

Zeus (Greek) living. Mythology:
chief god of the Greek pantheon.

Zeusef (Portuguese) a form of
Joseph.

Zev (Hebrew) a short form of
Zebulon.

Zevi (Hebrew) a form of Tzvi.
Zhvie, Zhvy, Zvi

Zhane **G** (English) a form of Zane.

Zhang (Chinese) jade tablet.

Zhao (Chinese) vigorous.

Zhe (Chinese) philosopher.

Zhek (Russian) a short form of
Evgeny.
Zhenechka, Zhenka, Zhenya

Zhen (Chinese) genuine.

Zheng (Chinese) honest.

Zhen-Juan (Chinese) precious;
beautiful.

Zhìxin (Chinese) ambitious.
*Zhi, Zhihuán, Zhipeng, Zhi-yang,
Zhiyuan*

Zhong (Chinese) middle brother; loyal.

Zhora (Russian) a form of George.
Zhorik, Zhorka, Zhorz, Zhurka

Zhou (Chinese) to help.

Zhuàng (Chinese) strong.

Zia **G** (Hebrew) trembling; moving. (Arabic) light.
Ziah

Zigfrid (Latvian, Russian) a form of Siegfried.
Zegfrido, Zigfrids, Ziggy, Zygfryd, Zygi

Ziggy (American) a familiar form of Siegfried, Sigmund.
Ziggie

Zigor (Basque) punishment.

Zikomo (Nguni) thank-you.

Zilaba (Luganda) born while sick.
Zilabamuzale

Zimra (Hebrew) song of praise.
Zemora, Zimrat, Zimri, Zimria, Zimriah, Zimriya

Zimraan (Arabic) praise.

Zinan (Japanese) second son.

Zindel (Yiddish) a form of Alexander.
Zindil, Zunde

Zion (Hebrew) sign, omen; excellent. Bible: the name used to refer to Israel and to the Jewish people.
Tzion, Zyon

Ziskind (Yiddish) sweet child.

Ziv (Hebrew) shining brightly. (Slavic) a short form of Ziven.

Ziven (Slavic) vigorous, lively.
Zev, Ziv, Zivka, Zivon

Ziyad (Arabic) increase.
Zayd, Ziyaad

Zlatan (Czech) gold.
Zlatek, Zlatko

Zoami (Japanese) artistic figure.

Zoe **G** (Greek) life.

Zoé (Hindu) life.

Zoey **G** (Greek) a form of Zoe.

Zohar **B** (Hebrew) bright light.
Zohair

Zoki (Japanese) literary figure.

Zollie, Zolly (Hebrew) forms of Solly.
Zoilo

Zoltán (Hungarian) life.

Zorba (Greek) live each day.

Zorion (Basque) a form of Orion.
Zoran, Zoren, Zorian, Zoron, Zorrine, Zorrion

Zorya (Slavic) star; dawn.

Zosime (French) a form of Zosimus.
Zosyme

Zósimo (Greek) he who fights.

Zosimus (Greek) full of life.
Zosimos, Zosymos, Zosymus

Zótico (Greek) of a long life.

Zotikos (Greek) saintly, holy. Religion: a saint in the Eastern Orthodox Church.

Zotom (Kiowa) a biter.

Zsigmond (Hungarian) a form of Sigmund.
Ziggy, Zigmund, Zsiga

Zuberi (Swahili) strong.

Zubin (Hebrew) a short form of Zebulon.
Zuban, Zubeen, Zuben, Zubon, Zubyn

Zuhayr (Arabic) brilliant, shining.
  Zyhair, Zuheer

Zuisho (Japanese) literary figure.

Zuka (Shona) sixpence.

Zuriel (Hebrew) God is my rock.
  Zurial, Zuryal, Zuryel

Zygmunt (Polish) a form of
  Sigmund.
  Zygismon, Zygismond, Zygismondo,
  Zygismun, Zygismund, Zygismundo,
  Zygysmon, Zygysmond, Zygysmondo,
  Zygysmun, Zygysmund, Zygysmundo